ISBN 978-0-331-20535-0
PIBN 11027443

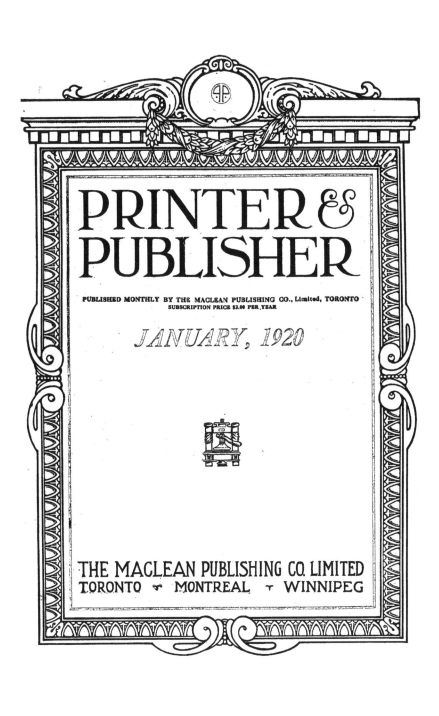

PRINTER & PUBLISHER

PUBLISHED MONTHLY BY THE MACLEAN PUBLISHING CO., Limited, TORONTO
SUBSCRIPTION PRICE $2.00 PER YEAR

JANUARY, 1920

THE MACLEAN PUBLISHING CO. LIMITED
TORONTO ⚜ MONTREAL ⚜ WINNIPEG

PRINTER AND PUBLISHER, January, 1920, Vol. 29, No. 1. Published monthly at 143-153 University Ave., Toronto, by the MacLean Publishing
Co., Ltd. Yearly subscription price, $2.00. Entered as second-class matter at the Post Office Department at Ottawa, Canada. Also entered as
second-class matter July 1, 1912, at the Post Office at Buffalo, N.Y. U.S.A. under Act of March 3rd, 1879.

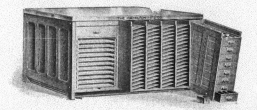

SATISFIED, *That's All*

After thirteen years of continuous satisfaction Phillips & Van Orden Co., San Francisco, California, ordered new equipment to bring their Monotype plant up-to-date.

PHILLIPS & VAN ORDEN CO.
PRINTERS
PUBLISHERS
SAN FRANCISCO

September 16, 1919

Monotype Company of California,
San Francisco, Cal.

Gentlemen:

When, in 1906, we installed our first Monotype it was somewhat of an experiment for us, but we were soon convinced that we had made no mistake. The following year, to meet increasing business, we added another keyboard and casting machine.

Our work consists of catalogs, booklets, general job work and commercial printing, direct advertising matter, and quite a volume of railroad tariffs. In all this miscellany we have found the versatility and adaptability of the Monotype of great advantage.

We are satisfied; why say more? Our satisfaction is most forcibly expressed in the order that we have just given you for replacing our Monotype equipment of two keyboards and two casting machines with new machines embodying all the latest improvements.

Cordially yours,

PHILLIPS & VAN ORDEN CO.,

per *C. H. Van Orden*
Secretary.

It creates business
May, 1908, after two years' use, they write:
"It is a peculiar circumstance, but it is a fact, that the Monotype is a creator of work; for we have been just as busy on two machines as we were on one."

Simply indispensable
March, 1912, after six years' constant use, they write:
"We have been using Monotypes for the past six years. The equipment has proved so helpful that it has simply become indispensable. If we were not able to duplicate it, you couldn't get it away from us with a Gatling gun."

It is unnecessary to say more

Lanston Monotype Machine Co., Philadelphia
NEW YORK   BOSTON   CHICAGO   TORONTO

Monotype Company of California
SAN FRANCISCO

266

This Advertisement set in Monotype Series Nos. 150 and 721, and Monotype Rule

BABCOCK

UNIVERSAL EQUIPMENT

The Shortest Endorsement Letter on Record

A successful Advertising Printer using five OPTIMUS presses recently received this inquiry:—

"Will you kindly tell us how you manage to print your half-tone work on bond paper on an ordinary cylinder press?"

Below is a reproduction of his reply.

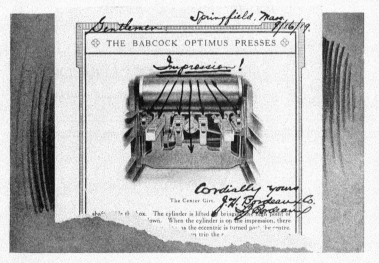

The catalogue from which this page was torn is unique, in that it is the only flat bed cylinder press catalogue issued, in which individual mechanical advantages are detailed.

If you have a copy, read it; if not, write for one.

Our Best Advertisements Are Not Printed,—THEY PRINT!

" The demand for BABCOCK PRESSES is double that of any precious year."

The Babcock Printing Press Manufacturing Company

NEW LONDON, CONN.   NEW YORK OFFICE, 38 PARK ROW

Barnhart Bros. & Spindler, General Western Agents, Chicago, St. Louis, Dallas, Kansas City, Omaha, St. Paul, Seattle.
John Haddon & Company, Agents, London, E. C.
Miller & Richard, General Agents for Canada: Toronto, Ontario, Winnipeg, Manitoba.

Cromwell
Tympan Papers

Give Cleaner Impressions with
a Minimum of Make-Ready

SAVING time on make ready, and securing sharp impressions are the two great things your press foreman has to strive for. With Cromwell Traveling, Shifting and Cylinder Tympan Papers, his draw sheets are always tight—no swelling—and they need not be oiled. They are also moisture-proof, protecting the packing against dampness.

You can turn a rush job quicker with Cromwell Tympan Papers because they resist offset, enabling you to back up reasonably wet sheets. Quick delivery is often your best selling argument.

Cromwell papers will take more impressions without replacing, and they *never* rot.

We especially recommend Cromwell Tympan Papers for trade journal and magazine printers where long runs are necessary without interruptions. It is ideal for book work and the highest grade of printing. Job printers will find it an excellent tympan paper for printing bond, linen and covers.

We carry Cromwell Tympan Papers in stock ready for quick shipment in rolls from 36 to 66 inches wide. Order to-day and secure the perfection and economy in printing that Cromwell Tympan Papers give.

Send us the size of your press, and we will forward free of all cost to you, Sample Sheet of our Tympan Paper.

The Cromwell Paper Co.
Department P.P.   Jasper Place, Chicago, U.S.A.

Trade   Mark

OLIVER CROMWELL

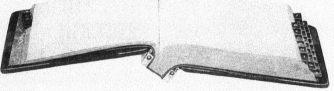

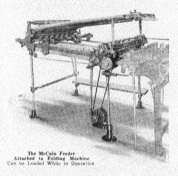

FOR SALE!

MIEHLE PRESSES
IN EXCELLENT CONDITION

Are you in the market for any or all of the presses listed below?

Miehle Two-Revolution, Four-Roller Press fitted with sheet and fly deliveries and spiral gear equipment. In first-class condition—size of bed 43″ x 56″, arranged individual motor drive.

—or—

Miehle Two-Revolution Four-Roller Press fitted with sheet and fly deliveries, size of bed 33″ x 46″, complete and in excellent condition, arranged for individual motor drive.

—or—

Miehle Two-Revolution Rour-Roller Press, size of bed 39″ x 53″, all complete with sheet and fly delivery, equipped for motor drive—splenddid shape.

If Interested, Apply to Box No. 664, PRINTER & PUBLISHER

Press Room Profits are derived from the money saved as well as from the money made in the operation of the presses. Whether Type presses or Offset, no presses built produce more work or better work than

The PREMIER
TWO-REVOLUTION 4-ROLLER PRESS

The WHITLOCK PONY
TWO-REVOLUTION 2-ROLLER PRESS

The POTTER OFFSET

The POTTER TIN P'T'G PRESS

．．．

Every mechanical device that makes for the production of the finest quality in the greatest quantity at the lowest operative cost is incorporated in these presses.

Every printer should know about them.

PREMIER & POTTER PRINTING PRESS CO., Inc.
SUCCEEDING THE WHITLOCK AND POTTER COMPANIES
1102 Aeolian Bldg., 33 West 42nd Street
NEW YORK

Canada West:	*Canada East:*	*Maritime Provinces:*
MANTON BROS.	**GEO. M. STEWART**	**PRINTERS SUPPLIES LTD.**
105 Elizabeth St.	92 McGill Street	27 Bedford Row
Toronto, Ont.	**Montreal P.Q.**	**Halifax, N.S.**

PRINTER AND PUBLISHER
Devoted to the Interests of the Printers and Publishers of Canada

Bread and Butter of the Printing Business
Knowledge of Costs is a Vital Thing

THE following is the first of a series on Printing Costs. The matter is prepared by a thoroughly competent student of the business. He is using the figures in the last issue of PRINTER AND PUBLISHER as a basis from which to work. This paper welcomes full discussion on this matter. It is of supreme importance to the job printer. If you have a good way of estimating costs, let us hear of it. If you care to send in a job to be analyzed for costs we will be pleased to render this service, with the idea, of course, of making use of the material in PRINTER AND PUBLISHER. In asking for estimates, give some idea of wages in your locality, or the basis on which to work.—Ed. P. & P.

AT the conclusion of the article in last month's PRINTER AND PUBLISHER relating to the bids on the Victory Loan job—"Be Safe"—it is stated that a knowledge of costs in printing is the "bread and butter of the printing business," and that many employing printers would gladly welcome more information on this important subject. It is an apt phrase; for a knowledge of costs is one of the essential tools of the estimator, the man who, by his judgment or lack of it can make or mar a business. The boss may be a good business man; he may have an up-to-date plant and efficient help, but if he has no proper methods of gathering cost data in his plant, his estimator will be no more and no less than a "guesstimator," and it will be more by good luck than by good guidance if the firm makes enough money to feed and clothe the boss and his wife and family and provide them with a few of the frills and folderols so dear to the ladies' hearts, and which seem to be enjoyed by the wives and daughters of successful men in other lines of business endeavor.

The article referred to shows the menace to our bread and butter in the present system of competitive bidding on jobs of printing. In it we can see that there is evidently no proper system or standard method of estimating in the various plants in the country, notwithstanding the fact that for the past ten years the Standard Cost-Finding System for printers has been available to any-one who desires to know where he is at with regard to costs and who has enough courage to install it and stay with it till he has mastered it thoroughly. It is chart

and compass to the printer who has installed it and who has faith in it, and every printer should have it, if he expects to keep clear of the business reefs and shallows as he steers along to his objective—a business that will give him a good return for his investment of time and money.

I will have something to say about the cost system later. Meantime, I would like to examine the article in the December issue and make a few remarks thereon, which I hope will be helpful. My only desire is to point the way, in the hope that other printers will get down to the actual study of the subjects that are so closely related to their bread and butter—namely, costs and estimating.

The article makes the astounding statement that in the actual bids on 200,000 four-page folders, printed and folded (stock and plates supplied by customer) the prices ranged from $130 to $300—a difference of 130 per cent. And *all the bids were from Toronto firms*, as far as could be learned.

Now, it has long been a sore point among country and small city printers that their worst competitors were the big city printers, who would make an occasional trip into their territory and quote prices on some classes of work so ridiculously low as to leave with the local man's customers the feeling that the local printer has been playing a hold-up game with him. And this feeling persists in spite of all that has been said to the contrary. The bid on this Victory Loan work shows that the city printers can make themselves look ridiculous by bids varying over 130 per cent. between the lowest and the highest, and this on a simple piece of printing like that under discussion.

The editor of PRINTER AND PUBLISHER, knowing my interest in the matter of costs and estimating, and my twenty-odd years' experience in all branches of the business from the P. D.'s job to manager and editor, and especially my knowledge of the country printers' problems, gained by actual experience, has asked me to write a series of articles along these lines. He suggested that I make a start by analyzing the estimates in the December issue, and to make my articles of interest generally to the craft, and more particularly to the small city and town printers, who form the major portion of the profession. I will endeavor to obey his behest as best I can, and if I can interest 60 or 70 per cent. of the printers in this bread and butter proposition, my work will not be entirely in vain.

In examining the article in the December issue, it will be found that there was evidently some tall guessing done to arrive at the prices quoted. Before proceeding to examine the estimates, let me point out that the tabulations at the end of the article show a common mistake which one is liable to make in dealing with printers' estimates—due to lack of one system in making these. Under the caption, "Some Comparisons," lockup, press-work, and folding and cutting in estimates A, B and C are compared. This is misleading, because A set down his selling figures, B set down his cost figures and added 9 per cent. while C used cost plus 15 per cent. in his. Just to show the lack of uniformity, I will set down the various percentages added in these estimates, as follows:

A figured .... selling price
B added .... 9 per cent
C added .... 15 per cent
D added .... 20 per cent
E figured .... selling price
F added .... 25 per cent
G added .... 20 per cent
H .... No detailed estimate
K added .... 40 per cent

In table No. 1, which accompanies this article, I have shown the charges for the various departments in selling price figures—that is with the above percentages added. This is for the sake of uniformity and ease of comparison. An examination of this table is interesting.

Estimate.	Stock Handling.	Composition.	Presswork. (Ink and MKR.)	Folding.	Cutting.	Packing and Del.	Total Bindery.	Charge.
A..	$10.00	$5.00	$100.00	$ 70.00	$19.60	None	$ 83.60	$198.60
B..	27.50	7.04	122.65	*110.00	.....	$11.00	121.00	276.00
C..	28.75	5.75	108.18	184.00	18.40	None	202.40	343.05
D..	None	7.20	99.00	120.00	†30.00	.....	150.00	256.20
E..	16.15	7.00	81.38	190.00	36.00	8.00	142.00	250.00
F..	18.26	6.20	60.94	75.00	61.85	24.00	160.88	250.00
G..	11.89	None	76.25	150.60	9.00	None	168.60	278.00
H..	No detailed estimate							250.00
K..	14.00	5.04	70.20	112.00	6.72	25.20	143.92	233.66

*Includes cutting.   †Includes handling and packing.

Under the heading of "Stock," the figures vary from $10 to $28.75. The only estimate showing how the figures are arrived at is that of E, who, however, makes the mistake of not charging a profit on the cost of handling. It is a labor charge almost entirely and should yield a profit. D's estimate lumps cutting, handling and packing together for $30, which is just about enough for cutting, according to his way of running the job (a phase which I will touch on later).

Composition is fairly close, running from $5 to $7.20. G has evidently invented a process whereby the plates walk into his shop and accommodatingly lay themselves on the press, all set for make-ready. The unpacking, checking and examining of cuts has to be done by some-one, and should be charged for over and above the charge for lockup.

Presswork column includes make-ready and ink, these were separated by some and lumped together by others. A detailed estimate like that of E takes no longer than the other kind and is better for checking purposes. The presswork runs from $60.94 to $122.65 (just 100 per cent of a spread). It must be explained, however, that the lowest, F, figured only half the number of im-pressions necessary. In handling stock and in cutting he mentions 33 reams, but in presswork he figured just enough impressions for one side of the paper, instead of two. He evens up on make-ready, however, by charging about three times more than is necessary for this class of work.

In the bindery, we naturally have the most variations, as it is here that the average printer knows least about costs and output. Prices for all operations vary from $83.60 to $202.40 (or about 150 per cent of a spread), and here again the lumping together of the various items makes it hard to analyze. Figures for fold-ing range from $70 up to $184. B combines cutting and folding at $110. There are two ways of folding this job. In my estimation, the better way is to lock up the form so that when completed the job can be folded 2-up, either by machine or hand. This brings in a variation in the next item—cutting. Some of the estimates figure cutting at a price per ream. A figures 68 reams at $13.60. (I do not know how he gets the 68 reams—his presswork figures are O. K.) C allows $18.40; D charges $30 for cutting, packing and handling. E charges $36; F, $61.88; G, $9, and H. $6.72. Now, to fold 2-on necessi-tates an extra cut after folding, and considerably more handling. It has to be taken from the cutting bench to the folding machine or table and back to the cutter. This extra handling has to be taken care of, besides the increased cutting time which it entails over the time necessary to cut the whole stock down to single leaflet size. So that while folding 2-up is a decidedly quicker way to handle the job, it does not save as much in cost as one would suppose, as it puts more work on the higher-priced operator and machine. Two hundred thousand folders takes some handling and E seems to be nearer the mark than any of the others. His cutting charge was $36.

Packing and delivery were considered comparatively unimportant items by some, who no doubt would have arranged to have some of the Victory Loan officials come in and take the leaflets away, as they left the cutting bench—at least, they omitted cutting and packing altogether.

The consensus of opinion, as shown in the estimates, is that the job is worth $250, and that is the price I think would be fair to both parties—buyer and seller.

I will now show how this job would be estimated accord-ing to the Standard Price List, published by the United Typothetae of America. The first part is from the list dated July 1, 1919, while the bindery items are from list revised August 1, 1919. The estimate is as follows:

Stock-handling (using E's basis) .... $ 16.15
Add profit 3.22
Cut handling 2.00
Lockup, 2.7 hours at $2.65 .... 7.15
Presswork, make-ready, $5.10; run $2.40 per hour,
  $81.60 .... 86.90
Ink, 17.29 lbs. book black at 25c, plus 25 p.c... 5.40
Folding, $1.25 per first 1,000, 60c per 1,000 on
  subsequent 1,000's, less 5 p.c. on whole quantity. 115.25
Cutting, 33 reams, at 50c 16.50
Packing and delivery 10.00
                        $262.57

This shows 5 per cent. higher than the Canadian price above, which I agreed was a fair one.

The Franklin Printing List, which is gaining a large degree of popularity in Canada, sets the price of this work at $274.94 or 10 per cent above our figures. This list is revised to November 10, and accounts for the slight increase. The figure worked out from lists 9 and 10 are as follows:

Stock-handling (using E's basis) .... $ 16.15
Composition, handling and lockup 7.00
Press make-ready, 3.5 hours, at $3 .... 10.50
Run 160 per M 81.60
Ink, 17 lbs. at 25c 4.70
Folding 80.00
Cutting 12.00
Packing 8.00
                        $219.95
Add 25 per cent 54.99
                        $274.94

Figures Showed Need of More Cost Study
Montreal Firm Had No Chance to Tender

Editor Printer and Publisher.

Sir:—From the job printer's point of view, your December number is the best we have had for some time, in view of the valuable data given regarding prices secured by the Dominion Publicity Committee on their four-page folder.

From the wide difference in figures it is evident (1) that the average printer still has a lot to learn about costs, and (2) that those who have undertaken to bring about greater uniformity in the matter of price have not been nearly so successful as they would have those who prefer to be guided by their own experience believe.

The Dominion Publicity Committee did not think it worth while getting quotations in this city. They evidently think that while Montreal is a good enough place to sell Victory Bonds, Toronto and vicinity is the only part of the Dominion in which the money at their disposal ought to be spent. This company, at any rate, did not have an opportunity of figuring on the job. Had we been asked to quote, our price would be $215, arrived at as follows:—

MATERIAL

34 reams M.F. book, 25x38-50 (value $161.50) supplied		
Handling and profit, 20 per cent.	$ 32.30	
5 lbs. black ink at $1	5.00	
Profit, 20 per cent.	1.00	
		$ 38.30

COMPOSITION

Lock-up, 2 hours at $2.50		5.00

CUTTING

Trimming, etc., 5 hours at $2	$ 10.00	
Jogging by cutter, 4 hours at $2	8.00	
		18.00

Carried forward		$ 61.30

PRESS WORK

Make ready, 3 hours at $3.00	$ 9.00	
Printing, 34M. Impressions (1250 per hour) 28 hours at $2.00	56.00	
		65.00

FOLDING

200M folds at 40c per M		80.00

PACKING

6 hours at $1.00		6.00
Total		212.30

(Would quote $215.00)

The unit prices herein used yield in the aggregate a net profit of 20 per cent., with which we are content. They are arrived at by adding to the actual cost of chargeable time 50 per cent. for non-productive labor and 150 per cent. for overhead expense. These percentages are not estimates, being based on a year's actual disbursements. That they are sufficient, and will stand analysis, is readily ascertainable by working upon the initial cost of each operation.

For example:—The Union scale for a cylinder press feeder in this city is $22.00 per week of 48 hours, or 46c per hour. Adding 23c for non-productive labor and 69c for overhead, we arrive at a total cost of $1.38. In charging $2.00 per hour for a feeder's time, therefore, a profit of 62c, or 45 per cent., is realized. The value of other operations is worked out in like manner.

We add a minimum of 20 per cent. to the value of material used no matter who supplies it. It is noticeable in the instances given by you that this is not generally done, in consequence of which an unfair advantage is given those who supply their own paper, and, incidentally, necessitates the charging of a higher rate for labor.

It would be interesting to know how the time of a cutter (who receives $8.00 per week more than a press feeder) can be sold for $1.20 per hour, or how a rate lower than $2.50 per hour for a compositor yields a profit.

The whole question being of vital importance to all, it is to be hoped the matter will not be allowed to drop until a definite conclusion is reached. The fear of being considered a controverser should not deter anyone who is in a position to throw any light on the subject from expressing his views.

Yours faithfully,
Henry Lipton,
President.

Too Much for Her

Unobserved and unannounced, the president of a church society entered the composing room of a newspaper just in time to hear these words issue from the mouth of the boss-printer:

"Billy, go to the devil and tell him to finish that 'murder' he began this morning. Then 'kill' William J. Bryan's youngest grandchild, and dump the 'Sweet Angel of Mercy' into the hell-box. Then make up that 'Naughty Parisian Actress,' and lock up 'The Lady in Her Boudoir.'"

Horrified, the good woman fled, and now her children wonder why they are not allowed to play with the printer's youngster.—Philadelphia *Public Ledger.*

The Saskatoon *Phoenix* has been securing some good page business on the "Babies' Gift Page" idea. Merchants advertise various things they will give to the first baby born in the New Year. Others take different dates. In fact, an assortment of things from a five-pound piece of lamb to a silver drinking cup make up the list.

Commenting on last week's jump in the price of newsprint paper, on labor's demand for more wages and on other advances in the cost of newspaper production, the Halifax *Herald* suggests a possible subscription price increase from seven to nine dollars per year.

Rev. Charles N. Sheldon, one of the most widely-known preachers in America, has become editor of the *Christian Herald.* Since 1889 Mr. Sheldon has been pastor of the Central Congregational Church, of Topeka, Kans. Mr. Sheldon is the author of "In His Steps," which holds a record sale of ten million copies. After the publication of the book in 1898 the author accepted an invitation to become editor of the Topeka *Capital* for one week and run it as he believed Jesus would. The experiment attracted wide attention and the *Capital's* circulation jumped from 12,000 to 36.000.

The past year has seen an increase of over 5,000 in the business population of Vancouver, according to Wrigley's British Columbia directory, which came from the presses. It records a still larger increase in the interior country and Vancouver Island. The gazetteer lists the name and occupation of every available business man in 2,042 communities throughout the Province and in the case of places without a local directory the list is a complete residential one as well.

The System of the Vancouver Daily Province

No Friction in the Editorial Room There

By E. H. Scott, Winnipeg

"WHAT is the best managed newspaper from an editorial standpoint in Western Canada?"

Several months ago I asked that question of a representative of the Toronto *Star*, who had just returned to Winnipeg after visiting all the larger papers in the Western Provinces.

"The Vancouver *Province*," he answered without hesitation.

"Why?" I asked.

"Because," he replied, "in my opinion it plays up the news the best. That is to say it maintains an ideal balance, featuring invariably the strongest stories of the day, and heading up in their true proportion the mediocre dispatches; those which are based on rumor, or those which have the yellow tinge. In its dress the *Province* maintains a high-class standard in much the same manner that the dress of a gentleman distinguishes him from the common individual. It bars scare-headings; it bars slang headings; it bars cheapness of any kind. The whole paper from front to back page has a finished look, it has the appearance of having been edited by some very sane men of quiet good taste."

Moreover he remarked that the paper seemed to be produced with the minimum of friction and the minimum of effort, while at the same time it maintained a small staff and was handled apparently at a very low expense.

Since my talk with the Toronto man I have had the privilege of working for a few months on the *Province*. I am not with the paper now. I hold no brief for it, but I believe that Canadian newspapermen will be interested in the system as operated in its editorial rooms, and that is the only reason why I am writing this article.

I never will forget my first peep into those editorial rooms, rather I should say the editorial room, for the entire news staff, including editors and reporters, occupied a space about 20 x 30 feet in one large room at the rear of the second floor. There were other quarters in the building for the managing editor, editorial writers, society editors, sporting editors and financial editors and the cartoonist.

The news staff looked ridiculously small to turn out a paper the size of the *Province*. Around a broad semi-circular table was grouped five men, including the city editor and the telegraph editor. One of the five was Roy Brown, the news editor, who sits right in at the game and handles the entire paper at close range. The other two were copy readers. All copy, whether local or telegraph, is handled at this desk. There is the closest kind of co-operation, and the fluctuating news situation from day to day is adjusted to a nicety without any of the rushing and fussing and misunderstanding that is a feature of many offices.

In one corner of the room was grouped a half-dozen reporters, comprising the entire staff. A lady stenographer made up the personnel of the room. All told, a dozen people to get out three editions a day; handle the Canadian Associated Press and United Press news services; two or three British cable services, as well as feature services from Canada and the United States; a big grist of suburban news, running to three or four columns a day; all the local news, and all the extra features for Saturday. Besides this one of the desk men was the music and dramatic critic, and the city hall reporter, who happened to be an expert with a brush, made up bulletins for the front of the office.

There are many news staffs in Canada composed of from 20 to 40 people which do not handle any more work, nor handle it with such dispatch.

The editorial office of the *Province* is handled with clock-work system, and system it is well known is a lost art in most editorial rooms. The office may be said to be standardized, every man has his place and his work, the whole system of heading up stories and featuring them is mapped out for the guidance of all copy readers. There are no freak heads, nor anything else for that matter; nothing is left to chance, with the result that the paper which will be issued next Thursday cannot fail to look as trim and high-class as that which was issued to-day.

It is wonderful what system will do to create a smooth operating news room at a minimum of expense and a minimum of labor. When one considers the speed at which the modern newspaper is put together, and the mechanical difficulties involved, the wonder of it is that the larger newspapers get through with even more than the severe strain and brain storms to which they are now subjected. It would be well if some of these papers would study and emulate the system on the *Province*.

Rather it should be said that they should emulate the system of Roy Brown, for he is the presiding genius who has brought the *Province* system into force during the past ten years. Mr. Brown, it should be stated in passing, reflects in his personality the make-up of his paper. He is a tall, calm, quiet, young man with a reserved manner, who seldom talks and who speaks in a modulated tone when he does so. He has the friendship and confidence of his staff.

The *Daily Province* is of course an exclusive afternoon paper and is perforce up against the same problem as other afternoon papers to dovetail into the fresh news of the day all the events which have transpired since the day before and which has been carried in the morning papers. In the case of the *Province* its circulation far exceeds that of any paper in Vancouver, and it is in duty bound to give its readers all the news. This problem is solved by putting on a night editor and some linotype operators to set the matter he turns in to them. So that the preparation of the afternoon paper really begins the night before.

This night editor handles all the night string of the Canadian Associated Press, and his position serves a double purpose, for he is right on hand to start a big extra on the way should big news break in the evening. During the war and since the war the *Province* has quickly gathered its staff together by the use of the telephone to get out many of these evening extras.

In the average editorial office of an afternoon paper the night telegraph string starts the whole works off on the wrong foot each morning. Editors and compositors start work about the same hour and the day starts off with the strain of trying to dissect 30 or 40 pages of flimsy in order to glean the hot news in the shortest possible form so that the linotype machines may be supplied. What the telegraph editor on a morning paper takes hours to accomplish the day telegraph editor tries to shove through in half an hour. Usually he clips the morning paper, and at the very inception of the day clogs the machinery with long-winded reports which are already ancient news by the time the afternoon readers get it. A hurried glance through the night string, and he lets it go at that, for already the day telegraph copy is beginning to pile in on top of him. The whole process is confused, unsatisfactory and unfair, not only to the mechanical force, but to the reading public.

What a contrast on the *Province!* The night editor, a

trained and trustworthy man, receives the entire associated press night string page by page and, in the familiar language of all editorial offices, "trims it to the bone." With an eye to the fact that all of this matter appears in the morning paper, it is his duty to put the night telegraph copy into the briefest possible form. He has plenty of time and he does his work thoroughly, in many instances rewriting stories a column in length to a couple of sticks or less. Where in his judgment a story warrants it, he lets it ride for all that the wire will bring.

But this is not all his work. On the *Province* it is so arranged that all local events transpiring in the evening, from dramatic criticism and sporting affairs to civic or political meetings and the general run of local news, shall be written up and turned in to the night editor. It makes a hard game for the reporting staff, but an effort is made to divide the work evenly, and the man with a night assignment does not turn up until late the next morning. In addition to the general run of local news it is planned that all of the suburban news for the next day's editions will be turned in during the evening. As Vancouver is surrounded by small communities this matter runs into a considerable volume.

The net result of all this preparation is that when the news editor appears on the job in the morning—and it should be said in passing that Mr. Brown is always in the office before 8 o'clock—he has before him galley proofs of all the night telegraph string, and the local news right up to the minute. Moreover all of these stories are headed up, and the compositors can begin at once the make-up of the inside pages and have them put away early out of the way. The galley proofs go back to them marked for the various pages on which they are to appear.

With the decks cleared for action at this time of the morning the production of the three issues of the day proceeds with the utmost ease and comfort. In fact the editorial room of the *Province* is usually as serene and unruffled as a Government office.

Does it pay to have a night editor and to pay night rates for compositors? The *Province* has found from experience that it does. It has found that this system eliminates many of the problems of the afternoon paper. When the night staff is not busy setting up the telegraph and local news they prepare time copy for the Saturday issue, and one of the strongest features of this system is in connection with the service to the advertising department. Wherever possible all advertisements are set at night, and the proofs of these ads. are on the advertising manager's desk in the morning. He is not only able to submit these proofs to the merchants, but is in a position to make corrections in the ads., to improve their typographical appearance, and otherwise see that they are presented to the public in their most attractive form. In addition to all this the early preparation of these layouts insures that the mechanical staff will have leisurely time to place them in the exact positions called for in the contract. There is a minimum of correspondence from angry clients with regard to advertisements not given position, or left out altogether with a consequent loss in both instances. All of this helps to pay for the night staff. An element of gain that must also be taken into consideration is that this superior service satisfies merchants and leads to their taking more and more space. The fact that confusion is eliminated from the composing room with consequent avoidance of mistakes and delays is another important factor, and it must also be taken into consideration that there is a saving in many ways through the paper coming out on time each day. It is an unheard of thing for the *Province* to miss a train or boat.

But to get back to the editorial room. One of the finest features of its system is that it uses exclusively solid type, both for headings and for matter. On the wall, within plain view of the copy readers, is a style card of headings which takes in everything from a big single column "Flash" heading with three or four decks to two, three

and four column heads, and for smaller stories the uniformity extends down to 10 and 5 point type. McFarlane italics are largely used in the heads larger than one column in size, giving a trim, clean, dignified appearance to the sheet day in and day out.

The front page of the *Province* is essentially a telegraph page, although a few good local stories are featured. Attention is called to the best news stories of the day on the inside pages by a display originated by the *Province* and which is set eight columns wide just under the title. This space is divided into three sections, and in lines of uniform length the announcement of inside stories is made.

A distinguishing feature of this paper is that the dress of the inside is uniformly as good as that of the front page. The large, single column flash heads are used with great frequency, also two column italic heads.

One could go on indefinitely telling of the many splendid features of the *Province*, including its daily cartoon on page one, almost always of a humorous nature; its intimate column of local comment under the heading "Street Corners," its intensely conservative editorial policy, with leaders lofty in tone and having a very marked effect in preserving public balance in this Western hot-bed of labor unrest and its column of pointed editorial paragraphs. One of the strongest features of the *Province*, and one that gives it undisputed leadership as much as anything else, is the vast amount of money spent on special services. During the war it carried the London *Times* service through the Philadelphia *Ledger* as well as the *Mackenzie* and *Windermere* services. It is also supplied by several Canadian and United States exclusive services. In the case of all these stories the *Province* never fails to feature prominently a by-line such as "Special service of the London *Times* exclusively to the Vancouver *Daily Province*." A marked impression is undoubtedly made on the public by the use of so many special features.

Perhaps the one item that contributes mostly to the success of this coast paper is that its editorial staff is hand picked. Kids and amateurs are barred. There is not a man on the desk but could get out and rustle a big news story full of fire and vigor if the occasion warranted it, while in the case of the reporters they are all old experienced men who handle the news of the city as thoroughly and as accurately as any staff in the country. Their connection with the desk seems to be automatic. There is never any jangling, or arguments; in fact there is little talking or excitement of any kind on the *Province*. It all moves along like a well-oiled machine, and as I said before, just like a Government office—along about the lunch hour.

Hamilton *Spectator*, Jan. 2.—As a result of a strike of about 75 pressmen this morning, the output of all the union job printing plants in this city is stopped. The strike was decided on by the job pressmen's union on Wednesday night, although it is claimed that the wage committee recommended taking the same action as the job printers and bookbinders, to defer striking till an officer from the International Union headquarters could come here and try to effect a settlement. At the conference between representatives of the employing printers and a committee of the Allied Printing Trades on Wednesday, the employes agreed to leave the dispute for settlement to the International officers, in view of the fact that the wages demanded were in excess of the union wages prevailing in neighboring cities whose print shops compete with the Hamilton firms.

The pressmen demand an increase from January 1 from $28.50 to $35, and after July 1 the scale is to be $37. They were offered $33 a week along with the other two trades, but they declined this unless the hours were cut from 48 to 46 per week. Already printing jobs are being sent out to Dundas and Oakville, where open shops are run.

Standardizing News Sheets

The question of standardization of news sheets is being taken up by the papermakers. It is understood that there is going to be sufficient time to make the changes, and that they will not be of such a drastic nature as will necessitate new presses or equipment calling for any very serious outlay.

The chances are, though, that the papermakers are going ahead with their programme of standardization, but they are taking the matter up with the Weekly Association before doing so.

For instance, here is a group that will be standardized at 30 inches by 44 inches (50 lbs.) At present they are: 29x45, 30x45½, 30x43, 30½x44, 30½x44½, and 31x42. It is likely that the makers will continue to turn out about six standard sizes, although it was the wish of several of the makers that this should be further reduced to four. Representations were made by the Association asking for at least half a dozen sizes, and it seems possible that this will be done.

A Well-written Appeal

The Acton *Free Press* makes a strong appeal for new subscribers in a space three columns across by 16 inches deep. The method taken is particularly attractive, in that it puts the appeal in the form of a local story. The reading matter of the story is as follows:

PAST, PRESENT, FUTURE.

The column presided over by "The Old Man of the Big Clock Tower" has been a marked success.

Letters of congratulation to this versatile old writer have been numerous. When this venerable old gentleman requested space for a contribution every week, some months ago, we were just a little dubious as to how our readers would take to this kind of writing, but the result has been wonderful. One day we asked him how long he considered he could continue his writings and historical happenings of the town; and, to use his own words, he informed us: "As long as my rheumatics behave and Mary doesn't register a kick. It'll take me a year at least at the rate I'm going."

And as long as he cares to write, we will certainly be delighted to give our readers his jottings from week to week.

There is assured one solid year's contributions by this writer, along with our usual interesting local features. To get the full benefits of "The Old Man's" writings, it seems as if not a single number should be missed. We are now besieged for back numbers by friends. The only sure way of not missing an issue is to subcribe for the *Free Press* at once. Back copies of issues are uncertain, and single copies are not always available. Tell your old friends about the features of the local paper—the *Free Press*—show them a copy of the "Old Man's" writings, and the results will help us continue to encourage the "Old Man" and give him more space, if the response justifies it. It will mean about 75 columns of purely local history within the next year. Wouldn't your old friends appreciate knowing about this?

A conference between the employing printers and representatives of the Hamilton journeymen compositors, printing pressmen and bookbinders proved futile in arriving at a settlement respecting an increase in wages. The master printers refused to go beyond their offer of $33 per week.

Owing to higher cost and scarcity of print paper, three of the four daily Albany papers have increased their advertising rates and the fourth will put higher rates into effect on January 1.

Farm. and Home, Vancouver, is doing effective full-page advertising in the coast papers. In one of these ads. there is a particularly good phrase brought out, as follows: "The Richest Population Lives Between the Cities."

Firm Shares Its Increase.

The Dominion Press, Ltd., Montreal, at Christmas paid a bonus to each employee, accompanied by the following letter:

A marked improvement in the year's output, and incidental profit, warrants the payment to shareholders of an increased dividend of 5 per cent.

In the hope that it will promote regularity and stimulate employees to still greater effort, it is proposed to grant a like bonus to them, based on their respective salaries or wages for the year.

Under this profit-sharing plan, there is coming to you $......., cheque for which is herewith enclosed. Wishing you and yours a Merry Christmas and a Happy New Year, I remain,

Sincerely yours,

(Signed) HENRY UPTON,

President.

The total amount so distributed was $1,001.37.

The increase in output for eleven months (December not yet closed) is 48 per cent. as compared with the same period last year, the increase in net profit being 169 per cent.

The regular dividend to shareholders is 10 per cent. The dividend this year (including bonus above referred to) will be 15 per cent.

The reserve at date is double the capital actually paid up.

Ye Ed Loses His Payroll

(From the Watertown, Wis., *Times.*)

Lost—Ninety cents in change in Main street. Return to *Times* office.

The *Farmers' Sun* announces that, commencing with the issue of January 20, that publication will appear semi-weekly, that is on Tuesday and Friday. Mr. J. C. Ross, for some time the Montreal representative of the *Globe,* assumes the editorship of the *Farmers' Sun.*

"I have been instructed by the village council to enforce the ordinance against chickens running at large and riding bicycles on the sidewalk."— Red Deer *Advocate* (Alberta).

The Nanaimo *Herald* announces an increase in advertising rates.

The Oak Lake *News* announces that it is contemplating putting its subscription price at $2 per year. It is $1.50 now.

Using the Suggestion Box

A suggestion box has been placed in the office of the Lethbridge *Herald.* The card over it is as follows:

HOW CAN WE DO IT BETTER?

Members of the staff are invited to offer suggestions which will help us—

1. To produce a better paper, and to get more business.
2. To make our organization more efficient.
3. To improve the system in any department.
4. To take a pride in our institution.
5. To foster good fellowship among ourselves and to take pleasure as well as profit out of our work.
6. To maintain the present high morale both in and out of office hours.
7. To win on our merits as the best and most aggressive paper in Canada.

Recognition will be given suggestions which are adopted.

Arranged Settlement on Voters' List Prices

Range of Charges Was a Very Wide One

THE publishers of Ontario, especially those in the towns and villages, have a great variety of prices to put up to the Government in regard to the payment for the publication of Voters' Lists for the recent referendum vote. PRINTER AND PUBLISHER has received several letters on the subject, but it is not necessary to publish them, as the matter has been settled in the meantime, and no good purpose would be served by airing views that afterward turned out to be without very much foundation in fact.

The impression seemed to have gone abroad, however, that an attempt was being made by the Provincial Government to pay off the printers on the basis of about 6½ cents a name, because, as one publisher puts it, "one Lambton price came in at four cents and one Toronto figure was put down at six cents."

GREAT VARIETY OF STYLES

As a matter of fact, there was nothing much to go by in the preparing of the lists in the first place. Printers received the work from the county judges, and they went ahead and got it out as best they could. In some cases, a great deal of care was taken, and rules were used, the same as in the getting out of the municipal lists. In other cases, the work was all run in, there being no justifications to make. This was the method pursued in the majority of cases. On this page is a specimen page showing how one of the Simcoe lists was prepared. There was some space placed between the letters of the alphabet, but the composition was of the straight-ahead, run-in kind.

There could be little surprise that the Government was amazed when the bills started to come in. There was such a range that there was no possibility of reconciling the figures on the ground of the difference in locality, wage scales, etc. In fact, the prices billed against the Government ran from 4½ to 15 cents a line. Make this on a large scale and it becomes more noticeable. It meant $450 against $1,500. The bills ran all the way in between. Some came as low as six cents, more at eight, a lot at ten, a few less at 12, and, one at least, asked 15 cents. For this last-named chap it should be said that he took a lot of pains with the work, put in rules and was liberal with his space.

GOVERNMENT SETTLES IT

The Department of Justice sought legal advice on the matter, and, according to what PRINTER AND PUBLISHER learned, the publishers would have a hard time were they to try to sue for collection, in the event of their accounts being refused. It is practically a case of not being able to sue the Government without its permission, and the chances of securing this were decidedly small.

The legal advisers of the Government met with the manager of the Weekly Publishers' Association and went over the matter at some length. There was an evident desire on the part of the Government to deal fairly with the prices, but it was felt that it was not possible to reconcile the spread between 4½ and 15. After considerable discussion, and an explanation of the whole circumstances under which many of the lists were produced, it was finally decided that the publishers' bills would be paid as presented, while cases that were considered high enough to be contentious would be put through at ten cents per line.

A certain allowance, regarded as being very fair, is made for headings and blank space.

As far as PRINTER AND PURLISHER can learn, the settlement negotiated by the manager of the Weekly Publishers' Association is quite satisfactory, and several publishers have written, stating their appreciation of the fact that the trouble was so amicably settled.

A Bit of Romance

Hunting for his fiancee, Miss Gladys Bell, in Christmas shopping crowds, and finding her at the entrance of a Boston store, was the exciting experience of F. Beverly Owen, editor of a Prince Edward Island newspaper and a captain in a Gloucestershire regiment, in the British army, during the war. Captain Owen telegraphed Miss Bell that he was coming to Boston for the holidays. When he reached her home she was out on a shopping tour. He made inquiries about the marriage regulations here, and, after obtaining the consent of the court to waive the five-days' residence law, was informed he had but an hour to bring his fiancee to the court house for the necessary paper. Captain Owen made a hurried exit and started on a hunt for Miss Bell and succeeded in finding her at the entrance of one of the big stores. Explanations followed and they arrived at the court house with time to spare. The marriage took place shortly after at a Presbyterian church.

Polling Sub-Division No. 5, Town of Midland

Name	Place of Residence	P.O. Address	Occupation
Chew, Beverley,	King St.,	Midland,	Lumberman, M.F.
Chew, Edith,	King St.,	Midland,	M.W.
Cave, William G.,	King St.,	Midland,	Printer, M.F.
Cave, Elizabeth,	King St.,	Midland,	M.W.
Courtemanche, Alfred,	King St.,	Midland,	Clerk, M.F.
Courtemanche, Rose,	King St.,	Midland,	S.
Courtemanche, Irine A.,	King St.,	Midland,	Clerk, S.
Courtemanche, Clarence,	King St.,	Midland,	Sailor, S.F.
Courtemanche, Mary A.,	King St.,	Midland,	S.
Campbell, Harriet,	Horrell Ave.,	Midland,	M.W.
Copeland, Albert E.,	Midland Ave.,	Midland,	Miller, M.F.
Copeland, Laura,	Midland Ave.,	Midland,	M.W.
Cambell, William,	Queen St.,	Midland,	Carpenter, M.F.
Campbell, Margaret J.,	Queen St.,	Midland,	M.W.
Carter, Silina,	Queen St.,	Midland,	M.W.
Cronier, Frank,	Midland Ave.,	Midland,	Machinist, M.F.
Cronier, Eva,	Midland St.,	Midland,	M.W.
Cambell, George,	Queen St.,	Midland,	Labourer, M.F.
Campbell, Janet,	Queen St.,	Midland,	M.W.
Cambell, Willis,	Queen St.,	Midland,	Carpenter, S.F.
Campbell, Herbert,	Queen St.,	Midland,	Pool Room, S.F.
Cataleno, Joseph,	King St.,	Midland,	Fruit Merchant, M.F.
Cataleno, Pauline,	King St.,	Midland,	M.W.
Cusson, Alphonse,	Queen St.,	Midland,	M.F.
Cusson, Bernedetta,	Queen St.,	Midland,	M.W.
Carr, Naomi,	Queen St.,	Midland,	M.
Carr, Roy C.,	Queen St.,	Midland,	Insurance Agent, S.F.
Carr, Frederick H.,	Queen St.,	Midland,	Labourer, S.F.
Campbell, Joseph,	Horrell Ave.,	Midland,	Labourer, M.F.
Cadieux, Thomas,	Manley St.,	Midland,	Labourer, M.F.
Cadieux, Malena,	Manley St.,	Midland,	M.W.
Church, Morriss E.,	Russell St.,	Midland,	Labourer, M.F.
Church, Ada,	Russell St.,	Midland,	M.W.
Cloose, William,	Russell St.,	Midland,	Labourer, M.F.
Cloose, Katherine,	Russell St.,	Midland,	M.W.
Coombes, Elizabeth,	Russell St.,	Midland,	M.W.
Coombes, John,	Russell St.,	Midland,	Labourer, M.F.
Campbell, Alexander,	Yonge St.,	Midland,	Labourer, M.F.
Campbell, Alice,	Yonge St.,	Midland,	M.W.
Carruthers, Theodore,	Yonge St.,	Midland,	Longshoreman, M.F.
Carruthers, Louisa,	Yonge St.,	Midland,	M.W.
Chappel, Albert,	Princes St.,	Midland,	Labourer, M.F.
Chappel, Gertrude,	Princes St.,	Midland,	M.W.
Carroll, Thomas,	Hugel Ave.,	Midland,	Watchman, M.F.
Carroll, Ellen,	Hugel Ave.,	Midland,	M.W.
Carroll, John,	Hugel Ave.,	Midland,	Labourer, M.F.
Carroll, Stephen,	Hugel Ave.,	Midland,	Pipefitter, S.F.
Carroll, Nellie,	Hugel Ave.,	Midland,	Clerk, S.
Carlton, Stanley,	William St.,	Midland,	Labourer, S.F.
Carlton, Irine,	William St.,	Midland,	M.W.
Carlton, James,	William St.,	Midland,	Labourer, M.F.
Carlton, Eveline,	William St.,	Midland,	M.W.

Printer & Publisher

Published on the Twelfth of Each Month.

H. A. NICHOLSON   -   -   -   Business Manager
A. R. KENNEDY   -   -   -   -   -   -   Editor

SUBSCRIPTION PRICE—Canada, Great Britain, South Africa and
the West Indies, $2 a year; United States, $2.50 a year; other
countries, $3 a year. Single copies, 20 cents. Invariably in
advance.

PUBLISHED BY

THE MACLEAN PUBLISHING CO.

Established 1887   Limited

JOHN BAYNE MACLEAN   -   -   -   -   -   President
H. T. HUNTER   -   -   -   -   -   Vice-President
H. V. TYRRELL   -   -   -   -   -   General Manager
T. B. COSTAIN   -   -   -   General Managing Editor

Head Office, 143-153 University Avenue   -   TORONTO, CANADA
Cable Address: Macpubco, Toronto; Atabek, London, Eng.
Also at Montreal, Winnipeg, New York, Chicago, Boston, London,
England.

Vol. 28.   PRINTED AT TORONTO, JAN., 1920   No. 1

CONTENTS

That Voters' List Business

A GOOD deal of criticism has been made, and some of it is no doubt warranted, in regard to the great difference in prices charged by the printers for turning out the voters' lists for the recent Provincial referendum and election.

The prices, judging by the bills sent to the Government for payment, run all the way from 4½ cents per line to 15 cents. Almost every figure is represented between these two extremes.

It is going to do little good to state that there is room for a lot of work in the matter of costs. Other people have said that same hackneyed thing in so many ways that the chances are that no person believes it now, though all know it.

The man publishing a paper in the community is, rightly or wrongly, looked to for a certain amount of leadership. He, at least, should know a very great deal about his own business. The publisher who is not master of his own calling stands a poor chance of taking the place in the community that is always awarded the progressive newspaper man.

Let some of the Ontario publishers put themselves in the place of the Ontario Government—a new concern—new, in many ways, to the methods of business. The Government knows that a large amount of printing has been done all over the Province in order that the elections might be held. The bills arrive. That printing, to the Government, is much the same as a barrel of apples or a horse, no matter whether produced in Kent or Bruce or Middlesex. Certain it is, if there were a spread of from four to fifteen in the prices of apples or horses from one county to another, the press would no doubt be asking for an investigation.

Now, in way of justification, there is something to be said. Many of the publishers did not want the business. They were filled up with other work; they

were short-handed. In one case that PRINTER AND PUBLISHER knows of the judge and the sheriff of a county went to a publisher and made it quite plain that his office would have to take on the work, and also that it would have to be turned out in fourteen days. It was also necessary to work night and day, and in some cases to secure permits to operate the plant on Sunday. Other work had to go begging, the issues of the papers that were turned out in these offices were more or less neglected, and the whole concern was turned on end for the time being.

But even the knowledge of these facts does not warrant the difference in prices. It might tend to raise the standard of the whole for that particular job, but it would not make a case for one office doing the work for almost one-quarter of what another one asked.

PRINTER AND PUBLISHER would be pleased to have offices where this work was done discuss the matter fully in the columns of this paper. The Weekly Association did a good stroke of business, through their Toronto office, in getting in touch with the proper authorities in the Government at once, and explaining the whole situation to them. The weekly publishers should see to it, though, that there is little of this sort of explaining to be done. The section should not turn its general manager into its general explainer.

A thorough knowledge of costs is the solution. Know what your work costs you, know why, and know what you have got to charge for it, in order to make a decent living.

The Sins of the Reporter

COMING from Ottawa is a signed statement from W. F. O'Connor, of the Board of Commerce, to the effect that the doings of the board have been grossly misrepresented in the daily press of the country: Mr. O'Connor goes further. He not only makes the general statement, but he points out the actual instances.

"It is very regrettable," said Mr. O'Connor, "when the same are inaccurately reported to the public as they frequently are, and especially in attempted summarization for telegraphic service. Notwithstanding precautions instituted by the Board, really in defence of itself and members, the misreporting of its doings and sayings has continued. For instance, no member of the Board ever suggested that farm products should be embargoed to cause a reduction in prices. There never was any 'forty-day milk order' prohibiting raises in prices of milk for forty days, yet even a Cabinet minister, misled by press reports, stated in the House that there was.

"These two matters out of many are mentioned only because they served to occupy the time of a whole day's session of Parliament. The Board obviously cannot take time to read all the Canadian newspapers to correct all misstatements which are made with respect to it, whether in newspapers or otherwise."

Of course, there is nothing unusual in a man claiming that he has been misreported. In fact, no man is truly great unless he has been misreported a couple of times. But, apart from that, there is reason to believe that Mr. O'Connor has reasons for a kick.

The system adopted in many papers does not give a speaker a chance to have his meaning correctly placed before the public. The reporter, in many instances, is not a shorthand writer. He knows how much he wants to fill in his paper. He may have been told to get a column out of a speech that would, if fully reported, fill six or seven columns. He undertakes the running story. There are reporters — bless 'em — who can get the drift of what a man is saying. They are able to pick out his best points and use them, and sometimes improve on them. In that way his message gets a proper hearing. There are other reporters who have not the gift of writing a running story, and they can never acquire it. They—to use a poor phrase—make a mess out of the whole thing. Their paper gets its column of copy and the story and the speech end at the same minute. A dozen lines by way of introduction, and the work is through. Any paper can well afford to be delivered from the reporter who imagines he has mastered the art of writing a running story.

The standard of reporting in Canadian daily papers is not improving. It is necessary to keep on bringing in new, untrained and untrained men. The way to find out if a man is going to make a reporter is to send him out and put him to work. If he is going to prove a failure the assignments that he has been put to work on in the meantime have to bear the brunt of his experimental stage.

Canadian papers would do well to recognize, even from a selfish point of view, that Mr. O'Connor has provided a great deal of good copy for them in the past few months. When he comes out and gives specific cases where he has been misreported, and where the findings of his board have been contorted, he should be seriously and fairly considered in what he has to say.

The old slogan of "Get It Right" that used to adorn a good many desks in editorial rooms, could well be brought back and given a 1920 frame.

Newspapers Blamed For This

NEWSPAPERS are shouldered with much of the responsibility of labor unrest in an article by George A. Amyot, president of the Dominion Corset Company, in a recent edition of the *Canadian Courier*. Manufacturers, according to Mr. Amyot, are being hurt in this country by the attitude of the press in picturing them as making great fortunes, and as being in the class of profiteers.

Dealing with the press in particular, the writer says:

"Newspapers take exactly the same attitude. They play to the gallery. They print what the masses—workers—want to read, without any thought of the consequences. Recall the strikes in Vancouver, Winnipeg and Toronto. They were played up in big type in all their details, from coast to coast. I claim such publicity is detrimental to labor, and to the country at large. Newspaper publishers are vested with serious responsibilities, and should take a different stand in matters of this sort."

It is not a very hard matter for any person to make such a general statement as that. The reception it receives depends largely on the prominence of the man making it. But at its best it is only a general statement, one that would carry no weight in a court of law, where evidence is weighed according to its fact value.

Reduced to fact, it would be fair to assume that what Mr. Amyot wants is censored news. There are certain happenings that he would seek to keep out of print, and the strike events of 1919 would be numbered with these. Publicity was what was needed more than any other thing to let the people of the Dominion see just what was going on at Winnipeg. The Reds in that city did all they could to keep out the news of what was going on. It was right in line with their purpose that nothing should get into print without their sanction, but journalistic enterprise defeated that idea.

The newspapers made it possible for Eastern Canada to know what was going on behind that curtain that the strikers would draw over the whole mess in the West.

The function of the paper is to print the news that is fit for the people to read: to keep its pages clean enough for any member of the family to read; to comment on these current events, and to try and interpret their meaning aright. On top of all this there is the ever-present problem of keeping the news and editorial pages bright enough to be attractive.

The Wetaskiwin *Times* announces an increase in advertising rates. The Renfrew *Mercury* did the same thing a few weeks ago, and the *Bulletin* and *Enterprise*, of Collingwood, have also increased rates.

Do Not Apologize For Collecting

THE publisher of a weekly paper in Ontario has an editorial announcement in a recent issue, in which he appeals for a paying-up spirit to rest upon his readers.

The one big fault is that he heads the article "A Whisper."

When a publisher makes an appeal for payment of debts that are honestly owing to him he should not call it "A Whisper." There is no good reason that he can bring forward as to why he should whisper about such a matter.

The men who sell paper to him do not whisper about their bills. They send the bills along, and they have to be paid by a certain date. The printers in his office do not treat the matter of their wages as a whispering event. They know they are to be paid on Saturday, or some other day, and they take it for granted that the cash will be forthcoming. If he pays rent for his office or house, his landlord does not whisper about the matter. The rent is due on a certain date, and he has to pay it.

Now, why should a publisher not get the same view? The men who get out weekly papers, and have a hard time making collections, find that they are up against a tradition that has caused people in general to believe that they are hard up and willing to wait for money, and for this feeling they are themselves largely to blame.

There are weekly publishers in Canada who do not keep a proper set of books. There are offices where you can go in and order work. Your order will be put down in a book. If you pay for the work when you get it, all right, the word "paid" is written after the deal. If you do not that book is thumbed over some weeks after to send you a bill. If you drop in after that again and ask how much you owe, the same old book is thumbed all over again until the date is found when you placed the order, and that magic word "paid" is not there. No other record is kept.

The paper that puts itself on a respectable basis is going to be respected. The community will accept the publisher pretty much at the valuation he places on himself. Put that valuation high enough and then come up to it.

ABOUT TIME.

THE RE-SET ADVERTISEMENT

 Specimens Taken at Random From Canadian Papers
By H. A. Nicholson, Manager Printer and Publisher

STRANGE to say, two of the most important requisites of effective typographical display are not universally appreciated by compositors. We refer to the use of white space and the grouping of parts.

White space has the power to give more effect to a twelve-point line of type than twenty-point line of type crowded by other display lines; white space, properly used, can give more effect to eighteen-point type than thirty-six-point type minus white space relief.

There are many compositors who have been setting type of all kinds for years who never give any particular thought to the white space and the value of this important element of display. There are other compositors who appreciate its value but are timid about using it. They are inclined to the opinion that unless the advertiser expressly asks for white space display it dare not be brought into play to any great extent, as the advertiser (in the mind of the compositor) might conclude he was being cheated. This is a delusion. The great majority of advertisers are appreciative of value of white space. They are witnessing more and more forceful and artistic typography today in magazines and newspapers than ever before, and they are not slow to see that white space is the big element behind these appealing typographical effects.

Where one would see one or two white space advertisements in an issue of the metropolitan dailies a few years ago, there are now a score or more to be seen. The compositors who pay indifferent attention to this element in the setting of advertisements are behind the times.

White space, however, to be most effective, must succeed in making the parts of the advertisement stand out clearly—in practice this is technically called grouping.

By taking the various parts of an advertisement and separating them with the amount of white space the eye dictates, the most readable and effective advertisements may be produced.

As an example of the merits of proper white space and grouping of parts the reader is referred to two advertisements on this page. Both read alike, but one represents crowded display while the other represents group display with white space relief. There is no question as to which is the more satisfactory advertisement.

RESET ADVTS.

The advts. chosen for criticism this month either show a lack of proper proportion of white space or are not as effective as they might be if the parts were grouped.

Advertisement No. 1.—Here is an instance of timidity in the use of white space. The compositor who set the advt. evidently knows the value of white space, judging by the amount he distributed in arranging the items for sale, but he showed a lack of courage in carrying out his convictions by putting a black rule beneath the headline. The black rule dominates the display, crowds the matter, and proves a stumbling block to the eye in reading the message. There is too much rule work throughout the advertisement, as a matter of fact. It intrudes at the bottom to a disadvantage, as well as at the top.

While we may seem to have commended the central portion of the display by referring to the white space brought into play,

there is room for improvement here as well as in the other portions of the arrangement. Our idea of a more effective advertisement is shown in the *reset* on a following page.

Advertisement No. 2.—Being considerably reduced in size the reproduction on the opposite page hardly displays some of the faults apparent in the original set-up, which was two columns wide by 9¾ inches deep. By visualizing the reproduction in its original size it will be seen that the arrangement is rather clumsy, or in other words overdisplayed. The words "Christmas Gifts," no doubt, give due emphasis, but the tone of the advertisement suffered through this breach of harmony. No particular objection may be found with making the words stand out. In bold type, but a type-face more in harmony with the Caslon series used throughout the rest of the advertisement would have been more appropriate. Monotonous spacing of lines is also apparent; in fact, lack of proper spacing forms the seat of the most faulty features of this and countless other advertisements seen in weekly and daily newspapers everywhere one looks.

Our *reset* aims to show how much easier it is to read an advertisement where the parts are grouped, and how much neater is the whole effect when type and border harmonize. It may also be noted that the topmost line appearing in the original advt. has been eliminated; it is superfluous and a pirate of space.

Advertisement No. 3.—It must be admitted that the manner in which this advertisement is displayed quickly informs the reader that it has much to do with toys. But a compositor should never be satisfied with accomplishing one object alone in setting an advertisement. Neatness in display is essential, also; a feature lacking in this case. The arrangement is common-looking. It would appear, too, that the message alone referred to toys. As a matter of fact, cut glass and Community plate is being advertised also, and being so divergent from toys should no doubt have received some distinction in the set-up. In our *reset* we have taken the liberty of introducing a heading and in other respects changed the arrangement, which is held to be advantageous to the effectiveness of the advertisement.

Advertisement No. 4.—Rather a good-looking display as it stands as far as tone is concerned, but there are some faults about this advertisement which may well be considered. Attention may be called to the disadvantage of crowding type, compared with the advantage of grouping various parts of an advertisement. It will be noted the parts fail to stand out separately and distinctly. How much more pleasing to the eye if each group were separated with a suitable amount of white space, or if they were in some other manner separated in units?

We have commended the tone, but this feature, it may be said, is not altogether harmonious. The text letter used in the line at the top is permissible with the Caslon series, especially for a Christmas advt. but the name set in Roycroft at the bottom is out of harmony. Caslon italics would have served the purpose nicely.

Our *reset* gives our idea of a more attractive and effective arrangement of dislaying this advertisement.

Advertisement No. 1.—Reproduced from the Maryfield News, (Sask.) Original size, 3 columns wide by 9 inches deep.

Advertisement No. 2.—Reproduced from The Economist, Shelburne, Ont. Original size 2 columns wide by 10 inches deep.

Advertisement No. 3.—Reproduction from The Mail, Milestone, Sask. Original size 2 columns wide by 6 inches deep.

Advertisement No. 4.—Reproduction from the New Era, Victoria Harbor, Ont. Original size 3 columns wide by 5¾ inches deep.

SALE SUGGESTIONS!

Ask the Clerk for a Ticket on the

Free Gram-o-phone
with each Dollar Purchase

Boots and Shoes

Don't overlook our bargains in Felt Footwear, Overshoes, etc.

Overshoes and Rubbers

15%
Discount

Felt Footwear, all sizes

25%
Discount

Dry Goods

Remember, all lines of Dry Goods, including Dress Goods, Flannelettes, Prints, Ginghams, Underwear, Overalls, Blankets, Comforters, are subject to

20%
Discount

GROCERIES

Our stock is complete with all lines of Fresh Groceries. Now is the time to stock up. The following 10% discounts are too good to miss:

Kellog's Cornflakes
2 for .... **25c.**

Tomatoes, 2½-lb. tins
5 tins for **$1.05**

Black Tea
1-lb. package .... **55c.**

Peas, 6 tins
for **$1.15**

Sale Lasts till December 20---Buy NOW

H. O. FOWLER
General Merchant
Maryfield

Reset Advertisement No. 1

Reset Advertisement No. 2

TOYS!

Call at Thorburn's Store and look over our Christmas Goods. We have the most complete line of Toys ever offered in Milestone.

Cut Glass and
Community Plate

We also have a fine assortment of Cut Glass and Community Plate to choose from, in fact we have a suitable gift for every member of the family.

Don't Forget to Bring the Kiddies

Thorburn's Hardware

Reset Advertisement No. 3

The Ottawa Valley Association List

LETTERHEADS
(Padding Included)
Bond 20 lbs., at 20c
250 ....$3.00
500 .... 4.00
1000 .... 6.00
1000 additional 4.00

Printing Only
250 ....$2.75
500 .... 3.00
1000 .... 3.50
1000 additional 1.25

NOTEHEADS
Bond 20 lbs., at 20c
250 ....$2.50
500 .... 3.00
1000 .... 4.25
1000 additional 2.50

Printing Only
250 ....$2.25
500 .... 2.50
1000 .... 3.25
1000 additional 1.25

BILLHEADS
No. 5 (5 in. deep)
250 ....$2.50
500 .... 3.00
1000 .... 4.25
1000 additional 2.50

No. 7 (7 in. deep)
250 ....$2.75
500 .... 3.25
1000 .... 4.75
1000 additional 2.50

No. 11 (11 in. deep)
250 ....$3.00
500 .... 4.00
1000 .... 6.00
1000 additional 4.00

No. 14 (14 in .deep)
250 ....$3.50
500 .... 4.50
1000 .... 6.75
1000 additional 4.75

STATEMENTS
250 ....$2.50
500 .... 3.00
1000 .... 4.25
1000 additional 2.50

ENVELOPES
No. 7 at $1.50
250 ....$2.00
500 .... 2.75
1000 .... 4.00
1000 additional 3.00

No. 8 at $1.75
250 ....$2.25
500 .... 3.00
1000 .... 4.25
1000 additional 3.25

Printing Only
250 ....$1.25
500 .... 1.50
1000 .... 1.80
1000 additional 1.20

POSTERS
Full Sheet (24 x 36)
50 ....$6.00
100 .... 8.00
Ad'l 100's, per 100 .... 2.50
Colored ink (one color 25%
extra minimum charge. 2.00

Half Sheet (18 x 24)
25 ....$3.50
50 .... 4.00
100 .... 5.00
200 .... 6.50
Ad'l 100's, per 100 .... 1.50

Quarter Sheet (12 x 18)
25 ....$2.50
50 .... 3.00
100 .... 3.75
200 .... 4.75
500 .... 6.75
1000 .... 9.50
Ad'l 100's, per 100 .... .60

Eighth Sheet (9 x 12)
50 ....$1.75
100 .... 2.50
250 .... 2.50
500 .... 3.50
1000 .... 5.00
Ad'l M's, per M 3.00

Sixteenth Sheet (6 x 9)
100 ....$1.50
250 .... 1.75
500 .... 2.00
1000 .... 3.50
Ad'l M's, per M 2.00

**BUSINESS CARDS AND AD-
MISSION TICKETS**
100 ....$1.50
Subsequent 100's .... .25
1000 .... 3.50
Ad'l M's, per M 2.50
For Stub Tickets, add 25c for
first 100 and 5c per 100 subsequent

WINDOW CARDS
Based on stock costing 3c to 5c
per sheet
(11 x 14)
1 ....$1.25
25 .... 2.75
50 .... 3.75
100 .... 5.25
Extra color, $1.50 addl.
(14 x 22)
1 ....$1.50
25 .... 3.75

50 .... 5.50
100 .... 8.00
Extra color, $2.00 addl.
(22 x 28)
1 ....$1.75
12 .... 3.25
25 .... 4.75

SPECIAL CARDS
Such as "Notice," "Trespass,"
Etc., containing only a few
lines, proportionately lower.

POST CARDS
Printing on Government Post
Cards
100 or less $1.50
Ad'l 100's, per 100 .... .35

VISITING CARDS
Ladies' or Gents'
50 ....$1.00
100 .... 1.50

Black Bordered
50 ....$1.25
100 .... 1.75

INVITATION CARDS
25 ....$2.00
50 .... 2.50
100 .... 3.25
200 .... 5.00
300 .... 7.00
Ad'l 100's. each 2.00
Gilt-edged cards, 25c extra per
100; Unprinted cards, 25c
per dozen; Envelopes, 10c
pkg., 35c 100

WEDDING STATIONERY
25 ....$3.25
50 .... 4.00
75 .... 5.00
100 .... 6.00

MEMORIAL CARDS
12 ....$2.00
25 .... 2.50
50 .... 3.50
100 .... 4.25

FUNERAL NOTICES
Note Size
15 ....$1.50
25 .... 1.75
50 .... 2.00
100 .... 2.50

Letter Size
15 ....$1.75
25 .... 2.00
50 .... 2.50
100 .... 3.50

TAGS
Work Only
Add stock at list price plus
40%.
250 ....$1.25
500 .... 1.40
1000 .... 2.00
1000 additional .... .60

FRENCH FOLIO
Letter Size
500 ....$ .85
1000 .... 1.50
Add'l 1000's 1.25

Note Size
500 ....$ .60
1000 .... 1.00
Add'l 1000's .... .75

HAND COMPOSITION
Per hour $1.50

MACHINE COMPOSITION
Per hour $2.00

PRESS WORK
Cylinder, per hour $2.00
Platen, per hour 1.20
Based on 1,000 impressions per
hour as an average

CUTTING MACHINE
Per hour $1.50

WIRE STITCHER
Per hour ....$ .80

GIRLS' HAND WORK
Per hour $0.50

FOLDING
Hand 75c per thousand folds
for the first fold, and 50c per
thousand folds for each subsequent fold.
Folding cover, 75c per thousand

INSERTING
50c per thousand sections
handled.

TRIMMING
Paper Cutter Rates
Signed by: The Advance,
Kemptville; The Courier,
Perth; The Chronicle, Arn-
prior; The Central Canadian
Carleton Place; The Expositor,
Perth; The Era, Lanark; The
Gazette, Almonte; The Herald,
Carleton Place; The Journal,
Renfrew; The Mercury, Ren-
frew; The Observer, Pem-
broke; The Record-News,
Smith's Falls; The Review,
Carp; The Sun, Cobden; The
Standard, Pembroke; The
Watchman, Arnprior.

For Making Up Standard Page

A handy little contrivance was noticed in one of the large shops a few days ago. It was in the form of a gauge for pages. It fits on the top of the date and name line at the top of the page and also on the outside of the chase. When it comes to spacing out, all that is necessary is to put on this gauge and put in enough leads along with it to make it reasonably tight. The number of leads or other spacings can then be left on each page, and put in before the adjustment or locking takes place. Not only is it quick in this way, but it keeps the page heads well lined up, even better then using a straight edge on them. It is not a difficult matter to make these gauges, and they come in very handy where standard pages are used.

The Murray Printing Company, of Toronto, will spend a quarter of a million dollars in a new printing house, to be erected at 192-4 Spadina Avenue. The building will be six storeys high, and contain 60,000 feet of floor space. Construction will be started early in the new year. The site is 60 feet by 210 and runs back to Cameron Street.

Collier's Weekly has changed hands under a . contract by which the Crowell Publishing Company became owner of the weekly, as well as all other publications issued by P. F. Collier and Son. No changes in the personnel of Collier's are contemplated at present, it was announced. Finley Peter Dunne is editor.

At one session of the Ontario Laundry Owners' Asso- ciation in Toronto, the value of publicity was impressed upon the delegates by Mr. W. B. Haggerty of Ohio, who pointed out that the dealers could readily double their business if they would only make the husbands see through the medium of publicity, that the wives "should be released from the drudgery of the washtub."

The Best of the Holiday Greetings
Received by Printer and Publisher

WHEN PRINTER AND PUBLISHER receives a piece of printing from the Mortimer Company of Ottawa, a feast for the eyes in artistic effects is assured. The Mortimer Yuletide Message this year is right up to the Mortimer standard in originality and good taste. It consists of an eight-page folder of superior antique deckle-edged stock, printed in two colors. A printing office interior scene of an early master of the art is illustrated on the front page, and below a short Christmas Message is printed in prominent hand-lettered text in red and black inks.

A New Year Message is tastily printed in Bookman Caps on one of the inside pages. The other pages are entirely blank, and it may be said that the richness of the stock in itself is pleasing to look upon and requires no embellishment.

Another similar folder of eight pages was received from H. W. Reeder, editor and publisher of the Kerrobert *Citizen*. The front page only is devoted to the Christmas and New Year's message, which is printed in green and red inks. Holes punched at the top admit a green ribbon bow which gives distinction to the whole effect. The stock used is crash buff with deckle-edge.

We have never seen anything more original and more appropriate than the holiday message from the Toronto Envelope Company. When we took this greeting out of the wrapper in which it was enclosed we at first concluded that we were in receipt of a new envelope stock, for there was no printing on the outside to give a clue as to the contents, and the stock was of exceptional quality, kid finish as a matter of fact. Closer examination revealed that the flaps were all loose, and when turned back a neatly engraved greeting was revealed. On each of the side flaps beautiful Christmas ornaments in red and green appeared. The centre of the fold contained the greeting and the lower flap a New Year's quotation from Dickens' Chimes. The top flap was, in good taste, left blank. The Toronto Envelope Company are to be congratulated.

Some of the most artistic Holiday Messages we received contained but a limited amount of red ornamentation, which goes to show that in order to produce an appropriate Yuletide Message it is not necessary to flash strong colors before the eye of the recipient. We have a beautiful eight-page folder from the *Border Cities Star* in green and red on white antique stock. There is a short quotation from Johnson, along with the word "Greetings" on the front page. Only the two pages are used for printing and both carry a double rule border in green and red. The green border is two points in thickness, and the red one point. An initial "A" in 24-point is all that appears in red outside the border on the front page, and on the inner page only the one-point border appears in this color. The effect is very artistic.

Another unique design in Holiday Greetings was received from Charles P. Doughty, publisher of the Hastings *Star*. It is in the form of a folded card. The ends are folded in to meet at the centre. When folded down the word "Greetings" and the name of the paper and the name of the publisher is seen between from the lower left-hand corner between wavy rules top and bottom. Then on the inside the holiday greetings of the publisher are printed.

The Lanston Monotype Machine Company are noted for their artistic publicity matter. Their four-page folder in black, green and red, bearing Holiday Greetings, fully upheld the reputation of the company's publicity department. The feature of the folder is seen in the two inner pages where two Christmas trees are displayed. A happy

printer who has adopted "The Monotype Way" is seen gazing upon one of the trees with evident satisfaction, as it is laden with signs of prosperity. Then another, but dejected, printer is shown gazing on the other tree labelled with signs of misfortune; the inference being that he is in need of a Monotype. The folder is of bristol board stock and has a typical Canadian appeal with the picture of a beaver on the front cover and the maple leaf on the back cover, the latter containing an inset picture of the Toronto office of the company.

Think of an illustrated Christmas card of kid finish in eight colors, all beautifully blended, the colors being black, blue, light-green, purple, red, golden-brown, and flesh, all on a background of gold. This combination of artistic effects represents the Christmas Greeting of the Gazette Printing Company, Limited, Montreal, and forms a splendid color-scheme study. The illustration shows an old-time carol-singing scene, comprising a boy singer, bass violin and flute players. The card measures 9 x 6 inches and is folded once. The illustration appearing on the front page is only 3 x 2 inches, but an abundance of white space displays the design to excellent advantage on the finest of heavy kid-finished stock. Beneath the design "Christmas 1919" appears in large gold letters of hand-lettered text, and the right-hand inner page bears the Christmas message of the firm in hand letters of one color. Recipients of this card will undoubtedly retain it.

A remarkably fine specimen of offset lithography has been turned out by the Royal Print and Litho. Company of Halifax. It is in panel form and on one side is "In Flanders' Fields," and on the other "Victory," the one being in answer to the other. In the first is the misty spirit of a soldier rising from the poppy-covered fields of Flanders, while in the "Victory" panel the soldiers of the Allied nations pass over the same poppy fields. The whole idea is remarkably well planned; the coloring is soft and all registers perfectly done. The Royal Print have been so anxious that nothing should be done to spoil the effect that the only trace of any mark is their imprint behind one of the panels. The whole production is truly artistic and thoroughly representative of a refined taste in this field of work.

The lad came into the office the other morning with something over his shoulder that looked like a piece of eavetrough. We had a suspicion that it was in reality the monster calendar that the Estevan *Progress* turns out at the start of each fresh 365, and such was the case. The furniture in the building had been previously moved around a bit, so there was no trouble in getting the big Westerner in. The *Progress* has hit upon a great picture this year in Thomas Moran's "Allegheny Trout Stream." The picture is one that lends itself easily to a wealth of color and a warmth of atmosphere that is pleasingly realistic, especially when one gazes upon a Summer scene at 12 below zero. The numbers used are large and plain, and can be easily read at a distance. In fact, the Estevan production could well be classed as a community calendar.

New Mailing Machine

A new label pasting machine has been put on the market by Chauncey Wing's Sons, Greenfield, Mass. It is constructed of aluminum and weighs only two pounds. The frame and all the castings to hold bearings and gears have been made in one piece, insuring unusual strength and freedom from trouble. Because it has the exact "hang," combined with its extreme lightness, it is claimed that this new machine can be used in either right or left hand with unusual facility.

Bud Fisher is the Highest Paid Artist

How He Got His Start with the "Strip"

CAPT. BUD FISHER, creator of Mutt, and Jeff, has the reputation of earning more money than any other cartoonist. Ben Mellon, writing in *Editor and Publisher* recently, tells something of Fisher's work and fancies:—

"Mutt is derived from mutton-head," he said in reply to a question. "When I first went to work on the *Chronicle* in San Francisco I did general assignments. In racing season I was always sent down to the track in the afternoon. It was not unusual for me to get a fire in the early evening and a banquet of preachers or a prize fight at night. Those were busy days. In my trips to the races—which I did not object to—I noticed a great crowd of persons who would rush down to the betting ring with about $4—hard-earned money. We came to call them soft-heads or mutton-heads. Mutt is my composite idea, legs included, of all the mutton-heads who threw their hard-earned cash away.

"Mutt made his first public appearance in the *Chronicle* in October, 1907," he continued. "He was then already a year old. I made my first Mutt strip in 1906. It was of the regulation seven-columns length and practically the present depth. I had six of them on hand, made in spare moments. The first one went upstairs about 6 o'clock and about 6.20 the foreman of the engraving department, the superintendent of the composing room and the make-up man were down in our department shouting that my new sketch could not be used. They said my strip was a make-up impossibility. What they said went and Mutt went into retirement for one year.

"I continued my regular work during the year that followed," said Mr. Fisher, "but I never forgot Mutt. By steady plugging I gained a public following that won respect for my wishes on the *Chronicle*. It was then that I tried another Mutt streamer. This one was 5 columns wide and very narrow, just running a few inches in depth. It was the first strip of the kind ever run in this country and made a hit, although the space was small."

HOW JEFF WAS NAMED

"What about Jeff—and why Jeff?" I asked.

"Well, it was this way. Mutt had been going pretty much alone and seemed to be going good but I could see that he needed company. To meet this condition I turned the inmates of an institution for the insane loose on him. I introduced one or two a day. If one seemed especially good I kept him for several days. James J. Jeffries was at the height of his glory then and I brought out a little wee bit of a guy—a direct opposite—and had him represent himself as James J. Jeffries—I mean brought him out from the institution for the insane. The people seemed to like the new character. I made him a partner of Mutt and they have been traveling together ever since."

Bud Fisher is the regular name of the great newspaper artist, although when signing official documents, he makes it "H. C." He acquired the name of Bud when aged about three years and has held to it pretty closely ever since. He likes it. If somebody yelled "Hello Harry" to him tomorrow he would not know they were hailing him. The C. in his name stands for Conway. Bud Fisher, contrary to popular belief, was born in Illinois. His parents started West with him a few weeks after the event and he grew to manhood and fame in California. Bud Fisher has a sister who is a few years older. They were raised together. Bud was taught to say "sister" but she could not master "brother" and the result was "Bud."

While he was born in Illinois, Bud Fisher passes over that as a mere happening and gives all credit to California and the metropolitan atmosphere of San Francisco and especially its newspapers for the ability that has made it possible for him to make millions of Americans laugh from day to day and into years. In relation to this he made an interesting remark about newspaper art as it is affected by locality.

"When you see a picture or cartoon that includes a boy, a stick and dog," he said, "you know, if you are a student of newspaper art, that the artist who made the drawing was from the Middle West. If you see drawings that show barrooms, race tracks, shipwrecks, or the oddities of local characters—moving drawings that seem to breathe action and reflect life in all its phases—you know that artist is from the Pacific Coast and in all probability from San Francisco.

GEOGRAPHY INFLUENCES ART

This is no reflection on the men who do not come from San Francisco, nor on their work. That a majority of the present day successful newspaper artists are from San Francisco is a well-known fact. I believe this can be easily explained. The newspapers of the Middle West travel on a line—the atmosphere of the Middle West is conservative. The Pacific coast is progressive. San Francisco looks out on the world, welcomes persons from every corner of the world and goes the limit to make them feel at home. This is reflected in the newspapers which, I believe, are more metropolitan than the newspapers of any other city in this country. They try to make a special appeal to every element in the great community. This gives the staff man a wide vision, a wide range of action. The quickly changing conditions to meet changing human elements have created an active newspaper art as represented by more than a dozen men that I could name off hand."

Bud Fisher denies that he is temperamental and attributes almost all of his daily acts to habit. He lives on Riverside Drive right next door to William Randolph Hearst, who brought him East the first time. He says that he sees Mr. Hearst "once in a while." They have several little differences that the courts have been trying to decide for the last three years.

Bud Fisher's favorite color is blue—he always wears blue socks and blue neckties—and he used it pretty freely, almost as freely as works of Japanese art, in decorating and furnishing his apartment. Two of the bedrooms, including his own, are done entirely in Japanese. The Fisher home is in complete charge of a Turk. His name is Gregory—Bud Fisher renamed him that a long time ago. When he says "no" you don't even get a chance to look into the front door.

PREFERS NIGHT WORK

The maker of Mutt and Jeff in his own words, "Hates to go to bed and dreads getting up again." That is his excuse for doing all his work at night and sleeping most of the day. He blames this practice on his early newspaper training. The San Francisco *Chronicle* is a morning paper, and it was there, he says, that he got the habit of working all night and he has never been able to break himself of it. He also hates to eat. His one real meal every twenty-four hours is breakfast. It is always a real meal. Dinner he looks upon as a necessity and not a function; banquets he refuses to attend; dinner parties—those attended by about twelve persons—he considers the great crime of the age.

"I never attended one in my life at which I was not bored to death and I think everybody else felt the same way," he remarked, then added, "When it comes to eating I would just as soon have a slice of cheese or ham and piece of bread as a porterhouse steak, provided I have had my regular breakfast."

There was a time, which newspaper editors remember, when Mutt and Jeff would fail to arrive in time to make editions. That, however, was under the old schedule of habit of Bud Fisher. Nothing like that could happen now. The English Army changed all of that. When Bud Fisher became Captain Fisher of the British Army he was told he could mail Mutt and Jeff on Tuesdays and Fridays. When he arrived back home the practice was an established habit.

TWO LABOR NIGHT

The Mutt and Jeff strips are now made on Tuesdays and Fridays only. Along about 9 o'clock at night—which is early in the morning for Bud Fisher—work is started and it is continued until the famous pair of newspaper funmakers have been put through enough stunts to last until the next night of labor.

Fisher draws a monthly salary of more than the life wealth of any of the old masters; he keeps a studio downtown, but does most of his work in the smallest room of his apartment; he buys no ideas and receives very few from friends that are of any value to him; he is 34 years of age, smiles easily and has a twinkle in his eyes that indicates that the humor of Mutt and Jeff will continue for sometime.

His favorite breakfast dish is a large platter heaped high with pork chops. His chief life ambition, he said, is to live in Los Angeles.

HIS STUPENDOUS EARNINGS

One of my objects in seeing Bud Fisher was to ask him if the rumor was true that he is now the highest paid newspaper or any other kind of an artist in the known world. I found him to be a little hazy on the point and I assumed, rightly or wrongly, that this was a sort of delicate subject with him—something that he might know about, but would be disinclined to blurt to strangers. I did not make headway with him, but I know, just the same. He is the highest paid newspaper artist or any other kind of an artist extant. His syndicate sales, I have reason to believe, are $3,900 per week, or about $200,000 per calendar annum, for his newspaper work alone and then—Mr. Fisher does very well indeed with such as movies, theatrical performances, books and what-not-ramifications of his comic characters.

Agency News

Miss M. Pennell of the Toronto office of J. J. Gibbons, Limited, advertising agents, has just returned from Winnipeg and announces considerable expansion in the organization for Western Canada of J. J. Gibbons, Limited. The Winnipeg office of this well-known firm, which has lately occupied extensive premises in the *Tribune* Building, welcomes a new addition to the staff in the person of Bruce Campbell, a prominent figure in Western Canada business circles. Mr. Campbell is vice-chairman of the Convention and Publicity Bureau of the Winnipeg Board of Trade, and is publicity counsel to the boards of a number of philanthropic and charitable organizations.

The Winnipeg offices of J. J. Gibbons will now have an executive staff of five widely-experienced men, including Gordon E. Hunter (manager), Bruce Campbell, D. Frank Tees and E. J. Budden. Activity in Western Canada commercial enterprise is fully expected in the near future, and J. J. Gibbons, Limited, are preparing to meet all demands for advertising service.

Carnation Milk advertising space has been increased for 1920. Where one hundred to three hundred line space has been used in the past, six hundred to one thousand lines are being used. The Baker Agency is placing the copy.

Toronto wholesale coal dealers are running a campaign in Ontario dailies. Their aim is to exploit the advantages of buying coal at Toronto, rather than at the mine or from the American wholesaler. Dominating space is being used for this campaign, which is being conducted by the Baker Advertising Agency, Toronto.

The Baker Agency has secured the account of the Dominion of Canada Accident and Guarantee Insurance Company, and announce that this is the first company of its kind to go in for big space in newspapers in a casual or definite way.

Various Want Ads

Editor PRINTER AND PUBLISHER:—

In reading the advertisement for help as classified in the daily newspaper, the expression, "A two-thirder," is frequently noticed. The phrase, as included therein, implies two things particularly: (1), that before finishing a term of years with the man started with, an apprentice is given an offer of another job; (2), the use of the other man's training is to be taken advantage of when his protege is becoming proficient at the trade.

Following up the same column of advertisements for one week in anticipation of getting a suitable position, the eye caught a notice as follows:

"Practical printer and reporter to take charge of small weekly newspaper while publisher is South; or would lease paper to absolutely reliable man. Box 760, Globe."

That was the job for me, as during the summer the same thing had been done satisfactorily for a publisher in just such a predicament, with commendation at the close, and also the request to correspond if at liberty a year hence. The advertisement inserted here appeared Tuesday, with immediate reply given to the box number, and requesting some response at an early date. The most surprising part of the incident to me was the re-appearance of the same notice and box number (without receiving answer to what had been previously inserted), in the Saturday edition of the paper. Common journalistic courtesy would have commanded a reply, just as much as authenticity was involved.

Whatever may be the impressions prevailing in regard to any man, if capable of filling a position satisfactorily, it ill-becomes anyone with self-respect to ignore what is done in good faith by others. Tolerance with conviction often moderate the view of a pre-possessed individual, and underhand inquiry, when found out, is just as condemptible as when done. Intervention by parties not concerned with a deal, like a fictitious advertisement, is a breach of business etiquette.

A "Want Column," in general terms, is placed that the needs of those concerned may be filled, particularly by the one who calls for assistance. A newspaper is justified only upon being neutral, not daring to suspect anything else than that such is the case; any difference between an applicant or an advertiser relevant to what actuates their motives in making terms one with the other, should concern themselves entirely, their parties being left out of the question.

A pioneer undertaking of importance to Canada is the organization of a Canadian company known as Leo Feist, Limited, with headquarters in Toronto. The object of this company is to print and develop the songs of the parent company, Leo Feist, Incorporated, of New York City, whose publications are well known the world over. The Canadian company, in addition to the regular American catalogue, will publish songs by Canadian writers. The company is managed by Mr. Gordon V. Thompson, formerly of the Thompson Publishing Company, which has been absorbed by the new organization. Professional offices have been opened in the Heintzman Building.

The Calgary *Albertan* has put in a new Goss Acme press. This is the fourth press used for publishing the *Albertan*. The first was a Whafdale press, hand fed, which printed four sheets of an eight-page paper, at the rate of about 500 an hour. This paper after doing fairly good service for three or four years was replaced by a Miehle, a very excellent press of its kind. The *Albertan* outgrew this press in a few weeks. The *Albertan* purchased the Goss perfecting press, which it has just discarded, in March, 1906. It was a serious venture, for these presses cost an amount of money, and the cost of operation is much greater than the smaller presses. At the present time there are six such presses in this Province alone.

THE PERSONAL SIDE OF IT

 We'd Like To Get Items For
These Columns

British Columbia

Will A. Elletson, jr., has been added to the managerial staff of the *Herald*, Cranbrook, as assistant manager.

Owing to W. A. Elletson having to devote some of his time to his new paper, the *Herald*, Cranbrook, he has secured Thos. H. Fawcus as assistant editor of the *Miner*, Rossland.

Jas. Ellis of the *Herald*, Merritt, who was East for the Press Association meeting in November, spent a month renewing old acquaintances in Middlesex and other Ontario haunts.

T. A. Love, of the *Gazette*, Grand Forks, as a visitor in Vancouver at the end of December, accompanying Mrs. Love and family that far on their trip to California, to spend the winter with her parents.

The Kaslo *Kootenaian* is twenty-five years old this month, and Editor Grier claims it is the oldest paper published continuously in the Kootenay. In the boundary country Gus. Evans of the *Sun*, Grand Forks, is claiming similar honors for himself.

R. T. Lowery of the *Ledge*, Greenwood, is again wintering in California. Being leap year the Colonel, with commendable foresight, advises the ladies that if any of them wish to propose they will have to do it by mail for the present.

Commencing the first of the year the *Daily News*, Nelson, advanced its subscription price on city delivered papers a matter of $1.50 a year. At outside points the rate is still $5 per annum. The *News* is now a member of the Audit Bureau of Circulation.

The No. 19 linotype at the *Kootenaian* office, Kaslo, has been purchased by the *Daily News*, Nelson, and H. W. Power, former *Kootenaian* editor, was at Kaslo last month, helping the *News* machinist knock down and move the machine to Nelson. With the advent of the machine the *News* has quit hand-setting its heads.

About six years ago a former owner of the *Review*, Revelstoke, had a circulation contest during which quite a number paid subscriptions a matter of ten years in advance. The new ownership of the *Review* have just discontinued all these, the high price of newsprint being responsible for their disclaiming further liability in the matter.

Moose Jaw *News*:—Farmer Hines, of Wales, has determined to branch out into new lines. In the first place he has determined to enter the ranks of newspaper proprietors, having purchased the Liberty *Press*, of which he is now sole owner, and which will produce the first number under his editorship immediately. The special feature of its editorial columns will be the advocacy of the sale of wines and beers in the Dominion. Mr. Hines has also purchased the Liberty hotel and he will take over the establishment as from January 1.

Chester E. Moffet, who was on the advertising staff of the Saskatoon *Daily Star* for fourteen months, has transferred his services to the Saskatoon *Morning Phoenix*. It will be recalled that Mr. Moffet was the first salesman to travel in Western

On Sunday, Jan. 4, the diamond wedding was celebrated of Mr. and Mrs. Mundy, Oshawa. Mr. Mundy has for years been one of the best known figures in weekly journalism in Canada, and congratulations have been literally showered upon him on the occasion of his 60th year of wedded life. Mr. Mundy is 83 years of age, and his wife is 80. Both are blessed with an unusual degree of good health. Mr. Mundy, although relieved now from his duties at the *Reformer* office, still takes an interest in the business, and is down at the place of publication almost every day.

The day was made the occasion for several presentations. C. M. Mundy, on behalf of the family, presented his father with a handsome gold-headed cane, and Mrs. Gumpricht, on behalf of the other members, presenting her mother with a beautiful gold watch chain. Mr. and Mrs. Mundy responded in well-chosen words, and to equal the kindness shown by the children, Mr. Mundy presented each of them with a handsome cheque. Mr. Mundy purchased the *Reformer* on July 1, 1878, from Messrs. Samuel Luke and J. S. Larke, the publications then being a little more than seven years old. From 1878, Mr. Mundy piloted the fortunes of this journal through the various vicissitudes of newspaper life, retiring from the active editorship on April 1st, 1910, when the paper was sold to the Reformer Printing and Publishing Company, Limited,

MR. AND MRS. EDWARD MUNDY

of which Mr. Mundy became President, which position he still holds. But Mr. Mundy's newspaper career extends to days before the existence of the *Reformer* was thought of. He served his apprenticeship in the office of the *Globe*, the *Leader*, the *Colonist*, and the *Echo*, all of Toronto, before moving to Prince Albert, Ontario, where he edited the Ontario *Observer*. A few years after he started the publication of the Ontario *Advocate* in Uxbridge. This paper continued for several years under the auspices of the late Thomas Paxton, and others. He removed the printing plant to Port Perry and conducted the Port Perry *Standard*. In 1878 the Ontario *Reformer* was purchased and for some time he conducted both papers. In 1889, he disposed of his interests in the *Standard* to his son, Mr. E. J. Mundy, and moved his family to Oshawa, where he has since resided.

Mr. Munday has always taken an active interest in publishing circles outside the confines of his own business, and in all matters that had to do with the advancement of his community.

Members of the family present at the diamond wedding were: Mrs. Jessie Gumpricht, Oshawa; Mrs. E. L. Cull, Orillia; Mrs. G. R. Weir, Denver, Col.; Mrs. Chas. Drew, Ardock, North Dakota, and Chas. M. Mundy, business manager of the Ontario *Reformer*, Oshawa. The absentee from the family circle was Mr. E. J. Mundy, of Pueblo, Col.

Canada by aeroplane. Last May he accompanied pilot Stanley McClelland to Rosetown, where he was given several orders by local merchants. The flight was made in the interests of the A. G. Low Company, hardware specialists, Saskatoon. The trip was made to Rosetown in 50 minutes and copies of the *Phoenix* were distributed in the town en route.

A number of changes have occurred in the editorial staff of the Regina *Daily Post* in the past few months. As now constituted it includes Lieut. J. W. Fairley, who was with the *Province* before the war, as city editor; Lieut. C. B. Pyper, who served almost five years with the Imperial army, and who was an editorial writer for the *Province* before the war, as telegraph editor; I. D. Moyer, also a returned man, as sporting editor; Mrs. E. L. Storer, whose father was a pioneer publisher at Battleford, edits the woman's page; Hamilton Butler, formerly of New York *Herald*; Fred O'Malley, formerly of Ottawa *Journal*, and J. Arthur Gibson, a returned man who before the was was on the *Province* and the Saskatoon *Phoenix*, are reporters. W. L. McTavish, assistant publisher, is in charge of the editorial end.

Alberta

Thomas B. Malcolm has started the publication of the *Gazette* at Verwood, Alberta.

A new scale is reported from Lethbridge—Newspaper, book and job (day)—Handmen, operators, $40. Eight hours. (Night)—Handmen, operators, $42. Seven and one-half hours. The contract covers a period of one year—October 1· 1919 to October 1, 1920. Increase—Newspaper, book and job, $10.

Fred J. Slight, for three years. employed with the Camrose *Canadian*, and Miss Ila Henry, employed for three years with the *Canadian*, and for the past two years assistant editor, were married in Camrose on Christmas Day, leaving on December 26th for their home in Erskine, where Mr. Slight is now proprietor of the Erskine *Review*. Mr. Slight enlisted in January, 1915, won the Military Medal, and returned to Canada in May,

Mr. Will D. Mackay, who before going overseas, where he served with the 29th (Vancouver) Battalion, was publisher of the *News* at Alderson, Alta., has lately taken a lease of the Provost *News* from the owners, the Provost Publishing Co., Ltd. Associated with Mr. Mackay is another returned man, Jno. R. McLauchlan, M.M. In fact, the whole staff of the *News* to date were in khaki during the late war, Mr. Frank J. Schumacher being the other ex-soldier not heretofore mentioned. The *News*, ever since its establishment in 1917, has enjoyed a very pleasant prosperity and the new management hopes to carry on, and possibly add a few wrinkles of their own in the future.

Secretary Bellamy, of No. 451, Medicine Hat, writes as follows in a letter dated Dec. 10, to the *I.T.U. Journal*:—"Scale has not yet been signed, but agreement has been reached; Minimum, $37.50 per week of forty-eight hours, with same wage for forty-four hours in four months of summer; matter of payment for holidays will be taken up at a provincial conference of employers and employees at Calgary; night work, $39.50, forty-two hours; machinist-operators, 50 cents per machine per day extra; apprentices to receive $12 to start, with gradual raise every six months; foremen to receive at least $6 per week over minimum."

Saskatchewan

Gerald T. Humphrey has purchased the Nokomis *Times* newspaper business and took possession on Jan. 1. This newspaper has been owned and published for the last nine years by J. A. McGowan. The new home of the Nokomis *Times* was erected in 1918 and just recently a newspaper press, new cabinet and other equipment were installed. The new proprietor, has ten years' newspaper experience and was in France during four years of the war.

W. F. Herman, proprietor of the Regina *Post*, Saskatoon *Star*, and *Border Cities Star* (Windsor, Ontario), was bereaved by the death at Victoria, B.C., of his only daughter, Ruth Knox Herman, aged 22. Mrs. Herman and Miss Ruth had gone to Victoria to spend the winter. Mr. Herman has been with them during his daughter's illness which extended over several weeks. Pneumonia was the cause of death.

Members of the executive of the Saskatchewan branch of the Canadian Press Association, met at Regina and decided that the annual convention and short course in Journalism should be held at the University of Saskatchewan on Thursday, Friday and Saturday, May 27 to 29, inclusive. It is proposed this year to carry out the plans provided for last year in every way and to make the three-day course of real interest and benefit to the publishers of the province. In addition to several well-known Saskatchewan newspaper men who will be on the program, some publisher of national or. even international prominence will be secured to give an address at the convention

and short course. A program committee was appointed and ιrther announcements will be made later regarding the program. Those present at the meeting, included C. R. McIntosh, North Battleford *News*, president; S. N. Wynn, Yorkton *Enterprise*, secretary; Charles Hynds, Lumsden *News-Record;* Hon. S. J. Latta, Govan *Prairie News*, and W. F. Kerr, the Regina *Leader*.

Ontario

Lieut. J. Vernon McKenzie, associate editor of *MacLean's Magazine*, has been appointed Canadian Trade Commissioner at Glasgow, for which point he will leave after making a study of business and export conditions in Canada.

McKen-  zie has had a wide and varied experience in the world of newspapers, and when we say wide and varied we mean exactly what we say. In fact, McKenzie confided to the writer one day that his score card read: "Hired 23, Fired 7, Stayed Fired 1.

Mr. McKenzie's newspaper spark was flamed in 1904, when the Pickering *News* published a classic from his pen that ran thusly: "The following are the new scholars at Pickering College this year . . . . ."

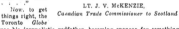

LT. J. V. McKENZIE, *Canadian Trade Commissioner to Scotland*

Now, to get things right, the Toronto *Globe* was his journalistic godfather, becoming sponsor for something he got across on the" juvenile page in 1898.

McKenzie might easily have fallen into a good medical practice from his father, but the newspaper game and $6 per week were stronger drawing cards, and he made his kick-off in 'Frisco in 1904, doing police for the *Post*. If there be any records left they will show that McKenzie gouged that paper for $6 per week for nine months. Other records — if the city editor ever penned any — will show that McKenzie was likewise fired — canned — discharged — relieved of his duties — or whatever you care to call it — nine times in nine months. At one time he remained fired for a week, but a spell of smallpox, typhoid, fever and ague hitting the office, the staff was so reduced that the good health of the fired cub was his greatest asset. He demonstrated that he could work on the paper and not get sick. When he jumped to the 'Frisco *News* to do waterfront for $17 per week he scratched Crœsus off his speaking list.

A mixture of academic and newspaper education followed from 1905 to 1909. 'Varsity and the Toronto *Star* and *News* figured largely. Among other things, McKenzie was helping "Bill" Scanlon (killed at Vimy) to do the Kinrade case. The years of 1909-10 were Westerns, when the now Trade Commissioner was on the Seattle *Times*, Tacoma *Tribune*, Spokane *Press*. Coming back to Canada, McKenzie admits that he stuck to the Lethbridge *News* six months or so, until he anchored the paper for a libel suit, owing to the fact that he said the local hangman, conscience-stricken, spent his blood-money on champagne to drown his sorrow — whereas the headsman was a man whose foot had never pounded the brass rail, and whose fingers had never reached across the mahogany toward the free lunch.

Charlie Hayden on the Calgary *News-Telegram* took him on, and in 1911 McKenzie was working on the Toronto *Star* trying to put reciprocity across. Whether McKenzie had anything to do with bringing in the famous Buffalo bologna we don't know. It may be that here he got his first desire to tackle import or export matters. The next mixture of school and paper over, took him at Boston and Ottawa, intermittently, Boston at Harvard and the *Journal* at Ottawa. McKenzie and W. B. Meldrum organized a European trip in here. Went over on a cattle boat and came back on a freighter; net cost going $5.50, returning 60c; amount on hand on landing in Montreal, 24 cents. The *Herald* office was still intact and "Bill" Scanlon was interviewed to the extent of $10, which he borrowed from the cashier. A hard-luck sob-story written on his experiences caused the city editor to advance transportation home for fear of a series.

Montreal *Star* for eight months; with Main Johnson for N. W. Rowell in the 1914 election; a short stay in Alaska and also a short hunt for stories in Chihuahua, Mexico, in 1905, as well as odd times on the Winnipeg *Telegram*, 1907 and 1908, end the list.

Lieut. McKenzie enlisted in 1915 — went overseas and every-one said he was too old and too heavy — 30 and 215 — to fly. So being too old and too heavy for flying, he proceeded to fly. Spent considerable time riding around in a Handley-Page bomber. Got lost in a fog one night after being seven hours up. Crashed in behind American lines. Pilot was killed, but Lieut. McKenzie escaped with a crushed leg.

Returning to Canada, Lieut. McKenzie joined *MacLean's* as associate editor of *MacLean's Magazine*. Shortly after this he led into existence No. 15 of the MacLean group, *Canadian Motor, Tractor and Implement Trade Journal*, lovingly known around the premises as Mac's "M. T. I." At other times the paper serves to distinguish the man, and he goes here as "M. T. I. McKenzie." Said paper was a success right from the start, and it won its place in short order, and gave the editor a great chance to come into close contact with the industrial field in Canada.

J. J. Hunter, Mayor of Kincardine, is the way it reads at pres-ent, and they do tell that the publisher of the Kincardine *Re-porter* won out against one of the best known citizens of the place by a majority of 61. Mr. Hunter has been a good booster for his town, and a hard worker for every-thing that comes along in the way of public or national work. He has never been a community slacker. In fact the only poor piece of news that has drifted in to PRINT-ER & PUBLISHER from that corner of Bruce during the past few months was a thrilling episode in which the Mayor-pub-lisher played the lead-ing role and ran his

J. J. HUNTER
Mayor of Kincardine.

garage into the front end of his car, with results similar to the page that gets shoved off the stone with the quoins sleeping at the switch.

The Strathroy *Despatch* published no paper Christmas week. The Uxbridge *Journal* announces an increase in advertis-ing rates.

The annual review number of *Canadian Machinery* has come out, and this year grew to 446 pages.

W. A. McIntyre, formerly city editor of the St. Thomas *Journal*, has been elected an alderman of St. Thomas.

Miss Foley, who is a sister of the editor and proprietor of the Orangeville *Sun*, was elected by acclamation to the municipal council.

Thomas E. Walsh, formerly advertising manager of the London *Advertiser*, has opened an advertising agency at Windsor.

Claude Sanagan, formerly of the Toronto *Globe* editorial staff, has been appointed advertising manager of the Willys-Overland Co., Toronto.

Sixty-four pages is the mark put up by the Kingston *Whig* in its Christmas number. The reading matter covered a wide range. The advertising patronage was liberal.

Acton *Free Press*:—Albert Laing, formerly of Acton, is now editor of the Vermont *Issue*, the representative of the Vermont Anti-Saloon League. It is published at Burlington, Vermont,

and has for its motto now "A Dry World in 1930." Its earlier motto was "A Dry America in 1920."

The Toronto *Star* presented each of its employees with an ex-tra pay Christmas week. If there had been overtime in the mechanical department, the whole thing was doubled.

According to reports, the newly-organized Newswriters' Union in London is making some progress and expects to have an agreement in shape to present to the employers shortly.

Ross Munro, news editor of the *Globe*, is in New York and other American centres, in connection with news services and features for the *Globe*.

F. M. Chapman, editor of *Farmers' Magazine*, Toronto, is delivering a course of addresses on Journalism at the Agricul-tural College in Guelph this season.

Miss Isabel C. Armstrong has joined the staff of the To-ronto *Star*. She was formerly on the editorial staff of the London *Advertiser*, doing many large assignments, generally of an interest to women.

The idea of Christmas greetings from merchants was worked for three pages of business in the *Border Cities Star* the day be-fore Christmas. The advts. were well illustrated with timely cuts.

Dundalk *Herald*:—W. H. Glendinning, who recently sold the Morden (Man.) *Times*, arrived in town Tuesday from the West on a visit. He has purchased the Parry Sound *Canadian*, to get possession 1st January.

James S. Carlton, publisher of the Creemore *Star*, died on January fifth after a severe illness. Mr. Carlton learned his trade in the office he afterward owned, having purchased it from the late A. H. Watson.

Charles Clarke, who has been the advertising manager of the *Christian Guardian* for the last twelve months, has resigned his position to become the representative of the Columbia Graphophone Company in the West.

The death took place of Charles R. Watson, at the Sydenham Military Hospital, Kingston. He was formerly manager of the Madoc *Review*, owned by his father, M. A. R. Watson. The father's health is also in a very poor condition.

The Toronto *Globe's* annual survey number was well done this year. M. O. Hammond did a good many things before he became a financial editor, but he has demonstrated clearly dur-ing the past year that a good newspaper man can do anything.

Lucan *Sun*:—Editor W. Bryant of the Thedford *Tribune* an-nounced in his last edition that he will accept subscriptions to the *Tribune* for six months only. The regrettable fact is that Mr. Bryant is not enjoying good health and he may have to re-tire from newspaper life.

The Record-News Press of Smith's Falls, Limited, has re-ceived a provincial charter with a capitalization of $40,000. The incorporators are: George F. McKimm, Harry Sutton, Mrs. Annie Lavinia Sutton, Mrs. Helen Frost McKimm and Charles Harwood McKimm, all of Smiths Falls.

The industrial expansion edition of the *Border Cities Star*, 40 pages, appeared on December 31. The principal features were centered around local industries and opportunities. Advertising patronage from factories and real estate firms was generous, and well displayed.

The Druggists' Weekly is the name of the sixteenth paper to be issued by the Maclean Publishing Co., University Avenue, To-ronto. It made its appearance at the first of the year and will come out weekly. It caters to the business and interests of the retail druggist.

Bram. Thompson, of the Irish and Saskatchewan Bar, will shortly assume the editorship of the *Canadian Law Times*, ac-cording to an announcement in that journal. He will succeed A. T. Hunter. Mr. Thompson is known in legal circles for his writings on "Parliamentary Divorce in Canada."

Three members of the staff of the Ottawa *Journal* were the recipients of cheques for $1,500 each at Christmas time. Editor-ial, business and mechanical departments were included in the big honors. Other members of the staff were also remem-bered by bonuses.

The Toronto *Telegram* gave each of the members of its staff—all departments—an amount equal to their week's pay the ghost-walk before Christmas. One report has it that the *Tele-gram* used to give turkeys, but this year not being able to pur-chase turkeys, they took the cheaper method of giving a week's wages.

E. Roy Sayles has taken over the work of looking after the management of the Canadian Weekly Publishers. For the pres-ent the office adjoining the premises used by the daily papers is being used. Mr. Sayles is still retaining his paper in Port Elgin, preferring to see what the new field looks like before burning the bridge to Bruce.

The new year edition of the Halifax *Chronicle* was 56 pages this year and a great deal of attention was paid to the resources and development of the Maritime Provinces. Advertising patronage was particularly good, a casual summing up placing the amount carried in this issue at about 275 columns.

Dave Johnson, foreman on the London *Morning Free Press* for a number of years, has gone as make-up man to the *Border Cities Star.* He was given a pipe and pouch by the chapel before leaving. Jack McLean, who held the position some years ago, is said to be billed for the *Free Press* post.

Renfrew *Mercury*: Among Ontario's new mayors will be found Dan A. Jones, editor of the *Pembroke Observer*, and J. J. Hunter, editor of the Kincardine *Reporter*. Both are progressive newspapermen and should make splendid presiding officers for their respective towns.

The Port Arthur *News-Chronicle*, on the Saturday before Christmas, brought out a 34-page number. A good deal of attention was given to letters of little folks to Santa Claus, the little writers being residents of the city, giving a local appeal to the feature. Advertising patronage was good for some 135 columns.

The Christmas tree given by Col. Maclean to the children of the families of the staff took place the Saturday before Christmas. Some 160 children were remembered and about 500 were in attendance. There was a Punch and Judy show, ice cream booths, and all other forms of entertainment for the children, as well as other features for the parents.

The management of the London *Free Press* distributed among their employees, numbering upwards of 150, a Christmas box in the form of a full week's pay. For years it had been the custom of the firm to distribute turkeys, but this year they materially increased the value of the gift individually, even taking into account the advanced value of the bird of the season.

The *Sun-Times* of Owen Sound announces that Mr. S. H. Pearce has been appointed editor in charge of the news and editorial pages of the paper. Mr. Pearce has been associated with the paper for some years. Mr. Howard Fleming will now devote his whole time to the business end of the paper.

Mr. Cowan, new editor of the Niagara Falls *Review*, has received news that his youngest brother, Major William Cowan, had been killed in action December 31, last year. Major Cowan, who was only 19 years of age, enlisted in the British Army in 1917, when only 16 years of age, and gained a commission the following year.

Captain Fred Hubbs, formerly editor of the Hastings *Star*, has returned home. He enlisted with the 4th C. M. R., was wounded, taken prisoner and held by the Germans for two years. Later upon being released he returned to Canada and re-enlisted for service after spending several months on duty in that country, having given over five years to military service.

Financial editors in Toronto have now permission to go on the floor of the Toronto Stock Exchange, a privilege extended in very few centres. It gives them a good chance to see all the brokers, the only drawback being that very often it is not convenient for the brokers to spend much time with the financial scribes.

The Drayton *Advocate* has undergone a change of ownership. For the past thirty years it has been published by Mr. Iabez Coram, who previous to going to Drayton published a paper in Fergus. Mr. Coram has sold his residence, office and entire printing plant to Mr. J. B. Garbutt, who has been foreman in the office for nearly nineteen years.

Alderman R. J. Moore, formerly proprietor of the Fenelon Falls *Star*, and later manager of the Lindsay *Free Press*, was elected deputy mayor of Saskatoon by the city council. Besides being deputy mayor, Alderman Moore is a member of the legislation and by-laws committee, secondary in importance to the finance committee, and is one of the representatives of the city council on the Board of Trade.

Arthur Baxter has left for London, England, where he will take a position as editorial writer on Lord Beaverbrook's paper, the *Daily Express.* During last year *Chamers's Journal* featured his short stories a number of times, and these will shortly be published in book form entitled: "The Blower of Bubbles." His first novel, "The Part Men Play," is now completed, and after publication in *MacLean's Magazine* and *Chambers's Journal* will be published in book form. Mr. Baxter hopes to return to Canada next winter to work on a second novel.

Frank Levick, who has been the accountant of the Woodstock *Sentinel-Review* for several years, has accepted a position with the business department of the Detroit *News* and has left, together with his wife and daughter, to take up his residence in the American city. The staff of the *Sentinel-Review* presented him with a handsome leather travelling kit. The presentation was made by Stanley Ross and Spenser Hunter, advertising manager. Mr. Levick is succeeded on the staff of the *Sentinel-Review* by A. Thomson of Hamilton, who was formerly on the staff of the Regina *Leader*.

GLOBE advertising rates are the highest in Canada, yet they are lower, per thousand of circulation, than those of similar dailies in the United States.

There are twenty-one morning papers in the United States with circulations between 50,000 and 150,000 and they have an average rate per thousand of circulation, of .24 cents per agate line. The Globe's rate is .172 cents per agate line.

If The Globe rates were on a par with the rates of these American papers, its 5,000 line rate would be 20¾c a line, instead of 15 cents.

The Globe

"Canada's National Newspaper"

TORONTO

Windsor scale is now:—Newspaper, book and job (day)—Handmen, operators, $38. (Night)—Handmen, operators, $41. Eight hours, day or night. The contract covers a period of one year—January 1, 1920, to December 31, 1920. Increase—Newspaper, book and job (day)—January 1, 1920, Handmen, $10; operators, $8. May 1, 1920, $1. (Night)—January 1, 1920, Handmen, $11; operators, $8. May 1, 1920, $1.

Several well-known advertising men attended the annual staff conference of the McConnell & Fergusson Advertising Agency, The representatives included Messrs. D. C. Coutts, manager of the Winnipeg office, and Lionel Benison, manager of the Montreal office. Mr. Walter E. Gunn, the newly-appointed manager for the Toronto office of the firm, was presented to his new colleagues by Mr. J. E. McConnell and Mr. M. M. Fergusson.

W. S. Johnston, president of the firm of W. S. Johnston & Co., Ltd., printers and publishers, 108 Adelaide St., West, Toronto, who is leaving for an extended tour of the West Indies and South America, was presented by the employees with a magnificent set of marine glasses. In making the presentation Mr. Barry spoke of the cordial feeling that had always characterized Mr. Johnston's relations with his employees and hoped that the trip would be a safe and pleasant one.

Walter J. Blackburn, president and general manager of the London Free Press Publishing Co., died at his home, Richmond street, following an illness that had become acute in the last few weeks. Mr. Blackburn had devoted his life to the interests of the newspaper with which his family name has been connected since its inception. He was the eldest son of the late Josiah Blackburn, who founded the daily issue of the London *Free Press* in 1855. He was second vice-president of the Canadian Press, Limited, upon the formation of that organization to take over the Associated Press in Canada.

Hon. W. L. Mackenzie King, leader of the Opposition, issued the following statement: The position of editor of the political literature of the National Liberal Organization Committee has been accepted by Mr. John Lewis, of the Toronto *Daily Star.* Mr. Lewis has had an experience of some thirty years as editorial writer on the Toronto *Globe*, the *Star*, and other journals. He is the author of the biography of George Brown, in the Makers of Canada series, and also of the political history of Canada since Confederation, in the work known as "Canada and Its Provinces."

Bradford *Witness*—When Mr. Wm. McDonald, member for North Bruce and editor of the Chesley *Enterprise*, was defeated in the October election the *Witness* felt sorry because he was a man whose absence from Parliament was going to be a distinct loss to the province. We learn now that the U.F.O., whose opponent he was in the election, have appointed him to an office in the Government and he has sold out his newspaper to take charge. This is proof positive that the U.F.O. are using no "red tape" but are picking out the men of worth.

Frank Rolph, dean of Canadian lithographers, was the guest of honor at a dinner in the National Club, Toronto, given by the directors of Rolph, Clark, Stone, Ltd., to mark the seventy-fifth anniversary of his birthday and his sixtieth year in business. In addition to the directors of the lithographing company a number of Mr. Rolph's old friends and business associates were present, and in the after-dinner speeches and toasts paid their tributes to the long and honorable business record of the man who blazed the trail and opened the way for the greater development of the lithographing industry in Canada.

The death occurred quite suddenly at the General Hospital at Guelph, of Herbert William Philp, son of Prof. and Mrs. William Philp, 38 Northumberland Street. Until two weeks ago he had been working on the editorial staff of the *Mercury.* He was in his thirty-first year. He worked for some time on the Guelph *Herald,* later taking a position as sub-editor on the Stratford *Herald.* At the outbreak of the war he was among the first to answer the call, enlisting August 12, 1914, with the original First Contingent. He spent forty-three months in France with the 8th Battalion of Winnipeg, known as the "Little Black Devils." He was a member of the Guelph Musical Society's band and the G.W.V.A.

The will of the late William J. Douglas, general manager of the Mail Printing Company, Toronto, filed for probate deals with an estate of the total value of $192,847, made up as follows: Real estate, $1,271; stocks, $172,108; life insurance and cash on hand, $17,968, and sundries, $1,500. The late Mr. Douglas bequeathed the income from the estate to his widow for life. After the death of Mrs. Douglas the estate will be divided equally among the three sons, William, James S., and Howard R. Douglas, subject to the following legacies: Mrs. Adams, $400; and Mrs. J. E. Riordon, Mrs. M. B. Sherwin and Mrs. C. E. Townsend, $1,500 each.

In the Non-Jury court at Osgoode Hall, Toronto, Mr. Justice Logie gave judgment for the *Industrial Press,* represented by J. M. Ferguson, against *Jack Canuck* for $2,414.58, balance of account for printing, trimming and binding the weekly paper. The *Industrial Press* took the contract for five years from 1915, and last September, when pressed for payment, the *Jack Canuck* launched an action to recover $8,000 damages from the *Industrial Press,* alleging that that firm had failed to properly "trim" the publication. That action is now dismissed.

John Lewis has quit daily newspaper work after forty years' service. He is one of the veterans of Canadian journalism and in the course of his brilliant career has covered every assignment in the business from a revival meeting to the diamond jubilee of Queen Victoria. He has seen Toronto grow from a small city served by horse cars to a bustling metropolis of half a million people. For the past fourteen years Mr. Lewis has been one of the editors of the Toronto *Daily Star.* He is the author of the "Life of George Brown," and also of the political history of Canada since Confederation in the work known as "Canada and Its Provinces." He severs his long connection with daily journalism to accept the position of editor of the political literature of the National Liberal Organization Committee at Ottawa.

A sad ending came to the young life of Walter Purdy, who was about out of his apprenticeship with the MacLean Publishing Co., Toronto. No authentic account is available of his demise, but it is surmised that he undertook to heat his room during the night by means of a gas stove, from which he was asphyxiated. The body was identified at the morgue by one of the members of the MacLean composing room, the company sending with him a request that the remains be turned over to them for burial. However, this had been attended to by the Grand Army shortly before. Walter Purdy came from Chesley, and had been in the Maclean composing room for about a year after returning from overseas. He was a young man of good habits, quiet and industrious.

Shortly before 11 o'clock on January 18, the residence of L. G. Morgan at Port Dover was discovered to be on fire. Owing to the dense volume of smoke the fire was hard to locate, but was at last found to be in Mr. Morgan's bedroom, where there was an oil stove, which is supposed to have been the cause of the fire. After the flames were subdued somewhat Mr. Morgan's body was found badly burned, and his remains were removed to another room in the house. Meanwhile his

two sisters had been rescued with difficulty. Mr. Morgan began his career as a public school teacher in Shand's school, 55 years ago. Later he taught in the Port Dover high school. He had been editor and proprietor of *The Maple Leaf* for the past 38 years, retiring from active life last September. It was generally conceded that Mr. Morgan was one of the best masters of English in Canada. In addition to the sisters mentioned, one brother, Cosbie, survives. Deceased was in his seventy-third year. He was an Anglican, and a Mason.

The death took place in Parkhill on January 18 of William Dawson, for many years publisher of the *Gazette-Review.* Mr. Dawson's health had been poorly for some time. He was in his sixty-second year. On the death of Malcolm McKinnon, about twelve years ago, Mr. Dawson purchased the Parkhill paper. Shortly after that he took over the Parkhill *Post,* which was then owned by W. E. Clothier, who also published the Ailsa Craig *Banner.* Mr. Dawson, prior to going into the publishing business, had taught school, conducted a general insurance business and looked after other interests. He was a life-long resident of that section of the country. His wife, who was a daughter of the late Mr. Cameron, formerly editor of the Hamilton *Spectator,* has always been of great assistance to her husband in turning out the paper. A grown-up family survive.

Around the holiday season, E. Roy Shantz, manager of the Merchants Printing Company, Kitchener, was agreeably surprised by the staff, who presented him with a gold signet ring. The foreman was spokesman and voiced the sentiments of all the employees by saying that, owing to increased business, Mr. Shantz had made lately large purchases in machinery and equipment. This was all very well, but better yet was it to know that he had the entire good-will of the employees of the Merchants Printing Company, who knew by past experience that his welfare was theirs as well, and assured him of their wholehearted support in the future. Mr. Shantz thanked the staff in a few words and told them that the sentiment they had expressed would assist him greatly toward the goal he wished ultimately to reach.

The death occurred very unexpectedly at Vancouver on Tuesday, of Eric Ross Goulding. While having his dinner in a restaurant he suddenly collapsed and died a few minutes later. Mr. Goulding was forty years of age and first became known in newspaper circles through his work for the London, Ont. *Advertiser.* He wrote a number of special articles and considerable poetry. When the war started he enlisted with the 7th Canadian Mounted Rifles, but later transferred to the 33rd Battalion and went overseas with that unit. At the battle of Courcellette in 1916 he was terribly wounded by being caught in a barrage fire. He lost one eye, his nose and portions of his chin and forehead. It is believed that his sudden death is a direct result of the injuries he sustained. Notwithstanding that at times he suffered most intensely from the after effects of his injuries, Mr. Goulding was always one of those "cheery Englishmen" that it was a real pleasure to know. For a time after returning from overseas he worked on the London *Advertiser,* later going to Windsor on the old Windsor *Record.* From there he went to the coast and wrote special articles for both the Vancouver *Province* and the Victoria *Colonist.* There is an element of pathos in his death in that his passing marks the last of a family of five, all of whom gave their lives in the war. Two brothers went from India and two sisters who went as nurses made the supreme sacrifice.

Quebec

The *McGill News,* is the name of a new publication of the McGill University Graduates' Society. Seven thousand copies are at present being dispersed through the mails, a copy going to every living graduate of the university as far as such a course has been humanly possible.

H. L. D'Hellencourt, who for a number of years has been editor-in-chief of *Le Soleil,* the official Liberal organ in Quebec, was tendered a reception by Hon. J. N. Francoeur, Speaker of the Legislative Assembly. The members of the press gallery, several members of the House, intimate friends of Mr. D'Hellencourt, and Mr. C. F. Delage, superintendent of public instruction, were the guests. Mr. D'Hellencourt is returning to France, his country, after having spent some 13 years in Canadian journalism.

Montreal Typographical Union, No. 176, did honor to its soldier members with a complimentary banquet at the St. Lawrence Hall. Over two hundred covers were laid and an excellent menu and an extensive musical programme made for a thoroughly enjoyable evening. The guests of honor were Lt.-Col. Clarke-Kennedy, V.C., and Mr. E. F. Slack, managing director of the *Gazette.* Mr. Thomas Black, president of M. T. U. No. 176, presided. About seventy returned men, in whose honor the banquet was given, were present. A total of ninety-one members of the organization enlisted for active service, and of this number, eighty-one went overseas. Seven journeymen and four apprentices lost their lives in battle and their memory was observed with a silent toast.

Maritime.

D. Richard has joined the writing staff of the St. John *Standard.*

The St. John *Evening Times* has added a four-page comic supplement to its Saturday issue.

The Art Engraving Co. is a new concern which has started business with an extensive plant in Halifax.

Percy Clancy, who has been for years associated with the Imperial Publishing Co. of Halifax, is gone with the Ross Print.

W. A. Creighton, advertising agent for the Canadian National Rys., was in Halifax on publicity business during the early part of December.

T. M. Fraser, who was formerly with the staff of the *Morning Chronicle*, and is now with the Publicity Department, Ottawa, was in Halifax in December.

The United Farmers are planning on the issue of a weekly publication devoted to the interests of their party, with offices and plant in Moncton. First publication is expected soon.

The members of the different printing trades are presenting a demand for increased wages which they ask to become effective early in the New Year. Their request is now being considered.

Wm. Gould, who has recently been appointed secretary of the Canadian Manufacturers' Association, was formerly on the writing staff of the St. John *Telegraph* before going to the Montreal *Star.*

J. B. F. Livesay, manager of the Canadian Press, was in St. John recently on a tour of inspection and for purpose of organization in connection with local and Maritime newspaper services.

Fred T. McGuire, who has been a member on the writing staff of the *Daily Telegraph*, has joined the staff of the *Business Review and Maritime Retailer.* His place has been taken on the *Telegraph* by F. L. Barber.

S. K. Smith, proprietor of the *Business Review and Maritime Retailer*, has started an advertising agency under his own name in addition to his other publication. He was formerly city editor of the *Telegraph.*

George D. Macaulay, a former member of the *Times'* writing staff, was in St. John recently on a holiday visit from New York. He was overseas with a British unit formed in Boston and served with the 8th Royal Scots.

The Typographical Union has asked for a large advance on their scale from the 1st of January, and the employing printers consider the large advance asked for is entirely unjustified, and cannot meet the increase asked for, but they will probably come to some amicable arrangement.

Some of the printers in Halifax are using unfair means to take away hands from other printing offices and offering them wages which scarcely can be earned. The large volume of work being done, the shortage of help, and employing printers not working together is largely responsible for this.

James Drury, of Montreal, representing the International Typographical Union, announced that a new contract and wage agreement had been entered into between the publishers of five daily newspapers in Halifax and ten printing establishments. The minimum day wage is $30 and nights $35. The old scale was $25 and $27.

A new departure in the annals of the printing trades is the bonus system adopted by A. E. Powter, proprietor of Powter's Printery, Montreal, when each of his employees received a handsome bonus on the year's work. Mr. Powter, in the course of his address to the employees, said it was his intention to adopt this system annually to stimulate the efforts of his help, and he trusted it would be as much benefit to them as the annual week's holiday he had given them for the past ten years.

Many friends throughout the newspaper world will hear with interest of the wedding of F. Beverley Owen, editor of the *Pioneer* and the *Island Farmer*, of Summerside, P.E.I., which occurred this week in Boston. His bride was Miss Gladys Bell, to whom he was married in Boston by Rev: Isaac Ward. They passed through St. John on their way to their future home in P. E. Island. The groom is a native of Ottawa, and was at one time a member of the writing staff of the London *Times*. He served in the war as a captain in a Gloucestershire regiment.

Mr. J. Drury of the International Typographical Union of Montreal was in Halifax over Xmas.

The printing business in Halifax is a little slow at the present time, but at the same time there is no printer out of work.

The Richmond Paper Co. of Halifax was completely burnt out on Sunday, the 11th January. The loss was $100,000. A large amount of this was covered by insurance.

Early in January the Ross Print had a small fire in their plant. One time it threatened to be serious, but fortunately they got it under control before it made headway.

It is with considerable satisfaction we have to state that there never has been a strike in Halifax in the job printing plants, as the conferences for readjustment between the employing printers and the Typographical Union have always been satisfactorily settled.

After several friendly conferences the Employing Printers and the Typographical Union have agreed to the following scale for the year: January 1st to April 30th, 8 hours per day. The minimum weekly scale: Operators, machinists and handmen $30.00 (day), $35.00 (night). Machinist-operators $32.00 per week.

Owing to the increase in wages and very material advance in writing and bond papers, printers in the Maritime Provinces will have to raise their prices accordingly, and we sincerely hope that the printer in estimating up his cost will not forget the fact, and figure on the wage list and the old paper scale. Printers who repeatedly figure on work without properly estimating the cost are neither helping themselves nor their employing printers.

The Montreal *Star* has ordered a lockout of all its union reporters and editors to take effect New Year's Day. The lockout is announced in a letter to each member of the staff, signed by C. F. Crandall, managing editor. Mr. Crandall, after recapitulating qualifications and "special aptitude" necessary to make journalists, declares that on account of the duty owed to the public by newspapers, it is impossible to allow the news to be written or edited by men who are allied with any particular section of the community, in this case organized labor. Accordingly he announces no member of the News Writers' Union will be retained on the staff after the end of the year. At the same time he says senior men on the *Star* editorial staff will, commencing the New Year, be "paid at least as much as the mechanical staff."

The *Iron Age* issue of December 18 has the following: "James E. McDonald has been appointed resident editor at Cincinnati of the *Iron Age*, succeeding Mr. Smith. Mr. McDonald comes to this journal with ten years' experience in newspaper work, chiefly at Sydney, Nova Scotia, and five years, mechanical experience in machine shop work, and since the war has been steel inspector for Robert W. Hunt & Co. On leaving the newspaper field he joined the Dominion Bridge Co. at Montreal as a mechanic and became foreman of the shell shop of that company, from which he gained appointment as superintendent of Lymburner Ltd., Montreal, manufacturers of shells there for two years until the armistice was signed. He had supervision of a plant employing over eighteen hundred persons, including tool room, machine shop and electrical departments and had charge of the building of about two hundred machines of various types. For the last nine months he has been most of the time inspecting steel at the works of the Algoma Steel Corporation at Sault Ste. Marie, Ontario."

Presentation to Acton Burrows

As a token of respect and an appreciation of long service to the members of the Canadian Electric Railway Association presented Acton Burrows, Toronto, with a handsome Sheffield server of antique design. For some fifteen years Mr. Burrows has been honorary and acting secretary of the Railway Association, but pressure of other business forced him to resign this position a few months ago. It came to the knowledge of members of the Railway Association that Mr. Burrows was particularly enamored of a fine piece of Old Country plate in the collection of an antique dealer, and it was also whispered that he had counted over his surplus dollars and tens of dollars, always ending the performance with a sigh and an unspoken "not yet." Recently Mr. Burrows was called to the Albany Club, where the railwaymen were in waiting, also the much wanted piece of Sheffield plate. The presentation was made, and it goes down as a matter of local history that it was the first time that Mr. Burrows was so surprised that he could not come back with a speech.

Frank Munsey Buys The New York Herald

New York is about to see the most interesting experiment in newspaper ownership in its history. This is the result of the purchase of the New York Herald by Mr. Frank Munsey, who is also the owner of the Sun. For a newspaper owner to buy a second competing paper and merge it with his own property is an almost everyday occurrence. When Mr. Munsey bought the Sun in 1916 he was already the owner of the New York Press, and he merged the Press in the Sun. That he would sink the powerful individuality of the Sun in the Herald or extinguish the fame of the Herald in the Sun is not to be thought of. For more than a generation the Herald was the best-known abroad of any American newspaper, and it has not wholly lost this earlier distinction. The Sun, on the other hand, has a distinctive genius of its own. Readers who like the Sun methods would not like the Herald methods, and those who have been brought up on the Herald tradition would not read the Sun. The papers are as distinctive as the Globe and The Mail and Empire. So we are likely to see the experiment of two first-class metropolitan newspapers, both owned wholly by one man, in strenuous competition.

MR. MUNSEY'S CAREER

Mr. Munsey is a publishing genius. He began life as a telegraph operator, went to New York as a youth and started the Golden Argosy, a boys' magazine, to which he was a large contributor. He had no capital, no backing, but the venture prospered and continues to-day as the Argosy. Later on he established Munsey's Magazine, for a long time the leading ten-cent American magazine, and at the present time he owns the Railroad Man's Magazine and the All Story monthly. His first venture in the newspaper field was when he bought the Baltimore News, and greatly improved it. Later he became the owner of the New York News, but abandoned it in a few months after vainly trying to make it pay. Shortly afterward the paper went out of existence. Previously he had owned the New York Star, whose name he changed to the Continent, and this he sold as a going concern. Its name was changed to the Advertiser and later on it was merged with the New York American. For a number of years Mr. Munsey owned the Washington Times, the paper whose sale to Arthur Brisbane, of the Hearst papers, financed by a number of German-American brewers, was the subject of a Congressional investigation in the course of the war.

THE FAMOUS HERALD

The New York Herald is one of the most remarkable of American newspapers. The story of its founding and career is a romance. It was established by James Gordon Bennett, an American of Scottish-French descent, eighty-five years ago. In its early issues it was a four-page paper, smaller than a handkerchief, and was written almost entirely by the proprietor. It sold for a cent, but such was Bennett's amazing industry and sense of news that after five years it was netting the proprietor $100,000 a year. Bennett was the greatest of news experts, though he was by no means a great editor, in the sense that Greeley and Dana were great. It was Bennett who made one of the greatest of newspaper discoveries, namely, that people like to read about what they have seen. The idea which he shattered was that if a man saw a fire he felt he knew all about it and would not bother reading about it in the paper next day. It was in reporting a fire that Bennett discovered that the most eager readers of his story were the people who had been eye-witnesses.

THE GREATEST REPORTER

He was the first of the sensationalists. His journalism was intensely personal. He was continually attacking, exposing and insulting. When he was chastised for his articles he faithfully reported the encounters, which must have been painful to him. He had no respect for the editorial page, and was just as well pleased if in the hurry of getting the paper to press the page containing the editorials was left out. The result was that for many years the editorials of the Herald were indescribably feeble. Indeed it is only in the past fifteen years or so that they have been worthy of an important newspaper. But as a newspaper the Herald was great, and even to-day it has the most shipping news of any American paper. The Herald would pay more for news than any of its rivals, and consequently for many years the Herald had more news. The circulation went up, and up went the advertising rates. From first to last Bennett made millions out of the Herald.

FROM FATHER TO SON

His son inherited the paper, and for many years edited it from France by cable. James Gordon Bennett the second had much of his father's genius, but gradually he abandoned personal journalism for the impersonal. He also established the Paris edition of the Herald, a unique and valuable contribution to journalism. He founded a London edition, but it was short lived. The second Bennett rarely visited the United States. He became a Frenchman in all but name. Through the war he and his papers were fiercely pro-Ally. He died in May, 1918, and the chief item in his will, the Herald properties, was left to maintain a home for broken-down newspaper workers. The will did not forbid the sale of the paper, and the money that Mr. Munsey paid for it—several million dollars, it is said—will be used to found and maintain the home.

The "Sold" Prospect

THERE is a better understanding among advertising men on what the word "sold" means. Fred Millis, assistant advertising manager of the Indianapolis News, is against specials, but emphatic on having the advertiser really "sold" on the broad line of knowing that he can get results from his advertising. Mr. Millis' view is this: "He must be placed in a clean, wholesome paper. His story must be told in a straightforward, readable, interesting way. He must not be sold ads. He must be sold advertising. Your salesmen must be big enough to sell him this idea. They must have enough intelligence to teach him how to advertise right."

An advertising man from one of the larger Canadian houses had just succeeded in getting his prospect to sign his name "on the dotted line." He pocketed the contract and sat for a few minutes talking about things in general. Before going the advertiser asked to be allowed "to see that contract for a minute." He no sooner had his hands on it than he tore it into ribbons and threw it in the waste basket.

That brings out the point:—

There is a vast difference between having your prospect sold on sound general lines and inducing him to put his name on the "dotted line."

That "dotted line" stuff has been sinned against until it should be forever cast out. It has been used in correspondence school talk and in other places that should know better.

Don't be content to have any of your advertisers hanging on. Do not leave them at the point where they advertise because their opposition does. Get them SOLD, and more than half your trouble is over.

Midland Angus:—Simcoe and York Publishers' Association have been called to attend a meeting in Barrie to discuss important matters in connection with the publishing business. On account of the rapid advance in the price of papers and other materials used by the publishers, it is believed the meeting will decide upon a considerable increase in present prices. Nearly every week advances are being made upon the price of all classes of material used by the newspaper man, until the business has become one of the most burdensome to carry and many newspapers as a result have been forced out of business. There appears to be no means of getting away from a general advance in the price of job work, and it would appear that it will only be a short time before the weekly newspaper will have to increase its subscription rate to $2.00 a year as well as advance the price of advertising to a considerable extent.

The editor of the Bradford Witness has been appointed fuel controller for his district. Time was when the editor was admitted to be an A1 judge of cordwood, but we thought those days had gone for keeps.

Danger From Foreign Press

New York.—With the conviction of Gust. Alonen and
Carl Paivio, editors of *Loukkataistelu*, a New York Finnish
newspaper, on charges of anarchy, attention of State and
Federal officers was turned to more than 50 other publications in 16 alien languages. Thirty-five of these are now
being published in New York City, one was formerly published here, and is now printed in Chicago, and one is printed in Milan, Italy, and sent here through the mails. It is
known that Attorney-General Palmer has in his possession
complete evidence that each of the publications referred to
has from time to time, since July last, published editorials
and news articles of an anarchistic character; almost every
issue of the publications referred to contained articles ad-
vocating the overthrow of the United States Government.

Where the Extremes Meet

Cornelius Vanderbilt, Jr., son of Brig.-Gen. Cornelius
Vanderbilt, has turned his back upon the Newport season
and gone to work as a "cub" reporter on the New York
Herald. The heir to numerous millions was hired the day
before yesterday at a salary of $25 a week. Young
Vanderbilt obtained the job on his own initiative by a letter
he wrote to the city editor of the *Herald.* For the last two
days his work has been limited to the handling of the
"cheese" assignments that are the lot of the novitiate in
newspaper work. These have not dulled his enthusiasm for
the craft. "I wanted to be a reporter," he explained, "because I have always found newspapermen to be the brightest and most alert people I know. When I was in France
with the 27th Division I noticed that any duty calling for
resource and initiative was nearly always given to a
former newspaper man."

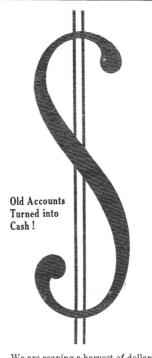

MANTON BROS.

Printing Inks

An unrivalled experience and technical knowledge enable Manton Bros. to produce Printing Inks of the first quality for the latest processes and with the greatest range of colors. We are prepared to supply in any quantity.

Printers' Rollers

If you are to get maximum production from your presses you must have first-class rollers. Manton Bros. make rollers free from pin holes and oil marks and they have that resiliency and spring so necessary to good printing.

Printing Machinery

SELLING AGENTS FOR

THE PREMIER TWO-REVOLUTION PRESS

THE WHITLOCK PONY

THE POTTER ROTARY OFF-SET PRESS

THE POTTER LITHOGRAPH PRESS

THE POTTER ROTARY TIN PRESS

THE STANDARD HIGH-SPEED AUTOMATIC JOB PRESS

Standard High-Speed Automatic Job Press

A Number Recently Sold and Now Running in Canada

One Standard Automatic will do the work of four hand-fed job presses. This new press is a genuine labor-saver, cost-cutter and profit-maker. Can you afford to be without one? Write for full description.

Rebuilt Machinery and Repair Work

We still have a number of rebuilt newspaper and job presses for sale. Let us know your requirements. Expert repair work done on all kinds of printing machinery. Electrical equipment and repairs.

MANTON BROS. - TORONTO

Montreal   Winnipeg   Calgary

Don't Overlook Printer & Publisher Want Ads.

RELIANCE ENGRAVING TORONTO

*E*ngravings

A complete engraving plant fully equipped for intelligent service and the finest production of half-tones and line engravings.

The RELIANCE ENGRAVING Co

CORNER EDWARD ST. AND CENTRE AVE., *Toronto.*
PHONE ADELAIDE 4094.

Who Sells The Line You Are Looking For?

Very likely you can find it in the Buyers' Guide Columns of P. & P.

Another Reminder!

LUSTRE BLACK

The Best Black Ink To-day for Half-Tone Printing

The BLACK that is ALWAYS THE SAME

Shackell, Edwards & Co.
LIMITED
Canadian Factory:
127 Peter Street, Toronto, Ont.

Buyers' Guide

Buyers' Guide

PRINTER AND PUBLISHER

Printer and Publisher Want Ads.

2 cents a Word—10 cents extra for P. & P. box number
Invariably in Advance

INDEX TO ADVERTISERS

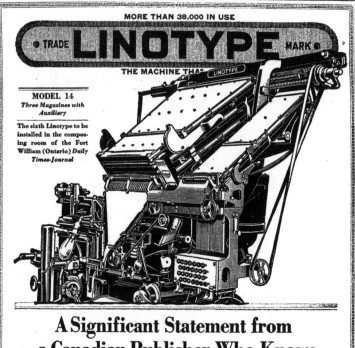

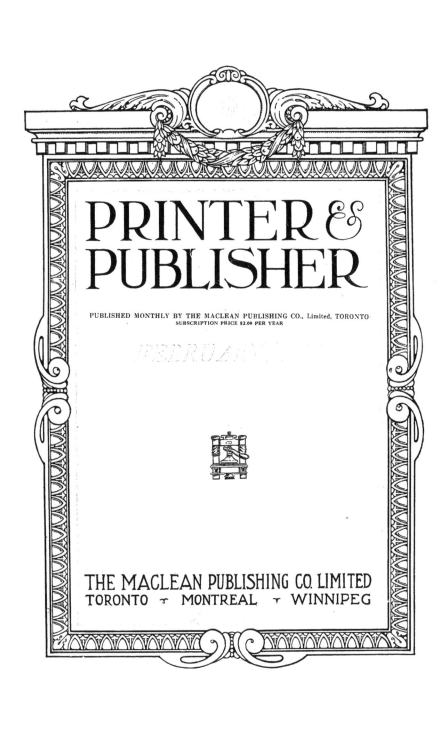

PRINTER & PUBLISHER

PUBLISHED MONTHLY BY THE MACLEAN PUBLISHING CO., Limited, TORONTO

SUBSCRIPTION PRICE $2.00 PER YEAR

THE MACLEAN PUBLISHING CO. LIMITED

TORONTO ⲧ MONTREAL ⲧ WINNIPEG

ART PHOTO BOOK

The Paper Which Stands as a Distinct Credit to Canadian Paper-Making Industry

There is more capital represented in paper (the raw product and the finished article) than in any other industry in Canada. Paper is Canada's big specialty. So it is not unnatural to see a Canadian mill put upon the market a book paper outclassing in *quality* and *value* the book papers of other countries. Such is *Art Photo Book.*

Prominent printers who are using *Art Photo Book* say they like it because of its uniformity of finish, good printing surface, strength, color and rare BULKING qualities.

A notable feature of *Art Photo Book* is its adaptability to color printing — neither curls nor stretches. For half-tone work there is no bookpaper can serve the pressman to better advantage in bringing out the various lights and shades. The finest half-tone screens can be used to perfection.

One of the most valuable services a printer can render to his customer is to recommend to him a paper he can always rely upon — a paper dependable in quality, strength, weight, cleanness, a paper that is moderately priced.

Art Photo Book is just such a paper the printer can unhesitatingly recommend.

Let us send you sheets for a Dummy of your next catalog. Stocked in all regular sizes and weights.

Made in Canada by

CANADA PAPER CO. LIMITED

PAPER MAKERS

TORONTO   MONTREAL   WINDSOR MILLS, P.Q.

Western Agents:
Barkwell Paper Co., Winnipeg, Man.

PRINTER AND PUBLISHER, February, 1920, Vol. 29, No. 2. Published monthly at 143-153 University Ave., Toronto, by the MacLean Publishing Co., Ltd. Yearly subscription price, $2.00. Entered as second-class matter at the Post Office Department at Ottawa, Canada. Also entered as second-class matter July 1, 1912, at the Post Office at Buffalo, N.Y. U.S.A., under Act of March 3rd, 1879.

HAMILTON EQUIPMENT

WOOD AND STEEL

For Nearly Forty Years the Standard in Every Department of the Printing Plant

While material and workmanship are important factors—jealously guarded to keep them on a high plane—of equal or greater importance are the features of time and space saving that are worked into every piece. If you are crowded or you feel or know that your plant is not producing what it should per dollar of pay roll—it will pay you to investigate Hamilton equipment.

Full information sent promptly on request.

The Hamilton Manufacturing Company

Hamilton Equipments are Carried in Stock and Sold by all Prominent Typefounders and Dealers Everywhere.

Main Office and Factories, TWO RIVERS, WIS.　　Eastern Office and Warehouse, RAHWAY, N.J.

CANADIAN SELLING AGENTS

Toronto Type Foundry Co., Limited—Toronto, 70 York Street; Montreal, Beaver Hall Hill. Ern. J. Goodland, Box 177, St. Johns, representative for Newfoundland. Stephenson, Blake & Co., Toronto. American Type Founders Co., 175 McDermot Ave., Winnipeg. George M. Stewart, Montreal. Miller & Richard—Toronto, 7 Jordan St.; Winnipeg, 123 Princess St. Printers Supplies, Ltd., 27 Bedford Row, Halifax, N.S.

A VALUABLE LINE GAUGE, graduated by picas and nonpareils, mailed to every enquiring printer.

Monitor Machinery Cuts the Cost of Production

MONITOR MACHINES deliver more work; lose less time through breakdowns; cost less to operate and maintain; last longer, depreciate less and command a higher trade and resale value than any other machines of their kind.

MONITOR MACHINES are built to endure. Designed right, built from the best material and with the highest grade of workmanship, they can always be depended upon to produce the work most efficiently.

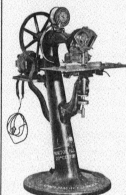

No. 1 Monitor Wire Stitcher

In Use Nearly 100% of the Time

No. 1 MONITOR WIRE STITCHER is in operation a greater number of hours per day than any other size Wire Stitcher because of its adaptability to almost any stitching job.

This protects you against unproductive time and earns you a profit when machines of limited capacity are idle.

THE REASON:

Capacity, 2 sheets—⅞ inch; wire used, No. 30 to 25 round and 20 x 25 flat. Speed, 150 R.P.M.

Buy this machine of general utility! Save on floor space and idle machinery.

Extra Heavy Perforator

Speed and Durability

The MONITOR EXTRA HEAVY PERFORATOR combines these two essentials. Equipped with Feed Gauge and Back Roll Delivery it is possible to make all parallel lines of perforation at one handling of the stock through the machine, thereby eliminating resetting the gauges and many handlings of the stock. The DIE PLATE in the machine is made of hardened tool steel. The STRIPPER is of heavy T bar iron with brass facing, insuring perfect alignment of the pins with the Die Plate without friction on the pins. The PINS are also hardened, but not as hard as the Die Plate. The PINS can readily be replaced at small cost in your own plant.

Sold in Canada by

H. J. LOGAN, 114 Adelaide St. W., TORONTO

Monotype Essential *in* Every Composing Room

The advertisement reproduced herewith speaks volumes and tells the story better than anything that we can say. This ad appeared in *The Pacific Printer* for October, 1919.

Franklin Linotyping Company
A. F. HEUER

Has installed ready for operation a complete, modern, up-to-the-minute

Monotype Plant

Franklin Service is too well known in San Francisco to require any comment, and besides modesty forbids—notwithstanding which fact the response to our efforts in this regard, backed by

Franklin Enterprise, have warranted us in giving to San Francisco a metropolitan composition plant second to none in the West. Because we recognized our shortcomings in the past, we also recognized that only in one way could

Franklin Efficiency be improved. Complete service was the answer, and we place at your disposal a plant that measures up in every way with the trade-composition plants of the big eastern cities. This plant can supply you with a variety of composition that will meet any requirement you may have in tabular, straight, or display matter. To do the work quickly, do it well, and in any face or size you may need—that is our aim in bringing our plant to its present capacity, and while we may be premature in this investment we are confident that our customers will appreciate the improved service, and because of it increase their business—so that ultimately our confidence will prove to have been warranted.

FRANKLIN LINOTYPING COMPANY
A. F. HEUER

509 SANSOME STREET
DOUGLAS 4854
SAN FRANCISCO

*C*OMPOSITION *for* PRINTERS
Monotype : Linotype
Makeup : Lockup

Lanston Monotype Machine Company
PHILADELPHIA

NEW YORK   BOSTON
CHICAGO   TORONTO
Monotype Company of California
SAN FRANCISCO

This advertisement set in Monotype Series No. 137 and Monotype Rule

A Few Facts for the Fair-Minded

ENGRAVINGS have not advanced in selling price during the past few years to the same extent as other products employing equally skilled labor.

Increases in charges have not, in fact, kept pace with increases in production costs.

Schedule "F," for example, is based on labor and other costs as of last summer. These costs have since gone up materially.

The new scale is actually lower in some instances in the rate per square inch, above the minimum size plate, than the prices in effect two years ago.

To compare selling prices of zinc and half-tone engravings 3 columns wide by 10 inches deep—70 square inches—required for a page in the average trade journal:

	Size	1918	1920
Zinc etching	70 sq. in.	$ 7.00	$ 9.00
Half-tone, square finish	70 sq. in.	15.40	16.20
Three-color half-tone	70 sq. in.	94.20	127.50

In the same period production costs have gone up about fifty per cent. How has this increased cost been met by the engravers?

It has been made possible by a **readjustment** of the selling prices based upon extensive cost records kept over a long period.

It was discovered that certain types of engravings, particularly minimums, were being sold at an actual loss, which necessitated an increased price on the larger size work, but now the subject of selling price has been readjusted on a fair basis to the buyer, so that every type of engraving bears its proper proportion of cost, and has made possible the selling of engravings of 70 square inches at a very slight increase over the price of 1918, even in face of enormous increase in the cost of manufacture.

Published by the Cost Committee of the

Manufacturing Photo Engravers of Canada

An organization formed several years ago, embracing all Canada, consisting of manufacturers of all types and kinds of engravings. As an Association it neither manufactures, buys, nor sells. Its sole purpose is to assure for the mutual benefit of the industry and the buying public the best class of engraving that scientific knowledge and human skill can produce at a fair price.

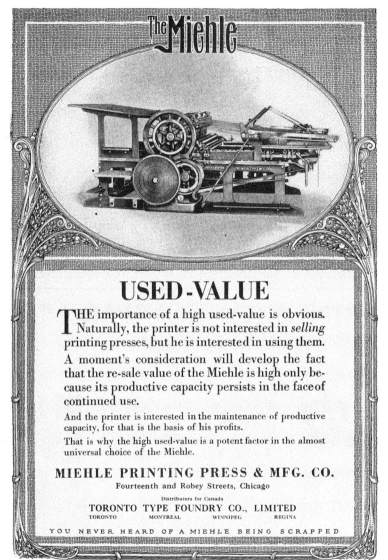

USED-VALUE

THE importance of a high used-value is obvious. Naturally, the printer is not interested in *selling* printing presses, but he is interested in using them.

A moment's consideration will develop the fact that the re-sale value of the Miehle is high only because its productive capacity persists in the face of continued use.

And the printer is interested in the maintenance of productive capacity, for that is the basis of his profits.

That is why the high used-value is a potent factor in the almost universal choice of the Miehle.

MIEHLE PRINTING PRESS & MFG. CO.

Fourteenth and Robey Streets, Chicago

Distributers for Canada

TORONTO TYPE FOUNDRY CO., LIMITED

TORONTO   MONTREAL   WINNIPEG   REGINA

YOU NEVER HEARD OF A MIEHLE BEING SCRAPPED

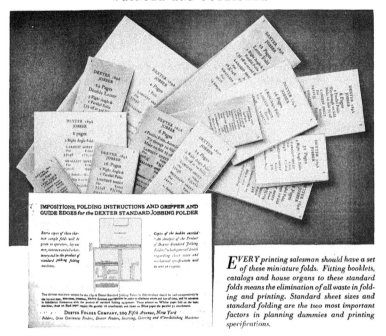

EVERY printing salesman should have a set of these miniature folds. Fitting booklets, catalogs and house organs to these standard folds means the elimination of all waste in folding and printing. Standard sheet sizes and standard folding are the two most important factors in planning dummies and printing specifications.

Send for this set of Miniature Sample Folds

The envelope contains the impositions, folding instructions and gripper and guide edges for the thirteen standard folds that fold on the Dexter Standard Jobbing Folder.

A careful analysis of folding requirements made by this company showed that more than 98 per cent. of booklet, catalogue and house organ folding comes within these thirteen standard folds.

Extra copies of these folds will be gladly given to your stonemen, compositors, layout men and bindery operators. Write today for your sets.

DEXTER FOLDER COMPANY
200 Fifth Avenue, New York
Folders, Cross Continuous Feeders, Dexter Feeders, Inserting, Covering and Wire-Stitching Machines

BABCOCK

UNIVERSAL EQUIPMENT

The Shortest Endorsement Letter on Record

A successful Advertising Printer using five OPTIMUS presses recently received this inquiry:—

"Will you kindly tell us how you manage to print your half-tone work on bond paper on an ordinary cylinder press?"

Below is a reproduction of his reply.

The catalogue from which this page was torn is unique, in that it is the only flat bed cylinder press catalogue issued, in which individual mechanical advantages are detailed.

If you have a copy; read it; if not, write for one.

Our Best Advertisements Are Not Printed,---THEY PRINT!

" The demand for BABCOCK PRESSES is double that of any previous year."

The Babcock Printing Press Manufacturing Company

NEW LONDON, CONN.   NEW YORK OFFICE, 38 PARK ROW

Barnhart Bros. & Spindler, General Western Agents, Chicago, St. Louis, Dallas, Kansas City, Omaha, St. Paul, Seattle.
John Haddon & Company, Agents, London, E.C.
Miller & Richard, General Agents for Canada: Toronto, Ontario, Winnipeg, Manitoba

Cromwell
Tympan Papers

Give Cleaner Impressions with a Minimum of Make-Ready

SAVING time on make ready, and securing sharp impressions are the two great things your press foreman has to strive for. With Cromwell Traveling, Shifting and Cylinder Tympan Papers, his draw sheets are always tight—no swelling—and they need not be oiled. They are also moisture-proof, protecting the packing against dampness.

You can turn a rush job quicker with Cromwell Tympan Papers because they resist offset, enabling you to back up reasonably wet sheets. Quick delivery is often your best selling argument.

Cromwell papers will take more impressions without replacing, and they *never* rot.

We especially recommend Cromwell Tympan Papers for trade journal and magazine printers where long runs are necessary without interruptions. It is ideal for book work and the highest grade of printing. Job printers will find it an excellent tympan paper for printing bond, linen and covers.

We carry Cromwell Tympan Papers in stock ready for quick shipment in rolls from 36 to 66 inches wide. Order to-day and secure the perfection and economy in printing that Cromwell Tympan Papers give.

Send us the size of your press, and we will forward free of all cost to you, Sample Sheet of our Tympan Paper.

The Cromwell Paper Co.
Department P.P.   Jasper Place, Chicago, U.S.A.

Trade   Mark
OLIVER CROMWELL

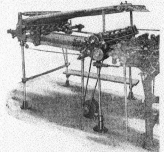

EASTERN AVE. PLANT, TORONTO

Mr. Printer:

Approximately 65% of the white metals sold in Canada last year were made in the plant shown above.

Think it over. What's the answer? There are three of them.

1st—QUALITY
2nd—QUALITY
3rd—QUALITY

Try a sample lot of Linotype, Intertype, Monotype, Stereotype, or Electrotype.

HOYT METAL COMPANY

MONTREAL **TORONTO** **WINNIPEG**

MEDIUM TONING LIBERTY RED, No. 9954

"THE ONLY INK HOUSE IN THE WORLD"

that manufactures all the materials entering into its Lithographic and Letter-Press Inks and with its large staff of expert chemists and ink makers offers the printing trade

THE BEST IN THE WORLD

Every Ingredient

Acids   Dry Colors

Chemicals   Intermediates

Aniline Dyes, Varnishes, etc.

Manufactured in Our Own Factories

The Ault & Wiborg Company

of Canada, Limited

MONTREAL   TORONTO   WINNIPEG

TORONTO VARNISH WORKS

TORONTO INK WORKS

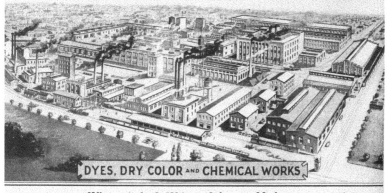

DYES, DRY COLOR AND CHEMICAL WORKS

Where Ault & Wiborg Inks are Made

Earnscliffe Linen Bond

White and Eight Tints

Azure, Blue, Pink, Buff, Golden Rod, Russet, Green, Tuscan

These new "Earnscliffe" colors have been enthusiastically received, both by consumers and printers. If you haven't already received one of the new sample books showing all the colors with printing examples, let us send you one.

EARNSCLIFFE LINEN BOND
is made in Canada and supplied by wholesalers throughout the Dominion.

THE

ROLLAND PAPER COMPANY
LIMITED
MILLS AT
ST. JEROME AND MONT ROLLAND
OFFICES AND WAREHOUSES
MONTREAL AND
TORONTO

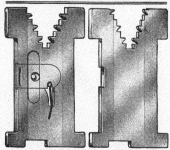

PRINTER AND PUBLISHER

Devoted to the Interests of the Printers and Publishers of Canada

The Bread and Butter of the Business

Business Policy vs. Editorial Expediency

ABOUT a dozen years ago a clever young printer, who had a thorough training in his calling, who was energetic, ambitious and full of enthusiasm, accepted a partnership in a good country newspaper and job printing business, which had been bought by a trio of politicians from the executors of a deceased publisher's estate in a town of about 6,000 not a thousand miles from Queen City, Ontario. Bill Caxton, as he will be called, was to be allotted a fifth interest in the business in exchange for an option he held; he was to be one of the working partners, pay his share out of the profits of the business, and he was to be paid a wage as foreman. His other working partner was a competent pressman, who came in on the same terms. The others in the company were three professional men with political aspirations.

Through industry and their all-round knowledge of the mechanics of the business, Caxton and his partner were able to make a very good showing the first year, and a handsome profit resulted. At the annual meeting, however, Bill had his first lesson in business practice. Without much discussion the directors decided that they would write off $2,000 to clean up the mailing list, which was found well padded with deadheads, place $2,000 to reserve and divide up $2,000 equally among the five shareholders. Caxton's share was $400. He was disappointed. He felt this was not enough for all the extra hours he had put in (without extra pay) to make this big profit possible, and the more he thought the sorer he became.

There were other things that made him feel that way. He had up to this time worked in printeries which were up-to-date in every way, with modern equipment, and every time he looked at the old umbrella machine (as he scornfully referred to the old-fashioned typograph) and its chum, the stubby monoline, he craved for a linotype of the latest model. He waxed eloquent about the superiority of the Merg. to the managing director of the company (a professional man who had once represented the riding at Ottawa, and who still had hopes). Caxton's enthusiasm impressed the M.D., who called the company together and they discussed the matter from all angles. The President was M.P.P. for the riding, and he had in the course of his varied career worked at one time in a country newspaper office and could sling type a little, and he posed as an authority on things typographical. He asked young Caxton how much matter could be set on a linotype and was told that a fair output would be from 3,000 to 4,000 ems an hour. The M.P.P. scoffed at this and said, "In my young days I knew a man who could set 5,000 ems an hour by hand." No amount of argument would convince the other men that the M.P.P. was wrong and the printer right. And—it killed the linotype proposition right there.

That was not all. In his zeal to get all the information he could to put before the company, Caxton had received from the linotype agent of that time the price his company would allow for the typograph and monoline machines in part payment on the lino. The figure was ridiculously low—something like $400 for the two, which stood on the plant inventory at $1,200. At the next annual meeting these smart politicians, out of a nice bunch of profit, wrote these machines down to $400,

the cylinder press down to near scrap iron value, and the rest of the plant down to near the vanishing point. The profit left to divide up was $250, of which Bill Caxton received credit on his stock account of $50; and because he did not know much outside the mechanical department, he thought he was being robbed, and his resentment grew more than ever.

Being diplomats, and knowing that the business as it was being run was of the hen-that-laid-the-golden-egg variety, the directors offered the management of the business to Caxton. Bill was inclined to accept before doing so. The paper was Conservative in politics and had, up to the death of the former owner, been a faithful supporter of the sitting M.P. The new company, however, were out after his scalp, and at the party convention held shortly before this an attempt had been made to win the nomination for the managing director, a "has-been" in Federal politics, who thought he could "come back." The attempt failed, the M.D. getting 18 out of 800 votes. Caxton was too busy, nor had he the inclination, to dig into politics—he had, in fact, no use for the kind he saw around the office. He looked at the situation from a purely business standpoint, and gave it as his opinion that the M.P. could outgeneral all comers and was so strong politically that he would never be defeated as long as he wanted to run—(he is still on the job, too,)—and it was poor policy to be slamming him all the time. It made enemies for the business, and he wanted to build on friendship. Caxton was curtly told that the editor would attend to that department of their affairs, and it was up to him to look after the business part.

Bill Caxton asked time to think the matter over. He was confronted with the eternal problem of running a business made up of conflicting interests. Its revenue was fairly evenly divided between subscriptions, advertising and job work, and there was a tendency among its erstwhile political friends, since the convention especially, to send their patronage elsewhere, rather than give it to a "bunch of knockers," as they dubbed the company now. Bill thought he would be better off away from the political scramble, and he talked the matter over with the other working partner (the pressman), who was also feeling sore—but for other reasons. They decided to resign and start a job office, being confident that the big profits which they had been earning would be surpassed when they were relieved of the weight of the other three partners, who were driving away business anyway. Their partnership agreement stipulated that on severing their connection with the business they must first offer their shares to the company. They each had $450 to their credit, and $900 in those days would be an ample first payment on a job plant valued anywhere up to $8,000 or $9,000. (This was another business practice which is directly responsible for much of the sickness of the printing business to-day.) They reckoned too soon, however, for when their resignations had been accepted they were offered $300 each for their shares, and after some legal advice they accepted that sum.

A visit to a type foundry was made and a small plant, consisting of a No. 2 Gordon, an 18-inch hand power cutter, a nice assortment of type, rules, cases and so forth, was selected, valued at about $800, on which they made a first payment of

$150. An upstairs room was rented at $5 a month heated, a motor was installed (2-h.p.) at a cost of $75, and a few weeks later another smooth supply man sold them a 14 x 22 Colts and a wire stitcher—on the instalment plan.

About a month after they started, the printing situation in that town took an abnormal turn. There had been two newspapers up to then and both had job departments as profit-producing adjuncts. Now another paper loomed up. The local option party were preparing to dry up the town and the liquor men could not induce either paper to give them the support they thought their business warranted them in expecting. The result was a liquor sheet, The *Daily Wail*—with a job department attached. This made three daily papers and four job plants in a town of 6,000. Then started a merry war, in which the main features were low prices for everything. Advertising space went begging at 2c an inch, while job work was practically given away. And no one was worse than the other. This went on for about eight months and the temperance party began to see signs that their opponents were weakening. The fact was that the liquor men were finding the sport of running a daily paper a very expensive proposition; and when the local optionists showed no signs of forcing the issue, the liquor interests arranged with the Conservative sheet whereby they could get all the space they were willing to pay for when the time came. Their *Daily Wail* made its exit at the early age of ten months.

At the death of the *Daily Wail* the situation was serious from a job printer's point of view. In the blind cut-and-slash competition which was being indulged in, shrewd business men saw an opportunity to stock up on all kinds of office stationery —the kind the small job printer especially goes after. The Caxton job office had been turning out real classy work, so good that *Printer and Publisher* gave the men several good-sized puffs; even the *American Printer* and the aristocratic *Inland Printer* saw merit in their work and reproduced specimens which came from their little print shop. They were up against the financial game good and proper, however. Their plant was only half paid for, everybody was stocked up, and few orders in sight. It was hard, uphill work to get the people of that town to pay any more for the real printing these men were producing than for the mediocre kind the others were getting away with. A lot of educational work was required, and meanwhile two families had to be provided for. After two years' struggling, during which other factors entered to aggravate the situation, Caxton bought out his partner and attempted to swing the business to safety alone.

About this time the First Printers' Cost Conference became history and the secretary of the C.P.A. visited town, bringing with him a lot of small cards and a few charts and gave the printers of the county a talk on costs. To Bill Caxton the talk was a revelation. It showed him that there was more to his job than the mere mechanical excellence, desirable though that

certainly was, which he was ever striving after. It "wised" him to the fact that he must study the books more, and at least learn the rudiments of bookkeeping. He had a friend who was accountant in one of the factories, and he asked his advice. The accountant offered to keep the books for him for $5 a month until Bill could take them over himself. Thus began the study of costs. Month after month Bill strove to increase his output to bring the turnover up to the point where he could feel at least safe. But the bad methods he and the others had been following for the past three years had cut deeper than could be imagined and each monthly statement looked worse than the former.

He found that his composition was costing him over a dollar an hour and his platen presswork about 80c., but he could not get any business at these prices on a competitive basis, and only a few jobs came in on a no-price-asked footing. In fact, he had generally to figure out every $2 or $3 job, and that was a great time-wasting system. The other printers were in the same boat. They were all guessers and the lowest guesser got the work every time. And Bill could not get away from the feeling every time he got a job that he had left something out, or had made a mistake in figuring stock, or omitted it altogether.

Well, to finish the introduction to Bill Caxton's career as a printer until circumstances forced on him the study of costs, let it be said that the statement which his accountant friend made for him every month—and for which he religiously collected his $5 per—showed Bill that the only way he could do justice to his family was to sell out and go back to the case and a steady income. He took a job on a small city daily as superintendent, and it was not long before his ability as a writer of good, newsy reports came to the fore and he was made news editor. The manager was not a practical printer and was only interested politically, and when the Second Printers' Cost Conference was held in Toronto in 1912, Bill was sent as representative of the paper. Some progress had been made in the three years that intervened between the first and second conferences and a pretty complete system was presented to those printers who thought it worth while to attend. In fact, so well had the Cost Commission done its work that the system presented in 1912 is practically the same as is being used to-day in an increasingly large number of offices in Canada and the United States—to say nothing of the fact that it has been adopted by the Federation of Master Printers of Great Britain. The impetus given to the study of costs at the Toronto meeting in 1912 has, however, spent itself, and there is ample evidence on every hand that the influx of newcomers into the great game, and other reasons, are causing a drift back to the rotten conditions of a decade or so ago.

The reason Bill Caxton's experiences are here chronicled is because they are typical, and embody several conditions that require drastic remedies, and an attempt will be made to point out these remedies in future articles.

The Shop With the Low Price Got These Jobs

Total Difference of 38 Per Cent. in Figures

THE question of costs continues to be one of absorbing interest. *Printer and Publisher* received a few days ago the following letter from William Fox, of the A. E. Long Co. Ltd., Toronto, makers of folding boxes, printers and embossers.

Mr. Fox states:

"Having taken great interest in the articles published in the November, December, and January issues of the *Printer and Publisher*, relating to the price quoted on the Government Folder, and noting that many others have also taken the same interest, I am taking the liberty of sending to you an instance of the same trouble that we are having on the smaller class of work.

"You will find enclosed a few samples of labels, etc., together with the prices we quoted, and the prices the customer bought them at from from some other printer. I might state that each one was figured separately, as the customer would not order the same labels together later on, and always expects his goods

at the same price as last, if not ordered too far distant apart. The ink has to be a special shade of brown and green, the price of the brown is $2.00 per lb., and the green $1.50 per lb."

Printer and Publisher went carefully over the work with Mr. Fox, being given every chance to go over the cost sheets that were used on every job. It would be interesting to reproduce the labels, but that cannot be done as they are the property of a well-known medicine company in Toronto. Plates were supplied in nearly every case, only one of the jobs requiring any composition.

Job No. 1 was a 2-color label for an average size bottle. It was done on special label stock, finished on one side. The price of this material is $7.65 per ream and the size is 25 x 38. The size of the label is 8 1-8 x 9 5-8. One set of electros was supplied, and another secured by the firm, so that the job was run two-on. In this job 660 sheets would be necessary.

Here are the figures used on this work:

600 sheets (profit added)	$11.56
Ink, 3 pounds	5.61
Wrapping paper	.05
Locking up	1.40
Cutting	.35
Press make-ready	1.80
Press, run 2 on	5.40
Jogging	.50
Trimming	.70
Packing	.25
Counting	.25
Electros	5.59
	$33.46
Add profit	8.36
Total	$41.82
Per thousand	8.36

For reasons best known to the firm in question, this job was quoted at $7.85 per thousand. *Printer and Publisher* believes that $8.36 was a very fair price. In fact there are offices where a higher figure would be justified. Cutting charges are low and presswork is low.

But how did Mr. Fox happen to lose the job, even after having his estimate lowered?

Simply because a Toronto print shop printed those two-color labels, and supplied the stock, turning them over to the buyer at $4.75 per thousand. They were done in a shop of very ordinary equipment, and it has no place in the establishment to indicate that they were printed in a place so well equipped, that they would be rushed out at a 5,000 an hour rate.

Then How About the Next One?

Job No. 2 is a label 2 1-2 inches square. It is printed from a plate with a good quality brown ink used. Stock is the same as in the preceding instance. The customer supplied the plate, so it was simply a case of stock and press work. Here are the figures that Mr. Fox used in this connection. The run was 2,000.

Stock	$ .60
Ink	.55
Wrapping paper	.05
Lock-up	.58
Cutting	.20
Make-ready	.60
Feeding	1.86
Jogging	.15
Trimming	.30
Packing	.20
Cost	$5.09
Add	1.25
	$6.34
Per thousand	3.17

The price quoted on this work was $3.35 per thousand. We fail to see where Mr. Fox was too high in his charges. It is simple work. Granted. No composition. Granted. But it takes up the time of part of a plant, and it must help to bear its share of the overhead or it has no place in the establishment. What happened to No. 2? Why, it went along the same way as No. 1. A Toronto job printing house came along and carried off the bacon at the handsome price of $1.85 per thousand.

What Happened to No. 3?

By way of variation, we will take here a hand-set label in two colors, that Mr. Fox gave a figure on. The customer wanted 2,000 of these. The colors used were red and gold. The gold was done in ink, not size and bronze. There is a fair amount of composition, and the way the borders are arranged would classify it as rather "fussy." The stock used was the same as the others, and the size of the job 3 1-8 x 3 3-4.

Here are the figures that were on the cost sheets as shown the *Printer and Publisher*:

Ink	$ .75
Stock	.80
Composition	3.50

Lock-up	.70
Cutting stock	.25
Press make-ready	1.80
Press running	3.00
Jogging	.25
Trimming	.35
Packing	.10
	$11.50
Add	2.87
Total	$14.37
Per thousand	7.18

The price that was given to the customer on this was $14.50, or $7.25 per thousand. There is certainly nothing exorbitant in Mr. Fox's figures. There are two wash-ups in this work. There has to be a good register or there would be shortage.

The figure of $7.25 per thousand did not get the work. The job shop referred to before got the work at $4.50 per thousand, or $9 for the whole thing.

Now, Here is the Last One

No. 4 is done in brown, one plate being supplied by the drug company, size 2¾ x 4¼.

The customer wanted 5,000—and got them—but not at Mr. Fox's price. Here are the figures we found on his cost sheet. He secured an extra electro at a cost of 96c., which was justified by the saving in press work.

Stock	$1.80
Ink	1.10
Wrapping paper	.06
Electro	.96
Make-up	.58
Cutting stock	.25
Press make-ready	.66
Feeding (2-on)	2.40
Jogging	.26
Trimming	.66
Parcelling	.25
Counting, etc.	.25
	$9.17
Add	2.35
Total	$11.52

This makes a price of $2.30 per thousand. "On this job," remarked Mr. Fox, "we quoted exactly $2.40, and I thought we were giving a very fair price, and one that would be hard to beat on a fair basis. Well, we didn't get that one, either, because a job shop took that at $1.85 per thousand. In other words he beat me by 23 per cent. That 5,000 was done for $9.25."

Uses His Own Cost Sheet

The cost sheet used by Mr. Fox in his department is comprehensive and simple.

For a place that handles a wide variety of work the printing costs are well looked after, and it cannot be said that any of the quotations given above are high. In fact, *Printer and Publisher* believes they are low if anything.

"Meet much of this sort of competition?" we asked Mr. Fox. "Almost every day," was the reply. "It is one of the worst things in the trade. It has been that way for a long time and shows little sign of any betterment. The only thing is that it does not make so much difference now as nearly all the plants that pay attention to costs can get all the work they need at a fair price."

To summarize the whole thing, here are the prices quoted and the prices per thousand at which the job was done:

	Quoted	Cut Price
No. 1	$ 7.85	$ 4.75
No. 2	3.35	1.85
No. 3	7.25	4.50
No. 4	2.40	1.85
	$20.85	$12.95

Or, to get a good look at the thing, take the totals for one thousand of each job, $20.85 against $12.95. Or the successful bidder was on an average 38 per cent. below Mr. Fox.

Ottawa Claims Lead in Guesstimating Now

A Spread From $1.15 to $4.85 Per Page

A CORRESPONDENT at Ottawa, writes as follows:
  The printers of Ottawa have followed with much interest the publicity and subsequent instructive analysis given in your December and January numbers regarding the estimates secured by the Dominion Publicity Committee on a small folder.

It would appear that neither Montreal nor Ottawa were invited to take a hand in this interesting transaction, and the writer, in view of his knowledge of local conditions, can only regard this as a very unfortunate oversight on the part of the Dominion Publicity Committee.

Leaving your special correspondent, whose excellent article and comprehensive analysis appeared in the January number, to deal with the waywardness of the Toronto Printer, the writer would like to give an instance showing what Ottawa Printers can do in the matter of estimating when opportunity offers and to show that in the matter of "Spread" we have our Toronto competitors hopelessly outclassed.

A few weeks ago, the Corporation of the City of Ottawa called for tenders for its departmental annual reports. The total number of pages of these combined reports amount to about 460, consisting of approximately 345 pages of tabular matter set in 8 point and the balance of 115 pages set in 10 point on 12 point body. There are 8 individual departmental reports, and 200 copies of each report are printed, 160 copies of which are bound in paper covers for each of the 8 different departments, and 40 copies are delivered loose. These 40 copies are reserved for binding in full leather and form no part

10

of the contract in question. The size of the book is 8½ x 5½, and the pages are set 25 ems wide by 45 ems deep. Inside stock consists of No. 1 Book, 24½ x 36½—50 and the covers of assorted colors, are cut from 22 x 28—60 and cost roughly $12.50 per ream. Specifications called for a flat rate per page, regardless of the size of the type.

Five bids were put in for the work with the following remarkable results:—

A quoted $1.15 per page.
B " 1.70 "
C " 2.98 "
D " 4.20 "
E " 4.85 "

As an instance of "guesstimating" this must surely be regarded as a classic and under the circumstances the printers of Toronto who figured on the Dominion Publicity folder should not feel too badly concerning their efforts in connection with the job which provoked the present discussion.

Both jobs were for institutions fully prepared to pay a fair price for services rendered or work performed. The heavily burdened taxpayer of the country, and of this city in particular, surely owes a debt of gratitude to the unselfish and self-sacrificing attitude of these patriotic printers for even such a small contribution to the relief of their already pressing burdens and incidentally of their help in modifying, to some degree, the present H.C. of L.

We have in this city a Master Printers' Association and at present a somewhat considerable class are attending a course of instruction on estimating conducted by a very able exponent from Montreal. It is only charitable to suppose that the efforts of both this organization and the school of estimating have not had sufficient time to yield the desired results, but we may only express the hope that it will come quickly.

The Purchasing Agent at our City Hall once assured the writer that even with his limited knowledge of the printing business he was quite certain that practically all orders for printing placed by him were performed at less than actual cost. Unfortunately there are only a few printers in this city who are operating a reliable cost system, and to those who obviously have no knowledge of their costs, a very comprehensive, effective, and most profitable guide may be secured by investing in a copy of the Franklin Pricelist. This is a book of easy reference and one which moreover will ensure to every printer, who will live up to its teaching, a fair margin of profit.

NEW YORK PRINTERS

The 6,000 compositors in the Union book and job offices in New York City will receive $45 a week, an increase of $9 a week over their old scale, it was announced, through a new agreement made by the employing printers and the "Big Six" Typographical Union. The new scale calls for a 48-hour week until May 1, 1921, and the increase is retroactive to January 1.

As a mark of personal esteem, two hundred friends tendered a banquet to Mr. Dallas on the occasion of his giving up his work as New England representative of the International Typographical Union, which had extended over a number of years, to become affiliated with the sales organization of the Lanston Monotype Machine Company.

ESTIMATING THE LOSSES

Lack of business acumen cost printers in 65 American cities a "lost profit" of $28,000,000 last year, according to results of business surveys cited before 800 employing printers at a "survey mass meeting" in New York. Joseph A. Borden, general secretary of the United Typothetae, declared that although no business offers greater opportunities for money-making, 73 per cent. of printers in the United States "are irresponsible and have no credit." Referring to labor conditions, Mr. Borden declared that printing labor would disappear within 35 years unless replenished by men from the present number of apprentices.

Ailsa Craig Banner:—Few can realize the struggle we are having each week to get the Banner out with our present help. We are compelled to drop next week's issue to try and catch up with our work. We regret that this and last week's Banner were so late.

Getting Business Out of a Wreck

Great interest was manifested in the rescuing of the Powhattan at Halifax. The Halifax *Herald* cashed in on this in a way that pleased a man who really wanted publicity. In fact, there is a full page ad. in the issue of the *Herald* on January 28th, telling of the merits of a certain make of rope that finally stood the strain and pulled the stranded steamer to shore. How did that ad. come? Well, here's how W. H. Dennis tells the story:

The towing of the Powhattan to Halifax is the biggest sea story that has been broken in the North Atlantic since the sinking of the Titanic. Several attempts had been made to take her in tow but the lines parted.

On Saturday morning last, the manager of the Consumer's Cordage Co., a local industry, called up and asked us to mention the fact in our reading notices that the lines used by the Lady Laurier, the Canadian Government steamer which was assisting the Powhattan, were manufactured in their plant. We asked for an opportunity to tell the story in a full page display in the *Herald* and the *Mail*, stating that if he would favor us with a piece of the cordage similar to that of the Powhattan tow we would have a cut made. The particular make of their cordage is "Lion Brand," so we had our staff artist make up two lions' heads.

Well, a paper that can grab pages of advertising copy out of a wreck deserves the business.

Motors in Canada has issued a volume called "Facts" giving a comprehensive survey of the automobile and automotive equipment situation in Manitoba, Saskatchewan, Alberta and British Columbia. A very large amount of useful information has been gathered and put into very readable form.

The Pulp and Paper Industry

A preliminary report on the pulp and paper industry in Canada has been compiled by the Dominion Bureau of Statistics for the calendar year 1918. The statistics are represented for each class by number of mills, as follows: Pulp mills 37, paper mills 31, pulp and paper mills 26, or a total of 94 mills.

The total capital invested in the industry was $241,344,704, of which $12,520,765 was invested in paper mills, $71,708,223 in pulp mills and $157,115,716 in pulp and paper mills.

The number of persons employed, male and female, by classes of employment, and the amount paid to each, were as shown in the following tabular statement:

	Male	Female	Amount
Officers, superintendents and managers	462	2	$1,807,450
Clerks, stenographers and other salaried employees	1,164	391	1,888,151
Employees on wages, average No.	23,086	848	23,278,606
Totals	24,712	1,151	26,974,226

The number of persons employed in paper mills was 1,775 males and 531 females, with payments of $2,050,615; in pulp mills the number was 7,328 males and 105 females, with payment of $7,508,834 and in pulp and paper mills 15,609 males and 516 females, with payment of $17,414,776.

Women in Newspaper Work

Two newspaper women of Western Canada have been spending a short time in Toronto, Miss Cora Hind, who is agricultural editor of the Winnipeg *Free Press*, and Miss Jean Grant, formerly of Stratford, now business manager and associate editor of the *Market Examiner* of Calgary. Miss Cora Hind has acquired a reputation that extends to many countries in connection with the annual crop survey and prediction which her paper runs for Western Canada. She is also a well-known contributor to many financial and special papers on the business conditions of Western Canada.

Miss Grant is a daughter of Mr. and Mrs. John Grant, Stratford. Several years ago she went to the Calgary *Herald*. Her own venture is best told in her own words:

"There was a big demand in the West among stock men for a reliable market paper. You know, Alberta is the great stock country. There, in the foothills, it is possible to keep cattle out all winter. Stock people, grain men and farmers were handicapped because they did not know the actual prices being paid for their products. Ignorance of these resulted again and again in their being bitten by buyers. Prices paid by buyers were frequently practical stealing.

"My paper, which goes out every Friday all over the Province, contains lists of the prevailing prices, not only for stock and grain, but for butter, fowl, all farm products. A letter I received shortly before coming East illustrates the importance of this. A stock breeder wrote me that a buyer came and offered him a certain figure. The breeder told him he'd see

the prices in the *Market Examiner* before deciding to accept. Immediately, the buyer offered him $300 more."

SHE KNOWS LIVE STOCK

Does the woman editor-manager-proprietor of an agricultural market paper know live stock as well as market prices? "Yes," was her prompt reply to this question. "I don't know definitely why or when I began to acquire a practical knowledge. I never lived on a farm. I was born and brought up in Stratford. After I went West, I began to get interested in our wonderful pure-bred stock out there. My interest was increased through going to the exhibitions, then I had the opportunity of seeing wonderful round-ups, and the stock on the farms and ranches around Calgary. Recognizing the need of a paper such as I am publishing, I stepped into the field, and it is still going after three years. The stock yards are right inside the city of Calgary and I get authoritative information from all over."

Miss Grant has associated with her a former Saskatchewan newspaper woman, Mrs. Ellis, at one time of Prince Albert, whom she trained herself in the fine points of live stock and marketing, and has placed her in Edmonton to take charge for the paper there.

The St. John Typographical Union, No. 85, recently elected the following officers for the ensuing year: E. H. Toole, president; Otto Hahn, vice-president; F. W. Stanton, recording secretary; H. T. Campbell, secretary-treasurer; C. Morgan, sergeant-at-arms; G. H. Maxwell, J. Longon, and G. T. McCafferty, trustees.

Here is a front page that stands as a distinct credit to the publishers of the St. Maurice Valley *Chronicle* (weekly). The news stories have been "played up" with attractive headings, and a pleasing balance has been maintained throughout the page without altogether resorting to symmetrical arrangement, which, when adopted, too often possesses the fault of appearing stiff. While all newspaper publishers are not in favor of a "flashy" front-page make-up it must be admitted that, in its particular style, the make-up presented above has been handled with skill seldom reflected in weekly publications. The inside pages of the St. Maurice Valley *Chronicle*, too, are well arranged. The pyramid style of make-up prevails and a good deal of attention has been paid to uniformity in tone and style in which the advertisements are displayed.

Printer & Publisher

Published on the Twelfth of Each Month.

H. A. NICHOLSON   -   -   -   Business Manager
A. R. KENNEDY   -   -   -   -   -   -   Editor

SUBSCRIPTION PRICE—Canada, Great Britain, South Africa and
the West Indies, $2 a year; United States, $2.50 a year; other
countries, $3 a year.   Single copies, 20 cents.   Invariably in
advance.

PUBLISHED BY

THE MACLEAN PUBLISHING CO.

ta   Esblished 1887   Limited

JOHN BAYNE MACLEAN   -   -   -   -   President
H. T. HUNTER   -   -   -   -   -   Vice-President
H. V. TYRRELL   -   -   -   -   General Manager
T. B. COSTAIN   -   -   -   General Managing Editor

Head Office, 143-153 University Avenue - TORONTO, CANADA
Cable Address: Macpubco, Toronto; Atabek, London, Eng.
Also at Montreal, Winnipeg, New York, Chicago, Boston, London,
England.

Vol. 28   PRINTED AT TORONTO, FEB., 1920   No. 2

CONTENTS

Don't Cheapen Your Paper

A WESTERN paper carries a half-column story to the effect that one of its readers dropped into the office a few days ago to have a smoke. Picking up the broom to secure a straw, subscriber saw that the broom was shot to pieces. He thereupon took pity on the publisher, and paid for his paper so that the office could afford a new broom. That is used as a plea on which to hang an appeal for readers in general to come along and pay up their arrears.

There is a certain amount of color to the story, but it has no place in an appeal for paying up arrears. It has been a procession of this stuff that for years has made it hard work and unsatisfactory labor to get people to pay up for their papers in some districts. Very often the editors have allowed their sense of humor to ride over the business acumen they should have in order to bring their affairs to a state of decency and financial stability.

Why should a weekly paper set itself up as saying this: "We're hard up. We need a new broom. We need some shoes for the children. We need a suit of clothes. Now come along in and spend half a day and see for yourself how badly we need the cash. Pay up a couple of the years you are in arrears." A little exaggerated? Not much. There are many of the papers all across Canada putting up week after week the most miserable sort of apologetic bids for the payment of arrears.

Why not take this attitude: "We are in the publishing business to make a living. You ordered the paper to be sent to you. We did so, fully expecting that we would be paid in advance for the service. You owe us for this service, and it is necessary that our bills should be paid if we are to continue in business. You owe us—and we will thank you for remitting it to us at once."

Never apologize for asking a man for what he owes you. You weaken your case the moment you begin to treat your should-be assets as a matter for joking. Your readers begin to realize that you do not take the matter very seriously, and they begin to let you slide down toward the bottom of their list of accounts payable.

The weekly publishing business has itself to blame for much of the trouble that it encounters in the collecting of amounts due

it. Columns have been written about editors fainting at the sight of a ten-dollar bill, of prostrations being reported when a subscriber paid up for three years in advance, and all such stuff. Gentlemen—quit it! It is poor business on your part.

Paid Advertising and Free Space

NO small amount of feeling has been brought to pass in some of the weekly offices throughout the country in connection with the manner in which the advertising for the Church Forward Movement was placed. To put the case in short, it amounted to this: The appropriation was used up in the daily papers, while the weekly papers were given an assortment of free readers and plate matter for which no payment was made.

Now with the decision of the Forward Movement to do their advertising in the daily papers we have no quarrel. It reflected good salesmanship on the part of the dailies to have the committee handling the appropriation convinced that they could cover the ground through the daily papers alone.

But the point is here: Why pay the daily papers for space, and then send along a supply of readers and free plate to the weekly papers? The weekly papers have a right to take objection to such treatment. If they were not included in the paid list, they should have been ignored as well in the plea for free space.

Several of the weekly publishers have been placed in a peculiar position in this way. In one case the remark was made by a weekly man that he was asked to subscribe to the fund, and was glad to do so, but that when they had any money to spend, the daily papers got it all. By the time the gentleman in question was quoted as saying that he had not received any advertising, therefore he would not subscribe. Nothing could be further from the truth.

Weekly newspapers should not feel particularly aggrieved that they were cut off the appropriation in the first place. Their way to meet this is to produce better papers, and sell the advertiser on the idea of their usefulness in the community. The weekly papers have reason, though, to feel slighted in that they were treated to free readers and free plate while the daily papers were getting the paid material.

A SAD EFFECT.

Aside from the wages and rent paid, there is no more important item in the figuring of costs than the value of machinery and equipment. It is a sad fact that but few manufacturers, including printers, actually know the value of their plant, and yet they attempt to do business, figure costs, and say they are making money.—(Roy T. Porte, in "How to Figure Costs in Printing Offices.")

ABOUT TIME.
Copyrighted by the International Feature Service.
—Coffman for the International Feature Service.

Three Cheers for Mac!

ADVERTISING is a fine art in many ways. People who have anything to sell, advertise it. They tell all its good points, and they sing in print of the things it will do, or should do. And so it is that a friend drew our attention a few days ago to the advertising that a drug store was doing in the northern part of Ontario. The part that appealed to him very strongly was as follows:

"Mac's Louse Killer is Guaranteed—Every Person Who Uses It Comes Back for More."

Of course the question will at once be asked, "Why should a person be coming back for more?" It may be that having routed their own cooties they want to dust it on others, or it may be that the first application only makes them dizzy or wobbly.

Small wonder that some are puzzled by the working of the thing. Why should people have to go back a second time for a good louse killer? Honest to goodness, we don't know, do you?

Stiff Rates — Smaller Papers

THE problems that confront publishers of daily papers are not by any means decreasing. Costs continue to go up and every effort that is made to get more revenue to meet the increased cost simply works out to aggravate, rather than soothe the situation. Papers are caught up in the never-ending circle of trying to keep ahead of the game of increasing costs and increasing revenue.

Does the solution rest in a stiff increase in rates, and a smaller paper? It is safe to start from this point: The present craze for greatness, for big issues, for bulky editions, is putting a premium on the things that the daily papers themselves must in turn buy. They demand more type, and still more type. They demand it at a great rate of speed. They are in the market for all the newsprint they can secure. In fact the demand for this has made the problem of selling one that the mills have not to consider at all. The increasing demand for type makes it possible for the man who can produce type to sell his labor in a very advantageous market.

A big increase in rates, with the deliberate idea behind it of forcing advertisers to use less space, would make no inroad in the revenue of the office. On the contrary it would increase it. It would make less demand on the mechanical possibilities of the plant. It should make it possible to turn out better-appearing, better-edited and more readable papers.

It may be very satisfactory for a publisher to thumb over his edition as it comes from the press and look at the big number of pages. He may have an 18 or 24 page issue. He could have covered his field just as well in a 12 or a 16 with the advertising cut down, with streamers removed from the top of pages, with display headings pruned a bit, and with a more compact make-up for his whole paper. If he could secure the same revenue from the 12 or 16 as he could from his 18 or 24 he would be ahead. He would be helping to reduce the abnormal demand for newsprint, and he would also be doing a part in easing off on the demand for newsroom capacity and efficiency.

The matter is one that has received considerable attention recently by the publishers in various parts of the country. It will take no little courage to start this procession, but there are great possibilities in the field, and in these great possibilities are included the solution to several troubles that are becoming larger and more insistent every day.

Analyzing a Market

The Winnipeg *Free Press* has made a survey of the automobile and truck market of Western Canada, in order that the automobile trade in its various branches may have a good idea of the business to be done in that country.

The *Free Press* presents to the trade a great array of facts that the trade wants to know. The prospective advertiser will be impressed with the fact that the Winnipeg *Free Press* understands the Western markets for cars and trucks, and that it has gone to no small trouble to get together its facts and figures.

A publication that analyzes the market for the producer deserves to get the business.

More and more it must be recognized that service to the advertiser will get for the advertising department what service

to the readers gets for the editorial and circulation departments. The prospective advertiser of today does not want his time taken up by solicitors who want to "give him a talk" on the value of advertising.

The prospective advertiser will generally be glad to grant an interview to the man who can analyze the problem and show him what business there is in sight and how he can reach and influence it.

An advertising salesman—not an order-taker—must be a student of market conditions. He can never secure too much information on the lines he is handling.

A newspaper that can furnish the information that will help an advertiser to intelligently plan his advertising campaign for the year is going to get the business. It deserves it.

Election Cost $1,500,000

Toronto *Globe* (news item):—The last Provincial election cost the Province between $1,250,000 and $1,500,000 as against $148,000 in 1914, $119,000 in 1908, and $84,000 in 1905. The Government, while it has in no way criticized the expenditures authorized in connection with the October election, feels that the increase is far out of proportion to the need, and it is probable that some radical changes will be made in the methods employed in making up the voters' lists for the Province, so that the expense may be lessened at the next election.

TOLEDO HOUR COSTS

Toledo hour costs for November, 1919, and the average for the year, were announced as follows by the Toledo Typothetae:

	Nov.	Average
Hand composition	$2.77	$2.88
Linotype	2.12	2.11
Job presses, 10 x 15, or smaller	1.60	1.43
Larger than 10 x 15	1.66	1.64
Mech. Feed Jobbers	1.10	1.22
Cylinders, Smaller, 25 x 38	2.36	2.14
Larger, 25 x 33	3.13	3.00
Cutters	1.43	1.45
Ruling Machines	1.58	1.75
Folders	1.94	4.08
Bindery A	2.42	3.25
Bindery B	1.43	1.73
Bindery C	1.24	1.07
Bindery D	1.01	71

THE QUESTION IS—"WHEN WILL THEY GET DIZZY?"

New Association Has Been Organized

Canadian National Newspapers and Periodicals Association

ORGANIZATION of the Canadian National Newspapers and Periodicals Association was completed at sessions held in the King Edward, Toronto, on January 16 and 17.

Directors were named as follows:

Acton Burrows—Canadian Railway and Marine World
John Weld—Farmers' Advocate.
Lionel Davis—Continental Publishing Co.
Rev. S. W. Fallis—Methodist Book and Publishing House.
Hugh C. MacLean—Hugh C. MacLean Publications.
Lt.-Col. J. B. Maclean—MacLean Publishing Co.
C. D. Stovel—Stovel Company.
J. A. Beaudry—Le Prix Courant.
R. M. Burns—Catholic Record.
F. E. Dougall—John Dougall & Sons.
Rev. R. Douglas Fraser, D.D.—Presbyterian Publications.
H. T. Hunter—MacLean Publishing Co.
T. J. Tobin—Canadian Countryman Publishing Co.
T. S. Young—Hugh C. MacLean Publications Co.
H. V. Tyrrell—MacLean Publishing Co.

Members of Standing Committees Nominated by Sections

Advertising Policy and Promotion.—Agricultural—H. V. Tyrrell, MacLean Publishing Co., 143 University Ave., Toronto. Business—J. A. Beaudry, Le Prix Courant, 80 St. Denis St., Montreal. Magazine—W. G. Rooke, Canadian Home Journal, 71 Richmond St. W., Toronto. Religious—E. M. Shildrick, Methodist Book and Publishing House, 299 Queen St. W., Toronto. Technical—B. G. Newton, MacLean Publishing Co., 143 University Ave., Toronto.

Circulation.—Agricultural—F. O Campbell, Canadian Farm, 181 Simcoe St., Toronto. Business—Gordon Rutledge, MacLean Publishing Co., 143 University Ave., Toronto. Magazine—C. C. Campbell, The Veteran, 224 Sparks St., Ottawa. Religious—F. E. Dougall, John Dougall & Sons, 220 Craig St. W., Montreal, Que. Technical—J. J. Salmond, Monetary Times Printing Co. of Canada, 62 Church St., Toronto.

Editorial.—Agricultural—W. Porter, Farmers' Advocate, London, Ont. Business—G. D. Davis, MacLean Publishing Co., 143 University Ave., Toronto. Religious—Augustus Bridle, Canadian Courier, 181 Simcoe St., Toronto. Religious—Mrs. Campbell MacIver, Woman's Century, 157 Bay St., Toronto. Technical—W. R. Carr, Hugh C. MacLean Publications, 347 Adelaide St. W., Toronto.

Mechanical Production.—Agricultural—C. D. Stovel, The Stovel Co., Winnipeg, Man. Business—T. S. Young, Hugh C. MacLean Publications; 347 Adelaide St. W., Toronto. Magazines—Murray Simonski, Continental Publishing Co., 259 Spadina Ave., Toronto. Religious—W. L. Cope, Methodist Book Room, 299 Queen St. W., Toronto. Technical—H. V. Tyrrell, MacLean Publishing Co., 143 University Ave., Toronto.

Membership.—Agricultural—E. W. Hamilton, Canadian Power Farmer Motor in Canada, Winnipeg, Man. Business—S. K. Smith, Business Review and Maritime Retailer, St. John, N.B. Magazines—G. H. Tyndall, MacLean Publishing Co., 143 University Ave., Toronto. Religious—Rev. J. M. Duncan, D.D., Presbyterian Publications, 341 Church St., Toronto. Technical—H. T. Hunter, MacLean Publishing Co., 143 University Ave., Toronto.

Paper.—Agricultural—John Weld, Farmers' Advocate, London, Ont. Business—A. B. Stovel, The Stovel Co., Winnipeg, Man. Magazines—Lionel Davis, Continental Publishing Co., 259 Spadina Ave., Toronto. Religious—Rev. J. M. Duncan, D.D., Presbyterian Publications, 341 Church St., Toronto. Technical—Lt.-Col. J. B. Maclean, 143 University Ave., Toronto.

Postal and Legislation.—Agricultural—G. F. Chipman, Grain Growers' Guide, Winnipeg, Man. Business—H. T.

Hunter, MacLean Publishing Co., 143 University Ave., Toronto. Magazines—F. E. Dougall, John Dougall & Sons, 220 Craig St. W., Montreal. Religious—R. M. Burns, Catholic Record, London, Ont. Technical—Acton Burrows, Canadian Railway and Marine World, 70 Bond St., Toronto.

Chairmen and Secretaries of Sections

Agricultural.—John Weld, Farmers' Advocate, London, Ont., Chairman; T. J. Tobin, Canadian Countryman Publishing Co., Toronto, Secretary.

Business.—G. D. Davis, MacLean Publishing Co., Toronto, Chairman.

Magazines.—H. V. Tyrrell, MacLean Publishing Co., Toronto, Chairman; F. O. Campbell, Canadian Farm, Toronto, Secretary.

Technical.—T. S. Young, Hugh C. MacLean Publications, Toronto, Chairman; B. G. Newton, MacLean Publishing Co., Toronto, Secretary.

Religious and Educational.—Rev. R. Douglas Fraser, D.D., Presbyterian Publications, Toronto, Chairman; W. J. Dunlop, The School, Faculty of Education, Bloor St. W., Toronto, Secretary.

The election of officers and executive resulted as follows;
President—Acton Burrows.
Vice-President—John Weld.
Members representing the various sections:
Agricultural—C. D. Stovel.
Business—Hugh C. MacLean.
Magazines—Lionel Davis.
Religious—Rev. S. W. Fallis.
Technical—Lt.-Col. J. B. Maclean.

These five representatives, together with the president and vice-president, constitute the executive of the Association.

The matter of securing a manager was also taken up, and advertisements are now appearing, calling for a high-class man to take over this work.

The schedule of annual membership fees shall be as follows; based on advertising and subscription revenue:

Not exceeding $25,000			$ 50.00
Over $25,000 and not over $37,000			75.00
" 37,000 " " " 50,000			100.00
" 50,000 " " " 75,000			125.00
" 75,000 " " " 100,000			150.00
" 100,000 " " " 150,000			200.00
" 150,000 " " " 200,000			250.00
" 200,000 " " " 300,000			300.00
" 300,000 " " " 400,000			400.00
" 400,000 " " " 500,000			500.00
" 500,000 " " " 600,000			600.00
" 600,000 " " " 700,000			700.00
" 700,000 " " " 800,000			800.00
" 800,000 " " " 900,000			900.00
" 900,000			1,000.00

Annual fees for second members, $5.00

The National Steel Car Corporation, Limited, recently organized under a Dominion charter, has taken over the plant, business, equipment, assets and liabilities of the National Steel Car Company, Hamilton, Canada. The new company is purely Canadian in every sense of the word, having as president, R. J. Magor, a former Montrealer. The National Steel Car Corporation, Limited, will continue to manufacture railway cars and the motor truck department will have a greatly increased capacity. The minimum production for 1920 is placed at 1,500 motor trucks. An extensive advertising campaign, including newspapers, magazines, farm publications, and trade papers, is now being placed through the Hamilton Advertisers' Agency of Hamilton, Canada.

Some Ideas That Are Worth Passing Along
Suggestions That the Weekly Man Can Think About

IS there an opening for a good advertising salesman to sell his services to various weekly newspapers in this province and in other provinces?

We do not mean to suggest that he should go out and solicit for a group of papers, but that he should spend his time, week by week, or month by month, with individual publishers helping them to cultivate their own local field.

In other words there would probably be a number of answers to such an advertisement as the following:

Experienced advertising solicitor, who understands the weekly newspaper field, will place his services at the disposal of publishers at — per week, or — per cent. of the business written.

Yes, the chances are that there would be quite a few answers to such a proposition. Many of the publishers are coming to realize that their greatest chance to do more business is by plowing the local field a little deeper, by picking up the odds and ends that have been let pass, and by interesting those who have been chronic non-advertisers. Not only so but it is being more and more realized that selling advertising is a business that can become a specialty and a science, and the smaller publisher, who is fortunate enough to get the services of a good man for a short time, can learn much of the ways used by a successful man. He can, if he cares to accompany his solicitor, learn his method of approach, his arguments, his reasons, the way he meets objections, and best of all the manner in which he is able to actually close the business and sell the space. That last is the greatest of all selling arts. There are numerous very good canvassers, but the real salesman is not often met with.

Printer and Publisher knows of one weekly paper in Ontario that secured the services of a man who was representing a very reliable publishing house in Toronto. He had some spare time, and the publisher bought it. He worked on a commission basis, and in one week was able to bring back some $700 worth of business, none of it from sources that the publisher would otherwise have secured. This man was a real salesman. He wrote some of the first ads. for non-advertisers, advised them to have certain window displays for the day following the appearance of the ad. in the paper, and gave them quite a few good suggestions for weeks to come. The new advertisers were pleased with the results. They were convinced that advertising paid, and they became the best kind of advertisers, viz., they advertised certain specific things each week, and not their whole stock in general, and they back up their ad. with a window display.

FINDS STATIONARY FITS IN VERY WELL

ANOTHER weekly publisher sends this along, and while there may be some who disagree entirely, still the idea is genuine and we simply pass it along as it may help some in the same position as our correspondent:

"I would like to know how many publishers of weekly papers ever tried running a stationery stock in connection with their business. Some have tried it and quit, but I have found that it is good business. In fact I would not think of going out of it, and it looks as though my best chance for expansion were in the direction of enlarging that end.

"How does it help the printing business? Well, here. When a customer comes in and wants writing paper or envelopes we suggest that printed ones look much better. It is surprising the number of the farmers who are getting a name for their farms and getting it put on their writing paper. In some cases they have a photo of the house, or in cases of those who specialize in stock, they have a view taken in their pastures or sheds. This business is growing all the time. Once they have the cuts made they are going to come back for a repeat order. I generally manage to retain the cuts on the understanding that they are to have the advantage of a cheaper price next time.

"Then we used to have our share of the people who used a rubber stamp on their stationery. We have cured most of them. We specialized in this line of work. We had several fonts of type that made particularly good work. We used a good ink, and to my certain knowledge we have not a single rubber stamper left in the community. They are buying better paper than they did before.

"Another thing. We printed up quite a lot of writing paper with the name of the town on it and a little picture of one of the streets that made a very good impression. We put these in pads. We also got out a paper for the local Collegiate Institute, as there were a large number of out-of-town pupils attending there. We sold a lot more in this way. I will admit that the bookstore in town kicked and took out his ad. But he was a miserable little advertiser at the best and I was mighty glad when he pulled out his little announcement, for it opened the way for me to go ahead and advertise the stationery end of my business good and proper. I have since added scribbling books and note books and am satisfied with the move. It all fits in very nicely provided you have the space to house the lines and the help to sell them."

HELPING THE CORRESPONDENTS TO WORK

STILL another. This friend prints a paper in a community that is largely rural. He says:

"I read some time ago in *Printer and Publisher* how to interest the rural correspondent, and decided to try some of the ideas out. I want to say that they worked. Here is the case in point: I have had more or less trouble getting my correspondents to give me real stuff, and to get away from the trivial gossip of the community. I do not belittle that, for it interests them. But I wanted something of more general interest. To put it another way, I wanted to get some stuff from my country correspondents that my town readers would pay attention to. I read where some speaker or preacher in Toronto had been making an attack on the farmer for the prices that we were paying for things we buy. Formerly I would have blazed away at this myself in the form of an editorial item. But I changed around and did this: Sent a letter to the correspondents enclosing a reprint of the clipping of the attack on the farmer. I told our correspondents that I wanted them to show to the community where this man's views were wrong and why. I placed a limit of some two hundred words. Well say, perhaps that didn't get them. What they didn't do to that preacher or teacher was not worth doing. It was the greatest stuff we ever had in the country news. And, believe me, the correspondents themselves were proud of the way they had come to the defence of their own folks. I am going to work this about three times a year—toss out some live suggestion to the correspondents and keep their interest up in that way."

Justifies the Ten-Cent Rate

C. W. Rutledge, of the Markdale *Standard*, writes as follows: The Markdale *Standard* was visited by the County Judge, re printing of Voters' Lists for the Referendum and Provincial Elections last July. Having a linotype and two competent operatives, the Judge supposed we could do several municipalities. The staff was consulted, and we mutually agreed to do what we could to help out. The time being short it would be necessary to do this rush work, largely by overtime, so we arranged to divide up this revenue with the staff. Nothing was then said about price. To get the work done speedily was the chief object. After the printing of lists for five municipalities was complete, delivered, and O.K.'d, we concluded that ten cents a name would be fair remuneration, which rate was also O.K.'d by the Judge. Are we not entitled to further consideration for the long wait for our pay?

Our County Press Association schedule for voters' list work is $2.00 a page for a 25-name page, which is 8c. per name. I was giving my staff twenty-five per cent. of this as an encouragement to do the work and do it speedily. I added this to the 8c per name, which made it 10c per name. This was surely just and fair all around.

C. W RUTLEDGE.

The Babcock Co-operative Plan

The Babcock Printing Press Mfg. Co., New London., Conn., are now operating their plant largely on the co-operative plan. James E. Bennett, president, speaking of the plan, states:—

Over two years ago we formed a Committee consisting of the members of the various departments. This Committee met one night a week and its session usually lasted from two to three hours. It discussed all kinds of factory and office problems, which ordinarily would have been settled by the head of that department, or the executive officers of the company. Such settlement, however, often resulted in many misunderstandings because they would not be known to the members of the other departments, and a lack of co-ordination would result. Under this present plan there is almost perfect co-ordination in the operation of all departments throughout the office and factory. A record is kept of the discussions made at each meeting, and these minutes are read at the subsequent meetings and permanently preserved. Of course, the general policy of the company has been and still is outlined by the directors, but a large number of details affecting the various departments are all handled by this Departmental Committee.

One of the fundamental rules upon which this Committee is working is that nothing shall be taken for granted, the facts and figures shall always be presented in writing, if possible, and that each member of the Committee will present all the objections as well as points in favor of each proposition, and that we must "disagree without being disagreeable." Inasmuch as this has worked so satisfactorily we later organized a factory advisory council, which consists of all of the foremen or heads of the factory sections, together with the departmental heads. This makes quite a large body of men, and at their own election they meet one evening a month and the session lasts from eight to ten o'clock. Cigars are furnished and the men come to the meeting dressed in their street clothes and with their minds free from any worry which they might have if the meeting was held during factory hours. The meeting is quite informal and every member of the Council has an opportunity of making any suggestion. The officers of the company on their part agree that they will carry out and put into effect any plans adopted unanimously by the council, and that they will not put into effect any plans for factory management which are disapproved by the factory council. These conferences have developed a close co-operation between the officers, the heads of the departments and foremen, and through them with the workmen with the result that the entire working force is rapidly growing into a family, held and actuated by a feeling of mutual confidence and responsibility and each has the right to believe that he is a necessary part of the establishment, and that his opinions will be given due weight and consideration in the effort to develop the best kind of a working organization.

This also works out socially, as was evidenced at the dinner on July 17th. The wives of the men seemed to be as deeply interested in the welfare and progress of the company as their husbands.

A factory baseball team is making a good record, and those who do not play are enthusiastic fans.

An Athletic Association is being formed, which will have basketball and bowling team during the winter.

The employees have themselves formed the Babcock Printing Press Mutual Benefit Association, of which they have full control and management. They pay weekly sick benefits, death benefits, make floral offerings to the sick and at funerals, provide an annual banquet for their men and maintain a small factory store for the accommodation of the workmen. Money is raised by the assessment method and of the total amount assessed the company pays one-third.

Anyone visiting the factory is impressed with the idea that the men appreciate the confidence that is reposed in them by the officers.

The Montreal *Standard* is out with a circular on its increase in circulation. It now has 84,086.

Fate and —

Peterboro *Review*:—Ex-Ald. Dobbin has in a recent issue of the PRINTER & PUBLISHER an article written in his characteristically breezy vein, in which he deals with an eventful chapter in his own life. When Mr. Dobbin was a youth of tender years, his father, of whom he speaks with commendable filial regard, was an ardent follower of the Liberal party. There were at that time in Peterborough the same two papers that are now published here. One day Mr. Dobbin's father told him to go to the newspaper office and get a job as printer's devil. The future city alderman and publisher had already established a visiting footing with the *Review's* staff of printers, through personal acquaintance with one of its members. In his mind the "printing office" meant one place and one only, a delusion with a difference. He got a position with the *Review* and was already well started on his career before his father, to his unbounded amazement, found that the boy had got into the wrong pew. The former had had the rival establishment in view for his son all the time. But the die was cast. The young printer grew up a Conservative, departing from the political creed of his ancestors.

The lessons from this incident are obvious. From the beginning ex-Ald. Dobbin manifested a tendency to take the better part. A kindly fate took him by the hand just when he needed assistance, and directed him into the straight pathway of life. With the circumstance in his memory, Mr. Dobbin must now be convinced that "there's a destiny that shapes our ends, rough hew them how we will." And no doubt, as he reflects on his narrow escape, he is truly and humbly grateful.

Exporting Canada

Port Arthur *News-Chronicle*:—One hundred thousand cords of pulpwood was cut in the Port Arthur district during the past winter season, and the rivers and streams emptying into Thunder Bay, Black Bay and Nipigon Bay are still covered with thousands of cords of wood on its way to the greater water, where it will be loaded into ships and taken to United States ports.

Every year for more than a quarter of a century, pulpwood running into many thousands of cords is shipped from the north shore of Lake Superior to American mills, which would otherwise be closed and the machinery removed to Canada.

A number of years ago the Government adopted a law which prohibits the exportation of pulpwood cut from Crown Lands. For the length of time required to work out schemes to overcome the law, exportation dwindled, but that time was not long. Those engaged in cutting for export found unscrupulous individuals who, for a slight consideration, were ready to locate on free grant lands and turn them over, in effect, if not in fact, to the manipulators. Other concerns bought up batches of veteran's script for a mere song and secured wood. Others again by themselves and through compliant hirelings located on so-called mining claims and overcame the provisions of the Act.

By various and devious way the intention of the Act was brought to naught, nor was action taken to circumvent the schemes until recently, when a regulation was adopted prohibiting the cutting of timber on locations taken up for mining purposes. Yet the country is filled with "timber farmers," who, taking up a location proceed to cut the timber and then abandon the location.

But with this phase of the matter we do not propose to deal at the present, but to point out the great injustice that is being done to Canadians and Canadian interests by the policy which permits practically unlimited exportation of pulpwood in its raw state.

It is admitted on all sides that Ontario is pursuing a policy that will ultimately impoverish her timber resources and is receiving the very least reward in the shape of returns.

The true policy for Ontario is to prevent any of its wood to leave the country unmanufactured into paper.

THE RE-SET ADVERTISEMENT

 Specimens Taken at Random From Canadian Papers .

By H. A. Nicholson, Manager Printer and Publisher

WHEN the printing apprentice in the up-to-date office tries his hand at "display" one of the first principles of good typography taught him is harmony.

"Type" harmony is now generally recognized as desirable in nearly all classes of printing. The compositor who commences an advertisement with this in mind and is determined to practise the principle of harmony makes a step in the direction of artistic results. Should an advertisement be faulty in several respects (within certain limits) but still retain the virtue of being harmonious in its type and border display it is bound to appeal to the artistic taste in some degree. This truth forced itself upon the writer when turning the pages of a newspaper recently. One of the pages contained a five-column, ten-inch department store advertisement. The entire advertisement (referring to the display lines) was set in one series of type; namely, the popular Caslon series. To be more specific Caslon Bold and Bold Italics were the faces used. There was something attractive about this advertisement in spite of the fact that it required but little effort to spy out many deficiencies in its construction. It possessed one distinct virtue, a virtue which covered several faults. That virtue was contained in the harmonious effect produced by the use of one series of display type throughout the entire advertisement.

While the virtue of harmony in display, as it pertains to type, is general known among the printing craft it is a fact that printers are not practising the principle as one might expect. This is patent to everyone who reads newspapers, and is observant of type styles of the various advertisements. The reason for this lack of harmony is due to several reasons; the chie reason probably lies in the fact that compositors have not at their disposal a sufficiently complete series of any one family of type. Another reason for the diversity in style may be laid at the door of compositors' inability to see that harmony in display is good practice; every compositor is entitled to hold to his own good views, but it is worthy of note that the master typographers of this and every other generation agree without exception that the best results in type are only to be secured by adhering to display elements that harmonize in character.

It has been often pointed out that advertisement or any other kind of type display is not an exact science. For instance, it may help to give desirable expression to a particular piece of work by the introduction of a type line that is not of the same series as the balance of the display lines. When the occasion prompts it is well to remember that dangerous ground is being trod and artistry is apt to be sacrificed for facility, which may or may not tend to the best results. When the introduction of an "off-series" line or two is decided upon for type composition it should be borne in mind that the closer one sticks to the character of type which forms the basis of the work the better. For example French Old Style and Caslon make a good combination. But either of these faces, particularly in their larger sizes, clashes with Cheltenham or Gothic.

Reference has been made in the foregoing to harmony in display lines only, but harmony in some cases may be extended to the body matter, too, with superior effect. An advertisement of almost any kind might appropriately be set in Caslon series, using the bold face for the display lines and the light face for the body matter. Then on the other hand it would be somewhat ridiculous to set another class of advertisement in all Adstyle, as the lightest Adstyle face would be too heavy for its consistent use, particularly where there are many parts to the advertisement containing lengthy text matter. However, some excellent composition is seen in all Adstyle; it is a matter of judgment for the compositor, or whoever is responsible for the style adopted.

Appropriateness

There is another important point in typography worthy of note. This is appropriateness of display in respect to the article being advertised.

Gilbert P. Farrar, the eminent advertising man, has some interesting things to say apropos this feature of typography. He refers to it as harmony. Undoubtedly there is value in it.

Mr. Farrar offers some proof in the following words addressed to a convention of advertising dignitaries:

"A masterpiece is something in which every element of its composition is related, either by its harmony of thought or its harmony of relation. And a masterpiece usually has behind it a big boss who knew his job.

Webster says that 'Art is a system of rules and principles for obtaining a desired end.'

Your prospect is attracted first by character of your display. If this same character is reflected in the copy that this prospect reads the display helps the copy and vice versa.

In order to be more concrete, I will try to explain what I mean by the possibility of attracting and holding the attention and making the message penetrate.

Somehow I came across one of the booklets for the new Bethlehem motor truck. Now what does a buyer want to know all about a motor truck? Will it stand up?—Is it strong?

I hadn't become acquainted with this booklet ten seconds before this idea of strength was suggested to me by the display. The type was bold throughout as well as the illustrations. It was strong stuff, but I have been told that it was successful and I don't see any reason why it shouldn't be.

This booklet may not suit the aesthetic tastes of advertising men who are selling women's wear or jewelry. But the success of this campaign proves to a degree that the message in the booklet got across with a rush.

Here's another case:

A jeweler came to me for a set of four newspaper advertisements that would help him do a bigger business. But he also wanted the advertisements to create a better feeling toward his store, because he had a competitor who had been in the field many years ahead of him and the people of the town did not think that my advertiser's store was as 'classy' as that of his competitor.

So, it was a case of suggesting quality rather than just a statement of quality. The advertisements had to have quality sticking out of them to the extent of making quality the first thought in the onlooker's mind. In fact, the quality suggestion was more important than the quality talk.

Therefore, I selected a style of illustration that was refined but with a touch of attractive strength. I then selected a type that reflected quality and also harmonized with the drawings.

What was the result?

The jeweler sold four times as many diamonds as in the same period the year previous—and we weren't advertising diamonds in our copy. The high quality display suggested diamonds. I have the actual figures taken from his ledger as to the results, and I know that the client feels that the excellent quality of new business was the suggestion of quality in the display.

Would this style of frail quality sell the motor trucks? And would the crudely strong poster style sell diamonds when we are not talking diamonds?

Yes, these unrelated displays do sell some goods. And that's the answer that I get when I plead with an advertising man to change his methods. But do such effects sell as much as they should? That's the question.

I have tried the same copy with both related and unrelated display in order to prove that it does pay to harmonize all the elements of display so that they reinforce the message by suggesting the message or the spirit of the message, and I've never failed to get better returns with the related display. What you should be after is not just results but maximum results."

Note Reset Ads.

The reset advertisements on the following pages carry out the principles advocated in the preceding remarks. Compare them with the original advertisement placed immediately adjacent.

BIG REDUCTION

In Prices of Groceries

For Thursday and Friday

Dairy Butter, Choice, 2 lbs. for $1.25
Creamery Butter, Sask., 2 lbs. for 1.45
Shredded Wheat. 7 pkts for 1.00
Rolled Oats, Tubes, 3 for 1.00
Macaroni, Ready-Cut, Columbia, 11 pkts for 1.00
Pineapple, No. 1 Pack, Sliced or Grated, 3 tins for 1.00
Plums, Lombard, Heavy Syrup, 5 tins for 1.00
Tomatoes, 5 tins for 1.00
Corn, 5 tins for 1.00
Pork and Beans, 1½'s, Clark's, 7 tins for 1.00
St. Charles or Carnation Milk, talls, 6 tins for 1.00
Pacific Milk, talls, 6 tins for 1.00
Lennox Soap, 17 bars for 1.00
Dingman's Electric Soap, 11 bars for 1.00
Ivory Soap, 11 bars for 1.00
Fairy Soap, 9 bars for 1.00
Lifebuoy Soap, 11 bars for 1.00
Royal Crown Soap (cartons, 6 bars), 3 cartons for 1.25
Sunlight Soap, (cartons, 4 bars)), per carton 30
Palm Olive Soap, 9 bars for 1.00
Soups, Campbell's or Van Camp's, 6 tins for 1.00
Soups, Evaporated, Goug's, 4 for 25
Sopade, large package, 2 for 75
Raisins, Seeded or Seedless, 11 oz. packets, 5 for 1.00
Cooking Onions, choice, 7 lbs. for 50
Jams, $1.50 for, pail 1.35
Jams(Pure, 4's, Greengage, Red Plum, Cherry, Apricot and
   Peach. Regular $1.25 for, pail 1.10
Corned Beef, Fray Bento's, 2 tins for 1.00
Japan Tea, Bulk, Reg. 80c lb., 2 lbs. for 1.45
Nuts, whole mixed, 3 lbs. for 1.00
Apples, Jonathan, wrapped, to clear at, box 3.00
Currants, Bulk, per lb. 30
Casup Relish, 4 bottles for 60c, 9 bottles for 1.00

There are many other articles on our bargain table at greatly reduced prices, too numerous to mention

We have a line of Stoneware consisting of Mixing Bowls, Pitchers and Bean Crocks which will be sold at a very big reduction.

Saunders-Fullerton Ltd.

54 High St. W.   Phones 3627 - 4627

Diamonds !

Good Diamonds bought right are an investment not an expense.

We have a very complete stock of these preciou gems at prices substantially lower than elsewhere.

Come in and let us explain market conditions to you.

F. H. Nettleton

Jeweler and Optician

GORDON & WALTERS

January Clearance Sale

10 only Ladies' Suits to clear Wednesday morning at $45.00
Material of Gaberdine and fine French Serge; beautifully lined and styles up to the minute; regular values $69.00. A snap at $45.00
5 only Silk Poplin Dresses; regular value $25.00 Special clearance $17.50
Special sale of Wool Sweater Coats at $10
All Shades.

642 COLUMBIA STREET

Three two-column (reduced) newspaper advertisements selected at random from various newspapers. Note "resets" on the following page.

Reset advertisements—originals appear on opposite page.

The Church Page of The Saskatoon Star

Feature of Western Paper That is Well Conducted

AN article appearing in a recent issue of *Printer and Publisher* stated that the Winnipeg *Free Press* was the first paper in Canada to have a church editor. This paper made a mistake—quite unintentional—as the Saskatoon *Star* has paid particular attention to this department for some time. In fact, for over three years Miss Clara Holmes has run a Saturday feature.

What is of perhaps more outstanding importance in these

=== THE CHURCH AND ITS WORK ===

days of dollar-chasing and increasing costs is the fact that the Saskatoon *Star* has never yet charged a cent for printing the church announcements. *Printer and Publisher* may be in error, but we do not know of another paper doing this.

The page conducted by Miss Holmes is well edited—the stories are well headed, and the matter well laid out. A reproduction of some of the headings used will give an idea of the kind of matter carried.

Saskatchewan Social Service Congress To Convene Next Monday

INCLUSIVE PROGRAM IS ARRANGED WITH TOPICS OF VITAL IMPORTANCE TAKEN BY RECOG NISED AUTHORITIES

Praise to God Voiced in Weird Music of Old Syrian Tunes in Awakening India

THIRTY THOUSAND ATTEND THE LARGEST CHRISTIAN CONVENTION IN THE WORLD—FERVOR NOT MERELY EMOTIONAL—ECHO OF APOSTOLIC TIMES

Local Auxiliary of Christian Women's Board of Missions to Take University Drive Service

TASK OF CHURCH TO RADIATE NEW AND IDEAL SPIRIT

Rev. S. R. Laidlaw and Dean Tucker Address Vancouver Convention

Sermons For The Times Announced By Mr. Freeman

Evangelist Has Remained Here For 2 Services

Rev. Dr. Dix And Mr. Coates Preach Sun. At Mayfair

Calgary *Herald's* New Rates Out

The Calgary *Herald* is sending out well-arranged publicity on its circulation figures. Its distribution is as follows:

Alberta	9,188
Saskatchewan	192
British Columbia	903
Scattered	784
Calgary	16,837
Total	27,904

The new rate card is as follows:

Are You Connected?

The following is from a Nova Scotia paper under the editorial heading, "Are You Connected With the Town Sewer?"

So far as we know the numbers of the present Town Council have no desire to stir up hard feeling or to hold anyone up to public censure or ridicule, but it may be taken for granted right now, in order to save argument, that where the town sewer passes a man's door he will be expected to become connected up with it. If this public intimation is not sufficient then there will come the personal, polite request. Then if there is still no action a list of the people who should take sewerage and who have failed to do so, will be published in the *Tribune*. Failing to secure action from any of these methods then the wheels of the law will be set in motion to secure obedience to obvious and necessary requirement.

Please bear in mind that no favorites will be played. The rich and the poor, the high and the low, the good-looking and the ugly, the good-natured and the cranky—all will come under the operation of the sewerage law. A fair deal will be meted out to everybody.

If you have neglected the sewer matter, better make application to the Town Clerk right now. Delays are frequently dangerous.

THE WAY TO BRING IT DOWN

St. Louis "Star."

*And the Board of Commerce might help "Everybody" by telling how to handle
the weapon.*

The right kind of a strike

What One Office Follows as Its Style
To Ensure Uniformity in All Its Pages

1. Capitalize titles preceding names, as Chief of Police Smith, Professor Jones, General Logan. But lower-case titles standing alone or following names, as the chief of police; Dr. A. Ross Hill, president of the University of Missouri; William Jones, professor of economics; *except* President and Vice-President referring to the President and the Vice-President of the United States, and the titles of the national Cabinet officers, as Secretary of War, which are always to be capitalized. *Presidency* and *presidential* are not capitalized. (See also "Titles.")

2. Do not capitalize *former* preceding a title, as former Senator Wilson. *Former* is preferred to *ex-*.

3. Lower-case *king* and all such words when not used with the name of a specific person, as the king of England. In general, all such foreign titles follow the rules for American titles.

4. Capitalize epithets affixed to proper names, as Alexander the Great.

5. Capitalize *Union, Nation, Republic*, the *States* when referring to the United States. But do not capitalize adjectives derived from such names, as national, etc. Do not capitalize *government*.

6. Do not capitalize *state* referring to one of those in the United States.

7. Capitalize *constitution* referring to that of the United States. But state constitution (lower-case).

8. Capitalize such terms as Stars and Stripes, Old Glory, Union Jack, Stars and Bars, etc.

9. Capitalize *League of Nations* and also *League* referring to the League of Nations.

10. Capitalize the names of national legislative bodies, as Congress, House of Representatives or House, Senate, Parliament, Reichstag, Chamber (France). Do not capitalize names of committees of these bodies.

11. Capitalize *state Legislature* and synonymous terms (*legislature, assembly, general assembly*) only when the Missouri Legislature is meant. Capitalize *senate, house of representatives* and *house* when referring to the houses of the Missouri Legislature.

12. Capitalize *city council* only when referring to the Columbia City Council; lower-case *council* used alone.

13. Capitalize the names of federal and state departments and bureaus, as Department of Agriculture, State Insurance Department, Bureau of Vital Statistics. But lower-case municipal departments, as fire department, water and light department, street department.

14. Capitalize *Federal Reserve Bank* and *Federal Reserve District* in referring to a specific bank or district; otherwise use lower-case. Capitalize *Federal Reserve Board*, but lower-case *federal reserve system*.

15. Capitalize specific names of courts of record, as Boone County Circuit Court, Kansas City Court of Appeals, Missouri Supreme Court. Capitalize *circuit court*, standing alone, only when the Boone County Circuit Court is meant. The same rule applies to *county court* and *probate court*. Do not capitalize *police court*.

16. Capitalize *county* only when used in a specific name, as Boone County, County Mayo.

17. Capitalize the *East*, the *West*, the *Middle West* and other terms used for definite regions of the United States, but do not capitalize *east, west*, etc., when used merely to designate direction or point of compass, as "west of here." Do not capitalize *westerner, southerner, western states* and other such derivatives.

18. Capitalize sections of a state, as Northern Missouri,

Central Missouri, etc., but not *the northern part of Missouri*, etc.

19. Capitalize the full names of associations, clubs, societies, companies, etc., as Missouri Equal Suffrage Association, Tuesday Club for the Prevention of Cruelty to Animals, Star Publishing Company. *The* preceding such a name is not to be capitalized. Do not capitalize *association, club*, etc., when not attached to a specific name. When not using exact title of firm, write the *S. H. Jones shoe store*.

20. Capitalize *university, college, academy*, etc., when part of a title, as University of Missouri, Central College, Missouri Military Academy. But do not capitalize when the plural is used, as the state universities of Missouri, Kansas and Ohio.

21. Capitalize *building, hall, house, hotel, theatre*, etc., when used with a distinguishing name, as Nowell Building, Parker House, Athens Hotel, Star Theatre.

22. Capitalize *room*, etc., when followed by a number or letter, as Room 31, Academic Hall; Parlor C, Grandview Hotel.

23. Do not capitalize *postoffice, courthouse, poorhouse, council chamber, city hall, armory, president's house, army, navy, marine corps, cadets, fraternity* (as Phi Delta Theta fraternity), *police court, women's parlors*.

24. Capitalize the names of all political parties, in this and other countries, as Democratic, Republican, Socialist, Liberal, Tory, Union, Bolshevist. But do not capitalize such words, or their derivatives, when used in a general sense, as republican form of government, democratic tendencies, socialistic views, bolshevist ideas.

25. Capitalize the names of expositions, congresses, conventions, etc., as Panama-Pacific Exposition, World's Press Congress, Journalism Week. But do not capitalize such words as *third annual, biennial*, etc., in connection with these names.

26. Capitalize *Boy Scouts*. Make *Campfire* (referring to the girls' organization) one word, capitalized.

27. Capitalize *pole, island, isthmus, cape, ocean, bay, river*, and in general all such geographical terms when used in specific names, as North Pole, South Sea Islands, Cape Hatteras, Hudson Bay, Pacific Ocean, Mississippi River, Isthmus of Panama.

28. Capitalize, when used with a distinguishing name, *ward, precinct, square, garden, park*, etc., as First Ward, Eighth Precinct, City Hall Square, Madison Square Garden, Forest Park.

29. Do not capitalize *street, avenue, boulevard, place, lane, terrace, way, road, highway*, etc., as Ninth street, More's boulevard, Maryland place, Rosemary lane, Old Trails road, Ashland gravel road.

30. Do not capitalize *addition, depot, elevator, mine, station, stockyards*, etc., as Wabash freight depot, Yellow Dog mine, Clover Leaf station, Kansas City stockyards.

31. Capitalize the names of French streets and places, as Rue de la Paix, Place de la Concorde.

32. Capitalize *church* when used in a specific name, as Wilkes Boulevard Methodist Church, First Christian Church. But a Methodist church, a Christian church.

33. Capitalize the names of all religious denominations, as Baptist, Quaker, Mormon, Methodist.

34. Capitalize names for the Bible, as the Holy Scriptures, the Book of Books. But do not capitalize adjectives derived from such names, as biblical, scriptural.

35. Capitalize all names used for the Deity, including personal pronouns.

36. Capitalize the names of holidays, as Fourth of July, Dominion Day, Columbus Day, Washington's Birthday.

37. Capitalize the names of notable events and things, as the Declaration of Independence, the War of 1812, the Revolution, the Reformation, the Civil War, the Battle of the Marne.

38. Capitalize titles of specific treaties, laws, bills, etc., as Treaty of Ghent, Eleventh Amendment, Workmen's Compensation Act, Good Roads Bill. But when the reference is general use lower-case, as the good roads legislation of the last Congress.

39. Capitalize such names as Triple Alliance, Triple Entente, Quadruple Entente, Allies.

40. Capitalize the fanciful titles of cities and states, as the Mound City, the Buckeye State.

41. Capitalize the nicknames of baseball, football and other athletic teams, as Chicago Cubs, Boston Braves, Tigers, Jayhawkers.

42. Capitalize distinctive names of localities in cities, as West End, Nob Hill, Back Bay, Happy Hollow.

43. Capitalize names of military organizations, as Eighty-third Regiment, Company B (do not quote letter), Company F (but headquarters company), National Guard, Grand Army of the Republic, Missouri State Militia, University Cadet Corps (but University cadets).

44. Capitalize the names of races and nationalities, except the negro, as Italian, American, Indian.

45. Capitalize college degrees, whether written in full or abbreviated, as Bachelor of Arts, Doctor of Laws, Bachelor of Science in Education; A.B., LL.D., B.S. in Ed. (When the year is given, use the form: A.B.'09—no comma between degree and year.)

46. Capitalize high school when used as in Moberly (Mo.) High School (but the high school at Moberly, Mo.)

47. Capitalize, but do not quote, the titles of newspapers and other periodicals, as the Evening Missourian, the New York World, the Outlook, the Saturday Evening Post. Do not capitalize the.

48. Capitalize and quote the titles of books, plays, poems, songs, speeches, etc., as "The Scarlet Letter," "Within the Law," "The Man With the Hoe," "The University and the State." The beginning a title must be capitalized and included in the quotation. All the principal words—that is, nouns, pronouns, verbs, adjectives, adverbs and interjections—are to be capitalized, no matter how short; thus: "The Man Who Would Be King." Other parts of speech—that is, prepositions, conjunctions and articles—are to be capitalized only when they contain four or more letters; thus: at, in, a, for, Between, Through, Into. The same rules apply to capitalization in headlines but not to scriptural texts or formal subjects for debate, in which only the first word is capitalized.

49. In titles of books, plays, etc., and in headlines capitalize prepositions that are attached to or compounded with verbs: "He Was Voted For by His Party."—"He Was Stared At by the Crowd."

50. Capitalize the first word after a colon in giving lists of officers; thus: "The following were elected: President, William Jones; vice-president, Frank Smith," etc. In general, however, the use of capital or small letter after the colon is dependent upon the sense. Use a capital when the passage after the colon would have an independent meaning. Use lower-case when the passage is dependent upon the preceding clause. There is no hard and fast rule.

51. Capitalize adjectives derived from proper nouns, as English, Elizabethan, Germanic, Teutonic. But do not capitalize proper names and derivatives whose original significance has been obscured by long and common usage. Under this head fall such words as India rubber, street arab, pasteurize, macadam, axminster, gatling, paris green, plaster of paris, philippic, socratic, herculean, guillotine, utopia, bohemian, philistine, platonic.

52. Capitalize the particles in French names, as le, la, de, du, when used without a Christian name or title preceding, as Du Maurier. But lower-case when preceded by a name or title, as George du Maurier. The same rule applies to the German von: Field Marshal von Mackensen, but, without Christian name or title, Von Mackensen. Always capitalize Van in Dutch names unless personal preference dictates an exception, as Henry van Dyke.

53. Capitalize only the distinguishing words where two or more names are connected, as the Wabash and Missouri Pacific railroads. (In singular form, Wabash Railroad.)

54. Do not capitalize senior, junior, sophomore, freshman. And remember the adjective form of freshman is freshman, as the freshman football team, freshman girls (you wouldn't write sophomores girls).

55. Do not capitalize the seasons of the year unless they are personified.

56. Do not Capitalize a. m. and p. m. except in headlines.

Oiling Keyboard

If there is one place where care is a virtue, it is in the use of oil on keyboard cams. Some machinist-operators "squirt" oil on pivot points of the keyboard cam yokes. Most operators know that a little oil on keyboard cams goes a long way. Heavy machine oil should never be used for this purpose. A light clock oil is best. Cams should be oiled about once in three or four months. Oil should be applied with a broom straw to the pivot on the cam yokes—it should never be squirted on with an oil can. Bearings of keyboard rubber roll shaft should be oiled only once a week, and then sparingly. All surplus oil should be wiped off. If too much oil is used, it will come in contact with the ends of the rubber rolls, and rot them. If rolls are washed with soap and lukewarm water once each week, and thoroughly dried, they will retain their resiliency and insure keyboard cams turning properly. Observing the above points will insure a good working keyboard—J. H. Westcott, Ottawa, Kansas.

More About Rubber Rollers

From time to time I have heard complaints from operators about the difficulty involved in replacing the cam rubber rollers. With my method of replacement it is very easy to make this change—and with dispatch. First: Place the new roller over the stock or core, and give it a start by pushing it down on the core about six or eight inches; then place the palm of the right hand firmly over top of the rubber roller to form a vacuum, and pushing downward gently the roller will almost jump into place on the stock. Holding the palm of the hand over the end causes the air confined in the roller to expand the opening around the stock, permitting the rubber roller to slip on easily. After the roller is in place and stretched to proper length, coming flush with end of core, a little liquid glue placed on the stock so it will come under the roller about one-half inch on each end will hold it in place and also prevent the excess oil from creeping under the end of the rolls, causing them to rot.—N. W. Key, Richmond, Va.

Driving-Clutch Leathers

Recently, in setting wide-measure slugs, the machine stopped at the point of ejection, the clutch not being able to pull the cams over. I examined the knives—they were properly set; tested the clutch spring—it had the proper tension. Sandpapered the clutch leathers, but it would not pull cams over on slugs over 22 ems. Finally, I moved the old leathers and applied new ones secured from the factory, which did the trick. I found that clutch leathers become oil-soaked in time, which makes them unfit for use. A new pair is recommended. —R. G. Albright, Souderton, Pa.

The Largest Printing Plant In the World

How U. S. Bureau Is Efficiently Handled

THERE is, apparently, a very great difference between results achieved from the Government Printing Bureau at Washington and the one at Ottawa. The U. S. Department passed through a period of tremendous work at high pressure, and through it all the work came out on time and at minimum cost. That is about as good a test as can well be made of any concern.

A writer in a current publication devotes considerable space to showing how the Washington Bureau of Printing is conducted, and to giving some idea of the amount of work passing through what is probably the largest printing office in the world.

Referring to the manner in which the department went through the war period, the article says:—Under the able management—the improved systematization, shrewd, foresighted buying in an unsettled, understocked market, practical all-round economies, executive ability, both as a matter of handling the working force and in keeping it up to the required muster despite depletions due to the inroads of the draft and the lure of higher wages—under the direction of Mr. Ford, and the impetus of hearty, patriotic co-operation on the part of employees throughout, the reserve of the Government Printing Office was skilfully and diligently tapped to the utmost and made to absorb the incalculable pressure of war work. Item after item that ran into millions of questionnaires, thrift cards, notices of classifications, and what not else having to do with the construction of a vast war machine, not to mention orders from single departments for copies of miscellaneous jobs (100,000,000 entered in one instance on the same day) and other millions of drill books, handbooks, regulations, etc.—a literal deluge of additions to the regular work of the office was taken on, executed, job by job, with singular steadiness, accuracy, and dispatch, and promptly delivered at minimum cost.

Let us see what component parts of this colossal institution are, and something of what it does when it has nothing else to do, so to speak:

Some 5,200 persons are employed, and the divisions of actual production are as follows: Job Room—117 employees—modernly equipped throughout. Handles 45,000 jobs a year. Section of Machine Composition—This is the department of the batteries of linotypes and monotypes—far and away the largest of its kind in the world. The bulk of all the straight-matter is set on the former. The output of the section is nearly if not quite 2,500,000,000 ems a year. Hand Section—190 employees, engaged in correcting, make-up and imposing. Proofroom—290 employees—editing, preparing, reading, and revising. Foundry—125 employees—thoroughly equipped; produces about 17,000,000 square inches of plated matter a year. Pressroom—660 employees—145 modern presses that handle 280,000 forms a year and turn out over 12,000,000 chargeable impressions every twenty-four hours. Presses range from the smallest, with capacity of 5,000 impressions an hour, to the largest of web presses, taking 64 quarto pages. Presses are equipped with automatic feeders. Best of elevating trucks for loading paper on presses are in use, and other overhead runs facilitate handling of roll stock. 130,000 pounds of inks are made each year in the ink-room, and about 3,600 rollers—containing 30,000 pounds of composition—are made each year in the roller-room. Bindery—1,700 employees, complete modern machine equipment for all kinds of pamphlet and bound work. A number of smaller divisions handle special work such as postal cards, money-order blanks, etc.

The Government Printing Office consumes about 50,-000,000 pounds of paper stock a year; and, while its capacity is still adequate in the sense of the reserve capacity aforesaid, the increasing demand upon it for printing and binding has continued so steadily that already extensive systematizing of production methods has become necessary. An idea of the meaning of this increase is to be gained by a comparison of the amount of blanks, schedules, postal cards, money-order forms, envelopes, and similar matter printed during the fiscal year of 1880 and the same total for 1918. For 1880, the total was 131,000,-000 copies; for 1918, it was about 5,000 000,000 copies. Book work has increased proportionately—to a grand total of about 1,800,000 type pages a year. Average production in the division of book composition is 7,000,000 ems a day; and it has been estimated that, if occasion arose, a publication of 2,000 pages could be set up, read, printed, bound into copies, and delivered in a single day. The output of postal cards runs about 4,000,000 a day. The cards are counted in 50's, banded, boxed in lots of 500 in cartons and containers, and shipped to points designated by the post office officials. About 140,000,000 money-order forms are printed each year, and delivered in books of from 50 to 200 each. The daily "Congressional Record" is printed each night during sessions of Congress, and varies in sizes from 8 to 225 quarto pages. Copy comes in late at night—some of it as late as 2 a.m. Type must be set, plates made, 33,000 copies printed, folded, gathered, wire-stitched, and addressed in time to catch the early morning mail. The "Official Bulletin," issued by the Committee of Public Information (16 to 48 quarto pages in size, and to the number of 117,000 copies), is also printed each night and mailed from the office. About 18,000,000 copies of the *Farmers' Bulletin* are printed for the Department of Agriculture. Some 25,000,000 copies of speeches are printed annually for members of Congress and paid for by them. 25,000 bills and resolutions of Congress are printed during each session. They vary in size from 2 to 200 pages, and in quantity from 200 to 800 copies each. Bound "Congressional Records," covering complete proceedings of each Congress, are printed in this office. The one for the 63rd Congress, Second Session, made nineteen volumes. 61,030 copies of each volume were printed and bound, making a total of 116,470 volumes. The total annual expense of the Government Printing Office is about $12,000,000. The appropriation to cover this outlay is divided and allotted by Congress among the departments and the various bureaus of the Government in accordance with their size and needs for printing, each being allowed printing and binding only to the amount of its allotment. Existing law requires this printing and binding to be done at cost, and charges, based on a fixed scale of prices, regulated by a modern cost system, are rendered for each piece of work produced. About 80,000 bills are rendered annually—to a total of about $12,000,000.

Employees are on an 8-hour per day basis, they receive compensation that compares favorably with union wages paid throughout the country, and each is allowed thirty days' vacation, with pay, during the year. Most divisions run night forces throughout the year. Employees working at night receive a 20 per cent. advance over corresponding day rates.

An emergency hospital for employees is maintained in the new building. The hospital is directly in charge of a medical sanitary officer. Here, an average of 2,500 surgical and medical cases are treated each year.

Digby Courier:—If you want to settle in a wide-awake community, all you have to do is to look at the local newspaper. A wide-awake, well-supported home newspaper is always associated with good schools, churches, active business and intelligent people. It never fails. No business man or pioneer in any community makes any better investment than in the support of a home newspaper.

The Work in Saskatchewan

The Saskatchewan Division of the Canadian Press Association is sending the following letter to its members:—

Owing to the increased cost of newsprint and ready-print, together with the continuously rising prices of type, machinery, wages and all other production costs, a number of weekly newspapers throughout the province have decided to increase their subscription rates from $1.50 to $2.00 per year.

This matter was discussed at a recent meeting of the executive of this Association and it was unanimously agreed that an increase in subscription rates was not only justifiable, but absolutely necessary in the interests of the publishers of the province. It was also felt that the present was an opportune time for such a move and that it would be advisable if all increases became effective about the same time. Therefore, if you are contemplating increasing your subscription rates, we would suggest that you make an announcement covering the matter immediately, and, if possible, arrange for the increased rate to become effective on March 1st.

We also wish to remind you that arrangements are now being made for holding the 1920 convention of the Saskatchewan Division, Canadian Press Association, at the University of Saskatchewan, Saskatoon, on May 27, 28 and 29. This will be along the lines of last year's convention, which, in spite of the small attendance on account of the serious strike situation at that time, was nevertheless one of the most successful and profitable gatherings in the history of the weekly press of Canada. Further particulars will be sent you later but this preliminary notice is to remind you to reserve these dates for this gathering. Arrange to bring your wife along, as ample accommodation will be provided at the University at a nomina cost.

At a meeting of The Canadian Paper Trade Association, held at Toronto, Friday the 6th inst., the following resolution was passed by its members:—"Owing to the extremely adverse rate of exchange existing against Canada we strongly recommend that the members of our Association refrain from purchasing in the United States (wherever possible) until the rate of exchange becomes more normal."

The Barrie *Examiner* in a recent announcement, makes the following reference to its price: " The price remains the same as last year—$1.50."

Canadian District of Monotype organization. Taken at their annual "Get Together" in Toronto.

Rear row, left to right—George Philip, office assistant; F. W. Forster, production expert; T. H. Griffin, B. C. and Alberta, salesman-inspector; W. G. Mould, chief instructor, Toronto school; F. F. Smith, Sask. and Manitoba, salesman-inspector; T. Strickland, Quebec, inspector; A. Shepherd, general inspector; A. F. Dennis, Ontario, inspector.

Front row, left to right—L. W. Beatty, Ontario, salesman; F. F. Esler, special representative; H. F. McMahon, Canadian Manager; G. H. Clark, office manager; Romeo Bourque, Quebec, salesman; H. E. Mountstephen, Ontario, salesman.

THE GREATEST ESSENTIAL

We have expended in recent years a great deal of time, a great deal of money and the thought of the very best brains in the printing business in studying costs; in finding and devising the most efficient methods of production; in inventing new labor-saving machines and refining methods of manufacture; in the training of efficiency experts, cost finding experts, but we have not as yet given the measure of thought and study necessary to that other fundamental, which is the more essential of the three—the selling of the product.—("Dad" Mickel, in "What Shall it Profit You?")

Harold Flammer, music publisher, 56 West 45th St., New York City, has brought out something new in the line of decorated music. One is accustomed to seeing all sorts of illustrations on the outside of a song, but the inside pages are generally kept clear for printing. The new songs brought out by Harold Flammer carry the illustrations both on cover and inside. The effect is artistic, but to the musician who reads the music it may be rather confusing.

The Jarvis *Record* has been sold to a group of local men, who took over the property on the first of the present month. For the past 18 years, Mrs. Elva Rogers has owned and managed the property.

Woodstock, N. B., *Press*:—The Aroostook *Daily News*, the first daily paper Aroostook ever had, was first issued Monday, published at Houlton by the Aroostook Publishing Company, of which Simeon L. White of that town, formerly of Caribou, is the president, and many prominent Houlton business men are stockholders. A gentleman named John Page, who comes from Texas or some other place in the South, is the editor and also the business manager.

The Edmonton *Journal* has been carrying a good amount of special advertising pages in recent weeks, including a 16-page Aviation Section, eight-page Book Supplement, ten-page Music Feature, and a four-page Shopping Special, which latter was sold for three insertions.

The Brantford *Expositor* had a successful Dollar Day recently. Harris Walsh, of the *Expositor* staff, was the mysterious Dollar Bill of the day. In order to get the $10 reward it was necessary to first find the man and then say this: "Pardon me, mister, but are you not the mysterious Mr. Dollar Bill for whom all the Dollar Day Shoppers of Brant and Norfolk Counties are looking?" We had no idea any person could keep their head under water for that length of time, but a Brantford woman said it all—easily.

The Toronto *World* was fined $100 in a libel suit with a Toronto detective. Ida Webster (Mrs. Charles George), who wrote the article, was acquitted.

On February 15th, the West Lorne *Sun* put up its price from $1.00 to $1.50 per year.

Hamilton *Times*, Jan. 29th:—A meeting of the leading newspaper publishers of Ontario was held yesterday in the Royal Connaught, this city, at which the chief subject for discussion was the subscription price of the papers. There is a general feeling that the newspapers cannot continue to be sold at the present low rates. The publishers of the smaller dailies are meeting in Toronto to consider the same subject. United action is looked for in a short time.

The Govan (Sask.) *Prairie News* announces an increase of rates to $2.00 per year. Annual subscriptions therefore paid on and after March 1st next will be $2.00 to points in Canada and $2.50 to points outside of Canada.

Stratford papers were tied up on the first of February. Lack of power was the trouble.

The *Border Cities Star* announced that the price of the paper would be increased to three cents, commencing Monday, February 2nd.

The Edmonton *Bulletin* has had "The Mysterious Mr. Raffles" around the city. A page of advertising—paid kind—announces in what stores he will be at various hours. A prize of $20 was hung up for his capture.

GENTLEMEN—QUIT THIS!

Hartland, N.B., *Observer*:—But our Woodstock contemporary tangles itself up awfully when it says: "The big pay roll was not sufficient to set the County Council proceedings as the *Observer* borrowed the ready-set type from the *Sentinel*, which will probably appear in the *Observer* this week." Stung, ol' boy! The *Observer* is not printing the Council report at all. The funniest part of all is that the *Press* had not the facilities for setting the said report and for two weeks has been printing it from "ready-set type borrowed from the *Sentinel*."

THE PERSONAL SIDE OF IT

We'd Like To Get Items For These Columns

York and Simcoe County Association

A most enthusiastic meeting of the York and Simcoe County Press Association took place on Friday, January 16th, in the Board-room of the Public Library at Barrie. A very low temperature prevented a large attendance of members of the Association, but the meeting was very representative of the pressmen of these two counties, and excellent progress was made during a meeting that lasted from 2 to 5 p. m. Mr. McLaren, president of the Association, presided.

The major portion of the time was taken up with a revision of the price list. The list underwent a considerable revision upwards and as it now stands should meet the requirements of the pressmen in this district. The list is in the hands of the printer and two copies will be sent to each member of the Association.

W. G. CAVE,
Midland "Argus," President of the Simcoe and York Co. Press Association.

On motion, the Association will be known as the York and Simcoe Press Association, the joining fee is $3.00 and the annual subscription for each member $2.00.

Since the last meeting of the Association the following members have passed away: George Hale, Orillia *Packet*; Erastus Jackson, Newmarket *Era*; H. F. Blackstone, Orillia *Times*, and J. S. Carlton, Creemore, and the secretary was directed to write a letter of sympathy to the families of the deceased.

The next meeting of the Association will be held in June, the time and place to be decided by the Executive.

The members present at the meeting were the guests of the Barrie *Examiner*, at luncheon in the Allandale Restaurant.

British Columbia

Two outstanding figures in the weekly journalism of British Columbia are Col. Lowry and "Dad" Simpson, now of Kamloops. The following reference to the latter appears in a recent issue of the Merritt, B.C., *Herald*, and will no doubt be of interest to Western readers especially:

Journalism in British Columbia will be poorer by the loss from its ranks caused by the retirement of F. E. Simpson (universally known as "Dad" Simpson), editor of the Kamloops *Standard-Sentinel*. We deeply regret to note that failing eyesight has necessitated the step that the genial "Dad" has decided to take, and sincerely trust that his retirement may soon have the effect of improving the condition of his eyes, and that some day he may again be wielding the mighty pen for the enlightenment of his many readers.

"Dad" Simpson has been in the newspaper business for more years than some of us would care to admit, and has thoroughly earned his retirement had it been for any other reason than that mentioned above. Let us wish for him years of solid comfort. Below we give a letter he sends to his associates:

"Owing to the condition of my eyes, which have been growing worse for the past year, I am forced, much against my will and natural inclination, to relinquish for good, so far as I know

now, newspaper work or go blind. I want to say just a word of good-bye to the boys and an expression of regret over leaving their ranks. Many of you I have known for years, some for a shorter time, and a few only by your papers. I have never had an unkind word from any of you. I owe all of you the deepest debt of gratitude for your uniform courtesy and kindness to me. You have honored me in your editorial association; you have been more than good in your references to me during the twenty-two years that I have been in this business in the province. I want you to know that I am sincerely thankful to you for what you have done for me, and that I wish all of you the prosperity that is coming to you and the happiness that is your natural inheritance for the sacrifices you have made.
Sincerely yours,

January 17, 1920.   F. E. SIMPSON."

In the recent school trustees election at Penticton, R. J. McDougall of the *Herald* headed the poll.

Users of "insides" from Regina were treated to another boost of 4 cents per quire at the first of the year.

Editor Grier of the Kaslo *Kootenaian* is taking time by the forelock. His rate on poetry is 20 cents a line, cash with copy.

Alex. F. Wallace has left the Cowichan *Leader* to become sporting editor of the Vancouver *World*.

A. Hope Herd, owing to ill-health, has disposed of his interest in the Comox *Argus* to his partner, Ben Hughes.

Mr. Forester, editor of the Oakville *Star*, has gone south on an extended trip to Kentucky, Tennessee, Florida, and other points.

McConnell-Fergusson Winnipeg branch are offering B. C. weeklies contracts on Eaton advertising on a space of not less than 1,000 inches a year.

In the run for aldermen in Ward 2, Grand Forks, T. A. Love of the *Gazette* defeated his rival, Gus Evans of the *Sun*, by quite a respectable plurality.

Walter Jordan of the *Review* was Revelstoke's delegate at the annual convention of the Associated Boards of Trade of Eastern B. C. at Trail this month.

L. J. Ball of the *News*, Vernon, has been chosen Knight Commander of a chapter of the Knights of Columbus covering the Okanagan country, which will have its lodge-quarters at Vernon.

J. McD. Torrance, business manager of the Lethbridge *Herald*, who has gone to California for the winter, was a few days' visitor at Revelstoke, en route south, the guest of his old friend, Walter Jordan of the *Review*.

Blairmore *Enterprise*:—E. T. Saunders, owner of the Pincher Creek *Echo*, and formerly in the newspaper game at Lethbridge, died at San Diego, California, leaving a wife to mourn his loss. Mr. Saunders was about 65 years of age.

Robert G. Marshall has taken over the management of the Kamloops (B. C.) *Standard-Sentinel*. Mr. Marshall was with the mechanical department of the Vancouver *World* for a number of years and has had experience throughout various parts of Canada as a printer and publisher.

J. B. Daniell is now editing the Prince George *Citizen* and is identified with the Company which has taken over the business from three old time newspaper men, J. G. Quinn, W. A. Stillingfleet and G. C. Dyment. Mr. Daniell founded the Fort George *Herald*. He served in the R.A.F. and spent some time in German prison camps.

Kamloops *Standard*:—Charles E. Smitheringale, once a well-known newspaper man in the interior, but now making honest money in Vancouver, was recently married to Miss Violet L. Hoole. It is a good thing that Mr. Smitheringale got out of the newspaper business or this little romance would not have materialized.

The Penticton *Herald* announces an advance in subscription to $2.50 a year, effective March 1st. The *Herald*, Merritt, recently put the same rate in effect, while the Cranbrook *Courier* established that rate when it was revived a little less than a year ago.

Linotype installations are becoming quite frequent in the interior. In addition to the No. 19 secured from the *Kootenaian*, Kaslo, the Nelson *Daily News* has also just put in a new No. 14. Machines are also being installed this month at Princeton *Star*, Summerland *Review* and the Rossland *Miner*.

F. E. Simpson, better known as "Old Man" Simpson, retired as editor and manager of the Kamloops *Standard-Sentinel* on Feb. 1st, and is succeeded by Robt. Marshall, his assistant in those positions for the past eighteen months. Mr. Simpson is opening a swell confectionery and ice cream palace in Kamloops.

The Trail *News* has a kick on the economical habits of the aldermen-elect of that town. Following their election they went in all together on a united card of thanks which got the *News* about $1.75 on the 10 cent a line rate, instead of each of the seven of them running individual "thank yous" at a dollar a throw.

A. E. Darby, who joins the staff of the Vancouver *Daily Sun*, has had considerable experience as an editorial and political writer in Canada and the Old Country previously. He was born in Sheffield, England, in 1880, the son of W. Evans Darby, D.D., LL.D., who may be remembered by many readers in Vancouver in connection with his activities for international peace and arbitration. Early in his career, Mr. Darby identified himself with the political issues of the day, taking an active journalistic part in all political and economic subjects. He joined the *Free Press* in 1912 and associated himself with John W. Dafoe, editor-in-chief of that paper. The editorial columns of the *Free Press* have been recognized as a big factor in influencing and building up Western Canada, so that Mr. Darby's association with the *Sun* will no doubt prove a boon to Coast journalism and add considerable prestige to this paper, which has made progress during the past two years. Surrounding himself with a group of active young men, Mr. Cromie, owner and publisher of the Vancouver *Sun*, has in the past two years built up the morning paper situation in Vancouver into what is regarded by newspapermen as a very fine property.

Alberta

The Granum (Alberta) *Herald* has discontinued publication. Major W. A. DeGraves, former Calgary newspaperman, who enlisted in the ranks in the army service corps and performed such distinguished service that he was twice decorated, has sailed for England. He has been asked by the *Daily Express* to go to Russia.

Lethbridge *Herald*:—It took a good deal of courage to establish a newspaper in Lethbridge in 1885. The population was sparse, the future uncertain, and material in the nature of press, type and paper had to be hauled from a long distance, for there was no railroad in those days. Despite all this E. T. Saunders began the publication of the Lethbridge *News* and was its owner until about 1907. He came here with more experience as a printer than as an individual possessed with capital. He faced many ups and downs, but the years of toil and his faith in Lethbridge earned him a competence that enabled him to spend his later years in comfort and recreation. Old-timers like "Si" Saunders are not properly valued until they pass away. The part they played in those early pioneer days can never be justly estimated. Their faith in the country was an asset that meant much. Adversities there were many, but they remained and fought the battles and we, the late comers, are reaping the reward, living in a city with modern comforts and assurance of greater development.

Saskatchewan

Following the lead of many large industrial concerns in the Dominion, the Times Publishing Co. Ltd., publishers of the Moose Jaw *Evening Times*, has adopted the plan of insuring the lives of all its employees. The announcement was made on January 28th by the company that each married employee of the company would be insured for $1,500 and each single employee for $500. This insurance is a straight gift from the worker remains in the employ of the company, becoming operative as soon as the worker joins the staff.

Manitoba

William Menzie, credit manager of the Winnipeg *Tribune*, and a well-known newspaper man, died Sunday after a few days' illness. He was 42 years of age.

J. Ellison Young, managing editor of the *Border Cities Star*, at a recent meeting of the Rotary Club of Windsor, gave a talk on "The Making of Newspapers." He went into the details, showing the method of collecting, editing and printing news, editorial and other matter.

W. J. Healy, assistant editor of *Grain Growers' Guide*, and formerly associate editor of the Winnipeg *Free Press*, has accepted appointment as Provincial Librarian. Mr. Healy

will take over control of the Library Department about March 1st. Mr. Healy represented the *Mail* of Toronto in the Press Gallery.

Mr. and Mrs. J. F. B. Livesay, both well known in Western newspaper circles, who are leaving Winnipeg after a residence of many years, were the guests of honor at a gathering of the Women's Press Club. The club presented Mrs. Livesay with a pair of earrings. Mr. and Mrs. Livesay are leaving for Toronto, where Mr. Livesay takes over-general managership of the Canadian Press Ltd.

Here is something to show the conditions in Winnipeg on February 11th: To-day's issue of the *Tribune* is "adless" for the reason that only enough paper for a six-page edition was on hand at press time. The *Tribune* regrets keenly that it must disappoint its advertising patrons and its host of readers, who "shop in the *Tribune* before they shop in the stores." Only dire necessity compels the elimination of advertising which, as it must be obvious to readers, entails a considerable loss to the *Tribune*. It is believed that a supply of paper will be received in time to permit the publication of a normal edition to-morrow.

Some important changes are taking place in newspaperdom in the county of Hastings. D. H. Morrison, who has long and successfully conducted the *Times* at Bancroft, disposed of his interests there some time ago to Harry Price. Mr. Morrison has now purchased the Tweed *News* from O. M. Alger, who has been publisher and proprietor of that journal for about 15 years. Mr. Morrison has already moved to Tweed, and taken possession of the *News*. Mr. Alger intends to remove to Oshawa, where, it is stated, he will found and establish a newspaper to be called the Oshawa *Telegram*. He will also conduct a large job printing plant. He expects to get the new business at Oshawa under way by March 1. It was on the Tweed *Weekly News* that W. J. Taylor, publisher of the Woodstock *Sentinel-Review*, and president of the Canadian Press Association, 1918-19, began his journalistic career, starting first as editor and later becoming publisher and proprietor. Mr. Taylor disposed of the business to Mr. Alger.

Ontario

Oliver Watson is sending out notices informing the trade that he has opened an office at 81 Peter St., Toronto. Mr. Watson has been recently connected with the mechanical department of the MacLean Publishing Co.

Collingwood *Bulletin:*—Mr. C. H. Hale of the *Packet* was re-elected chairman of the Water, Light and Power Commission of Orillia. Mr. Hale has given good service to this department of municipal affairs and his re-election is a further mark of the confidence in him of his colleagues.

The Canadian Press Photographers' Association held their annual meeting and banquet at the Florence Cafe, Toronto, when the election of officers for the ensuing year took place. The following officers were elected: President, C. Roose; vice-president, L. J. Turofsky; secretary-treasurer, C. Brid.

"Uncle Dud" Mason, publisher of the Prescott *Journal,* is now Mayor of the town. He says concerning the transition and its subsequent feeling: "Well, it's all over now and the same old hat still fits our dome." . . . . . 'From the cradle to the Mayor's chair in 46 years,' will be the title of the next book we publish."

The remains of John G. Reid, Woodstock, a printer, who died in Windsor, following a short illness from pneumonia, were sent to Woodstock. Deceased, who was about 36 years of age, was born in Woodstock. Until eight years ago he was engaged in newspaper offices there. Since then he has been employed in London and Windsor

Prescott *Journal:*—W. L. C. Jento, who for the past nine months has held several consignments on the reportorial staff of the Montreal *Herald,* severs his connection with that publication this week and goes to Sherbrooke, P.Q., where he has secured the position of city editor of the *Daily Record.* Here's wishing you every success, "Bill," and may your shadow never grow less.

E. H. Gourlie, publisher of the monthly journal, *Six Bits,* at Hamilton, after putting this paper on a very profitable basis, both in advertising and circulation, has presented this valuable asset to the Men's Association, which has the object of preserving the identity of the 75th Battalion, independent of any other militia unit.

Almonte *Gazette:*—Mr. A. D. Jones, of the Pembroke *Observer,* is a good sport. He writes in his paper as follows: "Town readers of the *Observer* may be expecting in this column this week some comment on the Mayoralty contest, but as the editor is figuring as one of the principals in the race, and as his opponent is not in the position of having a newspaper at his command, we feel that to urge the editor's claims editorially might be in the nature of taking an unfair advantage, hence we leave the matter in the hands of the citizens without any comment."

Listowel *Standard:*—The many friends in Listowel of Mr. Ed. Loney will be pleased to learn that he has received an excellent position in Toronto as day editor for the Canadian Associated Press, Ltd. Mr. Loney's promotion in the newspaper field has been very rapid owing to his exceptional ability. Less than two years ago he started in newspaper work with the *Sentinel-Review* at Woodstock, where he soon won a name for himself. He later went to the Toronto *Times* and after that paper ceased publication he went to the Hamilton *Herald.* When the Canadian Associated Press wanted a day editor for Western Ontario they chose Mr. Loney.

Mr. Gordon Butler, son of Mr. and Mrs. F. H. Butler, of London, died very suddenly in Detroit. Influenza was the cause of his death, and the first intimation of his being ill was in a telegram informing the parents of his death. Prior to going to Detroit, Mr. Butler was a captain in the W. O. R. here, and was well known locally. He was at one time sporting editor of the *Advertiser,* and had also worked in the Merchants Bank here. In Detroit he was connected with the Lakeside Foundry Company.

A beautiful window has been put in the Church of the Messiah, Sherbrooke and Simpson streets, Montreal, in memory of the late Anson McKim. Rev. Frederick R. Griffin, an old friend of Mr. McKim's, came from Philadelphia to conduct the service. Professor Dubois played the 'cello and Merlin Davies sang the solo in Gounod's Sanctus, the music in the service being under the direction of Mr. George Brewer, the organist of the church.

A valued and highly regarded member of the Toronto *Globe* editorial staff passed away in the death of Mr. Sydney Hood, assistant financial and commercial editor. Mr. Hood had been ill only eight days and was a victim of influenza, followed by pneumonia. A gallant fight was made to save his life, but without success. Mr. Hood was thirty years of age. He was born in Toronto, being the son of Mr. Ebenezer Hood of Yonge street. He took to newspaper work early in life, his chief connections being with the Toronto *Daily Star,* the *World,* the *Financial News Bureau* and the *Globe.* He joined the Financial Department of the *Globe* early in 1918 and had special charge of the reports from the live-stock market and the Mining Exchange. Mr. Hood, who passed away at his home, 382 Eglinton avenue east, is survived by his wife and four small children. His father and two brothers and two sisters also survive.

Miss Mary Hallam, of St. Marys, formerly of Wyoming, has become a member of the *Advertiser-Topic* staff of Petrolia.

E. J. Penny, for many years a reporter with the *London Free Press,* has just been appointed assistant secretary of the London Chamber of Commerce.

Since the death of Walter J. Blackburn, manager of the London *Free Press,* Mr. A. S. Blackburn has been filling the position of manager as well as that of secretary.

Reorganization of the editorial staff of the London *Morning Advertiser* has resulted in the placing of Joe Maloney in the position of night editor, T. L. Smith as financial editor, and W. J. Yorke Hardy as Western Ontario editor.

Bert Perry, advertising manager during its lifetime of the London *Week-End Mirror,* and previously with the London *Advertiser,* is now with the advertising agency of McConnell and Fergusson, with which firm Wallace J. Laut, proprietor of the *Mirror,* had previously accepted a post.

W. Stewart, editor of the *Sunday World,* has gone to Detroit to do feature work on the Detroit *Journal.* Mr. R. F. Choate, formerly of the Toronto *Times,* will get out the *Sunday World.* Mr. Choate first broke into the newspaper business at Peterboro, and has had a wide experience both in United States, Eastern and Western Canada.

The London Newswriters' Association has a membership composed now of 100 per cent. of the reporters and desk men of the London *Advertiser* and London *Free Press,* and a union charter granted by the International Typographical Union. A negotiating committee is now engaged in discussing an agreement with the employers. Stated hours of work, a higher scale of minimum wages, and a closed shop are some of the clauses in the agreement being presented. The officers of the Newswriters' Association are: President, J. Stronach, city editor *Advertiser;* vice-president, T. R. Elliott, Western Ontario editor, the London *Free Press;* secretary, Joe Maloney, night editor, the *Advertiser.*

After a very brief illness of influenza followed by pneumonia, Miss Eleanor Milloy died at her home in Toronto. A sister, Mrs. P. Moffatt, her parents and a host of sorrowing friends mourn the loss, not least of these being her associates on the *World* staff. The late Miss Milloy, who was only 19 years of age, was a gifted vocalist, with an exceptionally sweet contralto voice, and was at times soloist and a member of St. James' Square Presbyterian Church choir. The pastor, Rev. D. N. Morden, conducted services at the house and at Prospect Cemetery. Many floral tributes were laid on the coffin by her friends and associates, among them being a wreath from the *World* staff, which was represented at the funeral by Mr. F. Richards, Mr. A. N. Bastedo and Mr. Charles Meek.

John Curran, the veteran newspaperman of Orillia, died of pneumonia at his home on February 17th. John Curran was born in Armagh, Ireland, in 1839, and therefore was in his eighty-first year. He came to Orillia about forty-five years ago, and in 1884 founded the Orillia *News-Letter.* His first journalistic venture was the Essex Centre *Chronicle,* which he conducted from 1880 to 1884. He returned to Orillia, bringing the *Canadian Workman* with him. This paper was made the official organ of the Ancient Order of United Workmen in 1895, since which time Mr. Curran has devoted his energies exclusively to that publication, editing the February edition, which is now being printed here. He was twice married, and is survived by his wife and family of twelve. His sons are : George and John of the *News-Letter;* James W., proprietor of the *Daily Star,* Sault Ste. Marie; Robert, ex-Mayor of Orillia; William S., Sault Ste. Marie; Dr. Ernest T. of Brighton, England; and Walter, Orillia; the daughters: Mrs. J. W. King, Toronto; Margaret, Orillia; Mrs. A. H. Arens, Akron, Ohio; Mrs. Wm. Webster, Sudbury; and Mrs. Chas. F. Gray, wife of Mayor Gray of Winnipeg.

The Owen Sound *Sun-Times* has an interesting story in a recent issue regarding Duncan McMurchy, a member of the mechanical staff of that paper, who has been for 60 years working at the trade. As a lad he developed a fondness for the printing business and left school to go to work with Pat. Lowrie, who had a printing office on Union Street (8th St. E.) Owen Sound), where Shean's tea store was until recently. This was in the late 50's and after a short time there learning the rudiments, Mr. McMurchy went back to school. About that time the *Comet* was being published by the late Owen Van Dusen, in the premises now occupied by Mr. Simon Bomalick on 3rd Ave. E., and Pearce and Culbertson had a printing office about opposite the Pacific Hotel property. They published the *Pioneer.* After a further short period in school Mr. McMurchy went to work as a clerk with Mr. Bothwell in a store opposite the Clifton House, the firm later moving to the stand now occupied by Mr. T. W. Douglass. But his love of the printing business stuck and Duncan left his clerkship to take a position on the *Advertiser.* He stayed with that paper till the *Times* was taken over from the late Richard Carney by Messrs. D. Creighton and John Rutherford. This was about

1863. He was still there when the Fenian Raid occurred and when No. 1 Company left for the scene of hostilities, Mr. McMurchy was one of those who rushed into uniform and became a member of No. 5 Company of the Grey regiment. He stayed with Messrs. Creighton and Rutherford until that combination dissolved partnership, when he again returned to the *Advertiser* as right-hand man to the late James H. Little. After ten years he was back again on the *Times* and served that paper well and faithfully until 15 months ago when it was absorbed by the *Sun*. Since then Mr. McMurchy has been a valued and valuable member of the *Sun-Times* staff.

Quebec

Alf Rubbra, a well-known newspaper man in Toronto, is now getting out a magazine, *"Business Methods."*

Clark E. Locke is now with the Robert Simpson advertising department. He formerly did the Legislature for the *World* and *News*.

E. H. Scott, formerly of the Winnipeg *Free Press*, is now in charge of one of the T. Eaton Co. advertising departments in Winnipeg.

W. E. Playfair has gone to the New York office of the A.P. He has been with the Montreal *Star* for some time, previous to which he was overseas.

E. F. Slack, president of the Canadian Press, Limited, and general manager of the Montreal *Gazette*, died at his residence, 658 Grosvenor avenue, Westmount. He was taken ill with influenza a couple of days ago, and this developed into double pneumonia, to which he succumbed. Mr. Slack would have completed his fifty-second year in 1920, having been born at Waterloo, Quebec, in 1868. He was educated at the Waterloo Academy and joined the staff of the Montreal *Gazette* in 1885 as a reporter. He was successively telegraph editor, city editor, editorial writer and managing editor, finally becoming manager-director of the *Gazette*. He organized the Canadian Press, Limited, in 1891, of which he was later made president. Speaking of Mr. Slack, the Ottawa *Journal* says:—"The sudden death of Mr. E. F. Slack, of the Montreal *Gazette*, is a heavy blow to Canadian papers from the Atlantic to the Pacific. His work in connection with the Canadian Press, Limited, of which he had been president for a number of years, was of a most generous character, and he was animated largely for the need of a closer intimacy between the people of the East and the people of the West. Mr. Slack had recently brought almost to completion plans for a direct cable news service from Britain to Canada. The papers of Canada generally will extend sympathy to the Montreal *Gazette* in the loss of so fine a gentleman.

Maritime Personals

The plant of the *Casket*, published at Antigonish, N. S., suffered by fire recently.

Amos Mantle has been made a member of the writing staff of the St. John *Standard*.

F. W.W. Bartlett, of the writing staff of the St. John *Evening Times*, is ill at his home in Hampton, N.B.

John T. Hawke, editor and proprietor of the Moncton *Transcript*, who has been ill at his home, is reported improved in condition.

Richard O'Brien, managing editor of the St. John *Globe*, is at his desk again after having been laid up for a little while with poisoning in his foot.

The warehouse of the Richmond Paper Co., owned by Orr Brothers, in Halifax, was destroyed by fire recently with a loss of $175,000, the better part of which is insured.

The Halifax *Herald* was visited by a disastrous fire. The chief sufferer was the Royal Print & Litho. Despite the flooded condition of the premises the *Herald* came out with an eight-page issue the same day.

F. J. Hardiman, who has been office manager for the Telegraph Pub. Co., St. John, was recently presented with a morocco wallet containing a substantial sum by his associates there, prior to his departure for the West.

The master printers of St. John and others interested held an informal dinner this week at the Clifton House, when about twenty were present. E. Allan Schofield presided and after the dinner an interesting discussion of business conditions and problems of the printing trade took place. The affair was greatly enjoyed.

Friends in the printing and publishing business throughout Canada, especially those of the older generation, will regret to learn of the death of Joseph Shaw Knowles, aged 85 years, which occurred recently at his home in St. John. He had won much popularity as a humorous writer, and published different papers, among which might be mentioned "The Gripsack" and "The True Humorist," while he also wrote for several publications. He retired from active business about ten years

ago. Mr. Knowles lost a son killed in action and was badly shaken over it as he was an only boy. His wife and three daughters survive.

An interesting event took place on February 14th, when the various staffs of the Halifax *Herald* made a presentation to Senator William Dennis, who has been associated with the paper from the time of its first issue, 45 years ago. The *Morning Herald* appeared first on January 14, 1875, and a junior reporter on that issue was William Dennis. One other man who helped to bring out that issue is still with the paper, John Trider, the head pressman, who at that time was a press boy. The presentation took the form of a sterling silver loving cup, accompanied by an address. His colleague of that time last evening handed the cup to Senator Dennis, on behalf of the staffs. The Senator made an appropriate reply to the address. Mrs. Dennis was presented with a bouquet.

The death is announced, at Halifax, of William A. Monaghan, for many years correspondent in that district for *Printer and Publisher*. Mr. Monaghan was badly injured in a street car accident while on the way home to lunch, and never regained consciousness, although receiving every attention at the Halifax General Hospital. He was for over forty years in the employ of T. C. Allan and Co., and at the time of his death he was the manager of that firm. Years ago he was secretary of the Young Men's Literary Association, and he was at one time secretary of the Charitable Irish Society. He was a member of the Knights of Columbus, the C.M.B.A. and the Mayflower Curling Club. He was an enthusiastic militia man, and for thirty-five years he was attached to the 63rd Rifles. In 1885, accompanied by his brother Edward, he went to Western Canada with the battalion at the time of the rebellion. He was 57 years of age, and a son of the late Patrick Monaghan, who was prominent in temperance work in this Province. The deceased leaves a widow, three sons and two daughters.

At a large attendance of the International Pressmen and Assistants' Union, No. 36, recently in St. John, Alex. Ellison was elected president; J. Maxwell, vice-president; W. Ward, recording secretary; W. R. Green, financial secretary; P. Brown, treasurer, and C. Finlay, sergeant-at-arms.

Demand versus Acceptance

Editorial in "Printers' Ink"

A prominent retail merchant walked into the office of "Printers' Ink" the other day and asked us to advise advertisers to go easy on the you'll-have-calls-for-my-goods argument. According to this man, this plea does more harm than good.

He says that too often it is the concern that advertises only in flashes for the sole purpose of impressing the retailer, that is the loudest in talking about calls. The buyer discounts these promises, because he knows from experience that the few calls that such advertising may produce can be safely ignored.

When an article is well advertised, it may be taken for granted that the retailer will receive calls for it. But to emphasize this too much is dangerous. There is nothing easier than for the buyer to declare that he is not receiving calls. That is always his pet objection, and an overmastering one it is. Most salesmen give way before it.

As a matter of fact, the call argument is fallacious, both from the standpoint of the man who uses it to make a sale and also from the standpoint of the prospect who tries to get out of buying by saying he never had a call. Demand is not always expressed vocally. Advertising accumulates a host of desires in most persons that they do not express until a favorable occasion for the purchase of the desired article arises.

The chances are they may never ask for the product at all. Some time when they see it displayed, they will buy it merely by saying, "I will take one of those." Every experienced advertiser knows that advertising is vastly more potent in creating consumer acceptance of a product than it is in bringing oral demand for that product.

Recently one of Hart, Schaffner and Marx's largest dealers told us that it is seldom a man comes into his store and asks for this brand of clothes. This retailer is widely known as a Hart, Schaffner and Marx distributor. Customers who come in take it for granted that they will be given these clothes. They do not call for the brand; they accept it. Nine times out of ten that is the way advertising works.

It is a mistake to pin too much faith on the "call" theory. It is rarely a reliable guide. We heard a druggist not long ago say that he had greatly increased his sales since he stopped waiting for "calls" and began to handle everything that he thought his trade should buy. One illustration that he gave is graphic. He declared that he always carried dental floss, but did not display it because "there were so few calls for it." In an entire year he sold only a gross of floss. However, a salesman one day induced him to group all his dental goods in an imposing display. The sale of all this merchandise immediately increased. Almost everyone who came in picked something off the counter. The increase in the floss sales was particularly noticeable. Picking up a package his customers would say, "My dentist told me to use this. I did not know that you handled it." He now sells twenty-four gross of dental floss in a year. In this one case waiting for calls was euchring this druggist out of about 96 per cent. of his possible floss business.

REBUILT MACHINERY

No. 1827—Two-Revolution Cottrell, bed 33½x 50, four rollers, interchangeable, table distribution, front fly delivery, four tracks, back-up.

No. 202—25 x 34 Whitlock Drum Cylinder, table distribution, rear tapeless delivery, two form rollers, four distributors, back-up.

No. 338—24 x 32½ Diamond Cylinder with power fixtures.

No. 1829—Two-Revolution Cottrell, bed 25x30, two rollers, tapeless delivery, air, table distribution, power fixtures.

No. 376—Six Col. Quarto Two Revolution Campbell, front fly delivery table distribution, four form rollers, and four distributors.

No. 132L—36" Childs Acme Automatic Paper Cutter with two new knives.

No. 395—13 x 19 Universal with Hot Embossing attachment, four chases.

No. 401—10x15 W. & B. Gordon, power fixtures, treadle, long fountain.

No. 399—10x15 W. & B. Gordon, power fixtures, treadle and fountain.

No. 341—13x19 W. & B. Gordon with treadle and power fixtures, 2 chases.

No. 392—10 x 15 W. & B. Gordon with fountain.

No. 235—10" Bradley Card Cutter.

No. 237—32" Cloth Piper Ruling Machine, 1 beam striker, receiving box and power.

No. 115L—S.K. White Power Paging Machine, with six wheel steel figure head.

Full Details on Request

STEPHENSON, BLAKE & CO.

C. H. CREIGHTON
Manager

60 Front St. West
TORONTO

Opposite
New Union Depot

Brass Rule Made to Order   *Roller Composition and Casting*

GEO. M. STEWART

PRINTING and BOOKBINDING MACHINERY
TYPE and SUPPLIES

92 McGill Street, Montreal, 'Phone Main 1892.

Thoroughly Rebuilt Cylinder and Platen Presses, Paper Cutters and Machinery of all kinds for Printers, Bookbinders, Box Makers, etc. Write and state your requirements.

RELIABLE

Tinned Stitching Wire

You will eliminate trouble on your stitching machines and ensure satisfactory work by using this Canadian-made product.

Sold by Leading Jobbers

THE STEEL COMPANY OF CANADA
LIMITED

Sales Offices : Hamilton   Toronto   Montreal   Winnipeg   Vancouver   St. John

Quality
and
Service
Built An
Extensive Business

Thirty-five years ago W. G. Harris, president of the Canada Metal Co., had an idea — namely, that a service and quality metals, combined with ability and a keen, earnest interest in the patrons' business, would prove successful beyond the average — and he had the courage to found the Canada Metal Company, Limited, on that idea. Certainly his judgment was right. Time and results tell a true story. In a nutshell it is this:

Canada Metal Company products include 90% of the typemetal used in Canadian printing and publishing offices. It is used exclusively by offices big and small for typesetting and stereotyping purposes.

The struggle for supremacy was trying. It required ceaseless pounding away to impress upon some printers that the service policy went beyond the office of the president, down and up into every branch and man of the organization.

The president's work still goes on. Thirty-five years ago Mr. Harris gave personal attention to the requirements of every buyer of a pound of his metal. To this day Mr. Harris gives the same personal service. If a buyer of Canada Metal Company products has a metal problem to solve Mr. Harris aims to go right to the seat of trouble and investigate the problem right on the spot where the trouble occurs. If the distance is too far from the head office in Toronto, there are other expert metallurgists working under Mr. Harris' supervision at the Canada Metal Company plants at Montreal, Winnipeg and Vancouver, as well as thirty representatives on the road.

Ability to look after Printers' wants has made Canada Metal Company Metals - for - Printers supreme—these metals include:

IMPERIAL LINOTYPE
IMPERIAL INTERTYPE
IMPERIAL MONOTYPE
IMPERIAL STEREOTYPE
IMPERIAL ELECTROTYPE

The Canada Metal Company, Limited
Toronto   Montreal
Winnipeg   Vancouver

At it 35 years and still going strong.

W. G. Harris, President

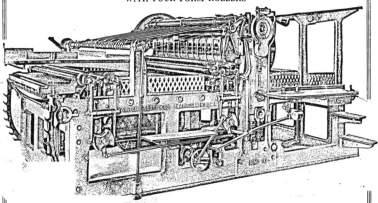

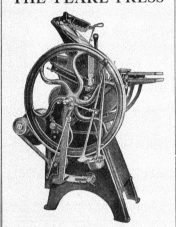

Buyers' Guide

BUYERS' DIRECTORY

ADDRESSING MACHINES
The Challenge Machinery Co., Grand Haven; Mich.
BALERS, WASTE PAPER
Golding Mfg. Co., Franklin, Mass.
Logan, H. J., 114 Adelaide St. West, Toronto.
Stephenson, Blake & Co., 60 Front St. W., Toronto
Stewart, Geo. M., 92 McGill St., Montreal.
BINDERY SUPPLIES
Logan, H. J., Toronto, Ont.
Morrison Co., J. L., Toronto, Ont.
BOOKBINDERS' MACHINERY
Logan, H. J., 114 Adelaide St. W., Toronto.
Miller & Richard, Toronto and Winnipeg.
Morrison, J. L., Co., 445 King St. W., Toronto.
Royal Machine Works, Montreal.
Stewart, Geo. M., 92 McGill St., Montreal, Que.
Stephenson, Blake & Co., 60 Front St. W., Toronto
BOOKBINDERS' WIRE
The Steel Co. of Canada, Hamilton.
CHASES—SECTIONAL STEEL
The Challenge Machinery Co., Grand Haven, Mich.
COLLECTION AGENCIES
Canadian Mercantile Agency, 46 Elgin St., Ottawa.
Publishers' Protective Association, Goodyear Bldg.,
154 Simcoe St., Toronto.
COUNTING MACHINES
Stephenson, Blake & Co., 60 Front St. W., Toronto
CYLINDER PRESSES
The Challenge Machinery Co., Grand Haven, Mich.
CROSS CONTINUOUS FEEDER
Morrison, J. L., Co., 445 King St., Toronto.
CUTTING MACHINES—PAPER
Golding Mfg. Co., Franklin, Mass.
Morrison, J. L., Co., 445 King St. W., Toronto.
Stephenson, Blake & Co., 60 Front St. W., Toronto
The Challenge Machinery Co., Grand Haven. Mich.
ELECTROTYPING AND STEREOTYPING
Rapid Electrotype Co. of Canada, 229 Richmond
St. W., Toronto.
Toronto Electrotype & Stereotype Co., 111
Adelaide St. W., Toronto.
ELECTROTYPE AND STEREOTYPE BASES
The Challenge Machinery Co., Grand Haven, Mich.
EMBOSSING PRESSES
Golding Mfg. Co., Franklin, Mass.
Stephenson, Blake & Co., 60 Front St. W., Toronto
ENVELOPE MANUFACTURERS
Toronto Envelope Co., Toronto.
W. V. Dawson. Ltd., Montreal and Toronto.
ELECTROTYPE METAL
British Smelting & Refining Co., Ltd., Montreal.
Canada Metal Co., Limited, Toronto.
Hoyt Metal Co., Limited, Toronto.
FEATURES FOR NEWSPAPERS
International Syndicate, Baltimore, Md.
GALLEYS AND GALLEY CABINETS
Stephenson, Blake & Co., Toronto.
The Challenge Machinery Co., Grand Haven. Mich.
The Toronto Type Foundry Co., Ltd., Toronto.
GUMMED PAPER MAKERS
Jones, Samuel, & Co., 7 Bridewell Place, London
England, and Waverly Park. New Jersey.
HAND PRINTING PRESSES
Golding Mfg. Co., Franklin. Mass.
INKS
Reliance Ink Co., Winnipeg, Man.
JOB PRINTING PRESSES
Golding Mfg. Co., Franklin, Mass.
JOB PRESS GAUGES
Golding Mfg. Co., Franklin. Mass.
Megill, Ed., 60 Duane St., New York City.
LEADS AND SLUGS
Stephenson, Blake & Co., Toronto.
The Challenge Machinery Co., Grand Haven, Mich.
The Toronto Foundry Co., Ltd., Toronto.
LITHOGRAPHERS
Goes Lithographing Co., Chicago, Ill.
MAILING MACHINES
Chauncey Wongs Sons, Greenfield, Mass.
Rev. Robert Dick Estate, 157 W. Tupper St.,
Buffalo, N.Y.
MAILING GALLEYS
The Challenge Machinery Co., Grand Haven, Mich.
METAL FURNITURE
The Challenge Machinery Co., Grand Haven, Mich.
METAL FOR TYPESETTING MACHINES
British Smelting & Refining Co., Ltd. Montreal.
Canada Metal Co., Fraser Ave., Toronto.
Great Western Smelting & Refining Co., Van-
couver.
Hoyt Metal Co., 356 Eastern Ave., Toronto.

Buyers' Guide

BUYERS' DIRECTORY

PAPER MANUFACTURERS AND DEALERS
Buntin, Gillies & Co., Ltd., Hamilton, Ont.
Canada Paper Co., 112 Bay St., Toronto.
Dickinson & Co., John, 25 Melinda St., Toronto.
Don Valley Paper Co., Toronto, Ont.
Eeleeck Mfg. Co., Turner's Falls, Mass.
Hails Paper Co., Ltd., Fred H., Toronto, Ont.
McFarlane, Son & Hodgson, Montreal, Que.
Niagara Paper Mills, Lockport, N.Y.
Paper Sales, Limited, Bank of Hamilton Building, Toronto.
Provincial Paper Mills Co., Telephone Building, Toronto.
Rolland Paper Co., Montreal, Que.
Ticonderoga Pulp & Paper Co., 200 Fifth Ave., New York.
United Paper Mills, Ltd., Toronto.
Wilson Munroe Co., Limited, Toronto.
Whyte Paper Co., A, 55 Bay St., Toronto.

PATENT BLOCKS
The Challenge Machinery Co., Grand Haven, Mich.

PHOTO ENGRAVERS
Reliance Engraving Co., Toronto, Ont.

PRINTING INK MANUFACTURERS
Ault & Wiborg Co. of Canada, Ltd., Toronto, Ont.
Canada Printing Ink Co., 15 Duncan St., Toronto.
The Columbia Printing Ink & Roller Co., Hamilton St., Vancouver, B.C.
Dominion Printing Ink Co., 128 Pears Ave., Toronto.
Manton Bros., Toronto, Ont.
Reliance Ink Co., Winnipeg, Man.
Shackell, Edwards & Co., Ltd., 127 Peter Street, Toronto.
Sinclair & Valentine, 233 Richmond St. West.

PLATE MOUNTING EQUIPMENT
The Challenge Machinery Co., Grand Haven, Mich.

PRINTERS' FURNITURE
The Hamilton Manufacturing Co., Two Rivers, Wisconsin.
The Challenge Machinery Co., Grand Haven, Mich.

PRINTERS' IRON FURNITURE
The Toronto Type Foundry Co., Ltd., Toronto.
Stephenson, Blake & Co., Toronto.
The Challenge Machinery Co., Grand Haven, Mich.

PRINTING PRESSES
Babcock Printing Press Co., New London, Conn.
Goss Printing Press Co., Chicago, Ill.
Hoe & Co., R., 504-520 Grand St., New York.
Linotype & Machinery, Limited, London, Eng.
Manton Bros., 105 Elizabeth St., Toronto.
Miehle Printing Press & Mfg. Co., Chicago.
Premier & Potter Printing Press Co., Inc., New York City.
Stephenson, Blake & Co., Toronto.
The Challenge Machinery Co., Grand Haven, Mien.
The Mann Litho Press Co., 58 Walker St., New York City.
Walter Scott & Co., Plainfield, N.J.

PRINTERS' PRICE LISTS
Port Publishing Co., Salt Lake, Utah.

PRINTING PRESS MOTORS
Kimble Electric Co., 635N Western Avenue, Chicago, Ill.
Manton Bros., Toronto, Ont.

PRINTERS' MACHINERY AND SUPPLIES
Manton Bros, Toronto, Ont.
Royal Machine Works, Montreal
Stephenson, Blake & Co., Toronto.
The Toronto Foundry Co., Ltd., Toronto.

PRINTERS' ROLLERS
Canada Printing Ink Co., Limited, 15 Duncan St., Toronto.
The Columbia Printing Ink & Roller Co., Hamilton St., Vancouver, B.C.
Manton Bros., Toronto, Ont.
Sinclair & Valentine, Toronto, Ont.
Winnipeg Printers' Roller Works, 175 McDermot Ave., Winnipeg.

PROOF PRESSES
Stephenson, Blake & Co., 60 Front St. W., Toronto.
The Challenge Machinery Co., Grand Haven, Mich.

"REDUCOL"
Indiana Chemical Co., Indianapolis, Ind.

REGISTER GAUGES
E. L. Megill, 60 Duane St., New York.

REGISTER HOOKS, BLOCKS AND CATCHES
The Challenge Machinery Co., Grand Haven, Mich.

ROTARY PRESSES
Goss Printing Press Co., 16th Street and Ashland Ave., Chicago.
Hoe & Co., R., 504-520 Grand St., New York.

ROLLER SUPPORTERS
The Challenge Machinery Co., Grand Haven, Mich.

RULED FORMS
Matrix Ruled Form & Tabular Co., Fort Worth, Texas.

STEREO PAPERS
L. S. Dixon & Co., Ltd., 38 Cable St., Liverpool, England.

SECTIONAL BLOCKS
The Challenge Machinery Co., Grand Haven, Mich.

STEREOTYPE METAL
British Smelting & Refining Co., Ltd., Montreal.
Canada Metal Co., Limited, Toronto.
Hoyt Metal Co., Limited, Toronto.

TYMPAN PAPERS
The Cromwell Paper Company, Chicago, U.S.A.

TYPE-HIGH MACHINES
The Challenge Machinery Co., Grand Haven, Mich.

TIN FOIL PAPERS
J. & W. Mitchell, Birmingham, Eng.

TYPE FOUNDERS
Stephenson, Blake & Co., 60 Front St. W., Toronto.
Toronto Type Foundry Co., Ltd., Toronto, Montreal, Winnipeg.

THE NEW ERA PRESS
A Multi-Process Printing, Punching, Perforating, Cutting and other operation machine. Manufactured by The Regina Co., Rahway, N.J., U.S.A.

TYPE-SETTING MACHINES
Canadian Linotype, Ltd., 68 Temperance Street, Toronto.
Miller & Richard, Toronto and Winnipeg.
Lanston Monotype Machine Co., Lumsden Bldg., Toronto.
The Linograph. Stephenson, Blake & Co., 60 Front St. W., Toronto.

TYPE-HIGH GAUGES
The Challenge Machinery Co., Grand Haven, Mich.

Printer and Publisher Want Ads.

2 cents a Word—10 cents extra for P. & P. box number
Invariably in Advance

Manager Wanted for Canadian National Newspapers and Periodicals Association

To act also as Secretary-Treasurer, and carry on the Association's general work, under the direction of the President and the Board of Directors, study the interests of the various classes of publications in the Association, and plan and carry on promotion work in their interests. Applicants should understand advertising and merchandising.

Apply in writing only, stating age, full details of experience, and salary expected. Application will be treated as confidential.

Address Acton Burrows, President, Canadian National Newspapers and Periodicals Association, 70 Bond Street, Toronto.

SITUATIONS VACANT.

WANTED—FOREMAN FOR PRESS ROOM. Capable man with knowledge of duplex press preferred. Apply to the "Reformer," Oshawa, Ont. (p1p)

WANTED

WANTED — USED HALF-PAGE CASTING box. Send particulars and price to Kitchener "Daily Telegraph."

FOR SALE

FOR SALE—DEXTER FOLDING MACHINE, sheet sizes 36x49 to 20x30; this machine has automatic feeder for side insertions. Continental Publishing Co., 259 Spadina Ave., Toronto, Ont. (p2p)

PRESS FOR SALE

FOR SALE — COLT'S ARMORY PRESS complete, size 14x42; three chases; ink fountain. Write or wire, Telegraph Printing Company, Quebec, P.Q. (p2p)

CORRESPONDENTS WANTED

WANTED — CORRESPONDENTS ALL parts Dominion to report attractive store window displays; regular spot cash market assured for right stuff; send sample bunch of windows arranged by local merchants. Box 665, Printer and Publisher.

LINOTYPE MACHINE FOR SALE

FOR SALE—ONE MODEL NO. 6 (CANADIAN) Linotype in good running order; Very suitable for country printer; snap; terms. 106 Sixth Ave., West Calgary, Alberta. (p3p)

MONOLINE PARTS FOR SALE

MONOLINE PARTS FOR SALE—INCLUDING pawls, distributor wires, molds, spacebands, etc.; approximately $300.00 in Value; will exchange for paper cutter over 24 inch cutting surface. Write Drawer 106 Cranbrook, B.C. (p2p)

BUSINESS CHANCES

FOR SALE — NEWSPAPER AND JOB printing plant at a bargain; a well equipped and established business in a thriving industrial Nova Scotia town will be disposed of at a right price; large advertising and job printing income; only newspaper in a large and prosperous community. Apply at once for particulars to Box 666, Printer and Publisher, Toronto, Ont. (p1p)

SNAP—NEWSPAPER AND PRINTING plant for sale, consisting of good Cottrell bed press, Gordon quarter sheet press, gasoline engine, make up stones, seVeral cases of type, ten point, six and eight, with some twelVe point, and some twenty other fonts, etc. All in good condition. Price $1,000.00 en bloc, or will sell separately. If interested write P.O. Box 107, Scott, Sask. (p1p)

ONE OF THE BEST LOCAL WEEKLY newspapers and job offices in Alberta. First-class equipment, with gasoline power. Side-lines of stationery and musical goods. Best of reasons for selling. The Press, Daysland, Alberta. (p1p)

FOR SALE

1—10 x 15 Westman & Baker Press, power and foot fixtures complete.

1—8 x 12 C. & P. power and foot fixtures complete.

1—30-in. hand leVer Oswego Cutter, 2 kniVes.

1 Hand and Foot Stitcher complete.

1—13 x 19 Colt Armory Press complete.

Above machines 100% first-class.

ROYAL MACHINE STOCKS

Presses and Bookbinding Machinery and Special Machinery.

738 ST. PAUL WEST, MONTREAL

WEEKLY NEWSPAPER WANTED

WANTED TO BUY WEEKLY NEWSPAper; good support in town about twelVe hundred. Western Alberta preferred; new location accepted. Box 29, Newburgh, Ontario. (p1p)

EQUIPMENT WANTED

PLATEN PRESS, 15 x 21, FULL EQUIPment. Must be in good order. Apply Gazette, Norwich. (p1p)

COLLECTIONS

SEND US YOUR LIST OF DELINQUENTS. We will turn Debit into Credit. Publishers' Protective Association, Toronto.

SITUATIONS VACANT

LEARN THE LINOTYPE — WRITE FOR particulars. Canadian Linotype, 68 Temperance St., Toronto.

INDEX TO ADVERTISERS

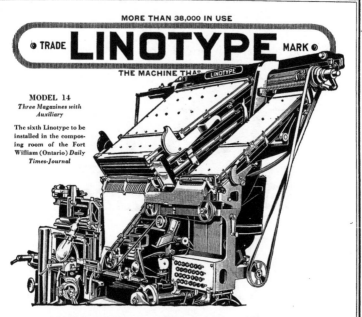

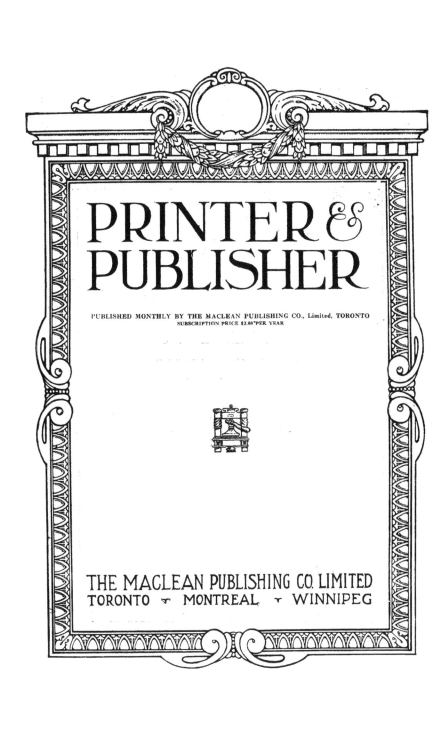

PRINTER & PUBLISHER

PUBLISHED MONTHLY BY THE MACLEAN PUBLISHING CO., Limited, TORONTO

SUBSCRIPTION PRICE $2.00 PER YEAR

THE MACLEAN PUBLISHING CO. LIMITED

TORONTO ⊤ MONTREAL ⊤ WINNIPEG

BUY
FIBRESTOC COVER

You Not Only Save Import Duty
But High Exchange Rate

**Made
in Canada**

PRINTERS of Canada! When you bought imported cover papers in the past you had to foot the bill (indirectly) for duty on imported goods. Now you not only have to pay high duty but have to meet a high exchange rate too.

Why pay big prices for imported cover paper when you can secure a made-in-Canada cover suitable for the highest class of printing at a much lower price.

FIBRESTOC escapes import duty—it escapes exchange rates—it saves you real money.

FIBRESTOC is made in all the popular colors. It has the desired strength and bulkiness which makes it a desirable cover for catalogue covers, booklets, mailing folders, post cards, etc. Permits the finest of color combinations and embosses deeply.

In every respect FIBRESTOC qualifies as a high-grade cover—yet it is moderate in price. Use it and save money.

This design a
guarantee of quality

**Other Good
C.P. Co. Covers**

*Wove Mill
Cashmere
Derby
Tinted Art S.C.
Tinted Art Suede*

DISTRIBUTED BY

Barber-Ellis, Limited - - - -	Calgary, Alta.
Barkwell Paper Co. - - - -	Winnipeg, Man.
Buntin, Gillies & Co., Limited - -	Hamilton, Ont.
Buntin, Gillies & Co., Limited - - -	Ottawa, Ont.
Canada Paper Co., Limited - - -	Montreal, P.Q.
Canada Paper Co., Limited - - -	Toronto, Ont.
Schofield Paper Co. - - - -	St. John, N.B.
Smith, Davidson & Wright, Limited -	Vancouver, B.C.
Smith, Davidson & Wright, Limited -	Victoria, B.C.
L. P. Turgeon - - - - - -	Quebec, P.Q.

MADE IN CANADA BY

CANADA PAPER CO. LIMITED
WINDSOR MILLS, P.Q.

COLORED PAPERS OF ALL KINDS A SPECIALTY

PRINTER AND PUBLISHER, March, 1920. Vol. 29, No. 3. Published monthly at 143-153 University Ave., Toronto, by the MacLean Publishing Co., Ltd. Yearly subscription price, $2.00 Entered as second-class matter at the Post Office Department at Ottawa, Canada. Also entered as second-class matter July 1, 1912, at the Post Office at Buffalo, N.Y., U.S.A., under Act of March 3rd, 1879.

HAMILTON EQUIPMENT
WOOD AND STEEL

For Nearly Forty Years the Standard in Every Department of the Printing Plant

While material and workmanship are important factors—jealously guarded to keep them on a high plane—of equal or greater importance are the features of time and space saving that are worked into every piece. If you are crowded or you feel or know that your plant is not producing what it should per dollar of pay roll—it will pay you to investigate Hamilton equipment.

Full information sent promptly on request.

The Hamilton Manufacturing Company

Hamilton Equipments are Carried in Stock and Sold by all Prominent Typefounders and Dealers Everywhere.

Main Office and Factories, TWO RIVERS, WIS.   Eastern Office and Warehouse, RAHWAY, N.J.

CANADIAN SELLING AGENTS

Toronto Type Foundry Co., Limited—Toronto, 70 York Street; Montreal, BeaVer Hall Hill. Ern. J. Goodland, Box 177. St. Johns, representative for Newfoundland. Stephenson, Blake & Co., Toronto. American Type Founders Co., 175 McDermot Ave., Winnipeg. George M. Stewart, Montreal. Miller & Richard—Toronto, 7 Jordan St.; Winnipeg, 123 Princess St. Printers Supplies, Ltd., 27 Bedford Row, Halifax, N.S.

A VALUABLE LINE GAUGE, graduated by picas and nonpareils, mailed to every enquiring printer.

Every Time the Clock Ticks

one Monotype Type-&-Rule Caster will make one inch of strip material— leads, slugs, or rules. Sixty inches, five feet, every minute. Three hundred (300) feet every hour.

Half-a-Mile a Day

Do you realize what this means to you? One-third of the average job or ad is blank space. You can fill it with Monotype strip material at less cost than by any other method.

This is but one of the many advantages of the versatile Monotype Composing Machine and Type & Rule Caster.

Lanston Monotype Machine Co.

PHILADELPHIA

NEW YORK, World Building   BOSTON, Wentworth Building
CHICAGO, Plymouth Building   TORONTO, Lumsden Building
Monotype Company of California, SAN FRANCISCO

268

This Advertisement set in Monotype Series No. 150 and Monotype Rule

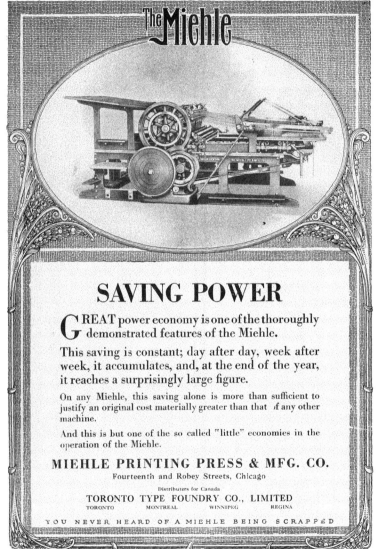

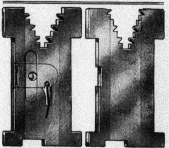

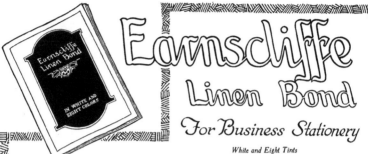

BABCOCK

A Cylinder Press is only as efficient as the weakest link in its chain of operating advantages. This handicap frequently offsets the economies possible from the good features of a press.

The head of a printing concern, whose high grade catalog work is known all over the country, was recently asked by a prospective purchaser of a cylinder press:

"What are the Weak Points of the

OPT·IMUS"

"I don't know of any weak points in the Optimus," replied the executive. "We have been doing high-grade work on our oldest Optimus for more than twenty years."

In operating economy, that "oldest one" does not begin to compare with the owner's more modern Babcocks. But it is the wearing qualities suggested in the owner's reply, *plus the perfection of Babcock Universal Equipment*, that makes the Optimus what it is today—the most profitably-operated cylinder press in the world.

Our Best Advertisements Are Not Printed—THEY PRINT!

THE BABCOCK PRINTING PRESS MFG. CO.
NEW LONDON, CONN.   NEW YORK OFFICE, 38 PARK ROW

BARNHART BROS. & SPINDLER, *General Western Agents*, Chicago, St. Louis, Dallas, Kansas City, Omaha, St. Paul, Seattle.

MILLER & RICHARD, *General Agents for Canada*—Toronto, Ontario, and Winnipeg, Manitoba.

JOHN HADDON & COMPANY, *Agents*, London, E. C.

1 Positive Delivery Fingers

2 Perfect Automatic Delivery

3 Universal Roller Control

4 Accessible for Makeready

5 Multiple Perforators and Slitters

6 Rigid Impression

7 Quickly Handled Rollers

8 Safety Feed Board

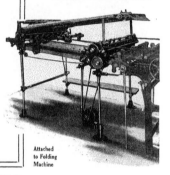

PRINTER AND PUBLISHER
Devoted to the Interests of the Printers and Publishers of Canada

It is Foolish to Tinker With a Cost System
And Yet It Has Been Done In Many Cases
By Peter Wilson, Supt. of Woodstock Sentinel-Review

IN the preceding article, attention was drawn to some of the rotten practices which have crept into the printing business. "Crept" is the right word, for they have come in either innocently—the innocence of the child in business—or with malice aforethought, like a thief in the night. There was first the party politician who was in the game for his own ends, and whose financial control influenced the editorial policy to the detriment of the business as a business. There was Bill Caxton and his working partner with the mistaken notion that because they were good mechanics there was' little possibility of failure. There was also the practice of the type founders of that time being so keen after sales that they did not scruple to hang a mill-stone, in the shape of a printing plant, around the neck of anyone who could put up a twentieth part of its value, irrespective of the fact that the field was well covered already and that their action would not only prove a detriment to those already there, but would result in a cut-rate war among the printers of the place, who in turn would find it harder than ever to keep their place in the business, until the inevitable would happen when one of them went under. Then it would be found that prices had sunk so low that it took years to recover, and while recovering the printers who stayed were so hard up that the typefounder, who might under normal conditions have sold them a tidy annual bill of goods, was held at arm's length until he quit coming around altogether. The type-founder's argument was that he got enough out of the rental which he received (in the shape of part payments) before he took the plant back, that it was worth while. They know now that that kind of business would surely prove a boomerang, and while occasionally one may have broken out of late years, the supply business, along with other businesses, has been in such a chaotic condition through the war and its after effects that the danger of such transgression in the future is almost *nil*. In fact at the recent U.T.A. convention in New York one of the salesmen of the American Type Founders Company advised the printers to try and get along with their present equipment for some time to come, and especially not to buy machinery.

The Subscription Contest

We left Bill Caxton at the beginning of his gropings after light on the question of Costs, and after attending the Cost Conference in Toronto, he returned to his home filled with the spirit of the evangelist who had been called to preach the gospel of Costs to every printer creature. The manager of the plant in which Bill filled the dual position of superintendent and news editor was not a practical printer, nor did he claim to be a smart business man, but (with that seemingly inherent perversity of politicians in dealing with this best of all callings) he had been appointed over the head of a real printer who was also a good business man. This manager had been appointed to assist as canvasser in one of those gambols—no, gambles— (which is it?)—a subscription contest, and because he succeeded in piling up a good round sum, half of which was spent in cleaning up overdue accounts (the other half going to the promoters) this outsider was given charge of one of the most intricate of businesses, full of details and everlasting pitfalls, while the

competent printer was sidetracked. This printer has since proved his ability both as a craftsman and as a business man by building himself into a substantial niche in the affairs of a Western city, where he has gained both substance and honor.

Mortgaging Future Business

The subscription contest eased off a critical situation for the plant in question, but there were so many paid-in-advance subscriptions to carry and nothing to carry them with that the whole thing turned out to be a costly business blunder and the financial backers soon had to go dipping again to keep things going. This was a Liberal paper, and as there was a Liberal Government in power at Ottawa it received a small amount of party patronage in the shape of advertising, but not enough to make any appreciable effect on the budget. There were conferences continually being held between the directors, the manager and the banker, and much frenzied financing to keep the payroll up every week.

The Cost System Underdone

Bill Caxton thought he saw what was the matter with the business and suggested the installing of the Standard Cost System, which he was sure would prove a panacea for its numerous and ever-increasing ailments. He was told by the manager that they had "that fool thing but it had never been any good—didn't make us any money!" Bill had great faith in it, however, and set out to combat this attitude of the manager towards the cost system, and after much talk he was allowed to see "the fool thing!" Imagine his surprise when he saw that while the cost clerk had done her best to post the time from the time sheets to the individual job records, no attempt had been made to gather the data necessary to carry the system to its logical conclusion and to summarize this information on what is known as Form 9H—the key to the whole system. Bill pointed out this state of affairs to the manager, but got little thanks for his pains. He asked permission to go back at nights and try to work out the summary, but was told the books had to go in the safe at nights. It was the old dog-in-the-manger policy and it made Bill feel sore to think that his offer made solely for the good of the business was turned aside on such a petty pretext. He got busy of his own accord, however, by cultivating the friendship of the bookkeeper, was given the details he required for his summary. His first task was to take an inventory of the plant, for he found there wa;; no such thing in the place, or at least was told so. This was a tedious job, but he had lately been owner of a plant and could strike a comparatively close valuation, which would be near enough for his purpose. This done, it was fairly easy to watch the fluctuations of the hour costs in the different departments, but it entailed a lot of tedious figuring to separate the job work from the newspaper, as the two branches of the business were run as one.

County Minutes at 65c Per Page

Under the scrutiny which Bill was able to give the various jobs several wonderful things came to light. The printing for the county was contracted for, and while Bill imagined that prices had reached rock bottom in his former town, he found new low levels in this place. The minutes for the county, a 6x9 page set in solid 10 pt., with a slug between pars., sold for 65c a page! (Printers of to-day will hardly credit this, but it is a fact that less than twenty years ago the minutes of this county sold at 37c a page.) The township voters' list—an example of extravagance in time and effort, full of rules and printed on one side of the sheet only, was billed at 85c a page. Examples like this were found all through the records, and after collecting enough for his purpose, Bill Caxton summarized them and showed alongside each other the prices received and the prices which the hour costs as shown by Form 9H called for.

How the Printer Reasoned in Those Days

Voters' lists at 85c and county minutes at 65c a page were no doubt low, but there was a reason for this. Most of the town printers who handled these jobs had a certain amount of plant for the production of the great family journal and anything that was produced over and above this was "velvet." (Needless to say their wives never wore any of that kind of dress goods.) Depreciation of plant worried them not at all till they tried to sell it, and found that the prospective buyer was not inclined to buy a junk heap.

A Flat Rate for Farmer's Sale Bills

Another colossal farce in those days was the habit of charging a flat rate of $2.50 for 50 farmer's sale bills, irrespective of whether it contained a small amount of copy, or whether there was a list long enough to keep a man busy setting for from four to six hours, and sometimes longer, besides taxing the plant to its utmost to scare up enough Great Primer to tell the pedigree of this and that great stud horse. Bill Caxton started charging according to the size of the list and managed to bring the average up to about $5, and thought that was pretty good. Here is how he figured on a moderately long list:

Stock—27 sheets white news at 2½c lb.

(80c a ream)	$ .05
Composition, 4 hrs. at 75c	3.00
Presswork, ½ hr. at $1.00	.50
Cutting, ink, and wrapping, etc.	.10
	$3.65
Profit, 25 per cent	.92
	$4.57

Let us see how this works out at present day figures, as these articles are intended to have an application in this way. The hour costs are very moderate and no one will accuse the writer of attempting to inflate the estimate.

Stock—27 sheets white(?) news at 6c a lb., $2.10 a ream, plus handling

	$ .15
Composition, 4 hours at $1.50	6.00
Press-work, ½ hr. at $1.80	.90
Cutting, ink, packing, etc.	.40
	$7.45
Profit, 25 per cent	1.87
	$9.32

How many printers who handle farmer's sale bills get anywhere near $9.50 to-day? Yet that is about the price that should be charged. And there are more reasons than merely rising costs for this. In the good old days before the linotype became part of the equipment of every ambitious printer, the setting of the newspapers week after week by hand developed a speed in composition in the average printer that is almost an unknown thing to-day, so that we have, hand in hand with higher wages and shorter hours, a race of slow-moving type slingers that would have made the old-timer blush for very shame. There are of course some country-bred printers who can throw together a half-sheet bill in quick time and also put it on the press and run it off. If it is a quarter sheet he may run it on the No. 3 Gordon and cut down the cost a little there, but even then it will work out fairly high:—

Stock—present price 6c and going up, 15 sheets at $2.10 a ream, plus handling, is 8c, but it is unwise to charge less than

	$ .10
Composition, same copy as half sheet would likely be done at a saving in time of 20 per cent., 3.2 hrs. at $1.50	4.80
Press-work, platen, ½ hr. at $1.00	.50
Cutting, ink, packing, etc.	.20
	$5.60
Profit, 25 per cent	1.40
	$7.00

To produce sale bills in Bill Caxton's cost experimental days took time and money that could never be recovered by a flat rate unless it was high enough to cover every conceivable contingency, and the same applies to conditions to-day. In Bill's time the sale list was as follows:

50 quarter sheet sale bills	$2.00
50 half sheet sale bills	2.50
50 full sheet sale bill	4.00

To-day some printers' associations have adopted the following flat rate, which the writer contends is not enough to cover the average as he experiences them:—

50 quarter sheet sale bills	$4.50
50 half sheet sale bills	5.00
50 full sheet sale bills	8.00

When Bill summarized the results of the various jobs, he placed the result in the hands of the manager for his guidance, but this individual refused to be guided. He knew that a change was pending, as the reciprocity election had changed the Government and switched the patronage to the other paper, and it was not long before Bill was informed that the two papers had amalgamated, and that if he desired he could take a job in the one alley. This did not suit him, however, as he saw the possibilities of specializing along cost lines, so he hit the road once more.

The Cost System Overdone

This time Bill thought he had landed the right kind of job. He found himself in a job plant in the city that Hamilton delights to call Baconsville. The firm made a specialty of looseleaf work and office supplies, and because they specialized in these lines they kept their cost system up to the highest point of development, and in fact carried it beyond the realm of utility. The cost system will give information on any detail of the business which may be desired, but if it is so overloaded with detail that it costs more to get the information than the saving it will accomplish, then it defeats its purpose. In this plant, cost finding had run mad. Not only that, but the proprietor reasoned that a cost system and a good executive could run any business successfully with the cheapest kind of help. Bill, although he had never handled a job like this before, was not worrying about that phase, but set out to learn all he could about the various operations. He was specially interested in the Bindery, as it was there he would fall down, if he tumbled at all. He was not openly opposed in his endeavors to learn, but he did not get much assistance either. But Bill's natural ability for picking up the mechanical operations of a job and his analytical faculty, which had been steadily developing with study, helped him to hang on to a job whose only redeeming feature was that he had the run of the factory and would learn more in this way than in a dozen other more specialized shop. The farce of having a highly ornamented cost system in the front office and the cheapest kind of help in the factory, that were here to-day and away to-morrow, was one more proof that if the cost system is not accomplishing all it should, it will be found that the fault lies in the manner in which it is run, and not in any weakness or imperfection in the system itself.

A year in this plant sufficed, and Bill voluntarily joined the procession of superintendents who came and went. This time he joined the staff of an old-established weekly paper, which did considerable job work and could boast of having installed the Standard Cost system. Here again he found the system carried to a certain point and no further. In the year he spent with this firm he saw all the outward signs of cost keeping, but not once was the key-stone of the system put in shape. Form 9H was not filled in once in that year. The accountant, who was office manager, was more like a message boy and general factotum than anything else, and he never had time for the most important function in the business. The rates charged were the rates which the Printers' Board of Trade considered were proper for that city.

In three years Bill Caxton worked in three different shops, each of which had adopted the Standard Cost system as their sure and certain guide to profitable printing, and all three had fallen down in the working of it. The first did not understand it, simple though it is. The second knew to a nicety what each sold hour was costing, but failed to recognize the connection between the cost system and the necessity of having efficient and well-trained help. The third went through all the motions of keeping the records except the main motion—that of properly filling out the summary every month and comparing results.

These cases are typical of the uses and abuses of the Standard Cost Finding System and have called forth requests from some printers to have the system modified or simplified to suit their special needs. The lazy man will not find a simpler system; the honest man will find the system will reward him by telling him the truth; and while it is simplicity itself it is capable of the most elaborate expansion—in fact it is adaptable to the small one-man business and also the largest organization—it is only a matter of how much or how little the printer desires to know. Simplification is unnecessary and modification to suit individual whims works against its main purpose—STANDARDIZATION. The Standard Cost Finding System, where it is run with plain, common-sense and an honest attempt is made to run the mechanical departments efficiently, is the only system to use. Bill Caxton was sure of this when he first started to study costs and the Standard estimating class which he joined while in Baconsville, Ont., convinced him he was right. The next article will tell of this estimating class, and what Bill got out of it and what he gave to it.

The Saskatchewan Market

The Regina *Leader* has prepared a careful analysis of the Saskatchewan market, and has it in attractive form to send to advertisers and prospects who want to reach the people of that province. Here are some headings that indicate the scope of the work.

"72.74 per cent. of Population occupy Rural Districts of Province."

"Greatest Production, Per Capita, in the World."

"Saskatchewan is First in Average Size of Farm."

"Saskatchewan Entering the Dairy Class."

"Second Largest Railroad Mileage in Canada."

The *Leader* gives very careful attention to all detail that would in any way be of value to the producer or distributor who wants to get into its market.

Bruce Out for $2 Rate

Walkerton.—The Bruce Press Association held its annual meeting in the Town Hall, Walkerton. Representatives from eight newspapers in the county were present. Mayor J. J. Hunter of Kincardine, publisher of the *Reporter*, who has filled the office of president for several years, asked to be relieved of the office, and the members accepted his resignation with great reluctance. "J. J." is a hard hitter, but has a heart as big as a house and possesses the confidence and respect of his fellow craftsmen to a high degree. Mr. Hunter was succeeded in the chair as president by Lorne A. Eedy, of the Walkerton *Telescope*. Mr. D. McKenzie, the secretary, retains his office for the coming year. Considerable business was dealt with and a social hour spent, after which the meeting adjourned to meet in May at the call of the chair. The meeting was practically unanimous for raising the weekly subscription price to $2.00, but it was decided to meet again in April at the call of the president, when it is hoped there will be a full representation of all the papers to deal with this important question. Those present were:—Ernest E. Shortt, Southampton *Beacon*; Lloyd Logan, Wiarton *Canadian Echo*; John A. Johnston, Mildmay *Gazette*; J. J. Hunter, Kincardine *Reporter*; Arthur Rogers, Kincardine *Review*; J. A. Wesley, *Herald-Times*, Walkerton; Lorne A. Eedy, *Telescope*, Walkerton; D. MacKenzie, *Advocate*, Paisley.

A Handy Estimating Form

The John Martin Paper Co., Ltd., of Winnipeg, have prepared a concise estimating form, which they invite the trade in their territory to make use of. The reproduction here is filled in to show how the system works. The form is not by any means complicated, and should give the job printer an easy line to follow to make sure he is not missing anything in putting in his figures.

ESTIMATE BLANK

Compliments
JOHN MARTIN PAPER CO. LTD.
Printers' Papers Exclusively
WINNIPEG   CALGARY

_____ July 8 __ 19 __

NAME Manitoba Coal Co. Ltd., Winnipeg

DESCRIPTION OF JOB 2000 Delivery Forms in triplicate to a sheet—

(Original, Duplicate and Stub). Perforate two cuts. Number in triplicate. Bound in 20 Books of 100 sheets each, quarter flush. Marble sides. Size of sheet 10½x4.

	2000		1M Add		5000	
Stock. Walrus Bond 17x22-16 lb.-8 out; 265 sheets at $3.42 per						
Ream	1	85		95	4	65
Percentage on Stock (one third)		60		30	1	55
Machine Composition ✓						
Hand Composition 2 hours at $2.00	4	00			4	00
Make-up ✓						
Lock-up 1 hour at $2.00		50				50
Press Make-ready 1 hour at $1.10	1	10			1	10
Impressions 2000 at $1.10	2	20	1	10	5	50
Ink Black		25		05		40
Ruling ✓						
Binding 20 Books at 15c	3	00	1	50	7	50
Perforating on press						
Punching ✓						
Numbering 6000 numbers at 50c	3	00	1	50	7	50
Gathering ✓						
Folding ✓						
Stitching ✓						
Padding ✓						
Drawings ✓						
Cuts ✓						
Electros ✓						
Cutting ½ hour at $1.50		25		05		40
Delivery ✓		25		05		40
Quoted	17	00	5	50	33	50

NOTE—Three price columns are shown for the purpose of taking care of a request for first and additional quantities—that is, first column is for original request of say 2000, second column for additional 1000, third column for say 5000; or, third column may be used to show difference in estimate when two kinds of stock are asked for. When request is made for additional quantities, be sure the second column, it is only necessary to add stock, press, ink, etc. make-ready, being included in first column.

Renfrew *Mercury*:—Announcements last week are to the effect that the Delhi *Reporter* has ceased publication and been incorporated with the Simcoe *Reformer*. Thus a town that used to support two papers now has none published in the town. The Collingwood *Bulletin* also announces the amalgamation of the Barrie *Advance* and the Barrie *Pointer*.

From the Bureau of Standards of U. S.:—"As a result of tests upon approximately 150 samples of paper, stored since March, 1909, it is noticed that bonds and ledgers containing 100 per cent. rag did not deteriorate in bursting strength as much as printing, writing, and similar paper containing wood-pulp. The loss in bursting strength for the first class of paper tested was about 11.9 per cent., while the bursting strength for the second class was 20.4 per cent. less than when tested 10 years ago. While these conclusions have been derived from tests on about 150 samples, as noted above, a large number of additional samples will be tested soon and the results studied to determine, if possible, the cause and amount of the deterioration of paper in storage."

Yes---A Lot of Things Happen in Fifty Years

Thirty of These With The Brantford Expositor

By A. R. Kennedy

THIRTY years ago a very faithful and well-behaved cylinder press rumbled away for the best part of an hour each lawful day, and disposed of the afternoon edition of the Brantford *Expositor*, which the counter declared to be between seven and eight hundred. Today a modern perfecting press is tuned up to the job in half the time, turns out some 10,200 papers. Of course in that time the field has grown, but not in proportion to the *Expositor*.

Thirty years ago this month T. H. Preston reversed the order of things by leaving the West and coming East. There were three daily papers then, the Brantford *Courier*, published by Henry Lemon, with the assistance of F. D. and R. H. Revi le, who afterwards took over the paper. The *Courier*, after being form-

ed into a joint stock company, went out of business about a year ago, being sold to the Southam interests, from whom the *Expositor* purchased the circulation list, after which the paper was discontinued. The *Telegram* was also in existence in Brantford at that time, conducted by J. A. Miller, who had been a working printer previously, and who had for a time on his staff J. Bruce Walker, then a

fresh arrival from the land of cakes, and afterward with the *Expositor*. Mr. Walker is now Dominion Immigration Agent at Winnipeg.

The *Expositor* was then owned by Messrs. Watt and Shenstone. The files of the paper show that the new proprietor made a short and concise bow to his clientele, and proceeded at once to serve them. It is stating a fact to mention that Mr. Preston has a broad idea of the place a newspaper holds in the community. He never looked upon it as a purely private venture, realizing always the responsibility that the unwritten franchise to publish in this community carried with it. It is not necessary to go into details about the growth and development of the *Expositor*. That paper has always been a good purchaser in the way of equipment, either in

THE OTTAWA PRESS GALLERY OF FORTY YEARS AGO

Standing, left to right — J. T. Hawke, Ottawa correspondent Toronto "Globe," now publisher of the Moncton "Transcript"; Albert Horton, Toronto "World," now chief of Senate Hansard; J. E. B. McCready, St. John "Telegraph"; the late H. Pingle, head of the Press Bureau of the Dominion Telegraph Company, afterward superintendent of Ontario division of the C. P. R. Telegraph Company; the late George Johnson, Halifax "Herald," afterward Dominion Statistician; O. Higman, head of the Press Bureau, Montreal Telegraph Company, and now of the Inland Revenue Department; the late George Eyvell, Toronto "Globe," and Hansard.

Sitting, left to right — Arthur Wallis, "Mail," afterward editor of that paper for twenty-one years, now clerk of the Surrogate Court for York County; A. C. Campbell, "Globe" and Hansard; the late George B. Bradley, "Mail," and Hansard; W. T. R. Preston, London "Advertiser" and Port Hope "Times"; T. H. Preston, Ottawa "Free Press," now publisher Brantford "Expositor"; E. J. Duggan, Montreal "Gazette," Hansard, now Seigneur Murray Bay.

the composing room, press room or in the matter of securing news service. The *Expositor* has made money, and money has been put back into the business in generous proportions.

The Personal Side of the Paper

Printer and Publisher, for the purpose of this article, desires to devote more space to the man than to his business, not an easy matter in this case, for like many another publisher, Mr. Preston has been so wrapped up, tied up and welded to his paper that he seems to consider that the personal side of it should refer to a combination known as T. H. Expositor. However there are many ways of securing information about men and their successes and failures.

It was fifty years ago last January that T. H. Preston was indentured to R. McWhinney, Jr., who was then publishing the Woodstock *Sentinel*. The *Review* part of the paper came along later. The *Review* then lived in Princeton if we mistake not. Wages were not fabulous at that time, but hours and duties were.

The first year the sum of $20 in cash passed to the apprentice, and the next year it was doubled and became $40. Of course thrown in with this was the board, which was served up at the house of the proprietor. Mr. Preston, referring to his experiences there, once remarked, "I had all the work of the apprentice to do. Lighting fires early in the morning, washing rollers, sticking type, turning the press, carrying a route in town, delivering bills and pasting some of them up." Great times, but deliverance was at hand. The business was sold by McWhinney after Mr. Preston had been with the firm a couple of years. He was not included with the chattels in the deed of sale, so he considered that his binding papers were done for, notwithstanding the fact that the third year he would have received $60 and $80 the fourth.

An uncle, William Buckingham, was running the Stratford *Beacon* at that time, and with him he stuck type, reasoned with the presses and figured on the pay-roll, but for only a short time. The wanderlust was sprouting and the two-thirder finally reached Toronto where he held down a case on the *Christian Guardian*. Shortly after he was "subbing" on the *Globe*, when the famous George Brown strike, as it is referred to yet, took place. The union printers wanted more pay and a short-er day, fand at the instance of George Brown action was taken against some of the leaders. The de-mands of the men look quite reasonable, viewed in the light of present day inflations, as they asked for 30 cents more day and 33 night. Mr. Pres-ton was not out of his time then, but the union decided to recog-nize him as a journey-man, and so he had the chance of having the rather unique dis-tinction of striking from the mechanical department of a paper on which he afterward held an important editorial position.

Transportation was also offered by the union to printers who desired to leave the city, and as a result of this the now fully unionized and journeymenized Preston secured a "case" in Indianapolis, and afterward in Toledo, moving from there to the Springfield *Republican*. All the time he was keenly in-terested in the editorial policy and the news columns of any and all of the papers on which he worked, and his term on the Springfield *Republican*, then under Sam Bowles, in the days of the great Massachusetts Senator, Charles Sumner, gave him a good opportunity to become conversant with that phase of American history connected with Horace Greeley's "Mugwumps." The year 1874 found him on the make-up of the Worcester *Press*.

Then a chance came to make the break from the com-posing stick to the pen. Wil-liam Buckingham was appoint-ed confidential secretary to Alexander Mackenzie at Ottawa, and from him he learned of a chance to go on the reportorial side of the Ottawa *Free Press*, then published by C. W. Mit-chell. Ottawa had two other papers then, the *Morning Times* and the *Citizen*, a morning paper, published by C. H. Mack-intosh, who afterward

EXPOSITOR BUILDING

became ,Lieutenant-Governor of the Northwest Territories.

Mr. Burgoyne of the St. Catharines *Standard*, writing in his paper a few days ago on the thirty years of the *Expositor* under Mr. Preston, recalls the days in Ottawa, saying, "In offering heartiest greetings to the Brantford *Expositor*. ' . . . it is to an old friend with whom the editor of the *Standard* began an acquaintanceship now nearly 45 years old, when both, together with Mr. John H. Thompson, of the Thorold *Post*, were employed on the Ottawa *Free Press*, Mr. Preston as a reporter and the other two as compositors. It was on March 28, 1875, that the two young typos set out from St. Catharines for the Capital, to take "cases" on the *Free Press* under the late C. W. Mitchell, but Mr. Preston was already on the paper. These three with another comp. on the *Free Press*, Mr. R. Uglow, now conducting a prosperous book and stationery emporium in Kingston, all boarded at the same house on Salter Street, and the friendships made in those days have always been cherished. . ,"

Shortly after Mr. Preston joined the *Free Press* he was sent to the Press Gallery for his paper, and it was about 1880, the group was taken which is shown on another page of this article. There was no official *Hansard* then. It was not possible for members of the House to talk for hours with the sure and certain knowledge that they could get the whole speech for distribution to their constituents before the next voting day came around. Members of the House had to depend on the reporters then. Mr. Burgess, who afterwards became Deputy Minister of the Interior, got out a report of the proceedings of the House, taking his matter entirely from the reports that appeared in the papers. It was in 1875 that official *Hansard* came to life, and on it T. J. Richardson was chief reporter; others were George Bradley, who had been in the Gallery for the *Mail*; and the Horton brothers, Albert and Edward.

Among the press representatives in the Ottawa Gallery at that time were the now Hon. Thomas White, for the Montreal *Gazette*; M. J. Griffin, now Dominion Librarian, for the Toronto *Mail*; Arthur Wallis, who was afterward editor of the *Mail* for 21 years, and is now registrar of the Surrogate Court for York County.

"Those were interesting days," remarked Mr. Preston. 'There were many of the Fathers of Confederation in the House. Sir Wilfrid Laurier at that time was a young man, starting his political career. He was looked upon as one sure to develop. He was always of a most lovable disposition. I will never forget the night he came to Ottawa after winning Quebec East. There had been a bye-election following his defeat, and on this second occasion he was victorious. The Liberals of the Mackenzie Government had arranged a torchlight procession from the old St. Lawrence & Ottawa Ry. station. I was one of the reporters assigned to cover that story. Well, they paraded, and they burned broom-sticks, and it rained. It has never rained so hard since. Of course the reporters felt they 'had to stay with it, and we were wet through to the skin by the time the performance was over. No — I shall not forget the night that Wilfrid Laurier came back from his win in Quebec East. He

had been made Minister of Inland Revenue in the Mackenzie Government, and this necessitated an appeal to his old constituency of Drummond and Arthabaska, which rejected him."

The desire to own a paper caused Mr. Preston to leave Ottawa in 1881, and take over the Walkerton *Telescope*. He did not stay there long, as the lure of the daily was too strong. He was able to dispose of the property in a few months, and John T. Hawke, now publisher of the Moncton *Transcript*, offered him the position of night telegraph editor of the *Globe*, of which paper Mr. Hawke was then news editor, Gordon Brown being the editor. The paths seemed destined to lead back to Ottawa, for he was sent there as permanent Ottawa correspondent of the *Globe* on the resignation of the late J. P. McCready, who went back to his paper, the St. John *Telegraph*.

It was during one of his stays in Ottawa that Mr. Preston went along on a little jaunt staged for the benefit of Lord and Lady Dufferin by E. J. O'Neill, then superintendent of the Dominion Police. O'Neill had a bit of a boat that ran up the Du Lievre, a feeder of the Ottawa, on which there is some magnificent scenery which the skipper O'Neill wished the Dufferins to behold. All went well until the wee craft struck some rapids, when all went wrong. The skiff made for the shore and the cargo — human — with the exception of Lord and Lady Dufferin and the engineer, was dumped on the shore. Just as they put out into the stream the current took the boat and started it as though a bit of cork directly for the opposite side, where the banks were steep and a landing not in sight. The reporters were witnesses to the sight of Lady Dufferin throwing herself in the arms of her husband, while the engineer tinkered for dear life with the mechanism of the boat. Tinkering succeeded, and the Dufferins, Lord and Lady, were spared a plunge into the water. By special request no mention of the incident was made in the press. So even forty years ago the "Keep this out" chant was set to journalistic music in Canada.

The Western Field of Journalism

The newspaper situation in Winnipeg around 1882-85 provides some remarkably interesting reminiscences. Mr. Preston can tell many of these, and so can Mr. Acton Burrows of *Railway and Marine World*, Toronto. In 1882 the call to go West came in the form of an offer to take editorial charge of the Winnipeg *Sun*, which at that time was being conducted by W. H. Nagle, formerly a reporter on the Ottawa *Free Press*. Mr. William Buckingham was also in Winnipeg at that time engaged in the lumbering business. When the changes were being made at the *Sun*, J. C. McLagan was secured from the Guelph *Mercury* and given charge of the mechanical department: Some time later Mr. McLagan went on West; and in the end founded the Vancouver *World*. The *Sun* later on had Edward Farrer as an editorial writer, and Rev. W. F. Clarke, who from the agricultural flavor in his contributions was often dubbed as "Rhubarb Clarke." Senator Dennis, now owner of the Halifax *Herald*, was a reporter on the *Sun* for a time, also R. L.

T. H. PRESTON   W. B. PRESTON

The business management of the *Expositor* is in charge of Mr. W. B. Preston. W. B. has been schooled in the newspaper business, and has been an apt scholar. He spent some time at Toronto University, but it has been in the business management of a daily paper that he has found real scope in which to work. W. B. Preston has always taken a keen interest in affairs of the C. P. A. and is now chairman of the Advertising Promotion committee of the C.D.N.A.

Richardson, M.P. Then there was the now Honorary Lt.-Col. George Ham of the C.P.R. In 1882 he was a reporter on the Winnipeg *Times*. The *Free Press* was under control of W. F. Luxton, who was quite a prominent man in the journalistic and political life of the West. J. W. Dafoe was getting his start there, and John Lewis was also a Winnipeg Westerner, as well as J. T. Hawke and A. C. Campbell. B. W. Thomson was another, who was later known on account of his work on the Boston *Transcript*. W. E. McLellan, afterward school inspector for Nova Scotia, edited the *Free Press* then. F. B. Wood, re-named "Big Thunder," was chief justice of Manitoba. Hon. Jos. Cauchon was Lieutenant-Governor, Government House being held at the Hudson Bay Co. post inside the walls of old Fort Garry, most of which was still standing. C. J. Brydges, afterward head of the G. T. R., was Hudson Bay Company's commissioner.

"Winnipeg was a very ordinary looking place then," remarked Mr. Preston to the writer. "It had a population of about 20,000. There were no paved streets and the sidewalks were wooden. The C.P.R. had not reached the city and the passengers had to be transferred from the St. Boniface side of the river. The telegraph service," he continued, "was not by any means as efficient as we have it at present. The wires had the habit of growing cold every hour or so, and nothing would come in on them. The service, by the way, came around by Chicago and St. Paul. Well there was to be a hanging in Sherbrooke, Quebec, one morning at the usual time. The Winnipeg *Times*, to be ahead of the other papers on the street with the story of the event, had it all in type good and early. Something went wrong with the wires that day, but the *Times* was not going to be hindered in getting on the street first. So they had a good story about the way the prisoner ate his last breakfast, told how he slept well in the night, walked with a firm step to the gallows, and never quaked when they put the noose around his neck. If I mistake not they had his last words to his spiritual adviser and friends. About four o'clock they rushed their paper out on the streets with the story of the Sherbrooke hanging. A few minutes after the wires came to life again and almost the first story was one stating that the condemned man had cheated the gallows by hanging himself during the night."

When the boom began to break in the West there were changes made in newspaper control. Acton Burrows, who was then Deputy Minister of Agriculture for Manitoba, bought the *Sun*, and also came into possession of the *Times*, which he amalgamated, calling the combination the *Manitoban*. Just here it might be mentioned that the *Manitoban*, which was conducted then as an afternoon paper, was afterward the *Morning Call*, subsequently absorbed by the Winnipeg *Free Press*. When Mr. Burrows came into possession of the *Manitoban*, Mr. Preston went in with him as managing editor, on the understanding that he was to have nothing to do with the editorial page, which was Conservative in its flavor.

Mr. Preston recalls with a great deal of interest the events that crowded themselves into newspaper life during the strenuous days of the rebellion of 1885. The Winnipeg *Free Press* at that time was satisfied that it had a news service that could care for anything that might break, and so made use of the phrase on its front page, "When Nothing Is Reported in The *Free Press*, Nothing Has Happened." Just to show how wrong newspaper slogans can be, the *Sun* went out and bought up the services of the operator at the telegraph office at Clarke's Crossing, near Batoche. When the news of the battle at Fish Creek came through the *Sun* got it about 4 o'clock in the morning, and at 6.30 was out with an extra carrying the only account of the fight. Just to make it a little more pronounced the *Sun* went to the trouble of getting C. E. Hamilton, then mayor of Winnipeg, to ring the bells and have a celebration. The *Sun*, by the same method, secured another memorable beat when the Battle of Batoche took place. That was on a Sunday, and when the congregations were coming out of church the *Sun* was there with an extra—yes, a Sunday paper in Canada even that far back.

And here is a little item that has not come into print before. There may be some shooting done as the result, but in these days of excitement that matters little. W. E. McLellan was then the editorial writer on the Winnipeg *Free Press*, Liberal and morning. He would turn in his matter for the morning paper of the Liberal persuasion, and then turn immediately to the task of writing the answers to many of the problems and theories for use in the *Manitoban*, the afternoon Conservative

paper. When the *Manitoban* office was opened in the morning one of the first duties of the day's routine was to pick up the editorial matter for the day which had been carefully pushed under the door by the editorial writer of the *Free Press* during the night.

There seemed to have been a failing for the name *Sun* in Mr. Preston's newspaper career, for following the 1885 rebellion he started the second paper by that name, having the backing of some local men. R. L. Richardson was interested in the venture, and others were J. H. Ashdown, the hardware man; Hon. C. H. Campbell, and several others. Lt.-Col. C. D. Keenleyside, now of Regina, was the business manager of the paper. That paper ran for three years and it paid from the first issue. It was capitalized at $15,000, and at the end of three years negotiations were opened for its purchase, with the assurance that it would be continued as an independent newspaper. These were successful. The sum of $45,000 was paid for the paper, and inside of a week after the sale, W. F. Luxton, of the *Free Press*, came into the *Sun* office one morning and announced that he was the owner of the property with the C.P.R. behind him. He stated his intention of closing out the paper, which was done at once. R. L. Richardson went in soon after and bought the plant for $7,000, and all that Mr. Luxton had for his $38,000 was the mailing list. Mr. Preston was not at all anxious to quit the Western field, but under the terms of sale, which were made before he knew the real buyer, he was bound not to again enter the Winnipeg field for a term of five years.

"So it was," concluded Mr. Preston, "that I turned to the East. My parents were living at Mt. Pleasant, a short distance from here. It was in March, 1890, that I bought the *Expositor*. What has happened since you know about."

Mr. Preston has not only been a successful publisher, and a good citizen of Brantford, but has ever been ready to interest himself in provincial and national matters. For several sessions he represented South Brant in the Ontario House, at that time taking a keen interest in labor matters and any legislation of benefit to the masses of the people. Also in connection with the Ontario Parole Board—Mr. Preston has been a member of that body since its inception.

Close to the Hundred Mark

The Brockville *Recorder-Times* is nearing the century mark, having made its 99th year. Frank B. Allen, writing in the *Daily News-Chronicle* of Port Arthur, says:—No matter how many years may have passed from the time he was the imp in a print shop, when he washed rollers, washed up the press, ran errands and subbed for a carrier boy who had failed to put in an appearance, the old-timer likes to hear of the continued success of the paper he first worked on. It is, therefore, with the kindliest feeling that the writer learns of the passing of the ninety-ninth birthday of the Brockville *Recorder*, now published under the style *Recorder and Times*. It was back in the last period of Col. David Wylie's connection with the *Recorder* that the writer honored the office with his presence and learned the rudiments and technique of the printer's trade from Wallace Wright, the foreman. Looking back on those days it is a matter for wonder that Mr. Wright did not commit murder. He surely must have had a super-supply of the article that made a reputation for one Job, who had only to endure boils and other minor plagues. Mr. Wylie was also a man of marvellous patience. We did not realize what wonderful control he had of himself until years later. We do not know whether some of those young imps who infested the office have received their just deserts, but if not the fact stands to the credit of a merciful Providence. The *Recorder* was old even in those days, but vigorous and fearless. Its staff was faithful to its interests, for every man felt that the whole work was resting on his individual shoulders, and the fellowship of the old-time printer prevailed in the composing-room and press-room. The writer was the first employee of the Brockville *Times*. Thad. Leavitt was the first editor of that paper and was followed by N. B. Colcock, who afterwards became Ontario representative in London. The *Times* grew in influence politically, becoming the hub from which radiated all Conservative activities in the riding. With the incoming of the war the Brockville papers felt the depression in the newspaper business and finally made an arrangement to amalgamate, and so in its hundredth year the *Recorder* finds itself coupled up with the comparatively youthful *Times*, and may the infusion of new blood send the old one on to its second century of usefulness.

It Was Easier to Break In Than Stay In

By J. Vernon McKenzie, Now Canadian Trade Commissioner to Glasgow

OCTOBER, 1904, I was attending a Quaker School in Canada; November, I was covering the police beat in San Francisco. Breaking into the game was accomplished almost prosaically; the trick was to *stay* in.

I landed in 'Frisco one Saturday with nine bucks. I paid for a room for a week, bought a meal-ticket, and Monday morning braced Y.M.C.A. Employment Secretary Davis for a job.

"What do you want to do?"

"Write."

"No experience?" And he glanced at my yet-to-have-its-first-shave-chin.

"None."

I was hired at $6 per week.

"All right," said Davis. "Take this card to the *Post* and ask for Charles H. Warren."

I hunted up Warren. In five minutes I was hired at $6 per; in twenty, was taking down voluminous notes at a ministers' meeting. Warren, who was City Ed., glanced over my copy and—didn't fire me. I got a few "one-heads" in the paper that week, and learned that the *Post* was being run on an economical basis—two or three "star" men, the rest $6 to $9 cubs. .

There was a shake-up in the staff. The police reporter was fired, and in desperation Warren said:

"Here, you lanky Canuck, get down on 'Police'."

Soon I got so mixed up in four lower courts, three Superior courts, coroner's office, morgue, police and detectives' offices, that I didn't know whether I was on my head or my heels. How I managed to be left there for a week, Providence only knows. Chiefly, I think, because the *Bulletin* and *Examiner* chaps were sorry for me, and gave me "hand-outs."'

Then this news broke: Judge Hebbard had been shot at by a prisoner, Selby, whom he was trying. Three bullets went into the judge's chair.

It didn't make much impression on me, as 'Frisco was having a suicide a day and a murder every week. A little thing like shooting up a judge in open court I took for an every-day affair! I sat down and wrote—*almost a stick!* (Not that I had heard of a stick, then.) The copy went to the office.

I was called to the 'phone.

"You're fired!" exploded a voice.

"Who's talking?" I shouted.

"Warren, you addle-pated fool."

Then I heard a chuckle—"Why don't you interview Selby?"

I knew not that reporters were forbidden to talk to prisoners in the cells. Experienced newspapermen didn't even try, then. I wandered up to the top floor of the Hall of Justice, asked a 'trusty' where Selby's cell was, and, being a mere kid, I suppose it didn't occur to any official to ask my business.

I had bull-headed luck. I saw Selby, talked with him freely for fifteen minutes, and got such a yarn as I have often hoped for since.

I wrote in a sort of daze, not knowing what was wanted. "Write, write!" commanded Warren, and the *Post* came out with a column exclusive interview with Selby. I wasn't fired again—that week.

I was fired again !

A few weeks later I was fired, on Saturday. My room rent was over-due; the landlady locked me out. Saturday night I slept in the——Methodist Church, finding pews hard. Sunday night I tried a verandah hammock, but about 2 a.m. a dog ripped me, none too gently, and I vacated the hammock hastily. The remainder of the night was spent, rather comfortably, on a pile of shavings in a lumber yard. My food Sunday was a dime tea at the Y.M.C.A.

Monday, I was lounging around "Y"—dashed hungry. Davis spotted me, and said: "Go down to the *Post*."

"J—— has been arrested," said Warren, "in connection with the Sacramento scandal. L—— is on a drunk. You may be better than nothing. . . . I'll give you $9."

I took it, and was hired and fired alternately for the next six months. There were several one-meal days, and two more nights on the shavings. To *get* into the game seemed easier than to *stay* in. However, I managed to stick until I had the immense satisfaction of *resigning* six months later, to go to the *News*.

Candid Opinions Were Given

The Hamilton *Spectator*, in its Saturday Musings, has the following about Thomas McQueen, an ancient Hamilton editor:—"James Mitchell, an ancient printer, and now an accomplished Government attache in the Ontario archivist's department, has kindly furnished the Saturday Muser with a copy of the Goderich *Signal*, containing a chapter of conditions, political and editorial, in Canada 70 years ago. Mr. Mitchell is a graduate from the London *Free Press*, where he learned the printing art, and afterwards was an editor and publisher in Goderich, which he still calls home. Thomas McQueen was the founder of the Huron *Signal* in 1848. He was a rabid Reformer, and had no idea that a Tory would ever enter heaven. 'Old Tom McQueen,' as he was known in those old days 70 years ago, was a stone cutter by trade. All Scotchmen were Reformers in those days. After he had been in Goderich about a year, he was invited to sell out his interest in the *Signal* and go down to Kingston and assume the editorship of a Reform paper in that town. Here is the venerable Scotchman's opinion of Kingston: 'I sincerely trust that the paper in Kingston may succeed, but the place is such a miserable, lifeless hole that I cannot but regard the undertaking as a hazardous speculation. Besides, the number of newspapers, such as they are, already established in Kingston, throws the success of a new one entirely upon the energy and originality of the editor. The competitors are certainly not the most formidable in the world.' '' ·

The daily newspapers of London, Ont., announced that owing to the high cost of newsprint the charges will be $7.80 per year for delivered papers and $5 per year for mail editions. The papers will sell on the streets at 3 cents per copy.

Pulp and Paper Magazine:—Enquiry at the Customs Department as to whether books printed in the German and Austrian languages were admitted free into Canada while those in English were subject to a duty, confirmed the truth of this statement. Item 172 in the Canadian tariff provides for the free admission "of books printed in any language· other than the English and French languages, or in any two languages

How Much Depreciation? Advance List

Two Questions That Are Very Important

PRINTER AND PUBLISHER, at instance of several publishers, has asked several offices questions on two points, first, what amount of depreciation should be charged and secondly, as to the desirability of insisting upon a strictly paid-in-advance circulation. The question of depreciation becomes a live one owing to the greatly increased replacement value of machinery, etc.

H. B. Donly, Simcoe *Reformer*:—The first of your queries was much debated when cost-finding conferences were in vogue. My recollection is that the consensus of opinion settled for cost-finding on two figures: on type 20 or 25 per cent., other plant 5 per cent. It may be argued that this is too low for typesetting machinery. On the other hand it is a fact that a great deal of a printing shop's equipment, speaking more particularly of a town or village plant, will, with reasonable care, last almost indefinitely.

As to the matter of a strictly paid-in-advance subscription list for a weekly, it is, without question, possible, for Bro. Moore of Acton tells us that he accomplishes the seeming miracle. But, personally, I prefer the middle way. It has never appealed to me as a pleasing possibility to have to face a man, possibly a life-long friend, possibly too a very solvent personage, just after having refused to trust him to two or three shillings worth of newspapers. Remember, however, please, I said the middle way. It is an exceedingly foolish thing to permit the chronic dead beats to work one. The publisher who has come to know his people need have but little care over the problem, if he spares an hour once a quarter to look over his mailing list, and is not afraid to use his pencil where his judgment tells him he should.

H. P. Moore, Acton *Free Press*:—1. Depreciation of plant. For years I have allowed a deduction of 10 per cent. for depreciation. This, I think, is a fair average. Type to-day will not last ten years. Presses will undoubtedly give longer service, if properly looked after. The Linotype, however, has little value in ten years and will be comparatively obsolete in that time, owing to the many and valuable labor-saving improvements which are being constantly added.

2. Cash-in-advance subscriptions. From a business standpoint the cash in advance plan is ideal. It is practical and can be operated even by a small weekly like my own publication. For sixteen years I have adhered to this plan. It requires careful cultivation of the subscription lists and demands more attention than is usually accorded the average weekly newspaper. From an advertising standpoint I have sometimes thought there is a disadvantage. The go-as-you-please subscription list has the advantage of a larger circulation to talk to the advertiser than the paid-in-advance newspaper of the same class can honestly show. It seems to me, however, that the newspaper man with a list padded with subscribers years in arrears and numbers of deadheads who will invariably creep in under the ordinary plan of careless collections, must violate his conscience somewhat in stating or swearing to his circulation.

W. Gibbens, Cornwall *Standard*:—With regard to allowance for depreciation on plant, we are of the opinion that a very small percentage will suffice if the proper amount of care is taken of the plant. We have our machinery looked over at regular intervals by a competent machinist and find that it is money well spent. On this part of the plant, therefore, we feel an allowance of 5 per cent. sufficient and on the type, which is now a comparatively small matter, 10 per cent.

As to the question of paid-in-advance circulation, we do not think it is impossible, but we would not care to try the experiment with a country weekly paper. We have to make a clean-up occasionally, but on the whole we find that the great majority of our subscribers have enough appreciation of the paper to pay for it, even if they sometimes lag a little.

W. R. Davies, Renfrew *Mercury*:—We have been charging up 10 per cent. on depreciation. I do not know whether this is too much or too little. Type wears out very quickly but machinery lasts a long time. I am afraid that some weekly publishers do not take this matter into consideration at all. If they do they surely would not be able to do work at the price they do and still show profit. Reliable information received recently shows that a great many printers are still doing auditors' reports for $1.50 and $1.75 a page. Just how it is done is one of the problems we have not yet solved. I am looking forward with a great deal of interest to reading the views of other publishers on this matter of depreciation.

Regarding a paid-in-advance circulation. I operated a strictly paid-in-advance system in connection with our subscription list on the Thamesville *Herald*. We served the subscriber with three notices: one 10 days before the subscription expired; one 10 days after it had expired; and a final notice about the 20th of the month. If he had not then paid at the first of the following month we struck his name from the list. This method worked fairly satisfactorily, but I do not know after five years' experience whether it is wise to be quite so rigid. It is hard to keep from hurting the feelings of some people who are perfectly good risks and who have no intention of stopping the paper, though they failed to respond to either of the three notices. It has one great advantage, it rids you promptly of the man who is always with us: who will take the paper for three or four months, then put it back in the Post Office and mark it refused; and will then walk in quite blithely the following fall and sign up until the end of the year. The argument mentioned in your letter against a paid-in-advance list does not seem to me to be well taken. Because a list is paid-in-advance it is not necessarily all paid in December. While a great many subscriptions do expire at the end of the year, on our paper a great many expire every month and paid-in-advance simply means that they pay before or immediately after expiration. With the increasing cost of newsprint the necessity of close collections becomes imperative as newspapers cannot afford to be carrying a lot of subscribers two, three, four and in some cases five years old. At the present time on the *Mercury* we are busy cleaning up the lists and hope soon to have it on a basis as nearly paid in advance as seems practical with a large circulation. I have often wondered if it would be a good thing for the newspapers if the Post Office Department would refuse to carry papers more than six months in arrears.

C. Kerr Stewart, St. Maurice Valley *Chronicle*: — Printers generally are familiar with the fact that the cost of machinery and material is going higher from year to year, and that to replace the plant they bought a few years ago, would mean the expenditure of many more dollars than had been originally invested.

One of the items, therefore, which should have a little more attention is depreciation, and the question arises, "What amount should be written off each year so that a plant may be kept up to a high standard for the production of good work economically?"

Many printers make the mistake when closing their books at the end of the year, of not allowing the proper amount for depreciation, and in that way disillusion themselves as to their profits.

Just to illustrate what is meant, take for instance the matter of type. Every printer knows that good type is a necessary factor in turning out good work, and that worn type takes much longer to make ready and does not produce the same results even with the extra time spent in the press room. Yet how many printers neglect to keep their type up to a high standard, simply because they have not allowed the proper amount for depreciation so that it can be replaced. To my mind new type should be added from time to time so that you have a complete renewal of faces every four years, which mean that 25 per cent. should be written off for depreciation every year on type alone.

But type is not the only thing which depreciates in a printing plant. Modern printing machinery costs more to-day than it did a few years ago, and here again the printer is confronted with the bugbear depreciation, and it is right here that a mistake is often made. If your business shows an increase over the previous year, you will no doubt find on investigation that your presses have been running more steadily. Now just think a minute—does that not mean that there has been more wear on your presses than the previous year—then why not increase your percentage allowed for depreciation?

Suppose we say a press, or any other piece of machinery, is good for ten years, then why not allow ten per cent. depreciation and increase this percentage from year to year as the machinery prices advance, so that you will have the necessary reserve fund to replace it when business demands a more modern machine.

The above is, I think, a fair way to allow a proper percentage of depreciation, and if the output of a plant is being sold at a profit, after having ascertained your cost, there is no reason why printing plants should not be kept up to a high standard of efficiency.

One of the troubles with the printing business in past years has been the lack of applying everyday business methods to the industry. The printer of to-day should study modern business methods as applied to any other manufacturing business, and if this is done it would be but a short time till printing plants were on a better basis financially and also better equipped than the majority are at the present time. Spend a little time investigating your own plant and business methods and you will have no trouble arriving at the proper amount that should be allowed for depreciation.

County Association Can Help a Great Deal
To Get Prices on an Honorable Basis

Kincardine, March 12,1920
To the Editor of *Printer and Publisher*.

Sir:—Will you permit me through your excellent paper to address my fellow-printers and publishers of the rural districts? The question I desire to bring before them at this time is the vast spread in prices for job work. This has been brought out most forcibly by the recent printing of voters' lists for the Ontario Government. As you know from four cents to twenty cents a line was quoted by those doing the work. Is it any wonder that the Government thought that some of the printers were holding them up? Yet this was not the case. Had the printers actually gone into the matter they would have found that 12 cents a line was a fair price to ask. When the job came up I took the matter up with the County Judge of Bruce. I found out what was required and I then got in touch with a printer who had done the work for a bye-election. He received 8 cents a line and at that time made what he considered a fair profit. After figuring the work from all angles, with overtime and night work, missing at least one issue of a paper, and the fact that the work had to be out in fifteen days, I, after consulting with some other printers, decided that the work was worth 12 cents per line.

I then called all the printers of the County of Bruce together at Walkerton, submitted the proposed price, giving them my figures. The Bruce Printers' Association were asked if they could do the job by the Board appointed by the Government. We replied that we could, and an agreement as to price, size of page, number of copies and other details was entered into, and the job accepted by the Association and the Board.

The work, which was for the three ridings of Bruce, was then allotted to the various offices. After all had taken what they thought they could handle, the riding of West Bruce was found to be untouched. The Kincardine *Review* and the Kincardine *Reporter* agreed to tackle this riding, and as you know Bruce was the first and only county to deliver the lists on time, you can understand what it meant to us in the way of extra work.

Now, what I want to come at is the haphazard way the country printers are going about their business. Had there been county associations such as Bruce has, there would have been no need of such a discrepancy in prices quoted, and the printing trade held up to ridicule. What the country printer wants is closer co-operation with his neighbor. Also be prepared to show the reason why you get the prices. The man with high prices need not be afraid to let his competitor know what he is getting, for the fellow who is not getting good prices will reason that he is as good a printer and his work is worth as much as the other fellow's. Don't be afraid to instal some kind of a cost system into your job department. Don't be afraid to ask the price when you know you are right and the work is worth it. Last month's issue of *Printer and Publisher* will be an eye-opener for some country job printers, if they read the article on costs on Page 17. Printers, for heaven's sake have a little confidence in one another. Don't take it for granted that the customer is the only truthful man and that when he tells you he can get it done for so and so at your neighbor's, that he can. Trust your fellow-printer first and hold out for your price—if it is honest.

This voters' list printing has shown that we have some poor business men in the publishing game. Just here I want to say that the Bruce Printers were paid 10 cents a name. True it was a cut of two cents a name, and we accepted it, because we placed the matter in the hands of the manager of the Canadian Weekly Newspapers' Association, with power to act. He was conversant with every phase of the work, and I desire to say that we are well satisfied with his efforts. True he did not get the full amount, but he was able to save us the costs of an expensive litigation. Right here I want to say that Mr. Sayle's work justifies the Canadian Weekly Newspapers' Association being separate from the Daily Association, and I would appeal to every Weekly man to join. If we would make the country publisher occupy the place he should, we can only do it by being united and making our Weekly Publishers' Association the medium through which we voice our strength.

Yours for the betterment of the Weekly publisher,
J. J. HUNTER.

Liberal Daily at Ottawa?

At the annual meeting of the Ottawa Reform Club in the club rooms Mr. A. R. McDonald announced that a new Liberal party daily paper would be started soon in that city. It would be a national Liberal newspaper. Mr. D. D. McKenzie, M.P., former Leader, is president of the new company, and appeals are being made for $60,000 stock subscription.

A Worth-While Specimen Book

The Rolland Paper Co. have issued a neat specimen book showing uses to which their colored bond is being put by various commercial houses. The various specimens are intended to cover a range showing offset and flat-bed lithography, letterpress printing from zinc etching, etc. The title cover is well done, a light buff stock being used. A heavy block in blue black, with an outline of light blue, makes a striking ground in which to plant their lettering, which is cut out of the tint block. It would be good business for printers generally to secure samples of such specimen books as they contain fine specimens of well-designed and well-balanced letterheads. Although many of these are hand-lettered, there is much for the average office to learn from them in the way of design, display and relation of ink-color to stock.

Cutting Down N.Y. Papers

Immediate reduction of ten per cent. in consumption of newsprint by all newspapers and a request to advertisers to reduce their space ten per cent. "during the present emergency" were urged in a resolution adopted at New York by the board of directors and the paper committee of the American Newspaper Publishers' Association. The general sentiment of publishers attending the meeting, the resolution states, was that the situation, while serious, does not justify Government action or the passage of any of the various measures which have been introduced in Congress, the belief being that the results already achieved, the higher prices for spot paper and the adoption by newspapers generally of the spirit of the resolutions above will finally meet the situation.

Toronto Telegram to Build New Press Room
Secure Site to Duplicate Capacity

THE Toronto *Telegram* will shortly begin the erection of a press-room on Dupont street North Toronto, where it will duplicate the plant it already has at the corner of Bay and Melinda. The *Telegram* has been facing the question for some time, and believes that the solution arrived at will be the best for all purposes.

When one considers the lay-out of Toronto, it can readily be seen that the situation of the *Telegram* office is not one that is going to assist a quick exit of trucks for delivery purposes. The paper is at the extreme south side of the city, and the growth is toward the north, east and west. The city is growing in three directions away from the *Telegram* office, and the problem of quick distribution to the readers will be one that will increase every year.

Two options were open to the *Telegram*. The one first considered was of buying more property near their present office. This would have cost them a lot of money, and it would have meant that they would have to go ahead burrowing under the ground to get the press room capacity they needed. To have gone ahead with such a plan would have cost the office at least a million dollars. Even when this was finished it would not help out the distribution problem, which was about as serious as increasing the running capacity of the press room. They would still have the "neck of the bottle" proposition to deal with in getting out their trucks quickly.

So the other proposition was taken up, that of purchasing a site at some outlying point, and Dupont street was chosen. Work will be started shortly on the erection of a press-room there that ought to give the *Telegram* all the press-room space it will need for the next half century or so. It is proposed to make duplicate plates and rush them to the Dupont plant in motor trucks. In this way, it is believed that the presses at the Dupont office can be started within ten or fifteen minutes of the presses at the corner of Bay and Melinda. Distribution will be made to a large area from the northern office, and considerable time will be saved in reaching the readers in that part of the district. It is quite easy to see that from a half hour up can be saved in this way in getting the papers on the streets and to the dealers.

The *Telegram* may not stop with the securing of more press-room capacity in the northern office, but may duplicate the entire plant, so that no matter what happens .they will not be tied up in the matter of mechanical equipment to turn out the paper.

Could You Meet This Price?

Could you print 1,400 books, 64 names per page, 25 eight point across, for $40? There are 21 set pages, each page having about 2,600 ems. Cover is fairly good manila, and stock in the book is a fair book paper, about 50 pound.

Printer and Publisher reproduces one of the pages here. It is good machine composition; the operator has taken care to do his part well. There are no spaces between the leaders, and the justifications are nicely made.

This job was done in Nova Scotia. One office figured on it this year but lost, as it was done for $40. No, that's not a mistake—Forty.

What is the job worth? Why not figure this out and see for yourself? There are 1,400 copies, and the paper is about.50 pound book, between 12 and 13 cents a pound. The figures for wages were not given, but we are using something slightly lower than Toronto rates.

Stock	$20
Cover Stock	5
Composition	42
Hand Composition	8
Make-up and Locking	7
Press work on both the book and cover	15
Jogging and Stitching	10
Delivery and Packing	2
	$114

There is nothing added to the above for profit. Taking a very nominal figure of 20 per cent. we have $23, which makes it $137, against the $40 charged

MacLennan, Chas. S., Scotsburn, R. R. 2 ,..,.Nov—12, 1918	800
MacLellan, Geo. W.., Pictou..R. R. 2 ....June 19, 1919	1,000
MacLellan, Robert, New Glasgow ....Oct. 22, 1920	500
MacLellan, Wm. F., Scotsburn. R. R. 2 .....Nov. 12, 1919	1,000
MacLennan, Wm. F., Scotsburn R. R. 2 .....Nov. 12, 1019	1,000
MacLeod, Alex. S., Scotsburn, R. R. 2 .....May 14, 1921	2,000
MacLeod, Alfred P., Westville ....Nov. 29, 1920	700
MacLeod, Archie & Jas. McK, Hopewell R.R 1 Mar. 30, 1920	1,100
MacLeod, Arthur, West River ....Jan. 13, 1920	700
MacLeod, David, Denmark ....Feb. 7, 1920	1,200
MacLeod, Geo. Falls, ...July 12, 1920	1,000
MacLeod, H. D., Woodfield ....June 11, 1921	600
MacLeod, Hiram H., Westville ....July 22, 1920	600
McLeod, Mrs. Hugh, Scotsburn. R. R. ? ......Jan. 5, 1921	600
McLeod, Hugh J., Scotsburn. R. R. 2 ......Nov. 3, 1920	1,500
McLeod, Jas. A., Westville. R. R. 1 ....Jan. 19, 1921	1,000
McLeod, John, Carriboo River ....Nov. 29, 1919	1,000
McLeod, John, Westville ....May 9, 1920	900
McLeod, John, The Falls, ...Aug. 2, 1920	1,800
McLeod, John, Hopewell ....April 29, 1919	500
McLeod, John W.,.R. John ....April 13, 1921	1,000
McLeod, John W., Westville. ....July 24, 1920	800
McLeod, Archie & Jas. McK, Hopewell ......Jan. 25, 1920	400
McLeod, Robert G., Lansdowne. R. R. 1 .....Aug. 26, 1921	700
McLeod, Simon A., Pleasant Valley ....Aug. 23, 1919	700
McLeod, W. A., Meadowville ....Dec. 7, 1919	600
McLeod, Malcolm G., R. John ....Dec. 20, 1921	2,600
MacLeod, Wm. Scotsburn. R. R. 2 ....Nov. 30, 1919	2,00
McLeod, Wm, Hopewell ....March 20, 1920	1,300
MacLeod, Wm. D. Watervale ....Aug. 15, 1921	1,000
MacMaster, Alex. H., Seafoam ....June 28, 1919	400
MacMaster. Hugh. Seafoam ....Dec. 6, 1919	1,000
McMillan, Duncan. Pictou. R. 3 ....Dec. 14, 1921	700
McMillan, Herbert. Scotch Hill ....June 22, 1919	1,300
MacMillan, John, Springville ....April 15, 1921	700
MacMillan, John, Garden of Eden ....June 5, 1921	700
MacMillan, Roger, Woodfield ....June 11, 1921	500
MacMillan, Finlay, New Glasgow, R. 2 .....Dec. 25, 1921	2,000
McNeughton, Jas., Eureka ....Aug. 13, 1919	700
McNeil, F. M., Little Harbor ....March 15, 1920	1,000
McNeil, Thomas, Westville ....April 18, 1921	700
McNutt, Rufus, Sandville ....Aug. 21, 1921	1,000
McPhail, Edward, Alma ....Oct. 10, 1919	1,000
McPherson, Alex. F., Hopewell. R. R. 1 .....July 12, 1921	800
McPherson, Angus, Garden of Eden ....June 23, 1921	500
McPherson, Arthur M., Lansdowne, R. R.. 1\..Aug. 27, 1921	900
McPherson, Duncan, New Gairloch ....July 25, 1920	600
McPherson, John H., W. River Sta., R. R. 2 ..Aug. 15, 1921	1,000
McPherson, Robert O., New Glasgow. R. R. 1 .Oct. 22, 1920	1,000
MacPhie, Duncan, Hopewell ....May 4, 1921	700
MacPhie, W., Avondale ....March 5, 1921	1,000
MacPhie, John, Sunny Brae ....May 22, 1919	50
MacPhie, Mrs. M. J., French River ....March 14, 1920	800
MacPhie, John W., Stellarton, R. R. 1, ...March 9, 1920	1,000
McQuarrie, J. and J., Avondale ....Oct. 3, 1920	700
McQuarrie, Mrs. Mary F., Caledonia ....June 12, 1921	600
McQuarrie, James, Sunny Brae ....May 22, 1919	50
McQuarrie, Mrs. Mary F., Caledonia ....June 12, 1921	500
McQuarrie, Samuel L., Caledonia ....June 11, 1921	500
McQuarrie, Wm., Sundridge ....July 13, 1920	500
McRae, Alex., King's Head ....April 14, 1921	800
McRae, Allister, Trenton ....Aug. 31, 1921	2,000
McRae, Thos., Trenton ....July 15, 1920	1,000
McRae, Mrs. Sarah J., Granton. ....Aug. 31, 1921	1,000
McTavish, Mrs. Elizabeth, Meadowville, R.R. 1 Aug. 16, 1920	1,000
McTavish, Wm. H., Meadowville ....Nov. 26, 1919	500

What After July First?

New Glasgow *Eastern Chronicle*:—After seventy-five years of continuous service the Montreal *Weekly Witness* has had to temporarily suspend publication owing to the shortage of newsprint paper. The Montreal *Herald*, also a very old paper and a daily, has had to suspend for the same reason. How long other papers like the *Eastern Chronicle* can struggle along is a question that we can not decide. Last week the firm from which we have purchased all our supply for many years and paid for every pound advised us that they had made arrangements to supply us until July 1st, 1920, and this was contingent on that we used no more than we did in a like period last year. They warned us that only a certain allotment could be secured and if we exceeded this quantity they could not take care of us. There is nothing in the premises that we can do but patiently wait until the specified time arrives and see what the paper mills can do for us. We are not partners of the present situation, merely victims.

Printer & Publisher

Published on the Twelfth of Each Month.

H. A. NICHOLSON   -   -   -   Business Manager
A. R. KENNEDY   -   -   -   -   -   Editor

SUBSCRIPTION PRICE--Canada, Great Britain, South Africa and
the West Indies, $2 a year; United States, $2.50 a year; other
countries, $3 a year.   Single copies, 20 cents.   Invariably in
advance.

·PUBLISHED BY

THE MACLEAN PUBLISHING CO.

Established 1887   Limited

JOHN BAYNE MACLEAN   -   -   -   -   President
H. T. HUNTER   -   -   -   -   -   Vice-President
H. V. TYRRELL   -   -   -   -   General Manager
T. B. COSTAIN   -   -   -   General Managing Editor

Head Office, 143-153 University AVenue   -   TORONTO, CANADA
Cable Address: Macpubco, Toronto; Atabek, London, Eng.
Also at Montreal, Winnipeg, New York, Chicago, Boston, London,
England.

Vol. 28·   TORONTO, MARCH, 1920   No. 3

CONTENTS

Do Not Delay Increase Too Long

PRINTER AND PUBLISHER has never advocated "soak-ing" the reading public. It can adhere to that course, and advise the publishers of weeklies and dailies alike to get their subscription prices adjusted to meet the uncertain conditions that may prevail after July 1st, past which there is no guarantee as to the price of paper.

Occasionally we read of some courageous publisher who is threatening to put his paper to $1.50 per year, and at the same time waving to the countryside to crowd in at $1 per head. When he is about it he might as well make the price $2 and be done with it for a· while. If some of his subscribers wished to drop out he would be better off with a slightly smaller circulation and a bigger price.

It is not necessary to become an alarmist in this case, but there is evidence that some of the publishers do not appreciate the seriousness of the paper situation as far as they are concerned. With prices where they are now, and in view of the further increases that seem likely, the subscriber who pays $1 a year for his weekly paper is not carrying his share of the cost of publication. The $2 weekly is here, and in some places where publishers insist on keeping up their standard of excellence a charge of $2.50 will be necessary.

It is poor policy to put off until the increases are on your heels. If that is done it takes months before you start to get returns on your increased rates, as your circulation will have many papers that are running on the old rate.

The End of the *News-Times*

GOING, going, gone! Such was the requiem· that was chanted at the clearing out of what was left of the fixtures at the office of the Toronto *Times*, formerly and better known as the *News*.

The story of the closing up and selling of the plant forms a chapter unique in Canadian journalism. At the time of the crash the paper was carrying more advertising than it had for some time past, and it looked as though matters were in better shape financially than they had been for months.

The story was freely circulated, perhaps through inspiration,

that the paper's policy on the referendum on liquor business was the rock on which the ship was wrecked. There have been denials of this quite as emphatic as the story.

There is not a case on record in Toronto or elsewhere, as far as we can learn, where a paper came to such an abrupt ending. It was tragic, as far as the staff was concerned. One reporter burned the oil far into the night turning in a night assignment. On his way home he got a morning paper and found that his own paper was through, and that his night's work was in vain. The staff, business, editorial and mechanical, were all on hand the following morning. It was then they received the first intimation that the paper was through.

How much money was sunk in that venture? We don't know, and the few who could furnish the information are not telling, although estimates at times have placed the figure as high as $1,500,000.

There is not much sentiment in business now. The hammer of the auctioneer knocked down desks and typewriter tables to the buyer who would part with the greatest amount of cash for them. The countless stories that were written on them were forgotten—the struggles of the cub to get his first efforts across—all swallowed up in the hurry to clear them out so that the so-much-per-hour trucks would not be kept waiting.

Several negotiations were attempted with a view to taking over the property intact, but they did not come to a successful issue. There was a chance there for any interested parties to go ahead with their threats to start a new paper. As long as they had the price· they could have made the plant whistle, Tory or Farmer. One rumor was that a well-known Canadian publisher would have gone in had he been able to secure recognition as the organ of the U.F.O., but that body was already tied up with the *Farmer's Sun*, and apparently had nothing to gain by identifying itself with the defunct Toronto paper.

A Situation That Grows Worse

THE newsprint situation dces not become any better. Nor is there anything in sight to indicate that it is going to become better. Many publishers—old customers—do not yet realize the seriousness of the situation. Not long ago one of them was not satisfied with the quality of the paper he was getting. He wrote to another company, stating that he was thinking of changing, and intimating that he was open for a call from one of their men.

You know what happened. He was told quite courteously that if he were securing an adequate supply of print, he had better stay with it, as there was not the remotest chance of the company taking on any new customers.

A writer in a current paper has this to say:—

"Why do not all publishers, both large and small, agree to run not more than fourteen pages during the week and not more than forty pages on Sunday, cut out fiction, comic sections, rotogravure sections, magazine sections, cut the size of the social section, give the people a newspaper, not a story book? In this way an enormous amount of white paper would be saved.

"Most publishers will laugh when they read this, but·some will not laugh before the end of 1920."

So far publishers have not shown any real desire to go ahead and cut down on newsprint. There is still the circulation ·contest, the extra pages on Saturday, the full page splashes of prepared miscellaneous pages. They all take paper and still more paper.

Without going into details, it is safe to assert that the newsprint situation is worse than it was a year ago. If there are signs showing an improvement, we would like to be optimistic enough to point them out.

There are counties in Ontario that are not organized. In them, we are reliably informed, voters' list and auditors' reports are printed from $1.15 to $1.25 per page, with $1.50 as positively the last word. Business cards, it is stated, are turned out for $3.00 for 2,000. It seems a little hard to make some sections see the great light, although present prices of paper and labor may in time act as the barn-lantern for some of these offices.

THE RE-SET ADVERTISEMENT

 Specimens Taken at Random From Canadian Papers
By H. A. Nicholson, Manager Printer and Publisher

Hamilton School Making Typography an Art
Third Annual Ad. Contest is Successful

IF any of our readers entertain a doubt as to the value of the trade school for the development of printing apprentices their attention is directed to the exhibition of work on the following page. The work represents an advertisement setting contest conducted by the printing class of the Hamilton Technical and Art School.

The *Printer and Publisher* staff acted in the capacity of judges, and it may be said that in establishing the winner and in grading the advertisements according to their typographical merits the judges found themselves confronted with a difficult task, so uniform in merit are the great majority of the advertisements, which, all told, are twenty-one in number.

The first advertisement shown in the reproduction on the next page was awarded first honors. The other advertisements appear in order of merit, reading left to right.

It should be stated here that the reproduction represents the appearance of the advertisements after they were reset in accordance with suggestions made by the judges; the changes effected were not drastic in the majority of cases; not sufficient to warrant space for the reproduction of the originals.

A Practical Competition

Before proceeding to discuss the lesson to be taken from this very creditable work an idea of the manner in which the competition was conducted is probably in order.

The contest was decidedly practical in every respect. Twenty-one Hamilton merchants submitted paid advertisements for the occasion. The copy was prepared in the usual way by each merchant, just as copy is prepared for insertion in the daily papers. This copy was placed at random on a copy-hook at the school, each apprentice "taking from the top" in accordance with the usual shop practice. The competitors then went to their respective "cases" and proceeded to work in regular composing-room style.

Printer and Publisher was not informed as to a time-limit for setting, but quite a number of other interesting restrictions were enforced according to information given out. The contestants had no choice in changing copy and the selection of type was restricted to Cheltenham Light, Caslon Light, and the Chippendale series. It rested with them to select the salient points for display. Their instructors, however, pointed out that there should be three things to emphasize—*the article, the price, and the name of the advertiser*. The contestants were also told to bear in mind that there are three factors underlying an effective advertisement—*black, grey, and white* (the black tone given by heavy face type, the grey tone given by light-face type, and the white space produced by the background). It was further pointed out that only by *massing* and *grouping* the various parts of the advertisement could the best results be secured.

Benefit of Scientific Principles

Printer and Publisher, of course, is anxious to pay due tribute to the excellence of the work produced by the students of the printing class of the Hamilton Technical and Art School, but the main reason for giving special prominence to this contest is to emphasize the importance of the practising of the principles of display as set forth time and again in these columns, principles which are identical with those that have guided the students of this school in this contest.

The advertisements were inserted en masse in the Hamilton *Herald*, Hamilton *Spectator*, and Hamilton *Times* as indicated in the reduced full-page reproduction. It is safe to say that no other newspapers in Canada, or elsewhere, carried on the same day as these productions appeared, such a galaxy of attractive-looking advertisements on one page, viewing the display collectively.

What is the secret of the pleasing results obtained? *The restriction of type faces employed to a minimum number of readable styles all very much alike; adherence to the other principles of display heretofore referred to—grouping and massing, in particular.*

Printer and Publisher is not disposed to acclaim these productions of the Hamilton Technical and Art School students as masterpieces of the highest grade of typographical excellence, but the work certainly merits high praise, as splendid examples of every-day ad-setting.

Refer to Following Pages

Some of the ads. of the contest might still be changed to advantage. With this in view four of them may be changed by *Printer and Publisher* and are shown alongside of the original on the following pages.

Two examples of the changes in display suggested by the judges are also given.

Method of Judging Explained

It may be interesting to observe the method which guided the judges in establishing the merits of the various advertisements. Twenty points was made the greatest possible number in each case — five points each for grouping, massing, white space, and general display, treatment. The results follow:

No.	Grouping	Massing	White Space	Display	Total
1	4	4	4	4	16
2	4	3	3	3	13
3	4	4	3	4	15
4	1	2	3	2	8
5	2	2	3	4	11
6	2	2	2	3	9
7	5	5	4	4	18
8	3	4	3	4	14
9	2	2	3	3	10
10	3	3	3	4	13
11	3	3	3	3	12
12	5	5	5	4	19
13	4	4	3	4	15
14	3	3	3	3	12
15	3	3	3	4	13
16	3	3	4	4	14
17	4	4	4	3	15
18	4	4	4	4	16
19	3	4	4	4	15
20	2	3	2	3	10
21	3	3	3	4	13

It should be remembered that the results above are not representative of the advertisements as they appear in the reproduction on the following page, as the reproduction shows the advertisements after they were changed in accordance with the suggestions by the judges.

A Newspaper's View

A Hamilton paper in announcing the results of the contest made the following comment:—
Continued on page 33

Advertisement contest recently conducted by the Hamilton Technical and Art School, twenty-one students competing. The PRINTER AND PUBLISHER staff judged the competition and suggested changes in each case where it was thought an improvement could be effected. The reduced full-page reproduction above shows the advertisements after being changed according to the judges' suggestions, but are shown in the order of merit (reading from left to right from the top left-hand corner) established by the judges in the first instance. By limiting the styles of type to Caslon Light, Cheltenham Light and the Chippendale series (type faces of the same weight yet sufficiently different in character to escape monotony in effect) a pleasing tone has been given to the whole arrangement. Each advertisement, too, has been made effective in itself by skilful use of white space, grouping of parts and massing of tones.

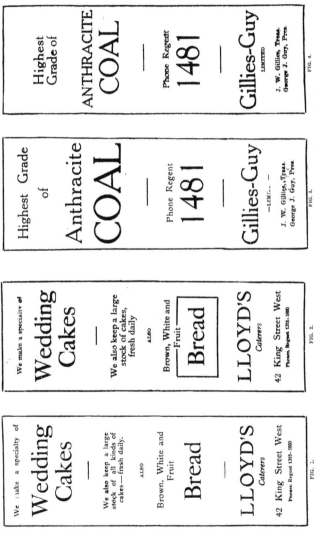

Hamilton Technical and Art School Advertisement Competition

We make a specialty of

Wedding
Cakes

We also keep a large
stock of cakes,
fresh daily.

ALSO

Brown, White and
Fruit

Bread

LLOYD'S
Caterers

42 King Street West
Phones, Regent 1363-5880

FIG. 2.

We take a specialty of

Wedding
Cakes

We also keep a large
stock of all kinds of
cakes—fresh daily.

ALSO

Brown, White and
Fruit

Bread

LLOYD'S
Caterers

42 King Street West
Phones, Regent 1363-5880

FIG. 1.

Highest Grade
of
Anthracite
COAL

Phone Regent
1481

Gillies-Guy
—LIMITED—

J. W. Gillies, Treas.
George J. Guy, Pres.

FIG. 3.

Highest
Grade of
ANTHRACITE
COAL

Phone Regent
1481

Gillies-Guy
LIMITED

J. W. Gillies, Treas.
George J. Guy, Pres.

FIG. 4.

Figures 1 and 3 give an example of the appearance of the advertisements as originally displayed by the
students. Figures 2 and 4 show the advertisements after being changed in accordance with suggestions offered by the judges of the competition.

Hamilton Technical and Art School Advertisement Competition

Cylinder Grinding

We have installed an up-to-date HEALED GRIND-ER which enables us to grind a tobile, motorboat and motor-cycle cylinders with ut-most accuracy

The HEALD is designed especially for internal grinding and possesses great advantages over the ordinary method of grinding and reaming.

Following are a few reasons why you should send your work to us:

1. Travels the work horizontal—ways properly oiled and protected from grit.
2. Is fitted with micrometer which insures absolute accuracy.
3. Produces a better finish.
4. Grinds accurately and faster, because handier.

Oversize Pistons and Rings made to fit

WORK GUARANTEED

Write to-day for prices.

Wing & Son
32-34 Bay Street North, Hamilton, Canada

FIG. 1.

Cylinder Grinding

We have installed an up-to-date

HEALD GRINDER

Which enables us to grind

Automobile, Motorboat and Motorcycle Cylinders

The "Heald" is designed especially for internal grinding and possesses great advantages over the ordinary method of grinding and reaming.

Following are a few reasons why you should send your work to us:

1. *Travels the work horizontal—ways properly oiled and protected from grit.*
2. *Is fitted with micrometer which insures absolute accuracy.*
3. *Produces a better finish.*
4. *Grinds accurately and faster, because handier.*

Oversize Pistons and Rings made to fit

WORK GUARANTEED

Write to-day for prices

Wing & Son
32-34 Bay Street North
Hamilton, Canada

FIG. 2.

Royal (Tailored) Suits

Measured by every standard, whether it be the materials, workmanship, styles or patterns, our suits

Prove Their Superior Worth

—prove that they are the faultless productions of men who have made the designing and making of men's high-class clothing their life study.

There is refinement in every detail—in the appropriateness of the color effects and in the fashioning of the labels—in the graceful back lines of the coats and in the perfect set of the trousers:

—THE—

Royal Tailoring Company
M. SILVERMAN, Prop.
229 King St. East

FIG. 3.

Royal Tailored Suits

Measured by every standard, whether it be the materials, workmanship, styles or patterns, our suits

Prove Their Superior Worth

—prove that they are the faultless productions of men who have made the designing and making of men's high-class clothing their life study.

There is refinement in every detail—in the appropriateness of the color effects and in the fashioning of the lapels—in the graceful back lines of the coats and in the perfect set of the trousers.

The
Royal Tailoring Company
M. Silverman, Prop.
229 King Street West

FIG. 4.

Figures 1 and 3 show two advertisements selected for reset purposes by "Printer and Publisher." Figure 2 presents figure 1 in more attractive style; figure 4 presents a heading more in keeping with the refinement of the message than is seen in figure 3.

Hamilton Technical and Art School Advertisement Competition

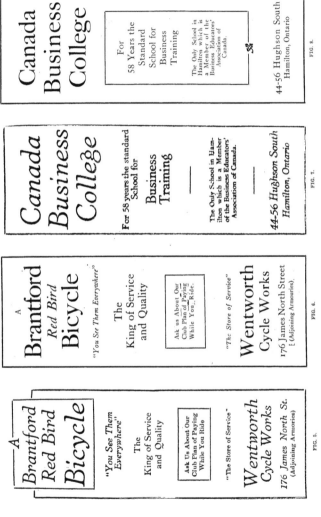

FIG. 8.

FIG. 7.

FIG. 6.

FIG. 5.

Figures 5 and 7 show two more advertisements selected for reset purposes. Figures 6 and 8 have been slightly varied in style to make the message more readily assimilated. Fine points in typography are thus presented which are worthy of close study.

Price List Adopted by the Norfolk Association

PRICES charged in Bruce, Ottawa Valley and Norfolk should not vary a great deal. To begin with, the publishers in all these places buy from a common market. Labor costs are not a great deal different, and the same industries are served.

Take three district Associations, Bruce, Ottawa Valley and Norfolk. How do prices compare? On letterheads, practically the same. On envelopes, based on a No. 7 for 500:—

Bruce	$3.25
Norfolk	3.25
Ottawa Valley	2.75

Dodgers are common stock in trade. The sixteenth is priced thus for 500:—

Bruce	$3.00
Norfolk	3.00
Ottawa Valley	2.25

Quite a little difference there, as in the envelopes, with the Ottawa people a fair charge behind.

The quarter sheet auction sale bill is a regular customer.

Bruce (50)	$4.50
Bruce (100)	5.00
Norfolk (50)	4.00
Norfolk (100)	5.00
Ottawa Valley (50)	3.00
Ottawa Valley (100)	3.75

Below is given the new list adopted by the Norfolk Association. Printers should keep these published lists. Especially if your territory is not organized, in this way you will have the advantage of the experience of men who have gone carefully into the whole field, and are willing to put down in tabulated form their conclusions.

Letterheads

[Based on stock costing $2.00 a thousand]

250	$3.00
500	4.00
1000	6.00
Each extra thousand	4.00

For two colors add $2.00 to $3.00, according to work.

For more expensive stock add to these prices accordingly.

Billheads

8vo. Post	— 500	$3.00
	—1000	4.50
Quarter Cap	— 500	3.50
	—1000	5.00
4to Post	— 500	4.25
	—1000	6.50
Half Cap	— 250	4.00
	— 500	5.00
	—1000	7.25

100 of any of above $2.50 to $3.50.

Noteheads, Memo Heads, etc.

[Based on stock costing $1.00 to $1.50 per thousand]

Noteheads	— 500	$3.00
and Memos	—1000	4.50
Each extra 1000		3.00
Statements	— 500	3.50
	—1000	5.00
Each extra 1000		3.50

Envelopes — No. 7

[Based on stock costing $1.50 per thousand]

500	$3.25
1000	4.50
Each extra thousand	3.50

No. 8

[Based on stock costing $1.75 to $2.00]

500	$3.50
1000	5.00

Business Cards

[Based on stock costing $1.00 per thousand]

100	$2.00
250	3.00
500	4.00
1000	5.50
Each extra thousand	3.50

Admission Tickets

100	$1.50
Each additional 100	.40

Printed with coupon, 50c extra

Receipts, Notes, Etc.

[About 10x4; perforated. Put up in books, 50 or 100 to a book. Tag or cover paper bound. Average composition]

100	$2.50
250	3.50
500	4.00
1000	6.00

Funeral Cards

12	$2.00
25	2.50
50	4.00
75	5.00
100	6 00

Shipping Tags

[Based on No. 5 ordinary Commercial Stock, costing about $1.75 per M]

250	$2.25
500	3.00
1000	4.50

Other sizes in proportion; extra charge for better qualities of tags.

Government Post Cards

[Printing only: cards supplied by customer]

100	$1.50
Each additional 100	.25

Cards supplied by printer, charge 10 per cent. on cost.

Private Post Cards

[On Government post card Manila or equal stock]

500 printed on two sides	$4.00
1000	6.50

Visiting Cards

50	$0.75
100	1.25

Wedding Invitations

15, $3.00; 25, $3.50; 35, $4.00; 50, $4.75; 75, $6.00; 100, $7.25

For more expensive stock, add in proportion.

Dance Invitations and At Home Cards

[On kid-finished Bristol; size approximating 3 x 4]

50	$2.50
100	4.00

Printed both sides, 50 per cent. extra. Larger sizes in proportion. Prices include envelopes to match.

Ballots

[Ten names or less. Bound in books for polling divisions]

300 ballots	$5 00
Each additional name	1.00
Each additional 100	.75

Route Cards

[Display card on 6-ply Printers' Blanks]

Half Sheet	— 25	$6.00
	— 50	8.00
	— 100	10.50

Route Folders

7 x 7½	— 100	$7.50
Each additional 100		1.50

For heavy tabulated pedigree, charge extra according to time consumed.

Window Cards

[Prices for black ink only; any other one color add 75c]

Quar. Sheets	— 1	$1.50
	— 25	3 00
	— 50	4.00
	— 100	6.00
Half Sheets	— 1	2.50
	— 25	5.00
	— 50	7.50
Whole Sheet		$2.00 to $5.00
Each extra card		30c

For a second color add 75 per cent. to above prices.

Prize Lists

200 copies, $2.00 per page; 25c additional for each extra 100 copies; cover to count four pages.

Financial Statements

Size of page, 5½ x 8½; type 8-point, 24 ems by 40 ems. 200 copies, $2.50 per page; double charge for all tabular matter Each additional hundred, 25c per page. Cover to count four pages.

Voters' Lists

On basis of an average of 25 lines to a page; set in 8-point, without rules, $2.25 per page for 200 copies. Cover to count as four pages.

Books, Pamphlets, Constitutions, By-Laws, Minutes, Etc.

Size of page, 5½ x 8½; set in 8-point; 100 copies for $1.75 per page; 25c additional for each 100 copies; cover to count as four pages.

Circulars and Forms

⅛ Post and ¼ Cap	— 100	$2.50
	— 250	3.50
	— 500	4.00
	—1000	6.00
¼ Post	— 100	3.00
	— 250	4.00
	— 500	5.00
	—1000	7.50
½ Cap	— 100	3.50
	— 250	4.50
	— 500	6.00
	—1000	8.00

Add 66 2/3 per cent. to prices of ¼ and ½ Cap when endorsed.

Real Estate and Farm Stock Sale Bills

Sixteenths (6x9)

100	$2.50
200	2.75
300	3.00
500	3.50
1000	5.00

Eighths (9 x 12)

100	$3.00
200	3.50
300	4.00
500	5.00
1000	7.00

Quarter Sheets (12 x 18)

25 or less	4.00
50	5.00
100	6.00

Half Sheets (18 x 24)

50 or less	6.00
100	7.00

Posters and Heralds for Meetings and Entertainments

6x8 16th Sht.	— 100	$1.75
	— 200	2.00
	— 500	3.00
	—1000	4.00
Each extra 1000		3.00
6x12(12th Sht)	— 100	$2.00
	— 200	2.50
	— 500	3.50
	—1000	4.50
Each extra 1000		3.50
9x12 (8th Sht)	— 50	$2.25
	— 100	2.75
	— 200	3.25
	— 500	4.00
	—1000	5.50
Each extra 1000		4.00
Quarter Sheet	— 25	$3.25
	— 50	4.00
	— 100	5.00
	— 200	6.00
Half Sheet	— 25	$4.50
	— 50	5.00
	— 100	6.00
Whole Sheet	— 50	$2.00
	— 100	10.00

For heavy composition and colored paper add to these prices.

Bills Printed Off Advertisements

Sixteenth Sheets

500	$2.00
1000	3.00

Eighth Sheets

500	2.75
1000	4.00

Quarter Sheets

100	4.00
Each additional 100	.75
1000	10.00

Half Sheets

100	4.00
Each additional 100	.85
1000	12.00

Mercantile Posters

(Stores sales not used as advt. in newspaper)

Quarter Sheets

500	$10.00 to $15.00
1000	12.00 to 18.00
Each additional 100	.60

Half Sheets

500	$15.00 to $20.00
1000	20.00 to 25.00
Each additional 100	.85

Great care should be exercised in quoting prices in advance on these bills, as there is much latitude for differences in cost depending on amount of copy, condition in which it is furnished, and layout demanded by the customer.

Butter Wrappers

"Pure Dairy Butter," per 100 sheets	$0.50

With Maker's Name

500	$4.00
1000	6.00

Bold Effort to Control Editorial Policy

Low Tariff Papers Were to Be Penalized

INTEREST has been aroused by a remarkable document prepared by G. M. Murray, at one time general manager of the Canadian Manufacturers' Association. It has been brought to light and published, first in *Marketing*. It is of such vital interest to Canadian publishers that *Printer and Publisher* reproduces the article in full. It was prepared last October and has had a very careful and confidential circulation:

When an unscrupulous scoundrel employs his knowledge of certain facts to enrich himself at the expense of some poor devil to whom the suppression of the truth is a matter of vital moment, we call it blackmail.

When a newspaper lashes a community into a frenzy of indignation over certain abuses which exist mostly in its imagination, and then undertakes to allay the ugly temper of the people by counter propaganda, for which the so-called "big interests" are induced to pay, it is customarily referred to as clever journalism by those who desire to avoid a libel action for calling it what it really is.

In the Spring and Summer of 1918 a certain Canadian daily, which had frequently championed the cause of the Socialists in municipal politics, began featuring to an unusual degree news that in any way reflected unrest or discontent. The fire-eating radical who addressed a small audience of malcontents at some labor meeting was generally honored with a liberal amount of front page space, while counsellors of moderation who addressed large audiences or sober-minded citizens from public platforms were accorded nothing more than inconspicuous paragraphs among the locals.

It pilloried the courts for the harshness of sentences imposed upon men who were preaching sedition. On one occasion it sent a special staff reporter over 100 miles to write up in harrowing style, and with all the local color possible, an illustrated article describing the mournful Christmas of a family whose father had been arrested a few days previously for circulating revolutionary literature. In one way and another it played up the alleged menace of Bolshevism until the ranks of the discontented had become greatly widened and solidified. Then, after carefully sowing the seed in its news columns for a big crop of trouble, it considerately offered to plow the whole thing under provided the banks, manufacturers, wholesalers and others with large businesses at stake, would subscribe a fund of $31,200 ($600 a week for 52 weeks) to enable it to publish every Saturday for one year a series of full-page, illustrated advertisements denouncing Bolshevism.

The proprietor of this particular publication would assume an air of injured innocence if anyone were to venture the remark that his action was dishonorable. In his editorial columns he frequently denounced as a profiteer the business-man who by hard and honorable work achieves success in the conduct of a perfectly legitimate enterprise—yet in order to earn an additional profit for his own business venture, he did not hesitate to persist in an agitation which caused his community to seethe with discontent. He glories in the freedom and independence of the press—yet by his very action he shows that he was willing to sell out the public in order to line his own pockets.

By reason of the large circulation his paper enjoys, it stands high in the favor of advertisers. A score of space-users are known to have expressed their digust at its editorial policy, yet they keep right on advertising in it, apparently content to buy space and circulation as such and oblivious to the fact that in doing so they are merely feeding more ammunition to an enemy that seems intent upon injuring if not actually destroying them.

Towards the end of May last, another Eastern daily ran a series of editorials dealing with the Winnipeg strike. Long after the real motives behind the strike had begun to appear, it consistently supported the "One Big Union," it approved of the sympathetic strike as a legitimate means to enforce compliance with labor demands, it endorsed the principle of collective bargaining in its broadest and most objectionable form, all the while denouncing the tariff as the fundamental cause making for industrial unrest, and insisting upon its elimination as the price to be paid for industrial peace.

If a newspaper persistently giving expression to such views were to lose the advertising patronage extended to it by Canadian manufacturers it would probably occasion no surprise. Certain it is that if all manufacturers were to withdraw from it, it would not long survive. Yet by actual measurement of the advertising space used by Canadian manufacturers in this paper they were giving it on an average of $200 worth of business every day that this campaign of slander and revolution was kept up.

The business end of any newspaper will always try to influence the editorial end, at least to the extent of seeing that the latter does not offend and drive away the customers whom the former spends good money in securing. The phenomenon just referred to must, therefore, find its explanation in the fact that advertisers pay so little attention to editorial opinion that they do not know enough to be offended and driven away — they just naturally stick, no matter how hard the editor pummels them.

Just after the Canadian Manufacturers' Association issued a tariff statement last January, a prominent Western daily came out with the following choice sample of editorial spleen:—

"The people of Canada have listened to many a wailing appeal from the manufacturers of Canada in the years that have elasped since the Conservative Party, away back in the seventies, committed this country to the pernicious policy of high tariff protection. . . . . .

It is questionable, however, if during all these years the manufacturers ever issued such a palpably dishonest, snivelling, disgusting appeal as that handed out this week by the General Manager of the Canadian Manufacturers' Association, by direction of the Executive Council of that body. It is worthy of the despicable, unspeakable Hun who, having plundered, destroyed and mutilated to the limit of his ability, throws up his hands when the hour of retribution comes, and like an arrant coward shrieks 'Kamerad! Kamerad!' The present wailing appeal of the manufacturers indicates how thoroughly frightened they have become on account of the rising tide of national indignation against the present high tariff which is robbing the people and draining the very life-blood of the nation into the pocket books and safety vaults of the big interests magnates."

Considering the fact that some 3,500 manufacturers, including all the large advertisers, are members of the Canadian Manufacturers' Association, and presumably interested in maintaining its prestige and influence, one would be justified in supposing that an attack like the above would cause widespread resentment, and be followed by the wholesale cancellation of advertising contracts. But not so. The enterprising editor who wrote this tirade still dips pen in vitriol, and the easy-going manufacturers, whose advertisements cram his columns, still provide him the wherewithal to keep up his pernicious campaign of poisoning the mind and embittering the heart of the West against the East.

A few months ago all the Canadian manufacturers of a certain article joined together in an advertising campaign to create an increased public demand for their commodity. In one Canadian city they had the choice of two mediums—one, a paper which has always shown itself a fearless champion of the cause of success of Canadian industry, the other a paper which in season and out of season advocated free trade and never neglected an opportunity to denounce manufacturers as a privileged class, who were a burden that all the other people of Canada had to bear. The rates charged by these two papers were exactly the same, yet the syndicate of manufacturers in question deliberately chose the hostile paper in preference to the friendly paper, for no other rather than that the former claimed a circulation 5,000 in excess of the latter.

Had they considered the matter a little more carefully, they would have recognized that their decision was tantamount to saying to the hostile paper: "Abuse us all you like, be as unfair to us as you like; we will continue to buy your space just so long as you have the larger circulation." and to the friendly paper: "Do not imagine that we are going to buy your space just because you have a good word to say for us; all we are interested in is circulation, and you cannot talk business to us until you get up into the same class with the other fellow."

Considering the utter lack of discrimination displayed by industrial corporations, banks, insurance companies and other business institutions in the allocation of their advertising patronage, what possible incentive is there to a publication to champion their cause? Surely business men must realize that it is to their advantage to have the press of the country fair to them, and that it is to their disadvantage to have the press unfair. They could have a very much larger section of the press favorable to them if, when placing advertising contracts, they would show a little more consistency, and take more pace in the papers that support their cause, than in those which oppose their cause. It is the future they should look to, rather than the present. They may reap an immediate advantage in the form of increased sales by utilizing the hostile paper with a larger circulation; similarly, they may forego an immediate advantage by deliberately choosing a friendly paper with a smaller circulation. The important point they overlook, however, is that a paper can only build up a circulation by the liberal expenditure of money. Papers are sold on their merit rather than on sentiment, and it is the paper which is carrying the most news, attractively presented, and accompanied by the largest amount of feature and copyright material, that is favored by the public, and it can only give this service in proportion as the revenues from advertising make it possible. According as advertisers buy more generously of space in friendly papers, and more sparingly of space in unfriendly papers, they will enable the former papers quickly to overtake and supplant the latter; but according as they continue to favor the unfriendly paper and force the friendly paper to be content with the crumbs of their patronage, they perpetuate a situation which can only add to their troubles.

The newspaper that is fond of showing editorial bias against the manufacturer is usually prone to display the same bias in its news columns. A woollen manufacturer, when giving evidence a few months ago before the Cost of Living Committee of the House of Commons, submitted figures to show that on the previous year's business he had made profits equal to 72 per cent. of his paid-up or nominal capital. While he made it clear that he was employing in his business a reserve that had been accumulating during thirty years, until his real capital was twice the amount of his paid-up or nominal capital, and while he also stated that for fifteen years he had paid his shareholders no dividends at all, the reporters and head-line writers dressed up this item of news so as to show the manufacturer in the most unfavorable light possible, giving the item still more prominence by putting it on their front page. Had they wished to be fair, they would have reported the profits as 36 per cent. instead of 72 per cent. of the capital actually employed. Had they wished to be fair, they would have added that this abnormal profit was largely made on export business, which brought foreign money into Canada. Had they wished to be fair, they would have congratulated the company on its good fortune in getting out of a very bad hole. But they did not wish to be fair; they wanted to arouse the indignation of the people by making them believe that the high price of woollens was due entirely to the greed of the manufacturer. So far were their reports from reflecting the conditions of this case fairly that the Chairman of the Committee felt called upon to issue a statement in correction. The papers could not very well refuse to reproduce the Chairman's statement, but they did not give it anything like the same prominence that they gave the incorrect report, and so far as subsequent editorials were concerned, they were nearly all based upon the details as first supplied, showing very clearly animus which even the Chairman's announcement could not remove.

A newspaper actuated by a desire to see that the public is given correct information about the broad, general conditions in any line of business can do a real service to the country at large; a newspaper that has no higher ideal than to be a scandalmonger, featuring all that is bad or questionable, and manipulating partial truths in such a way that wrong conclusions will be drawn, is hampering legitimate business and retarding the growth of the country.

True, the latter policy may enable it to sell more papers; true also, that the more papers it sells the more it is able to charge for its advertising space. But it does not necessarily follow that just because it has a big circulation its space is always going to be in demand. Advertisers are only human. Like the buyers of any other commodity, they expect to receive value for their money. Newspaper space is to them like so much seed which they sow in the expectation of reaping a harvest. If they ever get the idea that the seed they are buying from a certain newspaper will not germinate because of the editorial poison with which it has been sprinkled, they will naturally stop buying from that particular newspaper.

If the unfair type of newspaper has thus far prospered in Canada, it has not been because of its own astuteness, but rather because of the forbearance of its advertising patrons. The wonder is that the constant goading of successful business men, indulged in by a large section of the press of Canada, has not long since driven them into some sort of co-operative movement, having for its object the influencing of more business to those publishers who play fair, and the withdrawal of business from those other publishers who deliberately and persistently play unfair.

For why should not advertisers have recourse to this means of self-protection? Co-operation is one of the characteristics of the age in which we live. If workmen feel that an employer is unfair, they resort to team play in order to force him to discontinue his unfairness. If advertisers believe that a newspaper is unfair, it should be equally legitimate for them to resort to team play in order to force a change of editorial policy.

The publishing of a newspaper is fundamentally a business proposition. It is a venture undertaken for the purpose of

making money. Its salaried editor may hold pronounced views on certain subjects, but its shareholders will permit him to ventilate those views only so long as it is apparent that he is not. imperilling the paper's financial success by so doing. What the shareholders are most concerned about is maintaining a comfortable excess of income over outgo. The income from circulation is a negligible quantity, for it is all eaten up in the cost of paper, composition and printing. It is the income from advertising that counts, and no shrinkage ever takes place in that item without a searching investigation as to the cause. Should the shareholders find that the shrinkage is due to an editorial policy which the paper's advertising customers resent they will order a change of editorial policy. If their orders are not carried out, they will secure a new editor. Dividends must be protected, but more important than dividends, invested capital must be protected, and in the publishing game, as those who have tried it very well know, capital has a tendency to disappear with remarkable rapidity unless the paper makes a hit among advertisers.

It is probably well within the mark to say that the manufacturers, banks, insurance companies, wholesalers and brokers of Canada spend $9,000,000 a year for newspaper publicity. If it were possible to shepherd this expenditure in some way, if it were even possible to secure from the advertisers recognition of and adherence to the principle of rewarding fairness and discouraging unfairness, the grounds which business men now have for complaint against the press would largely disappear and other troubles associated therewith would be relieved in proportion.

Apart from the benefits of this kind, which would, of course, be the main consideration, there is no good reason why the advertiser should not gain financially through giving the movement his support. In the field of Canadian journalism there are many publications that are freely patronized by business firms, not because the latter want to, but because they feel that they have to take space. In many cases, when the manufacturer gives a contract to a trade paper or when the insurance manager gives a contract to a financial journal, he feels that he is being held up. He does not expect to receive value for his money. What induces him to sign up is the fact that his competitor is advertising in the medium under consideration, coupled sometimes with the fear that if he refused, the paper might say something to the disparagement of his business. There are, of course, legitimate trade papers just as there are legitimate financial papers, and legitimate labor papers. But generally speaking, it is a fact that many publications in Canada are parasites pure and simple; they live off the business man without rendering him any adequate service in return. The disappearance of such papers would quickly follow the reaching of an understanding among advertisers that they would restrict their patronage to useful and legitimate mediums.

Some business men would no doubt shudder at the very thought of attempting anything so bold as the project here suggested. They might say that at the first sign of pressure, the press itself would expose the whole movement. They might instinctively shrink from the public indignation that would be aroused at what might be described as a gigantic effort to muzzle the press. They might fear that in some way or other they would be rendering themselves liable to prosecution for conspiracy, or to an action for damages at the hands of such papers as might be made to suffer.

But such fears are really groundless. They are based on the supposition that an elaborate organization would be necessary, operated more or less secretly and by hard and fast rules, with the ever present danger of a Court investigation out of which they might emerge as criminals. Far from that being the case, the whole thing can be put under way easily, quietly, safely and with every prospect of quick results, by the simple expedient of subscribing to a Bureau which, for a stipulated consideration, will furnish reports upon the editorial policy of any or every paper published in Canada, and advise in every case as to the desirability of commencing or discontinuing the use of space, or of increasing or decreasing such space as is already used. The Bureau's relation to the advertiser would be that of a lawyer to his client; the latter would retain it to give specialized information and advice, and would be free to follow or reject the advice received, according as circumstances or his judgment might direct. The head of the Bureau would, of course, need to be a person well known to advertisers, one who understood their problems, and whose advice would be taken as dependable. Under the direction of such a person, the Bureau should be able to show results after one month's work, increasing its usefulness in proportion as advertisers worked themselves free from existing contracts and were at liberty to follow the Bureau's advice. Commencing with the New Year when it could make its full impression on the allotment of advertising appropriations for 1920, the Bureau would attain its maximum usefulness, and exercise an influence which no publication could afford to ignore.

The proposal here outlined for influencing editorial policy has been discussed with a number of advertisers, all of whom are 'of the opinion that it offers an easily workable method of effecting a much-needed reform. From a close study of the detail connected with the undertaking, the writer is absolutely convinced that the plan can be put into execution promptly and effectively, provided those who are most concerned in converting the press of Canada to safe and sane policies will line up behind it and give it their unqualified support. The question is—will they do it?

G. M. MURRAY.

912 C.P.R. Building,
    Toronto, Oct. 1st, 1919.

THE UNDERSIGNED hereby employs G. M. Murray for a term of ....

commencing..and ending...........................

(a) To ascertain by careful and systematic review, and to determine as correctly as he can, the editorial policy of every daily newspaper published in Canada (foreign language papers and papers published in the Yukon territory excepted):

(b) To ascertain by careful and systematic review, and to determine as correctly as he can, the editorial policies of such other Canadian publications as the undersigned may hereafter specify, or as said G. M. Murray may deem it wise in the interest of the undersigned to embrace within the scope of his investigations;

(c) To furnish information on record in his office or obtained within the period covered by this agreement, concerning the editorial policy of any Canadian publication upon which the undersigned makes demand in writing for a report;

(d) To furnish without the formality of a demand in writing, reports upon the editorial policies of such Canadian publications as, in his judgment, it is in the interest of the undersigned to receive;

(e) To advise, with respect to any Canadian publication (except as aforesaid) carrying advertisements for the undersigned, as to the desirability of continuing, increasing, reducing or discontinuing the space used therein;

(f) To advise, with respect to any Canadian publication not patronized by the undersigned for advertising purposes but apparently suitable therefor, as to the desirability of contracting for space therein;

IN CONSIDERATION of the work to be performed and the service to be rendered, the under-signed hereby agrees to pay G. M. Murray the sum of....................dollars ($) at the commencement of the above mentioned term.

It is further expressly agreed by the undersigned,

(1) That all information, whether printed, written or verbal, furnished voluntarily or upon demand by G. M. Murray to the undersigned, shall be held in strict confidence, and shall never be revealed to the owners or officers of any publication reported upon, except in such cases and under such restrictions as may be authorized in writing by the said G. M. Murray.

(2) That, while the said G. M. Murray undertakes to exercise good faith, due diligence and care in the performance of the duties herein specified, he does not guarantee the correctness of the information supplied, and shall not be liable in damages to the undersigned in respect thereof.

(3) That the said G. M. Murray reserves the right to terminate this agreement at any time, by refunding to the undersigned the unearned portion of the above-mentioned consideration.

(4) That upon the expiration of the term set forth herein, this agreement may be renewed for a like term by the undersigned again paying to G. M. Murray the above-mentioned consideration, in which event, even though no new agreement shall have been signed, all the conditions embodied herein shall be deemed as continuing in effect.

(5) That the duplicate of this agreement in the undersigned's possession shall be held in strict confidence, and that without the said G. M. Murray's consent, no third party shall either during the currency of this agreement or at any time thereafter, be shown the agreement or made aware of its existence or informed directly or indirectly concerning any of its contents.

(6) That upon the termination of this agreement the duplicate of it shall forthwith be returned by the undersigned to the said G. M. Murray.

(7) That the reports and other printed matter or written advices referred to herein shall be deemed to have been satisfactorily delivered by the said G. M. Murray when mailed, postage prepaid, under personal and confidential cover to...

....
    (Insert name of individual and such address as will always ensure delivery).

Signed...
    (Must be signed by proprietor or by responsible officer of a corporation.)

Dated at...this............................day of

......................................19....

This is the Murray Agreement which Many Manufacturers Have Signed

Results of Catalogue Competition

One year ago the T. Eaton Co., Limited, announced a competition, open to Canadian artists, for which 13 prizes were offered, with a view to securing a suitable catalogue cover design for fall and winter, 1919-20.

This competition proved so successful in bringing new talent to the fore, and in securing a catalogue cover of unusual excellence and appropriateness, that it was decided to conduct another competition this year, with the object of securing a cover design suitable for the catalogue for fall and winter, 1920-21.

Three subjects were suggested, along which lines a design would be acceptable:

1. A design conveying the idea of Canadian growth and progress—that we are on the eve of the great era of Canadian development; or
2. A design illustrating a typical phase of Canadian outdoor life in fall or winter, or
3. A purely ornamental design of new and arresting character.

The method of the competition was that of inviting each artist to submit not more than two miniature sketches, 5½ x 7 inches upright.

From these were chosen twelve designs, which, in the opinion of the judges, were most mer torious, and the artists were requested to make full-size drawings from them.

For these twelve final competitors prizes were offered as follows:

First prize............................	$500
Second prize..........................	350
Three prizes at.....................	250
Four prizes at.......................	150
Three prizes at.....................	100
Total.............................	$2,500

The competition was held under the auspices of the Society of Graphic Art, with Herbert S. Palmer, A.R.C.A., as secretary. The following gentlemen acted as judges:

Frederick S. Challener, R.C.A.; Albert H. Robson, president Society of Graphic Art, and Henry Sproatt, R.C.A., architect.

The number of entries in the competition was even greater than that of last year. One hundred and twenty-eight miniature sketches were entered by artists in various sections of the country, from Montreal to Winnipeg.

Following are the names of the winning artists:

1st, Arthur Keelor, Toronto; 2nd, Francis H. Johnston, Toronto; 3rd, J. E. Sampson, Toronto; 4th, H. R. Perrigard, Montreal; 5th, Charles Simpson, Montreal; 6th, Frank Carmichael, Toronto; 7th, J. E. H. Macdonald, Toronto; 8th, Stanley F. Turner, Toronto; 9th, Andrew Lapine, Toronto; 10th, Charles F. Comfort, Winnipeg; 11th, James Crockart, Montreal; 12th, Geo. F. Charles, Toronto.

William Shaw, member for Forfar, in the British House, intends to ask the Premier if he will institute an enquiry into the profits of the great newspaper trusts in England. The *Express* declares there is not a daily paper here to-day showing a profit, taking commodities at their present prices.

The price of newsprint on International Paper Company contracts will be five cents per pound for the second quarter of 1920, against 4½ cents per pound for the first quarter, an increase of 11 per cent. Canadian companies will no doubt follow suit.

Cheapest in the World

Charlottetown *Examiner:*—On March 1st the subscription price of the Charlottetown *Daily Examiner* will be increased to two dollars per year. The reason for the advance it would hardly seem necessary to state. The cost of white paper is to-day much more than double what it was four years ago, and every other cost entering into the production of a newspaper has very largely increased. The *Examiner* at two dollars a year will still be a good deal lower in price than any other daily newspaper published in Canada—or the world.

St. Thomas *Times-Journal:*—The result in the present rise in the price of newsprint and the one that will be made next July, will undoubtedly be the suspension of many papers during the coming year. One result will be that those newspapers that desire to live will have to raise their subscription price to $2

at least. In the United States the price of many weeklies is $2 and $3 and some weeklies in Canada have also adopted this rate. Certain it is that under prevailing conditions it will not be possible to survive long at the $1.50 rate, while twice-a-week papers may have to raise their price to $3.

Making Typography an Art
(Continued from page 29)

The first page of twenty-one advertisements set by apprentices in the printing department of the Hamilton Technical and Art School, Wentworth street north, appeared in the three local newspapers yesterday. To-day the same advertisements appeared on page 6, revised and corrected, to correspond with criticism for improvement as set forth by the judges. The advertisements are arranged to-day in order of merit, the first eight being prize-winners. This is the third annual ad. setting contest, and this year's pages show a decided improvement over the two previous years, and reflect great credit upon the instructor, Fred Atkinson. The judges this year are men of recognized authority on the art of printing—A. R. Kennedy, editor of *Printer and Publisher*; O. J. Hutchinson, typographical artist of the MacLean Publishing Company, and H. A. Nicholson, advertising manager of *Printer and Publisher*.

In announcing their decision, the judges wrote: "We wish to congratulate the students upon the excellence of their work. There is not an advertisement among those submitted that does not come closer to the principles underlying effective typography than 50 per cent. of the advertisements appearing in the various media of publicity throughout the country to-day.

"Your school has the right idea. Good and much needed work is being accomplished. It is, in fact, schools that know their business—practical schools such as the Hamilton Technical School—that are going to lift typography to a higher plane.'

The winners are as follows:—

First advertisement, No. 12—A. M. Cunningham; set by Ronald Taylor, employed by Spectator Printing Company.

Second, No. 7—The Right House; set by Joseph Allen, employed by Spectator Printing Company.

Third, No. 1—B. Harris: set by Cecil Pond, employed by Barnard Stamp and Stencil Company.

Fourth, No. 18—Minnes Bros.; set by Albert Stroud, employed by Spectator Printing Company.

Fifth, No. 19—John Lennox; set by George Thurston, employed by Kidner Press.

Sixth, No. 13—Culley & Breay; set by Frank Clarke, employed by Times Printing Company.

Seventh, No. 17—A. C. Turnbull; set by A. Toll, employed by Spectator Printing Company.

Eighth, No. 3—Fred L. Kickley; set by W. Crocker, employed by Spectator Printing Company.

Ninth, No. 16—Canada Business College; set by George Elford, employed by Times Printing Company.

Tenth, No. 8—Gillies-Guy; set by Vincent Smith, employed by Herald Printing Company.

Eleventh, No. 10—Carl J. Jenning; set by F. Obermeyer, employed by Herald Printing Company.

Twelfth, No. 2—Wentworth Cycle Works; set by Fred Reed, employed by Herald Printing Company.

Thirteenth, No. 15—Oak Hall; set by Roy Crocker, employed by Spectator Printing Company.

Fourteenth, No. 21—Strand Theatre; set by Robert Carroll, employed by Times Printing Company.

Sixteenth, No. 14—Nordheimer's; set by John Marr, employed by Seager's Press.

Seventeenth, No. 5—Lloyd's; set by William Smart, employed by Times Printing Company.

Eighteenth, No. 9—Wing & Son; set by Russell Wray, employed by Herald Printing Company.

Nineteenth, No. 20—Howell Bros; set by Lloyd Shelton, employed by Spectator Printing Company.

Twentieth, No. 6—Royal Tailoring Company; set by C. V. Harris, employed by Herald Printing Company.

Twenty-first, No. 4—Spencer Heating Company; set by J. Kelly, employed by Davis Printing Company.

Compare to-day's paper with the one published yesterday and you will readily see the improvements made in each advertisement.

THE PERSONAL SIDE OF IT

 We'd Like To Get Items For
These Columns

Quebec

Alfred Michaud, a well-known Quebec newspaperman, died at the Civic Hospital at Quebec from pneumonia, which had developed from influenza. Mr. Michaud was telegraph editor at *Le Soleil*.

Another new publication is the *Union Worker*, published by the Trades and Labor Congress, with A. D. Colwell managing editor. It is devoted to the cause of labor and unionism in these parts.

The Quebec Telegraph Printing Company is at present making big changes in its office accommodation, spending about $25,000 in the way of improvements and new cut-cost equipment. An efficiency man is remodelling the plant.

There has recently been formed in Montreal an association known as the "Montreal Association of Printing House Executives," the object of which is to promote good-fellowship and the study of improved methods of manufacture and the general betterment of the printing and allied trades.

Maritimes

S. D. Granville, accountant of the *Standard*, has purchased the St. Croix *Courier*, published in St. Stephen, N.B., and will remove their plant about May to take up its management.

Francis I. McCafferty, city editor of the St. John *Times*, was recently bereaved by the loss of his father, and Bruce S. Robb, city editor of the St. John *Telegraph*, by the death of his brother.

The St. John Standard Publishing Co. held their annual meeting this week. After the meeting H. V. McKinnon, managing editor, said that he had purchased the paper. The directors say it has not changed hands. No announcement has been as yet made in its columns of a change in ownership.

A glimpse into the methods of the dark ages was had by workers on one of the St. John morning newspapers a short while ago. The electric-lighting power in the city went temporarily out of commission and the paper was produced under candle light, though with much difficulty.

The St. John *Standard* recently conducted a successful contest for amateur photographers, offering a prize of $25 for the best photographs of ice scenes taken during a big storm which visited the city and lower parts of New Brunswick. W. H. Golding and Rev. D. H. Loweth acted as judges and there were many entries.

Congratulations have been extended to John N. Golding of St. John upon his 80th birthday, a few days ago. He is a veteran in the publishing business in St. John, having spent sixty years in it, fifty of which were with J. and A. McMillan. Mr. Golding is the father of W. H. Golding, a former well-known newspaper man in St. John.

A loving cup was recently presented to Senator Wm. Dennis of the Halifax *Herald* by the members of its various staffs in honor of the forty-fifth anniversary of his association with the paper. He has been with it from the time of its first issue. John Trider, the only other member of the staff who was with Senator Dennis at that time, and who was then a press boy, made the presentation and read an address accompanying it. Mrs. Dennis was presented with a handsome bouquet.

British Columbia

K. L. Rauk, accompanied by his wife and two little girls, left Prince Rupert on the Princess Beatrice for Vancouver. He is going to obtain medical treatment for the eldest girl and may go East. He will resume the printing business in the city on his return in a month or so.

Fire destroyed a portion of the building in which the Creston *Review* at Creston is located. The entire business office portion of the building, which is located near the C.P.R. depot, was burned away from the mechanical department. Fortunately for Editor Hayes, the mechanical end of the business was not seriously damaged.

Prince Rupert *News*:—E. E. Chandler Robertson, arrived in the city and left for Terrace. He has just purchased the printing plant at Terrace which was formerly used by the Terrace *News-Letter* and will publish a weekly paper in the fruit town, to be known as the Terrace *News*. Mr. Chandler

is a practical printer, a young man with plenty of enthusiasm. He believes that Terrace will become an important town and he will do his bit to help bring it to the fore. He says that there are a large number of new settlers coming into the Terrace district this year and he looks for great improvements there. Mrs. Chandler accompanies him to the new location.

Alberta

Macleod is to have another weekly newspaper, to make its initial bow to the public shortly. The company responsible for the new publication have already issued their prospectus.

The Jas. W. Young Printing Co., Calgary, has undergone some reorganization in the fact that Mr. Young has sold his interests in the business to his partner, J. Dichmont, who will continue the business under the old name.

M. J. Hutchinson, formerly a widely-known Ontario newspaperman of Toronto and Peterborough, and also for several years advertising manager of the Regina *Leader*, and who has for the past four years been business manager of the Edmonton. *Bulletin*, has resigned his position and will be at the head of an organization that is being formed for the purpose of establishing a chain of confectionery stores in Edmonton and district.

Saskatchewan

The Milestone *Mail*, on the first of March, raised its price from $1.50 to $2.00 per year.

In a fire at Star City (Sask.) Thursday afternoon the Star City *Echo* office, the barber shop and the confectionery store were destroyed. The fire was caused by a gasoline explosion in the barber shop. All buildings were insured.

Word was received in Regina of the death in Macleod, Alta., of Hubert Galbraith, a member of the R.C.M.P., and brother of F. D. Galbraith of the *Daily Post* advertising department. He was ill only a few days. On learning of his illness Mr. Galbraith, accompanied by his wife and mother, left Regina for Macleod. Death was due to influenza.

Manitoba

W. H. Glendenning, former publisher of the *Times*, Morden, Man., has purchased the Parry Sound, Ont., *Canadian*.

R. L. Brindley, formerly city hall reporter for the Winnipeg *Free Press*, has accepted a position with the Canadian Press, Ltd., and will soon come to Ottawa.

R. Thornton, who has been associated with the *Western Canadian*, Manitou, Man., for several years, has purchased the newspaper and plant from W. J. Rowe.

W. A. Tutte, until recently day telegraph editor on the Winnipeg *Free Press*, has returned to his old position as Legislature reporter for the Winnipeg *Tribune*.

M. C. Lane, formerly of the Houston, Texas, *Chronicle*, has accepted a position as day telegraph editor on the Winnipeg *Free Press*. He came to Winnipeg from overseas, where he had served with the Canadian Expeditionary force.

Mrs. Stead, wife of Hay Stead, editorial writer of the Winnipeg *Telegram* staff, died recently. She was a gifted woman and had done some valuable newspaper work, although latterly she had been in poor health. Mrs. Stead had a large number of friends in Winnipeg's newspaper fraternity.

Manitoba sheep-breeders paid a tribute to Miss Cora E. Hind, commercial editor of the Manitoba *Free Press*, when George Gordon, Oak Lake, Man., Manitoba director of the Canadian Co-operative Wool Growers' Association, on behalf of the breeders, presented her with twenty-six ewes.

Saskatoon *Phoenix*:—The newspaper world of Western Canada lost one of its most popular figures, when Thomas Bowers MacDermott, a well-known news writer of Winnipeg died in King Edward hospital, following a length illness from tuberculosis. "Mac," as he was affectionately known to his fellow-newspapermen, was born in Dublin, Ireland, 22 years ago, and came to Winnipeg in 1913. Prior to that he gained considerable fame as a police reporter in St. Paul and Minneapolis. He served on all three Winnipeg dailies, and for two seasons prior to his death was press agent for the Pantages and Winnipeg theatres. Saskatoon knew MacDermott in 1915 when he acted as telegraph editor and dramatic critic for the *Phoenix*. He returned to Winnipeg in 1916.

Ontario

Mr. McKinnon, of the staff of the Beeton *World*, died from influenza.

The Kincardine *Review* was tied up through an outbreak of the "flu," and no paper was issued for a week.

Mr. Arthur Blackburn, acting general manager of the London *Free Press*, has been seriously ill for a few weeks but is recovering.

Allan Baxter, for some years city editor of the *Border Cities Star*, has resigned to accept a position with an advertising firm in Detroit.

Charles Thompson, formerly of the Hamilton *Times* business office, has been appointed provincial auditor of the Workmen's Compensation Board of Manitoba.

Mr. Moss Winters, formerly of the Windsor *Record*, has been appointed inspector for the Children's Aid Society in the Windsor district. He has been overseas for some time.

The Department of History at Toronto University is to issue a quarterly, entitled *The Canadian Historical Review*, in place of the former historical magazine published annually.

Zed Lafontaine, editor and proprietor of the Tweed *Advocate*, died at an early hour on March 3, from pneumonia. He had been ill only a couple of days. He is survived by a wife and family.

J. L. MacNichol, who was assistant paper controller under R. A. Pringle, K.C., has been retired from the position. Mr. MacNichol's operations were chiefly confined to Fort Frances, Ont., mills.

Mr. Joseph Collins has rejoined the staff of the Guelph *Mercury*. He was for some time in the post-office department, also serving overseas. Before this he was on the reportorial staff of the *Mercury*.

Harold Tanton, of the Canadian Press telegraphers' staff at London, is back at work after 10 days' illness of influenza. His place was taken during that time by Charles Case, who worked night and day for the whole time. ·

J. R. Bone, managing editor of the Toronto *Daily Star*, has been chosen as a director of the University of Toronto Alumni Association in succession to the late Lieut.-Col. John H. Moss, B.A., K.C., who died on February 9.

Maxwell B. Cody, telegraph editor of the London *Morning Free Press* has gone to Ottawa to represent the London *Free Press* during the session of Parliament. The *Free Press* will also send a staff man to the Legislature this year.

The death is announced of H. C. Jones, for 23 years editor of the *Eastern Ontario Review*, Vankleek Hill. He was previously connected with the Ottawa *Journal*, and Ottawa *Citizen*. The funeral took place on March 4th at Vankleek Hill.

Ed. F. Weekes has left the St. Marys *Journal* to go to Toronto to take the foremanship of the mechanical department of R. G. McLean Limited, Toronto. In Nov. 1913, he left the Acton Publishing Co. of Toronto, to take the foremanship of the St. Marys *Journal*.

Bradford *Witness*:—The Creemore *Star* lost three editors by death in a very short time. Mr. Carlton died a few weeks ago. He was succeeded in the editorial chair by Mr. J. E. Cave, of Beaverton, who died three weeks after assuming his duties, Mr. A. H. Watson, a former owner, died a couple of years ago.

Application for probate of the will of the late Walter James Bell, former wholesale paper merchant, who died in Toronto on February 9, was made to the Surrogate Court. The estate is valued at $74,719 and, after a bequest of $20,000 has been made to the daughter, the remainder of the estate is left to his widow.

Tom Walsh, lately assistant manager of the advertising department of the London *Advertiser*, resigned recently' to start into the advertising agency game for himself in Windsor. He went to the Border City but was unable to get an office for immediate use, so necessarily postponed his venture there for a few weeks.

T. Howard Jarrett of Trenton, succeeds Mr. Ed. F. Weekes as foreman of the mechanical department of the St. Marys *Journal*. Mr. Jarrett is a son of Mr. Thos. Jarrett, recently one of the publishers of the Trenton *Advocate*. He resigns the position of foreman of the Port Hope *Times* to take his present position with the *Journal*.

L. J. Salton, who has been secretary of the Stratford Chamber of Commerce since its inception last summer, has resigned his position, and will be succeeded by E. W. Tobin, of the editorial staff of the *Beacon*. The change takes effect from March 1.

Mr. Tobin is well known in Western Ontario newspaper circles, and has been with the *Beacon* for a number of years.

Photo Engravers, Limited, have bought from Messrs. William Leibel and Abe M. Schiffer, Nos. 249 and 251 Spadina avenue, Toronto, two houses on the south-east corner of Spadina and Grange avenues, and expect to erect a five-storey factory on the site in the near future. The work of tearing down the houses has begun. There is a frontage of 40 feet on Spadina avenue and 140 on Grange avenue.

Charles Parsons has rejoined the staff of the London *Advertiser* as news and city editor. Mr. Parsons left the *Advertiser* about a year and a half ago to join the editorial staff of the MacLean Publishing Company, his work being mostly on *Hardware and Metal* and the trade papers of the company in general. Mr. Parsons began his newspaper work on the London *Free Press*, going from there to the *Advertiser*.

The death occurred at his home, 164 Duchess street, Toronto, after two weeks' illness of influenza and pneumonia, of James E. Gordon. Deceased was foreman of the Toronto *World* mailing room and had been employed by that journal for 25 years. He was formerly in the employ of the old *Empire*. The late Mr. Gordon was a member of the Orange and Masonic Orders and was widely known and respected. He is survived by his wife and one son.

After a week's illness William Stothers, 239 Emerson avenue, Toronto, died from bronchial-pneumonia. He was born in Grand Valley, but had resided in Toronto the greater part of his life. In his younger days he was a well-known lacrosse player and athlete and was a member of the Orangeville lacrosse team for many years. He was a printer with the *Mail* and *Empire* for twelve years and with the *World* for six years. He was in his 47th year and is survived by his wife and four children.

R. A. Lawrie, of the *Gazette* and *Chronicle* staff, Whitby, received notice that he had been awarded the Military Medal for service during the war. This is the first official announcement that he has received on the subject, and the information was something of a surprise to him. His name had appeared in the London papers some time ago, but not having had any further word, he had concluded that it referred to some other man with the same name. The medal is only now being forwarded to him.

Simcoe *Reformer*:—Arrangements have been completed between the *Reformer* and Messrs. Hickling Bros., publishers of the Delhi *Reporter*, by which the *Reporter* will in future be incorporated with the *Reformer*. Beginning next week subscribers to the *Reporter* will be supplied with the *Reformer*. It is proposed to carry on the *Reporter* as a department of the *Reformer*. The Messrs. Hickling will continue in business as merchants and job printers. They will act as representatives in Delhi for the *Reformer*.

A fire broke out at Wallace's printing office, Cork street, Guelph, the origin of the fire being unknown. The flames spread rapidly through the printing room, where a large quantity of paper was stored, and on the arrival of the fire department the room was in flames. Chief Smith immediately put into use the 30-gallon chemical tank, which is carried on his car, and soon extinguished the blaze, making it unnecessary to have to use the water lines. The machinery in the building was not damaged, and the loss was light.

Wade Toole has left the O.A.C. at Guelph to become managing editor of the *Farmers' Advocate* at Winnipeg. He was a graduate of the O.A.C. in 1911. For seven years he was on the staff of the *Farmers' Advocate* at London, Ont. He went to the O.A.C. staff about two years ago, but has, through contributed articles, kept up a close touch with the farm press. Another change also takes place on the O.A.C. staff, Jack Neil, who has been assistant to Prof. Leitch, joining the staff of the *Farmers' Magazine*, with the MacLean Publishing Co., Toronto.

Albert E. Smythe has resigned from the Toronto *World* to do editorial work for the Canada Newspaper Service, an organization which will handle syndicate matter and aim to release Canadian newspapers and publications from their present dependence on similar material supplied from the United States. Mr. Smythe has been connected with the *World* since 1903, except for a brief period on the *Globe*, and for ten years he has been the *World's* chief editorial writer. He is a journalist of wide information and scholarly attainments and is an admirable writer.

Chatham *Planet*:—Miss Edna Howie, who for a number of years has been the social editor of the *Planet*, left for Windsor where she will assume the duties of social editor of the *Border Cities' Star*. Miss Howie has made rapid progress since her entry into the field of journalism and she has a large number of Chatham friends who will be interested to learn of the change she has made in her field of work and who will join in wishing her every success in the future. The *Planet* has secured the services of Miss Marion Estlin of this city, who will take over the duties of social editor of this paper.

February *Labor Gazette*:—A strike of job printers and pressmen in nearly all the shops in Hamilton occurred during the month. The strike commenced on January 2, when the employees' demands for an increase of from $28 to $35 and subsequently $37 per week was refused. However, work was resumed three days later on a basis of $33 per week pending further negotiations. The negotiations did not prevent a second strike, which resulted on January 27 and terminated on January 29. It was settled by compromise, the printers resuming work at $34 per week with a further increase effective at the end of a year.

The annual meeting of the parliamentary Press Gallery was held at Ottawa for the election of officers, when the following were returned: President, Ernest Bilodeau, *Le Devoir* (acclamation); vice-president, H. E. M. Chisholm, Manitoba *Free Press* and Toronto *Star* (acclamation); secretary, M. Grattan O'Leary, Ottawa *Journal*; executive: Thos. Blacklock, Montreal *Gazette*; W. Gauthier, *Le Droit*, Ottawa; M. J. Shea, Canadian Press, Ltd., Ottawa; W. Marchington, Toronto *Star*; W. Wallis, *Mail and Empire*, Toronto. Votes of thanks were extended to Messrs. Wallis and Chisholm, retiring president and secretary, and the other retiring officials. Several new members were welcomed by the meeting.

Orillia Packet:—A story from Creemore this week is pathetic. The editor and proprietor of the local paper there succumbed to an attack of grip. His widow applied to Toronto for a man to carry on the business until permanent arrangements could be made. As the only one in the Soldiers' Re-Establishment School for linotype operators experienced in all departments of the business, Mr. Cave, a returned soldier, volunteered to go. Soon he, too, was taken down, and died of pneumonia. The young man was the eldest son of Mr. J. J. Cave, editor of the Beaverton *Express*. The soldier spirit burned brightly to the end, and shortly before his death, he said to his father: "Tell mother I put up a good scrap."

John Law, secretary-treasurer of the Tillsonburg *News*, formerly proprietor of the Tillsonburg *Observer* until January of this year, when the *Observer* united with the Tillsonburg *Liberal* into one paper, died at his residence on Broadway, in his fifty-seventh year, of a severe illness of three weeks' duration. He was one of the best-known newspapermen in Western Ontario, a man of high moral standing amongst his business associates, and one of Tillsonburg's most congenial citizens, always interested in anything pertaining to the good of the town and the public in general. He had been in the newspaper business during his entire life, and was a member of the Canadian Press Association. He leaves a wife.

After nearly 40 years of service in the *Globe*, Mr. D. W. Waddell has been forced by ill-health to abandon his work as cashier, for a protracted rest. The members of the staff joined in bidding him *au revoir* and wishing him a speedy return to his former state of health. To their good wishes they added a cheque, which represented contributions from every department in the institution. An impromptu reception was held in the business office, whereat many of the representative members of the staff expressed the high esteem in which Mr. Waddell had always been held during his long term of office. Mr. Waddell joined the staff of The Globe Printing Company in October 1881, as a clerk, and assumed the duties of cashier in 1904.

Walkerton Herald:—The Hespeler *Herald*, owned and conducted by Mr. George E. Hudson, was totally destroyed by fire, entailing a loss of $10,000. The fire originated from an electric motor in the basement of the building and was beyond control when discovered. Mr. Hudson had only been in Hespeler about a year, he moving there from Cayuga, where he formerly conducted a paper. Mr. Ed. Bauman, grandson of Mr. and Mrs. James Brislan of town, was foreman in the Hespeler office. George, who is publishing his paper *pro tem* from the office of his brother, Ed., in Beamsville, has already taken steps to reopen a new printing plant in Hespeler, which on account of the increased cost of machinery and material will be an expensive undertaking.

The death took place in London, under distressing circumstances, of John Stronach, news and city editor of the London *Advertiser*. Within 48 hours both he and his wife passed away, victims of influenza, folllowed by pneumonia. The late Mr. Stronach was a graduate of Edinburgh University, and coming to this country, did his first newspaper work for the Woodstock *Sentinel-Review* at Ingersoll. His work was a success from the start and it was not long before he was taken on as city editor of the paper. Leaving there some six years ago he joined the staff of the London *Advertiser*, and has worked in various capacities there, at the time of his death being city and news editor of the paper. He had also done considerable editorial writing for the paper. The funeral of the deceased and his wife was attended by all the newspaper men of the city of London.

The death occurred at Guelph, of Ranald Macdonald, a well-known newspaperman, following an illness of about three weeks. He came to Guelph from Scotland a few years ago and was a student at the O.A.C., later going into newspaper work on the staff of the *Mercury*. He enlisted in 1914, and served all through the war with the 18th battalion, being once wounded. He returned about a year ago and conducted a news bureau until he was taken ill. He was a son of Angus Macdonald, of Edinburgh, Scotland, and was born in that city nearly thirty-nine years ago. His brother, George A. Macdonald, resides in Peterboro. Ranald Macdonald, or "Big Mac" as he was better known, had writing ability in no small degree. While on the staff of the *Mercury* he covered most of the Winter Fair one year, and on that assignment turned in copy that was about the finest and most readable ever extracted from that annual event.

The Charters Publishing Co. of Brampton celebrated its 47th birthday by a banquet. This company publishes the Brampton *Conservator*, the Weston *Times and Guide*, the Port Credit *News*, the Mimico *Advertiser* and Mt. Dennis *Express*. Mr. Charters, in speaking of old days, recited some amusing facts connected with his experiences as printer's devil on the *Conservator*. The one that appealed most strongly to the hearers, among whom were several pseudo devils, was the fact that in those days the devil began work at 6 a.m., his first duty in the winter being the starting of a fire in the box stove. As the wood used was invariably green, the devil's difficulties were not hard to imagine. Another duty falling to the lot of the devil was the pasting, on blank walls and fences throughout the town, of bills containing various advertising matter. The salary for three months was $10.

The Stratford *Herald*, referring to the appointment of E. W. Tobin, as secretary of the Chamber of Commerce in that city, says:—Mr. Tobin has for several years without a break—in fact since he left school—been on the editorial staff of the *Beacon*, and is very well known in the city. Born in Stratford, he was educated in the Roman Catholic Separate School and the Collegiate Institute, taking up newspaper work as a profession. "Ed." was for several seasons a hockey player of ability, and still takes an active interest in sports of all kinds. He joined the benedicts a couple of years ago. The new secretary has youth, a thorough knowledge of the city and some years of experience in publicity work as valuable assets. It is understood that some other Stratford men, who learned of the vacancy, also went after the position, as well as a number of outsiders, but the committee selected Mr. Tobin, who accepted the secretaryship."

Picton *Gazette*:—A Picton boy who has made a marked success in the newspaper world is Mr. H. N. VanDusen, son of Capt. T. L. and Mrs. VanDusen, of Queen St. Mr. VanDusen began his newspaper career with the *Post-Standard* of Syracuse some twelve years ago with Mr. James A. Walker, also of this county, who was then circulating manager of this journal. Shortly after, he went to Minneapolis, Minn., on one of the Metropolitan newspapers. After some experience here, Mr. VanDusen spent some time at Joplin, Missouri, afterward securing the position of agency manager of the Capper Publications, which included the Topeka *Daily Capital*, and some six or seven farm journals circulating in the Western Middle States. Mr. VanDusen has just accepted a lucrative position with the American Fruit Growers of Chicago, which promises splendid financial advantages, as well as opportunity for advancement.

By working along novel lines, thieves plundered the home of C. H. J. Snider, managing editor of the Toronto *Evening Telegram*, at 499 Keele street. Acting on information obtained from Cleveland and other American cities, warrants were applied for at detective headquarters and evidence submitted by a detective agency. Mr. Snider has been in poor health for time, and is at present in Jamaica. He leased his house furnished to people giving the name of Kirks and Curran. There were four persons in the two families, and they stated that they were Americans from Cleveland. To neighbors they afterward gave other names, the man and woman giving the name of Curran, stating that their name was Curtis. The house was leased some weeks ago, and since that the tenants have evident-

ly moved furnishings away piecemeal. As Mr. Snider is still in Jamaica, and left no inventory, it has been hard for his relatives to find out just how much has been taken.

Kenora *Examiner*:—By a destructive fire the office of the Rainy River *Record* was destroyed, and to resume publication the plant of the *Gazette* was bought. Consolidation in these days of high cost of production could be followed to good advanatage in other towns. In its new issue the *Record* said:— "Out of the ashes of last week's fire, the *Record* emerges stronger and more energetic than ever."

Wallace M. Findlay, for the past five years connected with the advertising department of Willys-Overland, Inc., Toledo, Ohio, has rejoined J. J. Gibbons, Limited, Toronto. Mr. Findlay was a member of the Gibbons organization for three years previous to going to Toledo, for a time at Toronto and later at Montreal. He rejoins the Canadian advertising agency as a member of the executive department at the head office in Toronto. Previous to entering advertising work Mr. Findlay was engaged in newspaper editorial work on leading Canadian dailies, working in Hamilton, Guelph, Brantford and Toronto. Since arriving in Toronto, Mr. Findlay has been receiving the glad-hand from old friends of former newspaper days. If we are not mistaken Findlay and Gordon Rutledge, now business manager of *Financial Post*, were yoked together as reporters on the old Toronto *News* on a novel stunt. They were to invade local option territories together, one to prove that local option was a success, the other to show its failures and follies. It was in this connection that the anti-writer reached out and dusted off that famous Byron phrase, "There was a sound of revelry by night." For some time past Mr. Findlay was in the U. S. Army. He tried first to enlist in Canada, but failed on account of eye-sight.

Quality
and
Service

**Built An
Extensive Business**

Thirty-five years ago W. G. Harris, president of the Canada Metal Co., had an idea — namely, that a service and quality metals, combined with ability and a keen, earnest interest in the patrons' business, would prove successful beyond the average — and he had the courage to found the Canada Metal Company, Limited, on that idea. Certainly his judgment was right. Time and results tell a true story. In a nutshell it is this:

Canada Metal Company products include 90% of the typemetal used in Canadian printing and publishing offices. It is used exclusively by offices big and small for typesetting and stereotyping purposes.

The struggle for supremacy was trying. It required ceaseless pounding away to impress upon some printers that the service policy went beyond the office of the president, down and up into every branch and man of the organization.

The president's work still goes on. Thirty-five years ago Mr. Harris gave personal attention to the requirements of every buyer of a pound of his metal. To this day Mr. Harris gives the same personal service. If a buyer of Canada Metal Company products has a metal problem to solve Mr. Harris aims to go right to the seat of trouble and investigate the problem right on the spot where the trouble occurs. If the distance is too far from the head office in Toronto, there are other expert metallurgists working under Mr. Harris' supervision at the Canada Metal Company plants at Montreal, Winnipeg and Vancouver, as well as thirty representatives on the road.

Ability to look after Printers' wants has made Canada Metal Company Metals - for - Printers supreme—these metals include:

IMPERIAL LINOTYPE
IMPERIAL INTERTYPE
IMPERIAL MONOTYPE
IMPERIAL STEREOTYPE
IMPERIAL ELECTROTYPE

The Canada Metal Company, Limited

Toronto   Montreal
Winnipeg   Vancouver

At it 35 years and still going strong.

W. G. Harris, President

SALE OF MILITARY AND
OTHER GOVERNMENT STORES

Equipment and Supplies for Hospitals, Institutions, Bunkhouses, Camps, Dining-Rooms, Kitchens, etc.

Bedsteads, Furniture, Hardware, Dry Goods, Rubbers, Overshoes and other Footwear, Blankets, Sheets, P.llows, Baskets, Woodenware, Brushes, etc.

CONSTRUCTION EQUIPMENT AND MACHINERY— AMBULANCES.

The Stores are located at various places throughout Canada

Instead of or in addition to sales by sealed tender

PRICE LISTS WILL NOW BE ISSUED

for most articles—the goods being offered in lots for purchase by wholesale houses, jobbers, and the trade generally.

TRADE ONLY SUPPLIED

except that arrangements previously announced for sale to returned soldiers and sailors and widows and dependents of same through the G. W. V. A. and similar organizations and to hospitals and philanthropic institutions will be continued.

SALES WILL CEASE IN MARCH. Any balances left will be cleared by public auction shortly thereafter. This advertisement will not be repeated. Those interested should therefore apply AT ONCE for price lists and other information to the

SECRETARY OF THE WAR PURCHASING COMMISSION, BOOTH BUILDING, OTTAWA

February, 1920

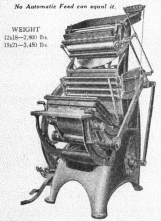
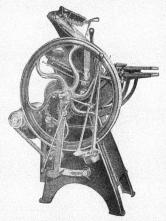

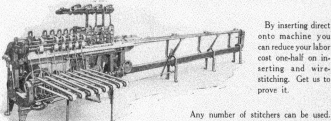

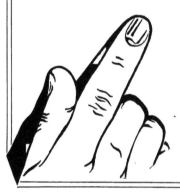

Buyers' Guide

BUYERS' DIRECTORY

ADDRESSING MACHINES
The Challenge Machinery Co., Grand Haven, Mich.
BALERS, WASTE PAPER
Golding Mfg. Co., Franklin, Mass.
Logan, H. J., 114 Adelaide St. West, Toronto.
Stephenson, Blake & Co., 60 Front St. W., Toronto
Stewart, Geo. M., 92 McGill St., Montreal.
BINDERY SUPPLIES
Logan, H. J., Toronto, Ont.
Morrison Co., J. L., Toronto, Ont.
BOOKBINDERS' MACHINERY
Logan, H. J., 114 Adelaide St. W., Toronto.
Miller & Richard, Toronto and Winnipeg.
Morrison, J. L. Co., 445 King St. W., Toronto.
Royal Machine Works, Montreal.
Stewart, Geo. M., 92 McGill St., Montreal, Que.
Stephenson, Blake & Co., 60 Front St. W., Toronto
BOOKBINDERS' WIRE
The Steel Co. of Canada, Hamilton.
CHASES—SECTIONAL STEEL
The Challenge Machinery Co., Grand Haven, Mich.
COLLECTION AGENCIES
Canadian Mercantile Agency, 46 Elgin St., Ottawa.
Publishers' Protective Association, Goodyear Bldg.,
154 Simcoe St., Toronto.
COUNTING MACHINES
Stephenson, Blake & Co., 60 Front St. W., Toronto
CYLINDER PRESSES
The Challenge Machinery Co., Grand Haven, Mich.
CROSS CONTINUOUS FEEDER
Morrison, J. L., Co., 445 King St. W., Toronto.
CUTTING MACHINES—PAPER
Golding Mfg. Co., Franklin, Mass.
Morrison, J. L., Co., 445 King St. W., Toronto.
Stephenson, Blake & Co., 60 Front St. W., Toronto.
The Challenge Machinery Co., Grand Haven, Mich.
ELECTROTYPING AND STEREOTYPING
Rapid Electrotype Co. of Canada, 229 Richmond
St. W., Toronto.
Toronto Electrotype & Stereotype Co., 111
Adelaide St. W., Toronto.
ELECTROTYPE AND STEREOTYPE BASES
The Challenge Machinery Co., Grand Haven, Mich.
EMBOSSING PRESSES
Golding Mfg. Co., Franklin, Mass.
Stephenson. Blake & Co., 60 Front St. W., Toronto
ENVELOPE MANUFACTURERS
Toronto Envelope Co., Toronto.
W. V. Dawson, Ltd., Montreal and Toronto.
ELECTROTYPE METAL
British Smelting & Refining Co., Ltd., Montreal.
Canada Metal Co., Limited, Toronto.
Hoyt Metal Co., Limited, Toronto.
FEATURES FOR NEWSPAPERS
International Syndicate, Baltimore, Md.
GALLEYS AND GALLEY CABINETS
Stephenson, Blake & Co., Toronto.
The Challenge Machinery Co., Grand Haven, Mich.
The Toronto Type Foundry Co., Ltd., Toronto.
GUMMED PAPER MAKERS
Jones, Samuel, & Co., 7 Bridewell Place, London
England, and Waverly Park, New Jersey.
HAND PRINTING PRESSES
Golding Mfg. Co., Franklin, Mass.
INKS
Reliance Ink Co., Winnipeg, Man.
JOB PRINTING PRESSES
Golding Mfg. Co., Franklin, Mass.
JOB PRESS GAUGES
Golding Mfg. Co., Franklin, Mass.
Megill, Ed., 60 Duane St., New York City.
LEADS AND SLUGS
Stephenson, Blake & Co., Toronto.
The Challenge Machinery Co., Grand Haven, Mich.
The Toronto Foundry Co., Ltd., Toronto.
LITHOGRAPHERS
Goes Lithographing Co., Chicago, Ill.
MAILING MACHINES
Chauncey Wongs Sons, Greenfield, Mass.
Rev. Robert Dick Estate, 137 W. Tupper St.,
Buffalo, N.Y.
MAILING GALLEYS
The Challenge Machinery Co., Grand Haven, Mich.
METAL FURNITURE
The Challenge Machinery Co., Grand Haven, Mich.
METAL FOR TYPESETTING MACHINES
British Smelting & Refining Co., Ltd., Montreal.
Canada Metal Co., Fraser Ave., Toronto.
Great Western Smelting & Refining Co., Van-
couver.
Hoyt Metal Co., 356 Eastern Ave., Toronto.

Buyers' Guide

Printer and Publisher Want Ads.

2 cents a Word—10 cents extra for P. & P. box number
Invariably in Advance

BUSINESS CHANCES

NEWSPAPER
FOR SALE

A newspaper is offered for sale in one of the most thriving towns in the Annapolis Valley, Nova Scotia. Only a moderate capital required. The business is in good condition, but the owner has good private reasons for selling. Apply to O. K., c/o Printer and Publisher, Toronto, Ont. (P 5 P)

NEWSPAPER AND JOB PRINTING PRESS office in divisional junction town of 500 population on C. N. Railway; one of the best centres in Southern Saskatchewan for live practical printer; comfortable cottage adjoining; also government telephone agency in same building will be transferred to the purchaser. Satisfactory reasons for selling. Apply to Box 667, Printer and Publisher. (P 4 P)

FOR SALE — NEWSPAPER AND JOB printing plant at a bargain; a well equipped and established business in a thriving industrial Nova Scotia town will be disposed of at a right price; large advertising and job printing income; only newspaper in a large and prosperous community. Apply at once for particulars to Box 666, Printer and Publisher, Toronto, Ont. (ptfp)

FOR SALE

FOR SALE—GORDON PRESS, 7 x 11; GOOD condition. The Owen Sound Advertiser, Owen Sound, Ont. (P tf P)

FOR SALE—ONE MODEL NO. 6 (CANA-DIAN) Linotype in good running order; very suitable for country printer; snap; terms. 105 Sixth Ave., West Calgary, Alberta. (p3p)

FOR SALE

FOR SALE—JOB PRINTING PLANT AT Sarnia for immediate shipment, comprising the following:
Galley Universal, complete with fountain, extra rollers, etc.; size 14 by 22.
Challenge Gordon, used less than one year, with Buckeye fountain, extra rollers; size 10 x 15.
Small-size Gordon, Westman & Baker, with extra rollers.
Diamond paper cutter, power or hand, 32-inch, with extra knife; a fine machine and in the best of condition.
Numbering machines, hand stitcher, round-cornering machine, padding outfit and tools.
Three-horse motor, new, 25-cycle, with shafting, pulleys, belts to all machines, ready for use.
Stands and stones, racks and cases, dust-proof cabinets, best of type, script, texts and gothics, also display and body type, enough for every purpose, brass rule, slugs, leads and borders, ink, ink knives and everything needed to get out first-class work.
The plant is being sold to make room for newspaper work. Write at once, making offer on plant complete or in part, giving references. Canadian-Observer, SARNIA, Ontario. (P 3 P)

POTTER NEWSPAPER PRESS, 7-COLUMN, two-revolution; Mentges folder, cutter, stitcher, all kinds cases, tools and types. Price and terms right. Thomas H. Cook & Co., Sarnia, Ont. (P 3 P)

MONOTYPE EQUIPMENT, CONSISTING of two casters and three keyboards, all in first-class condition and ready for immediate use. For full particulars apply to E. R. Whitrod, Montreal Star, Montreal, Que. (P 5 P)

LINOTYPE METAL POT, IN A1 CONDI-tion, replaced by electric pot. Also No. 2 and No. 3 W. & G. job presses, and a quantity of wood type. Apply to Advertiser-Topic, Petrolia, Ont. (p5p)

FOR SALE—36-INCH UNDERCUT PAPER cutter; ideal press for four pages, six-column folio; cylinder press, hand and power fixtures, takes two pages six-column folio; Gordon press, 10x15; all cheap for cash, or will sell on time to good party. Apply Record, Rainy River, Ont. (P 3 P)

COLLECTIONS

SEND US YOUR LIST OF DELINQUENTS. We will turn Debit into Credit. Publishers' Protective Association, Toronto.

FOR SALE

1—10 x 15 Westman & Baker Press, power and foot fixtures complete.

1—8 x 12 C. & P., power and foot fixtures complete.

1—30-in. hand lever Oswego Cutter, 2 knives.

1 Hand and Foot Stitcher complete.

1—13 x 19 Colt Armory Press complete.

Above machines 100% first-class.

ROYAL MACHINE STOCKS

Presses and Bookbinding Machinery and Special Machinery.

738 ST. PAUL WEST, MONTREAL

EQUIPMENT WANTED

WANTED—PAIR SECOND-HAND SIX-column twin chases. The Tweed News, Ltd., Tweed, Ont. (P 3 P)

LINOTYPE WANTED FOR CASH — FULL particulars to Record, Rainy River, Ont. (P 3 P)

SITUATION WANTED

PRINTER — RETURNED SOLDIER, 5 years' experience in country newspaper and job offices wishes situation in office with chance to learn linotype. Apply Box 668, Printer and Publisher. (p3p)

SITUATIONS VACANT

LEARN THE LINOTYPE — WRITE FOR particulars. Canadian Linotype, 68 Temperance St., Toronto.

INDEX TO ADVERTISERS

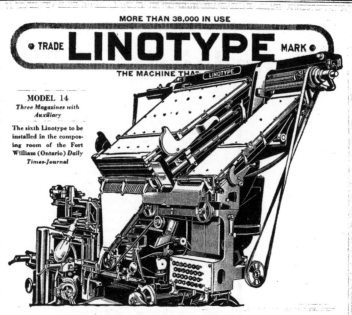

MORE THAN 38,000 IN USE

● TRADE **LINOTYPE** MARK ●

THE MACHINE THAT LINOTYPE

MODEL 14
Three Magazines with Auxiliary

The sixth Linotype to be installed in the composing room of the Fort William (Ontario) *Daily Times-Journal*

A Significant Statement from a Canadian Publisher Who Knows

"This makes the sixth Linotype we have purchased and we have yet to find cause for complaint, either in the machine or business dealings with your Company."

Manager, Fort William (Ont.) Daily Times-Journal

Canadian Linotype Ltd., 68 Temperance St., Toronto
Mergenthaler Linotype Company, *New York, U. S. A.*
San Francisco   Chicago   New Orleans

This Advertisement, Including Border Ornament, is Composed Entirely of Linotype Material

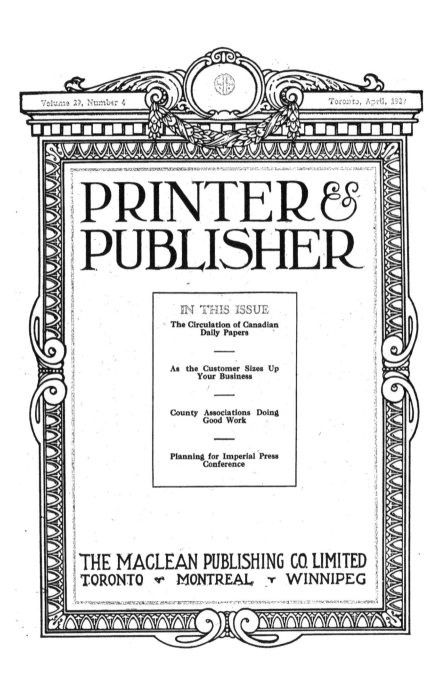

Volume 29, Number 4

Toronto, April, 1920

PRINTER & PUBLISHER

THE MACLEAN PUBLISHING CO. LIMITED
TORONTO ❦ MONTREAL ❦ WINNIPEG

PRINTER AND PUBLISHER, April, 1920. Vol. 29, No. 4. Published monthly at 143-153 University Ave., Toronto, by the MacLean Publishing Co., Ltd. Yearly subscription price, $2.00. Entered as second-class matter at the Post Office Department at Ottawa, Canada, also entered as second-class matter July 1, 1912, at the Post Office at Buffalo, N.Y., U.S.A., under Act of March 3rd, 1879.

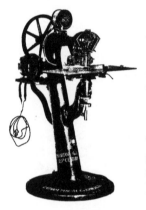
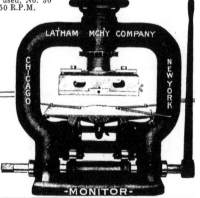

Monotype Composition
for every purpose

 The Monotype is the only composing machine that will handle economically all classes of composition.

 Straight matter and intricate tabular work are equally easy for the Monotype.

 Catalog, booklet, and other special work requiring combinations of type faces offer no difficulty to Monotype users.

 With the new Plate-Gothic Unit more than one-half of the small job work can be composed on the Monotype and cast in justified lines.

 The Monotype Type-and-Rule Caster provides all the type, rules, leads, slugs, and spacing material to make every hand compositor 100 per cent efficient.

 There is a place for the Monotype in every printshop.

Lanston Monotype Machine Company
PHILADELPHIA
NEW YORK, World Building   BOSTON, Wentworth Building
CHICAGO, Plymouth Building   TORONTO, Lumsden Building
Monotype Company of California, SAN FRANCISCO

This Advertisement set in Monotype Series No. 150 and Monotype Rule

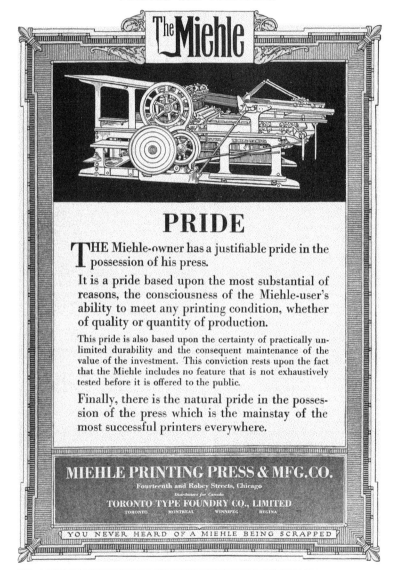

PRIDE

THE Miehle-owner has a justifiable pride in the possession of his press.

It is a pride based upon the most substantial of reasons, the consciousness of the Miehle-user's ability to meet any printing condition, whether of quality or quantity of production.

This pride is also based upon the certainty of practically unlimited durability and the consequent maintenance of the value of the investment. This conviction rests upon the fact that the Miehle includes no feature that is not exhaustively tested before it is offered to the public.

Finally, there is the natural pride in the possession of the press which is the mainstay of the most successful printers everywhere.

MIEHLE PRINTING PRESS & MFG. CO.
Fourteenth and Robey Streets, Chicago

Distributors for Canada

TORONTO TYPE FOUNDRY CO., LIMITED
TORONTO   MONTREAL   WINNIPEG   REGINA

YOU NEVER HEARD OF A MIEHLE BEING SCRAPPED

Ask Your Jobber For

THORNCLIFFE COVER

A lightweight, durable cover at a moderate price
carried in the following colors : Shrimp, Nile Green,
Cadet Blue, Buff, Watteau, Platinum, Lavender.

Made in Canada by

THE DON VALLEY PAPER CO., LTD.

TORONTO, CANADA

BLANK BOOKS

IN ALL

RULINGS AND BINDINGS

Line 25

Line 25

Bound Imitation Red Russia Leather back and
corners, raised bands, heavy black cloth sides,
gilt finishing. One of our best sellers. Have
you placed your order?

Manufactured and Sold by

W. V. Dawson, Limited

MONTREAL AND TORONTO .

BABCOCK

A Cylinder Press is only as efficient as the weakest link in its chain of operating advantages. This handicap frequently offsets the economies possible from the good features of a press.

The head of a printing concern, whose high grade catalog work is known all over the country, was recently asked by a prospective purchaser of a cylinder press:

"What are the Weak Points of the

OPTIMUS"

"I don't know of any weak points in the Optimus," replied the executive. "We have been doing high-grade work on our oldest Optimus for more than twenty years."

In operating economy, that "oldest one" does not begin to compare with the owner's more modern Babcocks. But it is the wearing qualities suggested in the owner's reply, *plus the perfection of Babcock Universal Equipment*, that makes the Optimus what it is today—the most profitably-operated cylinder press in the world.

Our Best Advertisements Are Not Printed—THEY PRINT!

THE BABCOCK PRINTING PRESS MFG. CO.
NEW LONDON, CONN.   NEW YORK OFFICE, 38 PARK ROW
BARNHART BROS. & SPINDLER, *General Western Agents,* Chicago, St. Louis, Dallas,
Kansas City, Omaha, St. Paul, Seattle.
MILLER & RICHARD, *General Agents for Canada*—Toronto, Ontario, and Winnipeg,
Manitoba.
JOHN HADDON & COMPANY, *Agents,* London, E. C.

Image labels: 1 Positive Delivery Fingers; 2 Perfect Automatic Delivery; 3 Universal Roller Control; 4 Accessible for Makeready; 5 Multiple Perforators and Slitters; 6 Rigid Impression; 7 Quickly Handled Rollers; 8 Safety Feed Board

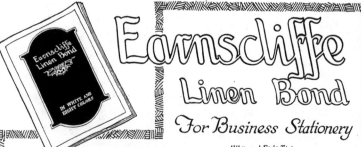

For Business Stationery

White and Eight Tints

The Earnscliffe Linen Bond illustrated above shows specimens of this very fine Canadian-made Paper—with some attractive letterheadings. You should have one. Let us send it.

THE

Made in White and Eight Contrasting Colors.

ROLLAND PAPER COMPANY
LIMITED  MONTREAL

The "R SHIELD" Watermark   guarantees "ROLLAND QUALITY"

A
COMPLETE
STOCK
OF
BOND PAPERS

ALL ORDERS
SHIPPED
DAY RECEIVED

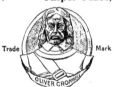

PRINTER AND PUBLISHER
Devoted to the Interests of the Printers and Publishers of Canada

As the Customer Sizes Up Your Business
He Must Always Be Kept in Mind

EDITORIAL men may sit around and plan what is good for their paper. They have their own conceptions and ideas. They have been trained and schooled along certain lines. They may pride themselves that they have news instinct and sense, that they understand the proper editorial conduct of every department—and along these lines they work.

Advertising men in their sphere do the same thing. With the service and art departments they plan to bring their display and classified pages to a certain typographical standard.

And so with the ad compositor or the job compositor. He has served his time and has followed the study of correct display. He is an artist in his own way. He has made it his business to study type and white space and he knows and appreciates what is right and what is wrong.

Now then, with that for a starting place, what happens? The editorial men, the advertising men and the job and ad. men too often leave out of their reckoning a very important personage, viz: the party who is going to buy the finished product, the reader, the advertiser or the purchaser of job printing. Just this week a newspaper man from an Ontario city said: "I know there are mistakes in the make-up of my paper, but it is a fact that there are only certain limits to which we can go to correct them. There are advertisers who want their ads. set a certain way. They have signatures and borders that we know are not correct from a study of good typography. We have a fish merchant who glories in the cut of an old fish at the top of his announcement. He says it

gets him more business than anything else. The same works with quite a bit of the job work. Stores and hotels have a certain style of letterhead they have used for years and they have no desire for a change. So while you are pointing out the right way all the time, just remember occasionally that there are quite a few things that may not appear on the surface to account for much of the work that is done."

As the Space Buyer Reasons

For the purpose of getting a new and very important viewpoint, PRINTER AND PUBLISHER this month discussed the matter with several large space buyers. The idea was to find out how they sized up the various media they intended to use, and if there were two in a field how they would decide which to patronize. For the purpose of this article we are using material secured from Wm. Stewart, advertising manager of the Goodyear Tire & Rubber Co. In a general way this firm uses large and small dailies, magazines and special papers. Some idea of the way in which they buy space may be gathered from the fact that they use double-page spreads in every number of "MacLean's" and other publications are patronized on a similar scale.

"As a general thing," stated Mr. Stewart, "we consider the following points: the general make-up, the A.B.C. audit, the way in which the circulation is secured, the subscription price and the general tone and sanity of the editorial policy. Taking the first thing, the general appearance and make-up. It goes quite a distance in influencing an advertiser. We would not be inclined to consider a paper that was sloppy, with the news not well placed or arranged. We do not like to use a paper that has medicine ads. on the page we use, and we also object to advertisements of a boomster nature, such as mining stocks of doubtful character, for which very large claims are made. We like to deal with publishers who censor their advertising columns as closely as a good editor would censor his news and editorial pages. We take it that publishers who exercise this care over their advertising columns have a rather high conception of their business, and it follows that a discriminating public will place confidence in what they read there. We have had cases where manufacturers in a distant place write here and say they saw our announcement in a certain paper, and because they did they are favorably inclined toward our product. They say so themselves, so I don't know what better proof we can ask.

Reliable Circulation Figures

"When there are two papers serving the same territory, and where we are in doubt, we will give the business to the paper furnishing us with an A.B.C. statement. We are using now only four papers or magazines that do not give us these statements. We take it that the publisher who asks the A.B.C. to come in and audit his circulation lists has nothing to conceal. It is only fair to the buyer of space that he be given some independent statement regarding circulation. We put the A.B.C. figures above the sworn statement of the publisher.

"Then," continued Mr. Stewart, "we consider the quality of the circulation as far as possible, and the way in which it is secured.

I have known papers that put on a contest of some kind or other and gather up a lot of new readers. In a short time they are down here asking for a rate based on the size of their new list. We do not place much weight in the contest form of securing circulation. A good deal of it is secured because some person wants votes for some prize or trip. It is not selling the paper on its merits. Some of this circulation may be retained, and no doubt is, but our point is this: the paper will not retain as much of it as is claimed when the new rate is asked for before the time has come for it to shrink. We prefer papers that get and hold circulation on the merits of the publication, and nothing else.

"Now when I state that we consider the sanity and general tone of the editorial policy of a medium we intend using, do not think that we use or leave papers on account of their political leanings. In no case have we done this. The political color of the editorial page, or its policy, does not influence us as space buyers. But we do like to see a well-conducted editorial page, with the same feeling reflected throughout the paper. We like to see papers stand for a good general tone in the community. We like to see them treating intelligently the big general questions and the matters nearer home. It is well that they should show evidence of study and intimate knowledge of all these things. They all count in helping the buyer of space to size up whether he will or will not use that medium."

HE more people do, the more they can do. He that does nothing renders himself incapable of doing anything. While we are executing one work, we are preparing ourselves to do another.

—HAZLITT

The Circulation of Canadian Daily Papers
Information of Interest to Many People

IN the office of Miss Pennell at the J. J. Gibbons Agency, is a most ingenious blackboard arrangement for posting the latest information in regard to daily papers, trade, and class publications in Canada. The basis is the latest A.B.C. statement, where such can be furnished, and failing that, the publisher's statement. As new figures come in they are changed on the blackboard. There are columns showing the trend of circulation, for this purpose the present and two preceding circulation statements being used.

At a glance one can find out the total circulation of any paper, its local and outside distribution, whether it has an A.B.C. audit, and if the advertising rates have been increased this year.

Through the kindness of Miss Pennell, *Printer and Publisher* is able to give most of the information gathered in regard to the daily papers. The first column shows the name of the city, the next the papers, while the third and fourth columns give the total circulation and the local distribution.

There are papers that no doubt have right now a larger circulation than is shown in these figures, and in this way some A.B.C. papers may appear at a slight disadvantage, in that they do not immediately get the credit from the A.B.C. for their increased circulation.

*—A.B.C. Papers
† Have increased advertising rates this year.

City	Paper	Total Circ'n	Local Circ'n
†Truro............	News............	1,172	1,100
Yarmouth........	Post............	....	....
Charlottetown....	Examiner........	1,500	....
Charlottetown....	*Guardian.......	8,557	987
Charlottetown....	Patriot..........	4,547	1,700
Brandon.........	Sun.............	4,723	....
†Portage la Prairie.	Graphic.........	1,300	....
†Winnipeg........	*Free Press......	73,050	36,525
†Winnipeg........	Telegram........	33,416	18,911
†Winnipeg........	*Tribune........	33,451	20,335
†Moose Jaw......	*News...........	6,181	2,674
†Moose Jaw......	*Times..........	6,474	2,642
Prince Albert.....	Herald..........	4,875	1,600
Regina..........	*Leader.........	20,006	5,872
†Regina..........	*Post...........	12,934	5,380
Saskatoon.......	*Phoenix........	5,860	1,675
†Saskatoon.......	*Star...........	22,975	5,865
Calgary.........	*Albertan.......	14,079	5,143
Calgary.........	*Herald.........	25,833	14,900
Edmonton.......	*Bulletin........	9,574	4,025
Edmonton.......	*Journal........	18,659	12,644
†Lethbridge......	*Herald.........	5,541	2,428
†Medicine Hat....	*News..........	2,677	2,021
Nelson..........	*News..........	5,072	1,025
New Westminster.	Columbian.......	3,200	2,500
Prince Rupert....	Empire..........	1,955	1,224
†Vancouver.......	*Province........	57,271	25,082
Vancouver.......	*Sun............	20,041	11,109
Vancouver.......	*World..........	17,770	6,568
†Victoria.........	*Colonist........	10,178	7,580
†Victoria.........	*Times..........	9,376	7,917
†Toronto.........	*Telegram.......	90,048	86,299
Toronto.........	*World..........	29,684	18,897
Toronto.........	*Globe..........	86,041	21,257
†Toronto.........	*Mail-Empire....	72,100	28,031
†Toronto.........	*Star...........	88,165	53,210
Toronto.........	Hebrew-Journal..	13,223	8,911
Windsor.........	*Star...........	12,379	9,270

City	Paper	Total Circ'n	Local Circ'n
†Woodstock........	*Sentinel-Review...	6,046	....
†Montreal..........	*Gazette..........	31,366	22,981
Montreal..........	*Herald..........	15,010	10,424
†Montreal..........	*Star.............	107,509	71,042
Montreal..........	*Le Canada......	12,747	8,896
Montreal..........	*Le Devoir......	14,662	5,318
Montreal..........	*La Patrie.......	28,081	12,865
Montreal..........	*La Presse.......	123,713	73,069
Montreal..........	Jewish Eagle....	12,571	8,092
†Quebec...........	Chronicle........	15,867	11,319
†Quebec...........	Telegraph........	11,202	7,680
Quebec...........	L'Action Cath....	10,979	3,490
Quebec...........	L'Evenement.....	19,155	9,510
Quebec...........	*Le Soleil.......	41,266	18,112
†Sherbrooke......	*Record..........	9,866	1,929
Sherbrooke......	La Tribune.......	8,660	....
Fredericton.......	Gleaner..........	6,081	....
Fredericton.......	Mail..............	....	....
Moncton..........	Times............	3,620	....
Moncton..........	Transcript.......	4,131	....
†St. John.........	Globe............	7,000	6,500
St. John..........	Standard........	14,087	2,823
†St. John.........	*Telegraph........	14,789	4,370
†St. John.........	*Times...........	14,390	12,832
†Amherst..........	News............	1,904	1,644
Glace Bay........	Gazette..........	5,825	4,511
Halifax...........	*Chronicle........	14,331	3,031
†Halifax..........	*Echo............	10,984	3,402
Halifax...........	*Herald..........	10,996	2,475
†Halifax..........	*Mail............	16,374	11,593
†New Glasgow....	News............	3,386	1,400
Sydney...........	*Post............	6,036	2,570
†Sydney..........	Record..........	4,543	....
†Belleville........	Intelligencer.....	2,652	1,675
Belleville........	Ontario..........	1,975	....
†Brantford........	*Expositor........	9,336	6,574
†Brockville........	Rec. and Times...	4,445	2,225
Chatham.........	News............	2,505	1,536
Chatham.........	Planet...........	2,723	....
†Cobalt...........	Nugget..........	5,693	1,623
Fort William......	Times-Journal....	4,948	4,200
†Galt.............	*Reporter........	4,003	2,750
†Guelph..........	Herald..........	2,900	....
†Guelph..........	*Mercury........	3,625	3,072
†Hamilton........	Herald..........	18,907	13,330
Hamilton........	*Spectator.......	30,347	22,338
Hamilton.........	Times...........	11,300	8,000
Kingston.........	*Whig...........	5,919	3,488
†Kingston.........	Standard........	5,087	3,309
Kitchener........	*News-Record....	3,512	3,252
Kitchener........	Telegraph.......	3,197	2,055
Lindsay..........	*Post............	2,147	1,316
Lindsay..........	Warder..........	2,300	....
London..........	*Advertiser......	41,881	6,352
London..........	*Free Press......	41,204	10,449
†Niagara Falls.....	Review..........	3,203	....
†Ottawa..........	*Citizen..........	28,894	20,242
†Ottawa..........	*Journal..........	23,295	13,551
Ottawa..........	*Le Droit........	8,661	3,970
Peterboro........	*Examiner.......	5,999	4,415
Peterboro........	Review..........	3,270	2,450
Port Arthur.......	News-Chronicle...	4,135	2,950
†Port Hope.......	Guide...........	....	....
St. Catharines....	Journal..........	....	....
†St. Catharines....	Standard.........	7,599	4,756
St. Thomas.......	*Times-Journal...	8,662	3,515
Sarnia...........	Can. Observer...	3,500	2,900
Sault Ste. Marie...	*Star............	4,175	3,508
†Stratford........	Beacon..........	3,136	1,670
†Stratford.........	*Herald..........	3,100	1,734

The County Associations Doing Good Work

Several Meetings Held During the Month

ESSEX and Kent Press Association met at Crawford House, Windsor, on Monday, March 22nd, at 2 p.m. Those present were R. V. McGuire, the *Herald*, Thamesville; E. V. Bingham, the *Dominion*, Ridgetown; J. M. Denholm, *News-Tribune*, Blenheim; B. A. Lane, *Post*, Leamington; R. N. Epplett, the *Journal*, Wheatley; E. E. Lancaster, the *Herald*, Comber; W. E. Hellems, the *Reporter*, Kingsville; C. H. Whitehead, *Reporter*, Kingsville; Mr. Brett, *Free Press*, Essex; Mr. Jno. Auld, *Echo*, Amherstburg; Mr. Marsh, *Echo*, Amherstburg; Mr. Woodward and Mr. Stephenson of Chatham; Mr. Clark of Walkerville, Mr. Seguin, Mr. Kuhlman, Mr. Percy and Mr. Jack of Windsor, Messrs. Young and Graybiel, of the *Border Cities Star*, were also present and presented an invitation to the publishers to be the guests of the *Star* at dinner at 6.30.

Mr. Woodward of Chatham opened the meeting and proceeded with the election of officers, which resulted as follows: President, W. H. Hellems, Kingsville; vice-president, J. N. Denholm, Blenheim; sec.-treas., A. W. Marsh, Amherstburg; executive, B. A. Lane, Leamington; J. E. Young, Windsor; Ross McGuire, Thamesville; A. C. Woodward, Chatham; Messrs. Seguin and Kuhlman, Walkerville.

The president, on assuming his duties, said that the Association would be called together more frequently and for a while at least he would ask the members to come together three or four times in a year.

The manager of the C.W.N.A., Mr. E. Roy Sayles, was present and was asked to present to the meeting the proposed work of the C.W.N.A. and also to open up the discussion on the increased subscription rates and higher rates for job printing and advertising. A very interesting discussion on these subjects was taken part in by all present, and especially regarding job printing prices. Increased costs of job papers and newsprint was also the subject of much comment. A strong committee was appointed to revise the job printing price list on a basis of existing costs, with power to proceed with the printing of the list at the earliest possible moment. A committee on advertising rates, both local and foreign, was also appointed to make recommendations at a further meeting of the Association which will likely be held in May, when the matter of the $2.00 rate will also be finally decided upon. A favorable feeling existed among the publishers present that subscription rates must be increased, although it was felt that a raise from $1.50 to $2.00 on the part of small weeklies would be more serious than the raise from $1.00 to $1.50. It was thought advisable that in the raise to $2.00, semi-weeklies should be asked to raise to $2.50.

President Hellems made an appeal to those present who had not paid their membership fees in the C.W.N.A. to do so at once and to use their influence to bring all publishers into the Association.

At 6.30 the visiting publishers were entertained at dinner by the management of the *Border Cities Star*, at which a pleasant time was enjoyed, J. Ellison Young, managing editor of that paper, acting as chairman.

ST. CLAIR DISTRICT MEETING

ST. CLAIR District Press Association was held at the Vendome Hotel on Friday, March 19th. The meeting was called for at 2 o'clock. Only seven members were present when the meeting was called at 1 p.m. owing to the fact that a snow storm tied up a train upon which other publishers were coming and they did not arrive until 4.30 p.m., when those who arrived early in the day were scheduled to leave for their homes. Mr. H. J. Pettypiece, president of the Association, presided, while Mr. Dunlop of the Forest *Standard* officiated as secretary. The manager of the C.W.N.A. was present and presented to the publishers the work of the C.W.N.A. since the New Year and also took up the matter of increased subscription rates and job and advertising rates. Those present spoke favorably towards the move for $2.00 subscription, but in view of the fact that the storm had hindered the attendance it was decided to call a meeting in May, when final action will likely be taken.

The Association also decided to print a job price list and to send it to each of the members. The president and secretary are to consider the matter of increase in advertising rates, both local and foreign, and to present recommendation at the meeting in May. A resolution of condolence was passed and presented to Mrs. Dawson, who has been bereaved of her husband, late proprietor of the Parkhill *Gazette*. Members present also expressed their appreciation of the visit of Mr. E. Roy Sayles, manager of the C.W.N.A., and tendered their thanks.

OTTAWA VALLEY PRESS ASSOCIATION

THE Ottawa Valley Press Association met at Carleton Place on Friday, April 9, with sessions morning and afternoon. The meetings were held in the office of the Central Canadian, Mr. F. A. J. Davis being the secretary. Mr. D. A. Jones, of the Pembroke *Standard*, president of the Association, had charge of the meeting. The papers represented were the Perth *Expositor*, W. G. Dickson; Arnprior *Watchman*, A. E. Bradwin; Carleton Place *Herald*, W. H. Allen; Pembroke *Observer*, D. A. Jones; Pembroke *Standard*, Thomas Whalley; Renfrew *Mercury*, W. R. Davies; Almonte *Gazette*, James Muir; Renfrew *Journal*, Mr. Samson. Mr. E. R. Sayles, manager of the C.W.N.A., was present at the meetings.

The morning was taken up with a revision of the price lists, corrections being made in many cases. Each section of the list was considered. Mr. Davis gave real service in this matter, having copies ready for the members with all the corrections made, for the afternoon meeting. The manager of the C.W.N.A. took up the serious situation in regard to newsprint. The fact that there would be great advances in the price of newsprint and the demands made by labor warranted an immediate raise of the subscription rates to $2. The members after due consideration unanimously decided to raise the rate from $1.50 to $2, to take effect on the first of June. Members of the Valley Association not present were communicated with by the secretary, and their co-operation was secured in this matter. The advertiser must also carry his share of the increased costs in all departments, and a revision upwards of the advertising rates was decided upon.

On Saturday some of the Valley men not present at Carleton Place were at Renfrew. The membership of the C.W.N.A. was increased by the coming in of several new papers.

WEEKLY ASSOCIATION HAS NEW OFFICE

THE Daily Newspapers Association requiring the offices which were temporarily occupied by the Weekly Association at 901 Excelsior Life Building, the C.W.N.A. had to seek other quarters at once. The rooms at 45 Jarvis St. are being occupied temporarily. Permanent offices have been secured in Manning Chambers, corner Queen and Teraulay Streets, and after May 1 the central office of the weeklies will be 305 Manning Chambers.

No Apology is Needed

Commenting on those weekly papers which apologize for raising the subscription rate to $1.50 or $2.00, the Bowmanville *Statesman* says: "Whoever heard of producers apologizing for asking $6 a barrel for apples they used to sell at $2; 70 cents a pound of butter they sold at 10 cents; $3.06 for wheat for which they were once glad to get a dollar; and $1.50 for a fat chicken that sold for 30 cents; or a merchant asking $75.00 for a suit that sold at $25 and so on? No apology is necessary, Brer Publisher. At the rate paper has been advancing since 1920 began publishers of weekly papers will be compelled to advance their price to $2.00 or $2.50 a year before many moons."

The Boston *American* has raised its advertising rates to 45 cents a line, and is accepting annual contracts at that price. The *American* has made several advances, intended to cut down advertising, in order to get within its tonnage of newsprint.

Price List of York and Simcoe Seems Too Low
But Meeting Will Revise These in Short Time

Letterheads
[Based on stock costing $2.00 per thousand]
250 .... $2.75
500 .... $4.00
1000 .... $6.00
Each extra 1000 .... $4.25
For two colors add $3.50 per 1000.
For more expensive stock add to these prices proportionately.
Padding, 50c per 1000

Billheads
8vo Post — 500..... $3.00
—1000..... $4.50
Extra 1000.. $3.00
Quarter Cap — 500..... $3.25
—1000..... $5.00
Extra 1000.. $3.25
4to Post — 500..... $4.25
—1000..... $6.00
Half Cap — 500..... $5.50
—1000..... $7.25
Padding, 50c per 1000
100 any of above $2.00 to $3.00

Noteheads, Memo Heads, and Statements
[Based on stock costing $1.00 per 1000]
500 .... $3.00
1000 .... $4.50
Each extra 1000...... $3.00
Padding, 50c per 1000

Envelopes
100 .... $1.50
250 .... $1.75
500 .... $3.00
1000 .... $4.50
Extra 1000 .... $3.25
For more expensive stock, add to these prices proportionately.

Business Cards
[Based on stock costing $2.00 per 1000]
50 .... $1.50
100 .... $2.00
250 .... $2.75
500 .... $3.75
1000 .... $5.25
Extra 1000 .... $3.25

Shipping Tags
[Basis No. 5 tag, costing $1.60]
500 .... $2.50
1000 .... $3.75
Extra 1000 .... $2.50
Other sizes in proportion.

Tickets
[On 120-lb. Bristol]
100 .... $1.50
Each additional 100 .35

Government Postcards
100 (printed only) $1.75
Each additional 100 .35

Receipt and Order Books
[Bound in 100s]
          100   500   1000
3½ x 8½ $2.25 $3.50 $5.00
3¼ x 11 .....$2.50 $4.00 $6.00
Extra for heavy composition

Window Cards
[Based on card costing 5c sheet]
11 x 14 — 12........ $2.50
— 25........ $3.00
— 50........ $4.00
—100........ $5.50
Extra color, $2.00 additional
12 x 22 — 25........ $4.00
— 50........ $5.75
—100........ $8.50

Extra color, $3.00 additional
22 x 28 — 12........ $3.50
— 25........ $5.00

Sign Cards
1/6 or ¼ Sheet— 6...... $1.50
, —12...... $1.75
Half Sheet — 6...... $2.00
—12...... $2.50
Full Sheet — 6...... $3.00
—12...... $4.00

Dodgers
1½ x 6 (32nd)— 200.... $1.50
— 500.... $2.25
—1000.... $3.00
Extra 1000 $1.75

WHAT has become of the salesman who used to tear around the country taking orders for printed envelopes at $1 per thousand ?

6 x 9 (16th)— 100.... $1.75
— 200.... $2.50
— 500.... $3.00
—1000.... $4.00
Extra 1000 $2.50
— 250.... $2.50
— 500.... $3.50
—1000.... $4.75
Extra 1000 $9.75

6 x 12 (12th)— 100....$2.00
— 250.... $2.50
— 500.... $3.50
—1000.... $4.75
Extra 1000 $9.75

9 x 12 (8th)— 50.... $2.50
—.100.... $3.00
— 250.... $3.50
— 500.... $4.25
—1000.... $5.75
Extra 1000 $3.50
10 per cent. extra for colored paper.

Posters
[White News Print]
Quar. Sheet — 25........ $3.00
— 50........ $3.50
—100........ $4.50
Each add. 100 $1.50
Half Sheet — 25........ $4.00
— 50........ $4.50
— 75........ $5.00
—100........ $5.50
Each add. 100 $2.00
Whole Sheet — 50........ $7.00
— 75........ $8.25
—100........ $9.50
Each add. 100 $3.50

For heavy composition or for colored paper, add 10 per cent. to these prices.
Color Work—For one color, add 25 per cent.; 2 colors, 50 per cent. extra.

Auction Sale Bills
Quar. Sheets — 50...... $4.00
—100...... $5.00
Half Sheets — 50...... $5.00
—100...... $6.00
Full Sheets — 50...... $9.00
—100......$11.00
Farmers' sale dodgers, $3.00 for composition, 50 cents per 100 for printing.

Mercantile Posters
500 .... $7.00 to $10.00
1000 .... $9.50 to $12.50
HALF SHEETS
500 ....$12.00 to $16.00
1000 ....$16.00 to $20.00
Each additional 100 ....$ 1.00

Note and Letter Circulars
Note 8vo — 100...... $2.50
— 200...... $2.75
— 500...... $3.50
—1000...... $5.00
Extra 1000 $3.50
Letter — 100...... $2.75
— 200...... $3.50
— 500...... $5.00
—1000...... $7.00
With blank flyleaf add 30 per cent. Full note or letter, double above prices.

Funeral Cards
[Based on stock costing $2.00]
12 .... $1.75
25 .... $2.25
50 .... $3.50
An extra charge of 50 cents where memorial verse is used.

Visiting Cards
50 .... $1.00
100 .... $1.50

Wedding Invitations
[Based on stock costing $1.00 per Cabinet]
25 .... $2.50
50 .... $3.50
100 .... $5.50
For more expensive stock, add proportionately.

At Home Cards
Small — 50...... $2.50
—100...... $3.50
Large — 50...... $2.75
—100...... $3.75
Extra 100... $1.00
Two sides, $1.50 to $2.00 extra

Butter Wrappers
500 with maker's name.. $2.75
1000 with maker's name.. $4.50
"Dairy Butter," per 100.. $0.40
"Dairy Butter," per 500.. $1.75

Half Cap Circulars and Forms
100 .... $2.50
250 .... $3.50
500 .... $4.50
1000 .... $6.00

Route Cards
Cards, 14 x 22 — 50.... $6.00
—100.... $8.00
Folders, 7 x 7½ —100.... $4.75
Each add. 100 .75
For extra heavy or tabulated pedigree charge extra.

Ballots
10 names or less—
300 ballots $5.00
Each additional 100 .... $1.25

Private Postcards
[Based on stock costing $2.00 per 1000]
500 .... $3.75
1000 .... $7.00

Prize Lists
Per page, 200 copies...... $1.75
Per page additional for each extra 100........ .20

Financial Statements and Auditors' Reports
Size of page 5½ x 8½; type 24 ems by 40 ems, 100 copies, $2.00 per page. For each additional 100 add 35 cents per page. Cover to count as four pages.

Voters' Lists
On basis of an average of 25 lines to a full page, $2.25 per page for 200 copies. Where average is higher, add to price per page proportionately. For 300 copies, $2.50 per page.

Books, Pamphlets, Constitutions, By-laws, Minutes, etc.
200 copies. 8 point solid, $1.75 per page; 20 cents per page additional for each 100 copies.

Labor
$1.00 per M for hand composition.
75 cents per M for machine composition.
For semi-tabular, add 50 per cent.
For tabular, add 50 per cent.
$2.50 per hour, cylinder press.
$1.50 per hour, platen press.
(Including washup and make-ready.)

Canadian Division of United Typothetae

By J. B COWAN, Vancouver, B. C.

WHEN a number of thinking employing printers living in widely-separated parts of Canada, and doubtless of varying temperaments, arrive at the same conclusion about the same time, one cannot get away from the feeling there is an idea abroad. Any time a real, honest-to-goodness idea in the printing business is without a home and wandering forlornly about, for heaven's sake let us grab it and take it in.

This big idea that has been agitating the minds of the more progressive Canadian employing printers is the idea the time is ripe—rotten ripe, say some—for the formation of a Canadian Employing Printers' Association extending from Halifax to Vancouver, and from the American boundary to the North Pole if need be. An idea is like the organization bug: once it lodges in the minds of certain men it leaves them no peace until something has been accomplished—or attempted, at any rate. There is no other bug quite so active and indestructible as the germ of organization once its takes hold. All progress in any line of endeavor can be traced to this activity. Men possessed by it are the missionaries and pioneers of human achievement.

The idea as it first suggested itself to a few printers on this Western frontier was the formation of a Western Canadian Association; and when that had become a reality, to broaden the scope of influence of that organization, invade the East, and try to develop some bond of common interest and plan some method of co-operation and education. to benefit all Canadian printers. Our problems, whether in East or West, are becoming increasingly the same. There is only one way of meeting these problems—organization!

Last August the Vancouver Printers' Board of Trade, possessed by this idea, communicated with printers in various Western cities outlining some such plan. Replies received were sympathetic and favorable. The matter should have been followed up, but we were in the throes and unsettlement of wage scale negotiations from that time until the end of the year, and the greater issue was left in abeyance while the local affair was being grappled with. These wage scales have been settled after a fashion and the Canadian Association idea is again on the rampage.

Now, why should there be a Canadian Employing Printers' Association? Should it be a Canadian Division of the United Typothetae of America? How can it be accomplished?

We have printers in Vancouver who can build beautiful organization structures and work out large plans without materials of any kind—in the fairy-wand fashion. Presto!—it is done. Just like that! Doubtless other cities are similarly afflicted. Soberer minds know that associations—and particularly printers' associations, and *more* particularly *Canadian* printers' associations—are built in no such airy fashion. Before proceeding with an outline of this idea and any suggestions for its accomplishment, for the benefit of those East of the Rocky Mountains let us give an abbreviated history of organization work among printers in British Columbia.

So far as I can learn—though the East doubtless still thinks "no good thing can come out of Nazareth"—British Columbia at the present time has more co-operation and better organization among its employing printers than any other Canadian province. That statement may be refuted. I hope it can be—for we have yet a long way to go! It started in Vancouver in August as late as 1918: not the first Printers' Board of Trade in that city by any means, and perhaps not the only one existing in B. C. at that date; but the present Vancouver organization, from which the influence and necessary information and enthusiasm have gone out to smaller Boards throughout the province to help weld divergent elements together and create associations. Prejudice dies hard and the printer is skeptical of any scheme designed to help him. The noble few, hard-bitten by the organization bug and driven by necessity, came together most naturally, the right man was secured as secretary, and growth rewarded their efforts. The Vancouver Board was singularly fortunate in having chosen as its secretary a man of excellent judgment, extensive knowledge and practical training. William Brand is competent, thorough and courageous; is stronger on brains than beauty, and greater in wisdom than

words; he is an artist-printer as well as a competent estimator; and being a diplomat, possessing the respect of all who know him, he guided the craft though its early, troublous days. Mr. Brand has accomplished much. Quiet men frequently do. Vancouver Board Printers have used for many months a price list of Mr. Brand's compilation that is the simplest, most accurate, fairest printers' price-list in use to-day. That statement and that list (now undergoing revision on account of recent wage-scale increases) will bear analysis and not be found wanting.

Printers' associations have within the past year or so b en organized, or have been strengthened, in Victoria, New Westminster, Nanaimo, Cumberland, Prince Rupert, Nelson, in the Kootenays and in the Okanagan Valley. Most of these organizations are using the Vancouver price-list. There is much correspondence between these various associations and the Vancouver Board and a friendly spirit has grown up. The Okanagan association comprises the towns of Vernon, Kelowna, Armstrong, Enderby, Summerland and Penticton. It is a live organization, and recently a permanent secretary, who devotes his time to travelling over his field looking after the interests of its members, was appointed.

That is where British Columbia printers are to-day in organization· work. Naturally—being Westerners—they are ambitious and desirous of extending their influence.

Getting back to our test, why is there need for a Canadian printers association? So far as Ontario is concerned the December issue of *Printer and Publisher* answers that query.

Estimates were asked from Eastern printers for printing 200,-000 booklets, conforming to certain specifications, for the Victory Loan campaign last autumn. These estimates, according to the story, ranged all the way from $130.00 to $300.00 for this work. Does that need comment as being cause suf ficient for greater education and the formation of printers-organizations in the East. Judging by the published figures, even the rudiments of estimating had not been grasped by a large number of the firms estimating. Perhaps the work in this instance had been left to bright office boys. All printers in Vancouver are not Board members, yet I do not believe such a variation would be found here. What would probably happen on such a job would be that of ten figures submitted nine would be in the neighborhood of $300.00 and one would be somewhere about $150.00. The guesstimater would not be a Board member—need I explain? There are still freaks of that type extant, though the tribe is rapidly thinning. It is axiomatic one cannot violate economic laws with impunity and long survive.

The economic revolution taking place the world over is creating problems that printers, as others, must face. Before long, in the matter of wages for instance, whether we like it or not, the East is going to have no advantage of the West. A uniform scale will some day be a fact. Why should we not, therefore, line up shoulder to shoulder and face our problems as a unit?

In the minds of Canadian printers, more particularly of Eastern Canadian printers, there seems to be prejudice against the United Typothetae of America. Certainly there is not the co-operation and confidence between us there should be; certainly we in Canada are not taking advantage of what the U. T. A. offers. The United Typothetae, no matter what prejudice there may be, has been the salvation of the printing industry in America—and in Canada no less. It is to-day a forceful, beneficent, wise and effective organization. Many years of missionary work resulted last year in almost one hundred per cent. increase in its membership. If printers had not got together in the years gone by, and if there had been no Typothetae, can you imagine the chaotic condition the printing trades would be in to-day? Just dwell on that a moment. And its work is not yet completed.

Of late years the United Typothetae has more or less neglected the Canadian field. Why that should be I do not know. Perhaps we gave them little encouragement. Yet any time assistance was asked of them, was it not promptly given?

It must be confesse l in some respects the United Typothetae does not meet the Canadian printers' needs as effectively as it does those of the craft in the United States. Its methods of organization, for one thing, do not meet with the approval of the more conservative, less demonstrative Canadian: a difference in temperament perhaps. For another, the U.T.A. emblem used so effectively over there is altogether unsuited to use in Canada. The distance to U.T.A. conventions generally is much too great for an adequate attendance from Canada to make Canadian influence felt in its deliberations. Perhaps also there is the feeling that with the administration offices all confined to American territory and its officers almost entirely from that side of the line, its good works become less effective among the printers and buying public here. As these things can not all be changed to suit us, some other method must of necessity be found.

It seems to me any attempt to duplicate in Canada the machinery for organization and education that already exists in the U.T.A. would be foolish, extravagant and unnecessary. What we in the West would recommend is the creation of a Canadian Division of the U.T.A., in affiliation and working in harmony with that vigorous body, but with a Canadian office, manned by Canadians for the most part trained under U.T.A. guidance, and with Canadian organizers for work on this side of the line; local conventions to be held to discuss Canadian problems and to formulate policies for discussion at the greater U.T.A. conventions. The beaver might be substituted for the eagle on the U.T.A. emblem, and the words "Canadian Division" added. By these things we can perfect an organization among ourselves and at the same time become a real factor in United Typothetae councils.

Such an ambitious plan requires capital and great thought and care in working out. The first step would naturally be the formation of local associations, the larger fighting force being composed of these units.

If these plans were perfected and laid fully and intelligently before the U.T.A. executive, we are certain they would receive a sympathetic hearing and perhaps the unqualified support of the only organized force that ever helped establish the printer in the class of sane business men, made him a factor in the community, and gave him the data and inspiration to acquire self-respect and a little money.

Any move in any direction towards organization is infinitely better than our present disorganization and stagnation.

Notes for the Pressman

Answering queries in a recent issue of the *American Pressman*, the editor gives the following information:

The trouble you are having with perforating rules can be partly overcome by using corks along side of the rules, just high enough to have a tendency to push the sheet away from the rule. You failed to state whether or not the perforating rules were in the form of type and of course we would have to have this information before we could give you the correct solution.

You can make your inks dry out glossy by adding a gloss varnish to them. The ordinary varnish will not be satisfactory, and it is necessary that you buy a gloss varnish from the ink maker. When too much varnish is used, the ink will not lay well and is therefore inclined to mottle. For that reason we must use discretion in handling it.

Gasoline has a tendency to harden composition rollers and if used continuously shortens the life of the roller. It has no immediate bad effect on the composition, at least this effect is not discernible, and for this reason many still cling to the idea of washing rollers with gasoline. Kerosene is better, but yet it does not wash the rollers as clean, as it leaves a greasy residue. This grease is good for the rollers but not for the printing. Mix the two together and you will have an ideal wash.

To make your black ink darker, you must have good distribution and possibly add a touch of good strong bronze blue. If we knew more about the nature of your work and the inks you have used, we could be more specific.

In regard to the kind of packing you should use for linen paper and for handbills, would advise that theoretically speaking, a hard packing is the best for all classes of work, because it enables the pressman to get a good sharp impression. Hard packing should always be used for hard papers, such as bonds, covers, etc., and because handbills must be printed in a hurry, without the proper makeready, it is necessary that a softer packing be used so that the inequalities of the form and press will be taken up without the necessity of makeready. When hard packing is used more pressure is necessary but shows less on the back of the sheet and obviously more makeready is required. Bearing these facts in mind, a pressman should be able to determine the packing best suitable for his presses.

Watch the Ink and Rollers

When you have a job that you have real hard cash tied up in —a job that has absorbed high-priced labor, expensive illustrations on it? Is it not just as important that you should have the very highest quality of ink that can be secured in order that your finished product should be high grade throughout? Many a job has been reduced in quality because of an apparent saving in the price of ink used.

New rollers should always be carefully and evenly set. In dry weather, rollers will shrink, slightly, and in damp weather they swell. Proper setting produces proper inking and lengthens the life of the roller.

Rollers should not be stored against damp walls where they can absorb moisture, nor in direct sunshine. In hot weather rollers in racks should be turned over occasionally to prevent sagging.

One roller that melts on the press may spoil three or four other good rollers. If ink does not carry to end of the rollers, a few drops of oil will prevent overheating. Rollers should never be allowed to run "dry" on the press.

—From "Passing Show," London.

Lloyd-George: "Hold your noise! I've brought you here to enjoy yourselves, and enjoy yourselves you shall."

THE OTHER PUBLISHERS' BUSINESS

 Special Advertising, Circulation and
Editorial Plans

St. Marys *Argus* had a Dollar Day in March, the third of the kind in that town. It still retains its attraction as a good local merchandising event.

On April 1st the subscription rate of the *Ontario Reformer* delivered by carrier in Oshawa or by mail anywhere in Canada will be advanced from $2.00 per year to $2.50 per year and in the United States from $3.00 to $3.50 per year. The United States rate is higher than the rate in Canada to cover additional postage.

Writing of the experiences of the Barrie *Examiner*, with its methods of circulation, Mr. J. A. MacLarin, says:—"The paid-in-advance plan is no doubt very desirable in many ways, yet we question if a circulation can be as well maintained if this system is strictly adhered to. It is much easier to lose a subscriber than to pick him up again. Most publishers are willing to pay a certain percentage to get new subscriptions. It surely is equally good business to spend a few cents to hold old subscribers who may be inclined to be tardy. By our system of looking after subscriptions we have no great difficulty in keeping our list in good shape. The close of our last financial year showed only a comparatively small percentage of arrears in our list of over 3,700."

In February of this year a meeting was held in Toronto of most of the publishers of the smaller dailies of Ontario to discuss ways and means of meeting the critical situation in the newspaper business, and a scale of minimum advertising rates per 1,000 of circulation was adopted. It was as follows:

Circulation	Minimum Rate per Line
2,000 to 3,000	1½
3,000 to 4,000	1½
4,000 to 5,000	1¾
5,000 to 6,000	2
6,000 to 8,000	2¼
8,000 to 9,000	2½
9,000 to 10,000	2¾
10,000 to 11,000	3

Dollar Day Still a Success

The Parkhill *Gazette* held its third successful Dollar Day on March 17th. At a meeting of the merchants held in the *Gazette* office, the cost of the necessary half-sheet, two page supplement to the paper was discussed, and agreed upon. The cost of this was divided among the twenty-four merchants in town according to the amount of business they expected to do on that day. Dry-goods merchants paid a greater proportion than others in different lines, as groceries, furniture, etc.

Pennants and price cards were printed. The pennants for window decoration, the price cards about 6 inches by 5 inches, to give the stores a uniform appearance. When the public saw that card they looked for a Dollar Day bargain.

It was agreed to by the merchants that the bargains offered were to be genuine reductions in price. This policy has been followed during the three years since Dollar Day was inaugurated here, with the result that this year the stores were crowded. The turn-over of goods was the greatest in the history of the town, one merchant reporting that his sales exceeded $1,500 on that day.

The *Gazette* also shared in the general good business. The supplement, the pennants, the price cards, the increased ad-

vertising for two weeks previous and the large number of subscriptions paid on that day, all helped to make Dollar Day worth while.

Outside of their sales, the merchants look on Dollar Day as good advertising. Many people enter every store, searching for Miss Dollar Day or for bargains, who usually confine their purchases to one store when in town. This in itself is a sufficient return for the money expended and eventually brings new customers.

The bills for Dollar Day advertisements and other work were all payable at once and were kept separate from regular accounts.

A Novel Motor Page

The Phoenix (Ariz.) *Republican* has a new advertising idea that has many attractive features. It is called the *Busy Motorist*.

The *Busy Motorist* feature contains eighteen advertisements, and runs for a period of eighteen weeks. Each week the *Republican* photographer photographs some person in an automobile on the street without his or her knowledge. This picture is reproduced in the *Busy Motorist* page, and the person who was shown is presented with a $10 order on one of the advertisers, so that during the eighteen weeks every one of the advertisers is presented with an order from one of the *Busy Motorists*.

This feature is sold at a rate sufficiently high to pay for the promotion space, prizes, costs of taking the pictures, etc., besides paying for the space occupied by the advertising.

It not only gets some extra business, but it carries with it a reminder to the advertiser that the plan has a tendency to bring a new customer to his store. It also creates much interest and comment among motorists.

The Calgary *Herald* announces an increase in rates, to take effect on June 1. A new rate on classified comes in on May 1, as follows:—Casual rates:—

Under any heading per count line per day	.12
Under any heading three consecutive days per count line	.30
Under any heading six consecutive days per count line	.50

Classified Display Casual Rates:—

One day per inch	$1.56
Three days per inch	3.90
Six days per inch	6.50

Minimum space for classified display, one inch.

Borders may be ordered for classified display only as per sample on following page. No classified display advertisement less than two inches can be set with border.

All advertisements for insertion on the classified pages are confined to single column width.

Toronto *Globe*:—In its efforts to conserve newsprint, the *Globe* has lengthened its columns by a little less than half an inch, or five-fourteenths of an inch, to be exact. To do this new plate-casting machinery has been installed, and the cylinders of the presses have been adapted.

The change, which simply leaves less margin at the top and bottom, does not alter the size of the page, and, perhaps, will be imperceptible to the reader. Yet this narrow strip, formerly left blank, is worth, as white paper, more than $8,000 a year. It will give to *Globe* readers each day an average of nearly three columns of additional reading matter.

The H. K. McCann Co. is sending out contracts to weeklies for 300 inches advertising Imperial Oil Products.

Press Agency Bureau sent out two 30-inch advts. for Jewish Relief to 95 weekly papers.

Desbarats Advertising Agency of Montreal is placing contracts for 1920 for the Borden Milk Company.

A number of the weekly papers in various parts of the Dominion have increased their rates recently. The following are noted:—The *Confederate and Representative*, Mt. Forest, both local and foreign increases; the *Mercury*, Renfrew; the *Examiner*, Barrie; the *Recorder*, Gore Bay, Manitoulin Island; the *Reformer*, Oshawa; the *Despatch*, Alameda, Sask.; the *Enterprise*, Bolton, Ont.; the *News*, Vernon, B.C.; the *Free Press*, Forest; the *Union Advocate*, Newcastle, N.B.; *L'Action Populaire*, Joliette, Que.; the *Herald*, Miami, Man.; the *Register*, Norwood, Ont.; the *Post*, Thorold, Ont.; the *Mail*, Milestone, Sask.; the *Telescope*, Walkerton. The *Herald*, Alliston, Ont., in announcing new rate card prints: "Discounts to bonafide agencies recognized by the C.W.N.A., 25 per cent. Terms net monthly or quarterly."

The Charlottetown *Guardian* has sent out a pamphlet pointing out the buying power of the people of Prince Edward Island. The following gives an idea of the sort of material used:—Prince Edward Island has a land surface area of 2,134 square miles, or roughly 1,250,000 acres. It is the most thickly settled and one of the most productive of the provinces of Canada. At last census the population was 93,728, an average of 43 to the square mile. The population has no foreign element in it whatever, the people being of pure Scotch, Irish, English and Acadian stock.

The Winnipeg *Free Press* is paying special attention to its automobile section, having an editor to do that work. In connection with this feature it has issued a special folder on "Automobile Publicity—Its Uses and Abuses."

The Lowe Printing Company, of Hamilton, will build an additional storey to its present building at John and Rebecca streets, estimated to cost $3,000.

The Indian Head *News* sports quite a novel heading for its editorial page, being the head of an Indian gazing at a newspaper equipment on the opposite side of the cut. Said equipment could look quite like either an ink-bottle or a paste pot.

The Orangeville *Banner* increased its price to $1.50 per year at the first of March.

The Windsor City Council at its meeting, by vote of 6 to 5, definitely rejected request from local Board of Commerce for a grant of $4,200. The board said they wanted the money to "advertise the town." Some of those opposed to the grant declared that no "advertising" was needed now, as many people had been compelled to live in tents because they could not find houses to live in.

Belleville "Ontario" 50 Years

THE Belleville *Ontario*, on March 26, celebrated its 50th anniversary, and in its issue of that date published much material bearing on the journalistic ventures, successes and failures, in that city. The first newspaper to be established in Belleville was called the *Anglo-Canadian*. This was 89 years ago, or in February, 1831. Belleville was then a lusty village, boasting of 1,000 inhabitants. The editor of the *Anglo-Canadian* was Alexander T. W. Williamson, and associated with him as publisher was W. A. Wellse. The subscription price was rather high for a weekly as compared with present standards, four dollars a year being the price asked. The *Phoenix* was the

second. It began publication a few months later than the *Anglo-Canadian*. It passed away July 3, 1832, aged one year. In 1834, George Benjamin founded the *Weekly Intelligencer*. Thirteen years later, Mr. Mackenzie Bowell, who had served an apprenticeship with Mr. Benjamin, became a partner in the business. Next year or in 1848, Messrs. Bowell and Moore became proprietors of the paper. The partnership lasted for three years and a quarter when Mr. Moore retired and Mr. Bowell became sole proprietor.

The *Sun* began life in 1835 but lasted only a brief period. A Mr. Hart started the *Plain Speaker* in 1836. It was friendly to the "rebel" cause of William Lyon Mackenzie. Those were exciting days in the little burg and the editor of the *Plain Speaker* appears to have led a life consistent with the period in which he lived. He was finally landed in the Kingston penitentiary for an attempted raid on a bank at Cobourg. "Soldiers" afterwards marched to the office of the *Plain Speaker*, threw the type fonts into the river, and trailed the manager through the snow and slush. This raid was occasioned, it is said, because the paper appeared one day with the British coat-of-arms upside down.

In 1870 Messrs. J. W. Carman and Jacob Yeomans formed a joint-stock company, known as the Ontario Publishing Company. On Saturday, March 26, 1870, they issued the first number of the *Daily Ontario*. The following week, the first number of the *Weekly Ontario* appeared. The Ontario Publishing Company continued to issue the paper for five years, when Mr. T. S. Carman, who had founded the Napanee *Express*, moved to Belleville and acquired the property. He retained the services of his brother as editor. Mr. Carman held control until April 15, 1910, when the present publishers, Messrs. W. H. Morton and J. O. Herity, purchased and took over the business.

Business is Developing

Canadian pulp and paper exports for the month of January reached a total value of $9,151,266, compared with $6,885,319 in January 1919, a gain of $2,265,947. The details:

January	1919	1920
Paper and Manfs. of	$4,429,803	$5,519,718
Woodpulp, chem. prop.	2,193,194	2,658,974
Woodpulp mech. ground	262,322	972,574
	$6,885,319	$9,151,266

The paper exports during the month included 1,152,508 cwt. of newsprint, valued at $4,471,799; paper boards, valued at $459,935; 32,761 cwt. of kraft wrapping, and roofing paper valued at $89,645.

Paper and woodpulp exports for the first ten months of the fiscal year reached a total value of $83,576,178, compared with $67,403,247 for the corresponding period in 1919, and $51,923,419 in 1918; a gain of $16,172,931 over 1919, and of $31,652,759 in 1918, as follows:

Ten mos. ending Jan.	1918	1919	1920
Paper and Mfs. of	$30,295,563	$37,099,163	$49,717,824
Woodpulp:			
Chem. prop	15,963,707	26,268,144	26,509,626
Mech. ground	5,664,149	4,035,940	7,348,728
	$51,923,419	$67,403,247	$83,576,178

Exports of unmanufactured woodpulp amounted to 59,789 cords, valued at $615,101 in January 1920, compared with 97,915 cords, valued at $972,129 in January 1919. Exports of pulpwood for the ten months period were as follows:

	Cords	Value
Ten months ending January 1918	907,131	$ 7,419,272
Ten months ending January 1919	1,303,370	12,567,357
Ten months ending January 1920	738,457	7,417,390

Fergus *News-Record*:—The Dundalk *Herald* in a wedding report, made a small but peculiar and embarrassing blunder. A young couple were reported as "united in matrimony," but the "t" and "i" changed places in the type and it was printed "united in matriomony." The editor sees the humorous side of the situation but thinks it better to explain that the happy young couple were not seeking divorce.

Printer & Publisher

Published on the Twelfth of Each Month.

H. A. NICHOLSON - - - - Business Manager.
A. R. KENNEDY - - - - - - Editor.

SUBSCRIPTION PRICE—Canada, Great Britain, South Africa and the West Indies, $2 a year; United States, $2.50 a year; other countries, $3 a year. Single copies, 20 cents. Invariably in advance.

PUBLISHED BY

THE MACLEAN PUBLISHING CO.

Established 1887   Limited

JOHN BAYNE MACLEAN - - - President.
H. T. HUNTER - - - - - Vice-President.
H. V. TYRRELL - - - - General Manager.
T. B. COSTAIN - - - General Managing Editor.

Head Office, 143-153 University Avenue - TORONTO, CANADA
Cable Address Macpubco, Toronto; Atabek, London, Eng.

Also at Montreal, Winnipeg, New York, Chicago, Boston, London, England.

Application for A.B.C. Audit.

Vol. 29   TORONTO, APRIL, 1920   No. 4

CONTENTS

No Control on Paper Now

IT was not necessary to wait until the first of July to find out whether or not there would be any paper control after that date. A decision handed out at Ottawa this month puts a quietus on anything that might look like control in any form. The ruling says that newspapers and publications in general are not necessary to existence, in the same way as food, clothing, fuel, etc., and on that ground there never existed any real ground for control of output or price.

It means that there is an open market for paper, and that sooner or later every paper in Canada, big or small, will be in direct competition with the buying power of the great metropolitan papers of United States.

From what information *Printer and Publisher* has been able to gather there is nothing by which to gauge future prices. It seems unlikely that the makers of paper wish to see any of their old customers in want, but the big dominating fact is that the big market of United States is right at their doors, with its tremendous buying power.

Papers have done little or nothing at all toward trying to save newsprint. There are cities where afternoon papers dash out on the streets with three or four half-baked editions per day, where the field would be well served by one well-edited edition, and a lot of paper could be saved.

There is something lamentably wrong when one paper can say that it has not got to trouble about the paper situation, while another is at the point of suspension because it cannot get supplied.

Publishers of daily papers especially will have to come to the point where they will show more common sense than they have ever done if they are going to continue in business. They should start with the idea of having better-edited, smaller papers. The average large paper could be trimmed. Despatches could be boiled. Editorials would be just as pithy shorter, and more forceful. In fact the cutting out of the wind-up would save many a column.

Unless all signs fail newspaper will be faced with the poor option of HAVING to go on rations for print, and paying a stiff price for their product. When any group of makers get their consumers in the attitude of bidding for the product the price is going to be where the bidders put it, and at present the bidders are keen.

He Could Not Get a Foreman

THE publisher of a weekly paper was in Toronto for several days this week looking for a foreman. He had advertised in one of the morning papers for several days, and the answers came here. It was his intention to get in touch with applicants by telephone as he was very much in need of help in his office.

He had a few applications, five or six, and he started to run them down. He ALMOST got one man, but before he closed he had signed up with a city daily. The publisher in question thing is up-to-date, and he has a good town in a good district. He went back without any sign of getting his man.

Had he been able to secure a foreman it would have meant that he would simply have transferred his own worries and troubles to some other office.

It may be a blunt way to put the question, but how long will it be before there are no more printers?

It is one of the most serious propositions that the trade has faced for a long time. It may be that a slump would throw a number of men out on the road, but that is a poor way to face the issue.

Printer and Publisher may be wrong, but we believe that the city offices are training more apprentices per capita employed than those in the country. A number of publishers in towns have given us the information that they have no apprentice in their offices. In several instances the claim was that they had to pay their foreman so much that it did not pay to take up his time teaching an apprentice how to shoot.

Go over all this ground, and nothing will show up to point the way out. It is a fact that the printing industry is woefully short of competent mechanics now. The man who goes to take charge of a good country office must be a good man. He must have a knowledge of newspaper work, of good newspaper typography, of job work, press-work very often, of binding in certain stages, estimating and the general management of the country office. The point is here: These men can be trained only in the country office. Men who graduate from a city office are not used to the class of work they do in the smaller places. On the other hand the man trained in the weekly office can quickly adapt himself to any of the specialized work of the big daily or the big publishing house.

Too Many Pocket Editions

AN increasing number of Canadian municipalities have Chambers of Commerce or Boards of Trade that seem obsessed with the idea that one thing they must do is to get out a little paper of their own and fill it up with this, that or the other thing about the place calculated to be of some "boosting" merit.

How much real service is given by these little sheets? They are probably sent out to firms in far-off cities with the idea of impressing them with the importance of the place as a manufacturing centre. There are better ways of doing this than by sending out these pocket editions. There are a goodly number of recognized Canadian publications that have access to the offices of some of the largest and best American industrial concerns, because they are carrying the advertising of these American firms. A paper where a firm is spending its money is going to have a preferred position when it comes to opening the mails, and any message there from Canadian municipalities is likely to get a hearing.

Apart from that it seems that some of the publishers of these special papers have the idea that the papers already printed in the community have never done anything in the line of calling attention to the merits of the place, whereas for years they have been doing their best, very often unaided and unthanked, to keep the home fires burning, and to try and have the people at home show the confidence in their own home—

towns that they now expect to instil in others who have never seen the place.

Papers that are already in existence need support. They do not need nor do they deserve to have their field of legitimate revenue cut into on the assumption that they are not filling the bill. These little publicity sheets may serve as a vehicle for many of the leading citizens to get some heavy thinking off their chests and into print, but the sum total of real service they perform is mighty close to the zero point.

Hints in Advertising

A FULL page advertisement appearing in Toronto papers recently was started by a story of the late Sir John A. Macdonald getting a shave in a barber-shop. The barber had the statesman by the nose, just ready to shave, when a friend remarked that this barber was the only man who could take him by the nose. The late Premier is said to have replied that he had a handful when he did so.

Then the ad. writer goes on to state that had Sir John been living at the present time he would undoubtedly have been using some certain kind of razor to take off the heavy beard that would be almost certain to grow on such a face.

This was followed by a long list of distributors of this razor. This part of the ad. was quite right and proper, but the top part was not.

It would be small wonder were some relative or admirer of the late Sir John to take action to see what could be done in such a matter.

There are certain well-prescribed limits, unwritten no doubt, but it is dangerous to pass them in the preparation of advertising copy.

Some of the large daily papers are finding it necessary and desirable now to undertake large campaigns for the purpose of protesting against the extravagant statements that have been made in much of the automobile advertising that has been issued.

People are not convinced by freak notions, or by exaggerated and twisted conceptions of things. In the last analysis successful advertising has its strong points in honesty and service to the consumer.

Some Plain Truths Here

SO true are some of the things contained in a recent interview with Hon. Josephus Daniels, secretary of the U. S. Navy, that they command and deserve attention. In a recent issue of *Editor and Publisher* is an article recounting experiences of Mr. Daniels in the publishing business in his early days, when he was finally owner of a weekly paper in a small town.

Especially can publishers of small daily papers and of weeklies take seriously what Mr. Daniels has to say:—

"It is all right to print the news from the national capital and from Europe, but if your paper doesn't touch the life of your community, if it doesn't think and talk in their language, and if it doesn't interpret the thoughts and ideals of your community, it will fail.

"Another thing I learned early in the game was to train my subscribers to pay in advance for a year. Before long 90 per cent. of my subscribers were paying in advance. There were two reasons for this: If a man has paid in advance, even if he gets mad at what you say in the paper, he isn't going to stop his paper; then, too, a man values your paper less if you seem apologetic about asking him to pay for it. In other words, people value what they pay for.

"You cannot run a paper successfully without the paper having a heart and soul, and that means you must put your own personality into it. You can't sit on the fence—you have to take sides. I always tried to get into every fight. I fought hard, but I fought fair. Unless two-fifths of my readers hate my paper like sin, I feel that I have fallen down in making my paper interesting. The other three-fifths of your readers will swear by the paper and work for it, while the two-fifths that don't like it continue to take it to see what new mischief you are up to and what you are saying about them and their party."

The editor of any paper can well take some of that seriously. "If your paper doesn't touch the life of your community, it will fail."

Do you believe that? Some people do not, and they fail. Others do believe and they succeed. It is all right to gaze longingly on the big world news, to imagine that which is going to make your paper great—and when all this distance gazing is going on it is also easy to curtail, leave over and forget local stuff that does not seem very important.

We can recall only a short time ago meeting the editor of one of the snuggest little dailies in the Dominion. His first remark was that on a recent day they had published a paper on the front page of which there wasn't a single date line article—everything home-brew. He counted that a real accomplishment, and that man is a real newspaperman.

There is a great truth in this:—"Then, too, a man values your paper less if you seem apologetic about asking him to pay for it."

Secretary Daniels is so right that there is no chance for an argument in that matter.

If you want to weaken your ability as a collector just assume the "Well, you might let me have a little on this" attitude. You will find that there will be plenty to meet you on that ground.

IT is probable that a more complete and effective organization of the Master Printers of Toronto will be brought about shortly. The matter has been discussed at various times, and in view of the vast amount invested here it is felt that the business warrants a central office in charge of a competent organizing secretary. Figures show that Toronto is about the seventh city on the continent in the publication of all kinds of printed matter, and the volume is constantly on the increase. There are many matters that are of common interest to the Master Printers, and the need for a clearing office for information and adjustment is being felt more now than ever before.

One of the first moves is likely to be a survey of all the publishing houses in the book and job class. This will take some considerable time, and will call for quite an expenditure, but it is felt that such an appraisal will give statistics and information that will put the Master Printers in a much stronger position in many ways. It is understood that it is the intention of the Association to secure a competent secretary and manager, and that the work of organizing on the new lines will be completed inside of the next two months.

Planning For Imperial Press Conference
Noted British Journalists to be Present

ARRANGEMENTS for the Imperial Press Conference which is to be held in Canada this summer are now nearing completion and there is every indication that the event will be a huge success.

In 1909 a conference of editors and publishers from different parts of the Empire was held in London to discuss matters of mutual interest, which proved so successful that it was decided to hold one every five years. The war delayed plans, but the Empire Press Union, representing the publishers of Great Britain and most of the overseas dominions, this year accepted the invitation of the Canadian Press Association to hold the second conference in Canada.

The Canadian newspapers will entertain about one hundred visitors, sixty from Great Britain, including Lord Northcliffe,

Itinerary of Imperial Press Conference Tour of Canada, 1920

Miles	Place	Prov.	Day of Trip	Day of Week	Month	Day	Ry. or SS.	Local Committee Chairman	Remarks
	Ar. Halifax	N.S.	1	Sunday	July	25	E. of F.	G. Fred Pearson.	
	Lv. Halifax	N.S.	2	Tuesday	July	27	D.A.R.		
130	Ar. Annapolis	N.S.	2	Tuesday	July	27	D.A.R.		
59	Ar. Kentville	N.S.	2	Tuesday	July	27	D.A.R.		
7	Ar. Wolfville	N.S.	2	Tuesday	July	27			Motor Kentville to Wolfville.
77	Ar. Truro	N.S.	2	Tuesday	July	27	D.A.R.		
43	Ar. N. Glasgow	N.S.	2	Tuesday	July	27	C.N.R.		
181	Ar. Sydney	N.S.	2	Wednesday	July	28	C.N.R.		
224	Ar. Truro	N.S.	3	Wednesday	July	28	C.N.R.		
123	Ar. Tormentine	N.B.	4	Thursday	July	29	C.N.R.		
11	Ar. Borden	P.E.I.	4	Thursday	July	29	C.N.R.	J. R. Burnett	Motor to Summerside and
11	Ar. Tormentine	N.B.	4	Thursday	July	29	C.N.R.		Charlottetown.
164	Ar. St. John	N.B.	5	Friday	July	30	C.N.R.	F. B. Ellis.	
	Lv. St. John	N.B.	6	Saturday	July	31	C.N.R.		
80	Ar. Fredericton	N.B.	6	Saturday	July	31	C.N.R.		
63	Ar. Woodstock	N.B.	6	Saturday	July	31	C.N.R.		
360	Ar. Quebec	Que.	7	Sunday	Aug.	1	C.N.R.	Sir David Watson.	
	Lv. Quebec	Que.	8	Monday	Aug.	2	C.N.R.		
83	Ar. Grand'Mere	Que.	8	Monday	Aug.	2	C.N.R.		
120	Ar. Montreal	Que.	8	Monday	Aug.	2	C.P.R.	Lord Atholstan.	
	(Windsor St. Station)								
	Lv. Montreal	Que.	10	Wednesday	Aug.	4	C.P.R.		
	(Windsor St. Station)								
21	Ar. St. Annes	Que.	10	Wednesday	Aug.	4	C.P.R.		
91	Ar. Ottawa	Ont.	10	Wednesday	Aug.	4	C.P.R.	P. D. Ross.	
	Lv. Ottawa	Ont.	12	Saturday	Aug.	7	C.P.R.		
265	Ar. Toronto (Union)	Ont.	14	Sunday	Aug.	8	C.P.R.		
81	Ar. Queenston	Ont.	14	Sunday	Aug.	8	C.S.L.		Trolley to Niagara for night.
	Lv. Niagara Falls	Ont.	15	Monday	Aug.	9	G.T.R.		
43	Ar. Hamilton	Ont.	15	Monday	Aug.	9	G.T.R.		Motor back to Toronto.
	Lv. Toronto	Ont.	17	Wednesday	Aug.	11	G.T.R.	J. E. Atkinson.	
48	Ar. Guelph	Ont.	17	Wednesday	Aug.	11	G.T.R.		
	Lv. Guelph	Ont.	18	Thursday	Aug.	12	G.T.R.		
124	Ar. Sarnia	Ont.	18	Thursday	Aug.	12	G.T.R.		Two nights on boat.
542	Ar. Port Arthur	Ont.	20	Saturday	Aug.	14	N.N.C.		
	Lv. Fort William	Ont.	20	Saturday	Aug.	14	C.P.R.		
426	Ar. Winnipeg	Man.	21	Sunday	Aug.	15	C.P.R.	John W. Dafoe.	
	Lv. Winnipeg	Man.	23	Tuesday	Aug.	17	C.P.R.		
56	Ar. Portage	Man.	23	Tuesday	Aug.	17	C.P.R.		
50	Ar. Carberry	Man.	23	Tuesday	Aug.	17	C.P.R.		Motor to Wellwood and
28	Lv. Brandon	Man.	24	Wednesday	Aug.	18	C.P.R.		Brandon.
226	Ar. Regina	Sask.	24	Wednesday	Aug.	18	C.P.R.	W. F. Kerr.	
42	Ar. Moose Jaw	Sask.	24	Wednesday	Aug.	18	C.P.R.		
383	Ar. Gleichen	Alta.	25	Thursday	Aug.	19	C.P.R.		
51	Ar. Calgary	Alta.	25	Thursday	Aug.	19	C.P.R.	J. H. Woods.	
	Lv. Calgary	Alta.	26	Friday	Aug.	20	C.P.R.		Motor to Banff, picnic-lunch
82	Lv. Banff	Alta.	28	Sunday	Aug.	22	C.P.R.		on route.
35	Ar. Lake Louise	Alta.	28	Sunday	Aug.	22	C.P.R.		
	Lv. Lake Louise	Alta.	29	Monday	Aug.	23	C.P.R.		
106	Ar. Glacier	B.C.	29	Monday	Aug.	23	C.P.R.		
132	Ar. Vernon	B.C.	30	Tuesday	Aug.	24	C.P.R.		Day motoring Okanagan
	Lv. Vernon	B.C.	30	Tuesday	Aug.	24	C.P.R.		Valley.
46	Ar. Sicamous	B.C.	30	Tuesday	Aug.	24	C.P.R.		
335	Ar. Vancouver	B.C.	31	Wednesday	Aug.	25	C.P.R.	John Nelson	
	Lv. Vancouver	B.C.	33	Friday	Aug.	27	C.P.S.		
83	Ar. Victoria	B.C.	33	Friday	Aug.	27	C.P.S.	B. C. Nicholas.	
	Lv. Victoria	B.C.	35	Sunday	Aug.	29	C.P.S.		
83	Ar. Vancouver	B.C.	36	Monday	Aug.	30	C.P.R.		
	Lv. Vancouver	B.C.	36	Monday	Aug.	30	C.N.R.		
258	Ar. Kamloops	B.C.	36	Monday	Aug.	30	C.N.R.		
276	Ar. Jasper	Alta.	37	Tuesday	Aug.	31	C.N.R.		
241	Ar. Edmonton	Alta.	38	Wednesday	Sept.	1	C.N.R.	M. R. Jennings.	
	Lv. Edmonton	Alta.	39	Thursday	Sept.	2	G.T.P.		
127	Ar. Wainwright	Alta.	39	Thursday	Sept.	2	G.T.P.		
287	Ar. Prince Albert	Sask.	40	Friday	Sept.	3	C.N.R.		
87	Ar. Saskatoon	Sask.	40	Friday	Sept.	3	C.N.R.		
472	Ar. Winnipeg	Man.	41	Saturday	Sept.	4	G.T.P.		
837	Ar. Timmins	Ont.	43	Monday	Sept.	6	T.N.O.		
195	Ar. Cobalt	Ont.	43	Monday	Sept.	6	T.N.O.		
186	Ar. Huntsville	Ont.	44	Tuesday	Sept.	7	G.T.R.		Boat trip to Bigwin Inn and
146	Ar. Toronto	Ont.	45	Wednesday	Sept.	8	G.T.R.		return.
	Lv. Toronto	Ont.	46	Thursday	Sept.	9	G.T.R.		
220	Ar. Prescott	Ont.	46	Thursday	Sept.	9	G.T.R.		
120	Ar. Montreal	Que.	46	Thursday	Sept.	9	C.S.L.		Boat trip.
160	Ar. Quebec	Que.	47	Friday	Sept.	10	C.S.L.		Boat trip.
	Lv. Quebec								

8555—Total Mileage of Tour.

Lord Burnham and Lord Riddell, and the rest from Australia, New Zealand, South Africa, Newfoundland, India and the other parts of the Empire.

The executive committee of the Canadian Press Association in charge of the preparations is composed of: Lord Atholstan, Montreal *Star*, chairman; J. E. Atkinson, Toronto *Star*; P. D. Ross, Ottawa *Journal*; Oswald Mayrand, Montreal *Presse*; W. J. Taylor, Woodstock, *Sentinel-Review*; and C. F. Crandall, honorary secretary. William Wallace is secretary and the executive headquarters are in the Star Building, Montreal.

The arrangements in the different provinces are in the hands of local committees. The chairmen of these committees are: Nova Scotia, G. Fred Pearson, *Chronicle*, Halifax; New Brunswick, F. B. Ellis, *Globe*, St. John; Prince Edward Island, J. R. Burnett, *Guardian*, Charlottetown; Quebec City, Sir David Watson; Quebec, Montreal, Lord Atholstan; Ontario, Ottawa, P. D. Ross, *Journal*, Ottawa; Ontario, J. E. Atkinson, *Star*, Toronto; Manitoba, John W. Dafoe, *Free Press*, Winnipeg; Saskatchewan, W. F. Kerr, *Leader*, Regina; Alberta, northern, M. R. Jennings, *Journal*, Edmonton; Alberta, southern, J. H. Woods, *Herald*, Calgary; British Columbia, Vancouver, John Nelson, *World*, Vancouver; British Columbia, Victoria, *Times*, Victoria.

The party will arrive at Halifax on July 25 and will sail from Quebec on the return journey about September 15. The meetings of the Conference will be held in Ottawa on August 5, 6, and 7.

The overseas delegates will be taken on a tour across Canada and return on two special trains. They will start from Halifax on July 27, visit the Annapolis Valley, then to Sydney, go to Prince Edward Island, then to St. John and Fredericton, to Quebec and Montreal, where they will spend two days, August 2 to 4. They will then go to Ottawa for the sessions of the Conference.

From Ottawa the party will go to Toronto August 8, visit the Niagara District and Hamilton, leaving Toronto August 11, visiting Guelph and going to Sarnia to take the boat for Port Arthur and Fort William.

They will be in Winnipeg August 15 to 17, and will then visit in turn Portage, Carberry, Brandon, Regina, Moose Jaw, Gleichen and Calgary, arriving at the latter place on August 19, leaving on August 20 and visiting Banff, Lake Louise, Glacier, Vernon and the Okanagan Valley, arriving at Vancouver August 25, spending two days there and two at Victoria.

Leaving Vancouver on the return journey on August 30 they will proceed to Kamloops, Jasper and Edmonton, then to Wainwright, Prince Albert and Saskatoon, arriving in Winnipeg again on September 4. They will visit Timmins, Cobalt, and Huntsville, stop at Toronto on September 9 and take the boat from Prescott to Montreal and Quebec.

There may be some changes made in the itinerary of the party as published here.

Saving Claimed in Printing

The report of the Editorial Committee for 1919, which was tabled by Sir George Foster in the House of Commons, shows some remarkable reductions in public printing. Last year was the first complete year of the committee's operations. The members of the committee consist of Fred Cook, chairman; F. C. T. O'Hara, and P. C. C. Lynch. With regard to departmental reports the committee passes not only upon the number to be printed, but upon the text of the manuscripts also. Three years ago the number of departmental reports printed was 325,365; last year the number was 151,425. The number of printed pages in the former year was 210,000,000; last year 56,000,000. Similarly with regard to supplementary reports to Parliament, the number of copies printed has been reduced from 222,000 to 56,000, and the printed pages from 61,000,000 to 11,000,000. For this class of publicity alone, the cost of printing has fallen from $343,301.00 to $188,966.00.

Ferdinand Rinfret, editor of *Le Canada*, the official Liberal organ in Montreal, was the choice of the Liberal convention held at Desalaberry School Hall in Montreal, to be the Liberal candidate at the bye-election in the St. James Division of Montreal for the Federal Parliament in April next. Ten candidates were proposed, but two dropped out and eight names went before the convention. In the four ballots taken, Mr. Rinfret's name polled the most votes each time.

Are You Fooling Us Now?

Picton *Gazette*:—The local merchants are ready to meet competition as to quality and price from any source. This is the attitude of the *Gazette*. We are ready to meet prices from Toronto firms, or firms from any other place. Here is an instance. The *Gazette* did a certain printing job for a local business man. Our charge was $12. To be sure he was not overcharged the customer wrote a Toronto printing firm for prices. They quoted him $107.50 for exactly the same job, a saving of $95.50 on one small job alone buying at home. The *Gazette* has taken some pains to investigate printing prices. The result is that it was found that the prices of Toronto firms were invariably higher than those quoted by Picton printers. The moral is, buy your printing and other requirements at home, and at the same time give employment to the local mechanic, workman and tradesman.

He May Have to Answer

Ottawa newspapers are having some fun with Professor W. F. Osborne, of the University of Manitoba, who, in addressing the Montreal Canadian Club, denounced the press of Canada and declared that "the general run of people suspected its news was either suppressed or else tinctured for propaganda purposes, with the result that the people had lost their old-time confidence in the newspapers." Just before making this address, Professor Osborne was in Ottawa taking an active part in the meetings of the National Council of Moral Education. At the close of the series Professor Osborne paid a tribute to the excellent reports of the discussion that had appeared in the newspapers. The reporters, he said, had been fair and accurate, and had used admirable judgment in the preparation of their summaries.

But with still more interest is recalled the fact, the Ottawa *Journal* says, that Professor Osborne was partly successful, after much personal importuning of news editors, in getting "suppressed" the report of a paper read to the Council by Mr. Cudmore, the Dominion Statistician. Prof. Osborne strenuously contended that Mr. Cudmore's facts about the exchange rate should not be made public. Was it the blunder of the Ottawa newspapers in acceding to Professor Osborne's request that led him to denounce the press of Canada as either suppressing or tincturing the news for propaganda purposes? The professor seems to have overlooked his own act when he launched forth on a wholesale denunciation of newspapers. If some of the newspapers cared to, they could point out a lot of inconsistence between the acts and the words of certain men in high places.

Kingston *Whig*:—Coming home to Kingston, the situation at times has been very serious. The *Whig* has on several occasions since the advent of 1920 faced the possibility of having to suspend publication. On no less than three occasions a supply of newsprint has arrived only in the nick of time. There has never been any guarantee that the supply would be kept up and would be available at such intervals as would ensure continued service. The situation is not improving, but is rapidly growing worse. When newsprint control ceases in Canada on July 1st, no newspaper will be able to tell where its next supply of newsprint is to come from. The whole output of Canadian mills will be thrown on the open market, to be sold to the highest bidder, and there will be such a competition as will probably double the present price, which is already over one hundred per cent. greater than in 1915. There will be a wild scramble for newsprint, and the papers which are not able to secure a share will be in a very serious and unfortunate position. Many small newspapers will be forced out of business. There is no other alternative.

Charles Dana Gibson, the artist, has bought a controlling interest in *Life*, the weekly humorous paper, and will take charge on April 1. On Tuesday last Mr. Gibson purchased the majority of stock from the widow of John A. Mitchell, the former editor. Thirty-four years ago Mr. Gibson sold his first drawing to *Life* for $4. It was called the "Moon and I." That night he went home and drew twelve more sketches, all of which the magazine rejected the following day. Later he became a frequent contributor.

Uniform Style Needed in Printing Trades

Confusion Results from Present Practice

THE carelessness and sometimes ignorance of those who write for the press is notorious and patent to all who are engaged in producing printing. In speaking, people punctuate unconsciously; in writing, they seem unconscious of the fact that punctuation exists at all. Modern usage favors the elimination of much that was formerly thought indispensable, such as accents, italics and punctuation marks. The theory seems to exist that an educated reader can supply the punctuation for himself, while an ignorant person would not understand it anyway. Therefore it obtains that punctuation is one of the most vexing problems of editors and proofreaders, while it is an expensive item to the printing department.

Though this theory of what might be termed "indifferent punctuation" on the part of authors and writers is a good excuse for careless work, it becomes dangerous if carried too far. For instance, the question of using a comma before a conjunction is very questionable, and largely depends on the proofreader's judgment. According to rules of grammar, a conjunction is used to join two words together, while a comma is used to separate two words. If the two are used together a paradoxical question suggests itself in this way: Can a thing which is joined be separated? I merely ask the question without pretending to decide the matter.

Unfortunately punctuation, capitalization, and the use of hyphen (both dividing and compounding words) can be agreed upon by no two people.

The result of this variance may seem trivial until we come to calculate the amount of lost time that is caused in the printing business by corrections. There are few industries in Canada which suffer such an enormous waste through lost time as does printing, through corrections! This is due to several causes. Difference of opinion existing between proofreaders and editors and poor copy. Both of these causes could be eliminated very easily. First of all, all copy should be edited before going to composing machines. This would eliminate all doubt from the operator's mind as he could be instructed to "follow copy" to a dot. Then the author or editor should have enough trust in the proofreader to let him edit the copy and read it. An understanding could be reached as to "style" and then let the proofreader be responsible for the rest. There can be no go-between. Either he has free rein, or else he must "follow copy" absolutely. He must not be allowed to vary from copy at one time and not another. Of course, he is always expected to correct "glaring errors" regardless of copy, but the term "glaring" in this case is very ambiguous.

Only one dictionary should be used. An editor once having determined whose spelling he will follow, should not change. By this I mean that the editorial room should not be equipped with Webster's and the proofroom with Cassell's. Dictionaries are very confusing. Some of the later ones are a study in themselves, a study in "how not to do it." They are veritable circumlocution offices when it comes to divisions and compounds. "Who can decide where all pretend to know?" The editorial department are the people who write the articles. They should know better than anyone else what they want. Could they not be persuaded to give a little attention to consistency? Finally it figures down to this: Will a publishing firm save money if they tolerate carelessness by editors and writers and leave it all to the printing department. Surely it is obvious that the oftener a page is handled the more the cost of production. Some newspapers and publishing houses will not accept poor copy and any deviation from even good copy must be paid for by the customers.

Style is the bugbear of all compositors and proofreaders. Even in the same office one will find two different spellings of certain words, for two different publications. Much time is lost when strangers handle type and have not been instructed as to style. Of course, probably no one outside of a printer ever notices these defects, but isn't that enough?

Is it sane to presume that no expense will be saved to make a magazine perfect in every detail and that the spelling and punctuation should be neglected? Think it over.

In Spain there is, I believe, the Spanish Academy, in France the French Academy; and England the Royal Society to decide questions governing the language of their countries. Could we not follow their example? With the large influx of foreigners coming to our shore, it is going to be increasingly difficult to keep our language to any kind of standard. It is a trend of this age to standardize everything, why not the language? A living language must grow, and it should be trained. It must not be allowed to grow up in a haphazard fashion, and perhaps, who knows, eventually lose its identity entirely.

Would it not be possible for the different Printers' Boards of Trade to become interested in this subject in conjunction with the various Canadian Universities and Education Departments? A commission of Canada's most scholarly men could be appointed (minus spelling reformers) who would standardize capitalization, pronunciation, division, etc., of words. The benefit derived from such an undertaking would be universal. The expense need not be great as the men serving on this commission would do so for the honor attached to the position. Besides being a boon to the printing business it would make for better and sounder scholarship throughout Canada.

EUGENE J. ROBERTS,

Proofreader with Continental Publishing Co.,

Toronto.

There is a point in this letter of Mr. Roberts' that ought to receive attention from some central body, such as the Canadian Press Association. It might seem arbitrary to tell offices what style they shall adopt in their composing room, and that they shall keep up certain things and keep down others. They might rebel at first, but there is a big community of interest to be served, and there would be much to gain by having a standard style card.

Operators going from one office to another—and they still do these things—find that they face a queer proposition for some days on the new job. They cap those things which should not be capped, and they keep down those things which should have been kept up, and according to the proofreader, there is no good in them at all.

One standard style, adhered to, would settle much of this.

Mt. Forest *Confederate and Representative:*—We find that conditions of conducting a country newspaper office have become such that it is necessary for us to make a moderate advance in our advertising rates of from 20 to 35 per cent. according to the class of advertising. The advance of 50 per cent. in subscriptions took care of our increased expenses to some extent. In no case will the rates exceed the combined rates when there were previously two papers, and in some respects they will be considerably less.

REVIEW OF JOB SPECIMENS

 If You Want An Opinion On
Your Work, Send It In

PRINTER AND PUBLISHER wants the co-operation of job printers in making a department for their use and assistance. If you are turning out work that you consider well up to the standard, let us have specimens. Do you ever want an outside opinion on a job, apart from the cost of the thing? We will be pleased to go over your work, and offer suggestions or suggest changes if they seem to be necessary. For the time being at any rate the re-set ad. department will be discontinued. It has served a good purpose, and publishers in several cases have told us that the re-set ads. were regularly torn out and posted in their composing room.

The study of job work is interesting to ad. men as well as job printers. Especially in the smaller centres where job and paper offices are nearly always combined, the specimens will be of special interest. The success of the department depends on the amount of co-operation. If you think you have turned out something a little different or a little better than usual, let the rest of the printers have a chance to get the benefit of your good ideas. Withholding them will not make you richer, neither will giving them away make you any poorer.

There is unquestionably a very keen demand for knowledge of costs. It is well that printers should pay a great deal of attention to this matter in these days of rising prices. Make sure that the costs do not get the start of you, and that you are not too long in putting in new prices to keep up to them. It is a serious thing, in the race of increasing costs, to keep your prices a couple of hurdles behind the increases.

FIGURE A—This was done in the job department of the Kingston *Whig*. The original was done in grey suede finish stock, in purple and gold. The panel and rule work were in gold, and the lettering and figure in purple. The long rule in gold was striking in effect, bleeding off the edge top and bottom. To look at the reproduction, it really seems heavier and more ponderous than the original, as the black stands

out much more than the gold. The programme has the menu on one side, with the toast list on the opposite page. The back was punched and tied with white cord.

FIGURE B—This job is also from the Kingston *Whig* job department. It is used here to show two different treatments of the same kind of work. The colors used were purple and gold, while the stock was buff cover. The grouping and composition are pleasing. The designer of this work has been careful in the spacing to avoid the flat effect of having either lettering or figure in the centre of the space allotted to them. The rule of three to five is a very safe one to follow in this regard. This sort of an event does not lend itself to anything startling or overly original in design, and the compositor can do his best work by devoting his attention to grouping and a judicious use of white space. The tieing of this job was also attended to with commendable attention to detail.

FIGURE C—Cover design as used on a little booklet issued by the Lanston Monotype Co., regarding the work done in training returned soldiers on keyboard and caster. The corners all through are perfect. It would be hard to suggest a change that would improve the lay-out of this cover. From the size and shape (oblong) of the job the figure used looks better centred than otherwise. It is a style that could be used for reference in a number of jobs, not necessarily confined to book covers.

FIGURE D — Rather an unusual design from a printing house in United States. It is given here to show a use that is being made of panels and rules, which are coming into use more in many offices. No doubt there will be a difference of opinion in regard to the running of the panel through the word. Orange and black were used in the original, the orange being the rules on the inside and the little ornament. Taken as a whole, the idea is good. There is a lot of white space, but it is used to advantage. It is a departure from the usual lines followed for a cover.

125th
Anniversary

1794   1919

Banquet

The Ancient
St. John's Lodge
No. 3, A. F. & A. M.
G. R. C.

City Hall
Monday, December 29th
1919

FIGURE A

FIGURE E—This Vancouver specimen is the centre of an invitation folder. The top and bottom had pithy little mottoes relative to the trade. The original had a touch of color by doing the two little ornaments in red, giving just that touch of color needed to make the entire announcement stand out. The compositor has succeeded remarkably well in getting a lot of wording in a limited space, and still avoiding any appearance of solidity or crowding.

FIGURE F—This cabaret programme cover was part of the publicity work done by the mechanical department of the MacLean Publishing Co., in connection with an evening's entertainment provided for the rest of the staff. The stock used was India tint ripple finish cover stock, and the ink was sepia. The grouping of the lettering top and bottom is in good taste, while the use of the ornament forms a connecting link between them.

YOU ARE MOST CORDIALLY INVITED TO ATTEND

A BANQUET

arranged through the kindness of Mr. Jos. C. Nicholson, Vice-President
Vancouver Printers Board of Trade, and Dean of U. T. A.
members in British Columbia, in the

ROSE DUBARRY ROOM :: HOTEL VANCOUVER
THURSDAY EVENING, MARCH 4th, 1920
at 6:45 o'clock

Mr. JOS. A. BORDEN
General Secretary of the United Typothetae of America
WILL SPEAK

Kindly use the enclosed card at once and tell the Banquet Committee whether you can or can not be present.

FIGURE E

else, it is necessary to keep the type of a fairly legible sort. Too often a memorial card is jammed through the printing department with the same speed as a quarter sheet. There is a form standing, with the furniture left all around it. All that is needed is to change the name of the person and the date and place of the funeral, simply a few lines on the machine.

TWO requests were received this month for criticisms of funeral cards. In order to explain what is hard to put in words, we have had set up a card which we consider conforms to the requirements of good typography, modesty and yet sufficient dignity to meet the case.

The custom of using the cards for the dual purpose of putting in windows and mailing is not so common as formerly, but at the same time it is well to keep in mind that these cards are often used for window display, where they are read at some distance, and where, above all

---

Cabaret

given by the employees of the Mechanical Departments of The MacLean Publishing Company to the Executive, Office and Sales Staff of the Organization.

HELD AT THE OFFICE OF
THE COMPANY
143-153 UNIVERSITY AVE.
MARCH 18, 1920

FIGURE F

Festival
of St. John the Evangelist

Annual Banquet

The Ancient St. John's Lodge
No. 3, A. F. & A. M., G. R. C.

Hotel Randolph
Friday Evening, December 27th
1918

FIGURE B

THE MONOTYPE SCHOOLS
IN CANADA

WHAT THEY ARE DOING FOR CANADIAN PRINTERS AND RETURNED SOLDIERS IN PARTICULAR

FIGURE C

Too many of the cards that are turned out bear that look of haste. Remember that the card is an announcement of a death, and any announcement of this should have something in it that you do not give to the auction sale. It is a matter of common courtesy to look upon the funeral card in this way. In the card that is reproduced here we have placed the two sides one on top of the other, because it would have meant too much reduction to bring it down to across the page size. Under the word "Died" and again under the word "Funeral" there might be a very small and neat ornament. If your office has one like a hollow square, not larger than a 6-point, try it. To your taste it may improve the general appearance a little. But be careful. Funeral cards do not call for ornamentation, and anything you do in this line should be carefully considered and weighed.

"Color Types" is High Class

If there is one thing more than another that the average printer has neglected to post himself thoroughly on it is the advances in designing, photo-engraving and illustrating. The old established firm of engravers and printers, Brock-Haffner Press, Denver, have recognized the need for disseminating knowledge in this respect and have just launched a 24-page monthly magazine called "Color-Types," which is sure to prove popular among the printing fraternity of America. Color-Types, properly speaking, is a "house-organ," but since it contains much general information of interest to printers it may be appropriately dignified by the term "magazine." A feature of the magazine is seen in the display of striking examples of halftones and color printing. Besides many helpful ideas it contains instructive articles and hints of interest to printers.

The following item was taken from Color-Types:

Investigators have made careful tests to determine the legibility of colors. The distance, size and form of type used, and other facts being identical, the following list shows their findings in the order of legibility:

1. Black letters on yellow paper.
2. Green letters on white paper.
3. Blue letters on white paper.
4. White letters on blue paper.
5. Black letters on white paper.
6. Yellow letters on black paper.
7. White letters on red paper.
8. White letters on green paper.
9. White letters on black paper.
10. Red letters on yellow paper.
11. Green letters on red paper.
12. Red letters on green paper.

For the Machine Operator

I was watching an operator in an office a few days ago working on twin slugs. He claimed that it did not pay him to change liners for a short take. He had a 30-em mold, and wanted a 36 line, so worked it from two 18's, which measure he had on previously. He was making use of a piece of brass rule to make sure of his right and left line. About every fourth line he would pull this rule out and put it in ahead of the last line, and it was fairly warm handling too. Of course there is nothing new in using the piece of brass rule, or an old slug of longer length than the one being set, but there used to another way of keeping tab on these lines, although it seems to have fallen out of use. Did you ever use your foot to keep count of right and left lines when working on twin slugs? Don't laugh; it is quite easy and plenty of the best of the old school operators used that trick. The right foot was placed on the leg of the base, only an inch or so from the floor. When the line was started the foot was placed up and when the division was made and the last half of the line was in the assembly box the foot was allowed to slip off on the floor. It became quite automatic. In fact I have seen operators in the old days when it was not easy to change liners and molds, working twin slugs, hour after hour and never miss their count. The foot was the indicator, and a real one. When the toe rested on the leg of the machine it was an unwritten sign that a new line was starting, and when that one went into the

---

$$\mathfrak{Died}$$

in Any Town on Monday, March 22, 1920

$$\mathfrak{John Alexander Doe}$$

Husband of Margaret Blank
in his Seventy-fifth
Year

$$\mathfrak{The Funeral}$$

Will leave the residence of his son-in-law,
P. T. Blank, Broad St., on Wednesday,
March 24th, at 2.30 p.m. Service
at the house at 2 o'clock.

Interment in
the Brown Cemetery.

Friends and acquaintances will
please accept this intimation.

Funeral Card described on Page 32.

Announcement

To printers whose trade demands the best it is within the gift of man to produce

FIGURE D

is not a good word, as it is safer to use a sharp splinter, or a toothpick. Be careful of course not to let any oil get on the surface of the cam. Fortunately the foolish habit of cutting down the size of the wheel on the end of the cam rollers in order to speed up the operation of the releasing mechanism is passing away, if it has not entirely disappeared already. This practice was popular, especially on the old Canadian machine where the roller moved a trifle slow. The idea was carried too far, though, and it did not use to be an unusual thing to see these wheels cut down to the size of a Canadian copper. The result of course was that there was a great strain and jerk on the releasing mechanism, and many of the smaller verges could not stand it, so they cracked off. The linotype, as it stands now, should not be monkeyed with in this regard. The keyboard rollers run fast enough for the proper speed of the machine. Careful fingering and a little common sense will get out a great deal more and a great deal better work than can be accomplished by any other method.

The St. Catharines *Journal* has been devoting attention editorially to the paper situation, placing much of the blame for the present shortage on the large dailies. The series is attracting considerable attention, especially from the smaller dailies.

The Ellis Embossing Method

The Ellis "New Method" of embossing is attracting considerable attention in Canada. By it printing and embossing are done in the one operation, and much of the intricate processes surrounding successful embossing are eliminated.

Embossing produces an effect that can be secured in no other way. Unconsciously a person passes a finger over a piece of work and mentally remarks "Embossed." The Ellis method puts the embossing business within the reach of the average office. The Canadian representative can be addressed at 9 James St. N., Hamilton, while Mr. Ben Cross, 89 Queen St. West, Toronto, is the Toronto agent.

The company announces that it has just prepared a book of designs and dies for the use of its licensees.

elevator the toe slipped to the floor and the right hand end of the twin slug was being attended to. There may not be much demand for twin slug work now with such improvements in molds and lines, but it is a kink worth knowing. It requires a little practice and it becomes an established habit. Just in passing it might be mentioned that too much care cannot be taken in having full ends when doing twin-slug jobs. When a machine runs along on single column stuff—and we are speaking particularly of machines in small offices where there is no machinist—it is not undesirable to have about a hair space to keep the type a little off the column rule. Watch this when doing twin-slug jobs. It is very easily adjusted. There is no excuse for having a white line down between the two lines, as is too often the case.

What to do With Rollers

What do you do with rollers when they do not seem to make a quick connection with the cams?

Rollers sometimes get so hard that there is nothing for it but to put them away. Sometimes they will, under climatic conditions, regain some of their spring, but as a general thing this will not be the case. If your rollers do not seem to be susceptible to the rough surface of the cam, try a little sandpaper. To make sure that you have them clean use a little gasoline to take off any dirt or oil. Sandpaper often helps. A file has been used at times, but that is too rough. Next try your cams. It has sometimes been found that a very fine three-cornered file will do a lot here. Sharpen the teeth a little, and by so doing you remove any accumulation of dirt that may be hindering the cam from gripping on the roller when released by the operation of the key. It takes a little time to go over your keyboard, front and back, this way, but it will give results right straight off. When you are doing this it is a good chance to drop the least bit of oil on the pin where the cam turns. "Drop"

The PRESSMAN

The Pressman is a fine adjuster of variable surfaces. His job is to secure pleasing impressions upon varying surfaces of paper stock, from varying surfaces of metal moving at varying speeds, on presses of varying characteristics.

¶ TYPE, engravings, inks, paper, stock—are as different as the men that make them. A Form of type is a plateau of hundreds of points and ridges: A Halftone in surface is as indeterminate as the lights and shadows which determine it. Paper is a rolling plain of pulp, wooded with tiny forests of fibre. Paper flirts with "static," and is as sensitive as a Southerner to temperature. Ink has a fluid nature —fickle, inconstant, makes a splendid impression when treated with consideration and understanding.

¶ AND COLOR — color lies at the rainbow's very ends. Presses are dumb, mechanical entities, individual and demanding deference. These are the friends—and enemies—of the pressman.

¶ THE PRESSMAN adjusts his form; a form, like conscience, must lie easy. Mixes his inks and distributes them in the fountains and on the rollers; they must be prepared to assume well a good position in life. The form must be "made ready"—a blanket built up like a landscape gardener's plan—hollows for high faces and soft cushions for letters of a retiring disposition, polite pressure for sensitive screens.

¶ THIS BLANKET becomes the common ground on which TYPE, INK and PAPER meet, that good may come of their union. And lastly, the press must be forced to realize that it is expected to be swift without being careless.

It takes a good pressman to do such a job—a better craftsman; who has the skill and the desire to "do best what many do well."

THE PERSONAL SIDE OF IT

 We'd Like To Get Items For
These Columns

Quebec

Fernand Rinfret, editor of *Le Canada*, a Liberal daily in Montreal, was elected to the Federal House in the bye-election for St. James constituency.

J. L. Pepper, specializing in printing plant production, addressed the Rotary Club of Quebec on efficiency. He treated on many points, such as ventilation, light, methods, material, etc.

James D. Morrison passed away in Montreal at the age of 51. He was on the *Gazette* as marine reporter from 1892 to 1900. He afterward went to the *Daily Witness* in the same capacity. In 1907 he went to the composing room of the *Star*. About a year ago his health failed and he was sent to the Printers' Home. His health showed some improvement, but the shock of his son's death at the front was too much for him, and after that he failed rapidly.

At the annual meeting of the Montreal City Hall Press Gallery Henri Rodier, *La Presse*, was elected president; R. Homes Parson, the *Star*, and A. Goyer, *Le Canada*, vice-presidents; C. E. Parrot, *Le Devoir*, secretary, and P. H. Lefebvre, *La Patrie*, as treasurer. The officers with Messrs. Grant Smith, *Herald*, and T. Lonergan, *Gazette*, were appointed as the members of the council. A hearty vote of thanks was accorded Mr. Lonergan of the *Gazette* for his services as president for the past two years.

The death of Robert Alexander Becket occurred at 84 York avenue, Westmount, where he has been living for some time past. Mr. Becket was 75 years of age, and was the last direct member of his family. He was a son of the late J. C. Becket, and, in partnership with his brother, succeeded to the father's printing business on St. James street, the firm being known as Becket Brothers. The Beckets were among the pioneers in the printing business in Montreal, being the original printers of the *Witness*. Mr. Becket was born and lived all his life in Montreal.

Maritimes

G. W. Rhodes has resigned as foreman of the Halifax *Chronicle* because he could not get a house to live in.

A. H. Case has rejoined the editorial staff of the St. John *Standard*. He has been engaged with this journal before but has lately been with other businesses.

George Bidlake has joined the St. John *Standard* writing staff as editor. He has had a wide experience in newspaper work with English and Canadian publications.

The death of Wm. H. Kelley, for thirty-two years a valued employee of the Telegraph Publishing Co., St. John, occurred recently. He was foreman of the composing room for many years.

Resolutions condemning the Hearst publications have been passed by meetings of different bodies in St. John and elsewhere through the Maritime Provinces recently. Among those asking that they be barred from the mails were the G.W.V.A. and the I.O.D.E.

The plant of the Aroostook Pulp and Paper Co., at Keegan on the St. John river near Van Buren, Me., has been purchased by the International Paper Co., which operates mills in Quebec, Maine, New York, and other centres. The company, it is said, plans to make some additions to the plant, including the building of a kraft paper mill.

E. Allan Schofield, of the wholesale paper house of the Schofield Paper Co. Ltd., St. John, has been nominated for the mayoralty of that city. So far no opposition has appeared against him and it is regarded as likely that his election will be unanimous. Mr. Schofield has long been prominent in civic matters and has been connected with any movement tending to promote the betterment of the city and the advancement of its welfare.

Stanley D. Granville, who has for some time been accountant with the St. John Standard Publishing Co., has purchased controlling interest in the St. Croix *Courier*, published at St.

Stephen, N.B., and will take up his residence there and management of that paper about May 1. He will direct the business management of the paper, while H. M. Webber, who has been with the *Courier* for some time, will continue in the editorial department.

British Columbia

Rube Hull, a few years ago editor of the *Gazette*, Grand Forks, has started the *Miner* at Heyder, Alaska.

Gus Evans, of the *Sun*, Grand Forks, is reported to be planting an acre of his ranch property to peanuts this year.

W. Curran, who has been on the Nelson *News* reportorial staff for a number of years, has retired to go into another line of business at the coast.

The *Daily News*, Nelson, is now setting its editorial double-column measure—the only paper in the province to follow other than single column style.

Commencing this month the Vernon *News* subscription rate is $2.50 per year. The *News* is invariably twelve pages, even columns, and without doubt the best weekly in the whole of B. C.

Quite a number of the weeklies in the Kootenay are carrying the Eaton advertising, recently offered by the Winnipeg branch of McConnell & Fergusson. It is of generous proportions—usually ten inches by three columns.

The Creston *Review* resumed publication after missing two issues due to its recent fire. The blaze was disastrous to the extent of $1,000, but the worst feature was the loss of the news-paper fyle covering the past ten years.

In order to be able to continue issuing at $2 a year the Kaslo *Kootenaian* is now only issuing two pages of home print to six of patent. By adopting this policy, and thus having more time for job printing, Editor Grier hopes to avoid raising his subscription rates.

At a meeting of the executive of the B. C. Division of the Canadian Press, Inc., last month, a move was made to have the B. C. *Gazette*, the Government's official publication, revise its advertising rates, which have never been altered since 1906. On standard notices such as certificates of improvements, water notices, etc., the *Gazette* rates are at least 25 per cent. lower than the weeklies.

C. F. Hayes of the Creston *Review* was a guest at the annual meeting of Cranbrook Board of Trade, taking the response to the toast to Publicity. Mr. Hayes is one of the three representatives on the East Kootenay Publicity Association that is conducting a vigorous campaign to divert American tourist traffic from the south to come via the Kootenay route on the trip to or from Banff.

Alberta

Bert Laing, late of the Kamloops *Standard-Sentinel* staff, has left for Prince Albert to accept the foremanship on the Prince Albert *Herald*.

The Edmonton *Journal* has bought the northwest corner of College avenue and 101st street, Edmonton, and is clearing the ground for what is expected to be one of the finest newspaper buildings in the West.

Mr. J. J. Duffield, who has been associated with the Vulcan *Advocate* for some time, has accepted the position of managing editor of the *Advocate* in succession to Mr. Ganoe, who will engage in some other line of work in town.

The new scale signed at Vernon is as follows:—Newspaper, book and job—Handmen, $6.50 per day. Operators, $6.50 per night. Seven and one-half hours. The contract covers a period of eleven months—February 2 to December 31, 1920. Increase—Newspaper, book and job—$1 per day. Representative Stoney assisted.

According to the report in the *Typographical Journal*, Calgary printers are out for a big increase. The report says:—That the members of No. 449 are ready to fight for a scale commensurate with the present cost of living was demonstrated at February meeting. The committee's recommendation of $50 for day and $55 for nights was amended to read $55 and $60. When one takes into consideration the purchasing price of the dollar to-day compared with that of 1914, the demand is not outrageous. Calgary has been laboring under the handicap of a low scale all during the war and it is the intention of the members that this is going to be remedied when the next agreement is signed. The present scale of prices terminates May 1, 1920 for the job men, and May 15 for the news.

Saskatchewan

Emory Marshall Young, son of Mr. and Mrs. J. M. Young of Regina, has been appointed associate editor of the *Financial World*, of New York, which is one of the highest positions in the financial newspaper world. He will start in on his new position on April 1. Although not born in Regina, Mr. Young was educated there and for some time studied law. He left Regina to work as a reporter on the 'Frisco *Examiner* and later became editor of *Prospector*, a financial journal.

The proposed Labor paper to be published in Moose Jaw was discussed at the Trades and Labor Council. A report from the Moose Jaw council stated that the paper was to be run under the direct supervision of a committee from the council. The Moose Jaw council urged the need of such an organ on the ground that Labor could not get fair play from the capitalistic press. The matter was referred back to the locals. The president of the council said he believed he was expressing the sentiment of the council when he said that the local Labor people were very well treated by the Saskatoon press. Their meetings were well reported.

Actions for injunctions and damages have been entered in the court of King's Bench at Regina, by the Toronto Type Foundry Co., Ltd., against the proprietors of six weekly publications in Saskatchewan. These publications are the *Lawson Post*, the Mawer *Tribune*, and the *Beacon*, published at Central Butte, by S. W. Juckes; the *Standard Press*, published at Brownlee by S. P. Leach; and the *Municipal Chronicle*, published at Milden by H. R. Griffen. The Toronto Type Foundry Company, Ltd., claims in the actions against Juckes that on December 28, 1918, it entered into a contract with Juckes to supply ready-prints for his three papers for a term of three years. In the statement of claims the plaintiffs set forth that in February this year the defendant ceased to take the ready prints which they supplied and is now using ready prints supplied by some other firm. The plaintiffs further claim that the defendant agrees in the contract made December 28, 1918, to use their ready prints exclusively for the term of three years. The actions against Leach and Griffen are taken on similar grounds. The plaintiffs want injunctions to restrain the proprietors of these publications from using ready-prints by other firms.

Manitoba

R. Murray McBean, Winnipeg, who was a *Tribune* pressman for 10 years and on the *Free Press* mechanical staff for 20 years, has left for British Columbia, to take up his residence in the Okanagan valley. Mrs. McBean and a daughter, Dorothy, will follow. Mr. McBean has lived in the West since 1883, and in Winnipeg since 1886. Mrs. McBean is prominent as an I.O.D.E. worker.

Ontario

Verne D. Wall, late of the Ottawa *Citizen*, is now doing city hall work for the *Border Cities Star*, Windsor.

W. J. Sharpin, mechanical superintendent of the Arnprior *Chronicle*, was laid up for a month with the "flu."

B. L. H. Bamford, editor of Listowel *Standard*, has been appointed town clerk at $600, just double the amount paid previously.

Mr. Lemon, formerly on the staff of the *Border Cities Star*, has purchased a machine and is setting type for the trade. He is busy.

John Grant, for over 30 years a citizen of London, died as the result of a paralytic stroke which he suffered. He was the father of Jean A. Grant, the Western Canada journalist.

Henry M. Wodson, of the Toronto *Telegram* staff, has been appointed by the police commissioners to succeed the late Wm. Banks, sr., as police censor of local theatres. The salary is $2,000 per year.

Bertram N. Scott, for many years mechanical superintendent of the Detroit *News*, died at his home in Detroit following a brief illness. Mr. Scott was born in London, Ont., and for some years was in the traffic service of the C. and G.T. Rail-

way, with headquarters at Port Huron. Mr. Scott was 61 years old.

Peterboro Union has signed a new scale with the employers: Newspaper, book and job—Handmen, operators, $30. Eight hours. The contract covers a period of fifteen months—February 1, 1920, to April 30, 1921. Increase—Newspaper, book and job—$9.

Roy Evans has left the *Journal Dailies*, Ottawa, to become a member of the advertising staff of the *Border Cities Star*, Windsor. Mr. Evans will devote all his efforts in the Border Cities to the local field. During the war he served overseas with the 3rd Canadian Siege Battery.

The A. McKim Limited Advertising Agency has opened an office in Hamilton, Ont., which will be under the direction of B. B. Stewart, who has been connected with the Toronto office for eight years. McKim's now have offices in Montreal, Toronto, Winnipeg, Hamilton and London, England.

It has been proposed by the University board of governors that the Toronto University press be moved from its present quarters, in the basement of the library building, to a new building which will be built on the west side of the University grounds, adjacent to the Physics building, and will cost between $50,000 and $60,000.

Fred C. Hastings, of Dunnville, son of David Hastings, publisher of the Dunnville *Gazette* and a former well-known Hamilton newspaperman, has been appointed general secretary-treasurer of the students' administrative council at the University of Toronto, succeeding C. C. Grant, B.A. This office is one of great honor, the incumbent of which is business manager of the University publications, including *Torontonensis* and the *Varsity*.

The Brantford *Expositor* announces the adoption of an insurance plan. All employees who have been with the *Expositor* for one year are entitled to a policy for $1,000, and for each additional six months of service $500 of insurance is added until $3,000 is reached, the length of service being retroactive. There are quite a few who have been in the service of the *Expositor* for the necessary period of time to be entitled to the $3,000 policy, and they are well pleased with the action of the *Expositor* management.

Mr. James Gairdner, for several years foreman of the Toronto *Mail and Empire* composing room, has severed his connection with the paper to take a vacation in the West for the benefit of his health. He was presented with a handsome travelling bag by members of the composing staff. The presentation was made by Mr. Harry Clark, chairman of the *Mail* Chapel, who referred to the kindly relations existing between the members of the staff and the retiring foreman. Mr. Gairdner made a suitable reply.

C. A. Goodfellow & Son, Whitby, have erected an addition to their office building during the fall months, size 20 x 30, which is used almost entirely as a bindery. In December they installed a second Intertype, and about April 1st installed a No. 1 Miehle Press. They have at present a Whitlock Premier cylinder, so that with these two presses they will have a pretty good pressroom equipment. In addition, they have within the past year installed a new power cutter and power stitcher.

A few friends of J. Vernon MacKenzie, the newly appointed Trade Commissioner to Glasgow, gave him a dinner at the Ontario Club prior to his departure for Glasgow. Several addresses from friends who have followed his successes in academic life and in his newspaper experiences, referred in appreciative terms to his work on the MacLean publications, his work in the Air Force at the front and his wide acquaintanceship with industrial conditions and trade magazines in Canada. Mr. Gordon Rutledge, of the *Financial Post*, occupied the chair.

J. Ellison Young, jr., only son of J. Ellison Young, managing editor of the *Border Cities Star*, died on March 11 after a few hours' illness of convulsions. The little lad's body was taken to St. Thomas, where the funeral services were held from the home of Mrs. Young's parents, Dr. and Mrs. FitzSimons, with interment in the family plot in St. Thomas Cemetery. Rev. Canon Carlisle said prayers at the family home in Windsor, while Rev. J. W. J. Andrew officiated at the services in St. Thomas. There were many lovely floral tributes, including a number from Mr. Young's newspaper associates.

James Henry Westman, of the firm of Westman & Baker, died at the family residence, 26 Rose avenue, Toronto, after a short illness. Mr. Westman, who was in his 72nd year, was born in King township, but came to Toronto in his early youth. He was a life member of King Solomon's Masonic Lodge, and has been a member of Sherbourne Street Methodist Church for more than thirty-five years. He survived his wife but a short time, she having died in February. The late Dr. Samuel H. Westman was his son. Four daughters are left to mourn their loss: Miss Minnie E. Westman, Mrs. Gordon Dallyn, Mrs. Arch Brown, and Mrs. John M. Millar.

Durham *Chronicle:*—Mr. J. Wilfrid Greenwood, son of Mr. and Mrs. Thomas Greenwood, has taken over the editorial work in connection with the Alliance (Alberta) *Argus* and is now pushing the editorial quill. Alliance is a small place about 100 miles east of Edmonton on the C.N.R., on Battle River, and has sprung into existence since 1915. In 1916 the *Times* newspaper was established there, and as no mention is made of the *Argus* in McKim's Directory of last year, we presume this is the second paper to be launched in the little Western town.

Lawson & Jones, Limited, lithographers and printers, have purchased about an acre of ground on York street, just west of Rectory street, London, Ont. It is understood that the company has purchased the property with a view to the erection of a large plant for the manufacture of paper boxes. The transaction includes three properties on York street, Nos. 739 to 748, and a strip of property of the Geo. H. Belton Lumber Co., running back to the G.T.R. The purchase of the Belton property will give the company shipping facilities on the G.T.R. The Lawson & Jones firm will have a frontage on York street of more than 100 feet.

A pleasing event took place at the offices of the Monetary Times Printing Company, Toronto, when the employees from the several departments assembled to do honor to two of their number, Mr. W. J. Poole, city representative, and Mr. William McCullough, foreman of the printing department, who are severing their connection with the firm to enter business for themselves. Mr. Charles Honeyman, on behalf of the employees, presented them with a handsome office desk, and spoke of the high esteem in which they were held by all who had been associated with them. Mr. Joseph Black, secretary of the company, wished Messrs. Poole and McCullough every success in their new venture.

M. McIntyre Hood, for some time on the editorial staff of the *British Whig*, Kingston, has left to take the position of manager of the "Associated Editors" Newspapers Syndicate, Chicago, Ill., distributing newspaper and magazine features, especially for school boys and girls. Mr. Hood enlisted with the 59th Battalion in June, 1915, and went overseas in a draft in November of the same year. He was wounded three times, and returned to Canada in the fall of 1917, and was under treatment in Queen's Military Hospital and Cobourg Military Hospital until October, 1918, when he was discharged. The same month he was taken on the *Whig* staff as a reporter, and on Feb. 1st, 1919, he was promoted to assistant editor.

Book and job office printers in Toronto may go out on strike. This has been intimated by officials of the International Typographical Union, who point out that the employers in the trade have so far refused to negotiate with the union upon the demands of the men. "A conference was called for a month ago," said an official yesterday. "Since that time the employers have done nothing at all, not even replied to our communications. Apparently they rest their case upon the fact that the present agreement was signed to hold until 1921. We all know that since the agreement was signed wages have risen all along the line, and the cost of living has increased. The men are asking for an increase over the sum now received, $32 a week."

The staff of McConnell & Fergusson, London, Ont., has been augmented by the appointment of E. G. Hogarth, advertising manager of the Ford Motor Company of Canada, Limited, Ford, Ontario, to an important position in the agency's personnel. Mr. Hogarth, who is well known to advertising men as a director of the Association of Canadian Advertisers, spent two years with McConnell and Fergusson, later being placed in charge of the Windsor branch. He again advanced to this chosen field and for the last two years has been in complete charge of the advertising, motion picture and photographic department of the Ford Motor Company, directing this work for Canada, Australia, New Zealand, India, Africa and other British possessions, as well as the Dutch East Indies.

For the purpose of supplying "ready-prints" to weekly newspapers, and with a capital stock of $200,000, the Canadian

Newspaper Service Limited has been incorporated by the Ontario Government. Official notice of the incorporation appears in the *Ontario Gazette.* In addition to supplying ready-prints, the company will publish a new weekly newspaper in Toronto, to be called the *Toronto Free Press*, and it has power also to buy and sell feature articles for syndicating to Canadian newspapers, to conduct a news gathering and distributing bureau, and to start an advertising agency. Mr. W. Nelson Wilkinson, formerly managing editor of the Toronto *World* and of other Canadian newspapers, is general manager of the new company. Mr. Albert E. S. Smythe, formerly chief editorial writer for the *World*, is editor of the service, and Mr. G. R. Shibley, formerly on the editorial staff of the Toronto *World*, is manager of the advertising and service department of the new company. The *Toronto Free Press* will be published by the company as a "checking sheet" for advertisers in the "ready-print" and will be sold in Toronto for five cents a copy. It is understood that many features formerly published in the *Sunday World*, including Crusts and Crumbs, Advice to Girls, the Boys' and Girls' Corner, will be published in future in the *Free Press.* These and many other feature articles, comics and editorial comment are now appearing in country weekly newspapers to which the Canadian Newspaper Service Limited supplies ready-prints. The head office of the new company at present is in the Manning Chambers, Toronto.

St. Marys had a Dollar Day on Thursday, March 4, and a nice volume of business was carried. The *Argus* had a Mysterious Miss Dollar, for whose capture $5 was paid.

To place the merits of Saskatoon and its business advantages before a greater section of the public, the Board of Trade have made arrangements for a half-page advertisement and a skyline cut of the city to be inserted in the Manchester *Guardian* at a cost of $670.00.

Publishers of Los Angeles announced that the price of morning papers would be advanced on May 1 from 3 cents to five cents, and two afternoon papers from two cents to three cents, while a third afternoon paper, now selling for one cent, would advance to two cents.

Geo. Bidlake of Fredericton, formerly acting clerk of the Legislature of New Brunswick, has been appointed editor of the St. John *Standard*, and has already gone to St. John to take up his duties there. Before coming to Canada, some years ago, Mr. Bidlake was a London barrister.

That all newspapers, pamphlets, advertising, political campaign literature and similar publications printed and published or circulated in Canada in any other language except English or French should have an English or French translation in parallel columns is urged in a resolution which Brig.-Gen. W. A. Greisbach, Edmonton, will introduce in the Commons.

A small fortnightly bulletin, in the form of a magazine devoted to civic betterment and the interests of the organization has been started by the Commercial Club of St. John, entitled *It's You.* It is the intention to have contributions of articles by members of the club, that the paper will contain reports of committees and that it will contain an outline of matters to come up before each meeting. The paper is to be self-supporting, and is to be published by S. K. Smith, formerly city editor of the *Daily Telegraph.*

Winnipeg *Telegram:*—The members of Typographical Union, No. 91, Toronto, have made a request that their wages be increased from $32 to $40 per week for day men, the night men to receive the usual $2.50 extra per week. A preliminary meeting with the employers was held, but nothing definite done. The representatives of the employers promised that a general meeting of the employers would likely be held on Wednesday, and their answer would be sent the printers immediately.

TINNED
STITCHING WIRE

You will eliminate trouble on your stitching machines and ensure satisfactory work by using this Canadian-made Product.

Sold by Leading Jobbers.

THE
STEEL COMPANY
OF
CANADA
HAMILTON   LIMITED   MONTREAL

The Albion
SILKY COTTON
CORDS

The Cords of a hundred uses for the Artistic and Progressive Stationer and Printer.

A wide range of sizes and colours always in stock.

Send your enquiries direct or through indent agent to

THE ALBION SEWING
COTTON CO., LTD.

Fawley Mills,   Tottenham Hale,
LONDON, N. 17

The Ellis
"NEW METHOD"
Embo$$ing
(PATENTED)

Has the following original claims:

1—You can make a die in 30 minutes.

2—You can take a good proof by hand without a press.

3—You can readily correct, alter or modify a die.

4—Your light press is able to emboss by this method.

5—A die is "made ready" in 5 minutes—ready to run.

6—It is less costly than using a second color.

No "Free" Demonstration but—
Your Order is given on condition that these claims are made good.

Price : $150 cash
(or terms)

which includes personal instruction and license to use the method (patented) with all tools and appliances needed.

Booklet telling the tale, 10c

NO METAL   NO ACID   NO POWDER

The Ellis "New Method"
Embo$$ing Co.

140 W 38 New York City
Chicago   Seattle
9 James' St. N. Hamilton, Ont.
Canada

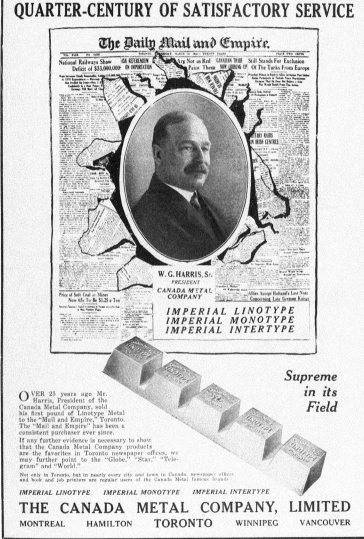

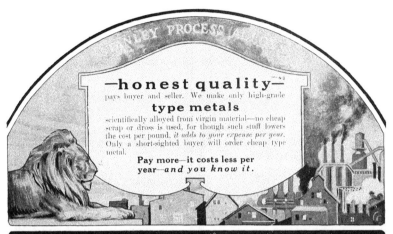

Go to Goes for

Stock Certificates
Both Regular-Litho and Steel-Litho Designs
Stock-Certificate Binders
Bordered Blanks

Diplomas   Certificates of Award
Bonds   Mortgage Notes
Charters   Insurance Policies
Marriage Certificates and Licenses

Bound and Loose-Leaf Corporation Record-Books
Lithographed Calendar Pads
Art Advertising Blotters
Art Advertising Mailing Cards
Art Advertising Calendar Cards

Samples of any of these Goes Printers' Helps upon request

Goes Lithographing Company
Chicago

Interwoven Cover
Now Carried in Stock

Single Thick
20 x 26—50   65
23 x 33—95

	Reams	500 lbs. and over
Antique Finish	29c	28c
Ripple Finish	31c	30c

Double Thick
20 x 26

	100 Sheets	1000 Sheets and Over
Antique Finish	$9.25	$8.50
Ripple Finish	9.75	9.25

Colors: White, Blue, Lawn Green, Dark
Brown, Neutral Brown, India,
Quaker Grey, Neutral Grey.

UNITED PAPER MILLS
LIMITED
TORONTO   HAMILTON
Exclusive Distributors for Ontario

CATCHING THE MAILS

—greatly depends upon
the speed of your mail-
er. Gain time by adopt-
ing the

New Wing
Aluminum Mailer

Extremely light, simple
and accurate, and can
be operated with greater
speed than any other
hand-mailer. Weighs
only two pounds. Built
on new lines. Write for
full description and
price.

Chauncey Wing's Sons
Greenfield, Mass.

When the Village Belle Marries
She needs wedding announce-
ments. You need the engrav-
ings. We make them.
Write us.
Wilson Engraving Co., Winnipeg

Electrotyping and Stereotyping at any one of
our three plants. All orders filled promptly.
Service and quality on every order.

RAPID ELECTROTYPE CO. of Canada
MONTREAL   TORONTO   LONDON   WINDSOR

METAL EDGING
(TINNING)

FOR YOUR CALENDARS, ADVERTISING HANGERS
DISPLAY CARDS, ETC., ARE PROMPTLY
AND CAREFULLY HANDLED BY

THE COOPER CALENDAR
METAL COMPANY
12-16 PEARL STREET - TORONTO, ONTARIO
PHONE ADELAIDE 5547

THE ONLY SPECIALTY OF ITS KIND IN CANADA

WE ARE COMPLETELY EQUIPPED FOR, AND SPE-
CIALIZE IN METAL EDGING AND METAL SLIDES, AND
SOLICIT YOUR PATRONAGE. . . . . . TRY US ONCE—
YOU'LL CONTINUE TO.

Electrotypes
and Stereotypes
Best Service in Toronto

Toronto Electrotype & Stereotype
Company, Limited
122 Adelaide Street West, Toronto

L D Phone   R. C. ELDER
Adelaide 1636   *Manager*

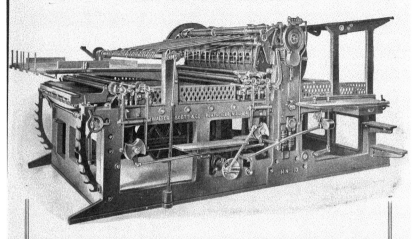

New Scott Cylinder Presses

READY FOR IMMEDIATE DELIVERY

Two No. 4 Presses, bed 26 x 36 inches, matter 22 x 32 inches, two form rollers, Front Fly Delivery.

One No. 4 Press, bed 26 x 36 inches, matter 22 x 32 inches, four form rollers, Printed-Side-Up Delivery.

Two No. 5 Presses, bed 29 x 42 inches, matter 25 x 38 inches, two form rollers, Front Fly Delivery.

One No. 5 Press, bed 29 x 42 inches, matter 25 x 38 inches, four form rollers, Front Fly Delivery.

One No. 4 Press, bed 27½ x 36 inches, matter 22 x 32 inches, four form rollers, Front Fly Delivery.

One No. 7 Press, bed 38 x 51 inches, matter 33 x 47 inches, two form rollers, Rear Fly Delivery.

One No. 8 Press, bed 41½ x 52 inches, matter 35 x 48 inches, four form rollers, Printed-Side-Up Delivery.

One No. 10 Press, bed 47 x 62 inches, matter 41½ x 58 inches, four form rollers, Front Fly Delivery.

The Scott Two-Revolution Presses

that we offer are substantially built machines guaranteed to give an unyielding impression and register to a hair. ¶ Each machine has four tracks, geared roller distribution, two air chambers on each end of machine, type bed driven by our direct drive movement, and satisfies the exacting requirements of the trade. ¶ The space occupied by these presses is required for other machinery.

WALTER SCOTT & COMPANY

Main Office and Factory: PLAINFIELD, N.J., U.S.A.

NEW YORK OFFICE: 1457 Broadway
CABLE ADDRESS: Waltscott, New York

CHICAGO OFFICE: Monadnock Block
CODES USED: ABC (5th Edition) and Our Own

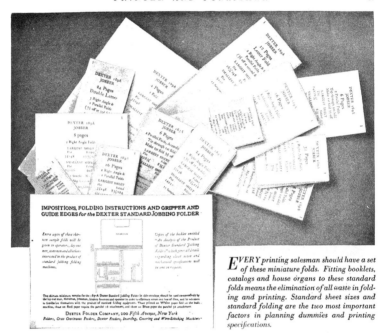

*E*VERY *printing salesman should have a set of these miniature folds. Fitting booklets, catalogs and house organs to these standard folds means the elimination of all waste in folding and printing. Standard sheet sizes and standard folding are the two most important factors in planning dummies and printing specifications.*

Send for this set of Miniature Sample Folds

The envelope contains the impositions, folding instructions and gripper and guide edges for the thirteen standard folds that fold on the Dexter Standard Jobbing Folder.

A careful analysis of folding requirements made by this company showed that more than 98 per cent. of booklet, catalogue and house organ folding comes within these thirteen standard folds.

Extra copies of these folds will be gladly given to your stonemen, compositors, layout men and bindery operators. Write today for your sets.

DEXTER FOLDER COMPANY
200 Fifth Avenue, New York
Folders, Cross Continuous Feeders, Dexter Feeders, Inserting, Covering and Wire-Stitching Machines

PERFECT PRINTING PLATES

We have the facility & skill gained thru years of experience to produce any Plates required for the best printing.

Give us a trial and be satisfied.

The RELIANCE ENGRAVING Co
Corner Edward Street and Centre Avenue ~ Phone Adelaide~ 4094

Used
Printing Machinery

For Sale
Cheap

One Wesel Proof Press, 18½ x 37.

Two Canadian Linotype Machines. Will set from 4 to 30 ems, 6 to 12 point, with one magazine each, also Jenny D.C. motors.

These machines are in good condition and would give good service in a newspaper office and will be sold at a bargain. Can be seen at our office.

The J. L. Morrison Co.
445-447 King Street West - Toronto, Ont.

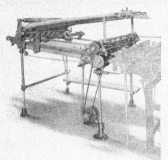

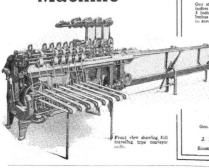

54

Buyer's Guide

TICONDEROGA PULP AND PAPER CO.

Machine Finish, Ticonderoga Finish and Antique Finish

BOOK, MAGAZINE, COATING, LITHO-GRAPH AND MUSIC

PAPERS

Mills at Ticonderoga, N.Y.

Sales Department

Rooms 934-936, 200 Fifth Avenue, New York

J. R. WALKER

267 WELLINGTON ST., MONTREAL

Specialising in All Grades of

Printers' Waste Paper
Books, News and Writing Papers

In Connection With

J. R. Walker & Company, Limited

35 Common St., Montreal

Manufacturers of Felt Paper, Fibre Board, Etc.

HIGH SPEED PAPER DRILLING

Do not "punch" round holes.

The Berry Round Hole Cutter

"cuts" them ten times as fast!

Clean holes cut in paper, cardboard—any bindery stock. *Ask for booklet.*

BERRY MACHINE COMPANY
101 N. 3D ST. ST. LOUIS. MO. U.S.A.

METAL FURNITURE
The Challenge Machinery Co., Grand Haven, Mich.

METAL FOR TYPESETTING MACHINES
British Smelting & Refining Co., Ltd., Montreal.
Canada Metal Co., Fraser Ave., Toronto.
Great Western Smelting & Refining Co., Vancouver.
Hoyt Metal Co., 356 Eastern Ave., Toronto.

PAPER MANUFACTURERS AND DEALERS
Buntin, Gillies & Co., Ltd., Hamilton, Ont.
Canada Paper Co., 112 Bay St., Toronto.
Dickinson & Co., John, 25 Melinda St., Toronto.
Don Valley Paper Co., Toronto, Ont.
Eslieck Mfg. Co., Turner's Falls, Mass.
Halls Paper Co., Ltd., Fred H., Toronto, Ont.
McFarlane, Son & Hodgson, Montreal, Que.
Niagara Paper Mills, Lockport, N.Y.
Paper Sales, Limited, Bank of Hamilton Building, Toronto.
Provincial Paper Mills Co., Telephone Building, Toronto.
Rolland Paper Co., Montreal, Que.
Ticonderoga Pulp & Paper Co., 200 Fifth Ave., New York.
United Paper Mills, Ltd., Toronto.
Wilson Munroe Co., Limited, Toronto.
Whyte Paper Co., A. 55 Bay St., Toronto.

PATENT BLOCKS
The Challenge Machinery Co., Grand Haven, Mich.

PHOTO ENGRAVERS
Reliance Engraving Co., Toronto, Ont.

PRINTING INK MANUFACTURERS
Ault & Wiborg Co. of Canada, Ltd., Toronto, Ont.
Canada Printing Ink Co., 15 Duncan St., Toronto.
The Columbia Printing Ink & Roller Co., Hamilton St., Vancouver, B.C.
Dominion Printing Ink Co., 128 Pears Ave., Toronto.
Manton Bros., Toronto, Ont.
Reliance Ink Co., Winnipeg, Man.
Shackell, Edwards & Co., Ltd., 127 Peter Street, Toronto.
Sinclair & Valentine, 233 Richmond St. West.

PLATE MOUNTING EQUIPMENT
The Challenge Machinery Co., Grand Haven, Mich.

PRINTERS' FURNITURE
The Hamilton Manufacturing Co., Two Rivers, Wisconsin.
The Challenge Machinery Co., Grand Haven, Mich.

PRINTERS' IRON FURNITURE
The Toronto Type Foundry Co., Ltd., Toronto.
Stephenson, Blake & Co., Toronto.
The Challenge Machinery Co., Grand Haven, Mich.

PRINTING PRESSES
Babcock Printing Press Co., New London, Conn.
Goss Printing Press Co., Chicago, Ill.
Hoe & Co., R., 504-520 Grand St., New York.
Linotype & Machinery, Limited, London, Eng.
Manton Bros., 105 Elizabeth St., Toronto.
Miehle Printing Press & Mfg. Co., Chicago.
Premier & Potter Printing Press Co., Inc., New York City.
Stephenson, Blake & Co., Toronto.
The Challenge Machinery Co., Grand Haven, Mien,
The Mann Litho Press Co., 58 Walker St., New York City.
Walker Scott & Co., Plainfield, N.J.

PRINTERS' PRICE LISTS
Port Publishing Co., Salt Lake, Utah.

PRINTING PRESS MOTORS
Kimble Electric Co., 635N Western Avenue, Chicago, Ill.
Manton Bros., Toronto, Ont.

PRINTERS' MACHINERY AND SUPPLIES
Manton Bros., Toronto, Ont.
Royal Machine Works, Montreal
Stephenson, Blake & Co., Toronto.
The Toronto Type Foundry Co., Ltd., Toronto.

PRINTERS' ROLLERS
Canada Printing Ink Co., Limited, 16 Duncan St., Toronto.
The Columbia Printing Ink & Roller Co., Hamilton St., Vancouver, B.C.
Manton Bros., Toronto, Ont.
Sinclair & Valentine, Toronto, Ont.
Winnipeg Printers' Roller Works, 175 McDermot Ave., Winnipeg.

PROOF PRESSES
Stephenson, Blake & Co., 60 Front St. W., Toronto.
The Challenge Machinery Co., Grand Haven, Mich.

"REDUCOL"
Indiana Chemical Co., Indianapolis, Ind.

REGISTER GAUGES
E. L. Megill, 60 Duane St., New York.

REGISTER HOOKS, BLOCKS AND CATCHES
The Challenge Machinery Co., Grand Haven, Mich.

ROTARY PRESSES
Goss Printing Press Co., 16th Street and Ashland Ave., Chicago.
Hoe & Co., R., 504-520 Grand St., New York.

ROLLER SUPPORTERS
The Challenge Machinery Co., Grand Haven, Mich.

RULED FORMS
Matrix Ruled Form & Tabular Co., Fort Worth, Texas.

STEREO PAPERS
L. S. Dixon & Co., Ltd., 38 Cable St., Liverpool, England.

SECTIONAL BLOCKS
The Challenge Machinery Co., Grand Haven, Mich.

The Toronto Star Weekly

has placed an order for our

Children's Page

Also used by

WINNIPEG FREE PRESS
EDMONTON BULLETIN
HALIFAX CHRONICLE
SHERBROOKE RECORD

And Others.

The International Syndicate

20 Years of Unfailing Feature Service

BALTIMORE, MARYLAND

WHILE-U-WAIT

RUBBER STAMP-MAKING OUTFITS

Require only eight minutes to make rubber stamps. Will also make Hard Rubber Stereotypes for printing. A few dollars buy complete outfit.

Send for catalog

The Barton Mfg. Co.

83 Duane Street   New York, N.Y.

Printers, Paper-Makers, Publishers and Manufacturers

Can reduce their "collection expenses" to a minimum by using

NAGLE

ONE PER CENT

DRAFT-SERVICE

Why pay 10 per cent. or 15 per cent. on accounts you can have collected at 1 per cent.? Save money. Investigate this system. Thoroughly reliable. Established 1909. Send for supply of 1 per cent. drafts to-day.

The Nagle Mercantile Agency

Laprairie, (Montreal), Que.

STEREOTYPE METAL
British Smelting & Refining Co., Ltd., Montreal.
Canada Metal Co., Limited, Toronto.
Hoyt Metal Co., Limited, Toronto.

TYMPAN PAPERS
The Cromwell Paper Company, Chicago, U.S.A.

TYPE-HIGH MACHINES
The Challenge Machinery Co., Grand Haven, Mich.

TIN FOIL PAPERS
J. & W. Mitchell, Birmingham, Eng.

TYPE FOUNDERS
Stephenson, Blake & Co., 60 Front St. W., Toronto.
Toronto Type Foundry Co., Ltd., Toronto, Montreal, Winnipeg.

THE NEW ERA PRESS
A Multi-Process Printing, Punching, Perforating, Cutting and other operation machine. Manufactured by The Regina Co, Rahway, N.J., U.S.A.

TYPE-SETTING MACHINES
Canadian Linotype, Ltd., 68 Temperance Street, Toronto.
Miller & Richard, Toronto and Winnipeg.
Lanston Monotype Machine Co., Lumsden Bldg., Toronto.
The Linograph, Stephenson, Blake & Co., 60 Front St. W., Toronto.

TYPE-HIGH GAUGES
The Challenge Machinery Co., Grand Haven, Mich.

Say you saw it in PRINTER AND PUBLISHER

CLASSIFIED ADVERTISEMENT SECTION

TWO CENTS A WORD, including the "Printer and Publisher" box numbers; minimum charge is $1.00 per insertion, for 50 words or less, set in 6 pt. type. Each figure counts as a word. Display ads., or ads. set in border, are at the card rates.

NEWSPAPER FOR SALE

A newspaper is offered for sale in one of the most thriving towns in the Annapolis Valley, Nova Scotia. Only a moderate capital required. The business is in good condition, but the owner has good private reasons for selling. Apply to

O. K.
c/o **Printer and Publisher**
Toronto, Ont. (P S P)

FOR SALE

FOR SALE—GORDON PRESS, 7 x 11; GOOD condition. The Owen Sound Advertiser, Owen Sound, Ont. (P tf P)

MONOTYPE EQUIPMENT, CONSISTING of two casters and three keyboards, all in first-class condition and ready for immediate use. For full particulars apply to E. R. Whitrod, Montreal Star, Montreal, Que. (P 5 P)

FOR SALE—AT NOMINAL PRICE, RULING machine and binder's finishing tools. Sutherland Press, St. Thomas. (p5p)

OPPORTUNITIES ARE OFFERED EVERY MONTH ON THIS PAGE—WATCH THEM

BUSINESS CHANCES

FOR SALE — NEWSPAPER AND JOB printing plant at a bargain; a well equipped and established business in a thriving industrial Nova Scotia town will be disposed of at a right price; large advertising and job printing income; only newspaper in a large and prosperous community. Apply at once for particulars to Box 666, Printer and Publisher, Toronto, Ont. (ptfp)

NEWSPAPER AND JOB PRINTING PRESS office in divisional junction town of 800 population on C. N. Railway; one of the best centres in Southern Saskatchewan for live practical printer; comfortable cottage adjoining; also government telephone agency in same building will be transferred to the purchaser. Satisfactory reasons for selling. Apply to Box 667, Printer and Publisher. (P 4 P)

WANTED

WANTED — 8x12 or 10x15 JOB PRESS. Must be in good condition. Also ¾ or 1 H.P. motor. Apply Box 670, Printer and Publisher. (p4p)

WANTED—GOOD SECOND-HAND RULING machine. Apply Box 669, Printer and Publisher. (p5p)

WANTED TO PURCHASE — A DAILY newspaper in town or city, not less than six thousand population. Forward full particulars to D.M., c/o Printer and Publisher. (p4p)

SITUATIONS VACANT

PRINTER WANTED — AN ALL ROUND man, qualified compositor and pressman, must be serious, sober and pushing, one having outside connection preferred. If desirable up-to-date printing plant, in a city of 15,000 population, near Montreal, Canada. Good business can be done with the right man. References exchanged. Apply at Lachine Printing, 24 Twelfth Ave., Lachine, Que.

FOR SALE

1—10 x 15 Westman & Baker Press, power and foot fixtures complete.
1—8 x 12 C. & P., power and foot fixtures complete.
1—30-in. hand lever Oswego Cutter, 2 knives.
1 Hand and Foot Stitcher complete.
1—13 x 19 Colt Armory Press complete.
Above machines 100% first-class.

ROYAL MACHINE STOCKS

Presses and Bookbinding Machinery and Special Machinery.

738 ST. PAUL WEST, MONTREAL

SITUATIONS VACANT

LEARN THE LINOTYPE — WRITE FOR particulars. Canadian. Linotype, 68 Temperance St., Toronto.

THE MONOTYPE KEYBOARD OPERATOR has the easiest and best position in the composing room. There is always steady employment at good wages. Why not learn Monotype operating? Tuition is free in the Monotype schools in Philadelphia, New York, Chicago and Toronto, and it only takes a few weeks for a good compositor to learn the work. Apply to the nearest city. Lanston Monotype Machine Co. (p4p)

COLLECTIONS

SEND US YOUR LIST OF DELINQUENTS. We will turn Debit into Credit. Publishers' Protective Association, Toronto.

INDEX TO ADVERTISERS

FOR SALE

TYPGRAPHY

MACHINE and MAN

MERE Machine may replace the mere labor of a man. It cannot do anything more. It cannot do a noble work. That is left to the Instrument which does not displace a man, but only liberates his energy, his ingenuity and his creative spirit. To free the human worker from everything that hampers his achievement of the best that is in him, is the true economy, for nothing in industry is so truly productive as is the human factor. It is the liberated, thinking, unharrassed human factor who produces quality, for quality can be won only by human care and skill. Cost-saving is wholly interlocked with Quality-maintenance. A cost-saving that reduces quality is an exchange of a good dollar for a counterfeit.

CANADIAN LINOTYPE LIMITED
68 Temperance Street, Toronto

MERGENTHALER LINOTYPE COMPANY
NEW YORK, U. S. A.

SAN FRANCISCO   CHICAGO   NEW ORLEANS
646 Sacramento Street   1100 So. Wabash Avenue   549 Baronne Street

This Advertisement, Including Border Ornaments, is Composed Entirely of LINOTYPE Material with the Exception of the Initial

RINTER &
UBLISHER

IN THIS ISSUE

The Building of a Type
Page

Organizing Toronto on
Typothetae Lines

Annual Meeting of the
C.P.A.

Be Careful of the Flat
Rate Price

MACLEAN PUBLISHING CO. LIMITED
TO ⊤ MONTREAL ⊤ WINNIPEG

PRINTER AND PUBLISHER, May, 1920. Vol. 29, No. 5. Published monthly at 143-153 University Ave., Toronto, by the MacLean Publishing Co., Ltd. Yearly subscription price, $2.00. Entered as second-class matter at the Post Office Department at Ottawa, Canada, also entered as second-class matter July 1, 1912, at the Post Office at Buffalo, N.Y., U.S.A., under Act of March 3rd, 1879.

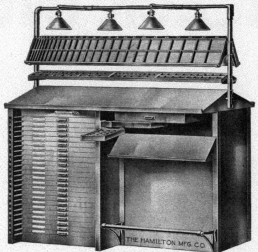

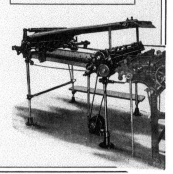

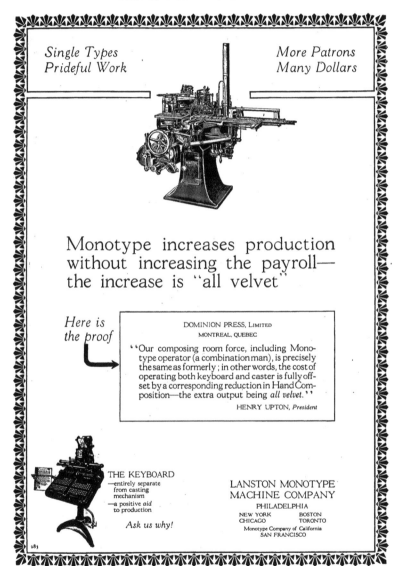

Single Types
Prideful Work

More Patrons
Many Dollars

Monotype increases production without increasing the payroll— the increase is "all velvet"

Here is the proof

DOMINION PRESS, Limited
MONTREAL, QUEBEC

"Our composing room force, including Monotype operator (a combination man), is precisely the same as formerly ; in other words, the cost of operating both keyboard and caster is fully offset by a corresponding reduction in Hand Composition—the extra output being *all velvet*.' "

HENRY UPTON, *President*

THE KEYBOARD
—entirely separate from casting mechanism
—a positive *aid* to production

Ask us why!

LANSTON MONOTYPE
MACHINE COMPANY
PHILADELPHIA
NEW YORK   BOSTON
CHICAGO   TORONTO
Monotype Company of California
SAN FRANCISCO

283

This advertisement set in Monotype Series No. 38, Border No. 251, and Monotype Rule

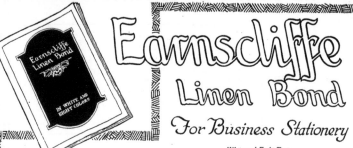

The Miehle

Pledges of Friendship

12,000 MIEHLES now in use, all purchased in about thirty years, proclaim the realization of the desire of printers generally for a durable, speedy, convenient press, capable of producing the finest grade of work.

The recognition of this fact, as well as the generous appreciation and co-operation of printers everywhere, has made this widespread distribution possible, and as Serial No. 12,000 leaves our factory, we pause to acknowledge our gratitude to all of our customers—every one of whom we feel to be a friend.

MIEHLE PRINTING PRESS & MFG. CO.

Fourteenth and Robey Streets, Chicago

Distributors for Canada

TORONTO TYPE FOUNDRY CO., LIMITED

TORONTO   MONTREAL   WINNIPEG   REGINA

YOU NEVER HEARD OF A MIEHLE BEING SCRAPPED

The Brown Folder

Most Successful Machine of its Kind

The Brown Folder has come to the front because it is simple and sturdy in construction and gives the greatest all-round satisfaction. Adapted to a great variety of work. WRITE FOR FULL DETAILS.

For Sale by

H. J. LOGAN

114 Adelaide Street West, TORONTO

Sole Agent
BROWN FOLDING MACHINE CO., ERIE, PA.

Sole Agent
LATHAM MACHINERY CO., CHICAGO

LATHAM

MONITOR Multiplex

PUNCHING MACHINE

A Modern Machine for Modern Conditions

Conditions of to-day are making it plain that old methods of production won't do. Modern requirements require modern machines—appliances that save labor and produce work rapidly.

The Latham MONITOR Multiplex has won an enviable reputation for efficiency and economy. Heavy, rigid, simple, fast and built to last.

No Tools Required for Locking Punch Head in Position.

Sold in Canada by

H. J. LOGAN 114 ADELAIDE STREET WEST TORONTO

LATHAM MACHINERY COMPANY

NEW YORK   CHICAGO   BOSTON

When You Know What These Men Know About REDUCOL You Too Will Use It—Regularly. Read What They Say:

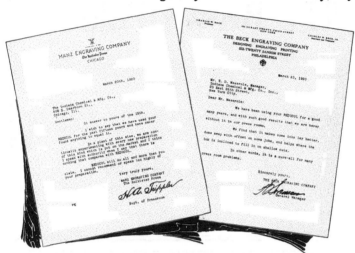

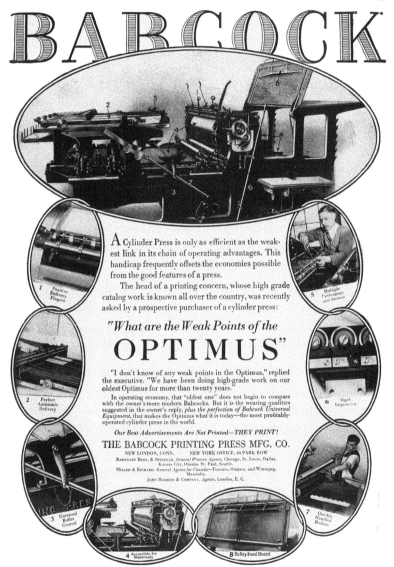

A Cylinder Press is only as efficient as the weakest link in its chain of operating advantages. This handicap frequently offsets the economies possible from the good features of a press.

The head of a printing concern, whose high grade catalog work is known all over the country, was recently asked by a prospective purchaser of a cylinder press:

"What are the Weak Points of the OPTIMUS"

"I don't know of any weak points in the Optimus," replied the executive. "We have been doing high-grade work on our oldest Optimus for more than twenty years."

In operating economy, that "oldest one" does not begin to compare with the owner's more modern Babcocks. But it is the wearing qualities suggested in the owner's reply, *plus the perfection of Babcock Universal Equipment*, that makes the Optimus what it is today—the most profitably-operated cylinder press in the world.

Our Best Advertisements Are Not Printed—THEY PRINT!

THE BABCOCK PRINTING PRESS MFG. CO.
NEW LONDON, CONN.   NEW YORK OFFICE, 38 PARK ROW
BARNHART BROS. & SPINDLER. *General Western Agents*, Chicago, St. Louis, Dallas,
Kansas City, Omaha, St. Paul, Seattle.
MILLER & RICHARD. *General Agents for Canada*—Toronto, Ontario, and Winnipeg,
Manitoba.
JOHN HADDON & COMPANY. *Agents*, London, E. C.

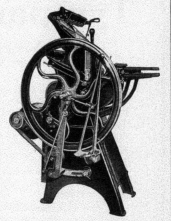

One Way of Cutting Costs These HCL Days

(Alternating Current Only)

Consume power only in proportion to the **speed** at which they are operated.

Half maximum press speed means a 50% cut in current consumed.

Ordinary A C Motors consume maximum current at **all** speeds; speed reduction being accomplished by interposing **resistance** which converts power to heat.

What's more, Kimble Motors offer such perfect and easy **control of speeds**, that the feeder increases speed as he "warms up" to his work. This means more output and less spoilage.

Job Press Motors
Cylinder Press Motors

also motors for monotypes, stitchers, folders, cutters and other equipment.

SEND FOR OUR CATALOGUE

KIMBLE ELECTRIC CO.

CHICAGO, ILL.

GREAT WEST ELECTRIC CO., LTD., 57 Albert Street, Winnipeg, Man., for all points west of Port Arthur and Fort William.

MASCO COMPANY, LTD., 87 Queen St. East, Toronto, Canada, for all points east of Port Arthur and Fort William.

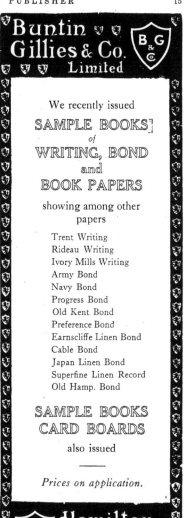

Buntin Gillies & Co. Limited

We recently issued

SAMPLE BOOKS
of
WRITING, BOND
and
BOOK PAPERS

showing among other papers

Trent Writing
Rideau Writing
Ivory Mills Writing
Army Bond
Navy Bond
Progress Bond
Old Kent Bond
Preference Bond
Earnscliffe Linen Bond
Cable Bond
Japan Linen Bond
Superfine Linen Record
Old Hamp. Bond

SAMPLE BOOKS
CARD BOARDS

also issued

Prices on application.

Hamilton
and
Montreal.

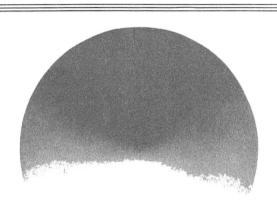

PERSIAN ORANGE No. 10388

"THE ONLY INK HOUSE IN THE WORLD"
that manufactures all the materials entering into its Lithographic and Letter-Press Inks and with its large staff of
expert chemists and ink makers offers the printing trade

THE BEST ON EARTH

Every Ingredient

Acids   Dry Colors
Chemicals   Intermediates
Aniline Dyes, Varnishes, etc.
Manufactured in Our Own Factories

The Ault & Wiborg Company
of Canada, Limited
MONTREAL   TORONTO   WINNIPEG

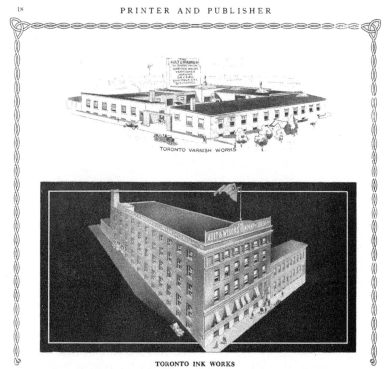

TORONTO VARNISH WORKS

TORONTO INK WORKS

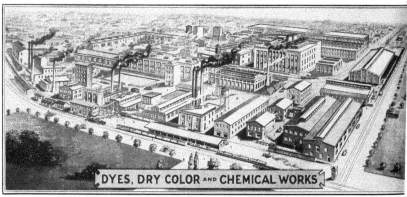

DYES, DRY COLOR AND CHEMICAL WORKS

Perfection Brown No. 10205

A Frank Talk on Buying Type Metals

"Blind Buyers" is a term which we believe it is permissible to use, to emphasize the lack of insight of some buyers when purchasing Type Metals. The buyer is not expected to be a Metal expert, and for this reason he will not know the technical facts in regard to Type Metals. We are, therefore, pointing out a few fundamental facts which will open his eyes to the economy of buying properly made Type Metals, and we believe he will be glad to secure this information.

SCRAP or virgin metals—that is the question. Whether to buy the cheap-priced, so-called type metals—mixed from dross metal and scrap; or

To buy an alloy, *made from prime virgin metals*, at a fraction more per pound, which has honesty in back of it—in the very fact that it *is* what it purports to be.

This is the manner in which a buyer *should* argue with himself. However, few consider what is put into a type metal. They usually figure that "metal is metal," and to them the only distinction is that of price per pound.

Most buyers know that metal houses are invariably anxious to buy their dross—because it enables them to turn out a product at about 75% the cost of new metals; you will agree this allows a very nice profit.

We offer you a 100% product of full efficiency—without question the only virgin type metal made in Canada—which is uniformly the same in each and every batch.

You may believe you are getting satisfactory results. Remember that there are degrees of satisfaction and degrees of economy. We offer the highest degree of both—on a frank and open basis. You owe it to yourself to compare our alloys with those you are using.

Less Dross per Melt Means Lower Cost per Year

A trial case will convince you that you can economise best by using

STANLEY PROCESS
LINOTYPE — MONOTYPE — INTERTYPE — STEREOTYPE — CASTERTYPE

TYPE METALS
VIRGIN METALS ALLOYED UNDER A SCIENTIFIC PROCESS
INSURING NON-SEPARATION AND LONGER
SERVICE WITH LESS WASTE

BRITISH SMELTING & REFINING Co. Limited.
Drummond Building 〜 Montreal.

PRINTER AND PUBLISHER
Devoted to the Interests of the Printers and Publishers of Canada

The Building of a Good Type Page
"Order is Nature's First Law"
By Edward D. Berry

I F more printed matter on the subject of composition were devoted to the fundamentals of building a type page and less to "higher education," better results would be achieved. Most printers who are known as being capable and artistic know little of the underlying and inviolable rules. Their quickness of perception has trained the eye to see, but opportunity has not been offered for analytical reasoning.

Columns of instruction in the trade papers are devoted to discovering the origin of type faces and tracing their development; article after article is devoted to the laws of balance, and tracing their origin; page after page is devoted to comparisons of poor jobs with good ones, pointing out the good and bad points and suggesting how poor jobs may be improved. All of which is of great value if the printer has already mastered the laws of composition.

Only occasionally have I found any schooling in the basic elements of correct composition —geometrical figures and their relation to each other; and color. And even in some of those cases the presentation is not elementary. Elementary knowledge is necessary to all printers, whether they are beginners or have acquired a certain degree of proficiency.

There are just two ways for a beginner to learn to set type—by imitation, that is, by observing the methods and results achieved by more or less proficient workmen; and by discovering and applying the science of correct composition. That the latter method is the better is obvious.

The resetting of jobs to show errors in composition is certainly commendable and highly educational, but if it is not illustrative of precepts that are common knowledge or that had been previously expounded in the same medium of instruction, a large part of its value is lost; the compositor is again in the imitative class instead of the scientific.

Correctness in composition contemplates not so much an originality of concept as a perfect, usable knowledge of inviolable rules. Good composition results from the ingenuity of making type faces conform to the rules of art. The nearer these rules are adhered to the better the picture and the more effective the printing. Originality lies almost entirely in the treatment of the whole.

The same laws apply to a text page and a display page, but they are more evident in the

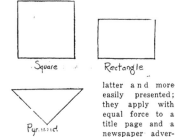

latter a n d more easily presented; they apply with equal force to a title page and a newspaper advertisement. The main difference between these two is in boldness of design.

There are many geometrical figures of possible use in composition, but three are used most frequently: the square, the rectangle and the pyramid. These are forms; the other element is color.

The Selection of the Border

By color is not meant, in this instance, the varying hues and shades of the prism, but weight or depth of tone. After these shapes of type-sections are arranged in pleasing and correct proportion on the layout, the picture is ready to be painted by the distribution of tones of different weights throughout the page. The central "figure" in the picture should be a concentration of mass-tones proportionately heavier than any other portion of the page—selected according to importance of its text; the other figures should have decreasing weight of tone according to importance and so placed in the area as to present perfect balance. If a border is used it should be slightly heavier than the average tone of the page; one of bold design

certainly would require a heavier border than one of delicate content. If border is too heavy, it not only offends the eye by lack of unity, but overshadows the important display lines.

An illustration may be found in picture frames. A six-inch frame around a small canvas, or a moderately sized one of delicate tints and in which there are no heavy masses, would obviously be out of place; a picture with heavy masses and bold design requires a heavy frame to "hold it together."

The correct and most pleasing shape of a page is a parallelogram of approximately 5 in. x 8 in.; if there is a single panel or section of type in the page its dimensions should be as near as practicable to the proportion of the page itself. If there are several sections of type matter, the general contour of all of them should bear the same proportion. For instance: on a page 5 in. x 8 in., a single panel, or section of type, 4 in. wide by 2 in. deep, would be out of proportion; if there is another panel in the lower part of the page and the outline of the two taken together conforms to the shape of the page, then proportion is correct. In other words, the general outline of all shapes within an oblong should be in direct proportion to the oblong itself. (See Figs. 1 and 2).

By the same reasoning, extended type is unsuitable to a narrow page, and vice versa.

To a page which is entirely filled with composition, such as a page advertisement, other forms may be added in the blank space without disturbing the general proportion, which may be accentuated by increasing the depth of tones in the central oblong. (See Fig. 6). Any section of a page which apparently separates itself from contiguous parts of the page are here considered separate forms.

If a page were divided into three parts by three equal forms, it would appear flat and uninteresting—geometrically, but not optically, correct or pleasing. If the forms are of varied sizes, the page is still geometrically correct and far more pleasing. (See Figs. 3 and 4).

Getting the Proper Balance

The distribution of tones is equally as important as correct proportion and very closely allied to it. In setting a job containing one line of type of black face, or heavy mass, of far greater prominence than any other in the page, it should be placed in the optical centre of the whole, or above it, depending upon the weight of other parts of the page. If there are two important figures, one of slightly more importance than the other, they are placed at distances from the optical centre, determined entirely by their

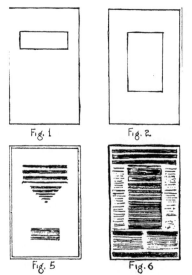

Fig. 1   Fig. 2

Fig. 5   Fig. 6

Figure 1 is out of proportion; occasionally on a title page with only two lines of type it is difficult to treat it otherwise; on a page of this kind, however, it is better to endure this lack of proportion than to insert an ornament that has neither proper shape, correct tone, nor suitability of character.

Figure 2—Notice how much deeper and more pleasing is this than Figure 1.

Figure 5 is Figure 1 reset in good balance, with the addition of other matter.

Figure 6 is Figure 2 reset with the addition of other sections to make it a solid page of composition, such as appears in newspaper advertisements; notice that the panel of Figure 2 is preserved in the heavier tones in Figure 6, thus preserving the proportion.

"weight." If they are very nearly of the same weight they are nearly equi-distant from the centre. If one is much heavier than the other it is placed close to the centre and the other enough farther away as to balance perfectly.

This may be illustrated by a scales for weighing heavy articles. The article is balanced on the scales by moving the balancing weight farther away from the fulcrum which is attached to the timber supporting the scales. The distance it must be moved along the bar to secure balance is of course determined by the weight of the article, and vice versa. Imagine the optical centre of the page to be the fulcrum of the scales and place all tones in a page so that if they really had weight there would be a perfect balance on the centre. Of course there can be no rules determining whether or not there is balance; but the eye rapidly acquires facility in this regard if aided by a knowledge of the science underlying it. For instance, a section of solid 8 point may have more weight than a line of 36 point, especially if the 8 point is surrounded by matter of light tone and there is a stronger tone surrounding the 36 point line.

A single spot of solid color has a weight all out of proportion to the area covered, in a page made up of lighter tones. It is for this reason that great care should be had in selecting an initial or ornament for a page. An initial which is heavier than the average tone of the text matter is not only in poor taste, but it throws the page out of balance. There are ways of correcting this error in balance—moving the section of type matter off the centre of the page, inserting an ornament in an opposite direction, etc.—but the error in unity cannot be corrected. How great the disparity of tone is determines whether the use of the initial is allowable. Of course, few shops have such an assortment of initials that just the proper one can be used at all times—except a letter of a large size of the same type; but if there is too great a difference of tone, it is better to omit it entirely. It is very easy to overdo ornamentation; as a general rule, simplicity is the best ornament.

The optical centre of a page is in the exact centre horizontally; vertically, it is above centre, about in proportion of 3 to 5.

It is above the real centre because the eye cannot see two halves of a page in exact proportion, the top half appearing larger; the eye naturally comes to rest at this point. If it is drawn away by intensive objects to another point, that point must be balanced on the centre so that there may be unity in the whole.

If there are several sections on a page, position is determined by the combined weight of the sections on the several sides of the centre; the relative position of each is determined by its weight in comparison to the weight of the other sections in its part of the page.

It is most important that compositors exercise the imagination that they may visualize the completed job or advertisement before beginning the actual work. There is no faculty more responsive to training than the imagination and the best way to exercise it, in this regard, is to make a sketch, no matter how crude, of each job; in a short time that will be unnecessary.

But in sketching or visualizing, it is necessary to keep always in mind "these few precepts" of balance and form.

Fig. 3   Fig. 4

Fig. 7.   Fig. 8

Figures 3 and 4—Figure 4 not only has more depth than Figure 3, but is more pleasing to the eye; it also gives better opportunity for display and balance, for the heavier tones are logically at the beginning and at the end of both pages, the heavier at the top.

Figure 7—Notice how the three heavy lines in the centre of the ad. stand out on account of the lighter tones surrounding them; the cut in the lower middle of the left side is balanced by the two heavy signature lines on the right.

In Figure 8, the price column on the left is balanced by the heavy panel on the right, which is a cut or may be a panel of heavy black type.

These sketches are made merely to show principles; it is seldom that copy is received which can be arranged just as desired, but if the cardinal principles are kept in mind in laying it out and selecting type for the different parts of it, much better ads. will result.

Organizing Toronto on Typothetae Lines
Jos. Borden, General Secretary, Speaks About the Work

"YOU know how it is in a good many cases. I have heard a lot about it since I came into this room. A man comes into your shop and asks how much a certain job will cost. You grab for the first old envelope you can reach, and put down a few figures. Then you look your customer in the eye, and if he is looking at you pretty hard you quit and reckon you've put down enough figures. The customer knows you are lying and you know it yourself."

In these words Mr. Joseph E. Borden, general secretary of the United Typothetae of America, got in on the ground floor at a mass meeting of the printers and bookbinders of Toronto. The meeting took place at the King Edward Hotel on May 4, and it was undoubtedly the largest and most representative gathering of the employing printers and their executives that has ever been brought together in this city. The banquet room, where the meeting was held, had a real "cost-finding" atmosphere, the walls being covered with reports of surveys that had been made in all corners of United States, and these were carefully scrutinized by many in attendance before the address of the evening was given, so that when Mr. Borden came to refer to them, many in the audience were able to follow very closely the drift of his reference to these various cities. Accompanying Mr. Borden were his son Edward and Mr. I. R. Knowlton, both of whom will be engaged for some time in Toronto making a survey of the printing industry.

Mr. Q. B. Henderson, president of the Master Printers' Association, was chairman of the evening. "When Mr. Borden was here some three months ago," he remarked, "he told him that he was addressing the largest meeting of employing printers ever held in Toronto, but to-night we can tell him it is the largest ever held in Canada. This is in reality a mass meeting under the auspices of the Master Printers' Association. Mr. Borden, I feel, has done more for the printing industry in America than any other individual, and his best qualification for speaking on the subject is that he began business with $300 and in 25 years was able to retire in comfort."

Mr. Borden, on rising to speak, was given a splendid reception. When he left his own business the United Typothetae had asked him to help them with some special work. That was four years ago, and the special work was still going on. "This work is a joy to me," began Mr. Borden, "because the whole industrial fabric is changing, and the printing industry must lead."

Mr. Borden made ready use of a lot of data kept on cards for his address, and laughingly referring to these remarked, "After giving an address on the question of cost-finding one Omaha printer stated: 'Anybody could make a speech if he had a pinochle deck like Joe Borden.'"

The Purpose of the U.T.A.

The U.T.A., now 34 years old, is simply an organization of 5,000 printers who are devoting a great deal of their time to make business conditions better. "It is not," asserted Mr. Borden, "a massive octopus sucking the life blood out of the general public. Its scope is, and has been for a long time, to take in the whole of North America, Canada as well as United States, and for that

This design for a Canadian Division comes from Vancouver

reason I want you up here to refer to it as 'our' Association. There is one member in Mexico, and there might be more were it not for the fact that it is not quite safe for an organizer to work in that country now. The U.T.A. is only one of four hundred other organizations doing similar work for the various industries on this continent. We are working shoulder to shoulder with all the others, and they are more and more looking to us for leadership in this movement. More than one hundred of these organizations have put in cost-finding systems along the same lines that we employ. We want you to feel that the U.T.A. belongs to you—that it is a big democratic institution."

Mr. Borden referred to the cost-finding conference at Philadelphia some years ago. The reports gathered at that time showed that competition was unfair, and that printers had high prices and low ones, but they also found that a definite, certain cost-finding system could be brought into operation by all following the same methods in their work. The United Typothetae for 12 years have pushed that work, and thousands are using it now, and they are all making money out of it. There are still too many printers afraid of having their case analyzed, they are afraid of the true costs, they are afraid they won't be able to cut and get the job away from the other fellow. But when they study conditions, and when they come to realize that it is their own pocket that is being hurt by a cut, they get past that stage and rise to a position where they can do justice to themselves, their business and their families.

A Financially Sound Family

The U.T.A. issue what is termed as a composite report, each year, covering a very wide range of offices, in which the payrolls amount to $30,000,000 per annum. These offices are all checked by Dun's or Bradstreets. "It might interest you," continued Mr. Borden, "to know the class of men who are contributing the information that is given out in these yearly composite reports. Eighty-four per cent. of them are classed as A1; fourteen and one-third are in class 2, and one and two-thirds per cent. in class 3, while there is not one in class four or five. These men are in good, sound financial condition, and many of them owe it to the fact that they put in the Standard Cost-Finding System and stayed with it. The Federal Trade Commission passed on this system. It was submitted to 16 of their accountants, and they said, after a careful examination, that it was a sound and proper basis on which to work. This enables us to issue a Standard Price List of every conceivable article that can pass through your printing plant. It is based on production figures, and you can sell on it safely and with the certain knowledge that you are charging your customer only a fair amount above the actual cost of your product.

"Now then," continued Mr. Borden, "there is something that we do not pay enough attention to. There is no industry in the world that requires more executive skill, or a greater knowledge of costs than the printing industry, and there is none in which there are a greater number of pitfalls into which it is so easy to fall. So, to our cost charge must be added a service charge for brains,

JOSEPH BORDEN

experience and ability. Perhaps we can't collect for this like the man who opened the vault door in the bank. He submitted a bill for $100, and the manager of the bank insisted on it being itemized. (There was a splendid laugh when Mr.. Borden likened this to the demands made for itemized statements from the printer.) So the mechanic sent in a bill for $5 for opening the vault and $95 for knowing how. It is time the printers valued their 'knowing how' at something."

The Same Thing the Same Way

Mr. Borden then proceeded with an explanation of the Three-Year plan. Four years ago in Chicago conditions in the printing industry were bad, disastrous in fact. Why? Because the great majority of the firms had no real definite knowledge of their business. They thought they knew, but they didn't. The thing there, as here, was to find a cure and it could be found, and had been found, in standardization and uniformity. "For instance," said the speaker, "Mr. Rose here and Mr. Southam may have a very good system in their plants, but if it is not uniform we are not going to get the results we want. And then if the offices here were working on the same plans, they would be different to Montreal, Ottawa, Vancouver or Winnipeg. The one sure way is to find the right way and stay with it. Let us all do the same thing in the same way. It has taken us some time to get the present campaign under way, and it has taken some money too. Some time ago we figured that we would need $250,000, and it took us two years to get it. Conditions in the printing industry have been chaotic because we did not have a good foundation, because we did not dig down deep enough. We have got to build from the foundation up, stone by stone, one by one, and the cap-stone will be the one we call profit. The trouble with many of us has been that we grab that cap-stone, and try to bolster it up on a wobbly foundation, but it won't stay, and it never will stay until it has the proper structure below it."

"The whole plan is practicable and can be worked," declared Mr. Borden; "it is not simply an ideal that we have evolved. It is, as one writer has so well put it, 'Ideals entertained are without value unless expressed in practice.' The printers who were pessimistic in the first place know now that our plan is workable and possible and real, and they know this because they are using it. Our first step is to establish districts, and in each of these districts the same kind of work will be carried on. Some years ago I had a vision of printers all the way from Vancouver to Jacksonville, Florida, doing things the same way, and it looks as though it would come true—in fact it has come true. Each district must have a permanent man to keep the work going. We are going to start our survey and start it at once. We will show your investment, your mechanical payroll, your sales, and you will be able to go before the public or before your Legislature if necessary, and show where you stand in the community and the country. We will endeavor to do away with that condition that makes it possible for one man to say of business, 'Oh—it's bad,' while the next one says, 'It's fine.' There will be the master chart and the segregated classes."

Profits that Had Been Missed

Mr. Borden explained some of the things that had been found in the analysis of 74 cities. The payroll was $63,000,000, the overhead $66,000,000, and the stock cost, etc., $83,000,000, or a total of $212,000,000. The selling price of the work had been $219,000,000, or 3½ per cent. profit. Ninety per cent. of the shops made no profit at all. The ten per cent. who did knew their business. Add 25 per cent. to the cost of production and the selling price would have been $53,000,000, in other words they sold for $43,000,000 too little.

The Three-Year plan is being asked for in many places. Vancouver, according to information which Mr. Borden received, was now 100 per cent. organized, and they are ready to start on the standard programme. That means that every plant shall put in the Standard Cost-Finding System, and absolutely and without fail maintain it for three years. They can then know, month after month, where they are at, what they are doing, and they can make money at it.

"After the survey of a city or district has been made, come the educational courses. The drawback to this is that we have

not men enough to take up this work. The Standard Cost-Finding Course is to teach men to become expert cost clerks. We would place 2,000 of them right now if we had the trained men, so great is the demand. These courses are not the whims of crank printers. They are practicable, so much so that they are used in Harvard, in the Technical School at Pittsburgh, in our own U.T.A. school—in fact it will be taught all over the North American continent.

'How are we going to keep this thing up? It is up to you to run your own business," stated Mr. Borden in answer to his own question. "You need one or more cost supervisors to see that this end of the work is kept up. The Standard Accounting Course comes in next. There are too many people in the business who still persist in keeping their books on a spindle. I know of one man who, when a job is finished, puts the envelope in the left hand drawer of his desk, and when it is paid for he changes it over to the right hand drawer, so he always knows just how he stands." (Laughter.)

Estimating and Salesmanship

The speaker then came to the old question of estimating. "Since I have come into this room I have heard the old story about this and that job going to some other printer. You are all the same; it makes no difference where you happen to be located. You know how it is in a good many cases. A man comes into your shop and asks you how much a certain job will cost. You grab for the first old envelope you can reach, and put down a few figures. Then you look your customer in the eye, and if he is looking pretty hard you quit and reckon you've put down enough figures. The customer knows you are lying and you know it yourself. The Standard Estimating Course for printers teaches you how to estimate alike. I am not afraid to say that out of our 3,000 graduates there would not be a difference of five per cent. in their figures on a piece of work.

"How about salesmanship? In too many cases, it is simply peddling a price. We should train our men to sell jobs at a profit over our costs and we should remember that the salesman of printing owes a duty to the public. The buyer of printing does not always know what he needs. He may think he does, but it should be part of our business to act as his adviser. A friend of mine in San Francisco, Mr. Shaddock, a dealer in type and supplies, wanted some printing done to move stock that had been in his warehouse long enough. So he called in a printer. The printer came in and asked what kind of a job he wanted. The buyer replied that he didn't know, and the printer went off with the remark that he would get him up something. He did, and here it is. (Mr. Borden here held up a very ordinary looking four-page folder set solid and with no cuts or display to speak of.) That printing was wasted. It brought no results. Mr. Shaddock was certain that there would be a demand for his goods, and he called in another printer, who had taken the course in Salesmanship. He discussed the proposition with Mr. Shaddock, and found out what he wanted to do with his circulars. He at once made the suggestion that it would be better to use an enamel stock and a few good half-tones to illustrate the stuff, to which the customer agreed. Then he brought up the question of special envelopes. 'Let us get you something so you can ship these out flat. They will look much better than being doubled in a small envelope,' and that was quite satisfactory too. Engravings were considered quite all right. The salesman's next move was to suggest that he should use a card in order to trace the results he might get from the folder, and this card would need an envelope. All right. The customer was out to sell his goods, and he wanted some real service. 'Any letters from satisfied customers who have used any of these lines?' Certainly there were. Well, then, these could be made up into a very nice little insert to go with the circular. 'Now, look,' concluded the salesman, 'there is a great deal of this kind of material that is thrown into the waste paper basket before it is ever opened. How would it be if we got out a letter a week or so before mailing the circular telling the prospect to be on the lookout for this material, as it will certainly be to his interest?' This seemed to fit in very nicely.

"So," remarked Mr. Borden, "that salesman, instead of taking away an order for the circulars, as the first printer had done, secured eight different orders, and he gave real service to Mr. Shaddock that produced results.

The U.T.A. has no controversy with the advertising agency, but we do hold that the printer is, or should be, the proper man to give advice in matters of printing and publicity, and for that reason we have the Standard Advertising Course, but only for those who have taken the others. Printers are not good advertisers of their own business. They believe others should advertise, but do you know that on the whole printers spend only one-tenth of one per cent. of their turnover, while they want others to spend from two to three per cent.? The advertising bureau will give the printer assistance in advertising his own business. Then there is the House Organ campaign for the benefit of customers, and individual and collective newspaper advertising. In Minneapolis they use a splendid three-column ad each week, one that stands right out and hits the reader in the eye. It carries the names of all the printers interested in the work. It is time we came out of our shell. We should make use of our trade journals to sell our product."

Mr. Borden spent considerable time in dealing with the proper training of the apprentice, and of the importance of getting the young printer to have a proper respect for the dignity of his calling. "Many of the men now at the trade have never had a chance to be properly trained. The educational course for the apprentice, given by the U.T.A., aims to supply an all-round training. There are two lessons devoted entirely to creating a feeling of pride in his calling, respect for his fellows, and for his place of employment. The U.T.A. is also connected with the National Industrial Conference Board, members of which have in their respective plants eight million employees. The whole idea of this association is to make better citizens and to fight the rebel and the Bolshevik element whenever it shows its head." Reference was also made in passing to the recent outlaw strike in New York. "I am afraid that we hardly realize what we are up against in the printing industry unless we pay more attention to the training of apprentices. Unless we do much more there will not, at the end of 34 years, be a printer left at the trade."

The Business Administration course is for the scientific and sane management of your plant.

Put In If You Would Take Out

In all these things it has been our experience that the little fellow benefits in proportion with the big one. Does it pay? The first survey in Richmond a year ago showed a profit of 3½ per cent., and in the first year after that they gained $360,000, and are now showing 13½ per cent. In St. Louis the first survey showed that there had been two million dollars on the year's business that the printers should have had. The other records are before you to-night and they are authentic and conservative.

How is all this work to be financed? Every member pays a lump sum based on his payroll, and this is sufficient to take

care of the budget which has previously been figured out. There are no extras. The small plant with the minimum outlay gets the same service and benefit as the larger plants. Some of the lower ones, based on the experience in other cities, would be from $8.00 to $15.00 per month. Now, if a man cannot get 35 cents' worth of benefit out of this plan for every working day, he ought to quit. Every printer will make a profit, and when all are making a profit there will be no disturbers. Toronto is a union town. The U.T.A. takes no sides for or against the union, but I want to bring home to the men here to-night that you are paying several times more through International dues than it would cost you to run the best business organization on the North American continent. A firm going into the U.T.A. signs a definite, legal binding document.

"A year or so back I went into Salt Lake City on the way south. The first printer I met I asked him how business was, and No. I said it was rotten. He volunteered the information that the printers in city were a lot of skunks and cut-throats. Well, I called on the whole 28 in that place, and every one told me the same thing. So I went to work and asked them all for confidential data on their business, and it did not take long to show them that there was $28,000 dead loss in the last year. Then the question of organization came up, and they said at once that they wouldn't go into any association that would be made up of the hyenas in the printing business in Salt Lake City. I went to a lawyer and he produced an agreement that would be binding on them all. They all came in and the first year they played the game fair and together and gained $160,000. It ties every man up so that he's got to do it. He may kick and try to get out, but he can't. The result is that they all hang together instead of separately.

"We want to do the same thing in Montreal, Ottawa, Toronto, and right through. The locals swipe our trained men in almost every case when we send them out to make surveys, but we are glad to see them going, and we have simply to keep on throwing new men into the hopper. The printers of the United States in the last 15 months have pledged $840,000 for this work, or at the rate of $2,500,000 for the three-year term. Three hundred men met in Chicago just recently and raised their budget from $35,000 to $70,000; Portland, Spokane, and Oregon have increased by fifty per cent. Milwaukee was a mess at the start, and showed a real loss. We found there it would cost $18,000 to carry on the work. We got $22,000, and now they are raising it to $30,000 in order to intensify the efforts there."

Many Other U.T.A. Efforts

The Industrial Relations work of the U.T.A. was gone into at some length by Mr. Borden, reference being made especially to the situation in New York a few months ago when the pressmen pulled out from the recognized body, and where the members of the I. T. U., because they could not strike, took a "holiday." The Bureau tries by all means to bring the

Map of N. America Showing U.T.A. Districts

truth to both sides. "I would advise you strongly to use this service," stated Mr. Borden; "it will help you to avoid many pitfalls, and it will also come in handy when a local union gets you by the throat and makes you dance."

"Now, what are we going to do about it?" remarked the speaker in conclusion. "Unless we all buckle down and each one does his part we will never get any place. Come out into the open and tell the public what you are doing. Make it perfectly plain that our idea is to get a fair profit over and above the cost of every piece of work that goes out of the shop. You have nothing to conceal. Put your best efforts into this business, and the best will come back to you. It may require a little shifting of the mental gears. Here is what we want, and I am using a phrase that was coined by one of our men, 'Interlocking comradeship.' I have heard, and you will hear some person say, 'What do I get out of this?' You get out nothing unless you put in something. Don't you see that the man who is unwilling to put his energy and his time into this is in a position where he cannot receive any benefit from it? I should hold no enmity or ill-will in this business toward any of my fellows that I am not willing to forget on the display of a like spirit on his part. Apply the Golden Rule to this business, and you will find that nine-tenths of the misdeeds of others that you have heard about never took place, and you will discover also that ninety-nine per cent. of your own troubles never existed."

At the conclusion of his address Mr. Borden was given a splendid round of applause, and the thanks of the gathering was expressed by Messrs. George Brigden and Atwell Fleming, Sr.

Then Came the Questions

Mr. I. R. Knowlton, who came with Mr. Borden, stated that he believed it would take six weeks to get the required information from Toronto shops. He made it clear that all the information given would be regarded as strictly confidential.

On an invitation to ask questions, Mr. Brigden put the following to Mr. Borden: "How is it that people managed to live in the cities where the survey showed that they were running at a loss? How did the people of Milwaukee live and lose at the same time?"

Mr. Borden: "At the outset that may look like a hard question, but it is simple. One office in Chicago had a big tombstone painted on the wall, and on it were posted a lot of bills and papers. A customer came in there and asked for a figure on a job, which was given at $500, to which the customer replies that he can get it down the street for $300. Whereupon the proprietor asks the customer to sit down where he can see the tombstone effect. He enquires what all the bills are pasted up there, and receives the answer that they are sheriff's announcements of forced sales of printing offices. (Laughter.) Some of the concerns which seem to exist are growing less and less every day. You must remember that there is a big mortality rate in the printing business, and no doubt there are numerous examples in Toronto. In Baltimore we found that 54 had gone out in two years. You have, I suppose, about 250 shops in Toronto, and I dare say in that there will not be over 25 that have in operation a good cost-finding system. In our own business we always made some money. The Standard Cost-Finding System showed us where we were losing, and it also saved any customer from being charged too much."

Mr. Atwell Fleming wanted to know more about the survey, as to what information would be required, and if it would be possible to have it prepared beforehand. He was willing to give evidence to the fact that there were numerous changes in Toronto. "Mr. A. T. Hunter sent a car to our place," said Mr. Fleming, "to get some work done. We did the work and the cut was taken away. Then the war came and Mr. Hunter went overseas. When he came back he wanted to get that cut again and came to us for it. We looked up our records and told him where we had sent it and when. He traced it and found that the office that we had sent it to had changed hands four times while Mr. Hunter was away."

Further explanation was given as to what information was required in the survey. It will take in the number of employees, the presses, kind, feeders, equipment, total investment in machinery and fixtures, payroll of the shop, but not of the office. Overhead could be figured in many ways. It was also stated

that offices should not be afraid when the question was asked as to what salary the "boss" took out of the business. In some cases, it was stated these were ridiculously low. 'If a man's own business can't pay as much as someone else can pay him, it's time he got out," was the answer to this last condition.

Payroll and Overhead Charge

In answer to Mr. Bell of Business Systems, information was brought out about the relation of overhead to mechanical payroll. It is possible to secure this information even in shops making surveys that the records of 25 or 30 shops in a city where records are kept will apply to all the places. It is a mistaken idea to imagine that the large shop had the large overhead. It has been proven time and time that the small shop needed as much return to produce the same work as the large place. In the small office a man's time was broken attending to many things, while in the larger place there was constant pressure on production. In this connection the following figures were taken from the charts on the wall showing the relation of mechanical payroll to overhead. Taking the payroll as 100 per cent. the figures are:

U. S. (U.T.A.).....	126%
Detroit, Mich.......	117%
Cincinnati, Ohio...	117%
Syracuse, N.Y......	100%
Cleveland, Ohio..	117%
Pittsburgh, Pa....	131%
Toledo, Ohio.......	114%
Rochester, N.Y.......	117%
Grand Rapids, Mich......	125%
Baltimore, Md.........	107%
Atlanta, Ga.........	129%
Lincoln, Neb.........	133%
St. Louis, Mo......	133%
Kansas City, Mo...	94%
Albany, N.Y.........	86%
Fort Worth, Tex..	98%
Buffalo, N.Y.........	111%
Jacksonville, Fla......	149%
New Orleans, La.	113%
Birmingham, Ala......	125%
Mobile, Ala.........	132%
Chattanooga, Tenn...........	110%
Knoxville, Tenn....	133%
Montgomery, Ala......	122%
New York City......	96%

Mr. Wm. Telford gave information regarding the number of shops in Toronto, stating that there were 322 at present, and of these to his knowledge 32 of them were operating the cost-finding system under the supervision of Mr. Jones.

Mr. Robert Croft: "What is the proper selling expense?"

Mr. Borden referred to the figures of the composite report, and found that in a business of $20,000,000 the selling expense had been $1,200,000, or six per cent.

Mr. Lewis of the Southam Press asked if Mr. Borden were kidding them when he mentioned 25% above cost, and whether it would be possible to justify such a figure, to which the answer was given that 25 per cent. was the mark to aim at. If the shops earning less were taken out the losses in the charts would be greater.

Mr. Atwell Fleming, Sr., hoped the printers present realized that they were going in on a large scheme, and one that would take some money to finance—more in fact than they had ever put into any similar move in this city. "I won't be with the game very many more years," continued Mr. Fleming, "but before I quit I would like to feel that the trade had benefited by the example I have tried to set. I went off for a holiday of some weeks not long ago, and when I came back I was greeted with the remark several times 'Helloo, I thought you had gone out of business.' I replied to this every time, 'I will bury a lot of you chaps yet.' (Applause.) I want to die in the harness. When that time comes I want to be able to have it said as Ben Franklin wrote for his own epitaph, which was never used as such:

" 'Here lies the body of Ben Franklin, like the cover of an old book, its contents torn out, and stripped of its lettering and gilding, food for worms: but the work itself shall not be lost, for it will, he believes, appear again in a new and more beautiful edition, corrected and amended by the Author.' "

Mr. Snider of the Colonial Printing Co., wanted to know what protection members had by the U.T.A. against the practice of price-cutting. The explanation was that there was no protection, outside of the fact that members would be shown by the courses that when they were cutting prices they were putting their hands in their own pockets. The experience of other places had been that the price-cutter vanished, and in his place a good business man appeared. When all work along the same lines all make money.

Those attending the banquet were:—K. B. Allison, Andrew Cobean, Thomas B. Palmer, C. S. Acton, J. Pascoe Beel, Acton Publishing Co.; George Good, John Maidlow, Jr., The Acme Press; W. E. Apted, W. H. Apted; F. W. Duggan, J. C. Acton, R. G. Tress, Acton Publishing Co., Ltd.; W. R. Houston, Alan S. Houston, W. R. Houston; H. B. Donovon, Jr., Business Printing Co.; L. L. Clogg, Brown & Searle Printing Co.; B. A. Booth, Booth Bros.; J. Bell, G. A. Lumbers, Business Systems; Wm. H. Brigden, Geo. Brigden, Brigdens, Limited; Alex. W. Waraill, Alex. Innes, Daniel D. Mann, George H. Weld, Bryant Press Limited; W. R. Woodland, F. F. Clarke & Co.; Robt. D. Croft, Mackenzie Wright, Croft & Wright; Chas. E. Clifford, Copeland-Chatterson, Limited, Brampton, Ont.; F. F. Clarke, F. F. Clarke & Company; Maurice Levy, Crown Printing Co.; C. Wilford, R. H. McBride, Carswell Co., Ltd.; Victor M. Brown, B. H. Brown, Frank M. Brown, College Press Limited; S. Snider, The Colonial Printing Co., Ltd.; J. Bolander, Crane, Newall & Selby, Ltd.; G. Dudley Thomas, The Copp Clark Co., Limited; G. M. Thornton, Dudgeon Thornton; T. J. Conlin, Conlin Press; Robert E. Roddy, Charles Roddy; Althea S. DeWitt, DeWitt-Fenton; Wm. C. Moran, Peter M. Pratt, The Dundas Press; Charles Dickinson, 20 Temperance St.; S. C. Cross, Q. B. Henderson, Geo. A. Davis, L. A. Henderson, F. H. Green, Davis & Henderson, Ltd.; Fred P. Daville, F. E. Moore, Daville Press; Sam. J. Crealock, The Diamond Press; Charles Dawson, Charles Dawson; L. E. Bowerman, Dominion Loose Leaf Co., Ltd.; Charles Priestman, Dudgeon & Thornton; Chas. W. Fenton, DeWitt-Fenton; John J. Lynch, Espie Printing Company; D. W. McGregor, Enterprise Printing Co.; Atwell Fleming, Jr., W. E. Harrison, Atwell Fleming, Atwell Fleming Printing Co.; A. G. Parker, W. J. Gage & Co., Limited; Ernest J. Grand, C. A. Ray, W. W. MacDonald, W. J. George, Grand & Toy, Ltd.; H. Irwin, J. E. Burns, Greenway Press; H. F. E. Kent, W. J. Gage Co., Ltd.; Wm. W. Brown, Haynes Press; Fred W. Rose, E. R. Popham, The Hunter Rose Co., Ltd.; Wm. W. Harvey, W. R. Harvey, Harvey & Company; Geo. M. Rose, Hunter, Rose Co.; P. Bell, F. Harpell, Industrial & Technical Press; Fred Moss, Jackson, Moss & Co.: Jas. J. Kew, P. G. Kew, The Kew Printing Co.; J. P. Kenneally & Co.; P. C. Soules, A. E. Long & Co.; H. Pettitt, Lakeside Press; H. E. Pearen, Lyon & James Ltd.; T. W. Langstone, De La Salle Building; A. B. Green, T. W. Langstone; J. B. Lawrason, Lawrason-Doughty Co.; William Fox, A. E. Long & Co., Ltd.; H. W. Nelson, Ralph L. Lovell, R. J. Lovell, The R. J. Lovell Co.; S. Kling, United Press; W. R. Adamson, Mono-Line Typesetting Co., Ltd.; W. J. Telford, S. H. Moore, Fred J. Craddock, John Riley Curzon, Moore-Telford, Limited; Douglas Ford, The Monarch Press; George N. Hudson, Miln-Bingham Printing Co.; F. H. Ellins, W. J. Sheahan, William Hunter, A. N. Kirby, Methodist Book & Pub. House; Joseph Black, Monetary Times Printing Co.; Horace Mundy, Print-Craft; Robt. F. Wilson, William Baker, Miln-Bingham Printing Co.; A. E. Jennings, Monetary Times Printing Co.; Harry E. Baird, Chris. D. S. Murray, Joseph A. Murray, Murray Printing Co., Ltd.; J. M. Gardner, J. C. MacMillan, P. G. Cherry, C. A. Mills, Might Directories, Limited; O. J. Hutchinson, MacLean Publishing Co.; J. C. Anderson, P. Ferguson, R. G. MacLean, Limited; G. K. Kenyon, J. E. Mitchell, Major A. E. Nash, H. V. Tyrrell, MacLean Publishing Co., Limited; The McKinnon Press; O. B. McLeod,

C. L. Kenney, McLeod & Kenney; A. B. Kerr, The MacLean Publishing Co.; T. H. Garwood, G. S. Young, G. C. Young, Hugh C. MacLean, Limited; A. R. Kennedy, Herbert D. Tresidder, MacLean Publishing Co.; *Printer and Publisher*; Ernest A. Creed, Noble Scott, Geo. J. Marshall, Noble Scott, Limited; Jas. F. Doughty, W. E. Bishop, J. L. Nichols Co., Ltd.; J. Smyth Carter, H. G. Hocken, Ontario Press, Limited; Fred Hancock, Print-Craft; Geo. A. Gribble, Publishers, Ltd.; Charles Robinson, Robinson Press; C. W. Rous, H. L. Rous, F. Waterbury, Rous & Mann; Jas. G. Wilson, E. L. Patchet, A. C. Smith, Saturday Night Press; Albert Smith, Albert Smith Printing Co.; G. G. Sheppard, Service Press, H. F. Chandler, Southam Press, Ltd.; D. Tulver, S. H. Sandler, Superior Press; Walter J. Wood, Ernest J. Call, W. M. Oulster, A. L. Lewis, R. Southam, Southam Press; Horace C. Corner, Copp Clark Co., Ltd.; W. F. Stott, James J. Nightingale, Stott Press; M. W. Shepard, Geo. Shepard Printing Co.; H. Hobson, F. E. Pearsall, Sovereign Press; Geo. W. Shepard, Geo. Shepard Printing Co.; Edward Caldwell, W. G. Cumming, W. E. Miller, Strathmore Press; F. J. Giroux, Geo. J. Bell, Sterling Printing & Pub. Co.; W. R. Woodruff, Toronto General Hospital; F. S. Thomas, F. S. Thomas & Co. (Bookbinders); E. M. Wilcox, York Press, Ltd.; F. E. Galbraith, West Toronto Printing House; H. C. Woods, A. F. Rutter, Warwick Bros. & Rutter; William Powell, Waverley Press; Ed. H. Borden, U.T.A. Special Representative; Jos. A. Borden, Gen. Sec. U.T.A.; T. Noble, Welch & Quest; Wm. L. Powell, Waverley Press; N. A. Welch, Welch & Quest; I. R. Knowlton, Special Representative U.T.A.

Thinks Organization Essential

Winnipeg, May 10th, 1920.
Printer and Publisher,
   143 University Avenue,
      Toronto, Ont.
Gentlemen,

I was much interested in the communication appearing in your April issue by Mr. J. B. Cowan of Vancouver on "Canadian Division of the United Typothetae" and trust that the same will receive serious consideration from the printers of Canada.

That the printing industry in Canada should be more thoroughly organized is unquestionable, and it seems to me the most effective way of doing this would be by forming one or more division of the United Typothetae of America and thus take advantage of the missionary work performed by that Institution.

      Yours truly,
         JOHN STOVEL.

Northcliffe Not Coming

Owing to continued throat trouble, Lord Northcliffe will be unable to join the Press Conference to Canada. The agenda of the conference is being arranged so that discussions shall not be confined too narrowly to special newspaper interests, the English delegation desiring to hear views from Canadian representative men on matters of broad interest. An invitation has just been received from several influential bodies in New York for the conference to visit that city. This matter has been passed on to the Canadian committee to consider.

Standard Paper Sizes

Sheet news will in future be supplied as follows:
Minimum Basis—24 x 36, 33, including wrappers and twine.
Minimum Size—24 x 36.
The following shall be standard publishers' sizes:

24 x 36	35 x 45
27 x 41	35 x 48
28 x 42	38 x 48
30 x 44	42 x 56

Where sizes other than these are required and where they can be accepted by the mill, an extra charge for cutting shall be made, as follows:

2 or more tons........................$3.50 per ton
Cars (20 tons or over)...................2.00 per ton
Not less than two tons of any odd size shall be cut. All papers put up lapped.

Advertising vs. Subscription Rates

By Miss M. Pennell of J. J. Gibbons Ltd.

PRACTICALLY the only, and certainly the livest, topic of conversation between publishers and agencies now is the question of rising costs. We all thought that with the end of the war troubles in this regard would be over, but as a matter of fact publishers are now facing a graver crisis than they have ever faced. If it were not for the fact that, for one reason or another, the volume of advertising is greater than it has ever been, many publishers could not continue in business a month.

I don't suppose that by June 30th there will be a daily in Canada but what has advanced its advertising rates since February. Many have done so at least once before during the past few years.

What are they doing about raising subscription rates?

I have looked casually over the history of the dailies which are members of the A.B.C. I picked these out for analysis because one can fairly assume that they represent a progressive type of paper, although I am not going to get into any argument as to the merits of the A.B.C. Some of these papers not classed as non-progressive, although I may have my own opinion about that. Many of these papers have not increased their subscription rates since the beginning of the war. This may seem incredible, but it is nevertheless true.

Getting $2.00 by Mail

There is a daily published in Ontario, not 100 miles from Toronto, that is getting $2.00 a year by mail for its paper and it lays the blame on its contemporary who cannot see eye to eye with it on this question. Of course I may be all wrong, but if I were that publisher I would run such an educative campaign in my paper about the high cost of producing the paper the subscriber now gets for ¾c a copy that would not only get me the higher rate, but would make my contemporary look "sick." It's suicidal, that's all! I can quite understand that up to a certain point there MAY be some justification in building up a volume of circulation on a low subscription rate, but I am not convinced that the public are so devoid of sense that for the sake of an extra ½c or 1c. they are going to give up a paper they have been taking constantly for years.

Of course the smaller papers, with some justification, blame the whole thing on the metropolitan daily whose cost of production is less per 100 or 1,000 than his own. Some Western papers get $5.00 by mail, one or two $4.00 and the Eastern papers as a rule $3.00, and of course this is not net, in many cases, to the publisher. Less than 1c per copy for printing and distributing a paper of from 10 to 24 pages! Isn't it time that the publishers woke up to the fact that something will have to be done to get more for their finished product? Surely they have a very low estimate of their own value. It is generally conceded that the present volume of advertising is not going to keep up, and publishers say they would rather lose some advertising and get out a smaller paper. That is all right now, but how about two and three years from now? It is all very well to plaintively say "We are losing money—we haven't declared a dividend for years"—then lay your plans so you can, but keep your paper to a standard that will make it easy for you to get a fair rate both from the subscriber and the advertiser— and—and this is most important—that will enable you to attract to yourself advertising when it is not so readily obtainable as it is now.

Worry about what is going to happen July 1st, but do some constructive worrying.

Get What Paper is Worth

Many papers are considering the insertion of a clause in contracts providing for an arbitary advance in rate at the discretion of the publisher, depending on what he has to pay for newsprint, etc., this summer and fall. This is dangerous ground, and a fairer basis would be to figure out what it costs to deliver the paper to the subscriber's door and make him pay for it. The cost of the white paper per year for one large daily is $10.00 per subscriber, yet he gets $3.00 by mail and 2c in the city.

It would be invidious to list the papers which are the biggest offenders in this direction of low subscription cost, but it would be enlightening—particularly to a curious advertiser who really delved into this subject, and one of these days that is just what is going to happen. You say the advertiser calls for publicity. All right, most of you have it, and quality too. Then charge for it, even if you do drop a few names from your list who object to a slightly higher rate.

It's the easiest thing in the world to find an excuse, and some sound pretty good, too, for delaying this step, but with conditions as serious as they are, it is no time to bring them out.

There never was a time when the papers had such a good case to get higher rates, and are receiving such hearty co-operation from all sides. Then push for all you're worth—but remember to divide your costs between your subscriber and advertiser. Nobody values the thing he gets too cheaply.

Bruce and Grey Ask $2 and Adopt New List

AT a largely attended meeting of Bruce and Grey counties publishers at Hanover on Friday, April 30th, it was unanimously decided to charge $2 per year as a subscription rate for their papers. The order goes into force in all the offices on July 1st.

Mr. Lorne A. Eedy of the Walkerton *Telescope* is the president of the Bruce Association, and invited the Grey County publishers to join in the meeting held at Hanover. Lunch was had by the visitors at the Reid House, while the business sessions were held in the council chamber, arranged for by Mr. Geo. Mitchell, proprietor of the Hanover *Post*.

Much deliberation was given to the increase in subscription rates, but after counting the costs there was no other course open. A special committee revised the job price list and new copies were furnished each office. The matter of advertising rates was also taken up by another committee, and increases recommended. The meeting was most enthusiastic. The manager of the Canadian Weekly Newspapers' Association was present, and there were five additions made to its membership.

The publishers present were:
Lorne A. Eedy, the *Telescope*, Walkerton Ont., President.
H. A. Vandusen, the *Leader*, Tara, Ont.
J. J. Hunter, the *Reporter*, Kincardine, Ont.

A. Rogers, the *Review*, Kincardine, Ont.
Wm. McDonald, the *Enterprise*, Chesley, Ont.
A. Nolan, the *Enterprise*, Chesley, Ont.
D. McKenzie, the *Advocate*, Paisley, Ont., Sec.-Treas.
A. W. Wesley, *Herald-Times*, Walkerton, Ont.
J. A. Wesley, *Herald-Times*, Walkerton, Ont.
J. A. Johnston, the *Gazette*, Mildmay, Ont.
E. R. Sayles, the *Times*, Port Elgin, Ont.
A. D. McKenzie, the *Sentinel*, Lucknow, Ont.
Howard Fleming, Owen Sound *Times*, Owen Sound, Ont.
Stewart Fleming, R. B. & W. Co., Owen Sound, Ont.
Mr. Finlay, the *Advertiser*, Owen Sound, Ont.
Mr. Hugh McCullough, Chatsworth *News*, Chatsworth, Ont.
W. Irwin, the *Chronicle*, Durham, Ont.
P. Ramage, the *Review*, Durham, Ont.
Geo. Mitchell, the *Post*, Hanover, Ont.

The Ottawa *Citizen* has been running a bicycle page. A good line of bicycle news is used along with the advertising. The usual points of health, exercise and time-saving are brought out in the news articles on the page.

Artistic Lay-Out and Design in Printing

By Harry L. Gage

Of the Department of Linotype Typography, Former Head of the
Department of Printing, Carnegie Institute of Technology

CONTRARY to popular belief, there are no hard and fast rules in Art. The successful craftsman or artist is he who knows all rules, and yet can skilfully break them. The student of design is often inclined to adhere too closely to each newly observed principle, but he will gain by it in the end because his conception of his problem thus grows, item by item, until his work finally becomes a well-rounded embodiment of all of the traditions. Because

elements of design. Design governs the arrangement of dots, lines, and masses, to secure the qualities of beauty and of fitness to purpose.

Any piece of work which is so planned is called (in the abstract) "a design." Thus, we may speak of a printed page, a complete book, a piece of furniture, or a building, as a design. The relationship of its various parts, the lines of its construction, its color, and the manner in

FIGURE 1
The Photograph Shows Depth or Distance

FIGURE 2
Figure 1, Made Into a Flat Design

of this, basic principles will be emphasized here, but rigid rules and hard and fast formulae will not be given.

There can be no true utility without beauty. This axiom is the basis of civilization. Hence, all manufactured products for the use of mankind must be not only useful but also pleasing to the eye. If an article be pleasing in appearance, its making will have involved some of the

which it is decorated depend first upon its purpose, but are guided by certain almost universally recognized traditions which we call the principles of design.

Fitness of purpose in the printed page is, in part, a mechanical problem. Beauty depends upon those qualities which appeal to the eye, and mind, through the consideration of: Harmony (of shape, tone, and color) ; Proportion ;

Balance; Opposition of elements; Ornamentation and Decoration.

These elements of design enter not only into the arrangement of printing but into every problem of construction or arrangement. Thus, the problem of layout in design and printing gives us a common ground with the workers in all of the fine and useful arts. In the printed page, design is concerned with the arrangement of typographic elements (type masses, borders, headbands, illustrations) as parts of a pattern on a flat surface—the face of the printed sheet of paper. Hence, design in printing considers two dimensions only: width and height. The third dimension, depth, or thickness, which must be considered in the design of all but flat surfaces, can only be suggested on the printed page. The means of showing depth is really an illusion by which the eye sees various tones printed upon the page, which convey a pictorial impression by means of light and shade.

It is important to note that pictorial representation and decoration serve each a different purpose in printing. Because the mechanical means for producing either one is the same (a printing surface), confusion sometimes exists as to their use. The pictorial is used as an illustration for the text, or for its own interest. Decoration, or ornament, may be used to beautify the page, as a pattern on its flat surface, and may be related to the text, but very rarely serves as an illustration to express its thought.

Figure 4 is a section of a decorative headband designed for use with the Benedictine type series. The leaves, stems, and flowers of which it is designed are arranged as a flat pattern. These same leaves, etc., have been drawn as a picture in Figure 3. This picture not only shows the form of the natural objects but it suggests depth, or thickness, through the illusion of light and shade.

A photograph of these same forms, reproduced, would be still more realistic. The flat treatment of Figure 4 depends for its interest upon the arrangement of masses of black and white, and the graceful flow of line throughout the surface. It is purely decorative.

Figure 1 is reproduced from a photograph which might be used as an illustration.

Figure 2 has been redrawn from this photograph as a design, an arrangement of flat masses which lies flat upon the surface of the paper, and yet tells the story conveyed by the photograph.

The accompanying illustrations are given as a warning against the use of pictures, however pleasing, as decorative material. The same masses of shadow and light which express roundness or depth in a photograph or other picture, may be arranged into decorative flat masses, and thus be embodied in the design of a page. The page of type and decoration must appear flat upon the surface of the paper.

Unfortunately, much of the so-called "decorative" material heretofore supplied to printers has been merely pictorial in its representation of natural forms. One of the most useful characteristics of Linotype Typography lies in the studied decorative quality of the ornaments which are a part of the system. Derived from architectural bands and from natural leaves and flowers, each border or ornament has been reduced to pure decoration.

When the decorative arts of any nation or period lapse into the mere reproduction of natural forms, they decline into mediocrity. Typographic design in America has just emerged from such a period, and it is the understanding of these fundamentals that is helping to accomplish the re-birth of typography.

Figure 3—Natural Source of Figure 4.

Figure 4—Section of a Flat Decoration.

Printer & Publisher

Published on the Twelfth of Each Month.

H. D. TRESIDDER - - - Business Manager.
A. R. KENNEDY - - - - - - Editor.

SUBSCRIPTION PRICE—Canada, Great Britain, South Africa and the West Indies, $2 a year; United States, $2.50 a year; other countries, $3 a year. Single copies, 20 cents. Invariably in advance.

PUBLISHED BY

THE MACLEAN PUBLISHING CO.

Established 1887 Limited

JOHN BAYNE MACLEAN - - - President.
H. T. HUNTER - - - - - - Vice-President.
H. V. TYRRELL - - - - General Manager.
T. B. COSTAIN - - - General Managing Editor.

Head Office, 143-153 University Avenue - TORONTO, CANADA
Cable Address Macpubco, Toronto; Atabek, London, Eng.
Also at Montreal, Winnipeg, New York, Chicago, Boston, London, England.
Application for A.B.C. Audit.

Vol. 29   TORONTO, MAY, 1920   No. 5

CONTENTS

Where the Newsprint Goes

THERE are statements coming forward from time to time that throw an interesting light on the shortage of newsprint. One of these was the word of Jason Rogers, publisher of the New York *Globe*, when appearing before the Senate committee investigating the shortage of paper.

Mr. Rogers brought to light an advertisement in the Chicago *Tribune* last winter which boasted of the fact that one Sunday *Tribune* edition used more paper than all the dailies in Canada in two days.

Don't Be Too Enthusiastic

ALTHOUGH the newsprint situation is becoming more serious, there is no evidence of a sincere desire on the part of Canadian publishers in general to reduce their consumption. On the other hand papers are going ahead pretty much the same as usual. Some of them are putting on circulation contests, offering pianos, cars and tours. They are reaching out after a sort of circulation that the large advertiser is always inclined to discount.

In one column they are telling the public of the serious situation facing them, while on other pages they are calling for more readers to help aggravate the same.

Papers would be much better advised were they to spend their surplus energy telling their readers real facts, and getting their circulation and advertising rates in shape to stand any surprise that may be in store for them in the very near future.

Piling on circulation at a price that does not pay for white paper and distribution is such poor business at present that the wonder is that any sane publisher indulges in it.

And yet we have big, reputable papers out peddling water sets and other premiums in order to take on more readers.

This paper does not want to be pessimistic, but the prospects look as though some of the plungers will wake up some morning to find that their feet have been frozen overnight.

Censor the Advertising

THERE are papers in Canada which, if they intend to preserve their decency, should go after the moving picture ads. with an axe.

Here is one taken from a reputable daily paper:—

FASTER! FASTER!

Slaves of Pleasure, lost in the spell of Broadway's lights and laughter. Driven by the lash of unfulfilled desires—on and on—dancing, loving, thirsting for new sensations —beyond the law—beyond virtue—into the abyss.

A vivid lavish drama of human souls that drank of too much "life" on New York's Great White Way.

Every Scene a Sensation

And if that is not suggestive enough, here is another:—

At the Daily Matinees for Ladies Only,

ALICE STERLING

(A woman with a past) will address the single, married and divorced ladies, those in love and those contemplating marriage, on the subject of

"THE DUEL OF THE SEXES"

During her address she will endeavor to make clear the question: Whether or not it is best to tell of your past life before marriage.

Is that the sort of junk and rubbish you want your paper to stand for? Well, there are the extracts, taken from Canadian papers circulating in large, respectable communities.

No newspaper can maintain its self-respect if it does not censor its advertising columns just as closely as its news pages. These ads. bark like the shouter on the midway of a circus who tells passers-by that his is no Sunday-school entertainment.

He suggests certain things. They are neither clean nor respectable. These suggestively worded ads. of moving picture houses do the same thing.

R. Hoe & Co. have moved their Chicago office from South Clark Street to Room 827 Tribune Building. The Chicago representatives are Messrs. H. S. Mount and E. L. Johnston.

G. J. Ainger & Co., on account of largely increased business, have moved to larger premises at 521-523 West Monroe St., Chicago. Their index tabs are having a large run, and they expect in their new premises to be able to carry on a much greater volume of trade.

—Racy in Montreal "Star."
... "Two souls with but a single thought."

Don't Get Caught on the Flat Rate Idea

Half Sheet Bills Have Big Variety of Price

By Peter Wilson, Supt. Woodstock Sentinel-Review

Mr. Wilson, in this article, shows the poor wisdom of calling every half-sheet a half-sheet as far as the price is concerned. The tracing of costs will show where the charge should be made. It is a fact that the flat price for a quarter or half-sheet, for pages of voters' list, for almost anything that can be named, has led to a lot of poor practices in many shops.—EDITOR.

A FARMER comes in for 50 half-sheet posters and after looking at the long list we pluck up courage to tell him that it will cost him $9.00. (Put it at the ideal present-day price so that the student will become used to the idea of charging that much—it will have to come anyway.) The first thing to do is to take the job ticket—and enter the particulars of the job. First the date received and the date wanted, customer's name and address, number of copies, stock (news or colored poster), ink and finally shipping instructions (whether bills go to the customer by mail or are to be called for, or perhaps they are to be sent to the auctioneer). For convenience in keeping track of the copy and for filing away after the job is finished the job ticket should be printed on a manila envelope, 9 x 12, open end. On the reverse side may be printed information for the guidance in the mechanical departments and for keeping track of big jobs.

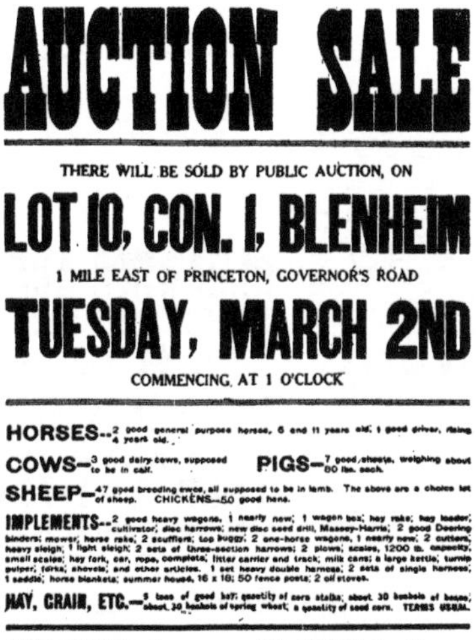

AUCTION SALE

THERE WILL BE SOLD BY PUBLIC AUCTION, ON

LOT 10, CON. 1, BLENHEIM

1 MILE EAST OF PRINCETON, GOVERNOR'S ROAD

TUESDAY, MARCH 2ND

COMMENCING AT 1 O'CLOCK

HORSES--2 good general purpose horses, 6 and 11 years old; 1 good driver, rising 4 years old.

COWS—3 good dairy cows, supposed to be in calf.

PIGS—7 good shoats, weighing about 80 lbs. each.

SHEEP—47 good breeding ewes, all supposed to be in lamb. The above are a choice lot of sheep. CHICKENS—50 good hens.

IMPLEMENTS--2 good heavy wagons, 1 nearly new; 1 wagon box; hay rake; hay loader; cultivator; disc harrows; new disc seed drill, Massey-Harris; 2 good Deering binders; mower; horse rake; 2 scufflers; top buggy; 2 one-horse wagons, 1 nearly new; 2 cutters; heavy sleigh; 1 light sleigh; 2 sets of three-section harrows; 2 plows; scales, 1200 lb. capacity; small scales; hay fork, car, rope, complete; litter carrier and track; milk cans; a large kettle; turnip pulper; forks; shovels; and other articles. 1 set heavy double harness; 2 sets of single harness; 1 saddle; horse blankets; summer house, 16 x 18; 50 fence posts; 2 oil stoves.

HAY, GRAIN, ETC.—5 tons of good hay; quantity of corn stalks; about 30 bushels of beans; about 30 bushels of spring wheat; a quantity of seed corn. TERMS USUAL.

JOHN COMMON, Prop. WM. PULLIN, Auctioneer

Figure 2—This sort of job comes into the office quite frequently. It is the ordinary half-sheet, and in this case there is not a great deal of composition on it. It permits of the use of greater display. In fact it is necessary to use the larger lettering if the half sheet is to be used in this bill. It took 2¼ hours to set it.

At the time the job ticket is made out the job is also entered on Form No. 2—the individual Job Record, which bears the same number as the job ticket, and information for the guidance of the bookkeeper or billing clerk. The price, if one was given, should be set down when entering the job, as this may avoid unpleasant wrangling afterwards.

Form No. 3—the Daily Time Sheet—has four kinds for use in the four generally recognized mechanical departments, namely, hand composition, machine composition, pressroom and bindery. When the compositor is handed the job he punches the clock, writes in the job number and customer's name, puts the figure 1 in the "kind of work" column, writes the time he has just punched in the column "time started," makes up his stick to the proper width of the form and "goes to it." **All these items are part of the job, and should be charged against the job—just as a plumber charges you for the time he spends walking from the shop to your house and back, and also for the time spent in going after a joint or a tool he has forgotten to bring in the first place.**

When a compositor starts a poster he generally can tell from a glance at the copy whether he can use very large display lines, or whether to set the list first of all in 18, 24 or 36 point bold and set the display afterwards. This latter is the safe way, and good practice. If he is a conscientious worker he finishes in good time, having combined the hand composition with the lockup of the form. He pulls a stone proof and hands it over to the reader, cleans up the leads and other material he has accumulated, and is ready for another job. He punches the clock again and this second punching shows the time the first job ended and the start of the second. He sets down the time in column "Time left off" and repeats the process of entering the second job, and commences work. By and by while he is at work on the second job, the proof of the first job comes in and it is found that he has left out two words which necessitates 15 minutes more work on job No. 1. He punches out again, this time using No. 14 for the kind of work. This indicates "office corrections" and is non-chargeable, as this work has been made necessary through his mistake or carelessness. We have now two kinds of time—one a charge against the job, and the other a charge against the shop—one "chargeable" and the other "non-chargeable." This process of recording time goes on all day, and at night the time sheet is scrutinized by the foreman, O.K'ed, and handed into the office. We now have entries something like those shown in the time sheet illustration. The chargeable and non-chargeable hours are divided as follows:—

Kind of work column to be filled in by using the No. to designate the work done.

Chargeable Time

1 Hand Composition
2 Author's Alterations
3 Makeup
4 Press Lockup
5 Foundry Lockup
6 Registering
7 Proofing
8 Monotype Keyboard
9 Monotype Caster
10 Monotype Auth. Alter.
11 Linotype Composition
12 Linotype Auth. Alter.
13 ....

Non-Chargeable Time

14 Office Corrections
15 Proof Reading
16 Copy Holding
17 Copy Revising
18 Distribution
19 Errands
20 Monotype Repairs
21 Monotype Clean Up
22 Monotype Oil Up
23 Monotype Caster Reps.
24 Monotype Delays (spec.)
25 ....

All classes of work, numbered 1 to 13, are "chargeable" and from 14 to 25 are "non-chargeable. When this extending of time elapsed is done the chargeable column is added and also the non-chargeable and the totals are added together. The total should agree with the clock punched time, and this is the time the employee expects to be paid for. This is the employee's bill against the business. The next proceeding is to enter each item of chargeable time against the respective jobs, and here is where the Individual Job Record comes in again.

The Payroll of the Chargeable Hour

So far we have dealt only with the individual items of chargeable time. We have now to take care of the totals of chargeable

AUCTION SALE
OF
Pure Bred Farm Stock
IMPLEMENTS, HAY, GRAIN, HOUSEHOLD EFFECTS, ETC.
The undersigned auctioneers have received instructions to sell by public auction on the premises
LOT 13 CON. 8 SOUTH NORWICH
1-2 mile west of Otterville, on
WED. MARCH 10TH.
1920 commencing at 9.30 o'clock, the following
M. L. HALEY, Sales Manager.
R. M. HOLMES, Prop
MOORE, DEAN & LONGWORTH, Auctioneers.
CATALOGUES WILL BE FURNISHED ON REQUEST.

Fig. 1—This is the same matter as the whole sheet, only this time used as a dodger. There is no doubt but that there are times when offices charge too much for these, when compared to the same price for a bill with a few display lines on it for door-to-door use. It is interesting to notice the way Mr. Wilson's records charged this bill.

and non-chargeable time, and we do so by transferring these items to Form No. 4, which is a combination Departmental Pay Roll Sheet and a record of the total chargeable and non-chargeable time of all the hand compositors (if there are more than one) for the particular payroll week. On this form, using a sheet for each department, we gather the following information—total chargeable hours for each department, total non-chargeable hours, total department payroll, average payroll cost per chargeable hour, and the ratio of non-chargeable hours to the payroll.

Accompanying this article are reproductions of three sale bills recently printed. They were set under good average shop conditions by men who are good average printers, and as such can be relied on to turn out the work in good average time. The following information will be interesting:

Job A-100 full sheet posters, 25x38, on S. C. book (quality of stock made necessary by two cuts asked for). The county lists show a rate of $11.00 for 100 full sheets. Allowing for extra time on make-ready and grade of stock, say $2.00 in all, the price asked would likely be about $13. The record of cost shown after the job was done is as follows:

115 sheets S.C. book, 25x38—60, at 12c, $7.20 ream (present price is 15c per lb.)	$1.66
Handling charge	.20
Ink	.15
Composition, including lockup, 6 hrs. at $1.50	9.00
Presswork—makeready and run, 1 hr. at $2.00	2.00
Stock, getting and packing, 15 minutes	.38
Cost of job	$13.39
Plus 25 per cent. profit	3.35
Selling Price	$16.75

Along with A was an order for 500 dodgers, 6x9, from the same copy. The list had to be set in 6 pt. to give room for the display, and the cost of this job was as follows:

Stock and handling	$ .35
Ink, ordinary news	.05
Composition, 1 hr. hand	1.50
1,500 ems, machine at 75c	1.15
Platen presswork, 45 min. at $1.20	.90
Getting out stock, cutting and packing	.20
Cost	$4.15
Plus 25 per cent	1.04
Selling Price, $5.25	$5.19

Job B-25 half-sheet posters, the lightest composition of this class listed in the county list at $4.50. The records show thus:

Stock and handling	$ .25
Ink	.10
Composition, 2¼ hrs. at $1.50	3.38
Presswork 20 min. cylinder at $2.00	.67
Stock, &c.,	.20
Cost	$4.60
Plus 25 per cent	1.15
	$5.75

Sold for $6.00

CLEARING AUCTION SALE
FARM STOCK
IMPLEMENTS, FEED, FURNITURE
THURSDAY, FEBRUARY 19
LOT 26, CON. 2, NORTH NORWICH
HORSES
CATTLE
HOGS
IMPLEMENTS
FEED AND SEED
FURNITURE
TERMS
Mrs. Jessie Allin, Prop.
Wm. Pullin, Auct.

Figure C—Here is another half-sheet bill, quite different from the one on the first page of this article. There is a great deal more work on this, and it is right that this bill should be sold for more than the other, because the buyer of this bill has taken up more of the working hours of the office, and working hours are what the office has for sale. Mr. Wilson says his cost sheets show that 4 hours were necessary to turn out the composition on this job. The point is also well made that when there is this amount of composition on the solid part of the bill it is well to set that part first and then the compositor is in a better position to see what he has left to work with in the way of display.

The New Postage Rate and the Papers
Various Views on Its Application

THE text of the resolution moved in the Commons by the Minister of Customs and Inland Revenue regarding newspaper postage follows:

"Newspapers and periodicals required to be transmitted by mail within a distance of forty miles from the place of publication, the publication of which is of no more frequency than once a week, which have a circulation by mail of not more than one thousand copies per issue, and which are published in any city, town or village which has a population of not more than five thousand persons, shall be transmitted free of postage within such area.

"Newspapers and periodicals which are required to be transmitted for a greater distance than is mentioned in the last preceding subsection, the publication of which is of greater frequency than once a week, shall be subject to a postage at the rate of one cent on and after the first day of January, 1921, and until the first day of January, 1922, and one and one-half cents thereafter for each pound weight or any fraction of a pound weight, and such postage shall be prepaid by postage stamps or otherwise, as the Postmaster-General from time to time directs."

Want a Reasonable Increase

The position of the Canadian National Newspapers and Periodicals Association was set forth in a memorandum to the Postmaster-General early in April, and the position has not changed. The Association claims that papers published by its members are largely educational in their character, and should be regarded in the light of technical schools, Government bulletins, etc. They also point out the fact that they are helping to encourage export trade, and are publishing such material as will increase the volume of business done in the retailing establishments.

The circulation of the papers in this class is computed as follows:

Agricultural	650,000
Business	180,000
Technical	79,000
Magazines	600,000
Religious and Education	900,000

Were the same increases applied to letter postage as is proposed to apply to these publications, we would have a letter postage of 12 cents in 1921, and 18 cents in 1922. The publication of magazine, trade and technical papers, religious periodicals, etc., has been built up under conditions that have been existing in the Postal Department, and it is claimed that the sudden reversal of these would be injurious in the extreme.

The magazine situation in Canada is a peculiar one. The attempt to build up general magazines of national circulation and standing in an effort to make a stand against the inroads of American publications has been a costly experience. There are approximately twenty million American magazines coming into Canada, against six million of Canadian published.

The National Newspapers and Periodicals Association do no object to an increase in rates, but they claim that it should be within reason. The purchasing power of the dollar has been cut in two, and on this basis they would be willing to meet the Postal Department, viz., a 100 per cent. increase. They view the present proposals as being ruinous and unfair.

On April 16 the C. D. N. A. submitted their views to the Postmaster-General. They admitted, in their memorandum, that there was some force in the agitation for an increase in second-class postal rates. The Dailies then made it clear that abuses of second-class mailing privileges should be done away with, such as stopping papers sold at a nominal price, sending papers to subscribers more than six months in arrears; denying postal rates of the second class to official organs of associations or societies. The dailies also object to the restrictions that prevent the mailing of newspapers in the half-fold as in United States.

The Dailies were also opposed to the zone system on the idea that it would encourage provincial rather than national ideas.

The Department's claim that as papers took up 60 per cent. of the floor space in the postal system, they should pay 60 per

Job C-50 half-sheets, composition a good average of this class of work. County list price, $5.00. Here's the actual record:

Stock and handling	$ .35
Ink	.10
Composition, 4 hrs. at $1.50	6.00
Presswork, 25 minutes at $2.00	.85
Stock, &c.	.20

Cost	$ 7.50
Add 25 per cent.	1.88

Total	$9.83

Sold for $9.00 as price was given in advance.

The most common fault of the average printer estimator is to over-estimate the output of men and machines, and the only safeguard against this fault is the installation of the cost system and the acceptance of the facts brought out by it. Do this cheerfully and philosophically, and profit will come to your business. And at the same time use the facts to point to improvement in methods and the gradual elimination of inefficiency in your workers.

Figure A—Here is a full sheet sale bill on good paper, the use of which has been made necessary by the fact that half-tones were used in it. There is a lot of heavy composition on this bill.

cent. of the cost, was not agreed to by any means. The subscribers to the memorandum were prepared to acquiesce in an increase in second-class postal rates up to a flat rate of one-half cent per pound, the increase to be effective from January 1, 1921. That would be an increase of 100 per cent. on the present flat rate of one-quarter cent per pound. The rate on sample copies should be increased in the same proportion, viz., from 1 to 2c. per pound.

It is understood that the Daily Association will put up a strenuous protest against the proposed cent a pound for 1921 and a cent and a half thereafter.

Where the Weeklies Come In

Some speculation was indulged in as to what the draft actually meant as far as the weekly papers are concerned. From what *Printer and Publisher* can learn it means that a paper published in a place of less than five thousand has a bonus of 1,000 free copies per week. If a paper had a circulation of 1,600, the new regulation would require them to pay postage rates at the rate of a cent a pound on 600 papers. Publishers of weekly papers in places of over 5,000 are at a loss to know why they are discriminated against. It has been intimated from Ottawa that further changes may be made in the draft regarding the Weekly newspapers.

The Small Dailies' Position

Printer and Publisher asked Mr. W. B. Burgoyne, of the St. atharine's *Standard*, regarding the position of small dailies. He said:

The new postal rates on second-class matter as proposed by the Dominion Government, to take effect on the first of June, 1921, of 1c per pound, to be increased in 1922 to 1½c per pound, will not mean very much to the Government in the way of increased revenue, nor will it tend to greatly improve the situation of which the daily newspaper publishers in the smaller cities have complained.

It is scarcely probable that the new postal rates would materially alter the conditions under which the smaller city newspapers are suffering to-day. Anything less than the adoption of a zone system such as the smaller city newspapers proposed in their memorandum to the Government will not improve the situation to any considerable degree. The new rates continue the enormous advantage to the big metropolitan newspapers which they have enjoyed for so many years, and under which they have become a serious menace to the prosperity and even existence of their smaller city contemporaries.

It is an undeniable fact that almost every big metropolitan daily makes a much lower rate by mail outside of the city in which it is published than it does within the city of publication, and this compels all the smaller papers to follow in the same path, even though it leads to their destruction, and in this the former have been aided by the ridiculously low rate of ¼c per pound, and they will still be aided in the future, even though the rate be 1c per pound in 1921. For instance, there is a Montreal evening newspaper which boasts a circulation of 110,000 daily. Over 24,000 of that circulation is beyond a 40-mile radius and materially affects many other daily newspapers within a radius of, say, a couple of hundred miles. It charges 40c per month within the city or where it can be delivered by its own carrier system. By mail its rate per month is 30c or $3.00 per year, made possible because the Dominion Government carries and delivers those papers at an admitted loss.

The postal zone system has been in effect in the United States for a couple of years, and has resulted in greatly increased revenues to the Government, while not materially affecting injuriously the circulation or subscription rates of the big daily papers, excepting to compel newspapers to charge a rate beyond their delivery limits equal at least to that which it charges at home. Take one of the leading newspapers of Cleveland as an example. It is a two-cent paper, but its subscription rate by mail per year in advance is $6.00. No extra charge is made for postage within the first and second federal zones, that is, a radius of 150 miles; but beyond the second zone excess postage is charged extra. Low postage rates enormously increase the circulation of these big metropolitan papers, increase their advertising space and command national advertising by reason of their wide circulation, which is made possible only by the generosity of the Dominion Government, or, in other words,

a subsidy granted by the Government which is paid by the people at large.

The newsprint shortage, or even famine, which exists to-day is brought about not alone by the big Sunday "Jumbos" of the United States papers, but by the daily "Jumbos" of a number of dailies in the larger cities.

The entire newspaper business in the United States and in Canada, outside of the metropolitan cities, is threatened by the almost unfettered development of these Jumbo papers. Because of their enormous consumption, U.S. papers are enabled to secure their paper supplies under contract, at least to an extent of 70, 80 and 90 per cent., and then go into the spot market and pay 10, 12 or even 15 cents per pound, which compels the smaller papers, which are unable to secure contracts, to pay the spot market price, and is thus forcing them out of existence or compelling them to merge with other local papers in order to keep alive. It is not alone the smaller city dailies, but also the weeklies who will ultimately be the sufferers, as well as the smaller papers in even the large cities. They are all being ground under the juggernaut of the unbridled Jumbo papers.

Ultimately it will be realized, but perhaps when it is too late, that the only effective way of bringing the consumption of newsprint within the capacity of the mills will be that the Government shall refuse the privilege of the second-class postal rates to any paper which charges a subscription rate less than the cost of the white paper consumed. There are Sunday papers in the United States which weigh 2½ and 3 pounds, the paper in which, even at contract price, would cost 12 or 15 cents per copy, and yet they are sold for 5, 7 and 10 cents. There are papers in Canada whose low subscription rates cause a loss on white paper alone of scores of thousands of dollars annually, which is made up from the increasing advertising patronage developed in the larger cities and which is not available to the smaller city publications.

In my estimation, the Government should charge the newspapers of the country rates which would meet the annual cost of the service to the Government, and newspapers as a class should ask no favor or subsidy from the Government of any nature. Should the Government adopt a course like that, it would put the newspaper business of the country, both in the larger and the smaller centres, on a better business basis which would enable them to live and to prosper. The big city papers are to-day the only ones which receive any considerable part of this Dominion subsidy, which is camouflaged under the guise of low postal rates. And they are the papers which can well afford to pay for the entire cost of the delivery of their publication beyond their local boundaries, as they do within. I make these statements as a publisher for more than one-third of a century, and as a student of the newspaper business for nearly half a century. In this connection, the evidence being taken before the United States Senate Committee, referred to, is very helpful. It suggests possibly the fear of national legislators of offending the newspaper publishers. To a suggestion of Senator Reed, the chairman of that committee, "If the committee should recommend a graduated tax to limit the size of newspapers, what do you suppose the newspapers would do to the committee and Congress?" Mr. Frank A. Munsey, publisher of the New York *Sun* and *Herald* and other papers, said, "I suppose there will be a great howl." "Much will be accomplished by getting the proprietors of the newspapers together to deal with the subject. The Government would be able to influence them and get results. If they refuse to co-operate, show them the picture of things as they will be 25 years hence." Mr. Jason Rogers, publisher of the New York *Globe*, stated to the committee, in answer to the Chairman's question as to the attitude the newspaper would take on the proposed tax on excessive use of paper: "Any remedial legislation will unfavorably affect only a limited number of metropolitan papers. The rank and file of the press of the country will see the public benefit of such legislation and will be behind it. It is the country newspapers that are influential. Of course the only publishers who have money to spend to come down here are the big ones, but they are not the ones who influence the public opinion of the nation." What these publishers say would apply to Canada as well as to the United States. The Dominion Government has an unprecedented opportunity to set an example even to the United States and to put the newspaper business of Canada on a plane of prosperity both in city and country that it has never before enjoyed.

REVIEW OF JOB SPECIMENS

If You Want An Opinion On
Your Work, Send It In

FIGURE A.—Much has been said about seeking "atmosphere" in advertising and job work. The artistic printer can do it just as successfully as the painter can do it, provided he has access to the proper facilities. This folder was prepared by the Thomas Todd Co., of Boston, for the Women's Educational and Industrial Union, and reproduces in type and effect much of the effect described in the reading matter of the little book. The original was done in brown and black, and produced a quaint effect that was entirely in keeping with the story the printed page had to tell. There is that little "touch" to the whole thing that places the maker of that job in the class of a thinking printer. It is more effective than any amount of splash and design. The brown was used in the border and cut, while the rest was in black. . The whole thing is highly suggestive of old books and quaint ways.

FIGURE B is the letter-head used by the Kitchener - Waterloo Typographical Union. The compositor has made good use of the sameness in the lines "Kitchener-Waterloo" and "Typographical Union," as they contain almost the same number of letters. Adding the hyphen in the first line makes them the same. The one objection to such a layout is that it may have to answer to the charge of being stiff and too square in appearance.

We have taken the privilege of having the letter-head reset in a slightly different way, using Caslon Old Style throughout. The two names in the corner are not, as is often done, run even at the flush end. Some might even prefer to reverse the names and have the long one on top in each case to carry out the pyramid suggestion that is used in the centre. Were we doing the job as indicated in

the reset the little book ornament would be done in a very light blue.

Other compositors will have plans at once that might impress them. Get in touch with this office or set the letter-head as you think it should be done, and send us a good proof. If possible hold your job in type, as we can get better results from your type than from a zinc reproduction of it.

FIGURE C.—This letter head of Harbinson & Allen is a good sample of plain, legible and dignified work. It is unfortunate that the zinc reproduction has lost quite a bit of the fine lines of the original, giving the whole thing a certain heaviness it did not have in the original. Commercial printers are finding that there is a lot of work among professional men who do not care to go into lithographed or embossed work. More and more users of printing are coming to see the beauty of plain type, artistic composition backed up by good press work and stock.

PAGE of letterheads.—Page 42 is the work of students at the Printing Class of the Technical School, Lippincott Street, Toronto, where Mr. Walter Handley is in charge. The samples shown here cannot by any means be said to be the best work of the school. They were picked at random from a lot of specimens that had been done some weeks ago.

Printer and Publisher representative, when visiting the school recently, had a chance to get a good idea of the way in which Mr. Handley tries to bring the apprentice ideas into conformity with the laws of good typography. It would be an easy matter

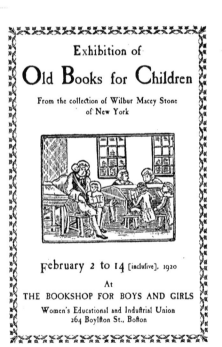

Exhibition of

Old Books for Children

From the collection of Wilbur Macey Stone
of New York

February 2 to 14 [inclusive]. 1920

At

THE BOOKSHOP FOR BOYS AND GIRLS

Women's Educational and Industrial Union
264 Boylston St., Boston

Figure A

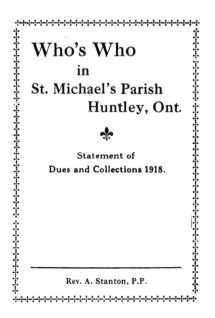

Who's Who

in

St. Michael's Parish

Huntley, Ont.

⚜

Statement of

Dues and Collections 1918.

Rev. A. Stanton, P.P.

The Original Cover

apprentices in the artistic side of the business, to the extent cf having them follow the courses with real enthusiasm and personal interest.

None of the letter-heads shown here are easy to handle. There is nothing so easy to muss up as a letter-head that has a lot of composition on it.

There is a large variety of work done at the Technical School. It gives a boy from a book shop a good idea of commercial printing. Many of them are in offices where they get nothing but ad. work, and a few hours of work on letter-heads, designs for booklets, announcements, business cards, etc., gives them a training that is sadly lacking in other places. Apprentices attend several hours each week on the firm's time, and in the evening on their own time.

The general run of the work, black or in colors, that goes through the school, is highly creditable. It can be called good, sane printing of the type that would convey the message of the purchaser to the reader.

COVER for Booklet.—Some time ago a little church job was sent to this office for price. At the time the cover was torn off for future use. In order to give an idea of a wider range of work, *Printer and Publisher* decided to get the job reset outside of the office.

The one reset by C. W. Baughman, of Moore-Telford, is done in Della Robia, using 36 point, 18, 14, 12 and 8. There is perhaps too great a tendency toward ornamentation, and the little corner pieces add nothing to the design. The wording of the text "Who's Who" suggested the use of the book border to the compositor.

The other reset is by A. W. Hill, of the Moore-Telford Co. It was Mr. Hill's intention in the first place to run the rules all the way down, and cut out the space required for the working, but this was subsequently changed. He has used Cloister and Cheltenham. There is too much rule in the job as it stands. A good idea of this can be obtained by cutting some small strips of white paper and pasting over all the rules but the outside and panels. The effect then is more pleasing than it stands now. Both these compositors kept in view the purchaser of the printing, and such a design might be quite attractive to him.

The Style Changed.—The reset by J. H. Tufford, of the Croft & Wright shop, is a real departure from the original. We asked Mr. Croft to do with it what he pleased as long as he used the same wording as the original, but not necessarily in the same way. Mr. Croft's letter, accompanying the reset, is interesting:—

for an apprentice instructor to keep on correcting mistakes, but it would not make good printers out of the mistake-makers. Mr. Handley makes it a point always to get the apprentices to preserve their originality, encourages them to have ideas, and then seeks to let these operate along proper lines.

One apprentice had just finished a job, supposedly for a jewelry firm. He gave a very good idea of his reasons for following the lines he had, for using certain type faces and ornaments. He not only was arriving at the stage where he could put together a good job, but he knew why he was following the lines he used.

Mr. Handley finds that it is quite possible to interest the

KITCHENER-WATERLOO
TYPOGRAPHICAL UNION

WILLIAM G. JOHNSTON, PRESIDENT   GEORGE A. HAMON, SEC'Y-TREASURER
FRED POLLAKOWSKY, VICE-PRESIDENT   ROPER M. YOUNG, RECORDER

KITCHENER
ONTARIO

Figure B

Mr. Kennedy,
Printer and Publisher,
Toronto.

Dear Sir:—

The title page of the St. Michael's Parish job which you left with us was handed to one of our compositors with the request that he reset it and give his reasons for any changes in style or arrangement. When his proofs came into the office the top one had written on it "Reason why: How do you know a good-looking girl when you see one? Use your judgment in resets the same way."

Personally I cannot agree with this, as in the one case we need consider beauty only, whereas in the other we must have some consideration for the customer, his business and the purpose of his job. If I have a decided preference for red hair and big feet, then every girl with red hair and big feet will look good to me. Similarly if I am very fond of black face Gothic type every job set in that type would look all right to me. I would be entitled to my own preference. But when it comes to making a selection that would be considered good taste by a majority of average intelligent people I must consider something besides my own preference.

I cannot see why "Who's Who" appears in the page mentioned. Looking over the job it appears to be a plain statement of dues and collections and that is why I approve of the reset. As copies will be sent only to members and adherents of St. Michael's Parish there is no necessity of undue emphasis of the name. I think "Who's Who" could be entirely eliminated with advantage to both the appearance and sense of the page. I also think that the plain rule and straight line borders are better taste, in most cases, than grotesque and ornate characters massed together in lines or rows. By the use of simple rule

𝔚𝔥𝔬'𝔰 𝔚𝔥𝔬

in

𝔖𝔱. 𝔐𝔦𝔠𝔥𝔞𝔢𝔩'𝔰 𝔓𝔞𝔯𝔦𝔰𝔥

REV. A. STANTON, P. P.

Statement of Dues and Collections 1918

HUNTLEY, ONTARIO

Composition reset by A. W. Hill
Moore-Telford Limited, Toronto

borders and legible type, properly graded in size and spaced with judgment, the ordinary office, with even a small range of type faces, can do very creditable work.

Sincerely yours,
R. D. CROFT.

THE Cabri (Sask.) *Clarion* submit copy of a telephone directory. The cover could be improved, we believe, by taking out the rules and bringing the wording to the centre, both top and bottom. The general style followed in the book is creditable. The office complains of a slur in the printing at the top of some of the pages. Mr. Pennie, writing of the work, says it was put on as 8 and turn. The slur might come from the cylinder not riding squarely on the bearings, but that would affect other parts as well. Some of the slurs look like washed-out ink or poor inking from the rollers, as there is sufficient impression and it meets the paper squarely enough. The slur has the same appearance as a line being slightly off its feet. If Mr. Pennie will give some more particulars about the press he uses and where the job was locked on the bed, he may get some suggestions that would help him.

THE Merchants' Printing Co., Kitchener, sent to this office several creditable samples of color work. One ingenious hanger has a color plate of the Kitchener fire department with the suggestive wording "Equipped for Rush Orders." A good selection of brown and red inks are used for the letterpress on an India tinted stock. Fire alarm box numbers and their location are included on the card which is about 12 x 8. The job is tied to a red card background, and is just such a bit of house printing as is apt to get a permanent place in the office.

WILLIAM G. JOHNSON, President
FRED POLLAKOWSKY, Vice-President

ROPER M. YOUNG, Recorder
GEORGE A. HAMON, Sec'y-Treasurer

The KITCHENER-WATERLOO
TYPOGRAPHICAL UNION

KITCHENER, ONT.

Figure B in Another Form

A Good Printer Had to Drop Out

Newcastle, N.B., Canada

The Editor,
Printer and Publisher.

. I have just finished reading your article in April *Printer and Publisher*, "He Could Not Get a Foreman," and while you put the question of the scarcity of printers very strong, you have made no effort at an answer. Why this serious shortage of printers for country offices? Does not the average country newspaperman expect too much from his foreman? I'll say he does. As you say, a country foreman "must have a knowledge of newspaper work, good newspaper typography, of job work, very often (I'll say always) of binding in certain stages, estimating and general management of country offices;" let me add "a general knowledge of the linotype,' for most country offices to-day are thus equipped. For all this knowledge, which generally takes from five to ten years to acquire he is paid (let me quote your figures, which I think are above the average) $32.00 per week for an eight hour day? Oh, no! The average country printer works from nine hours every day to twelve and fifteen on paper days and rush jobs. He is seldom, if ever, given an annual two weeks' vacation. He is expected to pick up all the local news he can find in his spare time, etc., etc. Compare the wages paid clerks, mill men, steam drivers, factory workers, railway men, city printers, and whoever you will, and you will find that the average country foreman printer is the hardest-worked and poorest-paid artisan in Canada to-day.

The writer, after fifteen years' service in country printing offices is to-day following another vocation, because the wages that have been offered me at the printing trade have been insufficient to support my wife and family, and within a few miles of this town I can give four or five other instances where good printers have laid away the stick and type to follow the hammer, shovel or rotary saw to earn an honest and respectable living.

Let the employing printers come back to earth and see the folly of expecting his foreman to be a mere piece of machinery. Let him pay him a wage in keeping with his knowledge and skill, and pass the extra cost to his customers for advertising, printing, etc., and in this manner will the printing problem be solved. The printing trade does not suffer nearly so much from the lack of apprentices as it does from the loss of men who have spent their best years serving at the trade, only to leave it when it has been mastered for an easier and better living at some other work.

Yours very truly,
R. A. N. JARVIS

There is something to think about here. *Printer and Publisher* knows something of the class of work Mr. Jarvis is capable of doing, several specimens of his having appeared in the pages of this paper. He could find plenty of openings, we are sure. He is a compositor who would be in demand, and yet he finds that it was necessary to quit the printing "because the wages that have been offered me at the printing trade have been insufficient to support my wife and family."

Who's Who

IN

St. Michael's
Parish

Huntley, Ont.

Rev. A. Stanton, P.P.

◘ ◘

STATEMENT OF

Dues and Collections
1918

Composition reset by C. W. Baughman
Moore-Telford Limited, Toronto

Will Printing Inks be Dearer?

British Printer, speaking of the tendency of ink prices, remarks in part:—*Blacks* are very largely obtained from the U.S. Exchange has put 30 to 40 per cent. on their cost during the past few weeks.

Dyes and Dye Pigments.¶ Contrary to expectation, Germany

has not flooded this market with dyes or dye pigments. There appears to be little or no stock of these articles in that country, and what there is has gone up 100 per cent., and even 200 per cent. quite recently. Further, the supplies available of British dyes and pigments added on to all that Germany can give us is entirely inadequate for the existing trade.

Linseed Oil to-day stands at about five times pre-war price and in all probability it will continue to increase in price. There seems little chance of a drop.

Resin and Mineral Oils are 200 to 500 per cent above pre-war cost, and hardening.

Tins and Drums are 200 to 300 per cent. dearer.

Labor. 100 to 150 per cent. up and will continue to cost more.

Fuel is at least 300 per cent. up.

Machinery is 300 per cent. at least, and appliances ditto.

The only surprise is that having regard to all these conditions printing inks are, generally speaking, not more than 100 to 150 per cent. dearer than they were in pre-war times,

Prices have advanced more since the above article was published than during any like period since the beginning of the Great War.

Illustrative, not only of the range of papers manufactured by the firm, but also because of the splendid printing possibilities displayed, the two books just received, entitled *Types* and *Better Paper*, issued by the S. D. Warren Co.. of Boston, are exceptionally interesting.

One Way to Stop Hearst

L. J. Taylor, proprietor of the Estevan News Store, has an 18-inch ad. in the Estevan *Mercury*, announcing that he will not handle any Hearst magazines, *Cosmopolitan, Hearst's, Good Housekeeping, Harper's Bazaar, Motor* and *Motor Boating*. The ad. states:—As a British subject I cannot continue to support a firm who are conducting an anti-British and anti-Canadian campaign throughout the United States. This will mean quite a loss to me as I have a large demand for these particular publications. But I hope and trust that the action which I have taken will be endorsed by British and Canadian subjects in Estevan and the loss involved will not be felt. If the Individual Dealers will all act there will be no need of aapproching the Dominion Government to suppress them.

Associated Advertising Club Convention

The 16th annual convention of the Associated Advertising Clubs of the World is to be held at Indianapolis, June 6–10. A number of Canadians are going to attend. Hotel reservations should be made as soon as possible. Correspondence about this or any other matter should be addressed to Associated Advertising Clubs, 110 West 20th Street.

The Canadian Club of New York City announce that it has decided to resume the issue of the club's monthly magazine, *The Maple Leaf*, on May 15. It will be enlarged to standard magazine size (7 x 10) inches and will give not only full Club news but also interesting matter of a more general character likely to be cf value both in the United States and in Canada. There will also be suitable illustrations to accompany the text. Arthur Elliot Sproul of New York, one of the members of this Club, has assumed the management of *The Maple Leaf* in its new form. Mr. Sproul is a New York journalist of experience and capacity, whose notable work in connection with American-Canadian matters, during the past year, has attracted deserved attention on both sides of the line.

The Kingston *Daily Standard* is running an interesting and unique full page, in colors, once a week for six months, in the form of a Telephone Page. It contains the announcements of over half a hundred Kingston merchants and others and, with the caption in red and the telephone numbers also in red, the remainder of the page being in black, it presents a very attractive appearance.

The Kingston *Daily Standard* on Saturday, May 1, in co-operation with the Automobile Dealers of Kingston, issued in connection with its regular daily paper a twelve-page section given over entirely to automobiles, tires and accessories. Every dealer in the city was in the number, some of them taking full pages. Special illustrations as well as reading matter had been prepared for the number, the entire issue being printed on the *Standard's* new 28-page Goss press, and presenting a fine appearance with its eight columns to the page—the *Standard* having increased its page size on the installation of its press some months ago.

Statement *of* Dues
and
Collections
1918

WHO'S WHO
IN
ST. MICHAEL'S PARISH
HUNTLEY, ONTARIO

▼

REV. A. STANTON, P.P.

Reset by J. H. Tafford, Croft & Wright, Toronto.

HENRY YOUNG, President   ANDREW BROWN, Secretary   JAMES MASON, Treasurer

REDMOND PRINTING COMPANY
FINE CATALOGUE BUILDERS
DESIGNERS : ENGRAVERS : ILLUSTRATORS : ELECTROTYPERS
PUBLISHERS OF THE IDEAL MONTHLy JOURNAL

Bathurst and Bloor Streets
Toronto, Ont.

J. HENRY JONES
President

JAMES M. SMITH
Manager

ASHDOWN PAINT COMPANY
EXCLUSIVE MANUFACTURERS OF
CROWN BRAND WHITE LEAD
PAINTS, OILS AND VARNISHES
TORONTO, ONT.

BRANCHES
MONTREAL AND WINNIPEG

ESTABLISHED 1857

OFFICE AND FACTORY
633-661 EASTERN AVENUE, TORONTO

A. R. CLARKE & CO., LIMITED
MANUFACTURERS OF
GLOVES, MITTS, MOCCASINS, MACKINAW AND
SHEEP-LINED CLOTHING, SHIRTS, ETC.

TORONTO,.................192.......

Embossing
Engraving

PHONE MAIN 248

Printing
Designing

ROBERTSON & McDONELL
Catalog, Book and Commercial
Printing
224 King St. West
Toronto, Ont....................................

Account of M...

Specimens of Work of Apprentices at Toronto Technical School

THE OTHER PUBLISHERS' BUSINESS

 Special Advertising, Circulation and Editorial Plans

The Hamilton *Review* is offered for sale.

The Brandon *Daily Sun* has a circulation contest on at present.

Le Devoir of Montreal announces that its price is increased from two to three cents.

The Rainy River *Record* on May 1st went to $2 per year for local circulation and $2.50 for foreign.

The *Daily News-Times* of Ann Arbor has announced an increase in subscription rates by carrier.

Calgary *Albertan* was offering a prize for the best story on 'How Would You Spend One Million Cold Dollars.''

The Wiarton *Canadian* announces an increase in its price to $2.00 per year, to take effect May 15th. The U.S. price is $2.50.

The Vancouver *Daily Sun* is conducting a Trip to Los Angeles contest for boys between 12 and 16 years of age. The contest is based on subscriptions as follows:—

Signed order for *Daily Sun* for 4 months, $2.00; Sunday *Sun*, 4 months, 50c; by mail, *Daily Sun*, 6 months, $3.00; by mail, Sunday *Sun*, 6 months, 75c.

The Manitoba *Free Press* has been using the bicycle page idea to secure good business. A strip 3 inches deep has a descriptive scene of bicyling in general for people of all ages and sorts.

New circulation rates for the Saginaw *News-Courier* have become effective. The Sunday issue is increased from 5 to 7 cents and the weekly price, by carrier delivery, from 15 to 20 cents.

The Winnipeg *Free Press* is conducting a contest for a "Commemoration Poem" in connection with the entry of Manitoba to the Confederation. Prizes are, first, $50; second, $25 and third $15.

The purchase of the *Western Morning News*, the *Times* of the West of England, by Sir R. Leicester Harmsworth, Bart., M.P., makes the 77th paper to pass into the hands of the Harmsworth family, a record in British journalism.

The Winnipeg *Tribune* is conducting a cooking-school at one of the large hotels. Admission to the classes is by coupons clipped from the paper. Well-known makers of food products are also represented in the exhibition, and special prizes are given in the school.

The St. Thomas *Times-Journal* gives notice of an increase in subscription rates. Delivered in St. Thomas, $6.00 per year by mail $4.50; delivered in Aylmer, $5.00 per year. Single copies of the paper, 3 cents. The new rate went in April 1, but old subscribers had until April 20 to get under cover.

The *Semi-Weekly Post* of Thorold is running a series of home-shopping material, showing that a great deal of business is going out of town that could and should be held by the home merchants. Note is made of the large number of people coming home on the trolley lines after doing their shopping in outside points.

Announcement was made that a deal has been closed whereby William R. Hearst of the New York *American* becomes owner of the plant of the Dexter Sulphite, Pulp & Paper Co. The deal is said to involve several million dollars. A timber tract of 20,000 acres was also included in the purchase.

The Halifax *Evening Echo* has a good page of business on the opening of the new St. Peter's Hall. Advertising matter was received from many who took part in its reconstruction, such

as electrical contractor, lumber company, plumbing, painters, iron columns and railings, architects, heating, shingles, etc. Are you making use of the "Clean-up and Paint-up Week" idea? Other publishers are. It comes around every year with new force, and can always be counted on to get business, provided you have some good editorial suggestions or story to tie your advertising to.

Chicago's New Selling Basis

These prices have been recommended to members of the Franklin Typothetae of Chicago by its Cost Committee:

Composing Room—Handwork	$3.50
Machine Composition—Slugs	4.00
Monotype Keyboard	3.00
Monotype Caster	2.75
Job Press, 10 x 15 and smaller	2.00
Job Press, larger than 10 x 15	2.25
Job Press, Mechanical Feed	2.00
Pony Cylinder, less than 25 x 38	3.25
Medium Cylinder, 38 x 50	4.25
Cylinder, larger than 50 inches	4.75
Kelly Press	3.25
Cylinder, Two-Color	7.50
Cutting	3.00
Machine Folder, Hand Feed	3.00
Machine Folder, Mechanical Feed	3.00
Bindery B (Men's Handwork)	2.50
Bindery C (Small Machines)	2.25
Bindery D (Girl's Handwork)	1.40

Advertising Classified Page

The Calgary *Herald* used a page recently to show the results that were secured from its classified section. The same style was followed throughout. The original ad. was shown, and the letter also cancelling the ad. as the article had been sold, the house rented, etc., in a short time. This ad. gives the idea:

Is the Day of the Repo

Taking the Prepared S

WHERE do reporters go? They quit the business—
better say "the game," for to the real reporter his work
is the greatest game imaginable. Of course, many of
them are promoted. They get desk jobs. They become
editorial writers. Neither of these chances is as good as that
of the reporter. A reporter on a good paper has the greatest
job going—bar none. There is not a good reporter out of the
business but looks back to his reporting days as the happiest in
his life.

Marquis James, in a recent issue of *Editor and Publisher*,
has an interesting review of the situation. He starts from the
way in which prepared statements are given by press agents,
publicity men and promoters generally.

"And so this is what the newspaper game is coming to," remarked the old-fashioned reporter. "No wonder more men
are getting out of it now than ever before in its history. What
is to hold them? The old fascination, which has always been
the greatest asset of the calling, is gone. When I broke into
the game twenty years ago a reporter had to get out and scratch
gravel for his stuff.

Then and Now

"The fact, figures, names and middle initials, statement of
eye-witnesses and what the police said — he had to get them
all himself, on the spot, and jot them down with his little
stub pencil.

"He wrote his story from 'notes,' cryptic and mysterious to
any but him. What does a reporter write his stuff from now?
Hand-outs. Mimeographed hand-outs which he doesn't
even have to go out and get. They are sent to his club. If
this keeps up for another ten years what will the reporter's
profession amount to when the old-timers begin to drop out?

"Suppose that after ten years of this sort of thing suddenly all
press agents should be suppressed and this elaborate private
propaganda system wiped out. How many of these reporters
de luxe would be equipped to go out and cover a story in
the old-fashioned way and then go into the office and write
it? All the city editor of that day will need are a few good
rewrite men who can read and transpose mimeographed print,
and a dozen or so uniformed messenger boys to make the
rounds and collect the hand-outs."

Betterment to be Doubted

Such is the old reporter's plaint; such the lament of the
patriarch who stands on the threshold of a new day—and a
part of what he says may be thus dismissed. An old order
never changes without regret from those who helped to make
it what it was and who cannot understand why it should not
endure forever. But there also is that in the old reporter's
lament which may not be thus dismissed. Many of the sweeping changes which have come to the metropolitan newspaper
profession within recent years will bear careful scrutiny before
we declare they are for the best simply because they are the
product of the new times.

No wonder men are getting out of the game, remarks the old-
fashioned reporter. Are they getting out? Two men who
chanced to overhear the foregoing soliloquy decided on a little
experiment. They sat down and wrote out the names of all the
newspapermen they could recall, out of hand, who had left
their jobs to go in the army. This hasty list was found to contain 36 names. Then they went over it and set down opposite each man's name his present occupation. The result
showed that only 9 of the 36 had returned to newspaper work.
Just one out of four. The tally on the remainder follows:

```
Publicity agents.......................11
Magazine writers.......................  4
Killed in action.......................  3
Trade journals.........................  2
House organs...........................  2
Magazine editor........................  1
Advertising writer.....................  1
Moving picture theatre manager.........  1
Job printing plant proprietor..........  1
Occupation not known...................  1
```

"An old school reporter, I see," laughed the other. "Not on to the curves of the new game. They don't see the boys like they used to. Statements are the thing. That's my job here. I wrote this statement."

"I know, that's all very well for the rest, but as you said, I'm of the old school. I want to see Blank. Will you take my name in?"

"I will, certainly," agreed Jerry, "and I will also inform you there is not a chance in the world of your getting by this door. When a statement goes out, that ends the discussion—until we have another statement. Oh, I know how it hits you. Hit me the same way, but I've been out of the o. d. since March—and out of the newspaper game since April, I may add."

Three "Statements"—and a Smoke

The reporter had no time to continue the discussion, for his compatriots had moved on to cover another angle of the story. He rejoined them at another downtown office, receiving another statement. He accompanied them to a third office and received a third statement. The reporter went to dinner and strolled into his office. On his desk he found an envelope filled with City News Bureau ticker and afternoon clippings. From these and the precious trio of statements he wrote his story. Then he refilled his pipe and had a long, thoughtful smoke.

He lasted on the old job just a week. Taking leave of the city editor, who was an old friend, he said:

"Boss, what you want is a messenger boy, not a reporter. But, after all, I am not really leaving your staff, merely going off the payroll. I'll have as much stuff in your columns as ever, because I am going to do publicity for Dot, Dash, & Co."

Bill is writing statements now and handing them out to the reporters. His principal mission is to keep Dot, Dash & Co. and the executive head thereof in a favorable light before the public. Under the present system the task is not difficult. He is making more money and enjoying better hours than he might expect to taking assignments from a city desk, and he was rated a good reporter and paid accordingly.

Wherever newspapermen foregather these days the changing times as reflected by channels through which a story reaches the copy desk is a topic of lively discussion. The exodus from the local rooms and the rapid development of the private propaganda field everywhere are commented upon.

Taking Care of Reporters

There is scarcely a great corporation without its publicity department, under that or another name. There is hardly a branch or bureau of the Federal Government at Washington without one. Personal press agents have become the style with a great many prominent personalities outside of the theatrical world. Rarely is there a meeting, conference, convention or assemblage of any sort at any place without a man or staff of men on the job to take care of the reporters.

To take care of the reporters. In the old days, and they were not so long ago, the reporters had to take care of themselves or they came out at the little end of the horn. Getting a story is easier than it used to be; getting *the* story is a good deal harder. It is a question whether so much solicitation is a good thing either for the reporter or the audience he addresses and instructs—the great public. Concerning this phase of the situation Frank A. Cobb writes in the New York *World*, of which he is editor:

"For five years there has been no free play of public opinion in the world. The Government has conscripted it, put it in charge of a sergeant, put it through the goose step, drilled it and made it stand at attention. Now we have nothing but private propaganda. There were 1,200 press agents before the war. I don't know how many there are now. Most direct sources of news are closed. We get the news sent out by the press agents of different organizations."

Commenting on Mr. Cobb's declaration, *Collier's Weekly* remarks with characteristic directness:

"He's right. The American people have difficulty even when there is no shortage in print paper in getting the facts about anything. Well-conducted propaganda and warmed-up personal opinion and the steaming advocacy of causes, worthy and unworthy, have been served up so long that the plain truth of hard, cold facts has almost been crowded off the dish. Most

of the great national reporters of yesterday, whose very names used to make the guilty tremble, have degenerated into two classes—those who write about themselves in relation to their opinions and those who write about their opinions in relation to themselves."

Fun Held the Old-Timers

In the old days an established percentage of the men who took up newspaper work could be relied on to stick and see it through. The pay and opportunities in the game provided about as liberal a return for talent as could be expected in most professional callings. A big factor was the fun a fellow got out of his work. For a lively interest from day to day and wholesome satisfaction in the end, the newspaper profession was hard to beat.

That day is in eclipse, if it is not past. Getting fun out of your work and leading an alert and picturesque life, desirable as they are, do not transcend the more material concerns of existence. Living costs have attained undreamed of levels. The private propaganda interests realize the tremendous value of publicity. They can afford to pay a big price for it and still turn a profit on the deal.

No newspaper man is going into the press-agent game because he prefers the work to work on a newspaper. He goes in because it pays more money, and incidentally affords shorter and more conventional hours of labor—but these are the lesser things. The money is the real attraction. In this day and age more of it is required to span the hiatus between pay-day and pay-day than ever before.

Want Skilled Men Only

The private propaganda interests require skilled men to carry out their enterprises, and they are getting them. The men who are abandoning the newspapers for this field rank high in their profession. Those who remain are the middling kind.

This is a very general statement and the specific exceptions which anyone may cite do not disprove it. Among the beginners the newspapers probably are getting as many promising youngsters as ever before. But will they stick? It is extremely doubtful. The ambitions of the young reporter of to-day are not those of the cub of 15 years ago.

The closing of direct news sources and the poisoning of the springs from which information trickles into the news columns through previously prepared channels presents an upset, the seriousness of which great editors have remarked. The stultifying effect on that mightiest of republican forces, public opinion, is the newspaper reporter. In this day of passing things is not the good going with the bad sometimes?

The old-time reporter, feared and fearless, who dug and wrote, dug and wrote, who pre-judged nothing, accepted nothing as a fact he could not establish to be a fact; who weighed words, men, motives and brought the news from producer to consumer without any aid of the pernicious middleman, or press-agent—has he gone the way of sailing ships, 50-cent table d'hotes, secret covenants and kings?

The Point System in Detail

Perhaps you know all these, and then again, you may have forgotten some of them:—

3½ point, Brilliant	20 point, 2-line Long
4½ point, Diamond	Primer or Paragon
5 point, Pearl	20 point, 2-line Small Pica
5½ point, Agate	24 point, 2-line Pica
6 point, Nonpareil	28 point, 2-line English
7 point, Minion	30 point, 5-line Nonpareil
8 point, Brevier	32 point, 4-line Brevier
9 point, Bourgeois	36 point, 2-line Great Primer
10 point, Long Primer	40 point, Double Paragon
11 point, Small Pica	42 point, 7-line Nonpareil
12 point, Pica	44 point, 4-line Small Pica
14 point, 2-line Minion	48 point, 4-line Pica or
or English	Canon
15 point, 3-line Pearl	54 point, 9-line Nonpareil
16 point, 2-line Brevier	60 point, 5-line Pica
18 point, Great Primer	72 point, 6-line Pica

Annual Meeting of C. P. A. Called for June 4

Weekly and National and Periodicals Meet June 3 and 4

THE annual meeting of the Canadian Press Association has been called for June 3rd and 4th in Toronto. The same dates are being used by the Canadian Weekly Newspaper Association and the Canadian National Newspapers and Periodicals Asso-

E. ROY SAYLES
President of the C.P.A.

ciation, while the Canadian Daily Newspaper Association will not hold its annual meeting until the 14th of October.

The daily papers claim that it is not convenient for many of their members from a distance to be in Toronto at this time. The annual meeting of the C.P.A. is to be held on the afternoon of the second day. Many of the daily members who are in Toronto or convenient to it, will no doubt be in attendance at the session, but the great bulk of the attendance will be made up from the Weekly and National Papers and Periodicals membership.

The Weekly Papers have had their programme arranged for some time back, and have a strong list of speakers. Special attention is being paid to the practical side of the business, and an effort is being made to eliminate the theorizing part of the discussion.

The Weekly programme, as mailed to the members, is as follows. It is worth noting that all the sessions are to be open to the press, and the blue pencil of the officials in censoring any reports that were to be published regarding the proceedings has been lifted. *Printer and Publisher* hopes to present a full report of the proceedings in the next issue.

THURSDAY, JUNE 3
10 a.m.

President's Address
Report of Board of Directors
Report of Manager and Treasurer
Reports of Committees
  Postal and Parliamentary—Rev. A. H. Moore.
  Circulation and Subscription—P. Geo. Pearce
  Job Printing and Estimates—A. R. Brennan
  Membership and Field Work—J. J. Hunter
  Advertising—W. R. Davies
  Paper—C. H. Hale
Imperial Press Conference
Correspondence re same and Appointment of Weekly Representatives
Appointment of Nominating Committee
"The Value of Verified Circulation Statements"
  Stanley Clague, of the Audit Bureau of Circulation, Chicago
Question Hour
  Presided over by H. P. Moore, the *Free Press*, Acton
Adjournment

2 p.m.

"The Cost of Producing Weekly Newspapers"
  E. K. Whiting, Owatonna, Minn.
"Job Estimating"
  A. R. Brennan, Summerside, P.E.I.
"How to Secure More Local Advertising for Weekly Newspapers"
  D. Maxwell Merry, B.A., Advertising Specialist

"A Talk on Typography"
  Axel Edw. Sahlin, Typographical Artist for the Roycroft Print Shops, East Aurora, N.Y.
Adjournment

FRIDAY, JUNE 4
9.30 a.m.

'Presswork'
  R. D. Croft of Toronto
'The Relation of the Weekly Newspaper to the Advertising Agency"
  Louis J. Ball, Vernon, B.C.
Report of Nominating Committee
Question Hour
  Presided over by C. H. Hale, the *Packet*, Orillia
Adjournment

2.00 p.m.

"What the C.W.N.A. is Doing for Its Members"
  J. J. Hunter, the *Reporter*, Kincardine
"Finding the Correct Cost of Job Printing"
  J. J. Hurley, Brantford
"Higher Subscription Rates"
  E. K. Whiting, Owatonna, Minn.

4.30 p.m.

General Session of the Canadian Press Association, Election of Officers, etc.

8.15 p.m.

Theatre Party

SATURDAY, JUNE 5
7.30 p.m.

Leave for Niagara Falls

Accompanying the programme is the following explanation, under the caption "Who's Who on the Programme":

Stanley Clague is a member of the Audit Bureau of Circulation of Chicago who is particularly well versed in his subject

E. K. Whiting is publisher of the *Journal-Chronicle* of Owatonna, Minn. He attended the Annual Meeting of the Canadian Press Association in 1915 and delivered two most interesting and illuminating addresses before the weekly section.

A. R. Brennan is publisher of the Summerside, P.E.I. *Journal*. He is second vice-president of the C.W.N.A., chairman of the Job Printing and Estimates Committee.

D. Maxwell Merry, B.A., is an advertising man of wide experience, at present doing free lance work in Toronto. Mr Merry was for many years connected with some of the largest New York advertising agencies. He has made a special study of the advertising possibilities of the weekly newspapers, from the viewpoint of the advertiser, the advertising solicitor, and the copy writer.

R. D. Croft is a member of the firm of Croft & Wright or Toronto, and is a pressman of acknowledged ability. He was formerly publisher of the Ailsa Craig *Banner*, and knows the weekly publisher's pressroom problems from practical exper ience.

Louis J. Ball is manager of the Vernon (B.C.) *News* Mr. Ball is one of the directors of the C.W.N.A.

J. J. Hunter is chairman of the Membership and Field Work Committee, and a former chairman of the weekly section of the C.P.A.

Axel. Edw. Sahlin is a native of Sweden and came to Amer ica early in life. For some years he has been connected with the Roycroft Print Shop at East Aurora.

Jas. J. Hurley is an alderman of the city of Brantford and manager of the Hurley Printing Company of that city. Mr Hurley has been managing large job printing establishments for 30 years.

THEATRE NIGHT

Arrangements are not yet definitely completed for the theatre night, but the management hope to have everything arranged in a few days. Full announcement will be made at the meeting.

TRIP TO THE FALLS AND EAST AURORA

The Programme Committee have completed arrangements for a trip to Niagara Falls on Saturday, the 5th, for the members and their wives, as guests of the Canada Steamships Company. They are trying to make further arrangements which will include a trip to the famous Roycroft Shops at East Aurora, N.Y., where lunch will be served. It is hoped as many as possible of the members will take in this social event, as the expense will be very low. Full announcement on meeting days.

The following is the official word that is going out announcing that the Daily Papers will not take part in the meeting as such:

"Requests of the Canadian Weekly Newspapers Association and of the Canadian National Newspapers and Periodicals Association, have been received to hold the annual meeting of the C.P.A. on June 4, as the above associations are holding their meetings on June 3rd and 4th. The Canadian Daily Newspapers Association will not hold their annual meeting until the fall.

E. ROY SAYLES,   JOHN M. IMRIE,
    President   *Acting Secretary*

Calgary "Herald's" New Clause

The Calgary *Herald* is sending the following letter to all the advertising agencies, asking also for an acknowledgment of receipt of same:—

"By our recent increase in rates and other steps toward economy in production costs we believe we have provided reasonably for the increase in newsprint, labor and other items with which the newspaper business is now faced. At the same time we cannot protect ourselves against any extreme situation which might arise particularly in regard to the supply and cost of newsprint. In order, therefore, to protect our business against such conditions we propose to stamp the following clause in each contract accepted:

"The *Herald* reserves the right to increase the rate of this contract on thirty days' notice in the event of abnormal or unforeseen increases in production costs. Such right will not be used otherwise, and the advertiser will have an equal right to cancel if he does not agree with the increase proposed.'

"It is far from the intention of the *Herald* Publishing Company to exercise the option given to it under this clause except in conditions of absolute necessity, of which you would be as fully informed as ourselves."

Minimum Prices for Printing, in Effect May 1, 1920

Adopted by the Bruce and Grey Associations

LETTERHEADS

20 lb. Bond at 23c.
(Padding 50c per 1000 extra)
250 ....$ 3 25
500 .... 4 50
1000 .... 7 00
Each Extra Thousand 4 50
For two colors add $2.00 per Thousand
For Extra Expensive Stock add to these prices proportionately.

BILLHEADS
(Padding 50c per 1000 extra)
No. 5—5 inch
8 to post— 500............$ 3 25
—1000............ 4 75
Extra Thousand 3 25
No. 7—7 inch
Quarter Cap— 500............$ 3 50
—1000............ 5 00
Extra Thousand.. 3 50
No. 11—11 inch
4 to post— 500............ 4 50
—1000............ 7 00
Extra Thousand.. 4 50
No. 14—14 inch
Half Cap— 250............ 4 25
— 500............ 5 50
—1000............ 7 50
100 of any of above..$2 50 to 4 00

NOTE, MEMO HEADS AND STATEMENTS
500 ....$ 3 50
1000 .... 5 00
Each Extra Thousand 3 25

ENVELOPES
Stock, $2.25
    250 500 1000 1000
No. 7..$2 50 $3 50 $5 00 $3 75

TICKETS
100 ....$1 50
Each Additional 100 50

GOV'T POSTCARDS
(Printing Only)
100 ....$ 1 75
Each Additional 100 50

WINDOW CARDS
11 x 14—1, $1.75; 25, $3.25; 50, $1.00; 100, $3.50.
Extra color, $1.50 additional
14 x 22—1, $2.25; $4.25; 50, $3.25; 100, $8.50.
Extra color, $2.00 additional
22 x 28—1, $2.50; 12, $3.50; 25, $5.25.

PRIVATE POSTCARDS
500, printed on two sides.$ 4 00
1000 .... 6 50

NOTE AND LETTER CIRCULARS
Note, 8vo—100, $2.75; 200, $3.25; 500, $3.75; 1000, $5.25.
Letter—100, $3.50; 200, $4.00; 500, $5.50; 1000, $8.00.
Add $2.50 to these prices for two colors. With blank fly leaf add 30 per cent.

HALF CAP CIRCULARS AND FORMS
100, $3.50; 250, $4.50; 500, $5.75; 1000, $8.00.

DODGERS
(White Paper; for colored paper add these prices.)
6 x 9 (16th Sheet)—100, $2.00; 200, $2.25; 500, $3.00; 1000, $4.00.
6 x 12 (12th Sheet)—100, $2.25; 200, $2.50; 500, $3.50; 1000, $4.50.
5 x 12 (8th Sheet)—50, $2.25; 75, $2.50; 100, $2.75; 250, $3.25; 500, $4.00; 1000, $5.50.
Each Extra Thousand, $3.25.

AUCTION SALE BILLS
Quarter Sheet—50, $4.50; 100, $5.25.
Third Sheet—25, $5.50; 50, $6.00; 100, $6.75.
Half Sheet—25, $7.50; 50, $8.00.

ADVERTISING FARM AUCTION SALES
10 cents per line for first insertion; 5 cents per line for subsequent insertion.

MERCANTILE POSTERS
Quarter Sheet
500 ....$ 10 00 to $12 50
1000 .... 12 00 to 15 00
Each Additional 100 60
Half Sheet
500 ....$15 00
1000 .... $20 to 25 00
Each Additional 100 ...... 1 00

OPEN DISPLAY POSTERS
(White Paper; for colored paper add 10 per cent. extra to these prices.)
Quarter Sheet—25, $3.25; 50.
$3.75; 100, $4.25.
Each Additional 100, $1.50.
Third Sheet—25, $3.75; 50, $4.25; 100, $5.00.
Half Sheet—25, $4.25; 50, $5.00; 75, $5.50; 100, $5.75.
Each Additional 100, $2.00.
Whole Sheet—50, $8.00; 75, $8.50; 100, $11.00.
Each Additional 100, $3.00.
For heavy composition add to above Prices.
Co-op. Work—For one color add 25 per cent.: 2 colors 50 per cent. extra.

PRINTING BILLS OFF ADVTS.
Eighth Sheet
500 ....$ 2 75
1000 .... 4 00
Quarter Sheet
100 .... 4 00
Each Additional 100 75
Half Sheets (6 or 7 Col.)
100 .... 4 00
500 .... 7 00
1000 .... 8 50
Each Additional 100 85
NOTE—The printing of bill off an advt. does not entitle the customer to any reduction in the price of his advertising.

SHIPPING TAGS
On basis of No. 5 Tag
500 ....$ 2 75
1000 .... 4 00
Other sizes in proportion
Additional 1,000 .... 3 00

MEMORIAL CARDS
50, $4.00; 75, $5.00; 100, $6.00.

VISITING CARDS
50, $1.50; 100, $1.75.
Black bordered, 50 per cent. extra.

WEDDING INVITATIONS
$2.00 Stock
15, $3.00; 25, $3.50; 50, $4.75.; 75, $6.00; 100, $7.25.
For extra expensive stock add proportionately

ALL PRICES SUBJECT TO CHANGE

AT HOME CARDS
Small—50, $2.00; 100, $2.75.
Large—50, $2.25; 100, $3.25.

BUTTER WRAPPERS
500, with Maker's Name..$ 3 75
1,000 with Maker's Name.. 5 50
"Daily Butter," 50c per 100 sheets.
Plain, 40c per 100; $1.75 per ream.

INVITATION CARDS
each additional 100, $1.25.

ROUTE CARDS
Cards, 14 x 22—50.........$ 7 00
—100......... 9 00
Folders, 7 x 7½—100......... 7 00
Each Additional 100 ...... 1 00
For extra heavy or tabulated pedigree charge $8.00 up.

RECEIPT AND ORDER BOOKS
          100 300 500
3½ x 8½..$2 00 $3 00 $3 25 $5 00
3¾ x 11.. 2 50 3 25 4 50 5 75

BALLOTS
10 Names or less, 300 ballots 5 00
Each Additional 100 ...... 1 25

PRIZE LISTS
$2.25 per page for 200 copies, and 25c per page additional for each extra 100 copies.

FINANCIAL STATEMENTS AND AUDITOR'S REPORTS
Size of page 5½ x 8½, type 24 ems by 40 ems. 200 copies, $2.25 per page. For each additional 100 add 25c per page. Cover to count as four pages.

VOTERS' LISTS
On basis of an average of 25 lines to a page, $2.50 per page for 200 copies. Where average is higher add to price proportionately. 300 copies $2.75 per page. Set without rules.

BOOKS, PAMPHLETS, CONSTITUTIONS, BY-LAWS, MINUTES, ETC.
100 copies, 8 pt. solid, $2.00 per page, 20c per page additional for each 100 copies.

A Canadian Typographical Union

A Montreal report states:—That the strike of the printers on the Montreal *Star*, which has failed and will be settled by return of the men on the terms offered by the newspaper, is not finished, but is part of a larger movement of a fight against the International Typographical Union, was indicated to-day. It is said that an effort is being made to form a Canadian Typographical Union; three cities—Winnipeg, Toronto and Montreal—have already taken into consideration this project, which may be given further support by the developments of the next few days in Toronto, where the printers have made demands for a wage of $40.80 a week.

Mr. W. B. Burgoyne, editor of the St. Catharines *Standard*, has had compiled in booklet form the series of editorial articles that have been running in the *Standard* in regard to the newsprint situation. In these Mr. Burgoyne has taken the stand that large city papers, by their cheap use of the mail service, have been giving an unnecessary service to districts some distance removed from their place of publication. To use a phrase from its own columns:—"The *Standard* believes that one of the most effective and most legitimate methods of saving newsprint and saving the smaller city dailies from destruction is for the Dominion of Canada to deny the privileges of the second-class mail to any newspaper which makes a lower subscription rate to the public than the actual cost of the white paper in its issues, plus postage at business rates. Advertisers should not be called upon to pay for losses caused by low subscription rates, nor should the Dominion be called upon to help these wealthy publishers in their work of avarice and destruction."

Convention Associated Advertising Clubs

The 16th annual convention of the Associated Advertising Clubs of the World is to be held at Indianapolis, June 6-10. A number of Canadians are going to attend. Hotel reservations should be made as soon as possible. Correspondence about this or any other matter should be addressed to Associated Advertising Clubs, 110 West 20th Street.

The Canadian Club of New York City announces that it has decided to resume the issue of the club's monthly magazine, *The Maple Leaf*, on May 15th. It will be enlarged to standard magazine size (7 x 10 inches) and will give not only full Club news but also interesting matter of a more general character, likely to be of value both in the United States and in Canada. There will also be suitable illustrations to accompany the text. Arthur Elliot Sproul of New York, one of the members of this Club, has assumed the management of *The Maple Leaf* in its new form. Mr. Sproul is a New York journalist of experience and capacity, whose notable work in connection with American-Canadian matters, during the past year, has attracted deserved attention on both sides of the line.

Illustrative, not only of the range of papers manufactured by the firm, but also because of the splendid printing possibilities displayed, the two books just received, entitled *Types* and *Better Paper*, issued by the S. D. Warren Co., of Boston, are exceptionally interesting.

British Printer, speaking of the tendency of ink prices, remarks in part:—*Blacks* are very largely obtained from the U.S. Exchange has put 30 to 40 per cent. on their cost during the past few weeks.

Dyes and Dye Pigments. Contrary to expectation, Germany has not flooded this market with dyes or dye pigments. There appears to be little or no stock of these articles in that country and what there is has gone up 100 per cent., and even 200 per cent. quite recently. Further, the supplies available of British dyes and pigments added on to all that Germany can give us is entirely inadequate for the existing trade.

Linseed Oil to-day stands at about five times pre-war price and in all probability it will continue to increase in price. There seems little chance of a drop.

Resins and Mineral Oils are 300 to 500 per cent. above pre-war cost, and hardening.

Tins and Drums are 200 to 300 per cent. dearer.

Value of Automatic Equipment

Speaking before the Chicago Club of Printing House Craftsmen, A. C. Hammond, vice-president and Western manager of the Dexter Folder Co., had this to say in regard to the use of automatic machinery in general, and feeders in particular:—

Several vital conditions must be considered by you, gentlemen, for the future. The industries of this country are right now, and will be for a long time to come, called upon to exert every ounce of energy to increase production. How? Not by the employment of additional labor—of which there is an existing shortage—but by increasing efficiency and by providing every means to increase it. You are the avenues through which your concerns and employers are depending to accomplish this result. Your subordinates are the manual producers, and it is up to you to suggest and provide ways and means that your employees may be aided in accomplishing this desired result.

Automatic equipment is one of your opportunities. You can advance the interests of your employers and improve your own working conditions physically and financially in no better way than by recommending the use of automatic feeders on practically every cylinder, folding machine and job press, as well as other ordinarily hand-fed equipment.

Don't forget that hand labor, however willing, cannot conscientiously approximate the accuracy of a machine. It is physically impossible to hand feed two sheets of paper precisely the same. It is a known fact that hand feeders are not being developed to-day as in years past, and no doubt you are experiencing difficulties in obtaining a sufficient number of such employees.

Are you going to limit the production of your plant by retaining old views and objections to automatic equipment, when your competitor is clamoring for these labor-saving and profit-producing devices? You know what the average output is on hand-fed cylinder presses and what it would mean to increase that product 20 or even 40 per cent. If an automatic can (and it will), you cannot very well stand in the way of producing a great volume of business turn-over, and you will agree that an increased output on your presses means a greater earning capacity through the entire plant, as each branch of the industry is dependent upon how much you can produce from the press room.

Put forth every effort there is in you to make working conditions better for your employee. Show him how he can produce, with modern improved methods, a greater number of dollars for you or his employer, which I believe you will approve that, in this period of high wages, becomes an economical and commercial necessity.

Recognition of Agencies

The C.D.N.A. has made a radical departure in the matter of recognizing agencies. Under the new basis recognition may be granted to parties possessing the necessary experience, equipment and financial resources even although they may not have one general advertising account. In other words, recognition may be granted to a party with the necessary experience, equipment and financial resources the day he starts in business. There is this important restriction, however, recognition when first granted and for the first six months will be of a limited character, covering only the handling and placing of NEW accounts. The applicant for recognition will be required to agree that during this period of six months he will not attempt to place any account handled by another recognized advertising agency during the currency of its existing contract. At the end of this six months' period, if the C.D.N.A. considers the new business developed warrants such action, the new agency may be accorded full recognition entitling it to place old as well as new accounts. As a precaution against the new agency slackening in its promotional work after getting full recognition a limit of one year is placed upon full recognition when first granted. When an application for extension of full recognition beyond that period is considered special attention will be given to t e nature, extent and results of the promotional work to dateh.

The business and executive offices of the Mergenthaler Linotype Company, long maintained in the Tribune Building, now occupy their new home in the eight-storey factory building

(extending from Nos. 15 to 45 Ryerson Street) which has been added to the group in Brooklyn. The new address is 29 Ryerson St., Brooklyn, N.Y.

Sees More Tombstones Sprouting

Simcoe *Reformer:*—One result of the present rise in the price of newsprint and the one that will be made next July will undoubtedly be the suspension of many papers during the coming year. Another result will be that those newspapers that desire to live will have to raise their subscription price to $2 at least. In the United States the price of many weeklies is $2 and $3, and some weeklies in Canada have adopted this rate. Certain it is that under prevailing conditions it will not be possible to survive long at the $1.50 rate.

"La Presse" Has New Rate Card

La Presse, Montreal, announce a new tariff of advertising rates, effective June 1st. An essential condition of all contracts is that space must be used, on a regular schedule, starting within sixty days from acceptance. Agency commission, 15 per cent. Cash discount, 2 per cent. Cash discount date, 20th of month following publication.

General Advertising—Per Line Agate.

Transient........................	$0.25
500 lines or more............................	.18
1,000 lines or more............................	.17
2,500 lines or more............................	.16
5,000 lines or more............................	.15
10,000 lines or more............................	.14

Display Classifications—Per Line Agate.

Amusements (general)........................	.25
Circus and Tent Shows......................	.50
Annual Reports and Financial Statements.............	.20
Dividend and Annual Meeting Notices	.12½

Classified (Undisplayed):
2c a word, cash with order; 3c a word, when charged. Minimum, fifteen words each insertion.

Franklin Club in Toronto

It is proposed to form a Franklin Club in Toronto of the present users of the Franklin Price List. A committee has been at work on the proposition and have already held several meetings. Another meeting is being held on the 19th of May at the Simcoe Club Rooms, Yonge St. Arcade, at which Mr. C. L. Jones will speak. The committee looking after the details are: Geo. A. Davis, chairman; P. Bell, Industrial and Technical Press, Ltd.; S. Snyder, Colonial Printing Co.; Don. Sutherland, Sutherland Print Shop.

A larger meeting is being arranged for June 7th, when R. T. Porte, of the Porte Printing Co., of Salt Lake City, will deliver an address on "Estimating and the Application of the Franklin Price List."

Honolulu, Hawaii, April 19.
Printer and Publisher,
145–149 University Avenue,
Toronto, Canada.
Gentlemen:

I have duly received your letter of the 12th inst., and your copy of *Printer and Publisher*, and I am very interested in this, Canada's National Printing Trade Paper.

Enclosed find a cheque for $3.00 of Bishop Bank of Hawaii for the subscription price of *Printer and Publisher* per year. So please send me the above paper from now on.

Yours very truly,
J. WATANABE, Importer.

Beginning May 3, the Jackson morning and evening papers advanced their rates to 20 cents a week. The Sunday edition of these papers hereafter will cost 7 cents.

THE PERSONAL SIDE OF IT

 We'd Like To Get Items For
These Columns

Quebec

The Montreal *Gazette* of May 1st referred editorially, at some length, to the discontinuance of one of their Saturday features. With this issue, the Saturday literary review, which for thirty-one years has appeared in the *Gazette* under the title "At Dodsley's," comes to an end. It is with reluctance and regret the announcement is made that no more will our readers revel in the brilliant writing, the trenchant criticism, the store of literary and historical knowledge poured out during that long period of time by the author, who half-concealed and half-disclosed his identity over the initials "M. J. G." To many no secret is revealed when we make known the author to be Mr. Martin J. Griffin, C.M.G., Librarian of Parliament, Ottawa. Mr. Griffin parts with his readers and lays down a willing and prolific pen with regret scarcely less than will be felt by those he has instructed and delighted for more than a quarter of a century, but the penalty of arduous work falls at some time on all, and impaired health compels him to cease the contributions which have given so much pleasure and profit. . . . . The title of his reviews was happily chosen. Robert Dodsley was the most celebrated bookseller and publisher in London in the eighteenth century. His name and work figure in the memoirs of that period as those of a man of industry, enterprise and talent. . . . . Of Mr. Griffin's personality a word suffices. He lives among his books, shunning the bubble reputation and garish light that falls upon celebrities. His early residence was in Halifax and his first profession that of the law, but his bent was literature, and as long ago as 1868 he accepted the editorship of the Halifax *Express*. In journalistic circles, however, Mr. Griffin is best remembered as chief editor of the Toronto *Mail* for five years previous to his becoming Librarian of the House of Commons in 1885, when he ceased from party political controversy and devoted his subsequent leisure to literature."

Maritimes

Leo Troy of Chatham, N.B., returned soldier, has joined the writing staff of the St. John *Standard.*

F. W. W. Bartlett, of the writing staff of the St. John *Times*, and Everett Chambers, of the writing staff of the St. John *Globe*, are graduates this year from the King's College Law School. They will go to Windsor in May to receive their degrees.

Woodstock *Press*:—John Wallace, the veteran printer, is very ill at his home here. Mr. Wallace, who is 74 years of age, came here from Fredericton over 50 years ago, and has resided here, with the exception of a year in Fredericton, continuously ever since. He is a good citizen and has many friends, who sincerely wish him a speedy recovery.

E. Allan Schofield, president of the Schofield Paper Co., Ltd., has been elected mayor of St. John. His victory was quite a notable one, as he scored a majority of almost two thousand over his opponent. Mr. Schofield has been active for many years in civic affairs and during the war was particularly energetic in patriotic endeavor. Through his activities much has been done to help promote the best interests of the city and port. His selection as chief magistrate of the city is expected to prove most popular.

British Columbia

Miss Glazer, recently telegraph editor on the *Daily News*, Nelson, has resigned, and gone to Vancouver to reside.

The *Herald*, Penticton, announces a raise in display advertising rates from thirty to forty cents, effective May 1st.

The *Ledge*, Greenwood, advanced its subscription price to $2.50 a year the first of the month—and gave no advance notice of the increase, either.

Geo. Kennedy, an old newspaperman in B.C., has taken charge of the editorial and news department of the *Herald*, Merritt. Editor Ellis of the *Herald* is Merritt's stipendiary magistrate.

The *Daily News*, Nelson, is running a circulation-gettin advertising campaign in the Kootenay and Boundary weeklie during April, May and June, using five and ten inch spac alternate weeks.

Ben Wallace, with the *Daily Entertainer*, which flourishe for a few weeks in the boom days of Cranbrook ten years ag was married at Fernie last month. He is now with the *Ech* Pincher Creek, Alta.

The *Saturday Miner*, Rossland, announces that if all change of advts. are in by Wednesday afternoon, composing roo operations can be so arranged as to obviate any raise in adve tising rates for the present.

The *News*, Trail, claims to have increased its circulation 8 per cent. since the first of the year. At present the *Dai News*, Nelson, is running a page of Trail advertising and readi matter in its regular issue each day.

Had it not been for the *Courier* staff lending a hand the *Heral* Cranbrook, would have had to skip its issue of the middle wee in April. Editor Elletson was taken suddenly ill and had to § to his home at Rossland to recuperate, arriving there only 1 find Mrs. Elletson also on the sick list.

H. W. Power, formerly of the *Kootenaian*, who for yea past had been Kaslo's foremost exponent of amateur histrion art, is treading the footlights of Spokane, where he is at prese with Mining Truth, playing the leading role there last week "A Night at an Inn."

The Prince Rupert *News* has the following announcemer about its advertising rates:—From now on, transient displa advertising will cost $1.25 per inch per insertion, and if require on the front page, $2.00 per inch. Reading notices will t charged at 25c per line per insertion and classified advertis ments 2c per word. The rates on the other particular class of advertising are shown on the new rate card, which may t had upon application.

Alberta

Because the Rimbey, Alberta, *Pioneer* published an adve tisement of a new Rimbey townsite company, advocates of t old site broke into the newspaper office and wrecked the presse

On April 21 the Macleod *Times*, a paper that started on three months ago, took over the plant and business of t Macleod *News*, an old established business. They report bus ness as very good, having secured every available advertise C. J. Dillingham and W. H. Day are the proprietors. M Day is a former alderman, who has a large grocery busines He went West from Ontario some years ago.

Saskatchewan

The Saskatchewan division of the Canadian Press Associ tion are holding a short course in journalism at the Universit of Saskatchewan, Saskatoon, on May 27, 28 and 29. W. / MacLeod, editor of Publications, is collecting a lot of inform tion about the rates charged by the papers of the province. I finds that many are not getting a living rate and an effort going to be made to standardize rates on a basis that will bri a profitable return. The Association has a big programme i hand, and a good time is being arranged for the spare momen

Manitoba

J. H. McCulloch, B.S.A., has been appointed manager edit of the *Farmers' Advocate and Home Journal*, Winnipeg, su ceeding R. B. Thomson, who has gone to Saskatchewan t operate his farm in the Indian Head district. Mr. McCulloc has been with the *Farmers' Advocate* for three years as associat and livestock editor, and was previously with the *Farm ai Ranch Review*, Calgary, for two years. He spent one year : district representative and superintendent of dry farmir stations in British Columbia. He came to Canada from Sco land in 1907 and is a graduate of Ontario Agricultural Colleg but took part of his training at Manitoba Agricultural College.

Ontario

The Leamington *Post-News* has started on the forty-sixth year of its publication.

Mrs. Kernighan, of Rockton, mother of Robert K. Kernighan, widely known as "the Khan," is dead.

Stephenson & Blake have moved their Toronto premises to larger and more commodious quarters at 130 Wellington Street West.

Port Hope *Times* has changed hands, Mr. H. M. Ryan, Newburgh, having purchased it from Messrs. Wright & Plummer.

T. N. Wells, publisher of the Dresden, Ontario, *Times*, underwent a critical operation on April 12th in the Toronto General Hospital.

The ninth annual convention of the Ontario and Quebec Conference of Typographical Unions will be held in Hamilton on June 14, 15 and 16.

Thomas Jarratt, a newspaper man of considerable experience, is contemplating the establishment of another paper in Trenton, to be called the *Sun*.

. Mark Minhinnick, who since returning from overseas has been a member of the staff of the London *Advertiser*, has severed his connection with that paper.

W. J. Duncan, who recently sold the *Mountain Herald* to H. Barry, has purchased the Vankleek Hill *Review*, formerly owned by Mr. Jones, who died recently.

Mr. Sam Hunter, the political cartoonist, who has been drawing pictures in the *World* for a long time, has joined the staff of the Toronto *Globe*, in which paper his work is appearing daily.

Barrie *Examiner*:—Beginning with the first issue of May, the price of single copies of the *Examiner* will be five cents. These are sold at the stationery stores and at the *Examiner* office.

The Allen Paper Co., formerly of 25 Melinda Street, announces the removal of the business to new premises at 105 Simcoe Street, Toronto. They are issuing from time to time warehouse stock lists, with prices.

It is understood that a proposal for the establishment of a Presbyterian weekly newspaper will be one of the recommendations of the Assembly's special committee on the co-ordination of church officialdom.

The Toronto *Globe* has placed a memorial tablet in its office, bearing the names of Harry C. Edmison, Jaffray Eaton, Michael Lyons and Robert Davey, who died in France or Flanders in the great war.

Mr. and Mrs. T. H. Preston have sailed from New York on the White Star Liner Adriatic for Southampton. Before returning they intend visiting the battlefields and more particularly the grave of their son, the late Lt. H. B. Preston, at Bourlon.

Ottawa *Citizen* has 45 small ads. on a page, the hidden name being the drawing card. Five women's names are taken at random from the city directory and inserted in various ads. Prizes are given at the stores on the page according to the volume of sales.

Maxwell B. Cody, assistant night editor of the London *Free Press*, who recently returned from Ottawa, where he was covering the House, is seriously ill with inflammatory rheumatism. His physician states that it will be six weeks before he can leave his bed.

Bert B. Perry, former sporting editor of the London *Advertiser*, and recently copy writer with the advertising firm of McConnell and Fergusson, has taken a position as Western Ontario traveller for a firm manufacturing adhesive paper for wrapping purposes.

J. E. Middleton has gone with the Provincial Hydro as publicity man, and editor of their house organ. Since the Toronto *Times* failed Mr. Middleton has spent some time doing publicity work for Victory Loan and latterly for the Church Forward movement.

Mr. E. G. Wilson, formerly secretary of the Ottawa Housing Commission, has been appointed manager of the Canadian National Newspaper and Periodicals Association. His office is at 70 Lombard Street. Mr. Wilson has had some newspaper experience, being at one time on the staff of Ottawa papers.

The Geo. Everall Printing Co. have acquired the building at 107 and 109 Jarvis street, Toronto, from J. M. Miller, for $27,500. It is a solid brick structure containing two storeys and basement, with a frontage of 35 feet 9 inches by a depth of 132 feet. A portion of the building has been occupied by the present purchasers for six years.

The People's Press of Welland, published by the Tribune Printing Co., has concluded an arrangement whereby it will publish a weekly cartoon dealing with municipal affairs. The cartoons will be drawn by Leslie McFarlane, a recent addition to the reportorial staff, who was formerly on the Cobalt *Nugget* and the *Haileyburian*.

International Bookbinders and Printers, at a very largely attended meeting held at the Toronto Labor Temple, decided by a unanimous resolution to make only yearly agreements with the master printers and bookbinders in the future. They also decided to ask the employers to grant increases adequate to meet the increasing high cost of living.

Bancroft *Times*:—The Minden *Echo* publishing business changed hands last week, Mr. Baker, the former proprietor, having sold to Mr. Wilmur Macarthur, a gentleman of ability and knowledge, covering several years in the printing business. The new proprietor is well known at Minden and in the county of Haliburton, having occupied the position of principal of the village school there for a number of years.

Shelburne *Free Press*:—The *Free Press* this week has passed another milestone in its career and has entered upon its 46th year of publication. Exactly 45 years ago to-day the first issue of the *Free Press* was published, and it is therefore now entering upon the 46th year of its existence, 37½ years of which it was under the able management of the late Robert Lee Mortimer, whose death occurred on Aug. 2nd last.

J. H. Woods, editor and managing director of the Calgary *Herald*, has been created a Chevalier of the Order of Leopold by King Albert of Belgium, and by order of His Majesty the Star of the Order was presented to him by M. De Burlet, Belgian consul at Calgary, at a public ceremony. The honor was conferred on Mr. Woods because of signal services during the war as secretary-treasurer of the Belgian Relief Committee for Southern Alberta.

The *Eastern Ontario Review*, of Vankleek Hill, conducted for many years by the late H. C. Jones, changed hands when Mr. W. J. Duncan, of South Mountain, Ont., acquired the plant and goodwill from the estate of the late Mr. Jones. Mr. Duncan was formerly editor and proprietor of the *Mountain Herald* and took part in municipal affairs, being a councillor for three years; also secretary of the Mountain Fair, and auditor for the united counties of Stormont, Dundas and Glengarry.

Rainy River *Record*:—J. A. Osborne, veteran editor of the Rainy River district, and latterly of the Radford *Journal*, Virginia, has thrown up the editorial pen and gone in for a large private business project. Mr. Osborne's papers have always been noted for their clean and wholesome editorials, and in losing Mr. Osborne, newspaperdom is losing a man who by his sterling character and his versatile pen has gained the confidence and friendship of the public.

Another morning paper is to be started in Winnipeg, if present negotiations for the amalgamation of the *Telegram* and *Tribune* go through. Davidson and Smith, Port Arthur men, are owners of the *Telegram*, and R. L. Richardson, M.P., backed up by A. A. MacDonald, millionaire grocer, own the *Tribune*. The idea is purely commercial, to make two papers better paying propositions in view of the future cost of news-print. The Hon. Arthur Meighen, it is also stated, is taking a deep interest in the *Telegram's* future.

A movement is on foot in Presbyterian circles, according to a Toronto report, for the establishment of an official church weekly newspaper. The only official organ of the Canadian Presbyterian Church in existence is the *Record*, which is published in Montreal under the editorship of Rev. Dr. Ephraim Scott. This is a small monthly periodical, which is distributed throughout the church in the form of a parish magazine. The *Presbyterian and Westminster*, which is published in Toronto, is owned by the Westminster Publishing Company.

Mrs. A. Cecil Gibson, widow of the late Captain A. Cecil Gibson, and the first editress of the "On Dit" column of the *Mail and Empire*, died at her late residence, 43 Elm Avenue, Toronto. Mrs. Gibson was the daughter of the late David Walker, who founded the Walker House Hotel in Toronto. She was born in Chatham, Ont., in 1866, but had been a resident of Toronto since her removal here at an early age. She took ill with influenza last February and never fully recovered. Mrs. Gibson was a member of St. Simon's Church. One daughter, Miss Marian, and one son, Capt. A. Cecil Gibson, and two sisters survive.

At the home of sister, Mrs. H. L. Chambers, 70 Stibbard Avenue, Toronto, Joseph Albert Warren died on Monday night from pneumonia. The deceased was 42 years of age, unmarried, and was employed on the editorial staff of the *Evening Telegram*. Enlisting with the Calgary Rifles in September, 1914, the late Mr. Warren saw much active service in France. He was twice wounded and finally discharged as medically unfit on June 27, 1919. Prior to the war he was connected with the Ottawa *Citizen* and the Calgary *Herald*. He was born and educated in Stirling, Ont., where the body was taken for interment.

Representative members and pastors of most of the Baptist churches in Toronto and its vicinity were present at a council held in the St. John's Road Baptist Church, when Mr. Dixon A. Burns, pastor of the church, was ordained to the Gospel ministry. Rev. Dr. Graham was the Moderator. Rev. J. R. Turnbull acted as Clerk of the council and conducted devotional exercises; the sermon was delivered by Rev. O. C. Elliott, and the charge to the church was made by Rev. J. B. Kennedy. Mr. Burns was formerly with the Toronto *Globe*. He is a graduate of the Toronto Bible College, and an under-graduate of McMaster University.

The following officers were elected by acclamation for Toronto Typographical Union:—President, Andrew Gerrard; vice-president, Walter Williams; secretary-treasurer, Samuel Hadden; recorder, George Murray; sergeant-at-arms, John McMahon; auditors, W. R. Steep, E. Webb, F. J. McNeillie; trustees, A. E. Thompson, Theo. Hopmans; delegates to Toronto District Labor Council, Messrs. Van Horne, Brayshaw, Webb, Beamish, Lucas, Simpson, Mance, Tolhurst, R. J. Stevenson, Burley, Kirkpatrick, Desmond W. Williams, McDougall, Burnham, Morrow, Monkman, Gerrard, McKay, Colgate, McCann, Elfreen, Lovess, N. M. Williams; delegates to Labor Educational Association, W. Turnbull, R. J. Stevenson, Walter Hardley. Delegates to the Trades and Labor Congress, I.T.U. convention at Albany and the Ontario and Quebec Conference of Typographical Unions and members of the Executive Committee and the Board of Relief remain to be elected.

J. W. Ferguson, now general manager of the *Editor and Publisher*, New York, has been appointed manager of the Advertising Promotion Department of the Canadian Daily Newspaper Association. Mr. Ferguson was born in Scotland, but came to Canada in his early youth and started newspaper work on the London *Advertiser*, with which paper he was connected for some time. In New York he was on the advertising department of the New York *Times*, and later became business manager of both the New York *Herald* and the New York *Telegram*. *Editor and Publisher* under his management has been an ardent advocate of the daily newspaper as an advertising medium. His appointment will strengthen the Canadian Daily Newspaper Association, of which John M. Imrie is the manager. Mr. Ferguson will enter upon his new duties on May 17.

Death removed a well-known and highly-esteemed resident of Paris, in the person of Charles Lawton, editor and proprietor of the Paris *Review*. Deceased was born in Yorkshire, England, in April 1860, and when 21 years of age came to Canada. Shortly after he went to Mount Forest, and was engaged upon the *Confederate*. Later he went to Beeton, where he was connected with the *World*. While there he married Miss Patterson, who predeceased him in 1899. After a short period spent on the staff of the Orillia *Times*, the late Mr. Lawton went to Toronto, where he filled the position of night editor on the *World*, later being day editor. This position he held till the fall of 1894, when he came to Paris, having purchased the *Review*. He was secretary of the Publicity Committee of the Board of Trade, and also secretary of the Patriotic League. In 1899 he was united in marriage to Miss Margaret Ames of Paris, who survives him, as also two sons, Claude and Nelson of Paris, and two daughters.

Globe, May 4th:—Fifty years ago yesterday W. J. Wilkinson, news editor of the *Mail and Empire*, and one of the best-known newspapermen in Canada, entered newspaper work. In the last half century he has worked on four papers, three of them in Toronto, and for the past twenty years he has been with the *Mail and Empire*. Mr. Wilkinson's father, Jonathan Wilkinson, was the founder of the Guelph *Advertiser*, now the Guelph *Mercury and Advertiser*, but before his son was old enough to take any part in the business he moved to St. Thomas and founded the St. Thomas *Times*. When eleven years old his son commenced to set type, and for the next ten years he not only wrote the news he gathered, but set it and then turned the press. Thirty years ago Mr. Wilkinson came to Toronto and joined the *World* as a reporter, but before he left, five or six years later, he was news editor. From the *World* he went as news editor to the *News*, and after a few years transferred to the *Mail and Empire*. Yesterday he received the congratulations of many friends upon his jubilee.

Newfoundland

Sir P. T. McGrath, editor St. John's *Herald*, has been in the United States all winter on a health trip.

W. J. Herder, proprietor St. John's *Telegram*, badly sprained his ankle early in February and was laid up for several weeks.

The *Workman* of St. John's, owned by W. J. Nichols, has been sold to Goodland and Ellis.

Hon. Alex. W. Mews, editor *Fisherman's Advocate*, St. John's, was also similarly treated shortly after the late general elections.

Hon. D. A. Campbell of the *Western Star*, Curling, has been appointed a member of the Legislative Council of Newfoundland and Minister of Agriculture and Mines.

The position of President Newfoundland Legislative Council, formerly held by Sir P. T. McGrath, from which he resigned last November, has been filled by Hon. J. D. Ryan.

Ed. L. Oke, son of Judge Oke, of Harbour Grace, succeeds Jas. D. Munn in the management of the Harbour Grace *Standard*.

Andrew Edward Wright, proprietor of the Times Printing Office, St. John's, died on 8th March of heart failure, in his fortieth year.

J. C. Puddester, business manager St. John's *Daily News*, was confined to his home for some time with la grippe. He is around again now, however.

At one time in March members of practically every printing office in St. John's were confined to their homes suffering from la grippe.

The St. John's *Evening Telegram* celebrated its 41st anniversary on April 21. That paper was started on April 21, 1879, by W. J. Herder, its present proprietor.

D. R. Thistle, formerly business manager of the St. John's *Daily Star*, from which he resigned to take a mercantile position, has since been appointed business manager of the *Trade Review*, the organ of the St. John's Board of Trade.

Hon. A. W. Mews, editor *Fisherman's Advocate*, St. John's, was confined to his home the early part of March with influenza. He has since been able to resume duties. At one time eight of the *Advocate's* staff were off through illness.

Dr. J. A. Robinson resigned the position of Postmaster-General after the resumption of present Government to power, and has taken offices in the *Daily News* building. Mr. Robinson is an experienced newspaper man, whose pen is a ready writer, in fact he is without a peer to-day in the Fourth Estate in Newfoundland, and he has done much in the past to uplift the general tone of journalism of the new Dominion. As Postmaster-General he put forward many reforms for the improvement of that branch of the public service.

Fred W. Halls, president of the Fred W. Halls Paper Co., Toronto, in a recent letter, seeks to point out to the trade the real situation, especially in regard to bonds and writing papers. The letter points out that the high pressure demand for paper will continue, and that printers and lithographers, in their own interests, should make provision for future needs. The circular goes into the matter of supply, demand and costs, stating it as the opinion of the firm that nothing is to be gained by staying out of the market in the hope of lower prices.

. London "Punch."

REBUILT MACHINERY

No. 376—Two-Revolution Campbell, bed 33x42, table distribution, front fly delivery, four form rollers, four distributors.

No. 436—No. 3 Scott Drum Cylinder Press, bed 24½x31.

No. 202—25x34 Whitlock Drum Cylinder Press, table distribution, rear tapeless delivery, two form rollers, four distributors, back up.

No. 338—Six column folio Diamond Press, bed 24x32½, power fixtures.

No. 1826—10x15 Falcon, good as new.

No. 368—10x15 Eclipse, throw-off treadle, six chases.

No. 418—13x19 Colt's Armory.

No. 433—7x11 Beaver, treadle, throw-off, two chases, roller mould.

No. 439—10x15 Gordon, with treadle, power fixtures and throw-off.

No. 412—8½x28 Roller Proof Press.

No. 405—No. 7 Brehmer Wire Stitcher, fitted with handle and foot power.

No. 390—No. 8 Brehmer Wire Stitcher, on stand.

No. 370—Breech Loaded Stapler.

No. 417—19" W. & B. Lever Cutter.

No. 434—19" W. & B. Lever Cutter.

No. 428—19" W. & B. Lever Cutter.

No. 427—26" W. & B. Lever Cutter.

No. 235—10" Bradley Card Cutter.

No. 237—Piper Ruling Machine, 32" cloth, 2 beam striker, lay-boy and power.

No. 391—No. 5 Steel Climax Baler.

No. .298—2 H.P. Century A.C. Motor, 550 volts, 25-cycle, 3 phase, speed 440.

A cordial invitation is extended to the printers
and publishers of Canada to visit our
NEW PLACE OF BUSINESS

130 Wellington Street West
TORONTO
Come and inspect our stock of printing machinery
and supplies at your first opportunity.

STEPHENSON, BLAKE & CO.
C. H. CREIGHTON
Manager
130 Wellington Street West, Toronto

Brass Rule Made to Order   *Roller Composition and Casting*

GEO. M. STEWART
PRINTING and BOOKBINDING MACHINERY
TYPE and SUPPLIES
92 McGill Street, Montreal, 'Phone Main 1892

*Thoroughly Rebuilt Cylinder and Platen Presses, Paper Cutters and Machinery of all
kinds for Printers, Bookbinders, Box Makers, etc. Write and state your requirements.*

Say

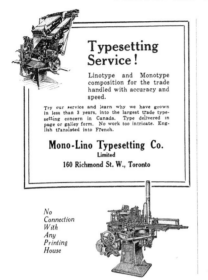
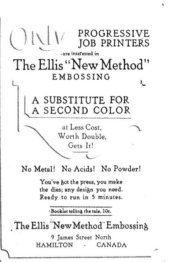

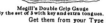

The Most Important Agency

In Producing Newspapers is the Mechanical Equipment

THE quality of newspaper printing depends in a great measure upon the plates. Improvement requires better plates, and for better plates HOE MACHINERY is essential. The newspaper halftone is no longer of necessity a smudge—it may be an attractive picture, and usually is when HOE MACHINERY is employed in making the matrices and finishing the plates.

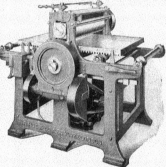

HOE DUO-COOLED EQUIPOISE CASTING MOULDS WITH DOUBLE PUMP FURNACE.
The last word in rapid plate-making equipment.

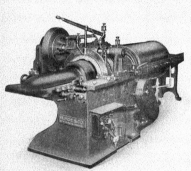

HOE AUTOMATIC PLATE-FINISHING MACHINE.
Trims, tail cuts, shaves, cools and dries six plates a minute.

HOE PNEUMATIC MATRIX-DRYING TABLES.
Make the best matrices in the quickest time and in the most economical manner.

HOE IMPROVED MATRIX-ROLLING MACHINE.
The strongest and most rigid roller made. Easy to control. Gives the most powerful and uniform impression.

There is nothing in the line of Printing and Plate-Making Machinery which R. Hoe & Co. cannot make at least a little better than anyone else and at the lowest price consistent with the highest grade of workmanship and materials.

R. HOE & CO.
504-520 Grand Street, New York

| 7 Water Street BOSTON, MASS. | 827 Tribune Building CHICAGO, ILL. | 109-112 Borough Road LONDON, S.E., 1, ENGLAND |

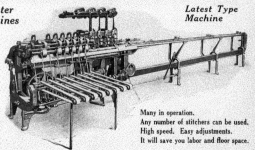

CLASSIFIED ADVERTISEMENT SECTION

NEWSPAPER FOR SALE

A newspaper is offered for sale in one of the most thriving towns in the Annapolis Valley, Nova Scotia. Only a moderate capital required. The business is in good condition, but the owner has good private reasons for selling. Apply to

O. K.
c/o Printer and Publisher
Toronto, Ont. (P5P)

BUSINESS CHANCES

FOR SALE — NEWSPAPER AND JOB printing plant at a bargain; a well-equipped and established business in a thriving industrial Nova Scotia town will be disposed of at a right price; large advertising and job printing income; only newspaper in a large and prosperous community. Apply at once for particulars to Box 666, Printer and Publisher, Toronto, Ont. (ptfp)

THE MONOTYPE OPERATOR IS THE man who is in line for advancement. Learn the Monotype and not only make more money, but be ready for future promotion. It only takes a short time in the Monotype school to make an operator of a compositor. There are schools in Philadelphia, New York, Chicago and Toronto, in which the tuition is free. Why not take up the Monotype? Lanston Monotype Machine Company.

LEARN THE LINOTYPE — WRITE FOR particulars. Canadian Linotype, 68 Temperance St., Toronto.

SITUATIONS WANTED

SITUATION WANTED — ALL ROUND practical printer, over twenty years' experience desires position as manager or foreman. Six years' experience as foreman and six years in own business. Apply to Box 105 Printer and Publisher, Toronto, Ont. (p5p)

COLLECTIONS

SEND US YOUR LIST OF DELINQUENTS. We will turn Debit into Credit. Publishers' Protective Association, Toronto.

EQUIPMENT WANTED

PAIR SECOND-HAND SEVEN-COLUMN twin chases. The Canadian Statesman, Bowmanville, Ont. (p5p)

MACHINERY FOR SALE

MONOTYPE EQUIPMENT, JOB PRESSES. Pony Miehle, One Wharfedale Cylinder Press and one Embosso Machine, Perforator Stitcher, Paper Cutter, Wood Type, Cabinets, Cases and various other supplies. Two offices amalgamated. The News-Record, Limited, Kitchener, Ont. (p5p)

SECOND-HAND DIAMOND CYLINDER Press. Power series and fixtures. Price and terms on request. The Eagle, Rosetown, Sask. (p6p)

TWO CENTS A WORD, Box Number as five words; minimum charge is $1.00 per insertion, for 50 words or less, set in 6 pt. type. Each figure counts as a word. Display ads., or ads. set in border, are at the card rates.

GOVERNMENT PRINTING BUREAU

FOR SALE
PRINTING MACHINERY AND EQUIPMENT

SEALED TENDERS will be received by the undersigned for the purchase of discarded Printing Machinery, Equipment and Supplies until the 25th of May instant inclusive. Lists and forms of tenders can be obtained from the undersigned on application by letter, wire or personally.

The articles offered for sale include:—

COMPOSING ROOM EQUIPMENT: 11 model 1 Canadian Linotypes; hand proof presses; imposing tables, iron and marble surface; type racks, single and double; type cabinets, soft stands with drawers; several type, galley and case cabinets; job and news cases; books, posters and heading chases; steel, zinc and brass galleys, single and double—(in quantity).

PRESS ROOM EQUIPMENT: 1 64-page Potter Webb press; several book presses; one Harris envelope press.

BINDERY EQUIPMENT: Sewing machines, bundling presses, tipping machine, folder; one duplex cutting machine, perforating machine, wire stitcher.

RULING EQUIPMENT: 1 double deck ruling machine.

STEREOTYPING EQUIPMENT: Routing machine, casting box, shaving machine, beveller, trimmer and saw, chipping block.

ADDRESSING EQUIPMENT: Two, each, Montague and Addressographs addressing machines.

Apply immediately to
KING'S PRINTER, Ottawa.

SITUATIONS VACANT

PRINTER WANTED — AN ALL ROUND man, qualified compositor and pressman, must be serious, sober and pushing, one having outside connection preferred. If desirable can purchase an interest in the business or buy the whole plant, in a well-established and up-to-date printing plant, in a city of 15,000 population, near Montreal, Canada. Good business can be done with the right man. References exchanged. Apply at Lachine Printing. 24 Twelfth Ave., Lachine, Que.

WANTED

WANTED—GOOD SECOND-HAND RULING machine. Apply Box 669, Printer and Publisher. (p5p)

WANTED—ROTARY PRESS

eight or twelve pages, seven column, in good condition. Send full particulars to Rotary Press, Box 54, PRINTER AND PUBLISHER, Toronto. (p6p)

FOR SALE

1—13 x 19 Colt. Practically new.
2—7 x 11 Pearl. Presses. Rebuilt.
1—No. 3 Scott Drum, 24½" x 31".
1—10 x 15 W. & B.
1—34½" C. & P. Power Cutter.
1—Bronzing Machine, 25" x 33".
1—Eclipse Folder, 35" x 44", with insert.

ROYAL MACHINE WORKS

Presses and Bookbinding Machinery and Special Machinery.

738 ST. PAUL WEST, MONTREAL

FOR SALE

FOR SALE—GORDON PRESS, 7 x 11; GOOD condition. The Owen Sound Advertiser, Owen Sound, Ont. (P tf P)

MONOTYPE EQUIPMENT, CONSISTING of two casters and three keyboards, all in first-class condition and ready for immediate use. For full particulars apply to E. R. Whitrod, Montreal Star, Montreal, Que. (P 5 P)

FOR SALE—AT NOMINAL PRICE, RULING machine and binder's finishing tools. Sutherland Press, St. Thomas. (p5p)

FOR SALE—OWING TO ILL-HEALTH OF its proprietor the Review, only newspaper in Carleton county, is offered for sale. Well equipped with linotype, cylinder and two platen presses, folder, cutter, stitcher, electric motor, plenty of type, etc. Circulation over one thousand weekly. Good job and ad. patronage. James A. Evoy, Carp, Ont. (p6p)

FOR SALE — NEWSPAPER COTTRELL press, 30 x 47, good condition. Furby St. Printery, Winnipeg. (ptfp)

FOR SALE—COMPLETE JOB PRINTING and newspaper establishment, including Cottrell newspaper printing press, paper cutter, folding machine, monoline, two job presses and type cases, stones, etc. For particulars apply C. A. P. Smith, Sault Ste. Marie, Ont. (p6p)

FOR SALE—WEEKLY NEWSPAPER AND Job Printing Plant in town in Western Ontario. Population 1200. No opposition. Excellent yearly turnover. Good equipment. Bargain for quick sale as proprietor is engaging in other business. Act now. Apply Box 513, Printer and Publisher. (p6p)

PERSONAL

FRANK KANE, NEWSPAPER CONTEST circulation builder, will soon tour "The Provinces." Publishers in the States regard Mr. Kane as one of the best in his line of work. Those contemplating increase circulation can address him Weldona, Colorado. (p6p)

OPPORTUNITIES ARE OFFERED EVERY MONTH ON THIS PAGE—WATCH THEM

Buyers' Guide

Newspaper and Magazine Accounts
EVERYWHERE

Send us your delinquent accounts, Let us turn them into cash for you. No Collection, No Charge—Prompt Returns

Reult - Reult

REFERENCES—The Bank of Nova Scotia and over 200 satisfied Canadian publishers for whom we have been collecting for the last nine years.

The Canadian Mercantile Agency
OTTAWA, CANADA

GREAT WESTERN SMELTING and Refining Co.,
P.O. Box - 1060
Vancouver, B. C.

TYPE METAL for All Purposes
Linotype Combination, Stereotype, Monotype, Electrotype.
Quality, Cleanliness and Analysis Guaranteed.

J. L. PEPPER
Printing Plant Production Expert
38 Toronto St., Toronto

Most efficient layout of office, composing room, pressroom and bindery.

Complete efficiency report on plant, recommending improvements for increasing production.

Accurate appraisals for cost accounting, perpetual inventory and insurance purposes.

ADDRESSING MACHINES
The Challenge Machinery Co., Grand Haven, Mich.
BALERS, WASTE PAPER
Golding Mfg. Co., Franklin, Mass.
Logan, H. J., 114 Adelaide St. West, Toronto.
Stephenson, Blake & Co., 60 Front St. W., Toronto
Stewart, Geo. M., 92 McGill St., Montreal.
BINDERY SUPPLIES
Logan, H. J., Toronto, Ont.
Morrison Co., J. L., Toronto, Ont.
BOOKBINDERS' MACHINERY
Logan, H. J., 114 Adelaide St. W., Toronto.
Miller & Richard, Toronto and Winnipeg.
Morrison, J. L., Co., 445 King St. W., Toronto.
Royal Machine Works, Montreal.
Stewart, Geo. M., 92 McGill St., Montreal, Que.
Stephenson, Blake & Co., 60 Front St. W., Toronto
BOOKBINDERS' WIRE
The Steel Co. of Canada, Hamilton.
CHASES—SECTIONAL STEEL
The Challenge Machinery Co., Grand Haven, Mich.
COLLECTION AGENCIES
Canadian Mercantile Agency, 46 Elgin St., Ottawa.
Publishers' Protective Association, Goodyear Bldg., 154 Simcoe St., Toronto.
COUNTING MACHINES
Stephenson, Blake & Co., 60 Front St. W., Toronto
CYLINDER PRESSES
The Challenge Machinery Co., Grand Haven, Mich.
CROSS CONTINUOUS FEEDER
Morrison, J. L., Co., 445 King St. W., Toronto.
CUTTING MACHINES—PAPER
Golding Mfg. Co., Franklin, Mass.
Morrison, J. L., Co., 445 King St. W., Toronto.
Stephenson, Blake & Co., 60 Front St. W., Toronto
The Challenge Machinery Co., Grand Haven, Mich.
ELECTROTYPING AND STEREOTYPING
Rapid Electrotype Co. of Canada, 229 Richmond St. W., Toronto.
Toronto Electrotype & Stereotype Co., 111 Adelaide St. W., Toronto.
ELECTROTYPE AND STEREOTYPE BASES
The Challenge Machinery Co., Grand Haven, Mich.
EMBOSSING PRESSES
Golding Mfg. Co., Franklin, Mass.
Stephenson, Blake & Co., 60 Front St. W., Toronto
ENVELOPE MANUFACTURERS
Toronto Envelope Co., Toronto.
W. V. Dawson, Ltd., Montreal and Toronto.
ELECTROTYPE METAL
British Smelting & Refining Co., Ltd., Montreal.
Canada Metal Co., Limited, Toronto.
Hoyt Metal Co., Limited, Toronto.
FEATURES FOR NEWSPAPERS
International Syndicate, Baltimore, Md.
GALLEYS AND GALLEY CABINETS
Stephenson, Blake & Co., Toronto.
The Challenge Machinery Co., Grand Haven, Mich.
The Toronto Type Foundry Co., Ltd., Toronto.
GUMMED PAPER MAKERS
Jones, Samuel, & Co., 7 Bridewell Place, London, England, and Waverly Park, New Jersey.
HAND PRINTING MACHINES
Golding Mfg. Co., Franklin, Mass.
INKS
Reliance Ink Co., Winnipeg, Man.
JOB PRINTING PRESSES
Golding Mfg. Co., Franklin, Mass.
JOB PRESS GAUGES
Golding Mfg. Co., Franklin, Mass.
Megill, Ed., 60 Duane St., New York City.
LEADS AND SLUGS
Mono-Lino Typesetting Co., Toronto.
Stephenson, Blake & Co., Toronto.
The Challenge Machinery Co., Grand Haven, Mich.
The Toronto Foundry Co., Ltd., Toronto.
LITHOGRAPHERS
Goes Lithographing Co., Chicago, Ill.
MAILING MACHINES
Chauncey Wongs Sons, Greenfield, Mass.
Rev. Robert Dick Estate, 137 W. Tupper St., Buffalo, N.Y.
MAILING GALLEYS
The Challenge Machinery Co., Grand Haven, Mich.

McFarlane, Son & Hodgson, Limited

WHOLESALE
PAPER DEALERS
AND
STATIONERS

14 ST. ALEXANDER STREET
MONTREAL

LIFE RESTORED
TO DEAD ACCOUNTS
Send us your list of delinquent subscribers to-day. No preliminaries necessary! ¶ We make collections without trouble and renew subscriptions.
No Results—No Charge.

Publishers' Protective Association
Goodyear Building, Toronto

THE NEW ERA
MULTI-PROCESS PRESS
Fastest Flat Bed and Platen Press on the market.
Unit Construction for any number of Colors on one or both sides and great variety of other operations. Roll Feed. Once through press completes job.

THE REGINA COMPANY
47 W. 34th STREET   NEW YORK, N.Y.

WE PAY
SPOT CASH
FOR
Type Metal Drosses
Old Small Type
Electros and Stereos

CANADA METAL CO.
LIMITED
Reclaiming Department
TORONTO

Buyers' Guide

INDEX TO ADVERTISERS

Say you saw it in PRINTER AND PUBLISHER

PRINTER &
PUBLISHER

Annual Meeting of Canadian
Press Association

Organizing Franklin Club
in Toronto

Press Room Problems of the
Weekly Office

Job Specimens and Designs
of Cover Pages

THE MACLEAN PUBLISHING CO. LIMITED
TORONTO ⚜ MONTREAL ⚜ WINNIPEG

PRINTER AND PUBLISHER, June, 1920. Vol. 29, No. 6. Published monthly at 143-153 University Ave., Toronto, by the MacLean Publishing Co., Ltd. Yearly subscription price, $2.00. Entered as second-class matter at the Post Office Department at Ottawa, Canada, also
entered as second-class matter July 1; 1912, at the Post Office at Buffalo, N.Y., U.S.A., under Act of March 3rd, 1879.

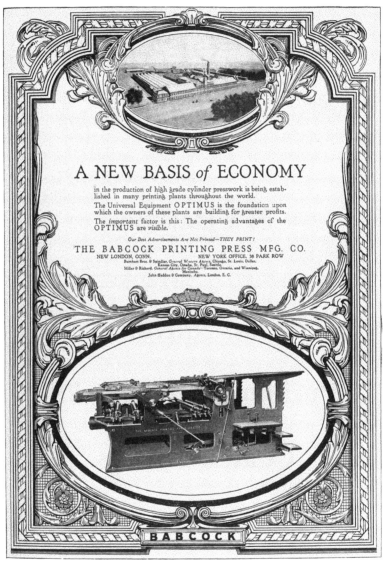

A NEW BASIS *of* ECONOMY

in the production of high grade cylinder presswork is being established in many printing plants throughout the world.

The Universal Equipment OPTIMUS is the foundation upon
which the owners of these plants are building for greater profits.

The *important* factor is this: The operating advantages of the
OPTIMUS are *visible.*

Our Best Advertisements Are Not Printed—THEY PRINT!

THE BABCOCK PRINTING PRESS MFG. CO.
NEW LONDON, CONN.   NEW YORK OFFICE, 38 PARK ROW

Barnhart Bros. & Spindler, *General Western Agents,* Chicago, St. Louis, Dallas,
Kansas City, Omaha, St. Paul, Seattle.
Miller & Richard, *General Agents for Canada—* Toronto, Ontario, and Winnipeg,
Manitoba.
John Haddon & Company, *Agents,* London, E. C.

BABCOCK

NON-DISTRIBUTION

Advertised by an Enthusiastic User

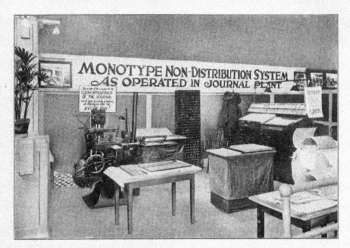

The Milwaukee *Journal* moved from its ad room a Monotype and Non-Distribution accessories to exhibit the system at the Milwaukee Advertising Show. Two operators were on duty demonstrating the Monotype System. The card tells why:

> This is one of the reasons for the clean appearance of the *Journal*. Fresh type is cast by a battery of Monotypes like this every day

Lanston Monotype Machine Co., Philadelphia

NEW YORK   BOSTON   CHICAGO   TORONTO

Monotype Company of California, SAN FRANCISCO

292

This Advertisement set in Monotype Series No. 150 and Monotype Rule

By Eliminating Ink Troubles in the Pressroom

REDUCOL

Helps You Keep Delivery Promises

The use of REDUCOL has eliminated the ink troubles of—

Beck Engraving Co.
  Philadelphia, Pa.
Chas. Scribner Press
  New York, N. Y.
Corday & Gross
  Cleveland, Ohio
Gugler Lithographing Co.
  Milwaukee, Wis.
H. S. Collins Printing Co.
  St. Louis, Mo.
Ketterlinus Lithographing Co.
  Philadelphia, Pa.
Magill-Weinsheimer Co.
  Chicago, Ill.
Manz Engraving Co.
  Chicago, Ill.
Strobridge Lithographing Co.
  Cincinnati, Ohio
U. S. Printing & Lithographing Co.
  Baltimore, Md.
Globe Printing Co.
  Denver, Colo.
Penick & Ford,
  New Orleans, La.
Rogers & Co.
  Chicago, Ill.
University Press
  Cambridge, Mass.
And hundreds more.

Modern advertising is scheduled as closely as the Chicago-New York Limited. Broadsides, folders and catalogs must be out on a certain day, in a certain mail.

There is no place in this scheme of things for the printer or lithographer who cannot be depended upon to deliver the job on time. He does not get the chance to break many promises to the worthwhile buyer of printing. He has a shifting, second-class, price-buying lot of customers. He lives a hunted, worried business life.

Printers and lithographers who use REDUCOL have found that it helps them wonderfully in keeping delivery promises. They have no ink troubles. Their press runs start promptly and finish on schedule time.

REDUCOL is the original ink reducer with a paste base. It works equally well under all weather conditions. It cuts the tack out of the ink without affecting the body, softens it instead of thinning it. It eliminates picking and mottling. It makes halftones, type and rules print up clean and clear.

REDUCOL does not affect colors. It gives impressions an excellent surface for perfect overlapping. It distributes the ink better, giving 10% to 25% more impressions. It has a marked tendency to cut down offset onto the tympan, slipsheeting, and wash-up during the run.

Send for a trial order of 5 or 10 pounds and see what a difference REDUCOL will make in your presswork.

INDIANA CHEMICAL & MANUFACTURING COMPANY
Dept. C6, 135 S. East Street, Indianapolis, Ind., U.S.A.

23-25 East 26th St., New York Cit   0 South Dearborn St., Chicago

Canadian Agents:

MANTON BROTHERS

TORONTO   MONTREAL   WINNIPEG

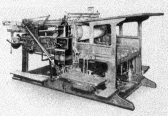

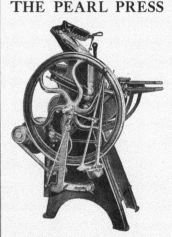

The Albion

SILKY COTTON CORDS

The Cords of a hundred uses
for the Artistic and Progressive
Stationer and Printer.

A wide range of sizes and
colours always in stock.

Send your enquiries direct or
through indent agent to

**THE ALBION SEWING
COTTON CO., LTD.**
Fawley Mills,   Tottenham Hale,
LONDON, N. 17

GOSS

The Name that Stands for
SPEED—
DEPENDABILITY—
SERVICE

The Goss "High Speed Straightline" Press
Used in the largest Newspaper plants in
U.S.A., Canada and Europe.

**The Goss Rotary Half Tone and Color
Magazine Press**
Specially designed for Mail Order, Catalog and
Magazine Work.

**The Goss "Comet" Flat Bed Web
Perfecting Press**
Prints a 4-6 or 8 Page Newspaper from type forms
and roll paper.

Goss Stereotype Machinery
A complete line for casting and finishing flat or
curved plates.

Descriptive Literature Cheerfully Furnished.

The Goss Printing Press Co.

Main Office and Works :   *New York Office :*
1535 So. Paulina St., Chicago   220 West 42nd Street

The Goss Printing Press Co., of England, Ltd., London

HOLLISTON
STANDARD
BOOK CLOTHS

Are you thoroughly acquainted with all grades of the Holliston Line?

Here are some leaders that may well come in for consideration at this time.

Library Buckram

The acknowledged standard binding for Library and Law Books.

The strongest bookbinding material on the market.

Caxton Buckram

A high-grade, medium-weight, medium-priced Library Buckram.

Supplied in all the popular Library Buckram colors.

Sterling Linen

The "Economy" binding.

Made in the popular Linen Finish. Used in increasing quantities for light-weight work of all kinds.

Rex Vellum

A low-priced cloth of splendid wearing quality. The ideal binding for school books, edition work and general job binding.

Up-to-date Sample Books of all or any grade on request.

THE WILSON-MUNROE CO.
SOLE CANADIAN AGENTS

TORONTO   106 York Street   ONTARIO

PRINTER AND PUBLISHER
Devoted to the Interests of the Printers and Publishers of Canada

How Do Your Rates Measure-Up to These?
Something for Publishers to Look At

THE special committee of the National Editorial Association appointed to study the selling price for advertising space in weekly newspapers based on known costs of production, recommends the following rates per inch:

For newspapers of   500 or less circulation 20c
For newspapers of 1,000 or less circulation 25c
For newspapers of 1,500 or less circulation 30c
For newspapers of 2,000 or less circulation 35c
For newspapers of 2,500 or less circulation 40c
For newspapers of 3,000 or less circulation 43c
For newspapers of 3,500 or less circulation 46c
For newspapers of 4,000 or less circulation 49c
For newspapers of 4;500 or less circulation 52c
For newspapers of 5,000 or less circulation 55c

After a thorough study of the present situation, the members of the committee were unanimous in the opinion that the prevailing rates for advertising in community newspapers are much too low and that these rates do not compare with the increased cost of other commodities.

After studying the costs of production as reported from newspaper offices in the different parts of the country the committee finds that only a small percentage of country newspaper publishers realize the perils which confront their future existence. In the mechanical departments labor costs have increased from 50 per cent. to 150 per cent.; machinery and materials have advanced in keeping with the rising costs and the newspaper publishers have not followed in the procession but have been deluding themselves into the belief that they are making a profit and that their future is as secure as their past apparently has been. It was found upon in-

vestigation that most publishers have a very in_adequate idea of the cost of producing their publications. Most of them have considered that the increased price of paper stock was the one item which should principally concern them. It is the one subject over which they have been especially alarmed. Since the circulation of most country newspapers is from 500 to 2,500 copies per week, the committee has felt that although the item of increased cost of print paper should have serious consideration it is of minor importance as compared to the increased costs of labor, machinery, materials, rent, insurance and the various other items of expense which are standard. It was found that a number of publishers who own their own building are not charging the item of rent in figuring what their publications are costing, nor have any considerable number been including interest upon the money invested in their plants as a part of the production cost of their newspapers. Others have been failing to put themselves upon their own payrolls for any adequate salary such as they might easily earn elsewhere, and from year to year have been laboring under the false delusion that they were making money. They have not taken into consideration the depreciation of plants and of the tremendously increased cost of replacement of machinery and still they have continued to sell space in their publications at rates which have prevailed for years.

The committee is strongly of the opinion that disaster and ruin face thousands of publications unless they immediately adjust themselves to the new conditions and rigidly adhere to the rates which the committee of investigation recommends.

First Gathering of Weekly Newspapers

The C. W. N. A. Showing Rapid Growth

THE annual meeting of the Canadian Weekly Newspaper Association was held at the King Edward Hotel, Toronto, on June 3 and 4, with the next day, the fifth, thrown in for good measure and a good time. Not only was the practical side of the business looked after in the arranging of the programme, but the social side, for the entertainment of the ladies of the party, was well provided for. The first day afternoon tea was provided by the Women's Press Club of Toronto, a theatre party being the entertainment in the evening. On Friday afternoon the entire party were the guests of Lieut.-Governor and Mrs. Clark at Government House. Saturday morning saw the party off on the boat for Niagara, from whence the trip was extended to East Aurora, the home of the Roycroft Shops.

Western Canada had a larger representation of weekly newspaper men present than ever before. There was undoubtedly a feeling among the weekly men, expressed openly at times, that they were now running their own business, and were mightily pleased with the strides that had been made in the few months since the organization became a separate body, the paid-up membership being at the date of the first annual meeting 342.

The receipts from the first of the year to April 30 were $5,668.53, while during the same period the expenditures were $2,776.51, showing a balance in the bank of $2,892.02.

Mr. Sayles, the manager of the Association, outlined the work of forming the organization at the start, pointing out that the movement was well under way now. Reports of the various committees were given as follows: Postal and Parliamentary, Rev. A. H. Moore; Circulation and Subscription, P. Geo. Pearce; Job Printing and Estimates, A. R. Brennan; Membership and Field Work, J. J. Hunter; Advertising, W. R. Davies; Paper, C. H. Hale.

The Imperial Press Conference

Some discussion took place when the question of representation on the Imperial Press Conference came up, and quite an extended correspondence was read, which had passed between the manager and the secretary of the committee which had been appointed by the Canadian Press Association. A letter was also read, which had been written by the president of the National Newspapers and Periodicals Association, protesting that no representative of that Association had been placed on the committee.

The feeling was expressed by several of the members that justice had not been dealt out to the various sections of the Canadian Press, and a resolution expressing regret at such action was passed. The Weekly Newspaper Association, as such will take no part in the proceedings of the Imperial Press Conference.

The service that the C.W.N.A. is giving to its members was explained at length by Mr. J. J. Hunter, Kincardine *Reporter*.

Mr. A. R. Brennan, Summerside, P.E.I., read an interesting paper on Job Estimating, showing the need for more uniformity. He advocated the use of the Franklin Price List for the shops of the size represented in the Association.

In opening the sessions, Mr. A. E. Calnan, of Picton, referred to the early history of the Canadian Press Association, which was organized in Kingston in September of 1859. "A list of the names of those present, with the papers they represented, reveals the fact that the weekly press was largely in the majority. No representatives of Toronto newspapers were in attendance, although three Montreal journalists were present. In fact the press of Toronto held aloof from the Association for many years. Among the country towns represented at this first press gathering were Cornwall, Barrie, Whitby, Milton, Dundas and Picton. . . . William Gillespie, of the Hamilton *Spectator*, was the originator of the movement and it was largely owing to his efforts that the Canadian journalists of that day were able to throw aside their political differences for the time. It was not financial betterment that was the mainspring of this early organization. . . An event of much interest and

pleasure was the annual excursion, some of them to far distan points, including the Philadelphia Centennial, the St. Loui Exposition, and one to the Canadian West in 1882 when th C.P.R. was building. In 1888 the real business meetings of th Association began to be held and permanent records kept."

Mr. Calnan paid tribute to the splendid work that was bein accomplished by Mr. Sayles in the position of manager of th Association during the early stages of its existence, when ther was no precedent to go by, and where every problem coming u had to be met and faced independently.

"The past year," stated Mr. Calnan, "has been a difficul one for weekly publishers. While business prosperity has con tinued throughout Canada, and this has been reflected in in creased advertising, job work and subscriptions, the increase revenue has not kept pace with increased costs. . . . Th Canadian Press Association has in the past been of inestimabl value to the general newspaper fraternity of Canada, but as business organization it has ceased to exist. Weekly newspape men should realize that the C.W.N.A. is the only organizatio that is to-day of any real practical aid and assistance to th weekly newspaper men of Canada."

Securing More Advertising

THE topic of "Securing More Advertising for the Weekl Paper" was handled by Mr. M. D. Merry, B.A. He in stanced several cases where publicity in the smaller paper had secured results for the advertiser after the national mediur had failed. One perfume company had $20,000 to spend som years ago. They spent $10,000 in national magazines, largel on monthly publication, and from this they secured no re sults and they were not getting the business. "They had $10, 000 of the appropriation left, and I advised that they concen trate on the New England States, and for that purpose use th daily papers and the weekly. In three weeks the firm ha orders, and to-day they are getting business from connection that were made there five years ago through the campaign i the weeklies and the smaller dailies.

"What is the reason?" queried the speaker, "of the negle of the weekly paper by the large advertiser. One reason, he stated, "is that they don't use mats, and another is th they do not want to handle a large number of small account One of the worst things that can happen to a weekly pap is getting a series of cuts to go with certain ads., as they a almost certain to get balled up. This does not refer to go cuts, which are very useful in making advertising more attra tive.

"The publisher should see to it that ads. are changed eve week. If this is not done remember the publisher will get t blame, and not the advertiser. Half the time your advertis does not know how to advertise, and it is the duty of the pu lisher to show him. In one case in an Ontario town qui recently we found a druggist who talked nothing but quality his ad. It didn't sell him a cent's worth because he was getting his message across in a human sort of way. He sho have gone about it to show the need for exactitude in the filli of prescriptions, or he should have showed that his turno was large, giving him a new supply of fresh drugs all the tin In that same store there was $400 worth of fishing tackle t was not selling. We induced that man to give advertising chance. We were out to give service so that the ad. stat there was a fishing expert in the store to give advice as to h and where to fish in the neighborhood. In three weeks per cent. of that stock was sold, simply because the advertis carried something seasonable, told in a human interest w There is something else," continued Mr. Merry, "and tha that the advertiser should never be allowed to state anyth in his ad. that he is not prepared to live up to. I believe special sales, for it gives the paper ᵣ great chance to prove w it can·do, and it is a wise publisher who will engineer thing that his paper is going to get credit for the selling that is don

The Editorial Page of the Weekly.

Mr. J. T. Clark, of the Toronto *Star*, in opening his address on "The Editorial Page of the Country Weekly," referred to the need for conserving newsprint by the regulation of the size of papers both in Canada and United States.

"Papers, if they are going to succeed, must be edited as well as published. Some weeklies are great, while others are not great simply because they depend on other papers. It is just possible that there is too much modesty in many of the papers, weeklies I mean, in discussing matters in their own community. That is where a great mistake is made, as they should seek to so thoroughly understand all the problems of their own municipality that they could speak with authority on them. In this province in the last few years we have seen so many things and movements spring from the smaller centres that we are coming to look more and more to them for leadership. There is the U.F.O. Government in the province, drawing its support from the very centres that are influenced by the weekly press. "The man who has a paper of his own should seek to give to it character and personality."

Mr. Clark referred to the trouble of setting aside a certain definite time each week to editorial work, going back to his own experience. He advised that the man on a weekly paper should put apart a certain time, say Tuesday morning, for the preparation of his editorial page, and should let nothing interfere with it.

Rather humorous references were made to his early days as a printer's apprentice in a weekly paper, where the copies of a neighboring paper were awaited each week in order that the work of producing the editorial page might be gone on with. The speaker, in conclusion, urged that the weekly papers should devote more time to their editorial work, believing that it was one of the strongest links by which the reader could be held.

Cost of Producing Country Newspapers
By E. K. Whiting, Owatonna, Minn.

THESE are indeed strenuous times for the country publishers of this continent. Costs have been pyramiding in a most startling manner, and even the publisher with an adequate cost accounting system has experienced the greatest difficulty in keeping up with these rising costs. If this be true of the publisher who KNOWS his costs, it can be readily seen that the publisher ignorant of his costs must indeed be in a most critical condition.

I have in mind a friend of mine who formerly operated a cost system in his shop and was thereby enabled to make a handsome profit not only from his newspaper but also from his job plant. Owing to the shortage of help during the war he failed to keep up his cost records and contented himself with using arbitrary hour costs which he felt would be shown by his cost system were it being kept up. He was even too busy to attend printers' conventions. As the result of this fact and his failure to keep in constant touch with his own costs he suffered an actual loss of over $2,000 last year. This publisher in times past had made extensive study of the subject of costs. Notwithstanding this fact he suffered an actual loss of over $2,000 in 1919 because he did not keep in touch with his costs from month to month. If that be the experience of a publisher who knew his costs prior to 1919, what must be true of the publishers who know absolutely nothing about their true costs of production?

Do Not Know Real Cost

From statistics gathered in the United States it is shown that only 5 per cent. of the manufacturing concerns know their costs and over 50 per cent. of the plants operated at an actual loss. Many publishers claim to be operating cost systems, while in fact they do nothing more than keep time records. Without accurate accounting methods and an adequate cost system it is utterly impossible to know one's true costs. Half-truths are very misleading and as a result much has been said and written upon the subject of costs which is little short of bunk. Just as an illustration let me cite the following from a prominent Western trade paper:

"The average hour cost in country newspaper offices is $1.25 an hour. The average country advertising can be set at the rate of forty inches an hour. This would make the actual labor cost, plus composing room overhead, about 3½ cents per inch."

Undoubtedly the above writer was honest in making the above statements, but as a matter of fact he was woefully misinformed as to his facts. The average hour cost for newcomposition in country shops will run $2.00 or more per hour and the number of inches of display advertising set by the average compositor will not run over about half the number given by the writer.

Production Costs of Journal-Chronicle

The following tables will give you an itemized statement of the production costs of my own paper for the years 1918, 1919 and the first four months of 1920. The small amounts charged to the editorial department during the last five months of 1918 and the first two months of 1919 was due to the fact that the war deprived us of our editor and his place was not filled until March of last year.

1918

	Edit.	D. Exp.	Mech.	Ad. C.	Inch	Page
January	136.00	80.07	472.65	74.88	1,644	38
February	137.68	130.87	416.12	92.68	1,589	40
March	174.75	200.65	424.27	27.20	2,365	52
April	139.09	114.10	355.31	69.64	2,170	42
May	172.07	166.36	482.30	108.22	2,554	52
June	137.14	161.76	421.95	85.47	1,921	40
July	136.54	145.53	413.09	83.80	1,485	34
August	71.17	165.73	520.32	47.12	947	40
September	52.35	114.84	526.33	50.68	993	32
October	52.38	142.40	597.20	62.13	800	32
November	70.78	190.27	601.06	88.09	1,652	44
December	54.00	163.58	477.30	92.43	1,257	34
	$1,333.95	$1,766.10	$5,707.90	$891.34	19,377	480

Ad. Composition	$ 891.34
Mechanical Cost	5,707.90
Total Mechanical Cost	6,599.24
Editorial, $1,333.95; D. Exp., $1,766.10	3,100.05
Total Cost	9,699.29
Pages 480	

1919

	Edit.	D. Exp.	Mech.	Ad.-C.	Inch	Page
January	57.42	145.25	594.47	64.41	991	42
February	99.44	151.27	510.28	58.21	1,293	38
March	174.78	144.44	412.56	64.61	1,853	40
April	200.52	142.17	401.46	55.13	1,939	42
May	243.03	168.25	411.42	108.62	2,066	48
June	193.76	185.82	398.18	141.61	1,803	40
July	199.22	201.90	454.00	80.62	2,077	42
August	276.09	185.12	559.70	132.52	2,682	56
September	213.46	113.41	511.28	113.23	2,496	44
October	236.02	145.00	590.75	79.80	2,488	52
November	168.02	138.86	534.57	123.84	2,433	46
December	192.45	134.81	567.75	160.68	2,919	46
	$2,250.01	$1,756.30	$5,934.43	$1,178.29	25,010	536

Ad. Composition	$ 1,178.29
Mechanical Cost	5,934.43
Total Mechanical Cost	7,112.72
Editorial, $2,250.01; D. Exp., $1,756.30	4,006.31
Total Cost	11,119.08
Pages. 536.	

Display Advertising Cost Journal-Chronicle	24.3c
1918 Page Cost Journal-Chronicle	$20.20
1919 Page Cost Journal-Chronicle	20.73
1919 Page Cost Northfield News	19.95
1920—4 months—Page Cost Journal-Chronicle	23.89
1920—3 months—Page Cost Northfield News	23.20

1920—4 Months.

	Edit.	D. Exp.	Mech.	Ad.-C.	Inch	Page
January	$238.00	$180.36	$ 781.79	$264.33	3,201	62
February	187.80	156.10	693.40	147.58	2,794	48
March	192.05	155.21	664.59	181.38	2,626	48
April	237.70	201.49	847.55	175.49	3,570	64
	$855.55	$693.16	$2,987.33	$768.78	12,191	222

Display Advertising Cost Journal-Chronicle—4 months, 1920..	25.4c
Ad Composition	$ 768.78
Mechanical Cost	2,987.33
Total Mechanical Cost	3,756.11
Editorial, $855.55; D. Exp., $698.16	1,548.71
Total Cost	5,304.82
Pages. 222.	

You will note by the above table that the display advertising in 1919 cost 24.3c an inch. The cost per inch for the first four months of 1920 is 25.4c an inch. This cost has been materially reduced by the fact that we carried 12,191 inches of display advertising during that period, as against 6,000 inches during the same period in 1919.

Watch the Page Costs

The page cost of your newspaper is an important thing to know, for without such knowledge a publisher is prone to add on two or four pages to his regular edition, thinking the increased

E. R. SAYLES
Manager C. W. N. A.

volume of advertising means increased profits. As a matter of fact it too frequently happens that the added revenue does not cover the additional cost, to say nothing of a profit.

In 1918 our page cost was $20.20; in 1919 it was $20.73 and for the first four months of 1920 the cost was $23.89. The Northfield, Minn., News, which operates the Standard Cost System, had a page cost in 1919 of $19.95 and for the first three months of this year had a cost of $23.20. Another Minnesota paper with 1,000 circulation has a page cost for 1920 of over $22.00 as contrasted with $13.80 in 1917 and $18.58 in 1919. An Iowa daily with 2,100 circulation has a page cost so far this year of $22.50 and an advertising cost of 23.4c an inch.

Comparing 1919 and 1920

For the sake of comparisons we will take the first four months of 1919 and corresponding months of 1920 and we find the following page costs by departments:

	1919	1920
Editorial	$ 3.23	$ 3.85
Direct expense	2.52	1.83
Mechanical cost	10.41	10.22
Print paper	1.43	3.23
Inches display advertising	6,076	12,191
Cost ad. composition	238.36	768.78
Pages printed	162	222

Production Costs per Issue

The following table will show you the mechanical costs for five issues during April, all being 12 pages with the exception of the issue of April 23rd, which was 16 pages:

	April 2	April 9	April 16	April 23	April 30
Print paper	$ 37.80	$ 37.80	$ 37.80	$ 50.40	$ 37.80
Linotype	48.76	59.78	55.12	59.86	55.97
Make-up	49.74	39.08	41.80	64.58	29.26
Presswork	17.99	20.05	19.27	26.27	19.28
Ad composition	37.26	25.72	25.56	61.01	25.94
Ink	1.00	1.00	1.00	1.00	1.00
Mailing	7.12	5.99	6.22	7.91	6.65
	$199.67	$189.42	$186.77	$270.73	$176.45

Advertising Rates for Country Newspapers

The National Editorial Association appointed a committee recently to formulate a schedule of advertising rates for country newspapers and in the report recently issued the following rates are recommended:

For newspapers of   500 or less circulation 20c
For newspapers of 1,000 or less circulation 25c
For newspapers of 1,500 or less circulation 30c
For newspapers of 2,000 or less circulation 35c
For newspapers of 2,500 or less circulation 40c
For newspapers of 3,000 or less circulation 43c
For newspapers of 3,500 or less circulation 46c
For newspapers of 4,000 or less circulation 49c
For newspapers of 4,500 or less circulation 52c
For newspapers of 5,000 or less circulation 55c

The above rates were made to cover 15 per cent. discount for advertising agency commissions, where all plate copy is run, 10c an inch being recommended as a charge for composition. In this connection you will be interested to know that the American Press Association, which represents over 6,000 country newspapers, recently announced in a full page ad. that it would refuse to represent any newspaper with a rate of less than 15c an inch.

Whither Are We Going?

Bradstreet and Dun showed that the printers of the States were down to 80th place in credit rating as an industry ten years ago. To-day we are in 34th place.

Bradstreet's and Dun's credit ratings of members of the United Typothetae of America who furnish annual composite statements are: 84 per cent. A-1; 14½ second rating; ½ per cent. third rating.

Bradstreet's and Dun's credit ratings for the printing industry as a whole: 27 per cent. good rating; 73 per cent. irresponsible with no rating at all.

The figures given above are exceedingly significant and point out forcibly the increased profit which has come to those printers operating cost systems and who KNOW their costs. The cost system may well be designated as a business compass. No mariner would think of attempting to cross the ocean without a compass, and it is equally necessary that printers and publishers have a business compass in the form of a cost accounting system that they may reach the harbor of financial success. It is absolutely necessary that the printer no longer continue to GUESS what his costs are. He must KNOW his costs if he is to make a profit and continue in business.

Costs are rapidly increasing this year and the printer must follow his costs up with increasing prices for his product. Country newspaper advertising rates have been ridiculously inadequate in the past, and in order that the country publisher may survive and function in his community as he should, he must draw adequate compensation for himself and in addition make a profit from his business. In no other way can the country newspaper effectively serve its community and the nation as a whole. The advertiser and the subscriber are willing that the publisher shall command an adequate rate for his services, but they will never pay more than the publisher has the courage and conviction to charge. The courage to ask an adequate rate comes most surely through true knowledge of one's costs, and every printer and publisher should KNOW and not GUESS.

I earnestly recommend the accompanying schedule of advertising rates for the benefit of yourselves, your families and your communities. Ask these rates and STICK, BROTHER STICK.

You should have them and you can get them for the asking

Getting Results From the Ordinary Job Press
By R. D. Croft, of Croft & Wright, Toronto

I DISTINCTLY remember a certain meeting of the Farmers' Institute, when I was living in Ailsa Craig, at which a young man from the Provincial Department of Agriculture gravely informed us that water ran down hill. About a month ago, when Mr. Sayles asked me if I would come here to speak to you about presswork, I felt that anything I could say upon this subject would be equally obvious.

On second thoughts, remembering how busy most of you are bowling and gardening in summer and curling in winter, I realized that a great many of you have very little time to devote to the study of your pressroom problems. This thought encouraged me to believe that at least a few of you would be able to get a suggestion or two which, as prohibition is still in force, would be of value to you on those rainy days when you cannot go fishing or indulge in any of the other sports for which printers and newspapermen seem to have such a strong inclination.

My remark regarding prohibition is not intended to be taken as an insinuation regarding the past history of any members of our craft. I was just thinking of the remark made seven or eight years ago by a young lady who worked in the Ailsa Craig Banner office. As the partition between the front office and the composing room did not reach to the ceiling, I could hear pretty well what went on at the back. One of the other girls was "jollying" this one about a young printer from Parkhill, and she indignantly replied that indeed she would never marry a printer, as all printers either drank or had big families. I am glad to say that I know a lot of printers who do not drink, and sorry to say that I know many more who are not blessed with large families.

Perhaps the best way for us to go into this question as to the best method of getting a clean and finished job off the press is to imagine that we have a Gordon press here and that we are putting a job on it. They say a printer's imagination is equal to anything. We shall go through the motions of putting on a very ordinary job such as any of you do on your presses every day of the week. As we go along we shall consider only the ordinary faults of the average pressman and endeavor to correct them. If we get considering all the things that might happen on unusual jobs or under extraordinary circumstances, we shall be here too late to take our wives to the theatre party this evening.

We will assume that the compositor has locked up this form, taking his usual care that the stone was clean, so that no dirt or foreign matter adheres to the back of the type; that it was planed down carefully both before and after tightening the quoins; and that everything in it is tight, so that we shall have no letters pull out on the press. To make assurance doubly sure we shall take a rag moistened with a little gasoline or coal oil and wipe off the back of the form. We shall also feel it to see that everything is tight. This is not meant as a reflection on the stone man, but most of us are a little Scotch and consequently cautious, and we know that the composing room has its failings too. Next we shall examine the face of the form to see if some careless printer has left ink on any of the type or cuts. If there is any dried ink on the face of the form we must get it off with a little gasoline, or alcohol if it has been on very long, as we cannot hope to get a nice black print from type or cuts in such condition.

Building Up the Tympan

Next we shall make sure that no dirt has been allowed to accumulate on the bed of the press. It is a good habit to have of wiping off the bed of the press every morning just before or after oiling the machine. It is surprising how much dirt will gather there and how much make-ready it will cause. It is sometimes necessary to scrape it well with a make-up rule. It is to be hoped that all these precautions are unnecessary, but I am assuming things to be rather worse than is at all likely.

Next, put on a thin, hard tympan and be sure to get it perfectly smooth. The platen should be set so that a thin card, four or five sheets of light weight paper, supercalendered preferred, and a manila top sheet is all the packing needed for the average job. Heavy forms would require an extra sheet or two

or even another thin card, while very light forms or average forms printed on cardboard would not require a card under the tympan sheets at all. If your tympan clamps do not grip tight enough to pull the tympan very smooth over the platen, they are probably bent and require to be taken off and straightened. It is of the utmost importance that we get the tympan on properly, as a soft or baggy tympan will cause slur and a consequent smudgy impression which all the grippers, strings and corks in the world, would not remedy. Very few pressmen realize the importance of this point. They think they are very clever to get the slur out of a job by using the grippers and all kinds of things tied to them, when as a matter of fact, there would never have been any slur there if they had put their tympan on properly.

The Proper Care of the Rollers

Now that the bed of the press is clean and we have a nice, smooth tympan to work on, we should, before running up our ink, examine the condition of our rollers. There are several conditions with relation to rollers which make it almost impossible to get satisfactory results. If the rollers are too hard—they will not roll the ink on to the type with that gentle pressure which leaves a smooth and even film of ink over the whole form and assures a thoroughly satisfactory print. Unless the ink is put on the form properly there is no use hoping that the form will transfer it to the paper with satisfactory results. When rollers are hard, a little temporary life can be restored to them by sponging with a wet rag, or if the pressroom is cold, a rise in temperature will be of material assistance.

If the rollers are too soft or "green" it is likely because they have absorbed too much moisture and the surface, instead of being smooth and tough, becomes tender and porous. Using rollers in this condition makes the form look as if it had been inked with a sponge. An improvement can be made in their condition by dusting them with powdered chalk and allowing

R. D. CROFT.

them to stand for a few minutes till the chalk absorbs a certain amount of moisture. If the roller is very soft from running on the press in hot weather what it needs more than anything else is rest and recuperation. Don't run till it melts on the press.

Another cause of roller difficulty is carelessness on the part of the pressman in using good rollers on rule forms, particularly forms having perforating rules in them, and also in not washing up carefully, thus allowing dried ink to accumulate on the rollers. Old rollers are plenty good enough for rule forms and attempting to do good work with rollers that are covered with dried ink is a hopeless undertaking. If you stop to think a minute you will realize that if dried printers' ink were the ideal substance for printers' rollers you would probably be able to sell the roller maker the accumulation of skin and dried ink which gathers around your shop so quickly and he would make your rollers of that material. They would then probably be a good deal cheaper than they are to-day.

The solution of all roller problems is to have summer rollers for the hot weather and winter rollers for cold weather. In this country of extremes of temperature, the rollers must suit the season in which they are used. Have them made as near the exact diameter of the roller trucks or journals as is possible and always have an extra roller or two on hand besides the set actually in use on the press. See that your rollers are washed clean but without any hard rubbing. Don't use gasoline or benzine except to remove something that coal oil will not lift. Use plenty of coal oil and do not rub too hard, as you are likely to rub the surface off and end what otherwise might have been a long and useful roller career.

The Ink is a Problem

Having attended to our rollers we are now ready to run up the ink. It is of vital importance to the results desired that we use a suitable ink. If the job is on coated paper we had better use a good half-tone color. We could get passable results with some other ink, but ink is cheaper than time these days and we are trying to do a good job in a reasonable time. It is therefore advisable that we have as many factors in our favor as possible. Few of the things we work with can cause us more trouble than the wrong ink. We must watch for offset, which is caused by unsuitable ink or an excessive quantity of ink. If we are to print our job on bond or cover paper we must have a stiff ink with sufficient body to cover well on the rough surface of such a paper. If we are using news, mill finish book or super-calendered we can use any soft ink we like, always remembering that the poorer the quality of the ink the more likely we are to have offset or some other trouble.

There are a great many jobs which require special inks. When you get a job of this nature and none of the ink you have will give satisfaction the best plan is to send a sample of the stock to your ink maker and let him supply you with the proper color. It is cheaper than wasting a lot of valuable time and expensive paper in purely experimental work.

Start on a Light Squeeze

Assuming that we have the proper ink, we run it up on the press, put on our form, adjust the grippers so that they will not run across it, and pull our first impression. From this first proof we decide what make-ready the form requires. It is possible that we have too much or too little squeeze to judge correctly. If too much we are unfortunate, as we may have damaged the type and most certainly too much squeeze on our first impression damages our tympan and we shall have to change it for a thinner one. If the first proof is light we can easily add a sheet or two to get the required pressure. If our form is small and our type in good condition we may not need to do anything but set our guides, have the job passed for reading and position and run ahead. It is a great mistake to assume that every job requires patching or levelling up. The trouble with most pressmen is that as soon as they see a job they form a preconceived idea that it cannot be made ready to run in less than a certain length of time and they will take that much time irrespective of how many things are in their favor to reduce it. At our shop we have had to dispense with the services of more than one pressman who could not put a business card on the press, set in all new type, without going to the make-ready board at one of the windows and spending half an

hour drawing lace curtain patterns all over the back of a proof. Just as it is desirable that the cuts and type of our form be perfectly level, so is it desirable that if they are not that way we should make them so. The only way to do this is by putting our patches or make-ready on the back of the form. It stands to reason that if the form is not smooth and even we cannot make it so by patching on the tympan to meet the inequalities of the form. A certain amount of making ready on the tympan is permissible, if the job is not too particular and it saves time to do it that way, but never on the top of the sheet. Generally speaking, the best system is to level the form from the back. This permits the rollers to exert a uniform pressure over the whole form and eliminates a number of troubles, such as slur, caused by making ready on the tympan. If the tympan and the form come together absolutely parallel at every point, with a solid impression, the result is practically certain to be entirely satisfactory, especially if the previous points mentioned have been attended to.

The fact that we have the form levelled up does not mean that our troubles are over. It may be that the sheet will not pull away properly. There may be some heavy type or cuts which need so much ink that the sheet will not pull away from them readily. Do not put a gripper on the sheet if you can get it to pull off by stretching elastic bands or tying strings across your grippers in such a position that they pull the sheet off without touching any of the printing surface. A gripper down one edge of the job is likely to cause slur along the other edge, especially if, as usual, it is put on the edge opposite the side guide. The gripper takes a tight hold of the sheet along the one edge while it still has a certain amount of air under it. When the sheet meets form it cannot flatten out on account of the gripper holding it on one side and the side guide on the other. The result is a slur. Running grippers on the sheet is a common cause of poor register, particularly if the grippers are not run in exactly the same position on each color. While speaking of register I might add that the guides should be set in exactly the same position with relation to the edges of the paper on every form or color on the job. Also the tongues of the guides should hold the sheet well down against the tympan and the form should be wedged to one side of the press to prevent the possibility of it shifting slightly during the run. Another reason for not running grippers on the sheet when coated paper is being used is that they pull the sheet away from the form so abruptly as to cause plucking or picking of the coated surface off the paper.

Having advanced our job this far we can generally leave it to the feeder with a warning to keep the color even throughout the run if it is a light form and if a heavy one we had better put the ink in the fountain and set it to give the proper amount of color, remembering that printing is not satisfactory that is done with ink only any more than it would be if done with impression only. A firm impression and just enough ink to give a solid color on the heaviest type in the form without filling up the small type is the ideal combination. The consideration of special problems is limitless and it would be possible for us to think of many difficulties which occur very rarely and only on special kinds of work. We need not worry about them here unless there is any particular trouble any of you are having just now that I could assist you to overcome.

Let me repeat, briefly, the few points I have already tried to bring out. These are the important things to remember First of all, a clean bed for the type to rest on, a smooth, hard tympan to print against, good rollers, suitable ink, the form properly levelled or made ready. Get the form ready to run with the least possible amount of work. It is a rare pressman who knows when he has the job made ready. Most of them

---

SOME OF MR. CROFT'S POINTS

IF YOUR JOB work is not as well done as you would like it, don't always blame the machine.

A SOFT OR BAGGY tympan will cause slur which all the grippers, strings and corks in the world would not remedy.

WHEN ROLLERS ARE HARD a little temporary life can be restored by sponging with a wet rag.

DON'T USE GASOLINE or benzine on rollers except to remove something that coal oil will not lift.

IT IS A GREAT MISTAKE to imagine that every job requires patching or levelling up.

want to keep on working on the form for half an hour to an hour after they get it ready. If these few points are kept in mind you will eliminate most of your trouble before you meet it—which, in my estimation, is the best way to do.

About Working on Cylinders

With regard to cylinder presswork I shall say very little. As I said before, if you have much cylinder presswork, you probably have a competent man in charge. To those who do some cylinder presswork themselves I have just one or two suggestions to offer. Use care in putting on your tympan. Get it tight. Don't give the grippers too much or not enough bite. On a modern, two-revolution press, a pica to a quarter of an inch is plenty. Many jobs can be run with less. On some of the older machines, especially drum cylinders, which are not so finely adjusted, the grippers may require a longer hold. If the form is set in such a position on the press that the grippers have too much bite they are likely to strike the edge of the sheet before taking hold, knocking it back from the guides and thus spoiling the register.

If you are troubled with slur along the gripper edge, if it is not caused by a baggy tympan, observe the point at which it is worst, loosen the nearest gripper so that it does not take a tight hold, and you may eliminate it in that way. If the slur is on the edge farthest from the guides it is probably caused by the reels being in a bad position. The idea is to have your reels set so that they do not cause the sheet to bulge between them as it runs into the press as the result is an air pocket which causes slur. Sometimes a slur will disappear by the simple expedient of turning the paper over, if it is not already printed on the other side. A particularly bad slur or crease can be removed ninety-nine times in a hundred by cutting two strips of heavy manila or wrapping paper about an inch wide and a little longer than the width of the sheet being printed, and pasting them, one on each side of the cylinder, so that they are placed close up to the edge of the type and extend a little beyond the edge of the paper. This has a tendency to pull the sheet out tight as the cylinder meets the form, and consequently it cannot buckle or crease.

The remarks I have already made regarding a clean bed, good rollers and proper ink apply equally to cylinder presses as to platens. Be careful to set your rollers so that they just rest of their own weight on the ink plate. If they are any lower the ink plate will strike them as it runs back and forth and, together with the fact that they are squeezing the form too hard, will soon wear them out. The system of making ready on cylinder presses is, of necessity, somewhat different from that used on platens. If, on pulling your first proof, you find some cuts low, unlock the form, take them out and underlay them. Or, better still, interlay them. That is, remove the metal from the wooden base, paste your make-ready on the back of the metal

and remount it on the wood. When underlaying cuts be very careful not to put any patching on in such a way that the cylinder of the press will rock the cut as it passes over it. If this occurs the surrounding spaces, quads and furniture will work up and nothing on earth will be able to keep them down. When cuts are high they should be taken out and planed down or the back of the mount rubbed down to type high on a piece of coarse sand paper. When the cuts are pretty well levelled up the balance of the making ready should be done on the tympan, preferably on a lower sheet. The make-ready should have at least four tympan sheets and a draw sheet over it. If the job is to register it is very necessary that your guides, grippers and register bars should work in perfect unison. Also the entire job must be run at the same speed, a variation in speed causing a difference in pickup and a consequent variation in register.

There is only one other thing I would, like to say about good presswork and that is that it should bring a good price. No doubt some other speaker will take up the matter of price but I can never say anything about printing without emphasizing the fact that, for the sake of our self-respect, we should realize our importance to the community and insist on a good price for all our work. We are all entitled to some consideration from the neighborhood in which we labor and should be like my wife and insist upon getting it.

You know about eight months ago we had another visit from the stork at our house. After the excitement was over we discovered that our third boy had arrived, giving a grand total of four children. Our oldest child, a girl, was attending school at the time and my wife thought it would relieve the nurse and housekeeper to some extent to have our oldest boy started to school also. He was a few months under the prescribed age but I took him down to the school, explained the circumstances and asked them to take him in. The teacher already had more than she felt she could attend to properly, so she demurred but consented to take him in for two weeks only until we could bring our household affairs back towards normal again. This didn't satisfy my wife, so she went down to the school about three weeks later and interviewed the principal about the matter. He regretted that he could not force more pupils on an unwilling teacher who already had her quota. "Well," said Mrs. Croft, "when I went to school I always thought the principal was boss." Moreover any person who has presented this country with three boys since the beginning of the war is entitled to some consideration, and I, for one, am going to get it." Needless to say the boy went back to school.

Now, Mr. Chairman, I think that is the attitude we, as printers, and particularly newspaper men, should take. Let us realize our importance to the community, and one of the best ways of convincing ourselves and the community also that we do count, is to charge a proper profit on all our work.

Axel Edw. Sahlin on the Art of Typography
A Great Field for the Student and Designer

ON BOTH days of the C.W.N.A. convention, Axel Edw. Sahlin, Typographical Artist of the Roycroft Print Shops, East Aurora, N.Y., was on the programme. The first day his subject was "A Talk on Typography," and the second "Roycroft Typography."

For this report we have selected the points that will have the most important bearing on the practical side of the business from the standpoint of the man in the business.

The design, balance, contrast, refinement—these four words possess much or little meaning to a printer, but the principles they represent may be in his brain and at his finger-tips. A good designer will, of course, fix his mind first on whether to proceed by a series of sizes of a certain face or by successive contrasting types. Certain kinds of work demand series treatment; many others, contrast.

One exception is to be noted at this point; the very lightest and most delicate work (in series) should be avoided. Just as in a painting composed entirely of delicate greys, greens and yellows, the eye is afforded no relief from a monotone, so in a weak series of thin and light-faced letters the vision finds over-

delicacy of type-matter to be really not much better than white space. A narrow panel advertisement with high, thin letters on a broad white page is in a way an example of such an effect. The moral of this is, if you wish to use a beautiful light-face, work it in where there can be a good (not too heavy) contrasting dark line at the centre or slightly above—never at top or bottom.

As to leading, margins, spacing of words and letters, the outlines of the job, ornamentation and all other minor points, ornaments in contrasted matter, they should generally not be quite as strong as the heaviest line, nor quite as light as the faintest type. A happy medium, for conventionalized leaves, fruits, flowers especially, is best, and the same applies if a band is used above and below.

Balance is the proper proportion of lines, the setting of initials, whether within the text or outside, the placing of display, the arrangement of wholly displayed lines in vase-shape, pyramid, or panels. Of course the wording must be studied and a man will readily find that if there is much matter to be set, a plane arrangement, with the display somewhat towards the centre—

or at top and bottom if it lends itself readily to that method—may be safely used.

One great advantage of panelling is that a plain rule or an ornamental border may be used, at the proper distance away from the type. The panel also looks well (if of fairly large type), unsupported by any border or rule; but how seldom is a good effect produced when rules are placed on an uneven display? Of course, the spindle-waist "hour-glass" shape must be avoided, and that equally funny form, the barrel-contour. Sometimes these queer things happen even in good magazines.

The setting of a large initial is not understood by many. I might say that the importance of the initial letter in the history of printing is not fully appreciated by typographers of our day, excepting indeed those who make a special study of the origin and evolution of their craft. The introductory letter of a chapter, paragraph or passage, in this age of the world, constitutes an integral part of the compositor's work. If the type measure is not very wide, it is well to let the initial project on the left a quarter of an inch or more and carry down a slight ornamentation; if color is used, however, the first letter may stand entirely outside.

Contrast is very poorly worked out by most printing houses, because their men do not familiarize themselves with old-style and modern faces. Caslon Text, Priory, Old English may be used, necessarily, only with old-style letters, because they have equally flowing and graceful lines. A man with the artist's eye would be shocked to see block letters used with Modern, Gothic, Scotch Roman, or even Jeneen or Goudy. Yet how many specimens we see every day of this inharmonious blending of types.

I do believe that each printing concern ought to subscribe to at least one of the best trade journals and to have a special place in the composing room for it so that each employee could get a chance to see it every month.

Because the trade journals contain a storehouse of knowledge, a mine of truths, and a lot of facts, from it he will be able to cull ideas and ideals, broaden his horizon, and widen his views.

From cover to cover the trade journal exhibits many interesting things for its readers and their business, and it gives inspiration, encouragement and advice, also education, uplift and self-respect. We know perfectly well that no man knows everything. We need to be continually verifying our opinions, and we need some vital information on subjects outside our ken. And we will find a lot of it in our trade journals.

At Roycroft, where they say things and also write them, criticize them, and perfect them, and then do them, every bit of printing has won some commendation—for boldness, good effect, individuality, general excellence. At times they are a little too striking for the timid, the "way back," or conservative. What matters it? The trade is coming to a clearer and better style, is gradually adopting the best of the East Aurora ideals, one of which is, DO NOT STICK TO ONE WAY of doing things; use all sorts of types, in the proper combinations. There is a chance for them all, even to the old-fashioned Monkish Text and the Satanic.

From His Second Address

I realize that many small job offices haven't got the same material as the larger ones, but there is no reason in the world why these shops couldn't get out artistic jobs as well as the larger one.

Good typography can be done with just one family of type and for decoration, rules can be used or no rules at all, or some ornaments. The main thing to be considered is the proper balance, grouping of text, right spacing and justification properly done and also get the right margin.

The spacing and leading out plays a big part on good typography, and good results can be obtained by giving thought, attention and study to the work.

Always plan out a job before it is set up, then there is a reason for what you are doing, and remember to use but one series of type and not too great variety of sizes if possible.

When display lines are set up in lower case, try to use lower case throughout; and when caps are used for display lines and I wish to introduce lower case as a variation, I prefer italic lower case rather than Roman, as I think it gives a more pleasing effect That is for a certain kind of work only.

If borders and ornaments are used, select those that harmonize and blend with each other, also if possible some that are appropriate for the job in hand.

Say for instance an ornamental border around an ad. for a manure-spreader, is incongruous, and a heavy rule looks bad around a jewelry ad.

And for instance when a job is set up for a florist we wouldn't select the same type face as was used for, say, a hardware store. In setting letterheads for special persons, as doctors and lawyers, I do not like to use too heavy, complicated designs; the job ought to be neat and delicate.

In suggesting colors for menus and programs take into consideration whether the job is to be read by natural or artificial light.

And last but not least the first thought should be considered in the harmony between paper and type, then arrangement of the type matter so as to carry out the principles of design, then the decoration.

There is a great fault found many a time in modern display typography by lack of taste evidenced in selection of type faces, ornaments and design, and the average compositor treats many jobs along the same lines, using types and ornaments without consideration as to whether they are in keeping with the tone or atmosphere of the work.

Great care should also be taken in regard to "whiting out"; all lines bearing any relation to each other should be placed closer together and separated by more "white." Many jobs have been lifted above the commonplace by the mere transposition of a lead here and there.

A layout can be made very easy by going over the copy twice and with a few strokes of the pencil indicating how the job is to be set; sketch in the main lines in their intended position, and the text matter may be grouped or centered and can be shown by lines, making them heavy and light according to strength required, then suggest harmonious borders and ornaments if needed. Then the job can be set up by even a young apprentice, and yet be of first-class character, and in as good shape as if set by an expert.

Many specimens that contain two, three and four colors would be just as good and sometimes better with one color only, if this color is properly selected. We do not always need to use black ink; we have blue, brown and many others, whereby good results can be obtained.

When I was setting type myself for posters, window-cards, etc., I always made my layout on the galley or stone, by setting up the whole thing line for line, without justifying the lines, only put in slugs and enough quads to prevent pi-ing, I could then easily make changes of lines and move them around until everything suited me, and I could get a good view of the job and see how it would look, at the same time it was time-saving.

I also think from my own experience that a young apprentice learns more in a small shop than in a large, because he gets more of a variety of jobs and it's more interesting to him. Some of the large printshops specialize on certain kinds of work and it becomes tedious, I believe, for a young apprentice.

Wage Scale in Five Principal Cities of the United States.						
	Compositors	Job Pressmen	Cyl. Pressmen	Job Feeders	Cyl. Feeders	Men Binders	Bindery Girls
New York ...	$45.00	$37.40	$46.00	$29.00	$36.00	$37.50	$27.50
Philadelphia	43.00	32.00	44.00	.....	32.00	38.00	18.00-$24.00
Boston	35.00	32.50	37.50	.....	30.50	31.50-$35.50	.....
Baltimore ...	39.00	28.00	39.00	22.00	30.00	35.00	18.00
Chicago	46.00	35.00	47.00	21.50-$23.00	39.00	41.00	20.50

The Advertising Agency and the Publisher

By Louis J. Ball, Vernon, B. C.

Mr. Ball, in his paper, brings out something that has been experienced by many publishers. They send their new cards to advertisers and agencies, and yet, some time after, get contracts offered at the rate they have discarded.

Remittances and measurements should call for very little trouble, but they sometimes do. An inch is an inch and a line is a line and a dollar is a dollar. With these to work from there should be very little friction.

THE subject which has been assigned to me, and on which I have been asked to prepare a short paper, "The Relation of the Advertising Agency to the Publisher," is one which is very difficult to handle in a manner which might be expected to be effective without a danger of causing offence. Criticism of the actions of others, no matter how true they may be, or how thoroughly they may be justified by facts, are bound to be unpleasant. I mention this in advance, and trust that what I am going to say may be taken in the proper spirit, my sole idea being to secure that harmony and co-operation between the advertising agencies and the publishers which the former express themselves as being so desirous of establishing, and which I am sure the publishers are just as anxious to see accomplished.

I have read with considerable interest, in recent Annual Reports, addresses which have been read by representatives of advertising agencies at conventions of the Canadian Press Association, and the noble sentiments contained therein, and the valuable suggestions offered to publishers, were masterpieces of their kind.

But I have failed to notice, on any of these occasions, any presentation of the publishers' side of the case, nor any suggestions or recommendations calculated to alter or correct the methods of most of the advertising agencies in their dealings with Canadian publishers. There are two sides to every question, and I have long felt that no harm could result from a presentation of the other side, if only to give more light on the matter and find out why some very unsatisfactory conditions continue to exist.

In a recent Bulletin from the C.W.N.A. were reproduced extracts from letters received from advertising agencies by the central office, such extracts dealing with a variety of conditions which agencies claim make it very difficult to do business satisfactorily with many of the publishers, mainly publishers of weekly papers. I will grant, since it is so stated by several writers, that many publishers of weekly papers do not have such information as agencies desire, compiled in a manner which is satisfactory to the agencies and fair to themselves. Publishers having service to sell should naturally have an established price for it, and should also have some literature outlining the value of such service, and some sound reasons why it should be taken advantage of. Therefore a publisher who has not a printed advertising rate card, together with a reasonable amount of good literature about his publication and the territory throughout which it circulates, fails in his first and most important duty to both himself and the advertising agencies. This fact can not be too strongly impressed on those publishers who have failed in this respect.

But—and this is where the other side of the story comes in—why, when all of this information has been supplied in simple form, complete in every respect, giving all the details which could be reasonably required, do most advertising agencies persistently and regularly disregard such information, and submit, time after time, incorrect contracts, as though they had no knowledge whatever as to a newspaper's rates or conditions? Why, when newspapers do their part faithfully and well, do the agencies persist in their efforts to get unfair rates, a position not provided for by the rate offered, or some other concession which they do not make provision for in the contracts which they submit? I therefore feel justified in claiming that those publishers who supply all the information required by the agencies should have their rate cards respected, and that contracts submitted should be based on and in accordance with such rate cards.

If the experience of other publishers is the same as mine, extending over a considerable number of years, I feel fairly safe in saying that of all the contracts submitted to weekly papers, not more than one-third are in the first instance such as can be accepted and placed on file without amendment. They are wrong either as to rate of advertising, rate of commission, position demanded, or contain vaguely worded clauses which are at times overlooked, but which later on are liable to cause disagreement. This should not be the case.

Nor is the trouble ended when a satisfactory contract has been arranged. Remittances are a constant source of worry, almost equal to the difficulty in getting satisfactory contracts. There is almost always a variation in measurement; if measurements are reasonably satisfactory, then insertions duly made have not been allowed, or have been missed in checking; granted that in these two respects the statement is correct, then the rate of commission is wrong; and it frequently happens that even the contract rate has not been adhered to.

Now I feel free to admit that to err is human, and all of us are prone to occasional mistakes; but in business there are supposed to be as few errors as are humanly possible. And it has frequently occurred to me that if the incorrect remittances are the result of purely clerical errors, then a house-cleaning of some of the office staffs would be in order.

Whether or not the foregoing conditions are exceptional in our case, or whether they are more or less general, I have no way of knowing; but I trust that the discussion which I hope will follow will bring out some facts either in support of my statements, or in criticism of them, just so that this matter may be properly placed before the advertising agencies, and that such representations may result in a better understanding and as between the publishers and the advertising agencies.

And in closing, I wish again to repeat that these remarks should be taken by all in the right spirit, which is a sincere desire to induce the advertising agencies to meet the publishers on the same basis as they suggest that the publishers should meet them, and to establish mutual confidence and fair dealing, harmony and good-will between advertising agencies and publishers.

—Thomas in the Detroit "News."
"City folks get themselves into the durnedest messes."

Finding the Correct Cost of Job Printing

By J. J. Hurley of Brantford

"The printer is a manufacturer. He buys costly and highly technical machinery, on which there is a high depreciation. He buys labor from one of the most highly organized labor unions in the world. . . He should know the cost of his product and how to sell it."—J. J. Hurley to the C. W. N. A. members.

I DEEM it a great honor and pleasure to be with you to-day and discuss the problems of the printing trade. It is a business of great importance to the public as well as ourselves. The printer is a manufacturer. He buys costly and highly technical machinery, on which there is a high depreciation. He buys labor from one of the most highly organized Labor Unions in the world. He transforms paper and ink into a finished article of a high technical quality, into which a large element of art enters. The printer ought to insist upon the dignified status of a businessman and manufacturer. He ought to be a good business man. He should know the cost of his product and how to sell it. He cannot, as do other manufacturers, take common laborers off the street. His employees must be skilled and educated men. Hence the necessity of well-devised methods in conducting a printing business, whether it be publishing a newspaper or commercial job printing or both. The slip-shod method of conducting the printing business in the past has been a disgrace. This is owing to an almost entire absence of proper methods, and lack of knowledge as to costs. No man can give a proper estimate on printing who does not know what his costs are in conducting his business from week to week or month to month. The wide variation in prices obtained on any given job has demoralized the purchaser's idea of values. This can only be overcome by the adoption of a cost system of some kind that will show us our selling hour cost.

Take the following as an approximate example. It can be varied to suit the local conditions of any present, whether your business is small or of fair proportions. It is an illustrative example of the cost of running your business for one week:

Salary of Self	$ 40.00
Insurance	3.00
Fire and Light	5.00
Rent	10.00
Office Assistance	15.00
Breakages and Repairs	5.00
Interest on Investment	10.00
Wages of 4 Employees:	
2 at $25.00 per week	50.00
2 at $12.50 per week	25.00
Total	$163.00

Here then is a plant that will require to earn $163.00 per week to just meet expenses. With four productive employees, how is this to be met?

Four employees at 48 hours per week .... 192 hrs.
Deduct ⅓ for non-productive time .... 64 hrs.
                                                  ———
Total productive hours sold .... 128 hrs.

You Can Sell Productive Hours

It will be seen that you buy 192 hours of labor. Do not make the mistake of supposing that you can sell the whole 192 hours. Experience has shown that you will have non-productive hours amounting to at least one-third. Non-productive hours must be carried into overhead. There is no other way of disposing of them. Receipts must cover expenses before profits can be earned. You have therefore a sale to your customers of 128 productive hours during the week.

One hundred and twenty-eight hours divided into 163 dollars gives you a cost hour of one dollar and twenty-seven and one-third cents.

This does not include (for purpose of simplicity) girls' time that may work in a bindery. You can safely estimate their time at 50 or 60 cents per hour cost.

Now you have a cost hour of $1.27. If your job does not return you this amount for every productive hour your men have put upon it, you have gone behind on that job. If, however, your job shows that you have earned the above for each hour and have gone 25 per cent. better, then you know for a certainty that you have made a profit of 25 per cent. above all your costs.

Your difficulties are not yet over, however. When estimating on a job, you must be sure to accurately estimate the number of hours it will take to do that job. Here is where too many of us fall down. We cannot escape the element of gamble here. You must have a pretty well-defined knowledge of the time it will take to set type—make up—make ready, and print, fold and stitch, etc. In this gamble you must guess safely or you lose.

Your known cost hour is a delightful thing on all jobs on which you do not quote. When your time sheet shows the number of hours on a job, it is an easy matter to arrive at your selling price, and this price will be just to you and just to your customer. It is, however, necessary that you should know how your quotations work out on those that you were obliged to quote upon. Your cost hour will show you whether you have made or lost money. If you have lost you have gained knowledge from experience, and will know better next time what figure to quote on that job or one like it. In any case you should know whether or not you have lost or made a profit. In estimating the number of hours it would take to do a certain job do not estimate on the skill of your best man. He may not do the job or only part of it. There is a great difference in the human element. Men's productive capacity will vary from 25 to 50 per cent. We have been told that we should get good, first-class men; that we can get them if we pay the price. This is not true. The available number of good men are limited. All the available printers of Ontario are employed—good, bad and indifferent, and when we want new help we must take what we can get. Therefore the average ability must be our basis of estimate.

Be Careful of the Overhead.

All our expenses should be taken into overhead. For instance the winter's coal supply cannot be met by increased prices in winter. We must apportion it over the whole twelve months or the 52 weeks. By observing closely the example I have presented anyone can readily arrive at their overhead costs. The press time should be charged for according to the number of hours the press is engaged under the job. The press charge per hour should include the rent of the press and the time of the operator. For example, let us suppose it take one hour to make a job ready on a Gordon, and you run it off. Here is a charge of two hours' press time. But suppose a belt breaks after the press has been running half a hour and it takes half an hour to fix the belt, and then the job is finished in the next half hour. Here would be two hours and a half. It will be obvious that this half hour fixing the belt cannot be charged as productive time. It must be show the time card as non-productive. Hence in justice to th customer only two hours' press time are to be charged again that job. This will illustrate why your press overhead mu usually charged at from $1.50 to $2.00 per cost hour. Gordo are usually charged at anywhere from 90 cents to $1.25 per co hour. This includes press time and operator's time. I estimating do not count on 1,000 per hour on your cylinders Gordons. You do not get it.

The weekly newspaper publisher is a great asset to our n tional life, and oftentimes much more so than he is an asset himself. Your work is a most important and responsible one. The ideals of the simple life must be persisted in, notwithstanding the rush city-ward. Our rural population must be maintained. It is your task to hold steady that grea: sane mass who people our farms and small towns and villages. On them depend the future greatness of our Dominion and our Christian civilization. That great trinity of races — the English, Irish, and Scotch—unmatched in the world—made this Ontario of ours the garden that it is. If these desert to the cities, and their places be taken by foreigners, our national life will reach lower levels. In California when the Jap moves in the white moves out. Your task at present is a difficult one. Only a few days ago many of the newspaper publishers were informed that their

supply of newspaper was about to be cut off. The *Expositor* of Brantford was among the number. In panic they rushed to Ottawa to save themselves from extinction. The United States claims our newsprint paper, and threats are made that unless they get it our coal supply may be cut off! And we only require for our domestic use 15 per cent. of our production! When one remembers the campaign of 1911 one is amazed at such a state of affairs.

Mr. Hurley closed his address by urging all to be steadfast in their duties and principles, and adopt better business methods in the conduct of their affairs, and insist upon demanding and maintaining that dignified place in the community which is rightfully theirs.

The President Appeals for Editorial Expression

IN INTRODUCING the new president, Mr. Calnan, the retiring president, said that he had very warm feelings for Mr. Davies. He had known him ever since he (the speaker) had first become a member of the C.P.A. He was an energetic and alert chap, who parted his hair in the middle, wore a bouquet in his buttonhole and carried a cane. He had been a constant attendant at the annual meetings, and had been an untiring and unselfish worker on committees, both in the Canadian Press Association and since the formation of the Canadian Weekly Newspapers Association. He felt that the nominating

W. RUPERT DAVIES
President C. W. N. A.

committee had chosen well, and he felt sure their choice would be popular with all the members.

When called on for a speech, Mr. Davies said he rose to accept the high office which had just been conferred upon him with mixed feelings. He realized and appreciated to the full the great honor which had been done him by his colleagues of the press, and wondered whether he would be able to fill such a responsible position to their satisfaction. He accepted it with a certain amount of diffidence because, having but recently assumed larger private responsibilities it would mean that they would have to suffer to some extent, but the one thought that was uppermost in his mind at that moment, was that the new position to which he had just been elected would open up greater opportunities for serving his fellow-publishers, and in serving

them he was always happy. The weekly newspaper men, said Mr. Davies, were the finest bunch of men on top of the earth, and he was sincere when he said so. He never went home from a convention of newspapermen that he did not wish it had been longer, so that there could have been more visiting with this one and that. "I feel that I am adopting a healthy seven months' old infant," continued the speaker, "and having a great love for children I naturally feel happy." It was seven months ago since the Canadian Weekly Newspapers Association was born, he said, and during those seven months Father Calnan had often looked very grave and Nurse Sayles had oftentimes shook his head and wondered whether the little "brat" was going to live. But it had lived and had now arrived at the time when it was necessary to take off the long clothes and put on short ones and teach it to walk. During the next year he said it would doubtless have the colic, the measles, the whooping cough, scarlet fever and all the other ailments which children seemed to be heir to, but he felt it would survive them all if it was well fed, well clothed and well tended. He hoped that when he handed it on to its next father a year hence, it would be a great big, lusty youngster, making quite a stir in the world.

Continuing, Mr. Davies said he would like to urge on every member, in view of the rapidly rising costs, the absolute necessity of charging $2.00 a year for his paper, and of raising his advertising rates to a profitable basis. Advertising rates were, he thought, altogether too low, and it was essential, if they were to stay in business, that they make very substantial increases in their advertising rates. They should, he said, realize, more fully, the dignity of their calling, and assume in the community the position which by virtue of that calling was rightly theirs. In this connection he strongly advocated an editorial page for every weekly newspaper, no matter how small. They had it in their power to be a great influence for good, not only in their own community, but in the country at large, and they should use it. An editorial page or column, in the opinion of the new president, gave a newspaper a position in the community that it could never otherwise occupy, and it was the duty of every weekly newspaper editor to prize the great heritage that had been handed down to him by the newspaper men who had moulded the opinion of Canada in days gone by, and helped shape the policies and laws of this great country. It was time we took ourselves and our work more seriously, he said, and impressed our honest convictions regarding public issues on our readers week by week, through our editorial pages. "Let us realize our great opportunity,", said the speaker, "and stop selling our birthright for a mess of pottage in the way of the few dollars we might make doing job work when we should be writing editorials. We have great opportunities before us. Let us use them, and let the people realize that in the weekly press of Canada they have a great power for good that cannot be reached or controlled by anyone except its owners."

Concluding, the new president said he wanted every member to go back home a booster for the C.W.N.A. They had had a grand convention and all that was needed now to make the association the splendid success they all wished to see it was more members. "Let us aim to double the membership by June 1921 he said. Browning had said: 'Grow old along with me, the best is yet to be," and he thought that as they grew old with the C.W.N.A. they would realize that the best was truly yet to be for the weekly newspapers of Canada.

Officers of C.W.N.A. and Members Present

President—W. R. Davies, Renfrew, Ont., *Mercury.*
Past President—A. E. Calnan, Picton, Ont., *Gazette.*
First Vice-President—V. C. French, Wetaskiwin, Alta., *Times.*
Second Vice-President—A. R. Brennan, Summerside, P.E.I., *Journal.*
Secretary—A. R. Alloway, Oshawa, Ont., *Reformer.*
Manager—E. Roy Sayles, the *Times*, Port Elgin.

Directors—J. A. MacLaren, the *Examiner*, Barrie, Ont.; Lorne Eedy, the *Telescope*, Walkerton, Ont.; F. A. J. Davis, *Central Canadian*, Carleton Place, Ont.; B. McGuire, the *Banner*, Orangeville, Ont.; L. J. Cowie, *News-Express*, Carberry, Man.; Roy G. Ashwin, the *Mail*, Milestone, Sask.; C. Kerr Stewart, *St. Maurice Valley Chronicle*, Three Rivers, Que.; Ed. Fortin, *L'Eclaireur*, Beauceville, Que.; F. Burton, *Globe*, Cardstone, Alta.; L. J. Ball, the *News*, Vernon, B.C.; Fred Stevens, *Observer*, Hartland, N.B.; F. A. Fisher, the *Advocate*, Pictou, N.S.

Directors on C.P.A. Board.—W. R. Davies, the *Mercury*, Renfrew, Ont.; D. Williams, the *Bulletin*,, Collingwood, Ont.; A. R. Brennan, the *Journal*, Summerside, P.E.I.; Mrs. Fielding, *Tribune*, Windsor, N.S.; J. C. Hebert, *Le Peuple*, Montmagny, Que.; S. N. Wynn, *Enterprise*, Yorkton, Sask.; J. A. Carswell, *News*, Red Deer, Alta.; J. M. George, *Times*, Deloraine, Man.; J. W. Ellis, *Herald*, Merritt, B.C.; H. B. Anslow, *Graphic*, Campbellton, N.B.

Advisory Board.—W. R. Davies, the *Mercury*, Renfrew, Ont.; A. E. Calnan, the *Gazette*, Picton, Ont.; A. R. Alloway, the *Reformer*,.Oshawa, Ont.; J. A. MacLaren, the *Examiner*, Barrie, Ont.; Lorne Eedy, the *Telescope*, Walkerton, Ont.; P. Geo. Pearce, the *Star*, Waterford, Ont.; F. A. J. Davis, *Central Canadian*, Carleton Place, Ont.

Advertising Committee.—Lorne Eedy, the *Telescope*, Walkerton, Ont.; J. A. MacLaren, the *Examiner*, Barrie, Ont.; D. Williams, the *Bulletin*, Collingwood, Ont.; J. F. Harvey, the *Express*, Newmarket, Ont.; A. R. Alloway, the *Reformer*, Oshawa, Ont.

Paper Committee.—F. A. J. Davis, *Central Canadian*, Carleton Place, Ont.; A. E. Calnan, the *Gazette*, Picton, Ont.; Edgar Laberge, *Le Spectateur*, Hull, Que.; J. S. Giles, *Watchman*, Lachute, Que.; W. W. Walker, *Courier*, Perth, Ont.; C. M. Mundy, the *Reformer*, Oshawa, Ont.; W. R. Young, *Freeholder*, Cornwall, Ont.

Membership Committee.—J. J. Hunter, the *Reporter*, Kincardine, Ont.; J. E. Hebert, *Le Peuple*, Montmagny, Que.; W. Jordan, the *Review*, Revelstoke, B.C.; A. R. Brennan, the *Journal*, Summerside, P.E.I.; Miss Forbes, *Tribune*, Windsor, N.S.; F. W. Galbraith, *Advocate*, Red Deer, Alta.; Roy G. Ashwin, the *Mail*, Milestone, Sask.; J. L. Cowie, *News-Express*, Carberry, Man.; F. E. Jordan, *Gazette*, Chatham, N.B.

Postal and Parliamentary.—A. H. Moore, the *News*, St. John's, Que.; F. A. J. Davis, *Central Canadian*, Carleton Place, Ont.; W. A. Fry, *Chronicle*, Dunnville, Ont.; Col. Hugh Clarke, the *Review*, Kincardine, Ont.; J. J. Pettypiece, *Free Press*, Forest, Ont.

Job Printing Committee.—F. B. Elliott, the *Herald*, Alliston, Ont.; A. R. Brennan, *Journal*, Summerside, P.E.I.; W. C. Walls, the *Examiner*, Barrie, Ont.;.J. H. Keefer, the *Register*, Norwood, Ont.

Editorial Committee.—C. H. Hale, the *Packet*, Orillia, Ont.; L. J. Ball, the *News*, Vernon, B.C.; H. T. Halliwell, *Progress*, Estevan, Alta.; Alex. Dunlop, *Press*, Neepawa, Man.; Geo. Gordon, *Herald*, Ponoka, Alta.; C. Kerr Stewart, *St. Maurice Valley Chronicle*, Three Rivers, Que.

Circulation and Subscription Rates Committee.—P. G. Pearce, *Star*, Waterford, Ont.; J. M. Marshall, *Review*, Weyburn, Sask.; John McKenzie, *Standard*, Strathmore, Alta.; J. Fortin, *L'Eclaireur*, Beauceville, Que.; Fred Stevens, *Observer*, Hartland, N.B.; E. E. Reynolds, *Banner*, Gravenhurst, Ont.; J. C. Bates, *Fraser Valley Record*, Mission City, B.C.

Members of the Canadian Weekly Newspapers Association registered at Annual Meeting, June 3rd and 4th, 1920:

Prince Edward Island.—Brennan, A. R.; Summerside *Journal.*

New Brunswick.—Fred. H. Stevens, *Carleton Observer*, Hartland, N.B.

Nova Scotia.—Arenburg, A. R., *Progress-Enterprise*, Lunenburg; Fielding, Mrs. J., *Tribune*, Windsor; Forbes, Miss A., *Tribune*, Windsor; Sodero, T., *News*, Sydney Mines; Smith, Mr., *Progress-Enterprise*, Lunenburg.

Quebec.—Carmichael, Roy, *Echo*, Verdun; Dechanes, Jos., *L'Eclaireur*, Beauceville; J. Ed. Fortin, *L'Eclaireur*, Beauceville; Sinard, A., *L'Eclaireur*, Beauceville; Giles, J. S.,·*Watchman*, Lachute; Girouard, A., *Le Canadien*, Thedford Mines; Hebert, Jos. C., *Le Peuple*, Montmagny; Laberge, Edgar, *Le Spectateur*, Hull; Legge, Geo., *Leader-Mail*, Granby; Moore, Rev. A. H., *News*, St. John's; Stewart, C. Kerr, *St. Maurice Valley Chronicle*, Three Rivers.

British Columbia.—Bates, J. A., *Fraser Valley Record*, Mission City; Jordan, Walter, *Review*, Revelstoke; Kay, D. A., *Courier*, Cranbrook; Morden, H. G., *North Shore Leader*, North Vancouver.

Saskatchewan.—Ash, Harry C., *Gazette*, Birch Hills; Ashwin, Roy C., *Mail*, Milestone; Hill, Mrs. W. P., *Herald*, Loreburn; Holmes, Ed., *Herald*, Carlyle; Keays, Thos. H., *Clarion*, Kindersley; Polley, Sydney R., *News*, Morse; Smart, Chas., *Review*, Imperial; Scott, Jno., *Herald*, Whitewood; Workman, E. S. H., *Star*, Lemberg.

Manitoba.—Cowie, Jas. L., *News-Express*, Carberry; George, J. M., *Times*, Deloraine; McMorran, R. W., *Plaindealer*, Souris; Munro, H. B., *Herald and Mining News*, The Pas; Pickell, W. G., *Herald.* Langruth; McFarlane, David G., *News*, Belmont.

Alberta.—Buchanan, J. E., *Conservator*, Fort Saskatchewan; Burton, F., *Globe*, Cardston; Evans, Geo. W., *Call*, Gleichen; Evans, Mrs. W. Park, *Call*, Gleichen; French, V. C., *Times*, Wetaskiwin; Housianx, Jos. A., *Review*, Coronation; MacKenzie *Standard*, Strathmore; Quayle, A. E., *Sun*, Carmangay.

Ontario.—Aylesworth, W. C., *Guide-Advocate*, Waterford; Aitcheson, *Express*, Clifford; Allen, Mrs., *Herald*, Carleton Place; Alloway, A. R., *Reformer*, Oshawa; Bennett, E. S., *Leader*, Stirling; Bingham, E. V., *Dominion*, Ridgetown; Blackstone, Geo. A., *Times*, Orillia; Boyer, Geo., *Muskoka Herald*, Bracebridge; Britton, B. O., *Reporter*, Gananoque; Brown, Geo. K., *News*, Teeswater; Calnan, A. E., *Gazette*, Picton; Cave, W. G., *Argus*, Midland; Cave, J. J., *Express*, Beaverton; Charters, C. V., *Conservator*, Brampton; Cliffe, W. W., *Central Canadian*, Carleton Place; Corson, R. J., *Economist and Sun*, Markham; Craig, W. Logan, *Star and Vidette*, Grand Valley; Currie, James, *News-Argus*, Stirling; Davies, W. R., *Mercury*, Renfrew; Davis, J. H., *North Hastings Review*, Madoc; Davis, H. D., *Advocate*, Mitchell; Davis, F. A. J., *Central Canadian*, Carleton Place; Denholm, J. M., *News-Tribune*, Blenheim; Donly, H. B., *Simcoe Reformer*, Simcoe; Dunlop, W. A., *Standard*, Forest; Eedy, Lorne A., *Telescope*, Walkerton; Eedy, John W., *Journal*, St. Marys; Ellis, A. W., *Advertiser*, Petrolia; Elliott, F. B., *Herald*, Alliston; Evans, F. L. E., *Age*, Strathroy; Evoy, Jas. A., *Review*, Carp; Fleming, Howard, *Sun-Times*, Owen Sound; Fry, W. A., *Chronicle*, Dunnville,; Gale, H., *Enterprise*, Colborne; Goodfellow, G. M., *Gazette and Chronicle*, Whitby; Hale, C. H., *Packet*, Orillia; Hale, W. M., *Packet*, Orillia; Harvey, J. F., *Express-Herald*, Newmarket; Harris, Elgin A., *Gazette*, Burlington; Hastings, Davis, *Gazette*, Dunnville; Hellems, W. H., *Reporter*, Kingsville; Hogg, W. A. *Enterprise*, Collingwood; Hudson, E. S., *Express*, Beamsville. Hunter, J. J., *Reporter*, Kincardine; Irwin, *Chronicle*, Durham Jarrett, Thomas, *Quinte Sun*, Trenton; Jackson, L. G., *Era* Newmarket; James, Geo. W., *Statesman*, Bowmanville; Johnston, J. H. F., Tillsonburg; Johnston, J. A., *Gazette*, Mildmay Keefer, J. G., *Register*, Norwood; Keefer, I. H., *Register*, Norwood; Landsborough, Jas. L., *Free Press*, Shelburne; Lancaster T. P., *Standard*, Havelock; Leavens, F. N., *Enterprise*, Bolton MacBeth, Malcolm, *Sun*, Milverton; McCullough, T. Hugh *News*, Chatsworth; McDonald, Wm., *Enterprise*, Chesley McGregor, Jean R., *Recorder*, Gore Bay; McGuire, R. V. *Herald*, Thamesville; McGuire, B., *Banner*, Orangeville McIntyre, J. R., *Herald*, Dundalk; McKenzie, D., *Advocate* Paisley; McKitrick, W. D., *Banner*, Orangeville; MacLaren, J A., *Examiner*, Barrie; McMahon, T. F., *Liberal*, Richmond Hill

Messecar, M., *Advance*, Burford; Mitchell, A, T., *Review*, Smithville; Mitchell, G. H., *Post*, Hanover; Monteith, C. B., *Express*, Aylmer; Moore, C. H., *Star*, Dundas; Muir, James, *Gazette*, Almonte; Mundy, Chas. M., *Reformer*, Oshawa; Naftel, Walter, F. A., *Star*, Goderich; Nolan, A. V., *Enterprise*, Chesley; Pearce, P. Geo., *Star*, Waterford; Pettypiece, H. J., *Free Press*, Forest; Reynolds, E. E., *Banner*, Gravenhurst; Rickaby, F. W., *Spectator*, Bruce Mines; Robinson, Wm. A., *Gleaner*, Cannington; Rogers, A., *Review*, Kincardine; Ross, Jas. H., *Press*, Winchester; Rutledge, C. W., *Standard*, Markdale; Sayles, E. Roy, *Times*, Port Elgin; Sabine, H. W., *Herald*, Marmora; Samson, W. D., *Journal*, Renfrew; Seim, O. M., *Witness*, Bradford; Semple, R. A., *Sentinel*, Tottenham; Short, Ernest, *Beacon*, Southampton; Shore, Harry J., *Citizen*, Port Colborne; Smith, A. G., *Advance*, Wingham; Southcott, J. M., *Times*, Exeter; Strachan, T. W., *Enterprise*, Belmont; Sutherland, A. E., *Transcript*, Glencoe; Templin, J. C., *News-Record*, Fergus; Thompson, John H., *Post*, Thorold; Thorning, Otto, *Northland Post*, Cochrane; VanDusen, H. A., *Leader*, Tara; Walker, W. W., *Courier*, Perth; Wallace, W. Y., *British Canadian*, Simcoe; Walls, W. C., *Examiner*, Barrie; Watson, James, *North Hastings Review*, Madoc; Watson, A. H., *North Hastings Review*, Madoc; Wesley, J. A., *Herald-Times*, Walkerton; Whalley, Thos. W., *Standard*, Pembroke; Williams, David, *Bulletin*, Collingwood; Wilson, Leslie, *Sentinel-Star*, Cobourg; Winterburn, J. S., *Gazette*, Norwich; Wright, A. W., *Representative*, Mount Forest; young, W. R., *Freeholder*, Cornwall.

The C. P. A. in Session

There was very little business done at the annual meeting of the Canadian Press Association on the afternoon of the second day. After the meeting had been in session some time John Imrie, acting secretary, informed the gathering that no quorum was present.

The chief topic of discussion was the "unfair representation" on the Imperial Press Conference Committee. Mr. A. Burrows said that to the five daily paper representatives should be added one representative of the trade journals and one of the weekly press.

Lt.-Col. J. B. Maclean explained that Sir Jno. Willison, the original chairman of the committee and himself as vice-chairman, had strongly favored the representation of weeklies, but J. E. Atkinson was strongly opposed and he "brought pressure to bear" on Sir John so that since the second meeting of the committee the weekly and trade sections "have been persistently excluded."

"That's as Sir John Willison told me personally," said Col. Maclean.

On motion of Messrs. Burrows and Williams a resolution was carried expressing the regret of the meeting that weekly and trade papers had been ignored.

The opinion was expressed that something should be done to discourage the importation of American publications which are "denationalizing Canadians."

Directors to the C.P.A. executive for the Canadian National Newspapers and Periodicals were elected as follows: Acton Burrows, Lionel Davis, Rev. R. Douglas Fraser, H. T. Hunter, Hugh C. MacLean, Lt.-Col. J. B. Maclean, H. V. Tyrrell, Jno. Wild, T. S. young and T. J. Tilson.

Decides in Favor of Publisher

The British *Whig*, of Kingston, contracted with the E. B. Eddy Co., of Ottawa, for the supply of 150 tons of newsprint approximately per year, being the whole of the publishers' requirements, over a period of three years. The first two years 472 tons were delivered, and the Eddy Company supplied 28 tons in the third year, holding that this more than completed the contract. The *Whig* was forced to buy at an advanced price to fill its requirements for 1918, and brought suit for $5,224.37 damages. Justice Middleton holds in favor of the *Whig* that each year must be taken by itself, and that the purchaser in the first two years having asked for and received more than he was entitled to, and this having been paid for, those accounts are closed. He declares the Eddy Company liable to pay damages based on the amount by which the delivery in 1918 fell short of 165 tons.

Death of Joseph Hays

Many publishers in Canada were acquainted with Joseph Hays, whose death occurred a short time ago. He was manager of the Typographic and Advertising Departments of the Lanston Monotype Machine Co. After completing his apprenticeship he worked in some of the best shops in Philadelphia, and later become foreman of the composing room of the Curtis Publishing Co.

When the movement for improving business conditions became interested and accepted a position of assistant secretary of the Printers' Board of Trade was in its infancy he tary of the Franklin Club of Philadelphia as it was then called.

In 1903 he went to Boston as secretary of the Printers' Board of Trade in that city and did such splendid work that he was

THE LATE JOSEPH HAYS

brought back to Philadelphia, in 1904, as secretary-manager of the Typothetae in Philadelphia, which had merged with the Franklin Club. His work in this position was so well done that he became known all over the country as a successful organization man. It was while here that he, in co-operation with one or two other enthusiasts, created the basis upon which the Standard Cost Finding System for Printers was built, a few years later. They also collected the data and figured out the first price list for printing.

Mr. Hays remained with the Typothetae of Philadelphia until October 1907, when he resigned to accept the position of assistant sales manager of the Monotype Company, with which company he remained until his death, receiving several well-merited promotions.

Denies the Montreal Report

In the May issue of *Printer and Publisher* an item appeared stating that, following the recent trouble in Montreal, a move was under way to form a Canadian Typographical Union, the cities of Toronto, Montreal and Winnipeg being the most interested. This item did not originate in this office, neither was there any comment passed on it. It was credited as being a Montreal report. Officials of the Montreal Branch of the I.T.U. have taken the matter up with this paper, claiming that there is no truth whatever in the report, and suggesting that nothing would be more pleasant to certain interests than to have a split in the ranks of the I.T.U. in Canada. *Printer and Publisher* can assure the Montreal officials that the item was published simply as a matter of news, and we just as willingly publish the contradiction of the report, thanking the president of the Montreal Union, Mr. Black, for calling our attention to the matter.

Franklin List Users Met in Toronto

Address by Mr. R. T. Porte of Salt Lake City

A S THE outcome of a meeting which was held in the St. Charles Hotel on Monday evening, the 7th inst., Toronto will soon have a Franklin Club, or some kindred organization composed largely of those from offices using the Franklin Price List.

The meeting at the St. Charles Hotel included several printers from out of the city who are using the list, as well as a large representation from Toronto. The speaker of the evening was Mr. R. T. Porte, of the Porte Publishing Co., Salt Lake City, Utah, a gentleman who has devoted a great deal of time and energy—and he has little of the former and plenty of the latter —to organizing the printing industry, and bringing actual costs and actual profits to the attention of the men in the industry.

During the course of his remarks Mr. Porte made mention of the changes in Canada in the carrying on of his business. Heretofore the Franklin Price List has been sold by Moore-Telford, but in the future Mr. Moore would be Canadian manager, the firm of Moore-Telford having been dissolved.

Mr. Porte, in opening, traced the development of the Franklin Price List, and traced the growth of the business of finding costs on the hundreds of jobs that come into an office that can be relied upon without estimating. He also made it perfectly plain that he was very much in favor of cost work, and advised all present to know and study their own costs in their own shops. He welcomed any move that could be made to check up the Franklin List by other cost systems.

"Here is something you should bear in mind," said Mr. Porte, "it isn't the printers that accept the list—it is the buyers of printing. The effect of showing the list has more to do with settling disputes between buyer and seller than anything else that can be done. I preached that point day and night." The work of finding average and reliable figures was a big task at the start, and Mr. Porte showed some of the difficulties that were encountered. With Mrs. Porte they had sat up night after night trying to get prices that would jibe, and finally the statement came from Porte that the trouble was in not using scales. "So the next day we laid plans for the adoption of scales and in three weeks we had them, and they were so perfect that they never had to be changed since. The effect of showing the list was to convince the customer that he was not buying in the dark. The customer was used to buying other commodities the same way and there was no reason why the same rule should not apply to printing. In the old way, when a customer wants a piece of printing, the printer starts to put down some figures, 18c, 36c, 75c, and so on. Then he scratches his head and goes all over the thing again. Then he announces that he can do the fob for $7, whereat the customer suggests that he can get the same thing up the street for $6, and in the end the printer announces that he'll do the job for $4.50."

Cost Systems Will Vary

"It makes no difference what you have in the way of cost systems," declared Mr. Porte; "even with the greatest care the results will vary as high as 25 per cent." He instanced a shop in St. Louis where there had been a difference of fifty per cent.

in the two prices quoted by one shop on the same job. The buyer had gone in and secured a figure from one man and short ly after had secured another price from another official in the same shop, with the difference above mentioned. "The human element is there all the time. You can put through a job to-day and three days from now you can put through the same job and there will be a difference in the costs. One time the buyer might get off easy and the next time he might get soaked. On one job a jobber sent us a letter saying that our cost was no good, as it was too low by ten per cent. on a loose leaf job he put through and in a few days he wrote saying that the list was all right because he had made a good profit by following the pric on another job, which he had checked up by his own cos finding system.

The Growth of Busines

Mr. Porte showed the car that had been taken to fin average prices that woul suit the average place in an part of the country, and th same effort also brought t light the great spread in thes figures in different centre They had asked for hot costs and wages from printer all over the country, and th replies received numbere 2,340, and the hour costs wer all the way from 50c to $4.5 These figures were compiled,- with the exception of th fifty cent cost, Mr. Por holding that there was r such thing to-day as a 5 per hour cost of time. The figures would be used for th next six months and wou form the basis for the pri list. "Our mail," remarked the speaker, "averages 500 lette a day. We have two men out visiting around the shops all over the country."

In the first place the list which is now the Franklin Printi Price List was intended merely for the use of Mr. Porte in l own printing establishment. Denver was the first city to ma application for it, and soon after a long, descriptive article w written in *Inland Printer*. Following this some two or th hundred copies of the list were applied for, and finally M Fish of the Western Newspaper Union heard of it and offer the use of his staff in selling it to the smaller printer in t States, "so we told him to go to it," remarked Mr. Por "The business has so increased that on December 1st of l year we organized the Porte Publishing Co. A year ago t office force consisted of my wife and a girl in the office. Th are 24 people there now and three men on the road."

Work was also being done in the same way for the sn country publisher to apply to advertising rates. There now 5,764 printers using the Franklin Price List, against 60 year ago. At a meeting of the National Editorial Associa a few weeks ago, Mr. Porte found that of 62 present 42 w using the list.

"The printer who gets the list at once becomes a mission At a meeting in Rochester not long ago practically the wl day was given over to a discussion of the Franklin Price lis The experience of Montgomery county was gone into. years there the country had told the papers what they w pay them for the county printing. Not far back a few spi bolder than the others had got together and taken it upon th selves to tell the county —in much fear and trembling—t their notices in future would cost them more money, and

MR. PORTE'S POINTERS

"I WOULDN'T RUN a shop for a second without a cost system.

IT ISN'T THE PRINTER who accepts the list. It is the buyer of printing.

THE EFFECT of showing a definite list is to settle the dispute at once.

THE HUMAN ELEMENT is there all the time and is sure to make mistakes in the estimating on a job.

THE SAME JOB done to-day and three days from now will show a difference on your cost sheets as high as 25 per cent.

THE CUSTOMER wants to know what he is going to pay before he orders the printing.

answer had been "Well, we'll pay it." So they called a meeting and organization was effected, and all but three of those people," declared Mr. Porte, "are using the Franklin Price List."

The Logical Thing to Do

"I have tried to put my own personal feeling into this matter. I went broke twice. I went into costs long ago when few people were thinking seriously about the matter, and then I preached them up and down the West, but we don't want costs after the work has been done, we want the costs before we start. The customer wants to know how much he is going to pay for his printing. You go into a shoe store and ask the price of a pair of shoes. Do you mean to say that the clerk gets out a pencil and starts to tell you what the shoes cost to get made, what the freight was, and what the selling costs are? He does not. He says the boots are $18.50 and you can take or leave them. Clothing is sold the same way. But what gets your goat is when someone gets for $4.50 what you have paid $5 for. That's why they go out shopping for printing. They look upon you as poor business men because of your variety of prices. If you can get orders without the price, do it, but be careful. When you use the Franklin List you do not care whether the price is asked for or given before or after the work is done. It is the same."

Mr. Porte remarked that some of the very best suggestions that had been received came from the printers themselves. Plans were in view for giving a much more comprehensive service than is included with the list now. The greatest suggestion they had received came from a small printer in Pittsburgh, and it resulted in bringing out the case for carrying samples in conjunction with the price list. Mr. Porte showed a sample of these cases. They consist of a series of large tough envelopes, fitted into a loose-leaf system, along with the various sections of the price list. By the use of this case the seller of printing is enabled to give not only a price at once on any job but also to give samples and show the customer what will cover his case. In this way the printer can walk out with the order for the business, and if he doesn't he hasn't spent half the day there estimating on work that doesn't come to his shop.

Mr. Porte also referred to other services that were available. They had brought out a perpetual stock inventory and a simple system of bookkeeping. We have an estimating department, "But get this clear, we won't give you an estimate on a job you haven't done, but on jobs you have done, all right." There is also a printer's advertising service, Mr. Porte giving it as his opinion that the printer as a general thing is the rottenest advertiser on earth. In conclusion he made it clear that he was prepared to stand behind the list. It could be used for sixty days in any kind of work, and it could be checked up by any system they cared to apply to it, and if at the end of that period the user was not satisfied with the list and with the service that went with it, he could return it and get his money back. At the conclusion of Mr. Porte's address, which was remarkably well received, several of those in attendance told of the way the list worked out. Peter Wilson, superintendent of the Sentinel-Review, Woodstock, stated that when they started to use the list in the first place they checked it with the Standard Cost Finding System, which they had in their office. This went on for three months, and the results were so much the same that we use the list almost entirely now for giving a price. A piece of work, a programme for a local theatrical, came in. It was 12 pages and 2,000 copies. Our price according to the Franklin List, which I used, was $150. The promoters stated they had secured the same work in Brockville for $85. After several more visits I offered to put my cost system on the job, and charge according to that, to which they agreed. In the end there were several advertising spaces not filled out, which made quite a little difference in the charge for composition, etc. Our figures this way showed $132 for the work, and if the programme had been the same as the one we were asked to estimate on in the first place, we would have found that our Cost Finding System and the Franklin Price List would give us about the same figure to a dollar.

Toronto Globe:—The tragic accident in the stereotyping room of the Evening Telegram yesterday brought speedy expressions of sympathy and offers of assistance in getting out the paper from the Telegram's contemporaries, which remember how quickly and unreservedly help has been tendered by the management of the Telegram in the past when things went wrong in any of the other offices.

Newspaper Service as Hosts

During the convention of the Canadian Weekly Newspaper Association in Toronto on June 3 and 4, weekly publishers using the new ready-print service supplied by the Canadian Newspaper Service Limited were tendered an informal dinner at the King Edward Hotel on the opening night of the convention.

W. NELSON WILKINSON
Gen., Manager Canadian Newspaper Service, Ltd.

Mr. W. Nelson Wilkinson, president and general manager of the new company, pointed out that in face of the newsprint crisis publishers using the ready-prints supplied by Canadian Newspaper Service Limited need not be at all concerned regarding their supply. It would be delivered every week without fail, as there was a sufficient supply of newsprint on hand to meet all requirements for many months and adequate arrangements had been made to supplement the supply whenever more newsprint was needed.

Mr. J. J. Hunter of the Kincardine Reporter, who was associated with Mr. Wilkinson on the Toronto World, called on some of the publishers to express their opinions of the service. This they did. All spoke very highly of the service and expressed their satisfaction. Mr. Hunter referred to the fact that no patent medicine advertising would be carried, claiming it was a step in the right direction.

Those who attended the dinner were:—Mr. and Mrs. A. E. Calnan, Picton, past president of the Canadian Weekly Newspaper Ass'n; E. Roy Sayles, manager of the Ass'n, and Mrs. Sayles; Mr. and Mrs. E. Sydney Bennett, Stirling Leader; Mr. and Mrs. McIntyre, Dundalk Herald; Mr. and Mrs. Reynolds, Gravenhurst Banner; Mr. and Mrs. McKenzie, Paisley Advocate; Mr. and Mrs. Brown, Teeswater News; Mr. and Mrs. McGuire, Thamesville Herald; Mr. and Mrs. Mitchell, Smithville Review; Mr. and Mrs. McBeth, Milverton Sun; Miss McBeth; Wm. Fry, Dunnville Chronicle; Mr. and Mrs. Sabin, Marmora Herald; P. Geo. Pearce, Waterford Star; J. H. Ross, Winchester Press; J. J. Hunter, Kincardine Reporter; G. R. Shibley, Mr. and Mrs. W. Nelson Wilkinson, Canadian Newspaper Service Limited.

Invitations were sent to about 50 publishers and their wives; but many found it impossible to attend the convention owing to pressure of work at home, while others had made previous engagements for their stay in Toronto.

Mr. Wilkinson will entertain his customers in the same way in Vancouver next year.

United Paper Mills' New Premises

The United Paper Mills, Limited, announce the removal of their executive offices and the Toronto warerooms to the second and basement floors of the new "Spadina Building," 129 Spadina Avenue, Toronto. This means that they have practically double the space that they formerly occupied, which, with increased staff and the carrying of a larger stock, facilitates an exceptionally efficient trade service. Printers and publishers, while in Toronto, might very well visit this establishment.

Printer & Publisher

Published on the Twelfth of Each Month.

H. D. TRESIDDER   -   -   -   Business Manager.
A. R. KENNEDY   -   -   -   -   -   -   Editor.

SUBSCRIPTION PRICE—Canada, Great Britain, South Africa nd
the West Indies, $3 a year; United States, $3.50 a year; otner
countries, $4 a year. Single copies, 30 cents. Invariably in
advance.

PUBLISHED BY

THE MACLEAN PUBLISHING CO.

Established 1887   Limited

JOHN BAYNE MACLEAN   -   -   -   President.
H. T. HUNTER   -   -   -   -   -   -   Vice-President.
H. V. TYRRELL   -   -   -   -   General Manager.
T. B. COSTAIN   -   -   -   General Managing Editor.

Head Office, 143-153 University Avenue -   TORONTO, CANADA
    Cable Address Macpubco, Toronto; Atabek, London, Eng.
Also at Montreal, Winnipeg, New York, Chicago, Boston, London,
                        England.
            Application for A.B.C. Audit.

Vol. 29   TORONTO, JUNE, 1920   No. 6

CONTENTS

The Future of the C.P.A.

THE meeting of the Canadian Weekly Newspapers Association was one of the most successful events that has taken
place in the history of organization movement in Canada as far
as the printing and publishing industry is concerned. It was a
happy combinattion of good times and solid business, with the
latter always in the foreground.

The Weekly Association is driving ahead now with the rather
ambitious goal of 700 members by June of 1921. The Association is working along lines that ought to give real service to the
weekly publisher, and show him something tangible for the
money he is putting in through his fees.

The fate of the Canadian Press Association, now that the
members are divided into three well-defined camps, is not so
certain. The Daily Papers do not meet until well on in the
fall, and until they appoint their directors to the C.P.A. it is
hard to see how they can go ahead and elect officers for the C.P.A.
The one chance the C.P.A. had of surviving was as a common meeting place for all the publishing interests in Canada,
and such a proposition seems to be almost out of the question
now.

There are not a few publishers, outside the ranks of the
Weekly members entirely, who would willingly see that C.P.A.
as such turned over to the Weekly Newspapers Association,
believing that it would in this way retain its identity to a greater
extent than by trusting to the hit-or-miss plan that now
threatens to take the remaining life out of the parent organization.

For years the first Canadian Press Association was kept up
almost entirely by the smaller publishers from Ontario, and it
would not be a radical departure were the fortunes of the Association entrusted again to the rapidly developing Canadian Weekly Newspapers Association. Membership would not necessarily
be confined to weekly publishers, and official representation
might be given to other sections, but it seems necessary to
find some fixed and organized body to look after the C.P.A.,
and the Weekly Association seems to be the logical place for
it to rest.

Editorial Work on the Weekly

BOTH the retiring and the incoming president of the C.W.N.A.
referred to the need for more hard work and concentration
on the editorial side of the weekly newspapers in Canada.

And both were right. There are papers all over the country,
many of them coming to our exchange table week after week,
that fail miserably to reflect the sentiment of either their
editors or the leaders in the community in which they make
their living. The editorial page, or for that matter the editorial
column, is not there at all.

Other papers make a weak effort. They ape the larger papers,
where specialists in editorial work do nothing else but grind out
editorial matter. These specialists have not half the chance of
serving their constituency as well as the editor of the smaller
paper who knows in detail—or should—the affairs of his community. Much of their material is at long range, covering a
wide range, and much of it fails to interest their readers.

The editor of the smaller paper has a far better chance. It
has been proved time after time. His readers have a fair knowledge of local conditions, and it is a safe rule to follow that people
like to read of things they have seen or heard of. If you see a
runaway or a fire, you look with interest to see what the paper
has to say about it. The fact that you have seen it does not
detract from your interest in the paper's account. On the
other hand, it tends to increase it.

That is in the realm of news, and the same thing holds good
in the matter of editorial comment.

Doing this work will make you a better digger, and it is the
digger who gets the worth-while material in his paper. When
you discuss local affairs don't guess. Know your facts and
speak as an authority. Cultivate the acquaintance of your
town officials, your clerk, treasurer and other civic heads who
can give you the truth and the figures to back it up.

If you are going to get $2 per year for your paper—and you
will have to do it if you are going to stay in business—make
your paper worth $2 a year.

If you can make your editorial page worth while your people
will read it. If you can't, they won't, and if you can't hold the
attention of your readers, then you are in the wrong business.

Knowing Your Own Business

THAT the advertiser is entitled to more information in
regard to rates is the claim of the *Advertiser's Weekly*, of
London, England. This point is brought out as follows—:

For a long time past publishers have been raising rates and
advertisers, tolerant at first, have at last become irritated. The
real reason for this irritation lay in the fact that, as we pointed
out in our recent articles on the subject, the advertiser had
been left in the dark in regard to matters in which he had a
real concern. He was not told what the publisher has to face
to-day in the shape of increased production charges. He was
simply informed that "owing to increased costs, etc.," it would
cost him more to publish his announcement and, naturally,
after several communications of this sort, he grew restive and
suspicious.

The publisher is poorly advised if he falls back on the "Well,
they're all getting it" plea.

Before the publisher knows what he should sell his space for
he must know what his production costs are.

Unfortunately there are a very large number of Canadian
publishers who do not definitely know their hour costs, page
cost, display and straight matter costs.

Not knowing these things, how under the sun can they put
up an intelligent and convincing case to the advertiser who
wants to know the reason of the several increases in rates?

It is not enough that he be told that paper, labor and postage
are increasing.

Know your business. Be master of your costs, and you can,
in printed statement, or by personal contact when renewals
or new contracts are up, convince your advertiser beyond all
question or doubt.

REVIEW OF JOB SPECIMENS

If You Want An Opinion On
Your Work, Send It In

IN LAST month's issue of *Printer and Publisher* we used as a job specimen a letterhead of the Kitchener-Waterloo Typographical Union, submitting on an opposite page a reset in a different style. The foreman of the office, the Merchants Printing Co., in which the work was done, in writing to this paper since, states that the work we had was only half-finished, as they were held-up for a large tint-block of the union label, which was to have been used 'as a background for the printed matter. This will no doubt have the effect of softening down any suggestion of stiffness or squareness that may have been present. Our Kitchener correspondent also had some well-timed suggestions and criticisms regarding the reset which had been made of their job. *Printer and Publisher* wants to make the Job Specimen department one of real service to the printers of this country, and it is only with assistance, co-operation and criticism that it can be done. There is nothing more interesting and entertaining to the real printer than to run into some kindred soul who takes a keen interest in the study of typography, whose originality is apt to kick over the traces at what certain leaders may have laid down as right and wrong, and who delights to pick a job to pieces to find where it went wrong, and where it can be made better.

If you have a good piece of work that has been done in your office let us see it. When you send it along give us a little note' on the subject. If you have selected a new or

particular style of grouping in your composition, tell us why you did it. If you want us to take your work and secure some resets of it in other offices, we'll undertake that. There's a real chance to study the business here. If you want to say anything about our resets, go ahead and say it. We want a department here helpful to and contributed to by the printers themselves.

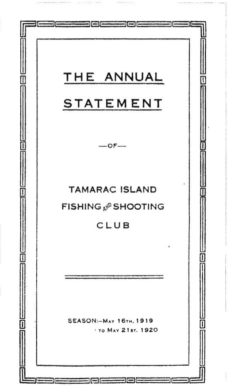

Figure A

FIGURE A—The annual statement of the Tamarac Island Fishing and Shooting Club. This sort of a job, roughly $3\frac{1}{2} \times 6\frac{1}{2}$, makes a splendid size to work in, especially where the printer is not worried with too much material. The original, Figure A, was sent to this office from a weekly newspaper and job shop combined, with the request that a reset be given, and some criticism of the original furnished.

The border is in good taste, and the spacing is fairly well done with the exception of placing of the "Tamarac Island Fishing & Shooting Club" too near a dead centre on the page. It tends to produce a flat appearance instead of following the oblong idea, which could be secured by taking the available space and dividing it by five and placing the wording in proportion to two from the top and three from the bottom. The rules should be taken out entirely. The ornamental "and" should be avoided.

The chances are that in turning out a report of this sort not many copies would be required. The printer should keep in mind that he can very often do a little good publicity work for his office by

The content inside the image (Figure A):

THE ANNUAL

STATEMENT

—OF—

TAMARAC ISLAND

FISHING AND SHOOTING

CLUB

SEASON:—MAY 16TH, 1919
' TO MAY 21ST, 1920

doctoring up a job of this kind, and putting a touch of color on the cover, or selecting a little better stock than usual. The report comes into the hands of members of a club. That means that they have some money to spend, and are apt to be influenced by a little piece of extra fine work. Many of the members may be from places where your work is unknown. In this way you have a chance to show them what you can do. Some of the best advertising a printer can do can be secured in this very direct way.

FIGURE B—This reset is furnished by Stanley Robertson, a fourth year student of the Toronto Technical School, and an apprentice on the mechanical staff of the Toronto *World*. The color was an afterthought, put in this office simply to brighten up the work, and show what can be done with a little extra work. Mr. Robertson is a pupil under Mr. Walter Handley. The job was set on the last day of the school term, and was put through in time that would be commercially successful. The Packard series is used throughout. There was no restriction as to what lines should be displayed and what should not. The reset leans to the idea that the Tamarac Island name is the dominating idea in the design. One might suggest that the strength of the design is a little too far removed from the top, as the eye at once travels down to the larger line.

FIGURE C—This reset was done by John Paré, a fourth year apprentice in the job department of the MacLean Publishing Co., and a student at the Technical School., although this job was done at the MacLean plant. The Artcraft series, not much unlike the Packard, has been used, although neither compositor had any idea of what was being used by the other. If a line were drawn right and left from the bottom of the floral ornament to the right and left corners of the top line it will be found that there is a well-formed pyramid in the design, long enough to keep the page from having any bunty or crowded effect. The squaring of the reading matter at the bottom is also desirable, as it tends to carry out the oblong idea, on which the whole page is built. If one complains that the ornament is too large, the compositor will tell him that it suggests the outdoor life, and is in keeping with the title of the book. It is fairly large but

its open design keeps it from dominating the situation in any way.

THE objection may be made to the resets that the style of type is not available in the smaller offices. That point was mentioned to the representative of *Printer and Publisher* several times during the gathering of the Press Association. It really makes little difference. Either of these jobs could have been put up just as effectively in any of the light Cheltenham or Caslon faces. Once the printer gets the idea of page building in his head he can apply it to a small cover the same as anything else. The selection of type must be part of that necessary thing, viz., a sense of proportion and effect, and the nature of the job must also be kept in mind. For instance an announcement of a sale calls for more strength than one telling that a bank is starting a new branch.

Many of the larger offices are confining their type faces more and more. The good old days when the comp. could romp all over the premises, gathering in fancy work, and running wild amongst the ornaments is gone for keeps. For instance in the composing room of the MacLean Publishing Co., where 16 different papers go through, some of them weekly, others semi-monthly and monthly, there are two families of type recognized outside of the job department. These are Cheltenham and Caslon, so no matter how many changes may take place in the ad. alleys there is not much chance of the new-comers altering the general appearance of the pages by the letting loose of any ideas they may cherish.

As a general thing, it is safe to keep your lighter faces for such a job as is under consideration. If you want to use a Gothic, pick a light one and stay with the Gothic all through for it is hard to put in another line that will jibe successfully

"THE Service Press", Brandon Man., has forwarded something rather out of the ordinary in the way of a blotter. I is a series of blotters showing various departments of th office. The first blotter, inside the one used for a cover, i devoted to the type setting equipment of the office, drawing attention to the service that can be secured on short notice there. The nex department taken u is the press room where the blotter shows the cut of cylinder • press an explains the scope work that can k turned out. Th

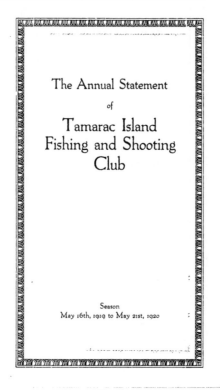

┌─────────────────────────────┐

The Annual Statement

of

Tamarac Island
Fishing and Shooting
Club

Season
May 16th, 1919 to May 21st, 1920

└─────────────────────────────┘

Figure B

bindery is represented by a power stitcher, while there is another sheet of blotter added summing up the case and also
telling of other lines such as counter check books, etc.

FROM the press of the Royal Print and Litho. Ltd., Halifax,
comes an artistic production showing the wealth of Nova
Scotia. The Dennis publications, the *Herald*, *Mail* and
Leader, are responsible for the book. The cover bears the
striking title "To Get Business Go Where Business Is," the
design being in two blues and gold. The stock throughout is
feather edge, and plate or antique finish. The press work is a
credit to the office and to the men on the job in the press room.
A wealth of information, concerning the possibilities of Nova
Scotia, its buying power and stability, is attractively presented.
The book is also a handsome advertisement for the office turning it out. We don't care whether they printed many or few,
neither have we been asked to estimate on the proposition, but
we feel that in sending us one of these copies, the publisher
has parted with about $2.

IN THE recently
published results
of examinations of
Toronto Technical
Schools, the follow-
ing were successful:
Typography, Class I.
(Norman Andrews,
Carson R. McClana-
than); (E. R. Craw-
ford, Geo. A. Page,
Frank E. Lawrence.
Class II. Cyril Sol-
litt, (Frank Miller,
Samuel D. Green.)
Typography,
(Special) Class I.
Hugh C. McGuigan,
Wilfred Tench, Ar-
thur Chadwick, Roy
Bradd, Arthur John
Baty, Ivor E. Grif-
fiths, J. Hubbard, K.
McLeod, John Pare,
Thomas A. Wood.
Class II: Percy R.
Webb, Stuart Rob-
ertson, Ben Levy,
Alfred J. Gilbert,
Simeon Frankel.
Class III. Albert E.
Ray, Athol Brown.

Typography II.
Class I. James Wil-
son, Jas. L. Parry.

The MacLean Pub-
lishing Co., and Mr.
D. J. Hutchinson,
mechanical superin-
tendent in particular,
are highly pleased
over the showing
made by the boys
from their compos-
ing room. Out of
the 27 passing, ten
are from the Mac-
Lean staff. Mr.
Hutchinson has al-
ways taken a com-
mendable interest in
the training of the
apprentice, and this
is reflected in the
splendid showing at
the Technical School
examinations.

Annual Statement

of

Tamarac Island
Fishing and Shooting
Club

SEASON

May 16th, 1919
to
May 21st, 1920

Figure C

FROM the office of the *Clarion* office, Cabri, Sask., comes a
copy of the "Pioneer Cook Book," the contents of which had
been prepared locally by women. The job runs into 64 pages.
The cover design bears out well the title "Pioneer," the centre
being a line sketch of the pioneer plowing with a yoke of oxen.
The type used on the cover is the Cloister series, and the general
composition and balance is pleasing. The plain black on the
buff stock makes the arrangement stand up well. The advertising pages, which are numerous, are set in a plain, legible
style, and care has been taken not to introduce too great a
variety of type face. For the size of the office, the *Clarion* can
feel satisfied with the work.

Chicago daily newspaper compositors were awarded $55 day,
$60 night—$1.15 an hour day, $1.25 night—by Judge Crowe,
arbiter. For those working five and one-half hours, after midnight, on a shift the time is reduced from eight full hours to
seven, including lunch time. Bonus operators are to set
4,000 ems an hour to be adjudged competent, and to get 96
cents day, $1.08
night. When they
set 4,500 an hour;
$1.06 and $1.18. All
above to be one cent
each hundred ems.
They may be limited
to a seven-hour day.

Newspaper pub-
lishers and the
Typographical
Union of Troy, N.Y.,
have reached an
agreement provid-
ing for increasing the
wages of printers.
The day workers will
receive $37 a week
and those who work
at night will be paid
$40. The rates apply
to compositors in
newspaper offices
and in book and job
printing establish-
ments. This is an
increase of $7 a
week, and a total
raise of $13 a week
in the last year.

A deputation of
Toronto printers
representing Cars-
well Co., Ltd., and
Noble Scott Ltd.,
have asked for a re-
vision of the three
years' contract ob-
tained by them one
year ago to handle
certain city printing.
They contended that
wages had advanced
46¼ per cent., and
materials 62½ per
cent. since the con-
tract was made and
they were therefore
losing money. The
matter was referred
to the city clerk for
a report.

When you cut a
price on a job it
may be that you are
putting your hand in
your own pocket.

FIGURES D and E.—Here are two widely separated styles of treatment for store advertising. This class of work is interesting to the job printer as well as to the ad. compositor.

Both these stores have secured the same stock cut for their ad., and the "Spring Exposition" line is apparently separate. In Figure E added depth has been given by lengthening the ad. at the top, and in so doing some of the good effect has been lost, by having white space out of proportion, and serving no good purpose. There is also in this ad. a questionable relationship

An upper and lower line of either Caslon, Cheltenham or Bodoni would have jibed with the line at the top.

When using a plate such as shown here great care should be taken in the treatment of the type around it. The design itself is so full of panels and circles and ornamentation in general that there is little left that the printer can do without running into trouble and clashing with these figures. Of course in considering the two ads., it must be borne in mind that they are published with two different ideas. Figure E is an ad. of a store that has the price message to get across to its readers, and it wants more of that peculiar thing called "punch" put into its message.

If the compositor has erred in this piece of work, it has been in using too many panels, or who knows but what this was all laid out for him in the store, and if this be the case, we beg his pardon.

The material in the bottom right-hand panel too is cramped, even in the original, and this effect is accentuated in the reduction in zinc. There is too much panelling in the design, which gives the broken-up effect. Neither can it be said that the panelling lends a great deal to the strength of the ad.

Figure D is a store in another Western city that selected the same design for their spring announcement. From the viewpoint of the advertiser, the appeal is made in an entirely different way. Right in the introduction it states that "Length of service, not initial expense, is the only basis for judging worth," and that idea is carried out all through the ad. There is not a reduction quoted, nor is there anything except one passing reference to price. It is a general appeal drawing attention to the manner in which the store is equipped to look after the wardrobe of the ladies of that community. The compositor who set the ad. and the person who laid it out

Figure D

in such a way as to give him a chance to work well, succeeded in carrying this idea into print.

When it comes down to practical typography and carrying out the wish of the store in the matter, there is hardly a change that could be suggested in the composition of this ad. It has dignity, the white space has been splendidly employed, and there is a certain refinement about the whole thing that brings to the reader exactly the impression that a store of that type wishes to convey.

Apart from the typography, it must be remembered, as stated before, that each ad. serves its purpose well. Both are well written and attractively worded.

between the outline letter used for the dates and the line at the top. More offices have good to seed on the wrong use of this style of type than anything else ever brought out. Papers that use and make it count toward the attractiveness of their paper, build pages along certain very definite lines, or if they use an outline on their classified pages they regulate the size and extent to which it shall be lost. We can name over offhand a number of offices where this style of type has been taken in for some special purpose, perhaps a special number, and then turned over as an addition to the ad. alley, where there is no relationship or harmony between it and the series already in use.

FIGURE G.—This is a group of three ads. that have been running in several of the newspapers. They represent a high type of design and execution, and the top one gives an exceptionally vivid picture of how one lower case hand-lettered line can stand out and tell its story. The wording "The Joy of Living" is in keeping with the idea of the sketch around the top and side. There is something more appealing in these ads. than all the red and yellow posters the railroads could ever post up. The story of the attractiveness of the country is kept to the front, and just at the end it is mentioned, almost casually, that the railroad service to that point is such. Interest the customer first and give him the details of the thing in conclusion.

There is something in these ads. for the job printer to study. There is grouping splendidly done, and in some of them there is a lot of reading matter without any suggestion of crowding.

EVERY printer, when asked to give a quotation on job printing, should remember that he cannot depend upon maximum efficiency in his shop at all times, but must consider averages. These will tell him:

That hand composition will average nearer to 600 than 800 ems per hour.

That linotypes will average nearer to 3,200 than 4,000 an hour.

That a good monotype averages 3,000 per hour.

That hand-fed job presses are doing well to average 1,020 an hour. Many do less.

That bindery girls generally average 750 folds an hour instead of 1,000 or 1,200.

That inserting runs around 1,000 to 1,200 an hour.

That 500 to 1,000 is a fair average for interleaving.

That the average girl will not do better than 1,000 to 1,500 in gathering.

That a girl and helper will average not over 20 stitches a minute for saddle back or 30 on side stitch.

That folding machines cannot be counted on ordinarily for more than 1,300 sheets an hour.

That a business card is not often set and locked up in less than an hour.

That billheads will average an hour for composition and lock-up.

That it will take an hour to set and lock up the average notehead or letterhead. Many take longer.

That it is always well to make allowances for something going wrong, and then be sure to charge enough.—*Printing Trade News,* Winnipeg.

INDIANAPOLIS.—The Board of Canvassers of International Typographical Union met here to tabulate officially the vote cast in the recent election for international officers. John McParland, New York, heading a "Progressive" ticket, was elected president by approximately 1,200 votes over Marsden G. Scott, who has served six years as president of the Typos, according to an unofficial tabulation announced last week. J. W. Hays, secretary-treasurer, and all other members of the present administration, have been re-elected.

Figure E

THOS. BLACK, *President*   JAMES PHILIP, *Secretary-Treasurer*

MONTREAL TYPOGRAPHICAL UNION

No. 176

TELEPHONE MAIN 7489   *Office of the SECRETARY-TREASURER*

ROOM 35 HERALD BUILDING

273 Craig Street West

MONTREAL

Figure F

THIS is a plain, readable, letterhead, used by the Montreal Typographical Union in its official correspondence. There is considerable matter in the job. One thing noticeable in its favor is the getting away from putting in "Montreal, Que.," or "Montreal, Can." in its date line. The larger cities are doing this and it is commendable. For instance it should not be necessary to write Hamilton, Ont., as Hamilton, Canada, is sufficient.

Not only does faulty makeready too often cause loss of register, but it quite as frequently is the source of slur. We enumerate some of the causes.

Loose, springy and poorly underlaid plates.

Over-makeready under plate or on cylinder; in other words, overpacking the cylinder.

Makeready too high above bearers.

Failure to reduce packing for very thick stock.

Last roller not in contact with vibrator.

Cylinder not hard enough on bearers.

Bands not tight enough to cylinder.

Form locked too tightly with bed clamps, causing spring.

Form locked with imperfect furniture or quoins, causing spring.

Feed tongues too high above tympan. This will sometimes cause sheet to buckle.

Poor justification and makeup.

Badly sprung chases.

Too much paste on overlays, or slovenly attached overlays to gripper edge of packing, or carelessly cut and attached underlays.

Loose or buckled tympan sheet, or spongy, springy packing.

Loose register rack or segment.

Form too large for press, or set too near front edge of bed, thus printing after bed has commenced to stop.

Knowing the cause, one should easily overcome the trouble. Examine your own work first, then the compositor's work, then examine the press.

THE Graphic Art Section of the Canadian Manufacturers' Association, Montreal, has submitted a comprehensive set of "Printing Trade Customs." There are several ideas that can well be copied in other centres. The idea is to make it certain that printing is an industry, and must have hard and fast rules the same as any other calling. The "Trade Customs" provide:

Orders:—Regularly entered orders cannot be cancelled except upon terms that will compensate against loss.

Experimental Work:— Experimental work performed on orders, such as

sketches, drawings, composition, plates, press work and materials will be charged for.

Sketches and Dummies:—Sketches and dummies shall remain the property of the printer, and no use of same shall be made, nor any idea obtained therefrom be used, except upon compensation to be determined by the owner.

Drawings, Engravings and Electrotypes: — Drawings made and manipulated by the printer, and plates made from the printer's original designs or from designs furnished by the customer, remain the exclusive property of the printer, unless otherwise agreed upon in writing.

Alterations:—Proposals are only for work according to the original specifications. If through customer's error or change of mind, work has to be done a second or more times, such extra work will carry an additional charge, at current rates for the work performed.

Standing Type:—All standing type matter held longer than thirty days is subject to a charge therefor.

Proofs:—Proofs, not in excess of two, will be submitted with original copy. Corrections, if any, to be made thereon and to be returned marked "O.K." or "O.K. with correction" and signed with name or initials of person duly authorized to pass on same. If revised proof is desired, request must be made when first proof is returned. No responsibility for errors is assumed if work is printed as per customer's O.K.

Press Proofs:—An extra charge will be made for press proofs. Unless the customer is present when the form is made ready on the press, so that no press time is lost, presses standing awaiting O.K. of customer, will be charged for at current rates for the time so consumed.

Postal Cards and Stamped Envelopes:—Being a cash expenditure, customers are expected to furnish these with their order. If they are not furnished, an extra charge of ten per cent. for additional services for securing will be made on the amount required to purchase them.

Handling Stock:—A charge of fifteen per cent. of the value of all paper stock furnished by customer will be made for handling and care of same.

Quantities Delivered:—Owing to manufacturing fluctuations, a variation of ten per cent. either in excess of deficiency shall constitute an acceptable delivery, the variation to be charged for or deducted at the pro rata rate for excess copies.

Customer's Property:— All plates, cuts, paper and other property are held at customer's risk, and printer assumes no responsibility for loss or damage by fire, water or from any other cause.

Agreements:—All agreements are made and all orders accepted contingent upon strikes, fires, accidents unusual market conditions, or causes beyond our control.

> THE more I see of rich men and the closer my insight into the workings of their minds and hearts, the more strongly convinced do I become that great wealth is no passport to happiness nor proof of true success.—*B. C. Forbes.*

The Purchasing Agent's Creed

INCE I believe that the position of the purchasing agent is honorable, worthy, responsible, and calls forth the highest ethical principles in relationship and dealings with men, I pledge myself to emulate in all of my daily duties the lofty, yet practical, ideals set forth in the following creed:

BELIEVE absolutely in honesty and sincerity—in thought, action and deed.

BELIEVE it my duty to elevate the standards of my profession—by study and service.

BELIEVE in the ideals embodied in the Golden Rule—"All things whatsoever that men should do unto you, do you even so unto them." Therefore, I believe in courtesy and good will toward all.

BELIEVE in the "square deal," toward the company I represent, with myself, and toward the men with whom I do business.

BELIEVE it a duty to refuse and renounce gifts or perquisites from those with whom I transact business.

BELIEVE in enthusiasm, progressive methods, and success; in the exchange of ideas and association among fellow purchasing agents and in fulfilling all my obligations like a man.

Ethics Committee, National Association of Purchasing Agents

Figure G

Midland Association Adopts the $2 Rate

Officers Elected at Oshawa Meeting

The semi-annual meeting of the Midland Counties Press Association was held at Oshawa on May 21, with an unusually large attendance. Nearly all of the publishers of newspapers in the several counties were present. Among the things discussed at the meeting were various measures that would meet the ever-rising cost of publishing a newspaper or running a job printing plant.

The meeting agreed to increase the subscription rate of weekly papers from $1.50 to $2 on account of the soaring cost of newsprint paper; the change takes effect in July.

A new schedule of prices for job work was also adopted by the majority of the producers of printing present.

D. D. C. DAWE

of the Peterboro' Examiner, Elected President Midland Co. Press Association.

Mr. C. M. Mundy, of the Ontario Reformer, Oshawa, president of the Association, occupied the chair.

The members of the Association were entertained at luncheon at Welch's banquet room by Mayor Stacey on behalf of the Town Council. Short speeches were given after luncheon by the Mayor, Dr. McKay, M.O.H., and the president of the Board of Trade, A. M. McLaughlin.

After luncheon the members of the Association were taken on a tour through the automobile plants of the town, visiting the Chevrolet, McLaughlin and Oldsmobile plants.

Officers Elected

At the afternoon session the following officers were elected for the next term: Hon. president, C. M. Mundy, Ontario Reformer, Oshawa; president, D. D. C. Dawe, Peterborough Examiner;

vice-president, J. C. Deyell, Lindsay Warder; secretary, Geo. W. James, Bowmanville Statesman; treasurer, W. H. Keller, Uxbridge Journal.

Among those present at to-day's meeting were: J. O. Herity, Belleville; George and Norman James, Bowmanville; G. M. Goodfellow, Whitby; S. Farmer, Port Perry; J. P. Cave, Uxbridge; T. P. Lancaster, Havelock; J. H. Keiffer and his son, Norwood; H. M. Ryan and F. Brisco, Port Hope; Leslie Wilson, Cobourg; H. H. Keyes, Colborne; Chas. P. Doughty, Hastings; J. A. Deyell, Lindsay; D. D. C. Dawe, Peterborough; G. P. Wilson and Roy Wilson, Lindsay; G. A. Knight, Campbellford; W. H. Keeler, Uxbridge; E. Roy Sayles, manager of Canadian Weekly Newspaper Association, Toronto; J. L. Pepper, Toronto; O. M. Alger, B. C. Colpus, C. M. Mundy, and A. R. Alloway, Oshawa.

Secured an Important Ruling

The Canadian National Newspapers and Periodicals Association is sending the following notice to its members:—

One of the resolutions of which the Finance Minister gave notice in the House of Commons on May 18 provided as follows:

"7. (a) That a tax of one per cent. in addition to the present duties of excise and customs be imposed, levied and collected on sales by manufacturers, wholesalers or on importations."

A Toronto daily paper stated on May 25 that a decision had been given at Ottawa that newspapers were considered manufactured articles and that there would be a sales tax on advertising space. An effort was at once made to obtain definite information for the Association's members, but it took considerable time to get it and in the meantime some Inland Revenue officials stated that the tax was in force.

Information having been obtained early this week that there was grave danger of the tax being imposed, the chairman of the Association's Postal and Legislation Committee, H. T. Hunter, went to Ottawa, and after encountering considerable difficulty, succeeded in obtaining a ruling that advertising in newspapers and periodicals is not subject to the tax.

In the meantime the Association's members are simply notified of the decision and that they should not add one per cent. to their advertising invoices. Details of the difficulties Mr. Hunter encountered will be communicated later, when it will be seen that through him the Association has been able to perform most important work for its members in this connection.

Members of Midland Co. Press Association photographed at last session in Oshawa.

The Cost System Shops are Money Makers

Result of U.T.A. Survey in Toronto

THE survey of the printing industry, conducted in Toronto under the auspices of the United Typothetae, shows that the firms made a profit—average—of 11 2-10 per cent. above their costs.

Shops operating the cost system were found to be on a much more secure basis than those running without a knowledge of costs. Thirty-three cost system shops showed profits of 15 2-10 per cent. above costs.

One hundred and seventy-six plants operating without cost systems showed a profit of 3 7-10 per cent. profit above their costs.

Mr. Knowlton, of the U.T.A., in presenting his report to the meeting of the Master Printers at the Prince George, stated that he had received the utmost courtesy during his work in Toronto, and that he was well pleased with the results, showing, as they did, that Toronto profits are well above those shown in other places where the preliminary survey has been made. The average in Toronto of 11.2 per cent. can be compared with the profits in other cities as found on their first survey:

Dayton	12	%
Memphis	8.2	%
Holyoke	15.	%
Worcester	9.2	%
Portland	6.7	%
Vancouver	10.2-10	%
New York City	2.6-10	%
Baltimore	5.7-10	%
Cleveland	2.8-10	%
Detroit	1.7	%

The Three-Year Term

Mr. D. V. Gerking, from the head office of the U.T.A., explained that lack of the proper knowledge of costs had always been found to be one of the reasons for losing money in the printing business. Lack of selling knowledge is another, when one man simply guesses high and another not quite so high. Creative salesmanship is necessary to a greater degree than ever before. The real salesman is not out scrapping for the existing business, but has ideas to sell, and there is no competition in ideas. The U.T.A. as a body is not organized for making money. All the money it takes in is given out in service to the members affiliated with it. We want to have in Toronto, stated Mr. Gerking, a definite organization with a definite programme. The organization of the U.T.A. aims to take in every place with five or more printing offices. Each organization has its own officers and standing committees to meet the needs of the locality. There are now 109 standard organizations, taking in 150 cities. It has been the experience of purely local organizations, not connected with any outside body, that they run off in one direction, and fail to get the well-rounded service that the U.T.A. can render. Under the three-year plan the locals have the opportunity of calling on the International at any time for assistance or counsel.

The introduction of the Standard Cost Finding System is the first step in the educational work, and this system has been endorsed by the Federal Trade Commission of United States as being correct and workable. It is, in reality, a statement of principles. All the members do not use the U.T.A. blanks, but these are recommended.

The experience of several cities was cited to bring out the fact that invariably those using the cost finding systems were making money, while those running without were making little or none. The Standard Cost Finding System is recognized in United States outside of the trade. When Camp Lee was established the Federal Trade Commission was asked where the printing would be sent, and without any hesitation the reply came that the work should go to a shop that was operating under the Standard Cost Finding System. It was also shown that volume of trade did not necessarily mean profit. In some cases a material production will mean an increase in profit. When all the Toronto plants get using this system it will be an easy matter to work out a local basis, and from this could be sent out local suggestive selling prices. Then there is the Standard Selling Price List. The Research Bureau gath information from a wide territory, and get thousands of returns, from which the average is taken. Revisions to th list are sent out every two weeks in order to keep it up to dat The book itself is invaluable as a selling guide. The estimatin and salesmanship courses are important factors in the chair as well as the training for cost clerks, business administration etc. Lessons written by the local students are sent to head quarters for examination, and certificates issued by those wh pass. The Advertising Bureau helps the printer take care his own business and the business of his customer. With i assistance he can map out an entire selling campaign, the sam as an agency would do. The Service and Research Bureau also at the disposal of the members for information on practic shop lines. Hard problems are worked out under actual sho conditions, as there is no guesswork about it. The checkin of estimates is also a very valuable service, and controversi which sometimes has reached the courts have been settled b this department. The Industrial Relations Bureau, M Gerking claimed, had done more to settle trouble than an other body. Unless asked to do so it never interferes, and will render the same service to the open or closed shops. puts the employer in possession of a great deal of informatio in the time when he is considering a new scale.

In conclusion it was stated that about $49,000 would be th amount needed to carry on the work in Toronto, and a favo able expression of opinion was given to going ahead with a ten tative understanding that those signing the agreements at th meeting were not binding themselves to affiliate with the U.T. until such a step had been considered and approved of by th Master Printers' Association of Toronto.

Employees of Toronto Shops — 200

Hand compositors	71
Machine compositors	16
Pressroom employees	86
Binderies	97
Miscellaneous	4
Total shop employees	2,76
Office employees	5:
Total employees	3,2:

Investment and Equipment

Total investment	$4,358,8
Typesetting machines	1
Platen presses, hand fed	4
Platen presses, mechanical fed	
Cylinder presses, hand fed	2
Cylinder presses, mech. fed	

Relation of Overhead to Mechanical Payroll

Mechanical payroll	$3,125,3
Overhead charges	3,110,8
Relation of overhead to mechanical payroll, 99.5 per ce	

Report on Shops with Sales of $10,000 and less—76 Firm

Mechanical payroll	$142,0
Department and overhead	173,3
Material and outside purchases	89,0
Total cost	$405,0
Total seeling price	377,0
Total loss	27,0
Loss, per centage	6.8-10
Relation of overhead to mechanical payroll	121.0

If these shops had been selling at a profit of 25 per cent. th would have made $129,201. In one case there was a profit of

Firms Doing a Business of From $10,000 to $20,000—30 Shops

Mechanical payroll	$161,071
Dept. and overhead	132,452
Material and outside purchases	120,132
Total cost	$413,655
Selling price	413,538
Loss	$117

Relation of overhead to mechanical payroll 82 per cent. Not all these shops show a loss. Seven show 25 per cent. or over profit. Seven show from 10 to 25 per cent. profit, while 13 show a loss.

Firms With Business from $20,000 to $40,000—27 Shops

Total mechanical payroll	$239,517
Dept. and overhead	232,251
Material and outside purchases	237,994
Total cost	$709,760
Selling price	724,331
Profit	$14,571
	or 2 5-10%

Relation of overhead to payroll—97 per cent. Four of these shops made 20 per cent.; eight between 10 and 25; 9 made under 10; one broke even and 5 lost. With 25 per cent. added to actual costs they should have showed added profits of $162,869.

Firms Doing a Business $40,000 to $100,000—21 Shops

Mechanical payroll	$400,273
Dept. and overhead expense	360,607
Material and outside purchases	379,873
Total cost	$1,140,753
Selling price	1,205,406
Profit	$ 64,653
	or 5 6-10%

Relation of overhead to payroll—90 per cent. Three of these firms made 25 per cent.; three from 10 to 25; ten less than 10 per cent, and five show a loss. These firms really lost, under the 25 per cent. over cost margin, $220,535.

Firms Doing a Business of from $100,000 to $200,000—12 Shops

Mechanical payroll	$529,723
Dept. and overhead	415,539
Material and outside purchases	505,946
Total cost	$1,451,208
Selling price	1,625,352
Profit	$174,144
	or 12%

Relation of overhead to payroll, 80 per cent. One firm made 25 per cent.; eight from 10 to 25; one less than 10; two lost money. They lost profits, based on 25 per cent. above costs, of $188,658.

Firms Doing a Business of $200,000 and over—11 Shops

Mechanical payroll	$1,332,428
Dept. and overhead	1,518,008
Material and outside purchases	1,983,720
Total cost	$4,834,156
Total selling price	5,612,455
Profit	$ 778,299
	or 16 1-10%

Relation of overhead to payroll, 114 per cent.

Three of these shops made 25 per cent.; four made from 10 to 25 per cent.; four less than 10. These shops lost, by not having 25 per cent. over costs, $430,240.

Trade Binders—8 Shops

Mechanical payroll	$130,974
Dept. and overhead	112,345
Material and outside purchases	109,240
Total cost	$361,559
Selling price	415,373
Profits	$ 53,814
	or 14 8-10%

Three of these places made 25 per cent.; two made 10 to 25 per cent. and 3 less than 10 per cent. Adding 25 per cent. to their costs would give them added profits of $36,575.

Trade Composition—9 Firms

Mechanical payroll	$55,935
Dept. and overhead expenses	50,327
Material and outside purchases	2,486
Total cost	$108,748
Total selling price	120,972
Total profit	$ 12,224
	or 11.4%

Relation of overhead to payroll, 90 per cent. Two of these places made 25 per cent.; two from 10 to 25; three less than 10; one showed a loss and one a profit of $6. They should have had, under 25 per cent. added to costs, an increased revenue of $14,963.

Specialty Firms

Mechanical payroll	$123,813
Dept. and overhead	115,508
Material and outside purchases	199,672
Total cost	$438,993
Total sales	480,717
Total profit	$ 41,724
	or 9.5%

Three of these places made 25 per cent.; three less than 25. Their added gain under the 25 per cent. margin would have been $68,024.

Relation of overhead to mechanical payroll, 93%.

Record of 167 Firms Operating Without Cost Finding System

Mechanical payroll	$1,164,752
Dept. and overhead expense	1,135,094
Material and outside purchases	1,080,325
Total cost	$3,380,170
Selling price	3,506,066
Profits	125,996
	or 3 7-10%

Relationship of overhead to payroll, 93 per cent. These shops lost a profit of $719,146 by not finding costs and adding 25 per cent.

Record of 33 Shops Using the Cost Finding System

Mechanical payroll	$1,960,612
Dept. and overhead payroll	1,975,224
Material and outside purchases	2,548,348
Total cost	$6,484,184
Selling price	7,469,779
Profit	985,595
	or 15.2%

Relationship of overhead to mechanical payroll, 108 per cent. These firms, by not adding 25 per cent. to their costs, passed up profits of $635,451.

Summary of the Shops Survey

Mechanical payroll	$3,125,364
Dept. and overhead charges	3,110,318
Material and outside purchases	3,628,672
Total cost	$9,864,354
Sold for	10,975,845
Profit	1,111,491
	or 11.2%

Average relationship of overhead to mechanical payroll, 99 5-10 per cent.

Total lost profits by not adding 25 per cent. to actual costs, $1,354,597.

Salaries Allowed to Proprietors.

Business	Salary
$10,000 and less	$1,413
10,000 to $20,000	1,964
20,000 to 40,000	2,112
40,000 to 100,000	3,240
100,000 to 200,000	4,909
Over $200,000	9,365

35 firms made 25 per cent. or more.

Brantford Typos Send Protest

The action of newsprint manufacturers in filling orders for export, and refusing contracts for Canadian publishers, has resulted in a strong resolution being framed by the Brantford Typographical Union for transmission to Premier Borden; Hon. Gideon Robertson, Minister of Labor; Sir Henry Drayton, Minister of Finance, and Mr. W. F. Cockshutt, M.P. for Brantford.

The resolution as forwarded by the local typos:—"Whereas we view with alarm the ever-increasing number of Canadian newspapers that are being forced to suspend publication owing to the unsatisfactory supply of newsprint and, whereas we believe a continuance of such suspension can only result in the acquisition of much influence and power by the individuals controlling the surviving newspapers, as well as throwing out of employment many operatives now engaged in the printing business, and whereas neither we believe to be in the best interests of the country in general and the printing industry in particular. Therefore, be it resolved that this meeting of Brantford Typographical Union, No. 378, go on record as urging such immediate action by the Dominion Government as will ensure an adequate supply of newsprint at a fair price for Canadian publications, to the end that the printing industry be not further embarrassed and that our situations be not placed in jeopardy."

Minimum Prices in Michigan

Advertising and circulation rates and the newsprint situation were the chief worries that the members of the Michigan Newspaper Publishers' Association brought with them to their annual convention. A committee was appointed to bring about as soon as possible a uniform circulation rate of 3 cents a copy, 15 cents per week delivered, and $6 per year.

Advertising rates should be increased, the meeting decided, to meet rising costs of newsprint and labor, and the following resolution was passed:

"Resolved, That this association consider the following minimum rates as the lowest at which national advertising should be sold in any quantity:

	Agate Line.
Papers of 1,000 to 2,000	1½c
2,500 to 4,500	2c
5,000 to 7,000	3c
8,000 to 10,000	3½c
11,000 to 14,000	4c
15,000 to 19,000	5c
20,000 to 24,000	6c
25,000 to 29,000	7c
30,000 to 35,000	8c

and that papers with rates of 2 cents a line and less should add composition charges of one-half cent per line."

Toronto Man is President

Canadian delegates have returned from the twenty-second annual meeting of the International Circulation Managers' Association held in St. Louis on June 1st, 2nd and 3rd. The consensus of opinion was that prices must be raised and that the practice of selling newspapers below the actual cost of the white paper must be discontinued.

Mr. William L. Argue, circulation manager of the Toronto Star, was elected president of the association. Mr. Argue, on the 26th of the present month, will complete 26 years of service with the Star. Mr. J. J. Lynch of the Cleveland Press was elected secretary-treasurer.

The Border Cities Era is running a circulation contest, with a car as the attraction.

The Oshawa *Reformer* has adopted the carrier boy system for delivering their semi-weekly edition. The results are very satisfactory. "The best feature is that we can give the merchants quick service. If they want to have a sale on Saturday morning we can run their ad. on Friday and have it in the homes of the whole town by supper time. In this way we can give them just as good service as any department store can get from a daily paper." That's the official explanation, and the plan, after a good trial, is regarded as a fixture.

THE PERSONAL SIDE OF IT

 We'd Like To Get Items For
These Columns

Quebec

An informal gathering between Montreal and Ottawa newspapermen was held at the Windsor Hotel, Montreal, the entertainment being offered by the Montreal News Writers' Union to the members of the Ottawa News Writers' Association. Among the speakers were A. E. McGinley, of the Ottawa Association; Stafford Green, the vice-president, and Mr. Julien, of *Le Droit*, Ottawa. T. P. Howard, president of the Canadian Manufacturers' Association, spoke at the meeting.

Three Rivers will, about the middle of July, have its own daily paper. *Le Nouvelliste* has been chosen as the name of this daily and it will be owned and controlled by La Compagnie de Publication Le Nouvelliste, Limited, a recently organized company which has purchased the *Le Trifluvien*, a weekly paper published for the last four years by Mr. J. A. Cambray, a Three Rivers lawyer. The new company has among its directors some of Montreal and Quebec's most prominent business men, among others, Mr. J. H. Fortier, managing-director of the firm of P. T. Legare, of Quebec. The manager of the new concern will be Mr. R. Bourque, till a short time ago Canadian representative of the Lanston Monotype Machine Co., of Philadelphia. Mr. Cambray will very likely remain on the editorial staff of the new daily. The offices and plant of *Le Nouvelliste* will be at 27 du Platon Street, Lebrun Building, where the plant of *Le Trifluvien* was in operation previously.

Maritimes

R. S. Cahill has joined the writing staff of the St. John *Evening Times*.

The *Mining News*, Stellarton, has temporarily suspended publication owing to the illness of the proprietor, A. C. Mills.

Robert C. Mills, a Truro newspaperman, has succeeded his father as publisher and editor of the Springhill *Record*.

Geo. W. Perry, manager of the Royal Print & Litho., had a ten-day business trip to Toronto this month.

Robert Nelson, until recently job department foreman of News-Sentinel, Limited, Amherst, N.S., has opened a well-equipped commercial printing office on King street, Amherst.

G. Fred Pearson, proprietor of the Chronicle Publishing Co., was the chairman of the Dalhousie College campaign for a Million Dollars, during the first week in June.

Geo. Vaughan, late foreman of the Royal Print & Litho., who has been confined for some months past to the Kentville Sanitorium, is expected back in the city shortly.

C. B. McDonald, of the *Atlantic Leader*, is on a three-week tour of Newfoundland in the interest of the circulation and advertising end of the *Leader*.

T. C. Allen & Co., booksellers and printers, were visited recently by fire. Outside of some stock being spoiled by water, the damage was not very great.

The Halifax *Herald* and *Evening Mail* are running an "Automobile and Movie Star Contest," as a means of boosting their circulation.

Chas. Lunn, of Truro, with characteristic vigor, has assumed the management of the *Headlight*, a Labor paper published at Truro.

R. M. Ross, whose newspaper training was obtained under his father, the late "Dave" Ross of the Amherst *Daily News*, and who has been doing general reporting on that paper, has become night news editor of the Sydney *Post*.

Cyril J. Fraser, who has been editor of the *Shipyards Times*, a house organ of Halifax Shipyards Limited, since the publication was established last October, has resigned his position to re-enter the insurance business, in which he was regularly engaged before he went overseas in 1916.

E. Geoffrey Stairs, a well-known Halifax newspaperman, who has been connected with Toronto and Ottawa papers, has become editor of the *Shipyards Times*, and publicity manager of

Halifax Shipyards Limited, of which concern the *Times* is a monthly house organ, issued in magazine form.

William Wilkie, president-elect of the National Editorial Association, one hundred members of which were visiting Nova Scotia, received word when in Halifax that his mother had been killed and his home at Grey Eagle, Minn., destroyed in a cyclone.

Dartmouth now has another newspaper, the *Independent*. Published weekly. Eight pages. The sheet is at present being printed in Halifax, but it is hoped, by the management that a plant will be installed in Dartmouth.

Eugene Cote, mechanical superintendent of the *Evening Mail*, was on an extended trip this month in the interest of the craft. Mr. Cote visited Montreal, Toronto, Ottawa, the Border Cities and Buffalo. It is felt that some further improvements will be noticed shortly in the mechanical department of the *Mail* office.

Harry Ervin, city editor of the St. John *Standard*, was recently honored by members of the St. John fire, police and salvage corps, who made a suitable presentation to him at a smoker held in honor of the anniversary of his connection with this body. He is very popular among its members and they took this occasion to express their appreciation of his services and worth.

Doctor J. D. Logan, better known as "Doc." Logan, has resigned his position on the *Evening Echo*, and gone into the insurance business with Thompson Adams Co. "Doc" will be remembered by many for his activities while serving with the 85th Nova Scotia Highlanders. "The *Thistle*, the newspaper of the battalion, while stationed at Halifax, was published by "Doc."

The Amherst *Daily News*, of which Geo. E. Herman has been editor since last fall, has been enlarged from a six-column to a seven-column sheet in order to meet the demand for more advertising space. The *Daily News*, which is the only daily published in its field, and of which the *News-Sentinel* is a semi-weekly edition, has lately added to its local popularity by championing the protests of Cumberland county mineral landowners against the proposal to dispossess them of their mineral rights.

The *Citizen*, Halifax Labor paper, celebrated its first anniversary in May. This paper, which is published under the control of the Halifax District Trades and Labor Council, has made exceptional progress since entering the news-paper field. The pessimists gave it only three months to live, but it looks healthier now than ever. The appearance of the sheet is very creditable. E. E. Pride is the manager, and Robt. L. Gaul advertising manager. Both men are practical printers.

W. R. McCurdy, well known throughout the Maritimes as a newspaper man, through his long connection with the Halifax *Herald* and *Evening Mail*, successfully underwent a very serious operation at the Halifax Infirmary recently. He had been in ill-health for some time, but it is felt that the result of the operation will be the restoration of his old-time health and vigor. At the time of his sickness, Mr. McCurdy was the editor of the *Atlantic Leader*, the new illustrated weekly published by the *Herald* and *Mail* people.

Ross Print Limited, Argyle Street, Halifax, who removed to their present address in August, 1918, have found it necessary to get more room to enable them to handle their rapidly expanding business, and have just taken possession of two additional floors in the building of which they have heretofore occupied the ground floor. The Ross plant now takes up about 8,000 square feet of floor space, and is considered one of the most modern establishments in the Maritime Provinces. A new Cottrell pony press has recently been installed, and a well-equipped bindery for small work has been opened. Practically all the firm's composition is done on a new and complete Monotype combination outfit. The names of twenty-two employees are now on the payroll. The business was started by John R. Ross, in a very small way in 1913, on Duke Street. Mr. Clancy, formerly with Imperial Publishing Co. Ltd., Halifax, is associated with Mr. Ross in the active management of the business.

The Sackville *Post* celebrated its fiftieth anniversary this month with the issue of a special sixteen-page feature number. It was nicely illustrated and contained reminiscences of the Sackville of fifty years ago, as well as interesting accounts of current matters in the town. W. C. Milner, now of the Archives Department, Ottawa, was the first editor of the *Post*, which came into being on May 12, 1870. E. Woodworth of Parrsboro, N. S., succeeded him in 1884, later returning to Parrsboro as editor of the *Leader* of that town. S. D. Scott, now editor of a large daily in Vancouver, B.C., and formerly of the St. John *Sun*, became the next editor and was followed by B. E. Patterson, now of Montreal. In 1895 A. H. McCready took charge of the paper from Robert King and has since been editor and proprietor. The first name of the paper was the *Chignecto Post*. Mr. McCready, who received his early journalistic education with the St. John *Sun*, has been the recipient of hearty congratulations upon his success with the paper and its anniversary.

British Columbia

D. A. Kay of the *Herald*, Cranbrook, represented Kootenay weeklies at the Press Association meeting at Toronto.

On June 1 the *Review*, Revelstoke, advanced its subscription rate from $2 to $2.50 per year.

R. T. Lowrey of the *Ledge*, Greenwood, who got back from his usual winter sojourn in California early in May, has been confined to the Grand Forks hospital suffering with kidney trouble.

Sid Duncan formerly part owner of the *Telegram*, Kamloops, has heard the "back to the land" call and has gone to Northern Alberta to spend the summer on a farm.

Golf is enjoying an unexpected boom at Fernie this year, and among the most enthusiastic players of the royal and ancient game are Jack Wallace of the *Free Press*, and Mrs. Wallace.

Rossland is about the quietest printer's town in the interior at present. Last month one paper house traveller failed to make a single sale in the city—the first time in a long experience.

The Provincial Lands Department is again having a three months' advertising campaign to reduce forest fire losses. It will run to about 150 inches with a minimum of 25 cents an inch, placed direct.

The *Courier*, Cranbrook, is crippled at present due to its new Anderson folder being smashed in a couple of places on the trip West, and cannot be used until new parts arrive. The *Courier* is also installing a new paper cutter.

The Granby Company is dismantling all its mining properties and abandoning Phoenix permanently, thus adding another graveyard town to the list in the province. The *Pioneer* ceased to publish there about three years ago.

After withstanding the blandishments of the syndicates handling comic feature, for these many years, the *Daily News*, Nelson, has at last capitulated and has just started using the "Bringing up Father" features.

The meeting of the B. C. Division of the C.P.A., which was called for the end of May, was cancelled by post card notification about a week ahead of the date originally set for the gathering.

At the East Kootenay Associated Boards of Trade meeting at Invermere on May 28 and 29 there was a distinguished assemblage of newspaper men, including Messrs. Sullivan and Williams of the *Courier* and *Herald* respectively, Cranbrook; F. J. Weston, *Daily News*, Nelson; and C. F. Hayes, *Review*, Creston. The toast to the Press at the annual banquet was most ably responded to by the quartette.

Alberta

Calgary *Herald*:—The death of Joseph M. Fullarton, formerly an employee of Calgary newspapers, occurred in the General Hospital, Edmonton, on Friday evening. Mr. Fullarton was known throughout the newspaper offices of the continent. He started as a printer at the age of 16 at Kalamazoo, Mich. Heart failure was the cause of death. Fred W. Grant of Victoria, B.C., writes of him to the Barrie *Advance*:—The deceased was indeed an old Barrie boy. He learned his trade at the *Advance* when it was published by William and Samuel Wesley. Like most other Barrie printers, Joe was a great traveller. I worked with him three years ago in the Calgary *Albertan*, and thirty years ago in the New York *Herald*, and like myself he has worked from the Atlantic to the Pacific on both sides of the boundary line."

Saskatchewan

Geo. M. Wilson, of Admiral, Sask., and Jno. V. Comstock, have opened a job shop in Moose Jaw known as the Quality Press.

It was unanimously decided at the closing session of the Saskatchewan division of the Canadian Press Association that Saskatoon would be the location of next year's convention, that if possible the association would take advantage of the offer of the University authorities and hold their proceedings in the University and that the date of the meeting would be practically the same as this year. With the election of officers a new office was created. It was felt by the members that the retiring president should be included on the executive and a motion to that effect created the office and made C. McIntosh, who has held the office of president for the past two years, a member of the executive. The result of the election was: Hon. president, Hon. S. J. Latta; president, W. F. Kerr, Regina; vice-president, T. M. Marshall, Weyburn; secretary-treasurer, R. G. Ashwin, Milestone; executive: S. N. Wynn, Yorkton; W. W. Smith, Battleford; C. Hynds, Lumsden; T. Scriver, Wolseley; W. E. Sharpe, Shaunavon. Representatives to the Dominion Association will be S. N. Wynn and T. M. Marshall. Advertising committee: W. A. MacLeod, Regina; J. McDonald, Unity; F. W. G. Sargant, Kamsack; C. McIntosh, Battleford, and Lee Bronson, Craik.

The following sketch of the life of Mr. Frank R. Munro, whose death took place at Vancouver May 18, is from the Publishers' News Service, Regina, of which the deceased was the manager. He was a son of Mrs. D. M. Munro of Clinton: "It is our melancholy duty this week to announce the death of Frank R. Munro, who since its inception has been manager of the Publishers' News Service, Limited. His early years were spent in the vicinity of Goderich, Ontario, and as a lad he was keenly interested in the political storms which, in the days of M. C. Cameron and D. McGillicuddy, seemed to centre around that town. He was naturally of a studious disposition and distinguished himself at Queen's University, of which he was a graduate. It was the habit of Col. Maclean, who controls *MacLean's Magazine* and other publications, to pick the members of his staff from the brightest students graduating from Queen's University. His choice fell upon Mr. Munro, and he was for a number of years associated with the MacLean publications and eventually came to Winnipeg as Western manager. During the ten years which he spent in the Manitoba capital he took a keen interest in public affairs, and contributed a number of excellent articles to various periodicals. He was for a short time engaged in real estate in Winnipeg, but eventually came back to the newspaper field. Two years ago he joined the staff of the Regina *Leader*; but some time ago resigned that position to take the management of Publishers' News Service, Ltd., of which he made a conspicuous success."

Manitoba

Officers of the Winnipeg local of the I. T. U. were elected as follows: President, Charles Ryan; vice-president, Robert Weir; secretary-treasurer, H. J. W. Powers. Members of the executive committee elected include: Job printers, F. W. Hastings, M. McKerracher and M. R. Lilly; news printers, G. W. Howard, and E. G. Smith. Messrs. Powers, Howard, McKerracher, Weir and W. McCormick were appointed delegates to the Trades and Labor Council, and Mr. Powers delegate to the Dominion Trades Congress.

Ontario

Ex-Mayor William Elliott, publisher of the Mitchell *Recorder*, dropped dead at a Masonic lodge meeting in his own town.

Mr. H. C. Lowrey, for several years a member of the *Globe's* advertising staff, is entering commercial business.

E. V. Corbett, formerly advertising manager of the Toronto *Times*, and more recently Toronto city salesman on the advertising staff of *Everywoman's World*, has joined the young Canada Publishing Company, publishers of *Rural Canada*.

The death occurred at Ottawa of Mrs. Bessie Smith, wife of E. Norman Smith, vice-president and managing editor of the *Journal-Press*, Ottawa, and president of the Canadian Press, Limited.

The Barrie *Advance* has a new editor, Mr. Frank Breckon of Toronto assuming charge recently. Mr. Breckon was editor of the Beeton *World* fifteen years ago and was also connected with the Orillia papers for some years.

Rural Canada announces to its readers that it will appear as weekly beginning with September, 1920. It is planned that th weekly edition will be a news supplement to appear each wee save for the seven-day period to be covered by the regula monthly edition.

Alf. Fraser, formerly of Huntingdon, Quebec, who for the past eighteen months has been satisfying his lust for travel, visiting and working in several of the large American printing plants, is now holding a "sit" with the MacLean Publishing Company.

Mr. G. K. Martin, formerly business manager of the King-ston, Ont., *Daily Standard*, has joined the advertising department of the *Globe*, Toronto. He will be in charge of financial and auto-mobile advertising. Mr. Martin has a long record of success as an advertising man.

J. M. Hunter, formerly of Kingston, Ontario, and for the past year employed by the Toronto *World*, is suffering from lung trouble, and has left for the Printers' Home in Colorado. His many friends and fellow associates hope he will be able to effect a speedy return to health.

Mr. H. J. Elder, formerly manager of the *Globe's* Eastern Office at Montreal, has been promoted to the Home Office. He is succeeded by Mr. J. R. Hamilton of Montreal, a former Toronto newspaper man. The *Globe's* Eastern Office is at 3[3 McGill Building, Montreal.

Mr. E. Roy Sayles has sold his paper, the Port Elgin *Times*, to Mr. S. R. Wesley, of Walkerton. He took possession a week ago. Mr. Sayles intends to devote his entire time to the work of the C.W.N.A., of which he is manager. He purchased the *Times* in January of 1910.

Halton's oldest newspaper, the *Canadian Champion*, is pub-lished at Milton, and with the last edition in May completed sixty years without missing an issue. The present editor and proprietor, Major William Panton, has been connected with this journal since 1882. The *Champion* was established here in 1860 by the late J. A. Campbell.

Parkhill *Gazette*:—The Thedford *Tribune* ceased publication with last week's issue. In his valedictory editorial Capt. Bryant states that owing to ill health and other causes this action has become necessary. The *Tribune* has been a bright, newsy, well-edited sheet and its weekly visit to the homes of subscribers will be missed.

Over forty employees from the composing room of the South-am Press, Toronto, gathered in their cafeteria at a compli-mentary banquet given to Mr. Wm. Harrison, who has been in the employ of the *Globe* for forty years. On behalf of his fellow-workers, Mr. S. K. Coryell presented Mr. Harrison with a beautiful leather easy chair.

William Crichton, aged 65, of 12 Browning Avenue, Toronto, was found dead in his office at the Buntin, Reid Paper Com-pany, 13 Colborne street, about 2.30 on the afternoon of May 15. Death is believed to have been due to heart failure. It is understood that no inquest will be held. The late Mr. Crichton was general manager of the company. He was discovered by the bookkeeper of the concern, dead in his chair.

Beaverton *Express*: — After sixty years of publication the Port Perry *Observer* has ceased to exist. Bro. Parsons was one of the oldest newspaper men in the province. The *Observer* was a staunch Tory paper and about the last straw was the Borden Union Government and the Farmer aggregation in Toronto. It is needless to say Bro. Parsons' name is not found in the list of millionaires.

Just after he had summoned the elevator in the Cosgrave Building, Mr. Herbert E. Sayers, of 84 Galley avenue, Toronto, suddenly collapsed and passed away before medical aid could reach him. He was about 58 years of age, and was very well known in newspaper advertising circles, having been with the Toronto *News* sixteen years before it was discontinued. For a time he was advertising manager on that paper.

His Excellency the Governor-General entertained the mem-bers of the Press Gallery of the House of Commons to lunch at Rideau Hall. Some 25 members of the Gallery were present. His Excellency, in extending a cordial welcome to the guests, emphasized the importance of the responsibilities which lay on newspaper representatives, especially at the present time, when unrest was abroad in the world.

Mr. J. B. Garbutt, editor and proprietor of the Drayton *Advocate*, was taken seriously ill with an attack of sciatica and rheumatism and has been bedfast ever since. It is thought, however, that he has passed the crisis and will soon commence to improve, but it will be some months before he will be able to resume full duties in the office. His medical attendant has ordered that he be kept as quiet as possible for a few weeks, which will restore him all the earlier.

Mitchell was saddened by the sudden passing of Mr. William Elliot, B.A., editor and proprietor of the Mitchell *Recorder*, one night recently at 11 o'clock in the Masonic lodge room. For twenty-five years the deceased was principal of the Mitchell High School, and for the past fourteen years he had published the *Recorder*, during which, he had never been absent one day

through sickness. The whole town is to-day grief stricken as the deceased was a man of sterling character, upright in all his dealings and loved and respected by all.

The death took place at his late residence, Norfolk street, Guelph, of Hugh F. Jones, one of the oldest printers in Ontario and superintendent of the Guelph *Herald* mechanical depart-ment. He had been failing in health for over a year. He started his career as a printer in the Milton *Champion* in 1867 and spent 53 pears at the trade. He was the dean of Western Ontario printers. He was chairman of the financial committee of the Grand Council of the Canadian Order of Chosen Friends, and a member of L. O. L. No. 1331.

Joseph T. Ma,ks, who has been editor of the *Industrial Banner* since it was founded twenty-eight years ago as a weekly paper in London, Ont., has placed his resignation in the hands of James Simpson, secretary- treasurer of the company which publishes the *Banner*. Mr. Marks has been appointed perman-ent secretary of the Labor Educational Association, and prefers to devote his entire time to this and propaganda work for the Independent Labor Party. Until the regular meeting of the directorate of the paper, Mr. Marks' position will be taken by Mr. Simpson.

The death occurred on June 2, of Thomas Jeffrey, one of the oldest printers of the Toronto *Globe* staff. He had been working as usual on Monday night, but on Tuesday complained of feeling ill. The end came quite suddenly. Mr. Jeffrey had been an employee of the *Globe* for about thirty-eight years, and for about twenty-five years was secretary-treasurer of the Globe Employees' Benefit Society. His work in connection with the latter organization had always been most faithfully per-formed. Deceased was 65 years of age, and is survived by wife and two daughters.

By the explosion of a steam table in the stereotyping room of the Toronto *Evening Telegram* office, John Dick, stereotyper, 45 Elmer avenue, was instantly killed and Edward Vitek, 342 Wellesley street, and H. Alderdice, 381 Church street, were in-jured. Dick was working over the table at the time of the explosion and was practically blown to atoms. Dick's face was blown off and he was hurled some distance. Vitek was badly burned about the face, arms, and legs, and he may lose his eye-sight as he received the full force of the explosion. The steam table stereotype equipment was completely wrecked. The explosion was heard several blocks. Dick had been on the staff of the *Telegram* for twenty years, and was popular with all.

At a meeting of the Bay of Quinte Press Association held at Belleville, the publishers passed a resolution recommending that in view of the enormous increase in the price of newsprint, the subscription price of weekly papers be increased to $2 a year, or 5 cents a single copy. Daily publishers present favored a proportionate increase in the price of dailies. The address of the day was delivered by A. R. Alloway, managing editor of the Oshawa *Reformer*, on problems affecting the weekly newspaper offices. The following officers were elected: C. G. Young, *Courier*, Trenton, president; A. P. Watson, *Review*, Madoc, vice-president; J. O. Herity, *Daily Ontario*, Belleville, secretary; executive: A. E. Calnan, *Gazette*, Picton; W. A. Statia, *Advocate*, Trenton; James Currie, *News-Argus*, Stirling.

The death occurred at Ottawa of John Henry Thompson, one of the oldest employees of the Printing Bureau. He had been employed at the Bureau almost since its organization, having been appointed in 1882 by Sir John A. Macdonald, of whom he was a friend and admirer. For many years he had been mechanical superintendent at the Printing Bureau. Ten years ago, when he attained the age of 70, he was urged to retire, but preferred to keep on with his work, and continued until a year ago, when he was superannuated on pension at the age of 79. His compulsory retirement caused him such un-easiness that he rapidly failed, and within a year he died, at the age of 80. He was one of the best known men of his craft in Canada, and had been a loyal employee of the Government, especially during various labor troubles at the Printing Bureau.

The third annual dinner of the Alpha Pi Chapter of the Pi Delta fraternity of the University of Toronto journalists, was held at the Walker House. William G. Colgate, the president, acted as toastmaster. The toasts included: "Canada and the Empire," "The Press and the University," Initiates," and "The Fraternity," and the speakers on these toasts were: Prof. Alfred Baker, former Dean of the Faculty of Arts; Bernard Sandwell, editor of the *Canadian Bookman*; Britton B. Cooke, Hector Charlesworth, Dr. W. T. Jackman of the Political Economy Department of the University; W. A. Craick, editor of *Industrial Canada*; R. Alan Sampson, Collier C. Grant, H. G. Stapells, N. A. McMurray and F. C. Mears of the *Globe*. During the evening the following were made hon-orary members of the chapter: Prof. Baker, Hector Charles-worth, W. A. Craick, Dr. Jackman and F. C. Mears.

At the annual meeting of the shareholders of the Toronto Globe Printing Company, with the president, Mr. W. G. Jaffray, in the chair, reports were presented indicating that the Globe continues to enjoy the confidence of the business community. The extraordinary increase of the cost of newsprint was referred to as a disturbing factor in the publishing business, affecting as it does the very existence of many useful daily and weekly papers throughout the country. The directors were re-elected by unanimous vote. The Board consists of W. G. Jaffray (president), A. F. Rutter, Rev. Robert Jaffray, G. Tower Fergusson, E. T. Malone, K.C., and Martin Love. A feature of the meeting was the presence of Dr. J. A. Macdonald, formerly managing editor of the Globe, to whom the president, on behalf of Dr. Macdonald's Globe friends, made a presentation of a sterling silver tea service.

Kingston Standard:—On and after June 1, Mr. Sherman T. Hill and Mr. Henry K. Hill, sons of Mr. W. R. Givens, will become stockholders and directors of the Standard Publishing Company and will be associated with Mr. Givens in the publication of this newspaper, thus taking from him a part of the ever-increasing duties in connection with the paper. Since his recent illness Mr. Givens has for some time contemplated such a change and it is with a feeling of satisfaction, therefore, that he is able to announce that these two members of his own family, who have been with the paper for some time now, are to be definitely associated with its publication. In this connection it may be said that, since his purchase of the stock of the original members of the Standard Publishing Co. shortly after its incorporation, twelve years ago, Mr. Givens has been the sole and only owner of the Standard. There has been no other money—not one single cent—in it, Governmental, political, corporation or otherwise.

John Donald Douglas, for fifty-two years in the employ of Miller & Richard, died at the residence of his son in Toronto on May 22. "Donald," as he was familiarly called, will not only be missed by his hosts of friends in Toronto, but his absence will also be felt by many outside publishers, who never visited the city without calling on him and talking over the days before the "point system" was introduced and the type-setting machine heard of. Up to within ten days of his death "Donald" was at his post, and although in his seventy-first year he was an expert in the art of handling the smallest varieties of type without the aid of spectacles. The widow, four daughters and three sons all reside in Toronto, the eldest son, Charles, being the city representative of Miller and Richard. Interment took place on May 24 to Prospect Cemetery, the many beautiful floral offerings bearing silent testimony to the esteem in which deceased was held, a magnificent pillow from the firm with which for over a half a century "Donald" had been associated with carrying the inscription For Your Fidelity and Worth.

JOHN DONALD DOUGLAS

When Calgary Was Young

The Calgary Herald, in a souvenir issue for the Hudson Bay Co.'s Pageant Anniversary, published the news of Calgary of 35 years ago. At that time (1885) the Herald had 200 subscribers at $1 a month. Some of the items give an interesting look into the early days of the now prosperous Western centre:

Mr. H. S. Cayley, editor of the Herald, was arrested to-day at noon by Deputy Sheriff Fitzgerald, on a warrant issued by Stipendiary Magistrate Travis, and directing that he should be held until the sentence in Queen vs. Cayley is delivered to-morrow morning. Mr. Fitzgerald hurried him away at a moment's notice, not even allowing him to eat his dinner, saying that he could get that all right at the barracks. Mr. Cayley was perfectly prepared to go to gaol to-morrow morning, but he was a little surprised at the summary method of disposing of him before his sentence was passed.

Later—It is now a little over three weeks since Mr. Cayley was sent to gaol by Mr. Travis for contempt of court. Yesterday, Mr. Travis was directed by the Minister of Justice that Mr. Cayley was to be released and his fines remitted.

Stip. Travis has stopped his subscription to the Herald.

We always wondered at his having subscribed to the "dirty, little, insignificant sheet" so long. There must have been some tall reading in it for him. He will now borrow his neighbor's copy, a's being less expense and more soothing.

Wm. Ramsey, agent for the C.P.R. Lands Department, has sold during the month of August ended, 2,080 acres of the company's land, averaging $3.50 per acre. This is an indication for the future of this district.

At 8 o'clock this morning the execution party on going into Riel's cell found him kneeling near the door leading to the scaffold, praying. At 8.05 sacrament was administered by Father Andre. He walked with firm step and head erect to the scaffold. There, while Fathers Andre and McWilliams prayed, Riel said: "I do ask the forgiveness of all men and forgive my enemies." He then prayed a short time. Exactly at 8.23 the drop fell and in two minutes life was extinct.

The Hants Journal, Windsor, N.S., announce a new rate card. On all new contracts and renewals of 500 inches or less (plate), we are obliged to quote 20 cents gross per inch and or contracts in excess of 500 inches, 18 cents gross per inch.

Canadian Press Elects Directors

At the meeting of Canadian Press Limited, in Toronto, more things were discussed than were given out in the prepared statement afterward. The directors were elected as follows:—
Maritimes Division—G. Fred Pearson, Halifax Chronicle; J. D. Black, Fredericton Gleaner.

Ontario and Quebec Division—H. Gagnon, Quebec City Le Soleil; C. F. Crandall, Montreal Star; John Scott, Montreal Gazette; E. Norman Smith, Ottawa Journal; T. Stewart Lyon, Toronto Globe; Irving E. Robertson, Toronto Telegram; T. H Preston, Brantford Expositor; H. H. Pickett, London Advertiser

Western Division—E. H. Macklin, Manitoba Free Press; R. L. Richardson, Winnipeg Tribune; Burford Hooke, Regina Leader; J. H. Woods, Calgary Herald, and Griffith Hughes Victoria Times.

At a subsequent meeting of the board of directors the following officers were re-elected unanimously:—

President, E. Norman Smith; first vice-president, E. H Macklin, second vice-president, G. Fred Pearson.

C. O. Knowles, general manager since the organization of the new association 1917, resigned to become assistant managing editor of the Toronto Telegram, and J. F. B. Livesay, assistant general manager since 1917, with headquarters in Winnipeg and acting general manager since last November, was appointed general manager in his stead.

Canada Gazette Shows Loss

The report of the Department of Public Printing and Stationery tabled in the Ottawa House showed the Government newspaper advertising bill for the fiscal year of 1918-19 to have been $433,116.62. This was the record figure for Government advertising contracts. Including the amount spent in Victory Bond advertising during the fiscal year ending March 3 1919, the total reaches $622,157.21.

The report showed the loss on publishing the Canada Gazette for the year to have been $7,589.22.

Toronto Civic Printing Problem

A deputation of Toronto printers representing Carswell C Ltd., and Noble Scott Ltd., have asked for a revision of t three years' contract obtained by them one year ago to hand certain city printing. They contended that wages had a vanced 46¾ per cent., and materials 62½ per cent. since t contract was made and they were therefore losing mone The matter was referred to the city clerk for a report.

The June bride, in her train, is bringing along a nice asso ment of advertising. Papers all over the country are mak special use of the "June Bride Gifts," and as a general th some very substantial advertising revenue is secured. advertising salesman, with a good layout, an attract heading, and a good assortment of cuts, can generally fill all the available space in short time.

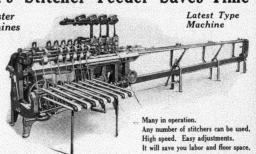

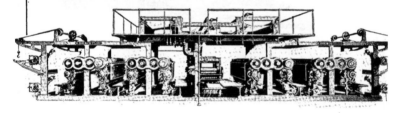

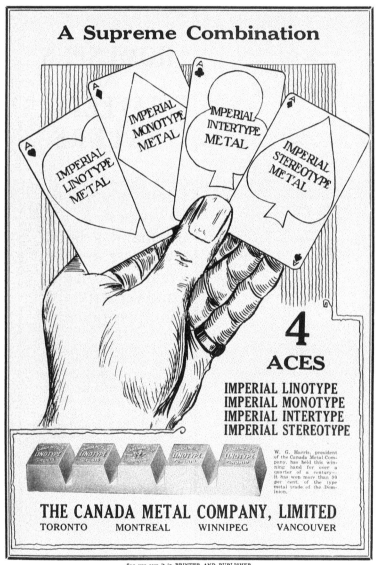

A Supreme Combination

4
ACES

IMPERIAL LINOTYPE
IMPERIAL MONOTYPE
IMPERIAL INTERTYPE
IMPERIAL STEREOTYPE

W. G. Harris, president
of the Canada Metal Com-
pany, has held this win-
ning hand for over a
quarter of a century—
it has won more than 90
per cent. of the type
metal trade of the Dom-
inion.

THE CANADA METAL COMPANY, LIMITED

TORONTO   MONTREAL   WINNIPEG   VANCOUVER

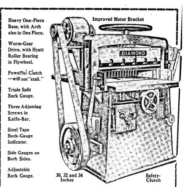

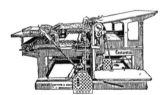

NEWSPAPER SERVICE LTD.

LONDON:
CROSS-ATLANTIC HOUSE
184 FLEET STREET, E.C. 4
Cables: "TERSENESS, LONDON"

NEW YORK:
134 WEST 36th STREET

A news gathering organization which provides special European correspondents and a London office for Canadian newspapers.

MONTREAL:
DOMINION NEWS BUREAU LTD.
171 St. James Street
P.O. Box 756
Cables: "DOMINEWS," Montreal

CROSS-ATLANTIC SERVICE
Provides Your Newspaper With

1. Full facilities of an European organization with special correspondents—your correspondents—all over Europe, available 24 hours daily.
2. Services of a staff of distinguished newspaper men with international reputations.
3. Daily cable service of exclusive special news.
4. Big news feature service by mail.
5. Special local news which you may order any hour of the day or night sent by cable or mail.
6. London office, Cross-Atlantic House, Fleet Street, where your readers can see a file of your paper and be advised or assisted with introductions and information.

The following representative Canadian newspapers are now subscribers to this service:—

Toronto Globe	The Manitoba Free Press
Montreal Herald	Vancouver Daily Province
Calgary Herald	Edmonton Journal
Halifax Chronicle	St. John (N.B.), Standard
Sydney Record	Lindsay Evening Post

Among the regular contributors to this service are:
W. Orten Tewson, former European manager for the Hearst newspapers. Hannen Swaffer, former editor Lord Northcliffe's "Weekly Dispatch." Col. A. N. S. Strode Jackson, the distinguished athlete. Lydia K. Commander, noted woman writer.

Sydney B. Cave,	Paul Brewster,	Grenville Vernon,
Col. A. T. Lynch,	Hugh Dryden,	Mark Zangwill,
Lewis S. Benjamin,	Edgar C. Middleton,	Hugh Curran,
Henry W. Francis,	Isabel Ramsey	and others.

Special contributions by such well-known writers as:

Marie Corelli,	Countess of Warwick,	Sir Hall Caine,
H. G. Wells,	Sir Conan Doyle,	and others.

If you are interested in securing this special service exclusive for your paper, write at once to

CROSS-ATLANTIC NEWSPAPER SERVICE
DOMINION NEWS BUREAU LIMITED
CANADIAN REPRESENTATIVES
171 ST. JAMES STREET

P.O. Box 756   MONTREAL, CANADA

Is There an Alien Menace in Canada?

IN THE years of war, people were quick to grasp the possibilities of danger that lie in Alien sympathies. But people quickly forget, and therein lies the danger for it is in the insidious breaking down of the ties of loyalty, that goes on in the piping times of peace, that makes the menace of the days of war.

In "The Stranger in Our Midst" the simple story of a school teacher's experience in foreign settlements in the West there lies a reproach and a warning, a reproach in that such things can be, and a warning that they may not happen again.

This is only one of the many stories and articles that make the June 15th issue of MacLean's Magazine of outstanding interest.

These are some other points of interest:

FICTION

"The Little Warrior"—Pelham Grenville Wodehouse's inimitable story.

"The Parts Men Play"—Arthur Beverly Baxter.

"The Sunset Homesteader"—Will E. Ingersoll.

"The Beetle and the Butterfly"—C. W. Stephens.

ARTICLES

"What Must Be Done?"—Mrs. Murphy's suggestions of a remedy for the drug menace.

"We Must Reform Dress"—Marian Keith.

"Gentlemen of the Fourth Estate"—The story of men who begin life in newspaper offices.

The Best From Everywhere

In the Review of Reviews department will be found the best articles from all magazines and periodicals the world over. Look at these titles and authors:

"Belgium Has Come Back"—by Frederick Palmer.

"How the English Came to Be"—by Rudyard Kipling.

"Eight Billions Wasted"—by Thomas V. Merle.

"Mankind Needs Change of Heart"—by Sir Philip Gibbs.

"Give Labor a Square Deal"—by Charles M. Schwab.

"The Slow Conquest of America"—by Forrest Crissey.

"Know Your Own Car"—by Alexander C. Johnson.

"Sending Pictures by Telegraph"—by Milton W. Stoddard.

MACLEAN'S
"CANADA'S NATIONAL MAGAZINE"

June 15th Issue Now on Sale at All Newsdealers

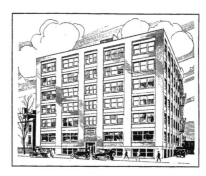

New Address

UNITED PAPER MILLS LIMITED
129 SPADINA AVENUE, TORONTO
Telephones: Adelaide 1343-1344

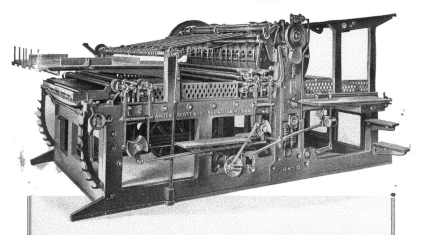

New Scott Cylinder Presses
READY FOR IMMEDIATE DELIVERY

Two No. 4 Presses, bed 26 x 36 inches, matter 22 x 32 inches, two form rollers, Front Fly Delivery.

Two No. 5 Presses, bed 29 x 42 inches, matter 25 x 38 inches, two form rollers, Front Fly Delivery.

One No. 4 Press, bed 27½ x 36 inches, matter 22 x 32 inches, four form rollers, Front Fly Delivery.

One No. 8 Press, bed 41½ x 52 inches, matter 35 x 48 inches, four form rollers, Printed-Side-Up Delivery.

One No. 4 Press, bed 26 x 36 inches, matter 22 x 32 inches, four form rollers, Printed-Side-Up Delivery.

One No. 5 Press, bed 29 x 42 inches, matter 25 x 38 inches, four form rollers, Front Fly Delivery.

One No. 7 Press, bed 38 x 51 inches, matter 33 x 47 inches, two form rollers, Rear Fly Delivery.

The Scott Two-Revolution Presses

that we offer are substantially built machines guaranteed to give an unyielding impression and register to a hair. ¶ Each machine has four tracks, geared roller distribution, two air chambers on each end of machine, type bed driven by our direct drive movement, and satisfies the exacting requirements of the trade. ¶ The space occupied by these presses is required for other machinery.

WALTER SCOTT & COMPANY
Main Office and Factory: PLAINFIELD, N.J., U.S.A.

NEW YORK OFFICE: 1457 Broadway   CHICAGO OFFICE: 1441 Monadnock Block
CABLE ADDRESS: Waltscott, New York   CODES USED: ABC (5th Edition) Bentley and Our Own

EASTERN AVE. PLANT, TORONTO

Every Pig and Ingot of genuine
HOYT typemetal bears our
name. If it's not HOYT
metal it's not the best.

HOYT METAL COMPANY

MONTREAL   TORONTO   WINNIPEG

SUMMER ROLLERS

Order Now

Specify

"Quality Brand"

S.V. & H. Inks and Rollers Form
a Happy Combination—Use Both

SINCLAIR, VALENTINE & HOOPS, LTD.
TORONTO
WINNIPEG   229-233 Richmond St. West   MONTREAL

Ask Your Jobber For

MAPLE LEAF BRISTOL

High Grade Bristol in White and following colors:
Pink, Canary, Green, Salmon, Blue, Cherry, Buff,
Lilac. Made up in index sizes on special orders.

Made in Canada by

THE DON VALLEY PAPER CO., LTD.

TORONTO, CANADA

Announcing Stock Line of Manilla Envelopes

TO BE KNOWN AS

No. 52

A LIGHT WEIGHT
"Quality" Manilla Envelope

Nos. 52, 69, 95

and Carried in Stock in

No. 69

A HEAVY WEIGHT
"Quality" Manilla Envelope

Nos. 7, 8, 9 and 10 O.S.

All the same Grade No. 1

No. 95

A MEDIUM WEIGHT
"Quality" Manilla Envelope

MANILLA

THIS STOCK ALSO CARRIED
IN STOCK FOR SPECIALS.

Don't Forget Our Whitewove
"LEADER"

Envelopes manufactured to *satisfy and please* not only you but *your customer*
will surely and steadily increase the envelope portion of your business.

□ □

TORONTO ENVELOPE COMPANY, LIMITED

"QUALITY AND SERVICE"

119 WEST ADELAIDE STREET, TORONTO, ONT.

Phone: ADELAIDE 3425   Manufacturers to the "Trade Only"

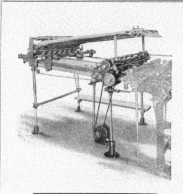

CLASSIFIED ADVERTISEMENT SECTION

FOR SALE

"St. Catharines Evening Journal"

Pursuant to the direction of a meeting of creditors of The Journal, of St. Catharines, Limited, there will be offered for sale by the Assignee, the entire business, goodwill and equipment of this newspaper, including printing presses, linotype machines, job printing outfit, office equipment, etc. For further information and terms, apply to the Assignee. Inspection of the property may be arranged by appointment with the undersigned. Dated at St. Catharines, this third day of June, 1920.

BURSON AND JOHNSTON
Solicitors, etc., Sterling Bank Chambers,
St. Catharines, Ont.

for ALBERT H. TRAPNELL,
Assignee, 25 Queen Street,
St. Catharines, Ont.   (P&P6)

BUSINESS CHANCES

FOR SALE — WELL-ESTABLISHED AND well-equipped printing business at a reasonable price. Reason for selling Mr. Sherwood's death. Apply Sherwood-Fowler Co., 709 First St. East, Calgary, Alta.   (p6p)

FOR SALE — NEWSPAPER AND JOB plant in Alberta, town of 25,000. Big outfit, type, machinery, etc. Good district. Would suit two men in partnership, splendid school, water system, electric light. Apply Box 528, Printer and Publisher.   (p&p6)

FOR SALE — NEWSPAPER AND JOB printing plant at a bargain; a well equipped and established business in a thriving industrial Nova Scotia town will be disposed of at a right price; large advertising and job printing income; only newspaper in a large and prosperous community. Apply at once for particulars to Box 666, Printer and Publisher, Toronto, Ont.   (ptfp)

THE MONOTYPE OPERATOR IS THE man who is in line for advancement. Learn the Monotype and not only make more money, but be ready for future promotion. It only takes a short time in the Monotype school to make an operator of a compositor. There are schools in Philadelphia, New York, Chicago and Toronto, in which the tuition is free. Why not take up the Monotype? Lanston Monotype Machine Company.   (ptfp)

LEARN THE LINOTYPE — WRITE FOR particulars. Canadian Linotype, 68 Temperance St., Toronto.   (ptfp)

COLLECTIONS

SEND US YOUR LIST OF DELINQUENTS. We will turn Debit into Credit. Publishers' Protective Association, Toronto.   (ptfp)

WHEN WRITING ADVERTISERS

PLEASE MENTION THIS

PAPER

TWO CENTS A WORD, Box Number as five words; minimum charge is $1.00 per insertion, for 50 words or less, set in 6 pt. type. Each figure counts as a word. Display ads., or ads. set in border, are at the card rates.

WANTED—ROTARY PRESS

eight or twelve pages, seven column, in good condition. Send full particulars to Rotary Press, Box 54, PRINTER AND PUBLISHER, Toronto.   (p6p)

FOR SALE

COLTS ARMORY PRESS FOR SALE, LATest model, inside chassis, 14 x 22. Complete with ten rollers, one distributor, two chases. Capacity 18,000 per hour. Write or wire manager, Telegraph Printing Co., Que.

FOR SALE—28 linotype molds for melting metal, all with handles in good condition. Write or wire manager, Telegraph Printing Co., Quebec.   (p&p7)

FOR SALE—DEXTER FOLDING MACHINE, No. 189, Job and catalogue, sheet size 28 x 42. In perfect condition, only used a few times. Dominion Loose Leaf Company, Ltd., 174 Wellington Street, Ottawa, Ont.

FOR SALE—OWING TO ILL-HEALTH OF its proprietor the Review, only newspaper in Carleton county, is offered for sale. Well equipped with linotype, cylinder and two platen presses, folder, cutter, stitcher, electric motor, plenty of type, etc. Circulation over one thousand weekly. Good job and ad. patronage. James A. Evoy, Carp, Ont.

FOR SALE—GORDON PRESS, 7 x 11; GOOD condition. The Owen Sound Advertiser, Owen Sound, Ont.   (P-tf P)

FOR SALE — NEWSPAPER COTTRELL press, 30 x 47, good condition. Furby St. Printery, Winnipeg.   (ptfp)

FOR SALE—COMPLETE JOB PRINTING and newspaper establishment, including Cottrell newspaper printing press, paper cutter, folding machine, monoline, two job presses and type cases, stones, etc. For particulars apply C. A. P. Smith, Sault Ste. Marie, Ont.

FOR SALE—WEEKLY NEWSPAPER AND Job Printing Plant in town in Western Ontario. Population 1200. No opposition. Excellent yearly turnover. Good equipment. Bargain for quick sale as proprietor is engaging in other business. Act now. Apply Box 513, Printer and Publisher.   (p6p)

OPPORTUNITIES ARE OFFERED

EVERY MONTH ON

THIS PAGE

Watch Them

FOR SALE

1—13 x 19 Colt. Practically new.

2—7 x 11 Pearl Presses. Rebuilt.

1—No. 3 Scott Drum, 24½" x 31".

1—10 x 15 W. & B.

1—34½" C. & P. Power Cutter.

1—Bronzing Machine, 25" x 38".

1—Eclipse Folder, 35" x 44", with insert.

ROYAL MACHINE WORKS

Presses and Bookbinding Machinery and Special Machinery.

738 ST. PAUL WEST, MONTREAL

FOR SALE

FOR SALE — ONE FONT HIGH-BASE STERCO. furniture, about 250 pieces. 100 California job cases. Font 9 point, 7 point, 6 point, 5½ point. Mats good condition, several very useful jobs fonts. Bargain. Apply Commonwealth Press, 1135 16th Ave., West, Calgary, Alta.   (p&p6)

SECOND-HAND D I A M O N D CYLINDER Press, Power series and fixtures. Price and terms on request. The Eagle, Rosetown, Sask.   (p6p)

CAMCO FEEDER FOR SALE—SIZE TO suit 00 Meihle; in perfect condition, can be seen in operation; used about eight months. The Reed Press Limited, Hamilton, Ontario.   (p&p6)

WEEKLY NEWSPAPER FOR SALE—IN heart of Peace River Country, Northern Alberta; plant, building and lot. Location excellent, building good, plant about half nearly new, annual turnover $4,800. Subscription rates, $2.50; display advertising, 22 cents to 3 0cents per col. inch. Price, $3,200, $2,000 down balance monthly payments. Write Box 6120, Printer and Publisher.   (p&p6)

SITUATIONS VACANT

WANTED—LINOTYPE OPERATOR. STATE experience and full particulars. Telegraph, Welland.   (p&p6)

PRINTER WANTED — AN ALL ROUND man, qualified compositor and pressman, must be serious, sober and pushing, one having outside connection preferred. If desirable can purchase an interest in the business or buy the whole plant, a well-established and up-to-date printing plant, in a city of 15,000 population, near Montreal, Canada. Good business can be done with the right man. References exchanged. Apply at Lachine Printing, 24 Twelfth Ave., Lachine, Que.   (ptfp)

PERSONAL

FRANK KANE, NEWSPAPER CONTEST circulation builder, will soon tour "The Provinces." Publishers in the States regard Mr. Kane as one of the best in his line of work. Those contemplating increase circulation can address him Weldona, Colorado.   (p6p)

Buyers' Guide

ADDRESSING MACHINES
The Challenge Machinery Co., Grand Haven, Mich.

BALERS, WASTE PAPER
Golding Mfg. Co., Franklin, Mass.
Logan, H. J., 114 Adelaide St. West, Toronto.
Stephenson, Blake & Co., 60 Front St. W., Toronto
Stewart, Geo. M., 92 McGill St., Montreal.

BINDERY SUPPLIES
Logan, H. J., Toronto, Ont.
Morrison Co., J. L., Toronto, Ont.

BOOKBINDERS' MACHINERY
Logan, H. J., 114 Adelaide St. W., Toronto.
Miller & Richard, Toronto and Winnipeg.
Morrison, J. L., Co., 445 King St. W., Toronto.
Royal Machine Works, Montreal.
Stewart, Geo. M., 92 McGill St., Montreal, Que.
Stephenson, Blake & Co., 60 Front St. W., Toronto

BOOKBINDERS' WIRE
The Steel Co. of Canada, Hamilton.

CHASES—SECTIONAL STEEL
The Challenge Machinery Co., Grand Haven, Mich.

COLLECTION AGENCIES
Canadian Mercantile Agency, 46 Elgin St., Ottawa.
Publishers' Protective Association, Goodyear Bldg.,
164 Simcoe St., Toronto.

COUNTING MACHINES
Stephenson, Blake & Co., 60 Front St. W., Toronto

CYLINDER PRESSES
The Challenge Machinery Co., Grand Haven, Mich.

CROSS CONTINUOUS FEEDER
Morrison, J. L., Co., 445 King St. W., Toronto.

CUTTING MACHINES—PAPER
Golding Mfg. Co., Franklin, Mass.
Morrison, J. L., Co., 445 King St. W., Toronto.
Stephenson, Blake & Co., 60 Front St. W., Toronto
The Challenge Machinery Co., Grand Haven, Mich.

ELECTROTYPING AND STEREOTYPING
Rapid Electrotype Co. of Canada, 229 Richmond
St. W., Toronto.
Toronto Electrotype & Stereotype Co., 111
Adelaide St. W., Toronto.

ELECTROTYPE AND STEREOTYPE BASES
The Challenge Machinery Co., Grand Haven, Mich.

EMBOSSING PRESSES
Golding Mfg. Co., Franklin, Mass.
Stephenson, Blake & Co., 60 Front St. W., Toronto

ENVELOPE MANUFACTURERS
Toronto Envelope Co., Toronto. ;
W. V. Dawson, Ltd., Montreal and Toronto.

ELECTROTYPE METAL
British Smelting & Refining Co., Ltd., Montreal.
Canada Metal Co., Limited, Toronto.
Hoyt Metal Co., Limited, Toronto.

FEATURES FOR NEWSPAPERS
International Syndicate, Baltimore, Md.

GALLEYS AND GALLEY CABINETS
Stephenson, Blake & Co., Toronto.
The Challenge Machinery Co., Grand Haven, Mich.
The Toronto Type Foundry Co., Ltd., Toronto.

GUMMED PAPER MAKERS
Jones, Samuel, & Co., 7 Bridewell Place, London,
England, and Waverly Park, New Jersey.

HAND PRINTING PRESSES
Golding Mfg. Co., Franklin, Mass.

INKS
Reliance Ink Co., Winnipeg, Man.

JOB PRINTING PRESSES
Golding Mfg. Co., Franklin, Mass.

JOB PRESS GAUGES
Golding Mfg. Co., Franklin, Mass.
Megill, Ed., 60 Duane St., New York City.

LEADS AND SLUGS
Mono-Lino Typesetting Co., Toronto.
Stephenson, Blake & Co., Toronto.
The Challenge Machinery Co., Grand Haven, Mich.
The Toronto Foundry Co., Ltd., Toronto.

LITHOGRAPHERS
Goes Lithographing Co., Chicago, Ill.

MAILING MACHINES
Chauncey Wong's Sons, Greenfield, Mass.
Rev. Robert Dick Estate, 137 W. Tupper St.,
Buffalo, N.Y.

MAILING GALLEYS
The Challenge Machinery Co., Grand Haven, Mich.

Buyers' Guide

TICONDEROGA PULP AND PAPER CO.

Machine Finish, Special Magazine and Antique Finish

BOOK, MAGAZINE, COATING, LITHO-GRAPH AND MUSIC

PAPERS

Mills at Ticonderoga, N.Y.

Sales Department
Rooms 800-816. 522 Fifth Avenue, New York

J. R. WALKER

267 WELLINGTON ST., MONTREAL

Specialising in All Grades of

**Printers' Waste Paper
Books, News and Writing Papers**

In Connection With

J. R. Walker & Company, Limited
35 Common St., Montreal

Manufacturers of Felt Paper, Fibre Board, Etc.

BERRY ROUND HOLE CUTTER

Drills or "cuts" clean holes through any paper or pasteboard stock ten times as fast as a die punch.

One to two inches drilled at an operation. Ask for proof.

Berry Machine Co.
300 N. Third St. St. Louis, Mo.

METAL FURNITURE
Mono-Lino Typesetting Co., Toronto.
The Challenge Machinery Co., Grand Haven, Mich.

METAL FOR TYPESETTING MACHINES
British Smelting & Refining Co., Ltd., Montreal.
Canada Metal Co., Fraser Ave., Toronto.
Great Western Smelting & Refining Co., Vancouver.
Hoyt Metal Co., 356 Eastern Ave., Toronto.

PAPER MANUFACTURERS AND DEALERS
Buntin, Gillies & Co., Ltd., Hamilton, Ont.
Canada Paper Co., 112 Bay St., Toronto.
Dickinson & Co., John, 25 Melinda St., Toronto.
Don Valley Paper Co., Toronto, Ont.
Esleeck Mfg. Co., Turner's Falls, Mass.
Halls Paper Co., Ltd., Fred H., Toronto, Ont.
McFarlane, Son & Hodgson, Montreal, Que.
Niagara Paper Mills, Lockport, N.Y.
Paper Sales, Limited, Bank of Hamilton Building, Toronto.
Provincial Paper Mills Co., Telephone Building, Toronto.
Rolland Paper Co., Montreal, Que.
Ticonderoga Pulp & Paper Co., 200 Fifth Ave., New York.
United Paper Mills, Ltd., Toronto.
Wilson Munroe Co., Limited, Toronto.
Whyte Paper Co., A., 55 Bay St., Toronto.

PATENT BLOCKS
The Challenge Machinery Co., Grand Haven, Mich.

PHOTO ENGRAVERS
Reliance Engraving Co., Toronto, Ont.

PRINTING INK MANUFACTURERS
Ault & Wiborg Co. of Canada, Ltd., Toronto, Ont.
Canada Printing Ink Co., 15 Duncan St., Toronto.
The Columbia Printing Ink & Roller Co., Hamilton St., Vancouver, B.C.
Dominion Printing Ink Co., 128 Pearl Ave., Toronto.
Manton Bros., Toronto, Ont.
Reliance Ink Co., Winnipeg, Man.
Shackell, Edwards & Co., Ltd., 127 Peter Street, Toronto.
Sinclair & Valentine, 233 Richmond St. West, Toronto.

PLATE MOUNTING EQUIPMENT
The Challenge Machinery Co., Grand Haven, Mich.

PRINTERS' FURNITURE
The Hamilton Manufacturing Co., Two Rivers, Wisconsin.
The Challenge Machinery Co., Grand Haven, Mich.

PRINTERS' IRON FURNITURE
The Toronto Type Foundry Co., Ltd., Toronto.
Stephenson, Blake & Co., Toronto.
The Challenge Machinery Co., Grand Haven, Mich.

PRINTING PRESSES
Babcock Printing Press Co., New London, Conn.
Goss Printing Press Co., Chicago, Ill.
Hoe & Co., R., 504-520 Grand St., New York.
Linotype & Machinery, Limited, London, Eng.
Manton Bros., 105 Elizabeth St., Toronto.
Miehle Printing Press & Mfg. Co., Chicago.
Premier & Potter Printing Press Co., Inc., New York City.
Stephenson, Blake & Co., Toronto.
The Challenge Machinery Co., Grand Haven, Mich.
The Mann Litho Press Co., 58 Walker St., New York City.
Walter Scott & Co., Plainfield, N.J.

PRINTERS' PRICE LISTS
Port Publishing Co., Salt Lake, Utah.

PRINTING PRESS MOTORS
Kimble Electric Co., 695N Western Avenue, Chicago, Ill.
Manton Bros., Toronto, Ont.

PRINTERS' MACHINERY AND SUPPLIES
Manton Bros., Toronto, Ont.
Royal Machine Works, Montreal
Stephenson, Blake & Co., Toronto.
The Toronto Type Foundry Co., Ltd., Toronto.

PRINTERS' ROLLERS
Canada Printing Ink Co., Limited, 15 Duncan St., Toronto.
The Columbia Printing Ink & Roller Co., Hamilton St., Vancouver, B.C.
Manton Bros., Toronto, Ont.
Sinclair & Valentine, Toronto, Ont.
Winnipeg Printers' Roller Works, 175 McDermot Ave., Winnipeg.

PROOF PRESSES
Stephenson, Blake & Co., 60 Front St. W., Toronto.
The Challenge Machinery Co., Grand Haven, Mich.

"REDUCOL"
Indiana Chemical Co., Indianapolis, Ind.

REGISTER GAUGES
E. L. Megill, 60 Duane St., New York.

REGISTER HOOKS, BLOCKS AND CATCHES
The Challenge Machinery Co., Grand Haven, Mich.

ROTARY PRESSES
Goss Printing Press Co., 16th Street and Ashland Ave., Chicago.
Hoe & Co., R., 504-520 Grand St., New York.

ROLLER SUPPORTERS
The Challenge Machinery Co., Grand Haven, Mich.

RULED FORMS
Matrix Ruled Form & Tabular Co., Fort Worth, Texas.

STEREO PAPERS
L. S. Dixon & Co., Ltd., 38 Cable St., Liverpool, England.

SECTIONAL BLOCKS
The Challenge Machinery Co., Grand Haven, Mich.

STEREOTYPE METAL
British Smelting & Refining Co., Ltd., Montreal.
Canada Metal Co., Limited, Toronto.
Hoyt Metal Co., Limited, Toronto.

TYMPAN PAPERS
The Cromwell Paper Company, Chicago, U.S.A.

TYPE-HIGH MACHINES
The Challenge Machinery Co., Grand Haven, Mich.

TIN FOIL PAPERS
J. & W. Mitchell, Birmingham, Eng.

TYPE FOUNDERS
Stephenson, Blake & Co., 60 Front St. W., Toronto.
Toronto Type Foundry Co., Ltd., Toronto, Montreal, Winnipeg.

THE NEW ERA PRESS
A Multi-Process Printing, Punching, Perforating, Cutting and other operation machine. Manufactured by The Regina Co, Rahway, N.J., U.S.A.

TYPESETTING
Mono-Lino Typesetting Co., Toronto.

TYPE-SETTING MACHINES
Canadian Linotype, Ltd., 68 Temperance Street, Toronto.
Miller & Richard, Toronto and Winnipeg.
Lanston Monotype Machine Co., Lumsden Bldg., Toronto.
The Linograph. Stephenson, Blake & Co., 66 Front St. W., Toronto.

TYPE-HIGH GAUGES
The Challenge Machinery Co., Grand Haven, Mich.

---

72 PRINTER AND PUBLISHER

JONES
Patent Non-Curling
Gummed Papers
Why Use the Curly Sort?

There is satisfaction and profit in using Jones famous Non-Curling Gummed Papers. They permit of any class of printing without the difficulty usually experienced with gummed papers which curl and stick together.

Over 100 years of experience has taught us how!

MILL No. 2
CAMBERWELL

ESTABLISHED 1810

Send Us Your Enquiries for

Gummed Paper   Flint Glazed Papers
Gummed Tape   Leather Papers
Stay Paper   Marble Paper
Sealing Machines   Fancy Papers

SAMUEL JONES & CO., LIMITED
MILLS:
CAMBERWELL, ENG.
NEWARK, N.J., U.S.A.
BRIDEWELL PLACE
LONDON, E.C. 4, ENGLAND

INDEX TO ADVERTISERS

 The " R-Shield " Watermark
The reputation built up in 40 years of High Grade Paper Making stands behind papers bearing the "R SHIELD" Watermark.
ROLLAND PAPER CO., LIMITED, MONTREAL
guarantees "Rolland Quality"

Say you saw it in PRINTER AND PUBLISHER

Economy in Pressroom Production

HALF TONE BLACK

"4480"

A High Grade Half Tone Black
that works clean and
dries with a finish.

Suitable for Highest Quality Catalogue Printing

MAIL ORDERS.

CANADA PRINTING INK CO.
LIMITED
15 DUNCAN STREET, TORONTO

TYP〈LINOTYPE〉APHY

A System for Correct Composition

Linotype Typography makes one sound system of the much confused accumulation of material that confronts the printer. It eliminates unsparingly that which is incongruous and wrong, but without limiting full variety of choice by the narrow canons of cold art. It simplifies the practice of ambitious composition, and as an actual part and result of that simplification, the Linotype user is provided with material for composition of a richness attainable heretofore only by inordinately costly and laborious hand work. Linotype Typography furnishes equipment that both guides and responds.

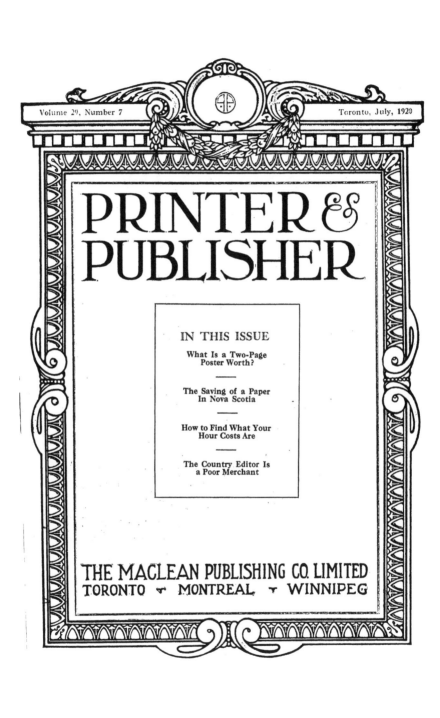

Volume 29, Number 7

Toronto, July, 1920

PRINTER & PUBLISHER

IN THIS ISSUE

THE MACLEAN PUBLISHING CO. LIMITED
TORONTO ▼ MONTREAL ▼ WINNIPEG

PRINTER AND PUBLISHER, July, 1920. Vol. 29, No. 7. Published monthly at 143-153 University Ave., Toronto, by the MacLean Publishing Co., Ltd. Yearly subscription price, $3.00. Entered as second-class matter at the Post Office Department at Ottawa, Canada, also entered as second-class matter July 1, 1912, at the Post Office at Buffalo, N.Y., U.S.A., under Act of March 3rd, 1879.

SINGLE TYPE

The best printing has always been
done from separate new type set up
one at a time—and always will be

The Monotype in the modern
composing room multiplies
the skill of the workers and
makes possible the production
of more good printing than
can be done in any other way.
Guided by the brain and skill
of the operator, *it sets new single
type one at a time*, retaining
all the excellence of the old
method with the addition of
modern productive efficiency.

Incidentally, it provides display
type and all the material required
for all the work that must be done
by hand, and eliminates the waste
of distribution.

LANSTON MONOTYPE MACHINE CO.
PHILADELPHIA
NEW YORK, World Building   BOSTON, Wentworth Building
CHICAGO, Plymouth Building   TORONTO, Lumsden Building
Monotype Company of California, SAN FRANCISCO

294

This Advertisement set in Monotype Series No. 150, Border 24 Point No. 65, and Monotype Rule No. 844

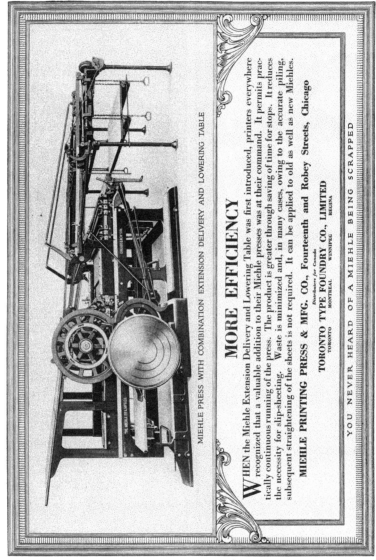

MIEHLE PRESS WITH COMBINATION EXTENSION DELIVERY AND LOWERING TABLE

MORE EFFICIENCY

WHEN the Miehle Extension Delivery and Lowering Table was first introduced, printers everywhere recognized that a valuable addition to their Miehle presses was at their command. It permits practically continuous running of the press. The product is greater through saving of time for stops. It reduces the necessity for slip-sheeting. Waste is minimized and, in many cases, owing to the accurate piling, subsequent straightening of the sheets is not required. It can be applied to old as well as new Miehles.

MIEHLE PRINTING PRESS & MFG. CO., Fourteenth and Robey Streets, Chicago

Distributors for Canada

TORONTO TYPE FOUNDRY CO., LIMITED

TORONTO   MONTREAL   WINNIPEG   REGINA

YOU NEVER HEARD OF A MIEHLE BEING SCRAPPED

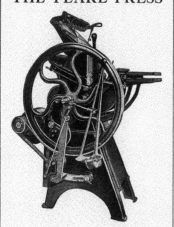

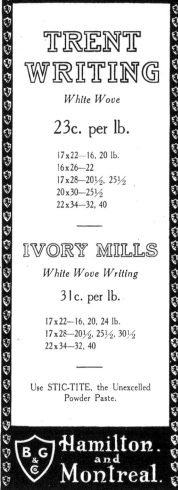

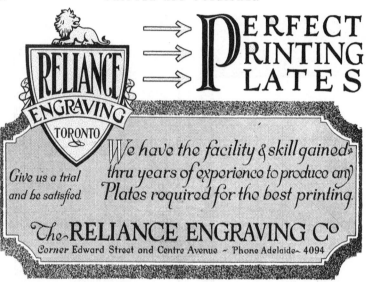

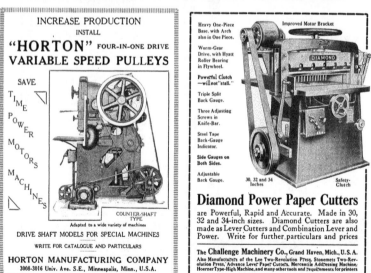

Say you saw it in PRINTER AND PUBLISHER

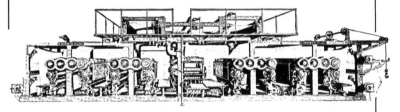

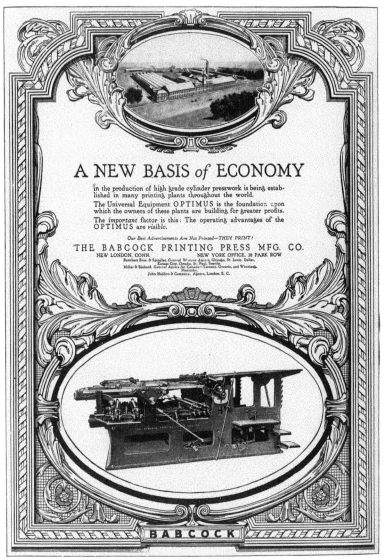

A NEW BASIS *of* ECONOMY

in the production of high grade cylinder presswork is being established in many printing plants throughout the world.

The Universal Equipment OPTIMUS is the foundation upon which the owners of these plants are building for greater profits.

The *important* factor is this: The operating advantages of the OPTIMUS are *visible*.

Our Best Advertisements Are Not Printed—THEY PRINT!

THE BABCOCK PRINTING PRESS MFG. CO.
NEW LONDON, CONN.   NEW YORK OFFICE, 38 PARK ROW

Barnhart Bros. & Spindler, *General Western Agents*, Chicago, St. Louis, Dallas, Kansas City, Omaha, St. Paul, Seattle.
Miller & Richard, *General Agents for Canada*—Toronto, Ontario, and Winnipeg, Manitoba.
John Haddon & Company, *Agents*, London, E. C.

BABCOCK

Cromwell
Tympan Papers

Give Cleaner Impressions with
a Minimum of Make-Ready

SAVING time on make ready, and securing sharp impressions are the two great things your press foreman has to strive for. With Cromwell Traveling, Shifting and Cylinder Tympan Papers, his draw sheets are always tight—no swelling—and they need not be oiled. They are also moisture-proof, protecting the packing against dampness.

You can turn a rush job quicker with Cromwell Tympan Papers because they resist offset, enabling you to back up reasonably wet sheets. Quick delivery is often your best selling argument.

Cromwell papers will take more impressions without replacing, and they *never* rot.

We especially recommend Cromwell Tympan Papers for trade journal and magazine printers where long runs are necessary without interruptions. It is ideal for book work and the highest grade of printing. Job printers will find it an excellent tympan paper for printing bond, linen and covers.

We carry Cromwell Tympan Papers in stock ready for quick shipment in rolls from 36 to 66 inches wide. Order to-day and secure the perfection and economy in printing that Cromwell Tympan Papers give.

Send us the size of your press, and we will forward free of all cost to you, Sample Sheet of our Tympan Paper.

The Cromwell Paper Co.
Department P.P. **Jasper Place, Chicago, U.S.A.**

Trade Mark

OLIVER CROMWELL

PRESS ROOM PROFITS are derived from the money
saved as well as from the money made in the operation
of the presses. Whether Type presses or Offset, no
presses built produce more work or better work than

The PREMIER
TWO-REVOLUTION 4-ROLLER PRESS

The WHITLOCK PONY
TWO-REVOLUTION 2-ROLLER PRESS

The POTTER OFFSET

The POTTER TIN PRINTING PRESS

❑ ❑

Every mechanical device that makes for the production
of the finest quality in the greatest quantity at the
lowest operative cost is incorporated in these presses.

Every printer should know about them.

PREMIER & POTTER PRINTING PRESS CO., Inc.
SUCCEEDING THE WHITLOCK AND POTTER COMPANIES
1102 Aeolian Bldg., 33 West 42nd Street
NEW YORK

Canada West:	*Canada East:*	*Maritime Provinces:*
MANTON BROS.	**GEO. M. STEWART**	**PRINTERS SUPPLIES LTD.**
105 Elizabeth St.	92 McGill Street	27 Bedford Row
Toronto, Ont.	**Montreal P.Q.**	**Halifax, N.S.**

PRINTER AND PUBLISHER
Devoted to the Interests of the Printers and Publishers of Canada

Don't Be Apologetic in Your Appeal
Present Prices Make a Good Case

NUMBER of papers in the Dominion, especially in the weekly class, are making a poor season for themselves in trying to explain why it is they are charging a living price for their papers.

In fact there are readers and appeals and warnings and threats that would make it appear that some vile influence had seized upon the papers and forced them into charging $2 a year for their papers.

It is a fact that the rate for weekly papers should have been at $2 a year long ago. The idea of getting together a good local paper, mailing it or delivering it by carrier, and getting from the reader $1 per year, has always been more or less of a joke to people who took the trouble to go seriously into the matter. The $1 weekly tied on to the country publisher all sorts of other things, and these other things helped to keep him, in too many cases, in such a hand-to-mouth state that he could not live decently, nor could he put money back into his business to improve his paper.

The weekly papers have themselves to blame as well for a lot of this $1 per year atmosphere in their business. For years they continued to fill their columns with half-baked jokes about the editor having seen someone else with a ten dollar bill and wondering what it was; about the payments they had to meet, and so please hump along with that little account and help us do this awful thing.

The country paper has it in its own power and in its own right to go ahead now, as it has always had the opportunity, and put itself where it wants to be. Necessity has been, in the last analysis, a kindness.

A number of papers are going to $2 per year at the first of July. They have been giving warnings, ringing bells, and throwing up sky-rockets for weeks and months in many cases.

They have been announcing that they did not want to do this thing, and that they want to get as many of their readers in at the old price as possible. In fact they create the impression that they can get along handsomely on the old rate, and they urge people to come along and pay up at the old figure.

There is no fault to be found with the publisher telling his readers why he has to increase his rates or his selling price. The publisher will find it much easier to get his price if he does t< the truth, and there is plenty of truth to be told at present in justification of a $2 or even a higher rate.

Do not make your announcements read as though $2 per year were the last high spot you would touch in the matter of subscription rates. If you have learned the lesson of the last year or so you will know that you may find $2 too small to run your business on.

And above all else stop this apologetic tone in announcing your increased rates.

Printer and Publisher has before it a number of clippings from weekly papers in Canada, some of them small, some of them large—so large that they ought to know better. It has been our intention to reproduce a number of these, but no good purpose would be served. They run the course all the way from wails and plaints to threats and coaxings.

Many of them demonstrate plainly that the owner of the paper does not know how to state his own case effectively. The publisher of the weekly paper ought to be the authority in the matter of clearly describing a situation, and in stating a case. He ought to be in a position to advise his merchants how to state their case to sell more goods; he ought to be able to state the case of the manufacturers and business men showing why they have the best community on earth. He does these things and he does them to advantage. Why, then, should he, when it comes to putting his own case before the public, stumble all over the premises, and wind up with a hat-in-hand attitude which is uncalled for and unnecessary, and largely useless as far as getting his price is concerned?

One of the best notices we have seen stated the case well. It showed the price of paper in 1914 and now, showed what the changes were in wages, ink, etc., stated plainly what it was anticipated doing to make the paper better, and

concluded by announcing that the new rate was the lowest figure that could be considered, and that it would come into force at a date about four days distant. That publisher made, it clear to his readers that he had a real case, that he wanted to take advantage of the new rate as soon as possible, that he intended to collect it as soon as possible, and that he had no desire to peddle his proposition for a month or so in order to do himself out of as many increased subscription rates as possible by getting in a lot at the old price. That notice was effective and it will bring results, as there was conviction and finality in every sentence.

An Addresser That Works Right on the Press
Mailer Brought Out by Paul F. Cox

THE "PRESS-ADDRESS MAILER,"illustrated herewith, and as the name rightfully indicates, is a very simple but neat and ingenious device which can be readily attached to any of the standard makes of web printing presses, though it is shown attached and working upon a "flat-bed" perfecting press and for which trade it is first being prepared and perfected.

The patent just granted states that "a primary object of the invention is to provide a novel addressing apparatus which can be attached to a web printing press and operated by and from the mechanism of the printing press in unison therewith, and which is preferably located at, or adjacent to the forms on the press and will apply successive addresses to successive news-

paper impressions descending the former; and which mechanism will not be in the way, or interfere with the threading of the press or the control of the press by the pressman, permitting him to run the press regardless of the presence of the addressing attachment the same as if the addressing attachment was not present. At the same time the addressing mechanism will be under control of the addressing-operator regardless of the operation of the press itself (other than that if the press should stop the addressing mechanism would stop) and the addressing mechanism can be put into and out of effective operation at the will of the addressing operator without stopping, or slowing, down, or otherwise affecting the operation of the printing press proper."

The Addresser attached to the Press.

While Mr. Cox, (whose mail address is at present, 5439 Winthrop Ave., Chicago,) has developed and patented "Strip" attaching and other devices of several kinds, the accompanying illustration shows the main patented device and system.

This is a close up view of the "Green-Address Mailer" detached from the press, showing the feed galley and the delivery or receiving galley, also the inking mechanism and the printing cylinder, safeties, and town marker devices.
The addresser is simple in construction and can be operated by one attendant when attached to a Web press, and will address newspapers at the running speed of the press when attached.

"THE PRESS-ADDRESS MAILER," attached to one of the well-known flat-bed web presses, applying the addresses direct to the outside top corner of the newspapers direct from the "line slugs," which are used with this system.
A series of slug galleys are employed with this system and device, the slugs being automatically handled by the machine in a most novel manner; being ejected from the feed galley into the Addresser, where it is inked and address is printed from the slug upon the margin of the paper (at the top, right hand corner of the first page) the slugs being ejected into a receiving galley after the printing operation; thus making a great saving in time and labor which would be otherwise wasted in handling the papers for hand addressing.
"Club" and "town-markers" have been cared for mechanically, in the several systems and devices Mr. Cox has produced, and with all of them the properly addressed papers are ready for bundling and wrapping as soon as they are taken from the packer-box of the folder.
There surely is a great prospective market for such a long wanted device, or "Attachment" and the publishers in general will quite certainly watch with interest the development of these latest inventions of Mr. Paul F. Cox.

The Sydney *Record*, in their issue of June 18, devoted a feature page, with two full columns of editorial matter, to the visit of the Empire Press Conference to that city on July 28. The editorial contains a précis of the proposed activities of the Press Conference and suggestions as to the civic and business reception in Sydney. The remaining space is filled by advertising some of the leading businesses in that city.

Will Collect the Damages

Arthur O'Leary, former president of the District Trades and Labor Council, of Toronto, who obtained a verdict of $1,500 in a recent libel action against James Simpson, editor of the *Industrial Banner*, stated that he had taken steps to collect on the judgment. Mr. O'Leary's decision has caused Mr. Simpson's friends within the Labor movement to rally to his support, but few of them are prepared to pay more than the costs of the action.
It was stated that Mr. O'Leary's solicitors, acting upon his instructions, placed a Sheriff in Simpson's home on Indian Road, but that the official was withdrawn upon security being provided until Mrs. Simpson would prove that it was her property. It was also said that Mr. Simpson's stock in the *Industrial Banner*, which secures him a seat on the board of directors of the paper, had been seized.
"Machinists are prepared to assist Mr. Simpson," said John Munro, business agent of one of the local unions of the craft. "We have struck off a committee for this purpose. I am surprised that Mr. O'Leary would attempt to collect the judgment. He must realize that anything that is paid will come from members of trades unions, and not from Mr. Simpson."
John Cottam, secretary of the Carpenters' District Council, said that several of the unions were prepared to assist Mr. Simpson.
"I have placed it in the hands of my solicitors for collection. I said I would go the limit. I did not ask Mr. Simpson to lay the charges," was Mr. O'Leary's statement.

What Chicago Survey Shows

That "ruthless competition" among Chicago book and job printers has injured the business as a whole, and that "improper division of attention between purchasing and selling" has been another weakness, are two major findings in a report just submitted by the Bureau of Business Research of Northwestern University School of Commerce to the Franklin Typothetae of Chicago. Prof. Horace Secrist was in charge of the survey, which covered several weeks of time and involved the use of half-a-dozen experts. That the competition "evil" is gradually being adjusted in Chicago is admitted, but the other weakness, Prof. Secrist says, "needs immediate attention." He continues:
"Printers have too frequently been indifferent to advances in costs of materials, merely passing them on to the customer. This has helped the paper interests to gain a closer control over the paper already largely monopolized and has put the printing business more and more at the mercy of the associations of paper manufacturers and dealers. Here again the group plan is the best instrument at hand with which to influence the situation."
The survey doesn't show that Chicago printers are paying extremely high wages save in a few instances. The average weekly earnings of 1,336 employees was found to be $30.62, but 28.4 per cent. earned more than $40 a week. Of the more highly compensated workers, 7.6 per cent. earned over $50 a week. The charts show, in this connection, that only six employees, all union men, received $65 or more. They are hand compositors of the highly expert class.
The fluidity of the trade is demonstrated by Prof. Secrist, whose bureau found that 64 per cent. of employees stayed on the job in the same plant only a month. The printer is a rover, as all the world has been taught, but the Franklin Typothetae survey has made this very clear.

Standard Sizes Are Urged

A standardized size for paper manufacturers' sample books is much needed in the present co-operative era in the production of printed matter.
The general attractiveness of the first sight of an artistically prepared sample book, and its "general publicity" qualities are not to be underestimated, but have limitations. Standardization on the other hand will save much time, money and energy for the printer and his customers. Standardization means ease of filing, and ease of filing means ease of finding, and thus constant reference. It benefits the customer, the paper manufacturer, and particularly the printer, who is seeking to give the best ideas, plans and advice to his customers in his efforts to excel in the quality of his service to them.

They Bought the Paper from the Sheriff

The Making of the Windsor, N. S., Tribune

(By J. L. Rutledge in MacLean's Magazine)

PLEASE God his intellectuals be not slipping," said Charles Lamb when his dog preformed antics that he could not understand. It was with something of the same sort of feeling that the townspeople of Windsor, Nova Scotia, received the news that the erstwhile defunct Windsor *Tribune* had been disposed of by the Sheriff to their fellow townswomen, Mrs. Jean Urquhart Fielding and Miss Antoinette Forbes.

Up to that time there had been no question of their sanity. Was not Mrs. Fielding the wife of a respected citizen and a housekeeper of repute, and was not Miss Forbes a graduate of Dalhousie University, and the vice-principal of the Windsor Academy; both citizens in good standing and apparently ready to follow the avocations that seemed to have been handed out by a kindly Providence?

Teaching and housekeeping are woman's work, said the townsfolk with unctious conviction, but who ever heard of a woman "sticking type?" Hands were raised in holy horror, and crusty old gentlemen were heard to mutter in their beards something about "petticoat government," combined with a pious belief that the business would not last over six months.

And all that happened something over sixteen years ago. The Windsor *Tribune* now owns and occupies one of the finest buildings in Windsor, is a prosperous and paying concern, with an influence over a wide field, and Mrs. Fielding and Miss Forbes are still in the saddle and judging from appearances and results their "intellectuals" have stood the strain of this deviation from the usual.

If you happen to live in a small town, and your husband, by reason of business calls, is away a good deal of the time, if you are not interested in gossip, and have the idea that Bridge is a game and not an afternoon business and have developed a prejudice against afternoon tea, then you will understand that Mrs. Fielding was ripe for a revolt against the conventional.

And if you happened to be a vice-principal of a school, with an idea that school teaching should be a life vocation, and suddenly learned that there was talk going round of pensioning teachers at an early age, at $50 a year or some such figure, whether the report was true or not, you might be pardoned for becoming a little restive. Therefore you will understand why Miss Forbes was ready to join the revolt.

They Decide to Buy

IT WAS round about this time that rumors began to circulate concerning the *Tribune*. It was not in a healthy state. It did not need a practitioner in newspaper diseases to tell this. It was a pretty sick paper; there could be no question of that. The *Tribune* needed careful nursing, and Mrs. Fielding and Miss Forbes knew that it was not getting it, and that the probabilities were that the obsequies were not far distant.

Up to the present the thing had not definitely entered their mind. It is possible that Miss Forbes and Mrs. Fielding, who lived together at the time, may have tried the idea out on one

another. "Wouldn't it be interesting to try to run that paper?" or "I wonder how much a paper like that would be worth?" or something like that, and there the matter would drop, for both were careful of their intellectual reputation, and were not anxious that the other should think that they were losing their mental grip.

Then one day Mrs. Fielding came home with the rumor that the *Tribune* was to be sold. Over the tea and muffins she tried this one on Miss Forbes. Miss Forbes was unquestionably interested.

"Why shouldn't we buy it?" continued Mrs. Fielding, expecting that Miss Forbes would immediately call the doctor.

"Well, why shouldn't we?" replied Miss Forbes imperturbably.

That finished any question in the matter as far as they were concerned. If Mr. Fielding could be made to see reason all would be well. For the ladies were contemplating purchasing that paper with comparatively few assets but enthusiasm and interest, and valuable as these are they are not as likely to appeal to the unromantic mind of a bailiff as readily as actual coin of the realm. Saturday afternoon they started off to see Mr. Fielding, who had considerable lumber interests and was in the bush a good part of the time. It was cold, and the drifts were deep, and it was sixteen miles back into the bush, and they were chilled in everything but their enthusiasm when they finally reached Mr. Fielding's camp. Mr. Fielding, who had in days past had some experience in rural newspaper work, and knew something of the pitfalls, proceeded to complete the chilling process.

He outlined all the ills that could befall a newspaper. He dwelt feelingly on the work entailed, and that a newspaper to be of service had to appear with a certain regularity, and that therefore it was a business rather than an entertainment. In fact if you had combined that melancholy trio, Eliphaz the Temanite, Zophar the Naamathite and Bildad the Shuhite, they could hardly have provided a more dolorous prospect than did Mr. Fielding. When he had finished the pessimistic picture he ended: "But if you want to try it, go ahead." Up went the spirits of the ladies again, the Bildad strains forgotten. All the way back over that sixteen-mile trip, they talked of their plans. They talked and planned well into the early hours of Sunday, and from daylight to dark on Sunday the conversation never strayed from the subject.

Bidding in the Paper

MONDAY morning was the morning of the sale. Miss Forbes had to go to her school, so Mrs. Fielding, alone and unassisted, strolled off to the court house. There the Sheriff was looking over a small gathering trying to locate someone who looked as though they were ready to adopt that bundle of trouble that is styled the local newspaper. Mrs. Fielding discovered the former owner in the assembly and enquired if he were going to bid the paper in. Apparently, however, he felt that his time could be better employed.

Mrs. P. M. Fielding, editor of the Windsor "Tribune," at her desk.

That point being settled Mrs. Fielding began to bid. There was a horror-stricken silence. The idea of a woman thinking of buying a newspaper! Very probably someone in the back row got off that old one about "Woman's place being in the home," and doubtless also it was hailed as quite a novel and weighty thought by the friends about. Certainly it stood out beyond question that no one in that gathering took Mrs. Fielding's bidding as a thing to be considered seriously, and no one for a moment believed that a woman could do anything with a newspaper. All of which gives point to the dictum of Mark Twain that, "The older we grow the greater becomes our wonder at how much ignorance one can contain without bursting one's clothes."

There wasn't a great deal of bidding because everyone but Mrs. Fielding was afraid that they might be left with a newspaper on their hands, and they were only eager to see it realize enough to pay their own private account against it. So finally the last competing bidder had been weeded out. Mrs. Fielding bid $2,100 and found that a whole newspaper had fallen in her lap. She gave a note for the purchase price and secured a deed for the property from the Sheriff, and went home to announce, somewhat breathlessly, to Miss Forbes that they were newspaper proprietors.

When they had time to look over their new kingdom they did not find it a particularly exhilarating sight. Two small rooms over a store, a flat-bed press and two small job presses, and an all too limited supply of type. They went home and talked it over some more. They were just as enthusiastic as they had been before and just as confident that they could make it a real paper, but they realized that it couldn't be done in a day. It's all very well to hitch your wagon to a star, but it is the part of wisdom to make sure that it is a fixed star before making the hitching too permanent. So it was decided that Miss Forbes should retain her position in the Academy as a sort of anchor to windward. Mrs. Fielding felt that she had not anything to lose, she had only been housekeeping for her husband, and that sort of job is not easily lost.

In justification of this solitary indication of uncertainty on the part of the owners of the Tribune it must be said, that its career had not been a rosy one, four or five times already it had been sold and on several occasions the Sheriff had been an interested party.

So it was decided that they should go on as they were, Miss Forbes coming in after school, and giving her evenings and Saturdays to the paper. Then came the first hitch. It was discovered that Mrs. Fielding, being a married woman, had to get her husband's official consent to her going into business. Of course she had that consent anyway, but she didn't like the idea of having to announce it to the world at large in an official document. So the lawyer who was drawing up the papers thought of a way out of the difficulty.

"You could form a Joint Stock Company," he said, "with three members." And so it was that it became the Windsor Tribune Publishing Company, Ltd., with Mrs. Fielding and Miss Forbes the actual company, and Mr. Fielding in the background supplying sympathy and occasionally advice, and the use of his name as the necessary third party.

It was Wednesday afternoon. Mrs. Fielding had spent two busy days in writing the first edition of the paper. It was mainly about the new management and what they intended to

do, and what attitude they intended to take. The printer had been induced to stay, on what he undoubtedly considered was a very dubious prospect of better times, and the five pages were in type. Miss Forbes dropped in cheerfully eager to get at her share of the work, when Mrs. Fielding met her with gloom dangling about her in great chunks.

"There isn't any paper," she said.

Now women in general are ingenious creatures, but no amount of ingenuity will get a newspaper out without paper, and this was Wednesday night, and the paper was supposed to be off the press on Friday. Consternation with the "C" was no chance of getting paper there in time. They were too new in the newspaper business to be very thoroughly imbued with the solemn fact that a newspaper must come out on time; but they were very conscious of the fact that their fellow townsfolk would be spilling "I told you so's" like a leaky kettle, if it did not appear. That was a thought that was not to be borne. Mere man in the shape of the foreman was called into conference It was the pessimistic gentleman. The news did not depress him further, that was impossible. However, he roused himself long enough to remark that sometimes paper was held up at the freight office owing to funds for its relase being unavailable. Both ladies felt that the foreman had been dowered at birth an almost superhuman intelligence. Their belief was confirmed when careful ivestigations unearthed the fact that there actually was paper at the freight office. The only difficulty was that the charges was fairly heavy, and they did not have the money. However they owed money on the newspaper, and there was no use picking on a matter of paper to put it before the public. Eventually the money was borrowed at

Antoinette Forbes, secretary and business manager of the "Tribune."

seven per cent. and the precious paper released.

The First Complaint

THE first issue of the Tribune brought its own troubles. It brought for one thing Mr. Jamieson, a dour Scotchman, who dropped in to demand a statement of policy. "I've been a subscriber to this paper for years," he said sternly, "because it was Conservative, and I'm not minded to see it change now. If you are thinking of changing I have come to tell you that I will discontinue my subscription and there are sixteen other Jamiesons taking it and they will stop too."

"Well," said Mrs. Fielding, "it won't be Liberal, and it will be temperance, and what else I'll have to let you know later." Mr. Jamieson went away with the scowl still on his face, and Mrs. Fielding sat down to make a little note regarding Mr. Jamieson's visit to town. Suffice it to say that not a Jamieson was dropped from the list.

There was another trouble, and that was in regard to a policy for the paper. Miss Forbes and Mrs. Fielding sat down to figure the matter out, and they decided that it didn't matter so much what the policy was as long as it was a fighting one. Politics is usually something that will stir the blood down in the Maritimes, but an election was just over, and they felt that the cream of the excitement was off for the time being. That would come later, but at the moment something else was needed. They were both temperance advocates, and that looked like a good cause.

Windsor was a Scott Act town, but despite that fact there were 15 saloons more or less openly retailing liquor. The two ladies sitting down together argued that there would probably be as much fight in this question as in any other that could be discovered, and they were certainly right. No sooner was this policy decided on than the *Tribune* appeared with a blazing attack on the liquor traffic in general and on the administration of the Scott Act in the town of Windsor in particular. They demanded that either the law be enforced or that the sellers be granted a license. They pointed out the insidious danger of this hole-and-corner business; told what it was likely to do, and pointed out some definite instances of what it actually was doing. If John Doe, the son of a prominent family in the town, was arrested for being drunk, when there was supposedly no liquor to get drunk on, John Doe's name appeared in print with the details of the case, but without comment. In this policy the paper has never varied. It gives the news and will not suppress names.

A Crusade Against Liquor

THE attack on the liquor interests, which were pretty strongly entrenched in the town, brought about a bitter fight. Even much of the better element in the town was only half in sympathy with the *Tribune's* campaign. Entrenched interests always gain a certain sympathy from the mollusc type of individual who hates a change of surroundings, and whose doctrine is always "let it alone."

Windsor stirred uneasily, and grew restive under the persistent argument that the "blind tiger" should be forced to go.

"Don't you think," said a friend of the two ladies dropping into the office, if you can speak of dropping in an office that requires a toilsome climb up stairs, "Don't you think that you are going a little too strong? There is a lot of feeling in the town."

"Well," said Mrs. Fielding, "that's what we were hoping for."

"But it's pretty strong feeling, and there are a crowd of people, a rough lot from the district, who might be troublesome. I'm afraid if you keep on, that they will raid the office and throw your plant into the street."

"As long as they leave us enough type to spell '"Temperance," Mrs. Fielding snapped back, "we will publish this paper."

It is not to be denied that it was a struggle, and Miss Forbes, who presides at the business end, found it pretty hard sledding. She had to see that there was enough money forthcoming to pay the weekly charges.

"Have we enough money to pay the wages?" Mrs. Fielding would ask on Saturday mornings.

"No, but we will have," would come the prompt reply from Miss Forbes, and she would start out and collect accounts till the necessary funds were in hand. That was hard business, but it was sound business, and no small part of the success of the Windsor *Tribune* has lain in the fact that its proprietors were not afraid to ask for the money that was due them.

A Hard Struggle

BUT as the campaign for temperance went on the collecting grew harder. One large advertiser discontinued his advertising entirely, because, as he said, the paper was "a dirty rag." It was a hard blow, but instead of backing down they redoubled their attacks on the liquor interests. They received threatening letters, and were solemnly warned time and again by their friends. But nothing happened, that is nothing happened to them. But gradually the town feeling began to turn to the side of the paper. The molluscs clambered off their rocks, and began to believe that there might be a worse catastrophe than a change, and one by one the "blind tigers" began to slink away till the mere name of Windsor was sufficient to parch the throats of the bibulously inclined.

And so gradually they won out. The advertiser who had thought the *Tribune* "a dirty rag," forgot that remark and announced proudly that it was the only paper with the courage to tell the truth. That typified the change in sentiment of the community, and ended the lean years. Working together steadily and persistently, for Miss Forbes had given up her school and was busy all the time drumming up business for the paper, they had made the *Tribune* a factor in the community. They worked together in this as they have done in all the business of the paper, although Mrs. Fielding has devoted most of her attentions to the editorial side and Miss Forbes to the business management.

A gentleman dropped in one day, in an embittered spirit. Something had displeased him, and he was bent on cancelling his subscription. He had doubtless announced his intention to his wife at the breakfast table, and had thus gained the desperate courage that comes of the bridges burned. He announced his complaints and outlined his intentions to Miss Forbes. Miss Forbes at once countered with a variety of reasons as to why he should not adopt the course proposed. Mrs. Fielding, scenting the battle from afar, drifted in, and added her arguments to those of Miss Forbes. For the moment the business and editorial departments ceased to function and all engeries were focussed on the circulation end. The man's protests were beaten down in a torrent of argument. He threw up his hands in despair, stopping only long enough to stick his head back into the office and announce, "I give it up, what the one of you doesn't think of the other does." But the name did not come off the list. That disgruntled gentleman had put his finger on the vital point in the success of the Windsor *T ibune*. "What the one of you doesn't think of, the other does."

A New Building Planned

THE business began to prosper, and there began to be a little money in the treasury, and their pride began to revolt at the little printing shop over the store.

There was a fine corner lot in one of the best locations in the town. It had formerly been the site of an hotel, but the hotel had been burned down some years previous, and only its blackened skeleton remained. The ladies pondered over the matter, and to them it seemed that it would be a fine touch of poetic justice if the old grog shop should give place to the temperance newspaper. Finally the lot came up for sale and Mrs Fielding again journeyed to the court house and bid it in. It lay idle for some time, and finally in 1914 they decided to build. They had nice plans drawn by an architect and paid $200 for them. They looked nice, but when Miss Forbes and Mrs. Fielding got together and discussed them, they did not seem just to suit, so it was decided to scrap them, and Miss Forbes herself drew others that took into account that it was a newspaper office, and that it needed a large side wall on which the name of the Windsor *Tribune* could be blazened forth in letters so large that he who walked, ran, or motored might read. For this was one of the outstanding ideals of the proprietors.

The plans were completed and the great war broke out at approximately the same time. The ladies were anxious to get right on with the work, but there were croaking friends who foresaw dire possibilities. "The Germans might come sailing up the river any day," they said, "and blow your new building into kingdom come."

The ladies, however, were not to be daunted by the bogey of a special German hate for the *Tribune*, and despite all arguments they decided to go ahead.

They contracted for the building. When they had secured the whole contract they went over it and decided that they were being gouged, and that the process was neither pleasant nor profitable. So instead of one contract they made several, with the bricklayers for construction work, for which they themselves placed the orders for brick; with the carpenters, plumbers and electrician. The building when completed was and is one of the finest in Windsor. They put in a new press and when they were located in the new building, they had paid the original mortgage and had a clear receipt for the new press as well. They have a circulation that covers a 20-mile radius about Windsor, and stretches farther afield. They have a business that has more than doubled even since they went into their new building, and ask either of these ladies and they will tell you that though they have worked hard, they have had a thoroughly good time.

Mrs. Fielding is a member of the Board of Trade, the first woman member on record. She is also president of the local Red Cross, and at the time of the catastrophe in Halifax spent six weeks there helping to organize the relief in her own energetic way, which entailed riding on loads of coal to assure their delivery, and similar decisive measures. During her absence Miss Forbes ran the paper.

They are both fighters, though in a different way. Mrs. Fielding wields a forceful pen, but is fortunately gifted with a legal type of mind that has been a protection against the possibility of libel actions, even in the most strenuous days of their campaign. Miss Forbes is the business end, a very keen, systematic and fearless business getter.

How to Figure Your Hour Costs Correctly

Some Real Information in This

By TUCKER E. MILLER, Oklahoma Advertising Bureau

A PUBLISHER writing to the bureau this week wants to know how he is to find a real selling price for display advertising. From the information he sends I have made out the following estimate, keeping as near to his data as possible. From this basis, others may wish to do some figuring.

If you do not know the average costs per inch of producing advertising you are taking long chances at any price, especially if you are operating a job department in connection.

If you do not know costs of production in your plant you can start none too soon to find out. I give the following estimate that others may compare it with costs in their plants.

Call On Bureau

If the bureau can be of assistance to you, call on us— it's yours.

To find the overhead expenses: rent, $360; taxes, $60; light, $30; telephone, $8.50; heat, $180; insurance, $130; salary, $2,400; interest on fixtures, $36; office supplies, $87; bookkeeping, $600; advertising, $50; postage, $54; expense of travelling in interest of office, $32; Press Association dues, $6; donations, $50; miscellaneous expense, $184; spoiled work, had accounts, etc., $104. Total $4,371.50.

Cost Per Week

Divide by 52, equals $84.10, the cost per week.

The cost of productive hours of labor: Three printers with an average of 32 productive hours in a 48-hour week, or 96 productive hours. One boy averages 12 productive hours, or a total for the four of 108 productive hours.

One printer for 32 productive hours receives $30 per week. His wage for one hour is therefore 94 cents. This rate per hour added to his pro rata part of the overhead hour cost makes a total of $1.68 as the hour cost for one printer.

Hand Composition Next

Then take up hand composition. The investment in type, cabinets, stones, etc., is approximately $2,000. Interest on this amount at 10 per cent. for one year would be $200 per year. Depreciation at 25 per cent., or $500 would total $700 a year, and for one week, $13.50.

Daily time cards will show about 24 hours of hand composition time, which would make this overhead charge come to 56 cents per hour. Add this to the $1.68 hour cost and you have $2.24 as the correct cost.

Then consider linotype composition. Figuring interest on cost of a $4,500 linotype at 10 per cent. gives you $450 for the year. Depreciation at 10 per cent makes another $450. Repairs and upkeep another $75. Power $192. Total $1,167, for the year, or $23 for the week, for an average of 32 hours of productive time. An average of 72 cents per hour to add to the $1.68. Total cost of operating your linotype per hour, $2.40.

Press Operation Cost

By the same process you will find that operating your cylinder will cost you not less than $2.25 an hour.

Costs other than for composition and press work for an eight-page, six-column weekly paper carrying 60 per cent. advertising, or 570 inches would be: print paper, $1,081.80; ink, $35; plate, $60; wrapping paper, $5; postage, $110; allowance for miscellaneous expense, $331; reporter and correspondents, $350. Total, $1,955.81. Average for 52 weeks, $37.62.

There are seven hours cylinder press work at an hour cost of $2.25, or $15.75; 30 hours linotype composition at $2.40, or $85.84. Cost of printing the paper for one week—$160.21. Adding 20 per cent. for profit, $32.40, or selling price of $192.60. Receipts from other than for display advertising paper. To make a profit on these figures, take the circulation of

1,500 at $1.50 per year. Collectible $1,200, or $23 per week. Paid readers and legals, average per week $18.

Cost Per Inch

Subtract this total of $41 from the cost per week, $160.21, gives $119.21 or a cost per inch of 21 cents. The $41 subtracted from $192.60, leaving $151.60 as selling price for display advertising.

With a weekly average of 570 inches a profitable display advertising rate would be 27 cents which includes 20 per cent. profit added to cost production.

Mr. Porte Appeals to Buyers

The Porte Publishing Company, publisher of the Franklin Printing Price List, is now extending its activities very significantly, going directly to the printing buyer in aiding users of its Franklin Printing Price List. *System*, The Magazine of Business, carries a full page advertisement in its July 1920 issue, the motive of this appeal to the business men apparently being to mold his confidence in the Franklin Printing Price List printer. Mr. Porte, the energetic president of the Porte Publishing Co., has applied one of the most forceful and potent means of the big magnate in his promotion work, by going directly to the consumer—the printing buyer in this case—with his message. Advice comes that this is merely a beginning; that in the future, this concern will utilize mediums, such as *System*, to further the interests of Franklin printers. Report is made that the response to the *System* advertisement mentioned above, has been gratifying to the Porte Publishing Co.

Hour Costs in Toronto

Hand Composition	$2.25	per hour
Monotype Keyboard	2.50	"
Monotype Caster	2.50	"
Job Press Hand	1.50	"
Job Press Miller	1.50	"
Pony Cylinder	1.75	"
Large Cylinder	3.00	"

Mr. Calnan, Please Stand Up!

Alliston Herald:—The editor of the Picton *Gazette*, Mr. A. E. Calnan, who was president last year of the Canadian Weekly Newspapers Association, got enough pleasure and profit out of the recent annual meeting to go home and write enthusiastically of the success of the meeting from his viewpoint. Mr. Calnan deserved all the enjoyment he derived, since it was he and the board of directors, of which Mr. J. A. MacLaren of the Barrie *Examiner* is one, who provided the program for the best convention ever held by the Canadian weekly newspapers. The addresses were held by experts on editing, advertising, typography, cost finding and accounting covered every phase of the weekly newspaper publisher's problems. The spirit of fraternity and sociability at this meeting was present to a degree far in excess of that which has prevailed at any meeting since the old days before the formation of the C.P.A. To Mr. Calnan a generous expression of thanks is due from Canadian weekly newspaper publishers for the pleasant and profitable time they had in Toronto a couple of weeks ago.

The Regina *Daily Post* is making good use of the vacation idea to take on a page of business. Firms represented include sellers of kodaks, books, ladies' outfits, tires and auto accessories, supplies for campers, etc.

What is This Poster Worth at Your Shop?

Interesting Study in Costs Here

THE cost of turning out a large double-page advertising poster is a matter on which various offices differ, and should differ. It would be well-nigh impossible for many offices to think alike in matters of policy in their papers, and the same thing applies to the turning out of the work. The only sin can be that sometimes some of them think too lowly in the matter of prices.

A few days ago *Printer and Publisher* saw a piece of work that had been done in the office of the St. Marys *Journal*, and about which some of the newspapermen were having a little discussion as to what it was worth. A zinc reproduction of the job was made, and sent to some of the weekly papers where this class of work would be done. The request was that they should give us an estimate on what the work would be worth from their office. It is hardly a fair thing to ask an estimator to go over a job that is greatly reduced in size, as it is rather confusing. Then, it works another way, too; it is easy to imagine that greater speed can be made when sizing up a reprint job than it is to tackle the original manuscript. There is always more or less preliminary work and experimenting to get a proper lay-out in a large piece of work such as this, and the man who looks at the finished product is apt to underestimate the time that can be taken—and is taken—up in this way.

It was not until we heard from Mr. Eedy of St. Marys that we knew the job was to be folded, so allowance has been made for this. Mr. Elliott of Alliston allowed for this and so does Mr. Eedy. The peculiar thing about the estimates is that they are lower than the office in which the work was actually done, as it must be borne in mind that the figures given by Mr. Eedy are those of the time actually spent on the work. Reference to the Franklin List gives $82.50 as the selling price of a bill that seems to have more composition on it than the one under review.

Mr. Eedy's price shows that it cost $96.25 without the folding and in his letter he mentions the figures as being "the cost of producing the job in our office," so from that it is inferred that he adds 25 per cent. to the figure as his selling price, which would bring his charge up to about $120 without folding, so it is seen that there is quite a spread between the estimates and the price charged by Mr. Eedy.

In his letter it will be noticed that Mr. Eedy brings up the matter of distribution, which is not usually included in an estimate, as his composition costs should be based on a price sufficiently high to take care of the distribution, which is reckoned as non-productive time, which cannot be sold to the customer.

The figuring of how long it would take to throw in this job is an interesting little study in itself. The job is about (type size) 36 x 21, which gives us 756 square inches, and from this it can be estimated that the thing should weigh 189 pounds. There are considerable pounds in the wooden type and linotype matter will go a little lighter than straight foundry type, and for this reason we will place the weight at 160 pounds. Figuring at $2 per hour a fast man will throw in type for six cents per pound, and a slower one will run up around 10 cents. Just to show what can be done in the matter of keeping up the cost of printing, cases are on record where it costs as high as 19 cents per pound to throw in ordinary type. This may be accounted for by too much running around on the part of the workman, and it is worth noting that on a job of this kind it is easy to waste a lot of time in the same way. In this job there is a great deal of linotype matter, perhaps some nine thousand ems, and the cuts take up a good deal of space. In a rough way, but one which will be found to be not far out, we will put the amount to be distributed at 80 ounces. If a galley is used to pick out all the type for the one case this should be thrown in at the rate of about 25 pounds per hour. This gives us a few minutes over three hours for the throwing in of this bill, and it is worked out on the same rule as by many of the larger shops. It is, we contend, much safer to leave out the price of distribution in the actual figures, and include in your hourly selling cost sufficient to take care of your productive and non-productive hours. These can be divided as follows:

Chargeable: Hand composition, machine composition, author's corrections, make-up, press lock-up, foundry lock-up, registering, proofing, press work.

Non-chargeable: Office corrections, proof-reading, copy-holding, copy revising, distribution, errands, repairs and delays to machinery, and keeping same in good shape.

In Mr. Eedy's bill he has made allowance for one hour for proof-reading, and he has also a 'change" marked up for one hour, which of course would not be included in the estimates of the others. The other offices probably include the proof-reading in their hour-costs.

The following figures shows what the work would be charged in several of the offices:

Renfrew *Mercury*	$76.40
Oshawa *Reformer*	84.30
Simcoe *Reformer*	80.00
Acton *Free Press*	78.10
Barrie *Examiner*	96.25
Alliston *Herald*	83.50
St. Marys *Journal*, cost without fold	96.25

If 25 per cent. were added to this it would bring the price of the St. Marys *Journal* to about $120 without folding. Here are the figures:

Replying to your letter of July 9, we beg to submit the following as the cost of producing the job in our office:

Linotype Composition	5	hours
Linotype Corrections	15	min.
Hand Composition	1	hour
Assistant	2	hours
Corrections	½	hour
Proof-Reading	1	hour
Change	1	hour
Make-Ready	1	hour
Wash Up	½	hour
Distribution	4¾	hours

26 hrs. at $2—	$52.00
4,000 impressions, 6 hours on press, $2.75	16.50
Folded on machine, 5 hours at $2	10.00
4,000 sheets stock at $7.50 per cwt	26.75
Ink etc.	1.00

You will note the item distribution is 4¾ hours. This may appear long, but in this case this time was actually taken. In some offices no doubt the distribution would have been easier and even, perhaps, considered as non-productive and therefore not chargeable time. Nevertheless it is part of the work which was necessary in connection with the job and in our estimation should be included in the quotiaton.

Many offices will guess at a figure for overhead expenses, instead of which we take the time each man is working, and charge for it at a sum which we know covers overhead and his wages.

Because a man is being paid twenty-five or more dollars per week it does not mean that we can sell his time at that price. We are all agreed that approximately 1-3 of the printer's time is non-productive, and even a one-third increase on what we are paying, in the charge to the customer, is inadequate.

The foundry here sent us a man last month to tighten a pulley on a shaft. The man took 2 hours to do the work. He received for those two hours 90 cents. We paid the foundry $3.00. No machinery was used, no type destroyed, or brass rule ruined, and yet $1.50 per hour was charged for the man's time. Why? Because there is a bookkeeper to pay, stationery to buy and a hundred and one other things not actually overhead in the mechanical department, but a part of the cost of employing that one man. So it is in the print shop. With the coming winter's coal at $17.00 per ton we must begin to increase the selling price of our producers' time, otherwise the rising price of newsprint will cease to give us worry.

Yours very truly,

JOHN W. EEDY

Alliston Herald

It is quite true I have pondered over this piece of work. There was just eleven hours disparity between my estimate and the time it actually took to put it in the chase. Then I set up a number of the headings and later put up a few lines of the machine composition. I am convinced that the form could, in a shop where there is plenty of good labor-saving material, be put in a chase, ready for the pressman, in nine hours, but to allow for all contingencies we will say eleven hours and estimate it as follows:—

Composition, 11 hours ($25 per week of 48 hrs).	$7.26
Lock-up, proof-reading, corrections, etc., 1 hr...	.66
Press work, 8 hours	5.28
Folding, 5 hours	3.30
Stock	30.00
Ink, gasoline, rags, wrapping	1.00
	$47.50
40 per cent. profit on $47.50	19.00
25 hours overhead at $1.00	25.00
	$91.50

Selling price, $92.00

F. B. ELLIOTT, Alliston.

As noted in the introduction to this article, we said Mr. Elliott's price for folding was being taken out. With its share of overhead the folding would make a difference of about $8 in his figure, bringing it to $83.50.

The Barrie Examiner

Would say that it is rather hard to make a correct estimate on the reduced size of the bill, but will do the best I can on it. Mr. Elliott had the original of the bill up here a week ago, but I hadn't much time to look over it. I have figured the cost as follows:—

Stock $30.00, plus 10% for handling, $3.00	$33.00
Linotype, 4 hours at $2.50 per hour	10.00
*Hand Composition, 5 hours at $2.00	10.00
*Hand Composition, assistant, 3 hours at $1.50.	4.50
Lock-up, half-hour at $2.00	1.00

Make-ready, 1 hour at $2.00	3.00
Cylinder Press, 5 hours at $2.50	12.50
Attendant, Cylinder Press, 1 hour	2.00
Ink	.50
Jogging and delivering	1.50
Total cost	$77.00
25 per cent. profit	19.25
Total selling cost	$96.25

Of course you will understand it is pretty hard to make a correct estimate on the time taken on a job of this size, as one office might get the job out in half the time another would, through having better system, better workmen or a better supply of material to work with. Regarding the Linotype Composition it would be better figured by the thousand ems, but in the reduced size of the sample sent it is impossible to figure the estimate on the number of ems. If you have the correct number of ems, you might substitute it for my estimate on the Linotype, charging it at $1.00 per 1,000 ems, including corrections and proof-reading, which I think is about the right charge for 10 point.

On looking up the Franklin Price List, I find that a bill with more composition than sample on 24 x 36 size is quoted at $82.50 selling price for 4,000.

Trusting this will be satisfactory.

I remain, yours very truly,

W. E. WALLS.

*Assuming that expert hand does the placing together and spacing, and assistant sets up the display lines and introduction.

The Acton Free Press

We estimate the price for the White and May job, St. Marys, as follows:—

Stock	$30.00
Machine Composition, 4 hours at $2.50	10.00
Hand Composition, 8 hours at $1.50	12.00
Lock-up, ½ hour at $1.50	.75
Make-ready, 1 hour,	1.85

This cut is greatly reduced from the original, which was a well-displayed 39 x 24 poster. There were 4,000 of them. Printer & Publisher put an arbitrary price of $30 as the cost of the stock. Franklin price list shows $82.50 for a bill that has more composition.

Cylinder Press and feed, 4 hours at $1.85......   7.40
Ink, 2 lbs. at 25c..........................   .50
$$\overline{}$$
$62.50
Percentage of profit 25 per cent...............   15.60
$$\overline{}$$
$78.10

Yours very truly,
H. P. MOORE

The Simcoe Reformer

Mr. H. B. Donly writes:—I showed your St. Marys job to my men. The hours are theirs. The prices are those used in our shop.

Machine Operator, 3½ hours, $2.00.......... $7.00
Ad. Compositor, 4 hours, at $1.50.............   6.00
Lock-up, Make-ready and Cylinder, 5 hrs., $2.50 12.50
Stock....................................... 30.00
Stock Handling............................ 3.60
Packing and Shipping...................... 1.00
$$\overline{}$$
$60.10
Sell...,...................................$80.00

The Oshawa Reformer

Mr. Chas. M. Mundy writes:—I am taking it for granted that the price of $30.00 for stock is cost price and as you will see is cost price and not the selling price. My estimate is as follows:—

Machine Composition, 3 hours at $2.50........ $7.50
Hand Composition, 5 hours at $1.75.......... 8.75
Lock-up 1 hour at $1.75..................... 1.75
Make-ready, 1 hour at $1.75 .... 1.75
Press work, 5 hours at $2.50 ....: 12.50
Handling stock 10 per cent. of $30.00........ 3.00
Wrapping and delivering at $1.50............. 1.50
Ink, 2 pounds at 35c........................   .70
Stock, $30.00............................. 30.00
$$\overline{}$$
$67.45

To this, of course, must be added profit. With us we add 25 per cent., which in this case would amount to $16.85, or total of $84.30 for the job.

We think it is a good idea for *Printer and Publisher* to take up estimates on different jobs like these, as we feel sure the printers are not charging enough for store bills. In the case of auction sale bills we honestly believe there is more money lost than made by the printers of Ontario in this particular line.

Renfrew Mercury

I am enclosing our estimate sheet which explains itself. If we were tendering on the job we would probably give $75.00 as our figure.

We have noticed a tendency on the part of printers to quote far too low a price on this class of work, not seeming to realize the amount of time and labor involved in setting it up.

Stock....................................$30.00
40 per cent. for freight, handling, profit........ 12.00
Machine Composition, 4 hours at $2 .... 8.00
Hand Composition, 8 hours at $1.50 .... 12.00
Make-ready................................ 3.00
Running................................... 8.00
Delivery.................................. 1.00
$$\overline{}$$
$76.40
W. R. DAVIES.

There is also some difference of opinion as to how long it would take for machine composition. Here are the estimates:

	Hours
St. Marys *Journal*........................	5
Barrie *Examiner*.........................	4
Acton *Free Press*........................	4
Simcoe *Reformer*.........................	3½
Oshawa *Reformer*.........................	3
Renfrew *Mercury*.........................	4

If any of the offices have any other points that should be brought out in connection with this matter, *Printer and Publisher* would be pleased to hear from them.

Bonds in This Editor's Safe

Oakville *Star*:—Some inexperienced, uninformed burglars made a desperate raid on the safe of Elgin A. Harris, publisher of the Burlington *Gazette*, one evening last week, and found a whole stack of bonds, debentures and such other foolish trash as an editor should know nothing about.

But as for cash. Editor Harris has a pair of pockets well able to take care of all the glittering coins and musty bills which pass through his fingers, and there the wealth is more safe than most any place else. Not that the pen artist does not dig down and bring forth liberally when the occasion demands, but because any nimble-fingered gent who attempted to dislodge said wealth would find himself surrounded by a maze of trouble.

So the filthy lucre the burglars collected was nil, and the bonds etc., were all registered and can be duplicated and therefore without intrinsic value to the intruders, who gained nothing but experience for their trouble and risk.

Mutt and Jeff in Chancery

Mr. Harry Conway Fisher, an American cartoonist, commonly known as "Bud" Fisher, brought an action in Mr. Justice Sargant's Court against Sir Alfred Butt and Messrs. Oscar Barrett, Leon Pollock and Larry Ceballos for an injunction to restrain them from infringing his copyright, by exhibition in dramatic form, of any scene or character representing or imitating the figures known as "Mutt and Jeff." The plaintiff complained of a performance last December at the Empire Theatre, London, of the Red Mill, which was produced by the defendants Pollock and Ceballos. His Lordship granted an injunction against Pollock and Ceballos and ordered them to pay the costs. By consent an injunction was granted against Sir Alfred Butt and Mr. Barrett, but without damages or costs.

Winnipeg Free Press Delivery

The Winnipeg *Free Press* has concluded an interesting contest, participated in by its carrier boys, as a result of which 22 of them are to take a trip to the coast and points between, extending from July 6 to 24.

The *Free Press* is now delivered daily to more than 35,000 Winnipeg homes, and the paper pays tribute to its carrier boys when it says that complaints about poor delivery do not amount to five per day. The *Free Press* has adopted the plan of selling papers direct to the boys, depending on them to make collections from their customers.

Real Meaning of "Two Bones"

One of the latest additions to the composing-room force of the *Press* of Bristol, Connecticut, is "Teddy," the Boston bulldog owned by Frank T. Chapin, linotype operator.

When machine copy ran out one morning not so long ago, Chapin turned away from his keyboard and spoke to the dog that had insisted on accompanying him to work : "Teddy, go downstairs and bring us up some copy."

To the surprise of many of the composing-room workers, the dog got onto his feet and trotted downstairs. He entered the editorial room and gave a loud bark. One of the staff recognized the dog as belonging to an operator, and instantly surmised what the dog was after. Some copy was placed in the mouth of Teddy, and he trotted back upstairs again.

Several times that day the faithful animal made the copy-carrying trip from the editorial room to the composing-room of the paper, and performed his task with skill and accuracy.

So attached have many of the workers of the paper become to the dog that they have made him an honorary member of the staff at the compensation of two bones a week.

The Winnipeg *Telegram* has a page of business that can be developed in any locality with a little selling behind it. There are eight letters omitted from certain of the ads., and of course the eight letters are tucked away all over the page. In order to find these letters, readers are going to read the ads, and win the prizes offered. Each week these amount to $10.00.

The Country Editor is a Very Poor Merchant
An Analysis of Western Conditions

A T THE annual meeting of the Saskatchewan Branch of
the Canadian Press Association, W. A. Macleod, editor
of Publications, Government of Saskatchewan, presented
a careful analysis of the position of the country editor as follows:—

This convention is dealing with the editor from many points
of view. One speaker has described him as a professional man
who deliberately chooses for his life work a poorly paid and
exacting profession because of the opportunities it offers for
public service. Another has described him as a missionary
laboring diligently in search of disciples and followers. The
reader's opinion of the editor and his work will be given us by a
prominent and discriminating critic. The editor as a community leader and moulder of public opinion will be described by
an authority on the subject, an authority who a few years ago
was just a common or garden variety of country editor and is
now a Cabinet Minister. The editor as the gatherer and distributor of news, a licensed, commercialized community gossip,
will be discussed by one of the ablest news gatherers in our
province, also a man who graduated from the ranks of the
country editor. My task is to deal with the editor as a merchant, his stock in trade consisting of white paper, the bulk
of which he has to sell twice, and whose whole stock must be
turned over 52 times a year.

The general public has no conception of the difficulties which
the country editor must overcome if he is to succeed. First of
all he should be master of at least two trades. He should be a
printer and a pressman. He should have the qualifications of a
good politician, but he should not interest himself too actively
in politics. It is not unreasonable to ask that he should also
know something about the newspaper business and should be
able to write advertisements as well as news and editorials.
The ideal editor on a small town, one-man, country newspaper
should be an expert printer, an A1 pressman, a man with good
judgment and pleasant manners, a clear thinker and a fluent
writer, a keen business man and an all-around good fellow.
It would add to his popularity if he had a private income of his
own so that he would not need to continually pester his subscribers and advertisers for the money they owe him. If
there are any ideal editors present I wish they would hold up
their hands. I would like to meet one.

I regret to report that the editor as a merchant is making a
rather poor fist of it. Many editors in Saskatchewan are making a fair living, but I believe that if they worked as hard in almost any other line of business they would earn more money.
The newspaper problem has been compared to the State of
Vermont, which some native sons described as "The best state
in the union to emigrate from." Some editors are making a
little money out of their job printing plant, out of the insurance business, by selling farm lands, or by farming, but I am
forced to believe that the majority of the editors of the province
are losing money on the newspaper end of the business. If this
is true, and I have gone into the question very thoroughly with
editors from all parts of Saskatchewan, this is a serious state of
affairs. If only a few merchants in the province were able to
make ends meet in their regular line of business, and had to
depend on side lines to keep out of bankruptcy, the Saskatchewan Retail Merchants' Association would unquestionably
decide that the first and most important duty confronting the
association would be to find a remedy for this condition. I am
no. Moses commissioned to lead you to the promised land, flowing with milk and honey; I am more like John the Baptist,
warning you that you are going to get into a peck of trouble if
you do not mend your ways.

Facing a Serious Proposition

The editor's business as a merchant is a very complicated one
indeed. He must first sell his advertising space to the business
men of his community or to national advertisers. He must
then secure these firms the raw material which he has to
manufacture into attractive advertisements, and he must then
sell the completed product to the readers of his community.
While all newspaper publishers have to do this, the editor of a
one-man newspaper has the most difficult task, and it is his

problem that we should consider first. The weekly papers in
our larger towns and cities are facing the same problem of cost
of production, continually advancing much faster than advertising rates or subscription prices, but we cannot cover the entire
field, and the man whose troubles I want you to consider first
is the editor of the one-man paper who collects the news, sets
the type, prints the paper, looks after the subscriptions and the
advertising, looks after the job work, and probably has one or
more side lines which he depends upon to eke out a decent
living. To prove to you that I am not exaggerating the situation I would like to read to you an extract from a recent issue
of a good little country weekly which suspended publication for
three months last winter and threatens to suspend publication
indefinitely unless the people of the community contribute
enough insurance business to give the editor a living income.

"We have stated before," this announcement reads,
"that it is impossible to publish a paper here without additional income, and through insurance is one way you can
be sure of having a paper here in the future. Every one in
the district, and especially the farmers, missed the paper for
the three months it was not published, and nearly all
were emphatic in asking for it again. The business men
cannot alone afford to support the paper, and it is up to
the farmers to do their share."

Figures that Bespeak Starvation

Another bright little weekly in a recent issue asks: "Do the
people of this community desire the continued publication of a
weekly paper in their village? If not, we would be glad to
know, without prolonging the agony needlessly. If so, are
they prepared to give it the support necessary to keep it up to a
dècent standard?" And a list of the business firms and institutions shows their average weekly outlay for advertising amounts
to only 56½ cents.

Here are some figures given me by different editors, giving the
cost of one week's issue: Wages per hour, at 50c, $18.00;
wages per hour, 30c, $10.80; total $28.80. Depreciation, insurance, taxes, newsprint, ink and printing, $42.55. Profit on
one issue, $3.45.

This editor can certainly escape the charge of being a profiteer.

The next gives the cost of one issue of one of our best country
papers, an eight-page home print. This paper reports a fair
profit of about $100.00 a month for the business, which you
will agree is considerably above the average for the publishers
of the province. The total cost for each issue was apportioned as
follows: Wages at $42.00 per week, $70. Stock, depreciation,
ink, heat and light; power, insurance, taxes, overhead expenses,
postage, collecting, $23.20. Total $93.20.

The following figures are for a six-column, eight-page paper,
four pages ready-print. These figures are a little high, as they
are allowing a salary of $40 per week to the two partners in the
business and this includes the job business as well. Fair
wages is all this firm apparently looks for, and they wisely made
sure of that first. Salaries at $40 each per week, $80.00;
newsprint, taxes, and insurance, depreciation on plant and
building, gasoline, freight, express, electric lights and other
incidentals, $38.00. Total weekly cost, including job printing,
(seven columns, ten pages), $118.00.

Another paper gives a total business for the year of $5,521.03,
$2,222.11 being general job printing; $2,879.57 advertising;
$419.35 subscriptions. This is an exceptionally well-edited
newspaper and owing to bad crops the subscription figures
for the last year are much lower than they would be for average
years. The total expenses were $5,357.65, leaving a net profit
of $163 38.

"Yearly contract display advertising, being the backbone,
the skeleton support of the business, if I may so term it, can be
sold at approximately cost," the editor writes. 'It enables thé
newspaper to stay on the ground so as to be in a position to
serve transient advertiser in case of need.

"Beginning Jan. 1st, 1920, we therefore set our contract rate
at 25c per inch. No new contracts will be made on the old
basis, but present ones will be carried out at the 20c signed for."

Another editor who publishes a five-column, eight-page newspaper has even a harder row to hoe, as his total income for the year for advertising and subscriptions is estimated at $1,650 and his expense at $2,433, so that his newspaper costs him $783.60 a year instead of earning him a profit, a weekly loss of $16.21. I am glad to say that this editor has made a radical revision upward of his rates and is getting away with it successfully.

Put Paper Through as a Job

I think that we should look upon the advertising end of the editor's business as entirely separate from his job printing business, and look upon the paper as just a job which should be charged for like any other job, and should not be printed for less than it costs, any more than the publisher would accept any other job to be turned out at a loss. Due allowance should be made for the job printing which the newspaper brings in, although this item is often overestimated. And if the editor thinks that his paper brings him in much job printing, I think he should take more pains than he does in advertising the job printing side of his business.

Why is it that the newspaper is so often the spoiled child of the printing business, gobbling down his full share of the porridge, then sticking his spoon into the job printing dish, while the editor pretends to overlook the fact that this greedy, perpetually hungry infant is gradually starving to death the patient, industrious, uncomplaining job printing member of the family? Perhaps it is because most of you are editors not for any financial rewards in the business but because you love the work and you are too proud to complain. But I think that this independence and this contempt for filthy lucre may be carried too far, and may seriously hamper you in your work. Take the public into your confidence. Tell them you are losing money on your papers, and why. I hope that this round table conference will prove a good old-fashioned experience meeting where everybody confesses his sins and promises to reform. Tell the facts to your readers and your advertisers. You can always trust the people, if they thoroughly understand the situation, to give everybody concerned a square deal.

Lack of Capital Keeps Them Down

Most of the grief in the newspaper business arises from the fact that only a few papers are able to come into the field well equipped with capital and with subscribers before they have to think of advertising. The *Grain Growers' Guide* is one of the fortunate few in this class, but the *Grain Growers' Guide* lost $60,000 in six years before it began to break even, to say nothing of making money. There are not many editors in this province who had $60,000 cash as a reserve to assist them in establishing their paper. If one of us ever got hold of such a sum, I am afraid we would be like the Irishman who landed in the Klondike during the gold rush without a cent and was told that no one ought to go there without at least a thousand dollars capital. "If I had a thousand dollars capital, what the divil would I be doin' in the Klondike?" he indignantly demanded.

Perhaps one big source of trouble is that it does not require much capital to start a country weekly, but it requires considerable to keep it going. The leading business men in a town decide that they must have a newspaper, and they capture an editor and promise him support. There are a few who do not, but he thinks they will come around. They never do come round, by the way; they are a thorn in his side as long as he is in the town until they go bust, partly because they do not advertise and partly in answer to his fervent prayers. But he generally starts in with his paper full of advertisements, with the fairest prospects, in the most promising centre in the whole province as he tells in his first editorial, but somehow or another he does not seem to prosper. Why is this thus?

It is partly his own fault and partly the fault of the business men of the town, more especially that obstinate, unprogressive minority in every town which holds aloof from the whole undertaking, throws cold water on the enterprise, secretly hopes to benefit from having a paper in the town, but embitters the soul of the editor by refusing to advertise.

The editor is to blame because he does not set a proper value on the white space which is his sole stock in trade. For purposes of illustration, let us take a six-column, eight-page paper, four pages, home print. The dailies and the larger weeklies have the same problems and the advertising question is one of the most important they have to face, but it is out of the question for me to attempt to cover the entire field, and we will consider how the average country editor conducts his business as a dealer in advertising and news.

For Sale—40 Feet of White Space

The editor of such a paper as I have described has for sale each week exactly 480 inches, or 40 feet, or 13⅓ yards of white space. Let us look on this space as a white ribbon, 13⅓ yards long, 2¼ inches wide, which is the editor's stock of raw material. It would not be so difficult if he only had to sell this once, but he must first dispose of the white space to the advertiser, then after many weary rounds he collects the copy and manufactures the advertisement, procures and sets up the news, arranges it all the best way he can and sells the completed product to several hundred people in the country, who have all tried to discourage him from starting a newspaper by declaring that "they have more papers now than they can read."

He makes the first mistake, commits his initial financial crime, by selling his white ribbon to the advertiser at too low a price, a price so low in many instances that he has to rob his country customers of several yards of news ribbon which rightfully belongs to them, and which in turn lowers the value of his advertising pages. And hardly any two editors charge the same price for their space. And this is not the worst of it. Instead of using to the best advantage the little ribbon that is left, he gives it away right and left like a drunken sailor. He gives half a yard to a man who does not even subscribe to his paper so that he can vent his spleen against one of the paper's best friends. He gives another half yard to some religious fanatic with a special revelation about the end of the world and some incomprehensible theory of Scripture interpretation. He gives a quarter of a yard apiece to three or four social organization that have beaten him down to cost price on their printing, and he gives a few inches to the churches, and a few inches more perhaps to some article sent him by the Department of Publications at Ottawa or the Bureau of Publications at Regina. If an editor has the space to spare and he considers the articles submitted him of interest and value to his readers, it would be foolish for him to reject them, but his first duty to his readers is to give them the local news. In a country weekly, local news should always have the right of way, provincial news second place. Most people look to their daily papers for the world news and we have in Saskatchewan seven excellent daily newspapers, some of them ranking high among the dailies of the Dominion.

The theory is that the reader is entitled to an even break of fifty-fifty news and advertising, but in actual practice 60 per cent. of advertising and 40 per cent. news is all right, but even on this basis the reader often gets the short end of the stick. If the editor charges 16 cents per inch for his advertising—and many are guilty of selling their advertising space for less—and only six columns of reading matter, this amounts to $5.76 per yard, a total of $57.60 for six yards of advertising. Instead of increasing his rate, the reader is robbed, and the reader consequently gets sore and turns a deaf ear to the editor's timid plea for a continuance of his custom.

I may be mistaken in believing that if the business men of our small towns realized how very little revenue the editor received from his newspaper business, they would be willing to co-operate in building up a bigger, better and more prosperous paper, but the number of successful country weeklies, some of the best and most prosperous in some of our smaller towns, proves my contention.

A Large List of Poor Advertisers

The business man is often to blame, because only a small proportion of our country merchants are good advertisers, and in every town there are business men who should realize that it is a good thing for the town to have a newspaper and that they benefit indirectly from having a paper published in their town, but contribute nothing to its support.

In stating that only a few country merchants are good advertisers, I did not mean that they did not pay for advertising. Some of the men who are good friends of the editor and pay him a large sum annually for advertising space, insult his paper by filling up their white space with something like: "Watch this space next week," which is treating the reader of the paper in the same manner as a minister would treat his parishioners if he got up one Sunday in the pulpit and told the congregation he had forgotten to prepare any sermon this week but perhaps if they came next Sunday he might feel more inclined to preach. Do you think many would come the next week? Week after week some merchants run the same stale, dry list of the goods they have for sale, without any attempt to attract the reader's attention or arouse his interest, and then when the editor tries to persuade them to run more up-to-date advertisements, they tell him they are not very firm believers in advertising anyway, but they think he is a pretty good scout, and just run the same thing again this week and they will have the copy for a new ad. ready for next week. Sometimes the editor falls down when entrusted with making up a convincing and satisfactory advertisement, as he may not get the merchant's point of view, or feature the goods which the merchant wants to get rid of, but in most cases the fault lies with the merchant. The Saskatchewan Retail Merchants' Association is doing splendid work along this line by organizing an advertising department in. charge of an expert with practical experience, to assist retail merchants in building up their business by the most up-to-date methods of advertising.

A Plea for Government Notices

I would like to speak briefly about Government advertising. Several editors have written me that they thought both the Dominion Government and the Provincial Government should pay at a rate of so much per line for all the news articles sent out by the Publications Branch or various departments of both Governments. If you give this a little consideration, you will admit that it would be a very dangerous policy. If the editor has sufficient space and believes some of these articles sent him would be of interest and value to his readers, it is good business to publish them. If his columns are full of local news and advertising, it is good business to drop these articles in his capacious. waste paper basket unless the matter is of sufficient . value to file for future reference. But if Governments began to pay advertising rates for straight reading matter, it would be an exceedingly bad thing for both the newspapers and the Governments practising this policy, as any benefit received by the paper from increased revenue would be more than offset by the loss of influence which would inevitably result from injurious suspicions that the papers had been bought up by the Governments, and the Governments would also suffer from the suspicion that they had something to conceal, and had bought up the newspapers to prevent their misdeeds becoming known to the public.

· Both the Dominion Government and your Provincial Government are beginning to use the advertising columns of the newspapers from a purely business standpoint, at a fair commercial rate, and this development of advertising is bound to continue. As far as Saskatchewan is concerned, the old patronage idea in giving out advertising does not exist, and where an advertisement appears in one paper in a town or city it appears in all papers where more than one paper is published.

The value of newspaper advertising was brought home to the Governments of all English-speaking countries during the war as never before, and the success of the Victory Loans and the various patriotic drives in Canada were due very largely to a liberal use of newspaper advertising and the generous co-operation of the editors of Canada, who gave liberally of their time and their space to every public cause.

Hon. S. J. Latta, my minister, has been going over our advertising rates, and believes, as many of you do, that it is time to revise upward the rate for both display advertisements and legal and official Government advertisements. If you have no objections, they will be revised. We can go into this more fully later on.

I hope that the discussion will bring out some practical suggestions which will result in some definite action to put this whole advertising question on a more satisfactory basis. For legal and official advertising as well as display advertising, I believe that this convention should endorse adopting the agate measurement of 14 lines to the inch as the basis of measurement, as this agate line basis has been adopted by all the advertising agencies in Canada, by nearly all the daily newspapers and most of the larger weeklies. I would strongly suggest the framing up of a model and uniform rate card by this convention, which should be submitted to all the publishers of the province and would serve the same purpose as the Winnipeg price list, which may not be followed by the job printer, but gives him a

good sound basis on which to do his figuring. I will read you the following extracts from a letter I received last week which puts the matter very clearly:

Should Have an Understanding

"In regard to advertising rates, I do hope something may come of your address on this subject and the discussion which may follow. The best way to solve it would be for the rural newspaper men form their schedule of advertising rates. And this was never so noticeable, perhaps, as just now, with the continued rise in costs. Newspapers, like other businesses, require to adjust their rates. How do we find our fellow newspapermen making this adjustment? In most cases we believe display ad. prices have been increased, but not in many cases in proportion to the rise in costs. However, we leave the display ads. and come to the classified ads., and we find more than fifty per cent. of the newspapers accepting classified ads. at 50c for first insertion and 25c for subsequent insertions — the same rate charged in 1914 — and a most unfair way to sell space — the man who uses a two or three line space is charged the same as a man who uses six or seven lines. In other words the small space user pays the piper for the bigger advertiser. Again, the commercial reader—an incident. Last week or two weeks ago the manager for a Ladies' Orchestra on tour asked us why we charged 12c per line for a commercial reader that he had inserted in all other papers at 10c per line? Our answer was that our pre-war price was 10c per line and that now it was 12c per line—and it ought to be 18c or 20c—else we were getting too much in pre-war times at 10c.

"A few weeks ago the Dominion Government sent us plate matter advertising in regard to the income tax telling us to charge them 16c per inch. We sent it back and told them we could not insert except at our quoted rates. · In the .meantime, however, we got in touch with two of our fellow newspaper men, with circulations about the same as our paper, we would judge, and we found that these advertisers dictated to them the rates that they should charge. There is surely lots of room to get together in regard to advertising rates. It is a knock on our trade and ability as managing newspapermen to continue to operate under such varied advertising rates. There can be some uniformity in rates, surely."

The editor as a merchant should have a dead line below which he will not publish any advertising and this dead line should be the lowest figure at which he can publish the advertisement at a profit. He should no more sell his advertising space below cost than a grocer should be expected to sell his sugar, tea or flour below cost. That ribbon of white space which is his stock in trade should no more be handed out to all comers—and these are ten begging for every inch of space he has to give away—than a dry goods merchant should sell his ribbons below the cost of production or give away yards of his stock to any person bold enough to ask for it. First, he should ascertain exactly what the selling price of his space should be and having this figure he should stick to his guns, and if he finds that he cannot publish his paper at a profit he should cease to publish it.

I would suggest that a committee of the best men in your association should be appointed to take up this whole question of advertising and prepare a model rate card to be submitted for adoption to all the papers of the Province, and that this Saskatchewan Branch of the Canadian Press Association thus take the lead in a reform which will be of service not only to the press of Saskatchewan but to the press of the entire Dominion.

The Saskatoon *Star* is getting advertising on the appearance of a Miss Raffles. Stores are offering special prizes should the mysterious young lady be found in their premises. But listen what must be done to identify the young lady:

"You must approach her in one of these stores, place your right hand on her left shoulder and say: "You are the *Daily Star's* Mysterious Miss Raffles who rides in an Overland car and who will see every performance of Khaym at the Empire theatre." Then you must take your captive to the office of the Empire where Mr. George Stuart will tell you whether or not you have the right Miss Raffles."

If a man were to start singing that song to the wrong woman she'd have time to go home and get her husband and an axe before he got through.

The Passing of Senator William Dennis

Halifax Publisher Dies Following Operation

THE death occurred of Hon. William Dennis, of Halifax, at the Massachusetts General Hospital, Boston. Senator Dennis, on the advice of specialists, had gone from Ottawa for an operation, which was performed on Friday. It was at first thought that the operation had been successful. Senator Dennis was 64 years old. He was born in Cornwall, England. He came to Canada and had been actively identified with the conduct of the Halifax *Herald* and the *Evening Mail* since the establishment of these papers. He was one of the best-known and most successful of Canadian newspapermen. A Conservative in politics, he conducted his paper in outspoken and independent lines. Though for years a victim of physical infirmities, Senator Dennis always exhibited a buoyancy and

SENATOR WILLIAM DENNIS

optimism that gave no hint to the outside world of the pain he suffered. The widow, one son and four daughters survive.

Hon. Arthur Meighen expressed deep regret on being informed of the death of Senator William Dennis at Boston.

The Prime Minister paid the following tribute to the deceased member of the Upper House: "I had known that Senator Dennis was to undergo a dangerous ordeal, and I am much distressed at its fatal termination. For many long years the Senator had endured recurrent intense suffering, but no physical handicap could dampen his courage or restrain his indomitable spirit. Indeed, his business enterprise seemed to increase as his afflictions multiplied. His life, through these latter years, was as fine an example of pluck as I have ever witnessed. Senator Dennis was a real man and a true friend, and he will be mourned by thousands."

An editorial from the Halifax *Herald* has the following reference to the late Senator:

"This morning there is imposed upon the Halifax *Herald* the duty of announcing the death of its revered chief, Senator William Dennis. The sad event occurred yesterday afternoon at the Massachusetts General Hospital, Boston. On Friday he underwent an operation which at first gave promise of being successful, but yesterday his condition became dangerous and the end came with startling suddenness.

He was 64 years of age. Born in Cornwall, England, on March 4th, 1856, he came to Nova Scotia when he was a lad, without a dollar, and by his own dynamic force advanced himself step by step from the position of newsboy to the proprietorship of the Halifax *Herald*, the *Evening Mail* and the *Sunday Leader.*

As he was himself proud to say he was "46 years in the public service," and the impress which he made on the public mind and heart will not soon be effaced.

His temperament was ever optimistic; his heart radiated kindness. In his long and testing career he was bound at times to arouse criticism and make enemies, but he never made response in the kind; he never permitted personal enmity to influence his attitude either in private or public life.

His business career was a wonderful march onward and upward. Leaving school at the early age of eleven years, he undertook, one year later, the responsibilities of a travelling salesman for an uncle's firm, the great business house of Parnell Brothers, of Bristol, but soon after that hearing of Canada, and believing that this country would enable him to work out the ambitious career which already he was mapping out for himself, he crossed the ocean and soon after his arrival in Nova Scotia he laid the foundation-stones of success by becoming a successful newsboy.

From that lowly beginning his career was one of conscientious devotion to tireless duty, always forward and upwards towards the goal of success which he fairly won.

From newsboy to reporter, from reporter to editor, from editor to manager, and from manager to owner of the Halifax *Herald*, were sure and certain results of his forceful character. Then the *Evening Mail* was established and the *Sunday Leader*, an acknowledged triumph in the publishing art, was recently added to his business victories. In addition to these great and successful undertakings he established the Royal Print, and Litho Limited, and the Dennis Realty Corporation, and was interested in many other useful and successful business ventures in the city of Halifax. Instead of making his investments outside of Halifax he devoted all of his means, as well as his energy, to the building up of his adopted city. His splendid pluck and his inflexible determination were proved when the disastrous fire of 1911 destroyed the newspaper building and plant at the corner of Granville and George streets. He was in Ottawa. It was midwinter. Immediately the news reached him he was on his way to Nova Scotia, and on his arrival here his plans were at once matured for the erection of the Dennis Building on the burned site; and the modern newspaper building plant on Argyle street, from which the *Herald*, *Mail* and *Leader* are now issued, and where the Royal Print and Litho. Ltd. is also housed."

Guess This Makes 53 Years

Grandview, Man.,
June 28th, 1920.

Publishers *Printer and Publisher*,
Toronto, Canada.

Gentlemen:—

In forwarding your renewal subscription to your valued publication, allow me to say it has ever been appreciated for its sterling worth, by not only myself, but every workman in my employ. The good pointers we have received through its columns have been worth many times its cost, and I trust it may continue to improve and prosper.

I notice from time to time the many "deans" of the printing art mentioned in your columns—many of whom I knew personally in the years that have passed into the discard. Might just mention that your humble servant is not one of the youngest of them—having commenced in the Fergus, Ont., *News-Record*, under J. and R. Craig, on the 1st day of April, 1867—and have been continuously at it ever since.

Yours truly,

A. G. GRAHAM.

Watching the Summer and Winter Rollers

It Pays to Give Heed to This Matter

THE question of the use of winter and summer rollers throughout the printing industry is one which has been reviewed, but which has not as yet been by any means exhausted or considered over seriously by one of the largest sections of the trade.

The printing trade can for this subject be divided into two classes; the city and rural. The city printer is running his presses to capacity day and night and his returns greatly depend on the amount he can get out of a press. Any stoppages during a run are most costly and it has been realised that every possible precaution must be taken, and absolutely no loophole, left for mechanical errors to occur.

This also applies to the rural printer, though his business differs in the respect that his presses have not to withstand the continuous strain imposed on those of the city printer.

Do Not Change Rollers

It has been a practice amongst a large percentage of rural printers to run their rollers to the limit, and only when an accident occurs, such as melting, to take any action. This invariably takes the form of rushing the damaged article to the roller-maker with the request that it be returned the same day or earlier if possible

As a result, most large concerns now keep a number of spare rollers and pay the greatest attention to the way they are affected by temperatures. This has resulted in the adoption of what are termed winter and summer rollers.

Summer rollers are "short-lived" because they are made as hard and tough as possible so as to withstand the heat, consistent with the method of manufacture.

To a great extent it is not the actual temperature which affects the rollers, but the friction they undergo, which is materially affected by the amount of "tack" in the ink and the adjustment and type of drive used for the rollers on the particular type of press in use.

Keeping Them Cool

Many systems have been tried for the cooling of rollers, such as having hollow cores and running water through; but this defeated its own purpose, for the "Sweating" of the metal where the composition joins the core soon "rotted" it to such an extent that it caused the composition to leave the core in which case "the remedy was worse than the disease."

Another more feasible system which has been to some extent successful, is that of placing a mechanical attachment for a fan on the drive side of a cylinder press, thus keeping a steady stream of cool air flowing on the rollers.

When all points have been considered the only way to be absolutely certain of uninterrupted output is to keep duplicate rollers. Storage is one of the most important points in the care of rollers and varies with the locality of the business, position of the presses and type of building used.

Get Out of the Cellar

Rollers should not be stored in a basement, as dampness is their worst enemy and it is difficult to guarantee perfect dryness in variable climate.

For the sake of saving labor alone, rollers should be stored in racks, in or as near the press room as possible, where they will be easily accessible, and in an even temperature to that in which they will be eventually required for use.

When rollers are taken off a press over hot, care should be taken not to cool them standing on end or they will become pear-shaped, also they should not be left resting in a horizontal position or they are apt to become oval.

If possible they should be kept revolving free of friction till cool enough to keep their shape.

It has often been asked, when rollers become too hot during a long run in Summer, what is the best course to take? The only really satisfactory course is to find another set and treat the ones removed as outlined above.

The time over which summer rollers are used is, roughly, from May to October according to the locality and average temperature for the year.

The next and most important point in the greater efficiency and cutting of costs which can be attained if there is sympathetic co-operation between printers and the ink and roller manufacturers.

If printers lay their troubles before the ink and roller makers and give them every opportunity to study the conditions under which their product will have to work they should receive goods suitable in every way to all the requirements of season or locality.

More can be done towards lengthening the life of rollers by close co-operation of this kind, than by hasty decisions and changing from one brand to another. Both printers and roller and ink manufacturers will do well to realize that they will benefit materially if the above feeling existed; the printers by the added efficiency of their press service and the length in the life of their rollers; the ink and roller makers by the increased business due to their reputation for reliability and good service and the minimum of stoppages and mechanical defects while using their products.

No Blanket Form of Goodness

Rollers may be advertised which are reputed to be good for an indefinite period regardless of climatic or other conditions but I am assured by one of the greatest experts in Canada on the ink and roller question that this is impossible, and that any firm advertising such a product is not to be relied upon.

Here are a list of points about rollers which will bear attention though many readers may be thoroughly conversant with the ground covered.

1. Rollers are much more apt to become hot and deteriorate at night than during the day; as the moisture hangs in the air, not being absorbed by the heat of the sun.

2. A hot moist day is more injurious to rollers than a hot sunny day for the same reason.

3. All colored inks are more injurious to the life of a roller than blacks because of the nature of the ingredients: the average colored inks being "ground" in litho (linseed) varnishes while most black inks are "ground" in rosin and paraffin oils, which contain less "tack," hence less friction, which means added life to the roller, as the greatest percentage of heat is derived from the friction they undergo in use.

4. The following should not be used as washes:—Lye, benzine, patent washes or turpentine as the latter is a drier and all the above compounds impoverish the face of rollers. Coal oil is the best washer for general use.

5. Keep your rollers in a steady temperature as near the average kept in the pressroom as possible.

6. Set your rollers lightly and to the "touch," not to a "flat," and be sure to re-set with varying temperatures as they shrink in the cold and fail to make efficient contact; they swell during heat which causes undue friction and destructive wear and tear.

7. If a roller does melt and scatters all over the other rollers, it can be removed quickly by taking a sheet of paper and placing it around the roller and then stripping same carefully.

It cannot be borne out strongly enough the benefit which will accrue to the trade by giving consideration to the added efficiency which will be gained by sympathetic co-operation between printers and the ink and roller manufacturers. The treating of the ink and roller makers as physicians and discussing ailments with them will be well repaid, as far as the sake of their reputation and continued business; they will in nearly all cases meet the printer half way or more. When one remembers that there are specialists in every branch of life it will be obvious that after having exhausted one's own resources one must turn for help to the specialists, who are the ink and roller manufacturers in the printers case: and they out of a lifetime's experience will advise to the added efficiency and repayment of the printing industry.

Printer & Publisher

. · Published on the Twelfth of Each Month.

H. D. TRESIDDER　-　-　-　- 　Business Manager. .
A. R. KENNEDY　-　-　-　-　-　- 　Editor.

SUBSCRIPTION PRICE—Canada, Great Britain, South Africa and the West Indies, $3 a year; United States, $3.50 a year; other countries, $4 a year. Single copies, 30 cents. Invariably in advance.

PUBLISHED BY

THE MACLEAN PUBLISHING CO.

Established 1887　　　　　　　　　　　　　Limited

JOHN BAYNE MACLEAN　-　-　- 　President.
H. T. HUNTER　-　-　-　-　-　- 　Vice-President.
H. V. TYRRELL　-　-　-　- 　General Manager.
T. B. COSTAIN　-　-　- 　General Managing Editor.

Head Office, 143-153 University Avenue　-　TORONTO, CANADA
Cable Address Macpubco, Toronto; Atabek, London, Eng.
Also at Montreal, Winnipeg, New York, Chicago, Boston, London, England.
Application for A.B.C. Audit.

Vol. 29　　　　　TORONTO, JULY, 1920　　　　　No. 7

CONTENTS

He's Only a Printer

DID you ever hear the phrase, "He's only a printer?" It used to be quite a common phrase, and men at the trade did little or nothing to kill it off.

The existence of that phrase, and of the atmosphere that made it possible for that phrase to live, rested largely with the printers themselves.

And so it was that many people did not care to have their boys learn the printing trade. They did not believe there was much of a future to it. They knew there was a certain amount of steady work, but they wanted to put their boys into something that had a promise and a chance in it.

Well, there is a chance in almost any calling, but said chance does not make a habit of coming around and pulling people out of bed.

We have in mind a case this week. A young man was a printer, and a good one, and he knew pretty much all that was to be known about press work. He could have stayed at his trade, and made a fair living, but he would have been building up for someone else, and at best would have been possessor of nothing much more than a job.

He started with a partner in business. They were both workers, and good planners. The first year they did about ten or twelve thousand dollars business; the second year this went up to twenty-four; the third year the mark went up to some thirty-three thousand, while this year it looks as though this firm would do fifty thousand, and the partners are making at least three times as much as they ever would on wages.

This case is stated to show what has been done, and to bring to the attention of printers that there are opportunities in the trade to advance and go ahead, just the same as there are in other lines of business.

"Only a printer." Yes, but able to build up a business in three years that pays him·between seven and eight thousand dollars a year.

"Only a printer." Yes, but able to look his banker square in the face, knowing that he is under no obligation to him.

"Only a printer." Yes, but building up a business, helping it grow to larger proportions year after year, putting more in and taking more out.

"Only a printer." Yes, but able to hold his'customers by the quality of work turned out, and find that his trade keeps on coming back to him.

Now that's only one case. There are others, lots of them, in newspapers and job offices, where printers have gone in and gone ahead. It may be reaching a little out of the territory, but it does no harm to remember that both the Democratic and the Republican nominees for President of United States served their time at the case, and that they have been on speaking terms with the pica case, and know enough not to throw the three-nick brevier in the two-nick case.

In the light of some of these accomplishments, the term "only a printer," loses a great deal that has been attached to it in the way of designating the commonplace and the ordinary.

The whole business is on the upgrade now, and it ought to be kept headed steadily in that direction.

Mr. Burgoyne and His Hobby .

A YEAR ago Mr. W. F. Burgoyne, of the St. Catharines Standard, placed $1,000 at the disposal of the Parks Board of his city on the understanding that it be devoted to starting a rose garden in one of the city parks. This year the garden is in existence and also in bloom. Mr. Burgoyne is putting in some more funds to carry the beautification scheme still farther. Recently a move has been made to take an unsightly place and make it worthy of the name "Oakhill" park. Mr. Burgoyne's daughter is also very much interested in this matter, and local gossip has it that Standard reporters receive instructions to decorate the front page of the Standard with notices about band concerts, shrub and bulb givers, etc., and that there is no option in the matter of dodging the issue. In fact a recent number of the Standard which came to Printer and Publisher had some five items concerning this particular public fix-it-up idea. Mr. Burgoyne and his friends in this work—and they all seem to be friends in St. Catharines—are accomplishing much. The idea is apparently contagious, for when a representative of Printer and Publisher took a walk around the city recently with Mr. Burgoyne, they came upon one of the citizens climbing a tree to remove a limb that had ceased to be a thing of beauty, and the Chief of the Fire Department was also on hand looking for a chance to squirt water on some new shrubbery. The Chief and his brave men may put out a few fires on the side, but the fix-it-up idea has him by the buttonhole.

Mr. Burgoyne has the community idea, and he is passing it along to a lot of other people.

Pass the Technical Papers Along

ONE Ontario publisher writes telling of the use he makes of the articles that interest him in Printer and Publisher and other papers that come to his office regarding printing and publishing. When he reads the paper, he makes note of the contents. When he comes to something that he thinks will interest his pressman, or his compositors or any of his staff, he makes a note of it and passes the paper along. Not only does he pass it along, but makes it a point to see that the articles are read.

One office that came to our attention made it a point to give the mechanical force time in the office hours to read certain articles in this paper that dealt with typography and the display ing of advertising and job matter. The office considered that they were not losing anything by this, but rather were they gaining. Their compositors would have ideas that had been passed on by good workmen in other good shops, and in that way would be more valuable.

The more your staff read about the business the better for them. Unfortunately there are offices, and quite a number of them, where papers such as Printer and Publisher are read in the front office and filed away there. On the other hand there are others where the paper is well thumb-marked before it is filed away. Thumb marks can be taken as evidence that the office is getting its money's worth out of the subscription. If you want to get good work, and more of it, and if you want ·your staff ·to be enthusiastic over their work, get them interested, help them to get a wider viewpoint, and you will find its pays over and over.

REVIEW OF JOB SPECIMENS

If You Want An Opinion On
Your Work, Send It In

THE Cliffe Printing Co., Sault Ste. Marie, Ont., forward a number of specimens from their job department. One of them is a mining company's report, done on twin slugs, and another book is a catalogue of the Espanola Library Association. The cover design of both jobs are in good taste, the compositor having stayed with a series pretty well all the way through. The cover stock used is a little hard to work on with black ink. It is about a Paynes Grey. A dedication service programme is very well done, red and blue being used on white stock and tied with blue. We are reproducing Figure B, another job sent from the same office, viz., a menu card. The original of this is done in blue and orange. In making up this cover design it should be remembered that the work is being done in a rectangular shaped space, no matter whether a border is used or not to indicate this. When working in this shape it is well to bear in mind that everything must conform to the general idea of giving length, rather than width to the effect. There are three general forms that the compositor can feel quite safe in following, viz., the square rectangle, and the pyramid. Of course there are numerous other plans and forms, but in a broad way it is safe to make your job, before you start to work,

SUCCESS

by

Frederick W. Taylor

Figure A

The press work on the card, as on the other jobs, is good, a nice clean impression being registered. To further illustrate the point in the form treatment of this job, we use two lay-out plans. Fig. 1 is the well-known rectangle, with the mistake made of introducing a breadth treatment. This might yet be saved by the use of a triangle treatment below to pull it down a bit. Figure 2 shows the same rectangle with the proper lay-out to conform to the lines of the design. The same rules apply to the menu card cover under discussion. In our reset Figure C care has been taken to avoid anything that would take up much time, so that it is quite possible to get it out without gouging the cost sheet. If any of the other offices have any idea of how it can be improved, let us have a set-up. If color were used in the reset the secondary color would be put on the ornament under the word "Menu" and the two cap "Cs" in City and Cafe.

FIGURE A—The reproduction of this cover gives the border a trifle heavier than the original, and in that way detracts from its good appearance. The original was in black and red on buff linen-finished Bristol, the rule and little ornament being done in red. The book was about a third larger than shown in our reproduction. One of its strong points has been the willingness of the compositor to let the job alone after he had made a good thing out of it. In less competent hands there might have been a tendency or desire to pitchfork something into the white space at the bottom, which would have been a dangerous, if not disastrous thing to do. Good display really consists of balance and design.

conform to one of these, or a combination of them, but be careful of the combination, for it is in the pyramid idea that the safest combination can be worked with the others. In this menu card the mistake is made of not keeping carefully to the front the idea that the design is a rectangle, and needs length treatment. The use of the frame around the word "Menu" tends to give an unnecessary and unwelcome breadth that is quite foreign to the rectangle treatment, and the top part is too scattered to be said to follow any particular lines. The introduction of Della Robia series for the words "Open Day and Night" is not desirable.

FIGURE F—The office of the Cabri *Clarion* turns out good, clean work, and that same office is interested in getting good ideas. In a recent letter to *Printer and Publisher* the question is

Fig. 1

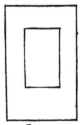

Fig. 2

put if we can suggest an improvement in their letterhead. We are not, in this issue, making any suggestions, but simply reproducing the letterhead as it appears. The office uses yellow stationery done in black. *Printer and Publisher* would like to be able to send out to Cabri a number of good suggestions regarding their letterhead. Why not take a little time off and draft a design and then set it, or have it set? *Printer and Publisher* would be pleased to get a number of these resets. Get interested in this class of work, and you will increase your circle of friends. If you are a good printer, this is a good way to let the printing trade know it.

FIGURE G—The particular reason for using this letterhead, the original of which is embossed, black on a good white stock, is to show a rather unusual arrangement of the wording at the left-hand side. It is easy enough to put up a good layout for the firm's name and address, but what to do with all the little disjointed words that must be carried—that's the real problem. Some compositors may be inclined to disagree with the bunching of the reading matter at the left-hand side, as is done in this case, but there is really much to commend the arrangement. The whole announcement is grouped in a plain, readable style, instead of being strewn or dropped in sections.

THE demand for dry colors in inks at the present time is good in most lines, and in some it is not possible to place orders, according to all reports, for deliveries nearer than fall. In some instances, it is difficult to buy anything to be delivered before next year. There seems to be a good demand for all of the standard manufactured colors, such as iron blues, chrome green, chrome yellow and para red.

Producers of ultramarine blues are said to be booked up for months ahead. The demand for blacks continues to be good. Prices are said to be holding steady and there seems to be little reason to change them at the present time. They continue to be high, however, and there are slim prospects of much cutting coming in the near future. Production costs are still advancing and no one in the trade ventures to make any predictions as to when they will start to take a drop.

It is believed, however, that should a large amount of German blues be dropped on market, domestic producers might be forced to cut to meet the competition, but there has been nothing in the importations yet to cause any uneasiness.

THE March meeting of the Milwaukee Typothetae was called to hear reports from the committees working on the printing survey of that city.

There was a record attendance of about 150, and the interest was intense, especially when Secretary W. G. Penhallow sprung on them a tabulated report of 42 estimates which he had secured from Milwaukee printers upon a set of three ordinary commercial jobs, giving the figures in detail of individual plants, but mercifully designating them by number, as there was in some instances 50 per cent. variation in price for the same job by members, as well as outsiders, or from $11.50 to $5.75.

Mr. Herman Beyer told in no uncertain way of his conversion to the Standard Cost System and the benefits and surprises it had brought him.

Mr. Chas. H. Hayward spoke for the new Trade Composition Branch and of the metal troubles of the composition houses and asked for closer co-operation.

A most important subject not only a live one but one affecting the very life of the printing business—was the report of the apprenticeship committee. They announced that the Boy's Technical High School had opened evening classes in printing, with a curriculum covering English, hand composition, imposition, machine composition, presswork, bookkeeping, estimating and cost finding. The committee also reported that they were canvassing the seventh and eighth grades for students in printing and had prepared a booklet setting forth the advantage of printing as a profession for distribution to select boys.

The Milwaukee Typothetae are conducting cost finding classes three evenings a week and two estimate class are forming, but they fully realize the present menace to the craft in the lack of desirable apprentices.

"RED letter" days on the Printing Industry Calendar this year are September 13-15, when the 34th annual convention of the United Typothetae of America will be held at St. Louis. Printers from far and wide sense the unusual in this meeting. Discussions of vast importance to the industry will come up and be disposed of, and any moves made and seconded by members of this gigantic international printers' association are bound to impress and be followed by every printer in the world. The program is being built around three absorbing subjects—the industrial situation, the paper situation and the Typothetae itself. Indications are that the attendance will be larger than at any previous convention. Last year it reached nearly twelve hundred.

THE
CITY CAFE

531 Queen St., E.   Phone 270
Sault Ste. Marie, Ont.

MENU

Open Day
and Night

We are not responsible for hats, umbrellas, or coats, left on the premises.

Figure B.

AN echo of the suspension two months ago of the *Evening Journal*, comes in the form of a writ in the Superior Court, issued by George M. Elson against the assignee, claiming $7,000. Elson claims he paid this sum for his brother, John M. Elson, the publisher of the paper, for wages and small sums, covering a period of several years. There are 123 items. The trustees of the estate after the assignment threw George Elson's claim out. Efforts are being made to start the *Journal* under a new name and by a new company, outside capital being interested.

AT a meeting of the Board of Directors of the Intertype Corporation, held Tuesday June 22, Harry G. Willinus was elected Assistant Secretary and Hammond Hardy was elected Assistant Treasurer.

J. J. HUNTER, editor of the Kincardine *Reporter*, visited this locality, and among other friends the editor of the *Free Press*. Last week in his paper had the following interesting article:—

"Its a long way back to the days when William Lyon Mackenzie published a paper in LittleYork, now Toronto. Yet there remains in excellent preservation at the present time the Washington Press upon which Mackenzie's paper was printed. Last week the editor of the *Reporter* had the pleasure of examining this press in the office of Mr. H. J. Pettypiece, Ex-M.P.P., proprietor of the Forest *Free Press*. The number of the press is 2334 and was built by R. H. Hoe & Co. During the troublesome times when Mr Mackenzie's printing office was raided, this press among other material was dumped into Toronto bay. Later it was recovered, and it was taken to Western Ontario, first to Parkhill, by the late Wallace Graham. In 1879 it was taken to Forest when the *Free Press* was established. Mr. Pettypiece's business is long past the days of the Washington press, but he values the old relic highly on account of its historic connection. It is also exceedingly useful around a printing office. Its history was compiled by Mr. Graham and the facts verified as far as possible. The Hoe people sent the press to Toronto in 1837 and it was during the rebellion of 1838 that

Mackenzie's office was wrecked. Mr. Pettypiece has been very modest about his possession of this piece of machinery around which historical events loom big. By it, was William Lyon Mackenzie able to place his propaganda before the people and the rebellion, which resulted in better conditions, fomented."—Forest *Free Press*.

S. J. FRAME, secretary-treasurer of the Canadian Paper Box Manufacturers' Association, 24 King Street, West Toronto, has sent a circular to the trade setting forth certain changes in the by-laws of the Association as they affect its claims and objects. These include the following:—

"By mutual co-operation among the members to uphold the standing of the paper box business, by educating the general public to a realization of the usefulness and increasing necessity of the paper box and the extent and size of the paper box industry.

"Raise the standard of general efficiency of those in the business whereby the capital involved shall have a proper return thereon, the management shall be adequately rewarded, the wages paid, and factory conditions shall be such as to attract a good class of labor, and to improve the quality of product turned out.

"Exchange information as to costs and other matters of general interest relating to the paper box business.

"Maintain and continue, by social intercourse, the good feeling at present existing among the trade and those supplying it."

A CHARTER has been granted the Peterborough Paper Box Company, Limited, Canada with a capital of $50,000 and headquarters in this city. Local capital is interested in the new enterprise and a general range of boxes will be turned out.

FIGURE D—This is a good example of a plain, yet dignified bit of stationery for a business where correspondence is carried on with a number of communities, and where the plain announcement of the nature of the firm's activities is all that is required. The original is engraved, black on a good white stock. The placing of the wording is well-balanced, and the fact that the firm name is off-centre adds to rather than detracts from the appearance of the job.

THE

CITY CAFE

531 Queen Street E.—Phone 270

SAULT STE. MARIE, ONT.

Menu

Open Day
and Night

We are not responsible for hats, umbrellas, or coats left on the premises.

Figure C.

Heaton's Agency.
Confidential Correspondents.

PUBLISHERS OF
HEATON'S ANNUAL &c.

32 CHURCH STREET,

Toronto, Canada

IN REPLY PLEASE REFER TO FILE NO.

Figure D.

Royal Print & Litho. Ltd.

PRINTERS   ENGRAVERS
LITHOGRAPHERS   BOOKBINDERS
DESIGNERS   PUBLISHERS
DIE EMBOSSERS   LOOSE LEAF DEVICES

SACKVILLE STREET
Halifax ~ Canada

Figure E.

The Cabri Clarion

THE BEST ADVERTISING MEDIUM ON THE
FAMOUS SWIFT CURRENT-EMPRESS
DIVISION OF THE C.P.R.

ROSS & PENNIE PROPS.

CABRI
SASKATCHEWAN

Figure F.

RIVET SETS
BRIDGE REAMERS   THE STRUCTURAL TOOL CO.
COUNTER SINKS
FLAT BEADED DRILLS   3160 WEST 106TH STREET
CHISEL BLANKS
PUNCHES & DIES   CLEVELAND, OHIO
SPECIAL TOOLS

Figure G.

FIGURE E—This is the letter head used by the Royal Print & Litho. Ltd., Halifax. The unusual feature is the success that has been met with in the grouping of the wording, on both sides of the decorative design in the centre. Were great care not taken with this it would have been an easy matter to add a stiff squareness to the whole design that is avoided in this way. The original is embossed in royal blue on a good white stock. It carries the message of the house very well.

THE PERSONAL SIDE OF IT

 We'd Like To Get Items For
These Columns

Quebec

Local 176, Montreal Typographical Union, will hold their annual picnic at Ste. Anne de Bellevue on August 7. Mr. J. J. Harpell of the Garden City Press has consented to provide equal, if not better, facilities for entertainment than last year.

A deputation composed of Burford Hooke, Regina *Leader*; W. F. Herman, Saskatoon *Star*; Hugh Pette, Moose Jaw *News*, and H. M. Heuston, Prince Albert *Herald*, arrived in Montreal on June 27, to represent the case of the newspapers of Saskatchewan to the Government and paper mill operators and to endeavor to obtain assurance of an adequate and steady supply of newsprint.

Maritimes

R. Drake has joined the writing staff of the *Daily Telegraph*. He was formerly with this newspaper but left to attend college.

The British Editorial Association is expected to arrive at Halifax around the 15th of July.

The Truro News Publishing Co. have installed a new large Golding Press.

E. L. Coleman, business manager of the Record Publishing Co., Sydney, paid a business trip to Halifax around the 1st of the month.

H. L. Harrison, who has been tending the mono caster since its installation at the Ross Print, has left Halifax to take a position on the Sydney *Post*.

The Lino Print, of Halifax, have moved to their new quarters on Buckingham St. A Whitlock Pony has been installed at the new office.

Jos. S. Wallace, former editor of the *Citizen*, has been nominated as Labor Candidate to contest Halifax County in the coming Provincial election, which will be held on July 27th.

Robt. L. Gaul, advertising manager of the *Citizen*, has charge of the publishing of the *Labor Annual* 1920, which is being issued by the Halifax District Trades and Labor Council, some time in August.

Geo. Scriven, who has been with the *Herald and Mail* composing room for a number of years, was recently operated upon for appendicitis. He is now back on the job again looking quite fit.

Owing to the ever increasing cost of paper, and everything that goes into the publishing of a daily paper, the *Morning Chronicle*, Halifax, has increased its subscription rate from $6.00 to $9.00 a year.

Members of the *Telegraph* and *Times* writing staffs have formed a baseball team, but went down to defeat upon their initial effort of the season in a game with local motion picture men by the small score of 14 to 13.

The Halifax District Trades and Labor Council have commenced work on a very elaborate *Labor Annual*, which is expected to be off the press around the end of August. This Annual will contain, besides able articles on local labor, numerous illustrations of the Empire port.

Shirley Ellis has joined the writing staff of the St. John *Globe*. He is a son of F. B. Ellis, editor, and a grandson of the late Senator John V. Ellis, a veteran of many years with the same journal. Mr. Ellis is taking the place of Everett Chambers, who has gone to Harvard to study.

Larry Healy, who will be remembered by many of the old time printers as a compositor on the *Recorder*, but for the past few years an operator on the *Evening Mail*, has returned to his first love—the *Acadian Recorder*. This is one of the few, if not the only daily paper in Canada that is still being set up by hand composition.

The *Independent*, a weekly newspaper which came into existence recently in Dartmouth, is showing healthy progress. The management expect to install a plant shortly, to escape the handicap of having the paper printed out. "Barney" Walker, formerly of the Weeks Printing Co., it is expected will be the mechanical superintendent.

During the month of June the American National Editorial Association visited Nova Scotia. A trip through the Land of Evangeline in apple-blossom time was very much enjoyed by all hands. While in Halifax the delegates were greatly impressed with the modern manner in which the city newspapers are published.

The *Splash* is the name of the paper issued this year by the compositors employed at the *Herald · and Mail* office. It consists of two eight-column pages, and contains humorous skits on the employees of the office. This issue was published in celebration of the annual picinc which was held by the employees on Sunday, July 4th, at Cole Harbor Dyke.

The members of the American press party now touring Canada in its Eastern parts were royally entertained in their visit to various parts of New Brunswick. They were heartily received at Moncton, Fredericton, Dalhousie, St. John and elsewhere, were feted and banqueted, given motor drives to points of interest and expressed themselves as delighted with the warmth of welcome accorded them.

The National Council of Women held their annual convention in St. John this last fortnight and among their delegates were several well-known newspaper women. Mrs. Jessie C. McIver, editor of the *Women's Century*, Toronto; Mrs. L. A. Hamilton, of the same magazine; Mrs. Graham of the *Echo*, London, Ont., and Mrs. E. M. Murray of the *Echo*, Halifax, N.S., were among the number. The delegates were nicely entertained during their stay.

At a special meeting of the shareholders of the St. John *Standard*, Limited, negotiations which have been in progress for several months, based on an agreement of sale made in February last, were brought to a conclusion. Effective immediately, the entire assets of the *Standard*, Limited, consisting of land and building, plant and equipment, supplies on hand, book debts, subscription lists, advertising contracts, etc., have been sold to Hadley V. MacKinnon. Mr. MacKinnon, the new owner of the *Standard*, has been its business manager for some years, working from sticking type to writing editorials on the paper.

British Columbia

R. J. McDougall of the *Herald*, Penticton, has just been gazetted a commissioner for taking affidavits, etc.

The *Interior News* of Smithers, B.C., has increased its subscription to $3.00 a year in Canada and $5.00 outside Canada with effect from August 1st.

F. A. Williams of Summerland, has joined the staff of the *Herald*, Cranbrook, as assistant manager, and the news columns of the paper show a decided improvement since his arrival.

H. W. Power, formerly of the *Kootenaian*, Kaslo, now with *Mining Truth*, Spokane, is spending July in the Slocan country gathering information on strike conditions in the mining camps of West Kootenay.

No less than seven returned men have taken their vocational training course with the *Daily News*—both mechanical and editorial. The last of them, J. F. Weston, was added to the permanent reportorial staff this month.

Commencing July 1st the *Daily News* raised its subscription price to mail subscribers from $5 to $6 per year. Alberta dailies coming into the same territory went to $8 a year the first of July. The *News* has also increased its classified advertising rates 50 per cent.

At a special meeting last month the Okanagan Master Printers' Guild decided to have Mr. Conrad of the United Typothatae make a thorough survey of the offices in that locality, with a view to definitely establishing costs. The Guild includes in its membership all the shops in the Okanagan Valley as well as those on the main line as far east as Revelstoke.

The compilation of a brand new voters' list in connection with the forthcoming liquor referendum, along with the legislation changing the rule of the road from "Turn to the Left" to "Turn to the Right" has brought the weeklies some additional

Government advertising this month. Twelve inches a week for four weeks were the instructions, at card rates for display.

The new weekly, the *Western Idea*, has started recently under editorship of A. C. Cummings. The *Western Idea* is topical and non-political in its policy. Those connected with the new paper are J. Templeton, G. B. Black and Captain R. M. Massie, late assistant secretary to the Manufacturers' Association of B.C. The title of the firm will be The Western Idea, Ltd.

Alberta

Calgary newspapers announce that because of the mounting costs delivery by carrier will be 25c a week and by mail $8 a year.

The Red Deer *Advocate* is increasing its subscription rates to $2.00 a year, effective from July 1, in consequence of the increasing price of newsprint.

The two upper stories of the Western Printing and Litho. Co., building in Calgary, Alta., were completely gutted early on the morning of July 5th. The loss is estimated at $60,000 and is fairly covered by insurance was stated by J. W. Renton, a director of the company.

The National Executive of the Imperial Order Daughters of the Empire at a meeting recently, passed a resolution to boycott the Hearst journals, to strongly support Canadian and British publications and to conserve the national pulp wood supply to this end.

The Calgary *Herald* announces a new subscription price: Delivered by carrier, per week, .25c; or $13 per year; by mail, per year, $8.00; 6 months, $4.25; 3 months, $2.50. The old rates were: delivered by carrier, per week, 15c, or $7.80 per year; by mail, per year, $5.00; 6 months, $2.75; 3 months, $1.50.

Saskatchewan

The Yorkton *Press* office moved its premises on July 1st to the Furby Building, Second Ave.

V. M. Snow has resigned his position as editor and manager Melville *Progress* for a position on the staff of the Yorkton *Enterprise*.

A new publication under the name of the Bruno *Leader* made its first appearance recently. This paper is edited and published by Jos. A. Tepe. Its size is of six columns and ten pages well filled with town and district news.

The Saskatoon Public Library are making arrangements to supply responsible persons with a maximum of 6 books to read during vacation period. Two works must be selected from non-fiction classes.

Members of the Kiwanis Club tendered expressions of regret at the departure of James Cruikshank recently from Regina, wishing him success in the new enterprise he is embarking on in the United States.

The outlook for Saskatchewan daily newspapers, which continue to publish under great difficulty, is bad, and unless there is some speedy action taken which will ensure a regular sufficiency of newsprint, they will not long be able to continue publication.

The newspapers of Western Canada have found it necessary to increase their subscription rates to 25c per week for city circulation and $6.00 per year for mail and rural. Saskatchewan papers advanced their prices some months ago and the advance by the Western papers was inevitable.

William F. Kerr, pioneer newspaper man of Western Canada and editor for nearly nineteen years of the *Leader*, Regina, has been appointed a Red Cross Commissioner for Saskatchewan, and will immediately take over his duties as chief executive officer of the Red Cross. He will sever connection with the Leader Publishing Company as soon as his successor is appointed.

The Toronto Type Foundry Co. has brought an action against O. W. Tukes and Mr. Leach, publishers of weekly papers, operating in different parts of the Regina judicial district, to restrain their using ready-prints from other companies. Various local newspaper men were called as expert witnesses to decide as to the efficiency of the "lay-out" of the newsprints supplied by the Toronto Type Foundry.

Manitoba

J. T. Hull, editor of the Saskatoon *Pheonix*, is retiring from that position and assuming the editorship of the *Grain Growers' Guide*.

E. H. Macklin was the guest of honor at a banquet given by the resident directors, heads of departments and members of the staff of the Winnipeg *Free Press* at the Fort Garry Hotel, to celebrate his attaining his anniversary of 40 years in news-

paper life. Mr. Macklin, now president and general manager of the Company, started his newspaper career in the office of a Toronto paper.

The announcement of the purchase of the Winnipeg *Tribune* by Wm. Southam and Sons, Ltd., makes another important addition to this already influential group of newspapers. Associated in the transaction is M. E. Nichols, who has just resigned from the position of Director of Information to the Department of External Affairs. Mr. Nichols will commence his duties as managing director on July 1st.

McCreary, Man., has a paper, the *Times*, starting on July 1. P. E. Lacey is the publisher. The advertising rates are announced as follows:—Display per inch each week, 25c; under one month, 50c; Legal and Muncipal per line, 10c; Political and Election per line, 10c; Condensed (For Sale, etc.), 50-25c; Locals, per line, 10c; Births, Marriages and Deaths inserted free. Memoriams and Card of Thanks, 10c per line.

After a brief illness, Doris Mary Metcalfe, eldest daughter of Mayor and Mrs. Joseph H. Metcalfe, of Portage la Prairie, passed away at the home of her parents at the age of 24 years. The deceased, who for the past five years had been a member of the editorial staff of the Winnipeg *Free Press*, was well and popularly known to a wide circle of young people in Winnipeg. After receiving her education in the public schools and collegiate at Portage la Prairie, the late Miss Metcalfe came to Winnipeg securing a position with the *Free Press* as reporter. In this capacity her vivacious and attractive nature won for her much popularity. About a year ago she became editoress of the Boys' and Girls' section of the *Free Press*.

Ontario

Alex. McGregor, former editor of the Peterboro *Review*, has accepted a position with the Renfrew *Mercury*.

The Bancroft *Times* and the Hastings *Star* have both increased their subscription rates to $2.00, effective from July 1.

The Durham *Chronicle* is advancing its subscription rates to $2.00 per year, effective from July 1.

Mr. Sam Hunter, the *Globe's* cartoonist, has left for his summer vacation amongst the Kawartha Lakes.

The Zurich *Herald* took its annual week off, the editor explaining that be"was going to rest up a bit during the hot weather and visit his friends."

The office of the Burlington *Gazette* was broken into on June 18, and a number of bonds and debentures, most of which were registered, were stolen.

At the annual meeting of the Chatham Canada Club, resolutions were passed strongly condemning the entry into Canada of the Hearst Publications.

The Hamilton office of the *Globe* has been removed to the Imperial Building on the northeastern corner of Main and Hughson streets.

The Toronto Women's Press Club held a trip to Niagara recently. During their stay they were the guests of Mrs. T. P. Rivett, Mrs. Edmund Phillips and Miss Servos.

The Tweed *Advocate* has been compelled to enforce a strictly cash-in-advance subscription basis, in view of the soaring of prices, otherwise an increase in rates would be inevitable.

The Milton *Champion* has just commenced its 61st milestone. Major William Panton, the present editor and publisher, has been in charge for thirty-two years.

Plans are under consideration for the enlargement of the press-room capacity of the *Border Cities Star*, as their present press-room is taxed to the utmost.

T. Arbuthnot, printer, has purchased the property at 150 Jarvis St., which he proposes modelling into a print shop. The purchase was made from A. E. Grier, 108 East Queen St.

The *Canadian Spoting Review*, Hamilton, has temporarily suspended publication, owing to the increasing cost of materials and shortage of paper.

Local No. 10 Pressmen's Union, Canadian Federation of Labor held a picnic at Centre Island recently. More than 500 members and friends were present and thoroughly enjoyed the many diversions provided.

The Wyoming *Enterprise* is ceasing publication at the end of June. The *Enterprise* is the seventh paper to drop out of the Lambton field and from the present outlook it will not be the last.

The Florence *Quill* has been forced to cease publication. This paper has been established since 1896 and is the second weekly to cease publication in Lambton during the past two weeks.

Sinclair and Allen, publishers, Toronto, have taken a long lease on the entire fifth floor of the new Hobberlin building at 366 to 378 Adelaide street West, and will get possession about August 1st.

Fred. P. Hambly, printer, of 338 Berkeley St., former chairman of the Board of Education, was chosen as successor to the late C. A. B. Brown as trustee for Ward 3 at a special meeting of the Board held yesterday.

J. M. Moore, who had leased the Georgetown *Herald* from R. D. Warren for ten or twelve years, has just bought the business and is now owner as well as publisher. Joe has made a success of the business.

H. P. Moore, of the Acton *Free Press*, who has been a Justice of the Peace for the past twenty-two years, has been gazetted Police Magistrate for Acton, this new office having just been created by the Attorney-General's Department.

The Niagara *Advance* is increasing its advertising rates with the exception of "Want Ads" from July 1. Subscription rates will in all probability have to be advanced shortly in view of the ever-increasing cost of paper and other materials.

W. J. Dunlop, B.A., business manager of the *Canadian Historical Review* and editor of the *School*, has been chosen to succeed Dr. A. H. Abbott as director of the Extension Department of the University of Toronto.

J. A. Osborne, former editor of the Fort Frances *Times*, has recently disposed of his interests in the Radford *Journal* and has purchased a weekly in Canton, North Carolina. His son, Hugh, is with him in the new venture.

The Kingston *Standard* in their issue of July 2nd used the fact that Kingston was to suffer from a gasless day on Sunday July 4th, to advantage, by securing a fine display of advertising placing before the public, concerns and their products, who were desirous of lessening the inconveniences of a gasless day.

Zurich *Herald*:—The home of Mr. and Mrs. Jos. May, London Road South, Usborne, was the scene of an interesting event on June 2, when their only daughter, Miss Florence A., became the bride of Mr. John M. Southcott, editor of the Exeter *Times*.

The St. Marys *Journal* has taken a step in the right direction by publishing extracts from the results obtained by advertisements inserted in their Lost and Found Section. The public do not realize what a powerful medium advertising is unless results are literally pushed under their noses.

A. S. Forster, of the Oakville *Star*, who spent a couple of months in travelling through the United States, in the South, is favoring his readers with a very interesting series of articles descriptive of the various points visited and historical reviews of incidents related thereto.

The *Border Cities Star* of Windsor, Ont., has issued a most attractive and well-arranged booklet, showing the field covered by them from an editorial and advertising standpoint. There is much useful general information contained in the booklet, as well as the clearly laid out data of the field covered solely by them.

J. B. Bryant, formerly proprietor of the *Advance*, has received an appointment to the editorship of the Gananoque *Reporter*, with which paper he has been for the past few weeks. B. O. Britton, the proprietor of the *Reporter*, is leaving for an extended trip to the Old Country and Mr. Bryant will assume editor's duties during his absence.

A bankruptcy petition has been filed against Lawretic Lyon, M.P. for Hastings, who came here some years ago from Toronto. He is a newspaper owner and was returned to Parliament at the last election as a Unionist. He was to have attended a function in his constituency on Saturday, but did not do so and is now reported by the newspapers to be missing.

John Hooper, Sen., London's oldest printer, died at his home, 491 Richmond street. Deceased was 86 years of age. In 1863 he came to Canada from Plymouth, England, and became foreman of the printing department of the London *Advertiser*. Until quite recently he had been able to go to his place of employment in the morning, despite his advanced age. For the past several years he was employed at the *Echo*.

Orillia *Packet*:—The naivete of the following paragraph in the Coldwater *Planet* is refreshing: "Having been appointed a Commissioner to the General Assembly of the Presbyterian Church, which meets at Ottawa this week, and as the honor does not come very often, we have decided to go, consequently there will not be any paper next week. The next issue will be June 17." Why can't we all be publishing papers in towns like Coldwater?

In accordance with instructions received from the Presbyterian General Assembly, the new General Board of the church and the Board of Publications, have decided to issue a weekly

church paper. Rev. Dr. Robert Haddon will serve as acting editor. Extensive changes are in contemplation during the autumn, when a permanent editor will be appointed. Presbyteries of the church have been called upon to make nomination for editorship.

J. Vernon McKenzie, now Canadian trade commissioner at Glasgow, Scotland, is spending part of his time writing on the chances of sending Canadian butter into Scotland, and the competition it has to meet from other countries. Now, that is very interesting, and Mac does it very well, but we can't help wondering what the same J. V. McK. would have said to any city editor, in his newspaper days, who would have salted him with such an assignment.

Col. R. F. Parkinson, D.S.O., managing director of the Ottawa *Journal*, has accepted the invitation of the committee of Canadian newspaper publishers to proceed to England to receive the delegation of prominent British newspaper publishers who are coming to Canada to attend the Imperial Press Conference. The delegation reaches Halifax July 25. There will be 60 delegates from the British Isles and 40 from the overseas dominions. The conference will be held in Ottawa August 4 to 7, and afterwards the visiting publishers will tour Canada.

The Acton *Free Press* has passed its 46th birthday, it being started on July 1, 1875. During the first four years the *Free Press* had three editors—Joseph H. Hacking, Steve W. Galbraith and T. Albert Moore. The present editor, Mr. H. P. Moore, dates his official connection with the paper from July, 1878. Upon retirement of his brother, Rev. Dr. T. Albert Moore, to enter the ministry in 1879, the present editor took the editorial chair. For forty-one years he has continued uninterruptedly in that position.

George W. Yates, who has been appointed Assistant Deputy Minister of Railways, is a native of London, Ont. He began work as a newspaper reporter in that city. He was a member of the *Globe* staff for some time, and left to enter the Provincial civil service as private secretary to Hon. E. J. Davis, then Commissioner of Crown Lands. He remained with successive Ministers, going with Hon. Frank Cochrane to Ottawa in 1911. He had a long experience in the Railway Department, to which he returns after a period as private secretary to the Prime Minister.

St. Catharines *Standard*:—Yesterday the third deck on the *Standard's* press was operated for the first time, and a 20-page paper printed at one run. Previously any issue beyond 16 pages required two runs, and the insertion by many hands of the first printed sections into that printed last—the outside section. The new deck is a great addition to the *Standard's* press equipment, and, with the new 25-horse-power motor required to operate the big machine, represents a capital cost of $11,000. To-day the entire press could not be installed for less than $35,000, an object lesson in itself of the large cost of equipment in the printing of a modern newspaper.

At an informal get-together meeting of the advertising men of the Western Ontario dailies, held at Kitchener, under the auspices of the Kitchener *News-Record*, an organization was formed which will be known as the Western Ontario Newspaper Association. An organization meeting will be held in Brantford during the third week in August. This afternoon's meeting was addressed by John M. Imrie, J. W. Ferguson of the C.E.N.A., Frank Adams of the London *Advertiser* and George Davis of the Hamilton *Herald*. Dinner was served to the delegates at Bridgeport.

The sixteenth annual meeting of the Canadian Association of Advertising Agencies was held at the King Edward Hotel, Toronto. Practically all the members were present. W. B. Somerset, the retiring president, occupied the chair. His report, which was received with great interest, surveyed the work of the association during the year and showed a very satisfactory advance. The new officers elected are as follows: President, J. P. Patterson, of Norris-Patterson; first vice-president, E. Desbarats, of Desbarats Advertising Agency, Limited; second vice-president, J. E. McConnell, of McConnell & Fergusson; secretary-treasurer, A. J. Denne, of Smith, Denne & Moore Ltd.; member of committee, R. A. Baker, of Baker Advertising Agency, Ltd.; immediate past president, W. B. Somerset, of A. McKim, Ltd.

Members of the National Editorial Association of the United States, who have just concluded an extended tour of Eastern Canada, were entertained in Toronto on Saturday, June 26. The party, numbering one hundred and twenty-five, were entertained by the T. Eaton Company at breakfast. The visitors then made a tour of the water front and viewed the activities of the Harbor Commission, who then entertained them to lunch at the Sunnyside Pavilion. During the afternoon the party had the pleasure of being received by Lieutenant-Governor and Mrs. Lionel Clarke at Government House, where a garden party was given in their honor. The National Editorial Association, on completing the tour of Western Ontario and the Niagara Peninsula, will have covered nearly 4,000 miles of the Canadian National - Grand Trunk Systems. Particular interest was shown in the Laurentide and the Abitibi pulp and paper mills, where much useful information in regard to the newsprint situation was collected.

The Wellington County Press Association is sending out the following notices:—

A meeting of the Wellington County Press Association will be held in Fergus on Friday July 23rd. There will be two sessions, at 10 a.m. and 1.30 p.m. Business of importance will be considered, including increased subscription, advertising and job rates, the postage and paper situations, etc. Every publisher in Wellington County and adjacent territory is urged to attend at least one session. Mr. E. Roy Sayles, Manager of the Canadian Weekly Newspapers Association, will be present, and would like to meet as many publishers as possible. He will be able to give valuable information and advice on many live matters. The following program is suggested in order to focus attention on various questions of interest. The publishers whose names are attached to the topics are asked to lead in the discussions:—1. The $2.00 subscription rate—Mr. Rixon Rafter; 2, Advertising Rates—Mr. W. A. Wright; 3. Job Rates—Mr. E. R. Mills; 4. The News Print Situation—Mr. J. C. Templin; 5, the Editorial Page—Mr. Hugh Templin; 6. Our Relations with Neighboring County Associations—W. Logan Craig, J. R. Aitchison. Rixon Rafter is President and A. W. Wright, Secretary.

Niagara Peninsula Press Association

The Niagara Peninsula Press Association met at Dunnville on Friday, July 9th, the meeting being held in the Dunnville Club, Mr. W. A. Fry presiding. Discussion took place regarding the counties to be included in the Niagara Peninsula organization. Mr. Donly of Simcoe, explained that Norfolk was allied with Oxford, because of better train facilities. It was moved, seconded and carried, that Lincoln, Welland and Haldimand be joined in an Association to be known as Niagara Peninsula Press Association.

The following provisional officers were then named:

President—W. A. Fry, the Chronicle, Dunnville.

Secretary—A. T. Mitchell, the Review, Smithville.

Executive—H. J. Shore, the Citizen, Port Colborne; Harry Davy, the Advocate, Cayuga; E. H. Brennan, the Advance, Niagara-on-the-Lake; W. B. Burgoyne, the Standard, St. Catharines J. A. Livingston, the Independent, Grimsby.

A general discussion took place on the $2.00 subscription rate, several publishers present deciding to announce the $2.00 rate to take effect September 1st. It was decided that a further meeting would be held at Welland on Friday, July 30th, for the purpose of giving proper consideration to a revised Job Price List, and also for the consideration of Advertising Rates and rate cards.

The Association will consist of the eighteen papers as follows: Beamsville Express, E. S. Hudson; the Bridgeburg Review, C. W. Johnston; the Grand River Sachem, Caledonia, H. B. Sawle; the Halidmand Advocate, Cayuga, R. H. Davey; the Dunnville Chronicle, W. A. Fry; the Dunnville Gazette, David Hastings; the Grimsby Independent, J. A. Livingston; the Jarvis Record, Mrs. Elva Rogers; the Port Colborne Citizen, Harvey J. Shore; the Smithville Review, A. T. Mitchell; Dunnville Reform Press, W. D. Patterson; the Niagara Falls Review, F. E. Leslie; the St. Catharines Standard, W. B. Burgoyne.

The visiting publishers were entertained at luncheon by Mr. W. A. Fry.

E. Roy Sayles, manager of C.W.N.A., attended the gathering.

Retires After Long Service

F. W. H. Crane, who has for over forty-one years been in the continuous service of R. Hoe & Co., and for the last four years president of the Company, has retired from the business because of a desire to be relieved from the burden and responsibility incident to the management of the business, and Richard Kelly, who has been in the continuous service of the Company for over thirty-four years and for several years vice-president and secretary, has been elected to succeed him as president and

general manager of the Company. Oscar Roesen, Sr., who has been second vice-president for some years and who is widely known as one of the foremost authorities on printing machinery, assumes the position of first vice-president and general superintendent of the shop, and Harold M. Tillinghast is the newly appointed secretary of the Company. Charles MacInnes and Otto L. Raabe continue in the offices of treasurer and assistant secretary respectively. The new president reports that the business will be conducted along the same conservative but energetic and progressive lines as heretofore.

Have Issued New Rate Card

The Oxbow Herald announces the following new advertising rates:

	Per Inch
Yearly contract, per issue	18c
Six months' contract, per issue	20c
Three months' contract, per issue	22c
One month's contract, per issue	25c
Single issue	25–30c

Government, League and Municipal Advertising:—

First insertion, per line ... 12c
Each additional insertion, per line ... 10c

Local readers:—

Locals, per line, each insertion ... 10c

Transient Advertising:—

This class of advertising includes advertisements such as "Lost," "Strayed," "For Sale," "Found," etc. Rate 50c per issue.

Plate matter, gross ... 20c
Flat rate for all ... 25c

Bank of Commerce Paper

Like the Canadian National Railways, the Canadian Bank of Commerce now has a magazine of its own. It is called the Caduceus and is different from the railway publication in that it is printed for the benefit of the members of the staff of the bank throughout the country and is not an official publication of the bank itself. It is a neat, well-illustrated and interesting little magazine, containing a variety of articles of special interest to bankers, as well as social and sporting news.

The Development of a Business

While it may be more or less true that there is nothing new under the sun, nevertheless, we are sometimes told an old story in a new and more attractive form. This is substantially what happened with the establishment of the Howell Cuts, 303 Fifth Avenue, New York, some two years ago. In scarcely two years the Howell Cuts have become popular and in demand not only in all the English-speaking countries but in such out of the way places as Sweden, Chile, the Strait Settlements and China. As a matter of fact the only resemblance this service bears to the ordinary one is that the drawings are supplied in matrix and electrotype form. The big difference lies in the fact that the drawings are all made and signed by Charles E. Howell especially for this purpose—which means pictures of known quality and reputation.

Another unusual feature of these drawings is that they are general in character, and while devoted to no one business, are elastic enough for any use where a picture is desired, which perhaps accounts for their widespread use among printers of all classes.

Le Perroquet, a new French weekly, was published for the first time in Ottawa recently. The aims of the new periodical are stated by the editor, C. R. Daoust, as being: to publish such truths as are not generally permitted to be included in the large newspapers.

Rev. Dr. George Peck Eckman, pastor of the Elm Park Church, formerly editor of the Christian Advocate, and a big figure in Methodism, died suddenly at Scranton, Pa., on June 28.

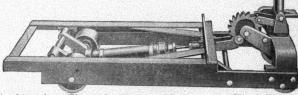

CROSS-ATLANTIC

Provides you with—

Your own special correspondents in London, Paris and other European centres.

Your own office in the heart of London's newspaper district.

Your own special cables by distinguished writers.

Your own special feature stories by mail.

In fact, everything, that your own private office in London could provide, but at a fraction of the cost.

ONLY ONE NEWSPAPER

in a city or town can have Cross-Atlantic service. Already the following leading newspapers have secured this service for their districts:

The Daily Province, Vancouver, B. C.
The Edmonton Journal, Edmonton, Alberta.
The Calgary Herald, Calgary, Alberta.
The Manitoba Free Press, Winnipeg, Man.
The Evening Post, Lindsay, Ont.

The Globe, Toronto, Ont.
The Herald, Montreal, Que.
The Standard, St. John, N. B.
The Chronicle, Halifax. N. S.
The Sydney Record, Sydney, N. S.

If you want this service, exclusive for **your** territory, write us for terms and full particulars.

CROSS-ATLANTIC NEWSPAPER SERVICE
DOMINION NEWS BUREAU LIMITED
CANADIAN REPRESENTATIVES
171 ST. JAMES STREET

P.O. BOX 756   MONTREAL, CANADA

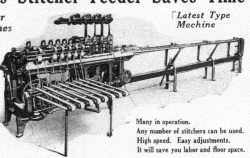

Brown, Blodgett & Sperry Co.
of St. Paul, Minn., commend

KIMBLE MOTORS

Mr. John J. Gleason, Treasurer and Manager of Brown, Blodgett & Sperry Company, whose famous printing, lithographing and engraving plant at St. Paul, is known to all, answers an inquiry as follows:

"We installed Kimble Motors on all of our machines requiring variable speed something over three years ago, and they have proved entirely satisfactory. We have had little or no expense in the upkeep or repairs, and the speed control is all that we could ask for.

"If the Motors continue to do the service and stand up as well in the future as they have so far with us, we would not hesitate to duplicate our order if we were putting in a new installation."

In equipping their plant some three years ago, they installed something like 75 motors, of which about half were constant speed, the rest of the equipment being KIMBLE Variable Speed Motors—all the variable speed motors purchased being Kimbles.

Their experience tallies with that of all Kimble clients—efficient, economical daily performance, combined with marked freedom from repair expense.

In these three years, the electricity saved by the KIMBLE VARIABLE SPEED MOTORS (which consume current only in proportion to speed) must have amounted to a good many hundreds of dollars. And the increase in output and saving in spoilage due to flexible speed control, would total up to a much larger sum.

Consult us on your alternating current motor equipment for

CYLINDER PRESSES
JOB PRESSES
FOLDERS, STITCHERS
AND OTHER SHOP EQUIPMENT

Whether you need only one motor or a "flock" of them.

SEND FOR OUR BULLETINS.

KIMBLE ELECTRIC CO.
N. Western Ave.
CHICAGO, ILLINOIS.

GREAT WEST ELECTRIC CO., LTD., 57 Albert Street, Winnipeg, Man., for all points west of Port Arthur and Fort William.

MASCO COMPANY, LTD., 87 Queen St. East, Toronto, Canada, for all points east of Port Arthur and Fort William.

34th
Annual
Convention
of the
U.T.A.

MEMBERS, make your hotel reservations NOW, for this greatest of U. T. A. conventions. Plan to spend three of the most resultful days of your business life in St. Louis—September 13th, 14th and 15th.

Problems vital to the interests of our trade will be dealt with; information and experiences that are invaluable will be exchanged; keenly interesting reports of growth and of plans for the future will be made.

No matter how busy you may be or whether you be member of the U. T. A. or not, you can ill afford not to take a three-day vacation for the purpose of meeting your fellow craftsmen at this convention. Arrange to be there, and come prepared for exceptionally interesting sessions.

*Non-Members cordially
invited to attend.*

To Be Held at St. Louis
Sept. 13, 14, 15, 1920
At the Hotel Statler

(Make your
own room
reservations
DIRECT)

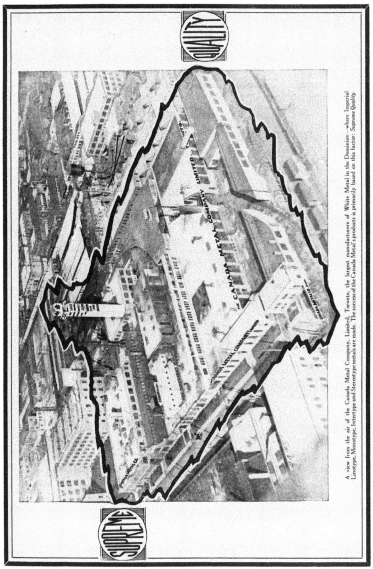

A view from the air of the Canada Metal Company, Limited, Toronto, the largest manufacturers of White Metal in the Dominion—where Imperial Linotype, Monotype, Intertype and Stereotype metals are made. The success of the Canada Metal's products is primarily based on this factor: *Supreme Quality.*

The Publisher's Page

TORONTO   July, 1920

Improving Our Service

THE Directors of the Canadian Press Association decided last year that the MacLean Publishing Company was the largest and most important newspaper organization in Canada and must therefore pay the highest annual fee to the Association. The Montréal **Star** with its two big weeklies comes second, but the **Star** group had been doing business for 18 years before the MacLean Company began. While we have not the details upon which the Press Association based their decision we understand they figured that the MacLean Company had a larger advertising revenue. This is not the case. Lord Atholstan's properties probably carry a third more advertising, use more paper and have a greater total circulation. The MacLean papers on the other hand get more revenue from circulation; have to pay perhaps three times as much in salaries and wages and show considerably less profit.

Extra good service to readers first and advertisers next has been the cardinal principle upon which Colonel Maclean has built during these 33 years. In this work every man, woman and junior apprentice on our staff has had a share. We have tried to gather about us and train the best experts in the country. Here is the latest example of what we are doing:

In the recent annual examinations of the Toronto Technical School, session 1919-20, in the Typography branch—that is the department where they learn how to set type—only 27 boys out of the whole city passed, of whom 10, or nearly 38 per cent. were boys of our own Composing Room, while in two out of the three classes MacLean boys stood at the head.

Several of our papers are the best of their class in the world but we are still far from satisfied with the service we are giving. As we can afford it, as the country grows, as our business grows, the service will be improved. We ask our readers to take these Technical School results as an evidence of our efforts to serve them better and better, for by giving a superior training to these boys we are laying the foundation for the still better work we hope to do in the future.

Readers can help us to give them a better service by sending in—direct to the President, Vice-President or General Manager—criticisms and suggestions.

PRINTER AND PUBLISHER

Montreal   Toronto   Winnipeg   Vancouver

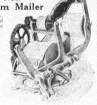

![Buyers' Guide]

CLASSIFIED ADVERTISEMENT SECTION

FOR SALE

PRINTING MACHINERY FOR SALE—HAV-ing sold the franchise of the Review, we have for sale 1 Cox Duplex Press, 1 Linotype Model 5, 1 Linotype, Model K. All the plant necessary for the publishing of a daily and weekly newspaper. Will sell enbloc or separ-ate. For particulars apply to the Peterborough Review Co., Peterborough, Ont. (p8p)

FOR SALE—JOB PRINTING AND BIND-ery plant, well equipped in one of the best manufacturing cities in Ontario. Good business, only one other office. Will require $10,000 to swing. For particulars apply Box 6920, Printer and Publisher. (p8p)

COLTS ARMORY PRESS FOR SALE, LAT-est model, inside chassis, 14 x 22. Com-plete with ten rollers, one distributor, two chases. Capacity 1,800 per hour. Write or wire manager, Telegraph Printing Co., Que. (p7p)

FOR SALE—28 linotype molds for melting metal, all with handles in good condition. Write or wire manager, Telegraph Printing Co., Quebec. (p7p)

FOR SALE—GORDON PRESS, 7 x 11; GOOD condition. The Owen Sound Advertiser, Owen Sound, Ont. (ptfp)

FOR SALE — NEWSPAPER COTTRELL press, 30 x 47, good condition. Furby St. Printery, Winnipeg. (ptfp)

WEEKLY NEWSPAPER FOR SALE—IN heart of Peace River Country, Northern Alberta; plant, building and lot. Location excellent, building good, plant about half nearly new, annual turnover $4,800. Subscrip-tion rates, $2.50; display advertising, 22 cents to 30 cents per col. inch. Price, $3,200, $2,000 down balance monthly payments. Write Box 6120, Printer and Publisher. (p9p)

TWO CENTS A WORD, Box Number as five words; minimum charge is $1.00 per insertion, for 50 words or less, set in 6 pt. type. Each figure counts as a word. Display ads., or ads. set in border, are at the card rates.

¶ Printer and Publisher is the only paper in Canada reaching the Printing and Publishing Trade.

¶ If it is to them you wish to advertise, there is no question but that Printer and Publisher is the medium you should use.

¶ Our Classified Advertisement Section is a result-getter.

SITUATIONS VACANT

PRINTER WANTED — AN ALL ROUND man, qualified compositor and pressman, must be serious, sober and pushing, one hay-ing outside connection preferred. If desirable can purchase an interest in the business or buy the whole plant, in a well-established and up-to-date printing plant, in a city of 15,000 population, near Montreal, Canada. Good business can be done with the right man. Re-ferences exchanged. Apply at Lachine Print-ing, 24 Twelfth Ave., Lachine, Que. (ptfp)

THE DEMAND FOR MONOTYPE OPERA-tors is always active—the number of Mon-otypes in use is daily increasing. This affords a chance for live printers and machinists to enter a profitable vocation. The Monotype Company maintains schools in Philadelphia, New York, Chicago and Toronto, where you can learn Monotype operating in a short time. Apply to the nearest. There is no tuition fee. Lanston Monotype Machine Company. (ptfp)

OPPORTUNITY FOR PRINTING SALES-men and Reporters to make a little extra cash for few hours work weekly. Reports wanted of unusual store window displays; all trades. Give store names; describe displays so that other merchants can use them. Send sample bunch of trims. Prompt payment and regular monthly order will follow if satisfac-tory. Ernest Dench, Sheepshead Bay, N.Y. (p7p)

LEARN THE LINOTYPE — WRITE FOR particulars. Canadian Linotype, 68 Tem-perance St., Toronto. (ptfp)

COLLECTIONS

SEND US YOUR LIST OF DELINQUENTS. We will turn Debit into Credit. Publishers' Protective Association, Toronto. (ptfp)

INDEX TO ADVERTISERS

TYPOGRAPHY

A System for Correct Composition

Linotype Typography makes one sound system of the much confused accumulation of material that confronts the printer. It eliminates unsparingly that which is incongruous and wrong, but without limiting full variety of choice by the narrow canons of cold art. It simplifies the practice of ambitious composition, and as an actual part and result of that simplification, the Linotype user is provided with material for composition of a richness attainable heretofore only by inordinately costly and laborious hand work. Linotype Typography furnishes equipment that both guides and responds.

CANADIAN LINOTYPE LIMITED
68 Temperance St., Toronto

MERGENTHALER LINOTYPE CO., New York, U. S. A.
SAN FRANCISCO   CHICAGO   NEW ORLEANS

This Advertisement, Including Border Ornaments, is Composed Entirely of LINOTYPE Material

PRINTER & PUBLISHER

THE MACLEAN PUBLISHING CO. LIMITED
TORONTO ❧ MONTREAL ❧ WINNIPEG

ART PHOTO BOOK
High in Quality—Low in Price

Wherever paper quality is mentioned these days we immediately associate with it high prices. This is the rule. But there is an exception to the rule. The exception is found in **Art Photo Book.** Here is a book paper of fine quality which sells at a comparative low price.

It is only by comparison that we can determine values. So we would recommend that you send for samples and prices of **Art Photo.** We will send you enough to provide for a catalog dummy. Compare it with any other higher priced book papers you may have on hand. The value represented in **Art Photo** will be clearly outstanding and easily appreciated. You will be struck by the uniformity of finish, fine printing surface, strength and color.

It will appeal to you as a paper that is adaptable for the best class of printing, and as a paper that will cut the cost of production.

Points to Remember

Art Photo Book is easy to print on, does not curl nor stretch and is, therefore, especially suitable for color work; it bulks well, and is a postage-saver.

Made in Canada by

CANADA PAPER CO. LIMITED
PAPER MAKERS

TORONTO   MONTREAL   WINDSOR MILLS, P.Q.

Western Agents:
Barkwell Paper Co., Winnipeg, Man.

PRINTER AND PUBLISHER, August, 1920. Vol 29, No. 8. Published monthly at 143-153 University Ave., Toronto, by the MacLean Publishing Co., Ltd. Yearly subscription price, $3.00. Entered as second-class matter at the Post Office Department at Ottawa, Canada, also
entered as second-class matter July 1, 1912, at the Post Office at Buffalo, N.Y., U.S.A., under Act of March 3rd, 1879.

THE LINOGRAPH

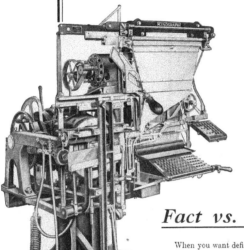

The LINOGRAPH Way is the Easiest Way

Fact vs. Guesswork

When you want definite, reliable information about anything, you naturally turn to someone who is competent to give you the proper information.

When you want to find out how a LINOGRAPH performs in actual operation, you naturally will ask someone who has used one enough to find out for himself.

LINOGRAPH users and operators are always very willing to tell you what results they obtain with a LINOGRAPH.

We are always willing to rest our case on what they may tell you.

The only suggestion we offer is that your inquiry should be directed to someone who *really knows* from *actual experience*.

THE LINOGRAPH COMPANY
DAVENPORT, IOWA, U.S.A.

ETABLISSEMENTS PIERRE VERBEKE
General European Agent
Rue des Boiteux 21
BRUSSELS, BELGIUM

PARSONS & WHITTEMORE, INC.
Agents for Australasia
30 Market Street
SYDNEY, AUSTRALIA, N.S.W.

"We have used slug-machine matter on our bookwork—*we now produce the same matter on our own Monotypes.* Not taking into consideration the many other Monotype advantages, our costs are less under the Monotype System."

—Canadian Advertising Agency, Montreal

Monotype is better on any kind of work—also cheaper!

The product of the Monotype—brand new single type

Every Monotype Job Sells Another

THE PRICE

WERE we to base our price upon the value of the Miehle to its users, it would undoubtedly be the highest priced press in the world.

On the contrary, the price of the Miehle is based solely upon its cost of production. And this cost of production is kept at a minimum by the employment of every device which will increase our efficiency without a reduction in the quality of the press.

And, therefore, we make use of the great economy in manufacturing, made possible by our large production, to maintain a price which secures to the printer the greatest possible return upon his investment.

MIEHLE PRINTING PRESS & MFG. CO.
Fourteenth and Robey Streets, Chicago
Distributors for Canada
TORONTO TYPE FOUNDRY CO., LIMITED
TORONTO   MONTREAL   WINNIPEG   REGINA

YOU NEVER HEARD OF A MIEHLE BEING SCRAPPED

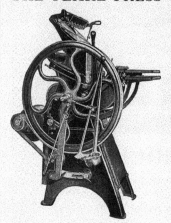

Red Letter Days
in Printing History

—September 13
14
15

THESE are the dates of the Typothetæ 34th Annual Convention at St. Louis.

Three intensely absorbing subjects will afford a program of prodigious value to printers — the industrial situation, the paper problem and the Typothetæ organization.

Keenly interesting reports of phenomenal Typothetæ growth will be presented — with plans for the future and suggestions as to how members can make their membership pay a manifold profit on their dues.

The industrial situation will be frankly discussed. Because action by this deliberative body is bound to affect the industry for years to come, you owe it to your own business to be present.

The paper situation is recognized for its importance, and speakers of authority will bring a message of tremendous value in planning your future printing operations over many months to come. Supplementing the program will be attractive printing, advertising and educational exhibits.

Every printer, even though not a member of Typothetæ, is cordially invited to attend, but reservations should be made quickly — headquarters hotel, the Statler. The largest attendance a U. T. A. Convention ever recorded should be registered at St. Louis.

To Be Held at St. Louis
Sept. 13, 14 and 15
At the Hotel Statler
Make your own room reservations direct

Cover Paper
That Counts

S ULTAN covers are not all there is to a good job of printing, but when used they improve the job's appearance no matter how good it might otherwise be.

SULTAN covers have a way of just adding that final touch to good printing that makes the printing buyer say "That's fine."

S U L T A N covers are made in nine Oriental shades and in two weights, 20 x 26 — 65 lbs., and 20 x 26—90 lbs. A lighter weight, suitable for fly leaves and box covers, may be had in six shades, 20 x 26—30 lbs.

If you have not a SULTAN sample book let us mail you one.

NIAGARA PAPER MILLS
LOCKPORT, N.Y.

IMMEDIATE DELIVERY
OF
GOSS STEREOTYPE MACHINERY

*The following new machinery we have on hand for shipment
AT ONCE. Compare with your needs.*

Combination Wet and Dry Matrix Rolling Machine.
Two Platen Steam Tables.
Pneumatic Head Steam Tables.
Double Page Form Pneumatic Head Steam Tables.
Automatic Gas Fired Steam Generators.
20"-21"-22" Col. Self-balanced Curved Plate Casting Boxes.
20'-21"-22" Col. Double Cooled Self-balanced Casting Boxes.
20'-21"-22" Col. Curved Plate Tail Cutting Machines.
20'-21"-22" Col. Curved Plate Shaving Machine.
20'-21"-22" Col. Curved Plate Trimming Blocks.
Metal Furnace—3500 pounds capacity.
One Pump Metal Furnace.
Two Pump Metal Furnace.
20"-21"-22" Curved Plate Routing Machines.
Flat Stereo Saws.
Flat Trimming Machines.
Flat Combination Saw and Trimmers.
Radial—Arm Flat Routers.
Jig Saw and Drills.
5-7 and 8 Col. Flat Casting Boxes.
Hand Power Flat Shavers.
Adjustable Head Flat Shavers.
Dross Refining Furnaces.
Paper Roll Trucks.
Ball Bearing All Iron Form Tables.
Elevating Form Tables.
Matrix Shears.
Ink Storage Tank and Pumping Equipment.

Send for Catalog "STEREOTYPE PLATE-MAKING MACHINERY"

THE GOSS PRINTING PRESS CO.
1535 SOUTH PAULINA STREET, CHICAGO, ILL.

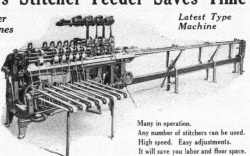

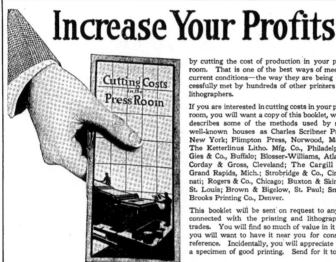

Increase Your Profits

by cutting the cost of production in your press room. That is one of the best ways of meeting current conditions—the way they are being successfully met by hundreds of other printers and lithographers.

If you are interested in cutting costs in your press room, you will want a copy of this booklet, which describes some of the methods used by such well-known houses as Charles Scribner Press, New York; Plimpton Press, Norwood, Mass.; The Ketterlinus Litho. Mfg. Co., Philadelphia; Gies & Co., Buffalo; Blosser-Williams, Atlanta; Corday & Gross, Cleveland; The Cargill Co., Grand Rapids, Mich.; Strobridge & Co., Cincinnati; Rogers & Co., Chicago; Buxton & Skinner, St. Louis; Brown & Bigelow, St. Paul; Smith-Brooks Printing Co., Denver.

This booklet will be sent on request to anyone connected with the printing and lithographing trades. You will find so much of value in it that you will want to have it near you for constant reference. Incidentally, you will appreciate it as a specimen of good printing. Send for it today.

Helps to Bigger, Better Production

Reducol
Reducol Compound adjusts inks to daily changes of atmospheric conditions and the varied grades of paper. It softens the ink, instead of thinning it. Eliminates picking and mottling. Does not affect colors. Neither a dryer nor a non-dryer.

Blue-Black Reducol
For use with blue or black inks when a toner is desired.

Paste Dryer
Dries from the paper out. Permits perfect overlapping. Positively will not crystall' 'e the ink, and dries on highly coated stock without chalking. Especially desirable for color work of all kinds.

Liquid Air Dryer
Transparent, and does not affect the color. Gives quick and satisfactory results.

Magic Type and Roller Wash
Marvelously effective and speedy. 1000% better than gasoline. Guaranteed not to stick type together, injure the hands, or damage engravings, type or rollers.

Gloss Paste
Makes any kind of printing or litho ink print extremely glossy on any kind of paper. Used as an after-impression, it makes labels and wrappers dust- and moisture-proof.

Electrical Destroyer
Eliminates static electricity completely nine times out of ten, and at least 75% in all cases.

Richter's Superior Metal Cleaner
Saves all valuable components of metal, restoring it to original condition, and greatly prolonging its life.

Further information about any of these specialties may be obtained from our home office or the nearest branch

INDIANA CHEMICAL & MFG. COMPANY, Indianapolis, Indiana
23-25 East 26th Street, New York City　::　608 South Dearborn Street, Chicago

Canadian Agents:

MANTON BROS., Toronto, Montreal, Winnipeg

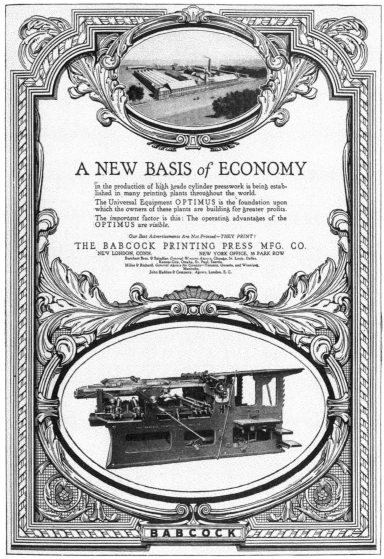

A NEW BASIS of ECONOMY

In the production of high grade cylinder presswork is being established in many printing plants throughout the world.

The Universal Equipment OPTIMUS is the foundation upon which the owners of these plants are building for greater profits.

The *important* factor is this: The operating advantages of the OPTIMUS are *visible*.

Our Best Advertisements Are Not Printed—THEY PRINT!

THE BABCOCK PRINTING PRESS MFG. CO.
NEW LONDON, CONN.   NEW YORK OFFICE, 38 PARK ROW

Barnhart Bros. & Spindler, *General Western Agents,* Chicago, St. Louis, Dallas, Kansas City, Omaha, St. Paul, Seattle.
Miller & Richard, *General Agents for Canada*—Toronto, Ontario, and Winnipeg, Manitoba.
John Haddon & Company, *Agents,* London, E. C.

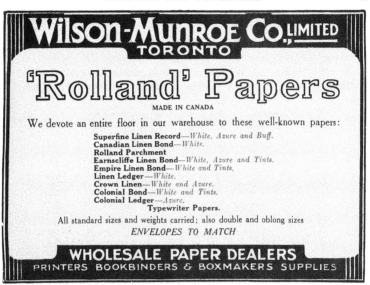

PRINTER AND PUBLISHER
Devoted to the Interests of the Printers and Publishers of Canada

The Actual Composition of a Type Page
By Edward D. Berry

OME time ago one of the readers of Printer and Publisher made the following inquiry of the composition department: "What is the best or most approved method by which a compositor may proceed in the task of setting an advertisement?"

The same method of procedure is applicable to the composition of an advertisement and a job.

Every workman has a method of his own, however crude, or at least an adaptation or variant of the method of someone else, whether he is cognizant of it or not. And who can say that any method is wrong by which satisfactory results are achieved?

To a man who can visualize a complete job or ad., with his mind's eye in proper 'focus to see and think in dimensions, and relations of tone, the principal concern is in selecting the method of greatest speed and facility of work. But all of us are not so gifted.

Many of us can draw a mental picture of the general appearance desired in the completed job, but usually find that the restrictions imposed by the unresponsive medium with which we work—type faces—makes it difficult to get the effect desired.

A rough sketch made in advance is of large usefulness, but until the compositor has attained the skill and accuracy that comes from the knowledge and practice of an experienced layout man, the same divergence between desire and accomplishment will exist, and from the same causes.

Unless an accurate sketch is prepared in advance either by the compositor or someone else, I should say that the first thing to be done after the size of the type page is determined, is to set the main display line—merely the letters, not spaced out, so that a possible change later will not waste so much time. In fact, time will be saved if none of the display lines are spaced until all of the other type is set and arranged.

It is a common practice to make up the border first, which is fundamentally wrong. A rule the exact size of the border placed around the page will aid in getting a proper distribution of white space and type sections, but the border to be used should be made up last, for the content of the entire inner page governs its weight and style. It is much easier to make a border that will conform to a page than it is to set the type to conform to a border previously selected, for obvious reasons.

A border which bears no relation to the enclosed matter, either in tone or character, is as offensive to the eye as a wrong font in a display line. How many pages are seen in which the border and type bear so little relation to each other that each might have been set by different compositors and assembled by chance?

After the main display line is on the galley, the next step is to determine the size of type of the principal straight matter section and the space it will occupy. Relative importance of different parts of the copy will govern this, but care should be used that its total weight does not overshadow the main display, for that is the signal which arrests the attention of the prospective reader.

After the main section is set, we have the two principal figures in the picture, which should stand out more prominently than any of the others. We are now ready for the smaller figures and the background—blank space. In a department store advertisement, where the total space is filled with type, the background is comparatively dim, only showing through and between the type lines. In this class of advertisement, it is therefore necessary that the other type sections be of comparatively even color—worked into the background as it were; for it is impossible to display the entire ad., efforts to do so having but one result—that nothing is displayed; it is practicable only to differentiate in distinction by headings of varied prominence—and care should be exercised in this also for the reasons just noted. Illustrations are an aid in calling attention to a subordinated section of an ad., but all ads. do not contain them. It is better to insure that the most important part of the ad. be assimilated than to lose even that by drawing the attention in too many directions at once. Everyone remembers the impossibility of watching three rings in a circus at one time and the sure result of attempting to do so—that of seeing very little of any of them.

When all of the type sections are set, the real artistry begins—assuming, of course, that type sizes and gradations of tone in the composition have been selected with due observance of the tenets here laid down—that of distributing the white space. This is really the most difficult part of composition. No matter how well the rest of the work is done, an injudicious placing of white will mar the job; and even a poor selection of type sizes and tones may be largely remedied by careful spacing. The prominence of display line or type section is in exact ratio to the amount of white space surrounding them and the proximity of competing attractions.

A leaded paragraph near to other type will not be so attractive as if it were set solid and the space thus saved surrounded it. It must be kept in mind that blank space is one of the important tools of composition; it should be considered an integral part of the job, to be handled just as carefully as the printing surfaces, for only by its careful distribution can the necessary contrasts of impelling attraction be produced and an invitation to perusal be extended to the observer.

If added weight is needed for a display line and there is not room for a larger size type, this may be secured by underscoring—the rules to be of the average weight of the stems in the letters. Care should be taken that there is more space below the rules than between them and the type line, for they would then take on the character of a cut off, which may not be in place, especially if there is a direct connection between the line and the following matter.

But any means of special attraction should be used sparingly and carefully, for each counter-attraction lessens the importance of each of the others. Overdone, they become irritants to the eye and usually result in none of the ad. being read.

An advertisement that is telling a single story, as ads. frequently do now, takes on the character of bookwork, and it is unnecessary to make it an assemblage of different tones; the narrative, if good, will itself sustain interest and it is unnecessary to continually re-arrest attention as it is in an ad. which is a collection of different and unconnected arguments.

When all of the type is set and the page spaced out, it is ready for the border. In determining the character of the border to be used, the general contour of the letters in the type series should be the first consideration; for instance, a flowing letter with pronounced connectives, and of ornate style, should not be surrounded by a border of which the general outline is square and severe. Neither should a square letter, such as we know as Gothic, have a border with fine and flowing lines. These are the two extremes which will serve to illustrate the point.

If it is decided to use a rule border, those errors may be avoided by a proper combination of tones. A page set in Gothic is properly surrounded, for instance, by two rules of equal width, with space between them of about half the width of the printing surface of the rules. For a page set in type of a flowing or ornate style, a rule border of graded tone is more suitable; for example, a heavy rule, the width of which is determined by the combined weight of the enclosed matter, let us say four point, outside of a one-point, a one-half point, and one or two hair-line rules, successively, the lightest face farthest from the heavy rule. The closer these rules are together the more apparent their gradation. It is also frequently necessary to add a light rule to the outside of the heavy rule to lessen its severity of outline.

It is never advisable to have the inmost rule of a combination rule border as heavy as the outer one, as the border will appear flat and uninteresting and the connection between it and the page will not be apparent. It should draw the eye inward to the reading matter.

The border should be just heavy enough to give the appearance of holding the page together; if it is too light, it seems to be attached to the page. If a drawn border is used, containing illustrations, or if it exemplifies the product advertised, the rules are frequently violated, and with propriety, for the border then has two missions to fulfill in the ad. But in the average advertisement it is well to remember that the advertiser is not selling borders; that the province of a border is not to call attention to itself, but to add to page attraction to induce a reader to pause and peruse the contents of the ad.; it should invariably seem to be a part of the whole.

The best and only true method of solving these problems is to take advantage of every opportunity to acquire a thorough knowledge of typography and the laws of art underlying it. The same general laws that apply to any of the forms of art apply to all of them, and it is necessary to master these fundamentals. A means that is open to everyone is a careful assimilation of the contents of the printing trade journals.

Watching the Fine Points in Typography
Attention to the Selection of Type

IT IS well that the question of hand composition should be revived. For a number of years it received very little attention. The apprentice was keen to get his hands on the keyboard of a typesetting machine. He was not keen to apply himself to the old case any longer than necessary. He was not particular to know and recognize much difference between thin, thick or hair spaces.

A writer in a current printing magazine claims that too much emphasis cannot be placed upon the importance of instructing apprentices in the principles and rules of good composition. In the days before machines were introduced, compositors observed many rules, most of which were based upon good common sense and sound mechanical practice. The production requirements of machine composition, together with the growth of a class of operators who know nothing of printing, has lowered the standard of straight composition in many departments of the business. The revival of interest in hand-set advertisements and book pages should bring a return to the observance of good style and good mechanical execution. Every apprentice should be taught to make his product correct mechanically—the artistic qualities will develop themselves.

Specimens reproduced in the trade journals should be models of excellence and no striving for artistic effect should be permitted to over-rule the issues of good style. A case in point is the unrestricted use of capitals—or, worse, italic capitals—without lower case.

Lower case is most easily read.

CAP LINES LACK LEGIBILITY

ITALIC CAPS ARE ILLEGIBLE

Of course, many squared-up effects require all-cap lines, but in general the use of too many capitals indicates weak design. Apprentices should be taught that all-cap lines lack legibility and that this condemns their use, except for definite display purposes.

Again, nothing can justify wrong division of words. True, there are different systems of division, but much printing of artistic merit is marred by word divisions that cannot be found in any dictionary. Another common fault is divisions of the elements of compound words. Such words are properly divided only upon the compounding hyphen. Another rule frequently disregarded forbids more than two consecutive hyphens at the ends of lines in bookwork. A little scheming will generally avoid this unsightly violation of good style. In work where time and layout allow, running the matter over in narrower or wider measure will often avoid bad break lines. A card recently seen, the product of one of the best typographers in America, had a three-line paragraph in the center of the card. The two first lines each ended in a divided word; the last line was not nearly full. Five minutes' work would have run the matter into a little narrower measure, avoided the break lines, and squared up the whole paragraph. On small work of this character, many compositors string out all their matter in one line, and then decide the measure to make best spacing and fewest breaks.

Good word spacing is a fine art. The tendency of late years has been to put very little space between words. Artistically this is justifiable, but here again legibility suffers, and proofs of such matter are frequently returned by customers with request to have spacing increased. Apprentices should be instructed to study the characteristics of the different type faces, and of the different letters of the alphabet, and to space for legibility always.

The printing industry to-day presents the greatest scope for the exercise of artistic talent, but we must not forget that it is based on mechanical and grammatical principles, and that work that will not hold together on the stone, or that is illegible, or that violates good taste, cannot be excused upon any plea of artistic value.

A BORDER which bears no relation to the enclosed matter, either in tone or character, is as offensive to the eye, as a wrong font in a display line. . . . . It is much easier to make a border that will conform to a page than it is to set the type to conform to a border previously selected.

—E. D. BERRY

W. F. Kerr, Long Time Editor of Regina Leader
One of the Successful Canadian Journalists

FROM telegraph messenger to editor of the leading morning daily newspaper in Saskatchewan is the record of Wm. Franklin Kerr, newly appointed Red Cross commissioner for the province. Mr. Kerr comes from a family of newspapermen. His grandfather, says the Regina *Post*, owned and edited one of the first papers in what is now the city of Ottawa and his father worked for many years as a compositor on the same paper.

It was as a youth that Mr. Kerr was first initiated into the mysteries of newspaper work, when as a telegraph messenger for the C.P.R., at Ottawa, his duties consisted in carrying press despatches from the correspondents in the gallery of the House of Commons. One of these correspondents later persuaded

W. F. KERR
For 19 years Editor of the Regina "Leader," now Red Cross Commissioner for the Province of Saskatchewan.

him to come West and in 1898 he went to the Winnipeg *Free Press* where he became an associate editor. In 1901 he represented the *Free Press* on the royal train which conveyed the present King and Queen across the Dominion. He was the only Western and the youngest newspaper correspondent on the train.

Joined Walter Scott

During his visit to Regina on that occasion he became acquainted with the Hon. Walter Scott, who was at that time Federal member of parliament and owner of the *Leader* and the *Times* in Moose Jaw. The late William Trant was at that time editor of the *Leader*. Mr. Kerr was invited by the Hon. Walter Scott to take over the active editorial and business management of the *Leader*, at that time a weekly publication. He agreed to do this for what was at that time the princely salary of $15 a week. In February, 1902, he arrived to take over his new duties. Hon. Walter Scott remained as president of the Leader-Times Company, Tom Miller was vice-president and editor and manager of the *Times* at Moose Jaw,

and Mr. Kerr was appointed secretary-treasurer of the company and editor and manager of the *Leader* at Regina.

Organized First Daily

It was in November, 1905, during the first provincial elections that Mr. Kerr organized the first daily newspaper published by the *Leader*. The Scott Government was returned to power and Hon. Walter Scott announced in the legislative assembly that he would sever his connection with the *Leader*. Mr. Kerr then organized the Leader Publishing Company, and became its first president, a position he held until the outbreak of war.

Mr. Kerr was a director of the Western Associated Press from the inauguration of that news collecting agency and one of the men who applied for the charter which created the Canadian Press Ltd. He was also at one time president of the Western Canada Press Association and last May was elected president of the Saskatchewan branch of the association. He is also vice-president of the Regina Press Club.

In 1918 Mr. Kerr was one of the Canadian newspapermen who visited the battlefields in France and Flanders as guests of the British and French Governments.

He was born at Goderich, on October 25, 1876, and was educated in the public schools of St. Thomas, Ont. On October 11, 1904, he married Sara Wilson Sharman, daughter of Joseph Sharman, of Russell, Man.

Well, Here's the Glad Hand!

Marmora *Herald*:—Trenton now has three weekly newspapers. The latest addition to the journalistic field is the Quinte *Sun*, and it is published by Jarrett & Son.

The editor is Thomas Jarrett, a journalist of several years' experience. In the opinion of most weekly newspaper men the proprietors of the new paper will deserve more credit for their courage than for their good judgment. When cities like Peterborough, Brockville, St. Catharines, Woodstock, and Brantford have only one paper, and the weekly papers in scores of live towns have amalgamated, while numerous others have dropped out of existence, it would look like a tempting of fate to start a third paper in a town like Trenton. In fact Trenton has had the reputation of being one of the poorest newspaper towns of its size in Ontario, as far as the financial returns to the papers are concerned. The result of the new venture will be watched with considerable interest.

Mr. Wm. C. Magee, for some time assistant to the late Mr. Joseph Hays, has been appointed to succeed him as Typographic Manager of the Lanston Monotype Machine Company. Gifted with the unusual combination of artistic temperament and executive ability Mr. Magee brings to his new position a thorough practical knowledge of high grade printing and experience in producing it. After an apprenticeship in one of the best printing offices in Philadelphia, several years' experience as compositor, monotype operator and foreman, he entered the employ of the Monotype Company as instructor in the Main School at Philadelphia. His ability was soon recognized and he was transferred to the Typographical Department, of which he has now become the head. A young man as years go, and full of energy, he will keep his department well to the front and monotype users can rest assured of continuation of the typographic service that has been a feature of the Monotype Company.

It is a well-known fact that hard paper will become smooth and take the ink readily when a little glycerine is added to the water used for wetting purposes. But it may be less known that the ink will also dry very quickly on paper wetted with glycerine water. Posters with large and full-faced types will be dry in a quarter of an hour, whilst the drying process, when the printing has been done on paper simply water-wetted, will require hours.

"He Profits Most Who Serves Best"

By Tres.

A T THE moment I do not know who coined this phrase—but 'tis mighty true.

Especially so in connection with Salesmanship.

* * *

Every Printing Salesman dearly loves to "land" the big order. Why not?

I remember on one occasion, when entering an establishment to solicit business, I was met at the door by a competitive salesman, and before I could say "Good-day," he warned me to "Keep off the job, this firm is our biggest customer and our firm does all the printing placed here."

I knew they were big buyers of printing and was desirous of getting some business from them. And why should I *not* have some of it?

I did not get "big business" there. My friend had them well sold, on price in any event.

But I have got big business from not a few firms; always on the basis of a sound policy—that of giving "real" service, as I understood that service to be.

I remember very well when my attention was first directed to Blank and Co. by their splendid and effective advertising matter. This firm were certainly "big buyers" of printing. I studied their printing. Was sure I could secure for them better results in some lines; could equal most of the other lines; while still others I was not so sure of. I would try for the business.

I did not go brazenly up to this firm and seek the opportunity of "figuring" on their work. On the occasion of my first call, the young lady at the enquiry wicket obligingly gave me the name of the general manager, who she said attended personally to all the advertising and printing. This was what I needed to know first of all. "He is very busy?" "Yes, and seldom sees travellers." "Oh, take my card in anyway;" and I underlined the word "Service" that appeared on my card. Back she came with that well known remark, "Mr. B— is too busy to see you to-day," handing me my card. I wrote across the back of the card the words, "Sorry, but I'll call again—I have some good printing dope to show *you*," underlining the "you." Then while the young lady was delivering my message, I beat it.

In the week that intervened before I returned, I studied that firm—who they were, the lines they sold, the class of advertising they used, etc. The young lady had told me that Mr. B— was "usually back from lunch at two and was easy to see then." I was there at two. Sent in my card. Was shown into his office, receiving a courteous but not any too encouraging a welcome. However I frankly told him my mission. I had admired his advertising, would like to show him how my firm's productions could compare with what he was using. We discussed several booklets, among them one printed in England which was well above the average of many of our Canadian productions. We discussed the question, and he firmly believed that the English houses could do better work than our Canadians could do. And it looked like it—at first. I had kept in reserve several jobs I considered "peaches." When I brought them out I pointed to our imprint on them. No more was said.

He said that every job he got out cost him hours of worry and work, because as a rule printing salesman did not appear to catch his viewpoint; and the printers were not giving sufficient attention to the details of the work—it was difficult to be sure of accomplishing first class results.

A pleasant interview closed at this phase, and I withdrew. I had learned that Mr. B— appreciated *good* printing, that he was a little dissatisfied with some of the results he was getting and that he dreaded the work and worry of getting out his copy. This provided me with my lead, which was certainly taken advantage of. I reported back to my chief and was promised all needed support in the effort to get his firm's account. A letter of appreciation for the interview was sent Blank and Co. and several points relating to the policy of our firm mentioned.

It is absolutely essential that the salesman have the enthusiastic support of the "house," from the general manager down—it will give him inspiration of a dynamic nature.

Next week Blank and Co. was the scene of a third visit.

Same time, same results—shown in to Mr. B—'s office. This time I was prepared to talk "Show and street car cards," having noticed his in the street cars. I hardly had the subject mentioned when he brought out a card he had just received from the printers. It was a good card—but it did not compare with the "style" he had told the printer to follow. The reason was not hard to discover. The "style" to be followed was a fine half-tone from wash drawing produced in two colors with process inks—beautiful. The printer had made zincs with some ben-day treatment, and the flat appearance of the finished product *was* disappointing when compared with the "style" to be followed.

I went to a great deal of trouble showing him the different methods of treating subjects for these cards: Wash drawings, photos, pen and ink drawings, half-tones, ben-days, zincs, etc., how different inks blended.

Salesmen will find it of great assistance to keep in touch with good engravers, learn the best methods, carry samples of ben-days, color work, half-tones, zincs, etc. I had all this in my sample case.

This interview ended in Mr. B—telling me about a show card he wanted prepared and I suggested that he permit me to work it out for him. He told me what he wanted and I *listened* (it pays to listen) to what he had to say, getting a mental picture of the effect he wanted created on this card.

I went to a good engraving house and explaining the whole situation secured in a few days a beautiful retouched and colored copy of this card. It *was* a beauty. The engraver gave me an estimate on the cost of art work and cuts. I prepared an estimate on printing in quantities and then telephoned Mr. B—, telling him I had the copy ready.

The interview that followed resulted in his OK-ing the copy with a few changes and giving me a good order; and note: without a price.

When I went back to the office I acknowledged his order, by letter, giving him the prices I had previously secured. The cost of the art work and cuts alone on this card was more than the whole cost of art work, cuts and *printing* on the previous card he had shown me. I think it *is* wise to acknowledge orders and if possible quote the price early in the process of the work.

When the cuts' were completed, proofs in several sets of colors were shown him for selection. This work was included in the first cost of art work and cuts, as "proofing of cuts." Mr. B— greatly appreciated these proofs, and framed copies are in his office to-day. Finally when the job was completed and delivered, Mr. B— called up the manager and complimented him on the work.

Order followed order, and Mr. B— was well sold on the *Service* basis. No price cutting was ever necessary. Our prices were seldom, if ever, the lowest, but with every quotation (if requested) went a dummy or suggestion, a tangible example of what was to follow.

Often Mr. B— would call for advice from our firm on matters that did not necessarily mean business, but it was part of the great plan of service, and he got it. The manager, the foremen, and the journeymen were all interested. They were told of Mr. B—'s appreciation and they appreciated that, too.

I kept in close touch with Mr. B— and we became good close friends. In a case of this kind it will be readily seen that "Confidence" had been established. Confidence in the salesman, confidence in the firm, confidence in the product of the firm.

Confidence is the basis of *all* real service and business, it is worth more than any other attribute of successful salesmanship —it is the *one* thing most necessary.

And the "profit" will come in the little things as well as in the large.

Let competition be confined to that of endeavoring to serve in every way that will contribute to the best interests of our customers and ourselves.

I think that *confidence* is really the fruit of certain ideals of character that can be woven into our business relationships.

But of that we will print more later.

The Newspaper Pressman and His Inks

He Has a Chance to Make Good Choice

By Chas. R. Conquergood

HAS it ever occurred to you that every system of printing, every style of printing press, and all the equipment in a modern or ancient print shop is built simply for the purpose of placing a little bit of Printing Ink upon the surface of some material, and repeating the film of ink as many times as desired. I read recently that the average coat of paint used on a building measured three one-thousandths of an inch in thickness, but if anyone has ever measured the thickness of the films of printing ink used, I haven't heard of it, and it doesn't matter anyway except to realize that this little bit of ink must possess in a very small compass several qualities which would cause us to marvel were it not such an everyday sort of happening, and so generally taken for granted. This tiny film, which only lays to the fraction of one-thousandth of an inch in thickness, possesses a bit of pigment of color of some sort, whose particles are bound together in an oil or varnish medium, so treated that it will dry either into or on the material used (generally paper of course.) In ordinary conversation, if we wish to express our idea of fineness, we frequently use the expression "as fine as silk," but this little film of ink cannot be described in any such language. It is ground between heavy rolls until every particle of pigment contains its mite of medium, and every particle of oil or varnish carries its load of pigment, and is as smooth and fine, as, well as—good ink should be.

As most of the readers of this issue of *Printer and Publisher* are for moment interested in newspapers, we will in this article discuss newspaper inks and leave inks for other purposes for later discussions.

Newspapers predominate with black; the color comic and illustrated supplements are specials rather than general.

Newspaper ink is made with black gathered by burning natural gas, the chief source of supply being the United States. Different grades of gas and different adjustments in the burners produce blacks of varying qualities and density, but, gen-erally speaking, the color is of a very brownish shade of black, and the ink will require the addition of blue to produce a dense black. The oils used vary but crude petroleum, which has to be specially treated to give it body, tack and drying qualities, before it is suitable for printing purposes, is the most popular.

Newspaper inks are made in different consistencies to suit the speed of the press used. The newspaper pressman has the largest share of control on the appearance of the newspaper. If ink is run sparingly, the paper will naturally present a grayish appearance, as small spots of white paper will show through the black ink, the combination of course making the gray. These spots are often so small as to be scarcely noticeable without the use of a magnifying glass. When too much ink is carried, the danger will be to give the paper a smudgy appearance, and sometimes cause a brownish stain to come through to the opposite side of the sheet, if a thin paper is used. The color of the sheet of paper used has a much greater effect upon the finished appearance of the paper than is generally supposed. The whiter the paper the better the result, but perhaps it did not occur to you that a sheet of newsprint is very seldom white, but generally gray.with a bluish or sometimes a creamy shade. To test this readily make a comparison of the newsprint with some sheets of white bond or coated papers. Complaints are sometimes made that newspaper inks are dirty or gritty. In about ninety-nine cases out of a hundred the trouble is caused by small particles of dust coming off the paper, which will be carried back by the rollers into the ink fountain. Best notify your ink maker of the trouble; a slight change in the formula may help. There is just this last item, if your newspaper is good in some pages and bad in others the trouble is not with the ink. Ink will be either all good or all bad. It will vary slightly with the variations of temperature in the pressroom. Little troubles will naturally creep into your ink fountain occasionally, but after all that little film of ink making the mark which carries the message has a story all its own.

A Profitable Convention

Members of the United Typothetae of America, with reason are expecting an unusually helpful program at the Annual Convention in St. Louis at the Hotel Statler, September 13-15.

Preliminaries in rounding out the program are rapidly going forward and thus far include the formal opening of the Convention at 9.30 Monday, September 13, by President William Green. The Mayor of St. Louis and A. B. Dewes, President of the Ben Franklin Club of St. Louis, will offer the addresses of welcome, to which Mr. Green will respond. Later, the latter will present his annual address.

Joseph A. Borden, General Secretary, will speak on "The Time for Action," and Edward T. Miller, Executive Secretary, is programmed for an address on "Typothetae, an Institution." Henry P. Porter, well known for his work as Chairman of the Typothetae Educational Committee, is forecast to deliver an exceptionally potent message on "The Educational Committee's Newest Contributions."

Not the least interesting feature will be discussions by department heads, of departmental services available to members, including F. A. Silcox, of the Bureau of Industrial Relations; Don V. Gerking, Assistant Secretary, on "The Relations of Fieldmen to Members"; F. M. Sherman, Director of the Trade Composition Department; A. J. Rich, on "Development of the Educational Program"; Chas. L. Estey on "Helping the Printer to Help Himself;" and Walter R. Colton, who will point out the technical and business services rendered by his department, the Bureau of Research and Service.

Bequests of Senator Dennis

By the will of the late Senator Dennis, which has been filed at the Registry of Probate, 55 per cent. of the capital stock of the Halifax *Herald*, Limited, publisher of the Halifax *Herald*, *Evening Mail* and *Sunday Leader*, was left to W. H. Dennis, nephew of deceased, and Vice-President of the company since its reorganization some years ago. Of the remainder of the stock, 35 per cent. is left to William Alexander Dennis, son of the deceased, and 10 per cent. to Andrew W. Robb, a son-in-law, in trust for his son, a grandson of Senator Dennis. To H. Wier, editor of the *Evening Mail*, for 40 years associated with the late Senator Dennis in the publication of his newspapers, is left $10,000; to W. R. McCurdy, an employee of 30 years' standing, is left $6,000; to John Trider, 46 years head pressman $1,000, and to Miss Alice Houston, an employee of 20 years' standing, $1,000. The public bequests include the sum of $100,000 to endow a chair at Dalhousie University, to be known as the "Eric Dennis Chair to Government and Political Science," in memory of Capt. Eric Dennis, M.C., a son of Senator Dennis, killed in the battle of Vimy Ridge; an additional $2,000 to be added to the endowment of the library at Dalhouse University, and $50,000 to be distributed as Mrs. Dennis, widow of the deceased, elects among the various charitable and philanthropic institutions of the city, Protestant and Roman Catholic. The residue of the estate is to be divided among Mrs. Dennis, to whom is left the Halifax residence and contents, and the children of the deceased, including the children of the late Mrs. Andrew Robb, as representing her.

WHY DO YOU ADVERTISE

When You Are Behind In Deliveries ?

❑   ❑

THIS seems to be a very natural question, and the answer involves the discussion of a vital policy of this business—a policy that is fundamental.

If we were building a business for to-day our policy would vary from day to day with the temporary changes with which every business has to contend.

But we are building for the time to come and we hope that this business will become many times greater than it is to-day. Without the proper foundation it would undergo violent changes dependent upon temporary national, local or even imaginary conditions.

If we should permit ourselves to become inflated with self-confidence when business conditions are favorable, restricting our selling and advertising activities, and go down in the dumps when conditions are not so favorable, this business would not amount to any more than the existing conditions would make of it.

We say right now, without reservations, that we hope, regardless of how aggressive and efficient our manufacturing department may be, that it will never be able to catch up with our selling organization.

If our efforts should be halted in the middle of the road in times of liberal buying to wait on the manufacturing department, there might come a time when the manufacturing department would have to suspend operations while waiting on the sales organization.

With such a policy we would be running around in a circle, disorganizing one day and reorganizing the next.

The greater the demand for our product, the quicker the turnover for merchants; and the more frequent the turnovers, the larger is the volume of profit.

In this business advertising is a sales policy—the same as our policy of maintaining a sales organization—and we might as well consider the elimination of one as the other. Neither will be eliminated, as this business needs both if we are building for the future.

We hope the idea will never creep into this organization that there will be any let-up in aggressive methods, which might suggest that when business is good there is no occasion for work and when business is poor it is too hard to get.

We constantly have in mind that the American people are much more concerned in their own affairs than in ours, and if we should restrict our selling and advertising activities they will begin to forget us—and this would be our fault.

We are going ahead with the idea of increasing the present momentum in favor of our goods; and if conditions should turn face about, our dealers and ourselves will be in a better position to hurdle obstacles than if we originated a policy for each condition as it arose.

Reprinted from "GRAPHITE," a monthly magazine published by Joseph Dixon Crucible Co., Jersey City, N.J.

Printer & Publisher

Published on the Twelfth of Each Month.

·H. D. TRESIDDER   - - - -   Business Manager.
A. R. KENNEDY   - - - - - -   Editor.

SUBSCRIPTION PRICE—Canada, Great Britain, South Africa nd
the West Indies, $3 a year; United States, $3.50 a year; other
countries, $4 a year. Single copies, 30 cents. Invariably in
advance.

PUBLISHED BY

THE MACLEAN PUBLISHING CO.
Established 1887   Limited

JOHN BAYNE MACLEAN   - - -   President.
H. T. HUNTER   - - - - -   Vice-President.
H. V. TYRRELL   - - - -   General Manager.
T. B. COSTAIN   - - -   General Managing Editor.

Head Office, 143-153 University Avenue - TORONTO, CANADA
Cable Address Macpubco, Toronto; Atabek, London, Eng.
Also at Montreal, Winnipeg, New York, Chicago, Boston, London,
England.
Application for A.B.C. Audit.

Vol. 29   TORONTO, AUGUST, 1920   No. 8

CONTENTS

The Exchange of Staffs

THE question of making an exchange of members of staffs of papers in various parts of the British Empire was brought up at the meeting of the Imperial Press Conference at Ottawa. There are greater possibilities in this than in the holding of any number of press conferences in various parts of the Empire. In the case of the latter a large number of those attending are not working journalists. Many of them, in fact, hold only a monetary interest. Even if they do hold a position where they can dictate or influence editorial policy, they are certain to fail in passing along anything worth while, for the very good reason that they have not absorbed any of the real national sentiment of this country.

Press conferences bring to mind banquets, after-dinner speeches, and civic welcomes, hurried visits to the show spots of the country, and a general excursion-hued impression of the entire Dominion.

It is not possible under such circumstances for a body of visiting journalists, with all due deference to their powers of observation, to correctly interpret the trend of Canadian feeling to their readers in other portions of the Empire.

By way of comparison, it is just as impossible for a newspaper man of eastern or central Canada to get in touch with the real West by a hurried trip through to the coast with stop-off privileges at the leading centres.

The interchange of staffs, to the exclusion of all but working journalists, is the best chance papers have of successfully carrying out this idea. Take, for instance a party of 50 from a wide-spread area in Canada, and place them on the staff of papers in various parts of the Empire in turn, their places to be filled here by journalists from other countries. Let these visitors have every opportunity of coming in contact with the various phases of existence here; give them a chance to study our labor problems, not only from the standpoint of labor leaders, but from the angle of the great majority of workers, who are not in any labor union; let them feel the pride we have

in the word Canadian as well as the manner in which we cherish the word British; in short, make an effort to let them enter into the real feeling of the people of this country.

A great deal of the world's troubles is caused by misunderstanding—the great mass of the people have not had a chance to see or khow each other. The world press can set itself seriously here to a worth-while task. It can make better use of its space than displaying the scandal and the rubbish of the irresponsible few, and introducing alleged comics that thrive from questionable suggestions or poorly concealed vulgarity.

Government grants could be much better extended to the interchange of staffs than to financing trans-continental trips of journalists that touch only the high spots, and result in little that will make for a better understanding between the people of the various parts of the British Empire.

The Shortage in Paper

THE development of the pulp and paper industry in Canada has been financed to the extent of 75 per cent. by American capital.

Trade follows the source of the capital as a general thing, so this 75 per cent. point makes a very good place from which to start any discussion of the pulp or paper industry.

The demand for paper increases by feet, while the supply increases by inches.

The Governments of Canada, Federal and Provincial, should be made to see the urgency of the situation, and newspapers would be within their rights in bringing every influence to bear on members of the various houses to see to it that Canadian publications are supplied.

There is no prospect, even at present figures, of a betterment in the situation. There seems to be no tendency on the part of publishers to cut down. Many of them feel that it is useless to make any individual or isolated attempt at curtailment, while other papers are firing ahead and turning out tremendously large issues that carry a large advertising revenue.

Unless a slump sets in, which would cause a falling off in the number of pages published, there is little prospect of the paper supply improving.

"What's the matter, doesn't he teeter?"
—Donahey in Cleveland "Plain Dealer."

Wellington County Press Association

Wellington County Press Association held a splendid meeting at Fergus on Friday, July 23rd. There were present publishers from the neighboring border counties as well. Those in attendance were: Messrs. H. P. Moore, and Arlof Dills, the *Free Press*, Acton; J. C. and Hugh C. Templin, the *News-Record*, Fergus; H. M. Donald, the *Progress*, Preston; George Hudson, the *Herald*, Hespeler; A. W. Wright, the *Confederate and Representative*, Mt. Forest; R. E. Mills, the *Express*, Elora; A. R. Aitchison, the *Express*, Clifford; W. Irwin, the *Chronicle*, Durham; A. H. Gardiner, the *Review*, Harriston; Rixon Rafter, B.A., the *Enterprise-News*, Arthur; John Foley, Orangeville.

A welcome was extended to the publishers by Reeve Ewing and Rev. Mr. Aitcheson, representing the town of Fergus, and Mr. Black, president of the Board of Tradde.

The first business under consideration was that of revising the advertising rates, for both local and foreign business. The association, after much discussion, finally drafted a minimum standard of rates for foreign advertising for circulations of a thousand, fifteen hundred and two thousand. A minimum standard for local advertising was also adopted. The revision of the job price list was left to a committee composed of Messrs. Templin, Mills and Wright, When completed the job and advertising rates will be printed, each publisher to be furnished with copies.

A lengthy discussion took place on the $2 subscription, and a resolution was passed recommending that the new rate be established as early as possible. A date will be decided upon later.

Mr. A. R. Aitcheson, of Clifford, read a very interesting paper, "Reminiscences." Mr. J. C. Templin, in a paper on "Newsprint" presented some useful information. A well-prepared paper on the value of editorial in the weekly newspaper was given by Mr. Hugh C. Templin.

Sessions were held at 10 a.m. and 2 p.m. The kindly hospitality shown by Mr. Templin and his family made the visit of the publishers a most enjoyable one.

Mr. R. E. Mills of Elora *Express*, was elected president, and Mr. A. W. Wright, Mt. Forest, secretary treasurer.

Get the Customer's Signature

The Employing Printers' Association of Chicago is doing a good deal of missionary work in order to consolidate the trade. Here is one of its little exhortations to printers, admittedly good sense.

Printer Jones was turning out a rush order for Brown & Company. At the last minute, just before going to press, Jones submitted a final proof to Brown for O.K. Brown made a lot of alterations on the proof—and failed to sign it! Jones made the alterations and produced the job on time, to Brown's entire satisaction. But when he presented a bill embodying an extra charge for those alterations, Brown refused to pay it! The case was taken into court. A lot of extra time had to be spent, and the foreman had to leave his work and come to court before the judge was satisfied. But payment was made.

Printer Smith had just completed the production of a large run of booklets for his customer, Mr. Green. All the booklets had been delivered excepting some ten thousand. So these ten thousand were packed and checked and delivered by Smith's driver one fine morning. But when Green came to pay the bill some time later, he denied absolutely all knowledge of this last delivery of ten thousand, and refused to pay for them. Now Smith had no receipt to show that his driver had actually delivered these booklets. So in his case Court action was taken. The driver was no longer in Smith's employ, and a lot of detective work and expense was necessary before he could be produced in court to testify to the delivery. But the amount due was recovered.

The moral of these two stories is plain.

Get the customer's signature for every alteration, make him sign for every delivery! Then if there is any misunderstanding or disagreement as to alterations or deliveries, in ninety-nine cases out of a hundred your possession of that signature will make it easy to straighten out the difficulty immediately.

Controls the Dennis Publications

W. H. Dennis, the new managing owner of the Halifax *Herald*, *Evening Mail* and *Sunday Leader*, is perhaps the youngest man in Canada to assume such a position. He succeeds the late Senator Dennis, by provision of the will of the latter, the Senator leaving him a controlling interest in the business.

W. H. Dennis became connected with the Dennis publications eighteen years ago, being then a mere boy, he being now only in his 34th year. The first eight years of his connection with the papers were spent in the mechanical, reportorial and business departments and ten years ago he was given a share in the active direction, eventually being appointed vice-president and manager. To-day he is managing owner. Under his direction the Dennis papers have become national institutions, enjoying

W. H. DENNIS

immense circulations and very extensive advertising patronage. Formerly political organs, they are now independent of party affiliation.

W. H. Dennis owes his success to his own personal efforts. While the fact that his being a nephew of the late Senator accounts for his being connected with the publications controlled in his life time by the Senator, that does not account for his elevation to the responsible position which he now occupies. He is a hard worker, always on the job, always ready to go after news himself if there is nobody else to go; always ready to consider a new idea and quick to execute it if it appeals to him. Of considerable personal magnetism and a good business head he proved just the man the Senator desired to carry on his work and to keep the publications in the front rank of Canadian journalism.

A Winnipeg Business that Grew

In the anniversary number of the Winnipeg *Free Press'* Stovel Company, Ltd., give an interesting story of the growth and development of their business, from the time of its inception in 1889. Then the firm used 750 feet of floor space and three men were employed. The growth of the Stovel trade is shown by the fact that one of the many interesting orders entrusted to the firm in recent years was that of supplying the Chinese Railways with passenger tickets. They supplied millions of such, and, as far as they can decipher the correspondence on the subject, to the entire satisfaction of the shrewd Chinese officials. The present Stovel plant extends from Dagmar to Ellen streets on Ballantyne Ave. It has 84,000 feet of floor space, and is 110 times greater than the original plant of 1889. The firm is still under the active management of its founders, Messrs. John Stovel, A. B. Stovel and C. T. Stovel.

REVIEW OF JOB SPECIMENS

 If You Want An Opinion On
Your Work, Send It In

NOVA SCOTIA turns out some pretty good printers. This week *Printer and Publisher* devotes a lot of space to specimens of G. D. Purdy, with the Truro Printing and Publishing Co. There is no apology made for the amount of space devoted, for a glance at the work will show a considerable amount of originality, a very good conception of grouping, and a well-defined idea of the part white space plays in display.

FIG. A.—The original of this was done on green stock with another color green ink and brown. The whole combination was pleasing. If a criticism were to be offered it might be

The little ornament, which in the original was in the lesser color, is quite in keeping with the subject treated, viz., a Citizens' Band. A compositor should always keep in mind the fact that any ornamentation should be in keeping with the nature of the job. If that is not possible, keep your decoration in line with your type faces. Above all else—if in doubt—leave it out. Mr. Purdy has done well in using groupings that add length to the appearance of his title pages, rather than width.

FIG. C.—This was done on cream stock ripple finish, in dark blue and red, the red consisting of the letter "S" inserted in the border, and the italic upper and lower in the top of the design. In its original form this piece of work was most creditable. If lines are drawn left and right from a point slightly below the words "for 1920" it will be found that a pyramid of almost perfect proportion is formed. In this page the compositor has shown that it is quite possible to have a

Figure A.

Figure B.

that the three words grouped at the top in caps seem rather harsh, and might stand a little toning down by using an upper and lower in part. The amount of type and the ornament—which looks much lighter in the original—is well used. Mr. Purdy has left the job alone at the right time. It is an effective cover even as it stands, and is not of such a character that it would unduly gauge the time clock.

FIG. B.—Buff stock was used in B with orange and black ink. There is a very ingenious use made of Italic in the upper grouping of B to prevent the job from being stiff and studied.

Announcing

The STRAND and
PRINCESS
POLICY

for 1920

SOUVENIR THEATRICAL
ANNOUNCEMENT
for the
NEW YEAR

Figure C.

good display by using nothing but white space. Had he used an ornament as he has done in the other two pages it would have shown a sameness that in this way is pleasantly avoided.

FIG. D. shows two posters or hand bills by the same compositor. There are many offices in smaller centres turning out sixteenth and eighth sheets in a way that is no credit to the compositor or the office. Apparently Mr. Purdy does not consider that a dodger needs any less artistic treatment than anything else. The one on the left was done in brown, while red ink on white stock was used for the other. In both cases the strength of the bill has been carried right from top to bottom. In too many cases a small bill has the fault of dwindling away toward the bottom. The use of the large ornamental "T" in the right hand bill is a particularly good treatment, and carries the eye interest of the reader right down, so that it will in all probability be read.

PYROXYLIN plastic, sold under various trade names such as pyralin, celluloid, fiberloid, French ivory, etc., is becoming very popular as a material to be used in place of cardboard for business cards, vest pocket schedules and calendars, interest and discount tables, etc.

Ordinary printers' ink does not adhere to the pol-

ished surface of this material. It requires a special printers' ink to give satisfaction. This special ink is made of a pyroxylin base of about the consistency of thick mucilage combined with the desired anilin color.

It is not desirable to try printing on the polished stock even with this special ink. Manufacturers of printed pyroxylin plastic novelties buy their sheeting unglazed. The printing is done on these unpolished sheets which are then thoroughly dried and afterwards polished by placing them between highly polished nickeled plates and subjected to pressure in a hydraulic press equipped with a heating unit. The heat must not exceed 190 degrees Fahrenheit. The cutting or shaping is done after the printing and polishing have been completed.

Many printers will wonder why this special ink serves the purpose better than ordinary printers ink. It is because the pyroxylin base and the "ivory" cards are made of the same basic substance, soluble cotton. This ink does not merely adhere to the surface of the card; it combines with it; sinks into it; becomes an integral part of it.

TO GET the required number of apprentices for the plants that are members of the Baltimore Typothetae, that association has begun an advertising campaign to induce the boy just out of grammar school to enter the printing industry, either as a printer, binder, electrotyper, photoengraver, or pressman, and sets forth the advantages that await the ambitious and studious boy who is looking to the trade of his livelihood. The advertisement shows that the ambitious worker can graduate into the foreman, the superintendent, the manager, or the office executive, and shows that there is a dearth of such material in the printing plants of Baltimore. It also shows that there is no limit to the possibilities of a young man with the will to succeed.

D. B. MORGAN, a printer on a Springfield, Mo., newspaper, who has always been rather pessimistic about old time slogans, has just about decided to change his mind. There is a reason. A short time ago he missed a $50 Liberty Bond. There had been a house cleaning around his home and it was finally decided that the bond had been thrown out with a lot of papers which were briskly burning in the yard of his home. It happened to be a rather windy day and when a search was made the bond was found a short distance from the fire with just a corner of the envelope slightly burned.

STRAND
Monday and Tuesday

WALLACE
REID

FEATURING in

"Too Many Millions"

The old question "What would you do with forty million dollars" is the tough problem that faces hero and heroine in a highly delightful picture

Extra!

New Motion Pictures of the

*Prince of
Wales'*

visit to Canada and the wonderful reception he received.

STRAND THEATRE
Monday-Tuesday
•

ANITA
STEWART
in her First Super-Picture

Virtuous
Wives

"Cosmopolitan" Magazine s
Greatest Story of all times.

THE TRUTH about married life in New York Society—A modern answer to "What is Virtue in a Wife?"—picturing in splendorous settings and by a great cast the story of "Virtuous Wives" from the two million edition book by OWEN JOHNSON

Showing in addition to a Short Subject
7.30 and 9.00. Prices 20c plus tax

Figure D.

Fifty Years of Service

Hamilton *Herald*:—In these latter times, more restless and changeful than the old, one rarely hears of such a thing as half a century of unbroken relations between employer and employed. Fifty years of continuous faithful service! It is so rare as to be noteworthy. That is the record of James R. Allan, advertising manager of the Hamilton *Spectator*. Fifty years ago he entered the service of the Spectator Printing Company as office boy, and for the greater part of the half-century he has occupied his present position. Mr. Allan is not only the oldest (in length of service) of all the numerous employees of Southam Limited in several cities, but has been connected with the *Spectator* for a longer period than Mr. Southam himself; for Mr. Allan had been a *Spectator* man for seven years and had grown to man's estate when Messrs. Southam and Carey came here from London to take over the old paper. Of those who worked on it and for it when he began his long career of service, not one remains. He has seen many—how many—come and go—some to take advantage of other opportunities in the newspaper world, some to take up other vocations, some to pass into the eternal silence; but he has stayed on. The old *Spec* owes not a little to his energy, industry, skill and fidelity. He is by far the best-known man in its service—and the best liked. An incurable optimist, full of the charity that thinketh no evil, with firm faith in the abiding goodness of human nature, it is not strange that the old *Spec's* "sunny Jim" has a friend in every acquaintance. His record of fifty years' service is honorable alike to him and to the *Spectator* company. May it be extended until the twentieth century is no longer young!

Additional Space for the Globe

The *Globe* (Toronto) has completed an addition to its building at the corner of Yonge and Melinda. For some years the Globe Printing Company has owned the lot to the south of its old property, but building operations were delayed on account of the war. Across Melinda street is the Head Office building of the Dominion Bank, covering a third of a city block. Across Yonge street is the Bank of Hamilton building, Toronto's first sky-scraper. Adjacent to the latter building is the Canadian Pacific Railway building, while on the corner opposite is the Royal Bank building, the highest office building in the British Empire. The *Globe's* addition will add 50 per cent. to its floor space. The new ground floor will be devoted to the president's office, the executive book-keepers and cashier's department. The second and third floors have been appropriated to the editorial staff and news room, and will provide much needed extensions. Another octuple press is being installed, and the stereotyping plant, which has been renewed, is now turning out plates 5 agate lines longer than previously. The paper thus used, which formerly was wasted in margins, has a value of over $10,000 a year. Lamson steel carriers will load from the presses to the mailing room which has been doubled in size. Several new linotypes have been purchased. The improved plant and increased floor space are urgently required to take care of present business and editorial conditions.

———

A piece of thin rubber sheeting of the kind used by dentists, will often satisfactorily soften the edges of an otherwise refractory vignetted half-tone when placed on top of the regular make-ready.

———

Cannot you quietly suggest to many customers that it is probable few of their letters or bills go out full weight of their postage allowance. Envelope and package "stuffers" can carry arguments or tell things that letters and bills must omit. They cost little and they can be made immensely attractive. If they help prestige, provoke inquiries or bring orders they have turned the waste places into profits. It is a good thing to do these days, and, incidentally, a useful field for the printer who can devise "envelope fillers."

———

The Quebec *Telegraph* has a subscription contest on at present, the prizes including two automobiles, piano player, and commissions to all on amounts turned in in excess of $25.00.

Can Export Canadian Paper

The following group of trade inquiries in regard to paper comes from the chief paper users of Rumania. L. D. Wilgress, Canadian trade commissioner at Bucharest, has apparently been in touch with many of these people who are now looking for a place to buy paper they used to secure in Europe. More particulars, together with names and addresses, can be secured by writing to this office or the Department of Trade and Commerce, Commercial Intelligence Branch, Ottawa, and mentioning the numbers used here:

1265—Paper. A newspaper in Rumania desires to receive samples and quotations from Canadian firms in a position to export newsprint paper.

1266—A newspaper in Rumania desires to receive samples and quotations from Canadian firms in a position to export newsprint paper.

1267—A newspaper in Rumania desires to receive samples and quotations from Canadian firms in a position to export newsprint paper as well as any other kind of book paper.

1268—A book printing house in Rumania desires to receive samples and quotations from Canadian firms in a position to export newsprint as well as any kind of cheap and finer papers.

1269—A printing firm in Rumania desires to receive samples and quotations from Canadian firms in a position to export all kinds of paper in general.

1270—A printing firm in Rumania desires to receive samples and quotations from Canadian firms in a position to export all kinds of paper.

1271—A firm in Rumania for sale of books and stationery in general desires to receive samples and quotations from Canadian firms in a position to export all kinds of paper.

1272—A firm in Rumania for printing and sale of books and stationery in general desires to receive samples and quotations from Canadian firms in a position to export all kinds of paper.

1273—A firm in Rumania desires to receive quotations and other particulars from Canadian firms in a position to export all kinds of paper in general.

Here's a Real Bouquet

Winnipeg *Telegram*:—As it is understood that our contemporary, the Manitoba *Free Press*, is associating its own history of progress with that of the celebration of the Province's golden jubilee today, we avail ourselves of the privilege of proffering the *Free Press* our sincerest congratulations upon its honorable career. So close is it to reaching its own fiftieth anniversary that it is most appropriate that the Province's celebration should, to this small degree at least, have associated with it this recognition of the sustained merit of the *Free Press*. The duty, as often without question the pleasure, of the *Telegram* has been to differ, and to differ very sharply from the *Free Press* in matters of public policy; but the Telegram has not yet found occasion upon which it could differ from its esteemed contemporary's conception of its journalistic function. We can only sincerely hope that the *Free Press* will continue its splendid record for another fifty years and more, so that the *Telegram* on the celebration of its own centenary again may be permitted to extend the hand of journalistic goodwill to its valuable colleague on the common ground and in the mutual service of serving the news, and striving rightly to guide public opinion in the fair province of Manitoba.

———

The Stratford *Herald* and the *Daily Beacon* announced an increase in subscription rates to $6 per year in the city and $4 by mail or 3 cents per copy. The reason given for the increase is the increased cost of newsprint and materials.

———

The Ottawa *Citizen* has been running a page of business on the lucky name idea. The names of Ottawa women are put in certain of the ads, said names being selected from the city directory. Prizes are awarded each week as follows, first $6; second, $4; third, $3; fourth, $2 and fifth, $1., the prizes being given in the order of their value to those whose cash receipt shows the greatest amount spent at the stores whose ads appear on the page. The same page runs for 13 weeks and the names are changed weekly.

What Should a Rate Card Have to Say?
Weekly Paper Should Be Careful of Facts

Mr. J. C. Holland of the Stanstead *Journal*, brings up the question of rate cards for weekly papers, a subject that has been receiving considerable attention. Mr. Holland apparently wants to get a model rate card, in which there are no faults. He writes as follows:—

Rate cards are among the things which sometimes make me wish I had been a preacher instead of a publisher. I suppose there may be consistent rate cards, but I have never happened to see one that could not be "shot to pieces" in a minute. Practically all of them read something like this:

1 inch or over	20c an inch			
50 "	"	" 14c "	"	
100 "	"	" 12c "	"	
200 "	"	" 10c "	"	
300 "	"	" 9c "	"	

These figures are taken from the rate card of a leading Ontario weekly, which I now have before me. I think you will recognize them as being similar to a number you have already published from time to time, although I have omitted most of the detail.

According to the above schedule, 45 inches will cost the advertiser $9.00, but he can buy 50 inches for $7.00; 95 inches will cost him $13.30 but he can buy 100 inches for $12.00; 195 inches will cost him $23.40, but he can obtain 200 inches for $20.000, and so on.

Are we business men?

Some years ago I got out a rate card, but I did not dare to let anybody see it—at least not for a long time. Then I got up courage and sent it to a few advertising agents from whom I sought advice. None of them vouchsafed a reply. Maybe they all dropped dead. I hope the editor of *Printer and Publisher* may not suffer such a fate, but I cannot resist the temptation to send him a copy of the card, not for publication, but for his personal information.

Another matter I would like to refer to is that of special positions. On the Ontario card above mentioned, I noticed this: "Preferred position 1 cent an inch extra. Top of column guaranteed 2 cents an inch extra." This is not particularly original; it is common to the majority of rate cards. Suppose it be a two-inch ad that must be given position at top of column. The make-up man would very likely be seriously hindered, and the appearance of the whole page might be marred, while the publisher would receive four cents gross, less agent's commission of 25 per cent., or three cents net. If the extra charge be on a percentage basis, it works out about the same. Since a first-class position must be sacrificed, it has seemed to me that the "extra" should be a "fixed" charge, but I must confess that the exact solution is beyond me.

Press associations maintain services for the benefit of newspaperdom. If they be manned by experts, what greater blessing could they bestow upon the craft than that of working out a consistent rate-card?

Yours truly,
Rock Island, Que.,   JOHN CALVIN HOLLAND.
July 26, 1920.

What the Agency Said

Printer and Publisher took this rate card up with several of the Toronto agencies, and asked them what they thought of it. "In the first place," answered the space buyer for one of these firms, "it is too complicated. It would be a very difficult matter to make use of such a card in checking up a paper. It would be much better to work on a flat rate. Then in the second place the card does not say what special positions are. The wording is simply 'Special rates for special positions.' The publishers ought to realize that this special position proposition is one of the hardest things we have to sell to an advertiser. After we get a man started in a paper he often comes along and suggests that he is not getting nearly as good a position on the page as some other firm, and very often the whole thing has been explained to him before. Then we have to go all over the special position business with him. So rate cards should state very plainly what the papers consider are special positions and what they charge for them.

The Rate Card Referred To

Printer and Publisher is reproducing the card used by Mr. Holland. It is 3½ x 5¼, black on buff stock.

THE STANSTEAD JOURNAL
Established 1845
Independent   Published Thursday

ADVERTISING RATES

Space	Per Inch Space	Per Inch Space	Per Inch Space	Per Inch Space	Per Inch
1″	42c	8″	35c	15″	28c	40″	21c

Space	Per Inch	Space	Per Inch	Space	Per Inch	Space	Per Inch
1″	42c	8″	35c	15″	28c	40″	21c
2	41	9	34	16	27	50	20
3	40	10	33	17	26	60	19
4	39	11	32	18	25	70	18
5	38	12	31	19	24	80	17
6	37	13	30	20	23	90	16
7	36	14	29	30	22	100	15

Figure "odd" inches above twenty at rate nearest space used, above or below, thus: 23 inches at 23 cents an inch, 27 inches at 22 cents an inch; 92 inches at 16 cents an inch, 98 inches at 15 cents an inch (five cents an inch less if plates are furnished ready for the press.

The above rates are for "display" advertising, and cover composition charge, weekly change.

When plates are furnished ready for the press, a deduction of 5 cents an inch is allowed.

When plates are unmounted or require the fitting of type in mortices, or addition of local names, deduct 4 cents an inch from the above prices.

When type is set up, but changed only occasionally, or not at all, deduct 4 cents an inch.

Rates given are for "run of paper."

Special rates for special positions,

Six months allowed for completion of any order or contract up to 100 inches.

Any order canceled before completion will be short rated according to above schedule.

Legal Advertising, Public Notices, Auction Sales, etc., 10 cents a line for the first insertion, 3 cents a line for each subsequent insertion.

Locals 10 cents a line for each insertion.

Sworn circulation six months ending————copies.

The Journal Printing Co., Publishers,
Rock Island, Que.

"Another objection I would have to that card is that it speaks in inches, whereas all the big advertisers are in the habit now of getting their space in lines. It might be better for him to use two separate cards, one for local and another for foreign.

Where Trouble Comes In

"And right here," remarked the agency man, "let me state that we get into a lot of trouble because there are better rates given at times to local dealers than would be extended to the national advertiser. Very often we have campaigns to put on in connection with a local dealer on a fifty-fifty basis. When the settling up time comes we bill the dealer with the rate charged us by the newspaper for our share of the advertising. I wish you could see some of the letters we get back from the dealers, telling us that we are robbing them because the paper has only charged them such and such a rate for the space they had to pay for, and wanting to know why we are billing them at an advanced rate. We write back showing the rate charged by the paper to us, which is higher than charged to the local dealer. The result is that the national advertiser gets disgusted at the whole thing and wants to drop the campaign entirely as far as these papers are concerned. I really believe that a number of larger advertisers are scared out of a number of papers on this account.

"Would there be any discrimination against a paper that charged a higher rate to all because it was turning out a good sheet that was worth the money?"

"No," replied the agency, "there would not. It is hard, though, to get a rate for papers that show too much difference. It is a fact, and a hard one too, that many a good weekly paper is kept back simply on account of the company it keeps. The publishers of the weekly papers, and some of the smaller dailies as well, have it in their own power to do a great deal to help themselves in the matter of getting their house in shape to go before the national advertiser with a suggested campaign. It is a hard matter for an agency to go into the merits of each individual paper with the advertiser, and if there were more strong weekly papers it would undoubtedly mean that there would be more of the national advertisers in the weekly papers."

There is also produced here pages 2 and 3 of the card of the Modeltown *Mail*, an imaginary paper published and supposed conditions. It meets with general approval by the agencies. Of course it has its defects, one of these being the way in which it slides over the special position part of the card, simply mentioning that a special price is charged. This card, it must be remembered, was prepared for weekly papers. The Weekly Press Association at several of its meetings has considered the matter of a standardized rate card for use by its members, and the chances are that it will bring out a rate card soon that will reflect the ideas of a good many of the best men in the weekly division.

The Modeltown Mail
ESTABLISHED 1880
MODELTOWN, CANADA

WEEKLY. All home print. Dated for Friday; goes to press Thursday afternoon. In politics, Independent Conservative. Latest sworn average circulation, 2,700. Present circulation, 2,800. 8 pages. 7 columns to page. Columns 21¾ inches long, 13 ems wide. Cannot use mats. Subscription rates $1.50 a year in Canada.

ADVERTISING RATES
Effective July 1, 1918.

DISPLAY CONTRACTS—PLATE MATTER

Agate measurement—14 lines to the inch.

1 inch and over —	cents per inch
50 inches and over —	cents per inch
100 inches and over —	cents per inch
200 inches and over —	cents per inch
	(No lower rate)

DISPLAY CONTRACTS — SET MATTER

cents per inch additional to above figures.

SPECIAL POSITIONS
The above rates are for run of paper. We always endeavor to satisfy our advertisers in regard to location, but when special positions are required, extra charges will be made according to position stipulated.

CONDITIONS OF CONTRACT
The rates quoted are for space to be used within 12 months of date of contract. If amount of space contracted for is not used within a year, the rate applying for the number of inches used will be enforced. If sufficient additional space is used to earn a lower rate, the lower rate will be given. All advertising subject to the approval of the publisher. The publisher not bound to insert over 40 inches in any one issue.

CO-OPERATION WITH ADVERTISERS
The Mail will extend all possible and reasonable co-operation with the advertiser and local dealer towards promoting the sale of any line of goods in Modeltown.

READING MATTER
In purely "local" column (first and fifth page), ...c. a line; 3 months' contract or over, with minimum of five lines a week, ...c. a line. On other pages, twice display matter rates. ....-point body type.

SPECIAL ADVERTISING
Financial and annual statements of banks and other corporations, ...c. an inch.
Political and election advertising, ...c. an inch.
Legal and formal Government and Municipal advertising, ...c. per line for first insertion; ....c. per line each subsequent insertion.

CONDENSED ADVERTISING
.... cent per word each insertion for first 4 insertions. Subsequent insertions .... cent a word. Minimum charge ....c. per insertion.

New Records Looked for at Canadian National Exhibition

"Work and Prosper" is the motto adopted for the 1920 Canadian National Exhibition and the entire machinery of the organization has been turned to the task of making the forty-second annual event a striking exemplification of the appropriateness of the slogan. Unwilling to rest on the standard of previous expositions the directors and management have utilized every resource of this mighty Canadian institution in the effort to make the position of the enterprise more noteworthy. Early indications point to new records in every department, perhaps also in matter of attendance which reached the magnificent total of 1,201,000 last year, a figure never attained even by the monster World's Fairs at Paris, London, Chicago, San Francisco, etc., in the same number of consecutive days. To be one of the crowd that establishes an even greater record this year will in itself be a thing to boast about, but even more important still will be the fact that all who come will see a field of marvels which will make the Big Fair undoubtedly the most remarkable and interesting array of activity and achievement ever presented.

Beware of New Paper Companies

Investment Items, published by the Royal Securities Corporation, has the following to say regarding new pulp and paper flotations:

"It must be borne in mind that the arguments which have been presented apply only to companies which are efficiently designed, that is to say, those which present a proper and well balanced combination of large supplies of cheap pulpwood, water power, mechanical plant and transportation facilities— and which are under efficient management both as to operation and marketing. There are a number of companies, and there will be more, which are radically defective in one or more of these respects, but which are pushing their securities into the hands of unwary investors under cover of the general prosperity of the pulp and paper business and the general popularity of its securities. Most particularly is it essential that the investor should satisfy himself as to the reserve of pulpwood available for future operations, since the supply of this raw material, in commercially convenient areas, is so limited that it may be utterly impossible in future years for any company to supplement its resources not only without paying greatly increased prices, but at any price at all."

THE PERSONAL SIDE OF IT

 We'd Like To Get Items For
These Columns

Quebec

The directors of *L'Evenement*, Quebec, announce the appointment of Florian Gortin, as managing director. Several other changes have been made in the organization.

Mr. J. H. Fortier of Quebec announces the foundation of *Le Novelliste*, the first daily paper to be published in Three Rivers, with Romald Bourque as business manager. Mr. Bourque was, until recently, associated with the Canadian office of the Monotype Co.

Maritimes

Mariner Ripley, linotype operator on the *Evening Mail*, has returned from his vacation, which was spent in Montreal.

Roy Fader, linotype machinist on the *Evening Mail*, is spending his vacation at Ingramport, N.S.

F. L. Yorke, of the *Evening Mail* Advertising Dept., is spending his holidays in Montreal. Mr. Yorke was formerly with the Ottawa *Citizen*.

Edgar Mason, foreman at the Royal Print & Litho., is spending his vacation in Halifax as he feels that his native city is as good as any other place in which to spend a vacation.

Dick Walsh, ad-setter on the *Evening Echo*, leaves shortly with wife and family for Orlando, Florida, where he will in future reside.

W. H. Dennis, nephew of the late Senator Dennis, who is now the guiding spirit of the Halifax *Herald* and *Evening Mail*, paid a visit to Ottawa recently.

M. M. McLean, editor of the *Canadian Brotherhood of Railway Employees' Magazine*, was in Halifax the latter part of July assisting the Labor Party in their election campaign.

James W. Power, news editor on the *Acadian Recorder*, of Halifax, enjoyed a motor trip through the province as far as Weymouth, during the latter part of July.

Mr. Edwin C. Young, business manager of the Chronicle Publishing Co, was on a business trip to Montreal early this month.

Alexander McMillan, head of the printing and publishing house of J. & A. McMillan, Ltd., has recently been honored in being appointed to the board of management of the St. John Hospital.

The St. Francis Xavier Press, at Antigonish, have recently issued a 250 page memorial to the Catholic soldiers and nurses from that diocese who served in the great war, The book is beautifully illustrated and a credit to the community issuing it.

W. R. McCurdy, who has been connected for over 30 years with the *Herald* and *Mail* newspapers, has retired from active service on these dailies, He is, however, still on the pay roll and is at present enjoying a well-earned rest at Gaspeaux.

The Nova Scotia Veteran Pub. Co. are busy compiling a book on Nova Scotia's achievement in the great war. The book is being edited by Capt. Hunt. and Dr. J. D. Logan, and will be printed by the Ryerson Press of Toronto. It is expected to be ready about August 30th.

Mayor McBride, of Brantford, Ont., who is by the way a member of the Typographical Union, spent some time in Halifax previous to the Provincial Elections which were held July 27th. Mr. McBride was a very able speaker on behalf of the Labor Party.

An Election Extra, consisting of two pages, was issued by the *Citizen*, the Halifax Labor paper, and 6,000 copies circulated in the interest of the Labor Party, previous to the recent provincial elections. It was a very creditable sheet and the only extra published during the campaign.

Sydney *Post*:—Jack McLellan, of the reportorial staff of the *Post*, who has been at East Bay spending vacation, came to the city last night and is at present at the home of Chief of Police McCormack, who is his uncle. Mr. McLellan, who has been ill for some weeks past, will be taken to St. Joseph's hospital, Glace Bay, for treatment.

Miss Helen Bissett, formerly of the *Evening Echo* staff at Halifax, who retired from her position for a season with the Boston English Opera Co., in which she was very successful, has returned to the *Echo*, replacing Miss Tyler, who has retired from newspaper work. It is understood Miss Bissett will rejoin the opera company on its opening for next season.

The announcement has been recently made that after negotiations lasting several months a special meeting of the shareholders of the St. John *Standard* has been held, at which the plant, equipment, etc., have all been sold to H. V. McKinnon, who has now assumed control. Mr. McKinnon is well known in newspaper circles, having been for some years past actively engaged in connection with newspaper management, both from a business and editorial standpoint. He is well qualified to be in full control.

The members of the Imperial Press Conference visiting Canada in organized party met with a hearty welcome in St. John. They were given a cordial reception, arriving here on the morning of Friday, July 30th, and leaving for Fredericton the following day. They were taken for a tour about the St. John harbor in the morning, then the ladies and gentlemen were taken to different places for the purposes of entertainment. The civic authorities tendered a luncheon at the Manor House. There was also a luncheon at the Riverside Golf Club and Mrs. F. B. Ellis, wife of Frank B. Ellis of the St. John *Globe*, was hostess at an enjoyable luncheon at the Royal Hotel for the ladies of the party. Dancing and music were enjoyed in the evening at the Golf Clubhouse. The delegates expressed themselves as greatly pleased with their stay in the city.

Montreal *Gazette*:—By the terms of the will of the late Senator William Dennis, the controlling interest in his newspapers, the Halifax *Herald*, *Evening Mail* and *Sunday Leader*, passes to Mr. W. H. Dennis, nephew of the late Dennis, although a relatively young man, has passed through practically every branch of the organization of which he is now the head, beginning at the foot of the ladder and winning his way to the top by industry, energy and the exercise of sound business judgment, qualities similar to those with which the late Senator Dennis was endowed. Mr. Dennis takes over a large responsibility, but one to which he is in every way equal, and he will be welcomed to the ranks of Canadian newspaper publishers.

British Columbia

The Creston *Review* is now in the $2.50 a year class—the second paper in West Kootenay to adopt the higher rate.

Kaslo *Kootenaian* has discarded the patent inside, and is now issuing four pages of home print.

Fred Roo of Elko, one of the best known Kootenay newspaper correspondents, died last month.

Walter Jordan of the *Review* is chairman of the committee handling this year's six day "Chautauqua" at Revelstoke.

R. T. Lowery of the *Ledge*, Greenwood, who has been in Grand Forks hospital the past two months, has almost recovered sufficiently to resume his editorial labors.

R. J. McDougall of the *Herald* is touring the interior investigating the city manager form of government on behalf of the Penticton council.

The Comox *Argus*, Courtenay, B.C., Ben Hughes, editor, have increased both advertising and subscription rates recently. Its circulation has increased 225 in three months.

Balance is the name of a new monthly publication that has just made its appearance at Vancouver. Its first issue was unique—it contained no advertisements of any sort.

East Kootenay supported just one issue of the *Labor News*, which got out its initial and only issue at Cranbrook last month. It was too red for most everyone but the editor, and the *Courier* refused to publish further issues.

J. A. MacKelvie, editor of the Vernon *News*, is mentioned as the possible successor to Hon. Martin Burrell, who has retired as M.P. for Yale. Another possibility is R. J. McDougall of the *Herald*, Penticton, who also has a paper at Princeton.

The *Gazette*, Grand Forks, is twenty-five years old. Since acquiring it nine years ago T. A. Love claims its circulation has trebled, despite the fact that the population on its territory has little more than held its own.

The *Review* office, Revelstoke, was the scene of a burglary early in July and an effort made to force open the safe. Editor Jordan had just recently sold his fruit ranch at Robson for $6,000 and it is presumed the knight of the jimmy and dark lantern fondly imagined the initial payment on the ranch was locked up in the safe.

Alberta

Calgary's Mayor, R. C. Marshall, is receiving congratulations on the birth of a baby boy. Mrs. Marshall was formerly Miss Daisy McGregor, City Hall reporter on the Calgary *Herald*, and previously society reporter on the Ottawa *Journal*. They were married a year ago.

Saskatchewan

T. Wayling, formerly city editor of the Prince Albert *Herald*, has been appointed advertising manager. Previously he was classified advertising man for the Winnipeg *Free Press*, going there from the city advertising department of the T. Eaton Co., Winnipeg.

Joint announcement is made by W. F. Herman, proprietor of the Saskatoon *Daily Star*, the Regina *Daily Post* and the *Border Cities' Star*, of Windsor, Ont., and by the Leader Publishing Company, Limited, which controls the Saskatoon *Phoenix*. The Regina *Daily Post* has been taken over by the Leader Publishing Company, Limited, and will in future be published from its office, and the Saskatoon *Daily Phoenix* has been taken over by W. F. Herman, and will in future be published from the office of the Saskatoon *Daily Star*.

Ontario

Essex and Kent publishers are going to put into effect the $2 per year rate on October 1.

Bert Penny, city hall reporter of the London *Advertiser*, is spending his holidays in Windsor and Detroit.

Charles Ramage, formerly of the Durham *Review*, has joined the reportorial staff of the *Border Cities Star*, at Windsor, Ont.

Haviland Nash, advertising manager of the London *Advertiser*, is spending his vacation in Muskoka.

J. A. Heidt, city editor of the Jacksonville, Florida *Metropolis* spent a week in London, Ont., recently visiting with friends.

The Watford *Guide-Advocate* took its annual holiday in July 23rd week.

J. W. Tibbs, news manager of the Canadian Press, spent a few days in Windsor this month.

Major Andrew Cory, late city editor of the Toronto *World*, is now telegraph editor of the *Border Cities Star*, Windsor.

C. V. Blatchford, editor of the Listowel *Banner*, and wife motored to Bruce Beach on Lake Huron recently and spent a very pleasant holiday with friends.

Mrs. T. Neelands, wife of T. Neelands, former proprietor of the Hensall *Observer* is spending her vaction with relatives at Oakville, Ont.

Norman Hibbert of the Petrolia *Advertiser-Topic*, spent his vacation with his parents, Mr. and Mrs. J. G. Hibbert at Walkerton, Ont.

Miss Helen McMillan, society editress of the London *Advertiser*, is spending her vacation at Bayfield. The society column is being looked after by Miss Marjorie Stevenson.

N. M. McLeod, at one time on the staff of the Toronto *Times*, is leaving the *Border Cities Star*, Windsor, to join the staff of the *Phoenix*, Saskatoon.

H. McCracken Morden, city hall man for the *Border Cities Star*, Windsor, is on the job again after a holiday at Jackson's Point.

The office of the Carp *Review* was swept by fire. The loss is placed at $12,000, with insurance of $5,000. Mr. A. E. Evoy is the owner.

Edgar Lindsay has taken the position of superintendent of the *Herald* office in Guelph. For some time past he has been on the mechanical staff of the Toronto *Star*, prior to which he was with the *Herald*.

A. Verne Wall, at one time on the staff of the Peterborough *Review*, and later with the *Border Cities Star*, Windsor, has lately been employed on the local staff of the Detroit *Journal*.

C. C. Rammage, at one time with the Oshawa *Reformer* and London *Advertiser* and later with the Cadillac Motor Car Company, Detroit, is now on the reportorial staff of the *Border Cities Star*, Windsor.

Members of the composing room staff of the *Telegram* presented T. E. Till, one of the veterans of the organization, with a club bag upon the eve of his departure for California. Mr. Till has been with the *Telegram* since the installation of their first machine and is a prominent member of No. 91, Typographical Union.

J. Frank Perkins, formerly proprietor of the Petrolia *Topic*, at Petrolia, Ont., has been appointed director of publicity for the Orton Motor Co. of Petrolia. Mr. Perkins recently returned after having served overseas with the 7th Canadian Mounted Rifles. He spent some time in England after the close of the war.

The Woodstock *Sentinel-Review* recently announced its new rates for subscription, as follows:—Delivered to the homes—single copies 3 cents; 15 cents a week when paid weekly; 60 cents a month when paid monthly; $1.75 for three months when paid quarterly; $3.50 for six months when paid half yearly; or $7.00 per annum when paid yearly.

The Guelph *Mercury's* subscription rates are as follows:—Single copies, from 2c to 3c; one week, from 10c to 15c; one month, from 45c to 50c; three months, from $1.25 to $1.50; six months, from $2.50 to $3.00; one year, from $5.00 to $6.00; by mail outside of Guelph (paper received by subscribers day following publication), $4.00 per year.

The Civil Service Federation of Canada has decided to abandon the *Civilian*, for the last nine years the official organ of the federation. The secretary of the federation is officially notifying Mr. Frank Grierson, proprietor, to this effect. It is understood that the Civil Service Association intends to issue a new publication.

Twenty-five newspaper men from representative Ontario daily papers were the guests of the Canadian National-Grand Trunk Railways for three days at the first of July, when they were taken over the line from Toronto to Kapuskasing. The trip was made from Toronto on the "National," the new schedule whereby the two railways are co-ordinated being used for the first time.

Yorke Hardy, president of the News Writers Union at London, Ont., left on Sunday evening for Albany to represent the organization at the annual meeting of the International Typographical Union. He will endeavor to obtain full support from the I.T.U. for other news writers' unions in Canada. Following the convention Mr. Hardy plans to spend a few days in New York City and Philadelphia.

The MacLean Publishing Co. have issued a revised price list of their papers as follows:—MacLean's Magazine, $3; Farmers' Magazine, $2; Financial Post, $5; Canadian Grocer, $4; Hardware and Metal, $4; Canadian Machinery, $4; Druggists' Weekly, $3; Printer and Publisher, $3; Dry Goods Review, $2; Men's Wear Review, $2; Bookseller and Stationer, $2; Sanitary Engineer, $2; Power House, $2; Marine Engineering, $2; Canadian Foundryman, $2; Motor, Tractor and Implement, $2.

By the terms of the award handed in to the minister of labor by the board of conciliation, which sat to adjudicate the wage dispute between the master printers and their employees, the members of the job printers' union in Ottawa, the latter, will in future, receive a minimum salary of $35 per week, in place of $32 as formerly provided for in their agreement, which does not expire until July next year. The increase is to be considered in the nature of a bonus, and is made on the conditions that no other change in the existing agreement shall be asked for, up to the date of its expiration.

Within the next month the American Baptist Publishing Society, a commercial organization, will occupy part of the ground floor of the Baptist Book Room at 223 Church street, Toronto. The Baptist Book Room will consequently use more space on the upper floors of their present premises. "The Publishing Society is a straight commercial

concern," said Mr. Fred Ratcliffe, "and is in no way connected with the Book Room. As they wanted to extend their trade in Canada and owing to the fact that we had more than enough room it was decided to rent a part of the main floor to them. The Baptist Book Room will still have a store on the ground floor."

Winners in the London *Free Press* circulation contest have left for a trip to Europe, including a tour of the western battlefields. They left Montreal on July 17 and are due back again on August 26. The members of the party are:—Miss Nettie H. Crosier, Woodstock; Miss Mamie Warrener, Goderich; Mrs. Ross C. Clark, London; Miss Florence P. Poole, Norwich; Mrs. Vera A. M. Fuller, Watford; Mrs. M. H. Lee, London; Miss Margaret Young, Wallaceburg; Miss Gladys Deviney, St. Marys; Mrs. E. M. Buchanan, Wingham; Miss Jessie Tuhill, Stratford; Mrs. M. L. Murdy, London; Miss Bertha A. Martyn, Alvinston; Miss E. W. Swift, Watford; Mrs. J. G. Anderson, Alvinston; Mrs. F. L. Edwards, London; Mr. M. L. Bushell, Norwich; Mr. Chauncey Poole, Norwich.

Elizabeth Ann Goodman, one of the oldest residents of Oshawa, died at her late residence, 25 Denison street, after an illness of eight months. She was the widow of the late Robert M. Goodman, a well-known newspaper man. who for many years was connected with the Oshawa *Vindicator* and the Oshawa *Reformer*, Mrs. Goodman was a daughter of the late John Doyle, a Disciples minister, who preached at Oshawa about 60 years ago, and two of her brothers took up journalism. One, the late J. E. P. Doyle, was an editorial writer on the New York *Herald*, under the late James Gordon Bennett, and another, the late Lieut. Frank N. Doyle, was connected with the Dubuque, Iowa, *Times*, and lost his life in the Civil War.

The last issue of *MacLean's Weekly*, a little house paper used by the MacLean Publishing Co., contains the following: Many of the members of the mechanical departments are taking holidays this summer. This is as it should be, providing the holiday is spent in such a way that a complete rest, physically and mentally, results. We are pleased to note that quite a number of men are enjoying two weeks' holidays with pay, a reward granted for faithful service to employees who have completed ten years of continuous service with us. The following employees will this summer enjoy this privilege: Arthur Hardy, F. MacNeillie, Jack Arthurs, Wm. Colgate, Sidney Metcalfe, Thos. McGillicuddy, Geo. Reeves, S. Snashall, C. Thackery, W. Cleghorn and Albert Armitage.

On Wednesday, July 21st, a quiet wedding was solemnized in the Methodist Church, Pembroke, Ont., when Miss Annetta Rosalind Whalley, M.A., only daughter of Thos. W. Whalley, proprietor of the Pembroke *Standard*, and Mrs. Whalley, became the bride of William Arthur Gayton, of Vibank, Sask., son of John E. Gayton, and Mrs. Gayton, Manitou, Man., and nephew of the Hon. Senator Turriff, of Ottawa, and also late lieutenant of the 15th Reserve Battalion The groom served four years over seas, and while a soldier in the 28th Battalion, C.E.F., was severely wounded at the battle of Paschendaele. The bride has until recently been engaged in literary work in Toronto with the MacLean Publishing Co., and is a member of the Canadian Women's Press Club. The Rev. W. H. Stevens of Pembroke officiated and the couple were unattended.

Chesley *Enterprise*:—A. V. Nolan, who has been a half-partner in the Chesley *Enterprise* for two years has purchased the Barrie *Advance*, the oldest paper in Simcoe County, and one of two papers in a town of 7,000 people, and has sold his interest in the Chesley *Enterprise* to his partner, Wm. McDonald, who was sole proprietor of the paper for 27 years and who will engage a competent foreman and give the business his whole time and attention. The partnership expires on the 31st of August as provided in the original terms of agreement. The most amicable relations exist between the partners and if Mr. Nolan, who is a successful business man and has made many friends in Chesley during his two years' stay, finds that the county town of Simcoe does not come up to his expectations he may be back to Chesley some day as the proprietor of the g. f. j. He has sold his house on McGaw Street to Con. Schaab.

The Chatsworth *News* has been purchased by the Owen Sound *Sun-Times*. Thirty-five years ago it was founded by the late G. J. Blyth early in 1885 and at first appeared as a small leaflet which gave in condensed form the news of the district. The press which printed the first copy of the *News* is still doing duty in the office, although not as a newspaper press. During the years the *News* was under the management of the late G. J. Blyth it attained a position among the weeklies of the district through its editor's pithy paragraphs and a place in the hearts of its subscribers from which larger papers have failed to dislodge it. After the death of its founder

the *News* was published for a couple of years by the members of his family, who sold it to Mr. A. Littlejohns who had served his apprenticeship with the Markdale *Standard*. After publishing the paper for a year Mr. Littlejohns sold it to the late A. C. W. Hopkins, son of Mrs. John Hopkins of this village, who, in 1916, enlisted with the 147th Battalion and found death on the battlefield in France. Mr. Hopkins, who learned his trade with the late G. J. Blyth, published the paper until early in 1915 when it was brought by T. H. B. McCullough.

Important News Service Started

Montreal.—The Cross-Atlantic Newspaper Service, Limited, which inaugurated a news, cable and mail service in March last for Canadian newspapers, announces that it has secured exclusive rights for Canada and the United States for the publication of the entire mail and cable service of the London *Daily Mail*, one of the most popular and important of the string of newspapers controlled by Lord Northcliffe.

Arrangements for this important addition to the Cross-Atlantic news-gathering facilities were completed July 23rd by W. Orten Tewson, founder of the Cross-Atlantic Service, and since that date the newspapers subscribing for this news report have been getting the enlarged service.

The Dominion News Bureau Limited, 1717 St. James Street, Montreal, is handling the Canadian end of the business and a very representative clientele has already been secured. As only one newspaper in a city or town is permitted to receive the service it makes it to all intents and purposes a specialized and exclusive European connection for each individual newspaper.

Mr. Tewson, managing director of the organization, is now en route from England to attend the Imperial Press Conference in Ottawa.

Making Illustrations Interesting

The art of illustration, says *British Printer*, enters very largely into all advertising work, and a study of its possibilities and the best methods of putting those possibilities into practice is a subject worth an infinite amount of study and attention. Here again we must emphasize that the main principle is to be interesting. An example will easily demonstrate this.

How perfectly void of interest to the average person is a mere mechanical drawing of an everyday article. The eye may be guided to the point of interest by an arrow running through a confusing maze of fine lines. Show this same part held in one hand, with the other pointing to the vital spot and you immediately introduce the "human touch." Undoubtedly this looks more interesting and will, in so far as it will appeal to non-mechanics, have a much wider effect. As a layman, most machinery looks much alike to you. If you are an expert the printed specification is sufficient, so that the illustration of the machine pure and simple has little value. Indeed quite a long treatise could be written on this point alone. Suffice it to say that the addition of anything that suggests "life" will vitalize an illustration of any inanimate object.

Has Had a Very Wide Experience

Although at this time it is rather uncertain just which one of two well-known printers will be chosen to sit at the key-board of the United States government, there can be no doubt that Senator Warren G. Harding, owner and publisher of the Marion (Ohio) *Daily Star*, still knows how to caress the keys of a linotype. Not long ago, when a representative number of American citizens were poised on tip-toe awaiting the publication of the Republican nominee's speech of acceptance, and a few linotype corrections were wanted in a hurry, the senator-operator peeled off his coat and got immensely busy with the key-buttons of one of his eight Mergenthalers. Incidentally, it is reported that the owner of the *Daily Star* strolled into a small-town print shop a year or so ago and asked for a job as a key-board man. After having demonstrated his ability as a manipulator of the linotype, and being assured of steady employment, the senator handed the proprietor of the shop one of his professional cards and both men had a good laugh over the matter! Harding still is a member in good standing of his local typographical union.

Mill No. 2—Camberwell

Established 1810

Jones'

Patent Non-Curling

Gummed Paper

There is only one kind of gummed paper that gives absolute satisfaction—that's Jones patent products. They have been universally preferred by printers for years. They are reliable in every respect — not like the curly sort.

Send Us Your Enquiries for

GUMMED PAPER
GUMMED TAPE
STAY PAPER
SEALING
MACHINES

FLINT GLAZED
PAPER
LEATHER
PAPERS
MARBLE PAPERS
FANCY PAPERS

Prompt Service Assured

Samuel Jones & Co.

LIMITED

Bridewell Place

MILLS:
CAMBERWELL, ENG.   London, E.C. 4,
NEWARK, N.J., U.S.A.   England

The

Imperial Press Conference

and

Our September Issue

PRINTER AND PUBLISHER will feature the Imperial Press Conference, containing a write-up of the tour, and covering items of importance dealt with by the Empire Press Union.

This will be a valuable record number.

Subscribers — Send your order for additional copies now for this issue.

Advertisers—Be sure your advertisement adequately represents you in this issue.

Printer & Publisher

Canada's National Publishing Journal

143-153 University Ave., Toronto, Canada

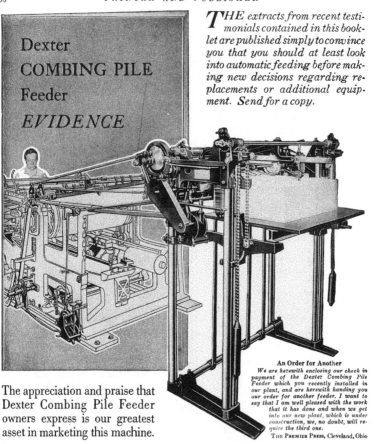

Dexter

COMBING PILE

Feeder

EVIDENCE

THE extracts from recent testimonials contained in this booklet are published simply to convince you that you should at least look into automatic feeding before making new decisions regarding replacements or additional equipment. Send for a copy.

An Order for Another

We are herewith enclosing our check in payment of the Dexter Combing Pile Feeder which you recently installed in our plant, and are herewith handing you our order for another feeder. I want to say that I am well pleased with the work that it has done and when we get into our new plant, which is under construction, we, no doubt, will require the third one.

THE PREMIER PRESS, Cleveland, Ohio

The appreciation and praise that Dexter Combing Pile Feeder owners express is our greatest asset in marketing this machine.

Every new installation adds to our list of friends and boosters. Let us put you in touch with Dexter Combing Pile Feeder users so that you may actually hear their enthusiastic opinion of automatic feeding. What our users say is a safe buying guide for you to follow.

DEXTER FOLDER COMPANY, 200 Fifth Avenue, New York

Folders, Cross Continuous Feeders, Dexter Feeders, Inserting, Covering and Wire-Stitching Machines

CHICAGO   PHILADELPHIA   BOSTON   DALLAS   ATLANTA   SAN FRANCISCO

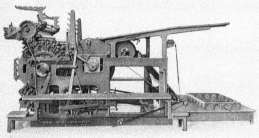

Manton Bros.

PRINTING INKS

Rollers and Machinery

Wide, practical experience has taught us how
to make good inks and rollers for all purposes.
Quick deliveries assured.

STEEL CHASES

Made-in-Canada

No better chases made anywhere than the steel
chases we are making in our own shops. Use
them and save duty. Why pay exchange rates?

◆

Selling Agents for

The Premier Two-Revolution Press
The Whitlock Pony
The Potter Rotary Off-set Press
The Potter Rotary Tin Press
The Standard High Speed Automatic Job Press

*If you are seeking a rebuilt
Job Press, let us know your
requirements. We have a
variety of machines on our
warehouse floors.*

*When anything goes out of
order with your presses, motors
or other pressroom equip-
ment notify Manton Bros.
Prompt and efficient service.*

MANTON BROS., TORONTO
Montreal   Winnipeg   Calgary

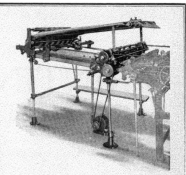
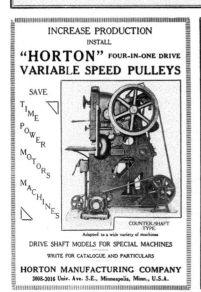
Say you saw it in PRINTER AND PUBLISHER

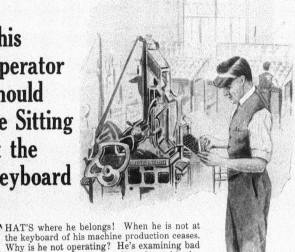

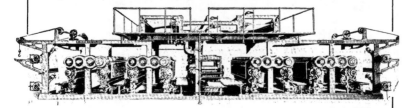

STANLEY PROCESS TYPE METALS
LINOTYPE — MONOTYPE -- INTERTYPE — STEREOTYPE — CASTERTYPE

Made in Canada

We offer you a 100% product full
of efficiency—without question the
only virgin type metal made in
Canada—which is uniformly the
same in each and every batch.

A trial case will convince you.

Less Dross per Melt Means Lower Cost per Year

BRITISH SMELTING & REFINING Co. Limited.
Drummond Building ～ Montreal.

THE J. L. MORRISON CO.
445-447 KING STREET WEST
TORONTO

We Are Prepared
to Equip Complete
Bookbinderies with
the Latest and Best
Machines for Every
Stage of the Work

Cutting Machines
Knife Grinders
Standing Presses
Stamping Machines
Paring Machines
Wire Stitching Machines
Ruling Machines
Feeding Machines
Folding Machines

Bookbinders' and Printers' Machinery and Supplies

THE FRED W. HALLS PAPER CO., LIMITED
invite you to inspect their
NEW WAREHOUSE
situated at
257-259-261 ADELAIDE STREET WEST
TORONTO

Make a Bigger Profit than Your Competitor!

How?

By lowering your production cost.
By and through the Matrix Ruled
Form and Tabular System

If **You** have this your competitor may bid at *his* cost—and leave you your normal profit.

If **His** bid embraces a normal profit to *him*, you may duplicate it, or cut slightly below it, and make a profit *above normal*.

The **Matrix Ruled Form and Tabular System** gives you, in short, *A Competitive Advantage.*

We are glad to hear from skeptics— we like *convincing* them. We save *money*, *time* and *labor* in your shop.

Coupon brings you such evidence and proofs as a practical man requires. It means PROFIT to mail it.

Matrix Ruled Form & Tabular Co.
Touraine Building, Fort Worth, Texas

Sign and Mail the Coupon

Matrix Ruled Form and Tabular System
Touraine Bldg., Ft. Worth, Texas

Gentlemen:
Please send me evidence and descriptive matter that tells all about your modern system of printing blank and tabular work at a big profit.

Name ....

Address..

Town .... State......................

Kind of Machine.....................................
PP7   (*Interlype or Linolype*)

SPECIAL ANNOUNCEMENT

CROSS - ATLANTIC NEWSPAPER SERVICE, LIMITED, announces that it has secured exclusive rights for Canada and the United States for the publication of the entire mail and cable service of the LONDON DAILY MAIL, the greatest of the more popular English newspapers, and the most important of Lord Northcliffe's string of newspapers.

This will enable the CROSS - ATLANTIC NEWSPAPER SERVICE to give its clients a wider and more extensive service of news of the world than heretofore.

Only one newspaper in a city or town can secure Cross-Atlantic Service. Write or wire at once if YOU want it.

CROSS-ATLANTIC NEWSPAPER SERVICE
DOMINION NEWS BUREAU LIMITED
CANADIAN REPRESENTATIVES
171 ST. JAMES STREET

P.O. BOX 756   MONTREAL, CANADA

PRESS
WANTED

**Cylinder Press
in good condition.
State make, size
and price.**

Box 7720
PRINTER & PUBLISHER
(p8p)

Just Order

"LUSTRE"
BLACK

and you will get

*"The Best Ink made to-day
for Half-Tone Printing"*

and

*"The BLACK that is
ALWAYS THE SAME"*

These are two remarks made by some
of our most Progressive Printers.

Shackell, Edwards & Co.
LIMITED
127 Peter Street   Toronto, Canada

MADE IN CANADA

CLASSIFIED ADVERTISEMENT SECTION

FOR SALE

PRINTING MACHINERY FOR SALE—HAVing sold the franchise of the Review, we have for sale 1 Cox Duplex Press, 1 Linotype Model 5, 1 Linotype Model K, 1 Waite & Sherde-Honley 2-strike Ruling Machine, 12' with 36" blanket. All the plant necessary for the publishing of a daily and weekly newspaper. Will sell enbloc or separate. For particulars apply to the Peterborough Review Co., Peterborough, Ont. (p8p)

FOR SALE—WEEKLY NEWSPAPER AND Job Plant in progressive Alberta town. Annual turnover over $8,000. Newspaper is eight pages, seven column, advertising rates from 25c to 40c an inch. Power plant and good assortment of job and advertisement type. Price $4,500, half cash, balance monthly payments or to suit purchaser. Apply to Box 7320, Printer and Publisher. (p8p)

FOR SALE—GORDON PRESS, 7 x 11; GOOD condition. The Owen Sound Advertiser. Owen Sound, Ont. (ptfp)

FOR SALE — COMPLETE TYPE OUTFIT for printing business, 150 fonts of type (several series weight fonts) and lots of biz type, rule, borders, spacing material, double column galleys, mailing galleys, wood type, lead cutter, miter, sticks, cuts, all in first-class condition. Some job and quadruple cases. Fine modern lay-out. Apply Box 72320, Printer and Publisher. (p8p)

WEEKLY NEWSPAPER FOR SALE—IN heart of Peace River Country, Northern Alberta; plant, building and lot. Location excellent, building good, plant about half nearly new, annual turnover $4,800. Subscription rates, $2.50; display advertising, 22 cents to 30 cents per col. inch. Price, $3,200, $2,000 down balance monthly payments. Write Box 6120, Printer and Publisher. (p9p)

FOR SALE — FEW CALIFORNIA JOB cases and rack. Can ship day order is received. Free Press, Midland, Ont. (p8p)

FOR SALE — ELECTRIC PROOF PRESS (good as new), two 10x15 Gordon presses, one 8x12 Gordon press, one hand embossing press, one calendar tining machine, three wall galley racks, one iron case stand, one twelve horsepower motor, three roll top desks, hangers, shafting, pulleys, etc. Saturday Night Press, 75 Richmond Street West, Toronto. (p9p)

Advertising Man
for New York Office

We want an advertising man to represent our several Trade Publications in the Eastern States. Office will be in New York.

The man we have in mind must be a real Canadian and know Canada. He would be single; 25 to 30; has experience selling advertising; of pleasing personality; initiative and constructive ability; he would be a gentleman, and of course honest, reliable, dependable and straight.

If you are such a man we would like to hear from you. Write, in first instance, please. Your letter will be held in strict confidence. Address N. R. Perry.

H. GAGNIER, LIMITED
73-81 RICHMOND ST. W., TORONTO

TWO CENTS A WORD, Box Number as five words; minimum charge is $1.00 per insertion, for 50 words or less, set in 6 pt. type. Each figure counts as a word. Display ads., or ads. set in border, are at the card rates.

¶ Printer and Publisher is the only paper in Canada reaching the Printing and Publishing Trade.

¶ If it is to them you wish to advertise, there is no question but that Printer and Publisher is the medium you should use.

¶ Our Classified Advertisement Section is a result-getter.

SITUATIONS VACANT

LEARN THE MONOTYPE AND MAKE more money. There are Monotype Schools in Philadelphia, New York, Chicago, and Toronto. There is no charge for tuition. It does not take long to learn. The benefits are certainty of permanent employment and a chance for advancement. Lanston Monotype Machine Company.

LEARN THE LINOTYPE — WRITE FOR particulars. Canadian Linotype, 68 Temperance St., Toronto. (ptfp)

MACHINERY LIST

1—10 x 15" C. & P. Press, complete.
1—10 x 16" Gordon Press, complete.
1— 8 x 12" Challenge Gordon.
1— 6 x 10" Gordon Press
2— 7 x 11" Pearl Press.
1—1¼ to 1¼" Rosbach Stitcher.
1—½" Rosbach Stitcher.
1—5/16" Perfection Stitcher.
All above Power and First-class.

1—5/16" Hand Stitcher Brehmer.
1—26" C. & P. Lever Cutter.
1—19" W. & B. Lever Cutter.
1—26" Oswego Lever Cutter.
All above hand power and first-class.

ROYAL MACHINE WORKS
738 ST. PAUL WEST, MONTREAL
Presses, Bookbinding and Box Machinery

SITUATION WANTED

AN ALL-ROUND PRINTER DESIRES change of location. Twelve years' experience. Married man. Would prefer small town office, in Ontario. Write P.O. Box 120, Lennoxville, Que. (p8p)

FOR SALE

FOR SALE—JOB PRINTING AND BINDery plant, well equipped in one of the best manufacturing cities in Ontario. Good business, only one other office. Will require $10,000 to swing. For particulars apply Box 6920, Printer and Publisher. (p8p)

FOR SALE—BRIGHT LITTLE ONTARIO weekly. Good circulation, splendid advertising and job patronage. Real, all-round printer-manager could develop $10,000 a year business. Price (including full equipment, building, etc.), $9,000. Address Box 8320, Printer and Publisher. (p9p)

EQUIPMENT WANTED

WANTED—HAMILTON TYPE CABINET, also about a 28-case Hamilton Wood Type Cabinet. State size, how many cases Cabinet will hold, condition and price. Advertiser. Topic, Petrolia. (p9p)

PRESS WANTED—CYLINDER PRESS IN good condition. State make, size and price. Box 7720, Printer and Publisher. (p8p)

WANTED—HAVING BURNT OUT, THE Carp Review wants some good second-hand equipment. Let us know at once what you have for sale, its condition and lowest cash price. J. A. Evoy, Carp, Ont. (p8p)

COLLECTIONS

SEND US YOUR LIST OF DELINQUENTS. We will turn Debit into Credit. Publishers' Protective Association, Toronto. (ptfp)

Are They Result Getters?
Do They Pull?---

The Maclean Publishing Co., Ltd.,
Toronto, Ont.

Dear Sirs:

Please cancel ad. (Diamond Cylinder Press for sale). We have disposed of same through the valuable assistance of the PRINTER AND PUBLISHER

Yours truly,

(Name on Application)

Buyers' Guide

Ask Your Jobber For

MAPLE LEAF BRISTOL

High Grade Bristol in White and following colors:
Pink, Canary, Green, Salmon, Blue, Cherry, Buff,
Lilac. Made up in index sizes on special orders.

Made in Canada by

THE DON VALLEY PAPER CO., LTD.

TORONTO, CANADA

INDEX TO ADVERTISERS

TYP☉GR APHY

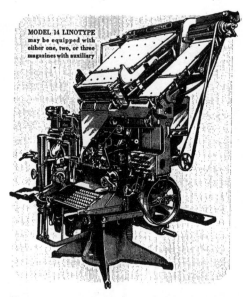

MODEL 14 LINOTYPE
may be equipped with
either one, two, or three
magazines with auxiliary

It is the "think" that counts in everything;
put the same thought into your Linotype
composition that you put into hand composition and you will be astonished at the result.

CANADIAN LINOTYPE LIMITED

68 Temperance St., Toronto

MERGENTHALER LINOTYPE Co., Brooklyn, N.Y.
SAN FRANCISCO   CHICAGO   NEW ORLEANS

This Advertisement, Including Border Ornaments, is Composed Entirely of LINOTYPE Material

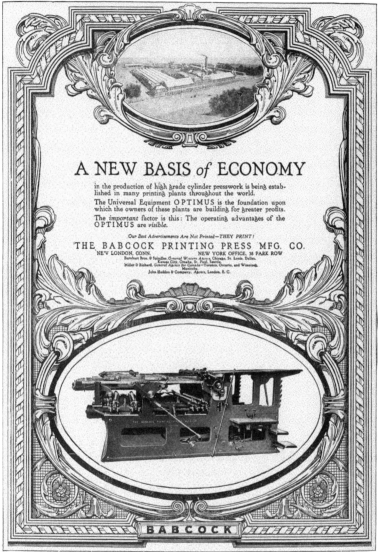

A NEW BASIS *of* ECONOMY

in the production of high grade cylinder presswork is being established in many printing plants throughout the world.

The Universal Equipment OPTIMUS is the foundation upon which the owners of these plants are building for greater profits.

The *important* factor is this: The operating advantages of the OPTIMUS are *visible*.

Our Best Advertisements Are Not Printed—THEY PRINT!

THE BABCOCK PRINTING PRESS MFG. CO.

NEW LONDON, CONN.   NEW YORK OFFICE, 38 PARK ROW

Barnhart Bros. & Spindler, *General Western Agents,* Chicago, St. Louis, Dallas, Kansas City, Omaha, St. Paul, Seattle.
Miller & Richard, *General Agents for Canada*—Toronto, Ontario, and Winnipeg, Manitoba.
John Haddon & Company, *Agents,* London, E. C.

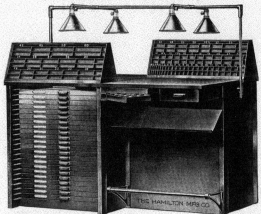

The Miehle

What's in a Name

THE name of a thing was anciently believed to be its essence or spirit.

But we know better now. And in the case of the Miehle, a name known everywhere and to many synonymous with "cylinder press," it is but the designation of a press which has won its way to pre-eminence by sheer merit.

A name may be popularized by advertising. And such advertising may bring *first* sales.

But this is not sufficient to account for the fact that, in practically every case, the purchase of the first Miehle removes all doubt as to future purchases—they are Miehles exclusively.

It's the press itself and not its name.

Onward! the Cry of Franklin Printers

Endorsed by the big paper supply houses, the big type foundries and the biggest men in the printing industry, the Franklin Printing Price List to-day ranks as the most potent influence in making for the prosperity of printers all over this continent that exists.

ORGANIZATION

How will organisation help you? Are you open-minded as to the plight of yourself and competitor or do you amble along with smug satisfaction, unresponsive to the trend of the times? You will find organization all around you, but do you recognize in it the potency of tremendous power? If not, better awaken!

Organization means power, for each and every member in it. "Let us organize and progress," should be your battle cry!

"Organization," a teeming monthly publication devoted to this phase of the printing industry, will be sent you for a year for Three Dollars. Subscribe to-day in this organization-promoter if you want to keep your fingers right on the pulse of printer's progress.

WHY are these big concerns and men so strongly endorsing the Franklin Printing Price List?

WHY are printers subscribing at the rate of about five hundred a month?

WHY are big corporations with private printing plants of their own adopting its use?

WHY are business men recognizing its power and seeking its users?

All because it is right in principle; and, furthermore, because it brings into existence a standard—a fair standard by which everybody is assured satisfaction, fair treatment and consistent quality throughout.

Because it eliminates the uncertainty of the printing business. Uncertainty, or lack of price knowledge, has been the factor directly responsible for the tremendous handicaps the industry has labored under in the past. Printers have not developed financial stability. Your big supply houses and printing men endorse and recommend it so categorically because they have seen its use demonstrated so positively that it spells prosperity for the craft—the big printer and the little printer—that they are using their own organizations to place it in every sh~ in the land.

In other words, it has made the printer prosperous—and this prosperity has been enjoyed by the allied trades.

And big corporations with private printing plants are adopting it to provide them with *absolutely definite knowledge of their costs of operation*. This shows their confidence in its utility—all *proved* to their utter satisfaction ere they made their decision to use it.

And the business man, he too is converted for the reason that he above all is the real judge of business principles. He recognizes in the Franklin Printing Price List the force that is going to improve the lot of the printers, to him meaning better service, which he is more than willing to pay for if he can but get it. The Franklin Printer is giving it to him. This printer is getting better prices; he can afford to give better service.

Mr. Printer—You Are In Danger!

Conditions are treacherous now for the printer. Onto you is foisted, to add to your already heavy burden, increased transportation costs on paper. The paper situation causes unlimited anxiety and no little loss of business and prestige. And on top of it all, a difficult labor problem confronts you.

Where is the printer at? you ask. What will be the outcome? Will it be insolvency, or must you grind soul out in the death struggle, sixteen to eighteen hours a day, merely to defer the day of reckoning?

There is, of course, no cure-all for these complexities. But what a deplorable and miserable condition for a printer to "carry on" under the old regime, the old order of things—charging before-the-war prices or even 1919 prices—like so many thousands are doing.

Are you one of the class which is paying toll to a weakness of not knowing what to charge for your product to make a profit; of lacking courage to *serve* for a fair and liberal profit; of living up to the ideals of the successful modern business man of to-day in demanding at least fair and impartial emoluments; of submitting to the temptations and coercion of shysters who would deprive you of birthright, subjecting you to humilities no creature called "man" should tolerate—or

Are you the counterpart of the other extreme—the Franklin Printer, who has been disillusioned and who is reaping the rewards of courage and sagacity, having adopted the most effective of all available forces to progress and to dethrone a spineless thing labelled "fear and ignorance?"

Just hear the voices of Franklin Printers speaking. Listen to their enthusiasm and appreciation; their confidence and assurance that the future is rosy, that all goes well with them.

This ought to be cheerful news to you, Mr. Printer, receiving this invitation to join the success-throng—the printers who are not slaving for a pittance, but getting a good margin of profit on their time and money investment.

Let us show you the way! Let us add inspiration to your equipment and encourage you on to getting a legitimate remuneration for your diligence and endeavors. Probably you only need some more real contact with that big fraternity of printers who are forging ahead. We will give you this contact.

Heed the call! Merely say that you are interested, and we'll do the rest. It entails no obligation on your part. Wait not, for to-morrow will be too late. Write to-day.

PORTE PUBLISHING COMPANY
S. H. MOORE, Manager
32 Temperance Street
Toronto, Canada

PRINTERS' CLEARING HOUSE

Mindful of the need for Practical facilities to make the printing office systematic, we have correlated the knowledge of widely experienced men covering the whole field of printing office conduct into Practical systems, and enumerate, among others, the following which have proved invaluable in obtaining extraordinary results for printeries:

Practical Sample Case for Selling

Practical Advertising System.

Practical Cost System.

In conjunction with the Franklin Printing Price List no printer need be unsystematic—for these systems and devices are available to all printers at a very nominal cost. Full particulars and samples supplied on request.

WHEN MACHINERY stops running and workmen stand idle—*that means loss.* STATIC ELECTRICITY is the cause of the slowing up of machinery and men—*every printer knows it.*

Get greater results, increased production, and better quality, by installing in your plant

The Chapman Electric Neutralizer

It will remove your static electricity troubles, and allow your presses and pressmen to work full time and at full speed.

It makes presses deliver light paper

LIKE THIS ↓   INSTEAD OF LIKE THIS ↓

Send for copy of "FACTS"

When in doubt use *Bronze!*

NO combination of colors of ink that the lithographer or printer can use will command the instant attention or produce the same effect of richness and quality that comes as though by magic with the glint of *bronze.*

U. P. M. Vacuum Bronzer

**Bronze for Emphasis
Bronze for Beauty
Bronze for Profit**

That's the triple title of a booklet we have published in behalf of bronzing. How many copies do you want?

United Printing Machinery Company

83 BROAD STREET, BOSTON   38 PARK ROW, NEW YORK   604 FISHER BLDG., CHICAGO

Centurette

Two-Revolution Press

SPECIFICATION

Size of Type Bed	39″ x 26″	Rollers:—		
Size of Sheet	37″ x 24″	Forme (two) . . (diameter)	3″
Nearest British Paper Size . Double Demy		Distributors (four) . "	2″
Size of Type Matter . . 35″ x 22″		Rider (one) . . . "	3″
Max. No. of Impressions per Hour . 3,000		Ductor (one) . . . . "	2″
Overall Length with Fly Delivery . 9′ 6″		Nett Weight . . . . . 7,280 lb.	
" " P.S.U. Delivery	10′ 7¾″	Power required . . . . . 3 H.P.	
Overall Width . . . . 6′ 10½″		Size of Fast and Loose Pulleys, 12″ x 2 5-16″	
Height with Feedboard raised . 5′ 8″		Size of Motor Pulley . . 24¾″ x 2½″	
Foundation Length . . . . 7′ 0½″		Driving Shaft Revs. per Impression . 7.26	
" Width . . . . 4′ 7½″			

Rollers covered with best composition; all gearing machine-cut from the solid; cylinder tripping mechanism; air buffers; flyer delivery or printed-side-up delivery; automatic jogging-up apparatus; circular cutter (adjustable to any part of the bar); steel ductor knife; locking-up bars; automatic counter; tool drawer (containing eight spanners, four tommy pins, two screwdrivers, and one oilcan). One extra set of roller stocks (unclothed) is supplied with each machine.

DRIVING FIXTURES

For INDIVIDUAL MOTOR DRIVE, the motor belt is connected directly with the flat flywheel, which is fitted with an inside rim brake.

For DRIVING FROM MAIN SHAFTING, fast and loose pulleys with belt shipper are fitted on the machine, and countershaft (with driving pulley, hanger, and four-speed cone pulley) and corresponding cone pulley for the user's main shafting are supplied.

THE CENTURETTE IS MANUFACTURED IN ENGLAND BY

Linotype and Machinery Limited, London

CANADIAN OFFICE:

LINOTYPE AND MACHINERY LIMITED
c/o CANADIAN LINOTYPE LIMITED
68 TEMPERANCE STREET, TORONTO

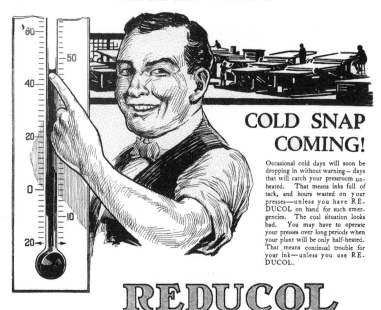

Photo Engravers

The "Horseshoe," Niagara Falls, Ontario

Sapphire Bronze Blue

MANTON BROS., TORONTO

MONTREAL   WINNIPEG   CALGARY

Makers of High-grade Printing and Lithographic Inks

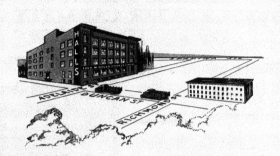

A Home of Our Own

THE FRED W. HALLS PAPER COMPANY LIMITED extend a cordial invitation to the Trade to inspect their new warehouse, situated in the very centre of the printing trade in Toronto. They now occupy one of the largest and best equipped premises devoted to the fine paper industry in Canada.

Remember the new address:

257-259-261 Adelaide St. West
TORONTO

All goods shipped same day order is received.

TORONTO VARNISH WORKS

TORONTO INK WORKS

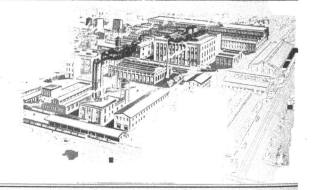

Light Liberty Red, No. 10850

ANTIQUE COVER

THORNCLIFFE COVER

EMPIRE ROPE BRISTOL   SULPHITE ENVELOPE

MAPLE LEAF BRISTOL   MANILLA ENVELOPE

POST CARD BRISTOL   SULPHITE TAG

BEAVER BRISTOL   MANILLA TAG

CHOCOLATE LAYER BOARD

TYMPAN

All the above in stock sizes, weights and colors.
Bristols and covers carried in stock in crash finish.
Specialties of all kinds made to specification.

Don Valley Paper Co.
Toronto, Canada

H.J.LOGAN

Bookbinders' and Printers' Machinery

Sole Agent

Latham Machinery Co.
Chicago

Manufacturers of the Famous

"MONITOR"

Bookbinders' Machinery

Sole Agent

Brown Folding Machine Co.
Erie, Pa.

Makers of the Most Reliable Folder
on the Market

*Put your machinery problems
up to H. J. Logan. Prompt
service. Expert on repair work.*

114 ADELAIDE STREET WEST
TORONTO

The WHITLOCK Pony Press

Two-Revolution   —   *Two-Roller*   —   *Front Fly Delivery*

NO CYLINDER PRESS is so profitable to the printer as *The* **Whitlock Pony**. Its reputation is world-wide. Smooth in its operation, even and rigid in impression, exact in register, easy to operate, simple and durable. Prints everything from an envelope to a sheet the full size its type bed will take. Produces heavy and light job work of the finest quality with minimum labor. It runs hundreds per hour faster than other ponies. It is the standard pony cylinder press of the world. Let us explain *The* **Whitlock Pony** fully---also the following well-known presses:

The PREMIER Two-Revolution 4-Roller Press

The POTTER OFFSET

The POTTER TIN PRINTING PRESS

Every mechanical device that makes for the production of the finest quality in the greatest quantity at the lowest operative cost is incorporated in these presses.

PREMIER & POTTER PRINTING PRESS CO., Inc.

SUCCEEDING THE WHITLOCK AND POTTER COMPANIES

1102 Aeolian Bldg., 33 West 42nd Street

NEW YORK

Canada West:	*Canada East:*	*Maritime Provinces:*
MANTON BROS.	**GEO. M. STEWART**	**PRINTERS SUPPLIES LTD.**
105 Elizabeth St.	92 McGill Street	27 Bedford Row
Toronto, Ont.	**Montreal, P.Q.**	**Halifax, N.S.**

PRINTER AND PUBLISHER

Devoted to the Interests of the Printers and Publishers of Canada

Press of the Empire See the Dominion

Coast to Coast Trip Lasted Six Weeks

WITH the possible exception of the Prince of Wales' tour through Canada last year, it is doubtful whether any trip ever undertaken in this country has been at all comparable with that recently completed by the delegates to the Imperial Press Conference. It was really an excursion de luxe, most complete in all its arrangements and so skilfully planned as to give the visitors the most thorough knowledge of the country to be obtained within the limits of their stay in the Dominion.

Commencing at Sydney, N.S., on July 27th, the trip lasted for a period of over six weeks, during which time the party crossed the entire breadth of the continent and returned as far East as Quebec. This involved a journey over 8,000 miles in extent. Notwithstanding the great length of the trip, it was accomplished without any serious mishap and perfect time was maintained by all the transportation companies participating in the service.

Diary of the Western Trip

The conference at Ottawa formed a natural division between that portion of the trip which took place in the Maritime Provinces and Quebec and the portion through Ontario and the Western Provinces. Immediately on the conclusion of the sessions at Ottawa, the party proceeded to Toronto and thence by boat to Niagara. Here a splendid opportunity was given to view the scenic wonders of the gorge and cataract and to inspect the power plants and other interesting features of the Niagara frontier. Returning to Toronto on the following day, part of the journey was performed by motor, enabling the visitors to view the fruit belt at close quarters, to see something of the industrial progress of Hamilton and to enjoy a run over the To-

ronto-Hamilton highway. En route, the whole company were entertained at luncheon by Mr. W. J. Southam, of the Hamilton *Spectator*, at his beautiful summer home, Kingsthorpe, near Bronte.

The stay of the press party in Toronto on August 9, 10 and 11 was marked by a series of entertainments, which included a civic banquet at the King Edward Hotel on the evening of August 9, a drive around the city on the morning of August 10, luncheon at Hart House at noon; a special convocation of the University in the afternoon and an inspection of the harbor, followed by a luncheon at the Royal Canadian Yacht Club on August 11.

It had been arranged that the water route would be followed to the West, the party sailing from Sarnia on the S. S. Hamonic on August 12. This precluded visits to other parts of Old Ontario, though en route to Sarnia. A stop of several hours was made at Guelph, where the visitors were entertained at the Ontario Agricultural College. At Sarnia a civic reception and drive were tendered, both of which were much appreciated. The sail from Sarnia to Port Arthur proved to be one of the most enjoyable features of the whole trip, the life on shipboard being particularly conducive to friendliness and good feeling. At the Soo, brief visits were paid to the mills of the Spanish River Pulp and Paper Co. and the Algoma Steel Corporation.

The twin cities of Port Arthur and Fort William co-operated to make the stay of the visitors at the head of the lakes a pleasant one. On the morning of August 14, a fleet of automobiles took the party for a tour round the cities, following which a civic luncheon was tendered at the Prince Arthur Hotel. In the afternoon, the company embarked on tugs and viewed the harbors, landing at Fort William, where a civic dinner took place at the local hotel. During the day Lord Burnham officiated at the

Left to right—Sir Gilbert Parker and Viscount Burnham, taken during the visit of the Imperial Press Party to Toronto.

R. A. Anderson is a Scottish Canadian. Born in Co. Cork, Ireland, 1861, he was educated at private schools in Ireland and became first official assistant to the Right Honorable Sir Horace Plunkett, K.C.V.O., F.R.S., etc. in 1889. He is a Director of the Irish Homestead Ltd., publishing the *Irish Homestead*, a weekly paper which is the organ of the Irish Agricultural Organization movement. He was wounded in the Irish Rebellion in Easter week, 1916. His three sons served in Irish Regiments in the Great War. Two were killed:

Lord Apsley is the eldest son and heir of Earl Bathurst. Lord Apsley's mother, Lady Bathurst is the only daughter of the late Lord Glenesk, under whose direction the *Morning Post*, the oldest London daily paper rose to the influential position in the British Press it now occupies. Born on August 3, 1895, Lord Apsley was educated at Eton and at Christ Church, Oxford. In the Great War he rose to the rank of Captain, gained the Military Cross in July, 1917, and was subsequently awarded the Distinguished Service Order.

the turning of the first sod for the plant of the Kaministiquia Pulp and Paper Co.

Winnipeg was reached on the morning of Sunday, August 15. No special program was provided by the local committee, though several private functions took place during the day. On the following morning, a motor tour of the city was arranged, terminating at the pavilion in Assiniboine Park, where a civic luncheon took place. This was followed by an inspection of the new Parliament Buildings, a visit to the Manitoba Agricultural College and, in the evening, by a government dinner at the Fort Garry Hotel.

Leaving Winnipeg on the morning of the 17th, a busy day was spent viewing the wheat fields of Manitoba. The first stop was made at Portage La Prairie, where hospitable citizens drove parties of the visitors for many miles through the surrounding country. After luncheon, the party moved on to Carberry, where at 2.30 the whole party were transferred to automobiles, for a run to Brandon. This gave an excellent opportunity to see the harvest fields close up. At Brandon, following a drive about the city, a dinner was given at the Prince Edward Hotel.

August 18th was devoted to visits to the cities of Regina and Moose Jaw. At the former, entertainment took the form of a drive around the city, a performance by the Royal Mounted Police on their parade grounds and a government luncheon at the Parliament Buildings, attended by the Lieutenant-Governor and presided over by the Premier of the Province. In the afternoon practically the whole party motored from Regina to Moose Jaw. At the latter point, the local committee entertained the visitors at a garden party, following the usual drive around the city streets.

Proceeding westward by night, the press party arrived in Gleichen on the morning of August 19. The visit here was signalized by the holding of an old-time stampede, which by reason of its novelty and exciting features, quite thrilled the delegates. It was preceded by a fifteen mile drive through the surrounding country and by the picturesque ceremony of creating Lord Burnham an Indian Chief. Leaving Gleichen at noon, the trains proceeded to Calgary, where the rest of the day was spent. The day's proceedings terminated with a civic dinner at the Hotel Palisser.

From Calgary, the excursionists moved on to Banff by motor, this being regarded as the most satisfactory way to introduce them to the wonders of the Rocky Mountains. The journey consumed the greater part of the day on August 20, a pause being made half way up for a picnic lunch on the banks of the Bow River. And now a day each was devoted to Banff and Lake Louise. Perfect weather conduced to the full enjoyment of the brief stops in these charming resorts, where the visitors bathed and golfed and rode and climbed and participated in the varied amusements provided for their entertainment.

Monday, August 23, was spent at Lake Windermere, inspecting the new settlement which has sprung up at this point following the building of the C.P.R. south from Golden through the Columbia Valley. Tuesday, August 24, was given over to the Okanagan Valley, headquarters being at Vernon, and on August 25 Vancouver was reached. Here another enjoyable program of entertainment was provided.

Commencing with a Canadian Club luncheon addressed by Lord Burnham, there followed an excursion to the logging camp of the Capilano Timber Co., north of North Vancouver, where the visitors saw giant trees felled, cut into logs, loaded on flat cars and hauled down to the waterfront. Then the huge sawmill of the Hastings Lumber Co. was visited at New Westminster and other industries inspected. Finally a civic dinner completed the round of entertainment.

On the morning of the 27th, the party took ship for Victoria, landing in the afternoon. They were almost immediately taken out to that famous show place, the Butcharts' sunken gardens and here afternoon tea was served. The evening witnessed the holding at the Empress Hotel of a state dinner by the government of the province, presided over by the Lieutenant-Governor. On the following day a trip to the town of Duncan over the beautiful Malahat Drive, a distance of 45 miles, was undertaken. The people of Duncan were warm in their welcome and entertained the visitors at luncheon.

Returning to Vancouver on Sunday, August 29, the eastbound journey by rail was commenced the next morning and all day the trains climbed the valleys of the Fraser and Thompson Rivers. In the evening a two-hour stop was made at Kamloops, where a civic reception took place. August 31 was

William Adrian Brennan, representing the *Argus*, Melbourne, Australia, was born at Sedgwick, near Bandigo (Victoria) on April 29, 1871. He entered the Public Service of the State of Victoria in April 1887. He joined the staff of the *Argus*, July 1901, and became leader of the Parliamentary Staff in 1906. In 1911 he became chief of the Reporting Staff and in 1916, was appointed a leader-writer occupying that position ever since.

D. D. Braham is the editor and delegate of the *Daily Telegraph* (Sydney, N.S.W.). He was born at Birmingham (England), January 23rd, 1875, and educated at Liverpool Institute and New College, Oxford. He became assistant to Sir Valentine Chirol, then head of the Foreign Department of the *Times*, 1907-1912. In 1912 succeeded Sir Valentine Chirol in that capacity, and was elected a Director of the *Times* Publishing Company. In 1914 he was appointed editor of the *Daily Telegraph* (Sydney.)

Augusto Bartolo B. Lit., L.L.D. was born October 17, 1883, and educated at Malta. He is a Life Fellow of the Royal Colonial Institute, London, and Associate of the Empire Press Union. For several years he edited the *Daily Malta Chronicle* the leading paper in Malta, owned by his father, Mr. Antonio Bartolo, M.B.E. He is a member of the General Council of the Malta University, and Examiner in English and Italian literature, Ancient and Modern History, Constitutional Law, Science of Law, and History of Legislation.

Sir Harry E. Brittain, K.B.E., cr. 1918, M.P. (C.U.) Acton since 1918, M.A., Barrister-at-law, born 24 Dec., 1873. Educated Repton, Worcester College, Oxford, B.A., 1896 (Honors in Law); M. A. 1898. Joined Sir Arthur Pearson and worked with him in the formation of the Tariff Reform League and the creation of the Tariff Commission. Joined the staff of the *Standard* and the *Evening Standard* in 1902; Director of the *Sphere* and the *Tatler*, 1906-1908. Originated and organized the first Imperial Press Conference.

devoted to Jasper Park and on the first day of September Edmonton was reached. Here the proceedings began with the ceremony of unfurling a flag, the gift of the school children of Edmonton, England, to those of Edmonton, Canada. This was performed by Lady Burnham. There was then a luncheon given by the Board of Trade at the University of Alberta and in the evening a government dinner at the Hotel Macdonald. On September 2, the party visited the Buffalo Park at Wainwright and on September 3 were guests of the citizens of Prince Albert and Saskatoon. The following day, ten hours were spent quietly in Winnipeg, after which the long run over the National Transcontinental to Cochrane was begun. On Monday, September 6, an interesting visit was paid to the Hollinger Gold Mine, while brief stops were made later in the day at New Liskeard and Cobalt. The next day was consumed in a trip through Lake of Bays to the new Bigwin Inn.

A visit to the Canadian National Exhibition at Toronto was paid on the 8th, while on the evening of the same day the Lieutenant-Governor of Ontario entertained the party at dinner at Government House. Leaving Toronto the same night by train, a run was made to Prescott, where a transfer was effected to the steamship of the Canada Steamship Lines and the rest of the journey to Quebec was accomplished by water.

As the trip neared an end, presentations were the order of the day and, if their number and value gave any indication of the feelings of the delegates, then indeed the whole undertaking was thoroughly appreciated. At Vancouver, A. B. Calder, who represented the Canadian Pacific on the tour, was made the recipient of an album containing the autographs of all the Imperial Press delegates. At Winnipeg, a similar presentation was made to C. K. Howard, who performed corresponding duties for the Canadian National Railways. At Prescott, when the party finally left the special trains, the crews were drawn up and thanked for their services and each man was presented with a handsome gratuity. Finally at Quebec, at a dinner tendered to the Canadian press staff and railway officials, a number of other presentations were made. Chief among these was one to C. F. Crandall, editor Montreal *Star* and honorary secretary of the special committee of the Canadian Press Association, to whom must be given the lion's share of the credit for the success of the trip. Mr. Crandall was made the recip-

ient of a solid silver tea service. Other gifts were made to Captain William Wallace, formerly of the Toronto *Star*, chief assistant to Mr. Crandall, and to Captain J. E. McEvoy, E. J. Moxley and W. A. Craick, assistant secretaries, as well as to a number of the railway officials.

No small credit for the success of the Imperial Press tour must be accorded to those Canadian newspapermen, who planned the local entertainment and assisted in carrying it out. In Nova Scotia, G. Fred Pearson, Halifax *Chronicle*; in New Brunswick, Frank B. Ellis, St. John *Globe*; in Quebec, Major-General Sir David Watson, Quebec *Chronicle*; in Montreal, Lord Atholstan, Montreal *Star*; in Ottawa, P. D. Ross, Ottawa *Journal*; in Toronto and Ontario, J. E. Atkinson, Toronto *Star*; in Manitoba, J. W. Dafoe, Winnipeg *Free Press*; in Saskatchewan, W. F. Kerr, formerly of the Regina *Leader*; in Alberta, J. H. Woods, Calgary *Herald* and W. R. Jennings, Edmonton *Journal*, and in British Columbia, John Nelson, Vancouver *World* and F. J. Burd, Vancouver *Province*, were prominent in this connection. W. J. Taylor, Woodstock *Sentinel-Review*, as chairman of Train No. 2, was with the party continuously throughout the trip and did splendid service in his capacity of host. John Nelson, Vancouver *World*, was chairman of Train No. 1, on the westbound trip and endeared himself to all on board. Lt.-Col. Macpherson, Portage la Prairie *Graphic*, accompanied the party from Winnipeg to the coast and back.

Some Outstanding Personalities

As leader of the Imperial Press party, Lord Burnham occupied a conspicuous position and it is not too much to say that he impressed everybody with the zeal and enthusiasm with which he devoted himself to the duties of leadership. He and Lady Burnham were among the first to rise in the morning. They were invariably on time for every function and exhibited an unflagging energy that won general admiration. Lord Burnham was called upon to speak on innumerable occasions and always seemed to possess the happy faculty of saying something fresh and to the point. He kept a close eye on his followers and is said to have known every delinquent who absented himself from the various functions. It was to him a matter of much concern that any delegates should have left the party before the whole program of Canadian entertainment had been

Sir Robert Bruce, Knt., Hon. L.L.D. University of Glasgow, Scotland, J.P., F.J.I., is editor-in-chief of the Glasgow *Herald*. Robert Bruce was born at Alloa in Clackmannanshire, Scotland, on Oct. 26, 1871. He began journalistic work on the Alloa *Advertiser*, and in 1892 joined the head office staff of the Aberdeen *Journal*. He is a Justice of the Peace of the City of Glasgow and received the honor of knighthood in 1918.

Miss Mary Frances Billington, was born at Chalbury in Dorsetshire. Her first journalistic contributions were to the *Globe*. Some article sent to the now defunct *Echo* attracted the approval of the late Mr. J. Passmore Edwards, who invited her to come to London and see how she liked the work on Fleet Street. Then followed a short spell with the *Daily Graphic*, and next a probationary period with the *Daily Telegraph*, followed by a staff appointment in the Diamond Jubilee year.

Taylor Darbyshire was born in Lancashire, July, 1875, went to Australia as a child and was educated at Brisbane Grammar School and Sydney University. He read for the Bar, but joined the Brisbane *Courier* in 1897. In 1903 he joined the staff of the *Age* of Melbourne, filling positions on the general and editorial staff. In 1919 he was offered and accepted his present appointment as London manager of the Australian Press Association.

Sir Emsley Carr, editor and part-proprietor of the *News of the World*, vice-chairman and joint managing Director of the *Western Mail*, and director of George Newnes Ltd., was born at Leeds on May 1, 1867. Sir Emsley Carr joined the staff of the *Western Mail* as a junior reporter and had a thorough and practical coaching in all departments. His chief work was in making the *News of the World*, with which he became connected in 1891; the most popular Sunday paper in the world.

completed and he himself voluntarily gave up a private expedition to Chicoutimi, which had been arranged to take place at the end of the trip, in order that the Quebec Government might be able to change the date of its official luncheon in honor of the delegates.

Lord Burnham was ably assisted in all the duties pertaining to his office by Lady Burnham, who was equally zealous in the discharge of the social obligations falling to her lot. On several occasions she was called upon to speak and she won the heartiest applause of her hearers by the clever and convincing way in which she expressed herself. Always cool and collected, she was able to meet every emergency. When officiating at the unfurling of the school children's flag at Edmonton before a crowd of 15,000 people, the ropes caught and the flag refused to unfold. It was an embarrassing moment, threatening to turn a solemn occasion into something of a farce, but Lady Burnham was equal to the occasion. She called out,—"It's the real old flag; it never gives in"; and the crowd cheered in appreciation of the sentiment. The tribute of esteem paid to Lady Burnham at the final dinner in Quebec reflected the feelings of all who participated in the trip.

Labor was represented in the Imperial Press party by T. E. Naylor, general secretary of the London Society of Compositors, and George A. Isaacs, general secretary of the National Society of Operative Printers and Assistants. Both enjoyed equal privileges with the rest of the delegates and were called upon to do their share of the speaking. As speakers they ranked high, eliciting hearty applause from their auditors. At Quebec, in expressing the appreciation of the labor delegates for their entertainment in Canada, Mr. Naylor referred to himself and Mr. Isaacs as the Bolsheviks of the party. He said that he had made a few converts in Canada and expressed the opinion that the next time they visited the Dominion, the labor element might be in the majority.

The philosopher of the party was probably R. W. Snelling, Egyptian *Gazette*, familiarly known as the "Egyptian." His comments, expressed in the driest manner imaginable, were most amusing. To him must be credited the saying that "the most extraordinary thing about this trip is that not one of the delegates has died." Speaking at Quebec, he congratulated the delegates on the fact that, after living together for

six weeks, they were still on friendly terms with one another, while their conduct throughout Canada had been quite irreproachable. To him both facts seemed to be hardly credible.

While in point of years the grandfather of the party, in spirit Lt.-Col. Sir Arthur Holbrook, M.P., was its youngest member. He was the life of Train No. 2 and kept the whole party in a perpetual state of merriment with his antics and stories. To dance was his delight and a Vancouver cartoonist pictured him as driving in an automobile and exclaiming, "Let's arrange another dance for to-night." Sir Arthur is the father of ten grown-up children and the grandfather of as many boys and girls. He was recently elected M.P. for Basingstoke, succeeding Sir Auckland Geddes.

For sheer pluck, the association of Alfred Langler, editor-in-chief of the *West Australian and Western Mail*, Perth, West Australia, with the party, was noteworthy. Mr. Langler is quite lame, being entirely dependent on the use of crutches. Yet he came all the way from West Australia and participated in practically every time of the excursion program. Naturally his fellow delegates gave him every assistance and he was well looked after wherever he went.

Mountain-climbing was the favorite amusement of N. Levi, Johannesburg *Volkstem*. Before reaching Canada he indulged in the sport in Europe for a few weeks. Here he was not afforded much opportunity to climb, but at Banff he scaled a considerable height within a few hours and again at Jasper Park, in company with J. D. Williams, *Cambria Daily Leader*, Wales, he ascended the famous Whistler Mountain. His exploits created considerable interest among his fellow delegates, none of whom, however, cared to follow his example. Mr. Levi was quite a linguist, holding the record in this respect for the party.

For versatility, Ernest Woodhead, Huddersfield *Examiner*, had few equals in the press party. Apart from being a newspaper man, familiar with both the business and editorial sides of publishing, he has been active in municipal affairs, is an ex-mayor of his home city and still a member of council. He was in earlier life an international football star. He is now a golf player of renown and an ardent pedestrian. He has decided gifts as an artist and is famous as a librettist of light operas, which have been played all over England. His jokes and

Hon. Charles Ellis Davies, M.L.C., J.P. of Lydnhurst, Hobart, is a member for Cambridge in the Legislative Council in the Parliament of Tasmania, being elected May 4th, 1897; and again in 1903, 1909 and 1915,for a further six years. He is managing proprietor of Davies Brothers Limited, proprietors of the Hobart *Mercury* and *Tasmanian Mail*. Founder of the Tasmanian Agricultural and Pastoral Society in 1874, he has been President for over twenty years.

John T. Clayton is editor and general manager of the Craven *Herald* and its allied industries. He is a member of the executive of the Institute of Journalists and this year he is President of the Yorkshire Newspaper Society. He had his newspaper training on the Preston *Herald*, Lancashire. Mr. Clayton is an active Mason a Past Master of Craven Lodge, 810, Skipton, and a member of the Bronte Lodge of Mark Masons, Haworth, Yorkshire.

David Davies, editor, managing director and part proprietor of the South Wales *Daily Post*, was born at Llanelly South Wales, November 30, 1862. He began his journalistic career on the Llanelly *Guardian* in 1879, joined the staff of the *Western Mail* Cardiff, in 1886, and between 1888 and 1893, was acting editor. In 1894, he established for the Conservative Party the South Wales *Daily Post*, Swansea, of which he is now editor, managing director, and part proprietor. He made an extensive tour of Canada and the U. S. in 1898.

William Davies, F. J. I., has been editor of the *Western Mail*, the oldest daily paper in Wales, since 1901. He joined the staff of the paper thirty-two years ago and eventually succeeded the late Mr. Lascalles Carr as editor in chief nineteen years ago. He was vice-president of the World's Press Parliament at St. Louis in 1904; he is a Justice of the Peace for the city of Cardiff and a Governor of the University College of South Wales and Monmonthshire. This is Mr. Davies' second visit to Canada.

songs formed no small contribution to the merriment of the press party, among whom Mr. Woodhead was exceedingly popular.

On the whole the excursion was completed without any serious mishap. The one real casualty was C. D. Don, editor Johannesburg *Star*, chairman of the South African delegation. In the drive from Carberry to Brandon, Mr. Don was the victim of a motor accident, which inflicted a nasty cut on his forehead. He was laid up on the train for a few days, then appeared for some time in bandages and eventually made a complete recovery. Apart from this accident, there were quite a number

of minor cases of illness, which gave the doctor and the two nurses, who accompanied the party, a good deal to do.

One of the most interesting members of the party was Dr. Augusto Bartolo, the representative of Malta. No country had a more loyal representative than he and woe betide the speaker who failed to mention Malta when enumerating the various portions of the British Empire. Dr. Bartolo was a fluent and humorous speaker and his speech in appreciation of the ladies in the observation car of Train No. 2 was reputed to be one of the cleverest things on the trip.

Opening Day of the Imperial Press Conference
Official Welcomes to the Visitors

THE official opening of the Imperial Press Conference took place in the Railway Committee room of the new House of Commons, on Thursday, August 5th. After the usual informal greetings between visitors and Canadian newspapermen, Lord Atholstan called upon the meeting to come to order and elect a chairman.

"As chairman of the Canadian Branch of the Empire Press Union," he said, "I have been asked to call the meeting to order. The first business is the election of the chairman. In 1909 the Motherland delegates recommended and the conference elected one of the overseas delegates. The choice was a man whom we all loved and whose death we all deplore, the late Sir Kippen Thompson. I am sure we all agree it is now the turn of the Motherland to be represented in the chair. It would require a man of ability, experience and tact, a man whose rulings will be respected, and whose election will meet with general approval. I have very much pleasure in presenting the name of Lord Burnham.

"This nomination has been seconded by every member of the Canadian executive, but I suppose as a matter of regular procedure there must be some obvious demonstration of its being accepted. Of course, other nominations are in order, but I

would ask those in favor of this nomination to kindly rise in their seats."

The proposal was unanimously carried, and Lord Atholstan handed over the chair to Viscount Burnham, who replied:

"Your Excellency, Lord Atholstan, ladies and gentlemen : It is with great diffidence but with no less pride that I accept this high honor which has truly been thrust upon me. I feel myself the chair should have been occupied by the head of the Canadian delegation. Canadian modesty, has yielded place to me and I shall do my best to fulfil the duties of the position. All I can say is that I will endeavor during these proceedings to show that sense of fair play which I honestly believe to be the essential characteristic of the newspaper press of the whole empire.

"I have the honor to ask His Excellency to open the second Imperial Press Conference."

His Excellency's Welcome

The Duke of Devonshire said in part:

"In the first place may I be permitted on behalf of the Government and people of Canada to extend to this conference a most cordial and hearty welcome?

Philip Davis is a director of the oldest Natal daily paper, the Natal *Witness*, published every morning and evening at Pietermaritzburg, the provincial capital. Mr. Davis was born at Pietermaritzburg in 1886, was educated at Hilton College, Natal, and Loretto School, Edinburgh, and entered the business of the firm in 1906. The *Witness* is strongly Imperialistic, its chief object in that sensse being to strengthen the ties between South Africa and the rest of the Empire, and to promote immigration and land settlement.

John Philip Collins, since 1901, London correspondent of the Cape *Times* and for the past five years chief London contributor to the *Civil and Military Gazette* (Labor). In the course of fifteen years on the *Pall Mall Gazette*, he acted as Leader Writer, Review Editor, and Special Correspondent. Since 1910 he has devoted himself to overseas correspondence, cable service, and special commissions for leading home dailies.

Mr. H. J. DeLisser of the *Daily Gleaner,* Kingston, Jamaica, was born in December 1878, in Falmouth. At 21 he became editor of the Jamaica *Times;* at 23 assistant editor of the Jamaica *Daily Telegraph;* at 25, editor of the Jamaica *Gleaner,* which position he still holds. In 1917, he became General Secretary of the Jamaica Imperial Association, representing the agricultural and mercantile interests of the colony. He was appointed a C.M.G. by the King on January 1st, "in recognition of public services."

Benjamin H. Dodd, editor *Daily Despatch,* East London, South Africa, was born at Widnes, south Lancashire, England. He was educated at Glasgow University; graduated M.A., 1892; went to South Africa, 1893, and for several years was engaged in teaching. He joined the staff of the *Daily Despatch* as reporter in January, 1901 and became editor in 1912.

"You have already had a week or ten days' experience of Canada, but I can assure you that the general reception you have received is only an earnest and a forerunner of what you will receive throughout the rest of your long tour. We in Canada are deeply grateful and sensible of the high honor which has been accorded to the Dominion by having been selected as the meeting ground of this second press conference. We trust that your tour will be a pleasant and illuminating and interesting one.

"We trust that during the course of your various peregrinations you will see something of that spirit which has either in peace of war done so much to place the Dominion in the position which it occupies to-day. I hope I may take it as a happy omen, that almost one of the first sights you saw on reaching the shores of Canada was a shipload of plates manufactured in Canada out of raw materials coming exclusively from British Dominions and intended for transhipment to other great British dominions overseas. (Applause.)

"You will have opportunities—and this is a specially favorable time for it—of seeing harvesting operations in full swing and I am glad that although we may not have reached as high as in 1915, the general indications are that the yield of the harvest will be a satisfactory one.

"It might perhaps seem an act of impertinence if I were to allude to paper or pulp. No doubt you will approach the consideration of the manufacture, supply, and what is more difficult—the price.

"I hope that your stay in this country will prove that in that great industry we are making valuable contributions to the supply which is so much needed not only in the Dominion itself, but throughout the world. But we in Canada are not merely going to take this conference as an opportunity of advertising our own pastures and our own wares. We look to this conference, in the conditions and under the circumstances in which it is meeting, as one in which we may get guidance and inspiration in dealing with the varied problems which we have before us. This takes my mind back to the time when the first conference was convened in the Old Country in 1909. The success which attended that conference certainly in the fullest degree justified its inauguration and the work which was accomplished then has been the means of doing much to help and guide

us through the critical and eventful years which have passed since then.

Power of the Press

"It is to you gentlemen that in these times we have to look, as I do, just now for guidance and inspiration. We must have faith in ourselves, we must have a vision and we must have confidence, and no body of men either individually or collectively are capable of having a wider and more far-reaching influence on public opinion than you have to-day. You are meeting with great responsibilities. We are standing at the turning point in our history. As we review, however, in a very inadequate manner, I am afraid, the past, we can with confidence say that British institutions have stood the test. They have shown adaptability and ability to stand the strain. And equal with their ability to stand the strain of war will be their ability to prepare for what I hope will be the better ties of peace.

From Broadest Viewpoint

"My Canadian friends I know will pardon me, but one of the things to which we look forward as a result of this conference is the still further awakening of the spirit of breadth and toleration than perhaps we ever knew before. And when I mentioned my Canadian friends just now, I was perhaps thinking too that we are sometimes inclined to place our local and almost parochial affairs possibly more in the limelight than the occasion calls for or justifies. More than ever it is for us at this moment to look to the solution of these many problems from the broadest standpoint and to know what is best for the whole is also best for the individual and the individual countries of the great British Empire.

Sir Robert Borden

"If I may be permitted to digress from the immediate subject, there is one subject on which I would like to touch. If you had met in this building a month ago, you would probably have seen on my left Sir Robert Borden. Governors-General have no politics, and although I take the greatest interest in the welfare and development of the political parties, I cannot interfere. I watch with the greatest interest and say it is the business of a Governor-General to see that the party which

---

Hugh Robert Denison, was born at Forbis, New South Wales, 11th November, 1865. He is a chairman and managing director of the *Sun* Newspaper Ltd., Sydney, chairman of directors of Heiron and Smith Ltd.; director of the London and Lancashire Fire Insurance Co., Ltd. (N.S.W. Branch), founder of the United Cable Service Ltd., (Australia). He was one of the N.S.W. delegates to the Chamber of Commerce Congress in London in 1912. He is a vice-president of the Royal Colonial Institute.

Robert Donald, chairman of the Empire Press Union and a member of the Committee which organized the First Imperial Press Conference, began his newspaper career as a reporter on the Edinburgh *Evening News.* About 1898, Mr. Donald joined the London *Daily Chronicle* as news editor, and a few years later became editor. Under his administration it became a great national newspaper. Mr. Donald has of late years devoted his time chiefly to a large group of provincial newspapers in which he has an interest.

Charles Davidson Don, chief editor of the *Star*, Johannesburg, was born at Bridge of Allan, Scotland, April 4, 1874. He joined the staff of the Cape *Argus*, Cape Town, in 1894. He was editor of the *Times* of Natal, Maritzburg, 1901-10; acting editor *Transvaal Leader*, Johannesburg, 1911; editor of the R h o d e s i a *Herald*, Salisbury, 1911-15; and has been editor of the *Star*, Johannesburg, since 1915. He has been a strong supporter for over 20 years of Imperial unity on the lines of a Britannic alliance rather than Imperial federation.

Edward Evan Edwards, B. A., who is attending the Empire Press Conference as the representative of the Telegraph Newspaper Company, B r i s bane, Queensland, was born in Brisbane. He was educated at Brisbane Grammar School and later proceeded to the University of Sydney, where he went into residence at St. Andrew's College, took an Arts course, and graduated B.A. In 1903 he visited Japan and the Far East at the period of the Great Osaka Exhibition. He is chairman of the directors of the Telegraph Newspaper Co.

has the greatest support in the country is the one from which the Government is selected.

"Sir Robert felt that he was entitled to ask for a rest, and as you are aware, about a month ago he formally handed in his resignation. His name will be handed down as that of a worthy successor of those prime ministers who have done so much to make this great Dominion what it is, and will find an honored place in that list. We all regret deeply that Sir Robert Borden no longer holds the place he so long adorned in public life, and we hope that his life will be long spared and he will be able to place his invaluable services at the disposition of Canada and the empire.

The New Premier

"We miss him on this occasion but I am sure that a hearty welcome is extended to Mr. Meighen, who has undertaken the heavy responsibilities of prime minister. I think we all know that Mr. Meighen is fully capable of carrying the responsibility in accordance with the best traditions of his office.

"I have now the honor and privilege of formally declaring this conference open."

Welcomed By Premier

Lord Burnham then proposed Lord Atholstan as honorary chairman and the latter in accepting remarked that "as an honorary chairman has no work to do I cannot escape by claiming no qualifications."

Premier Meighen next welcomed the delegates. "My first impulse," he said, "is to thank His Excellency for the graceful and cordial reference to the personal, not to the political career of the distinguished man whom I seek to succeed as prime minister. My words to you to-day are 'Welcome to Canada.' As you pass through this country you will find no disappointment in all you have been led to expect of the resources and hospitality of the people. You will find the bone and sinew very sound, the blood red and pure. You won't locate anything unhealthy in the body commercial. If the occasion were different I would say something of the soundness of the body politic. As you pass from point to point, you will be given keys to the houses and homes and possibly, in some provinces, to the cellars of our people. I give you the warmest of wel-

comes and trust that your work will be translated in abundant realization."

Leader to Leader

Hon. Mackenzie King joined heartily in the welcome to the Capital and the Dominion. He referred to the fact that it was the first occasion when in public he had met the new premier, whom he congratulated upon the high position to which he had succeeded as well as the felicity of his utterance. He would do his best, however, to make Mr. Meighen's tenure as brief as possible. (Laughter.)

"If I may be permitted," continued Mr. King, "there is one point I should like to raise, not in any spirit of criticism, but rather by way of inquiry and suggestion. It is concerning the use, if not the substitution, of the word 'Imperial' for the word 'British' in the characterization of this conference.

"There may be reasons for preferring the word 'Imperial' to the word 'British,' but may I submit, with the struggles of the recent past, the word 'Imperial' has come to denote a kind of centralization in all matters of organization, and in method autocracy rather than democracy, and as such is not adequately expressive of the spirit of the several democracies that comprise the nations of the British Commonwealth.

Only One British Empire

"The word 'British,' on the other hand, is suggestive of spirit rather than form. It speaks of an attitude that is synonymous with freedom, justice and liberty, fair play and right, and such it tends to give a larger and finer meaning and significance to everything with which it is associated. Moreover, it is all-embracing and world-encircling, and it is, above all else, distinctive. No nation or group of nations or peoples other than those comprised within the British Empire can appropriate it. There can be other Imperial entities, like those which have been swept away in the past, but there can be only one British people. It signifies all that is symbolized in the British flag."

'British' and '"Imperial"

Lord Burnham expressed his high appreciation of His Excellency in opening the conference and referred to the Duke of Devonshire as a national asset. The name of Cavendish covered with credit the best periods of British history. Refer-

Geoffrey Evan Fairfax is a barrister-at-law and s e n i o r director of John Fairfax & Sons, Ltd., proprietors of the Sydney *Morning Herald* and its associated illustrated weekly, the Sydney *Mail*. The Sydney *Morning Herald*, which journal Mr. Fairfax represents at the Conference, is a co-manager with the Melbourne *Argus* of the Australian Cable Association. Mr. Fairfax was born in Sydney, N.S.W., in 1861, and is the second son of the late Sir James Reading Fairfax.

John L. Greaves is a Yorkshireman born in Sheffield 50 years ago. He served apprenticeship on the *Derbyshire Times* and became chief reporter on that journal. Over 20 years ago he entered trade journalism as editor of one of the S. C. Phillips & Co's. publications, and subsequently was appointed chief of the editorial staff of the *Papermaker* and allied publications. He has been on the Council of the British Association of Trade and Technical Journals, Limited, since that association was formed.

Hon. Theodore Fink, lawyer, publicist, writer, and politician, was born in Guernsey, Channel Islands, July 3, 1855. In journalism, he is chairman of the directors of the Melbourne *Herald* and *Weekly Times* Newspaper Company Ltd., and other important companies. He was one of the Imperial Press Conference, 1909, and took part in the founding of the Empire Press Union. On the proclamation of the Australian Repatriation Act was appointed chairman of the State Board of Victoria, but resigned at the end of 1919.

James Henderson is the eldest surviving son of the late Sir James Henderson, M.A., D.L., J.P., managing proprietor of the Belfast *News Letter* and Belfast *Weekly News*, and one time president, Institute of Journalists, and a former Lord mayor and high sheriff of Belfast. He is a graduate of Dublin University and a member of the Irish Bar. For several years Mr. Henderson was Dublin correspondent of the Belfast *News Letter*, and also acting editor of the Dublin *Daily Express*. He is sub-editor of the Belfast *News Letter*.

ring to the name of the association, Lord Burnham said that, in spite of what Mr. Mackenzie King had said, the association would stick to its name. "We are proud," he said, "of Britain but not ashamed of the empire. It stands for liberty and equality and has nothing in common with ramshackle empires of the past. The reason we have adopted our name is because we include in our membership nations that are not British. There are representatives in this conference from the empire of India and the colony of Malta."

Lord Burnham concluded by hoping that the conference would have the gifts of "grace, wisdom and understanding."

Lord Burnham then read telegrams of greeting to the press conference, one from the 14,000 members of the Editorial Association of the United States and the other from the Southern Newspapers Association.

Cable Rates Reduced

A resolution was read and carried unanimously tendering congratulations to the Dominion of Canada and the authorities of the British West Indies on the signing of the new trade agreement.

Lord Burnham, in stating briefly the genesis of the conference, said that the first conference was held in 1909. It was also the last conference. As a direct result of that conference there had been obtained a great reduction in cable rates between different parts of the Empire. The Empire Press Union was established in London and it now extends all over the Empire, each branch being autonomous. In 1915 the Imperial Press Conference had been postponed for obvious reasons, and was now gathering in Canada for the first time. They were bound by no standing orders or bylaws in discussions, said Lord Burnham, and he would allow discussion on any point so long as it was relevant.

Urges Increased Grants

The discussion on cable rates was then begun. Mr. Robert Donald, vice-chairman of the British delegation, moved the resolution recommending the governments of Great Britain and the dominions to increase cable communication and to reduce the rates for news messages, so as to ensure the fullest interchange of news and opinions within the Empire. It also

recommended that these governments should make increased grants to cable companies, enabling them to reduce tolls without incurring loss, and that the governments should lay down new cables.

Worse Now Than In 1909

In supporting the resolution, Mr. Donald first spoke in discouragement of the suggestion the name be changed to British Press Conference. He was not afraid of the word "imperial." He said that since the last conference cable rates had been reduced, but conditions were worse than they were in 1909. Speaking of the work of the Empire Press Union, Mr. Donald said that it had succeeded in gaining for the press access to the foreign office and other "bureaucratic" departments in London.

Wireless as Supplementary

Mr. Donald, referring to the development of wireless, said it would inevitably be supplementary rather than a substitute to the cables. A uniform postal rate had been established for letters and why should it not be extended to newspapers and periodicals and why should there not be a uniform cable rate? The union and solidarity of Canada had been menaced by a break in communication between east and west, and it was suggested that it was undignified to ask and accept a government grant. He thought they simply showed appreciation of their responsibilities in the great work of helping east and west to understand each other, and he would suggest the same procedure in regard to the British Empire.

No Government Contract

J. W. Dafoe, (*Manitoba Free Press*) seconded the motion. It was the real business of the conference, he thought, as cables were the nerve system of the Empire. He wished to emphasize the feeling of the majority of Canadian publishers that they could not entertain the idea of a Governmental assistance which implied any sort of control or influence of news services by other than newspapermen themselves. In Canada the geographical barrier of the north shore of Lake Superior had been bridged by assistance from the Canadian Government, and had proved of tremendous assistance in unifying Eastern and Western Canada. It simply removed

John Clemmants Glendenning is the proprietor of the Derry *Standard*, Unionist newspaper, established in 1836, and published at Londonderry. He was educated at Foyle College, Londonderry, and succeeded his father, the late William Glendenning, in 1888, in the control of the *Standard*. He was president of the Irish Newspaper Society, 1918-19, and is at present vice-president of the Londonderry Chamber of Commerce.

Col. Sir Arthur Holbrook, K.B.E., M.P. for the Basingstoke Division of Hampshire, joined the staff of the Portsmouth *Times* in the 70's and in 1885 founded the *Evening Mail*, a daily paper that was later acquired by the Harmsworth Syndicate and amalgamated with the *Evening News*. Colonel Holbrook is Deputy Lieutenant of Hampshire and a Justice of the Peace for Portsmouth. He is a partner in the firm of Holbrook & Sons, the well-known publishers. Was elected M.P. for Basingstoke Division of Hampshire.

John Douglas Graham was born in Wolverhampton in 1871 the son of the late Mr. Thomas Graham, J.P., who was the proprietor of the daily and evening paper, *Express* and *Star*, and two weeklies, the Wolverhampton *Chronicle*, and the *Midland Counties Express*. All these papers circulate over a wide and thickly populated industrial district, including the whole of that famous coal area, Cannock Chase. During the war, the *Express* extended its great influence considerably by its vigorous propaganda work.

Patrick J. Hooper, the editor of *Freeman's Journal*, was born in Cork in 1873. He joined the staff of *Freeman's Journal* in 1892, and has since been connected with that paper except for a brief period in 1897 when he was on the staff of the *Irish Times*. After many years' service in the London office of the *Freeman's Journal*, and in the Press Gallery of the House of Commons, he was appointed London correspondent in 1912, and in July, 1916, was transferred to the position of editor. He was called to the Bar at Gray's Inn in 1915.

---

an obstacle of unproductive territory, with which the newspapers themselves had been unable to deal. But when a proposal was made to the membership of the Canadian Press Limited, at its last annual meeting that it accept a subsidy from the British Government for a cable service between Canada and the Motherland the newspapermen present had almost unanimously decided against the acceptance of that subsidy.

Dislikes Subsidies

Sir Roderick Jones, managing director of Reuter's Agency, also characterized Government subsidies as the last expedient to which newspapers should resort for the establishment of cable services. He supported Mr. Donald's proposal to aim at a penny-a-word cable rate though he was not sanguine of realizing it in the near future.

Alternative Resolution

G. E. Fairfax, chairman of the Australian delegation, moved an alternative resolution to the one before the conference. Its effect is practically that the Empire Press Union should use its influence to obtain Government assistance for the establishment of better cable or wireless facilities for the transmission of news.

H. R. Dennison (Sydney *Sun*) seconded the resolution, and urged that cheaper cable rates were absolutely necessary if the proletariat, or common people, were to be kept rightly informed on world affairs. This, too, was the best method of offsetting Bolshevism, which was stalking through the world to-day. Since the war cable business to Australia had nearly doubled, and both the public and Press were entitled to cheaper rates. One reason for an overloaded cable service was the filing of useless messages by Government officials.

After considerable further discussion the resolution was postponed until the next day.

Wireless Service

F. Crosbie Roles, chairman of the Asia and Near East delegation, moved that the principles should be at once established for providing the British Empire and the world with wireless and telegraphic and telephonic communication. The resolution also requests the Governments of the Empire to secure,

by public or by private enterprise, at an early date, adequate wireless services throughout the Empire.

Sir Campbell Stuart of the London *Times*, in supporting the resolution, said that newspaper people had a feeling of indifference toward news sent through a medium which might be tapped. He had feelings of altruism and brotherly love toward his fellow-delegates. None the less, he liked occasionally to get a scoop.

A. Burroughs, manager of the news department of the Marconi Wireless Company, then described what had been done in wireless development to secure secrecy.

Those In The Party

Train No. 1. Lord Apsley, London *Morning Post*; Robert Allister, *Cape Times*, Cape Town, South Africa; Miss Mary Frances Billington, London *Daily Telegraph*; W. A. Brennan, the *Argus*, Melbourne, Australia; Sir Harry E. Brittain, the *Sphere* and the *Tatler*; Viscount and Lady Burnham, London *Daily Telegraph*; Sir Emsley and Lady Carr, *News of the World*, London; John P. Collins, *Civil and Military Gazette*, Lahore, India; Taylor Darbyshire, Melbourne *Age*, Australia; Hon. Charles E. and Mrs. Davies, Hobart *Mercury* and Tasmanian *Mail*; David Davies, South Wales *Daily Post*; William Davies, *Western Mail*, Wales; Philip Davis, the Natal *Witness*, Pietermaritzburg, South Africa; Mr. and Mrs. H. R. Denison, the *Sun*, Sydney, Australia; Charles D. Don, the *Star*, Johannesburg, South Africa; B. H. Dodd, *Daily Despatch*, East London, South Africa; Robert Donald, the *Yorkshire Observer* and chairman of the Empire Press Union; Mr. and Mrs. G. E. Fairfax, *Morning Herald*, Sydney, Australia; Mr. and Mrs. John D. Graham, the *Express* and *Star*, Wolverhampton, England; James Henderson, Belfast *News Letter*, Belfast, Ireland; P. J. Hooper, *Freeman's Journal*; Levis Howarth, the *Yorkshire Post*, Leeds; Mr. and Mrs. Percy A. Hurd, the *Canadian Gazette*, London; Mr. and Mrs. E. Abbey Jones, Southland *Daily News*, Invercargill, New Zealand; Sir Roderick and Lady Jones, managing director Reuters; Mr. and Mrs. J. J. Knight, Brisbane *Courier*, Brisbane, Australia; Alfred Langlier, *West Australian* and *Western Mail*, Perth, Western Australia; C. D. Leng, Sheffield *Daily Telegraph*, Sheffield, England; N. Levi, *Volkestem*, Johannesburg, South Africa; Mr. and Mrs.

Henry Horton was born at Timaru, New Zealand, 1870. He is senior member of the firm of Wilson and Horton, proprietors of the New Zealand *Herald*, the only morning paper in Auckland, and of the Auckland *Weekly News*. Mr. Horton is a director and former chairman of the United Press Association of New Zealand, which controls the cable services of the New Zealand press. Mr. Horton, the son of the late Mr. A. G. Horton, a prominent New Zealand newspaper man, has been actively engaged in newspaper work his whole life.

George A. Isaacs is the general secretary of the National Society of Operative Printers and Assistants. He has served on the Executive Council of the National Printing and Kindred Trades Federation, of which he has been elected vice-president. The year before the war he paid a visit to Berlin as a delegate of the London Trades Council, and made a special study of trade union organization, and arranged the first agreement between the unions of England and America on trade union action.

Lewis Howarth, of the *Yorkshire Post*, Leeds, is in length of service the oldest member of the literary staff of that journal, having served under five editors. He gained his early journalistic experience on the *Halifax Courier* and the Bradford *Observer* (now the *Yorkshire Observer*). He is an original member of the Institute of Journalists, was at one time a member of the Council of that body and was successively hon. secretary and chairman of the West Riding (now Yorkshire) District. He is a life member of the Newspaper Press Fund.

Ralph Stapleton Ward Jackson is editor and managing director of the Rand *Daily Mail* and *Sunday Times*, Johannesburg. He was educated at Wellington College and Royal Military College, Sandhurst, and obtained a commission in the 11th Hussars in 1890. He became private secretary to the Right Hon. Sir West Ridgeway, Governor of Ceylon, and subsequently acted as assistant private secretary to the Right Hon. Ger. Balfour, chief secretary for Ireland. He proceeded to South Africa in 1904.

T. W. Leys, Auckland *Star*, Auckland, New Zealand and chairman of the New Zealand delegation; J. S. MacDonald, *Farmer and Stock Breeder* and *Morning Post*, London; T. B. Maclachlan, Edinburgh *Evening Despatch*, Edinburgh; Percival Marshall, *Model Engineer and Junior Mechanic*, London; William Maxwell, Aberdeen *Journal*; Sir Patrick T. McGrath, *Evening Herald*, St. John's, Newfoundland; Hon. Alexander W. Mews, *Evening Advocate*, St. John's, Newfoundland; Sir Frank and Lady Newnes, *Tit Bits, Strand Magazine, Country Life* and many others, London; Mr. and Mrs. J. O'B. Saunders, the *Englishman*, India; Roland W. Snelling, *Egyptian Gazette*, Bulkeley, Egypt; Sir Campbell Stuart, *Times* Publishing Co., London; L. Goodenough Taylor, *Times* and *Mirror*, Bristol; H. E. Turner, secretary Empire Press Union, London; Ernest Woodhead, the *Examiner*, Huddersfield, England.

Canadian newspapermen and others on the first train included C. F. Crandall, Montreal *Star*, honorary secretary Canadian Press Executive; William Wallace, Canadian Press; John Nelson, Vancouver *World*; Dr. S. G. Ross; Miss M. Schneider, G. S. Hensley, *Canadian Auditor*; E. J. Moxley and W. A. Crack, assistant secretaries; L. O. Thomas, government information bureau; F. G. Aldham, Canadian Press; A. B. Calder, E. Roberts, J. M. Gibbon, W. A. Gough, C.P.R.; J. M. Lindsay, H. R. Charleton and H. S. Ingram, Canadian National Railways.

Train No. 2: — R. J. Arnot, *Canada*, London; R. A. Anderson, the *Irish Homestead*, Cork; Augusto Bartolo, *Daily Malta Chronicle*, Malta; D. D. Braham, *Daily Telegraph*, Sydney, N.S.W.; Sir Robert Bruce, the Glasgow *Herald*, Glasgow; J. T. Clayton, the *Craven Herald*, Skipton, England; Mr. and Mrs. H. G. DeLisser, the *Daily Gleaner*, Kingston, Jamaica; E. E. Edwards, the *Telegraph*, Brisbane, Australia; Hon. Theo. and Mrs. Fink, Melbourne *Herald* and *Weekly Times*; J. C. Glendenning, the *Derry Standard*, Londonderry; Mr. and Mrs. John L. Greaves, the *Paper Maker*, London; Harold Harmsworth, the *Western Morning News*; John Harper, Glasgow *Record*; Col. Sir Arthur Holbrook, *Southern Daily Mail*, Portsmouth; Henry Horton, New Zealand *Herald*, Auckland; Mr. and Mrs. James Hutchinson, *Otago Daily Times*, New Zealand; Mr. and Mrs. George A. Isaacs, general secretary of the National Society of Operative Printers and

Assistants, London; R. S. Ward Jackson, *Rand Daily Mail*, Johannesburg; Walter Jeffery, *Evening News*, Sydney, Australia; N. K. Kerney, Rhodesia *Herald*, Salisbury, South Africa; Hon. J. W. and Mrs. Kirwan, *Kalgoorlie Miner*, Australia; Valentine Knapp, *Surrey Comet*, Kingston-on-Thames, and president of the Senior Newspaper Society of the United Kingdom; Hon. Arthur and Mrs. Lovekin, and Miss Lovekin and Miss Letcher, *Perth Daily News*, Perth, Australia; Major G. V. and Mrs. Lansell, *Bendigo Advertiser*, Bendigo, Australia; Walter Makepeace, Singapore *Free Press*; Major John and Mrs. Mitchell, *Dundee Courier*, Scotland; Ald. and Mrs. J. D. Morrell, director of companies publishing over 30 daily and weekly newspapers in the north of England, York, England; Dr. G. R. Mosdell, *Daily Star*, St. John's, Newfoundland; Miss Neall; T. E. Naylor, general secretary of the London Society of Compositors and editor of the London *Typographical Journal*; D. M. Olimeans, the Freuch Newspapers Limited, Bloemfontein, Orange Free State; Right Honorable Sir Gilbert Parker, Bart., London; J. Parker, *Wellington Post*, Wellington, New Zealand; Mr. and Mrs. Walter J. Penn, *Taranaki Herald*, New Plymouth, New Zealand; Dr. Ellis and Mrs. Powell, and Miss Powell, editor in chief *Financial News*, London; F. Crosbie Roles, the *Times* of Ceylon, Colombo, Ceylon; P. Selig, Christchurch Press Co., Christchurch, New Zealand; Alfred Gordon Sprigg, Leicester *Mail* and vice-president of the Newspaper Society, Leicester, England; Sir Charles and Lady Starmer, Birmingham *Gazette*, Sheffield *Independent*, Nottingham *News* and many others, Westville, Darlington, England; Sir George Toulmin, Lancashire *Daily Post* and others, Preston, England; Donald W. Vick, *Daily Mirror* and *Leeds Mercury*; Lieut. Col. Edward William Watt, *Free Press*, Aberdeen, Scotland; J. D. Williams, *Cambria Daily Leader* and *Herald of Wales*, Swansea, Wales.

Canadian newspapermen and others on the train included W. J. Taylor, of the Woodstock *Sentinel Review*, Canadian Press Train Chairman; J. W. Dafoe, *Manitoba Free Press*; J. H. Woods, Calgary *Herald*; T. L. McEvoy, assistant secretary; C. K. Howard, train director and F. L. Moore, secretary; Miss F. Thompson, nurse; T. Sherrin, of Dominion Government Information Bureau; W. C. Potts and L. L. Dougan of the Canadian National Railways.

Walter Jeffery is general manager and managing editor of the *Evening News, Sunday News,* and *Woman's Budget* of Sydney. He was born in Portsmouth in 1861 and educated there. He went to sea in 1876 until 1884. He then began journalism, and arrived in Sydney in 1886. He is a trustee of the Public Library of N.S.W., Sydney, and of the Mitchell Library. His publications include *A Century of Our Sea Story*, 1900; *The King's Yard*, etc., see Becke, Louis. He is a student of Australian and English naval history.

Percy Angles Hurd is a member of Parliament for the Frome Division of Somerset, entering the House at the General Election of December, 1918. He has been engaged in journalism in London for many years, and is London editor of the Montreal *Daily Star* (Winermere.) He was concerned in the establishment of the *Outlook* in 1898 and was its editor and managing director until 1904. Since then he has been well known as the editor of the *Canadian Gazette*, and as assistant secretary and later secretary of the Tariff Commission.

James Hutchison, editor of the *Otago Daily Times*, Dunedin, was born at Wanganui, New Zealand, 1867, the son of a journalist and politician of wide experience. He was educated at Wellington College and the University of Otago; entered the profession of journalism in 1886; joined the staff of the Otago *Daily Times* in 1898, and was appointed editor in 1909. He became honorary secretary in New Zealand of the Journalists' Institute (U.K.) He was married in 1893 to Anna Pearson, daughter of Jas. Copland, M.A., M.D., Ph.D.

Ernest Joseph Abbey Jones was born at Christchurch, New Zealand, 9th October, 1870; educated at Timaru High School. He obtained his early business training in a firm of stock and station and shipping agents. He became manager of the Oamaru *Mail* in 1906, and in 1909 assisted in the formation of a private company that purchased the Southland *Daily News*, Invercargill, N.Z., and occupying the position of general manager. For several years he has been on the executive of the Newspaper Proprietors Association of N. Z.

Joined in a Partnership of Consent
J. W. Dafoe's Vision of Empire Status

BEFORE the Imperial Press Conference on Friday morning Mr. J. W. Dafoe, managing editor of the *Manitoba Free Press*, expressed the view that the progress of events during the war had made it inevitable that future constitutional relations of the various nations of the Empire could be decided only on the principle "that British countries are nations of equal status joined in a partnership of consent."

This view was warmly endorsed by succeeding speakers, and Sir Harry Brittain proposed a permanent committee representing all British nations in London to discuss all matters of Imperial concern, unanimity being required before action could be taken. Mr. Dafoe's address and the debate reached the high-water mark of the conference, and was followed with intense interest.

Need Formal Affirmation

"They are equal or they are not," said Mr. Dafoe, "and the next step, the pressing duty which I presume will be dealt with at the Constitutional Conference when it meets shortly, will be to make that equality a matter of formal affirmation. I believe, and if I had time I could advance a powerful reason in support of my belief, that the definition should be made with least possible delay. I read a speech very recently by General Smuts, who, under very difficult circumstances, is fighting the battle for a unified Empire in the hottest corner of the British Empire. (Applause.) In this speech he said that this formal statement was vital and pressing, and I imagine that he knew what he was speaking about when he used those words in the Cape Parliament. I could, I think, demonstrate that we can never go forward with plans for Empire co-operation until the present indefinite status is cleared up and replaced by an understanding which will make clear not only to ourselves, but to the outside world, that the British Empire is a partnership of

nations of equal status united in a partnership of consent." Mr. Dafoe said that the situation in which the Empire found itself was not so much the result of the victory of one school of thought over another as force on the various Governments by a complexity of circumstances arising out of the exigencies of the war. Taking the steps forced on them from time to time, they had come to the point where it was abundantly clear that only this principle could be applied.

Heart of Whole Question

"I know there are people who are disturbed in their minds about all this. I have the greatest admiration for them, but they cannot get it out of their minds that if we are free to separate we will separate, although no formula could keep us together if we wanted to separate. That is the kernel and heart of the whole question. These people say, 'If it is partnership by consent, what will happen if the consent ceases?' Well, of course, if the consent ceases no constitution will keep us together. They think that with the cessation of a situation of dependence, which is our situation, in spite of after-dinner speeches about equality, the condition of independence begins."

They are quite unable to realize that the true alternative is not independence but inter-dependence.

The speaker quoted from interesting pages of Canada's history to quiet apprehensions. Canada had fought the constitutional battles for all the British Dominions and solved their problems. He quoted Lord Durham's report recommending responsible government, and the British Government's theoretical conceding of the point in 1840. They had "flinched" the issue when it came to the practical application supported by an influential body of colonists, who were wrong although quite sure they were right. When finally after 10 years of turmoil the British Government sent Lord Elgin to Canada

Sir Roderick Jones is chairman and managing director of Reuters. He entered the Reuter service twenty years ago as a junior correspondent in South Africa. In 1902 he was appointed the South African editor in London. Four years later he returned to South Africa with the rank of general manager, in charge of the agency's entire organization there. Meanwhile he travelled extensively in Europe, and on the death of Baron de Reuter in 1915 he succeeded him as head of the London agency.

Valentine Knapp is president for the year of the Newspaper Society, the senior organization dealing with the newspaper industry in the United Kingdom. Born in 1861, he was educated at Christ's Hospital, London—one of England's oldest public schools, founded by King Edward VI— he entered journalism in 1882. He became editor of the Surrey *Comet* at the early age of 26. With the conduct of the literary side of this journal for thirty-three years, he has combined many activities of a social and philanthropic character.

John James Knight is chairman of directors of the Brisbane Newspapers Company and editor-in-chief of that company's circle of papers. Born in Staffordshire, England, 1863, and arrived in New Zealand in 1874. He arrived in Queensland in 1884 and in 1900 was appointed editor of the company's *Evening Journal*, the *Observer*. He occupied this position for six years when he assumed the position of editor-in-chief of the whole of the company's journals.

T. Jones is editor of the *Times* of Ceylon, Colombo. After journalistic experience in the provinces in England he went out to Ceylon in 1905, and has been editor of the *Times* of Ceylon since 1912.

under instructions to recognize responsible government on the fullest terms, it was accepted in England as a matter of course that "it was the prelude of the separation of Canada from England." Most of the British statesmen of the time had so expressed themselves, and even welcomed the thought. Sixty years later the outbreak of the war gave the people of Canada an opportunity to demonstrate how strong were the ties of a common blood, language, literature and flag.

Mr. Dafoe believed the Empire nations had been enriched and strengthened by the experiences and sacrifices of the war. The common fight in a common cause must mean a permanent enrichment of all basic qualities of citizenship and would permanently reinforce the foundations on which the commonwealth rests in sentimental and spiritual ties by the common memories of the war.

War a Turning Point

"We have therefore the heritage of the past and we have the common sacrifices of the present to unite us and, more than that, we have the aspirations of the future. It has been the fashion to regard the war only as a great catastrophe. I think it is also open to us to believe, as I believe, that we will see the war is a great turning point in human history, and that it does make a definite break in the world order.

"The characteristic of the old order, which, I believe, is passing away, though dying hard, was the aggrandizement of peoples, nations, dynasties, in a military sense or commercial sense. The new order is for the enlarging of the individual life, of the life lived by the common man. If the British Governments, animated by that purpose, press forward to a common ideal, it will give us a very powerful point of union which will reinforce those historic ties which have proved their permanence.

"In that work of the future let us not forget a sister nation, kindred to ourselves, with the same blood strains drafted from the same sources, animated by the same purposes and who are of us by virtue of the past. I am sure that in the ampler atmosphere of the new world a little break in the historic continuity of these two peoples will seem a very little thing, and the fact that they express their national hopes in a different form of government will mean nothing at all, and that in this partnership of equal nations the time of common consent will come when, seated in pride of place by Great Britain, the first of equals, the great Republic of the United States may take its place."

Any Nation Can Withdraw

Sir Gilbert Parker said there never was a time when any other principle than that outlined by Mr. Dafoe had actuated the British Empire. Not a gun would be fired to prevent any nation withdrawing from the partnership.

Send Telegram of Sympathy

A standing vote of sympathy was taken by the conference in the death of A. E. Miller, editor of the London *Free Press*, and a telegram of sympathy was despatched to Mr. Miller's family. The vote was moved by Mr. T. H. Preston of Brantford, and seconded by Mr. G. E. Fairfax, chairman of the Australian delegation. Lord Burnham added his personal regrets, with a graceful reference to his meeting with Mr. Miller in London a couple of years ago.

Hon. Theodore Fink, of Melbourne, moved a resolution "that the Press remain independent of official and Government control and that privileges secured during the war be maintained." He suggested that there was a strong reason why the conference should go on record as opposed to any sort of fetter of officialdom being imposed upon newspapers. The war had secured to newspapers a greater recognition of its value and its dignity, but after a great war there was a tendency to official reaction.

Suspect Publicity Bureaus

The newspapers generally viewed with suspicion the mushroom growth of Government publicity bureaus with their crop of news despatches, sometimes with party politics. In Australia these usually found their way to the waste-paper baskets. There was also the duty which devolved upon newspapers to remove the suggestion that "the capitalistic press" was growing apace, and the belief in the minds of the industrial classes that newspapers were becoming "the rich man's plaything."

Referring to the censorship of the Press, Mr. Fink said that in Australia the censorship during the war had been ludicrous in principle and irksome to a degree.

Nicholas Knight Kerney was born in Dublin, Ireland, 1870; acquired the rudiments of journalism on the staff of the *Daily Express* of that city; went to London 1895; and was appointed London sub-editor of the Manchester *Courier*, and subsequently also financial editor of the same paper. Since 1911 he has been London editor of the *Argus* South African newspapers:—the *Star*, Johannesburg; the *Cape Argus*, Cape Town; the Natal *Advertiser*, Durban; the Bulawayo *Chronicle*, Bulawayo; and the *Rhodesian Herald*, Salisbury.

Alfred Langlen, governoring director of the West Australian Newspaper Co., Ltd., and editor-in-chief of the West *Australian* and *Western Mail*, Perth, Western Australia, was born at Ipplepen, Devonshire, England, 1886. He went on the editorial staff of the South Australian *Register*, Adelaide, 1890-95; after some years became actively concerned with the business management of the paper. Succeeded the late Sir Winthrop Hackett, K.C. M.G., as editor-in-chief of the West *Australian* and *Western Mail* in 1916.

Hon. John Waters Kirwan, J.P., M.L.C., is editor-in-chief and part proprietor of the Kalgoorlie *Miner* (daily) and *Western Argus* (weekly). He was born 2nd December, 1869, the second son of the late Nicholas John Kirwan of Sandymount House, Co. Galway. He has travelled extensively, did literary work for the London and Dublin press. He went to West Australia gold fields in 1895, and the same year became editor and part proprietor of the two papers that he has since controlled.

C. V. Lansell, was born in London in 1883, and arrived in Australia in 1888. He was educated at St. Andrew's College and the Church of England Grammar School (Melbourne). On the death of his father, Mr. George Lansell, he directed the estates — mining operations—besides sitting on the directorate of over fifty mining companies. He and his brother and sister bought out the mining interests from the rest of the family for half a million pounds. He is now a director of the principal financial institutions in the city.

The motion was seconded by Mr. D. D. Braham of the Sydney (N.S.W.) *Telegraph*. Mr. Braham said that Australians were emphatic against any form of Government control of the Press.

Amendment Offered

Amendment of the resolution was urged by Mr. Walter Makepeace of Singapore and representatives of Crown colonies. They took the view that there was a difference between self-governing communities able to judge news and the uneducated millions on the outskirts of the Empire.

Eventually an amendment was accepted providing that whatever assistance was given by the Government in the interest of the more extensive dissemination of Imperial news, the Press and all news service should remain independent of Government or official control.

Mr. N. Levi of Pretoria moved incorporation of another amendment providing that the Press should remain independent of Government control "except in so far as purely military exigencies may render censorship necessary in time of war."

On this the remark was made by an Australian delegate that in Australia the plea of "military exigencies" had been used in a most dishonest way.

Some Foolish Censorship

Mr. J. W. Dafoe of the *Free Press*, Winnipeg, remarked that during the war some things were done in Canada in regard to censorship which he thought were very foolish, but he was not prepared to take the responsibility of saying to those in authority that he knew the whole game. No doubt, Mr. Dafoe added, "we were all arm-chair strategists of great renown, pointing out errors to Generals in the field, but I think they knew more than we did." Mr. Dafoe was strongly in favor of the amendment.

Sir Campbell Stuart thought the Government would take care of censorship if another war arose. The conference was only weakening its case.

Col. Sir Arthur Holbrook, M.P., thought they should not question the power of the Government in regard to censorship. In the Russo-Japanese War, the Japanese lost two first-class battleships, but the news was withheld, and such action proved of inestimable benefit.

On a vote being taken, nine voted for the amendment, which was declared lost. The resolution was then carried without a dissenting voice.

Cable Rates Resolution

The conference then passed a resolution, dealing with cable rates. The resolution calls upon the Empire Press Union to take immediate steps to secure facilities for the better, quicker and cheaper conveyance of news throughout the Empire. It also urges the Governments of the United Kingdom, of the self-governing Dominions and India, to use their influence to increase cable communications, and to reduce the rates for news messages so as to insure the fullest interchange of news and opinion within the Empire; the Governments to assist in such provision, such assistance, however, to be limited to providing increased and cheaper cable, wireless and other facilities. Further, should any such assistance be given, it should appear specifically in the estimates of public expenditure. The resolution ends by expressing the belief that the full utility of cable and wireless communications as a factor in educating public opinion and in maintaining a good understanding between all peoples of the Empire will not be attained until rates, irrespective of distance, are reduced to a basic charge of one penny per word for press messages throughout the whole British Empire.

To Co-ordinate Efforts

With a view to the better distribution of news throughout the British Empire, a supplementary resolution was carried unanimously that "each delegation will impress upon its own Government the initiation of negotiations with the neighboring Governments of the British Dominions for such improvement of cable and wireless communication between them as would be to their mutual advantage. Each delegation will communicate with the Empire Press Union the result of such negotiations with a view to co-ordination of their efforts."

Sir Robert Bruce (Glasgow) then moved a resolution, which was adopted unanimously, putting the conference on record as opposed to any news carrier being concerned directly or indirectly with the compilation or distribution of news. Sir Robert asked the conference to endorse the principle involved. The subject had been placed on the agenda paper because the

James Smith Macdonald represents the large agricultural interests in technical and daily journalism. He was born in 1873 and served an early apprenticeship on the *Farming World* in Edinburgh, which was afterwards incorporated in the *Scottish Farmer*. He came to London in 1895 to take up similar editorial duties on the *Farmer and Stockbreeder*. Some twelve years ago Mr. Macdonald was appointed agricultural correspondent of the *Morning Post*, both of which appointments he now holds.

C. D. Leng, one of the directors of Sir Wm. C. Leng (Sheffield Telegraph Ltd.), is a member of the council of the Empire Press Union. His firm publish the Sheffield *Daily Telegraph* (the oldest penny morning paper in Great Britain) the *Yorkshire Telegraph and Star* (Evening), the *Weekly Telegraph*, the *Weekly News*, W. T. Novels, etc. and have one of the largest and most completely fitted newspaper offices in Great Britain. Mr. Leng is the eldest son of the late Sir Wm C. Leng, and nephew of the late Sir John Leng, M.P., of Dundee.

N. Levi, was born in Holland 1878, and educated at the Commercial High School, Amsterdam. He became the assistant editor of the first Dutch newspaper in Johannesburg, 1898, and was acting editor of the English-Dutch daily in Johannesburg during the Boer War up to the occupation of the British. He was in charge of the first completely bi-lingual Hansard in South Africa (Transvaal Hansard), 1907, and afterwards in charge of the Dutch Hansard of the Union Parliament at Capetown 1910-1915.

Walter Makepeace, F.J.I., has been editor of the Singapore *Free Press* since 1916. He was born at Coventry, Dec. 22, 1859, and educated for the scholastic profession at Birmingham and Midland Institute and Saltley College. He joined the Singapore *Free Press* on its resuscitation in 1887. He has been official reporter to the Legislative Council of the Straits Settlements on several occasions, Reuter's correspondent in Singapore since 1904 and correspondent of the New York *Herald* (Paris edition).

Wireless Press, Ltd., after the war, had undertaken the preparation and distribution of a news service.

They have since notified their subscribers that the Marconi interests were going out of the news distribution business.

In seconding the resolution, John Nelson of the Vancouver *World* said that the two objections to commercial companies engaging in the preparation of news were, first, that as a matter of common sense newspapermen must oppose the influence of any non-journalistic agency in the compilation of news services, and, second, that the distrust of the press, which was part of the modern unrest, could be only aggravated by the introduction of commercial enterprise into the preparation of news. The resolution carried without further discussion.

Tells of Paper Industry

Mr. A. L. Dawe of the Canadian Pulp and Paper Company gave an outline of the pulp and paper industry, introducing a paper which he had prepared for the use of the delegates. His speech earned him a warm tribute from the Chairman for the manner in which he had presented the case of the paper manufacturers, but individual members of the delegation were disappointed with his attitude. The Australian delegations were of the opinion that Canadian manufacturers of paper should give preference to newspapers in other parts of the Empire rather than to foreign consumers. Mr. Dawe explained that when Norwegian paper manufacturers failed during the war to meet the demand for newsprint in the United States, Canadian firms had "taken up the slack," and Mr. Dawe added, "We intend to keep it."

Mr. Dawe explained that, with the single exception of Russia, Canada was the sole remaining source of pulpwood in large quantities. A number of delegates from Australia and New Zealand plied Mr. Dawes with questions concerning prices, and when he failed to explain some seeming ambiguities Hon. Theodore Fink said that his address supplied all the information except that which the delegates really required.

Mr. P. D. Ross of the Ottawa *Journal* said the production of paper in Canada was in the hands of a few people who conceded to Canadian consumers no favors which other consumers did not enjoy. The manufacture of newsprint in Canada was

built up under the protection of a customs tariff which Canadian newspapers had paid to enforce. Canadian publishers thought it reasonable that they should get some privileges over other countries on this account. In regard to Empire needs, it seemed to him reasonable to ask Canadian manufacturers at least to give first choice to British countries in making contracts, although perhaps a concession in the matter of price was more than could be expected.

Resolution Carries

The following resolution was carried:

"The question of paper supplies being of vital importance to members of the Empire Press Union, steps should be taken to insure adequate supplies throughout the Empire; and that a standing committee be appointed to give effect to the above, such committee to consist of two representatives of the British Isles and one delegate appointed by each delegation and the President, who is to be Chairman."

Postal Rates Resolution

Sir Gilbert Parker introduced his resolution regarding postal rates, and it also was carried unanimously. The force of this motion is that all sections of the Empire Press Union are committed to work for the re-establishment of universal penny postage for letters throughout the British Empire. Sir Gilbert as well as Sir Frank Newnes, who seconded this motion, emphasized the point that every letter between British countries was a "missionary of Empire," and even if the carriage of letters at one penny did not pay in the monetary sense it would pay as an Empire asset.

Sir Roderick Jones introduced a resolution, which was carried, providing suitable committees for the enforcement of the resolutions already adopted concerning improved telegraph communication within the Empire.

Mr. J. P. Collins then presented an amended resolution concerning travel scholarships in journalism. In effect, it calls upon newspapermen to work with universities for the establishment of scholarships in journalism, providing students with the benefit of short courses in British and foreign countries.

Hon. Arthur Lovekin is a member of the Legislative Council of Western Australia. He was born in 1859, and educated at St. Edmund's School, Canterbury, England. He joined the staff of the Melbourne *Age* in 1880; the Adelaide *Register* in 1883; the Perth *Daily News*, in 1886; was editor and managing director of the Perth *Morning Herald* from 1896-1901, and became proprietor of the Perth *Daily News* in 1902. He is Justice of the Peace for the State of Western Australia.

Percival Marshall was born in London 1870, and educated privately and at Manchester Municipal Technical School and Owen's College. He was sub-editor of the *Hardwareman* in 1894; editor of the *Photographic News*, 1895. He founded the present business of Percival Marshall & Co., 1898. He is proprietor and editor of the *Model Engineer* (weekly), and *Junior Mechanics* (monthly), and a publisher of text-books on engineering, electricity, etc. He is chairman of the Council of the British Association of Trade and Technical Journals.

W. Maxwell has held the editorship of the Aberdeen *Daily Journal*, Aberdeen *Evening Express* and Aberdeen *Weekly Journal* since 1910. Previously he was news editor of the London *Standard*. He was news editor of the *Pall Mall Gazette* from 1902-4, and held a similar position on the *St. James' Gazette* from 1900-2. Before going to London, Mr. Maxwell was on the staff of the *Scotsman* (Edinburgh) for a number of years. The Aberdeen *Journal* was founded in 1748, and is the oldest newspaper in Scotland.

Alderman John Bowes Morrell, J.P., of Burton Croft in the city of York, is a man of many interests. He is interested in the production of newspapers and is chairman of the Birmingham *Gazette* Company, Limited, which publishes the city of Birmingham *Gazette*, an evening and a Sunday paper. He is chairman of the Lincolnshire *Chronicle* Ltd., which is one of the finest newspaper properties in Lincolnshire. He is also a director of the Nation Publishing Co., Ltd., and the Athenaeum Publishing Co. Ltd., of London.

Why There is a Shortage of Newsprint

John M. Imrie States the Case at Ottawa

THE newsprint situation in Canada is so closely related to and affected by the newsprint situation in United States that any intelligent discussion of the former must include consideration of the latter and the use of figures covering supply and demand in both countries.

Relation Between Supply and Demand

The present demand in Canada and United States is about 600 tons per day in excess of the combined production. Part of that production is not available for use in North America as 400 tons per day is exported to other continents. On the other hand, approximately 80 tons per day is now coming into United States from Norway and Sweden. Therefore, treating Canada and United States as one unit from a supply standpoint, the demand exceeds available supply by approximately 900 tons per day or 270,000 tons per year. That disparity would be much greater but for the fact that 300 tons per day is being produced temporarily on machines that have been diverted from other grades of paper because of the highly profitable prices now obtainable for newsprint in the spot market in United States.

Until recently a small portion of the excess demand was being met through the depletion of stocks on hand at the mills and in newspaper offices. A few newspapers had accumulated reserve stocks against such a situation as developed. But what relief was obtainable from such sources has been exhausted, and stocks on hand and in transit are now below the safety line.

The great bulk of the excess demand is simply not being filled. Certain mills have cut the requirements of their customers in United States by from 10 to 15 per cent. Some newspapers thus affected have been able to secure additional tonnage in the spot market, but many of them, and others which

have been caught without contracts, are making drastic temporary reductions in consumption.

Effect of Excess Demand on Selling Prices

These conditions have created a seller's market as regards price. Whereas newsprint was selling as low as $35 per ton at the mill in 1916, present contract prices, except in the case of three mills, are at an average rate of $120 per ton for the second half of 1920. Newspapers without contracts or with contracts for insufficient supply are, in effect, bidding against each other in the spot market for what little tonnage is available there. Individual sales in the spot market have been made at as high as $860 per ton, but current prices for the bulk of the sales are around $250 per ton. Large newspapers with contracts at $120 per ton for 85 per cent. of their requirements could pay $250 per ton in the spot market for the other 15 per cent. and get off with an average cost of $140 per ton. And with advertising offering in unprecedented quantities, or faced with the competition of a newspaper that has an ample supply, many publishers have been willing to increase their average cost to that extent in order to secure 100 per cent. of their requirements.

In Canada newsprint prices were under judicial control for the three years ending April, 1920. For the first eleven months of that period the price was $50 per ton; then, during the early part of 1918, it was $57 per ton. An increase to $66 per ton went into effect on July 1, 1918, and another increase to $69 per ton became effective December 1, 1918. That price remained in effect to December last, when the publishers and most of the manufacturers got together, composed their differences and agreed upon a price of $80 per ton to July 1st, and the lowest export price thereafter.

As the Canadian consumption is less than 15 per cent. of the domestic production, Canadian newspapers on the whole have

T. E. Naylor was born in London, March, 1868. He entered the printing trade at the age of 13 as compositor and passed from there to the reading room, and afterwards to the editorial department. He was elected general secretary of the London Society of Compositors, March, 1906, and still holds that position. He has been editor of the London *Typographical Journal* since 1906, when the *Journal* was established. He is chairman of London Printing and Kindred Trades Federation, and is well known as a writer and speaker.

Hon. Sir Patrick Thomas McGrath, K.B.E., was president of the Legislative Council of Newfoundland, 1915-19, and is managing director and editor of *Evening Herald*. He joined the reporting staff of the *Evening Herald* at the age of 21, and became acting editor in 1893, and editor in 1894. In 1907, he established the *Evening Chronicle*, and when in 1912 the *Chronicle* and *Herald* newspapers consolidated he became president of the United Company. He has been Newfoundland correspondent of the London *Times* since 1894.

This group was taken in front of the new Parliament

not had as great difficulty in securing supplies as the newspapers of the United States. There was extreme difficulty on several óccasions in Manitoba and Saskatchewan. In January all the daily newspapers of Winnipeg were suspended for five consecutive days, while other newspapers in Western Canada were on the verge of suspension. Subsequently, in June, 25 per cent. óf all the daily newspapers in Canada were facing the possibility óf suspension after July 1st owing to inability to secure any assurance of supply after that date even at current contract prices for export to foreign countries. The trouble then was largely confined to three mills. Two of the three later agreed to continue supplies and other manufacturers stepped in at great inconvenience to themselves to take care of the Canadian customers of the third mill.

It is generally recognized and frankly admitted that present contract prices bear little relation to cost of production. Reports of the Government Auditor under the recent Newsprint Control indicated that during the latter part of 1919 production costs in the more efficient Canadian mills were running around $50 per ton. December last is the latest month for which audits were made, and undoubtedly there has been a substantial increase in cost since then. But present prices are such as to take care of all increases in cost and yield hitherto undreamed of profits to the manufacturers. I am not saying that in a spirit of complaint. Canadian publishers agreed last fall to pay the current export prices after July 1st. They are good sports and will not welch on their agreement.

Immediate Cause of Present Situation

The immediate cause of the present situation as regards both supply and prices is an unprecedented increase in advertising during 1919 and 1920 to date, following closely upon a substantial increase in circulation during the war years.

In United States during the first two years of the war, 114 daily newspapers, each with a circulation exceeding 50,000

copies, had an average increase in circulation of 19 per cent. while ten foreign language daily newspapers, each with a circulation exceeding 50,000 copies, had an average increase of 67 per cent. Circulation continued to increase during 1917, the average increase during that year being about 13 per cent. There was a falling off during 1918, but towards the close of that year a period of unprecedented advertising volume commenced.

The advertising lineage in the newspapers of New York and Brooklyn was 37 per cent. greater in 1919 than in 1918; in Chicago the increase was 40 per cent.; in Detroit it was 42 per cent.

Individual newspapers in each of the cities mentioned had much larger increases than the average for the city as the following figures show:

New York Times......44%   Chicago Tribune.....49%
New York Sun......55%   Chicago American....70%
New York Tribune....95%   Detroit News........45%
                             Detroit Free Press....53%

Grouping the eighty-nine daily newspapers in the eighteen leading cities of United States, the increase in advertising volume during 1919 as compared with 1918 was 39.3 per cent.

That increase was continued and enlarged during 1920. Grouping again the eighty-nine daily newspapers in the eighteen leading cities in United States, the volume of advertising in the first quarter of 1920 was 39 per cent. greater than in the corresponding period of 1919.

But these increases, first in circulation and then in advertising, are but two phases of a gradually developing situation that has ultimately created the present disparity between supply and demand.

In 1880 the newsprint production in United States was approximately 110,000 tons and the consumption was about 75,000 tons. By 1899 production had increased to 570,000

Hon. Alexander W. Mews was born at St. John's, Newfoundland, May 26, 1882, and educated at the Methodist College, St. John's. He received a commercial training in the offices of Barrie, Johnston & Co., and the Standard Manufacturing Co. He is a contributor to the Newfoundland newspapers and magazines, and became editor of the Evening Advocate, the official organ of the Fisherman's Protective Union of Newfoundland in 1916. He was appointed to the Legislative Council in 1917.

Major John Mitchell, J.P., is editor of the Dundee Courier. He was born at Perth in 1860, and educated at Free St. Leonard's School, Perth, Chapelshade Seminary, Dundee, and Glasgow University. He was appointed Justice of the Peace of Dundee, in 1902; and was elected president of the Institute of Journalists, 1910. He retired from the Volunteers with the honorary rank of major, 1919.

Buildings at Ottawa at noon on the first day of the Conference

tons, by 1904 to 900,000 tons and by 1909 to 1,175,000 tons, consumption during 1909 being about equal to production. It was at this point that newsprint consumption in United States began to exceed domestic production. By 1914 production had increased by only 129,000 tons and the demand during that year necessitated the importation of 278,000 tons, exports being only 44,000 tons. During the next five year period, ending December last, the increase in production averaged only 1 per cent. per year, and during 1919 imports exceeded exports by over 500,000 tons. Production in United States during 1920 will be about 1,475,000 tons. At the present rate, consumption will be about 700,000 tons greater, and there will be an unfilled demand of about 270,000 tons.

The Newsprint Service Bureau is authority for the statement that the annual consumption of newsprint in United States has increased from three pounds per capita in 1880 to nine pounds per capita in 1894 and thirty-three pounds per capita in 1919.

Consumption By Sunday Newspapers

The development of the Sunday newspaper was an important factor in this increased consumption in United States. The term "Sunday newspaper" has quite a different meaning in Great Britain and United States. In Great Britain it is possible for one to buy a Sunday newspaper that is a newspaper. In United States, if one desires a Sunday newspaper he must accept with it a heterogeneous mass of illustrated pages, fashion plates, automobile supplements, book reviews, magazine sections, etc., aggregating in some cases as many as 150 or 160 pages.

The Chateau Laurier news stand has copies of only four of the latest issue of the Sunday newspapers of United States. Those four do not include all the more bulky ones, but at that they average 90 pages of standard newspaper size and their average weight is 1¾ pounds. Having regard to their respective circulations, they represent an aggregate consumption of

newsprint for the one issue of over 1,000 tons or over 50,000 tons per year.

Some Other Factors

But certain factors in addition to increased domestic demand have operated to bring about the partial dependence of United States on imported newsprint supplies to which I have already referred.

The first of these was that as a result of wasteful cutting and lack of adequate fire protection or any measure of reforestation, the pulpwood forests of the Eastern States are rapidly approaching exhaustion.

Another factor was the growing differential in production costs in favor of competing mills in Canada. As the pulpwood forests of the Eastern States became more depleted, cutting and driving costs increased and power and water difficulties were multiplied. Canadian mills on the other hand had large supplies of raw materials at their doors. As far back as 1911 that differential in production costs in favor of Canadian mills, according to the Tariff Board of United States, was $4.50 per ton—equivalent to about 15 per cent. of the then current production cost in United States mills.

These two factors acted as a deterrent on the extension of existing mills or the establishment of new mills in United States. As a result production in 1919, notwithstanding the diversion of machines from other grades of paper, was less than 6 per cent. in excess of 1913 figures—an average increase for the six years of less than 1 per cent.

Growth of Production in Canada

The development of the newsprint industry in Canada during the past ten years is quite a different story.

The Provincial Governments having jurisdiction over the pulpwood forests of Canada have encouraged development by leasing Crown Lands and water powers at nominal rates, by

Dr. Ellis Powell became managing editor of the *Financial News* in 1897, and acting editor in 1909. Since 1915 he has been editor in chief. He has discharged every function in a newspaper office from that of reporter to editor. Dr. Powell is a well known speaker on Imperial topics. He has been, for six years, a member of the Council of the Royal Colonial Institute. He was one of the delegates of the Royal Colonial Institute in the Halifax, N.S., celebration in 1912. Dr. Powell is a leading authority on questions of psychic research.

Alfred Gordon Sprigg, vice-president of the Newspaper Society, is manager and editor of the Leicester *Mail*. Born in Coventry in 1861, he was articled to the Coventry *Herald* and was afterwards on the reporting and editorial staffs of daily papers in Sheffield and Leeds. He started the Leicester *Mail* in 1910, and under his direction it has become one of the leading evening daily newspapers in the Midland area of England, a work recognized by his appointment as director of the company last year.

Thomas Banks Maclachlan was born in Glasgow, and educated at George Watson's College, Edinburgh, and Edinburgh University. He entered the press as reporter, and became consecutively, sub-editor of Edinburgh *Evening Despatch*, and editor of the *Weekly Scotsman*, and since 1909 he has been editor of the Edinburgh *Evening Despatch*. A number of years ago, while editor of the *Weekly Scotsman*, he inaugurated the custom whereby Scottish heather is collected and sent to every Scottish club and community in the world.

Walter James Penn, editor of the Taranaki *Herald* (daily) and the *Budget* (weekly), published at New Plymouth, the chief town and port of Taranaki, New Zealand, is a native of Worcestershire, England. Arriving in New Zealand in 1882, he spent about 3 years in gaining colonial experience in varied occupations. He joined the commercial staff of the Taranaki *Herald* in 1885, and ten years later was appointed editor, which position he still holds. The *Herald* was established on August 4th, 1852.

establishing fire protection systems, by building reservoirs at head waters, and by certain regulations as to the cutting of trees.

About ten years ago the Governments of Ontario, Quebec and New Brunswick amended the regulations covering leases of Crown Lands so as to prohibit the export of pulpwood cut on such lands except in the form of pulp and paper. Up to that time Canada's exports of pulpwood to United States had greatly exceeded her exports of pulp and paper to that country. In 1908 for example the exports of pulpwood were 900,000 cords, while the pulp and paper exported to United States represented only 250,000 cords of pulpwood. Since then the situation has been reversed until in the last fiscal year the exports of pulpwood were 840,000 cords, while the pulp and paper exported to that country represented over 2,000,000 cords.

These various factors contributed to a rapid development and expansion of the Canadian Newsprint Industry. Production increased from 150,000 tons in 1909 to 350,000 tons in 1913, 608,000 tons in 1916, and 807,000 tons in 1919. The production in 1920 will be almost 900,000 tons. These figures include certain quantities of newsprint used for paper-hanging.

Exports of Paper and Pulp from Canada

Members of this conference will be interested in the ultimate disposition of this enormous production.

The latest official figures of exports are for the twelve months ending March 31, 1920. During those twelve months approximately 100,000 tons were consumed in Canada and 713,625 tons were exported. 23,564 tons went to the United Kingdom, 32,173 tons went to Australia, 10,526 tons went to New Zealand, 4,226 tons went to British South Africa, and 629,152 tons went to United States.

Comparing this distribution of exports with the figures for the last fiscal year preceding the war, the exports to the United Kingdom show an increase of over 300 per cent., those to Australia an increase of 150 per cent., those to New Zealand an increase of 20 per cent., and those to British South Africa a decrease of 40 per cent. The increase in exports to United States was 460 per cent.

And now as to the remedies for the present situation, particularly as regards supply:

There is, of course, the possibility of a general curtailment of business which would have an immediate effect upon the consumption of newsprint. No person desires that remedy.

Apart from that, the situation would probably right itself in the course of time. The enormous profits in newsprint manufacture at present and prospective prices would attract capital and bring about greatly increased production. On the other hand, if prices continue to go up there must be eventually a contraction in consumption. With increases in subscription rates to 10 cents for Sunday newspapers and 3 cents or 5 cents for week day issues, there would be a lessening of duplication in circulation, particularly if the value of money were to increase and 10 cents or 5 cents were to mean anything like it did 6 or 7 years ago. There is a limit also beyond which advertising rates cannot be increased without materially reducing volume.

The real solution in my judgment lies in such an increase in production as would eliminate the spot market and create a surplus supply: Coupled with this there should be adequate measures of pulpwood conservation and reforestation. Most Canadian publishers would welcome such measures even although they did involve increases in newsprint prices for a time. They would effect economies in the long run and ensure continued supplies.

Prospects for Increased Production

Let us consider, then, the prospects for a remedy through increased production.

On the first of this month the rated daily capacities of Canadian and United States newsprint mills were 2,834 tons and 4,751 tons respectively—a total of 7,585 tons per day, or 2,275,500 tons per year. Three Canadian and two United States mills are scheduled to install new machines during the last five months of this year, adding 190 tons per day to Canadian capacity, and 150 tons per day to the United States capacity. During 1921 additional capacity of 580 tons per day is scheduled for Canada, and 225 tons per day for United States. If these installations take place as scheduled, and all machines now running on newsprint are retained on that grade of paper

Rowland W. Snelling was born at Sydenham, Kent, Dec. 15, 1869, the son of the late W. B. Snelling. He was educated at Dulwich College and New College, Oxford (Classical Exhibitioner, Honors Final Classical School). He was called to the Bar, Inner Temple, 1894. He was appointed editor and manager of the *Egyptian Gazette*, 1899. He is married and has two daughters. His residence is Bulkeley, Egypt.

P. Selig is general manager of the Christchurch Press Co., Ltd. (the *Press* and the *Weekly Press*). He is also chairman of the Newspaper Proprietor's Association.

Sir Gilbert Parker is known throughout the world. He comes to the Imperial Press Conference as one of the proprietors of a combine of newspapers. It is many years since he lived in Canada, but Canadians do not forget that since he produced his first play in 1888 he has given the world stories and novels of Canada, which have helped to make his fame, and have shown the more agreeable as well as the most adventurous side of Canadian life. He was knighted, given a baronetcy, and made a Privy Councillor.

Francis Crosbie Roles is the honorary secretary and Ceylon member of the Empire Press union. He is an original member (Fellow since 1900) of the Institute of Journalists. He was formerly editor, and still is a director of the *Times of Ceylon*, Colombo. He was born 1867, and was trained to journalism. He went to Ceylon in 1889. He obtained 48 hours copyright for foreign press messages in Ceylon, 1898. He was Ceylon Commissioner, International Rubber Exposition, New York, 1912.

the aggregate daily newsprint capacity on January 1, 1922, will be 3,604 tons in Canada and 4,976 tons in United States—a total of 8,580 tons, or 2,574,000 tons per year. That would represent an increase over present aggregate daily capacity of 995 tons per day, or approximately 300,000 tons per year. That increase is only 10 per cent. more than the present excess of demand over available supply in Canada and United States. It does not allow for any increase in demand during the next seventeen months, and, as already stated, it could take care of the present excess demand only if all machines now producing newsprint for consumption in Canada and United States continue to do so and all the new machines referred to above are used in producing newsprint for consumption on this continent.

If the present excess demand were to fall away to any appreciable extent, there would be withdrawn from the market part or all of the 300 tons per day now being produced temporarily on machines diverted from other grades. If that were not sufficient to maintain an excess of demand over supply, the manufacturers of this continent could easily do so under present conditions by yielding to the pressure for newsprint from other continents. I do not intend any offence to the manufacturers in that statement. Possibly publishers would do the same under similar circumstances. But it would be well for publishers to face the facts squarely and realize that there must be a very substantial increase in production before the present situation will be much improved.

As a matter of fact, it is reported that about 25,000 tons now being supplied in United States is to be diverted to Australia on January 1st, while it is known that part at least of the product of one of the new machines is to be shipped to England.

How North American Production is Marketed

In this connection a survey of the channels through which the newsprint production of Canada and the United States is marketed may be of interest as indicating what might be termed the potential mobility of the production.

The export business of five Canadian companies, producing 32 per cent. of the total Canadian production, is handled by and through the Canadian Export Paper Co. Ltd., which is an organization of the manufacturers themselves. The entire product of two other Canadian companies, producing 30 per

cent. of the total, is handled through Geo. H. Mead & Co., Dayton, Ohio. The export business of two other Canadian companies, producing another 17 per cent. of the total, is handled through an associated newsprint manufacturer in United States. These three groups represent 79 per cent. of the total Canadian production. Another 7 per cent. is produced by a mill owned by the Chicago *Tribune* and established to supply its needs; and another 5 per cent. is produced by a company that is a subsidiary of a newsprint company in United States and sells its export product through the parent company.

Turning now to United States, one company produces 27 per cent. of the total and another 15 per cent. Still another produces 7 per cent. but controls the distribution of a slightly larger tonnage produced in two associated Canadian mills. A fourth company produces 5 per cent. of the total production in the United States but controls the distribution of half as much more tonnage made by a subsidiary company in Canada. These four companies therefore produce 54 per cent. of the total production in United States, while two of them control in addition the distribution of 25 per cent. of the total Canadian production. It may be noted that another of those four companies is now building a mill in Canada that will commence operations next year and produce 7 per cent. of the then Canadian production.

Apart from these four companies and the 54 per cent. of the total production in United States which they produce, another 13 per cent. of the total production is not a factor from an export standpoint as it is produced in mills owned by newspaper publishers.

These facts regarding the ownership of Canadian mills and the channels through which the production in Canada and United States is marketed, coupled with the situation as to supply and demand, will throw some light on the question many members of this conference have asked, viz: why the publishers of other parts of the Empire are denied newsprint supplies when Canada is exporting over 700,000 tons per year.

There are other factors of a purely commercial character operating against the exportation of newsprint overseas.

The market in United States is close at hand, ensuring prompt deliveries, quick returns of cores and quick collections. There is no trouble about selling, as United States publishers are

D. M. Oilemans is vice-president of the Press Union of South Africa, member of the executive committee of the National Industrial Council of the Printing and Newspaper Industry of South Africa, and managing director of the Friend Newspapers Ltd., Bloemfontein, Orange Free State, proprietors of the *Daily Friend*, the *Farmer's Weekly*, the foremost farmers' paper in South Africa, and one of the largest agricultural newspapers in the British Empire; the *Motor Weekly*, and *De Vriend des Volks*, a Dutch newspaper.

Alderman Ernest Woodhead, senior partner of Messrs. Joseph Woodhead & Sons, Ltd., publishers of the Huddersfield *Examiner*, is deputy mayor and past mayor of Huddersfield; chairman of Finance, Education, and Parliamentary Committees, president of the Huddersfield Art Society, president of the "Mrs. Sunderland" Music Competition, Cornwall, chairman of the Congregationalist Insurance Society; and vice-chairman Municipal Mutual Insurance Society. He is famous as a librettist of light operas.

Sir George Toulmin is one of the governing directors of the firm of Messrs. George Toulmin and Sons, Ltd., proprietors of the *Lancashire Daily Post*, the Preston *Guardian*, the Blackburn *Times* and the Burnley *News*. The firm was founded in 1895 by the late Mr. George Toulmin, who purchased the *Guardian* from Mr. Joseph Livesey, the well known Preston temperance reformer. Mr. Livesey established the paper in 1844. Sir George is chairman of the Press Association for the second time, having been elected on the committee.

J. D. Williams is managing editor of the *Cambria Daily Leader* and *Herald* of Wales, evening and weekly journals, published at Swansea. He was born in 1878, joined the *Leader* at the age of 14 and has worked in every department of the paper from the job of errand boy, through the mechanical department into the editorial. During the war, rejected outright on physical grounds for active service, he joined the Y.M.C.A., being in the advanced Somme area during the offensive of 1916.

---

coming to the offices of Canadian manufacturers pleading for paper. Sales in the United States market are paid for in the funds of that country, which are at a substantial premium in Canada, and in most cases shipments are by rail, involving less trouble to the shipper and less cost in wrapping than shipments overseas.

Another factor is the partial dependence of the Canadian newsprint industry on United States for coal.

The Real Solution

The real solution of the present situation and a means of providing for the future pulp and paper requirements of the British Empire are suggested by the general topic for to-day's discussions at this conference: "Empire Partnership." There should be a partnership in pulp and paper development between Canada and the other parts of the British Empire—Canada providing the pulpwood and water power, and her people joining with the people of the United Kingdom and the Overseas Dominions in providing the capital for the develpment of those natural resources.

With a few notable exceptions, British capital which has been such a factor in other phases of this country's development, has played no part in the development of the Canadian pulp and paper industry. It has been stated by parties who should know that 75 per cent. of the capital invested in that industry is American capital.

British and Empire Capital

While appreciating to the full the benefits to Canada through the development of her pulpwood resources by American capital, the Governments and people of this country would welcome most heartily and co-operate in their further development through an Empire partnership such as I have suggested. And in promoting and themselves entering into such a partnership, the publishers of the Empire would be adopting what seems to be the only means of ensuring their future pulp and paper supplies. For I would like to emphasize this point: that serious as the present situation is it will assuredly become more serious as time passes and the pulpwood forests of the world are further depleted and production in United States diminishes.

This Empire partnership should be undertaken without delay. While Canada's pulpwood resources are vast, they are not by any means inexhaustible, and the more easily accessible areas are rapidly being acquired. One of Canada's leading foresters, Mr. Clyde Leavitt, has computed that, apart from annual growth and without allowing for further development, the commercially accessible areas of pulpwood in Quebec represent only 52 years supply, those of Ontario only 67 years supply and those of Nova Scotia only 39 years supply. Available supply in British Columbia is probably sufficient for a longer period at the present rate of cutting, but I have not at hand definite figures for that province.

In this connection one of the first statements of the present Premier of Quebec, following his election to that office a few weeks ago, is very significant, and will be endorsed by most publishers who, while realizing that the policy forecast would add to newsprint costs temporarily, realize also that it is the only means of insuring future supply. Premier Taschereau's statement was as follows:

"The time has come it appears to me to regularize the cutting on timber limits by fixing a maximum of the annual cut to prevent the destruction of the forests and a minimum to stop speculation, and to insure us a reasonable revenue from the cutting rights.

"Reforestation should be immediately undertaken and encouraged with energy."

A Vision of an Empire Industry

And so in considering the present situation and future prospects and looking for a solution of both of these and of the difficulties confronting the newspapers of the United Kingdom and the Overseas Dominions in regard to pulp and newsprint supplies, I see as in a vision a series of pulp and paper industries springing up in the pulpwood forests of this country, controlled by British and Empire capital, sending their product to every part of the Empire, insuring continued supplies for the Empire Press, creating another bond of interdependence, and strengthening the community of interest and unity of purpose and action among the component parts of the Empire. The opportunity is there: I commend it to your investigation, your consideration and your action.

Lionel Goodenough Taylor, cf the Bristol *Times and Mirror,* Bristol, was born July 16, 1871, in London. He was educated at Blundell's, Tiverton, Devon, and Exeter College, Oxford (M.A. 1895). He worked for two years on the *Western Morning News,* Plymouth, before serving thirteen years as London correspondent of the Bristol *Times and Mirror,* and political sketch writer in the Press Gallery, House of Commons. Since 1909, he has acted in Bristol on the directorate of that paper, being vice-chairman cf the board.

Edward William Watt, eldest son of the late William Watt, one of the proprietors of the Aberdeen *Free Press,* was born at Aberdeen, August 25, 1877. He served as reporter and sub-editor on the *Free Press* until 1902, and then went to the Press Gallery, House of Commons, remaining there until the close of the 1904 session. He returned to Aberdeen that year as chief sub-editor of the *Free Press,* and in 1906 was appointed editor of the *Evening Gazette.* He held this post until the declaration of war.

Out of Hours They Talked of Many Things

Sidelights on the Gathering at Ottawa

IN THE evenings at Ottawa some very pleasant meetings were held in a most informal way. One of these turned into a testimony and experience meeting of things that had happened in cub and young days in various parts of the world. One gathered then what a representative group of people were there, as they heard of happenings in the offices of England, Ireland, Australia, Canada, east and west, South Africa and other countries. This one, we believe, came from Mr. Jeffery of the Australian deputation:

In my early days I was sent by the chief to interview Sir John —— in regard to some land bill he was bringing into the House of Parliament. There were certain clauses that I was to get some more details about. I had been well warned that the house of Sir John was run on well-defined lines, so I prepared for the worst.

Upon knocking at the door, it was opened by a butler clad in the most immaculate knee breeches and all the rest of the outfit. I was told, with a long sweep, after presenting my card that I might come in and be seated and that Sir John would be down in a few minutes. He did come down, and I was invited to come over and sit down within shooting distance of him. Sir John looked at me and then looked at my card, and after doing all this beckoned to one of his men in the room. He responded with the alacrity that spells obedience, and the command was given in a voice that was just a trifle thick to start on:

"Whiskey and soda."

Just as the man turned to carry out the wish, Sir John snapped his fingers and called him back, adding: "Make it two whiskies and two sodas."

One of these was for me and the other was for Sir John. In the meantime I had been busy trying to recite to my man the reason for my trip, and had got along fairly well. "You see, Sir John, we want some more information about a certain part of the preamble to your bill, and also about clause four in particular. The editor considers it very important that. . ."

Another snap of Sir John's fingers brought the well-trained man to his elbow. "Whiskey and soda" chanted Sir John, and repeated the second snap the second time, and added "Pardon, two whiskies and two sodas."

The second whiskey and soda had been brought and duly polished off when I tried my best to get Sir John steered around to where he would give me some information along the lines I was after. I had not any too much time to get back to the office and turn the stuff in under the best of circumstances, and as the whiskey and soda was served in generous lots I was afraid that I would be bowled over before I ever got back to the shop.

So I made another attempt. Remember I was seated directly in front of his nibs, who was a very big man. He made a habit of sitting with his legs sprawled well apart and used his knees as resting posts for his hands. From this peculiar position he would look at me with something akin to amusement every time I started to tell him what I was after. So the third time the whiskey and soda wagon was run in I told him that I couldn't drink any more whiskey and stay sober, where-

upon Sir John looked at me and through me as no man had ever looked before, and then took up the card I had presented when I came.

"And so your editor sent you up here to interview me, did he?"

I admitted that such was the case, and gave Sir John to understand that there would be trouble in store for me if I fell down on the assignment.

"Well," drawled Sir John, focusing his rather bleary eye on me, "you take your card, sonny, and run back to your —— editor, and tell him when he sends any person out to interview Sir John to trot out a real man, not a child who can't hold is. Good-day." And thus the interview ended.

Another of the Australian delegation had served his time on one of the big London papers that devoted much space to scandal stories and divorce proceedings. In fact scandal stories always got the right of way.

"There had been a particularly sordid case in print for a couple of days and at last the city editor got tipped off as to where the man in the case was living. The circumstances were such that it was advisable for him to leave the premises he usually occupied, and he was on the third floor of what we call a tenement house, although around here you name them apartments; which sounds a bit better. So I was assigned to interview this man about what all the skunk stuff had been published.

"I was afraid I would be bowled over before I even got back to the shop"

"Well, I found the street and the house easy enough, and found that the scandal man lived on the third floor. The doors there opened abruptly off the top of the stairs, and there was no landing as there is in most of the houses now. So I knocked and waited. I didn't wait long for friend Scandal came right to the door. I told him who I was and that I was there to hear what he had to say for himself. I'll give him credit that he was fair enough, for he warned me to clear out before anything happened. But I had the honorable traditions of the paper to uphold, so far be it from me to show any signs of retreat.

'So just by way of showing that I was quite at home and intended to come in and talk the thing over leisurely, I made a move to step inside the door, explaining as I did so that it would be a good chance for the old top to put himself square with a great number of people who read our paper. I can quite well remember taking that step that was to put me inside the door, and then the next thing that I recollect is that something whacked me on the jaw and the back and the head all at once. It was a most peculiar sensation, and when it was all over I counted that I was one floor nearer the street than where I intended to have my sensational interview with the much-talked-of scandal centre. I was bally well bruised up in several parts and I guess I looked quite mussed as well. The man in question was sitting on the top of the stairs a flight up, and by this time he had fortified himself with an axe. He yelled at me to move out as quick as I could as he intended coming down in a minute with the axe.

"The whole thing looked too much like the retaking of Gibraltar for me to tackle. So I hurried off and caught a tram

Sir Campbell Stuart, K.B. E., deputy chairman of the Times Publishing Company, is the youngest son of the late Ernest H. Stuart of Montreal. He was born in Montreal, July 5, 1885. He was assistant military attache to the British Embassy, Washington, March 1917, and became vice-chairman of the London Headquarters of the British War Mission in the United States of America to January, 1918. In May, 1918, he became Deputy Director of Propaganda in Enemy Countries. He is a director of the Associated Newspapers Ltd.

ism to him had an autocratic sound, and brought back memories of Empires that had decayed and fallen because they forgot the rights of the people. But he didn't get away with it. Lord Burnham, the efficient chairman, was on his feet as soon as he got through and after addressing "your Excellency, My Lords, Ladies and Gentlemen," in a high-pitched voice, which reached to the farthest corner of the room and half way down to the Chateau Laurier, he reminded Mr. King that the British Empire had nothing in common with the ramshackle empires of the past, and the name Imperial had an all-embracing sound that British had not. Lord Burnham had the majority quite evidently with him, for there were many "Hyah, hyahs," and although Mr. King tried to look pleasant we imagine he felt a

where I sat outside and dusted myself off a bit. When I got back my eye was a beastly looking thing, my jaw was sore and some of the other corners of my anatomy were also horribly sensitive. So I went in to the editor looking a real mess. He had been having a few good shots that evening before he came to work and was living in the bravery that can come only from half-seas over.

"I must have looked like an ass as I sat down across from him and explained what had happened to me. He neither cursed nor raved. He got brave all at once. He rose to his full height and walked around the desk several times, finally pulling up across from me. 'You go back to that place, and tell that man that by —— he can't intimidate me by such actions.' "

A Real Bull Here

Perhaps one of the best stories of mistakes came from a visitor from India, Rustum Ghi. That may not be the way to spell his name but it sounds very much like it, unless one uses Gee for the Ghi. He is of the Parsee tribe in India, and has been a great traveller. He covered many countries speaking on what the British Government had done in India, in an effort to combat the tremendous and constant anti-British propaganda that has been carried on with such intensity during the last few years.

"I arrived in New York one evening," was the way he started his narrative to the evening loungers at the Chateau, "and it was not long after that a young reporter from one of the papers there called on me at my room. I was quite glad to see him and explained what I was in the country for, and told him a good deal about the real conditions in our country. Next morning I secure a morning paper at the hotel, and on opening it up was rather surprised to read that Mr. Rusty Jim, a Pharisee from India, was staying in the city."

What a Delegate Thought

W. R. Davies of the Renfrew *Mercury*, was, as president of the C.W.N.A., one of the delegates. In his paper he gives his impressions of the gathering in part as follows:—

Hon. Mackenzie King threw a monkey wrench into the works at the opening session, by suggesting that the word "British" Press Conference would sound better in the ears of the people in this democratic age than Imperial Press Conference. Imperial-

"He was standing on the top step and by this time had fortified himself with an axe."

bit uncomfortable. At the same time his viewpoint would doubtless appeal to the large majority of his fellow-Canadians.

Lord Burnham, owner of the London *Daily Telegraph*, was the chairman, and he was 100 per cent. efficient. He knew them all and as soon as a speaker got to his feet his lordship gave him an official announcement, and incidentally he is some announcer. If he had gone in for the operatic stage instead of journalism Caruso would have had to look to his laurels. He kept order too, and he missed nothing. He's a very clever man; not the kind of a lord our American cousins love to caricature, but an efficient, keen business man. Sitting up in the chair on the platform he reminded one of Old King Cole, who was a jolly old soul. He has an expansive smile and a genial personality, but beneath it all is an iron will and a strong determination. Lord Burnham seemed immensely popular with the delegates and has the reputation of being quite democratic in manner.

H. E. Turner became secretary of the Empire Press Union in the autumn of 1919, upon demobilization from the army. Prior to the war, he was for five years assistant secretary of the Newspaper Society. He left the society at the outbreak of war, and served in the infantry for five years in France, Belgium, Italy, Macedonia, and European and Asiatic Turkey. Recreation: yacht cruising and small boat sailing. (Writes on this subject.)

Sir Charles Starmer, J.P., of Westville, Darlington, is managing director of ten newspaper companies, which extend their influence over various counties in England in different groups. Sir Charles Starmer was born in 1870. In addition to his interest in newspapers, Sir Charles Starmer has devoted considerable time to public affairs. He was a member for the Darlington Town Council from 1903 to 1915, when he was made an Alderman. In 1907, he was unanimously elected mayor.

It is quite easy to distinguish members of this group. In the front are Sir Gilbert Parker, Lord Burnham, Robert Donald, Sir Robert Bruce; on the left, third line back is Capt. Henderson of Belfast; almost next to him is Sir Stuart Campbell.. This is taken on landing at Sydney.

Receiving Degrees at Toronto University—Left to right, Geoffrey Fairfax, Sydney Morning Herald, and chairman of the Australian delegation; Sir Robert Bruce, LL.D., Glasgow Herald; Robert Donald, chairman of the Empire Press Union; Sir Gilbert Parker.

Printer & Publisher

Published on the Twelfth of Each Month.

H. D. TRESIDDER   -   -   -   Business Manager.
A. R. KENNEDY   -   -   -   -   -   -   Editor.

SUBSCRIPTION PRICE—Canada, Great Britain, South Africa nd
the West Indies, $3 a year; United States, $3.50 a year; otner
countries, $4 a year. Single copies, 30 cents. Invariably in
advance.

PUBLISHED BY

THE MACLEAN PUBLISHING CO.
Established 1887   Limited

JOHN BAYNE MACLEAN   -   -   -   President.
H. T. HUNTER   -   -   -   -   -   -   Vice-President.
H. V. TYRRELL   -   -   -   -   -   General Manager.
T. B. COSTAIN   -   -   -   General Managing Editor.

Head Office, 143-153 University Avenue   -   TORONTO, CANADA
Cable Address Macpubco, Toronto; Atabek, London, Eng.
Also at Montreal, Winnipeg, New York, Chicago, Boston, London,
England.

Application for A.B.C. Audit.

Vol. 29   TORONTO, SEPTEMBER, 1920   No. 9

Now Is a Good Time

MANY publishers, especially in the weekly field, are still threatening to go into the $2 a year class. It does not require any courage to do this now. It did some months ago.

There are scores of publishers all over the country collecting $2 for their paper, so there is no experimenting to be done. It is an acknowledged fact that it can be secured without any difficulty.

Papers would be well advised were they to abbreviate very severely the period of contemplation.

To put the case plainly, publishers can get the $2 rate now. There is no doubt about that. It is not an exhorbitant charge, and costs as they are at present back up the publisher in his claim for the increased rate.

Conditions may not be as favorable in a few months from now. Publishers should not take a chance when they have nothing to gain by delay.

Do not make your announcement too far ahead. If your case is genuine, if your costs have increased to the point where you need an increase in rates, do not defeat your aim by a tub-thumping session in your columns, in which you appeal to subscribers to flock in at the old rate.

If you mean what you say, you are really asking your readers to come along and keep you from getting 50 cents per year on each paper, to which you are entitled.

Weekly men would be well advised to go to $2 at once.

Developing Big Men

THERE is a job that needs filling. The sorry part is that there are many such jobs all over the country. But here are the particulars:—

"We have a place for a young man in our establishment who has the ability and originality to get business without always to give a price.

"We don't mind giving prices to the concern who will give him their confidence and tell him when they want something but we hate like the devil to have him bring in every job for a quotation.

"We want a man who is versatile enough to get the customer's viewpoint and then go after what he should have and sell him from an enthusiastic dummy.

"If you know of such a man he can have a place in our office to hang his hat, we will also furnish him with a rag to rub the dust off his shiny shoes, and we will in addition help him to buy a good new home and an automobile."

Nearly any job is as big as you make it. There are many things that make men and jobs big, or keep them small.

As long as a firm regards a man as being small and ordinary, the chances are that he will be small and ordinary.

When a man feels that he has his firm behind him, that they appreciate him, and regard him as equal to any occasion, he is going to develop in nearly every case, and his job is going to develop with him, for it's a hard matter to pry a man from his job—it's hard to see where one stops and the other starts.

There are firms that never develop a big man. They are afraid that some of their men may grow into giants, bigger and better than anything the office has.

Big, capable men don't just happen to be so. They grow in an atmosphere that is congenial. They don't want petting or spoiling, neither are they asking for favors. They do want a decent chance, encouragement, the stamp of approval in the way of increasing pay, and a full share of responsibility and hard work.

Don't always look outside your own organization when a big opening is coming.

It's a negative tribute to your firm to reach outside when you have a big position to fill.

Living in the Past?

THE Smith's Falls Record-News, in a recent issue, discussed the custom that many papers follow now of running items from their files of 20 or 30 years ago, saying that:—

"But to tell over again the small matters of 20, 25 or 30 years ago indicates rather too much of a proneness to look backward rather than forward and shows that those interested in that sort of thing live to a considerable extent in the past. Communities thus peopled are not likely to be greatly marked by advancement. They ignore Longfellow's advice to "let the dead past bury its dead." And newspapers which do that sort of thing proclaim the undesirable quality of indolence, because anybody can reproduce matter from files. The work is easy and no initiative is required."

The success of building circulation is to find out what the people want, and then give it to them. This need not apply to the editorial page of a paper, but the editor who can successfully interpret in each issue the wants of his readers is going to have a big and a satisfied following. There are numerous cases where papers have picked out their clientele and then catered to it most successfully.

It is hard to agree with the Smith's Falls paper in regard to the value of the twenty or thirty years ago columns. There are many people who would willingly subscribe for a paper of their own town, which they have probably long since left, were they certain that each week they would get a dozen items of what happened there a quarter of a century ago. There is a weakness in human nature to hark back to the days that are gone; to the years when affairs in the town seemed more real than they do afterward when they have to stand comparison with the events in the various large centres to which these town boys drift. The man who does not like to talk about what he used to do twenty-five yers ago does not exist, and what people like to talk about they are apt to read about, so why not cash in on this trait of character?

The more a newspaper steeps itself in local history and events, ancient and modern, the more it is going to become a community institution that cannot be dispensed with, and remember, reader interest is the only safe way in which to build a paper for the future.

Replacing the Plant

HERE is a paragraph from the Carp Review, in reference to the rebuilding of its plant, which was largely destroyed by fire recently:—

"We cannot replace it to-day for at least twice as much as it cost, and in some cases four times as much."

Publishers should do well to give heed to this experience. The value of your plant is its replacement price. The trouble is that you seldom realize what a fair replacement price is until you are called upon by force of circumstances to find out.

There are few plants insured for anything like what it would cost to replace them. Every business ought to shoulder the expense of its own insurance, and earn the money necessary to meet the premiums.

It is poor policy to tinker with your insurance until some day you are called upon to poke among the ashes to see what can be saved from the ruins.

W. F. Herman Enters Morning Field at Windsor

Border Cities Sun Makes Its Appearance

WEDNESDAY, Sept. 8, saw the first publication of a new Ontario morning paper, the *Border Cities Sun*, owned by W. F. Herman, publisher of the *Border Cities Star*, the Saskatoon *Daily Star* and the Saskatoon *Morning Phoenix*. The *Sun* and the *Border Cities Star* are published from the same plant, with Hugh A. Graybiel as manager and J. Ellison young as editor of both papers. Already the *Sun* has a growing circulation list and gives every promise of taking as prominent a place in the morning field as the *Star* occupies in the evening.

The *Border Cities Star* was launched in September, 1918, succeeding the Windsor *Record* which Mr. Herman purchased from John A. McKay. Wonderful changes have been made in the Border Cities publishing field since that time. The *Star* is a modern newspaper in every respect, printing from 16 to 36 pages daily, and running each Saturday a four-page comic section in colors—printed in the *Star* office. The *Star* is the only paper in Ontario issuing a four-page colored comic section as part of a regular daily issue. The *Star* uses the full leased wire service of the Canadian Press and United Press Associations, besides having a large group of correspondents and taking various special news services. It carries probably more syndicate features than any paper in the province, and now has an A.B.C. circulation close to the 17,000 mark.

The *Sun* has been commenced to meet a definite demand for a morning paper in the rapidly-growing Border Cities (Ford, Walkerville, Windsor, Sandwich and Ojibway). At the present time London and Toronto papers do not reach the border in the early morning and up to now the only before-breakfast paper available was the Detroit *Free Press* which, naturally does not contain the news that Canadians desire to read. This was one reason for the starting of the *Sun*. Another was that train arrangements were such as to prevent the *Star* from reaching many outlying points on the day of publication. The *Sun* meets this problem.

The *Sun* is not a morning rehash of the *Star*, nor is the *Star* an evening rehash of the *Sun*. Each is a distinct and separate newspaper and not merely another edition of the other. The appearance is totally different, the features are different, the editorials are different. The heading of the new morning paper is most attractive, the words "The Sun" in distinctive black caps being separated by the Canadian coat-of-arms with maple leaves as a background. The full night service of the Canadian Press is carried, besides telegraphic contributions from special correspondents in London, Chatham

and elsewhere. In addition the *Sun* carries the special telegraphed financial service of the Philadelphia *Public Ledger*, including the contributions of Sir George Paish, B. C. Forbes, C. B. Evans, Richard Spillane and others, giving, altogether, an unusually fine financial page.

In matters political the *Sun* takes the same attitude as the *Star*, in that it is absolutely independent. The *Sun* announces that it will seek public support solely on one ground—that of being a good newspaper.

The publisher of the *Sun*, W. F. Herman, is one of Canada's best known newspapermen. His success in the direction of the Saskatoon *Daily Star* and the *Border Cities Star* is now a matter of Canadian newspaper history. He aims to make the *Sun* just as good, just as large, and just as great a factor in its particular field. Mr. Herman, a Nova Scotian by birth, has been in the printing business, in one form or another, since boyhood. His policy of "a square deal for all" and giving the public more than value for its money, has brought results which speak for themselves.

Mr. Graybiel, manager of the *Border Cities Star* and the *Border Cities Sun*, is a native of Caledonia, Mich., but has been associated with Mr. Herman for the past eight years. His whole newspaper experience was secured on the Herman papers. Mr. Young of the *Bordier Cities Star* and the *Sun*, was born in Aylmer, Ont., and spent a year in the office of the Aylmer *Express*, a weekly paper, before joining the staff in St. Thomas *Journal*, then under the management of F. W. Sutherland. Mr. young did city hall for the London *Advertiser*, spent some time in publicity and promotion work with Henry L. Doherty & Company, and then returned to St. Thomas as editor of the *Journal*, which position he held until the amalgamation of the *Journal* and the *Times*. He was connected with the amalgamated paper for a short time and then went to Windsor to join Mr. Herman's staff at the time of taking over the Windsor *Record*, succeeding Alfred J. West as editor when the latter resigned to become news editor of the now defunct Toronto *Times*.

The Rolland Paper Co., Ltd., of Montreal, Que., issue two compact paper sample booklets covering their products in, flat writing, bond, ledger, book and typewriter paper, and also envelopes, writing tablets, note papers and paperteries and linen bond in white and eight colors. The purpose of these booklets is to supply a handy pocket reference, which may be turned to for detailed reference about their products.

Union Earnings Increased 40 Per Cent.

Earnings of members of the International Typographical union increased 40 per cent. last year over the previous year, according to a report of Treasurer Hayes, given at the I.T.U. convention in Albany last month. The total earnings of the 74,179 members was $32,130,091. The total assets of the union are $1,986,903.50.

An amendment to the law providing compensation for members who perform service for the union was changed so that in the future those who do this work will receive $10 a day instead of $6.

An amendment providing for the regulation of initiation fees to $3 for candidates for membership who are twenty-five years old; $5 for those between twenty-five and thirty-five, $10 for those between thirty-five and forty-five, and $20 for those who are over forty-five was adopted.

The monthly per capita tax was changed from 45 to 55 cents, and this will change the per capita contribution to the printers' home from 20 to 30 cents.

The next convention will be held in Quebec.

New Paper in Peterborough

Peterborough is to have another weekly newspaper, the Peterborough *Weekly Chronicle*, published by the *Chronicle* Publishing Company in the plant formerly occupied by the Merchant's Press. The new company is being backed principally by labor subscriptions, and T. Tooms, M.P.P., is managing director. A press and machinery have been purchased and are now being shipped, and it is expected that the first edition will be published on Saturday, 28th August. Mr. Tooms stated Tuesday afternoon that though the new paper is being published by capital subscribed by labor, it will treat labor problems only on a broad basis, and will publish all news without fear or favor. Its editorial policy, Mr. Tooms said, would be based on broad and democratic principles. The *Chronicle* will publish weekly news and articles on subjects of importance. Its subscription list so far, according to Mr. Tooms, is satisfactory, as the various labor organizations are giving it their support. A job printing plant will be operated in connection with the paper, of which Mr. Alex. Miller is manager.

Cleaning Type Metals

From continued usage impurities will accumulate in any grade of type metal. These are caused by printing ink, dust and dirt from the metal sweepings on the floor, dirt and grit in the atmosphere and from other miscellaneous causes. The presence of a considerable quantity of such foreign matter is indicated by the sluggishness of the metal in the pot, or while being cast. It is advisable to keep the metal as clean as possible, but this can be overdone and a great deal of good metal wasted in the process.

Directions for Cleaning :—A flux to be mixed consisting of the following ingredients:—

Two parts of granulated sal ammoniac; 2 parts of powdered resin; 3 parts of beef tallow.

The above formula will answer the purpose, and should be used in the proportion of approximately one pound of flux to one ton of metal. Another formula which can be used which is more difficult to make up is as follows:—

Three parts of beeswax; 2 parts of granulated sal ammoniac; 2 parts of tanners hard grease, or tallow; 2 parts of powdered sulphur; 1 part of borax; 1 part of plumbago.

Reynolds, Ltd., Winnipeg, believe in the use of blotters, and they believe in putting two or three colors on them too. The making of a blotter into a calendar is of doubtful value. There is no doubting the wisdom, though, of using good taste and good printing in a blotter campaign.

THE PERSONAL SIDE OF IT

 We'd Like To Get Items For
These Columns

Quebec

It is announced that the Provincial Government of Quebec has decided to send two journalists of this province to Europe to complete their studies. The names will be announced shortly.

The Montreal *Gazette* announces that the paper will "on and after Wednesday, September 1, 1920," be sold at five cents, while the subscription price will be raised to twelve dollars a year. The announcement states that the new price represents an advance to subscribers of about one-third the increased cost of publication, and that the average percentage increase in costs has been 170 per cent. in the past six years.

The death occured in Montreal of Mr. Frederick Abraham, following a short illness from heart disease. He was born in Belleville, Ont., November 18th, 1870, of U.E.L. descent, his grandfather having settled in Bertie Township, Welland County, in 1779, the family being one of the oldest English families in the Dominion, and being to-day represented by many branches along the Niagara frontier to St. Thomas, Ont. Mr. Abraham was educated at the Belleville High School, and entered into newspaper work there, as editor of the *Daily Ontario*. From this he became associated with Mr. James S. Brierley, at St. Thomas, conducting the St. Thomas *Journal*. This association lasted many years, and Mr. Abraham came to Montreal in 1897 with Mr. Brierley, when they became associated in the conduct of the *Daily Herald*, then a morning paper, he being vice-president and secretary-treasurer of the *Herald* Company until 1913. At that time, when the change in proprietorship of the *Herald* occurred, Mr. Abraham dropped out of active newspaper work.

On the occasion of his fiftieth birthday opportunity was taken by a large circle of friends to pay a tribute to Louis Larivee, of the editorial staff of the Montreal *Star*. Mr. Larivee has been in active and continuous journalism in Montreal for nearly thirty years. During the course of thirty years he has played a part, and at times an important one, in many well-remembered events, especially so in the range of provincial politics, where, in particular, his friends are legion. It was to give expression to this feeling of friendship and comradeship that a considerable number of friends, including members of the Legislature, aldermen, brother newspapermen and friends generally, gathered to make a presentation to Mr. Larivee, and to offer him congratulations on the work he has been able to accomplish and the good he has been able to do in the past, and to wish him a still further measure of success in the future. During the course of his long career Mr. Larivee has served on the staffs of almost all the daily newspapers in Montreal, French and English, both in and out of existence. Among those who spoke were Edmond Robert, M.L.A. for Rouville; Dr. Ernest Poulin, M.L.A. for Laurier; Joseph Caron, M.L.A. for Hull; Amedee Monet, M.L.A. for Napierville; Ald. Lyon, W. Jacobs, and a number of others.

Maritimes

The *Carleton Sentinel*, Woodstock, N.B., has installed a Model L Linotype.

A Model No. 8 linotype has been recently installed at the office of the St. Croix *Courier*, St. Stephen, N.B.

The Sydney *Record* office has installed a Model 8 Linotype during the past month.

St. John, N.B., had a Dollar Day on Saturday, August 21, and a good line of advertising was carried by the papers.

H. V. MacKinnon, managing editor St. John *Standard*, has returned home after a pleasant vacation trip to Upper Canada.

Richard O'Brien, of the St. John *Globe*, and wife have returned after a holiday visit to Nova Scotia.

H. Harrison, formerly Maritime representative for the Lanston Monotype Co., is now mechanical superintendent on the Sydney *Post*.

J. Vernon McKenzie has been appointed editor of *MacLean's Magazine*, to succeed T. B. Costain, who has resigned to accept a responsible editorial post with the Curtis Publishing Company, Philadelphia. Mr. McKenzie, who was formerly Associate Editor of *MacLean's Magazine*, has been for the past year Canadian Trade Commissioner at Glasgow, Scotland. He served in the R.A.F. during the war and was wounded in a crash shortly before the Armistice was signed. Previous to going overseas he was engaged in newspaper work on various papers including the Montreal *Star*, Toronto *Star*, Ottawa *Journal*, *Leth-bridge Herald*, etc. He returns to Canada to take up his work the middle of October, his resignation having been forwarded to the department some time ago.

J. VERNON McKENZIE

Chas. H. Shaw, Maritime representative of the Canadian Linotype Co., was in Halifax recently. While in the city Mr. Shaw was instrumental in placing a Model 8 in the *Herald* office.

The Sydney *Post*, Sydney, N.S., has increased its subscription rate. Single copies now sell at five cents. Increase in the cost of production is given as the reason.

Mr. John Poole, linotype machinist with the Canadian Linotype Co., is in Halifax attending to some repair work on the *Herald*.

F. H. Kipp, formerly of the Montreal *Herald*, is expected in St. John in a few days to take up a supervising position on the editorial staff of the *Standard*.

The Sydney *Record*, the Sydney *Post* and the Glace Bay *Gazette* announce an increase in price to 5 cents a copy, effective from Sept. 1st.

F. I. McCafferty, city editor, St. John *Times*, has returned after a two weeks' holiday with his family at Loch Lomond.

B. S. Robb, city editor St. John *Telegraph*, with his family also spent his vacation at Loch Lomond.

The *Labor Annual*, 1920, published for the Trades and Labor Council by Robt. L. Gaul, advertising manager on the *Citizen*, was a decided success. It is planned by the Council to make this a feature every Labor Day.

Harry (Dutch) Ervin, news editor of the St. John *Standard*, accompanied the St. John oarsmen on their trip to Halifax, where they participated in the Annual Regatta held by the N.W.A.R.C. "Dutch" went into ecstasies when Belyea of St. John won the senior single with ease.

F. W. W. Bartlett, of the *Evening Times* writing staff, has returned after a vacation in Newcastle, N.B. A. M. Belding, editor of the *Times*, spent three weeks at Public Landing on the St. John River.

J. D. Black, for some years sporting editor of the Fredericton *Gleaner*, has met with much success in his recent appointment as manager of the Maritime Racing Association. They have conducted meets throughout the province which have been most satisfactory.

S. D. Granville, who has been for several years accountant and assistant office manager with the St. John *Standard*, left this week for St. Stephen, N.B., where he has purchased the St. Croix *Courier*. He will take over control at once. On his departure from the city he was tendered a luncheon by his associates on the *Standard* with whom he has been very popular.

Yarmouth *Herald*:—With this issue the *Herald* enters upon its 88th year, having been established by the late A. Lawson on the 9th August, 1833. It is the only weekly newspaper in the Maritime Provinces that has completed 87 years, with one exception, and so far as can be ascertained is the only paper in the world that has been continued by father and son for so long a period.

St. John *Standard*:—Members of the *Standard* staff met at the Sign o' the Lantern at a luncheon given in honor of Stanley D. Granville, previous to his departure to St. Stephen to take control of the St. Croix *Courier*. Mr. Granville, who has been with the *Standard* for a number of years and was a very popular member of the office staff, was the recipient of a cheque and a very appreciative letter from the *Standard* company. The young ladies in the business office presented him with a set of gold cuff links. Many friends in St. John will regret the departure from the city of Mr. and Mrs. Granville, and they will be followed by many good wishes.

British Columbia

According to an advertisement published in the Victoria *Times*, Griffith R. Hughes, proprietor of the *Times*, has made an assignment of his real and personal estate to David Leming and Eli Harrison for the general benefit of his creditors.

Vancouver *Province*:—Mrs. Evah McKowan, of Cranbrook, author of "Janet of the Kootenays," which appeared last year, is spending a holiday in this city and Victoria. Her new novel, "Graydon of the Windermere," is to appear this autumn, and will be, like her former work, a romance laid in a typical British Columbia setting. Possessing artistic as well as literary skill, Mrs. McKowan hopes to draw the cover design for her volume, that it may harmonize more perfectly with her conception.

The Vancouver *Daily Sun* recently announced an increase in the subscription rates of both the *Daily Sun* and *Sunday Sun*, with an intimation that a further increase is not improbable. The *Daily Sun*, delivered by carrier, was advanced from 15 cents per week to 20 cents per week. Price on street and newsstands is now 5c per copy, instead of 3 cents, as formerly. Concurrent with the change in the price of the *Daily Sun*, the *Sunday Sun* was advanced from 5 cents per copy to 10 cents per copy.

Farm and Home of Vancouver, Canada, published their first exhibition and harvest number on September 1st. It contained about sixty pages—the outside eight pages being printed in three colors on coated book paper. It is full of high class national advertising as well as several editorial feature articles by some of Canada's leaders in the agricultural field. Circulation was in excess of twenty-five thousand copies. This is a creditable showing for so young a publication, and shows the marked interest that is being shown in the agricultural and livestock industry in British Columbia.

Kaslo *Kootenaian*:—After nearly fifty years in the newspaper business, Colonel R. T. Lowery has retired owing to ill-health. It is eighteen years since the publisher of the *Kootenaian* went to work for the colonel in the beautiful town of New Denver on Slocan Lake. Afterwards in Nelson, then to the Fernie *Ledge*, and later the Greenwood *Ledge*, in all nearly eight years associated with the Colonel. We had the good times and the bad, the fat years and the lean years. The Colonel never got the big head or grumbled, and signed a check each week at $11.15 for the week's wages. Colonel Lowery was one of the easiest men in the world to get along with. He knew a day's work and expected it done, but never kicked. He was close in business, but liberal with employees, always paying the highest wages. As a writer he was independent and hit hard when he thought it was needed. His many friends throughout the interior will regret that he is compelled to quit the newspaper business and will be pleased to know that he has retired with a moderate fortune. "Billy" Smith, for the past nine years in charge of the mechanical end of the *Ledge*, has leased the busi-

ness. We wish him success and hope he will not have the strenuous times the *Ledge* had in its first two years in Greenwood, with politicians and other troublesome insects.

At a meeting of the members of the Okanagan Press Guild held in Vernon, the following officers were re-elected: Louis J. Ball, manager of the Vernon *News*, president; John Leathley, Kelowna *Record*, vice-president; Ralph E. White, Summerland *Review*, secretary-treasurer. Others present were M. D. Billings, Kamloops *Standard-Sentinel*; H. E. Moore, Salmon Arm *Observer*; H. M. Walker, Enderby *Commoner*; W. Watson, Armstrong *Advertiser*; G. C. Rose, Kelowna *Courier*; R. J. McDougall, Penticton *Herald*. The Princeton *Star*, Kamloops *Telegram* and Revelstoke *Review* were unable to send representatives. The Guild decided to take up the "three-year plan," which includes educational courses relating to the printing and publishing industry as prepared by the United Typothetae of America, an international institution, covering Canada and the United States and with which the Guild is affiliated. After considering the report of Mr. E. J. Conrad, the members all agreed that subscription rates must be advanced to help meet the cost of paper. Some of the publishers had already increased their prices and it was agreed that $2.50 or more should be charged. M. L. Jewell, who has been employed jointly since the first of the year by the several offices in the Guild, tendered his resignation, which was accepted with regret. E. J. Conrad, who with Mr. Jewell has been investigating the printing industry of the Okanagan, has left for Victoria to continue his work there. He has already organized Vancouver and New Westminster as divisions of the U.T.A.

Alberta

Commencing with a special Labor Day edition, the Alberta Federation of Labor is publishing its own newspaper, which will be known as the Alberta *Labor News*. The new venture is the result of an insistent demand for a Labor paper, which has expressed itself at the last three conventions of that body when the executive committee of that body was instructed to procure an official organ for Alberta labor. Henry J. Roche, a well known newspaperman, of Edmonton, will be the manager and Elmer E. Roper, representative of the International Printing Pressmen's Union, the editor of the new paper.

Milo Bert Huffman, manager and editor of the Delburne *Progress*, and Miss Gladys Irene McClure, youngest daughter of Mrs. James Sargent of Mannville, Alberta, were married at Red Deer on Saturday, August 7th, the Rev. Geo. A. Armstrong officiating. The bridegroom is the only son of Bert Huffman of Calgary, who was, before coming to Alberta, editor of the East Oregonian, Pendleton, Oregon, U.S.A. Mr. Huffman took over the Delburne *Progress* about one year ago and at that time was the youngest editor of any newspaper in Alberta, being only 19 years of age. He enlisted in the 187th Batt. when only 15, and served overseas with the Royal Northwest Mounted Police in Siberia and was discharged in June, 1919. He is at present president of the Delburne branch of the Great War Veterans' Association, for which he is a very ardent worker. Mr. Huffman, we understand, is shortly severing his connection with the *Progress*.

Saskatchewan

Yorkton *Press*:—Owing to increasing business and the necessity for enlarged accommodation the business premises and office of the Yorkton *Press* have been moved to the Furby Block, 24 Second Avenue, whence the business will in future be conducted. With the view of devoting more time to the newspaper end of the business it has been arranged that Messrs. Baimbridge and Zimmer, who founded the Caxton Press and have been operating it for the past year, will take over the job printing department of the *Press*. In future they will conduct their business in the same premises as the *Press*.

Ernest Wright, publisher of the Eyebrow *Herald*, has been running that business for the last couple of years, and even yet owns up to being on the sunny side of 19 years. He sent down a job in a hurry a few weeks past for the Brownlee Agricultural Society, there being 32 pages and cover in the book. It was turned out between Friday noon and the following Wednesday, four and a-half days. He has no help in the office and every bit was hand set. The composition throughout is fairly solid. There has been a commendable adherence to a few faces of type all through the advertising pages. He got $114 for the job, which seems like a fair figure.

Regina *Leader*:—Mrs. E. L. Storer leaves this morning for Moose Jaw, where she is joining the editorial staff of the *Times*. She was on the staff of the Regina *Daily Post* until a few days ago and has many friends in the city who are sorry to see her leave and all wish her success and a great deal of pleasure in work in the Mill City. Mrs. Storer is a member of the Canadian Women's Press club and of the press committee of the L.C.W. For some time she was secretary of the Women's Auxiliary of the G.W.V.A. and has been deeply interested in every movement that could benefit the returned men and their homes. She is also a member of the Forget chapter, I.O.D.E.

What is likely one of the biggest aerial showers staged by any one newspaper on the North American continent was conducted daily during the Saskatoon exhibition week by the Saskatoon *Phoenix*. Each day Chester E. Moffet accompanied aviator H. Stanley McClelland over the city in the aerobus owned by McClelland & Lobb. Parachutes were released which entitled the finders to free flights and cash prizes. Mr. Moffet sold over eight pages of space for this special. It will also be recalled that Mr. Moffet was the first salesman to be carried by aeroplane. That flight was made to Rosetown from Saskatoon on May 28, 1919. Copies of the Saskatoon *Phoenix* were delivered to the towns en route.

Moose Jaw *News:*—The second allied printing trades' picnic held at Kingsway Park on Saturday last was an unqualified success from every point of view, and from the time the first members of the local newspapers, with their wives and families, made their appearance, until the time the last had left the park there was not a dull moment. The sports program, which included almost every kind of race as well as swimming and water wrestling events, was eagerly contested, and a spirit of friendly rivalry was everywhere apparent. One of the dominant features of the whole afternoon was the evidence given of the friendly manner in which employer and employees get along together at all times. Both Thomas Miller, of the *Times*, and Hugh Peat, of the *News*, were on hand early in the afternoon, and both took part in everything that was going.

Manitoba

Winnipeg *Free Press:*—John Stovel, president of the Stovel Company, Ltd., who has returned from a holiday trip east, has announced that he had handed the provincial government his resignation as member of the Joint Council of Industry. The resignation, Mr. Stovel said, severed his official connection with the board, and he added that he had always regarded his connection with it of a temporary nature. "When I accepted office," said Mr. Stovel, "I was not aware there was any emolument attached to the position." Mr. Stovel's resignation has been rendered necessary on account of his return as one of the members for the constituency of Winnipeg at the last provincial election.

Ontario

Stratford had a midsummer Dollar Day on August 19.

Fred G. Griffin of the Toronto *Star Weekly* made the trip by airplane from Northern Ontario to James Bay.

R. J. Carson has issued a writ for slander against the *British Whig* Publishing Co., Ltd. for $20,000 damages.

The Shelburne *Free Press* took its annual holiday in the week of August 19.

Howard Neville, for the past year with *Marketing*, Toronto, left August 1 to join the sales department of the Chevrolet Motor Company, Oshawa.

Vincent O'Vernon, formerly of the *Evening Telegram*, Toronto, and at present reporter with the Oshawa *Telegram*, is on holidays trying to regain his health.

Mr. Arthur McLure, after matriculating from the Peterboro Collegiate Institute this year, joined the reportorial staff of the Peterboro *Examiner*.

During the summer months, Miss Hester Vokes, Oshawa, who is now teaching in Thorold, was associated with the Oshawa *Reformer* in the capacity of proof-reader.

Mr. J. H. Ormiston, for the past nine years with the Sudbury papers, has joined the staff of the Oshawa *Reformer* as news editor.

The Paisley *Advocate* recently decided to miss publication for one issue, in view of the fact that it was impossible in any other way to allow a staff holiday.

Mr. "Dolf" Wells, of the advertising agency of Gardiner and Wells, New York City, has just returned from a week's fishing in the Muskoka Lakes.

John R. Robinson, editor of the Toronto *Telegram*, was before the Timber Commission to explain certain statements in an editorial in his paper.

Mr. Chas. L. Reid formerly of the *Mail* and *Empire* and lately associated with the Oshawa *Reformer* as news editor has been forced to leave his position in Oshawa owing to ill health.

Mr. H. T. Harrison is no longer connected with Hugh C. MacLean Ltd., trade newspaper publishers; but with the

James R. Allan, advertising manager of the Hamilton *Spectator*, has completed fifty years of service with that news-paper. He began his career as message boy on July 16, 1870. learning the printing trade under the tuition of the late W. H. Cliff. Nowadays many young men regard a trade as useless or not worth possessing, but Mr. Allan states his early technical training proved of inestimable value to him in later years, that it was of benefit to advertisers and of profit to the newspaper he served. After serving his time in the jobroom he passed to the newsroom, and later became attached to the reportorial staff for a short period. A vacancy occuring in the business office, he was transferred to the advertising department, where he acted as solicitor for twenty-five years and for the past fifteen years filled the 'important post' of advertising manager and assistant to the managing director. The possessor of perfect health, it would not be surprising if Mr. Allan completed sixty years for the newspaper he has so long and usefully served.

JAMES R. ALLAN

Who has completed 50 years of service with the Hamilton "Spectator." He is advertising manager and assistant to the managing director.

A Hamilton "Old Boy," writing in the *Star Weekly*, makes the following reference to Mr. Allan:—Why not decorations for long service in newspaperdom? There's James R. Allan, of the Hamilton *Spectator*. He has completed fifty years with the "great family journal"—the name applied to it by the late John Robson Cameron. Think of it—fifty years, useful, profitable years, and continuous, too. Mr. Allan has been blessed with rare good health, which has enabled him to do his best for the paper he joined half a century ago, during the Lawson-McCullough regime, as message boy. Some of the old inhabitants are credited with saying that bashfulness, or some such form of masculine reluctance, almost kept him from entering the field in which he has been so successful. After learning the job printer's art and taking a sally into the newsroom, he essayed the role of reporter for a brief period. Then came the turning point. He was offered the position of advertising solicitor. He hesitated: misgivings as to his ability to fill the bill almost overcame his desire to try, but he accepted, stuck to his guns and made good, building up an advertising patronage which to-day fairly gorges the *Spec* pages. He has always been quiet and unassuming; he is no thrasher of the jungle in stalking his quarry; and no man in the newspaper business is more highly respected than the *Spectator*'s advertising manager. Best of all, he looks good for many years yet, and his friends are confidently looking to see him celebrate his diamond year of service.

Presbyterian Publications as advertising and subscription manager.

Arthur Raymond, who has been telegraph editor of the Toronto *Star*, has gone to Regina to take over the position of news editor of the *Regina Leader*, succeeding Mr. Cruickshanks, who has gone into newspaper work in Virginia.

Mr. Ralph B. Cowan, of Peterboro, formerly connected with the Peterboro *Review* and the *Canadian Horticulturist*, Peterboro, but who since April has been reporting for the Oshawa *Reformer*, left September 18 to enter the University of Toronto.

In his will, just probated, the late Thomas Jeffery, formerly a printer employed by the *Globe*, bequeathed the income from his $6,306 estate to his widow. On the death of the latter two daughters will inherit.

The marriage took place in Orillia, at the Presbyterian church, on September 10, of Chas H. Hale to Miss Mabel Maclean. Mr. Hale is a member of the firm owning and publishing the Orillia *Packet*.

Mr. T. B. Costain, editor of *MacLean's Magazine*, has accepted a position with the Curtis Publishing Co., of Philadelphia, as managing editor of the *Ladies' Home Journal*. Mr. Costain leaves about the end of the month to take over his new work. T. B. was started on his newspaper career on the Brantford *Courier* with Douglas Reville, then editor of that paper as master of ceremonies. Some months after he moved along the street and was with the Brantford *Expositor*. His first out-of-town change took him to the Guelph *Herald*, when Joe Downey was editor of that paper. Later he did general assignment work on the Ottawa *Journal*, going from there to the local staff of the *Mail and Empire*. He left Toronto for the Guelph *Mercury*, which he edited for a couple of years. He joined the MacLean organization some ten years ago, starting on *Hardware and Metal*. He made a success in the specialized field, and later held the position of general managing editor of the MacLean publications. About four years ago he took over *MacLean's Magazine*, and since then has centred his attention on this publication, and he has been largely responsible for the rapid national growth of that paper. In the MacLean organization Mr. Costain is deservedly popular. He was a leading spirit in the MacLean Club, especially fond of the social gatherings staged by this body, a keen debater and always interested in the development of a cordial atmosphere in the organization with which he was connected.

T. B. COSTAIN
Who Joins the Curtis Co.

There is a feeling of regret at his departure all through the MacLean staff that is mixed with one of pleasure at the compliment that has been paid to Mr. Costain and the firm with which he has been associated.

The many friends of Mr. W. A. Robinson, publisher of the *Ontario Gleaner*, Cannington, will be sorry to learn of the death of his aunt, Mrs. A. Hefkey, of Preston, who was killed by lightning during a storm in August, while sitting in the dining room of her home.

Mr. H. E. Wilmott, formerly on the *Globe* staff, but for some time secretary of the Conservative party in Ontario, has returned to active newspaper work, again with the *Globe* staff. He has been doing a resume of the radial situation for that paper covering a wide range of country.

Chester Fox, who for many years was the personal representative in London, England, of the late Charles Frohman, has joined the London organization of Cross-Atlantic Newspaper Service as Business Manager. Mr. Fox is widely known to newspapermen on both sides of the Atlantic.

Mr. E. Paul Redding, who has been assistant city editor of the Toronto *Globe* for some time, is leaving that paper shortly. He has accepted a position with the Reuter News Bureau, and will be stationed for the present at Shanghai, China. Mr. Redding served overseas with the Canadian Army.

The *News-Record* of Kitchener announces a new rate for subscriptions, as follows, effective September 1:—City Subscription Rate, single copies, 3 cents; per week, 15 cents; per month, 60 cents; per year, $7.00; Mail Subscription Rates—Three months, $1.00; Six months, $2.00; One year, $4.00.

The annual number of *Canadian Lumberman and Woodworker* has been issued by the Hugh C. MacLean Co., running into some 262 pages. Mr. Van Blaricom, the editor, has gathered together a representative editorial programme for this issue, and there is a very liberal patronage of the advertising pages.

The St. Catharines Typographical Union withdrew from the St. Catharines Trade and Labor Council, the cleavage being precipitated by the manner in which the Trades Council contracted for its printing for the Labor Day demonstration which, the typos claim, was not in the best interest of organized labor.

The Port Arthur *News-Chronicle* produced a page of special information in keeping with the visit of the Press Conference delegates. The following help-yourself line appeared on the top of the material:—"Editor's Note—Touring newspapermen are free to use any or all information contained in this article without giving credit. We have troubles of our own."

J. Lewis Brown, assistant sporting editor of the Montreal *Daily Star*, and formerly a Toronto sporting writer, has been appointed editor of *Golf Illustrated*, New York. Mr. Brown has been recognized as the premier golf writer in Canada for several years, and has done much to encourage the game in this country. He will take up his new duties on Sept. 1.

The "world's oldest reporter" celebrated his 101st birthday anniversary at St. Catharines, Ont., July 7. He is Dan Plumstell, who at the age of 101 is hale and hearty. Born in Prescott on July 7, 1819, Mr. Plumstell devoted the younger years of his life to newspaper work. He still follows the development of the daily press with keen interest and is considered one of the best posted men on topics of the day in Ontario.

The International Paper Company has notified its customers that it will make contracts for 1921 only on the basis of eighty per cent. of the allotment for the current year. An offer is made to supply print paper for 1921 on this basis under the same contracts now in effect; *i.e.* paper will be supplied up to an agreed tonnage, prices to be adjusted each quarter by an agreement governed by the cost of production.

The funeral of the late Thomas N. Wells, for thirty years publisher of the Dresden *Times*, was held in Dresden. Mr. Wells died in Toronto, having been under treatment for cancer. The Oddfellows had charge of the funeral, representatives being present from Florence, Tupperville and Chatham. Rev. Mr. Osterhout conducted the service at the house. The pallbearers were six members of Dresden Lodge No. 124, I.O.O.F.

Toronto *Star*:—Mr. Peter Donovan, one of the special writers on *Saturday Night*, whose clever and humorous articles signed "P. O. D." have earned him a reputation, has been offered a post on the London *Express*, and, it is understood, will accept it. The *Express* is controlled by Lord Beaverbrook who evidently has his eye open for Canadian talent. In Mr. Donovan he has made a find, and the *Express* will have a new interest for many in this country.

The members of the Kingston Typographical Union No. 204 held an enjoyable picnic at Collins Lake. The printers motored to this famed fishing ground and if other fishermen find that the lake is somewhat depleted they will begin to realize that printers are adept with the rod and line. The "boys" from the *Freeman*, the *Standard*, the Jackson Press, Hansons, Crozier and Edgar's and the *Whig* employed themselves immensely at fishing, cards, races and baseball. A fish supper was served.

Hamilton *Spectator*:—Alfred Frank, a former employee of the *Spectator*, has returned to the city after an absence of thirty years. Mr. Frank, who is now in charge of the proof department of the Rochester *Herald*, says that the *Spectator* building looks just the same as ever, but he misses the familiar faces in the workroom. Hamilton, at the time he left it, was only a city of 51,000 inhabitants, and Mr. Frank expressed great surprise and admiration as he learned of his native city's progressiveness.

Talbot Edward Torrance, for nearly half a century in newspaper and literary work, died at his home, 304 Wright Avenue, Toronto, in his sixty-fifth year. He began his newspaper work at the age of seventeen, when he joined the staff of the Stratford *Beacon*, and later went to Barrie, where he edited the *Advance*. Subsequently he was with the *Mail and Empire*, the Chatham *Planet* and Galt *Reporter*, closing his active newspaper career as owner and editor of the Paris *Review*. For the past four years he had lived retired.

Mr. Andrew ("Andy") Clarke is now city editor of the *Globe*, and Mr. F. C. Mears has been appointed as day editor at the office, an appointment that has not been filled for some time past, but which existed with considerable success some time ago. Mr. Clarke, since returning to the *Globe* from the London *Advertiser*, has, in addition to other work, been getting out the Retail Merchants Section of the *Globe*. This work has been turned over to Mr. Lloyd Moore, who is also responsible for the business page of the *Globe*, which appears every week.

After a prolonged illness, the death occurred at Brockville, recently, of Ralph R. Pelton, since 1903 editor and proprietor of the St. Lawrence *News*, a weekly newspaper published at Iroquois. Mr. Pelton was born at Innerkip, Ont., and began his journalistic career in the office of the Woodstock *Sentinel-Review*. He was successively connected with the Brussels *Post*, Blyth *Standard*, Deseronto *Tribune*, Atwood *Bee* (which he established), the Paris *Review* and the St. Lawrence *News*. He was a strong temperance worker. His wife and three daughters survive.

The Hamilton *Times* has been purchased by John M. Imrie, Manager of the Canadian Daily Newspapers' Association, Toronto, acting for himself and others associated with him. The properties acquired include the Hamilton *Daily Times*, the Hamilton *Semi-Weekly Times*, the *Times'* job printing department and the business of the Canada Ready Print Co. The new owners have taken possession and the business is being carried on in Mr. Imrie's name pending the incorporation of a company of which he will be President and General Manager, Mr. Imrie will not assume active management until October, when his resignation from his present position will become effective. The Hamilton *Daily Times* is one of the older newspapers of Canada, having been established in 1837 as a weekly newspaper. It has been published as a daily newspaper continuously since 1853. Mr. Imrie has been Manager of the Canadian Daily Newspapers' Association since its organization in December last. Prior to that date he was for nine years Manager of the Canadian Press Association, Inc. John M. Imrie is a Toronto boy, born in this city about 1883. His education was confined largely to the public schools and to that greatest of all institutions, the school of practical experience. He started the printing business at 13 years of age, and there was nothing unlucky in the number either. He has been at it in many capacities ever since. Prior to taking over the duties of manager of the Canadian Press Association he was manager of *Printer and Publisher*.

JOHN M. IMRIE

Friends of Mr. Peter O'Donovan, who is leaving the editorial staff of *Saturday Night*, to take a position on the London *Daily Express*, tendered a dinner to him at the Arts and Letters Club. About 50 were present and the occasion was marked by many generous tributes to the personality and literary ability of the guest of the evening. Mr. Augustus Bridle presided, and among the other speakers were Mr. Hector Charlesworth, Mr. George H. Locke, Dr. J. M. McCallum, Mr. Arthur Baxter. Original poems of much humor were read by Mr. Fred Jacob, Mr. J. E. Middleton and Mr. Baxter.

The Minister of Labor has established a Board of Conciliation to investigate the dispute of the Canadian Press Limited news service, with headquarters at Toronto and its telegraph operators. E. Norman Smith, president of the Canadian Press, Limited, will represent the news service on the board, and David Campbell, barrister, of Winnipeg, has been chosen to represent the operators. Messrs. Smith and Campbell will confer as to the selection of a chairman and in the event of their not being able to agree the Minister of Labor will make this appointment.

The Lindsay *Post* in its issue of August 23 says:—"Mr. H. B. Burgoyne, one of the publishers of the St. Catharines *Standard*, the very newsy and well-managed daily of the Niagara Peninsula, was a visitor in town on Saturday for a few hours. He was accompanied by Mrs. Burgoyne and young daughters, who with Mr. Burgoyne, were taking a motor trip through this district. It was Mr. Burgoyne's first visit to Lindsay, and he was very much taken with the width and appearance of our business streets, and the bright, up-to-date appearance of our business places."

The Lindsay *Daily Warder* and the *Weekly Post* ceased publication on September 1, and Lindsay is now served with one daily and one weekly paper, instead of two of each. The papers that remain are the *Evening Post* (daily) and the *Weekly Watchman-Warder*. In an announcement, signed by J. W. Deyell, for the *Watchman-Warder*, Ltd., and Wilson & Wilson, publishers of the *Evening Post*, it is pointed out that there has been no amalgamation, but an agreement between the publishers to drop the weekly edition of the *Post* and the *Daily Warder*.

"The enormous increase in the cost of every item incidental to newspaper publication, particularly with regard to newsprint," i given as the reason.

Globe Park at Port Dover closed for the season at the end of August. The season just closed has been a most successful one in every way. There are eight cottages and some 25 acres of ground in the park, and arrangements are under way now for a better service to the cottage holders for next season when a larger amount of land will be used in producing vegetables for the use of the *Globe* staff. Application is made for the cottages before the first of June each year, and then they are allotted for terms of two weeks or more, depending on the length of time required. All that is necessary is that each family take its own bedding and cutlery. *Globe* employees have had a splendid time this year at Globe Park.

Wiarton *Echo*:—The funeral took place at Hepworth, of Israel Poste, one of the veteran newspapermen of this district in his eighty-sixth year. Born in Postville, Ont., he came to Wiarton district in 1877 and was one of the principal members of the group who caused the Baptist Church to be established here. The late Mr. Poste was ever connected with the newspaper business in some capacity. A printer by trade he has been on the mechanical staff of the *Echo*, the *Canadian*, the *Bruce Peninsula News* and the Hepworth *Progress* at different times. He founded and edited the Wiarton *Encore*, a paper which lived for several years in the nineties under his management. He was an able writer and frequently contributed to various local papers in recent years, when too old to stand at the "case."

The *Christian Guardian* goes to the same size as *MacLean's Magazine* and *Saturday Evening Post* with the first issue in October. The circulation has grown to 32,000 from 20,000 a year ago. Mr. E. M. Shildrick, has charge of the circulation. He had no previous experience in this work, coming here from Edmonton where for some years he was musical director of Alberta College. He has taken to circulation work with a zest that puts it across. An appeal was made to the Methodist people through the ladies' organization in the churches, to stand behind the *Guardian*, and a commission was offered to them for new subscribers. The plan worked much better than expected, with the result that there was soon a fifty per cent. increase in circulation.

Goderich *Signal*:—Mr. W. H. Kerr has completed forty years as publisher of the Brussels *Post* and now is the "daddy" of all the newspaper men of Huron, every other paper in the county having changed hands at least once during the forty years. In referring to the anniversary, the editor of the *Post* mentions some compensations for the lapse of the years and one of them is that he has had a pretty little town to live in. The editor of the *Signal* was in Brussels for a few minutes the other day—the first time he had ever been in that town in the summer time —and was surprised and delighted to see the beautiful streets and the many handsome, well-kept residences with their air of substantial comfort. Brussels must indeed be a good town to live in, and we do not wonder that Editor Kerr has found the years passing swiftly over his head.

The Perth and Huron District Press Association met in Stratford on August 20. In the morning an admirable address by Mayor J. J. Hunter, of Kincardine, publisher of the Kincardine *Reporter*, reviewed the newspaper situation, dwelling on the necessity of increased rates if publishers are successfully to meet advancing costs. Subsequently officers were elected as follows: Hon. President, W. R. Davis, Mitchell *Advocate*; President, Malcolm McBeth, Milverton *Sun*; Vice-President, J. W. Vanatter, Goderich *Star*; Secretary-Treasurer, Alex. Abraham, Stratford; Executive: J. L. Kerr, Brussels *Post*; H. D. Davis, Mitchell *Advocate*; C. V. Blatchford, Listowel *Banner*. Mayor Stevenson formally welcomed and extended the freedom of the city to the newspapermen at the luncheon, over which Mr. Chas. Dingman presided, welcoming the gathering on behalf of the printers and publishers of Stratford. A number of impromptu speeches followed, those participating being: J. K. Kerr, J. J. Hunter, J. W. Vanatter, H. D. Davis, Hall, of the Gerlach-Barlow Company, C. V. Blatchford, M. McBeth, K. W. O'Beirne, Alex. Abraham and others.

Although it was not considered an opportune time to commence the publication of a daily newspaper, it was announced at an annual meeting of the United Farmers' Publishing Company, that before the end of the year, the *Farmer's Sun*, the official organ of the U.F.O., would likely be published three times instead of twice a week. Many leading farmers, who are shareholders in the company attended the meeting, which was held in the Labor Temple. Practically the same board of directors was re-elected. Hon. Manning Doherty is still a director, while W. A. Amos, vice-president of the U.F.O., was placed on the directorate to give the U.F.O. official representation as well as the Government. The officers elected were: President, Col. J. Z. Fraser, vice-president, W. A. Amos;

Selected from the "Best Advertisements"

"The work of a printing office, with

sufficient vision to keep a good lead on the demands of the times, requires a greater investment for up-to-date machinery than any other line.

"The business has grown so fast during Thorold's boom years that the new two-storey addition to the rear of the former office is now crowded to capacity up stairs and down, and Thorold may boast as well-equipped a printing plant as may be found anywhere.

"The new plant was purchased entirely from the old-established house of Miller & Richard, Toronto, the Canadian branch of the celebrated Scotch typefounders of the same name, who have the reputation of 'standing behind everything they sell,' whether of their own make or not, which has been clearly demonstrated in our dealings with them."

From The Thorold Post, July 16, 1920

secretary-treasurer, Harold A. Walters, directors, J. J. Morrison, W. C. Good and Hon. Manning Doherty. During the coming year the directors expected to have either $25,000 or $30,000 increased expenditure, said the president. This would naturally mean an increase in the price of the paper, an increase which the board is not anxious to incur, but which they believe will not be objectionable, he declared.

The meeting of the Simcoe and North York District Press Association at Barrie on Friday, August 20, was well attended. It was the third meeting of the district association since the beginning of the year. Consideration was given to the $2 subscription rate, and the publishers decided to put the $2 rate in force this fall, some with the first issue in October. There was a good deal of discussion on job printing prices, and it was the consensus of opinion that the association method of revising and printing a job price list was practically obsolete now. The fact that job stock and materials for job printing were increasing in price very frequently rendered the former method of price listing useless. The Franklin Price List was favored, and is being generally adopted. Advertising rates were also discussed. President W. G. Cave of Midland presided at the meeting, and there were present E. J. Hewson, of Penetang; J. A. MacLarin, W. C. Walls, A. V. Nolan, Barrie; R. A. Semple, Tottenham; F. B. Elliott, Alliston; D. Williams' W. A. Hogg, Collingwood; A. Wilkes, Midland; George Blackstone, C. H. Hale, Thomas King, Orillia; O. M. Seim, Bradford; G. L. Jackson, Newmarket.

Soccer in Toronto and throughout the Dominion sustained a severe blow in the death of Thomas ("Tom") Watson, the prominent soccer writer and critic. Mr. Watson died at his home, 2,059 Davenport road, following an illness of long duration. Born at Glasgow, Scotland, the late Mr. Watson was early interested in the national game of the British Isles. At the age of fourteen he was elected to a seat on the Scottish Association, and thus made soccer history as the youngest member to ever attain that honor. For fourteen years he was a member of the International Selection Committee, and was responsible for the formulating of the off-side rule as it exists to-day. At one time he played with the Queen's Park team, but as a player his fame was overshadowed by his brother, John, goal-keeper for the Rangers. In 1912 Tom Watson came to Canada, and in 1913-14 he was elected President of the D.F.A., and was one of the founders of the Provincial League. He was president of the O.F.A. at the time of his death. As a legislator in soccer he was held in high respect, and his articles on the game in the Telegram, with which he was connected as a sporting writer, were eagerly followed. He is survived by his parents and a son, Thomas Watson, jun., who served during the war with an Imperial regiment.

Alfred E. Miller, managing editor of the London Free Press, died at his summer home Bayfield. Early in June Mr. Miller felt symptoms of rheumatism, which he did not regard as alarming. A few weeks later it gave him some trouble. On July 1 he motored to Bayfield to spend a few days. On arrival there he complained of pain and went to bed. Rheumatic fever developed and on Wednesday pneumonia. This complication was too much for even his strong constitution. The late Mr. Miller was born on a farm in Perth County, near the birthplace of Premier Meighen, 49 years ago. His parents moved to London when he was a boy and he attended the schools here, being a graduate of Victoria School, of which Mr. MacQueen was then principal. After leaving school he entered the employ of the Free Press, learning the printing trade. Later he joined the reportorial staff. He was later successively city editor and managing editor. As a journalist he had a keen sense of news values and a fine insight into political and world affairs; as a writer he was vigorous, clear and convincing. He was chairman of the evening paper section of the Canadian Press, Limited, the big news gathering agency, which he did much to organize. Deceased went to Europe in 1918 with the Canadian press party and saw practically all the Western battlefront and some of the actual fighting. On his return he spoke at many points in Western Ontario on his experiences. Mr. Miller was a member of the Rotary and Canadian clubs, being vice-president of the latter. He was an enthusiastic horticulturalist and member of the Askin Street Methodist Church. Mr. Miller is survived by Mrs. Miller and two daughters, Misses Helen and Olga. Two brothers, George, of New York, and White, of New Mexico, also survive.

The Ottawa Citizen, in a recent issue, refers to Mr. Dan A. Jones, mayor of Pembroke:—There are a number of subjects upon which Pembroke citizens are in agreement; there is one upon which they are practically unanimous. That one is relative to this year's mayor—and the "answer" is a tribute to both his qualifications as head of a council and as a fine type of citizen. Mayor Jones is very popular with Pembroke people. Dan. A. Jones, born at Carleton Place, Ont., Dec. 7th, 1881, the son of the late John Jones and Mrs. Jones, now of Renfrew.

As a boy, he moved to Eganville with his parents, and was educated in the Separate school there. He served his apprenticeship at the printing trade in the office of the Eganville Enterprise, and afterwards spent a few years in the West. Returning east in 1902, he was for the next four years in charge of the Eganville Star-Enterprise, and in July, 1906, bought the plant and business, conducting it until the disastrous fire which destroyed the business section of the village in July, 1911, when the plant was completely burned. Mr. Jones then purchased the Pembroke Observer, a weekly paper whose fortunes were then at low ebb. It rapidly improved under his management, and soon attained a foremost place among the weeklies of the province. The paper has been a potent force in Pembroke affairs generally, and to its influence may be attributed in large measure the splendid civic spirit prevailing in the town, and the progress made by the community in the past decade. Mayor Jones is a Roman Catholic in religion and a Liberal in politics. He is Past Grand Knight of Pembroke Council, Knights of Columbus, and secretary of the North Renfrew Liberal Association; he was for several years secretary of the Board of Trade, and is now a member of the Board of Trade Council. At all times since making Pembroke his home, Mr. Jones has been actively identified with all civic movements. He was elected by acclamation for five years as a member of the town council for Center Ward, and in a contest last January was elected mayor.

Robert Munn Lays Down His Stick

An apprentice who has graduated from the Mail and Empire composing room wrote the following for Printer and Publisher: When the word was passed around that Robert Munn, or as he is more familiarly known among his associates as "Bob," had retired from ranks it brought forth many expressions of regret all over the Dominion, from printers both young and old. The writer of this article himself had the privilege and pleasure of learning to set his first line of type under the experienced eye of Bob, and feels that he owes much of success in after years to the careful training received. Many more of the younger members of the craft could tell of similar experiences. No matter how much we "pied" up his case or set a job up wrong, Bob never lost his temper, and always patiently explained the ins and outs of the craft. Whenever we were apt to bemoan our fate at the prospect of having to serve five years at very meagre wages, Bob would gently chide us and remind us of the fact that conditions were better by far than when he started. Then by dint of persuasion Bob would recount some of his experiences. At the age of eighteen Bob started his apprenticeship, which in those days consisted of a ten-year term with wages at a dollar a week at the start. The eight-hour day was not even thought of then, and the average day generally consisted of between ten and fifteen hours. After serving his apprenticeship in his home town, which was Montreal, Bob came to Toronto and joined what was then known as the Mail. The Mail at the time was only a four-page sheet, entirely hand-set. The wage system in vogue then was based on piece-work. The rate at that time being about $1.33 a column of eight-point, (four thousand ems), and you did not commence to earn money until you had distributed all the type you had set from the previous day, so it can be readily seen that it was necessary to work ten or fifteen hours in order to make any money at all. Bob, unlike many of the printers of the old school, was not possessed of the wanderlust that characterized the "prints" of those days, and he remained with the Mail, which some years ater became the Mail and Empire, until to-day—some forty-eight years of continuous service, broken only when Bob enlisted as a private during the Fenian Raid of '66. During that time he has witnessed many changes in the evolution of the printing industry. He well remembers when it was a common occurrence for an edition of the paper to be two days late in getting out on account of trouble with the presses. He saw the introduction of the Roger typesetting machines, and like most of the old school printers, was a firm believer that nothing could beat hand-set type. It was not until the introduction of the lino- type machines that most of the hand-set type disappeared from the news columns and this was one of the things that helped to bring about the abolition of the piece-work system. In spite of his seventy-six years Bob is hale and hearty, and would be still doing his daily "stint" at the case where it not for the fact that his trusty left, which held the "stick" with a deftness of long training, became affected with a partial paralysis, thus forcing into retirement one of the best exponents of the printing craft, who although he never travelled far in life, made a host of friends that extends from coast to coast, who cherish the memory of Robert Munn.

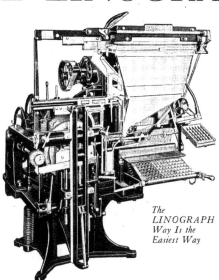

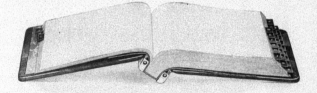

Canada Printing Ink Co., Limited

15 DUNCAN STREET

TORONTO CANADA

PRINTING LITHOGRAPHING

INKS

BUFF TINT NO. 16 VANDYKE BROWN

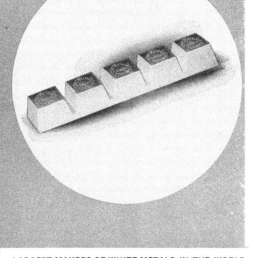

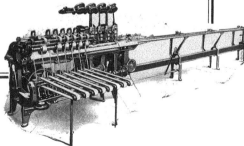

Cromwell
Tympan Papers

Give Cleaner Impressions with
a Minimum of Make-Ready

SAVING time on make ready, and securing sharp impressions are the two great things your press foreman has to
strive for. With Cromwell Traveling, Shifting and Cylinder
Tympan Papers, his draw sheets are always tight—no swelling—and they need not be oiled. They are also moisture-
proof, protecting the packing against dampness.

You can turn a rush job quicker with Cromwell Tympan
Papers because they resist offset, enabling you to back up
reasonably wet sheets. Quick delivery is often your best
selling argument.

Cromwell papers will take more impressions without
replacing, and they *never* rot.

We especially recommend Cromwell Tympan Papers for trade
journal and magazine printers where long runs are necessary without
interruptions. It is ideal for book work and the highest grade of printing. Job printers will find it an excellent tympan paper for printing
bond, linen and covers.

We carry Cromwell Tympan Papers in stock ready for quick
shipment in rolls from 36 to 66 inches wide. Order to-day and secure
the perfection and economy in printing that Cromwell Tympan Papers
give.

Send us the size of your press, and we will forward free of all cost
to you, Sample Sheet of our Tympan Paper.

The Cromwell Paper Co.
Department P.P.   **Jasper Place, Chicago, U.S.A.**

Trade   Mark

OLIVER CROMWELL

PUBLISHERS

:clusively Because They Give

reatest Dependability and Economy of Operation

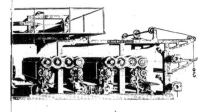

)CTUPLE PRESS

n, Combined with the Unit-Type Con-
the Plate Cylinders, Rollers, Inking

their visiting friends from Overseas to
Presses, that have been in successful
ʒe Hoe Rotary Presses of Unit, Super-
een installed or are now in process of
Offices in Canada:

.. Two Superspeed Decuples.
.. One Octuple.
.. One Intaglio and Color Press.
.. One Unit-Type Double Sextuple.
.. One Unit-Type Quadruple.
.. One Unit-Type Quadruple.
.. One Sixteen-Page Addition.
.. One Eight-Page Addition.

& CO.

reet, New York

IDON, S.E., 1, ENGLAND

Some of the HOE users in Canada

L'Evenement	......Quebec	....	1 press
Chronicle	........Quebec	....	1 press
Leader	............Regina	....	1 press
Beacon	....St. Andrews	....	1 press
Standard	.........St. Catharines	..	1 press
Standard	.........St. John	....	1 press
Globe	............St. John	....	1 press
Times-Journal	.....St. Thomas	.....	1 press
Star	.............Saskatoon	......	1 press
Post	.............Sydney	....	1 press
Le Nouvelliste	......Three Rivers	....	1 press
Globe	............Toronto	....	3 presses
Wilson Pub. Co.	...Toronto	....	1 press
Ontario Press	.....Toronto	....	1 press
Mail & Empire	....Toronto	....	2 presses
T. Eaton Co.	......Toronto	....	1 press
Star	.............Toronto	....	4 presses
Telegram	.........Toronto	....	4 presses
Sun	..............Vancouver	......	1 press
World	............Vancouver	......	2 presses
Times	............Victoria	....	1 press
Colonist	.........Victoria	....	1 press
Free Press	........Winnipeg	......	3 presses
Tribune	..........Winnipeg	......	2 presses
Telegram	.. ..Winnipeg	....	1 press
Sentinel-Review	....Woodstock	.....	1 press

NEWFOUNDLAND

Daily News	.......St. John's	......	1 press
Daily Star	.........St. John's	......	1 press

7 Water Street, BOSTON, MASS.

BY ARRANGEMENT *with*

LORD NORTHCLIFFE

CROSS-ATLANTIC NEWSPAPER SERVICE

has been granted the EXCLUSIVE right of publication in Canada and the United States of the world-famous news service of the great Northcliffe morning newspaper

THE LONDON DAILY MAIL

Here is Lord Northcliffe's authorization, given by him to W. Orton Tewson, founder of Cross-Atlantic

The Times
1785

Mr. Orton Tewson is authorized by me to state that the Cross-Atlantic Newspaper Service has the privilege of publication in the United States and Canada of the news service of the DAILY MAIL before any other American or Canadian news agency or journal.

(Signed)
July 21st, 1920   *Northcliffe.*

Client papers of CROSS-ATLANTIC will thus have available at no added expense the exclusive service of probably the best band of news-getters and special correspondents in the world.

"DAILY MAIL" CIRCULATION 1,121,700 DAILY	*In Addition* CROSS-ATLANTIC SERVICE *Provides Your Newspaper With*	THERE'S A REASON

1. Full facilities of an European organization with staff correspondents — your correspondents — available 24 hours daily.
2. Services of a staff of internationally-known newspapermen.
3. Daily cable service of at least 500 words.
4. Important signed correspondence by mail—at least seven columns a week.
5. Special foreign news and interviews local to your city and 24-hour protection on special queries.
6. Your own London office, Cross-Atlantic House, Fleet Street, where your readers can see a file of your paper and be advised or assisted in every possible way.

Write for exclusive rights for your city.

CROSS-ATLANTIC NEWSPAPER SERVICE
DOMINION NEWS BUREAU LIMITED
CANADIAN REPRESENTATIVES
171 St. James Street, MONTREAL, CANADA
LONDON   P.O. Box 756   PARIS

Everywhere the Union Jack Flies the Name of Brantford is Known

The Manufactured Goods of Brantford

Are Exported to All Parts of the World

THROUGHOUT the vast British Dominions, and in most foreign countries as well, the plow, the windmill, the harvester, the harrow, the tractor, the gasoline engine, the pulp machine, the sawmill, the motor, steel goods of every description, the blanket, knitted articles, in fact manufactured goods of many kinds, manufactured in this city, have found a market until "Made in Brantford" has become known everywhere the Union Jack flies. The manufacture of these articles, that have become so favorably known the world over, has helped to make Brantford the thriving industrial centre that it is, a city of 40,000 people, all prosperous and awake to the very newest and best in every walk of life.

In this busy city and the thriving district that surrounds it *The Expositor* is the only daily newspaper published, and, like its home city, it is alive and up-to-date, and is generally regarded as one of the foremost publications of the Dominion. No national advertiser would consider a Canadian campaign that did not include *The Expositor*.

The EXPOSITOR
Brantford's Big Daily, A.B.C. 10,300

To

Publishers
and Editors

It is a necessary part of your business or profession to keep well
informed upon business conditions in Canada. You should have
first-hand knowledge of the expansion and trend of affairs in the
industrial realm of the country. In no other way can you obtain
this information so well as by being a regular reader of Canada's
foremost industrial publications. They include:

POWER HOUSE

Twice a Month—$2 per year; foreign, $3.
The Power Plant Journal of Canada; keeps
its readers thoroughly posted on all things
pertaining to the electrical, steam, refrig-
eration and hydraulic field.

CANADIAN MACHINERY
AND MANUFACTURING NEWS

Weekly—$4 per year; foreign, $5.
Covers the metal-working field and is regarded as indispensable by those who wish
to keep posted on the machine tool industry of Canada; a first-class mechanical
and market paper combined.

CANADIAN FOUNDRYMAN.

Monthly—$2 per year; foreign, $3.
The only paper in Canada giving exclusive
treatment to foundry practice. It is
carefully edited; its news and views can be
relied upon.

MARINE ENGINEERNIG

Monthly—$2 per year; foreign, $3.
With the ship-building industry in Canada
claiming such wide attention Canada's
leading marine paper is especially valuable
to publishers and editors. Its news is up-
to-date and its views are authoritative.

Published by

The MacLean Publishing Company, Limited
143-153 University Ave., Toronto, Can.

A company whose idea of service has made it the largest publishing
house of its kind in the British Empire.

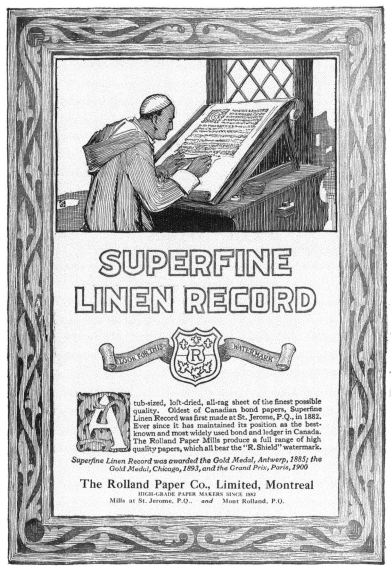

SUPERFINE LINEN RECORD

LOOK FOR THIS WATERMARK

tub-sized, loft-dried, all-rag sheet of the finest possible quality. Oldest of Canadian bond papers, Superfine Linen Record was first made at St. Jerome, P.Q., in 1882. Ever since it has maintained its position as the best-known and most widely used bond and ledger in Canada. The Rolland Paper Mills produce a full range of high quality papers, which all bear the "R. Shield" watermark.

Superfine Linen Record was awarded the Gold Medal, Antwerp, 1885; the Gold Medal, Chicago, 1893, and the Grand Prix, Paris, 1900

The Rolland Paper Co., Limited, Montreal
HIGH-GRADE PAPER MAKERS SINCE 1882
Mills at St. Jerome, P.Q., *and* Mont Rolland, P.Q.

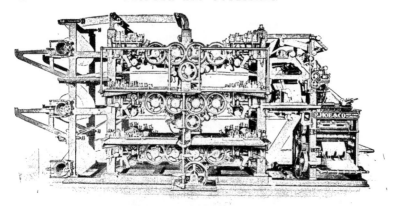

FOR SALE

Hoe Three-Roll Two-Plate Wide Newspaper Perfecting Press

With Rotary Insetting Folder, Complete with All Necessary Modern Stereotype Machinery Driven by Individual Motors, 16 Iron Top Tables, 1 Elevating Table and Sixteen Chases

This machine is specially suited for offices requiring a well-made, simple, compact, efficient and economical Stereotype Web Perfecting Press to print newspapers of a varied number of pages up to twenty-four, with cut-off 21½". Widest rolls 39". Folds to half-page size.

Among its advantages is the ability to turn out 14 and 18-page papers, with the sheets inset in book form, and 12, 16, 20 and 24-page papers either with the sheets inset or composed of two collected sections.

The running speed per hour is:

15,000 to 18,000 papers of 4, 6, 8, 10 or 12 pages with the sheets all inset from a double set of plates.

7,500 to 9,000 papers of 14, 16, 18, 20 or 24 pages, inset in book

form, composed of two collected sections, from a single set of plates.

12,000 papers of 16, 20 or 24 pages, composed of two collected sections, from a single set of plates.

There is no machine made that will give such a variety of products in so perfect a manner from three narrow rolls of paper and so few stereotype plates, composition rollers and working parts.

The number of columns can be varied at will.

The ink distribution is the same as in the most expensive Hoe Newspaper Presses, and the machine will turn out a higher grade of printing than any other press made to fill the same field.

DIMENSIONS (Approximate)

Length over bed plate .... 19 ft.
Width over bed plate .... 5 ft.
Height .... 10 ft.

The above described machine is equipped for individual motor drive and is operated by Westinghouse 25 h.p. motor, 220 D.C. with Koehler Push Button Control. We will sell the above machine at a bargain f.o.b. Regina, Sask. We bought the "Regina Post," which was printed on this press and was considered a most excellently printed paper. This equipment will sell for about half price and is in perfect condition in every respect and can be put into immediate operation. There is nothing broken or damaged in any way whatsoever, and press is as good as new for all practical purposes. If you need a press, do not let this opportunity pass. Immediate delivery can be given.

LINOTYPES— We have one Model 14 Linotype, Serial No. 23364, and one Model 19 Linotype, Serial No. 21645, with full equipment, each equipped with Electric Pot and individual motor drive for 110 volt, 60-cycle, single-phase. These machines have had very little use and for all practical purposes are as good as new.

Also one each Model 5 and Model 6 Linotype and Style A Intertype, with individual motor drive equipment to suit. Model 6 is in excellent running condition and the Model 5 and Style A Intertype have been rebuilt by one of the best Linotype experts on the Continent and we guarantee them for all practical purposes as good as new.

Each machine quoted includes full factory equipment and we have a lot of extra magazines, matrices and other equipment for the different machines.

TORONTO TYPE FOUNDRY CO., LIMITED

York and Wellington Streets, TORONTO, CANADA

Branches: MONTREAL, WINNIPEG, REGINA

Illustration of High Class Quadra-color Halftone, suitable for Calendars, Blotters, Counter-cards, Hangers Etc. We can furnish Photographic subjects. in color, or make Original Colored . . . drawings, suitable for all classes of . . advertising.

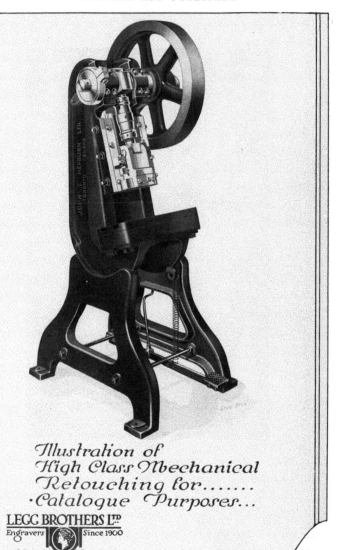

Say you saw it in PRINTER AND PUBLISHER

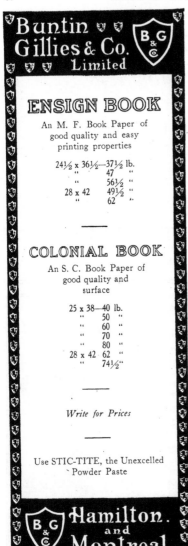

Buntin Gillies & Co. Limited

ENSIGN BOOK

An M. F. Book Paper of
good quality and easy
printing properties

24½ x 36½	37½	lb.
"	47	"
"	56½	"
28 x 42	49½	"
"	62	"

COLONIAL BOOK

An S. C. Book Paper of
good quality and
surface

25 x 38	40	lb.
"	50	"
"	60	"
"	70	"
"	80	"
28 x 42	62	"
"	74½	"

Write for Prices

Use STIC-TITE, the Unexcelled
Powder Paste

Hamilton
and
Montreal

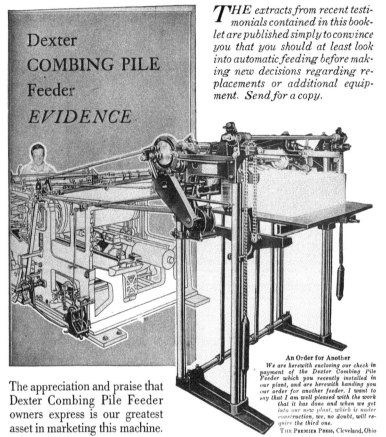

Dexter
COMBING PILE
Feeder
EVIDENCE

THE extracts from recent testimonials contained in this booklet are published simply to convince you that you should at least look into automatic feeding before making new decisions regarding replacements or additional equipment. Send for a copy.

An Order for Another

We are herewith enclosing our check in payment of the Dexter Combing Pile Feeder which you recently installed in our plant, and are herewith handing you our order for another feeder. I want to say that I am well pleased with the work that it has done and when we get into our new plant, which is under construction, we, no doubt, will require the third one.

THE PREMIER PRESS, Cleveland, Ohio

The appreciation and praise that Dexter Combing Pile Feeder owners express is our greatest asset in marketing this machine.

Every new installation adds to our list of friends and boosters. Let us put you in touch with Dexter Combing Pile Feeder users so that you may actually hear their enthusiastic opinion of automatic feeding. What our users say is a safe buying guide for you to follow.

DEXTER FOLDER COMPANY, 200 Fifth Avenue, New York
Folders, Cross Continuous Feeders, Dexter Feeders, Inserting, Covering and Wire-Stitching Machines

CHICAGO   PHILADELPHIA   BOSTON   DALLAS   ATLANTA   SAN FRANCISCO

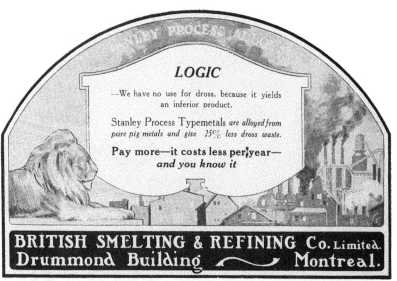

LOGIC

—We have no use for dross, because it yields
an inferior product.

Stanley Process Typemetals *are alloyed from
pure pig metals and give* 25% *less dross waste.*

**Pay more—it costs less per year—
and you know it**

BRITISH SMELTING & REFINING Co. Limited.
Drummond Building 〜 Montreal.

WHAT IS YOUR SPECIALTY?

IS IT COLOUR WORK?　Install a MANN OFFSET, which, owing to its special design, has established itself as the only Rotary Offset Machine capable of printing
successfully heavy solid colour work.

IS IT COMMERCIAL WORK, LETTER AND INVOICE HEADINGS, AND FINE
WORK ON HARD BOND PAPERS?　Install a MANN OFFSET, the simplest
in operation, enabling you to produce first-class work with no trouble and at a high
speed.

Whatever your work is, IT WILL PAY YOU to install a MANN OFFSET.　Over FIVE
HUNDRED have already been sold.

WE ARE SPECIALISTS TOO

We specialize in Offset Machinery of all kinds — Single-Colour Rotary Offset Machines
in sizes ranging from Demy Folio to Extra Eight Crown; Two-Colour and Perfecting
Rotary Offset Machines in sizes ranging from Double Demy to Extra Eight Crown;
Offset Proving and Reversing Presses in three sizes, etc., etc., and we shall be glad to
give you full particulars upon request.

THE MANN LITHOPRESS CO.
58 Walker Street, New York, U.S.A.

○ ○ ○ ○ ○ ○ ○ ○ ○ ○ ○ ○ ○ ○ ○ ○ ○

A Die for Every Purpose

Nelson Dies Are Unusual

both in their construction and performance. The punching members, after all, are the foundation of every punching equipment and the index to its earning capacity. Every Nelson die is built to the highest mechanical standard and warranted under an iron-clad Nelson guarantee which eliminates breakage, replacements, or inaccuracy of any kind.

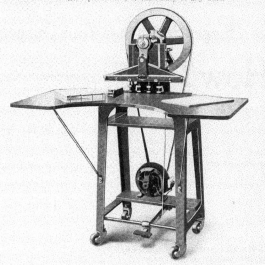

The Nelson Punching Machine

From standpoint of design as well as construction is a high-class tool, capable of producing the most exacting results.

Printers and Loose Leaf Makers buy their Nelson Press as an investment. They buy it as a known and established value, because they feel sure of it—sure of its performance, sure of its freedom from trouble, sure of every quality that makes a punching equipment thoroughly satisfactory.

Descriptive Literature for the asking

C. R. & W. A. NELSON

225 North Michigan Avenue, Chicago, Ill.

WRITE US FOR THE ADDRESSES OF OUR CANADIAN AGENCIES

Say you saw it in PRINTER AND PUBLISHER

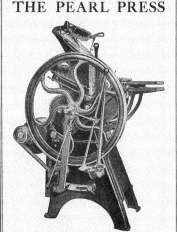

How About Your Pet Stock?

WHAT did the recent sharp decline mean as regards that stock in which you have money invested? Are you a little perplexed, perhaps a little worried?

THERE are facts you should know — facts regarding the influence general business conditions will have on profits. Perhaps there is some intimate information regarding the company unknown to you.

What Are You Going To Do About It?

WHY not do the obvious thing—ask about the stock? Ask some one who knows, or who can find out. Ask the editor of THE FINANCIAL POST.

EVERY week THE FINANCIAL POST prints scores of facts bearing on stocks, bonds and other investments. But it is impossible to deal with every security. If you want special information on something, write the editor. You will get a reply which will help you with your investment problem.

REMEMBER, this is an additional service THE POST offers every subscriber.

If you aren't already a subscriber hadn't you better take steps to become one at once? Fill in the coupon below and mail to us with any inquiry you may want to make. Remember there's no limit to the number of inquiries.

THE FINANCIAL POST

The Canadian Newspaper for Business Men and Investors

143-153 UNIVERSITY AVE.   -   TORONTO

$5.00 May Make or Save You $500.00 or $5,000.00

Annual Subscription $5.00.
THE FINANCIAL POST,
    143-153 University Ave., Toronto.
Please enter me a regular subscriber, commencing at once. I forward enclose $5.00 to pay for my subscription for the first year.

Name ....

Address ....
                    Please write plainly

CLASSIFIED ADVERTISEMENT SECTION

TWO CENTS A WORD, Box Number as five words ; minimum charge is $1.00 per insertion, for 50 words or less, set in 6 pt. type. Each figure counts as a word. Display ads., or ads. set in border, are at the card rates.

FOR SALE

FOR SALE—GORDON PRESS, 7 x 11 ; GOOD condition. The Owen Sound Advertiser, Owen Sound, Ont. (ptfp)

FOR SALE—ONE 30 IN. GOLDING CUTTER, extra knife, and sticks. Also one 24 in. Perforator. Wilson Methods, 43 Adelaide St. E., Toronto. Ontario. (p9p)

FOR SALE — NO. 11 IMPROVED PEARL Press, new, complete with friction belt drive and quarter horsepower A-K motor, 25 cycle A.C. G. Davis, 185 Richmond West, Toronto. (p10p)

FOR SALE—WEEKLY NEWSPAPER AND job printing plant in a prosperous British Columbia mining, fruit growing and lumbering district. Good schools, fine fishing and hunting with ideal climate the year round. $3,000. $1,000 down, balance on very easy terms. For particulars write H. W. Power, Box 582, Nelson, B.C. (p9p)

FOR SALE — JOB PRINTING PLANT, located in Toronto, established seven years and has good connection. Equipped with three Gordon presses, cutting machine and fine line of type ; cost about five thousand. Will sacrifice on account of bad health. For particulars address F. J. Martin, 185 Brookside Drive, Toronto. (p9p)

FOR SALE — ELECTRIC PROOF PRESS (good as new), two 10x15 Gordon presses, one 8x12 Gordon press, one hand embossing press, one calendar tining machine, three wall galley racks, one iron case stand, one twelve horsepower motor, three roll top desks, hangers, shafting, pulleys, etc. Saturday Night Press, 75 Richmond Street West, Toronto. (p9p)

PRINTING MACHINERY FOR SALE—HAVing sold the franchise of the Review, we have for sale 1 Cox Duplex Press, 1 Linotype Model 5, 1 Linotype Model K, 1 Waite & Sherde-Honley 2-strike Ruling Machine, 42" with 36" blanket. All the plant necessary for the publishing of a daily and weekly newspaper. Will sell enbloc or separate. For particulars apply to the Peterborough Review Co., Peterborough, Ont. (dh)

FOR SALE — A QUANTITY OF BRITE Light Furniture. A bargain. Southam Press, Toronto. (p9p)

MONOLINE FOR SALE—NEARLY NEW— Full set of mats. $30 worth of new mats never used. Hundreds of dollars' worth of new parts. Certified cheque for $200 takes all, f.o.b. Woodstock, N.B. As we need the floor space must be sold at once. Press Printing Co., Ltd., Woodstock, N.B. (p10p)

FOR SALE—BRIGHT LITTLE ONTARIO weekly. Good circulation, splendid advertising and job patronage. Real, allround printer-manager could develop $10,000 a year business. Price (including full equipment, building, etc.), $9,000. Address Box 8320, Printer and Publisher. (p9p)

LINOTYPE FOR SALE — CANADIAN model, sets 30 ems to 14-point; good working order; gasoline burner equipment; universal mold and stationary 13-em mold. Set of used 3-point two-letter mats goes with machine. Two-letter equipment. Will be sold cheap for cash. Address Lino, Box 8920, care Printer and Publisher. (p9p)

FOR SALE—WEEKLY NEWSPAPER AND Job Plant in progressive Alberta town. Annual turnover over $8,000. Newspaper is eight pages, seven column, advertising rates from 25c to 40c an inch. Power plant and good equipment of job and advertisement type. Price $4,500, half cash, balance monthly payments or to suit purchaser. Apply to Box 7320, Printer and Publisher. (p9p)

FOR SALE — COMPLETE TYPE OUTFIT for printing business, 150 fonts of type (several series weight fonts) and lots of big column galleys, mailing galleys, wood type, rule, borders, spacing material, double column galleys, mailing galleys, wood type, lead cutter, miter, sticks, cuts, all in firstclass order.' Some job and quadruple cases. Fine modern lay-out. Apply Box 72320, Printer and Publisher. (dh)

COLLECTIONS

SEND US YOUR LIST OF DELINQUENTS. We will turn Debit into Credit. Publishers' Protective Association, Toronto. (ptfp)

MACHINERY LIST

1—10 x 15" C. & P. Press, complete.
1—10 x 16" Gordon Press, complete.
1— 8 x 12" Challenge Gordon.
1— 6 x 10" Gordon Press
2— 7 x 11" Pearl Press.
1—½ to 1½" Rosbach Stitcher.
1—½" Rosbach Stitcher.
1—5/16" Perfection Stitcher.
All above Power and First-class.

1—5/16" Hand Stitcher Brehmer.
1—26" C. & P. Lever Cutter.
1—19" W. & B. Lever Cutter.
1—26" Oswego Lever Cutter.
All above hand power and first-class.

ROYAL MACHINE WORKS
738 ST. PAUL WEST, MONTREAL

Presses, Bookbinding and Box Machinery

SITUATION WANTED

COMPOSITOR—FOREMAN (LATE C.E.F.), who knows fine printing and how to produce it in every detail ; a good executive, capable of obtaining results at minimum cost, seeks a position in Canada. Union, M. C. Logan, 464 Eighth Ave., New York City, N.Y., U.S.A. (p9p)

SITUATIONS VACANT

LOOK AROUND YOU — MANY PRINTING office executives have found Monotype operating the stepping stone to advancement. You can do the same. Monotype schools are located in Philadelphia, New York, Chicago and Toronto. Apply to the nearest. There is no tuition fee. Lanston Monotype Machine Company.

LEARN THE LINOTYPE — WRITE FOR particulars. Canadian Linotype, 68 Temperance St., Toronto. (ptfp)

EQUIPMENT WANTED

WANTED—HAMILTON TYPE CABINET, also about a 28-case Hamilton Wood Type Cabinet. State size, how many cases Cabinet will hold, condition and price. Advertiser Topic, Petrolia. (p9p)

THE REVIEW, CARP., ONT., WISHES TO buy for cash the following used printing machinery : 6 col. Cylinder Press, 7x11, and 13x19 Gordons, 30 in. Paper Cutter, Paper Folder, Proof Press, and Dust-proof Cases, Racks, etc. Must be in first-class condition and cheap. (p9p)

HELP WANTED, MALE

SALESMEN WITH A FOLLOWING AMONG printers : ink salesmen preferred. Unusual opportunity to connect with a reputable house manufacturing product in great demand. Write territory now covering, merchandise handling. Replies treated confidentially. Printcraft Supply Co., 1400 Broadway, New York City. (p9p)

APPRECIATION

June 8, 1920.

Publishers "Printer and Publisher," Toronto, Canada.

In forwarding you renewal subscription to your valued publication, allow me to say it has ever been appreciated for its sterling worth by not only myself, but every workman in my employ. The good pointers we have received through its columns have been worth many times its cost, and I trust it may continue to improve our prosper.

I notice from time to time the many "deans" of the printing art mentioned in your columns—many of which I knew personally in the years that have passed into the discard. Might just mention that your humble servant is not one of the youngest of them—having commenced ....on the 1st day of April, 1867— and have been continuously at it ever since.

Yours truly,
(Name on application.)

Are They Result Getters?

Do They Pull ?---

The Maclean Publishing Co.; Ltd., Toronto, Ont.

Dear Sirs :

Please cancel ad. (Diamond Cylinder Press for sale). We have disposed of same through the valuable assistance of the PRINTER AND PUBLISHER.

Yours truly,

(Name on Application)

Buyers' Guide

THE firms listed in this Buyers' Guide are all advertisers in PRINTER AND PUBLISHER. Refer to the ads. by consulting the Index. Our interests are mutual—tell the advertisers you read their ad. in PRINTER AND PUBLISHER. Patronize PRINTER AND PUBLISHER advertisers—they are all definitely interested in the promotion of efficiency in equipment and service in Canada's allied printing trades.

ADDRESSING MACHINES
The Challenge Machinery Co., Grand Haven, Mich.
The Westman & Baker Co., Toronto.

BALERS FOR WASTE PAPER
Golding Mfg. Co., Franklin, Mass.
Logan, H. J., 114 Adelaide St. W., Toronto.
Stephenson, Blake & Co., Toronto.
Stewart, Geo. M., 92 McGill St., Montreal.
Westman & Baker, Ltd., Toronto.

BINDERY EQUIPMENT AND SUPPLIES
(See also CUTTING MACHINES)
Albion Sewing Cotton Co., Ltd., London, Eng.
Berry Machine Co., St. Louis, Mo.
Christensen Machine Co., Racine, Wis.
Dexter Folder Co., New York.
Golding Mfg. Co., Franklin, Mass.
Kallstrom, J., New York City.
Logan, H. J., 114 Adelaide St. W., Toronto.
Miller & Richard, Toronto and Winnipeg.
Morrison Co., J. L., Toronto, Ont.
Royal Machine Works, Montreal.
Steel Co. of Canada, The, Hamilton (wire).
Stephenson, Blake & Co., Toronto.
Stewart, Geo. M., 92 McGill St., Montreal.
Westman & Baker, Ltd., Toronto.

COMPOSING ROOM EQUIPMENT
(See also LEADS, SLUGS AND TYPE)
The following list covers Iron Furniture—
Eastern Brass & Wood Type Co., New York.
Hamilton Mfg. Co., Two Rivers, Wisconsin.
Stephenson, Blake & Co., Toronto.
The Challenge Machinery Co., Grand Haven, Mich.
The Toronto Type Foundry Co., Ltd., Toronto.
Westman & Baker, Ltd., Toronto.

CORDS, SILK, ETC.
Albion Sewing Cotton Co., Ltd., London, Eng.

COUNTING MACHINES
Stephenson, Blake & Co., Toronto.
Westman & Baker, Ltd., Toronto.

CUTTING MACHINES—PAPER
Golding Mfg. Co., Franklin, Mass.
Morrison Co., J. L., 445 King St. W., Toronto.
Stephenson, Blake & Co., Toronto.
The Challenge Machinery Co., Grand Haven, Mich.
Westman & Baker, Ltd., Toronto.

COLLECTION AGENCIES
Canadian Mercantile Agency, Ottawa.
Publishers' Protective Association, Toronto.
Nagle Mercantile Agency, Laprairie, Montreal.

EFFICIENCY EXPERT
Pepper, J. L., 38 Toronto St., Toronto.

ELECTROTYPING AND STEREOTYPING
Rapid Electrotype Co. of Canada, Toronto.
Toronto Electrotype & Stereotype Co., Toronto.

ELECTROTYPE AND STEREOTYPE BASES
The Challenge Machinery Co., Grand Haven, Mich.
Westman & Baker, Ltd., Toronto.

ELECTROTYPE METAL
British Smelting & Refining Co., Ltd., Montreal.
Canada Metal Co., Limited, Toronto.
Hoyt Metal Co., Limited, Toronto.

EMBOSSING EQUIPMENT
Automatic Ptg. Devices Co., San Francisco, Cal.
Ellis New Method Embossing, Hamilton, Ont.
Golding Mfg. Co., Franklin, Mass.
Stephenson, Blake & Co., Toronto.
Westman & Baker, Ltd., Toronto.

ENGRAVERS
Legge Bros., Ltd., Toronto.
Reliance Eng. Co., Toronto.

ENVELOPE MANUFACTURERS
Toronto Envelope Co., Toronto.
Dawson Ltd., W. V., Montreal and Toronto.

Buyer's Guide

ROLLERS
Canada Printing Ink Co., Ltd., Toronto.
Columbia Printing Ink & Roller Co., Vancouver.
Manton Bros., Toronto, Ont.
Sinclair & Valentine, Toronto, Ont.
Winnipeg Printers' Roller Works, Winnipeg.

RUBBER STAMP OUTFITS
Barton Mfg. Co., The, New York, N.Y.

RULED FORM
Matrix Ruled Form & Tabular Co., Forth Worth, Texas.

STEREO PAPERS
Dixon & Co., Ltd., L. S., Liverpool, England.

TINNING, ETC.
Cooper Calendar Metal Co., Toronto.

TYPE-HIGH MACHINES
The Challenge Machinery Co., Grand Haven, Mich.
The Westman & Baker Co., Toronto.

TYPE, LEADS AND SLUGS
DeCarle-Wareham Co., Toronto.
Stephenson, Blake & Co., Toronto.
Westman & Baker, Ltd., Toronto.
Toronto Type Foundry Co., Ltd., Toronto, Mont-
real, Winnipeg.
Miller & Richard, Toronto and Winnipeg.

TYPESETTING
Mono-Lino Typesetting Co., Toronto.

TYPESETTING MACHINES
Canadian Linotype, Ltd., Toronto.
Miller & Richard, Toronto and Winnipeg.
Lanston Monotype Machine Co., Toronto.
Linograph Co., Davenport, Iowa.
Stephenson, Blake & Co., Toronto.

WIRE (Tinned Stitching)
Steel Co. of Canada, The, Hamilton.

INDEX TO ADVERTISERS

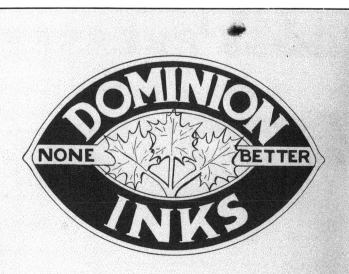

THE

DOMINION PRINTING INK

AND COLOR COMPANY, LIMITED

128-130 Pears Avenue, TORONTO, CAN.

Stocked and Sold by

JOHN MARTIN PAPER CO., LTD.

WINNIPEG   CALGARY   EDMONTON

CHAS. H. TICE, MANAGER FOR EASTERN CANADA

128 BLEURY ST., MONTREAL

PHONE: MAIN 5124

1920

VOLUME 29

NUMBER 10

PRINTER & PUBLISHER

OCTOBER

FEATURES IN THIS ISSUE:

What Editors Think About Their Reporters
Putting Character into Your Work
Much Depends Upon the Care of Inks

THE MACLEAN PUBLISHING CO. LIMITED
TORONTO - MONTREAL - WINNIPEG

PRINTER AND PUBLISHER, October, 1920. Vol. 29, No. 10. Published monthly at 143-153 University Ave., Toronto, by the MacLean Publishing Co., Ltd. Yearly subscription price, $3.00. Entered as second-class matter at the Post Office Department at Ottawa, Canada, also entered as second-class matter July 1, 1912, at the Post Office at Buffalo, N.Y., U.S.A., under Act of March 3rd, 1879.

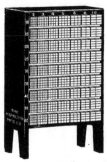

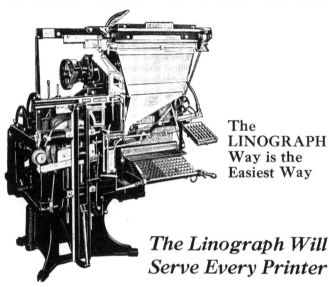

HOUSE BEAUTIFUL
ATLANTIC MONTHLY
CENTURY · ASIA · ST. NICHOLAS

These Five are the product of the Rumford Press, Concord, N. H.,

who also print twenty-five others—from the *Yale Review* to smaller scientific and technical publications—each of typographic excellence.

THESE MAGAZINES especially are treasured for their literary quality—the high-grade typography possible only from single types makes each of them a fitting addition to the finest libraries.

RUMFORD PRESS operates Monotype Composing Machines exclusively, as the only means of attaining the superiority of SINGLE-TYPE composition with the economy of mechanical production.

      MONOTYPE NON-DISTRIBUTION
IS, OF COURSE, AN INTEGRAL PART OF THE
RUMFORD PRESS EQUIPMENT

Lanston Monotype Machine Company · Philadelphia

NEW YORK ·   ·   BOSTON   ·   ·   CHICAGO   ·   ·   TORONTO
MONOTYPE COMPANY OF CALIFORNIA : SAN FRANCISCO

Form 304

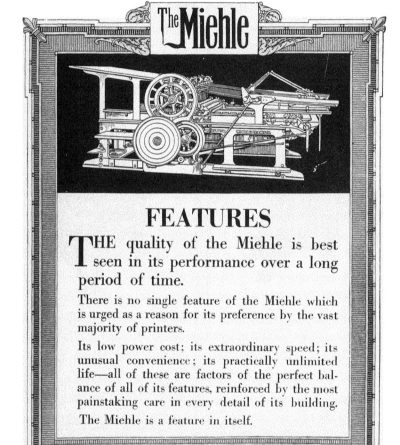

FEATURES

THE quality of the Miehle is best seen in its performance over a long period of time.

There is no single feature of the Miehle which is urged as a reason for its preference by the vast majority of printers.

Its low power cost; its extraordinary speed; its unusual convenience; its practically unlimited life—all of these are factors of the perfect balance of all of its features, reinforced by the most painstaking care in every detail of its building.

The Miehle is a feature in itself.

MIEHLE PRINTING PRESS & MFG. CO.
Fourteenth and Robey Streets, Chicago

Distributors for Canada

TORONTO TYPE FOUNDRY CO., LIMITED
TORONTO   MONTREAL   WINNIPEG   REGINA

YOU NEVER HEARD OF A MIEHLE BEING SCRAPPED

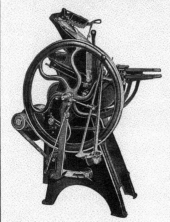

Dominion Printers Speak

This documentary evidence of the utility and high quality of the Franklin Printing Price List needs no further qualification. It is one chosen from hundreds of similar letters of commendation.

THE CAXTON PRESS LIMITED
1825 Scarth Street.
Regina, Saskatchewan, Canada.

Aug. 25th, 1920.

Messrs. Porte Publishing Co.,
32 Temperance St.,
Toronto, Ont.

Dear Sirs:—

We wish to express our appreciation of the Franklin Printing Price List, which is, in our opinion, far ahead of any other list ever issued.

Among the prominent features which appeal to us are the following: The extensive classification, the weekly issue of sections, the sample sheets of jobs listed, and above all the stock grading system, which enables us to follow advancing stock prices with the minimum amount of trouble. Then again, we have the satisfaction of knowing that in quoting a series of prices that our figures are correct, in other words that the prices agree as they increase, something that we have not found in any other list. Again, most other lists leave it to the individual as to charging out stock at the ream, case or ton price; the Franklin makes it clear that the ream price is the basis of figuring, irrespective of the quantity bought or sold and so on in all lines of stock.

The Franklin List is so good that we are tempted to keep it to ourselves, but in view of the great benefits that would result to the trade in general from its universal use, we feel every printing house should work from this list, and we attach hereto the names of the various firms in this city in the hope that you may be able to interest them in this proposition for their own good.

Wishing you all success, we are

Yours truly,

THE CAXTON PRESS, Limited,
(Sgd.) Jas. D. Simson.

You will want further information on the Franklin Printing Price List. A word from you will suffice to bring it. Don't defer the day of participation in its innumerable benefits.

Write Now!

PORTE PUBLISHING CO.

S. H. MOORE, Manager.

32 Temperance Street, Toronto, Ontario, Canada

This is a new set of testimonials--different from those which appeared last month in this magazine.

Just what the Doctor ordered ~

IF YOUR pressroom isn't doing as well as it should, try Reducol. The regular use of Reducol means better work, bigger production, and *lower* costs. These are actual facts, proved by hundreds of printers and lithographers.

BETTER WORK, because Reducol absolutely eliminates picking and mottling, two of the greatest enemies of good printing. Reducol takes the tack out of the ink without ill effects of any kind, because it softens the ink instead of thinning it. In color work Reducol is particularly valuable, because it gives a peculiar surface to each impression which permits perfect overlapping, and does not affect colors.

BIGGER PRODUCTION, because no matter what the weather is—hot or cold, dry or damp —Reducol will quickly put and keep your printing inks in perfect condition to do good work at high speed. Sometimes that means 25% more production from your presses in a single day. Furthermore, Reducol cuts down wash-up during the run to a minimum; and, although neither

a dryer nor a non-dryer, it has a marked tendency to cut down slipsheeting and offset onto the tympan.

LOWER COST, because it actually costs you more today to get along without Reducol than to use it on every job in the plant. Many users say 50% of the ink is saved; but suppose we put it at 20%. It does this by giving better distribution, which means increased impressions. And that's the least of the economies that Reducol makes for you.

Reducol has been used since 1903 by hundreds of printers and lithographers, both large and small. Charles Francis Press, Ketterlinus Litho. & Mfg. Co., Beck Engraving Co., Corday & Gross, Strobridge Litho. Co., Rogers & Co. and Walton & Spencer are a few of the regular users.

Reducol is unconditionally guaranteed. Send for 5 or 10 lbs. on approval, and try it out for thirty days. If it does not measure up to every statement here, there will be no charge.

INDIANA CHEMICAL & MANUFACTURING CO.
DEPT. C-10, 135 SOUTH EAST STREET
INDIANAPOLIS, IND., U. S. A.

Canadian Agents: Manton Bros.
Toronto   Montreal   Winnipeg

Say you saw it in PRINTER AND PUBLISHER

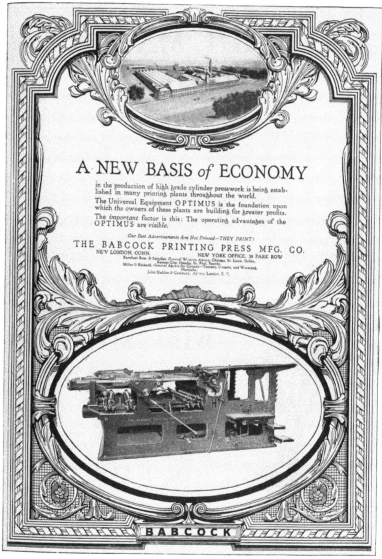

A NEW BASIS of ECONOMY

in the production of high grade cylinder presswork is being established in many printing plants throughout the world.

The Universal Equipment OPTIMUS is the foundation upon which the owners of these plants are building for greater profits.

The *important* factor is this: The operating advantages of the OPTIMUS are *visible*.

Our Best Advertisements Are Not Printed—THEY PRINT!

THE BABCOCK PRINTING PRESS MFG. CO.

NEW LONDON, CONN.   NEW YORK OFFICE, 38 PARK ROW

Barnhart Bros. & Spindler, *General Western Agents,* Chicago, St. Louis, Dallas, Kansas City, Omaha, St. Paul, Seattle.

Miller & Richard, *General Agents for Canada*—Toronto, Ontario, and Winnipeg, Manitoba.

John Haddon & Company, *Agents,* London, E. C.

BABCOCK

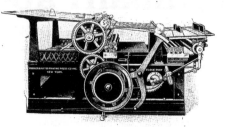

PRINTER AND PUBLISHER
Devoted to the Interests of the Printers and Publishers of Canada

Anything Wrong With the Reporters Now?
Some Defend Them—Others Whack Them

RE reporters to-day the equal of the reporters of 20 years ago? Printer and Publisher gathered the views of several newspaper men of wide experience, and their views differ—sharply in spots.

The reporter of to-day is keener than the reporter was 20 years ago. He has to work for several editions a day against one in the old times. He is called upon to dress his stories up for a taste that is widely different. He has to exercise more initiative in this way. The whole thing, to my mind, is changing, and changing very rapidly, and changing for the better. That is the way in which one well-known Toronto man looks at the situation, and he has been in the city for a quarter of a century.

"I am willing to admit that there is often a tendency to slop things over now that would not be allowed in the former days. This comes out especially in reports of meetings where men have made addresses. The habit of doing a running report story is largely to blame for this. There are reporters who have the rare gift of listening to a man, and being able to get his drift right from the start. They are able to discard a great deal of what he says, dress up the real stuff in his speech and the result is that he conveys to his readers in a comparatively short space what the speaker really said. The speaker reads the report, and he realizes at once that his real idea has been conveyed to the reading public. That reporter is a real asset to the paper. He has some sense of proportion; he saves re-writing and further work on his copy, and he makes friends for the paper every time he is sent out to cover an assignment. The trouble comes when a reporter who has not that keen interest in what is going on, or who fails to grasp the thought of the speaker, tries to interpret him in a running story. He gets as a general thing what he thought the man said. He may pick out some of the most inconsequential remarks, and around them spin his yarn. He does not get the reader the idea the speaker had in mind. In that case the speaker has a real kick. He imagines that all reporting is done in the same way because the brand that touched him happened to be particularly bad. It is a dangerous thing for many reporters to write a running story—in fact I think it taxes the ingenuity of the best of them. This class of work is really the penalty papers are paying now for not insisting that shorthand shall be part of the equipment that a reporter must have before he gets a chance on the staff."

The Shorthand Writer

Here is the way one good shorthand man sees the case, and his view is interesting no matter whether you agree with his conclusions or not. "I know some good-sized daily offices where the reporters boast that there is not a shorthand man on the staff. When I began reporting I studied shorthand and became a good shorthand writer. The benefit was that I was sent out to trail political tubthumpers all over the country. Whenever there was a big gathering in the city where important addresses were to be made there would I be in the midst of them, and it would be all night work at a terrific pace. I spent several sessions at Toronto and at Ottawa, and I found after some four years of hard, steady work that I was getting no further ahead. I was earning a little more money, but not much. The ordinary run of reporters could not touch the assignments that were pelted at me—all because I was a good shorthand man. I am not complaining of the work, but the system that penalizes the man by keeping him there because there is no other man coming along who can take his place. I saw before long that my best chance was to quit being a good shorthand man, and so that meant that I must start again in another office. I did this, and inside of a year I was on the desk at a great deal more money than I was getting as a reporter. Was I worth more on that desk than as a good shorthand man? Not for a minute, but the appreciation of the office was pinned to the desk job and the seal of approval in the way of increased pay was there also. I still make very good use of my shorthand, but believe me, a man's an ass to parade the fact that he can do 180 words a minute and do it well. My experience is that it gets him a job and all he has to do is stay right there, for the chances are that he will not go much higher. Now don't take my experience too seriously. It may not be the experience of other men at all. I am just stating the case as I went through it."

Another Shorthander

Speaking of shorthand men, here's the experience of another. This man is in the daily field in the smaller city class. "We got a reporter from a Toronto office. There is no question about the fact that he was a good shorthand man. The trouble was that he failed to couple up a certain amount of common sense with it. He would attend some affair in the evening that at best was good for a half column with heading. He would have yards and feet of what took place. Everything that was said would be correctly reported. But he did not seem to catch the idea of boiling down and giving a short account of what took place. It would take the time of an editor for an hour or so each morning to cut his stuff down. And it also took the chap so long he put his stuff in shape that he would often miss police court and other regular happenings in the morning. The chap was shorthanding us to death. He had no sense of proportion. The head of a big manufacturing concern happened to mention to me one day that he was in need of a secretary who would have to be a first-class shorthand man. "I've got your man," was my first remark, and the same day the reporter went over and got the job at quite a bit more than he was worth to me. He is still in that man's office, makes a very efficient private secretary. The truth is he should have gone into that work in the first place."

From the Composing Room

Still another, and this from a publisher whose city editor must be a reporter. There is another reporter kept in the office, sometimes two, but the reporter who is decorated with the title of city editor has to dig along with the rest of the flock. "We were in the habit of getting in a new man when the chance opened, believing that he would bring new ideas from other offices, and perhaps work harder for the reason that he was in a strange city making good. But it did not work out that way. If we brought a man from a city office we found very often that he would sit down and wait for the editor to find an assignment for him to cover. He could be taken over the beat from the city hall to police station, waterworks, gas and electric departments, government offices, law offices, court house, etc., but he couldn't get under the surface worth a cent. It took him some weeks to get to know even a few people. What did we do? Took a man from the mechanical department who had never done a day's work in an editorial room, and put him on the street. He made good from the first day. He was dead anxious to get a chance to go outside and do editorial work. He made the best reporter a paper could wish for. Best of all he had a good knowledge of the value of time and understood how the editorial department was generally looked upon from the composing room."

Says Ambition is Lacking

That the reporter of to-day lacks ambition is the view of the managing editor of a very large daily in Canada. In fact if it were possible to better conditions it might be imagined that he would like to clean house and start all over again. "Very seldom do we find the reporter of to-day digging out after his regular assignments are turned in, and trying to put across a feature that he can tie his name or initials to. Years ago we had a lot of that kind of work done in our office. The reporter of to-day strikes me as being carried away with the spirit of the times. He wants to get big money right away. I recall one case that happened only a few days ago. "We had an opening on the night side, made possible by the departure of one of our best men. On the day side there was a possible recruit from our own force, and we called him in and offered him an increase over what he was getting if he would try and make good on the position that was opening up for him. In fact we were bringing him up to within eight or ten dollars a week of what we had been paying. Say, he turned the thing down so cold and so fast that we were dizzy. We thought we were doing a good turn by offering him a chance to make good. Do you know what he wanted? Simply this, that he was to get the same money we had been paying to a high-class man the first day he went on the job, irrespective of whether he was capable of handling it or not. There was the chance for him to go ahead and show us that he was man enough to handle the work. When we had been satisfied on that point the money would have been quickly adjusted."

Lacking in Initiative

A good local staff swings pretty much on the city editor. If he is a dead one, or if he lacks the ability to get the best out of men, the staff is going to suffer. In the larger centres it is the hot corner of the office. Is there a shortage of good men for city editors? We are told that there is. One managing editor instanced a case where a man in his city was drowned in the States under rather unusual circumstances. He was almost struck dumb with surprise to see the item in the first edition running as a telegraph story, with no local connection. He was a prominent man in the city, and had large business connections. "Imagine a city editor

Waiting for the arrival of the Press Party at Sydney. In the centre is J. W. Dafoe of the Winnipeg Free Press. He was guide, friend and counsellor to the party, and one of the outstanding speakers at the conference in Ottawa.

worthy of the name letting a thing like that get away from him," was his only comment.

This group was taken on board the "Maid of the Mist" at Niagara Falls, and includes both visiting and Canadian pressmen. The figure in the rear, looking like a real honest-to-goodness sea salt, is J. D. Williams of Cambria, Wales. Others are, left to right, Auguste Bartalo, Malta; Valentine Knapp, president of the Newspaper Society; Capt. Wallace, Montreal Star; the lady in the picture is Mrs. Davis, and her husband, Philip Davis of the Natal Witness, stands next to her.

Bruce Printing List is Revised Upward

Also Add an Advertising Rate

THE Bruce County Printers' and Publishers' Association have issued a new list effective October 4th, 1920. It was compiled by Messrs. Lorne Eedy, A. Wesley, J. J. Hunter, A. Rogers and D. McKenzie. A note accompanying the list says:

"It was decided to base the new list on the figures given in the Franklin Price List, which is becoming the standard for printers very generally throughout the United States and Canada. It has been entirely adopted individually by hundreds of employing printers in Ontario, and collectively by some county and district associations in the U. S. As a basis for charging printers' products it is found to be the fairest to both

printer and patron. The committee of Bruce County printers and publishers who undertook to compile this latest price list could find no safer guide to follow. They feel, too, that it is only a matter of time until the issuing of a local list will be discontinued.

"A scale of advertising rates is also submitted in the last paragraph, which will be found reasonable. The adoption of this scale will bring about a uniformity in rates which will be much more satisfactory to advertisers than the wide variation that has appeared in the figures asked by different newspaper publishers in the came district for advertising of all kinds."

LETTERHEADS

20 lb. Bond at 35c.

250	$ 5 50
500	7 50
1000	11 00
Extra 1000	7 50

For two colors add $4 per thousand.

For extra expensive stock add to these prices proportionately.

BILLHEADS

No. 5—5 inch.

8 to post—	250	$4 50
	—500	5 75
	—1000	8 25
	—Extra 1000	4 50

No. 7—7 inch.

Quarter Cap—	250	$4 75
	—500	6 50
	—1000	9 25
	—Extra 1000	5 00

No. 14—11 inch.

4 to post—	250	$5 25
	—500	7 25
	—1000	11 00
	—Extra 1000	6 00

Half Cap—	250	$6 25
	—500	8 75
	—1000	13 75
	—Extra 1000	7 00

100 of any of the above, $4.25 to $6.00.

NOTE, MEMO HEADS AND STATEMENTS

20 lb. Bond at 35c

250	$4 00
500	5 25
1000	7 50
Extra Thousand	4 00

ENVELOPES

Stock $3.00

	250	500	1000	Extra
No. 7 ..	$3 00	$4 50	$7 75	$5 50

TICKETS

Concert Tickets with Coupons— 100, $2.75; each additional 100, 75c. Tickets without coupons — 100, $2.25; each additional 100, 50c.

GOV'T POSTCARDS

(Printing only)

100	$2 75
Each additional 100	50

PRIVATE POSTCARDS

100, printed on two sides	$5 50
500	7 00
1000	9 00

WINDOW CARDS

11 x 14—1, $2.75; 25, $4.50; 50, $8.50; 100, $7.

Extra color, $3.50 additional.

14 x 22—1, $3.25; 25, $6.50; 50, $8; 100, $10.25.

Extra color, $5 additional.

22 x 28—1, $4.50; 12, $6.50; 25, $8.75; 50, $11.

NOTE AND LETTER CIRCULARS

20 lb. Bond at 35c

Note 8vo—100, $3.25; 250, $4.50; 500, $5.75; 1000, $8.

Letter—100, $7; 250, $8.75; 500, $10; 1000, $12.25.

Add $3.50 to these prices for two colors. With blank fly leaf add 30 per cent.

HALF CAP CIRCULARS AND FORMS

100, $7; 250, $8.75; 500, $10.25; 1000, $12.50.

DODGERS

White Paper; for colored paper add 10 per cent. extra to these prices.)

4½ x 6 in. (32nd sheet)—100, $2.25; 250, $2.50; 500, $3.25; 1000, $4.50; additional 1000, $3.

6 x 9 (16th sheet)—100, $3; 250, $3.75; 500, $4.50; 1000, $6. Extra 1000, $3.25.

6 x 12 (12th sheet)—100, $4.25; 250, $5; 500, $6; 1000, $8. Extra 1000, $3.50.

9 x 12 (8th sheet)—50, $4; 100, $4.75; 250, $5.75; 500, $7; 1000, $9.25. Extra 1000, $4.50.

OPEN DISPLAY POSTERS

(White Paper; for colored paper add 10 per cent. extra to these prices.)

Quarter sheet, 12 x 18—25, $5.50; 50, $6; 100, $6.75. Additional 100, $2.

Third sheet, 12 x 24—25, $7.50; 50, $8.50; 100, $9.75. Additional 100, $2.25.

Half sheet, 18 x 24—25, $7.75; 50, $8.50; 75, $9.25; 100, $9.75. Each additional 100, $2.50.

Whole sheet, 24 x 36—25, $8.75; 50, $9.75; 100, $11.75. Additional 100, $3.75.

For heavy composition, add to these prices.

For extra color add 50 per cent.

AUCTION SALE BILLS

With List of Farm Stock, Implements, etc.

Quarter sheet, 12 x 18—25, $9.75; 50, $10.25; 100, $11.

Third sheet, 12 x 24—25, $11; 50, $11.50; 100, $12.50.

Half sheet, 18 x 24—25, $11.75; 50, $12.50; 100, $13.75.

Whole sheet, 24 x 36—25, $13.75; 50, $15; 100, $17.

ADVERTISING FARM AUCTION SALES

10 cents per line for first insertion; 5 cents per line for subsequent insertion.

MERCANTILE POSTERS

Quarter sheet, 12 x 18 — 250, $12.50; 500, $16.50; 1000, $22. Extra 1000, $7.

Half sheet, 18 x 24—50, $12.50; 100, $13.75; 200, $16.75; 500, $21.75; 1,000, $28. Extra 1000, $9.

PRINTING BILLS OF ADVTS.

Eighth sheet, 9 x 12—500, $4; 1000, $6.50.

Quarter sheet, 12 x 18—500, $5; 75c.

Half sheet, 18 x 24—250, $4.75; 500, $7.50; 1,000, $13. Each additional 100, 85c.

NOTE—The printing of bill off an advertisement does not entitle the customer to any reduction in the price of his advertising.

INVITATION CARDS

3¼ x 5½—25, $3.50; 50, $3.75; 100, $6.50. Extra 100, $3.25.

MEMORIAL CARDS

12, $3; 15, $4.50; 25, $4; 50, $5.25; 75, $7.25; 100, $8.75.

VISITING CARDS

50, $1.50; 100, $2.

Black bordered. 50 per cent. extra.

WEDDING INVITATIONS

$3 Stock—15; $4.50; 25, $5.25; 50, $7; 75, $8.75; 100, $10.50.

For extra expensive stock add proportionately.

AT HOME CARDS

Small—25, $3.50; 50, $3.75; 100, $6.50. Extra 100, $3.25.

Larger size—25, $3.50; 50, $5.75; 100, $6.25. Extra 100, $4.50.

BUTTER WRAPPERS

500 with maker's name, $4.75; 1,000, $7.50; "Dairy Butter," 75c per 100 sheets. Plain, 60c per 100, $2.50 ream.

SHIPPING TAGS

On basis of No. 5 Tag.

500, $5.25; 1000, $8. Additional 1000, $5. Other sizes in proportion.

ROUTE CARDS

14 x 22—25, $10.50; 50, $12.25; 100, $14.75. Additional 100, $4.25.

Folders, 7 x 7½—50, $7.50; 100, $8.50. Additional 100, $1.75.

For extra heavy or tabulated pedigree charge $10 up.

RECEIPTS AND ORDER BOOKS

3¾ x 8½—250, $5; 500, $6; 1000, $8; extra 1000, $4.25.

3¼ x 11—350, $6; 500, $7; 1000, $9; extra 1000, $4.75.

BALLOTS

3 names or less. 500 ballots..$7 50 Each additional 100 .... 1 50

Also add $1 per each additional name.

PRIZE LISTS

$2.75 per page for 200 copies, and 25c per page additional for each 100 copies.

FINANCIAL STATEMENTS AND AUDITOR'S REPORTS

Size of page, 5½ x 8½, type 2 ems by 40 ems, $2.75 per page. For each additional 100 add 25c per page. Cover to count as four pages.

VOTERS' LISTS

On basis of an average of 25 lines to a page, $3 per page for 200 copies. Where average is higher add to price proportionately. 300 copies $3.25 per page. Set without rules

BOOKS, PAMPHLETS, CONSTITUTIONS, BY-LAWS, MINUTES, ETC.

100 copies, 8 point solid, $2.50 per page. 25c per page additional for each 100 copies.

WORK LIST

Gordon press work, $2 per hour; hand composition, $2.50 per hour; cylinder press work, $3.50 per hour

ADVERTISING RATES

Legal advertising, 10c and 5c per line, agate measurement.

Locals, 15c per line.

Transient Display (1 to 4 weeks)

1 to 10 inches	50c an in.
11 to 20 inches	40c an in.
21 to 35 inches	35c an in.
36 to 50 inches	30c an in.
51 to 100 inches	25c an in.
101 in. and upwards	20c an in.

All Prices Subject to Change

Having Everything on the One Floor
The Plan Followed at Stratford Beacon

SEVERAL offices in Canada are considering new premises, and in some cases the work may even now be under way. In a subsequent issue more space will be given to this work, showing plans that publishers have found to be all right, and pointing out as well mistakes that have been made, and which should be avoided by others.

In this issue *Printer and Publisher* is giving a lay-out of the office of the Stratford *Beacon*, using it as a good example of something that is becoming more popular with many of the smaller daily and weekly publishers, viz., the one-floor idea.

The Stratford *Beacon* was planned largely by Mr. O'Bierne, the proprietor of the paper, and grew out of his conviction that the "everything on one floor" was the proper way to handle the work on a paper in a city the size of Stratford, where it is possible to get the room and the light necessary to carry the idea to successful completion.

Mr. Burgoyne of the St. Catharines *Standard* has his premises laid out on one floor, although the arrangement is quite different to that of the Stratford *Beacon*. But in the St. Catharines office Mr. Burgoyne's own office is so located that he is in touch with all departments, although to tell the truth he is closer to the composing room than to the till. He has plenty of light, a short distance to move forms and a quick way of getting latter to the stereotyper and on the press.

A glance at the plan of the *Beacon* shows that a lot of care has been taken in thinking out the details. The director of the paper, for instance, used to make his headquarters in the editorial room, although doubtless does so still, although our recollection of the office has more reference to the days before Mr. O'Bierne was stricken with sickness.

Seated in his office he could have the reportorial staff at his elbow almost, and his business establishment just a few steps away. The mechanical department was just at the end of the hall that separates the business office from the reportorial room.

I remember quite well being in the *Beacon* office some years ago when the afternoon paper was being put to bed. As will be seen by the plan the four machines dump on the bank directly behind. There is room to go between the machines. The last forms were being closed. Telegraph matter was handled right up to the last minute. It was set in small takes, dumped, pulled, corrected and dropped right in the form. When these were locked, they were simply lifted to the bed of the press. The type would not be cold when the first papers started to come from the folder.

There is a paper storage room in the basement, and the rolls are lifted with block and tackle through a trap in front of the press.

There is very little confusion with the route boys getting their papers and starting out. They came in through a door at the left and along the hall outside the reportorial room. There is a counter for them to be served. The front office is not disturbed with them.

The *Beacon* building is three stories, the top flats being rented for other purposes.

A very wise provision at the back is the reservation of a generous light area at the side of the building where the composing machines are placed. It is not always possible to do this, but it is an important point, and should always be kept in mind.

There is no question regarding the advantage of a one-floor office where such a thing is possible. For small daily papers and large weeklies it is quite often that sites can be found that will allow of such a building. In future issues we hope to go farther into this matter, trying to show advantageous lay-outs, and point out features that should be avoided. Correspondence and suggestions will be welcomed in this regard. If you have features that work well with you, let the others know of them. If you have tried something and found it to be not worth while, let us pass on the warning.—A.R.K.

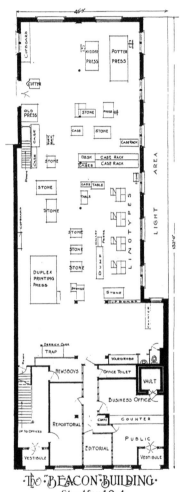

·ℑℎℯ ·ℬℰ𝒜𝒞𝒪𝒩·ℬ𝒰ℐℒ𝒟ℐ𝒩𝒢·
·Stratford Ont·

Sketch showing the layout of the Stratford Beacon editorial, business and news departments. The whole office is on one floor and is remarkably well arranged.

Chiefly About the Bobcaygeon Independent

A Paper that Had an Ideal and a Sick Press

By Frank H. Dobbin

BEING now of some mature years and beyond the days when if a good-sized composition roller, newly washed with lye and water, fell on the office floor and consumed much needed time in picking from its surface the basswood splinters that adhered so persistently, memory recalls incidents associated with the old-time handicraft and exigencies of each day's work. To-day the printer is more or less a specialist. In fact often a sort of glorified machine tender, a part on one whole that makes for what men delight to speak of as efficiency. Presently the all-round printer will be a being of the past, likely for his own good, too. But I take it to be true, (loud calls from the gallery of "No,") growing out of practice, application and experience, that the printing trade as followed, outside of the larger centres and as worked at fifty years ago, called for an application of more ingenuity and general resourcefulness than any other trade.

The plant, for instance, was sparsely supplied. Type was often, so to speak, worn down to the first nick before being discarded or replaced. The helps to speedy working that we now find set out so alluringly in the specimen and sample books of the type founders and supply houses, were absent. Dotted rule, for instance persisted in cutting the form rollers and all sorts of expedients had to be tried to combat the damage. The first coated paper that came to be used gave the press hands a fright. It seemed so impossible to do printing on such shiny stuff.

A moment before I referred to the attribute of Memory. A most wonderful thing, that stores in the cells of our brains the details of long forgotten incidents. But memory needs to be provoked in order to act. I, a few days ago burned a finger while wrestling with the kitchen range. Immediately recalled the fearful accident to a friend who lost his right foot by the overturning of a pot of melted iron on the foundry floor. Had not thought of the accident for thirty years but my trifling burn recalled the tragedy. So one night, while mending a hole in an otherwise perfectly serviceable coal scuttle memory digged up a happening of passed printing experience, and I place it on paper as in support of my contention that the printer of years ago had to be more resourceful than he now needs to be.

The Home of Obliging Fish

OFF from the north western edge of the county of Peterborough lies the village of Bobcaygeon. The name is a household word amongst the fraternity of those who go a-fishing

"The door stood wide open, for, mind you, there is no pay-as-you-enter sign on the door of the Bobcaygeon Independent."

for fish and occasionally buy what they do not catch. The village has had two industries, lumber and rod fishing. The latter survives as a sort of perpetual franchise. Men addicted to fishing, men from the big cities where they spend the days in among the tall buildings and long for the open shore of the lake, bring the implements of sport, inhabit the important hotels and spend the days in joyous piscatorial pursuit and the nights in statements that lack fact but redound in romance. Bobcaygeon owns a renown that passes far and near as a reliable fishing preserve, one that never disappoints and where fish bite and stay on the hook. If fish be not in the vicinity the inhabitants will go out prospecting and inveigle fish to come and locate.

Such shows true citizenship and a recognition of the financial fact that the professional angler is apt to be generous, and his habits are not to pause at trifles. He wants what he wants when he wants it. The village escutcheon is said to be that of four rods, rampant, two maskin-onge couchant, the whole entwined with eels and garnished with tackle galore. This presented in colors forms quite a halo.

The village is the home of the Bobcaygeon Independent, a paper of parts and prestige, one in a class by itself. Absolutely an enduring example of the personally conducted journal, that doesn't give a shoot for any politician, premier or potentate on this visible earth. It was started — that is the paper, not the earth — many years ago by Stewart I, who came out from the Old Country, an intense Radical, lugging with him a virulent animosity against crowned heads and titled persons. He is said to have used as a pen fluid a solution of acetic acid and gall, with a particularly biting effect. People delighted to sit down, open the paper and dwell on the process of vivisection, and to select issues of the paper in which some offender against public principles was immolated, and send copies to the victims across the pond who was or were under criticism. When Stewart I undertook to flay not his was the method of the rapier but rather he grasped the claymore. The swath he cut was markedly visible. Presently friends of the deceased called around to view the remains. It is even said that men sick of a fever and approaching convalescence, disdained to consume a tonic but asked for the Bobcaygeon Independent, first thing. All as an indication of a coming back to interest in personal affairs.

Now there are two newspapers in Canada that have from time immemorial blazoned at top of the page and under the title words defining the position of the paper and invoking the principles it upheld. One is the Toronto *Globe*, with its classic quotation, "The Subject who is loyal to the Chief Magistrate," etc., and another is the Bobcaygeon *Independent*, which in and out of season, amidst turmoil and clatter, in affluence or privation, inculcated that its chief mission in this life was to uphold the propagation of "The Good, the True and the Beautiful," whatever that means. Possibly, as one might say, it may have related to the discovering and retaining of excellence in fishing opportunity. Anyway there was the motto and there was found the virility and deftness to sustain it.

In process of years the paper came into the possession of Stewart II. Possibly it was entailed on him. He carried it on, adding to its columns the zest of infinite humor. Original, fresh, and kindly, inculcating a cheerful view of life and its involvements, the paper stood alone as one of a fast disappearing number such as the one-time Burlington *Hawkeye*, the Dansbury *News* and others, now only a memory. The *Independent* is still esteemed for what it says in its types, and for an occasional unique view of life. Especially so in the good old summer time when frequent and exhilarating paragraphs disclose of the exceeding luck of fishermen and notable catches.

Carried on with the newspaper is a general jobbing and printing business. This adds to the gaiety of nations, for the boys of the village come into the fold, become the cub apprentices, absorb of the handicraft and afterwards go out and take responsibility in printing offices up and down the land, and even further abroad. A long line of journeymen, several of them now opulent proprietors, have graduated from the Bob. office. By their works you will know them, grounded in the intimate mysteries of case and roller, in lock-up and justification, artists of the mallet and planer, brought up to work and the craftmanship of the hand-set press.

The Call from Macedonia

So sitting at my desk one day I opened a letter from Stewart II. It said, 'You are coming up this way in a day or two, drop in, I want to see you." Now I hadn't the slightest idea of going to Bobcaygeon, not being a fish fiend, but supposed that it was one of Stewart's jokes and that the answer would come along in due time, which it did. I had another letter from a resident of the village that the books in his library were getting under the weather and the worse for wear. and would I come up and prescribe.

When I got off the boat to go to the hotel to eat I passed the printing office. It was in the summer time, the hour being as after twelve, noon. The street was wide open, for mind you, there is no pay-as-you-enter sign on the door of the Bobcaygeon *Independent*. All hands and the boss were off to lunch. So I stepped in, rather allured by the quiet of the place and the warmth of the day outside. I loafed all around the room, taking in the surroundings, everything being thoroughly orthodox and true to tradition. The smell of the wet paper and the ink from the hand press distributor still hung about. Last issue proofs dangled from the nail at the side of a case rack, waving to and fro in the gentle breeze from the open door and windows. Handfuls of type, laid down when the staff hurried off to dinner, and the skeletons of the pages of the paper lay on the imposing stone. The office cat purred on the sill of the window overlooking Little Bob—as that arm of the river is named—flowing back of the office and which the rear of the building overhung. Recognizing in me a kindred spirit and one of the Craft the cat leaped down and came and rubbed against my ankles in a greeting of fraternal welcome.

In the Sacred Sanctum

Tacked up on the walls were specimen posters, the chef-d'oeuvres of past printers, thus leaving their work behind. One placard stated that A. Bottum had gotten in his stock of hoop skirts and corsets for the spring of 1869. Another intimated that the entirely desirable young stallion, Young Sir Tatton, was at the service of farmers for a moderate fee, with results almost guaranteed. A couple of announcements of by-gone political meetings and scraps were in evidence. The whole surroundings were so congenial that I at once one felt at home and tempted to slip off one's coat and go to work. Such is the allurement of association.

Over in a corner stood an old Oshawa Gordon press. These presses were the offshoot of the enterprise of one Erastus

Wiman, of early reciprocity fame, who in 1865 brought over the patterns, together with those of the old Taylor country cylinder, from the other side of the line. The machines were built at the Joseph Hall Works, in Oshawa, where they made the very first agricultural machinery turned out in Canada. They put together the reapers and mowers sort of loose jointed so that they could run over logs, sticks, stones, snake fences and silos and still keep up a decent working motion. Many of the presses, especially the Taylors, were of this kind. Often has a rural printing office resounded of a winter morning with imprecations and words of violence when the distributor rollers would be thrown across the room from the ink plate of the old Taylor press. The machines were a means to an end and only one jump removed from the hand lever press days.

At the Gordon press the hands had been working, running off a bill-of-fare for the local hotel. When I picked up a sheet to look at it I almost felt that I had tears in my eyes, the thing was so badly slurred. My feelings at once were of large sympathy. Well, I knew what was the matter. I too had passed under the rod. So I hunted up a strip of railroad board, drove the flies away from some paste that lay on a piece of paper on the imposing stone, trimmed the card and deftly stuck a couple of pieces on the projections underneath the feeding board, and where the gate that steadies the bed on the impression engages when the two parts come together. I left the sacred precincts and bade adieu to the cat.

The Miracle Had Happened

Having finished my errand as to the books, along in the afternoon I strolled back to the print shop. I found Stewart II. at the table grinding out copy. After greetings Stewart said. "It was about that old press in the corner that I wanted to see you. It has been slurring most disgracefully for the past week or so. Some one told me that you knew all about the cussedness of such and divers machines. To-day we thought we would give it another trial. Put on job and tried our darndest. We shifted the form from the middle to the side, then to the bottom and top of the chase, swore, pleaded, invoked all the saints, but no use. She still slurred. Just glance at that."

He handed me a sheet. It was about as bad as it well could be. His language was justified.

Then brightening up, he added, "Do you know, a most wonderful thing has happened."

"What was it, Stewart?" I asked. "Has some subscriber called in to pay in cash instead of produce?"

'No, it's not that," he said, "though that would be very good. We tried, as I have said, and gave it up and went to dinner. Coming back we gave her one more trial, and, by George, there she was all right. No slurring. Right as a trivet. Going along in great shape. Come and see."

Leaning back in his chair, he stuck one foot on the sill of the window, curled the other across the extended leg, poked his thumbs into the armholes of his vest and asked the question, "How would you explain that? Sorry to have bothered you about it, but it's all right now." Said it just as if he was proposing something of a poser, that would be unanswerable.

"Stewart," I said, "it seems to me that the only logical explanation is to assume that this is one of those Dispensations of Providence sent in recognition of the Good, the True and the Beautiful." And I led him over to the press and explained cause and effect.

"Gol darn it all," spoke Stewart, "and to think of it, that I have been monkeying around that piece of chaos for the last twenty years and never looked below the feeding board."

The outstanding speech of the conference was delivered by Mr. J. W. Dafoe, the brilliant and level-headed editor of the Winnipeg *Free Press*. Mr. Dafoe contributed a splendid address to the discussion on "Empire Partnership," in which he pointed out that the British Empire was an empire of nations by consent, made up not of independent nations, but of interdependent nations. He gave the Imperialistic ideals of some of the "Empah cementers" a rude jolt by declaring that an empire could not be held together by forcing the people to do obeisance to the all-high, but by mutual understanding and goodwill and common sense and effect. Mr. Dafoe was born at Combermere in Renfrew county. He is one of the big men of Canada to-day, and possibly this country's greatest editor.

Putting Character Into Your Work

How It Works in Selling Printing

BY TRES.

IN THE August issue of *Printer and Publisher* I closed my article on "He Profits Most Who Serves Best" by saying that "Confidence is really the fruit of certain ideals of character that can be woven into our business relationships."

I mean to infer this in connection with the salesmanship phase of the printing and publishing business.

Character must not be undervalued as capital. It has been said "When poverty is your inheritance, virtue must be your capital." Many a salesman has learned the truth of this maxim from personal experience.

Money is not necessary to start in business with—not altogether. There are men in business to-day making money, who did not have a cent to start with. They were industrious and had established "character" to such an extent that the word was spelled C-r-e-d-i-t, and very little difficulty was experienced in getting the financial and moral support necessary. I remember the instance of a young man who had learned the bakery business. One day he mentioned to a friend his desire to start in business for himself.

"But I have no money to start on," he said.

"Start on credit," his friend replied. "A dozen men in this town will start you, because they *know* you. Your ability, with the character you have, is better capital than ten thousand dollars would be to some young men."

A salesman, whom I know very well, preceded me on a call to a buyer of printing. The manager remarked:

"Do you know Mr. So-and-so, who just left my office?"

"Yes, I know him very well."

"Well, I always endeavor to place business his way. He's a good sterling fellow," said this business man.

I knew he was. Character did it. Unknown to him, it meant more to that salesman than money, advertising, boosting by his firm, etc. Character did all this and even more, for him.

Representing a big firm, being well-dressed, owning an automobile, being well supported by the firm's publicity, while all advantageous, will not of themselves secure confidence. They are contributing influences—mighty ones, too. Enough of some things will beget confidence in the pecuniary ability of a salesman, but these alone will not beget confidence in his moral ability. They are not a guarantee against misrepresentation. But character is.

Hence character is a peculiar kind of capital ever increasing in value, introducing the possessor to channels of influence and power he had not thought of.

Put Character in Your Work

It is in man's power to weave the ideals of good character right into his job, whatever that job may be.

The messenger boy, the "printers' devil," (a name, thank goodness, that is fast becoming obsolete,) the compositor, the pressman, the binderyman, the office man, the salesman—every-one of them can put the stamp of Character on their work. How? Do the job right. That's all. Put your real self—as you would have others see YOU—right into the work you are doing.

The firm will have confidence in you and grant you full scope for the exercise of your genius and initiative. How much that really means to any employee, but specially to a salesman! Confidence of fellow-workmen—assures co-operation. The compositor, the pressman, and the binderyman, all working to make the job or issue a "jim-dandy" thus backing up "Bill, our outside man," and boosting the firm.

Finally, the customer's confidence—valued most of all—follows as a matter of course, and the salesman in this will reap not a small share of the rich returns that will follow month after month and year after year.

The "certain ideals of character" mentioned will include:—
Truthfulness,
Cheerfulness,
Courtesy,
Cleanliness in speech and habit,
Punctuality,
The Golden Rule.

Truthfulness—Understood as easily as 2 + 2 = 4. Never "add color" unnecessarily. Boost your proposition to its limit, but sit four-square on the facts. Go as far as you *know* the firm will back you; and let them know how far you expect them to back you. If your firm don't make good, there are others that will. But remember—truthfulness.

This Chap Was Always Welcome

Cheerfulness—When I was associated with a certain firm in the capacity of buyer for their printing, engraving, etc., there were some salesmen I certainly appreciated having call, especially early in the day. They came in with a cheerful "Good morning, sir," that sent a good-natured thrill through me. Perhaps I needed it badly; at times anyway. But this spirit of cheerfulness is a mighty valuable thing to possess. You can't work it up. It must spring from a care-free heart and a clear conscience. Read "Marden's 'Every Man A King,' chapter 7, 'Mastering Our Moods.'"

Courtesy—Be apostles of politeness and so commend your society, and your firm, wherever you go. Courtesy is "Elegance or politeness of manners, or especially politeness connected with kindness." It has been said that this virtue "begins at home." But in business it "begins at the phone." Over the phone we often *are* misrepresented. Be *very* careful how you "look" over the phone—for at the other end as you speak a mental moving picture presentation is going on, illustrating your every move. In using the phone for making appointments, discussing business, etc., cultivate a refined, pleasant tone. Avoid discussing disputes over the phone—the other fellow has the advantage every time. Courtesy is a law in all well-appointed business firms to-day—from messenger to general manager.

Pleasant manners will gain for the salesman lasting popularity.

If there is right heart-attitude, there will be a ready expression of courtesy.

Cleanliness—"In speech;" nothing jars the refined senses like coarse or vulgar expressions. There is no necessity to emphasize a fact with a coarse adjective. No necessity to amuse with a vulgar story. Nobody enjoys either, and most people detest both. "And Habit"—avoid any habit that is offensive to "the other fellows."

One Way to Show Interest

Punctuality—Keep every engagement right on the dot. If you cannot get there, 'phone or get a message through somehow. Same thing is necessary with the firm. When they know a proof or a job cannot be furnished on time, let the customer or advertiser know *beforehand*. This will show that you are definitely interested. To the salesman, "Business before pleasure" every time. The salesman (or any employee, for that matter) who is always punctual, is the one who shares the confidence of the firm, and its customers—*because* he is on time in meeting his engagements, fulfilling his promises, discharging his office duties, and doing promptly the many things expected of a reliable member of the staff.

The Golden Rule—You can preach your own sermon on this text; but preach it every day in deeds, not words. We're only passing this way once—so let's do all the good we can, in all the ways we can, as often as we can. And the salesman appears above all men to have opportunities at every turn. Let's get after the whole six "ideals."

Just as I hand this to the editor, I have received a question from one of the readers of *Printer and Publisher*. Here it is:—

"I am a young man, a printing salesman, know the business mechanically, have taken a course in salesmanship, but I have certain deficiencies that apparently cripple my sales effort. How would you go about strengthening these deficient qualities?"

I am glad to receive this question and in next month's issue will endeavor to help my brother salesman by answering his question.

Free Press Recalls the Early Days in the West

Splendid Issue of Winnipeg Paper

THE Winnipeg *Free Press* went about it to celebrate the 50th anniversary of Manitoba. That province has been kind to the *Free Press*, and in turn it was quite proper for the *Free Press* to return the favor when the half-century mark was reached. The edition issued on July 15th contained 50 pages, a large part of which was taken up with reviewing the progress of firms, people and cities, and tracing the development of the province. Topics dealt with are as follows:—"Half a Century of Political Development," "Agriculture in 1813 and 1920," "Winnipeg in Music, Art and Culture," "From Pioneer Hamlet to Metropolis."

The whole issue is profusely illustrated throughout, and is a credit to the office issuing it, as well as to the city of Winnipeg and the province of Manitoba.

It is interesting to note that in referring to the history of newspapers in Winnipeg, some well-known personages are brought to light. The *Free Press* says in part:—

Early Papers

The *Manitoba Weekly Free Press* was first printed on November 9, 1872. "Volume 1, No. 1," of the *Daily Free Press* appeared on Monday, July 6, 1874. Harry Sloan, the well-known restaurateur of earlier days, was one of the builders of the first furniture used in the *Free Press* office, which in pioneer days was located on the east side of Main street, between Rupert and James, near the site now covered by the Strand theatre. William Code, ex-chief of the Winnipeg Fire Brigade, was one of the first pressman employed on the *Free Press*. James Whyte, now a veteran employee of the *Free Press*, began his typographical career in Winnipeg with the Manitoba *Gazette* in 1878. E. A. Blow, another veteran, was with the *Standard* in 1879.

William Coldwell, one of the men who started the first newspaper in Fort Garry, penned the opening words of this article in a paper read before the newspaper men of Winnipeg at a press dinner held in Clougher's restaurant during the year 1888. Mr. Coldwell gave this record of Winnipeg papers from the start:

1859 to 1870—*Nor'Wester*, published by W. Coldwell, W. Buckingham and Dr. Schultz.
1870—*New Nation*, by Major Robinson.
1870—*News Letter*, by P. G. Laurie.
1871—*Manitoba Liberal*, by Stewart Mulvey.
1872—*Manitoba Trade Review*, by A. Begg.
1872—*Manitoba Gazette*, by G. F. Carruthers.
1872—*Manitoba Free Press*, by Messrs. Kenny and Luxton.
1873—*The Nor'Wester*, by E. L. Barber.
1874—*The Standard*, by Molyneux St. John.
1877—*Manitoba Daily Herald*, by W. G. Fonseca and Begg and Nursey.
1878—*Manitoba Telegraph*, by Mr. Nursey.
1878—*The Gazette*, by Hon. H. J. Clarke.
1879—*Winnipeg Daily Times*, by C. R. Tuttle.
1879—*The Tribune*, by G. H. Ham.
1880—*Daily Times*, by Amos Rowe.
1881—*The News*.
1882—*The Daily Sun*, by W. Nagle.
1883—*The New Sun*.
1885—*The Daily Manitoban*.
1885—*The News*.
1886—*The Manitoba Daily Sun*.
1887—*The Morning Call*.

Mr. Coldwell noted in his paper that "all of these excepting the *Free Press* and the two last-mentioned have passed into the land where sheriffs are unknown."

Newspaper history, since Pioneer Coldwell's paper was prepared, is more familiar to the Winnipeggers of to-day. The *Morning Call* suspended publication, and for several years the *Free Press* and *Sun* held the field without opposition. In September, 1894, the *Free Press* (a morning paper since 1880) also began publication of the *Free Press Evening Bulletin*, as an evening paper. T. H. Preston disposed of the *Sun*, and the

printing of that paper was discontinued. For several weeks the only daily papers in Winnipeg were the morning and the evening editions of the *Free Press*. Then R. L. Richardson, who had been connected with the *Sun* since its birth, organized a new company and started the *Tribune* as an evening paper. The *Nor-'Wester*, established as a daily morning paper, was succeeded by the *Telegram*.

Outside Winnipeg the first paper published in Manitoba was the Portage la Prairie *Review*, by Thomas Collins. Other pioneer publishers of the West are: C. S. Douglas, Emerson *International*; James Hooper, Morris *Herald*; P. G. Laurie, Battleford *Herald*; Frank Oliver, Edmonton *Bulletin*; Alex. Dunlop, Neepawa *Press*; A. Weidman, Selkirk *Inter-Ocean*; C. Cliffe, Brandon *Mail*; W. J. White, Brandon *Sun*.

About Pioneer Papers

W. F. Luxton, who established the *Free Press* in 1872 in partnership with the late John A. Kenny, came to Manitoba from Strathroy, Ontario, in 1872, as western representative of the Toronto *Globe*. He was one of Winnipeg's first public school teachers, and took great interest in all educational, civic and legislative matters. He was a candidate for mayor at the first election held in Winnipeg, and was for several years a member of the Manitoba legislature. Mr. Luxton, who presided over the destinies of the *Free Press* for nearly a quarter century, died in 1907.

Geo. H. Ham was manager of the Whitby *Gazette* at 21. In 1875 he came to the Winnipeg *Free Press* as a compositor. In a very short time he was promoted to the local editorship of the paper, remaining in that position till October, 1878, when he established a paper called the *Daily Tribune*. This did not long survive, and was amalgamated with the *Daily Times*, with Mr. Ham as managing editor. He left newspaper work in 1882 to become registrar of the county of Selkirk. In later years and before joining the C.P.R. service Mr. Ham was again a member of the *Free Press* editorial staff.

William Coldwell and William Buckingham were the pioneer newspaper men of the West. They established the *Nor'-Wester* in 1859. Mr. Buckingham went back to Ontario before 1870. His widow still resides in Strathroy. Mr. Coldwell, after visiting the east, returned to Winnipeg and was engaged in journalistic pursuits for many years, latterly as legislative gallery reporter for the *Free Press*. He was an expert shorthander and was succeeded in his gallery work by Rev. T. E. Morden, another trusty pioneer, who has since gone to rest.

Some tribute must be paid in this Jubilee year newspaper review to that good old citizen and western "booster," Hon. James W. Taylor, United States consul at Winnipeg from 1870 until his death in 1893. Western newspaper men and Western Canada had a true friend in Consul Taylor. Just a word, too, in memory of another pioneer who "passed on" last year—dear old J. P. Robertson. "J. P." before his appointment as provincial librarian, was a newspaper man and had served on both *Times* and *Free Press* staffs. He never forgot his news training nor his newspaper friends.

Organizing in the West

A meeting of Central Saskatchewan papers brought about an organization known as the Central Saskatchewan Newspaper Association, with papers represented from Young, Govan, Strassburg, Imperial, Simpson, Viscount and Waterous. The officers elected are:—Hon. Pres., the Hon. Sam Latta, Minister of Highways; President, E. Garrett, Watrous; Vice-Pres., J. Small, Strassburg; Sec. Treas., C. Needham, Simpson. After an exhaustive survey of present conditions, and the intimations of still higher prices from the wholesalers, it was deemed expedient to put into effect at once a new scale of minimum advertising rates, as follows: yearly contract space, local display per inch, per issue, 30c; half yearly, 35c. Less than half yearly 50c. per inch per issue. General—Transient, 1 inch and under, 75c., each subsequent issue, 50c. Local readers, 25c per line per issue.

Much Depends Upon the Care of Inks

By Alton B. Carty

Portion of an address to Washington Club of Printing House Craftsmen

IN ALL large printing establishments the ink is kept in a room in charge of an employee, who is expected to guard against wastage, as well as to keep the stock in order and know something of the peculiar quality of the product, and its adaptability to the particular stock.

In the small establishment, as a rule, there is no especial care bestowed upon inks. Any employee has access to the "cabinet" and inks are handled in such a manner as to cause a degree of wastage that is nothing short of criminal.

The waste is usually caused by the method of removing the ink from the cans when a small quantity is to be used, as on the small jobs that are met with in the daily round of the average establishment.

Then, too, there is no effort made to preserve the labels on the cans, and frequently they are destroyed when the cans are opened, or the label is soon so badly smeared with ink as to be unreadable.

When ink can be supplied in collapsible tubes the wastage is reduced to a negligible quantity, but very stiff inks cannot be squeezed from tubes in the ordinary way, and this method of supplying inks must be confined to the softer varieties.

If ink is too stiff to remove from a tube through the cap end, the only other thing to do is to cut open the bottom of the tube, lay the tube on a slab, and press out the ink with a small piece of gas pipe. Cut off the end of the tube as the bulk of the ink is reduced.

A little care exercised in the handling of inks will not only reduce wastage, but will obviate much annoyance and loss of time, and aid materially in producing satisfactory results in the printed product.

There are a few simple directions that may be given for the care of inks that are so evident as to be generally known, and yet are so universally disregarded that a mild emphasis may prove of value, as well as be of interest.

Inks should be kept in a closed cabinet and separated according to colors; that is, the different colors should have separate apartments, and a further separation should be made according to grade and quality. Of course a purple copying ink should not be placed near a purple record ink, or where it would be liable to be taken out and substituted for the other ink.

All ink supplied in cans has a stout, oiled manila covering which is designed to prevent the ink from drying out and forming a hard, encrusted film; but when the paper is once removed it is impracticable to replace it. Some thoughtless pressmen simply raise the manila, dip a knife into the ink, take out what is required and press the covering back into place; but unless the remaining ink in the can is carefully smoothed over and the manila pressed closely to the ink, the air will not be excluded and a hard crust will be formed.

Some pressmen cover the ink with a sufficient quantity of cottonseed oil, while some use lard oil. Both of these oils are of the non-drying variety and are effective for the purpose. It is customary when either of the oils is used, to pour it off into the top of the can, remove the quantity of ink required for the job in hand, smooth over the ink remaining, pour back the oil, and replace the lid. The small quantity of oil that adheres to the ink that is removed from the can will mix readily with it and will not ordinarily impair its working qualities.

Perhaps the best way to deal with the problem is to remove the original oiled paper from the top of the ink by running a knife around the edge of the paper, work it into a ridge at one side, and with a firm grip peel it off and deposit it into the rubbish can to be burned.

Then secure a piece of old table oil cloth and lay the top of the can upon it, marking out the circle with a lead pencil; cut with scissors and lay on the ink in the can, and press down smoothly in order to exclude all air. It is best to have the fabric side of the cloth in contact with the ink. Do not oil the fabric as the cloth will then have a tendency to leave the ink.

The same piece of cloth can be used indefinitely if handled carefully.

In removing the cloth from the ink, press a portion of the edge together so as to form a ridge about a quarter of an inch high, and by a firm grip on the ridge with a pair of flat pliers, strip the cloth from the ink and lay clean side down upon a piece of paper.

Remove the quantity of ink desired and smooth over what remains in the can. With a small ink knife, pressed against the inked side of the cloth, lift it and when turned over, place in position in the can, with the knife between the ink and the cloth. Bear down upon the cloth with index finger of left hand in order to hold cloth in place, and pull out the knife. Press down cloth with a clean knife, being careful to have the cloth in close contact with the ink.

As the level of the ink lowers in the can due to the quantity removed from time to time, cut down the sides with a small pair of tinner's snips. It is a case of either preserving the can or the ink, and as the ink is the more valuable the can must be sacrificed. By this method all the contents of the can may be utilized and all wastage avoided.

The use of water or glycerin as a top coating for the ink in the can does not prove satisfactory, as the oxygen in these substances causes a thin scum to form on the ink.

All ink cans should be covered to prevent dust settling on the ink. When the tin cover, or lid, is lost or becomes unusable, it is a small matter to make a cover of stout manila stock by shaping it around the top and either tying a string around it or using a strip of gummed manila which is now found in almost every pressroom.

Be sure that somewhere upon either the can or the paper top, there will be a label or statement of the contents of the can, and the quality of the same. If there is a small quantity of ink in a number of cans in the cabinet, and there usually is, it will be profitable occupation to clean off the top and mix the remainder with a little balsam of copaiba to make it workable. Then put on an oil cloth top and the ink will be ready for the next job when that color is ordered. Where there are several cans, each containing a small quantity of ink of the same hue, it will be well to clean them up and combine them. If the ink is unusually hard it can be softened with a mixture of one part balsam of copaiba and two parts of benzol.

After the washing of the fountain cylinder at the shutting down of work in the evening, always cover the ink in the fountain with a full width strip of oiled paper, pressed evenly against the ink. In starting up in the morning, after removing the manila sheet, be careful to also remove all particles of dried or granulated ink that may remain in the fountain for it is the small particles that cause the filling up of forms. Never work dried ink into the body in the fountain, thinking by that method it has been gotten rid of.

Another questionable practice is to put fresh ink in the fountain on top of old ink. It is better to run the ink low and then clean out remainder before putting in fresh ink. Don't take ink out of fountain when changing color and put it back into a can of fresh ink. Put it into a can and label it. Attention to these little things makes work go along smoothly, and results in clean, sharp, satisfactory printing.

By a new system of accounting, recently installed by the Toronto *Globe*, it is possible to locate instantly any advertising under schedule from the time the copy is received in the *Globe* office until the account is paid. The system is said to run along new and modern lines as applied to newspapers. In setting up a system for the *Globe* advantage was taken of the experience gained in practical operation in the office of the *Free Press*, together with the excellent system of the Ottawa *Journal*, while refinements to both were secured by personal investigations in offices of leading newspapers in the United States.

Western Ontario Publishers in Session
Many Matters Discussed at Brantford

THE second organization meeting of Western Ontario publishers and advertising managers was held in Brantford on Tuesday, Sept. 14th, and proved perhaps an even greater success than the first meeting held in Kitchener early in July. About thirty newspaper men were present and were the guests of Messrs. T. H. and W. B. Preston of the *Expositor* during their stay in Brantford. After an address of welcome by Mr. W. T. Preston the visitors were taken for a drive around the city and out to the beautiful new club house being erected for the Golf Club, after which they enjoyed dinner at the Kerby House.

The afternoon session was marked by a delightful absence of formality and stiffness, and seldom has a gathering of newspaper men enjoyed a more beneficial get-together than was provided by the almost five solid hours of discussion which followed. Mr. W. B. Preston was a most efficient chairman and never allowed the proceedings to drag for a moment. A lengthy program had been drawn up and all the more important subjects in the list were covered.

Some discussion arose as to the matter of forming a permanent organization with a full staff of officers, but it was thought that the very informality of the present gatherings was a decided advantage, and the meeting voted in favor of continuing the organization in the same impromptu manner as at present, with meetings six times a year, the chairman in each case to be the publisher of the paper in the city where the meeting is held. T. H. Kay of the Kitchener *Record* was appointed permanent secretary.

Mr. H. B. Burgoyne of the St. Catharines *Standard* invited the gathering to hold the next meeting in St. Catharines, and the invitation was accepted, the meeting to be held in November.

An interesting report of various economies effected by individual publishers brought out a lot of beneficial information. Mr. J. W. Ferguson, promotion manager of the C.D.N.A., explained to the members the reason why they should secure the data and answer the questionnaires sent out by his department. After hearing Mr. Ferguson a resolution was unanimously adopted urging the members of the association to promptly fill in and return the questionnaires.

Mr. J. H. Johnson of the Brantford *Expositor* gave an illuminating address on the matter of selling "copy" rather than space. Mr. Johnson emphasized the point that the publisher's responsibility was by no means ended when the contract was signed, and by local instances showed how attention and help to new advertisers frequently meant the development of a permanent account. He illustrated his talk with examples of ads secured by the *Expositor* through writing copy.

Mr. Tate, classified advertising manager of the Toronto *Daily Star*, gave a splendid address on developing classified advertising.

The adoption of the Standard Rate Card and the standard of advertising practice as laid down by the Canadian Press Association was recommended to the members.

In discussing the amount of free reading matter allowed theatres a wide variation was discovered and a resolution was adopted recommending members to allow not more than one-half the amount in reading matter (or cuts) that is carried in display, *i.e.*, not more than one-half inch free reader for one inch paid display.

The percentage above the daily rate which advertisers using space once a week or as desired should pay also proved an interesting subject. Some publishers charge as high as 50 per cent. higher, and all the way from that to the flat rate. A recommendation that this class of advertising should be charged at not less than one-third higher than the daily rate was adopted by the meeting.

Other subjects discussed were "Agency relations,"; "Experience of those selling entire output to boys as against system of employing own route boys and making collections"; "Experience of those using motor trucks for delivery of papers to agents"; "Collecting accounts by sight draft at first of month," etc.

Those present were: W. L. Agnew, *Times-Journal*, St. Thomas; W. J. Motz, *Daily Record*, Kitchener; J. H. Johnson, *Expositor*; Brantford; Frank L. Watson, *Times-Journal*, St. Thomas; H: M. Gadsby, H. B. Burgoyne, *Standard*, St. Catharines; J. W. Ferguson, C.D.N.A., Toronto; R. B. Harris, Geo. Davis, *Herald*, Hamilton; Clive S. Bean, *Telegraph*, Kitchener; Stuart Cant, Henry F. Foster, *Reporter*, Galt; R. M. Hamilton, J. I. McIntosh, *Mercury*, Guelph; A. C. Woodward, *News*, Chatham; Chas. Dingman, S. B. Dawson, *Herald*, Stratford; E. S. Hunter, W. F. Tobey, *Sentinel-Review*, Woodstock; A. C. Shonk, *Herald*, Guelph; Frank L. Tate, *Star*, Toronto; T. P. Taylor, *Beacon*, Stratford; F. H. Leslie, *Review*, Niagara Falls; Geo. H. Wilson, Roy P. Wilson, *Post*, Lindsay; T. H. Kay, *Daily Record*, Kitchener; W. B. Preston, T. H. Preston, H. B. Christie, E. L. Strobridge, *Expositor*, Brantford.

Well, This from the Fruit Belt

MR. J. O. LIVINGSTON, editor of the Grimsby *Independent*, writing from the centre of Ontario's fruit belt and summer romances, tells as follows of happenings there:—

Printer and Publisher:—Just a line to let you know what "The Best Weekly in Ontario" is doing.

We have decided to raise our subscription rates on Oct. 15th to $2 per year. Should have done it long ago. Up to date we have lost no readers over the raise, but rather have had a regular flood of renewals at the old rate of $1.50. Also, on Dollar Days we offered the paper to new subscribers for one year for $1, and put on over eighty new readers. We believe that we have about convinced our readers that it is about as impossible to run a newspaper at a loss as it is to run a car without gasoline. We made no bones or offered no excuses for the raise. Simply told the people that we were in this business for a living and intended to get it. Explained the paper situation, etc., to them and left the matter in their hands.

On the same date our advertising rates raise, and so far have not had one complaint from our advertisers, and we have many of them. I enclose new rate card. These rates may seem a bit stiff when compared with other country weeklies, but we believe that we produce the newsy, best set, best dressed weekly in Ontario, and we have proven time and again that our advertisers get results. We give no special positions, but guarantee every adv. to be alongside reading matter or following reading matter.

On October 8th and 9th the merchants of this town held their second Dollar Day sale and it was very successful. When the writer first suggested the Dollar Day idea last winter it was not taken to very kindly by the merchants, but by hard work and persuasive talk a very successful day was held in March. It was so successful that the merchants immediately started talking about the fall sale, which they made a two day affair. In our Dollar Day issue of Oct. 6th, the total amount of space in our sixteen page paper was 1920 inches. We carried 1600 inches of advertising, and all at full rates.

Since October, 1919, the *Independent* has never been smaller than ten pages, except for two issues, and has run as high as twenty pages. Our advertising patronage has been exceptionally good and is getting better all the time.

Our job department has been very busy the past nine months, and is very much so now. We are getting good prices for all our work. When a man tries to beat us down in price we simply tell him that we cannot afford to do the job any cheaper. That he is in this world to make a living and so are we. We try to show him that when he gets a cheap price he also gets a cheap job. Nine times out of ten when they have taken their work elsewhere they have always come back and never have a word to say about price.

Newsprint is now costing us $240 a ton, so you can see that any weekly newspaper editor that keeps on selling his paper at $1.50 and continues to sell advertising space at the low rate is only preparing himself for a trip to the poor house.

Hoping that the *Printer and Publisher* will continue to be as welcome a visitor to our office as it has been, I remain,

Yours very truly,

J. ORLON LIVINGSTON.

Harks Back Over the Last Fifty Years
G. R. Pattullo's Memories of Woodstock

MR. G. R. PATTULLO, in a recent issue of the Woodstock *Sentinel-Review*, its fiftieth anniversary number, tells in an interesting and intimate way of events that have crowded into half a century living in Woodstock. Mr. Pattullo writes in part:—Fifty years ago the first day of. October, 1870,. I assumed control of the Woodstock *Sentinel*—editorial and financial. My editorial experience theretofore was limited to nine months as editor of the Paris *Transcript*. Prior to that I had been local correspondent at Drumbo for the same paper. I was teaching at the time, and at the close of the year the proprietor proposed that I should become a journalist and assume the management of his paper. This was how I drifted into journalism.

It will be seen, therefore, that my editorial experience was extremely brief and ill fitted me to fill the position that I had assumed. It was not surprising therefore that Mr. Alexander McCleneghan, then editor of the Woodstock *Times*, and who was an old newspaper man and a graceful and skilled writer, should welcome the new aspirant rather coldly though truthfully with the comment that it boded ill for both business and journalism that the *Sentinel* should have fallen in hands so inexperienced.

The *Review* was prior to October first, 1870, published in Princeton. Its publishers were Messrs. Clarke and Gissing. It having been announced at the time that the *Sentinel* had changed hands, and would appear on October 1st under Mr. Pattullo's management, the proprietors of the *Review* thereupon, upon a week's notice, decided to remove to Woodstock and to appear the same day as its former rival. Hence it was removed somewhat hurriedly and without formal farewell. Nor could its manner of going be described as very dignified. It was brought in a farmer's wagon. . . . The *Review* was printed on a Washington press which needed little room. How I often wished afterwards that the *Sentinel*, which had a powered press, had only a Washington hand press.

In the Wider Field

In the wider field of Canadian newspapers were Mr. George Brown, of the *Globe*, and his brother, Gordon, and A. H. Dymond; Billie Maclean of the Toronto *World*; James Beattie and Charles Belfore, editor of the *Leader*. In London there were the Blackburn brothers of the *Free Press*, and the Cameron brothers of the *Advertiser*; the *Times* and *Spectator* of Hamilton —A. S. Tyner of the *Times* and Mr. Freed of the *Spectator* being very well-known at that time; John Ross Robertson of the Toronto *Telegram* and latterly, J. S. Willison of the *News*, and J. E. Atkinson of the *Star*; E. J. B. Pense of the Kingston *Whig* and the Shannons of the *News*; William Buckingham of the Stratford *Beacon*, afterwards well-known as private secretary to the Hon. Alexander McKenzie, premier of Canada; M. y. McLean of the Seaforth *Expositor*; Gardner of the Brantford *Expositor* and Hamilton *Times*; C. D. Barr of the Lindsay *Post*; James Innes of the Guelph *Mercury*; Sir MacKenzie Bowell of the Belleville *Intelligencer*, and also the editor of the Belleville *Ontario*; James Young of Galt *Reformer*; Hon. Thomas White, of the Montreal *Gazette*; Archibald Blue of the St. Thomas *Journal*, and Donly of the Simcoe *Reformer*, who was succeeded by his son who still has it.

Impressions After 50 Years

"What would you say are your chief impressions with reference to journalism, and especially to local journalism, for the past fifty years?"

That it has made a distinct advance, and has a firmer hold on its respective communities than formerly. That is, where the local newspaper has continued to recognize the value of local news and the important place that local news has in a newspaper. In a general sense, I doubt if many local newspapers exercise as great an influence as they once did. Where the personality of the editor is specially marked, he may continue to exercise a great influence, otherwise the influence of the paper is very largely controlled by the city press.

In my day such local papers as the Guelph *Mercury*, under the control of James Innes, M.P., the Seaforth *Expositor* controlled by the McLean Brothers, the Stratford *Beacon*, edited by William Buckingham, widely known as the private secretary of the Hon. Alexander MacKenzie, the St. Thomas *Journal*, edited by Archibald Blue, afterwards chief statistician at Toronto and Ottawa, the Lindsay *Post*, controlled by C. D. Barr, still registrar at Lindsay, the Brockville *Recorder*, in my day controlled by a very old newspaper man, the daddy of us all, affectionately called "Father Wyllie", and latterly by the Hon. George Graham; the Belleville *Intelligencer*, controlled by the Hon. MacKenzie Bowell, and the *Ontario*, also of Belleville, were the leaders as local newspapers in the province of Ontario.

Among the other journalists whom I knew, but who have long since passed away, are Nicholas Flood Davin, the always brilliant, but rather erratic Irishman and familiarly known as the poet of "The Pile of Bones" (Regina); Hon. William McDougell, one of the finest writers on early Canadian journalism, but who had practically done his work as a journalist before my day; T. C. Patteson, of the *Mail*, and a neighbor in the county of Oxford; Martin J. Griffin, the scholarly but bitter editor of the *Mail*; and poor Ned Farrer, the most brilliant and versatile journalist Canada ever had.

Imperial Press Delegates landing from the tug in which they were taken off the S.S. Victorian, at Sydney on July 27.

Of Course These Things Do Come

Barrie *Advance:*—The head type sticker on the staff of the *Advance*, Mr. W. A. Whitney, left on Saturday with his wife and family on a week's holiday in Trenton and Toronto. He must have taken down the horseshoe from the door of the sanctum, for he took all the good luck along with him. Shortly after his departure, our linotype operator, Walter Bayliss, nearly lost three fingers by getting them crushed in a Gordon press. Our troubles were not to stop here, and to make sure "the devil" was after us, the only paid one we keep on the staff —the "Printer's Devil"—fell out of an apple tree and sprained his ankle so that he too is laid off. To lose three out of a staff of five in two days make the going pretty tough. Fortunately we were able to secure an operator from Oshawa and Miss Finlayson is now assisting to turn out the parent newspaper of Simcoe County. Miss Finlayson is a daughter of the late Mr. Hugh Finlayson, who conducted the *Advance* a few years ago for Postmaster Crew. In the course of a few days we expect the boss printer to return with the missing horseshoe, and we anticipate that the business will return to normal conditions next week.

Some suggestions give a pretty fair idea of what the finished article is going to look like. Here is one that would be easy to sell to a prospect. It has "stationery" atmosphere all around it, and would convey at once to the non-printer just about what the finished article would look like. The arrangement of the illustrations and the placing of the display is well done.

A correspondent asked a few days ago for the correct setting-up of a wedding card. This form is used and is unquestionably correct in every way.

Bruce Brains Boss Globe

☛ Some person started this, and now it has gone the rounds of the Bruce Press:—

The reason why the *Globe* so easily maintains its position as "Canada's National Newspaper" is easily understood when one considers where it got a lot of its best editorial timber. Mr. William Houston, perhaps the oldest editorial writer on the *Globe*, who is also a Senator of Toronto University and an ex-chairman of Toronto Board of Education, comes from the good old County of Bruce, Greenock Tp., to be exact. Ross Munro the clever news editor, late of the Ottawa *Journal*, was born at Port Elgin, where he served as printer's devil in his late father's printing office. Ewart Munro, a younger brother, and a native of this county, is also a *Globe* writer. H. B. McKinnon, whose articles on agricultural topics are so largely read, comes from next door to Bruce, his father being the veteran postmaster at Priceville. So does Finlayson, another member of the editorial staff, who is a son of the manse at Durham. All these and perhaps others too, who have a part in making the *Globe* what it is, are sprung from the good old pioneer stock which has made Bruce County famous.

The Spanish River Pulp and Paper Co. advises that they are installing a new paper machine which will be active by January 1st, 1921, and will increase the output of their plant at Sturgeon Falls by fifty tons a day.

The British House of Lords is putting through a measure covering a very drastic control of proprietary medicines. As a very large proportion of these preparations are American owned, the measure will be of particular interest to American advertisers who have found the English market a particularly responsive one.

Here is a message on a blotter. It is real, compelling and will not be tossed aside without the people who should be interested having an opportunity to read the message. The blotter was turned out at the office of Croft & Wright, Toronto.

Many Uses for the Initial Letter
Changing Styles are Much in Evidence

HAVE you ever seen an initial letter that hopped up out of the page and hit you right square in the eye as soon as you opened at its resting place? Perhaps it is not well to speak of the resting place of such letters, because they don't rest at all. They do not look comfortable enough to rest. They appear to be looking for the first chance for the next paragraph to get out of the road to make way for their escape. The initial letter, if used carefully and made to conform to the text, is a great asset in display. Very often it will break up a monotonous piece of white space, carry the reader's eye to some spot well down in the job which might otherwise lose balance.

OT long ago I first met the manager and salesman of a certain Middle Western printing concern. We met at an advertising convention, in fact. Perhaps he felt it necessary to explain why he was there, though increasing numbers of printers are going more and more into the advertising end of the business, and the more progressive are becoming real advertising counselors. "You see, Ram-

FIG. A

FIGURE A.—Here, for instance, is one of the standard uses in the better class of U. S. publications. The first line hugs the edge of the cut about as closely as possible, while the remaining lines have a set in of about a turn. That phrase, by the way, seems to be passing out, but in many print rooms in the case days the en and em were known as Nancy and Mollie. The phrase to-day calls for the en a nut quad. One might be inclined to call for another card or so at the bottom of this letter, but it is well done as it stands.

HEIR only thought to the finest axles, Eator neers go about their with the devoted patience etcher at his masterpiece. Fabı

FIG. B

FIGURE B is from one of the publications which circulates largely in Canada, the *Saturday Evening Post*. It is typographically correct, the matter in which it appeared being wider of course than is shown here, although the type face is not reduced. It is highly ornate for advertising purposes, and it might be dangerous for some offices where less care is paid to detail, to allow the use of such letters.

In this case the initial letter works out well. The type comes up very close to the edge, but this is partly offset by the

ITH the possible exception of the Prince of Wales' tour through Canada last year, it is doubtful whether any trip ever undertaken in this country has been at all comparable with that recently completed by the delegates to the Imperial Press Conference. It was really an excursion de luxe, most complete in all its arrangements and so skilfully planned as to give the visitors the most thorough knowledge of the country to be obtained within the

FIG. C

amount of white space between the lines, and by the distance from the "W" in the fourth line to the bottom of the initial.

FIGURE C is one of those mortised affairs into which it is possible to place an initial letter of any sort. If fault were to be found with this one, it would be in the fact that the letter itself is rather playing second fiddle to the ornate style of the surroundings. Also in this it is difficult to bring the initial letter up near enough to the top, and there is a somewhat hard white space as margin around the inserted letter. The spacing around this letter has been well done. It is even side and bottom, and the adjustment in the first line is so nice as to be beyond criticism.

LISTEN to cars in traffic or on hi is knock, knock, knock. Cylind cause spark plugs are fouled. valves cause loss of power.

FIG. D

FIGURE D—You're a mighty pleasing thing to look at, and I'd like to grasp the hand of the man who put you together. It looks as though great care were taken in cutting you out so as to make the type conform to the peculiar shapes in your make-up. Used in the usual way a cap "L" makes an abomination as an initial. The rest of the word that the "L" starts is very often put over a couple of ems or so, depending on the length of the lower extending portion of the letter. As Figure D stands now it is a pleasing piece of work. There is nothing common about it. It is real composition that gives a comp. pride in his work.

IN the installation of conduit for electrical wiring, gas, water, steam or air pipes, in the erection and re-erection of motors, generators, machine tools, crane runways, shafting, etc., in the fitting of steel door frames, window

FIG. E

FIGURE E—We knew that sooner or later we'd come to you. Ever see a letter stuck in like this? Oh, yes you have. He looks like a jag that has leaned against a lamp post and slipped down at the feet. In this case the "I" cannot slip down any farther because he's standing on the top of the slug that has the "tion" on the start of it. He's a bird, isn't he? It looks as though this matter were set eight point on a nine point slug, which takes up 27 points of space, while the initial letter is from some 24 point case, so there's a lead and a half room for the "I" to hop around in there, and in this case he has sunk rather than scrambled his way to the top of the heap. Don't let your stuff get away from you like that. It doesn't require much fixing, and any effort is well repaid in the added "good looks" of the job.

LATE CONVENTION OF U. T.

THE thirty-third annual convention of the Typothetæ of America, held at the Hotel

QUALITY and speed distinguish the work of Abbey Printshop, East Orange, N. J., so n

FIG. F

FIGURE F is an example of a tendency that is becoming quite marked in many offices, that of running the initial about the line. There are sharp differences of opinion regarding this practice. One must be careful how these are used. In the top part of Fig. F. the effect is open to question, owing to the length of the top heading. There is no space for the letter to lead off into.

FIGURES G and H show two more uses of the initial running above and they are rather pleasing. Fig. G. is well arranged. The heading is a sufficient distance from the paragraph and

The situation today

THERE are several anxious buyers for every new Marmon 34 being built. And there is by no means an overage of renewed Marmon 34's. In fact, a renewed Marmon 34 is extremely

FIG. H

THE exclusive tone control device on the Vocalion—the Graduola—lends an entirely new interest to the phono-graph and one that appeals strongly to all music-lovers.
This device enables one to control

FIG. G

the starting "T," though small, has sufficient room in which to sprout. The rest of the word hugs in close to the base of the letter, and gives it a desirable compactness. Figure H has no heading above it, but it has room, and the effect is pleasing.

The average family, especially in he food destined to spoil before it is cons

All that costly waste is stopped when Electric Cold Maker.

Melting ice leaves dampness in its wa germs multiply, food spoils.

FIG. J

FIGURE J is unusual. The compositor who stuck that in there was not afraid to take a chance on it; may be that some careful ad writer called for it. At any rate, it is unusual. Some of the old printers might be inclined to shy a bit at such an innovation, but as it looked in the ad, a page affair, it was very attractive and quite in order. It is another tendency that shows how successfully the starting of paragraphs may be changed to take away the monotony of a flush start or a few ems indention.

W E are constantly urging the looking into details, for they success or failure to the job a point in question—the m the plate square on the bloc the object assumes an uprigl and agrees with the printed page. You m

A GAIN brought into direct antagonism postal authorities, printers general make themselves acquainted with which may lead to the closing present-day outlet of much busines We refer to the picture post card, and as sum the whole question are asked to quote from *Telegraph* a special note by Sir Adolph Tuck Tuck & Sons, Ltd.). In this he states :—

FIG. K

FIGURE K—These initials are from a printing journal in England, and show the difference between their schools and ours. I do not fancy that a Canadian printer would agree that

they were correct. He would probably say that for a letter of this size he would avoid using foundry type, but would prefer a square ornamental one, as both the W and A are hard letters to reconcile to the matter adjacent. There is also a lot of white at the bottom that would hardly pass for good practice in this country.

Owners will tell you first high expectations by the distinct differenc

FIG. I

FIGURE I was taken from a high class publication where the work is correct. The use of the initial "O" in this case may seem to add very little to the scheme. It is just one of those little touches that make material more readable and attractive.

Conference at Hugh C. MacLean Co.

A conference of the executives, editors and travellers of the Hugh C. MacLean Publications took place in Toronto during a recent week-end. The interest shown in this conference was keen; in fact, it may be regarded as a splendid example of the advantages of gatherings of this kind for the exchange of business ideas.

The President, Mr. Hugh C. MacLean, in his opening remarks referred to the necessity of raising the standard of the business and trade press. "Why," he asked, "is the publishing business not on as high a plane as any other business or profession?" His answer was that the publishers themselves were to blame, because they were too often willing to sacrifice the dignity of the press. They have been lacking in independence and have not commanded respect as they should have done.

Mr. T. S. Young presented interesting figures showing the growth of the Hugh C. MacLean publications, also a paper on advertising rates and cost of production. The figures were illuminating and left no room for doubt as to the absolute necessity of getting higher rates for advertising and subscriptions. Production costs had increased over 100 per cent. within five years, while the increase in advertising and subscription rates of the Hugh C. MacLean publications had not been more than thirty per cent.

Papers on salesmanship, presented by different members of the staff, brought out many valuable points. The necessity of a salesman knowing his clients' products was emphasized.

The editorial policy of the paper was fully discussed, each editor submitting an outline of his proposed plans. Here the keynote was service to the subscriber. "The Co-ordinative Aspect of Editorial Work and Advertising in Trade Journalism" was the title of a paper which contained much food for thought.

Mr. George G. Colvin, of Winnipeg, gave a talk on "Western Canada as an Industrial and Distributing Field," emphasizing the importance of lumbering, agriculture and mining. The distribution of goods was in a large measure in the hands of the general stores, which number approximately 5,000.

Mr. P. T. Carre, of Vancouver, in reviewing the opportunities for the advertiser in British Columbia, referred particularly to the great future for the lumber industry of that Province.

Those in attendance at the Conference included: Messrs. George G. Colvin, Winnipeg; P. T. Carre, Vancouver; G. W. N. Day and W. H. Hughes, Montreal; E. J. Macintyre and S. H. Simpson, Chicago; F. W. Mar, New York; F. D. Bowman, Boston; Hugh C. MacLean, T. S. Young, Dr. W. R. Carr, B. L. Smith, T. H. Garwood, G. B. VanBlaricom, L. R. Wright, J. P. Russell, F. W. Sherbarth, C. G. Brandt, J. L. Currie, A. R. Whittemore, Andrew MacLean, W. W. Ingram, J. R. Thompson, Thos. Turner, W. Staples and Wm. E. Millson, Toronto.

The Hugh C. MacLean Publications include the *Canada Lumberman, Electrical News, Contract Record, Canadian Wood-worker, Footwear, Western Lumberman, Western Canada Con-tractor, Western Canada Coal Review* and the *Commercial,* Winnipeg.

The Weekly Paper Has a Field All Its Own

And It Gets Close to Its Readers

By T. R. Elliott, London Free Press

"THE day of the weekly is done," writes the editor of a well-known Ontario newspaper, "and with the scarcity of help in the job department, I have decided to quit the business."

In confirmation of his statements it must be noted that several weeklies of long standing in Ontario have given up the ghost. We feel inclined to doubt, however, that the usefulness of the weekly is at an end. Competition of the city daily no doubt will prove too much for still more of the weeklies located within the compass of the city paper's influence, but in the more sparsely populated districts the weekly publication must continue for a while longer to be the advertising medium and the source of information for the people. There would still seem to be plenty of room for both dailies and weeklies in at least some parts of Canada.

Considerable pleasure is denied to the reader of the big city paper by reason of the fact that space and style do not permit the chronicling of city happenings after the manner of the "country correspondent." It is now only the rural weekly papers, serving a limited field, which can afford the luxury of having extensive budgets of small-town news and "personals." On the metropolitan daily the news must be culled and condensed, sorted and discarded, and a small percentage of the news available to the editor sees the light of day on the printed page. Picayune paragraphs, of interest to only a few, must give way to the big news of the day, even though it comes by cable from thousands of miles away.

There are still papers in Ontario, however, which concern themselves not one whit with international intrigue or world-shaking disasters, filling their columns with hundreds of paragraphs about visitors to town, or doings of the rural communities which the paper serves each week. There are many weekly papers in Ontario with circulation of about 2,000, ninety per cent. of which goes into the rural free delivery boxes each Thursday or Friday. These papers are read with an interest which is never bestowed on the city daily, because the rural reader gets his own locality which can never hope to find space elsewhere. It cannot be argued that these papers do not serve a distinctive field, or that what they print is not real news. The very existence of the weekly paper proves the one point, and the oft-noticed scene in a city street car the other—the busy city-dweller delving into the weekly paper from "home" while the evening edition of his favorite daily lies ignored in his pocket. If the truth were known, he would like to read the news of his own city chronicled in just the same style as the news from "Hickman's Corners" in the *Argus*.

But who are the "rural correspondents" of these weekly papers, and how do they write? If you are from the country or some small town, and the chances are even that you are, you know already. They are doctors and schoolgirls, ministers and farmers, blacksmiths and merchants. And their literary styles are as varied as their occupations. Only the blacksmith usually writes better than the doctor. What he lacks in literary ability he makes up in volume.

Incidentally the editor of the weekly paper has a harder task than the copy-reader of the metropolitan daily if he wants to have his paper right, and all editors do. The editor of the daily has the copy brought to his desk typewritten, comparatively free from error, legible, and couched in more or less correct English. A glance, a few dashes of the pencil, a moment's deep thought for a "catchy" head and the copy is ready for the linotype. Not so the weekly editor. The chances are the budget from some outlying community comes to him written in dim pencil on two sides of tissue-paper, or butcher-paper. Of two evils, he would rather have butcher paper. The copy is hard to read, is badly spelled, and is full of names without initials. That is why the editor, after going all down one sheet striking out whole lines, comes to the last paragraph and leaves it because he hates to throw away the

whole sheet, and so some item like the following appears in the budget:—

Will McGregor of the fourth line has bought a new car and is frequently seen driving down the Gravel Road. Ah! there, Will!

It is easier for the country editor if he happens to be the compositor, too. Then he does his editing and correcting as he sets the type and inconsequential matter is easily omitted. Sometimes, though, the mind will wander, and the editor himself is probably surprised to see in the printed edition such items as:—

Wedding bells are ringing on the fifteenth concession.
Hal Robinson's colt is still very low.
Four new arrivals at the parsonage. Pups.

To turn contributions into standard English would be a task for a dozen copy-readers, and so it is not done. There are some correspondents who feel it incumbent on them to write in high-flown language, even about the most trivial occurrence. It gets in the paper as it is written for the reason that there is no one to re-write it. And besides, there are some contributors who consider that their offerings must be used word for word. There is the case of the Millchester correspondent of a certain weekly, who set forth a distressing accident as follows:—

'Walter Martin, Esquire, is suffering ostensibly from injuries inflicted vigorously by a ferocious bovine. He was attacked obviously by the infuriated monster while in the act of ministering to its wants, and the said animal excoriated and lacerated him immensely with both pedal extremities. Dr. Jackson reduced a compound fracture of the rib, and he will be confined ostensibly to his humble couch for an extensive period."

Then there is the man who "gets by" with some free advertising of himself by deceiving the editor:—

A. H. Pease was in Somville last week.
Mrs. Smith is visiting at the Pease residence on Main street.
Arthur Herbert Pease is installing a new cistern.

When Mr. Watson of Martindale gets only a free copy of the paper for his weekly budgets, it is quite legitimate, I suppose, to put in a free "liner" for himself occasionally. At any rate you often see it:—

"The weather has been rainy all week. New stock of rubbers at Watson Brothers."

Most of the subscribers to the weekly papers take a daily paper or two as well, because they must keep in touch with "affairs" but they could not do without the "Review" or the "Argus" because they must have the neighborhood news, even if they know it all long before it is printed. And if the truth were known there are many urban dwellers who would not be averse to getting the gossip in the same way if it were possible for the daily papers to handle it. Can you imagine the neighbors reading:—

"Dick Smith of 1123 Fourteenth street is all smiles to-day. It's a boy."

Brighton *Ensign*:—"You're all right—I'm wrong—good-bye and God bless you." These words will appropriately express my sentiments at the ending of my 35 years of life in Brighton. I do not desire that anyone misunderstands me—never have. I am simply heart sick of the town, and wish it no harm. The prospects of business here are at present the best I have ever known in over 20 years in business, and I am confident that my successor can do well financially. All that is necessary is a fair amount of business ability. The town is prospering and will continue to prosper better than ever before.

———

Big Employer of Labor

Regina *Daily Post*:—With the taking over of the Regina *Daily Post*, the *Leader* Publishing Co., Ltd., becomes one of the argest industrial employers in the province of Saskatchewan, both as regards the number of employees engaged and the total of wages paid.

At the present time the *Leader* Publishing Co, Ltd., has on ts payroll 221 employees, which number does not include news-boys or others engaged in work for the company outside of the Leader Building. The weekly payroll of the Leader Co. is 17,922 or $411,944 a year.

With the recent signing up of a new wage scale with the Typographical Union, new scales plus the taking advance in wages paid negotiated with all four of the trades unions with which the Leader Co. has relations, the average advance in wages paid under the new scales being just under 30 per cent., which fact partly explains the greatly increased total of wages paid by the company, the average yearly wage of the *Leader's* 221 employees now being $1,864.

As was explained in the announcement of the taking over of the Regina *Daily Post* by the Leader Publishing Co., Ltd., the tremendous increase in wages was one of the determining actors that brought about the arrangement whereby the two Regina papers are now published by the Leader Co.

The Situation in Lindsay

Toronto *Globe*:—In Lindsay, Ont., there are at present four papers, two weeklies and two dailies. It is possible that these are too many for a town of 8,000, but they found it impossible to continue under present conditions. There has been no amalgamation, but after September 1 the weekly edition of the Lindsay *Post* and the daily edition of the *Warder* will be discontinued. This arrangement will leave in the field the *Evening Post* as a daily and the *Watchman-Warder* as a weekly.

In making the announcement the publishers of these papers give the following "partial list of towns and cities which now have but one paper instead of two, three, four, or more as formerly: Brantford, population 30,000; Brockville, population 11,000; Fort William, population 20,000; Galt, population 12,000; Niagara Falls, N.Y., population 60,000; Peterboro, population 30,000; Port Arthur, population 15,000; Port Huron, population 32,000; Sarnia, population 16,000; St. Catharines, population 20,000; St. Thomas, population 22,000; Windsor, population 40,000; Woodstock, population 11,000."

Speaks of the Paper Markets

C. W. Dearden, advertising manager of Strathmore Paper Co., was one of the speakers at the recent convention of the Association of National Advertisers. He spoke on "Paper-making and Marketing Conditions."

Some of the points brought out in the address follow:

"It is estimated that the paper production for 1920 will be 10 per cent. over 1919 and 29 per cent. over 1914.

"The demand for paper of all kinds and conditions is unprecedented in volume. Orders received by the group of writing paper mills, which include sulphite to the all-rag papers, were 142 per cent. of the normal product of these mills for the first three months of this year.

"Stocks in store at the paper merchants are way below normal. In fact they decreased 11 per cent. in the first three months of the year and are still going down.

"How long this demand will continue varies according to the optimism or pessimism of the men approached. Some say six months and others five years. The majority, however, seem to think that it will be about two years.

"It is easy for the buyer, not knowing actual conditions, to conclude that paper prices represent mostly profit. The same thing comes to me when I buy a pair of shoes and a suit of clothes. As a matter of fact, prices for paper do not represent any larger, and in some instances as large, a margin as before the avalanche came."

Oxford and District Organize

On Friday, October 8th, Oxford County and district publishers were organized into a district Press Association, as a branch of Canadian Weekly Newspapers Association. Mr. E. Roy Sayles, of Toronto, manager of the C.W.N.A., was present and after the organizing preliminaries led in the discussions on subscription rates, advertising and job work rates. Publishers present also exchanged ideas on editorial work. Mr. H. S. Johnston of the Tillsonburg *News* was elected president and Mr. J. S. Winterburn secretary-treasurer. It was decided that all those having one dollar subscription rates should raise to $1.50 at once, while a date would be set shortly for the $2 rate to come into effect. A committee consisting of the president, secretary, and Messrs. Wilson (Woodstock), Monteith, (Aylmer) and Rae (Woodstock) were appointed to issue a price list for job printing, using the Franklin list as a basis. The Franklin Price List was also recommended to the weekly publishers. A committee was also appointed to decide upon a uniform rate for advertising. The sessions were held in the reading room of the local armories, and began at 10.30 a.m. Those present were: M. Messecar, Burford *Advance*; W. J. Walker, Paris; W. J. Taylor, G. S. Wilson, B. Ray, Woodstock; Mr. Monteith, Aylmer *Express*; L. W. Appel, Tavistock *Gazette*; D. E. Ritz, L. W. Ritz, New Hamburg *Independent*; J. S. Winterburn, Norwich *Gazette*; N. A. Willoughby, Ingersoll *Chronicle*; Geo. Janes, Ingersoll *Tribune*; A. A. McKinnon, Embro.

A third morning newspaper, the *Journal of Commerce*, will appear October 11. It will be a business man's newspaper, published by Andrew L. Lawrence, now publisher of the *Journal of Commerce* of San Francisco. Glen Griswold, western manager of Dow, Jones & Co., and the Wall Street *Journal*, will be business managers.

Number of Words to the Square Inch in Solid Type, and Type Leaded with 2-point Leads.

Square Inches	5-Point Solid	5-Point Leaded	6-Point Solid	6-Point Leaded	8-Point Solid	8-Point Leaded	10-Point Solid	10-Point Leaded	12-Point Solid	12-Point Leaded
1	69	50	47	34	32	23	21	16	14	11
2	138	100	94	68	64	46	42	32	28	22
3	207	150	141	102	96	69	63	48	42	33
4	276	200	188	136	128	92	84	64	56	44
5	345	250	235	170	160	115	105	80	70	55
6	414	300	282	204	192	138	126	96	84	66
7	483	350	329	238	254	162	147	112	98	77
8	552	400	376	272	256	184	168	128	112	88
9	621	450	423	306	288	207	189	134	126	99
10	690	500	470	340	320	230	210	160	140	110
11	759	550	517	374	352	253	231	176	154	121
12	828	600	564	408	384	276	252	192	168	132
13	897	650	611	442	416	299	273	208	182	143
14	966	700	658	476	448	322	294	224	196	154
15	1,035	750	725	510	480	345	315	240	210	165
16	1,104	800	752	544	512	368	336	256	224	176
17	1,173	850	799	578	544	391	357	272	238	187
18	1,242	900	846	612	576	414	378	288	252	198
19	1,311	950	893	646	608	437	399	304	266	209
20	1,380	1,000	940	680	640	460	420	320	280	220

THE OTHER PUBLISHERS' BUSINESS

 Special Advertising, Circulation and
Editorial Plans

The Tottenham *Sentinel* has increased its rate to $2 per year.

The Clinton *News-Record* is now charging $2 per year for its paper.

After October 1st, the Roland, Man., *News* will be $2.00 per year.

The Port Hope *Weekly Guide* has increased its price to $2.00 per year.

Barrie *Examiner* announces that it is now charging $2.00 a year for its paper.

The *World-Spectator* of Moosomin, Sask., on October 1, went to $2, per year.

The Provost, Alta., *News*, announces that on November 1, its price goes to $2 per year.

The *Morning Albertan*, Calgary, has a subscription contest on at present on a rather elaborate scale. Cars, visits to movie camps, etc., are among the prizes offered.

The Porte Publishing Company is conducting a vigorous campaign to place its Franklin Printing Price List in the New England States. A thorough canvass is now taking place.

The Autumn issue of *Canadaink*, published by the Canada Ptg. Ink Co., Limited, Toronto, is one of the most pleasing and effectingly arranged house organs noted for some time.

The Roland, Man., *News* went to $2.00 per year on October 1st. In justification it advertised that July, 1914, saw newsprint 3c per pound, while July, 1920, witnessed this commodity at 13c per pound.

The Fort William *Bulletin* is having a circulation contest in which an automobile, piano, etc., are given as prizes. There is also a guessing contest being run at the same time in which subscribers to the paper can participate.

It is announced by Frank A. Munsey, in the New York *Sun Herald*, that beginning with October 1st, the name of that amalgamated paper will be changed to the New York *Herald*, and the *Evening Sun*, will become simply the *Sun*.

The Winnipeg *Free Press* announces an increase in its morning rates to 25 cents per week delivered by carrier boys. The *Free Press* follows the policy of selling its papers to the carrier boys who in turn do the collecting. This is done every two weeks.

Notice is being sent out by the Collingwood *Bulletin*, and also by the *Saturday News* of the same place, that commencing October 1st the price of these papers will be $2.00. Additional charges are made for postage to U.S. and foreign countries, and only one year's subscription is taken at these prices.

The Owen Sound *Sun-Times* and the Oshawa *Reformer*, both of which have changed from twice to three times per week, have combined for the purpose of advertising in some of the larger papers. The idea is to reach the national advertiser and the point they want to make is that they should be included on the daily list.

The *Family Herald and Weekly Star* of Montreal has issued a new rate card. For general advertising there is a flat rate of fifty cents per agate line, with extra charges for preferred and special positions. Reading notices are charged at $1.00 per agate line. The paper claims that on the 30th of June it had a circulation of 156,385.

The *Weekly Courier*, of Riverhurst. Sask., is out with a new rate card. Its display contracts are from fifty cents to twenty cents per inch, depending upon the amount of space contracted for; transient advertising, fifty cents first insertion and twenty-

five subsequent; local readers ten cents per count line with a minimum of five lines; government or legal advertising 12 and 8 cents per line.

Calgary *Albertan*:—The collapse of *Turner's Weekly*, one of the ablest periodicals in all Canada, published in Saskatoon, is much to be regretted. The editor, a returned man, badly wounded in the war, also a member of the legislature, is a bright, able, fearless man, and his paper was one of the best edited papers of comment in all Canada.

At the meeting of the Washington State Press Association, held at Yakima, Washington, on Friday, August 13th, use of the Franklin Printing Price List was unanimously endorsed, and a campaign to effect organization in the various localities of the state begun, the Porte Publishing Company to give its active assistance in effecting it.

The Porte Publishing Company of Salt Lake City, Utah, publishers of the Franklin Printing Price List, are at the present time sending out to over seven thousand users of the Price List calls for information on cost records, production costs, together with plant and labor statistics. It is from the reports gotten from members that a large portion of information appearing in the Price List is obtained.

Collingwood *Bulletin*:—The current issue of *Printer and Publisher* is of general interest. It gives a very complete and interesting report of the visit of the Imperial Press to Canada, recording as it does many sides of this Empire party and its gatherings in the Dominion. Not only is it of special value to newspaperdom, but it has no small interest for the public generally. The editor is to be congratulated on his good work.

A branch office has been established at Toronto, Canada, by the Porte Publishing Company of Salt Lake City, Utah, publishers of the Franklin Printing Price List. Mr. S. H. Moore of the Moore Type Founders' Company, is manager of the Toronto branch and is making great headway in getting Canadian printers to adopt the Franklin Printing Price List, there being several hundred of them already under the Franklin banner.

A superstitious New Orleans man wrote an editor saying that he'd found a spider in his paper and asking whether that was a sign of good or bad luck. The editor replied, "Finding a spider in your paper was neither good nor bad luck for you. The spider was merely looking over the paper to see which merchant is not advertising, so that he can go to that store, spin his web across the door and lead a life of undisturbed peace ever afterward."

Renfrew *Mercury*:—The September issue of *Printer and Publisher* is one of the best that has ever been turned out. It consists of over 100 pages and contains, besides a special report of the Imperial Press Conference, about 50 pages of advertisements, every one of which is of interest to the printer and publisher. Editor Kennedy is keeping P. & P. up to a high standard, and making it more popular than ever with the newspaper men of Canada.

The Montreal *Daily Star* has issued a new rate card dated October 1st which becomes effective January 1st, 1921. The transient-run-of-paper advertising is from nineteen cents for 500 lines down to 14 cents for 20,000 lines, agate being the measure used. Classified advertising runs as follows in display: amusements, 25c per agate line, annual reports of banks and companies 50c; churches 12½c; circuses and tent shows, 40c; In the classified undisplayed such as "Board", "Found," "Rooms to Let," etc., two cents per word with a minimum charge of 30c and nothing under this item can be charged. The circulation of the *Star* according to the last statement is 104,736.

The Fred W. Halls Paper Co., Toronto, now occupy one of largest and best equipped premises devoted to the paper industry in Canada. They have moved to 257-261 Adelaide St., W., a situation that places them in the heart of the printing trade in Toronto. The new premises have been remodelled especially to fit the requirements of the paper trade. Fire protection is afforded through a sprinkler system. Special shipping facilities are also in the new premises to make it possible to get all orders out promptly.

The Richmond Hill *Liberal* had a pro-tem. editor, while the editor took a holiday. In explaining the situation the pro-tem. man used this:—"The writer will studiously eschew political questions, abstruse generalities; will avoid acrimonious personalities and all acrid and caustic remarks, so that friend McMahon will not be confronted with any libel suits on his return to the editorial chair. In chronicling the week's events we shall endeavor to adhere as closely to the truth as our reputation for veracity will allow." For the average man it would be much easier to say, "There will be no paper next week."

The Owen Sound *Sun-Times* is now being issued every Tuesday, Thursday and Saturday, and it looks as though this move were going to work out very well. In making the announcement of this change the Owen Sound paper says that "When the time is ripe for the publication of a daily edition in Owen Sound the *Sun-Times* will not shirk the responsibility, and as a matter of fact the plant of the newspaper is already equipped for such an undertaking." Some thirty years ago the *Sun* was established as a three times a week paper but it soon found that this was in advance of the town's requirements. For the present the *Sun-Times* is being sold at the same price of $2.00 a year, but it is announced that this price may soon have to give way to something higher.

The price of the Montreal *Gazette* having been advanced to five cents per copy and $12 per annum, that journal prints the following table showing some of its increased production costs since 1914, taking 100 as a unit.

	1914	1920	*Increase*
Wages.	100	180	80%
Paper.	100	300	200%
Other supplies.	100	200	100%
Delivery.	100	400	300%

Making an average percentage increase of 170% in the last six years. The new price to subscribers represents an advance of about one-third of the increased cost of publication.

The Kingston *Daily Standard* on September 23rd issued a special extra edition, 14 pages of which were given over to a Fair Refund Edition filled with advertising of the leading merchants of the city who had co-operated with the *Standard* in this Fair Refund proposition. One merchant alone took three full pages and the result was that during the week of the sale, from September 27th up to and including October 3rd, the Kingston merchants were unusually active and report one of the busiest weeks in their entire business careers. This Fair Refund Edition of the *Standard* has come now to be a semi-annual feature run by it exclusively in Kingston in co-operation with all the merchants and it has proven a decided business getter. Typographically and in mechanical arrangements this last issue of the *Standard* was an excellent one, the entire edition being run off on the *Standard's* 28 page Goss press.

The Oshawa *Reformer* is off to a good start with its every other day issue. The management of the paper is of the opinion that there can be no doubt as to the success of the venture, in fact they claim that they will be much better off than most small city dailies have been for the past few years. The first week of publication, the paper ran eight pages on Tuesday, sixteen on Thursday and twelve on Saturday. All of these issues are strictly local with the exception of a few features that are being introduced. The *Reformer* is charging three dollars a year and they intimate that this price may be increased to $4.00 for delivery by carrier on January 1st. They are also charging $1.50 a year extra for postage to U.S., apparently figuring that if the U.S. subscriber really wants the paper he will pay the additional postage.

A number of daily papers and some of the larger weekly ones as well are getting considerable business in the way of advertising supplies for hunters and campers who will soon be going

to the woods in the north, for the deer and duck season. Some of the pages carry a well written story or two in connection with experiences of campers, or advice from men who have spent a good many years in the bush. There is apparently no good reason why a reporter on almost any paper could not get out and secure the necessary stories to build up a page on this business. The firms that are using advertising space are quite varied and include hardware stores, sporting goods houses, boot and shoe stores that specialize in foot-wear for hunters, grocery stores that put up packages of canned goods and other necessary equipment. In some of the papers the drug stores have been brought in as well, their ads pointing out the necessity of carrying a few well-known lines of curealls, while the cigar and tobacco stores are also called upon to put their business before hunters.

A British Columbia Guide Book

The Sun Publishing Company, Ltd. Vancouver, B.C. have published a complete guide to the Province of British Columbia combined with a faithful record of conditions at the beginning of the year 1920. This year book is abundantly illustrated and contains a wealth of information about the staple industries of the Province, combined with much useful statistical information and comparative statements of the cost of living, covering the months June, 1919, and 1920. A synopsis of the contents are translated into the following languages:—French, Russian, Japanese, Spanish, Italian, Chinese.

Operators Accept Award

A strike vote taken by the Canadian Press, Ltd., telegraph operators resulted in authority being given to the representatives of the men to conclude a wage agreement. The board had recommended a flat increase of $5 a week to every operator in the service, which gave bureau operators $50 for day work and $51 for night; line operators in the Maritime division $42 for day and $42 for night; Ontario division men $45 and $46, and Western division men $46 and $47. This was rejected by the men, who stood by their first demands. The operators throughout the Ontario system will therefore get $45 per week for day and $46 for night service, with $5 extra for bureau men.

Who Wins Out Here?

The following has appeared in several weekly papers and one just wonders which party, the press or the tea company is getting the most advertising out of the notice:—"The Salada Tea Company, writing to the Owen Sound *Sun-Times*, gives an unqualified testimonial in favor of newspaper advertising, in preference to any other advertising medium. The company says: "The Salada Tea company never fails to give full credit to the daily and weekly press of Canada. For thirty years we have been consistent advertisers, and although we have tried practically every recognized advertising medium we have proved to our entire satisfaction that the newspaper gives by far the best results. The ever-increasing volume of our trade has resulted in the purchase of a new building in Montreal."

The Name "Gazette"

Toronto *Star*:—In Canada, as abroad, the name Gazette was the early favorite in the journalistic world, so much so that the first nine newspapers published in this country bore that name. They were: Halifax *Gazette*, 1752; Quebec *Gazette*, 1764; Nova Scotia *Gazette*, 1766; *Gazette Litteraire*, Montreal, 1778; St. John *Gazette*, 1783; Royal *Gazette* and New Brunswick *Advertiser*, 1784; Montreal *Gazette*, 1785; *Royal Gazette* (Charlotte-town), 1791; Upper *Canada Gazette*, (Newark), 1793. The first daily newspaper in Canada was the Montreal *Advertiser*, 1833. There is record of a *Royal Standard* published daily at Toronto in 1836, and the Kingston *Whig*, still flourishing, was a daily in 1849, in which year a *Daily Telegraph* had a short and unexciting career in Toronto. It is not generally known that the *Christian Guardian* is the oldest publication in Toronto, dating from 1828.

Handbook of Canadian Paper Industry

A most useful handbook on the Pulp and Paper Industry has been issued by the Canadian Pulp and Paper Association covering the trade from 1915 to 1919 inclusive. The main statistics for this report were collected and compiled during 1919 as for the calendar year 1918. There is a clear definition of the entire field covered by the trade, particular attention being paid to the growth of the export business during recent years. In all the handbook is most useful to those interested in the pulp and paper situation, there being a wealth of statistical information, and also a précis history of all the chief mills in the country.

Paper Situation and Job Printers

The paper market at the present time seems to show no change, being still universally tight. All mills are working to capacity and are booked ahead to the end of the year and further at prices prevailing at time of delivery. It is stated by an authority that there is small likelihood of there being any further advance in the price of higher grades of paper for some time.

European enquiries for paper are frequent, there apparently being very little manufactured in Sweden, France or Italy, but domestic bookings are so heavy that it is impossible to accept orders. Strenuous efforts are being made in England to adapt peat to the manufacture of paper but nothing can be definitely stated as to progress made. There are persistent rumors of a large merger in the pulp and paper interest in Quebec and it is noticeable the number of English interests who are devoting considerable attention to the securing of limits there.

Forty Years of Markdale Standard

The Markdale Standard took its annual holiday, missing the issue of August 25th. In its previous issue the Standard speaks of its forty years as follows:—

"The Standard takes its annual holiday next week; consequently this issue completes August, and ends the 40th volume. A book might be written, made up of interesting incidents and experiences covering those forty years, but ink is too expensive to thus squander it. We heartily thank all our patrons for more or less generous support, and especially would remember appreciatively our staff of correspondents for loyalty and excellent service all those years. Of the 16 publishers in Grey County forty years ago, C. W. Rutledge, of the Markdale Standard, is the only one now in business, and for aught we know he will also be gone before another 40 years passes."

Ink from Natural Gas

The entire printing industry is largely dependent upon natural gas for its supplies of ink.

Carbon black, obtained by burning natural gas, is the best color base for printing inks, carbon paper and black typewriter ribbons. It is also in great demand for the highest grade of phonographic records and automobile tires.

One pound of carbon black and eight pounds of mineral oil make the ink required for 2,250 sixteen page newspapers.

It is said that the addition of carbon black to rubber increases its tensile strength by from four to twenty-six per cent., depending upon the amount used. It is also is credited with giving tires greater resiliency.

Direct Appeal to Consumer

The September issue of the System contains one-third page follow-up advertisement by the Porte Publishing Company, on the potency of the Franklin Printing Price List in stabilizing the operations of its users—Franklin Printers—throughout the continent, and appealing to printing buyers to seek the Franklin Printer to do his printing. Such splendid results were obtained through the full page advertisement, used by the Porte Publishing Co., that it was decided to use this publication with frequency. The business of this concern is rapidly increasing, and the Franklin Printing Price List is attaining tremendous popularity. Hundreds of printers are adopting the Price List

each month. From every section of the country, organizations report the unanimous adoption of the Price List. In fact each weekly issue of the Business Printer contains resolutions passed by them for its adoption.

The Letter Writer Still Lives

Montreal Star:— Newspapers are continually being bothered with people suffering from various forms of dementia. For the last six months the Star has been pestered with one who has developed a novel form.

The person in question is a woman who seems to have an uncanny faculty at securing other people's stationery, especially if it happens to be monogrammed. Having secured a note sheet she immediately indites a note to the society editor of the Star giving some information usually with regards to a well known person. The woman seems to travel a lot for the "notes" come from points many miles distant.

The fact that none of her communications ever appear does not seem to daunt her, so the Star is endeavoring to find out in other ways who she is to explain to her that is a serious offence against the laws of Canada to sign other peoples' names to letters.

Turner's Weekly Suspends

The passing is announced of one of the brightest and most cleverly edited weekly periodicals in Canada. Turner's Weekly, of which Harris Turner, a blinded soldier, and formerly a member of the Princess Pats, was editor. Turner's has been driven out of existence by the rapidly increasing price of everything that enters into the publication of a newspaper. In one of his characteristic sermons to subscribers, "the last time I shall address you from the pulpit," as Mr. Turner puts it, the editor of the Weekly explains that: "The trouble has arisen over the parish magazine which I attempted to publish since the commencement of my pastorate. It has, unfortunately, been unable to compete longer with the cost of paper and the cost of ink and the cost of printers and the cost of printing machinery. In the space of two years it has passed a strenuous childhood, survived an exciting youth, blossomed into sturdy manhood, attained decrepit old age, and is now at the point of death. This is its last gasp. I pause to let those sob who take such things that way."

Western Weekly's New Card

The Grandview Exponent, with a circulation of 684, has the following rate card out now:—

Local readers, 12c per line each insertion.
Classified advts., 10c per line each insertion.
Legal and municipal advts., first insertion 12c per line; each subsequent insertion 10c per line; measured as per body type of advt.

Yearly contracts, per inch, per issue...........20c
Six months, per inch, per issue................25c
Three months, per inch, per issue.............30c
One month, per inch, per issue................25c
One week, per inch, per issue.................50c

Irregular insertions, or irregular sized advts., 15 per cent. additional. Foreign orders, cash in advance. Discount of 25 per cent. to advertising agencies recognized by Canadian Press Association. Orders and correspondence solicited, but no reduction in these printed rates will be considered.

Keeping Breaks Out of the Web

The Standard Steam Vaporizer has been placed on the market and its purpose can best be described by the following from the Houston, (Texas) Chronicle:—Mr. J. B. Collins has received letters patent on an invention that has been tried very successfully in the Houston Chronicle's press room and which is designed to be of especial aid to newspapers during the present scarcity of white paper. It is known as the Standard Steam Vaporizer, an apparatus for application to printing presses, and is to prevent the sheet of paper which goes rushing round the press cylinder from breaking or snapping while the big presses are revolving at the rate of anywhere from 20,000 to 50,000 printed papers per hour. When a big roll of paper starts revolving and the thin sheet flies forth, any break in what is known as the web means a delay of anywhere from two to, ten minutes, causing the destruction of several pounds of paper and is a general loss and nuisance to a daily newspaper office. The foreman of the *Chronicle's* press room concluded that if he could secure something that would throw a constant stream of vapor on the dry sheets as they revolved there would be little or no danger of the web snapping in two. Mr. Collins evolved an apparatus which he successfully applied to the *Chronicle's* two Goss octuple presses and as a result there is less waste and less delay in the Chronicle's press room to-day than ever before in its history.

Linking Up With the Past

THE Norwood *Register* is running a very interesting department under the caption of "My Norwood—Jottings from Memory, by T.M.G." The writer is apparently well known in the district because he goes back many years in a most interesting way, mentioning names of the boys and girls that lived in the town when all of the present generation of grown-ups were boys and girls. The publishers of the paper are certain, from the comment they have already heard about the material, that it is being read and appreciated.

For instance "do you remember" Walter Newell who used to live with his mother in the house between Mr. Pengelly's and Mr. McMullen's on King Street? was his name Walter? I'm not sure.

Do you remember Rhoda Boswell from Trent Bridge who lived with the Pagets? Of course you do! Rhoda was a daisy. But I'm not sure I didn't call her Miss Boswell in those days.

Then there was a Beavis family lived almost next to Mr. Squires—there was a boy—was his name Harold?

To the man who knows nothing about Norwood that would be passed over. Every town had its Walter or its Rhoda. But to the boy who knew Norwood years ago, that becomes real news.

Newspapers are slow to see the point that this paper has tried several times to make. It is this, there is a big field to which you can appeal for subscriptions beyond those living in your town and district. We know of one man who went and got the registers of the old school house and covered several years. He set about then to make inquiries as to where these boys and girls were. He found out a goodly number of them. He made a special effort to give them something that would interest them in the way of a dozen paragraphs of what was happening at the time when they were the young people of the town. He sent a form letter and a sample copy of the paper. He landed almost every one he went after. He followed this up with requests for letters now and then particularly when they were sending in their yearly subscription, telling of things that had happened in the old town, and he got real copy. There is a failing, and it's human and common to us all, to read of those things that happened years ago especially if we come from a village or a town where the community feeling has a chance to develop to the limit.

The Wiarton Echo's New Rate

The Wiarton *Canadian Echo* has issued a new rate card, based on a circulation of 2,000. Its foreign card shows the following:—

Display Contracts—Plate Matter.—Position—Alongside reading matter; space to be used at option of advertiser within one year; nonpareil measurement, 12 lines to inch. Any preferred position charged at preferred position rates.

One inch and over	50 cents per inch
10 inches and over	35 cents per inch
50 inches and over	25 cents per inch
100 inches and over	20 cents per inch
200 inches and over	18 cents per inch

Composition—Display matter requiring to be set, 10 cts. per inch, per insertion, additional on plate matter rates.

Preferred and Special Positions—Such as top of column and alongside, or alongside and following reading matter, or island position, from 25% to 33⅓% additional.

Special Advertising—Annual statements of banks and other financial corporations, whether having ordinary contracts or not, 40 cents per inch.

Political and election advertising, 40 cents per inch. This card, for the purpose of agency or national advertisers' use, should speak in lines rather than inches. The large advertiser is used to dealing in lines, rather than inches, and papers would be well advised to have regard to this when preparing their rate cards—*Ed. P. & P.*

The *Echo* is getting a fair rate for local business. Transient rates are:— 1 to 10 inches 50c inch; 11 to 25 40c; 26 to 50, 35c; 51 to 100, 30c; 101 to 150, 25c; 151 and over 18c per inch. Its other rates in detail are:—

Reading Notices—Entertainment—4 cents per word per insertion with a minimum charge of $1.00

Reading Notices — Entertainment or Meeting — for which there is no admission fee, 3 cents per word per insertion with a minimum charge of 75 cents.

Reading Notices—Such as Lost, Found, Maid Wanted, or Business Locals for regular advertisers, 2 cents per word with a minimum charge of 35 cents.

Legal and Government Notices—12 cents per line first insertion and 6 cents per line each subsequent insertion, nonpareil measurement; if set in 8 point, 8 cents per line 1st insertion, 4 cents per line each subsequent insertion.

Animals for Sale or Astray—$1.00 per inch first insertion, 50 cents per inch each subsequent insertion.

Government, Railway or Corporation Advertising—Display, 40 cents per inch per insertion; Reading Notices, 15 cents per line.

Property For Sale or Rent—$1.00 per inch first insertion 50 cents per inch each subsequent insertion.

Card of Thanks—2 cents per word, minimum charge of 75 cents.

Help Wanted—Male—4 cents per word per insertion, minimum charge of $1.00.

Political Advertising—Display, 40 cents per inch; Reading Notices, 15 cents per line.

Reports of Financial Institutions—Display, 35 cents per inch; Reading Notices, 15 cents per line.

Auction Sale Advertising—Set in body type of paper, 60 cents per inch, 1st insertion; 40 cents per inch, 2nd insertion; 25 cents per inch, 3rd insertion, with a minimum charge of $6.00 for two insertions of any sale.

Professional Cards—Not exceeding 1 inch will be inserted for $6.00 per year.

Tax Sale Advertising—Running 13 weeks—under 50 lots, 35 cents per inch each insertion; under 75 lots, 30 cents per inch each insertion; over 75 lots, 25 cents per inch each insertion.

Firms That Are Asking For Trade Openings With Canada

Information can be obtained by firms interested in the following lines, by communicating with this paper and mentioning key number.

2006—Pulp Boards—Irish merchant states that he is in a position to use large quantities of these if he can obtain them.

2008—Plywood—Canadian producers who are in a position to supply present at present time in Ireland can be placed in touch with firm in Belfast, who can handle large quantities.

2012—Kraft Paper—Irish merchant would like to hear from exporters of kraft paper.

2013—Newsprint.—Belfast merchant wants quotations from any Canadian company in a position to export whether now or in the near future.

2016—Paper of all Kinds—Wholesale and export manufacturing stationers desire to get into touch with producers; they hitherto have bought large quantities through London agents.

2015—Newsprint.—Irish importers state that they are in a position to handle large quantities of Canadian newsprint.

2018—Paper—The New Zealand Government Printing and Stationery Office require from 50 to 100 tons of M. F. printing paper. Sample of paper may be obtained from Commercial Intelligence Branch, Department of Trade and Commerce, Ottawa. They desire to know by cable how soon shipment can be expected, paper is to be standard weight; size will be stated when quotation is cabled.

THE PERSONAL SIDE OF IT

 We'd Like To Get Items For
These Columns

On October 23rd, Charles Christopher Jenkins quits his post as managing editor for the *Daily Times-Journal*, Fort William, Ontario, to join the staff of the MacLean Publishing Company, of Toronto. It is understood he has been engaged as a feature writer for *MacLean's Magazine*, to which he has been a contributor in the past. Mrs. Jenkins, who is also a writer, and their four children, will accompany him to Toronto.

Charles Christopher Jenkins was born in Hamilton, Ontario, of three generations of Canuck stock, and is a type as picturesque as some of the adventurous characters he has depicted in magazine short stories. His

CHARLES C. JENKINS

career as a journalistic soldier of fortune began about twenty years ago when he was eighteen years of age. Since then his wanderings have laced Canada from coast to coast and into the hinterlands of the north as far as canoe and pack trail would take him. His ruling passion has been to study the peoples and topography of his native country, and he is perhaps as well known among fur-traders and wandering tribes of the northwest as he is in marine circles on the great lakes or on the streets of Saskatoon, Winnipeg, Fort William, Windsor, Toronto and Montreal. Incidental to holding down posts as reporter, city editor and managing editor of well known dailies in eastern, western and central Canada, he spent one colorful year in 1911-12 writing motion picture scenarios for the Lubin Manufacturing Company, Philadelphia, and has had fiction and special feature articles published in *Munsey* publications, Boston *Evening Transcript*, *Motor Boat* (New York), *Yachting*, *Rod and Gun in Canada*, *MacLean's Magazine*, *Canadian Courier*, *Saucy Stories* and was a contributor to *Canada Monthly*, the *Century Magazine* and the *Trail Magazine* in their day. He has also written publicity booklets in story form. In Edward J. O'Brien's "Best Short Stories of the Year and Yearbook of the American Short Story," for 1918, three of Charles Christopher Jenkins' literary productions appear with stars from the well known critic attached, one story, "On the Wire," published in the Boston *Evening Transcript*, July 10, 1918, gaining the double star for exceptional strength and artistry.

It is understood that Mr. Jenkins will be succeeded on the *Times-Journal* by his associate for some years past, John R. Lumby, and that a new city editor will be appointed in the stead of Mr. Lumby.

Maritime

Frank Desmond, formerly of the Sydney *Post*, is now on the ad-side of the Halifax *Evening Mail*.

It is understood that the Truro *News* are now estimating their printing prices with the Franklin Price List as a basis.

A new wage scale has been signed up at New Glasgow with the able assistance of Organizer Drury. A twenty per cent increase has been granted.

The *Citizen*, the official organ of Labor in Halifax, is being placed on the co-operative basis, with shares selling at $12 each. It is the object of the present proprietors to have the workers own their paper and make it a province-wide newspaper.

Business throughout the Maritimes is very brisk at present, owing to the printing of the various voters' lists, which are being prepared for the referendum on the importation of liquor, to be taken Oct. 25th.

Mr. William MacNamara, formerly of the advertising department the *Morning Chronicle* and the *Evening Echo*, Halifax, has joined the Edwards Advertising Service. . Mr. MacNamara will have charge of the service department.

ᵉ The big Carnival Week held in Halifax from Oct. 4th to Oct. 9th was a decided success, and had many novel events. The greater part of the credit for this big event is due to the progressiveness of the Halifax *Herald* and *Evening Mail*.

James Drury, Canadian representative of the International Typographical Union, called at Halifax on his return from a ten days' stay in St. Johns, Newfoundland, where he was straightening out some difference in connection with the Typographical Union.

Miss Anne Merrill, who after returning from war work overseas, took over the women's page on the *Mail and Empire*, is turning out an interesting Saturday feature. The heading on the page, "For the Average Woman—and an Occasional Man," has a touch of something akin to anticipation that an occasional man might invade a woman's page in a newspaper. Apparently this is just what is happening for there are occasional—yes, quite frequent—letters from the sterner sex. The matter in the page is well selected, and the subjects treated are human and wholesome, while Miss Merrill's own material runs along in an entertaining and racy style.

Alberta

Circulation managers of western newspapers were in session in a two-day convention at Calgary. Delegates from all the western cities were present. Important topics relating to circulation building were discussed. Discussions centered round topics introduced by J. C. Thompson, *Morning Albertan*, who spoke on the question of "City Delivery"; by E. R. Folk, Regina *Leader*, on "Subscription Rates, City and Country"; by J. F. Sweeny, *Free Press*, Winnipeg, on "Collecting from City Subscribers"; J. A. McNeill, *Edmonton Bulletin*, whose topic was "Country Collection Methods" and J. K. Falconer, Vancouver *Sun*, who spoke on "Voting Contests." A banquet was held which was presided over by J. H. Woods, Calgary. Other speakers were H. W. Whitworth, Winnipeg *Tribune*; H. E. Fuller, Edmonton *Journal*; F. E. Henderson, Vancouver *Province*; W. E. Hamilton, *Western Home Monthly*, Winnipeg; W. H. Henderson, Moose Jaw *News*, and A. J. Hillker, Calgary *Herald*.

Saskatchewan

B. W. Nyson, of the Montreal *Star*, has been appointed editor of the *Export Journal of Canada*.

Netherhill is the newest town in Saskatchewan to have a paper, which has been brought out under the name of the *Optimist*. R. H. Heron is named as the proprietor and in the next line it states that O. R. Baxter is the editor, reporter, advertising and circulation manager, and printers' devil of this issue.

The executive of the Saskatchewan Press Association will take charge of the publicity side of a campaign that is being carried on in that province to raise three and a half million dollars. The purpose of the sale is to raise money for farm loans, and under the policy the more wealthy residents of the province will be asked to invest their savings for the benefit of the less well to do.

Mr. S. Oddsson, manager of the Wynyard, Sask., *Advance* had to take some rather drastic action lately in order to clear up his subscription list. There were a number of subscribers who were in arrears for some years. After other methods had failed he sued thirty-five of these dead-beats and was successful in collecting in every case. The accounts ranged all the way from six to ten dollars. Mr. Oddsson says that it is his intention to have the cleanest subscription list in the country. He also claims that they ran out of writs or they would have sued more of the delinquent subscribers.

Saskatchewan newspaper men from Young, Govan, Strasburg, Imperial, Simpson, and Viscount, gathered at Watrous last week, and together with the proprietor of the Watrous *Signal*, formed themselves into an organization under the name of the "Central Saskatchewan Newspaper Association." Hon. Sam Latta was elected Honorary President; E. Garret, of Watrous, president and C. Needham, of Simpson, secretary-treasurer. In reporting the organization meeting, the Watrous *Signal* said in part: "After an inexhaustive survey of present conditions and the intimations of still higher prices from the wholesalers, it was deemed expedient to put into effect at once a new scale of minimum advertising rates as follows: Yearly contract space, local display, per inch per issue, 30 cents; half-yearly 35 cents; less than half-yearly, 50 cents per inch, per insertion. General transient, 1 inch and under, 75c; each subsequent issue, 50c. Local readers, 15 cents per line per issue.

Manitoba

The Hudson Bay Company is issuing a paper called the *Beaver*, as a house organ. Some 5,000 copies are to be printed.

H. F. Weld was elected recently as vice-president and a director of the *Farmer's Advocate*, Winnipeg. He was with the *Farmer's Advocate*, London, from 1908 to 1915, at which time he became associated with the Winnipeg *Farmer's Advocate* in the capacity of advertising manager.

A board of arbitration settled the wages for job printers in Winnipeg. The men are to receive $44 a week for day work and $47 for night work. This is an advance of $9 a week over the old schedule and reverts to June 1. The 44-hour week is retained. Recently the newspaper compositors and the managements decided on a scale of $45 for day men and $48 for night men.

Alex. Stewart, one of the best known figures in the agricultural life of Western Canada, died at Winnipeg. He was live stock editor of the *Grain Growers' Guide* of late years. Mrs. Stewart, his wife, has been staying for the past year with her mother, Mrs. Stollery, of Edmonton, Mr. and Mrs. Stewart had been planning to leave shortly for a long holiday in Scotland, which is the native land of both.

Winnipeg *Tribune*:—W. N. Burkhardt, news editor of the *Tribune* for the last five years, has left Winnipeg for Detroit, Mich., where he has accepted a position as managing editor of the Detroit *Times*. He was accompanied by Mrs. Burkhardt and their young son Billy. Members of the *Tribune* reportorial and news staffs bid farewell to their retiring leader, when a handsome club bag, suitably initialled and inscribed, was presented to him. Mr. Burkhardt replied feelingly, declaring that he carried more than a club bag full of good wishes away from Winnipeg, and that he would leave as many behind. M. E. Adamson, business manager of the *Tribune* for the last eight years, is also leaving Winnipeg for Detroit, where he will become business manager of the Detroit *Times*. Mr. Adamson was presented with a beautiful diamond stick pin by members of the *Tribune* staff. He made a suitable response, thanking members of the staff for their co-operation.

Ontario

W. C. Brown, job printer, of Toronto, has accepted a position with the job department of the *Times-Journal*, Fort William.

The Mono-Lino Typesetting Co. are moving into larger quarters in the same building at 160 Adelaide St., West, Toronto.

Ald. A. R. Ford, night editor of the Ottawa *Journal*, has been appointed editor of the London *Free Press*, succeeding the late Alfred Miller.

H. Downman, of the Ottawa *Journal*, and latterly of the Montreal *Star*, has joined the publicity department of the Royal Bank at Montreal.

The Paris *Review*, formerly conducted by C. W. Lawton, has been disposed of by the estate of Mr. Lawton to Charles Nixon, editor of *Rural Canada*.

Miss G. E. Dell, who has been in charge of the Chatsworth *News* for some weeks, has gone to Port Elgin, to take charge of the printing plant of the Stephen-Hepner Co.

Miss Iola Plaxton has gone to New York where she will take a course in journalism in Columbia University. Miss Plaxton was in newspaper work in Toronto for several years.

After two days' illness from lock-jaw, Mrs. James Ridpath, wife of the editor of the Lakefield *News*, passed away. About a week ago she stepped on a rusty nail sticking up in a board.

John Chinn is now foreman of the *Globe* composing room, taking over that work a few weeks ago. He has been assistant foreman for some time, and his promotion is a popular one with the staff.

Shortly after landing in Canada. View of Imperial Press party taken at Sydney.

MR. W. NELSON WILKINSON has been appointed editor of the Hamilton *Times*, and has already taken over the duties.

Mr. Cal Davis, who for 20 years has been managing editor of the paper, remains with the *Times* as special municipal reporter and writer. Mr. Wilkinson's experience in the newspaper business has been extensive and varied. He was born in the St. Thomas *Times* office when his grandfather, the late Jonathan Wilkinson, owned the paper and his father, W. J. Wilkinson, now managing editor of the Toronto *Mail and Empire*, was managing editor of the paper. Eighteen years ago "Nels" joined the staff of the *Mail and Empire* as police reporter. He served as special political reporter for the *Mail and Empire*, was news editor of the Vancouver *World*, and on the staffs of other Western papers. In

W. NELSON WILKINSON

1908 he went to Halifax as news editor of the Evening *Echo*, and covered the federal election campaign in the Maritime Provinces for the *Morning Chronicle*. In 1912 he was appointed managing editor of the Toronto *Daily* and *Sunday World*. Mr. Wilkinson left the *World* to carry on some confidential investigation for the Dominion Government before going to Halifax as managing editor of the *Morning Herald* and the *Evening Mail*. He returned to Toronto to take charge of the publicity campaign for the 1919 Victory Loan, and on the first of January, this year, organized the Canadian Newspaper Service Limited, of which he is president and general manager.

Mr. T. Hugh B. McCullough, late proprietor of the Chatsworth *News*, has gone into the insurance business in Toronto. Mr. W. Hungerford, from the Meaford *Mirror*, is now editor of the *News*.

J. B. Hanna, of the *Spectator* staff, who is leaving to join the *Mail and Empire*, of Toronto, was presented with an illuminated address by the Canadian Club, of Hamilton, when he resigned its presidency.

Tommy Lowry, from the day side of the Ottawa *Journal*, has been taking over the work on the night side, formerly handled by Arthur Ford, who has gone to be managing editor of the London *Free Press*.

Lindsay Crawford, editor of the *Statesman*, Toronto, and one of the leaders in the cause of Irish Independence, has been threatened with "direct action" if he does not cease his Irish independence propaganda.

McConnell and Fergusson announce that Mr. A. R. Malton has become connected with their firm. For the past eighteen years he has been with the Bank of Toronto, the last five of which was spent at the Head Office.

The Sundridge *Echo* in its issue of September 16th announces that the business has been taken over by Wright & Co., publishers. For the past 27 years the *Echo* has been under the direction of Mr. J. Harper, who has taken up another line of work.

More than one hundred and sixty of the boys attended the annual picnic of the carriers of the *Mail and Empire* held at Bond Lake, and upon the conclusion of the program one and all declared it was the most successful outing that has been held by the carriers.

Albert Richea, until recently foreman of the Fort William *Bulletin* has returned to Toronto, where he will specialize on lay-out work for national advertisers, Mr. Richea having had several years' experience along this line before coming to the head of the lakes.

De-Witt Drake, advertisement compositor for a number of years on the *Times-Journal*, Fort William, but who is also an

artist of no mean ability, and a graduate of the Buffalo School of Art, has severed his connections with the above paper to practice his profession at Toronto.

G. W. Gorman, newspaper reporter, well known in Western Canada, having worked on several papers from Fort William to the coast, but who has been managing the Corona Theatre in Fort William since his return from overseas, has accepted a position with the Fort William *Times-Journal*.

G. B. Johnson, Canadian Trade Commissioner at Rio de Janeiro, has been transferred to Glasgow to replace J. Vernon MacKenzie, who resigned to become editor of *MacLean's Magazine*. Major McCall, of the Trade and Commission department at Ottawa, will be sent to Rio as commissioner. Mr. Johnson is a former resident of Belleville.

The wedding took place at Owen Sound of Samuel H. Pearce, editor of the *Sun-Times*, to Helen McQuaker, who has had charge of the woman's page in that paper for some time. Mr. Pearce was formerly a reporter on the paper, and served overseas, where he was seriously wounded. He took over the editorship of the paper shortly after returning from the front.

Hespeler *Herald*:—One of Hespeler's native sons in the person of George A. Martin has been made editor of the Kitchener *Telegraph*. Mr. Martin has been in newspaper work for some time, coming from the *Globe*, where for the past couple of years he has covered the parliamentary doings for that paper. Mr. Martin should make things hum on the *Telegraph*.

George Elms, of the composing room staff of the MacLean Publishing Co., Toronto, has been appointed assistant instructor of the typography branch at the Toronto Technical School. Mr. Elms learned his trade in Newfoundland, and came to Toronto 12 years ago. He has worked in most of the best job offices in the city, spending the last seven years at the MacLean Co. composing room, and latterly having charge of the make-up on *Motor, Tractor and Implement*, and *Printer and Publisher*.

H. N. ("Mike") Moore, son of Rev. T. Albert Moore, formerly European correspondent of the Montreal *Star*, and also with the Toronto *News* and Fort William *Times-Journal*, has been appointed managing editor and managing director of *Freeman's Journal*, Dublin. He covered a number of important assignments, including the Titanic, King George's coronation, went over as a correspondent with the first contingent, and afterward saw active service, and was also covering sessions of the peace conference.

A Toronto girl, Miss Irene Todd, of the publicity staff of the Canadian National Railways, left the Central Station at Ottawa for Toronto. Clothed in a suit of dungarees, with a fireman's cap perched on her head, Miss Todd, armed with the necessary authority from general headquarters in Toronto, climbed into the cab of the engine, which is one of the largest and most powerful on the road, and smilingly waved her hand as the train pulled out of the station on its two hundred and fifty-mile journey.

Uxbridge *Journal*:—The Uxbridge *Journal* loses the services of Mr. S. B. Griffith as foreman, a position he has ably filled since May, 1917. He came to the *Journal* from Uxbridge high school twelve years ago. During the past few years he has been preparing for the Free Methodist ministry and, having passed the necessary examinations, has been given an appointment at Odessa, in the Kingston district. Mr. Griffith has been a good citizen and many friends will join the *Journal* in wishing him success. The new man at the *Journal* office is Mr. Ed. Shell.

C. M. Dickinson, who established a small paper at the Canadian head of the lakes, known as the Fort William *Bulletin*, about eighteen months ago, the paper being published at noon daily, has disposed of his interests to other parties and will in future devote his entire time to the job end of the business, which is known as the Terminal Publishing Company. The new owners of the *Bulletin* have changed the time of publication from noon to a morning paper, under the same name, but published at Port Arthur by the *News-Chronicle*. The new editor is Leo Allen, of Port Arthur, son of F. B. Allen, editor the Port Arthur *News-Chronicle*.

Goderich *Signal*:—Mr. Arthur R. Ford, son of Rev. J. E. Ford, of town, has been appointed managing editor of the London *Free Press*, succeeding the late Alfred E. Miller. Mr Ford has had an extensive and varied newspaper experience. some time he was on the staff of the Winnipeg *Telegram*, later he was Ottawa correspondent for the Toronto *News*, and latterly he has been on the staff of the Ottawa *Journal* and has also been Ottawa correspondent of the London (Eng.) *Times*. As managing editor of the *Free Press*, he will have a position of great responsibility, but his friends are quite confident of his ability to hold the position with credit both to himself and to his paper.

An amalgamation has been completed between the offices of the *Tribune* Printing Company and the *Telegraph* Company, of Welland. The new paper, which will be known as the *Telegraph-Tribune*, already has made its appearance. The new *Telegraph* office at the corner of South Main and Avenue Place, which is now in the course of erection, will likely be sold, the new company moving into the *Tribune* office on Cross street. The two papers, formerly run as Conservative and Liberal, will now be run as one independent paper. The capitalization of the new plant will be $100,000, with L. B. Duff as editorial supervisor. The directors are T. J. Dillon, H. B. Sidey, Colonel Raymond and L. B. Duff.

The printers of Guelph are negotiating for a new scale. The present two-year contract now expiring calls for an eight-hour day and a minimum wage of $21 per week, with time and a half for overtime. In many cases, however, employers are paying considerably above the scale. The agreement now presented stipulates a week of 44 hours in job printing offices, and of 46 hours in newspaper offices, after May 1 next. The minimum wage is placed at $36 from October 1 to April 30. From May 1 to September 30 job printers are to be paid $36 per week of 44 hours, and those employed in newspaper departments $37.63 per week of 46 hours. The matter is not yet settled and the agreement made will probably be for six months only.

Hanover *Post*:—Hanover had its first experience of a "Sporting Extra" last Saturday evening when the *Post* had a paper on the street at 7 o'clock carrying the feature story of the final lacrosse match at St. Catharines that afternoon, in which our boys were defeated, the report being telephoned through by the editor of the *Post*, who was with the team. The extra also carried details of the St. Simons-Orangeville lacrosse game at Scarboro Beach, Toronto, the results of the world baseball series and the big Rugby games at Montreal and Toronto. One thousand copies of the extra were printed and distributed free all over town. The little sheet carried the advertisements of the local business men who accorded the innovation a friendly reception.

Citizens of Port Elgin and surrounding townships tendered to Mr. E. Roy Sayles a formal presentation and luncheon, prior to the departure of the family to take up residence in Toronto. An address and a handsome club bag were presented. H. H. Stevens presided, and the speakers were: Ex-Warden McConnell, Ex-Reeve Christie, John Rushton, Reeve Jamieson, Clerk Elliott, of the township of Saugeen, Reeve Cottrill, Clerk Geddes, Miss E. H. D. McClaren, A. F. George, G. McLaren, Principal Carter, Principal Cringle, and others of the town. Mr. Sayles has disposed of his newspaper, the *Times*, and assumed the responsibilities of manager of the Canadian Weekly Newspaper Association. During the week the women of the town presented Mrs. Sayles with cut glass.

Barrie lost a good citizen when Edgar G. Redditt passed away, after being confined to the house only a few days. Deceased was born at Richmond Hill and learned the printing craft in the Liberal office there. After being engaged in Toronto and Owen Sound for a number of years, he came to Barrie seventeen years ago and was a valued member of the Barrie *Examiner* staff. Enlisting in 1915, he went overseas as handmaster of the 157th Battalion, and when that unit was broken up was given charge of the band of the Canadian Forestry Corps with headquarters at Sunningdale, and received the rank of Warrant Officer. At the close of the war he returned and resumed his work on the *Examiner* staff. Previous to the war he was for some time bandmaster of Barrie Citizens' Band.

Hamilton *Spectator*:—The hosts of friends in this city of John B. Hanna, telegraph editor of the *Spectator* for the past ten years, will be sorry that he is leaving Hamilton to take up residence in Toronto, where he has accepted an important post on the editorial staff of the *Mail and Empire*. As a slight token of their esteem, his co-workers on the *Spectator* presented him with a handsome Sheffield silver tray. Mr. Hanna, since coming to this city from St. Catharines, has taken a deep interest in the welfare of the city, and has been an active worker in many organizations—civic, national and fraternal. He is president of the Canadian club and prominent in Masonic circles. In departing from this city he carries with him the best wishes of the entire newspaper fraternity and a very large number of citizens in all walks of life.

The Autumn meeting of the Midland Press Association will be held in Peterboro in the Council Room of the Peterboro Board of Trade on Friday, October 29th. Sessions will be held at 11 a.m. and 1.30 p.m. Addresses will be given on "Advertising Service" by Mr. J. G. Keefer, the *Register*, Norwood; "The Advantages and Savings Made Possible by the Monotype

System," by Mr. H. E. Mountstephen, of the Lanston Monotype Machine Co., Philadelphia; "The Evils of Propaganda," by Mr. E. G. McKeeley, city editor the *Examiner*, Peterboro; "Does it Pay to Put Modern Labor-Saving Machinery in a Country Printing Office?" by Mr. F. H. Dobbin, Peterboro; "Advantages of Adopting a Uniform Price List for the Association," by Mr. H. B. Johnston, Supt. of the *Review*, Peterboro; the printed price list of job printing will also be discussed. Through the kind permission of Mr. R. W. Cormack, Supt., a trip will be made by the members through the Quaker Oats Factory. Publishers outside of the Midland District will be made welcome at these sessions.

Mr. Alfred Logan, of Wiarton, and his daughter, Miss Jean Logan, were in town on their way to Nova Scotia to visit Mr. Logan's people. Miss Logan and her brother, Mr. Lloyd Logan (a former member of the *Globe* reportorial staff), both of them still decidedly youthful, have the unique distinction of "running" a paper, the *Canadian Echo*, together. Brother and sister do all the writing between them, and Miss Logan, who admits that she leaves most of the political editorials to her brother, says that sometimes she feels inclined to seize the editorial pencil and issue a few words of advice to women voters regarding the more useful use of the ballot, now that it has been won. Miss Logan, who has all the marks of a merry schoolgirl, has mechanical talents as well as literary ones, and can set type by hand or run a linotype machine with equal facility. One of Miss Logan's recent good deeds has been the unearthing and the writing up of some of the vast store of historical material that lies in Western Ontario.—From the Toronto *Globe*, September 16th.

A Kitchener despatch says:—"An important change in the personnel of the *Daily Telegraph* staff is announced. George A. Martin, of the editorial staff of the *Globe*, Toronto, has accepted the position of editor, and Allan A. Eby, who has been member of the editorial staff for a long term of years, will assume new duties in the advertising and business departments. Owing to his close association with the recreation and sporting activities in this city Mr. Eby will retain charge of the sporting page of the new paper. An advance in the subscription rate to $6 a year and three cents a copy is also anticipated. Extensive renovations to the *Daily Telegraph* plant are in course of completion. For a number of years Mr. Martin has been one of the *Globe's* most valued reporters. He has represented his paper in the Legislature Press Gallery and in the Press Gallery at Ottawa, and many of Canada's leading statesmen have been his friends. Mr. Martin has completed his work with the *Globe*, the editorial staff presenting him with a silver-mounted umbrella. Mr. Martin's wife was Miss Snider, formerly of the editorial staff of the *Telegram*.

Printers' Baseball Championship

At the end of the tenth game in the tenth annual tournament of the Union Printers' National Baseball League, held at St. Louis, Minn., from July 31 to August 6, the St. Paul team was declared the winner of the national championship, with the Detroit nine as runner-up. Teams from Boston, Chicago, Cincinnati, Cleveland, Indianapolis, New York, Pittsburg, St. Louis and Washington also participated. The final game of the tournament was played Friday afternoon, August 6, and was largely attended by St. Paul and Minneapolis printers and their friends. In the evening a reception and dance was given at the Armory. At that time President Joseph J. Dallas of Boston presented the members of the victorious team with the Garry Hermann perpetual trophy; gold-mounted fountain pens from the Lanston Monotype Company; gold cuff links from the Mergenthaler Linotype Company; a loving cup from the Intertype Corporation; and silver watch charms from the management of the St. Francis, the headquarters hotel. In addition, the members of the Detroit team were awared silver-mounted fountain pens, offered as the runner-up prize by the Mergenthaler Linotype Company. Several interesting side entertainments were enjoyed by attending typographers and their ladies. A special train was run from Chicago. The 1921 tournament will be held in Detroit.

This Is a Brick

Toronto *Globe*:—Nearly every week brings a new pulp and paper enterprise, and the announcement that another newspaper has been forced out of business by rising costs of material.

Where Your Message Fails

THERE are just as many waste paper baskets as ever, and they are seldom empty.

At a gathering like Toronto Exhibition, especially on Children's Day, when the free distribution booths are raided for literature all day, the grounds resemble a scrap sorter's yard. There is paper blowing around in ever direction. There are thousands upon thousands of printed sheets and booklets, paper bags and handbills—paper in every conceivable form. It may have had a short and fleeting existence in telling its message—but it seems very doubtful that such could be the case. The great bulk of that paper is wasted.

The same can be said of the jumbo editions of many daily and Sunday papers.

As far as the use of paper and ink and labor for turning out direct advertising matter is concerned, the meaning should be very plain, viz., there must be an excellence of product, and an appeal in the execution of the work that will keep it from being thrown into the scrap basket.

Printers and copy-writers must think more. Excellent as is much of the work now turned out, it must be better. If your printed matter is simply being glanced at and thrown away—it is not getting its message across in a lasting way.

Better stock, better printing, better thinking—these will do much to keep your advertising matter from going to the man with the truck and the garbage cans while the ink is still fresh on the message.

First Saskatchewan Paper

North Battleford:—Forty-two years ago this month the first newspaper was published in Saskatchewan. After a journey of 650 miles over boundless prairies and unbridged streams, the late P. G. Laurie, following the brigade of Red River carts which carried his plant, reached Battleford, the capital of the Northwest Territories, and printed the first edition of the *Saskatchewan Herald* on the 25th of August, 1878. It was a four-paged sheet 14 inches by 10, and contained as well as the news of the vast territories telegraphic communications from all parts of the world. The *Herald* has continued to publish weekly from that time to the present with the exception of during the Northwest Rebellion in 1885, when publication was suspended for six weeks while the late editor

did garrison duty in the fort. The late P. G. Laurie was the father of Mr. Wm. Laurie, barrister, now residing in Cardston.

The Pulp Wood Limit Deals

The following correspondence between the Canadian National Newspapers and Periodicals Association and Premier Drury relative to pulp wood limits, and the disposal of the product shows that fifteen per cent. of the product for Canadian publishers may mean a rather indefinite amount of protection for any particular section of the publishing business.—

The Canadian National Newspapers and Periodicals Association wrote to the Prime Minister as follows:—

Dear Sir:

We note that in connection with a recent sale of timber limits it was provided that the company must furnish at least 15 per cent. of the output of newsprint to Canadian newspapers. We should be pleased to know if you have also provided for the protection of the agricultural, business, educational and other publications which use half tone news and book papers.

We are informed that the product of this territory will be used almost entirely for the latter purpose and not for the production of newsprint.

We should also like to draw your attention to the fact that there is free trade in newsprint, while the book-paper manufacturers are protected to the extent of 25 to over 35 per cent.

We should like to suggest that before the matter is definitely closed you agree to see a representation from our Association. Possibly it might be convenient for you to do this early in September.

The Premier, Hon. E. C. Drury, replied as follows:—

Replying to your letter of the 11th instant with regard to the recent sale of timber limits wherein you state it was provided that the company must furnish at least 15 per cent. of the output to the Canadian press, I may say that the agreement with the Spruce Falls Pulp and Paper Company stipulates that this company shall be required to furnish to *Canadian Publishers* (not Canadian newspapers as you stated) a proportion not exceeding fifteen per cent. of their total output, as shall be determined by the Government from time to time. From this, you will note that no special mention is made of newsprint, but simply fifteen per cent. of their product.

As this agreement is now closed, further representation in this connection would serve no purpose. Trusting this is the information you desire.

Westman and Baker Reorganized

The firm of Westman and Baker, which has served Canadian printers since 1875, has been re-organized and incorporated within the last month by Walter T. Johnston, who is the manager and one of the principal shareholders of the new company Westman and Baker Limited. The few other shareholders consist of some of the most prominent and influential business men of Eastern Canada.

The firm of Westman and Baker was a partnership from its organization forty-five years ago until about ten years ago, when G. R. Baker retired. Mr. J. H. Westman carried on the business alone up to the time of his death last February. Both members of the original firm were machine designers and workmen of high

Left to right—Miss M. F. Billington, of the Society of Women Journalists; Robert Donald, chairman of the Union, and Percival Marshall, representing the British Association of Trade and Technical Journals. On the occasion of his visit to Toronto the second time Mr. Marshall was the guest of honor at a luncheon arranged by the Canadian National Newspapers and Periodicals Association.

ability. They built an organization with care and in the many years the firm has served the trade they earned a reputation for the highest integrity.

Mr. Johnston announces that the policy of the firm will be left unchanged and that the company will seek to enhance the reputation acquired by the founders. Mr. Johnston is an aggressive young man who needs no introduction to the printing trade. He is well known in Eastern Canada and he brings into the business the experience of three generations on both sides of his family. The late "Josh" T. Johnston, who was the founder and general manager of the Toronto Type Foundry Company, Limited, until his death ten years ago, was an uncle.

Westman & Baker Limited will carry on the old business of building printers' and bookbinders' machinery as in the past. In addition to their present line, the company expect to have ready for the market soon a new high-speed job printing press that can be operated with or without automatic feeder. It is said that embodied in the construction of this new press will be many improvements and time and labor-saving features that are not on any similar platen press now being imported. The printers of Canada will look forward to the coming of this press with interest. It is the intention of the management to also build trucks and other utilities for manufacturing plants in general.

In addition to the manufacturing business the company are now in the type foundry and general printers' supply business. They have established agency connections with a number of prominent American and British builders of modern profit-earning printing machinery and equipment. These lines along with the products of their own up-to-date manufacturing plant will enable the firm to supply the trade throughout the Dominion with anything from a font of type to the largest machinery.

The offices of Westman & Baker Limited are located at 165 Adelaide Street, West, Toronto.

An Interesting Knife Sharpener

J. Kallstrom, 1367 Broadway, New York, is commencing publicity in this issue of *Printer and Publisher* in the interests of his "Instanto" Paper Knife Sharpener. Any person with ordinary care can use this knife sharpener, although the better way is to take the knife out of the machine, yet the knife can be sharpened in the machine. This, of course, means a great saving of time. The patent is pending on this sharpener. We understand that already Mr. Kallstrom has manufactured very large quantities of this unique knife sharpener.

After Eight Years Leaves Moose Jaw

R. W. Beebe, one of the best known of the Western newspaper men, has severed his connection with the *Evening Times*, Moose Jaw, Sask., and is leaving the city with Mrs. Beebe to reside in Detroit, Mich. Mr. Beebe has been a member of the *Times* for eight years, during three of which he has acted as city editor. He is well known as a clever and able journalist. He carries with him from the city the esteem and well wishes of a large circle of friends and acquaintances by whom he will be much missed. His fellow newspaper men will join with his other friends in hoping for him every success in his future work.

Milton's Publicity Agent

F. L. White, who has been connected with journalistic work for a number of years, is now boosting Milton in outside points, showing the advantages of the town to the industrial world, he having been appointed Publicity Agent by the Milton Town Council.

The Indiana Chemical and Manufacturing Co., 135 South East St., Indianapolis, U.S.A., are issuing an advertising booklet for their product Reducol, entitled Cutting Costs in the Press Room. The booklet contains many useful bits and the clarity of definition in the printing and artistic cover make for a receptive market and good advertising of their products.

Recent Purchasers of Linotypes

The following is a list of recent Linotype installations:- Le Devoir, Montreal, two Model 14's; Napanee Beaver, Model 1 Bashaw, Sask., Star, Model L; Toronto Mail, two Model 14 and three Model 8's; Toronto Globe, four Model 8's; Slavoni Steamship Company, Toronto, Model K; North Sydne Herald, Model 8 and Model 14; Clinton News-Record, Mod L; St. Henri Printing Company, Montreal, Model 8; Cask Publishing Company, Antigonish, Model L; Forum Publishir Company, Winnipeg, Model 5; Poirier Bessette & Compan Montreal, Model L; Rouleau Enterprise, Model 8; Brantfor Expositor, Model 5; Montreal Gazette, Model 14; Guelp Herald, Model 14; Lindsay Post, Model 14; V. P. Aubi Ottawa; Model 8; Canada News, Winnipeg, Model 14; Walla Printing Company, Guelph, Model 8; Vankleek Hill Revie Model K; Moyer Printing Co., Brantford, Model K Fredericton Mail, Model L; F. J. Runge, Winnipe Model 8; Dominion Printing and Engraving Company, Mon real, Model 8; Trade-Review, St. John's, Model 4; Artist Print Shop, Montreal, Model L; Alger Press, Oshawa, Mod 14; Windsor Era, Model 8; St. Croix Printing Compan St. Stephen, Model 8; Guelph Herald, Model 8; Oshav Reformer, Model 8; H. H. Rans, Oshawa, Model 14; Jones McRae, Montreal, Model 5; Toronto Typesetting Compan Model 8; Eagle Publishing Company, Montreal, Model 14; Ingersoll Chronicle, Model 14; Sydney Record, Model Charlottetown Patriot, Model 8; A-One Printing Compan Montreal, Model 9; Sault Ste. Marie Star, Model 14; Ottav Printing Company, Ottawa, two Model 8's; Ottawa Recor Model 14; MacLean Publishing Company, Toronto, Model Owen Sound News, Model 8; Sentinel-Star, Cobourg, Model Fleming Publishing Company, Owen Sound, Model 8; Ca adian Printing Company, Sarnia, Model 8; Dundalk Hera Model 8; Hanson, Crozier and Edgar, Kingston, Model 1 Miln-Bingham, Toronto, Model 8; Israelite Press, Winnipe Model 8; Jackson Press, Kingston, Model 8; British Wh Kingston, Model 8; Dresden Times, Model 8; Bowmanvi Statesman, Model 8; Montreal Gazette, Model 8; Saskato Star, Model 14; Simmons Printing Company, Ottawa, Moc 8; Lethbridge Herald, Model 14; Colborne Express, Model Ashdown Hardware Company, Winnipeg, Model 9; Jor & McRae, Montreal, Model 14; Halifax Herald, Model Sentinel, Woodstock, New Brunswick, Model L; D. Wagn Niagara Falls, Model L; Parry Sound Canadian, Model Alger Press, Oshawa, Model 1; Tara Leader, Model L; Ow Sound News, Model K; Reynolds Limited, Winnipeg, Mo 14; Canada Weekly, Winnipeg, Model 9; Carleton Place Hera Model L; Le Droit, Ottawa, Model 9; J. G. Evans, Kingst Model 15; Gull Lake Advance, Model L; National Pre Winnipeg, Model 14; Le Progres, Sherbrooke, Model L; W ford Guide-Advocate, Model L; Kitchener News-Record, Mode

General Notes

At a recent meeting of the Society for the Protection New Hampshire Forests the subject of newsprint and its r material in future years was most fully discussed. La appropriations were advocated for forest conservancy. 1 Canadian stand in the pulp and paper question was most a handled by Mr. Edward Beck, of the Canadian Pulp a Paper Association.

The Kingston Daily Standard entered upon its 111th y on the 25th of September last—as fact that is strikingly bo out by the standing bordered announcement on the first p of the Standard to this effect:—"111th Year; Always boosti Never knocking."

Special trains for carrying newsprint will be run every ot day by the New York Central railroad from the mills in St. Lawrence division to New York so as to assure the N York and Philadelphia newspaper publishers of regular pa supplies.

A comprehensive and persistent advertising campaig shortly being launched by the United States Army for recrui purposes. The cost of the campaign will be approxima $240,000, and will be handled by the Advertising Agen Corporation of New York.

The initial publication of the proposed new Boston De cratic daily newspaper, the Boston Telegram, is still problemati but it is strongly rumored that it will get under way by the of October. Paper supply, circulation and necessary staff labor appear to have all been successfully arranged for.

A Long Record of Success

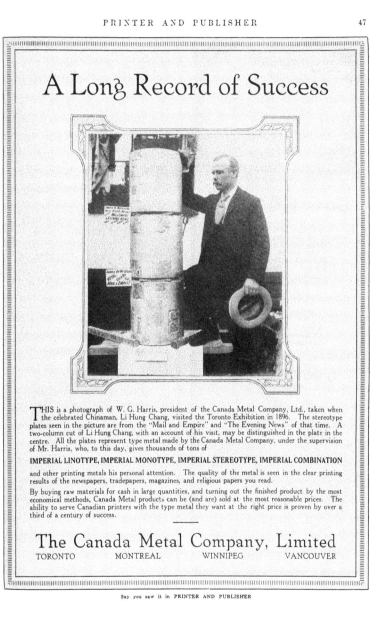

THIS is a photograph of W. G. Harris, president of the Canada Metal Company, Ltd., taken when the celebrated Chinaman, Li Hung Chang, visited the Toronto Exhibition in 1896. The stereotype plates seen in the picture are from the "Mail and Empire" and "The Evening News" of that time. A two-column cut of Li Hung Chang, with an account of his visit, may be distinguished in the plate in the centre. All the plates represent type metal made by the Canada Metal Company, under the supervision of Mr. Harris, who, to this day, gives thousands of tons of

IMPERIAL LINOTYPE, IMPERIAL MONOTYPE, IMPERIAL STEREOTYPE, IMPERIAL COMBINATION

and other printing metals his personal attention. The quality of the metal is seen in the clear printing results of the newspapers, tradepapers, magazines, and religious papers you read.

By buying raw materials for cash in large quantities, and turning out the finished product by the most economical methods, Canada Metal products can be (and are) sold at the most reasonable prices. The ability to serve Canadian printers with the type metal they want at the right price is proven by over a third of a century of success.

The Canada Metal Company, Limited
TORONTO   MONTREAL   WINNIPEG   VANCOUVER

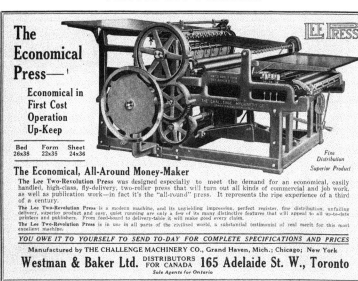
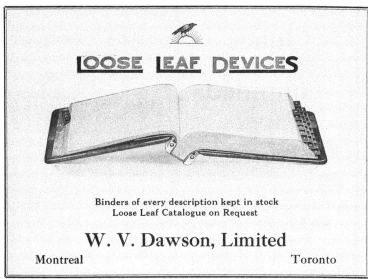

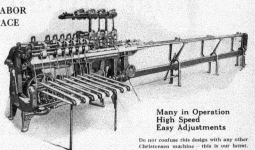

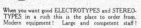

CLASSIFIED ADVERTISEMENT SECTION

TWO CENTS A WORD, Box Number as five words ; minimum charge is $1.00 per insertion, for 50 words or less, set in 6 pt. type. Each figure counts as a word. Display ads., or ads. set in border, are at the card rates.

FOR SALE

OR SALE — NO. 11 IMPROVED PEARL Press, new, complete with friction belt drive d quarter horsepower A-K motor, 25 cycle C. G. Davis, 185 Richmond West, Toronto. (p10p)

OR SALE—30" WESTMAN AND BAKER Paper Cutter in good condition. Kitchener legraph.

EWSPAPER FOR SALE—IN LIVE SAS-katchewan town, doing $500 business nthly. Practical printer can clear $300 per nth clear of expenses. $3,500 buys business d premises, only fair cash payment required, ance very easy, monthly payments. When swering state what cash payment can make. x 221020, Printer and Publisher.

OR SALE — CAMPBELL TWO REVOLU-tion cylinder press, 37x52. Apply Technical ess Limited, 426 Homer St., Vancouver, B.C. (p11p)

OR SALE—ONE 10 x 16 GORDON PRESS. one Washington Press prints 22 x 34, one 25 l case cabinet filled with good type, a large ortment of type, rules, leads, slugs, etc. ll sell in parts or the whole, worth $1,090. ll sell at a great discount if soon sold. rite for particulars. Box 10320. Printer and blisher. (p10p)

OR SALE—MILLER AUTOMATIC FEEDER for 12 x 18 C. & P., only used six months, thing broken, in perfect condition. Price, 000. Apply Box 10520, Printer and Pub-er. (p11p)

ONOLINE FOR SALE—NEARLY NEW— Full set of mats. $30 worth of new mats er used. Hundreds of dollars' worth of new ta. Certified cheque for $200 takes all, f.o.b. odstock, N.B. As we need the floor space st be sold at once. Press Printing Co., ., Woodstock, N.B. (p11p)

SITUATIONS VACANT

TRAVELLER WANTED FOR THE CITY OF Toronto by wholesale paper house. State experience and salary or commission required. Apply Box 10920. (p10p)

WANTED — SALESMEN THOROUGHLY familiar with foundry and coal mining trade. Box 10820. (p11p)

LEARN THE LINOTYPE — WRITE FOR particulars. Canadian Linotype, 68 Tem-perance St., Toronto. (ptfp)

MORE MONEY FOR EASIER WORK under more pleasant conditions. Would you like it? Then learn to operate the Mono-type. There are Monotype schools in Phila-delphia. New York, Chicago. and Toronto. Apply to the nearest. Lanston Monotype Machine Company.

COLLECTIONS

SEND US YOUR LIST OF DELINQUENTS. We will turn Debit into Credit. Publishers' Protective Association. Toronto. (ptfp)

POSITION WANTED

Young man experienced in selling space, advt. writing, and is a practical printer, desires a position as advertis-ing manager with a concern that has a future. Box 10220. (p10p)

MACHINERY LIST

1—10 x 15" C. & P. Press, complete.
1—10 x 15" Gordon Press, complete.
1— 8 x 12" Challenge Gordon.
1— 6 x 10" Gordon Press
2— 7 x 11" Pearl Press.
1—⅛ to 1½" Rosbach Stitcher.
1—½" Rosbach Stitcher.
1—5/16" Perfection Stitcher.
All above Power and First-class.

1—5/16" Hand Stitcher Brehmer.
1—26" C. & P. Lever Cutter.
1—19" W. & B. Lever Cutter.
1—26" Oswego Lever Cutter.
All above hand power and first-class.

ROYAL MACHINE WORKS
738 ST. PAUL WEST, MONTREAL
Presses, Bookbinding and Box Machinery

EQUIPMENT WANTED

WANTED — SEVEN-COLUMN QUARTO press in good condition. Apply Box 10820. Printer and Publisher. (P.T.F.P.)

Everybody Wants Something !

You may have just what the other fellow is looking for, and be only too glad to sell it to him. Let him know what it is through— The Want Ad Columns of PRINTER AND PUBLISHER. Many Canadian printers have succeeded in getting rid of idle equipment to good advantage by using this medium.

The rates are moderate

2 Cents a Word
Minimum Charge $1.00

What is the
PRINTER & PUBLISHER
to Canada ?

The National Printer-Journalist is the same to the United States

Send 25c. for a sample copy

National Printer-Journalist
(in its 37th year)
4610 Ravenswood Avenue
CHICAGO, ILL.

Live - Wire PRINTER

Do you want to de-velop into a salesman? I have a good oppor-tunity for the RIGHT man—who is of good appearance, not afraid of work and· who will really apply himself in the interests of the business.

Box 10120 (P10P)

Buyers' Guide

ADDRESSING MACHINES
The Challenge Machinery Co., Grand Haven, Mich.
Westman & Baker Limited, Toronto.

BALERS FOR WASTE PAPER
Golding Mfg. Co., Franklin, Mass.
Logan, H. J., 114 Adelaide St W., Toronto.
Stephenson, Blake & Co., Toronto.
Stewart, Geo. M., 92 McGill St. Montreal.
Westman & Baker Limited, Toronto.

BINDERY EQUIPMENT AND SUPPLIES
(See also CUTTING MACHINES)
Albion Sewing Cotton Co. Ltd., London, Eng.
Berry Machine Co., St. Louis, Mo.
Christensen Machine Co., Racine, Wis.
Dexter Folder Co., New York.
Golding Mfg. Co., Franklin, Mass.
Kallstrom, J., New York City.
Logan, H. J., 114 Adelaide St. W., Toronto.
Miller & Richard, Toronto and Winnipeg.
Morrison Co., J. L., Toronto, Ont.
Royal Machine Works, Montreal.
Steel Co. of Canada, The, Hamilton (wire).
Stephenson, Blake & Co., Toronto.
Stewart, Geo. M., 92 McGill St., Montreal.
Westman & Baker Limited, Toronto.

COMPOSING ROOM MACHINERY
(See also LEADS, SLUGS AND TYPE)
The following list covers Iron Furniture—
Eastern Brass & Wood Type Co., New York.
Hamilton Mfg. Co., Two Rivers, Wisconsin.
Stephenson, Blake & Co., Toronto.
The Challenge Machinery Co., Grand Haven, Mich.
The Toronto Type Foundry Co., Toronto.
Westman & Baker Limited, Toronto.

CORDS, SILK, ETC.
Albion Sewing Cotton Co., Ltd., London, Eng.

COUNTING MACHINES
Stephenson, Blake & Co., Toronto.
Westman & Baker Limited, Toronto.

CUTTING MACHINES—PAPER
Golding Mfg. Co., Franklin, Mass.
Morrison Co., J. L., 445 King St. W., Toronto.
Stephenson, Blake & Co., Toronto.
The Challenge Machinery Co., Grand Haven, Mich.
Westman & Baker Limited, Toronto.

COLLECTION AGENCIES
Canadian Mercantile Agency, Ottawa.
Publishers' Protective Association, Toronto.
Nagle Mercantile Agency, Laprairie, Montreal.

EFFICIENCY EXPERT
Pepper, J. L., 38 Toronto St., Toronto.

ELECTROTYPING AND STEREOTYPING
Rapid Electrotype Co. of Canada, Toronto.
Toronto Electrotype & Stereotype Co., Toronto.

ELECTROTYPE AND STEREOTYPE BASES
The Challenge Machinery Co., Grand Haven, Mich.
Westman & Baker Limited, Toronto.

ELECTROTYPE METAL
British Smelting & Refining Co., Ltd., Montreal.
Canada Metal Co., Limited, Toronto.
Hoyt Metal Co., Limited, Toronto.

EMBOSSING EQUIPMENT
Automatic Ptg. Devices Co., San Francisco, Cal.
Ellis New Method Embossing, Hamilton, Ont.
Golding Mfg. Co., Franklin, Mass.
Stephenson, Blake & Co., Toronto.
Westman & Baker Limited, Toronto.

ENGRAVERS
Legge Bros., Ltd., Toronto.
Reliance Eng. Co., Toronto.

ENVELOPE MANUFACTURERS
Toronto Envelope Co., Toronto.
Dawson Ltd., W. V., Montreal and Toronto.

Buyers' Guide

TICONDEROGA PULP AND PAPER CO.

Machine Finish, Special Magazine and Antique Finish

BOOK, MAGAZINE, COATING, LITHO-GRAPH AND MUSIC

PAPERS

Mills at Ticonderoga, N.Y.

Sales Department

Rooms 800-816, 522 Fifth Avenue, New York

J. R. WALKER

267 WELLINGTON ST., MONTREAL

Specializing in All Grades of

Printers' Waste Paper
Books, News and Writing Papers

In Connection With

J. R. Walker & Company, Limited

35 Common St., Montreal

Manufacturers of Felt Paper, Fibre Board, Etc.

ESTIMATING AND COST SYSTEMS
orte Publishing Co., Salt Lake, Utah, U.S.A., and 32 Temperance St., Toronto.

FEATURES AND READY PRINT SERVICE
anadian Newspaper Service, Ltd., Toronto.
ross-Atlantic Newspaper Service, Montreal.
ominion News Bureau, Ltd., Montreal.
lternational Syndicate, Baltimore, Md.
ublishers News Service, Regina, Can.

INK (PRINTING) MANUFACTURERS
(*Including Bronzing Powders.)
ilt & Wiborg Co. of Canada, Ltd., Toronto, Ont.
nada Printing Ink Co., 15 Duncan St., Toronto.
lumbia Printing Ink & Roller Co., Vancouver.
minion Printing Ink Co., Ltd., Toronto, Ont.
nton Bros., Toronto, Ont.
eliance Ink Co., Winnipeg, Man.
ockell, Edwards & Co., Ltd., Toronto.
nclair, Valentine & Hoops, Ltd., Toronto, Ont.

LEADS, SLUGS AND TYPE
:Carle-Wareham Co., Toronto.
sphenson, Blake & Co., Toronto.
sstman & Baker Limited, Toronto.
ronto Type Foundry Co., Ltd., Toronto, Montreal, Winnipeg.
ller & Richard, Toronto and Winnipeg.

LITHOGRAPHERS
es Lithographing Co., Chicago, Ill.

MAILING MACHINES
auncey Wong's Sons, Greenfield, Mass.
v. Robert Dick Estate, Buffalo, N.Y.
sedaumatic Co., The, Chauncey Wing's Sons, Greenfield, Mass.

MAILING GALLEYS
: Challenge Machinery Co., Grand Haven, Mich.
stman & Baker Limited, Toronto.

METAL
ır all kinds of Typesetting Machines and for stereotyping purposes.)
tish Smelting & Refining Co., Ltd., Montreal.
nada Metal Co., Limited, Toronto.
at West Smelting & Refining Co., Vancouver.
rt Metal Co., Limited, Toronto.

METAL FURNITURE
Carle-Wareham Co., Toronto.
no-Lino Typesetting Co., Toronto.
Challenge Machinery Co., Grand Haven, Mich.
stman & Baker Limited, Toronto.

MOTORS AND TRANSMISSION
Kimble Electric Co., 635N Western Ave., Chicago.
Manton Bros., Toronto, Ont.
Westman & Baker Limited, Toronto.

PAPER MANUFACTURERS AND DEALERS
Allen Paper Co. Ltd., Toronto.
Buntin, Gillies & Co., Ltd., Hamilton, Ont.
Canada Paper Co., 112 Bay St., Toronto.
Dawson Ltd., W. V., Montreal.
Dickinson & Co., John, 25 Melinda St., Toronto.
Don Valley Paper Co., Toronto, Ont.
Eslçeck Mfg. Co., Turner's Falls, Mass.
Halls Paper Co., Ltd., Fred. W., Toronto, Ont.
La Monte & Son. Ltd., George, Toronto.
McFarlane, Son & Hodgson, Montreal, Que.
Mitchell, J. & W., Birmingham, Eng.
Niagara Paper Mills, Lockport, N.Y.
Paper Sales, Limited, Toronto.
Provincial Paper Mills Co., Toronto.
Rolland Paper Co., Ltd., Montreal, Que.
Samuel Jones & Co., Ltd., 7 Bridewell Place, London, Eng., and Waverley Park, New Jersey.
Ticonderoga Pulp & Paper Co., New York.
United Paper Mills, Ltd., Toronto.
Whyte Paper Co., A., 55 Bay St., Toronto.
Wilson Munroe Co., Toronto.

PAPER, TIN FOIL
Mitchell, J. & W., Birmingham, Eng.

PAPER, TYMPAN
Cromwell Paper Co., The, Chicago, U.S.A.

PAPER, WASTE
Walker & Co., Ltd., J. R., Montreal.

PRESSES AND OTHER EQUIPMENT
(Includes Cylinder and Job Presses, Gauges, etc. See Embossing, Eq.)
Automatic Ptg. Devices Co., San Francisco, Cal.
Babcock Printing Press Co., New London, Conn.
Golding Mfg. Co., Franklin, Mass.
Goss Printing Press Co., Chicago.
Hoe & Co., R., 504-520 Grand St., New York.
Linotype & Machinery, Ltd., London, Eng., and 68 Temperance St., Toronto.
Mann Lithopress Co., The, New York City.
Manton Bros., Toronto, Ont.
McCain Bros. Mfg. Co., Chicago, Ill.
Megill, Ed., 60 Duane St., New York City.
Miehle Printing Press & Mfg. Co., Chicago.
Miller & Richard, Toronto and Winnipeg.
Morrison Co., J. L., Toronto, Ont.
Premier & Potter Ptg. Press Co., Inc., New York
Royal Machine Works, Montreal.
Scott & Co., Walter, Plainfield, N.J.

FEATURES

PAGES — Camera News, Fashion, Children's and Feature.

DAILY—Portraits, Puzzles, Fashion Hints and Useful Bird Citizens.

COMICS — O l d P a l s, Smiles and Noozie.

MISCELLANEOUS — Art Needlework, H o u s e Plans, Hints for the M o t o r i s t, Classified Boosters and The Ad-route.

The International Syndicate
20 Years of Unfailing Feature Service

BALTIMORE, MARYLAND

Printers, Paper-Makers, Publishers and Manufacturers

Can reduce their "collection expenses" to a minimum by using

NAGLE
ONE PER CENT
DRAFT-SERVICE

Why pay 10 per cent. or 15 per cent. on accounts you can have collected at 1 per cent.? Save money. Investigate this system. Thoroughly reliable. Established 1909. Send for supply of 1 per cent. drafts to-day.

The Nagle Mercantile Agency
Laprairie, (Montreal), Que.

WHILE-U-WAIT

RUBBER STAMP-MAKING OUTFITS

Require only eight minutes to make rubber stamps. Will also make Hard Rubber Stereotypes for printing. A few dollars buy complete outfit.

Send for catalog

The Barton Mfg. Co.

83 Duane Street   New York, N.Y.

Stephenson, Blake & Co., Toronto.
The Challenge Machinery Co., Grand Haven, Mich.
Toronto Type Foundry Co., Ltd., Toronto.
United Printing Machinery Co., Boston.
Westman & Baker Limited, Toronto.

PRESSES, ROTARY
Goss Printing Press Co., Chicago, Ill.
Hoe & Co., 504-520 Grand St., New York.

PRESSES, MULTI-PROCESS
A Multi-Process Printing, Punching, Perforating, Cutting and other operation machine. Manufactured by The Regina Co., Rahway, N.J., U.S.A.

"REDUCOL"
Indiana Chemical Co., Indianapolis, Ind.
Manton Bros., Toronto.

ROLLERS
Canada Printing Ink Co., Ltd., Toronto.
Columbia Printing Ink & Roller Co., Vancouver.
Manton Bros., Toronto, Ont.
Sinclair & Valentine, Toronto, Ont.
Winnipeg Printers' Roller Works, Winnipeg.

RUBBER STAMP OUTFITS
Barton Mfg. Co., The, New York, N.Y.

RULED FORM
Matrix Ruled Form & Tabular Co., Forth Worth, Texas.

STEREO PAPERS
Dixon & Co., Ltd., L. S., Liverpool, England.

TINNING, ETC.
Cooper Calendar Metal Co., Toronto.

TYPE-HIGH MACHINES
The Challenge Machinery Co., Grand Haven, Mich.
Westman & Baker Limited, Toronto.

TYPE, LEADS AND SLUGS
(Includes Type of all kinds—Wood, Brass or Lead.)
DeCarle-Wareham Co., Toronto.
Eastern Brass & Wood Type Co., New York City.
Stephenson, Blake & Co., Toronto.
Westman & Baker, Ltd., Toronto.
Toronto Type Foundry Co., Ltd., Toronto, Montreal, Winnipeg.
Miller & Richard, Toronto and Winnipeg.

TYPESETTING
Mono-Lino Typesetting Co., Toronto.

TYPESETTING MACHINES
Canadian Linotype, Ltd., Toronto.
Miller & Richard, Toronto and Winnipeg.
Lanston Monotype Machine Co., Toronto.
Linograph Co., Davenport, Iowa.
Stephenson, Blake & Co., Toronto.

WIRE (Tinned Stitching)
Steel Co. of Canada, The, Hamilton.

WOOD-TYPE
Eastern Brass & Wood Type Co., Inc., New York, N.Y.

LINOTYPE
INTERTYPE
MONOTYPE
ELECTROTYPE
STEREOTYPE

METAL

HOYT METAL COMPANY
MONTREAL   TORONTO   WINNIPEG

INDEX TO ADVERTISERS

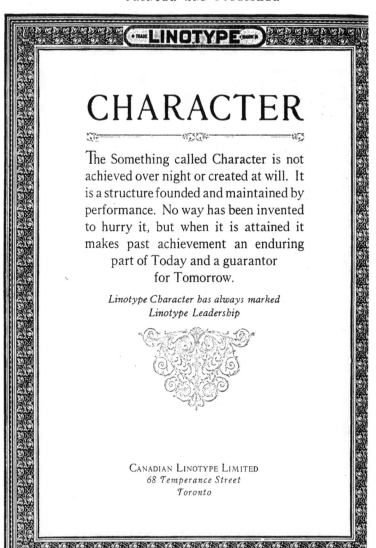

LINOTYPE

CHARACTER

The Something called Character is not achieved over night or created at will. It is a structure founded and maintained by performance. No way has been invented to hurry it, but when it is attained it makes past achievement an enduring part of Today and a guarantor for Tomorrow.

Linotype Character has always marked Linotype Leadership

CANADIAN LINOTYPE LIMITED
68 Temperance Street
Toronto

This Advertisement, Including Border Ornaments, is Composed Entirely of LINOTYPE Material

VOLUME 29   1920   NUMBER 11

PRINTER & PUBLISHER

NOVEMBER

Features In This Issue:

C. W. Young Writes of Old Days

Making Capital of High Rates

Success of a Unique Paper

THE MACLEAN PUBLISHING CO. LIMITED
TORONTO ᵥ MONTREAL ᵥ WINNIPEG

FIBRESTOC COVERS

The "Best Sellers" the Year Round

NOT for a period of a month (like the six best sellers in the bookstall) FIBRESTOC is the Best Seller of Canadian - made covers the year round.

Thus Canadian printers show their appreciation of a cover paper which represents the finest combination of *quality* and *moderate price* on the market.

FIBRESTOC Cover will save you many dollars per ream as against any other cover of similar quality.

It is bulky and strong, has a good printing surface and embosses deeply. Made in a variety of popular colors, suitable for catalogs, booklets, folders and private post cards. May we send you samples?

DISTRIBUTED BY

Barber-Ellis, Limited ....Calgary, Alta.
Barkwell Paper Co. ....Winnipeg, Man.
Buntin, Gillies & Co., Limited ....Hamilton, Ont.
Buntin, Gillies & Co., Limited ....Ottawa, Ont.
Canada Paper Co., Limited ....Montreal, P.Q.
Canada Paper Co., Limited ....Toronto, Ont.
Schofield Paper Co., Limited ....St. John, N.B.
Smith, Davidson & Wright, Limited ....Vancouver, B.C.
Smith, Davidson & Wright, Limited ....Victoria, B.C.
L. P. Turgeon ....Quebec, P.Q.

CANADA PAPER CO.
Limited
WINDSOR MILLS, P.Q.

Colored Papers of All Kinds a Specialty.

Other Good C.P. Co. Covers:

Wove Mill, Cashmere, Derby, Tinted Art S.C., Tinted Art Suede.

PRINTER AND PUBLISHER, November, 1920. Vol. 29, No. 11. Published monthly at 143-153 University Ave., Toronto, by the MacLean Publishing Co., Ltd. Yearly subscription price, $3.00. Entered as second-class matter at the Post Office Department at Ottawa, Canada, also entered as second-class matter July 1, 1912, at the Post Office at Buffalo, N.Y., U.S.A. under Act of March 3rd, 1879.

THE STORAGE PROBLEM

presents no difficulties to the modern printer whose plant is
equipped the "Hamilton" way. Illustration hereon is of our
Unit Galley Cabinet No. 657 (capacity 100 galleys, 8¾ x 13).
Each cabinet supplied with symbol letter and all galley openings numbered. Made in both steel and wood, and for various
sizes of galleys. A real example of composing room economy

Write for details

Manufactured by

The Hamilton Manufacturing Company

TWO RIVERS, WISCONSIN
Eastern House, RAHWAY, N. J.

Hamilton Goods are For Sale by All Prominent Type Founders and Dealers Everywhere

Is your printing easy to read? Is it read by enough people to warrant its production?

The answers to these questions decisively determine the worth of your product and are the measure of your business success. That is true today—it will be truer tomorrow.

Necessary to good printing are an inviting appearance and type that is read without conscious effort.

A contrast between type and background sharp enough to bring the type forward on a separate optical plane is inseparable from strong attraction and high legibility.

The only means of obtaining it is a condensation of the tones of a page by fitting the letters closely. Compact word-forms come forward to meet the vision; they attract the eye and, in reading, the background does not protrude between the letters to cause the slight nervous shocks of imperfect perception and thus affect assimilation.

This application of the psychology of reading is worthy of your careful consideration.

The *single-type* product of the Monotype Composing Machine reaches the highest point of compactness— and of attraction and legibility.

LANSTON MONOTYPE MACHINE COMPANY
PHILADELPHIA

NEW YORK   BOSTON   CHICAGO   TORONTO

Monotype Company of California, SAN FRANCISCO

This Advertisement set in Monotype Series No. 150 and Monotype Rule

If You Are a Printer

we can supply you with Scott Drum Cylinder or Two-Revolution Presses, as they are built in different sizes, with front fly or printed-side-up delivery, as desired.

If You Make Folding Paper Boxes

The Scott High-speed Direct-drive Cutting and Creasing Press should interest you. Several progressive folding box manufacturers in Canada have installed them, and in the United States, China, Japan and Australia they are also in operation.

If You Are a Lithographer

you should carefully investigate and inspect Scott Rotary Offset Presses. They embody so many good features and improvements that they are recognized the world over as the press that produces the maximum amount of work with the minimum amount of spoilage.

If You Publish a Newspaper

the Scott Multi-Unit Newspaper Press should interest you, as it is the only newspaper printing press of which it can truly be said, "It lasts a lifetime." No more trading out of presses, just add a section to meet increased circulation or advertising and if you take time before placing your order for another press to see the Scott Multi-Unit Press in operation you will purchase it.

WRITE US WHAT YOU WANT --- WE HAVE IT

WALTER SCOTT & COMPANY

NEW YORK OFFICE: 1457 Broadway   CHICAGO OFFICE: 1441 Monadnock Block

Main Office and Factory: PLAINFIELD, NEW JERSEY, U.S.A.

CABLE ADDRESS: Waltscott, New York   CODES USED: ABC (5th Edition) and Our Own

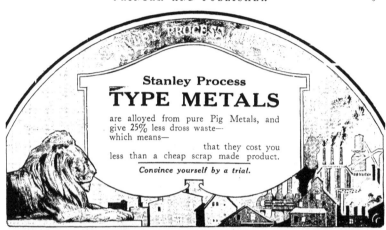

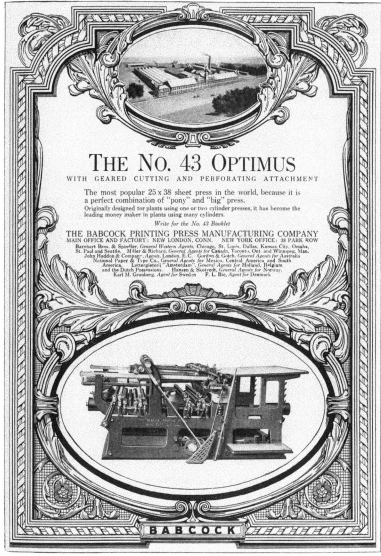

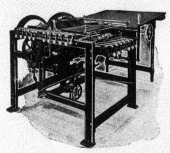

Cromwell
Tympan Papers

Give Cleaner Impressions with
a Minimum of Make-Ready

SAVING time on make-ready, and securing sharp impressions, are the two great things your press foreman has to strive for. With Cromwell Traveling, Shifting and Cylinder Tympan Papers, his draw sheets are always tight—no swelling—and they need not be oiled. They are also moisture-proof, protecting the packing against dampness.

You can turn a rush job quicker with Cromwell Tympan Papers because they resist offset, enabling you to back up reasonably wet sheets. Quick delivery is often your best selling argument.

Cromwell papers will take more impressions without replacing, and they *never* rot.

We especially recommend Cromwell Tympan Papers for trade journal and magazine printers where long runs are necessary without interruptions. It is ideal for book work and the highest grade of printing. Job printers will find it an excellent tympan paper for printing bond, linen and covers.

We carry Cromwell Tympan Papers in stock ready for quick shipment in rolls from 36 to 66 inches wide. Order to-day and secure the perfection and economy in printing that Cromwell Tympan Papers give.

Send us the size of your press, and we will forward, free of all cost to you, Sample Sheet of our Tympan Paper.

The Cromwell Paper Co.

Department P.P.   **Jasper Place, Chicago, U.S.A.**

Trade   Mark

OLIVER CROMWELL

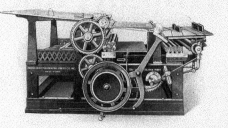

PRINTER AND PUBLISHER
Devoted to the Interests of the Printers and Publishers of Canada

There's an Art in Distributing White Space
Needs as Much Care as Any Display Work
By EDWARD D. BERRY

WHAT the average printer calls "whiting out" could more properly be called "condensation of tone"—that is, the arrangement of the black tones of letters with proper relation to the background of paper, so that proper contrast, proportion and balance may be attained.

The name by which this operation is known is immaterial, but the mental attitude is most important. If the attention is directed to the white space itself, the lettering receives second consideration when in reality it is the most important of the two, and the most attention should be directed to it, for then the white space should take care of itself. This may seem a distinction without a difference, but this reversal of the mental operation will prove itself of value.

An illustration of the virtue of tone condensation is of display lines of various sizes; if there is an equal space between them, they have not a good appearance, nor are they easily read, but if arranged in groups, the page takes on an entirely different aspect. Assembling the lines closely together gives them a preponderance over the background and makes them stand out and seem to come forward to meet the vision. That is also true, for the same reasons, of the closer they are fitted the heavier the tone of the word and the more concentrated the white space around it, which causes it to stand forward more distinctly. Composition done with single types offers better opportunity for this close fitting, because each letter may then be cast the exact size of the printing surface with no mechanical restrictions of interposed space between letters; the natural space caused by the letter terminations is sufficient in the majority of type faces without a shoulder on the letter.

Reading Without Conscious Effort

Letters and words are printed on a page with one purpose solely—they are to be read. If they present something of general interest, they may be read under almost any conditions, but, in advertising, with which commercial printers have most to do, readers are not interested until their attention is attracted and even then they will not read at length unless the matter keeps the interest, nor if it cannot be read without conscious effort. Then it is vitally necessary that matter that is expected to be read must have, first, an attractive appearance, and easy legibility. With these considerations in mind, condensation of tone, or distribution of white space takes on supreme importance.

You have observed how strongly a black cut or ornament stands out in a page of light-faced type; that is because the tones are condensed until the background barely shows through and a distinct contrast is formed with the surrounding white space, which is itself condensed in area. Many of you have noticed, also, that a strong, solid color, surrounded by lighter shades, seems to stand forward from its surroundings; in other words, it has strong attraction. That is just what we try to do with type—to make it stand out and draw attention to itself; the white space showing *through* letters makes close assemblage more necessary.

It should be clear that type stands out only in proportion to its contrast with the background of paper. In order to secure this contrast in sufficient degree, it is necessary that the combined weight of the type be greater than the combined weight of the background showing through and around the matter; in order to have each word distinctly legible it must have the same consideration. Thus, large, black-faced type stands out prominently because of greater contrast, especially if surrounded by type of much lighter tone or concentrated white space.

It follows, then, that in order to secure sufficient contrast and high legibility it is necessary to group letters and lines and that white space be not disseminated throughout the space. Attraction is the capability of arresting the eye by striking contrasts; legibility is in the immediate and sure discernment by the eye and unobstructed assimilation by the mind.

Proper placement of type tones is also responsible for balance in a page. Balance is secured by having a strength of tone, or weight, in opposite parts of a page that counterbalance. The

This ad. selected from a daily paper so well illustrates the points treated herein that comment seems unnecessary.

necessary weight is determined by distance from the center; in a page filled with type the total weight of any section or part must balance that diametrically opposite.

The weight of a part of a page can be lessened by the insertion of white space between the lines, or made greater by taking out space between them.

This layout is poorly spaced and therefore out of balance, it is heavy at the bottom. The optical center is about where the third of the heavy main display lines strikes, and there is more weight below than above it. With one exception, this page can be thrown into perfect balance without resetting anything (see No. 2.)
(No. 1.)

Working On Title Pages

On a title page in which there are but a few lines of type, which do not yield themselves readily to perfect balance, the arrangement of tones is the only recourse. For instance, in the majority of title pages there are two or three important lines in the top part of the page, which are the title of the book, and the matter is usually arranged in two sections, one in the upper and one in the lower part of the page. If the smaller section of type matter, at the bottom, is not heavy enough, set in the suitable size of type, nor is there opportunity to move it farther from the center of the page, space can be taken out between the lines, which will give it added weight without making the type larger and giving it undue prominence. On the other hand, if there is an unusual amount of matter at the bottom of the page—enough to overbalance the title lines—taking out space between the main lines in the upper part of the page helps to secure balance without unduly separating the lower part.

There are several other things to be kept in mind while this is being done. Sometimes this condensation can be carried so far, in order to secure balance, that the lines are placed too close together, giving them such a weight of tone that the background is almost obliterated and the words illegible, especially so if the type has many ascending or descending characters.

Attention must be given, also, to another element, somewhat more involved. In the ideal page, one series of display lines or one section of large type, has greater prominence than any other part of the page, and other parts are set in smaller type, and of a lighter tone, that they do not contest with the main section for prominence. In any case, there are a limited number that can compete for attention with any degree of success; as their number increases they detract from the main section in proportionate degree. Carried to an extreme, there are so many parts of a page striving for attention that one offsets the other and none has prominence. Excepting the selection of type faces or sizes for these sections, the distribution of tones governs the matter entirely.

Space Decreases the Prominence

Frequently, a section of straight matter closely spaced has more weight than a display line, especially if the line is widely spaced and not surrounded by an amount of white space.

Increasing the space between the lines lessens weight and gives greater prominence to other parts of a page.

It is well to set the main line or section first and space it closely, to give it strength, and proportion the other sections to it. This proportion of prominence could be achieved by wide spacing in sections which had been set without relation to the main section but it should not be done, for whiting out any section reduces its own contrast with its background, making it less attractive and harder to read. It is better to proportion the different attractions in a page so that each may be spaced to form proper contrast with its own background.

A section of type matter which will just fill the space allotted to it if leaded widely, will have much greater attraction if the extra leads are omitted and the space thus gained put around the section instead of distributed through it. Black-faced type should have more space between the lines than type of a lighter face; if black type is set solid, the background is not apparent in sufficient degree for requisite contrast; so it will be seen that there is a point where condensation of tone must stop; determining that point is one of the niceties of composition. But more errors are made in wide spacing than in close spacing.

Words and lines of type should be spaced just sufficiently to form the greatest degree of contrast with the paper; the tones of the page should be condensed and the white space assembled in units, and not disseminated throughout the page, for that will give the background too much prominence, which is not desirable.

No less an authority than William Morris abhorred a gray page, that is, one in which the type and background have almost equal prominence, that has necessarily a low degree of both attraction and legibility. The preceding should always be kept in mind; particular attention should be paid to proper condensation of tone—the background will then take care of itself.

Accompanying this article are some sketches and a clipping illustrating these precepts.

In this specimen the three large lines have been placed closer together, giving them added weight, and the lower straight matter sections moved upwards; also, the next to the last line, which may have been two or three lines of smaller type closely spaced, has been shortened showing more white at the bottom and thus giving more weight to the top, proportionately; the page is now in good balance.

But in securing this balance, another error has been committed. Note that the line next to the bottom seems, on No. 1 to conform better to the page. On No. 2, the shorter line, added to the effect of the inverted pyramid at the top, gives a general shape to the heavy lines of the page, which are the most apparent, that belongs to a vertical page. This page is oblong and the longer line in No. 1 is more in proportion to the shape of the page itself. This error could have been corrected by condensing the top display lines still more and not changing the bottom line. It was done in this way to illustrate a common error. (No. 2.)

Cashing in on the Increased Charges

You May be Able to Realize on Them

DO YOU ever make a serious attempt to link up current happenings and make it possible to form out of them a strong appeal for your local advertisers?

For instance, take the increase in freight rates and express charges. Perhaps you waded into this thing editorially in a pretty strong way, and got yourself all excited. Very well, now then for the constructive element that should get into every situation. What is there in these increases for you and your home merchants?

You have to pay more for your paper and supplies. What else? Does it not work out this way? It costs a shopper more now to take the train to some nearby city to shop. It costs more in that city than formerly to stop for any length of time. In this there is a strong appeal that the local merchant can make, and you should see to it that he makes this very appeal.

If there is any advantage in these conditions for the local merchant he will only get this advantage by some practical campaign that he puts into effect for taking advantage of these conditions. A live retail merchant is on the lookout at all times for subjects of this kind to be treated and enlarged upon, and it is out of such things that he should be encouraged to build his advertising campaign in your papers.

Don't waste your time by running foolish items about the mail order houses sending in large shipments of catalogues to your district. Don't bother telling your readers how much advertising from department stores you have refused in order to support the home merchant.

Put in some real constructive work, and you will find your merchant, if he is alive and aggressive, will respond. There is good reason for making such an appeal. It will help your merchants to fight the department store idea, and they want ammunition for that very purpose. They should bring out the idea very clearly in their advertising that the home price is the better now.

Included in this might be displayed just what it is likely to cost a customer to go away to do a day's shopping. Show it this way:

Railroad fare to Toronto..........................$00.00

Buy at Home		Buy at Home
	It Costs Too Much	
	To Buy Out of Town	

We Can Meet Big City Prices!

ARE you sure it's an advantage to habitually patronize metropolitan department stores? Are you sure you get better values? We doubt this! But even conceding better values are obtainable in the big cities, will they strike a balance with the high passenger rates now prevailing, and the other numerous incidentals of a trip to places where the cost of living is at high-water mark.

Unmatched Values in Silks and Fabrics

Shioze Silk

A washable silk that looks like taffeta and wears better, 36 inches wide, in white, pink, navy blue. Correct for waists. Selling in big cities for $2.50;

THE HOME PRICE - - **$1.98**

Coating Cloths

A big range of special coating cloths. All new weaves and colors. Big city price, $5.00;

THE HOME PRICE - - **$3.98**

Wash Silk

A heavy weight Habutai Wash Silk for dresses and waists, in black, navy, pink and white. 36 inches wide. Selling in the city for $2.50 or more

THE HOME PRICE - - **$1.49**

Plaids, Stripes

New materials for new skirts. They are very stylish wool fabrics in exclusive patterns. Big city stores are asking $12.00 for skirt lengths.

THE HOME PRICE - - **$9.98**

Splendid Values in Hosiery, Gloves, Underwear

Hosiery for Women— Pure wool full fashioned hose, seamless, reinforced heels and toes, in black, brown, cream. City price $2.25; the Home Price - $2.00

Silk Gloves – Women's Gloves of pure silk, heavy silk embroidered backs, all popular colors and sizes. You save 40 cents at the Home Price - $1.35

Children's Underwear— Natural color cotton vest and drawers. Drawers in ankle lengths, 4 to 12 years. The Home Price per garment - - - - 59c

Many bargains not advertised here—come and look around.

Johnson & James Co., Limited

Street cars and meals... .... 00.00
Incidentals...... 00.00

Other items would no doubt suggest themselves to you, and they could be worked into the appeal. On this page we have included a specimen ad showing one way in which the publisher might prepare copy for his advertiser, or suggest the preparation along these lines. Or it might be possible to go farther, and get your merchants to get together for such a campaign. At any rate the suggestion ought to be worth trying out.

Merchants will not resent suggestions from the publisher who knows his business, and is in a position to give intelligent advice to the advertiser. The publisher ought to get himself in a position where he will be looked to for suggestions in the merchandising business. He should be not simply a seller of news, and a seller of white space, but an authority in the proper way in which a merchant can make the best possible use of the white space he has for sale.

The weekly publisher in particular can take a lesson from the methods of the agencies and the business papers in this regard, which are well in advance of all others in the methods they employ for fully informing themselves of the nature of the business followed by the man or firm they seek to interest in their publication.

This side of the business is being more and more developed. If you can go to your merchant with definite knowledge of the field he wishes to interest; tell him the number of prospective customers he has; what their buying power is; the percentage of mortgage free firms; the number of automobiles, you can have an argument that will interest him just as it would the national advertiser, who intelligently makes use of all this information, and plans his selling campaign accordingly.

What we want to leave with the publisher is not a sample ad., but an idea that may mean many ads to him, viz., that there is something in many of the business developments and changing price conditions that can be turned to the advantage of the publisher who is on the alert to follow them up and reap the advantage.

Collect Arrears and Retain Subscribers

Claims it is Not an Impossible Thing

BY A. R. K.

IT IS one thing to get the money that a delinquent subscriber owes you and it is another and a better to keep that subscriber on your books.

Perhaps it has never occurred to you that there have been cases in which a subscriber has owed for 25 years, and where the account has been collected.

These thoughts and a few more like them prompted me to talk the matter of collections over with Mr. H. Goldstein, manager of the Publishers' Protective Association, Toronto. Rising costs in every line make it necessary for publishers to have money, and in fact the absence of money has caused a tombstone to grow in the office door of more than a score of them in the last year.

According to Mr. Goldstein, there are three very plausible reasons or excuses which are given by the delinquents. They run on these lines:

1. The publisher did not notify me that the account was due.

2. I subscribed for a year, and told the post office to stop sending it to me.

3. I intended to pay that account but it slipped my memory.

"As a general thing," stated Mr. Goldstein, "we do not find many people who are not willing to play square when we have taken the time and trouble to explain the position of the publisher to them, and explain how it is necessary that all available cash be turned in to keep his plant operating. We have found from a fairly long experience that it does not do any good to try to scare people into paying their accounts. A straight letter in which we set forth all the facts in connection with the case gets almost fifty per cent. of the money sent in. The second letter that is used gets perhaps ten to twelve per cent., and the subsequent letters vary in their drawing power."

"I suppose that most of the accounts you get sent to you have been pretty well drilled beforehand by the publishers?" was suggested.

"We take it for granted that they have," was the answer. "A publisher would hardly send us anything that he could collect himself. In fact they often write us to the effect that they are sending along their dead-wood, and insinuate that the picking will be pretty dry in it. We had one letter mentioning the fact that in the list that was being sent to us was one subscriber 25 years in arrears. We secured that man's cheque for the entire amount. I often wish that I had not let it out of my hands. It would have been a great piece of advertising material for me."

Many Let Lists Run

In spite of all that has been done in the way of education, Mr. Goldstein believes that there are many smaller papers who have not paid the attention to collections that should have been given.

"Papers that are large enough to have an organization to take care of these matters keep their lists in better shape than the smaller ones where there is no collection department. It surprises us to find the extent to which some of the smaller publishers will let their lists run. There is no need for this at all. A clean list is not an impossible thing, and it is not necessary to kill off a delinquent in order to get him to pay up.

"Much of the stuff that the subscriber writes to us about the publisher not having notified him of his arrears, is not to be relied upon at all," continued Mr. Goldstein. "The average publisher will not allow bills to run on and on without telling the subscriber that he is in arrears, and many of the papers are constantly containing references to the effect that the editor needs the money and asking the subscriber to look at the label on his paper and see when it is paid up to. Then the claim that the subscriber did not order the paper for anything over the year might hold water but for the fact that it has been explained away so often that every person who reads at all is familiar more or less with the newspaper law on this point. When a person keeps on taking a paper after the date of his subscription has expired, there is an implied contract that he intends to keep on taking it, and on that implied contract the paper can be continued and the reader is liable for a year's subscription. There are faults in that law, and I do not believe that it is generally appreciated. The publisher who is keeping his list clean is certainly not going to the trouble of hiding behind any such protection as that. It is much better to keep the collections well up, and not let the subscriber run behind. On daily papers where the subscription price runs up around $7 and $8 per year it would be much better to have the collections made every two months or so, as it is a great deal easier to collect a number of small amounts often than leaving it for the year."

Mr. Goldstein is convinced that it is quite possible to collect from a subscriber though the publisher has given him up, and still retain the good-will of that person for the paper to such an extent that the collected amount will include provision for the coming year's subscription. It has been our experience that it is poor policy to try and frighten a subscriber into paying his arrears. It is useless to try and browbeat him to the point where he will pay up. If common sense and reason are employed we find that it is not only possible to collect what he owes the paper in the way of arrears, but also to hold him as a reader of that paper. No," said Mr. Goldstein in conclusion, "collecting arrears for newspaper publishers is not nearly as much a hammer-and-tongs sort of business as a good many people imagine. It is simply the application of proven principles to known conditions, and from this combination it is quite possible for any subscriber to get at least 75 per cent. of all the arrears he has on his books."

Collections

Does the average publisher pay strict enough attention to the matter of collections?

With prices at their present level, and with banks not at all anxious to go very far in extending credit, money is needed to buy to advantage.

Collecting is something that a good many publishers dread. In many cases a good newspaper man is a poor collector.

Toronto Globe's New City Edition

The Toronto *Globe* is paying greater attention to the local field, and is turning out a city and suburban edition, which comes as a separate section of the paper. The regular edition for general distribution is run off first, and then the paper is remade for the city and suburban edition, by the inclusion of advertising by merchants who wish to reach the Toronto field rather than participate in a general distribution, and by the making up of a number of pages carrying strictly local reading matter. The city staff has been enlarged to turn in the material, and it gives a morning paper a greater opportunity to give attention to many matters that hitherto had to be much condensed or omitted entirely. At the outset it was more or less of an experiment, but so far, in fact from the start, the city and suburban edition has paid its way, and the *Globe* believes that the idea is possible of much greater development.

Old Traditions Are Being Shattered Here
Canso Breeze Runs On Novel Lines
BY JOHN S. SCOTT

FTER a lapse of twenty odd years, Guysboro county, Nova Scotia, can boast of a local newspaper. A paper was published at Guysboro town at one time, but it gave up the ghost a quarter of a century ago, and it is almost as long ago that Mr. Bourinot, who now directs the destinies of the Richmond County *Advocate*, at Arichat, N.S. left Canso, in Guysboro county, where for a brief spell he issued a weekly paper. Since Mr. Bourinot's departure the historic county has been as barren of newspapers as are some of its rocky hills of vegetation.

The newspaper, which is a real newspaper, too, of which the citizens of the county may properly boast, is published at Canso, and is called the Canso *Breeze*. The proprietor, publisher, editor, reporter, advertising manager and circulation manager is Cecil Boyd. Mr. Boyd is not what one would call an experienced newspaper man. He has never set type; has never been a reporter, has never sold advertising, and has never canvassed for subscriptions. And because of what he has not done some people would say the reason Mr. Boyd has started a newspaper in these days of sudden deaths of some papers, and lingering illnesses of others, is that he does not know anything about publishing a newspaper.

But He Doesn't Need Pity

Now you old, experienced, wise newspaper men, don't laugh at this budding Nova Scotia publisher, if you are cynical; and if you are soft-hearted, don't waste any commiseration on him. He doesn't deserve the one, nor need the other. In fact, Mr. Boyd, in spite of his lack of experience, appears to be pretty well equipped for the job of successfully publishing a country newspaper, and the way he has gone about the job indicates that he is well able to look after himself.

To tell the truth there are a lot of Canadian newspaper publishers who ought to be able to learn a great deal from Cecil Boyd and the Canso *Breeze*. For, while Mr. Boyd has not discovered any amazing secret to apply to the business of producing a newspaper, he is unquestionably putting into practice some sound business ideas that seem to be—or at least to have been—none too generally recognized by country weekly publishers.

First of all the father of the *Breeze* has a very firm conviction that the success of his paper depends fundamentally upon giving the people something they want. That something is local news. And so Mr. Boyd starts out by continually rustling local news. Perhaps he does not get it all. Most likely he does not. Who ever does? But he gets a lot of it. And he does not miss much.

Of course, the *Breeze* is not a general newspaper, and in the broad sense the class of news Mr. Boyd is after is not "important" news. That is the stuff in the *Breeze* is not calculated to set the world agog by dealing with the big subjects, and printing the big stories which find places in the dailies. But, when it comes to telling about the things that Guysboro folks do and say and think, and the events and conditions that directly and intimately affect them, the *Breeze* literally makes them "sit up and take notice." Not that there's anything of the "stormy petrel" type in the paper. Mr. Boyd does not aspire to achieve a reputation for sensationalism, for "knocking," nor for rabid criticism. He wants his paper to be simply a good, clean, bright, interesting and reliable local newspaper.

Well, it may be said, that is all very well for intentions, but having these fine ideas is one thing, and making them work is another. Quite true. And while I do not desire to pose as

CECIL BOYD

the discoverer of a great newspaperman, I believe I did find out in personal contact with *Breeze* subscribers in my four days sojourn in Guysboro county enough to warrant the conclusion that Mr. Boyd is "putting over" his ideas. The people there certainly do want, and do appreciate the *Breeze*.

Then, Mr. Boyd launched his journalistic craft with another good feature to keep it above water. And it really was a quite reasonable, and extremely simple idea. Nothing more nor less than that his subscribers should pay a reasonable price for the service he proposed to render.

And so he made the subscription price of the *Breeze* $2 a year. It is taking country weeklies a long time to get up enough spunk to ask that price, notwithstanding the clearly apparent fact that sooner or later they will have to get it—or the undertaker. So, Boyd, of the *Breeze*, not relishing a flirtation with disaster ribs up his craft with staunch $2 timbers.

Quite naturally, Mr. Boyd figured on carrying some advertising in the *Breeze*. Did he start out by crawling up to merchants and other prospective advertisers apologetically explaining that since he was only starting in, and didn't have much circulation, and was very anxious to have them put their ads. in the *Breeze*, etc., etc., he would make them a very low rate? He did—not. What he did was what any good business man would do. He figured out how much he would have to make the paper pay. And he made his advertising rates 20c an inch and upwards. Did he get the business? Well, for the four months the *Breeze* has been published it has carried an average of slightly more than three hundred inches of advertising an issue.

Not because he could not get it, but because he considered it good business not to do so, Mr. Boyd did not buy a printing plant in which to produce his paper. The *Breeze* is printed outside of Guysboro county. By whom, and at what price, it is not this connection that after totalling up interest on the necessary investment, if a plant were purchased; depreciation, rent, taxes, repairs, insurance and wages, Mr. Boyd concluded that he would be several hundred dollars ahead annually, to let an already established plant turn out his paper.

This leaf out of Boyd's book could be appropriated very profitably by many country weekly publishers who are going behind, or failing to go ahead, at the rate of hundreds of dollars every year simply because they persist in maintaining individual plants at an expenditure of money and time, out of all proportion to the value of the printed product they get from the plants. Throughout the country there are geographical groups of from five to a dozen papers in various sections that could be printed at one central plant, at lower cost, in better style and with more convenience to their publishers, than is now the case. The multiplicity of small, and often inefficient, printing plants is a tremendous drag on the country newspaper business. This is one pitfall that Boyd of the *Breeze* has overstepped.

Mr. Boyd is a native of the county which he has undertaken to serve through the Canso *Breeze*. He is thirty-six years old, and married. He was educated at the Canso public schools and then took up the vocation of telegraph operator from which such men as the late Senator Cox, Hon. J. D. Reid, Sir John Aird, Chas. R. Hosmer, Sir Herbert Holt, Edwin R. Pease, Senator Gideon D. Robertson and other notable Canadian men received the training that equipped them for successful careers in other fields. For years Mr. Boyd was employed as telegraph operator at the offices of the Postal Telegraph Cable Company at Canso, and during the war served as a censor at Canso.

Gatherings of Publishers In Recent Weeks

Daily, Weekly and Job Men Active

THE following officers and members of the Board of Directors of Canadian Daily Newspapers Association were elected at the first annual meeting in Toronto, on Friday, October 22nd, 1920.

President, P. D. Ross, Ottawa *Journal*; past president, M. R. Jennings, Edmonton *Journal*; vice-president, F. J. Burd, Vancouver *Province*; treasurer, Geo. E. Scroggie, Toronto *Mail and Empire*. Board of directors, H. V. McKinnon, St. John *Standard*; G. Fred Pearson, Halifax *Chronicle*; L. J. Tarte, *La Patrie*, Montreal; C. Pelletier, *Le Devoir*, Montreal; Lord Atholstan, Montreal *Star*; V. B. Merrill, Sherbrooke *Record*; T. H. Preston, Brantford *Expositor*; J. E. Atkinson, Toronto *Star*; H. Q. Graybeil, *Border Cities Star*, Windsor; W. B. Burgoyne, St. Catharines *Standard*; John M. Imrie, Hamilton *Times*; E. H. Macklin, Winnipeg *Free Press*; Burford Hooke, Regina *Leader*; J. H. Woods, Calgary *Herald*; Ben. Chas. Nicholas, Victoria *Times*.

Another resolution was as follows:—This general meeting of the Canadian Daily Newspapers Association takes this first

P. D. ROSS

opportunity of a general meeting of the Association to express the great regret of the members of the Association at the retirement from the position of General Manager of Mr. John M. Imrie. It is the unanimous feeling of the members of the Association that the services given by Mr. Imrie during his many years of connection with the newspapers of Canada, both in the present Canadian Daily Newspapers Association and in the Canadian Press Association, have been of practically inestimable value to the newspaper fraternity of Canada. They can hardly be measured in figures. We feel that the loss of Mr. Imrie is a very serious matter for the Association but we recognize that his first duty is to his own future. It is our earnest hope that Mr. Imrie will have every success possible in the new sphere of enterprise to which he has decided to go and we are confident that the qualities which made him so valuable in the newspaper fraternity in general will have a similar value to himself in his private undertaking. We desire to emphasize once more our deep appreciation of the ability, courage, untiring energy and unstinted industry of Mr. Imrie in the position of trust he has filled with us, and to express our earnest hope for his utmost success in the future.

This resolution was adopted by the meeting:—That the members of the Canadian Daily Newspapers Association on

this first anniversary of the birth of said association desire to express their great appreciation of the work of its retiring president, Mr. R. Jennings, in connection with its conception and inception and for the intensive labors on his part which have brought to it the large measure of success thus far achieved. He has been unsparing of himself in the work of upbuilding the Association and in his retirement from the office of president, we wish him to understand that we are not ungrateful.

Waterloo County Organized

Waterloo County publishers met at Kitchener. The meeting was held in the *News-Record* office. There were present: Geo. Hudson, Hespeler *Herald*; H. W. Kaufman, Wellesley *Maple Leaf*; W. V. Uttley, Elmira *Signet*; D. Ritz, New Hamburg *Independent*; W. Ritz, New Hamburg *Independent*; D. L. Motz, Kitchener *News-Record*; A. Beane, Kitchener *Telegraph*; A. W. Moir, Kitchener, J. W. Shantz, Kitchener. Mr. Malcolm McBeth, president of the Huron and Perth District Association, was present and addressed the gathering briefly on the work of organization. A district association was formed called the Waterloo County Press Association, affiliated with the C.W.N.A. The president is Geo. Hudson, Hespeler *Herald*; secretary-treasurer, H. W. Kaufman, Wellesley *Maple Leaf*; and executive: Messrs. Uttley, Ritz and Moir. E. Roy Sayles, manager of the C.W.N.A., was present and led in the work of organization and gave valuable information on publishing and printing problems. The meeting decided that all papers in the district charging $1 were to raise to $1.50 at once and those having the $1.50 were to raise to $2 at once, and further increase by the $1.50 men to $2 later on. The executive committee will meet in a few days to print a job printing price list and to revise advertising rates.

The Canadian Weekly Press Association now has 380 members, perhaps a few over, and they fully expect to reach the 400 mark by the first of the year. Considering that this organization started at zero, with no members and no funds at the first of the year, the going has been good.

Wellington Publishers in Session

A well attended meeting of the publishers of Wellington County was held in Harriston where the party were very hospitably entertained by Messrs. Dewar and Gardiner of the Harriston *Review*. The tariff of job work and advertising rates was revised to meet the radical changes which have taken place in paper prices of all kinds during the past month. In many instances, it was found that the material alone to-day costs more than the finished product sold for three years ago. A reduction in values, if it is really coming at all, has not yet reached the realm of paper prices, the increase which went into effect on the first of this month in newsprint quotations being one of the heaviest since the war, the present price being between four and five times higher than that prevailing before the war. It was unanimously decided to increase the subscription rates of Wellington County papers 50 cents per year. While this increase to each subscriber will be trifling, being less than 1 cent per week, in the aggregate it will greatly assist the publisher in carrying on. Newspapers of Ontario have practically gone through the war period without an increase in subscription rates. True, the $1.50 rate was adopted during the war, but it was essential and was in force in many newspaper offices before 1914. The $1.50 subscription price is really a pre-war price. $2.00 per year is now the prevailing price in the majority of newspaper offices in Ontario.

Toronto Typothetae Activities

The Toronto Typothetae, from its office, 1002 Royal Bank Building, is carrying on a progressive program in the interests of its members. Mr. Knowlton, the executive secretary, has his organization in good working condition, and the various courses that the Typothetae recommend are being carried out. These are largely educational in their scope, and the course in cost finding, which has been in progress for some weeks, has an average attendance of 85, showing a very healthy interest in the work. When this is through the organization is ready to go ahead with the estimating courses. These will be made up of members of the staffs of various firms in the city, estimators, travelling salesmen, etc. In many cases preference is being given to a printing salesman who, with his qualities as a salesman, can combine those of a competent estimator as it is often necessary to give a figure right on the spot, and it is not desirable to have to run back to the office every time a figure is asked for. Of course the fact is not lost sight of that the desirable way to sell printing is without an estimate.

The Toronto branch has already put in operation 45 cost-finding systems in city offices where no standard system had been used before, and it is likely that a movement will be undertaken to get some of the offices in the district to form district organizations, steps being under way now for the holding of a meeting in Guelph to include several of the centres in that direction.

The matter of presenting the case of the printing industry to the Tariff Commission has also been taken in hand by the Toronto Typothetae. For this purpose a questionnaire covering several salient points was sent to members, the following questions being asked:

1. Are you in favor of an increase in the present general tariff as it pertains to printed matter?

2. Are you in favor of a decrease?

3. Should it remain as it is at the present time?

4. Is there any point which you think should be changed? If so, please give details.

There was a very general response to the appeal for information.

The present tariff has the following items of interest to publishers:

Advertising and Printed Matter, viz:—Advertising pamphlets, advertising show cards, illustrated advertising periodicals, price books, catalogues and price lists; advertising almanacs and calendars; patent medicine or other advertising circulars, fly sheets or pamphlets, advertising chromos, chromo-types, oleographs, or like work produced by any process other than hand painting or drawing, and having any advertisement or advertising matter printed, lithographed or stamped thereon, or attached thereto, including advertising bills, folders and posters or other similar artistic work, lithographed, printed or stamped on paper or cardboard for business or advertising purposes: General Tariff, 15c per pound.

Tariff Item No. 179.—Labels for cigar boxes, fruits, vegetables, meats, confectionery, or other goods or wares; shipping, price, or other tags, tickets or labels, and railroad or other tickets, lithographed or printed or partly printed: General Tariff, 35 per cent.

Tariff Item No. 181.—Bank notes, bonds, bills of exchange, cheques, promissory notes, drafts and other similar work, unsigned, and cards or other commercial blank forms printed or lithographed or printed from steel or copper plates and other plates and other printed matter: General Tariff, 35 per cent.

The Employment and Welfare committee are also taking up with the local branch of the I.T.U. the matter of training apprentices, it being the feeling of the Typothetae that more attention should be given to this important matter.

The matter of having Toronto as the meeting place for the 1921 convention of the Typothetae was also discussed, and Mr. J. C. Acton has this matter in hand.

The officers of the Toronto Typothetae are as follows:—Q. B. Henderson, President; Douglas S. Murray, Vice-Pres.; F. M. Kimbark, Treasurer; J. C. Acton, Recording Secretary; Ira R. Knowlton, Executive Secretary. Executive Committee: H. L. Rous, Geo. M. Rose, R. T. McLean, A. L. Lewis, G. D. Thomas, R. D. Croft, J. J. Lynch, F. S. Thomas, Thomas G. Robinson.

Alberta Press Conference

The Alberta Press Conference met at Calgary a short time ago. F. W. Galbraith, of the Red Deer *Advocate*, reported on the activity of the Canadian Press Association in connection

with the price of paper, showing that there had been a saving of many hundreds of thousands of dollars. V. C. French, of Wetaskiwin, speaking of editorial work, stated: "Sometimes we fail to weigh the effect of what we write. It is sometimes a small thing to scribble something down, and put it into print, but we must consider that there are thousands who read our writings, and once gone out they can never be recalled. What may be light to us may mean grief and sorrow to others and in some cases financial injury. We would be traitors to our high calling, if we do not put our best thought and our widest charity into our writings."

Hon. C. R. Mitchell addressed the meeting, among other things pointing out his appreciation of the value of papers in sucessfully negotiating domestic and other loans. Hon. Frank Oliver spoke on the necessity of papers putting a high enough value on their own papers. Referring to the value of the local paper to the advertiser, Mr. Oliver said: "How could a merchant reach the field were it not for the local newspaper? If he attempted to circularize it every week in the same way, it would cost as much as the printing plant would cost. The difficulties are largely your own fault. You have not had confidence in the business side of the enterprise and have not pushed it in the way it should be pushed. The attention of the editor is often absorbed in the literary or news side, and not sufficient stress has been laid on the paying side."

Mr. D'Albertanson, of the Chauvin *Chronicle*, led in the discussion on advertising rates. He did not agree with the legal rates of Saskatchewan, which called for 12 and 8 cents. He advocated 15 and 12 cents. For financial statements he favored 50 cents an inch instead of 45 cents, plus 25 per cent. extra on account of tabular composition instead of 20 cents. The resolution was then carried, to reject the Saskatchewan rates and discuss a rate card to be brought in by the committee.

Coming to the election of officers, V. C. French, the retiring president, said that he would like to nominate J. H. Woods, of the Calgary *Herald*. He had shown a very keen interest in the work, and he was sure a more efficient or more honored president could not be had. There being no other nominations, Mr. Woods was declared elected by acclamation, and was given a round of hearty applause. Other officers elected were: First vice-president, J. H. Huntingford, Wainwright *Star*; second vice-president, Mrs. Annie H. Derrett, Pincher Creek *Echo*; secretary-treasurer, John McKenzie, Strathmore *Standard*; executive, H. D'Albertanson, Chauvin *Chronicle*; M. R. Jennings, Edmonton *Journal*; L. D. Nesbitt, Brooks *Bulletin*; Charles Clark, High River *Times*; and Mr. Whalen.

Some of those attending were:—V. C. French, Wetaskiwin; F. W. Galbraith, Red Deer; M. R. Jennings, Edmonton *Journal*; J. H. Woods, Calgary *Herald*; W. J. Watson, Calgary *Herald*; A. M. Terrill, Medicine Hat *News*; H. J. Ford, *Morning Albertan*, Calgary; H. E. and F. H. Osmond, Didsbury *Pioneer*; F. Burton, Cardston *Globe*; J. H. Salton, Granum *Advertiser*; F. H. Schooley, Claresholm *Review-Advertiser*; J. W. Johnston, Alliance *Times*; H. G. McCrea, Hanna *Herald*; L. D. Nesbitt, Brooks *Bulletin*; Mr. and Mrs. G. R. Westland, Innisfail *Province*; Mr. and Mrs. D'Albertanson, Chauvin *Chronicle*; Mrs. Annie H. Derrett, Pincher Creek *Echo*; Mrs. F. W. Galbraith, Red Deer; R. G. Jessop, Nanton; J. A. Carswell, *News*, Red Deer; W. J. Huntingford, *Star*, Wainwright; W. Park Evans, Gleichen *Call*, Gleichen; J. E. Buchanan, *Reporter*, Fort Saskatchewan.

Publishers Met at Milton

Halton, Peel and Wentworth publishers met at Milton, Ont. A district association was formed with the following officers: President: J. M. Moore, the *Herald*, Georgetown; Vice-president: H. G. Greene, the *Review*, Waterdown; Secretary-treasurer: E. A. Harris, the *Gazette*, Burlington, Ont. Executive: Wm. Paton, the *Champion*, Milton; Harry Moore, the *Star*, Dundas; G. G. Mitchell, the *News*, Oakville.

Other publishers present were:

Mr. H. P. Moore, the *Free Press*, Acton, Ont.; R. White, W. Blight, Milton; W. J. Fleuty, the *Record*, Oakville; A. S. Forster, the *Star*, Oakville, Ont.

It was decided to adopt the $2 rate for subscriptions, and a job price list will be printed for use. E. Roy Sales, manager of the Canadian Weekly Newspapers Association, was present and addressed the gathering. Several more publishers joined the C.W.N.A.

Space Grabbers Believe in a Free Press

Publishers Hold the Remedy Themselves

AT THE recent meeting of the Midland Counties Press Association, E. G. McKeeley, city editor of the Peterboro *Examiner*, discussed the "Evils of Propaganda." Mr. McKeeley said:—

In addressing the Midland Counties Press Association on the subject of the evils of "Propaganda" I may be a little out of place. It may be the members of this association are not victimized to the same extent as medium-sized dailies of from three to ten thousand circulation. However, I doubt if there is a paper in the country, weekly or daily, that can claim complete freedom from the free publicity pest. The late war produced many evils and one of them has been imposed on the publishers of this country in the form of publicity agents whose duty is to steal space from the newspapers. We have always boasted about a free press but not until the present era of free space lizards have we fully realized how free the press is. Press agents

E. G. McKEELEY

in their campaign of propaganda consume white paper, labor and rob publishers of a just revenue for advertising. The greatest space wasters in free publicity matter are the government, amusement enterprises, automobile manufacturers, charities and numerous others. Religious publicity agents appear to work on the theory that because their cause is religious the newspapers of this country must piously print their stuff regardless of its lack of news value. The automobile interests like the theatrical promoters by some strange process of reasoning establish the precedent that paid advertising commands an equal amount of free advertising.

Publishers of newspapers in some of the smaller towns and cities have been slow to realize that space is a commercial product and that the subscription paid by the subscriber is a retaining fee to print the news and not to advertise somebody else's product disguised as news. As an example of this we have the piffle sent out under the auspices of the Ontario Dental Society with the smug intimation that the articles in question are "sent to you without charge for use in your news columns." The articles presume to deal with the dental afflictions of mankind and carry with them the inference that the best way to secure relief is to visit a dentist. Very good advice we will ad-

mit but why should the newspapers of this country be asked to convey this information free of charge? If, as the dentists claim, it is unethical to advertise, then by the same token it should be unethical to steal space at the expense of the newspapers. A few months ago a dentist in this city informed me that business was very quiet. Strange to say a couple of weeks later an agent representing the dentists went through the country soliciting free space in the newspapers for the insertion of canned publicity extolling the wonders of the profession. One method employed in this case was to make the final appeal through the medium of a local member of the profession. In some cases the scheme worked and in many more cases it did not.

How A Campaign Worked

Perversion of viewpoint is not the only aim of many of the publicity sharps of this country. They do not hesitate to violate editorial integrity such as the shoe interests sought to do some time ago. Advertisements were first sent out calling attention to the shoe situation in which an appeal was made for public sympathy on behalf of the shoe manufacturers who were beginning to encounter hard sledding on account of falling prices. This was followed by a request for the insertion of free reading matter and especially prepared editorial matter. The insertion of the latter was sought through the influence of local shoe manufacturers whenever possible. The day upon which one of these editorial handouts appeared came a news despatch supplied by one of the news services calling attention to falling prices in the shoe trade. Papers that printed both the editorial and the news despatch on the same day supplied their readers with a strange conflict of opinion. The value of a press agent to his employer depends upon his ability to secure publication of what his employer wants to have appear and suppress what he does not want to appear.

As an example of what can be done locally in the way of free space grabbing I present the following so-called news item which appeared in one daily newspaper.

Charge For Lecture Hall in Library

"Owing to a clause in the new Public Libraries Act, the Library Board will be compelled in future to charge for the use of any room used by corporate bodies for patriotic, charitable and educational purposes. It is necessary therefore, that the Librarian be communicated with when any Society desires the use of one of the basement rooms or the lecture hall."

If the Public Library Board proposes to secure a revenue from the use of its room why should the newspapers not share in this revenue to the extent of the service it provides in the matter? Various organizations throughout the city will hold tag days and other events to raise funds for so-called charitable purposes and then expect the newspapers to turn around and thank everybody under the sun for contributing to the cause. If the Serbian Relief Committee, whose organizers recently swept through the country, paid for newspaper space in proportion to the amount they paid for some of the service they sought, very little money would remain for the Serbian orphans. A favorite method in connection with campaigns of this character is for an organizer to come into the locality, secure the services of some prominent citizen as chairman and a committee of overworked business men whose duty in turn is to overwork the newspapers for all the free publicity the traffic will stand.

In the Grave Now

I knew of one daily newspaper in this country that used cooked news, supplied by a free publicity bureau, on its front page headed up like real live telegraph matter. This particular brand of predigested opinion emanated from Winnipeg and was put out for the purpose of advancing the interests of a well known western corporation on the eve of a money-making anniversary. It pleases me to say that this newspaper has since found refuge in the graveyard of newspaperdom after long years of existence in the newspaper world. It deserved no better fate when it could not do better than give space and prominence to this class of sugar-coated propaganda.

One newspaper replied to space grabbers in the following terms:—

> Gentlemen:—If you desire effective publicity service in this district we offer you such service through the medium of our paper at regular space rates, but—
>
> If it is free publicity service you are seeking which is indicated by literature mailed to this office we suggest that you save your materials, labor and postage in the future.
>
> We are serving many patrons all of whom are paying for service rendered. We know of no reason why we should serve you without pay.
>
> Our representative for foreign advertising is so and so.

The remedy is in your own hands, gentlemen. Unity is strength and publishers will have to unite to win. It will be a hard fought battle and it is to be hoped that the rising costs will do something to inspire publishers to exterminate this pest. Make them come in through the front door. Make your advertisers understand that in buying space they are not buying editorial opinion. If they persist in sending you free publicity matter turn it over and use the other side for copy paper. So successful have been the press agents in this country that we find the government adopting a similar practice. Every year they send out canned comment by the ton and employ an army of scribblers to do this work. Press agents earn all they get. A press agent who can steal thousands of dollars worth of space from the newspapers is worth big money to any firm. A few examples of their handiwork are Orange Day, Prune Day, Mothers' Day and a host of others. The latter was created for the benefit of florists and others. Some of the demons of free publicity are to be found locally. The less some men do and the more they say through the medium of the local press the more awe-inspiring, conceited and selfish they become. A man must be born and he must be boomed and I have heard of one professional man who repeatedly advises his professional associates to play the newspaper for all they are worth as it will produce for them greater prestige and incidentally a larger volume of business.

Publicity bureaus are not created to send out free news but to steal free advertising. The best way to check this evil is to drop their products in the office wastepaper basket. It is the best thing I do in a day's work and I am proud of any success I may have achieved along this line although that success has been far from complete.

In closing I would ask how many publishers have ever stopped to find out how much it cost to finance the Victory Loans of this country and how much money the newspapers got for their share of the work? The figures are available if you want to look them up. The average local canvasser did better than most of the newspapers. It cost more money to produce the canned publicity matter than the newspapers of this country got for paid space. Under the guise of patriotism the newspapers of this country were urged to run screaming headlines, front page panels, daily bulletins and a mountain of other literature all of which made the task easy for the canvasser who went out and cleaned up more money in commissions in one month than he otherwise would have in three months.

Give Service—Then Charge Enough for It

And Be Careful of Extra Page Charges

ADDRESSING a recent gathering of the Midland Counties Press Association at Peterboro, J. G. Keefer, of the Norwood *Register*, said:—

In endeavoring to speak to you on this topic we wish to consider it from the standpoint of both advertiser and publisher. There are many ways in which we can give service to the advertiser, and one very important way is to endeavor to give him just what he wants—not what you want. Place your type, cuts and borders at his disposal and as far as possible meet his desires. Give him any position you have that is open that he may desire so long as he is willing to pay the price for it. Pull proofs of all the cuts you have in his line and give them to him.

Don't allow an advertisement to stand until it gets stale—if customer neglects to change his advertisement, call him up and ask for a change; if he is busy and cannot attend to it, offer your services. Ask him if you may draw up an advertisement for him and submit it. He will appreciate your interest in his welfare and you will impress him that you are awake and looking after your business.

If it is necessary to freshen up and improve the walls and interior of your home, is it not all the more necessary to constantly change and brighten up the advertising in your newspaper. *Even a good thing becomes tiresome*, and people become restless at seeing the same thing continually. Unlike some other things we might mention an advertisement does not grow better or more valuable as it grows older. To do its work effectively it must be continually changed. If the wording of an advertisement cannot be changed then change the setting of it occasionally. This will be appreciated by advertiser and reader alike and will help to keep up the fresh appearance of your paper, and thus you will render service to the advertiser.

Take pains in printing your paper. See that every advertisement prints up properly. A poorly printed advertisement is of little value to the advertiser and is a very poor advertisement for you. Carelessness in this regard means the loss of business and injures your prestige very materially.

We are convinced it is possible to make the advertising column of a paper as interesting—or nearly so—as the reading matter,

but this can only be accomplished by constant effort—but the reward will be worth while.

. . . . . I have not touched upon style of typography. An advertisement should be attractive and pleasing to the eye.

J. G. KEEFER

Keep your office clean and your surroundings neat and as orderly as possible. You expect merchandise to be sold over clean counters, is it not reasonable that the advertiser should expect when he enters your place of business to find similar conditions? The condition of some of our offices would often impress one adversely. There is no need of covering the office floor with velvet carpets, but it is important that the office have a clean, bright business air about it.

Having thus dealt with a few thoughts on service to the advertiser let us consider how we can be of better service to ourselves, and first we would say that business is done by solicitation and advertising, and advertising must be sold in a similar manner. Why should the local merchant feel that advertising is indispensable if the local publisher takes no pains to sell it to him? Advertising space is merchandise. As you value your advertising space, advertise that it is valuable. As you believe your paper is worth reading, advertise for readers. Sell your paper for money and your advertising for money and be sure you get what it is worth. The publisher who does not consider every type set word, whether reading matter or advertisements, as actual, definite, measureable, and positive merchandise, proves by his own words and actions that his advertising space has little commercial value. your paper and the advertising space in it are simply commodities necessary to the economy and progress of the business you represent. Nothing destroys the advertiser's respect for your commodity or adds to his appreciation of its worth more quickly than your own estimate of its value.

Sell advertising space as merchandise. The merchant wants to sell his goods more than the buyer wants to buy them. The merchant goes after the buyer. The publisher wants to sell his advertising space more than the advertiser wants to buy it. The publisher must go after the advertiser.

There is hardly a town or village anywhere where the merchants would not do more advertising if the seller of advertising tried as hard to sell his advertising as the seller of other things tries to sell those things.

The Price

Don't be afraid to ask the proper price. This should not be determined in any haphazard way, but should be based on the cost of the work. This gives you confidence in your own figures and you at once impress your customer with the fact that your price is right. If there is any doubt or guess work about it the customer is quick to discern it in your manner and although your figure may be lower than it should be, the effect is detrimental to you. Knowing your price and sticking to it makes you respect yourself and inspires the confidence of your customer and brings you more and better business.

What is a fair price per inch for a country weekly paper with a circulation of from 700 to 1,000 copies per week? We figure set display matter to be worth 20 to 25c. per inch—it costs 18c— and plate matter 15c. per inch minimum on all contracts of 100 inches and over. Less than 100 inches transient rates should apply. Transient rates should also apply on full page advertisements or advertisements necessitating the printing of a supplement, as this work cannot be profitably done at ordinary rates. In most cases a re-make up of your paper is involved, there is the extra press run, straightening, cutting, inserting, folding, postage and other little things to consider, which in these days all run into money. . . . In his admirable address before the C.W.N.A. at Toronto last June Mr. Whiting speaking along this line said: "The page costs of your newspaper is an important thing to know, for without such knowledge a publisher is prone to add on two or four pages to his regular edition, thinking the increased volume of advertising means increased profits. As a matter of fact it too frequently happens that the added revenue does not cover the additional cost, to say nothing of a profit." We have proved his words to be correct.

Fifty Years Ago In A Country Office

BY L. G. JACKSON, NEWMARKET "ERA"

WHEN I come to think of what they had to put up with half a century ago, in a country printing office, I wonder at the patient endurance of the old Jour. and the Printer's Devil.

Being "laid on the shelf" for a couple of weeks so far as moving around is concerned, and having caught up with the everyday routine of an editor I laid off my glasses and began to think of the old employees in a print shop 50 years ago and what they had to do. Perhaps some of these things would be interesting to the comps. of to-day and make them feel more satisfied with their lot.

In those days the boys of the office all boarded with the "boss," with the exception of the journeyman.

In summer the "devil" got up at six o'clock, put on the fire and waited around for breakfast. In winter, 5 o'clock was his rising hour, in order to have the office warm with a box stove when all the hands went to work at 7 o'clock. Work continued till six p.m. the year round, the only holidays being Good Friday, 24th of May and Christmas. When the 1st of July was added that was great luck.

There Was Pi In Those Days

Each man had his own appointed rack and his own set of cases for newspaper work; and with every size of type from nonpareil up to double english there was a case of italics to go with it, as in those days every newspaper and steamboat had to be set in italic. When the editor wanted to emphasize his remarks, italics were also extensively used.

I remember an experience one time that got me into trouble. An italic case was taken out of the accustomed rack and placed on the window sill for the convenience of general distribution. I was only a lad and going to the window to look out I placed my hands on the edge of the case. It had only been just nicely balanced and the result was that the case and contents tumbled over my head. There was "something doing" just then.

The devil had to sweep out after supper every night and the type picked up under each man's rack was put in his stick to distribute before he started work. Any stick that had an over-

dose was the subject of much grumbling, as the order was that each one should pick up his type when he dropped it.

L. G. JACKSON

One of the first things for an apprentice to do in his spare time was to make a composing rule for himself out of some discarded piece of brass rule and this he took pleasure in carrying wherever he went, like President Harding of the United States.

In those days one of the regular things for the devil to do was to wet down the paper every Saturday afternoon for the next week's issue. The paper came in quires of 24 sheets and each quire got two dips in a metal trough made for the purpose. In many other offices it was sprinkled with an ordinary watering can. Then on Monday morning the paper was turned so as to distribute the dampness more evenly and break the back of the paper.

What Real Press Work Was

The first side went to press Monday afternoon, as the type had to be distributed and reset for the inside. It fell to the lot of the apprentices in turn to pull the lever of the Washington press on the outside run as the jour. did the presswork on the inside, when dispatch was necessary. His stint was a token (240) an hour and it was always the ambition of the boys to get as near that mark as possible. The flying of the frisket was a great trick. And that reminds me that the frisket had to be pasted fresh every week or two to keep the edges of the paper from blacking. When the press was running the devil had his work cut out keeping the ink distributed on the roller and rolling the forms. If the roller handle should slip out of his hand and the roller go over the press upon the apron of the foreman, woe betide him. I have seen the devil chased all over the office and punched for the trick.

Then the making of the rollers out of glue, molasses and glycerine was an all-day job which nobody liked — especially the devil who had to keep up a roaring fire.

Good hardwood ashes were plentiful in those days and the forms were always washed with home-made lye, followed by lots of water to prevent the type from being slippery when distributing. This liberal allowance of water also made it convenient for the boys to show a "type-worm" to the new apprentice, but the practice was very dangerous to eyesight and never should have been allowed.

And Tallow Candles Too

With work ten hours a day it can easily be imagined that much artificial light was required through the winter months. This was supplied by tallow candles, 8 to the pound, obtained at the nearest grocery. Each man had his own, candlestick, moulded in lead, which was usually balanced in the lower case "e" box. Even after coal oil lamps were introduced, the candles continued to be the source of light for years, as lamp glasses were expensive and easily broken, besides the general fear of explosion of the coal oil.

For years the comps. were not allowed to sit down at the case, as that would make them lazy and round-shouldered; but gradually the seats came in—first a piece of board about 3 ft. 6 in. long with a short piece nailed on the top. The balancing was an easy matter after you got used to it. This was followed by the high desk office stool which the comp. had to provide at his own expense. $5 a week and board was good wages those days for those learning the trade and the term of apprenticeship was always five years. A journeyman at that time knew something about printing but we cannot say that about many of the so-called printers of these days.

As a rule boys from the country made better printers than village boys. They seemed to be more attentive to their work, appreciated the opportunity of reading newspapers and books accessible in a printing office, and were less concerned about the frivolities of the street.

When publication day came everybody had to stick at the job till the papers were printed, whether it was 8, 9 or 10 o'clock and no extra pay was allowed. The same about a day before or after a holiday—just so much had to be done and no extra pay. The wonder is that there were any printers sticking at the job.

When metal quoins came in, doing away with the shooting-iron and bevelled wood quoins, that was a great convenience and saved further chipping of the make-up stone. It seems from that time on every decade has lightened the drudgery of a printer's life, the climax of relief being the type-setting machine of to-day.

Editor's Note:—In the office where my apprenticeship was served, was a good old Scotchman who had read that a great many printers contract lead-poisoning from inhaling dust from the case, especially by sneezing over it. He conceived the

brilliant idea of having a notice placed over each case warning compositors not to cough or sneeze over the case. To make this campaign even more effective, he went to the drug store and got a small spray made up with some sort of an antiseptic solution that stunk like old Harry. We knew the boys in the drug store quite well, so the next time he went to get the squirter filled they doctored it up with a very pleasant smelling solution of toilet water and perfume. A few days afterward his wife happened to be in the office when he was making his rounds with the new squirter. She at once noticed the fine aroma that was coming from the mixture from the drug store, and she went right after the old boy—his name by the way was Malcolm—for spending his money on perfume to squirt on the printing cases, when she could not afford any such finery for her own use. That was the end of the campaign against germs, and we were left to the mercy of the lead-poisoning or anything else that might be crawling on the two-nick cases.

A Progressive Apprentice Plan

Three years ago, G. L. Sprague, principal of the Hamilton Technical and Art School, met in conference the representatives of the Hamilton Typographical Union, and, as a result of that conference, there came into force one of the most progressive apprentice agreements in Canada. The Typographical Union in conjunction with the Master Printers' Guild and the Publishers' Association agreed and have been sending their apprentices to the Technical School one-half day a week and six nights a month for instruction in the "Arts Preservative of Arts." That this instruction has proven of great value to the apprentice and the craft is conceded by some of the best authorities in the craft. The apprentices are required to pass an examination every six months and a final examination before they become journeymen. This examination committee is composed of the President of the Union, W. Mountjoy, A. Wilkins and F. Atkinson, instructor at the school.

A monthly report of the progress and attendance of each apprentice is sent to the employers and the Union. The attendance is practically one hundred per cent. in both the day and the evening classes.

Two returned soldiers who attended the school for a nine months' course are now earning thirty and thirty-four dollars a week respectively, as a result of the training received in this school. One of the men had three years' experience in a newspaper office and the other drove a brewery wagon.

While the school does not claim it can teach the trade in nine months, it does claim that it can teach an intelligent boy more in nine months than the average apprentice in a newspaper shop would receive in two or more years from the fact that he does not have to run messages, sweep the floors and put away leads and slugs day in and day out. Thus the school, if for no other reason, is of value to the employer in "breaking in" and giving the apprentice an insight into the fundamentals of the trade that the employer has not the time to do.

The school is equipped with a large and well selected assortment of type and materials, also two presses, a paper cutter, proof press and a modern Linotype and four keyboards. Instruction is given to journeymen who desire to become operators.

Real Wild Day in Bruce

Some of the Bruce publishers were in Kincardine a few days ago, and the *Review* says of them:— ". . . . . What appealed strongest to that bright mind of the *Herald-Times* was the twin beds as shown in a beautiful suite at the Malcolm factory and it would not surprise us to hear of Artie being comfortably tucked away in one of these this winter, while his better-half as she enjoys its mate will get away from that long-suffering of trying to warm Artie's feet while the cold chills are making their way up the spinal column. To send Dan McKenzie home without a visit to his old friend, Henry Coleman, would be worse than that of 'taking candy from a baby,' as these two are fast friends of long standing, and being aware of this, the party just allowed them to have their fling, which, by the way sent all to their various soup bowls thirty minutes late. Coming to the *Telescope* man we did not notice anything in particular about his actions, more than that as he gazed on the beautiful waters of Lake Huron, he began to wonder if he had not made a great mistake in pitching his tent in the sand hills at Walkerton before looking us over."

Price List Used By Oxford Association

District Is Working On A Fair Basis

AS A result of the meeting in Woodstock a few weeks ago, the Oxford County and District Press Association have issued their price list, with the following note attached:—

Enclosed find copies of Price List of Job Printing approved by the Job Printing Committee of the above Association. The prices have been carefully figured by this committee, and taking into consideration the cost of stock, wages and present conditions of the labor market in our business, they are considered fair minimum prices. It is the intention of the committee to revise the list from time to time, as conditions change, and it is hoped that the Job Printers will use the list as a basis for charging for their product until such time as they may feel justified in adopting the Franklin Printing Price List for this purpose.

Additional copies of the list can be procured from the undersigned, who will be glad to receive any suggestions which will help to extend the usefulness of this present effort.

We are indebted to the Bruce County Printers' Association for the basis of the list, and it will be found that the changes from their list are few. We would suggest that the list be framed and hung in a conspicuous place or laid under glass on the counter where the customer can see it. There will be little or no difficulty in securing these prices if the list is shown in this way.

Note the Sales Tax. Each printer is now required to pay a business license of $5.00.

PETER WILSON,
Chairman of Committee.

ALL THE ITEMS ON THIS LIST ARE SUBJECT TO A SALES TAX OF TWO PER CENT

LETTERHEADS
20 lb. Bond at 35c

250	$ 5 50
500	7 50
1000	11 00
Extra 1000	6 75

For two colors add $4 per thousand.
For extra expensive stock add to these prices proportionately.

BILLHEADS
(Grade 35)
No. 5—5½ x 8½

8 to post— 250	$ 4 50
— 500	5 75
—1000	8 25
Extra thousand	5 00
No. 7—8½ x 7	
Quarter Cap— 250	$ 4 75
— 500	6 50
—1000	9 25
Extra thousand	5 25
No. 11—8½ x 11	
4 to post— 250	$ 5 25
— 500	7 25
—1000	11 00
Extra thousand	6 75
No. 14—8½ x 14	
Half Cap — 250	$ 6 25
— 500	8 75
—1000	13 75
Extra thousand	8 50

100 of any of above..$4.25 to $6.00

NOTE, MEMO HEADS AND STATEMENTS, 5½ x 8½
20 lb. Bond at 35c

250	$ 4 00
500	5 25
1000	7 50
Extra thousand	4 25

ENVELOPES
Stock $3.00

250	500	1000	Extra 1000
$3 00	$4 50	$7 75	$5 50

TICKETS
Concert tickets with coupons—100, $2.50; each additional 100, 35c.
Tickets without coupons — 100, $2.25; each additional 100, 30c.

GOV'T POSTCARDS
(Printing Only)

100 (light form)	$ 2 75
Each additional 100	25

PRIVATE POSTCARDS—5½c Stock

100, printed on two sides	$ 5 50
500	7 00
1000	10 00

WINDOW CARDS
11 x 14—1, $2.75; 25, $4.50; 50, $5.50; 100, $7.00.
14 x 22—1, $3.25; 25, $6.50; 50, $8; 100, $10.25.
Extra color, $5 additional.
22 x 28—1, $4.50; 12, $6.50; 25, $8.75; 50, $11.

NOTE AND LETTER CIRCULARS
20 lb. Bond at 35c—10 pt. type.
250, $4.50; 500, $5.75; 1000, $8.
Letter 8½ x 11—100, $7; 250, $8.75; 500, $10; 1000, $12.25.
Add $3.50 to these prices for two colors. With blank fly leaf add 30 per cent.

MERCANTILE POSTERS
Quarter sheet, 12 x 18 — 250 $12.50; 500, $16.50; 1000, $22. Extra.
Half sheet, 18 x 24—50, $12.50; 100, $13.75; 200, $16.75; 500, $21.75; 1000, $28. Extra 1000, $9.

DODGERS
(White paper; for colored paper add 10 per cent. extra to these prices.)
4½ x 6 in. (32nd sheet)—100, $2.25; 250, $2.50; 500, $3.25; 1000, $4.50; additional 1000, $3.000.
6 x 9 (16th sheet)—100, $3; 250, $3.75; 500, $4.50; 1000, $6. Extra 1000, $3.25.
6 x 12 (12th sheet)—100, $4.25; 250, $5; 500, $6; 1000, $8. Extra 1000, $4.50.
9 x 12 (8th sheet)—50, $4; 100, $4.75; 250, $5.75; 500, $7; 1000, $9.25. Extra 1000, $4.50.

OPEN DISPLAY POSTERS
(White paper; for colored paper add 10 per cent. extra to these prices.)
Quarter sheet, 12 x 18—25, $5.50; 50, $6; 100, $6.75. Additional 100, $1.50.
Third sheet, 12 x 24—25, $7.50; 50, $8.50; 100, $9.75. Additional 100, $2.
Half sheet, 18 x 24—25, $7.75; 50, $8.50; 75, $9.25; 100, $9.75. Additional 100, $2.
Whole sheet, 24 x 36—25, $8.75; 100, $9.75; 100, $11.75. Additional 100, $3.75.
For heavy composition, add to these prices.
For extra color add 50 per cent.

AUCTION SALES BILLS
With List of Farm Stock, Implements, etc.
Quarter sheet, 12 x 18—25, $9.75; 50, $10.25; 100, $11.
Third sheet, 12 x 24—25, $11; 50, $11.50; 100, $12.50.
Half sheet, 18 x 24—25, $11.75; 50, $12.50; 100, $13.75.
Whole sheet, 24 x 36—25, $13.75; 50, $15; 100, $17.

PRINTING BILLS OFF ADVTS.
Eighth sheet, 7 x 8½, 8vo—100, $3.75; 1000, $6.50.
Quarter sheet, 12 x 18—500, $5; 1000, $8.50. Each additional 100, 75c.
Half sheet, 18 x 24—250, $4.75; 500, $7.50; 1000, $13. Each additional 100, 86c.
NOTE.—The printing of bill off an advt. does not entitle the customer to any reduction in the price of his advertising.

INVITATION CARDS
3½ x 5½—25, $2.50; 50, $4.50; 100, $6.50. Extra 100, $3.25.
Envelopes, 1c each extra.

MEMORIAL CARDS
$5.26; 75, $7.25; 100, $8.75.
Envelopes, 1c each extra.

VISITING CARDS
50, $1.50; 100, $2.
Black bordered. 50 per cent. extra.

WEDDING INVITATIONS
$2.50 100—12, $3.75; 18, $4.25; 25, $4.75; 50, $6.50; 75, $8; 100, $10.
For extra expensive stock add proportionately.

AT HOME CARDS
Small—25, $3.50; 50, $3.75; 100, $6.50; extra 100, $3.25.
Larger size—25, $5.50; 50, $5.75; 100, $6.25. Extra 100, $4.50.

SHIPPING TAGS
On basis of No. 5 Tag.
500, $3.25; 1000, $8. Other sizes in proportion.

BUTTER WRAPPERS
500 with maker's name, $4.75; 1000, $7.50; "Dairy Butter," 75c per 100 sheets. Plain, 60c. per 100, $2.50 ream.

ROUTE CARDS
14 x 22—25, $10.50; 50, $12.25; 100, $14.75. Additional 100, $4.25.
Folders, 7 x 7½—50, $12.50; 100, $8.60. Additional 100, $1.75.
For extra heavy or tabulated pedigree charge $10 up.

RECEIPT AND ORDER BOOKS

	250	500	1000	Extra 1000
3¼x8½	$6 00	$8 00	$4 25	
3¼x11	6 00	7 00	9 00	4 75

BALLOTS
5 names or less, 250 ballots..$ 3 75
Each additional 100 .... 25.
Also add 25c per each additional name.

PRIZE LISTS
$2.75 per page for 200 copies and 25c per page additional for each extra 100 copies.

FINANCIAL STATEMENTS AND AUDITOR'S REPORTS
Size of page 5½ x 8½, type 24 ems by 40 ems. 200 copies, $2.75 per page. Each additional 100 add 25c per page. Cover to count as four pages.

VOTERS' LISTS
12c per name for 200 copies. Set without down rules.

BOOKS, PAMPHLETS, CONSTITUTIONS, BY-LAWS, MINUTES, ETC.
100 copies, 8 point solid, $2.50 per page, 25c per page additional for each 100 copies.

STOCK CATALOGUES
200 copies, 6 pt. pedigrees, 6 x 9 broadside, $4 per page. Additional 100 copies, 25c per page.

WORK LIST
Gordon press work, $2 per hour; hand composition, $2.50 per hour; cylinder press work, $3.50 per hour.

ALL PRICES SUBJECT TO CHANGE

You Can't Sell Well If You Are Afraid

The Feeling Of Sure Victory Is Needed

LIEUT.-COL. W. A. MULLOY, the "Blind Trooper" of the South African War," at a Toronto gathering recently gave an inspiring account of how he, as a "returned man," had found his way back into civil life. The essentials on the part of the man himself, he said, were self-mastery, self-reliance, and purposeful self-direction. He described, step by step, his own fight from the moral despondency into which he was thrown by the information that his sight was forever destroyed to the position he has now attained on the repatriation committee at Ottawa. This hero soldier has won out in what is possibly the greatest battle any man has to fight in this life. He is an inspiration to every man and woman afflicted with that super-misfortune—loss of sight. On the occasion above referred to I venture to say that many persons made the resolve to master deficiencies that had previously been considered insurmountable but which when considered in the light of Lieut.-Col. Mulloy's experience fade very rapidly into insignificance.

I was very much interested in the question referred to at the conclusion of the article printed in last month's *Printer and Publisher*, under the caption "Putting Character into your Work. Here it is:—

"I am a young man, a printing salesman, know the business mechanically, have taken a course in salesmanship; but I have certain deficiencies that apparently cripple my sales effort. How would you go about strengthening these deficient qualities?"

Sit Down and Take Stock

The very first thing necessary is to recognize the deficiencies. This implies self-analysis. It's a mighty fine thing to sit down occasionally and seriously take stock of ourselves. Where are we strong? Where are we weak? Where do we win? Where do we lose? Write these down on paper. Look at them. Do these things really exist in our experience as day by day we go about our work? When ill, we go to a doctor; and we usually believe what he says, take his medicine and eventually pay the bill. And we thank the doctor. No wonder that in many a man glaring deficiencies exist, when from the very start they were allowed to take root, grow, and bear fruit. The more we neglect self-analysis, the more we neglect those things that need attention, the stronger will become the retarding influences that these same hindrances will have upon us and our service.

Our analysis will prove interesting. We will appreciate those qualities that daily contribute to success. Don't "worry" about the other deficient qualities but set to work to cast out, overcome or strengthen, as the case may be. Remember that thought without subsequent action is in itself worthless. Do the thing. Better action that is 50 per cent. right than inaction that is 100 per cent. perfect.

Take for instance one "deficiency" that is apparent, and which is undoubtedly our worst enemy: FEAR. Shakespeare says in "Measure for Measure:" "Our doubts are traitors, and make us lose the good we oft might win, by fearing to attempt." "Fear demoralizes character, destroys ambition, induces or causes disease, paralyzes happiness in self and others and *prevents achievement*," says O. S. Marden in his wonderful book "Every Man a King." It has not one redeeming quality. It is all evil. It lowers mental and physical vitality, and deadens every element of success. Buoyancy flees before it, and cheerfulness is unknown in its presence. Fear, fear, fear. It may have many degrees or gradations—but all along the line it is the same thing, as Dr. W. H. Holcomb says "a paralyzing impression upon the centres of life which can produce a vast variety" in effect in the ideals and actions of the one possessed of *Fear*.

The "Ordeal" of Soliciting

We know full well how fear operates in the daily routine of the average salesman. The very first thing in the morning, instead of going out in a buoyant manner, he rather dreads the "ordeal" of soliciting business. Even though the day may be bright with prospects, and the other fellows trip off in the full expectation of a real good day, our friend at the very beginning has a distinct and total eclipse in full operation. Entering the establishment of Jones & Co., he rather dreads meeting the sales manager. But he gets away with that, and is given an opportunity to present estimates on a certain job. Immediately he is afraid that Hiprice & Co., whom he represents, will be underbid by Messrs. Lofigur & Co. He worries the estimator about it and "gets him going." And he carries the same spirit into every detail of his activity for that day and every day. No wonder he fizzles along, and finds himself "hindered" at every turn. But he resolves to overcome this.

First understand what is at the foundation of fear. On the other hand, many salesmen are unprepared for their work—they have never shown concern regarding real training for this important phase of business—the result is when they meet the stiff resistance of competition and the necessity of man-to-man selling they are afraid. It may be that this is the *cause* of this *Fear*. Then he may be qualified in all these and yet have the problem of the fearing mood. It is usually if not always something that has not yet happened, will not happen, or seldom ever happens. No doubt the sales manager of Jones & Co. was ready to respond to a cheery "Good Morning," and reciprocate a smile—but. . . .

Many people are afraid to walk along a very narrow ledge high above ground. But mark a narrow line along a wide sidewalk, and it can be covered perfectly, never a thought of losing your balance. The only dangerous thing about walking along the ledge is the fear of falling. Steady-headed people are *fearless*; they do not allow the thought of possible danger to overcome them, but keep their physical powers under perfect control—and that's the secret. Special development is necessary for some feats; but a steady head is all that is necessary for most. The mind will have to be trained to throw off every suggestion of fear, and to avoid everything that contributes to it. In this instance it is a case of studying to crowd out the fear spirit and make room for that which will create confidence and assure strength of mind and heart. Right here Mr. Marden gives us the thought that "this same principle of crowding out the fear-thought by a buoyant, hopeful, confident thought can be applied to all the many kinds of fear that daily and hourly beset us. At first it will be hard to change the current of thought. An aid in the process is often advisable." He then proceeds to suggest diversion of thought or action as a good thing. Link up to some friend of a jovial disposition, have lunch with him, catch some of his happy spirit, for nothing is so contagious as happy enthusiasm. But whatever the means the task of conquering Fear is perhaps the most important of all in developing successful salesmanship. It will well repay any effort. Not until this is effectively accomplished will Confidence and a Right Attitude be established.

The same principle of application will be found necessary in the case of any other deficiency, but the same results are assured. "Where there's a will, there's a way."

Do not avoid your weaknesses, such as lack of tact, faulty introduction, inattention, unpreparedness, etc.—but give them immediate and earnest attention, for in so doing you will surely strengthen the essential qualities that make your sales talk and effort effective. Find out the opposite to your deficiency and steadily develop that to a state of efficiency.

Be determined to become master of every faculty and quality that will contribute to your sales success—in fact, no matter what your position in business, whether mechanic or salesman, keep the object of your ambition well in view and tenaciously work toward it. Few people ever reach the goal they have in mind—but the best any man can do is to show progress and get somewhere—and he will be infinitely nearer the goal than the man who is satisfied to let things go and never endeavor.

It is said that Edison discovered the incandescent light as the result of a rather unique experience with the gas company supplying his home. Completely absorbed in his laboratory experiments he had neglected to pay his gas bill, the gas was turned off, and when he found himself in darkness he vowed that he would invent a light and be independent of the gas company—hence the electric light. If fear, or anything else, turns off the supply of enthusiasm or self-confidence, get busy and invent something that will provide greater impetus to your job. Like Edison, don't be beaten.—*By Tres*.

Printer & Publisher

Published on the Twelfth of Each Month.

H. D. TRESIDDER   -   -   -   Business Manager.
A. R. KENNEDY   -   -   -   -   -   Editor.

SUBSCRIPTION PRICE—Canada, Great Britain, South Africa and
the West Indies, $4 a year; United States, $3.50 a year; other
countries, $4 a year. Single copies, 30 cents. Invariably in
advance.

PUBLISHED BY

THE MACLEAN PUBLISHING CO.
Established 1887   Limited

JOHN BAYNE MACLEAN   -   -   -   President
H. T. HUNTER   -   -   -   Vice-President.
H. V. TYRRELL   -   -   -   General Manager

Head Office, 143-153 University Avenue - TORONTO, CANADA
    Cable Address Macpubco, Toronto; Atabek, London, Eng.
Also at Montreal, Winnipeg, New York, Chicago, Boston, London,
                        England.

Application for A.B.C. Audit.

Vol. 29   TORONTO, NOVEMBER, 1920   No. 11

CONTENTS

The $2 Rate Is Needed

ONE Ontario weekly paper, well established in its district
announces an increase in subscription rates to $2 per year,
at the same time informing the readers that if there is a decrease
in the price of paper there will be a corresponding decrease in
the price of the paper, or the paper will be marked on that much
in advance of the date paid for.

A review of the conditions in the trade just now will make it
plain that this paper is making a mistake.

The adoption of the $2 rate for weekly papers, and the secur-
ing of a better price for their job printing has saved a number of
papers from going out of business. It has given them cash that
they could not have secured elsewhere, and without which they
could not have carried on much longer.

A number of papers may feel inclined to deny this, but in a
number of cases it was and is true.

The $1 a year for a weekly paper was not a joke. It was
something much closer to a tragedy. The community never
set that as the price it would pay for the service that a paper is
prepared to render. The price was set by publishers themselves, and it was never in keeping with the value of the article
supplied.

If papers find that they can turn out a good paper for less than
$2 a year, we would be pleased to have them send to this office
a copy of their paper, together with a statement that it could
not be improved, that they could not cover their district any
better, that they could not have a better typographical effect,
that they could not secure better press work, and that newer
equipment would not assist them in making their paper a
matter of personal and local pride.

The increase in the price of the paper should be taken as a
vote of confidence in the publisher, and he should be quick to
measure up to the new price with a better service.

The same thing holds good in the job printing trade of the
weekly papers. Offices that are getting the prices that are
shown in the columns of this paper from month to month should
do work in keeping with the figures.

There are specimens of job work turned out in some of the
offices that are not in keeping with the fair prices asked. The
better price should be met by the publisher with a determination that the quality of his output shall come up at once to the
standard in keeping with the price.

But do not apologize to your reader for charging $2 per year
for your paper. It may be necessary to apologize at times for
the paper itself, but you cannot turn out a good paper and make
a decent living on a lower figure.

Never slide back from the $2 rate. If papers have had the
good horse sense to pull themselves out of the $1 a week hole,
surely they appreciate their good fortune enough to let the
higher figure remain. There are papers that might get along
without that price, but there are hundreds that must have it.
When you have established the $2 rate, make your paper
worth the price. The public will pay it and think more of the
paper because it pays more for it.

Business Papers in Session

THE meeting of the National Conference of Business Paper editors, held at New York in October, gave those attending a
good opportunity to get new ideas for editorial work, and from
the standpoint of the Canadian it was a splendid chance to see
the extent to which the business community of United States
is sold on the business paper proposition.

Much of the material brought out could well be applied to
papers of any kind. All through the sessions speakers brought
out the idea of leadership in the community, or in the business
or trade, and not mere recorders of fact. Illustrating this a
point was given: When the railroad situation was serious a
few months ago one of the business papers immediately got
in touch with the best railroad men it could meet, and found
out the things that were necessary to put the roads back on a
good basis. The paper then assigned five of its editorial men
to the work of securing information along these lines—not with
the idea of making copy or of stringing out reports, but of
presenting facts. The result was that each article, cut to the
bone in length, was a real asset to the railroad men, and the
paper was made stronger than ever in its field.

The successful editor and editorial staff must be of the
agitator type, that is always ready to "start something." The
development of great initiative was continually brought home,
and the idea of forgetting precedent in many cases and launch-
ing out into new ways was advocated.

The editorial department should have a close contact with
the advertising and circulation staff. That was a delicate
problem at the start, and was introduced by A. R. Kennedy,
managing editor of mechanical papers of the MacLean Publishing Co. There was nothing in such a close working understanding to make it possible for any advertiser to secure consideration in the editorial columns. The field is changing
rapidly, and the editorial staff must be in contact with the men
who are on the outside if they wish to keep their policies in
shape to meet these changed conditions.

It was interesting to find the extent to which the American
business paper editors keep out of their offices. The idea that
an editorial position is a desk job is quite foreign to them. The
editor-in-chief of the greatest business paper on this continent,
if not in the world, spends at least two days a week out in the
markets, although the paper keeps a very large and highly
trained staff to attend to all this class of work. His explanation for doing this is interesting. "Our paper is supposed to deal
with the problems of our field. How can we know what these
problems are unless we get out and study the field, and meet the
men who are supposed to be facing these problems. Certain
it is they are not going to come around to our office and tell
their troubles and their problems. The only successful alternative is to get out and go to them."

The contact of the editorial department with the mechanical
section was discussed at length, dealing with the preparation of
copy, etc. An occasional "thank you" to the printer who had
turned out a good piece of work was recommended as working
wonders. It was also pointed out that a printing plant is
highly specialized for production, and in order to get full advantage of this organization copy must be in such shape as to pass
through readily.

Several members of the staff of New York University attacked
American writers and editors, claiming that the latter had
neither the soundness of the British nor the brevity of the
French. The opinion of the meeting can well be summed up
in this remark: "I would rather have an article written in
questionable or even poor English, but with some real ideas in
it, than one in the style of a Huxley, but barren of ideas."

Payment for contributed matter has increased from 25 to
40 per cent., although some editors claimed they insisted on
better material at the higher rates. A flat rate with increases
according to merit was recommended. That the higher rate
is not bringing in better material was the consensus of opinion.

The Mission and Purpose of the Bank Organ

By J. Herbert Hodgins

ONE of the outstanding phases of printing and journalism in Canada of recent months has been the development of the Bank magazine, which may be regarded as the super house organ of the present day. Ask any experienced newspaper man in Canada, or more to the point, any professional advertising man—be he ad-writer or ad-solicitor—and he will invariably tell you that our bankers are the hardest crusts to break. Where publicity and advertising are concerned they have long been regarded as ultraconservative. The more aggressive men among them of recent years and particularly since the war have decried "silk-hatted banking" methods, and, in their reaching out, have made determined, energetic pleas for the human element in banking. To what measure these modernists have succeeded in gaining their point in every-day business is of no immediate moment except that it were well to remark that banking within the Dominion has become increasingly competitive.

One of the more or less indirect results has been the bringing into being of the Bank "house organ." Patterned after its probably less pretentious brother, the house organ of commercial enterprises, the Bank house organ has a potential mission.

The house organ of industrialism for instance is in reality a glorified advertising medium when it is not educating the sales staff into a selling campaign. The Bank magazine is a simple thing, whose purpose in life is manifold, whose mission is as broad as propaganda in the broadest acceptance of the term, the while it is subtle in its educational influences. Undeniably the Bank organ opens up avenues for development of the bank's interior organization, for a development of an esprit de corps among individual bank staffs beyond ken.

Singularly enough two of the youngest of the Dominion's eighteen chartered banking institutions were first to launch the idea of the Bank magazine devoted exclusively to the interests of their own staffs. The Sterling Bank with *The Teller*, and the Home Bank with the *Home Bank Monthly* were Canadian pioneers in this form of publication. But their little staff booklets undertaken before the war were unpretentious though they have since been measurably expanded. Just as the vicissitudes and demands of the war period quickened the pulse of all financial advertising—because in no previous era was the sense of the human element more completely awakened in financial advertising and publicity—so, too, was there created a full realization of the possibilities of the Bank magazine as a regular institution.

Less than a year ago the Union Bank of Canada gave over to an experienced Canadian newspaper man the editorship of the *U. B. of C. Monthly*, an ambitious magazine modelled after the best of similar New York banking publications. In the great Wall Street district, it should be written here, the foremost banking institutions of America have developed the advertising and publicity booklet and the house organ to its highest present day conception. In less than a year the *U.B. of C. Monthly* has become a 40 page magazine, issued with newspaper promptness. While essentially a magazine and "for the staff," its contents embrace a wide range of subjects, though, quite naturally enough, concentrating upon financial and banking topics, with the dominant note at all times Union Bank.

Closely following this lead has appeared the new monthly organ of the Canadian Bank of Commerce employees, *Caduceus*, and even more recently there has been witnessed the debut of the magazine of the Imperial Bank of Canada. Other allied publications will doubtless follow. In fact it is divulging no secret to intimate that at least two among the remaining banks will start the issue of staff magazines before the close of 1920.

The Bank organ must therefore become an accepted institution among Canadian publications. Individually these can have no competitors and likewise their issue will not have a competitive effect upon any publication in the field. The reaction is neutral, so far as the publishing trade is concerned in a public sense.

The average publisher and newspaper man may not immediately guess the possibilities of this new bank organ movement—if it may be described in the larger sense of a movement. In actual practice the mission of the Bank organ may be tremendously broad. Canada's eighteen banks have 4,700 branches, which, allowing an average of ten clerks and officers at each branch, will give a combined circulation for these individual banking publications of nearly 50,000—a potential circulation indeed.

From an 'interior" standpoint the editor of the Bank organ has unusual, far-reaching chances for developing staff loyalty, for further educating the staff—and more particularly the junior officers—in banking practice, and in the larger aspect for broadening the banking vision of the readers, in a national and international sense. In short by adopting the more intimate terms of address embryo bankers, the younger element particularly, will be the more readily and quickly reached than by the highly technical banking journals.

A Bank organ is particularly desirable for a Canadian bank under the Canadian system of branch banks. By this medium the bank's representatives at the frontier posts may be kept in intimate touch with the passing events at the home office. The Bank organ may be made to fill much the same purpose as the small community weekly, whose item of news "Bill Smith has shingled his barn this week" is of more vital concern to the home town boy many miles removed from his native heath than the events duly chronicled in display headings on the front pages of our metropolitan dailies.

From the "exterior" or public viewpoint the coming of the Bank organ should not lightly be dismissed. The Bank organ unquestionably will accomplish much toward further improving the public service rendered by our banking institutions. As a literary contribution to our banking history they will no doubt exert their influences in due season, while at the same time they continue to offer a unique and interesting contribution to the art of printing and to the trade of publishing.

THE PRINTING OFFICE TOWEL

When I think of the towel,
    The old fashioned towel,
That used to hang up near the printing house door,
    I can think of nobody
    In these days of shoddy
That could hammer out iron to wear as it wore.

    The "Devil" who used it,
    The tramp who abused it,
The "comp" who got at it when these two were gone.
    The make-up and foreman,
    The editor .(poor man)
Each rubbed some grime off, while they put a heap on.

    In, over, and under,
    It was blacker than thunder,
Harder than poverty, rougher than sin,
    On the roller suspended,
    It never was bended
And flapped on the wall like a banner of tin.

    It grew harder and rougher,
    And blacker and tougher
And daily took on a still inkier hue
    Until one windy morning,
    Without any warning,
It fell on the floor and was broken in two.

REVIEW OF JOB SPECIMENS

If You Want An Opinion On Your Work, Send It In

FIGURE A.—The original of this was done in brown ink on buff stock with considerable body. The appearance was plain and substantial. There is no attempt at ornamentation—none is needed. There is quite a bit to be said on the cover and the wording states the case well. There are several fonts of type that could be used to give a very pleasing effect in this work. Cheltenham, Artcraft and Packard would make good work, but for the style attempted, there is not much room for criticism. The grouping of the central wording is well arranged. It gives strength, and is narrowed and bunched enough to add length to the job, which element is somewhat dissipated by the border lines at the top.

FIGURE B.—This is from the Hunter-Rose Press, Toronto, and was in the original brown on buff cover stock, but the size of the type page is not altered in the reproduction. The line on the top tends to give almost too much breadth to a job that is being worked the long way of the stock. The crest of the Home Music Club is artistic, if heavy, and rather dominates the situation. The rule at the bottom might be dispensed with and better use made of the wording "Constitution and Rules," which could then be brought up and not made to sit at the bottom so decidedly. The border effect top and bottom is fairly ornate for such a small piece of work, but has the redeeming feature of being open and not as ponderous as the size in points might indicate.

FIGURE C.—The first thing that would strike the critic in this work is the way the corners are joined up. The frame is perfect in this respect, and plain, and goes to show how all sufficient this sort of rule is in dealing with almost any kind of work. The whole appearance of the programme, which [has been slightly reduced, is pleasing, and quite in keeping with what one might expect for such an occasion. The crest is placed at the top of

this job, and for very good reason. Placing the title at the top with the crest under, is not good practice in this case, although the compositor might have the latitude to do the thing that way. This can very easily be determined by the reader if he will take the trouble to cut out the "Home Musical Club" line and the crest and reverse their position. He will decide that the arrangement as it stands is the best.

* * *

Home Musical Club

FOUNDED 1897

AT THE RESIDENCE OF THE HOSTESS

MRS. R. J. DILWORTH

BABY POINT

MONDAY EVENING, OCTOBER 25th, 1920

Programme

(a) Bach	- - - - - - -	Loure in G
(b) Ravel	- - - - - - -	Jeux D'Eau
	("The God of the Rivers Laughing at the Waters which Tickle Him")	
(c) Chopin	- - - - - - -	Barcarolle

Miss CECILE WILLIAMSON

(a) Grieg (Composed 1864)	- - - -	I Love Thee
(b) Grieg (Composed 1871)	- - - -	The Princess
(c) Elgar	- - - - -	Like to the Damask Rose
(d) Easthope Martin	- - - - -	Fairings

Mr. ERNEST MORGAN

(a) Ries	- - - - - -	Adagio (Opus 34)
(b) Cadman-Jost	- From the Land of the Sky-Blue Water
(c) Burleigh	- - - - - -	Fairy Sailing

Miss BEATRICE PREST

(a) Liza Lehmann	There are Fairies at the Bottom of Our Garden
(b) Felix Fourdrain	- - - - La Chanson Des Cloches
(c) Howard White	- - - - - - The Robin Song

Mrs. RUSSELL MARSHALL

FIGURE C

The *Canadian Courier*, the weekly magazine which has been regularly issued since 1906, has suspended publication, for the present at all events, although it is stated in certain quarters that a reorganization may be effected which will enable the periodical to make its reappearance. Mr. J. P. Langley has been appointed provisional liquidator.

When the *Courier* made its first bow to the public it was edited by Lieut.-Colonel John A. Cooper, who for many years previously had been editor of the *Canadian Magazine*. He continued to edit the magazine until early in the war, when he resigned, and his place was taken by Augustus Bridle, who had for some time been associate editor, and who has continued in charge until the present time.

* * *

Answer These:—

Are you drawing the salary of an executive who has invested his all?

Are you getting 25 per cent. net profit on your gross sales?

Have you considered the increased cost of new machinery, and are you insured to the full extent in case of loss?

Do you know what department has the most leaks?

Will you sign a special "Code of Ethics?"

Are you in favor of uniform trade customs and practices?

Should an effort be made to standardize shop practices and operations?

What are your views on a Standard Cost Finding System and a Uniform Estimating Form?

Where should the monthly group meetings be held and on what day and hour?
Wouldn't you like to know your competitor better?
Do you know your costs?
Are you interested in a minimum cost basis?
Do you know how much money you made last month?
Have you an efficient bookkeeping system?
Do you want to eliminate unfair and unequal competition?

* * *

It has been reported that on Sunday night, October 24, Alder Hewitt, linotype operator on the *Tribune*, of Salt Lake City, Utah, set a total of 82,500 ems of nonpareil composition in six hours and thirty-five minutes, an average of 12,540 ems an hour. If the facts in the case substantiate this report, the setting of this "string" has placed the name of Hewitt along with the names of the leading "swifts" of the world.

* * *

An interesting group of small job work samples was recently received from the Hunter Rose Co., Toronto. The typography on the whole is very pleasing. Particularly worthy of praise is the manner in which the Howard Russell concert announcement has been handled. The job is printed on light brown, linen-finish, deckeled edge stock, done in black ink, with just a touch of red on the two inner pages. The front page has a tip-on portrait of the singer, which, combined with excellent presswork,

another sample of fine press work, and leaves little room for criticism.

The letterheads submitted are neatly printed, but the First Unitarian Church heading could have been improved had

FIGURE B

Caslon Old Style been used in conjunction with the shaded text line in place of Plate Gothic.

While not submitted for criticism, we cannot lose this opportunity of expressing ourselves on the excellence of the Hunter-Rose letterhead, Caslon Old Style being used for the lettering, the ink-ball trade mark being embossed in relief, being further embellished with red, and H. R. printed in gold and embossed. The effect is original and pleasing.

* * *

The St. Maurice Valley *Chronicle* turned out a most creditable industrial number on October first. It ran up to 32 pages, and there are no weak spots. The financial returns must have been very satisfactory, as there is a fine volume of business carried. The features cover a wide variety of subjects, and the whole industrial life of the district is well represented.

Select New Art Director

On October first Mr. Frederic W. Goudy became art director of the Monotype Company, a position for which he is eminently fitted. There are probably few men of this generation who have done more to nurture and direct the growing aspiration now apparent in the printing world than this new member of the Monotype organization. It will be remembered that one of the earliest important type-faces designed by Mr. Goudy was the one that is known as Monotype No. 38. He will be employed in further extending and improving the range of Monotype faces and exhibiting their correct use in composition. In this larger field of endeavor his influence undoubtedly will be felt everywhere that good printing is appreciated.

FIFTEENTH ANNUAL
CONVENTION

Central Theme:

"Business Paper Leadership, Its Responsibilities and Opportunities"

The Associated Business Papers, Inc.

HOTEL ASTOR   NEW YORK

October 20, 21 and 22, 1920

FIGURE A

puts the job across with a punch. As a suggestion only, the tip-on might have been raised and moved to the left about a quarter of an inch. Another job neatly executed is the Voice-a-Phone catalogue, printed on white coated stock, with ripple finish used on the rule borders and decorative material. This is

THE OTHER PUBLISHERS' BUSINESS

Special Advertising, Circulation and
Editorial Plans

Acton *Free Press* went to $2 per year on November 1st.

Orillia *Packet* claims that 250 new subscribers came in at the $1.50 rate prior to the new $2 rate.

Hamilton afternoon papers have come up to 2 cents—something they should have done long ago.

The Cowichan *Leader* came out with a neat little special edition when the Imperial Press party visited that district.

The Canadian Order of Foresters are calling for tenders for the printing of their paper, the *Canadian Forester*. Tenders are to close December 10. The address is Drawer 940, Brantford, Ontario.

The Stratford *Herald* has had a window dressing contest. A number of the leading firms made special displays in their windows, and the *Herald* gives prizes for the best descriptions of these written by readers of the paper. Prizes run from $25 for first and $20 for second down to $1 for sixth to tenth.

A striking example of forceful advertising is found in the Sydney, Cape Breton, *Record* of October 16, when the president of the Dominion Coal Co. took the entire front page of the paper to lay his case before the miners who were on the eve of taking a strike vote. The matter was well prepared, and no doubt, apart from being a good paying proposition, would be read as eagerly by the subscribers as any news, local or foreign, the paper might otherwise have used on the page.

A Practical Cost System

The Porte Publishing Company of Salt Lake City, Utah, has just completed the revision and enlargement of the Practical Cost System for Printing Offices written some ten years ago by Mr. R. T. Porte, father of the Franklin Printing Price List. This will run in serial form in the *Publishers' Auxiliary*. According to Mr. Porte the subject of this book has been treated in a most clear and comprehensive way including the treatment of ideas and methods that have developed since the book was first written a decade ago. Mr. Porte was assisted by his corps of able assistants in the presentation of many forms and methods that have been found practicable for printing plants. The book is illustrated with specific examples of form usage.

Oshawa Reformer's New Card

The new foreign rate card of the Oshawa *Reformer* is as follows:—

Display Contracts Plate Matter—Space to be used at option of advertiser within one year; agate measurement (14 lines to the inch).

	Per Line	Per Inch
Transient (under 50 inches)	3	42
50 inches (700 lines)	2½	35
100 inches (1400 lines)	2	28
200 inches (2800 lines)	1½	21

Composition—Display matter requiring to be set, 7 cents per inch per insertion extra.

Reading Matter—Three times display plate matter rates.

Special Advertising

Annual Statements of banks, insurance companies, and other financial corporations, whether having ordinary contracts or not, 42c per inch (3c per agate line) per insertion.

Legal, municipal and government advertising 10 cents per line, first insertion; 5 cents per line each subsequent insertion.

Political and election advertising, 50c per inch.

Condensed Advertisements

One cent per word first insertion; one-half cent per word each subsequent consecutive insertion. Minimum charge 25c. Each initial letter, abbreviation, $ and c sign, figure, words of address, etc., count as full words. Box Number counts as 10 words.

Garden City Press Get-Together

The Garden City Press held its annual get-together and Thanksgiving dinner at Ste. Anne de Bellevue, Quebec, the guests being the heads of the departments at the Industrial and Technical Press on Adelaide Street, Toronto, and the members of the staff at the Toronto office of the Industrial and Educational Publishing Co., Limited. The latter organization controls the Industrial and Technical Press, and are publishers of educational and technical periodicals such as the *Canadian Mining Journal, Iron and Steel of Canada, Pulp and Paper Magazine, Canadian Textile Journal, Journal of Commerce* and others. These are printed at the Garden City Press in Ste. Anne de Bellevue, where the company, under the guidance and control of Mr. J. J. Harpell, president, has one of the finest publishing houses in Canada. Here in the historical and picturesque town of Ste. Anne, Mr. Harpell is working out a unique scheme of community service. A large number of houses have been built by the company for the employees and plans for further development and expansion along these lines are being carried into effect as part of a program looking towards the perfecting of a model publishing plant.

The workers from the Toronto departments were taken in hand by the President of the company immediately on their arrival in Ste. Anne on Thanksgiving morning, and entertained by him at luncheon at the golf club at noon. Part of the day's program of entertainment was a visit to Macdonald College. Then there was a visit to the grave of Simon Fraser, the discoverer of the Fraser River, whose remains lie in a quiet spot near the Senneville Road, followed by a hurried inspection of the big military hospital where hundreds of war-scarred men are being tenderly cared for.

The annual banquet was held at the New Clarendon Hotel, where most of the company's employees gathered and enjoyed a program of music and speeches under the chairmanship of Mr. Harpell. The chief speakers were Hon. W. S. Fielding, editor-in-chief of the *Journal of Commerce*; Dr. Harrison, principal of MacDonald College, the editors of the various publications and the heads of the departments in the Toronto plant. Brief speeches were given by the curé of the parish and the Anglican rector; T. W. Harpell, manager of the Industrial and Technical Press, H. W. Thompson, manager of the Toronto office of the Industrial and Education Publishing Co., and A. S. Christie, Montreal manager. Throughout the whole proceedings a fine spirit of co-operation and loyalty was shown.

Winnipeg Free Press' New Paper

The Winnipeg *Free Press* has started a Retail Merchants' Edition in connection with its other issues, the new departure to appear once a month. The first issue deals with merchandising problems, has sketches of the leading merchants of the Western metropolis, and contains as well a synopsis of business conditions in a large number of the towns of the West. Another department has paragraphs and personal items about the travelling salesmen who are known to the western trade. Good and bad advertising is also dealt with in a very interesting way. Bertram R. Brooker is the editor of the Retailers' paper, and the subscription price is fifty cents per year.

The Dean of Shorthand Writers

Court Reporter for 48 years, William C. Coo, says the *Globe*, may claim to be the dean of the profession in the Province of Ontario, particularly since the retirement of Thomas W. Bengough, the daddy of them all. Mr. Coo can tell many strange experiences during his close to half a century of reporting in courts, on commissions, and in Governmental inquiries.

At the present time he is handling the evidence given before the Public Service Commission and he estimates that the evidence from this will run to well over 2,000 pages of foolscap typewritten.

"I should judge that I have averaged well over 10,000 pages of typed foolscap a year since I started," said Mr. Coo. This means that a total of around 500,000 foolscap pages of typed evidence has been produced during his period of service.

"At one time I took a shorthand report of a play. Two of the actors turned ugly, the manager wished to discharge them but they refused to give up their copy of the parts they played. The manager had no other copy nor could he secure one. So he hired me to attend the play and to take a shorthand report. I had to be hoisted away up in the 'flies' and I had to take my report in the dark, but I got it. I was told that if the actors knew I was there they would have tried to kill me," said Mr. Coo, in relating this strange experience. Needless to say the two actors were turned loose next day.

Mr. Coo reported the investigation into the Toronto Jail under the Whitney Government. He reported the Sifton murder trial at London when the preliminary evidence went to 1,300 typed pages. He also acted as reporter for the Ontario Railway Board in their many inquiries and still is on the staff. At various times he reported the Senate speeches at Ottawa.

Perhaps a record might be claimed at Peterboro where Mr. Coo reported the trial of five men for murder recently, in which all five were sentenced to be hanged.

Mr. Coo started as Deputy Clerk of the County Court and as special shorthand examiner under Walter McKenzie, in which position he remained for 11 years. He then moved to London as Deputy Clerk of the Crown, but afterward returned to Toronto, where he has been employed ever since.

Failure of The Hamilton Times

The Ontario Newspapers Corporation, Limited, have made the following statement regarding the Hamilton *Times*:—

"It has been found necessary to suspend the publication of the Hamilton *Morning Times*. This has been brought about by a combination of circumstances, largely unforeseen and uncontrollable, which culminated to-day in the inability of the management to secure sufficient printers to make the issue of to-morrow's edition possible. It had been unable since Monday to publish papers of requisite size owing to this cause. The management, which had been paying a scale of wages in excess of the morning newspaper scale provided for in the agreement entered into between the Hamilton publishers and the Typographical Union, was unable to meet the demands which the union officials thought were fair under the circumstances, with the result as above stated.

"This is very much regretted by the Ontario Newspapers Corporation, Limited, but is the only action possible when all the facts are considered. The proposal to establish a morning newspaper in Hamilton, as it presented itself to the promoters a few months ago, seemed feasible, and even attractive as a commercial undertaking. Events, however, in the business world have of late developed so quickly and unexpectedly as to prejudice a successful operation of the enterprise which this company has undertaken.

"The management has, however, reason to be grateful for the encouragement accorded the new enterprise by a section of the city. Considering the appeal that was made, the response that was made from the advertising standpoint and subscriptions received, gave assurance that under normal conditions, and the co-operation that had been anticipated, ultimate success might confidently have been looked for.

"All obligations will be promptly met and money received for unearned subscriptions and advertising refunded immediately."

Newspaper Service Goes On

Mr. W. Nelson Wilkinson, managing editor of the Hamilton *Morning Times*, who also is president and general manager of the Canadian Newspaper Service, Limited, made the following statement:

"Canadian Newspaper Service, Limited, was separate and distinct from the Hamilton *Times*. The company purchased from the Ontario Newspaper Corporation Limited the plant and business of the Canada Ready Print Co. and amalgamated it with the Canadian Newspaper Service, Limited. The business of the Canadian Newspaper Service, Limited, is not affected by the suspension of the Hamilton *Morning Times*."

Following the issue by the management of the Hamilton *Morning Times* of a statement setting forth reasons for suspending publication, one of these being that a sufficient staff of printers could not be secured though more than the scale was paid, W. J. Mountjoy, President of the Hamilton Typographical Union, said:

"I desire to state emphatically that the Hamilton Typographical Union disclaims any responsibility for the Hamilton *Morning Times* having ceased publication. If individual members of the union did not consider they were to be sufficiently recompensed for their services, the union had no power to compel them to work."

Canadian Trip a Success

PRINTER AND PUBLISHER has received the following letter from Sir Harry Brittain, who was instrumental in organizing the Imperial Press Conference.

2, Cowley Street, Westminster,
October 15th, 1920.

Dear Sir,

All my best thanks to you for your most excellent September number giving so good an account of various aspects of the Second Imperial Press Conference to which I had the privilege of going as Chairman of the Arrangements Committee. To my very great sorrow I was only able to stay in Canada for the completion of the Conference itself, having to fulfil various engagements on the Continent towards the end of August which I had agreed to carry out many months previously. I should have enjoyed immensely the wonderful trip through the Dominion with our good hosts and my colleagues, even though it has been my privilege to have journeyed across Canada ten or twelve times. I much looked forward to getting in the visit to Toronto before the *Empress of France* returned, but that, alas, proved to be impossible.

I do not suppose that any of the visitors who went over were more gratified than I was in the permanent success achieved by this Second Conference for, as I think you know, the conception of the First was my own, the idea coming to me when in the Dominion some 13 years ago. Consequently I feel that the wonderful results of the Second Conference have finally set a seal on the effects of the First, thereby creating what must be a really permanent and invaluable institution to carry out the finest and most effective form of Empire work.

The organization of the First Conference took me the best part of two years; if it had taken the best part of twenty I should never have regretted it.

In conclusion let me suggest that during the months of August and September Canada set a pace in splendid hospitality and in continued and concentrated interest which the hosts for Conference No. 3, whoever they may be, will find extremely difficult to parallel.

Yours very truly,
HARRY BRITTAIN.

The Editor
Printer and Publisher,
Toronto.

Surely a Real Poster

Corona Hotel, Edmonton

Editor, *Printer and Publisher*,

Yesterday was voting on the Referendum in Alberta. One of the Returning Officers was Geo. D. Hunt, who before going overseas was one of those connected with the *Bulletin* at this place. He is a son of Mr. Hunt, connected with the Miller & Richard type supply house at Winnipeg, and is certainly a chip off the old block with perhaps a little height advantage. Mr. Hunt is now connected with a prominent real estate concern here. His being a returning officer perhaps does not convey anything remarkable, but accompanying this letter is a copy of a "notice to electors" issued by him which to my mind is out of the ordinary, in that it is a "solid" poster from start to finish, giving the polling divisions and other particulars in connection with the voting. It is believed that it is the largest poster of its kind ever issued in Canada. What would have been done in this case without the "machine" typesetter?

Yours truly,

H. C. STOVEL

The bill in question has solid composition of about 85,000 ems eight point. The stock is 48 x 32. The work is well done all through.—Ed. P. & P.

Too Much Foliage Here?

Editor, *Printer and Publisher*.

Sir:—On Press Day at the Canadian National Exhibition you will remember that the president of the Weekly Newspaper Association pleaded for a better and fuller understanding between the urban and rural press. He intimated they were beginning to understand one another more than they had in the past, but still had a long way to travel. It was not so many months ago that at least one Toronto daily published a column each Saturday of alleged wit and humor from the weekly publications, taking excerpts from some contributions of country correspondents, and reproducing local references and jibes.

The president of the Weekly Association remarked that while these clippings might appear ludicrous and perhaps ridiculous to the city readers, yet they were no more so than the recorded social events and society column of the metropolitan press were to the people of the farm and the smaller towns and villages.

Eliminating the names in the paragraph enclosed (from a Toronto daily of October 16) I submit that it might be reproduced in *Printer and Publisher* as illustrative of the inane chatter and frothy material that frequently masquerades as news in the press of Toronto and other large cities. It is certainly a *piece de resistance*, a bon mot, a veritable atom of ideality lost in verbal profundity.

Yours faithfully,

SANE JOURNALISM.

The clipping follows:—

"Mrs. —'s lovely little house away among the trees of Russell Hill road, was opened to a little group of "writing people" yesterday, by its chatelaine, who had, as her guest of honor, Mrs. —, the Canadian novelist. The house itself is instinct with charm. Every corner is inviting. A single pink rose, in a slender vase, stood on a bit of old mahogany in the hall, two lighted candles, in silver candlesticks, on either side seeming to pay its homage. Another perfect rose was on the grand piano, the deeper pink of asters further down the room forming a link between the summer and the out-of-doors, where, through muslin-curtained windows could be seen a fringe of trees, whose glory of autumn coloring was made still more glorious by the rays of the setting sun. The dining-room was bright with brass and marigolds and candle-light, and here Mrs. — and Miss — poured tea and coffee."

Howard Smith House Organ

The Crest, Vol. I., No. 1, the new house organ of the Howard Smith Paper Mills, Montreal, came to our desk the other day, and as first impressions are lasting, we hope it will be a regular visitor. The inside consists of 16 pages, printed on egg-shell finish book, while an egg-shell finish Bristol has been used for the cover. Cheltenham Old Style has been used for the text, done in black ink, while pale blue has been used for the second color. The whole job has been excellently gotten up and printed, and goes to show the excellent results obtained by mixing brains with paper, type and ink. *The Crest*, while primarily showing how paper fits into the general scheme of business, is by no means devoted to paper exclusively, but touches on many historical and business topics of particular interest to the printer.

Old Country Firm May Sell

Messrs. W. E. & J. Gomer Berry have made an offer for the purchase of Cassell & Co., Ltd., the celebrated publishing house, at a price of 22s. 6d. per share. This offer is conditional on its acceptance by shareholders representing 75 per cent. of the total issued capital within 28 days. The directors of Cassell's recommend acceptance, and as the shares have a market value of about 15s. at the present time there is every likelihood that the deal will be carried through. Cassell's have had a remarkable history in the publishing trade. John Cassell, the founder of the house, first began to issue in 1848, and his first great success was the publishing, in 1852, of *Cassell's Popular Educator*. The firm was known as Cassell, Petter and Galpin until 1883, when it became a limited company. Its greatest achievement on the book side was the issue of Cassell's National Library (1886-90), consisting of 214 reprints at a price of 3d. each. Writers such as R. L. Stevenson, Conan Doyle, Dean Farrar, and J. M. Barrie have presented their works, at different times, to the public through Messrs. Cassell.

The Editor Digs 12 pt. Spuds

North Bay—With the jingle of sleigh bells resounding from Cobalt to the north, J. J. Pratt, editor of the *Advocate*, with the assistance of a boy, dug fourteen bags of potatoes. The "murphies" were in excellent condition without the least sign of the rot that is prevailing amongst them this year. The atmosphere was as warm and balmy as a September morn.

Notes of the Agencies

Newspaper and magazine advertising for Dominion Chocolate Company, (Hooton's Chocolate) is being prepared and placed by Norris-Patterson Limited Advertising Agency, Toronto and Montreal.

The Norris-Patterson Limited Advertising Agency, is now placing the advertising of the McCrimmon's Chemicals Limited, Toronto, manufacturing liquid chemicals and disinfectants.

The next advertising campaign of the Eureka Vacuum Cleaner Company, of Kitchener, is being prepared by Norris-Patterson Limited, and will appear shortly in the daily newspapers.

Norris-Patterson Limited have been selected to handle the advertising of Hall Knitcraft Limited, Toronto, manufacturers of "Tosox."

The Master Cleaners and Dyers Association of Ontario are conducting a newspaper campaign in the daily press through Norris-Patterson Limited Advertising Agency, Toronto and Montreal.

General advertising on behalf of K. Farah & Sons, Limited, is being placed through Norris-Patterson Limited, Toronto and Montreal. Their products are the "Farabed" and the "Farahammock." The "Farabed" is a convertible folding single bed which can be converted into an invalid's lounge hospital cot and verandah couch.

Norris-Patterson Limited, Toronto and Montreal, are sending out advertising for Vox Pastilles, manufactured by Vox Chemical Company, Montreal, to a general list of papers.

L. R. Steel Service Corporation, operating a chain store system, have placed their advertising with Norris-Patterson Limited, Toronto and Montreal. Large sized copy has been sent out to a list of newspapers.

The Montreal office of Norris-Patterson Limited is now preparing and will shortly place a campaign in the daily papers for "Air-Peds" (Pioneer Products Limited.)

THE PERSONAL SIDE OF IT

We'd Like To Get Items For
These Columns

William Banks Leaves Globe

THERE was mild surprise in Toronto newspaper circles when it became known that William Banks had resigned from the *Globe* editorial staff. He had been there for 21 years and when a man's on the *Globe* for 21 years, folks don't look for his departure. Mr. Banks is now with the British and Colonial Press, Toronto, taking charge of the literary department there, a section which Mr. Batten expects to develop to a considerable extent, catering to newspaper features in the letterpress.

Mr. Banks entered newspaper work about 25 years ago as a reporter on the *Mail and Empire*, and for the past 21 years has been a member of the staff of the *Globe*. Since then he has covered many important assignments, including the British elections in 1918, and the early stages of the Peace Conference in 1919. He has also been a frequent contributor to Canadian and United States periodicals. As a mark of appreciation a cabinet of silver was presented to him, accompanied by many expressions of good-will from his old associates, with many of whom he had worked for years.

WILLIAM BANKS

Stewart Lyon, editor of the *Globe*, expressed his deep sense of the loss sustained through the resignation of Mr. Banks. During his long connection with the *Globe*, first as a reporter and later as parliamentary reporter, city editor, news editor and editorial writer, he had sought not only to serve the *Globe* with utmost faithfulness, but to give a square deal to the members of the staff under circumstances that, as in all daily papers, were frequently difficult and exacting. During the years of the war Mr. Banks, as news editor, had given absolutely invaluable services to the *Globe*. The news came in in such a way that the news editor had to be on his job morning, noon, night and Sundays, and all the credit for the manner of presentation of the news of the war in the *Globe* most was due to Mr. Banks as news editor.

W. G. Jaffray, president of the *Globe*, expressed his regret at the departure of Mr. Banks, who had served the paper faithfully and well during those years, and enhanced its reputation very much by his skill in the handling of news, and his knowledge of what would likely and what would not likely prove to be news. "He saved us many a difficult situation," said Mr. Jaffray. "Subsequently, as you will remember, Mr. Banks occupied the position of acting editor in Mr. Lyon's absence in France, and I came more closely into association with him than ever at that time. The question of the policy of the paper regarding the issue of conscription had to be dealt with, and when the decision was made that there was no other course for the *Globe* to pursue than to come out straight for conscription, Mr. Banks again served the *Globe* in a very valuable way. I would like to say that the directors of the *Globe* appreciate Mr. Banks' great service to the paper during these years, and to the message they have sent I would wish to add my personal regard and best wishes for every happiness and success in his new work."

Mr. Ross Munro, news editor, and Mr. M. O. Hammond, financial editor, expressed their regret at losing so esteemed a colleague after years of close association. Mr. Banks, in acknowledging the gift and the kind words expressed, spoke of the years of pleasant relationship with the members of the staff. Though there had often been differences of opinion, he felt that on both sides to each controversy there had been only one object, and that was the welfare of the *Globe*. He expressed his gratitude for the gift from his fellow-workers and for the recognition from the directors.

Quebec

Sir Campbell Stuart, who was born in Montreal and who raised the Duchess of Connaught's Irish-Canadian Rangers there in the early days of the war, has been appointed managing director of the London *Times* newspaper. He is 35 years of age.

Georges Pelletier, managing editor *Le Devoir*, Montreal; Fernand Rinfret, editor *Le Canada*, Montreal; and Noel Fauteux, associate-editor *La Presse*, have been recently appointed professors of journalism at the new Political and Social Sciences School, University of Montreal. Mr. Pelletier will lecture on newspaper editing and publishing, Mr. Rinfret will lecture on the social aspects of the press, and Mr. Fauteux, on the history of the press. The three new professors, who are still under forty years old, are former members of the Press Gallery, Ottawa; and M.M. Pelletier and Rinfret are especially well known among their English-speaking confrères of the Canadian press. Both M. M. Pelletier and Fauteux have formerly studied and practised law. Mr. Rinfret is Liberal member for St. James division, Montreal, in the Dominion Parliament. M. M. Pelletier and Rinfret have been elected last year members of the Royal Society of Canada.

Maritime

John D. McCallum, eastern representative of the Montreal *Star*, was in Halifax during the latter part of October.

Frank Desmond, who for a number of years was head adsetter on the Sydney *Post*, is now in Halifax with the *Herald*.

John Mitchell, reporter on the *Morning Chronicle*, Halifax, was on a two weeks' trip to New York the latter part of October.

'Gee' Ahern, sporting editor of the Halifax *Herald* and *Evening Mail*, was hurt recently in a football match and is nursing an injured ankle.

Farm and Home, Vancouver, British Columbia, has recently increased its subscription price from $1.00 to $2.00 per year. The circulation is now 24,000, published weekly.

Mechanical Superintendent Harrison, of the Sydney *Post*, was in Halifax during Carnival week. Mr. Harrison complains of a shortage of printers around Cape Breton.

The latter part of October saw the marriage of one of the most popular printers in Halifax, when "Pat" Doherty, foreman of the advt.-setting dept. of the *Evening Mail*, was united in matrimony to Miss Helen Lamrock, of Shelborne, N.S.

The credit for the promoting and making possible of the big Schooner Race, held off Halifax harbor, which has attracted so much international attention, is due to the energetic initiative of W. H. Dennis, who has succeeded his uncle, the late Senator Dennis, as proprietor of the *Herald* and *Mail* newspapers.

Jos. Garnet, who is employed at the Imperial Publishing Co., Halifax, recently attended the Annual Convention of the International Pressmen's Union held at Nashville, Tenn. Mr. Garnet was appointed organizer for the Nova Scotia district.

A book of poems entitled "Twilight Litanies" will be off the press around the 15th of November. It is to contain an essay by the author, Dr. J. D. Logan, on "Christ as Poet." The foreword is by Rev. Dr. Foley, Rector of St. Mary's Cathedral, Halifax. Cover design and illustrations are by Percy Covey. The printing and publishing end of the venture is being handled jointly by T. C. Allen & Co., Halifax, and Wm. Tyrrell & Co., Toronto. It is to be ready for the Christmas trade.

Dr. Mosdell, managing editor of the *Evening Sun*, St. John, Nfld., was visiting in Toronto. He has been asked by his government to investigate and report upon the workings of several public institutions in Ontario.

The employing printers of Halifax recently had a get-together to form an association for the betterment of conditions in the printing industry of the city. One of the main objects sought was the adoption of the Franklin price list. Under present conditions there is very little uniformity of prices among the various offices, and to remedy this condition is the object of the newly formed association. The temporary officers are: Geo. E. Perry, pres.; W. P. Allen, vice-pres.; F. A. Zwicker, secy.; Percy Clancy, treas.

The International Schooner Race held at Halifax early this month was responsible for the coming to Halifax of many well known newspaper men. Among the prominent ones were James B. Connolly, of the Boston *Post*, famous the world over as a writer of sea stories; Jas. T. Kinsella and George G. Holland, both of the Boston *Post*; three other Boston papers were represented: the *Globe* by Frank Palmer, the *Herald* by G. S. Hudson, and the American by A. C. Williamson, who will also cover the series for the International News Service.

British Columbia

Elmer Hall, of the *News*, Trail, was a visitor at Eastern Canada points for a few weeks last month.

Will Elletson, jr., business manager of the *Miner*, Rossland, is holidaying at Edmonton, Alta., this month.

Fred Smyth, for the past four years in charge of the *Star*, Princeton, recently resigned his position, and is now located at Kellogg, Idaho.

The Kelowna *Record* ceased publication last month, leaving the field clear for the *Courier*. This should give the town one really good paper.

L. P. Sullivan, of the *Courier*, was the government-appointed official agent of the "wets" in the recent prohibition plebiscite in the Cranbrook riding.

With a provincial election under way the weeklies with one accord announce a rate of 50 cents an inch for display political advertising, and 10 cents a line for reading matter.

W. K. Esling, until very recently owner of the *Miner*, Rossland, and *News*, Trail, is the Conservative candidate in the Rossland riding in the present provincial election.

H. H. Currie, news editor of the *Daily News*, Nelson, was a successful exhibitor in the poultry section at both Nelson and Creston fall fairs. His hobby is Rhode Island Whites.

Papers of Liberal leanings in the different assessment districts were favored with the advertising of the usual sales of lands and crown grant mineral claims in arrears for taxes last month.

The recent prohibition referendum necessitated the printing of new provincial voters' lists, which was paid for at the rate of $7.50 for a page of 70 names set straightaway. Newsprint stock was used.

G. W. A. Smith, has leased the *Ledge*, Greenwood, from R. T. Lowery. The latter, who has been a patient at Grand Forks hospital for almost four months, made his first visit to Greenwood last week.

When it comes to real economy the purchasing agent of B. C. is certainly deserving of at least a D.C.M. Until recently the cut of the provincial arms measured an inch deep. Last month new cuts were supplied and will hardly measure half the depth of the old ones.

Frank Phillips has been appointed news editor of the Vancouver *Sun*. He has been with this paper for some time, having recently accompanied Mackenzie King on his tour through a section of the West. Mr. Phillips was city editor of the Ottawa *Free Press* before going overseas, where he was wounded rather severely at Vimy Ridge.

Editor Elletson, of the *Herald*, Cranbrook, who also owns the *Miner*, Rossland, came in for considerable criticism in the temperance campaign due to the fact that at Rossland he accepted both "wet" and "dry" advertising, but at Cranbrook he editorially announced that he would have no truck or trade with "wet" publicity.

H. W. Power, who leased the *Kootenaian*, Kaslo, in July 1919, to Jas. Grier, in order to join the staff of *Mining Truth*, Spokane, has severed his connection with that journal and is

now operating the W. H. Jones job plant at Nelson under lease. He has added a linotype to the equipment and is doing considerable business setting type for the hand-set weekly papers in the Kootenay.

Warren Lambert, once editor of the Cariboo *Sentinel*, the sole newspaper of the Cariboo district away back in the middle sixties, was in Winnipeg a short time ago and gave the *Free Press* some interesting details of life in British Columbia in the stirring days of the great gold rush. Mr. Lambert believes his was the first press taken to the Pacific coast. It was a little implement, weighing less than 275 pounds, sent out by the Catholic church some time in the '40's for the use of the local bishop. Five years, 1862-7, were spent by Mr. Lambert on the Pacific coast, in a newspaper experience covering the Victoria *Colonist*, the Cariboo *Sentinel*, the Victoria *Chronicle*, and the Victoria *Evening Express*.

Saskatchewan

The Young *Journal* has recently been purchased by W. C. Needham, late owner of the Simpson *Lance*, and Mr. W. H. Willoughby of the *Signal* staff, Watrous, has taken over the *Lance*.

Manitoba

John R. Davidson, who for the last few years has been managing editor of the Hugh C. MacLean Co., Ltd., Winnipeg, publishers of the *Commercial*, the *Western Lumberman*, the *Western Canada Contractor*, and the *Western Canada Coal Review*, has resigned that position, and will on October 1st become affiliated with the Western Retail Lumbermen's Association, of Winnipeg, where wider scope presents itself for his long editorial experience. Trade journalism will not be entirely lost to Mr. Davidson, for included in his new work will be the management of the Association's new magazine, the *Prairie Lumberman*, which is the house organ of the retail lumber dealers in Western Canada, being published monthly. Fred H. Lamar is secretary of the Western Retail Lumbermen's Association, with offices at 406-9 Scott Block, Winnipeg.

Ontario

The Stouffville *Tribune* goes to $2. per year on December 1.

W. F. Herman, proprietor of papers at Windsor and Saskatoon, with Mrs. Herman, has left on an extended trip to Europe.

Rhys Crossin, formerly city editor of the Hamilton *Times*, has resigned, and is now acting as *Globe* correspondent in Hamilton.

Stewart McKenzie, son of Dan McKenzie, the *Advocate*, Paisley, Ont. has entered into partnership with A. V. Nolan of the Barrie *Advance*.

The *Globe* has taken on a trio of cubs in the persons of Calder, Munns and Loftus, the latter two being turned over to cavort around the sport pages.

Horace Bell is on the *Globe* staff again, doing local and general work. Since returning from overseas he has been in the north country for the last two years.

President W. Rupert Davies, of the Canadian Weekly Newspapers Association, was the speaker at a Board of Commerce luncheon at Montreal on Wednesday, November 3rd.

Hugh Ferguson, formerly a linotype operator on the *Globe* staff, has been taken off the mechanical end to hold down the city copy desk. He learned his trade in Walkerton, but has always been more or less interested in editorial work.

Prior to leaving the Fort William *Times-Journal* for the MacLean Publishing Co., Toronto, Charles C. Jenkins was presented with a handsome club bag by members of the staff. He had been managing editor of that paper for eight years.

Miss Dillys Jones was presented with a gold wrist watch by employees of the *Globe* business and circulation departments upon the occasion of leaving the circulation department staff to take a position in Los Angeles, California. Miss Jones has been five years with the *Globe*. The presentation was made by Mr. R. A. McCleary, circulation manager.

F. A. McLean, advertising manager of the Canadian Ingersoll-Rand Co., Sherbrooke, Que., went away into the woods to shoot up bear, deer, grouse, fish, or anything else that would stand still while he got the artillery steered in the right direction.

FEW men can claim an active connection of fifty years with any one newspaper, and fewer still have had such an intimate half-century connection as William M. Hale, founder of the Orillia *Packet*, and still actively connected with it. The *Packet* issued its fiftieth anniversary number on November 4th, and although the rest of the present day world was crowded out for the time being, a great deal of Orillia's history of the last half century was crowded in. The issue would make pleasant reading for any old time or present day Orillian. The *Packet* did not come into existence under the most auspicious circumstances. As a matter of fact it grew out of a variety of eventful happenings, Mr. Hale's own story of its first days concluding ".... On the bottom step I gathered myself together, and made my way to Mr. James Quinn, the local Conservative leader. He was not surprised to hear of the lock-out; he had been looking for it, as was everybody else in town. My offer to Quinn was that if he and his friends would advance me sufficient ready money to establish the needed line of credit, I would resume publication of the paper. A sum of money was raised, so small that I am ashamed to say how much, or rather how little. With this in my pocket I left the Orillia House on a cold winter morning, about eight o'clock, and, staging it through storm and drift, reached Barrie in time to catch the four o'clock train for Toronto, where the Gwatkins sold me a second-hand press and the rest of the meagre outfit with which the paper was soon got going again, in a building owned by the late Henry Boyes, about two doors south of the office of to-day. I did not have to advertise in the daily papers for printers. It was almost a case of 'Captain, crew, and bo'sun too, and cook of the *Nancy* brig.' My sole assistant was a youth named Taylor, Jim Taylor, a cousin of Mr. J. B. Henderson, and brother of Mrs. T. A. Main, who subsequently gained distinction in the publishing business in the United States, and my wages bill amounted to a dollar a week! About two years later I got rid of some of my worries and lessened my labor by taking my brother into partnership."

WILLIAM M. HALE

He spent most of the time shooting at a three-legged weasel and a few empty bottles. The weasel still has its three legs.

An X-ray examination has revealed the fact that John D. McGregor, of Trafalgar Township, near Milton, an orator and writer for one of the Toronto papers, who signs himself "Rob Roy," is suffering from cancer of the throat. He is now receiving special treatment with the Dr. Glover serum. Mr. McGregor has been writing the history of Halton County lately for a Toronto paper.

Listowel *Standard*:—The Mitchell *Recorder*, one of Perth's oldest newspapers, has decided to cease publication. It has been purchased by the Mitchell *Advocate* and from November 1 the two papers will be amalgamated. In making the announcement, the *Advocate* says that for a long time it has been felt that two papers could only exist in Mitchell, and in order that one might make a decent living, the *Advocate* has taken over the business of the *Recorder*.

Canadians attending the meeting of the Associated Business Papers Inc. in New York in October were Col. Maclean, president of the MacLean Publishing Co., G. D. Davis, B. G. Newton, A. R. Kennedy, of the same company, and Andrew McLean of the Hugh C. MacLean Co. The National Conference of Business Paper Editors was in session at the same time, and at the election of officers a place on the executive for the ensuing year was given to Mr. Kennedy.

The Oshawa *Telegram*, although not half a year old yet, is running up to a sixteen-page affair quite frequently. In a recent issue of 16 pages there were 70 columns of advertising, a

pretty liberal allotment for the edition. The paper is pretty much of a family compact type, Mr. Alger having his two sons, practical printers, associated with him. The $2 rate is being secured. O. M. Alger is editor, S. R. Alger, business manager and E. S. Alger, sales manager.

Samuel McCammon, after fifty-seven years of faithful service, has resigned his position as town clerk of Gananoque. He prepared the papers of incorporation in 1863, and became its clerk when the municipality was first formed a village. He was at one time prior to this on the business staff of the *Globe*, Toronto. He recently celebrated his 90th birthday. James Sampson, the present town treasurer, has been appointed to the position, the two offices having been combined.

E. E. Reynolds has sold the Gravenhurst *Banner* to Dass Brothers, both printers, and I formerly of that town. Mr. Reynolds took over. the Gravenhurst paper about two and half years ago, and made a notable improvement in the paper. Prior to going there he was with the Philip Davis Co., Hamilton, He was for some time on the mechanical side of the *Expositor* and *Courier* in Brantford, also with the Hunley Co. Mr. Reynolds is taking a rest from business for the present. The new proprietors have taken possession of the *Banner*.

The annual meeting of the Commercial Arts Association of Canada was held in Victoria Hall, Toronto. Mr. Frank Halliday was elected president. Mr. George Vanderbilt, the retiring president, remains on the executive. Appreciation was expressed of the valuable service rendered the association by Mr. Vanderbilt, under whose leadership over 90 per cent. of the professional artists of Toronto were recruited for the association. The other officers for 1920-21 are: vice-president, W. Phypers; secretary, C. F. Comfort; treasurer, J. Willson; executive, G. Vanderbilt, A. W. Cameron, T. McLean, H. Westerberg, P. J. Timmins and R. W. Capel.

Ottawa *Citizen*:—The members of the *Citizen* staff at noon honored one of their confreres, Charles Woods, on the twenty-fifth anniversary of his appointment as foreman of the composing room. The members of all departments of the newspaper organization assembled in the editorial rooms immediately the last form of the *Evening Citizen* had been sent to press and gave Mr. Woods the surprise of his life. An address of felicitation upon his quarter century of service was read on behalf of the staff by Horace M. Butler, at the conclusion of which Ernest Haddow presented the anniversary gifts of employees and management. Mr. Woods, though taken quite unawares, expressed his appreciation in concise but fitting terms, which the assembly broke up with a popular sing-song in his honor.

GENTLEMEN, we have with us to-day, Fred Elliott, of the *Alliston Herald*. Said fish are real, honest-to-goodness Muskoka fish, that look at one with the genuine cold eye of a dead fish.

Fred Elliott has ideas of his own. One is that his office should close two weeks each summer in order that there may be some real holidays. Another is that a weekly paper should have a cost system, and still another that weekly men should get in the C.W.N.A., of which he is chairman of the job printing committee.

He's fond of fairly long words, too, and they do tell that folks around Alliston, when they get stuck on a new word of ponderous length, put the thing in a cart and wheel it over to Elliott's office.

Not a bad chap as weekly publishers go. Pays most of his debts, is on speaking terms with his subscribers, and at gatherings of publishers gathers up the loose ends and writes resolutions with a hop-step and jump in them. That's about all we know of him. So hop along and clean the fish F. E.

MR. FRED ELLIOTT

St. Catharines *Standard*:—Archibald Fleming, aged 71, after spending five years in the Hospital for Incurables in Toronto, died there. Born in Thornhill, Ont., he was educated in Toronto, and in 1875 entered the *Globe* newspaper as sub-editor. After spending several years with them, he left for Toledo, where he continued in the newspaper business, afterwards working on newspapers for a number of years in various parts of the Union. For seven years prior to his illness which rendered him unfit for his chosen profession Mr. Fleming was a valued and conscientious member of the *Standard's* editorial staff. He was a newspaperman of the old school and practically all his acquaintances were numbered with his admirers. Since his confinement in the hospital Archie's trenchant pen refused to rest, and he occasionally contributed local items to the *Standard*.

Toronto press women bade farewell to Miss Daisy Cryer, of the *Telegram* editorial staff, who has left for her home in Caerphilly, Glamorganshire, Wales. Five years ago Miss Cryer came to Canada and entered the field of local journalism, where she has been very successful. She is well known as the editor of 'Shrapnel Corners,'' in connection with which she "covered" the first Parliamentary Commission on Soldiers' Re-establishment at Ottawa, and many other important developments in the interests of returned men and their dependents. During the past fortnight a number of farewell teas and dinners have been given in her honor, and among them a luncheon by the editorial staff of the *Evening Telegram*, when Miss Cryer was the recipient of numerous good wishes to carry with her across the sea, and a bouquet of pink roses. A reception was given by Mrs. E. B. Freeland, 27 North street; a dinner by Miss Florence Smith at the St. Regis Hotel, while others entertaining her were Mrs. Murray Muir, Balmoral ave., and the Misses Irene Todd and Beatrice Phipps.

After over 39 years of service on the staff of the *Globe*, Mr. W. Pitman Morse, treasurer of that newspaper, has resigned to enjoy a period of well-earned rest. Mr. Morse, before leaving, was summoned to the office of the president, where he found a large delegation from the staff awaiting him. On its behalf the president, Mr. W. G. Jaffray, presented him with a sterling silver table set, suitably engraved. Speaking for both the directorate and the staff, the president expressed the sense of loss experienced by the *Globe* in the retirement of its treasurer, and its deep appreciation of his long and faithful service. Mr. W. J. Irwin, the secretary; Mr. Geo. L. Wilson, of the business office staff, and Mr. Stewart Lyon spoke briefly, recalling outstanding incidents and events in the history of the paper with which Mr. Morse had been associated. Mr. Morse joined the business staff of the *Globe* on June 5, 1881, shortly after the assassination of Hon. George Brown, and has been in the service of the paper almost continuously since that time. For some time past he has been the treasurer of the Globe Printing Company.

The St. Marys *Argus*, founded over 60 years ago, ceased publication with the issue of October 8. The paper has been purchased by C. W. Eedy, publisher of the St. Marys *Journal*, and the *Argus* has been merged with the *Journal* under the title the St. Marys *Journal-Argus*. The *Argus* was first printed in January, 1859, when St. Marys was a village and before a railway had reached here, and has been issued continuously since. It was founded by the late A. J. Belch, who died at Winnipeg about ten years ago. The late J. J. Crabbe, of Toronto, owned and edited the *Argus* for about twenty years and it has changed hands several times since. A. C. Wood, customs officer, was the publisher at the time of his appointment to office. The paper has had a long and honorable career. Its absorption by the *Journal* is a direct result of conditions brought about by the Great War. The increasing cost of newsprint and all material entering into the production of a newspaper made it necessary for the present publishers, Messrs. Stewart and Grose, to dispose of the business. The *Journal* has been in existence nearly a half century, and is one of the most progressive country weeklies in Canada.

Mr. E. Grose, one of the publishers of the *Argus*, has been placed in charge of the mechanical end of the new business.

A New Rate Card

Messrs. Crossley & Turley, publishers of the Minnedosa, (Man.) *Tribune*, have issued a new rate card as follows:—

Display advertising: Transient 50 cents per inch first insertion; 35c thereafter, with no change.

Contract rate: 100 inches or more, not less than 2½ inches per insertion, the whole to be used within a year from date of contract, (plate) 35c per inch; (set) 40c per inch.

Classified Advertising: Not exceeding one inch, 50 cents each first two insertions, 25 cents thereafter.

Births, marriages and deaths: 50c each notice.

In memoriam notices: 50 cents up to one inch; 7 cents per count line above one inch.

Government, municipal and legal notices: 13 cents per agate line first insertion; 9 cents per agate line subsequent insertion.

Business locals: 25 cents per count line each insertion; (heavy type) 35 cents per line.

Local readers: 50 cents per inch each insertion.

Copy for ads. must be in the office Mondays to ensure insertion same week.

The contract rate is based upon a circulation of 1,100. The lists are open to advertisers at any time.

Position: the *Tribune* will not guarantee position.

No cash discount. The *Tribune* is a 4 page paper, all home print; each page is 7 columns wide, each column 22 inches deep, 13 ems wide.

"Miehle Service" is the name of a little book sent out by the Miehle Printing Press Co., of Philadelphia. In it is brought out the versatile nature of its mechanical plant which was able to turn at short notice to the manufacture of gun mounts and deliver them on schedule. The service the company is prepared to extend to users of the press is also emphasized. The printing and design of the book are up to the mark of Miehle excellence.

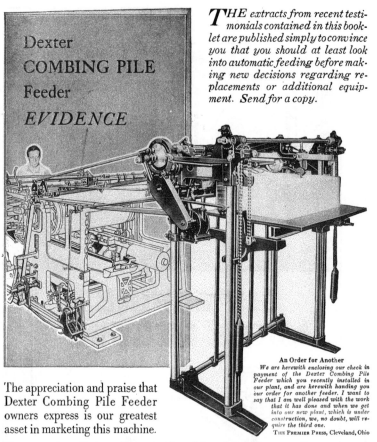

Dexter
COMBING PILE
Feeder
EVIDENCE

THE extracts from recent testimonials contained in this booklet are published simply to convince you that you should at least look into automatic feeding before making new decisions regarding replacements or additional equipment. Send for a copy.

An Order for Another

We are herewith enclosing our check in payment of the Dexter Combing Pile Feeder which you recently installed in our plant, and are herewith handing you our order for another feeder. I want to say that I am well pleased with the work that it has done and when we get into our new plant, which is under construction, we, no doubt, will require the third one.

THE PREMIER PRESS, Cleveland, Ohio

The appreciation and praise that Dexter Combing Pile Feeder owners express is our greatest asset in marketing this machine.

Every new installation adds to our list of friends and boosters. Let us put you in touch with Dexter Combing Pile Feeder users so that you may actually hear their enthusiastic opinion of automatic feeding. What our users say is a safe buying guide for you to follow.

DEXTER FOLDER COMPANY, 200 Fifth Avenue, New York

Folders, Cross Continuous Feeders, Dexter Feeders, Inserting, Covering and Wire-Stitching Machines

CHICAGO   PHILADELPHIA   BOSTON   DALLAS   ATLANTA   SAN FRANCISCO

EFFICIENCY AND ECONOMY

ARE BOTH VITALLY NECESSARY IN THESE DAYS OF HIGH OPERATING COSTS

Everyone who realizes this should investigate these two time and money savers.

DROSS REFINING FURNACE

No stereotype or electrotype foundry or linotype composing room can afford to be without one of these Dross Refining Furnaces. It will pay for itself in a very short time. By its use from sixty to seventy per cent. of the metal in the dross can be recovered.

The body of the furnace is of boiler iron lined with fire brick.

The spout is cast on to the pot and has a hinged yoke and cap which is closed when changing pans. Two pans are supplied with each furnace.

When the cap is screwed against the mouth of the spout the pot can be used for melting linotype or other metal. The pot has a capacity of 225 lbs.

The furnace is 29 inches high, and 24 inches in diameter at the base. The door in the hood is 11 inches in width.

Coal is ordinarily used for fuel, but when desired we supply a special gas burner.

A user writes:—"The furnace has been a more profitable investment than you claimed, as it more than paid for itself refining the first batch of dross we ran."

New Combination Curved and Flat Gas-Heated Matrix-Scorching Oven

This combination oven will dry curved matrices up to 24" x 28"—7 and 8 columns —for presses either with the columns running around or across the cylinders, as well as flat matrices up to 22½" x 25½".

As in our older model ovens, the matrix is placed face down in the drying chamber, so that all moisture is driven from the face through the back of the matrix, which is the correct method of scorching matrices.

The fact that it is possible to use this improved oven for scorching both curved and flat matrices is a feature which will be greatly appreciated, as it eliminates the necessity for an extra oven for making flat mats for the job department.

Every Stereotyper needs one.

R. HOE AND CO.

504-520 Grand St., New York City

7 Water Street	544-546 South Clark Street	109-112 Borough Road
BOSTON, MASS.	CHICAGO, ILL.	LONDON, S.E. 1, ENG.

"QUALITY"
ROLLERS

MADE FOR ANY SIZE OF PRESS

Have You Ordered Your
Winter's Supply Yet?
Let This Remind You!

*S.V. & H. Inks and Rollers make
a fine combination—use both!*

Sinclair, Valentine & Hoops
LIMITED
229-233 Richmond Street West
WINNIPEG   **TORONTO**   MONTREAL

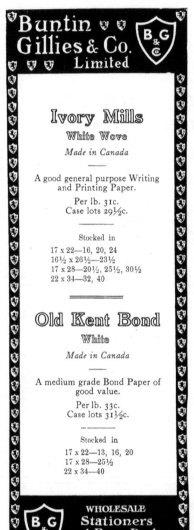

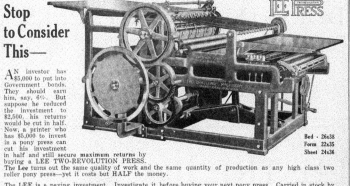

Say you saw it in PRINTER AND PUBLISHER

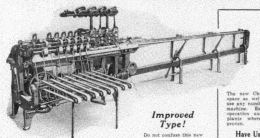
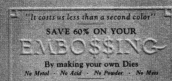

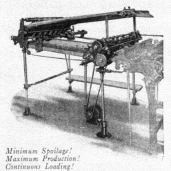

CLASSIFIED ADVERTISEMENT SECTION

TWO CENTS A WORD, Box Number as five words ; minimum charge is $1.00 per insertion, for 50 words or less, set in 6 pt. type. Each figure counts as a word. Display ads., or ads. set in border, are at the card rates.

FOR SALE

FOR SALE—MILLER AUTOMATIC FEEDER for 12 x 18 C. & P., only used six months, nothing broken, in perfect condition. Price, $1,000. Apply Box 10520, Printer and Publisher. (p11p)

FOR SALE—BRIGHT CENTRAL ONTARIO weekly. Good circulation, splendid advertising and job patronage. Annual turnover, $5,000. Good reasons for selling. Apply to Box 102520, Printer and Publisher. (p11p)

FOR SALE—CAMPBELL TWO REVOLUTION cylinder press, 37x52. Apply Technical Press Limited, 426 Homer St., Vancouver, B.C. (p11p)

FOR SALE—WEEKLY NEWSPAPER AND Job printing plant in a prosperous British Columbia mining, fruit growing and lumbering district. Good schools, fine fishing and hunting with ideal climate the year round. $3,000. $1,000 down, balance on very easy terms. For particulars write H. W. Power, Box 532, Nelson, B.C. (p19p)

PRINTING PLANT FOR SALE

MODERN, SMALL PLANT, WITH FULL equipment ; very little used ; Falcon and Gordon press and individual motor and control ; full line of type ; worth five thousand new ; sell twenty-one hundred, half cash. Mention "Printer and Publisher." Write Box 10, Globe, Toronto. (pfp)

SITUATION WANTED

ADVERTISING MAN WITH VALUABLE Eastern and Western newspaper training and experience, and first-rate war record, is open to discuss new proposition with publisher who seeks live, earnest worker for either local or foreign departments, or manager of both. Has all essential qualifications—soliciting, advising, preparation, lay-outs, copy, etc. Box 354, Postal Station H, Montreal, Que. (p11p)

COLLECTIONS

SEND US YOUR LIST OF DELINQUENTS. We will turn Debit into Credit. Publishers' Protective Association, Toronto. (ptfp)

What is the
PRINTER &
PUBLISHER
to Canada?

The National Printer-Journalist
is the same to the United States

Send 25c. for a sample copy

National Printer-Journalist
(in its 37th year)
4610 Ravenswood Avenue
CHICAGO, ILL.

SITUATIONS VACANT

Notice that "I" is at the centre of w-i-n.

MONOTYPE KEYBOARD OPERATORS OF ability always in demand. We offer you the opportunity to better yourself. By attending one of our schools for a few months the compositor fits himself for a position with better pay, better working conditions and a chance for advancement. We are selling keyboards as fast as we can make them, over 50 per cent. are for new plants, which means more operators wanted. Free schools in Philadelphia, New York, Chicago and Toronto. Write the city nearest you for information. Lanston Monotype Machine Company. (pfp)

LINOTYPE OPERATOR—EXPERIENCED ; steady job ; state wages. Write, mentioning "Printer and Publisher," to the Bulletin, Collingwood. (pfp)

PRESSMAN—GOOD ON PLATEN WORK, permanent. Apply, mentioning "Printer and Publisher," to Review, Niagara Falls, Ont. (pfp)

APPRENTICES—LOOK—I CAN HELP YOU make money in your spare time. Right in your own town. No experience necessary. Box 102220, Printer and Publisher. (p11p)

SUPERINTENDENT WANTED FOR JOB printing plant. Must understand the business in all branches, be able to meet customers and estimate. Franklin Price List used. Apply stating age, qualifications and salary to the Review Printing Co., Ltd., Peterboro. (p11p)

Machinery List

Two-rev. Cottrell, 4-roller, bed 33½ x 50, front fly delivery, table distribution, geared distributors, trip, back-up motion. Guaranteed in first-class condition. Price on application.
10 x 15 W. & B. Gordon, throw-off and power fixtures.
10 x 15 Universal (old style), throw-off, power fixtures.
18 x 19 Colts Armory (new style), throw-off, power fixtures, guaranteed.
18 x 19 Colts Armory, throw-off, power fixtures, in first-class condition.
7 x 11 Prouty, 4-form rollers, throw-off.
10 x 15 O.S. Gordon, throw-off, power fixtures and treadle.
30″ Peerless Paper Cutter, hand lever.
¼″ Rosback Power Stitcher.
¼″ Rosback Power Stitcher.
¾″ Morrison Stitcher Perfection G, Power.
¼″ Morrison Perfection, Power.
¼″ Morrison Stitcher (on stand), hand or foot power.
2—5-16″ Morrison Stitchers, hand or foot power.
20″ Round Hole Perforator, foot power.
Above machines guaranteed in first-class condition and for immediate shipment. Prices on application.
1—36 x 18 Harris Press with Fountain and Power Fixtures.
1—32″ Cloth Ruling Machine, Single Beam.
1—32″ Cloth Ruling Machine, Double Beam.
1—Washington Hand Proof Press.
1—Challenge Proof Press.
5—½ H.P. Type C.M., 1800 R.P.M., 230 volt, Crocker-Wheeler Motors, with starters, direct current. Suitable for driving presses.
1—½ H.P. Type C.M., 1650 R.P.M., 230 volt, Crocker-Wheeler Motor, with starters, new, direct current. Suitable for ruling machine.
3—Royal Shaft Straightening Presses.
New and Rebuilt Cylinder and Platen Presses, Paper Cutters, Stitchers, Perforators, Ruling and Punching Machinery and Supplies.

ROYAL MACHINE WORKS
738 ST. PAUL ST. WEST, MONTREAL

SITUATIONS VACANT—Con.

BE AN ARTIST—EXPERTS EARN $50 TO $100 a week ; we teach you at home in a few months ; our graduates are in demand ; one recently placed after just five months' study. Particulars, write, mentioning "Printer and Publisher," to Shaw Correspondence School, Toronto, Dept. G. (pfp)

BE A STORY WRITER — TURN YOUR ideas into dollars ; we teach you at home under an expert ; our students are successful ; one student earned $300 while studying ; we will sell your stories. Write, mentioning "Printer and Publisher," to Shaw Correspondence School, Toronto, Dept. G. (pfp)

BOOKBINDERS — GOOD JOB RULER wanted ; steady work ; this is a good position for the right man. Apply, mentioning "Printer and Publisher," to Mr. Johnson, Warwick Bros. & Rutter, King and Spadina, Toronto. (pfp)

PRINTING SALESMAN—WANTED FOR A real, live, job printing office. State experience, if any. Am willing to consider ambitious young man now in mechanical department. Box 102120, Printer and Publisher. (p11p)

BUSINESS WANTED

J. P. LAWRASON, 25 TORONTO ST., wants one chance to sell your business or property ; no matter what kind or where located. I can get you the last dollar. Write, mentioning "Printer and Publisher," or come in and talk it over. Advice free. (pfp)

EQUIPMENT WANTED

WANTED — SEVEN-COLUMN QUARTO press in good condition. Apply Box 10820, Printer and Publisher. (pfp)

DIRECT CURRENT MOTORS—ONE 2 H.P., 220 Volts, with Cutter-Hammer controller ; two ¾ H.P., 220 Volts ; one Monotype keyboard, Reliance ; one paper cutter, interlocking, 28½-inch cut ; about 100 type cases, upper and lower ; a number of California job cases ; about one ton Eddystone newsprint, 31x44, 51 lbs. ; three imposing stones, size about thirty-six inches by forty-six inches, for $25 each. Box 102720, Printer and Publisher. (p11p)

Printing Machinery for Sale

Amalgamation of the Tribune and Welland Telegraph finds the new owners, with the following duplicates:

4-roller 2-revolution Potter Press.
Bed 32x46.
Whitlock Drum Cylinder Press.
Pony Campbell, Bed 23x28.
30-inch W. & B. Lever Paper Cutter, with interlock.
Rosback Perforator (Treadle).
No. 2 Mentges Folder. Will fold 4, 6, 8, 10 or 12 pages.
Roller Proof Press.
Washington Hand Press, 26x36.
Fireproof Paper Baler

The items listed will be sold at very reasonable prices and terms.

Tribune and Telegraph Co., Limited
WELLAND, ONT.
(p11p)

Subscribe Today for "Printer and Publisher," $3.00 per year.

Buyers' Guide

*T*HE *firms listed in this Buyers' Guide are all advertisers in* PRINTER AND PUBLISHER. *Refer to the ads. by consulting the Index. Our interests are mutual—tell the advertisers you read their ad. in* PRINTER AND PUBLISHER. *Patronize* PRINTER AND PUBLISHER *advertisers—they are all definitely interested in the promotion of efficiency in equipment and service in Canada's allied printing trades.*

ADDRESSING MACHINES
The Challenge Machinery Co., Grand Haven, Mich.
Westman & Baker Limited, Toronto.

BALERS FOR WASTE PAPER
Golding Mfg. Co., Franklin, Mass.
Logan, H. J., 114 Adelaide St. W., Toronto.
Stephenson, Blake & Co., Toronto.
Stewart, Geo. M., 92 McGill St., Montreal.
Westman & Baker Limited, Toronto.

BINDERY EQUIPMENT AND SUPPLIES
(See also CUTTING MACHINES)
Albion Sewing Cotton Co., Ltd., London, Eng.
Berry Machine Co., St. Louis, Mo.
Christensen Machine Co., Racine, Wis.
Dexter Folder Co., New York.
Golding Mfg. Co., Franklin, Mass.
Kallstrom, J., New York City.
Logan, H. J., 114 Adelaide St. W., Toronto.
Miller & Richard, Toronto and Winnipeg.
Morrison Co., J. L., Toronto, Ont.
Royal Machine Works, Montreal.
Steel Co. of Canada, The, Hamilton (wire).
Stephenson, Blake & Co., Toronto.
Stewart, Geo. M., 92 McGill St., Montreal.
Westman & Baker Limited, Toronto.

COMPOSING ROOM EQUIPMENT
(See also LEADS, SLUGS AND TYPE)
The following list covers Iron Furniture—
Eastern Brass & Wood Type Co., New York.
Hamilton Mfg. Co., Two Rivers, Wisconsin.
Stephenson, Blake & Co., Toronto.
The Challenge Machinery Co., Grand Haven, Mich.
The Toronto Type Foundry Co., Ltd., Toronto.
Westman & Baker Limited, Toronto.

CORDS, SILK, ETC.
Albion Sewing Cotton Co., Ltd., London, Eng.

COUNTING MACHINES
Stephenson, Blake & Co., Toronto.
Westman & Baker Limited, Toronto.

CUTTING MACHINES—PAPER
Golding Mfg. Co., Franklin, Mass.
Morrison Co., J. L., 445 King St. W., Toronto.
Stephenson, Blake & Co., Toronto.
The Challenge Machinery Co., Grand Haven, Mich.
Westman & Baker Limited, Toronto.

COLLECTION AGENCIES
Canadian Mercantile Agency, Ottawa.
Publishers' Protective Association, Toronto.
Nagle Mercantile Agency, Laprairie, Montreal.

EFFICIENCY EXPERT
Pepper, J. L., 38 Toronto St., Toronto.

ELECTROTYPING AND STEREOTYPING
Rapid Electrotype Co. of Canada, Toronto.
Toronto Electrotype & Stereotype Co., Toronto.

ELECTROTYPE AND STEREOTYPE BASES
The Challenge Machinery Co., Grand Haven, Mich.
Westman & Baker Limited, Toronto.

ELECTROTYPE METAL
British Smelting & Refining Co., Ltd., Montreal.
Canada Metal Co., Limited, Toronto.
Hoyt Metal Co., Limited, Toronto.

EMBOSSING EQUIPMENT
Automatic Ptg. Devices Co., San Francisco, Cal.
Ellis New Method Embossing, Hamilton, Ont.
Golding Mfg. Co., Franklin, Mass.
Stephenson, Blake & Co., Toronto.
Westman & Baker Limited, Toronto.

ENGRAVERS
Legge Bros., Ltd., Toronto.
Reliance Eng. Co., Toronto.

ENVELOPE MANUFACTURERS
Toronto Envelope Co., Toronto.
Dawson Ltd., W. V., Montreal and Toronto.

Buyers' Guide

INDEX TO ADVERTISERS

Ebony Job Black No. 420 (for platen presses)
Ebony Cut Black No. 95 (for cylinder presses)

75c. lb.

*Mail orders and enquiries for Inks or
Rollers receive prompt attention.*

Canada Printing Ink Co., Limited
15 Duncan St.   TORONTO

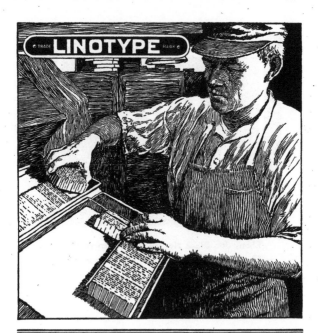

THE SIGNIFICANCE OF THE SLUG–I

AN ECONOMY
TOO OFTEN OVERLOOKED

The economy and ease of handling slugs, as compared with one type at a time, would alone be a sufficient reason for preferring the LINO-TYPE, even without giving consideration to the recognized economy of LINOTYPE composition

MERGENTHALER LINOTYPE
COMPANY

This advertisement, including border ornaments, is composed entirely of LINOTYPE material

Volume 29, Number 12   Toronto, December, 1920

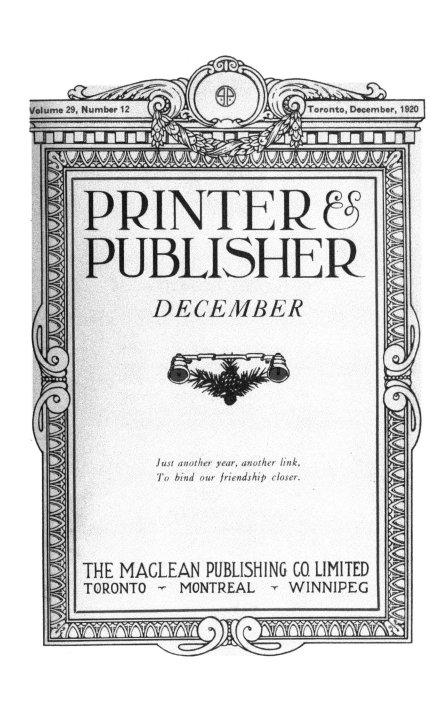

PRINTER & PUBLISHER

DECEMBER

*Just another year, another link,
To bind our friendship closer.*

THE MACLEAN PUBLISHING CO. LIMITED
TORONTO ~ MONTREAL ~ WINNIPEG

The Compliments of the Season

WE cordially extend to you and those associated with you Greetings of the Season, supplemented by the hope that during the coming year prosperity will outdistance your fondest expectations.

CANADA PAPER CO.
Limited
Toronto   Montreal   Windsor Mills, P.Q.

Colored Papers of All Kinds a Specialty

PERFECTION

A S there is in nature, so there is in applied art, a point of perfection. He who recognizes it, and is influenced by it, has a good taste: he who is not sensible of it, but is satisfied with what is below or above that point, understands neither art nor nature, and has no conception of scientific efficiency. —*La Bruyere: Of Works of Genius*

Our Rolling Galley Transfer Truck (No. 664) shown above, used in conjunction with Hamilton one-piece galleys, is an example of Hamilton efficiency. It is the present-day perfection of this composing room factor.

Our modernized line of composing room equipment makes an irresistible appeal to progressive printers.

The Hamilton Manufacturing Company
Eastern House: Rahway, N. J.   Two Rivers, Wisconsin

Hamilton Goods are For Sale by All Prominent Type Founders and Dealers Everywhere

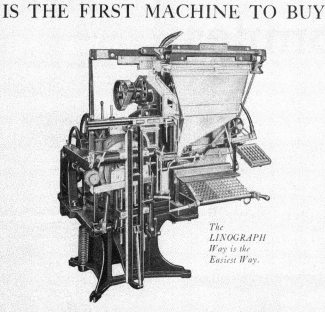

Who would reset a whole line when only one letter is wrong?

—who would use two men and a machine to make a correction that one man could make quicker, and without leaving his frame?

Typesetting machines were devised for composition; to use them for work which can be done economically only by hand is but to defeat the purpose for which they were intended.

Monotype Composing Machines are continually *producing*; the cost of the necessary evil of corrections is reduced to the minimum—*one man's time*.

The *one machine* system of
Non-distribution is solely a
Monotype activity.

LANSTON MONOTYPE MACHINE COMPANY · PHILADELPHIA
NEW YORK BOSTON CHICAGO TORONTO
Monotype Company of California, SAN FRANCISCO

This Advertisement set in Monotype Series No. 275 and Monotype Rule

Hope and Confidence

MORE than thirty years ago, when we began building the Miehle, our capital was mostly Hope and Confidence.

To-day, we have earned the confidence of those we have served and have realized our own hopes by fulfilling those of our customers.

MIEHLE PRINTING PRESS & MFG. CO.
Fourteenth and Robey Streets, Chicago

Distributors for Canada

TORONTO TYPE FOUNDRY CO., LIMITED
TORONTO   MONTREAL   WINNIPEG   REGINA

YOU NEVER HEARD OF A MIEHLE BEING SCRAPPED

If you had been a Colonial printer—

your work would have been much harder. You would have spent twelve hours a day pulling the bar of a handpress to print a few hundred sheets. Electric power and the modern press now do that in less than an hour. You wouldn't think of going back to the handpress.

Great improvements have been made in other ways. The Colonial pressman, when his ink was heavy and full of tack, had to thin it with boiled oils. Even today there are a few pressmen who stick to such crude reducing methods. But good pressrooms, large and small, now use Reducol. Instead of thinning the ink, Reducol softens it. It absolutely eliminates picking and mottling, at the same time preserving the full color.

Reducol is a great saver of labor and money. It gives much better distribution, which means easier, faster work, and a saving of 10% to 50% of the ink. On color work, Reducol prevents crystallization, thus permitting perfect overlapping. It is neither a dryer nor a non-dryer, but it has a marked tendency to cut down slipsheeting and offset on to the tympan. And it helps to keep rollers in good shape.

Put through an order for 5 or 10 lbs. at 65 cents per lb., and give Reducol a thorough trial for thirty days. If it doesn't come up to every statement we have made in this advertisement, tell us so, and we will cancel our charge. Reducol is absolutely guaranteed to make good.

INDIANA CHEMICAL & MANUFACTURING CO.

DEPT. C-12, 135 SOUTH EAST STREET, INDIANAPOLIS, IND., U. S. A.

23-25 East 26th Street, New York City   608 South Dearborn Street, Chicago

CANADIAN AGENTS: Manton Bros.
Toronto   Montreal   Winnipeg

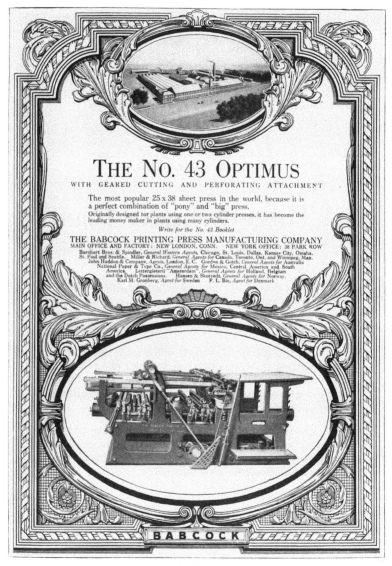

THE NO. 43 OPTIMUS

WITH GEARED CUTTING AND PERFORATING ATTACHMENT

The most popular 25 x 38 sheet press in the world, because it is a perfect combination of "pony" and "big" press.

Originally designed for plants using one or two cylinder presses, it has become the leading money maker in plants using many cylinders.

Write for the No. 43 Booklet

THE BABCOCK PRINTING PRESS MANUFACTURING COMPANY

MAIN OFFICE AND FACTORY: NEW LONDON, CONN. NEW YORK OFFICE: 38 PARK ROW

Barnhart Bros. & Spindler, *General Western Agents*, Chicago, St. Louis, Dallas, Kansas City, Omaha, St. Paul and Seattle. Miller & Richard, *General Agents for Canada*, Toronto, Ont. and Winnipeg, Man. John Haddon & Company, *Agents*, London, E. C. Gordon & Gotch, *General Agents for Australia* National Paper & Type Co., *General Agents for Mexico, Central America and South America. Lettergieterij "Amsterdam", *General Agents for Holland, Belgium and the Dutch Possessions.* Hansen & Skotvedt, *General Agents for Norway* Karl M. Gronberg, *Agent for Sweden* F. L. Bie, *Agent for Denmark*

BABCOCK

"Cross Continuous Feeders Run While You Load"

A Three-Cylinder Plant Entirely Cross Fed

"WE have not had a minute's trouble with the feeders since installing them over a year ago, and as I look back I wonder how we ever got along without them," says Orrin Terry of the Times Print Shop of Waterville, N. Y.

The illustration above is from a circular this concern mailed their customers to advertise their plant. The following quotation is taken from the folder:"The only large cylinder pressroom in central NewYork entirely equipped with accurate mechanical feeders."

The number of printers who are equipping all their presses with automatic feeders is growing. You should investigate the increasing demand for Cross Feeders. Write us for a list of users in your territory.

EXCEPTIONAL TYPESETTING
SERVICE

*Delivered
Anywhere
in Canada*

*Delivered
Anywhere
in Canada*

Monotype Key-
board and Cast-
ing Department

WE have made ex-
tensive provision for
the production of a large
volume of typesetting for
the trade. These illustrations show how efficient-
ly our plant is equipped.
Jobs of any size or style
may be safely
placed with
us—it will
surprise you
how quickly
and satisfac-
torily even the
largest job
will be com-
pleted.

EXPERT work-
men are en-
gaged for "make-
up" purposes —
accuracy in lock-
ing-up process is
assured, for the
reason that all
material used is
on the point-set
system. Think of
what this means
to you in time
saved in hand-
ling forms for
presses.

Make-up Department

A large range of Body and
Display Type Faces from
6 pt. to 36 pt.

LEADS, SLUGS, METAL RULES,
BORDERS & METAL FURNITURE

Manufactured and stocked for
immediate shipment.

Catalog Furnished on Request

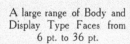

Storage, Lock-up and Linotype Department

NO CONNECTION WITH ANY PRINTING HOUSE

MONO-LINO TYPESETTING CO.
LIMITED

W. R. ADAMSON,
President and Manager

**160 Richmond Street West
TORONTO**

S. FRANK McMURRAY
Asst. Manager

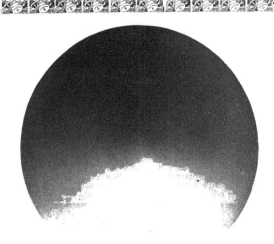

CHRISTMAS BRIGHT GREEN 11844

"T**HE ONLY INK HOUSE IN THE WORLD**"
that manufactures all the materials entering into its Lithographic and Letter-Press Inks and with its large staff of expert chemists and ink makers offers the printing trade

THE BEST ON EARTH

Every Ingredient

Acids   Dry Colors
Chemicals   Intermediates
Aniline Dyes, Varnishes, etc.
Manufactured in Our Own Factories

The Ault & Wiborg Company
of Canada, Limited
MONTREAL   TORONTO   WINNIPEG

TORONTO VARNISH WORKS

TORONTO INK WORKS

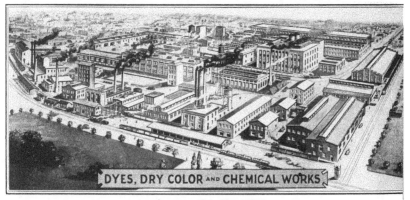

DYES, DRY COLOR AND CHEMICAL WORKS

CHRISTMAS RED, No. 10814

The WHITLOCK Pony Press

Two-Revolution   —   Two-Roller   —   Front Fly Delivery

NO CYLINDER PRESS is so profitable to the printer as *The Whitlock Pony*. Its reputation is world-wide. Smooth in its operation, even and rigid in impression, exact in register, easy to operate, simple and durable. Prints everything from an envelope to a sheet the full size its type bed will take. Produces heavy and light job work of the finest quality with minimum labor. It runs hundreds per hour faster than other ponies. It is the standard pony cylinder press of the world. Let us explain *The Whitlock Pony* fully—also the following well-known presses:

The PREMIER Two-Revolution 4-Roller Press
The POTTER OFF-SET
The POTTER TIN PRINTING PRESS

Every mechanical device that makes for the production of the finest quality in the greatest quantity at the lowest operative cost is incorporated in these presses.

———

PREMIER & POTTER PRINTING PRESS CO., Inc.

SUCCEEDING THE WHITLOCK AND POTTER COMPANIES
1102 Aeolian Bldg., 33 West 42nd Street
NEW YORK

Canada West:	*Canada East:*	*Maritime Provinces:*
MANTON BROS.	**GEO. M. STEWART**	**PRINTERS SUPPLIES LTD.**
105 Elizabeth St.	92 McGill St.	27 Bedford Row
Toronto, Ont.	**Montreal, P.Q.**	**Halifax, N. S.**

PRINTER AND PUBLISHER
Devoted to the Interests of the Printers and Publishers of Canada

It is Going to Cost More to Publish in 1921
How Various Papers View the Situation

PAPERS are carrying large volumes of advertising now, and much of this has to do with price reduction sales in many lines of merchandising. All this has a marked effect on the mind and temper of the merchant and the reader of the papers. They believe that the peak of prices has been reached, and that any change made now should be in the direction of lessened prices.

In such an atmosphere the advertising man has to go to the merchant now and explain his case, and it may be that he will have to go to his readers on a similar mission. Is it to be wondered at—on the surface of the thing—if he does not get a very cordial reception when he starts to name new and higher rates for the coming year?

There may be variations from the above case but in the main it sets forth the position that nearly all the Canadian daily publishers are facing right now.

Can they get more revenue for the same volume of business, or will they have to depend on increased business, which means increased mechanical expense in handling it? How near are present rates to the point where advertisers will go no further? These are questions that are turning over in the minds of many publishers now.

The Position As It Exists

Printer & Publisher asked this question of a number of representative publishers. Asked them what they had ahead of them in the way of increases and if they had any new way of meeting the situation. H. B. Muir, of the London Free Press, admitted that he had a tidy year's work laid out for him, but believes it can be done. Classified advertising, to his idea, can be still more developed by many papers, and he bears witness to the fact that it is a money-making department, as well as being highly interesting to the reader. Mr. Muir said:

"We have a nice little task ahead of us next year because we will have to find approximate-ly $100,000.00 more money to meet the increased costs made up of about $70,000 for white paper, $24,000 for postage, the balance for wages, etc. We have found it decidedly good business to work persistently for the greatest possible number of regular insertion contracts from local advertisers, large and small. Our solicitors do not readily accept an open space contract for the reason that they know they will have a hard job to have it accepted in the office. We have been increasing advertising rates gradually but persistently all year and expect to do so for another six months. It takes salesmanship but so does most every other business these days.

"We are getting our rates high enough where we can make rate inducements to advertisers who will run every day, every second day or at least twice a week and we find that the regular insertion fellows are the ones who can most easily be developed into larger space users and regular larger space users.

"Then, too, we are stressing the point to our merchants that the people generally take their cue from the leaders in business, said leaders being the merchants and manufacturers, and that if the merchants want to give the people the idea that business is quiet and buying is slow, a sure way to do it is to cut down their advertising. Travellers and merchants in London, who have taken the time to investigate a little in other and larger cities, tell me that retail business is better in London than any place in eastern Canada and from my own observation I believe this is true. Our Male and Female Help Wanted columns are a sure barometer every day that our factories are busy and looking for more help. When times begin to stress a little, the utility of the classified advertisement in the daily paper is more easily sold.

"I believe most newspapers are selling their classified advertising to-day at a price that makes them some money. I believe classified advertising should pay a profit the same as any other newspaper advertising. Thousands of dollars of extra revenue can be gotten during the coming year by every daily newspaper publisher out of his classified columns, provided he will show the people of his community how they can use the classified to their own profit. Classified is the "people's own" and it is largely the publisher's own fault that more of his readers do not use his classified columns oftener.

"We will develop more profitable advertising at home by having our merchants, wholesalers, manufacturers and commercial travellers spend more time attending conventions at home—conventions where the retail, wholesale and manufacturing business of our respective communities will be discussed at home rather than a few now and a few then, boarding a train and rushing off to some distant city to attend a 'whopper-up' business convention. Let's hold more of such conventions at home and get as many of our local business people to attend them as possible. See to it that good sense and sound guidance are given out at these meetings, all of which should be very carefully reported in the local newspaper.

"This is just another way of enabling the people of a community to get their cue of optimism, surety of progress and profitable advancement from the leaders in business in their community.

"The following clauses are from an advertisement published in the Free Press by Smith, Denne & Moore, Limited:

"Your livelihood and prosperity are bound up in the livelihood and prosperity of other men—you can't deny that point. There is nothing fundamentally wrong with the country —we have bountiful crops, ample money, capable heads and hands. But we can't survive a 'buying strike' nevertheless. Business is a gigantic organization, kept alive and active by trade coursing through its veins. When trade stops circulating—business dies. Your particular trade can't flourish in splendid isolation. The articles you make can't sell to men 'out of a job.'

"True thrift is always wise, but a stubborn refusal on the part of the Canadian public to buy the things they need NOW is simply slowing down the wheels of commerce that feed and clothe and house us ALL.

"If you are on a buying strike—'forget it'. Go out and buy today the things you need, for the prices ARE down. If you are waiting for them to come down further tomorrow or next day or next month, you may not **then** be in a position to buy.

"You are doing good work in establishing a forum of ideas—as Emerson says, 'Words and conversation are the laboratory, the workshop of thought.' We are going to need a good deal of constructive advertising thought during 1921 so perhaps it is a good plan to do some talking about it now."

Figures His Increases.

Another publisher in a good Ontario city, enjoying a monopoly: "As you perhaps know," he stated, "the price of newsprint has been fixed for the first three months of next year at $130 per ton. Assuming that this price will prevail for the year, it means that publishers will have to pay 33 1/3 per cent. more for their white

paper for 1921 than they did for 1920, since the average price for this year has been-$100 per ton. Added to this is an increase of 40 per cent. in freight charges. I would say that the freight means an average increase for Western Ontario publishers of $2.50 per ton, this over and above the 33 1/3 per cent. As the cost of paper is 44 per cent. of the whole cost of producing a newspaper, this is going to be a big item. For users of the telegraph service the additional charges for 1921 will be about 20 per cent. On January 1st there is an increase in postage rates of 300 per cent., and practically every publisher will have to face a decided increase in labor charges for next year. Every publisher is paying more for labor during the last three months of 1920 than he did during the first three months, and there is no reason to believe that the rate will be lower next year. Furthermore, there is a possibility of having to reduce the working time from forty-eight to forty-four hours."

There are publishers in one-paper cities who feel their position to be rather awkward. They know their costs—they know they must have revenue to meet the increased costs, yet they hesitate to move lest their customers come to the conclusion that they are taking advantage of the situation.

Costs Are Still Increasing

Here is another case of a one-paper city, and the hope is held that economy can be exercised along certain lines, thereby offsetting increases. A determination is also expressed to eliminate overtime—a commendable idea, but rather hard to follow week in and week out. Here are his views:

"Having just signed a new agreement with the Typographical Union which means a substantial increase in our present outlay, we are brought to a strong realization of the fact that costs are not yet decreasing in the newspaper business. The past few months have also seen increases in the cost of paper, ink, telegraph and features service and other component parts of a newspaper. In view of this—despite the general tendency towards lowering prices—we propose to effect every possible economy. White paper can be saved by setting reading matter solid where it has been the practice to lead it, and by increasing the ratio of advertising columns to reading matter columns in a given sized paper. We plan to cut out overtime as much as possible, and to encourage an increase in per diem production. Our special features, we believe, are not too many, but some newspapers might easily effect a saving on them.

"Economy only, however, will not be sufficient. We have already issued a new foreign rate card, increasing the minimum and 5,000-line rates one-quarter cent per line, and a small increase on our local rates will go into effect on January 1st. The advertisers who feel they cannot increase their appropriation for advertising will be invited to use less space, and we will save paper and labor.

"We believe that under the present conditions the increase in rates should be as small as possible, but where greater revenue is required to maintain solvency, we believe the rate increase should be put into effect without hesitation. Free readers, should, of course be cut to the limit, and all who can profit by the publicity a newspaper can provide should pay for what they get."

Advertising Rates at The Limit.

N. E. Morrill, managing director of the Sherbrooke Daily Record, believes that the advertiser has almost gone the limit in what he will pay for space, and that the reader should be called upon to pay the increase in postage. Mr. Morrill says: "I am of the opinion that newspapers, which are strong and successful to-day, after the trying periods of the past few years, have every reason to look to the future with confidence. The worst, it seems to me, is in the past. There is every reason to believe that the peak has been reached in the case of newsprint. Six months or a year should see a revision downward of present paper costs. With the decline in the cost of living, there will be no justification for further advance in the wage scales.

"It is true heavy postal charges are coming but the reader in all fairness should meet these and I believe will be quite prepared to do so. As to newspaper advertising rates, it seems to me that current rate cards should pretty nearly represent the peak in this regard. Most newspapers have met the advancing costs of the past few years by frequent rate card revisions. The cards, recently issued, are not now fully in effect but as contracts expire they will come into operation. The added revenue resulting should take care of increased costs in 1921."

No Objections to New Rate

Mr. J. J. McIntosh of the Guelph Mercury, has recently put out a new rate card, and has had no trouble in getting the new prices. Referring to the fact that his increased cost of publishing in 1921 will be around $15,000, he said

"We anticipated this increase and covered it by increase in advertising rates, changing our minimum local rate from 1 2/7 cents a line to 1¾ cents, and our foreign from 1½ cents to 2¾ cents per line, in the daily subscription from $5.00 to $6.00, and in weekly from $1.50 to $2.00.

"Recently the Porte Publishing Co., of Salt Lake City, who issue the Franklin Price List, which we are using in our job department, in one of their bulletins quoted a list of suggested advertising rates for weeklies of different circulations. This led me to write and ask if they had issued a similar list for dailies. They replied that they had not, and referred me to Will V. Tufford, secretary of the Inland Press Association, Clinton, Iowa, for information. Mr. Tufford in turn referred me to A. W. Peterson, manager of the Waterloo, Iowa, "Courier." Altogether I got from the correspondence material which stiffened up my back sufficiently to put up our advertising rates materially, in spite of the fact that they were then on a par with papers of our circulation in Western On-

tario. To date we have not met with a single objection from any advertiser.

"I thought I had done something worth telling about, and sent copies of our new cards to Mr. Tufford and Mr. Peterson. The former has since written giving me something further to think about. He says:

" 'I think you have your subscription nearer right than it has been, but that must be governed to some extent by your territory. Really, a daily delivered by a carrier should be $7.50 a year. Eventually I think you will have to come to a higher rate for your space advertising—local advertising. I don't believe it's possible to make much money below 35 cents, which includes composition, being your minimum per inch per issue. But you must figure, like we all do, that we are entering on a lean period, which will probably not be adjusted before the early summer, so that anything that you do in the way of changing rates you have done wisely before the first of the year, and I believe better not disturb your cards again before the middle of next summer.' "

Must Get More Revenue

D. Smith, manager of the Fort William Times-Journal, says something that will bring forth a hearty "Amen" when he mentions that the "paper mills are hitting the ball a little too hard." He sees no immediate relief for the publishers. Here are Mr. Smith's views:

"We do not see any way out except to advance prices in accordance with the requirements. There will probably be a reduced amount of advertising when the first flush of a panicky desire to unload passes away, and smaller papers will probably bring paper down somewhere near to what it ought to be.

"There is little use in watching and waiting, because the main items of costs are not going to fall for a long time, and the sooner everybody realizes this fact the better it will be for all.

"We believe the paper mills are hitting the ball a little too hard, and are driving good customers out and also training the newspapers to be economical, a policy which will react and hit the mills hard later on. But that's their business, and in the meantime we must meet the conditions and get higher prices for the service we perform.

"Labor will stay up for a good many years, and telegraph tolls will not be less, so that little relief is in sight, and newspapers will be obliged to charge more for both advertising and subscriptions than they ever thought possible a few years ago."

Are Dealing in Newsprint

Mr. E. G. Smith, manager of the Quebec Telegraph, has a good way of meeting the talk about lowered prices of commodities simply by stating that a paper does not thrive on commodities bought in a store, but largely on newsprint and labor, and neither of these show any signs of coming down. Mr. Smith sums it up like this:

"Your query suggests a question that has been in my mind for the last few weeks. 'I wondered would it be possible to obtain increased rates for advertising with the same complacency that has characterized contract giving for the past three or four years?' Obstacles are undoubtedly arising and such questions as the following are being put to us almost daily:

" 'Our prices are going down and you must lower the cost of advertising.' 'We will not renew except at a lower rate.' 'We refuse to give you a higher rate knowing that you will be glad to take our advertising in a short while, providing you do not accept now.'

"To these and sundry rejoinders we meet the arguments very simply by telling the customer that we are dealing with but very few commodities, chief of which is newsprint. Almost without exception the other material costs in the business, such as metal, furniture, machinery have not decreased in price, and we all know that both in the mechanical and clerical departments there is a general tendency upwards. We maintain that unless newsprint is reduced very much in price there would be little prospect of a lower rate for advertising.

"I can well understand there will be many difficulties to contend with during the next few months, and not a little business will be lost, but in the main I am satisfied that the adjustment will prove satisfactory, in that prices will be more stabilized and those manufacturers and business men using newspaper space will pay more regard to their copy end of it and attempt seriously to co-operate with their advertising plan.

"All the world knows that there is a tremandous waste going on in the way of promoting trade, expenses, selling costs and general extravagances, to which even advertising has not been immune. This will now require to be subjected to a closer scrutiny, when perhaps business men will pay as much attention to the selling end as they do to the manufacturing.

"Cases which have come before my notice recently would suggest that manufacturers are appealing to newspaper advertising to save themselves. Previously regarding branding their goods as suicidal; being quite satisfied to sell their brands under any name the jobber required, they may now appreciate how perfectly loose the system is, and subject to an overnight loss. Taken all in all, I believe the present readjustment in prices will be a good thing for newspaper advertising, and bring into the field many good converts who will regard advertising as a specialist's profession, and allow it to be directed by them instead of leaving it to sundry half-paid clerks and boisterous press agents."

Room for Some Economy

Here is one of the newer publishers in Ontario daily circles. He believes that the time has come for employees to call a halt in the procession of increased wages, holding that increases now should be as recognition of services or increased efficiency. Here are his views:—

"I must confess that I am somewhat at sea as to how the great increases in the cost of producing a daily paper are to be met in 1921. I have not come to any real decision in the matter because at present business is so strong that we have to carry on much as we have been doing. It appears to me that a great many newspapers will be able to lower their staffs—in some departments at least—for it is a fact that many of us are over-manned, encouraging inefficiency.

"Many of the smaller papers, in an endeavor to publish a metropolitan sheet in 'Punkey Doodle Corners,' are buying all sorts of syndicate froth that costs good money, but which adds little, if anything, to the value of a small city local newspaper. Such papers can, I believe, lower their overhead a good deal. But we have reached the point where the cost of living has started to go down hill, and I cannot see any ground at all for wage increases when conditions are as they are. The only justification for wage increases are greater efficiency and increased living costs.

"Unless the employees are willing to call a halt and stop calling for more, more, and more, then the publishers will have to continue their call on the advertisers for more, more and more, and my belief is that there will be a tremendous curtailment in advertising—possibly not at once because the merchants are exceedingly anxious to get rid of their stocks.

"We have made practically no advancement in advertising rates for a year, although our costs have gone up a great deal. On the other hand our business has greatly increased, and this has tended to offset the other increases. If possible we hope to continue at present rates, even if it is necessary to take a very small profit for a year or two. This decision is, of course, subject to revision."

The Case in Winnipeg

A recent notice in the Winnipeg Free Press states the position of the publishers there:

"Newsprint prices for the Winnipeg newspapers for the first six months of 1921 have been announced by the paper company which supplies this market.

"The price quoted is 7 cents a pound, or $140 a ton.

"This is an increase of $40 per ton, or 40 per cent. over the price paid for newsprint during the last six months of 1920.

"It is an increase of 75 per cent. over the corresponding price for the first six months of 1920.

"The increase of $40 a ton now announced is alone greater than the total price paid by the Free Press for newsprint as recently as May, 1916.

"The price is f.o.b. the mill, and to it the freight rate must be added. The freight now paid by the Free Press from its source of supply is $19.50, as against $10 a ton paid four years ago. This will make a total cost laid down of $159.50, as against $46.40 in 1916, an increase of $113.10—or over 243 per cent."

When The Apprentice Received $1 Per Week

Back In Early Canadian Papers

By C. W. YOUNG, Cornwall Freeholder

There may be publishers in Canada who are better known to the trade than C. W. Young of the Cornwall Freeholder, and there may be printers of the old school who have worked on more sets of cases than has the same C. W. Young. Then again there may be publishers who can attend press day at the Fair and wear more handsome red neckties than said C. W. Young, or there may be publishers who more thoroughly enjoy meeting the fraternity from all over the country. There may be all these things but we have never encountered them. Printer and Publisher asked Mr. Young to put some of his reminiscences in writing, and after considerable urging he has consented to do so.

IT SEEMS to me I was a very small boy when I first fussed with some old type that we got somehow or other at school, and tried to print from it in a kind of a press, and not so long after that the editor of the local paper taught me the case, and hoisted me up on a stool where I managed to set a stickful of type of which I took a proof and pasted it in my hat, and my joy when I saw it actually printed in the paper was as great as if I had won a war medal.

It was some years afterwards that I went to Hamilton to serve my time with Messrs. T. & R. White, who had recently come from Peterborough from the *Review* office and bought out the *Spectator*. Richard White (Whistling Dick) was the business man and Thomas White the editor and Ottawa correspondent. He wrote a very neat flowing hand, easy to read, but because he never finished his words and left the end of them to the imagination, White's copy was shunned by the compositor and classed as objectionable. It so happened that my education was rather better than that of the ordinary compositor, and I formed the habit of getting the sense of the article through my head, and so, very soon after I was able to set with some speed, this and other blind copy began to come my way.

I often think that boys of the present day would rebel against the treatment they used to receive in those old days. I got a dollar a week to start with, and my father paid three dollars for my board. The devil was supposed to do all kinds of chores. The composing room in the old· "Spec." office, which was on the corner of Main and Hughson Streets, was on the third storey and was heated with a big box stove, which took a cordwood stick, and the devil, which was me, had to carry up the wood.

Then on Thursday night he had to come back and carry the flimsy paper, sheet at a time, from the telegraph office to the editor, and when the daily went to press, curl himself up on a pile of papers under an imposing stone, and sleep till the daily was off, then help the foreman, who was Bob Gay (afterwards with the *Globe*,) to make up the weekly. This took till about 6 a.m., when the devil could go home to bed and have till noon off.

And Type Was So Scarce!

The equipment of the old 'Spec.' was rather scanty—hardly enough type to print the paper—bourgeois and brevier—and no one ever had a full case. In the last hours of the morning one was always down to bare boards and skirmishing for sorts was in order. Each compositor was allowed as much "dis" as he could lift and this sometimes led to disaster. I remember a printer named Theophilus from Philadelphia, who had hoisted five or six sticks on his left hand with the aid of a couple of reglets when the boys got him laughing and the handful fell into the case to the accompaniment of shocking profanity as was common talk those days. Then came the cutting remark: "How many did you throw?"

Printers of to-day will hardly understand the allusion, but in those days we used to gamble in a small way by "jeffing." Nine em quads were shaken in the hand and thrown down on the stone. All that came nick up counted for the player; if one fell on another it was a "cock" and didn't count either way. The stakes were moderate, five cents a throw or something of that kind, but a good deal of loose money changed hands.

Besides the news press, which did duty for book work in the day time, there was a small cylinder, which took a half sheet of royal, an old Alligator and a Washington hand press, on which posters were printed, and any one who has sweated on a day's work with such a contraption, whether inking the forms with a hand roller and getting smeared from head to foot, or pulled the lever, has good cause to remember it.

In due course the apprenticeship came to an end; the devil became a "jour" printer and landed first in Toronto, obtaining cases on the "Ould Layder" in Toronto, a small city in the late sixties. Those were the days of horse cars, which one used when there was no hurry, preferring to walk as a rule; when the city limits were at Bloor street, beyond was Yorkville; when the University was away out and Trinity College and the Asylum a Sabbath day's journey;

"The stakes were moderate . . . but a good deal of loose money changed hands in this way."

when the only theatre was the Royal Lyceum, standing back from King street, below the Rossin House; when Charlotte Nickinson flourished, when J. C. Myers and Spackmay were the lessees, when Den Thompson was the leading comedian, and later the Holman Opera Company leased the house. How well the old Lyceum is remembered, with capacity for a few hundred when the pit was on the ground floor, now the orchestra chairs, and the admission was a quarter; when Mrs. Holman at the piano was the entire orchestra and conductor as well, playing often an entire opera without glancing at the music. And what a wealth of operas we enjoyed—all the old favorites, Trovatore, Bohemian Girl, etc., and many others long forgotten. Sallie Holman was the prima donna, and the finest Grand Duchess that ever sang on any stage; Julia a spicy little devilette; Allie Holman was the tenor; Billy Crane, Billy Davidge, Charlie Drew, Chatterton (afterwards Signor Perugini) were apprentices to the drama and opera, and it was a good school. The Holman family lived in Richies' Terrace on Adelaide street, and fortunate indeed were the boys who were intimate enough to walk in of a Sunday afternoon and enjoy the fun and the music.

The Golden Lion, a leading dry goods store, was about where the King Edward now stands and one knew almost all the faces he saw on King street; strangers were spotted at once.

The Newspapers of that Time

The newspapers included the *Globe*, on King street, the editor George Brown; Howell was foreman of the news room and Bob Gay of the job office; the *Leader* business office was on King street on the corner of Leader Lane, the name of which survives; the composing and press room in the rear; Carrall was general foreman, and Henderson in the news room; George Gregg and Charley Belfors were editors, and E. P. Roden reporter. James Beatty, the proprietor, was to be seen most days in the business office, where Ed. Beatty was manager, and John Beatty a kind of utility man. The *Patriot* was a weekly edition of the *Leader* with Orange leanings, with Ogle R. Gowan as editor and I think a brother in the composing room. The *Mail* was in its infancy. I think Ed Farrar was the editor then or soon after. The *Leader* was absorbed by the *Mail*; the *Empire* came a good deal later and shared the same fate.

John Ross Robertson published the *Telegraph* on Bay street, later the *Telegram*.

John Cameron came from London and started the *Liberal*, which had a short life. The *Grumbler*, a semi-humorous sheet, used to make quite a sensation on its weekly appearances.

The union scale for printers in Toronto was $9 a week; 25 cents a thousand; the ads were set on time. The union was weak, and a good many of the printers were "rats;" all the shops were open. American money was at a discount, but we used to get a good deal of our pay in that coin, not daring to protest. Trying to work as a compositor on the *Leader* and at the same time pass the examination at the Military School brought on typhoid fever, and finished my career at the case in Canada.

Then He Started to Tour

When I started on the "grand tour," I lit out for Chicago, then the Mecca for printers—45 and 50 cents a thousand, and $21 a week, against $9 in Toronto, and whatever the boss could beat you down to in other places.

The *Tribune*, then as now, was the leading paper in the Windy City, the *Times* was its chief rival, but that was a "rat" office, as we used to call the non-union plants, and no self-respecting printer would work there. There was also the *Republican*—all three morning papers and one or more evening papers. I only remember the *Journal*, where I worked mostly.

I don't know whether the subbing system exists on daily papers nowadays with the linotypes, but it was a recognized institution then and a strange printer usually had to sub for a while before he got regular cases. My own luck was good in that respect. One day in the *Journal* office a regular named Paddy Collins told me to go on his cases while he went on a trip to his old home at Barrie, Ontario. The visit lasted some months, during which time I was to all intents and purposes a regular. It so happened that on a couple of other occasions I subbed for Collins during his prolonged absences for various reasons, and coming into the *Journal* office after the big fire of

1871 I was hailed, "Halloo, Brigham, are you after Paddy Collins' cases again?" '

When Tom and Jerry Lived

Talking about the fire recalls a rather funny incident. I did get Collins' cases once more—this was in October—and we set up the *Journal* and the *Tribune* for a few days in the same office on the west side, using the type of a directory plant until new outfits could be procured. The *Journal* was the first to get out an issue after the fire, which was the size of a small dodger, printed on a Gordon press. The first copy was seized and put in the archives of the chapel. At Christmas there was talk of some kind of a testimonial to the editor of the *Journal* and the first copy was framed, a gold-headed cane was bought, and an address was handsomely engrossed. The paper was pretty light on Christmas Day, perhaps it was a holiday, anyway there was a big bowl of Tom and Jerry and the boys all felt good. It fell to the lot cf the foreman, Hank Adams, to make the presentation, and the writer of this screed, and Mike Madden, another printer, accompanied him to the editor's residence where we were ushered into the parlor and greeted by the editor, who possibly had an inkling of.what was going to happen. Anyway he welcomed the party pleasantly when Adams, who was full as a goat, staggered forward, pulled the address out of his pocket, and began "Colonel Lorimer—(hic)—Dear Sir," This was as far as he got with his speech, which ended up with "—— it, Bill, here's the cane the boys sent you." The colonel appreciated the situation, and as the country correspondents say, he acknowledged the compliment in a few appropriate remarks.

There Were All Kinds Then

Most printers preferred to distribute their own cases, for obvious reasons, but if not, there were always some printers hanging around who would "dis" at a third the price of composition. One left a note on his case, and when he came to work, the type had been thrown in.

There were all kinds of printers among the subs, and naturally some "blacksmiths," as incompetents were called. I remember one fellow from Oshkosh, Wis., on the *Journal*, who was specially undesirable. The matter used to be cut up into takes

"He slipped down the street and picked up a half-drunken tailor. . . . He put a stick in his hand and told him to pick up those little things—type—and put them in there."

of not less than 200 ems, and the first take with more than three errors got the galley and corrected until he came to another take with three errors, when he passed it on. Pretty soon there were half a dozen galleys piled on "Oshkosh's" case and the "make-up" was in a sweat.

The foreman, who was notoriously profane, came over to the offender, and roared out, "Where in hell did you come from?" "Oshkosh," was the ready reply.

· "Well, if anybody asks you to sub for him to-morrow, tell him you'll be d—d if you do it. And now get back to Oshkosh and don't show your face again."

Printers were very scarce at times, and all sorts of expedients were resorted to to get subs. I recall one occasion on the New York *Tri'une* when a printer couldn't get a sub for love or money, and he slipped down to the street, and picked up a half-drunken tailor and brought him up to the composing room. He put a stick in his hand and told him to pick up those little things—type—and put them in there—the stick—and left the poor fellow to make the best of it. Very soon the trick was discovered, and the boozer kicked downstairs. The holder of the cases was a good workman and was not discharged, but he did not hear the last about his amateur sub for many a day.

While I was in Chicago a great event occurred—the completion of the Union and Western Pacific Railways, which for the first time bridged the continent between the great oceans. This was in May, 1869. The last spike was driven somewhere out in Utah, and the strokes of the hammer in the mountains were conveyed by wire to the big bell on the City Hall in Chicago, and repeated by everything that could ring in the city. There was a wonderful procession, miles long, and the biggest celebration the city had ever seen. Soon after that there was a monster excursion from San Francisco to Chicago, which included the Argonauts and Pioneers of the Pacific Coast, who 20 years before had braved the dangers of the sea passage and waded through the swamps of Panama, or dodged the Indians and sweltered through the sand deserts and froze in the mountains, and now made the trip in three or four days.

In due time there was a return visit to San Francisco, when such hospitality was extended by the citizens of the Golden Gate and all along the route as could hardly be imagined. In San Francisco one's money was absolutely no good, the excursionist's badge paid for everything. The city was wide open, and that meant a good deal for San Francisco.

It was not long before the boys began taking the long trail, for wages were good on the coast—75 cents a thousand, and those who got through made more money than they ever saw before. Denver was a small town, but some good printers went there and grew up with the city, quickly reaching affluence.

He Smites With Poetry

Council Bluffs, Iowa, and Omaha, Nebraska, on opposite sides of the Missouri, were as far as a good many printers got, many were stranded, and business became rotten. The bridge between the two cities was one of the first to cross the big river. The principal paper was the Council Bluffs *Nonpareil*, a beautiful sheet, realizing the conception of an artistic printer, and I think the Omaha *Bee* was established about the same time. The cities didn't love each other, as is usually the case under such conditions, and the editorial pages were particularly lurid. I recall a tramp printer, who was something of a poet, who set up some verses in the *Nonpareil* office, and left them in his stick on the case. The editor found them and printed them and they had a very wide circulation. They are worth recalling—I quote from memory:

"Hast ever been to Omaha,
 Where rolls the dark Missouri down,
 Where four strong horses scarce can drag
 An empty wagon through the town.

"Where sand is blown from every mound,
 To fill your eyes and ears and throat,
 Where all the steamers are aground,
 And all the houses are afloat.

"Where taverns have an anxious guest
 For every corner, nook and crack,
 With half the people going west
 And all the others coming back?

"If not, take heed to what I say,
 You'll find it just as I have found it,
 And if it lies upon your way,
 For — sake, stranger, go around it."

Anyone who knows what a beautiful city Omaha has since become, will hardly recognize the picture, but it was literally true in the last sixties.

Further out on the prairies and among the foot hills, where the thin lines of steel stretched out into space, there were some pretty hot towns at divisional points. Probably a rougher lot of men never were collected together than were assembled from the world over to work as laborers on the construction of the road, and the most lurid stories that have been written about conditions fall far short of the reality.

Cheyenne and Julesburg, I remember, were hells on earth. Each had its newspapers, and printers we met had lots to say about them. One story from Cheyenne I recall as characteristic. ·

A stranger from the east, waiting while the train stopped at Cheyenne for half an hour, strolled into a bar-room in the early morning, and found a man sweeping out. "Lots of grapes in this locality," he remarked. "Grapes, h—" was the gruff remark, "them's eyes. The boys had quite a frolic last night." The stranger fled.

Typothetae Activities in Toronto

At the executive meeting of the Toronto Typothetae, it was decided to secure the services of two additional experienced cost men from the U.T.A. for two months, and to engage locally two bookkeepers, specifically to assist in the actual upkeep of the cost system in the smaller shops. This will make a total of six cost men. In addition they have at present time Mr. Fillmore, the head cost man of the U.T.A., in an advisory capacity. It is felt that, with this force, it will be possible, within a very short time, to thoroughly cover the field amongst the members of the Toronto Typothetae. The cost finding classes which are being held each week on Tuesday afternoons at 3:45 p.m. and Thursday evenings at 8:00 p.m. at Room "G," King Edward Hotel, are coming to the most interesting stages, where the various forms and their uses are being taken up and explained.

Be Fair With the Readers

Editor, *Printer and Publisher*. While many publishers of weekly papers are now charging $2.00 a year, I think that every effort should be made to improve both the quality and the quantity of the reading matter. Many of them are giving too little for the money received. .

I was in a town of about three thousand the other day and happened to pick up a weekly paper, which was an eight-page, six-column edition. It might as well have been an advertising medium for all the news that it contained. Out of the forty-eight columns there were less than six of reading matter, and in the column and a half of the front page the item commanding the most central position referred to a "remarkable recovery' due to a proprietary preparation or, in other words, a patent medicine. On the second and third pages there was practically nothing at all, and scattered throughout the remainder of the publication were a few items, mostly set in six-point. It would not require ten minutes to peruse everything in the issue.

Until some weekly papers have a loftier conception of their service to the community and provide more news than did this one, they will find the city dailies encroaching upon their territory. The one stronghold which a home publication has is in conveying all the news of the district and having live correspondents at every post office who send in contributions regularly. On a newsprint paper when advertising encroaches so much upon the news columns, as in the case mentioned, two or, at least, four extra pages should be added.

Now that the publishers are charging more for their papers, they should see that the reader gets value and not seek to produce a mere advertising medium which is only a semblance of a real newspaper.

Sincerely yours,

IBEX.

The Printer-Editor President of the States

A Practical Man Around the Office

ACCORDING to reports, President-elect Harding is very much a printer and a thorough newspaperman in every way. He helped to pay his way through college by working in a printing office. It was in 1884 that the family moved to Marion, and with his father's help he became half owner of the *Star*, but the sheriff crowded him out shortly after, and Harding went reporting on the Marion *Mirror* at $7 per week. Politics apparently ran deep in his system, for he returned to the *Star* and staked another claim there.

His partner, "Jack" Warwick, now on the editorial staff of the Toledo *Blade*, sold out his interest to Harding, and the whole business, lean, lanky and wobbly, came over to camp with the now president-elect.

The story of Harding's struggle with that paper, and of the splendid assistance he received from his wife in those days, forms a story of determination and a resolve to build solidly and well that should be an incentive to others.

Apparently President-elect Harding's staff is behind him to the last man. They were ready for the win which they saw coming for their chief. A newspaper account of the scene of the presentation at the Harding home that night is as follows:—

Fifty-five pink candles were glowing on a birthday cake in the dining room of 389 Mount Vernon Avenue to-night when a blare of tin horns caused Mrs. Harding to pause as she was about to cut a thick wedge from the confection. The din was a summons to Senator Harding to make his first front porch speech as President-elect.

The Senator went out on the porch bareheaded. He had no idea he was going to make a speech. He had no idea, in fact, who his noisy callers were. When he came to the edge of the steps, he saw that the visitors were some forty of the employees of his newspaper, the Marion *Star*, Shoving one hand in his trousers pocket as a partial defense against the raw chill of the night, the editor of the *Star* called out greetings:

"Hello, Miller," and "Well, well, Bertie," and "Howdy; haven't seen much of you this summer."

President-Elect Harding's printing office, where the Marion "Star" is published.—(Courtesy American Printer).

One of the women holding an open box of chrysanthemums whispered to the Senator that they were paying a birthday call. Then all of them mounted the steps to the porch. A tall, thin man, a printer, began to read a presentation speech. He was acting for the long-whiskered man with steel frame spectacles who stood beside him holding a pasteboard jewelry box in one hand.

Then abruptly the presentation speech was finished. The whiskered man—it was Luther Miller, seventy-six years old and a *Star* printer for two-score years—shoved the little box into the Senator's hand. The Senator held it a minute. He appeared to be having some difficulty with his throat and eyes.

"Open it," directed one of the printers in a hoarse voice. The Senator did so, and found a gold make-up rule.

"Fellow members of the *Star*," began the editor, "you and I have associated together for a great many years. I know you and you know I wouldn't cheat you."

There the boss of the *Star* stopped. There could be no mistake about the tears in his eyes or the break in his speech.

"I am coming into very great responsibility if the election returns are interpreted aright. I don't know if I can meet them adequately. I know one thing: I can meet them with the same justice and fairness with which I have dealt with you."

Somehow "W. G." didn't seem much of an orator to-night. He paused again, his lips twitching nervously, and then went on:

"L. J., my old friend Miller—"

Miller's whiskers are more than a foot long and gray. This appendage began to wag absurdly. The aged printer was on the verge of tears, but not quite. It wasn't his birthday.

"The oldest employee on the *Star*," continued the editor. "We've been together thirty-six years. Sometimes the road was thorny. Sometimes I've known him to draw his pay and I'd have to borrow it from my mother. Other times I borrowed Miller's pay back from him in the morning.

"I'm just a plain fellow, but if I've been on the square with you I wouldn't cheat you. I'm going to be on the square with everybody."

"Somehow this has touched me—" again the editor had to pause.

Standing in the doorway were a couple of the Harding dinner guests—Colonel F. E. Scobey, of Texas, and Jess Smith.

President Harding is a rapid and clever make-up man. This photo was taken some months ago in the office of the Marion "Star."—Edmonston photo. Plate by courtesy of the American Printer.

of Washington Court House, Ohio. Both of them were using napkins to mop their eyes.

"I thank you for your call," continued the Senator. "I just want to say that my happiest moments always have and always will be those in the composing room of the *Star*, just before the presses begin to rumble."

The editor of the *Star* began to shake hands with his callers, again assuring them that on Thursday he was coming down once more to put the paper to bed.

Then Mrs. Harding was presented with the box of chrysanthemums and made her initial appearance as front porch speaker.

"I thank you very much," said the next first lady of the land· "You have made me very homesick for the old days when I worked each day in the *Star* office. Thank you, thank you."

In the *Star* office is a newspaper creed, to which Editor Harding has signed his name. It reads:

Remember there are two sides to every question. Get them both.

Be truthful. Get the facts.

Mistakes are inevitable, but strive for accuracy. I would rather have one story exactly right than a hundred half wrong.

Be decent, be fair, be generous.

Boost—don't knock.

There is good in everything. Bring out the good in everything, and never needlessly hurt the feelings of anybody.

In reporting a political gathering, give the facts, tell the story as it is, not as you would like to have it. Treat all parties alike.

If there is any politics to be played, we will play it in our editorial column.

Treat all religious matter reverently.

If it can possibly be avoided, never bring ignominy to an innocent man or child in telling of the misdeeds or misfortunes of a relative.

Don't wait to be asked, but do it without the asking, and, above all, be clean and never let a dirty word or suggestive story get into type.

M. L. Miller, thirty-six years a compositor on the "Star," who handed the gold make-up rule to the newly-elected president.
—International photo.

I want this paper so conducted that it can go into any home ·without destroying the innocence of any child.

President-elect Harding's *Star* is an eight-column, twelve-·page newspaper.

Advertising Agents in Canada

Editor, *Printer and Publisher*.

Sir,—Would it be asking too much to have you publish a list with the addresses of the recognized Advertising Agents of Canada? By recognition, I mean those recognized by the Press Associations. We are offered so many contracts from new agents these days that it is hard for the country editor to tell just when he should pay his full commissions.

Yours very truly,

THE EASTERN CHRONICLE

New Glasgow, N.S.

The following is a list of the agencies to which recognition has been granted in Canada. Some are recognized by all the press associations, but some are not. The following list, though, we believe to be approximately correct:—

Advertising Service Co., Ltd., The, 810-11 Drummond Building, 511 St. Catherine St., W. Montreal; Nordheimer Building, 220 Yonge St., Toronto.

Baker Advertising Agency, Limited, 184 Bay St., Toronto.

Canadian Advertising Agency, Limited, Unity Building, Corner of St. Alexander and Lagauchetiere Sts., Montreal.

Crawford-Harris Advertising Agency, 1422 Standard Bank Bldg., Vancouver, B.C.

Dean, E. Sterling, Advertising Agency, 8 Wellington St. E., Toronto.

Desbarats Advertising Agency Limited, Desbarats Building, 161 Beaver Hall Hill, Montreal, 43 Scott St., Toronto.

Federal Advertising Agency, London, Ont.

Gagnier Advertising Service (now being operated under name of Consolidated Advertising Service), 73 Richmond St. West, Toronto., 171 St. James St., Montreal.

Gibbons, J. J., Limited, 119 Wellington St. West, Toronto; Coronation Building, corner Bishop and St. Catherine Streets, Montreal; 404 Tribune Building, corner Smith & Graham Sts., Winnipeg.

Hamilton Advertisers Agency, Limited, the Hamilton Fire Insurance Building, 40 McNab St. South, Hamilton.

Imperial Publishing Co., Limited, 140-142 Barrington St., Halifax.

Massie, A.J., Limited, 700 Merchants Bank Building, Winnipeg; 60-1 Province Building, Vancouver.

McCann, H. K., Co., Ltd., 56 Church St., Toronto; 120 St. James St., Montreal.

McConnell & Fergusson, corner Dundas and Market Sts., London; Temple Building, corner Bay and Richmond Sts., Toronto; Confederation Life Building, Winnipeg; Bank of Toronto Building, Montreal.

McKim, A., Limited, Lake of the Woods Building, St. John St., Montreal; Jarvis Building, 103 Bay St., Toronto; Union Bank Building, Main St., Winnipeg.

MacPherson-McCurdy, Limited, Bell Block, corner Donald and Cumberland Sts., Winnipeg.

Muller, R. Sykes, Co., Limited, 128 Bleury St., Montreal.

Norris-Patterson Limited, 10 Adelaide St. E., Toronto.

Press Agency Bureau, Limited, 209-10 Dineen Building, Corner Yonge and Temperance Sts., Toronto.

Rowlatt, F. Albany, Tanner-Gates Building, 26 Adelaide St. W., Toronto.

Smith, R. C. & Son, Limited, 36-7 Imperial Bank Building, 171 Yonge St., Toronto.

Smith, Denne & Moore, Limited, 1007 Lumsden Building, corner Yonge and Adelaide Sts., Toronto; 400 McGill Building, Montreal.

Temporary recognition as advertising agents up to December 31, 1920, has also been granted to the following agencies:

Fisher, Jas. Co., Ltd., The, 384 Yonge St., Toronto.

National Publicity Ltd., 286 St. James St., Montreal.

"Well, that's enough to try the patience of Job!" exclaimed the village minister, as he threw aside the local paper. "Why, what's the matter, dear?" asked his wife. "Yesterday I preached from the text, 'Be ye therefore steadfast,'" answered the good man, "but the printer makes it read, 'Be ye there for breakfast'."

Wanted a Simple and Binding Contract
How Halifax Labor Paper Got It

N THESE days of the high cost of newsprint, with publishers everywhere raising the subscription and sales price of their papers, it is well to look to the advertising side of the publication to see if a remedy can not be found there.

In former days it was felt that, if a newspaper was divided fifty-fifty between news and advertising, it was financially solid. To-day, however, most newspapers are forced by necessity to modify the fifty-fifty basis in favor of inserting more advertising.

The above is particularly true in regard to the *Citizen*, published weekly at Halifax in the interest of labor generally. Unlike a number of other papers the *Citizen* seldom receives any outside financial support, and must make its own way. It is sold for five cents a copy, with the subscription price at $2.00 a year. So it can readily be seen that its advertising columns are its main source of revenue.

With over a year's experience in keeping the advertising columns of the *Citizen* in a healthy condition, the writer has come to the conclusion that the best method to employ is the contract form, to be signed by the party purchasing the space. By employing this method the paper is assured of a certain revenue and the trouble of visiting many advertisers weekly is avoided.

The matter of just how this contract form should be worded came in for considerable discussion on the part of the management, and may prove of some assistance to other papers of a like nature.

The heading of the contract is a reproduction of the heading on the paper itself. In fact, all the stationery and printed matter of the *Citizen*, where possible, bear this heading—the idea being to familiarize the name of the paper and style of its heading.

Incorporated with the contract is the advertising rate card, which we have been successful in keeping as simplified as possible. It was decided that the agate line system of measurement was not adaptable to our conditions, so all advertising is sold by the inch. Of course, in the case of paid readers, the agate line is the measurement used.

The word "consecutive" preceding "issues" was inserted to avoid the possibility of advertisers using their space irregularly. While this class of business is welcomed by the bigger papers having a large office staff, it was felt that in our case it would necessitate much work with no extra revenue arising therefrom. It was further found that if a prospective advertiser understood these stipulations it did not obstruct his signing the contract.

By inserting the words "cash, cheque or draft" it is readily seen when rendering statements whether the advertiser desires a collector to call or to have the bill mailed to him, or to be drawn on by sight draft. This method has saved time and annoyances.

To assist the advertising solicitor to rapidly calculate the

ROBERT L. GAUL
Advertising Manager Halifax "Citizen"

E. E. PRIDE
Business Manager Halifax "Citizen"

ment, and necessitated careful study. The underlying principle in its construction was that everything should be set forth in such a manner as to eliminate any possibility of misunderstanding on the part of the purchaser of space. The facsimile, herein reproduced, is the result of these deliberations

cost of a certain number of inches on a three, six, nine, or twelve month contract, a table has been compiled, a copy of which is pasted on the inside front cover of the contract book. Another table of equal importance will be found on the inside of the back cover. This table shows at a glance when a contract

A Journal Devoted to the Interest
of Workingclass—Male and Female

The Citizen

Endorsed and Controlled by the
Halifax Trades and Labor Council

Subscription $2.00 a Year. HALIFAX, NOVA SCOTIA Single Copies, Five Cents

54 Argyle Street
Phone: Sack 1218
Date........................192..

To the Publishers of THE CITIZEN,

Gentlemen,—

ADVERTISING CONTRACT

CONTRACT, per inch $0.40
TRANSIENT, per inch 0.60
FRONT PAGE, per inch 1.00

You are hereby authorized to reserve the space of.............inches in THE CITIZEN for an advertisement from the undersigned to appear in.........consecutive issues. This space is being purchased at your..........rate, each insertion being $......, which amount is payable monthly by cash, cheque or draft.

Contract commences................... Expires....................... Total Amount........

It is expressly understood that this contract cannot be cancelled, except by discontinuing in business. If for any reason whatsoever this advertisement is ordered discontinued before the expiration of this contract, the publishers can immediately draw on us for the balance of the amount of contract still outstanding. Verbal agreements will not be recognised by either Publisher or Advertiser.

Thirteen issues is the minimum in which the contract rate is obtained.

Failure on our part to furnish "copy" in time for publication in the current issue gives the publishers the authority to insert any copy of ours then in print. To insure change of advt., copy must be at the office of the publishers before 12 noon on Tuesday.

NOTE—Plates and Cuts to be furnished by Advertiser, or charged for at cost.

Advt. Accepted for the Publishers

Signed ....

By............................,
    Authorized Representative.

Business ....

Address ....

The above is a reproduction of the contract used by the "Citizen." It was impossible to reproduce it exactly as the color of the ink in which it was printed would not photograph for reproduction. In the original there is the label of the Halifax union, which is omitted in this job, as it was not available for use in this city.

expires that has been signed on a given date. Both these tables have proved invaluable as time savers as compared with the old paper and pencil method of calculating, which wastes the time of your prospective advertiser.

The clause making the contract binding is very necessary, and all prospective advertisers are urged to read same over very carefully before signing.

Failure on the part of some advertisers to get their copy to the office in time for publication in the current issue is a problem all newspaper men have to solve. The *Citizen* is trying out the method stated on the contract, the success of which can not as yet be very accurately estimated.

These contract forms are printed in duplicate, the original, which is white, remains in the book, while the duplicate is yellow is perforated and given to the advertiser.

The *Citizen* enjoys a very fair advertising patronage and is becoming very popular in Halifax and vicinity through its frank discussion of matters pertaining to the interests of the majority of citizens. In some cases this paper has been the first in the city to expose the reckless expenditure of public money; notably the case of the Highways Commission scandal which is now causing such a sensation in the courts. The *Citizen* is sincere in its mission and promises to some day be a power in the community for the welfare of all citizens.

Great ·thern Paper Co. has announced that its price for newsprint in ls, carload lots on contract for next year, will be 5 cents a po d. Great Northern's price last year was four cents. The co any makes a flat price for the year in advance. Considerab interest attaches to prices quoted by Great Northern, as it ւ the second largest producer in the United States.

The Artists Should Advertise

A. M. in Toronto *Mail and Empire:*—Miss Estelle Kerr, in the course of a talk on art at The Grange the other day, commented on what she referred to as "the great lack of ability in salesmanship among artists," and urged that the artists, the public and the press should consider exhibitions of pictures more in the light of sales. Miss Kerr might well have included without at all weakening her point other exhibits than those of pictures; and, being an artist, her criticism should be heard with respect.

It might indeed be well if all such collections were put frankly on a business basis and regarded (as Miss Kerr suggests) as sales; and if this were done, the press would have a more friendly feeling for them than can be said to exist in their present anomalous relations. There is a tendency on the part of many artists (merely through lack of consideration of business methods) to reach out after valuable newspaper space, for their own advantage, and as something entirely within their rights, without the slightest suggestion of recompense to the advertising office of the paper, and with hardly a thank you to the editor.

If an editor some day in Puckish mood, were to ask one of these artists for an oil painting, a "little picture," or even a simple statuette of bronze to top the editorial desk, the artist would probably die of shock. And yet they are continually asking from the newspapers, as gifts, that which is just as valuable to them, and to us, as their productions. No doubt these fashioners of beautiful things would be covered with shame if their business sense were ever awakened; but there are very few of them like Miss Kerr, with the journalistic, as well as artistic, experience that enables her to see both sides of the situation in their true proportion.

Trained Men To Sell Circulation

A Plan That Should Find Backers

By A.R.K.

PUBLISHERS are anxious to get all the good circulation there is in their district, but they are not anxious, at present prices and scarcity of paper, to take on additions to their subscription lists that represent numbers that are of no real value to their advertisers. It often happens that after a campaign for circulation there is an addition that does not represent real merit. The report is often sent out, and there is no reason to doubt it, that many of the accounts that are sent by publishers to be collected by an agency are those that have been secured through a contest. The reader was away from the real scene of the contest, his interest was not very great in the paper after the thing was over, but the paper kept on coming and he was billed. This is not imagination, but pure fact that can be substantiated from real letters.

Printer and Publisher discussed this matter with Mr. H. Goldstein, from whom we secured information last month regarding collections. Mr. Goldstein is an old circulation man, having at one time been in charge of one of the teams of the MacLean Publishing Co., and has a wide knowledge of the business. We know of one paper where he put on almost nine thousand in one year, and secured the cash for the entire amount.

"What is the best way to sell circulation?" was the plain question that was asked Mr. Goldstein.

"Common sense first of all, a little determination, and the ability to size up the person you are trying to sell. Given these qualities a man must have a good thing to sell, and he must sell it on its merits, without any premiums or any promises of anything else. There is little come-back or disappointment in this class of selling. Let me give you a case that is not all suppositious, but which can happen any place. Suppose you were asked by a rural paper to sell some circulation in their district, how would you go about it?

"In the first place the paper must be prepared to do its part before it ever sends a man on the road to secure subscribers. There must be a certainty that there is something worth while subscribing for. It is almost impossible to sell a paper to a man who is not in the least interested, and such a subscriber is not of much use to the paper. He is not a keen reader, he will not speak well of it, he will never mention it to an advertiser. Ask this question: Have we anything in the paper to interest the people of a certain given district? Have we in that section a good correspondent? Is that correspondent covering that territory for the whole people? If not get a good correspondent there, and have him working well before you ever start to sell circulation in there. It is so much easier to go to a man and be able to open right up to the news of his own territory."

Mr. Goldstein also took up the case of the paper that had not the income to allow it to put a man on the road all the time, or

---

CIRCULATION

There are times when publishers want to get increased circulation in certain districts, or in general. They do not want to put on a campaign, because they believe their paper is good enough to sell on its merits—and it should be.

They want a trained man, but they have no one around the office, nor do they think it worth while to put one on as they would have to provide for him after, as the chances are he would not be available for a few weeks or a couple of months.

Printer and Publisher has in mind that it is possible for a plan to be worked out whereby men could be trained in this line of work, and made available for service in any district on a commission basis. Men would have to be very carefully selected, as an irresponsible one could do a great damage in a short time. Mr. Goldstein's remarks are interesting, as he has had plenty of experience in selling circulation.

---

even part of the time as a general thing. He did not care to go to the trouble or worry of a contest, and it might be that he did not care for that way of securing circulation.

"Trained circulation men who would be available for a paper for a short period any time would be the most desirable service that these publishers could secure," was his analysis of the case. "The trouble is that many circulation men are not trained. They may train themselves in time, but very often it is an expensive proposition for the paper, and the paper that pays for the training very often fires them before they get to the stage where they can produce results.

Here is what happens in a good many offices, and I will take a chance that it is correct to any part of the detail. The proprietor has been thinking the matter over for some time and finally decides that there must be something done to dig up a little extra circulation. And so he talks the matter over in the office, and it is decided that someone shall be secured for this work. Who is the someone? Often a man out of their own office who knows nothing of the selling end. Sometimes a man around town who has been in the office asking if there is anything he can do. It is safe to wager that in almost every case the man selected is not an expert at the business. And so he is rigged up with a book in which to put down the business he writes, is given some sample copies, and before he starts out may look over the mailing list to see who are not taking the paper. As a last shot he may be given a little pepper and mustard talk by the proprietor who has never sold circulation himself, and therefore knows nothing about it. Then he starts out and does his best. Give him the benefit of the doubt, he has done his best, and he secures some business, but not much. There are places he cannot interest at all, there are little objections he cannot meet in a broad and general way. He quits right at the start, instead of being able to come back to the matter of subscribing two or three different times in two or three different ways. He has not been trained to know that many people say 'No' right off the bat when they are asked to subscribe for anything."

Printer and Publisher suggested the training of men for this work, and then have them operating from a central office wherever their services would be required. Mr. Goldstein thought such a plan would work out well enough, but the men would have to be trained, and there would have to be some plan devised in order to keep them after they had secured their training, "because," he continued, "you know as well as I do that the man who can get out and sell circulation is seldom looking for a job. Publishing houses and newspaper offices are looking for him.

"But it would be possible to train men in circulation work, and have them available for work outside such as we have mentioned. Such a person would preferably have some previous selling experience. It is easier to work with him after that. He has the fear taken out of him before, and he knows what disappointment is, and he is keen enough to be on the lookout for all the selling information he can gather in the new line he is undertaking. He should be schooled by actual work in selling to different kinds of people who might be brought in, different ones at different times, in order to make the work as varied as possible. Put him up against the person who will raise all sorts of little objections, and take an occasional slam at the paper—let him take these slams and objections and analyze them at once so that he can meet them, and at the same time do that most necessary thing—keep his temper. Never let him lose that, or it's all up. Let your prospect lose his temper if he will—keep cool. Let him get ready to shut the door on you—

never mind. Remember you are not there to fight, you are there to get that man's subscription on the merits of your case, and if the paper is all right, and he should be interested, the fault is yours if you do not sell him. The man who imagines that the fault is with the should-be subscriber or with the paper is not going to succeed. His biggest chance to build up his own case is to imagine that the fault is his and he must improve his selling methods. Those are lines along which men could be trained. There are many other things that go to make a good salesman of circulation, but what I have mentioned in the foregoing are the principal items. I believe there is an opening for such an organization in Canada right now, one that will go out and give a publisher the circulation he requires, and do it on merits of the paper without premiums or outside assistance."

How the A. B. C. Helps the Publisher
A Time Saver for the Salesman

By Stanley Claque, Man. Dir. A. B. C., Chicago

THE Audit Bureau of Circulations was established in 1914. At the first annual meeting, held in Chicago May 20 of that year, the business papers were strongly represented, and M. C. Robbins, then of the *Iron Age* and now of the *Gas Age*, and Fred D. Porter, then of the *National Builder* and now of *Buildings and Building Management*, were made directors. The business paper represented 10 per cent. of the total membership of the A. B. C. at that time, and has maintained its position of importance in the organization. To-day there are 246 members in that class, a group which I believe is the largest body of business paper publishers ever brought together in one organization.

The appreciation of the A. B. C. on the part of advertisers is leading publishers to come in. Advertisers are buying their space on a commodity basis rather than on faith, but while the A. B. C. is an advantage to the advertiser, it has proved equally advantageous to the publisher.

Membership in the Audit Bureau has made publishers appreciate their own property. Fewer publishers are throwing away or giving away copies of their papers. They are conserving paper stock in the present time of shortage. They are transferring unpaid copies into the net paid division, to the benefit of both publisher and advertiser.

Another important advantage to the publisher has been the improvement in methods of keeping records. They are maintaining them in better shape, with the result that they are saving money, while at the same time they are able to give advertisers more information about the circulation that they have to offer. Because records are in better physical condition, space salesmen representing publishers have more information to give advertisers, and hence are able to interest more prospects and make more sales.

The A. B. C., through putting circulation on a definite commodity basis, have given advertisers a keener appreciation of the value of circulations. They are willing to pay more per page or per thousand because they are more thoroughly sold on the value of the space represented by the circulation.

If there is any one thing done by the A. B. C. for the mutual service of advertisers and publishers it is making mandatory the answer to Paragraph 14 of the business paper form, relative to the occupational classification of subscribers. This provision went into effect July 1, and reports covering the period of July 1 to December 1 of the current year will include occupational statistics for all papers in the business paper division of the A. B. C.

This is information which is necessary to enable the advertiser properly to visualize the readers included in the circulation of a business paper. Since the character of the reader is

the big and important thing about business paper circulations it is evident that an A. B. C. report which tells quantity, but does not tell about character, is going only half far enough. Hereafter the A. B. C. report will tell the whole story.

The inclusion of this feature has developed slight resistance from publishers. They realize that it will be of advantage in enabling the editorial appeal to be made more definite, since it can be more intelligently directed after the subscribers are classified according to their occupations. At the same time the reader interest of the publication will be increased through the ability of the editors to serve the needs of readers more exactly.

The A. B. C. is rendering an economic service to publishers through saving the time of salesmen. The salesman who is armed with an A. B. C. statement of the circulation of his publication does not need to spend time in discussing circulation. The A. B. C. statement answers all questions on that score. There are easily 3,000 space salesmen calling on advertisers every day, and at least 10,000 buyers of space listening to their stories each day. If one stops to figure the time which would be wasted by these 13,000 people if circulation had to be argued in the old-fashioned way, and realizes that this time is saved and used to the advantage of the salesman and the space buyer by enabling other things of more direct profit to both to be discussed, it is easy to appreciate the greater effectiveness established by the A. B. C. statement.

The A. B. C. is more than an institution devoted to counting the number of papers distributed by publishers. It is going beyond those things to the bigger, broader and more vital aspects of the situation. It is these things that furnish attraction to me and to the directors of our board. They are among the most prominent advertisers and circulation men in the United States, and they are willingly giving their time nearly every month to come together in New York and Chicago to thresh out the problems affecting the industry at large. On Sept. 15 they journeyed to Toronto as a compliment to the Canadian members of the bureau.

The business paper is of special interest to the small manufacturer, who can address his merchants and customers through these publications. Many of the manufacturers using business papers are going into the advertising field for the first time. Some of them are struggling concerns, with limited amounts available for advertising. They must make the most of their appropriations in order to win the success that advertising can give them.

It is for these reasons that the small manufacturer should be especially interested in the A. B. C. He should select his mediums just as carefully as the large manufacturer, for while the latter is spending more money, the former has more at stake in proportion.

Printer & Publisher

Published on the Twelfth of Each Month.

H. D. TRESIDDER - - - Business Manager.
A. R. KENNEDY - - - - - Editor.

SUBSCRIPTION PRICE—Canada, Great Britain, South Africa and the West Indies, $3 a Year; United States, $3.50 a year; other countries, $4 a year. Single copies, 30 cents. Invariably in advance.

PUBLISHED BY

THE MACLEAN PUBLISHING CO.
Established 1887   Limited

JOHN BAYNE MACLEAN - - - President
H. T. HUNTER - - - - Vice-President.
H. V. TYRRELL - - - General Manager

Head Office, 143-153 University Avenue - TORONTO, CANADA
Cable Address Macpubco, Toronto; Atabek, London, Eng.

Also at Montreal, Winnipeg, New York, Chicago, Boston, London, England.

Application for A.B.C. Audit.

Vol. 29   TORONTO, DECEMBER, 1920   No. 12

CONTENTS

About the Space-Grabbers

AT a meeting of publishers in an Eastern city a few weeks ago one of the speakers took occasion to rake over the coals the space grabbers. When he lines up the space grabbers he takes in a lot of people, and when he hurls all his blame at them he leaves out a very interesting group which ought to be standing in and taking their share of the blame.

The publishers themselves had much to do in the first place with the raising and nursing of the generation of space grabbers they now seek to swat.

There is hardly a lad who ever went through his training time in the smaller offices but who remembers having set up auction sale bill notices, it being distinctly a part of the business that if an auctioneer got his bills printed at the office he would get a free notice in the column which was entitled "Sale Register" or something to that effect. And the publisher used to tell the people that the free reader had greater value than the bill itself. The same thing took place when some function was held that needed a few quarter sheets. All that was necessary was to come around to the office and get the bills and tickets printed and then there was sure to follow a bang-up free reader in the paper.

Why? The publisher had taught the general public to expect it. Why did the old free lunch flourish in the bars of the hotels? Not because the public demanded it. Because the proprietors put it there in order to get people to come in and spend their money. It was a miserable plan, and so was the idea of tossing

out a free reader to the man who had a little job printing done in the office.

This paper is not apologizing for the space grabber, but it must be recognized that he was nursed and trained and brought up for quite a spell by the publishers themselves, and the training and the nursing was done largely at the suggestion of the publishers themselves.

They are out to assassinate him now, but let the assassination ceremonies at times be tempered by the thought that the publishers themselves had much to do with making the assassination necessary.

That British News Service

THE Canadian Press Ltd., at a meeting held in Montreal a few weeks ago, decided to establish a direct British service. To do so some sort of a subsidy will be necessary on the part of the British government.

It is highly desirable that there should be a direct and very reliable news service between Canada and the British Isles, for it has often been charged in the past, and apparently with some degree of truth, that the British despatches appearing in the Canadian papers were more or less colored or distorted.

Allowing all that, it is equally desirable that the Canadian papers should keep away from anything that smacks of government assistance in the way of getting this service "at a price." The Imperial Press Conference at Ottawa wandered around in a maze on this point and arrived nowhere. They wanted a penny rate on cables. They wanted the news to be under no government control, they wanted to get this without having the service subsidized, and they wanted the whole thing without having to pay the price it would regularly cost.

Canadian papers must know that they are charged openly with being more or less subsidized by the government. When a statement like that is put in circulation it spreads and spreads rapidly. There is a certain conviction in some quarters that the money spent by the Canadian government in enabling the Canadian Press wire to be operated across unproductiver territory in the west amounts to a bonus to the papers.

Now, there is no bonus about it, but the bare fact remains that the papers do receive a news service in this way at less money than they could secure it for were they to finance it themselves. It is also possible to make out a very excellent case for the government assisting in bridging this unproductive territory, but it is impossible to get away from the idea of government assistance, and the public is quick and ready to pick this up and attach the whole enterprise to a plot for propaganda on the part of the government of the country, and participated in by the newspapers.

It would be highly advisable for the press of Canada to get past and beyond the place where it can be accused, directly or indirectly of being the beneficiary of any form of bonus, subsidy or official encouragement that could possibly find any reflex influence on the editorial or news freedom of the press of the country.

The most effective way by which the Canadian press can fight any attack on its integrity is to get its house in order, and place itself absolutely separate and apart from the reception of any government gift, no matter if it is called by the high-sounding name of a subsidy.

The Printer Minstrels Score

THAT the printer family in any concern is a many-sided and many-accomplished affair is evident from the second appearance of the MacLean Publishing Company Minstrels. The boys from the mechanical departments entertained some five hundred guests in the big ground floor department of the premises on University Ave. It was a real old-time minstrel show, in which the boys took a fling at every person around the office, from the president on down the line. The programme included very clever work by sleight-of-hand men, cornet solo, vocal solos, variety dancing and the usual run of material that makes a minstrel show just a little different from anything else under the sun, especially where the targets for the endmen are close at hand, and where all the references are understood locally.

The programme shows a neat design, nicely grouped, and with a little ornamentation that fitted in remarkably well with the border used. There is a point right here that many comps seem to overlook, or it may be that they have not the equipment in the office to carry out the idea, but there is much to be gained through having the border on the job in perfect harmony with any attempt at ornamentation. The stock used was a light blue tint cover with a linen finish. The ink was a dark blue. The type is Artcraft, and considerable care has been taken to secure a massed effect at the top in the square grouping of the wording there. Here again it is seen that although not working in that form, any pleasing arrangement can almost invariably be traced to some form of a triangle. In this case if a line is drawn from the bottom of the ornament, left and right to the ends of the long display line at the top, it will be seen where this shape has been conformed to, although the square has been used.

Printing Envelopes

A correspondent in a British paper sends the following:

Great difficulty is often experienced in printing envelope fronts, flaps and uneven surfaces. This is probably more noticeable where the matter is stereotyped or machine set, the metal being of a softer nature.

The difficulty can be overcome by the use of the rubber from an old inner cycle tube.

In printing the envelope front obtain position and make-ready in the usual way, cutting away all the portions which overlap. Then reduce the impression or remove the card from the platen dressing, carefully cover the rubber over the make-ready, tip the corners with an adhesive to keep in position, then cover all up with a light sheet.

By this method the printing will be sharp and clear, the type will not be damaged by the uneven gumming or "make up" of envelopes, and show little signs of wear after thousands of runs.

When working on small cylinder machines do not have the rubber too thick.

Securing a Close Register

In regard to close register a U.S.A. correspondent sums up a note on trade methods by stating that it is occasionally necessary to keep the sheet in contact with the tympan all the time. This can be done by attaching one end of a tape to the band rod, passing it in a margin under the cylinder and attaching it to the under side of the feed board.

When the machine is once adjusted so it will register properly, it will retain this adjustment. If it will register one day, it will register the next. It is not uncommon for machinemen to say that the machine registered yesterday and will not register to-day. Such trouble is not in the machine, but should be looked for in the paper or make-ready. Each form is different and needs different treatment. The movements of the machine are uniform.

A form for close register should not be locked or spaced with wood furniture, beyond a nonpareil reglet or such matter. Every change in temperature affects wood, either shrinking or swelling it, the same manner atmospheric conditions affect paper. Damp weather enlarges the sheet and dry weather contracts it. A thunderstorm may cause loss of register on next color and waste of register on stock as may be printed during the storm. Register may be lost over night because the weather has changed.

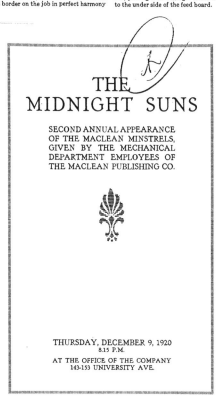

THE MIDNIGHT SUNS

SECOND ANNUAL APPEARANCE
OF THE MACLEAN MINSTRELS,
GIVEN BY THE MECHANICAL
DEPARTMENT EMPLOYEES OF
THE MACLEAN PUBLISHING CO.

THURSDAY, DECEMBER 9, 1920
8.15 P.M.

AT THE OFFICE OF THE COMPANY
143-153 UNIVERSITY AVE.

A PAGEANT
OF THE
Gild OF *Arts* AND *Letters*

wherein the BROTHERHOOD will
dedicate its

NEW HOUSE

which was built under the *Protection* of

Saint George of England

in the STREET *of the* ELMS
in the CITIE *of* TORONTO

¶ The BROTHERS will first meet together in an *Upper Chamber.*

¶ At the hour of *Seven*, the PRIOR of the *Gild*, the Sub-PRIOR, the SCRIVENER and the ALMONER will greet the BROTHERS and lead them in *solemn* procession to the *Great Hall.*

¶ When the *Companie* doth attain the *Hall*, the PRIOR will knock *thrice* upon the door thereof, whereupon it will *open.* Then after entering the *Hall*, will the *Companie* form *a great circle.*

¶ The PRIOR then will receive the Key of the House from *Saint George* his Knight.
[HERE, it is bruited, may be seen a *Dragon.*]

¶ THEN will certain Novices with great *solemnity* place *faggots* on the *hearth*, whereupon the MANCIPLE of the Gild will set *fire thereto*, and all the BROTHERS will give a mighty *shout.*

¶ Then at the bidding of the *Interpreter*, will follow a Colloquy on the *Master Builders*, during which Master Sproatt will be honoured by the BROTHERS.

¶ Then will the *Limners* and *Imageours* of the GILD adorn the Walls, and the *Chroniclers* and *Learned Clerks* will discourse *briefly* of Books.

¶ Then will the BROTHERS sing in honour of our LIEGE LORD the KING, and thereafter will take their appointed places at the Board and chant *Non Nobis Domine.*

House-Warming Programme

The original of this job was done in red and black on a russet rag stock with deckle edge at the bottom. The colors used were red and black, the former in the first three Italic display lines at the top, also for the paragraph signs. Owing to the peculiar style of the job it is impossible on our type page to reproduce it in its entirety. Considerable follows, but there is enough shown to give a good idea of the design, although the length of the work really adds to its quaint ap-

pearance. It might be expected that an organization such as the Arts and Letters Club would have something unusual in the way of printing, and in this they have lived up to expectations.

The wording is well chosen, and will be found to conform quite closely to the printing of some centuries ago. Caslon has been used throughout. The ornamentation, top, and bottom, as well as the ships, is in remarkably good taste. Much of the effect of the work is lost through reproduction in one color. The job was planned by members of the Arts and Letters Club and the work was put through by Rous & Mann, Simcoe St., Toronto.

Sales Tax on Engravings

A member of the National Newspaper Association submitted the following clause recently to a local Inland Revenue officer: "Advertisers, in sending copy for advertisements, frequently send photographs, and request us to have engravings made therefrom, and to charge the cost to them. We order the engravings from the engravers, who in invoicing us add 2 per cent. sales tax. We debit the advertisers with the face amount of the engraver's invoice, without adding any profit." The local Inland Revenue office submitted the matter to the Customs and Inland Revenue Department at Ottawa, which has given the following ruling:—"No additional sales tax is payable when the charge for engraving is passed on by the printer to the advertiser, as such is not a sale. The only sale, as regards the case as quoted, is from the engraver to the printer, as far as the engravings are concerned. In said cases there will be a sales tax from the engraver to the printer, but that tax will not apply when the tax is passed on to the advertiser."

The Paper Situation To-day

Buntin, Gillies & Co., of Hamilton, have issued in the form of a circular a little criticism of the present paper market by one of the officials of the company. The opinions expressed are interesting and timely, giving a careful, yet concise resume of the situation, and showing the danger of jobbers and printers going to the extreme of staying out of the market. The circular says in part:—

Paper as a commodity does not lend itself readily to extremes, either of consumption or conservation.

When general business is quiet the consumption of wrapping paper is naturally reduced. But this is counteracted by the increase in the consumption of paper used in advertising, in the hope of inducing more trade.

The use of fine paper for commercial purposes varies only slightly with changed business conditions. The pupils in the schools use just the same quantity of paper whether business is quiet or booming. Nor does the consumption of the household vary a great deal.

The war cut off our importations of paper, and for a time the scarcity was severely felt. The fact of being without stock induced buyers to purchase months ahead of their requirements. The mills were scrambling to get supplies of raw materials, and the natural result ensued. The conservatism recently developed in all lines of business has resulted in more cautious buying, and by the removal of this artificial demand danger of scarcity has been overcome, and we have probably seen the last of the extremely high prices.

A good healthy demand for paper continues, and there is every evidence that this will for a long time prevent any over-production or accumulation of large stocks.

Unless everyone runs to the extreme, and refuses to buy even bare necessities in the expectation of great reductions in prices, it seems reasonable to expect that whatever recession occurs in the paper market will come gradually.

The wholesale house exists to serve the printer, and the printer in turn to serve the consumer; to give good service should be the first aim of both. During the great scarcity this was impossible, but with a fairly sufficient stock such service has greatly improved, and the paper-dealer and the printer who bring this the nearest to perfection will surely be rewarded.

To give good service requires a large and well varied stock, and while prices may come down, we believe that neither paper-dealer nor printer should risk curtailment of business by allowing his stock of staples to become reduced.

Ontario Daily Publishers Meet At St. Kitts

Many Interesting Topics Were Discussed

 LTHOUGH there is no regular organization to hold them together, the publishers of the small dailies of Ontario are finding that the similarity of their problems provides all the binding that is necessary, and there is a community of interest quite sufficient to make up for other lack in the way of outward equipment, titles and officials.

These dailies met again in St. Catharines on Tuesday, November 30, special interest being attached to the meeting by the presence of Mr. Wil V. Tufford, secretary of the Inland Daily Press Association, which has its head office in Clinton, Iowa.

The publishers were the guests for the day of Mr. W. B. Burgoyne, publisher of the *Standard*, and of his son, Mr. H. Burgoyne. This in itself was sufficient to guarantee the nature of the hospitality that would be handed out to the visitors of the day. The party gathered at the headquarters of the Chamber of Commerce, from which a trip around the, city was commenced, ending at the office of the *Standard*, where the equipment of this office was inspected. Many of the publishers had a good opportunity to see the advantages of the one-floor plan for the small daily paper.

Luncheon—or to be correct a real honest-to-goodness St. Catharines dinner—was served at noon, and immediately following the business sessions were started. Mr. Burgoyne outlined the purposes of the meetings and drew attention to the fact that there was much that publishers of small city dailies faced now that required very careful study. Mayor Lovelace, a former newspaper man, once publisher of the St. Catharines *Journal*, extended a welcome to the visitors, taking occasion to emark that although he had quit the field of journalism some years ago, there were times when he had strong leanings toward his first love, and he could give no positive guarantee that some day he would not be coaxed back into the fold.

Hugh Bell, manager of the St. Catharines Chamber of Commerce, himself a former newspaper man, gave a brief outline of the way in which a Chamber of Commerce could work with a newspaper, and advocated the closest possible co-operation in order that the feeling of the entire business community, as centered in a Chamber of Commerce, could be correctly interpreted to the rest of the citizens.

From a Merchant's Standpoint

The St. Catharines gathering gave the publishers a chance to hear something they hear all too little, viz., the views of a man who buys space in the paper. Major George R. Bradley, owner of several grocery stores, started using a two inch space in the *Standard* years ago when his business was small, but he kept everlastingly at it, and made his two inches say something all the time. As he grew his space grew, and it is no unusual thing now to see Major Bradley using page space in the *Standard* to advertise his grocery business.

A reference in *MacLean's Magazine* to the attitude of the retailer to price reductions provided part of the text for Major Bradley's remarks. "Many people take the paper and scan the contents, noting all the reductions that have been made in Oshkosh, Timbuctoo, and other unknown corners of the world, and pay little or no attention to the reductions that are being made by their own stores. The merchants of far-off centres are held up as slashing prices, and the inference is given that the merchant at home is not doing so. The newspapers will find that their own merchants are willing to discuss their problems with them, and it would be a better thing for the editors of papers to become acquainted with the problems that their own merchants have to deal with especially in times like we are going through at this moment."

Major Bradley then went on to explain how the merchants had worked together on the "Get-Together Edition" of the St. Catharines *Standard*. The date for the selling was arranged, and that could be regulated according to the wish of the merchants themselves. In the first place the merchants had been called together at the Chamber of Commerce, and the plan outlined. They had decided the date and such details, and then came the matter of advertising. They wanted to get out a special edition of the *Standard*, and for the purpose of the sale had made arrangements for an extra 6,000 distribution, these papers being sent out house-to-house and in districts where the merchants thought they would do most good. The cost of this extra circulation was ascertained from the *Standard* office, and merchants were assessed pro rata on their contract for the extra space, so in this way it was fair to all concerned. They had turned out a 24-page paper on that particular occasion, and in order to do this it was necessary for some of the larger advertisers to use even less space than they would do on an ordinary day, in order that all the stores could have a chance to be represented in the publicity that was sent out.

According to Major Bradley there is still in existence a feeling of rivalry between a number of merchants. They like to watch the advertising of a competitor and slip in half a dollar under him.

"But right now merchants face a peculiar position. Many of them have large stocks, and they have more arriving. We can repudiate these orders, but we do not consider that a fair means of doing business. The other way is to keep up a continuous advertising propaganda. Forceful advertising can do for the merchant what nothing else can.

"Your merchants' organization or your Chamber of Commerce must help to sell the idea of a Get-Together Edition to the other merchants and they must knock out the idea that it is simply a money-making plan for the newspaper. In our campaign the advertising solicitor for the *Standard* went ahead and laid the proposition before the merchants, and signed up the business. After he had made the rounds he turned over to us

PUBLISHERS attending the meeting of the Daily Papers at St. Catharines a few days ago discussed their paper problems, and in this brought up the idea of collective bargaining for paper.

Printer and Publisher was able to get in touch with a paper maker from Wisconsin, who was in Toronto for several days during the week, in connection with their Canadian plant, and discussed the matter of collective bargaining.

"If the daily publishers were to get together and bring with them their paper orders, they could save a lot of money if I am not very much mistaken. This could be done by analyzing their business and sorting it out in sizes. If they could go to a mill with a good sized order for a certain kind, or with several that could be put through the machine at the same time, they ought to be able to buy to advantage. On some of the machines in our mills there is an overhead of as high as $800 per day, and that must be spread over the amount of paper that goes through. If it is kept full to capacity all the time the overhead per ton automatically moves down, but if it is turning out paper that does not take up the full capacity of the machine then the overhead must go up.

"It seems very probable that there will be cheaper paper before very long. The price has been too high, and there has been no necessity for the Canadian publishers paying the price they have. Allowing for high wages and all, and a fair profit on their investment, paper should sell in the Canadian market at four cents for rolls, and anything in excess of this is gouging the trade. There is more paper now on the American market than can be absorbed by the trade there, and some of the mills are at the point where they are closing off for want of business."

the list of stores that had turned him down, and we took them in hand, and got them. This year the advertising manager of the *Standard* sold the repeat business without any assistance from us, because they had seen the thing work out as a good thing the last time. We intend to go farther this year and refund half the railway fare of those who come to the sales. The financing for this is done by assessing each merchant at the rate of $1.50 for each employee he has in his store. The extra help that may be put on for such an occasion is not included in this count. If this is not sufficient we will make the assessment $2 per head, and if that is too much we will refund it pro rata. If you can get your merchants together you will be doing them a good turn, and you will be helping them to move more goods than they can do in any other way, and they will be unloading their stock, which is very necessary. When you help a merchant to do a good day's business you are helping yourself."

Major Bradley intimated that if any of the publishers desired additional information about the Merchants' Get-Together Edition, they could secure it from the Chamber of Commerce or any of the merchants, or from the publisher of the *Standard*. He was emphatic in commending the idea to other places as a perfectly feasible merchandising event.

The Inland Press Association

Will V. Tufford, secretary-treasurer of the Inland Daily Press Association, recounted the growth of that institution from 56 papers at $1 a year until at the present time they have 254 daily papers, with fees ranging from $15 a year for a paper with 2,500 circulation to $50 a year for the larger publications.

The Inland Association, he claimed, had been responsible for the settling down of the paper market. By its system of allocating newsprint some 74 papers had been saved from suspending publication. The print situation was still serious enough, and as evidence of this he produced several papers that had been turned out on sheets 11" x 8". In many cases the large publishers that had paper had shared it with those who had not been able to secure a supply. The association had also studied carefully the price of advertising and subscriptions, with the result that a good many papers that three years ago were not making a penny were now in the dividend producing class; they had helped some to cut their columns to 12 ems and add another column to every page, and in other cases the publishers had put an eight point face on a seven point body. They had been able to consolidate weak publications, and had brought publishers together on several occasions who had not been on speaking terms for years. "The Inland Press Association will work with you too if you have an organization," remarked Mr. Tufford. Referring to such gatherings as he was attending he advised that there should be an organization. "Don't sponge on any person," was his advice, "get organized, but don't have banquets. When you attend such a gathering as this have it a Dutchman's treat, bring your note books and get down to business early in the day.

"It is not fair that publishers should be dominated by union labor, but there should be a working together in every way. Some of our men have been driven to such lengths that they have gone to the open shop plan and they are operating under it sucessfully. The desirable thing is to keep close to your men. Know them and work with them."

Referring to the paper question he stated that many dailies were adopting a uniform size so that the mills could work to better advantage. He referred to the fact that the Great Northern had announced their price as five cents, the M. & O. were giving a ten year contract on an open price based on the average of a number of given mills. He could see no justification for the International charging 6¼ when the Great Northern had been making money at 4c. Freight rates had helped to make the paper makers' costs higher, and it should be remembered that on an average it takes three cars of raw material to make one car of paper, and so some of this material has to be hauled a long distance to the mills. Six shiploads of print from Germany had reached the American market at a time when the spot price was as high as 18 cents, and this German paper had broken the market. He could not promise that these shipments would increase or continue, or that they would come with enough regularity to warrant any publisher making a contract with that source, as each shipment was subject to the approval of some German official, and if that approval were withheld the publisher would be out in the cold. The New

York *World* and *Globe* were using this paper and they were well satisfied with its qualities.

The Subscription Price

Mr. Tufford went into the matter of subscriptions at some length. "Why," he asked, "are you sending papers out by mail for less money than you are delivering them in your city when it costs you more by mail?" He referred to the case of a publisher in Lansing who had made a very close study of the matter, and he came to the conclusion that it was not possible to deliver his circulation of some 28,000 under $7.50 per annum. The newsprint should always be charged against the circulation and not all handed over to the advertiser.

Referring to one shop where the foreman had a contract to set the type for the paper, the figures used to be 4½c per inch, but a careful survey raised this amount to six cents for the mechanical costs only, without taking in the overhead.

"There is not a paper publisher that can make money if it does not charge 35c per inch for its space as a minimum rate," stated Mr. Tufford, "and a number of rate cards that I have been receiving at my office within the last few days show that many of the publishers are going to that rate. Don't imagine because you have a small circulation you can come under that rate and get away with it. The very fact that you have a small circulation is one of the proofs of your needs for more revenue. Cultivate the want ad business. It pays well, at least fifty per cent. above any other sort of advertising you have in your paper, and it is desirable in that it has a great deal of reader-interest attached. Many papers are finding out that their display advertisers are requesting that they be given a chance to have their ads appear on the same page as the classified advertising."

Division of Revenue

Statistics covering a number of papers showed that of the revenue the average was as follows:—Advertising 60 per cent., circulation 32 per cent. Expenses were divided about as follows:

Editorial from as high as 21 down to 4 per cent., or an average of 8 7-10 per cent.

Departmental expenses, from as high as 29 to as low as 9, or an average of 13 5-10 per cent.

Advertising from as high as 15 to as low as one, averaging 6 4-10 per cent.

Circulation, averaging 8 per cent.

Mechanical from as high as 50 per cent. to as low as 26 per cent., or an average of 38 9-10.

General, from 32 down to 11, averaging 17 1-10 per cent.

Profits averaged all the way from as high as 36 per cent. to four per cent., or an average of 16 5-10.

The total expenditure compared to income averaged 83 5-10 per cent.

The speaker extended an invitation to the Canadian publishers to attend the meetings of the Inland Press Association which was being held in Chicago on January 15 and 16. "No matter if you are members or not," concluded Mr. Tufford, "come on over and get in on the discussions. We'll be glad to see you."

Several speakers expressed their appreciation of Mr. Tufford's remarks, and the chairman explained to him that the Canadian publishers had an organization, but they found at its sessions little opportunity to discuss the matters they had in common, and they had found that in these smaller gatherings they could get down to business in a much more satisfactory manner.

A Real Problem Here

"When I looked at the figures for the last car of paper we got and found that it was $2,800, and then added to that $150 for freight, and then included cartage and storage, and found the total was almost $3,200 I decided we had a real problem, especially when you put that figure up against the $700 that we were paying for the same amount three and a half years ago." That was the way Mr. Glover of the Peterboro *Examiner* started the discussion on the paper business, and it afforded a striking object lesson of the problem that all the publishers have to face.

"Against that," continued Mr. Glover, "we have increased our paper in the city from $4 to $6 by carrier, and from $3 to $4.80 in the mail, and single copies from two to three cents, but these increases in the revenue do not begin to let us out or help us to come up to the increase of almost four hundred per cent. to which I referred at the start."

Mr. Glover has had troubles of his own in getting sufficient paper. "I have seen us at eight in the morning with no paper in the office, but a car on the track, which we would have to get placed and trucked in order that we might publish. We have been helped out on several occasions by good friends in our district, and right now we are in difficulty for a sufficient supply of paper, and we would welcome any assistance that we can get now. These circumstances have led me to suggest that a move might be made toward collective buying of newsprint. We syndicate many things in the newspaper business, such as news, features, etc., and it works very well. I believe it is a matter that could very well be carefully considered."

The suggestion was also made that publishers should have more information about the contracts that are made with the unions. The question of the forty-four hour week was generally felt to be a very serious matter, one of the hardest propositions the publishers had yet faced, and in view of this movement it was necessary that they act together.

In this matter Mr. Tufford stated that statistics showed the average age of the present-day printer to be 35 years, and their average span of 57 years. The apprentices were not coming as in some places they now had it that there should be only one apprentice to every ten journeymen. Boys would not come in to learn the trade as they could make more money at other work at the start.

Reference was made to two contracts that had just been recently closed, one in Guelph at $32 for the eight hour day and the other in Galt for $31 for the eight-hour day, although in the first place the question of hours comes up again in May of next year.

The Eight Column Paper

Mr. Stephenson of the Chatham *Planet* had with him a dummy of a paper that he intended to get out next month, when he will have his paper in the eight column class with a 12 em width. The Detroit papers had been using this for some time and the sheet was a compact one of good appearance. "I did not get much encouragement in the first place,"

Here's the Real Difference Between 12 and 13 Ems

AT the meeting of the daily newspaper publishers at St. Catharines a few days ago, the matter of changing over to a twelve em column, and in this way getting eight columns on a page, with the same press and equipment that is now turning out a seven-column paper, was much discussed.

Mr. Stephenson, of the Chatham *Planet*, seems to have gone farther than the others in the matter of adopting the 12 em column, and says he intends to go ahead and use it in a few weeks.

In order to visualize the thing, Printer and Publisher has had the same matter set in twelve and thirteen em width, on an ordinary eight point face and body. The operator was requested to forget that there was any special reason for setting it both ways, but to space just as he would in ordinary matter, and it will be noted that this has been done.

The operator stated that he noticed very little difference in the setting—if any, it would be that the twelve em line would be a little more difficult to space, but it would not be sufficient to make a difference in the number of lines that could be put into the machine per minute. Where the operator would lose would be in the fact that each line would carry one pica ems less, and it is just as easy to feed in 13 em lines as it is 12 em. On a minion face, which many papers use, the spacing would be easier.

It will be noticed on measurement that the matter in the 13 has five inches, while in the 12 it amounts to 5½ inches. Suppose 20 inches made a column, it would mean that in 12 ems it would make 14 inches squeezed out to run into the extra eighth, leaving but six inches more to provide. So as far as the securing of material to fill the extra eight columns that would be added to a paper, the editorial department would have very little about which to worry.

(12-em column)

THEY WANT THE 12 EM COLUMN

Publishers Believe They Could Save Space and Produce Just as Good a Paper

The question of setting reading matter 12 ems might not stir up as much difference of opinion with the reader of the paper as with the advertiser and the agency. The advertiser, for instance, feels the same about it as the man who buys a No. 13 pair of shoes, only to find when he gets home that he has a No. 12. He may feel rather pinched for a time, but the chances are that he would not object very much. The reader on the other hand will not kick about the change. The agency will no doubt make a face when approached concerning the use of a twelve em column, as much of the plate matter that he has on hand has been made on the assumption that the regulation column of to-day is 12½ ems. Some of the publishers have approached the agencies intimating that they would like to break away from the old order of things in order to serve their high-priced paper, but for the most part the agencies have simply made a face at them and said, "Don't you dare to do this thing," and thereat the publisher has in most cases put the whole proposition in his hip pocket and done nothing more about it until he has met some brother publisher in the press gatherings, and there he again sprouts a new backbone and determines to start all over again. And so it is that some day twenty or more of these publishers may come together and say that on the first of some nearby month we will go in for an eight-column paper and make the columns twelve ems in width, in which case such twenty will be a real club to whack the head of the agencies and show them who is running the newspapers.

(13-em column)

THEY WANT THE 12 EM COLUMN

Publishers Believe They Could Save Space and Produce Just as Good a Paper

The question of setting reading matter 12 ems might not stir up as much difference of opinion with the reader of the paper as with the advertiser and the agency. The advertiser, for instance, feels the same about it as the man who buys a No. 13 pair of shoes, only to find when he gets home that he has a No. 12. He may feel rather pinched for a time, but the chances are that he would not object very much. The reader on the other hand will not kick about the change. The agency will no doubt make a face when approached concerning the use of a twelve em column, as much of the plate matter that he has on hand has been made on the assumption that the regulation column of to-day is 12½ ems. Some of the publishers have approached the agencies intimating that they would like to break away from the old order of things in order to serve their high-priced paper, but for the most part the agencies have simply made a face at them and said, "Don't you dare to do this thing," and thereat the publisher has in most cases put the whole proposition in his hip pocket and done nothing more about it until he has met some brother publisher in the press gatherings, and there he again sprouts a new backbone and determines to start all over again. And so it is that some day twenty or more of these publishers may come together and say that on go in for an eight-column paper and make the columns twelve ems in width, in which case such twenty will be a real club to whack the head of the agencies and show them who is running the newspapers.

admitted Mr. Stephenson, "but I am still of the idea that the eight column 12 ems is right. The agencies are very much set against making the change, but when I tell you that I was the first to use the typograph in this country, the first to use a Thorn typesetting machine and the first to try the Intertype, why it follows that I should go ahead with the 12 em paper. There is no reason why we should not do it. The *Planet* is having its chases cut at a machine shop. The Port Huron *Times* had no trouble either with the mechanical or any other department. Those who have made the change tell me that it is nothing but very satisfactory economy in every way." Mr. Stephenson had with him a number of letters from publishers who had made the change to the 12 em column in the United States, and they claimed there were very few cuts that would not go in that measure. Mr. Stephenson advised those present to measure up their own cuts and see for themselves, claiming there would be few cases in which they could not make use of the cuts in the narrow columns. "We should resolutely make up our minds that we are going to use the eight column paper," concluded Mr. Stephenson, "and then let enough of us go ahead and do the thing. It will be a great advantage, and I, for one, propose to start next month."

The question of increasing street sales prices came up here, Mr. Burgoyne remarking that when he put the *Standard* to three cents there was a loss of about two per cent. at first. Mr. Leslie of Niagara Falls stated that when the *Review* went to three cents there was no loss at all. The experience of the *Galt Reporter* was much the same, as they had gone from $4 to $6 in the city. They dropped a few at the outset, but they were practically all back at the new price.

Both Galt and London extended invitations to the publishers to hold the next meeting in their respective cities, but this will probably be decided by a vote of the members.

Those attending the meeting were:—

M. J. Gonder, Niagara Falls *Evening Review*; W. J. Motz, Kitchener *Daily Record*; H. M. Gadsby, St. Catharines *Standard*; Frank Adams, London *Advertiser*; A. R. Kennedy, Toronto, *Printer and Publisher*; H. B. Burgoyne, St. Catharines *Standard*; Hugh M. Bell, St. Catharines; Geo. R. Bradley, St. Catharines, merchant; J. J. McIntosh, Guelph *Mercury*; H. B. Muir, London *Free Press*; T. H. Kay, Kitchener *Daily Record*; Stuart H. Gant, Galt *Reporter*; Henry J. Foster, Galt *Reporter*; W. L. Agnew, *Times-Journal*, St. Thomas; R. M. Glover, *Examiner*, Peterborough; F. H. Leslie, *Review*, Niagara Falls; Wil. V. Tufford, secretary-treasurer I.D.P.A., Clinton, Iowa; W. B. Burgoyne, *Standard*, St. Catharines; E. J. Lovelace, St. Catharines; L. Stephenson, *Planet*, Chatham.

Getting Out a Weekly Paper

The publisher of the Colchester *Sun* sent an issue to this office for our opinion, particularly on its front page. One thing that is noticeable is that the paper carries a large amount of local reading matter—in fact nearly all the matter in the paper has a distinctly local bearing. On the seventh page is an objectionable feature, viz., half a page of advertising for the paper's own job department. There is too much the appearance in this of "Well, here's a page to be filled, now what are we going to do about it?" Avoid this as much as possible. If it can be done, take the two ads off the corners of the front page. It is not fair to your other advertisers to single these two out for front page treatment. A bank should be pleased, for instance, to have a chance to get a position on your back page, where there is a good showing of country and district news. Instead of running paid reading locals all through the paper why not collect them and work up a column in the form of a Buyers' Guide, which can be made attractive and profitable? Your front page is carrying plenty of home news. The large headings are well balanced, although we would use a smaller type in the lower part of the heading, perhaps breaking it up into two or three lines flush and two ems indent and followed by a cap line of the same size. The bottom half of the sheet is weak by contrast with the top, all the display having been thrown up there. On the outside column you have an eight point heading that reads this way:

TRANSFERRED TO
CAMPBELLTON

Avoid headings of that type. Change around to make one line. Headings always look better when the lines are full up.

6 point. Why not use an initial letter on your editorial page on articles carrying headings? The matter on this page is too largely taken from other sources. It may not be fair to judge from this one issue, but an editorial page is a great place to get acquainted with your readers.

Paper Makers Prosper at 6½

Definite announcement has been made that the price of newsprint for the first quarter of the year 1921 had been set by Canadian producers at 6½c per lb., or at the rate of $130 per ton, at the various mills.

The development was in line with current expectations, although for some time past reports have been circulated in the stock market districts that what price revision was in prospect would be on the downward scale. These rumors, however, received their quietus through the official statement. The 6½c rate, in the cases of several of the important producing companies does not represent any increase over the price set on October 10 last, or for the last quarter of 1920, although a number of other mills have been supplying newsprint on contract at well under that figure—in one or two instances as low as 5c per lb. The 6½c price set, however, will now apply generally and be uniform in the Canadian pulp and paper industries.

In confirming the statement that the 6½c rate had been decided upon for the first quarter of the coming year, an official of the Canadian Paper Co., Ltd., which acts as selling agent for a number of the most important paper enterprises in eastern Canada, said that, so far as his company was concerned, the rate was the same as the one presently in effect.

"The year 1920," he stated, "has been an excellent one for newsprint producers, the latter half of the year showing up exceptionally well. The outlook for 1921 is that conditions in the industry will prove even more prosperous."

THE PERSONAL SIDE OF IT

 We'd Like To Get Items For
These Columns

GEORGE M. ROSE, president of the Hunter-Rose Company, is running for alderman in Ward Three, Toronto. Mr. Rose is a successful business man, and takes a keen interest in public affairs, and is in a position to give valuable service to the community. Mr. Rose has been an energetic worker in the Toronto Typothetae, an organization that has already done much to bring about better conditions in the printing industry of Toronto. Previous to entering the publishing business, Mr. Rose had graduated from the O.A.C. at Guelph, and later was with the Williams, Greene & Rome Co., of Kitchener. It was in 1902 that he entered the present business, which his father had established years before, and in 1904 became president and manager of the company. Mr. Rose was in his younger days an enthusiastic lacrosse player. He is a member of the C.M.A. and Toronto Board of Trade, and is always interested in civic and national problems.

GEORGE M. ROSE

Quebec

The Montreal *Gazette* is securing five cents per copy, or $12 per year for its paper.

Charles W. Stokes, of the C.P.R. publicity department, is in England and France, delivering a series of lectures for the C.P.R. He was formerly in newspaper work in Calgary, Montreal, and other Canadian centres.

The plant of the Concord (N. H.) *Daily Patriot* was heavily damaged by fire which virtually destroyed White's Opera House block. The bulk of the loss estimated at $150,000 was sustained by Edward J. Gallagher, publisher of the newspaper, who also owned the building.

Bernard K. Sandwell has been appointed an associate in Economics with Prof. Stephen Leacock at McGill. He has been editing *Canadian Bookman* for some time, and it is not known at present whether this publication will be continued or not. Previously Mr. Sandwell used to write under the name of "Munday Knight" in the Montreal *Herald*, doing dramatic work.

When the fox exhibition was on in Montreal recently the *Star* saw the possibilities of fur advertising in the event. The exhibition was thoroughly covered from a reportorial standpoint, and a number of special articles were used dealing with the fur industry in general. The advertising patronage was very satisfactory, not only from dealers in furs, but also fox ranchers, fur coat salesmen, etc.

Considerable interest is being taken in the announcement made by *La Presse* that Sir Lomer Gouin had severed his connection with that paper, which he assumed at the time he gave up the Premiership of the Province. *La Presse* did not give a reason for his withdrawal. *Le Devoir* (Bourassa's paper) gives a reason, however. It is that Sir Lomer could not get on with Mr. Berthiaume, proprietor of *La Presse*, and that they split on the rock of authority, despite the fact that Sir Lomer had a three-year contract of $15,000 a year. Here is what *Le Devoir* says: It was solely over the division of authority that the disagreement between Messrs. Gouin and Berthiaume started. And the crisis, developing for some time, came to a head on Saturday. After a long conversation between Sir Lomer Gouin and Mr. Berthiaume, the former handed in his

resignation to Mr. Berthiaume, who intends keeping the supreme authority regarding his paper in his own hands.

Ontario

The Oakville *Star* announces an advance in its subscription price after Dec. 1st, 1920, from $1.50 to $2.00.

The Simcoe *Reformer* has gone to $2, and George Pearce at Waterford likewise collects a similar fee from his *Star* gazers.

A few days ago the morning papers killed Lord Desborough, but by the middle of the day the noon editions had him alive again.

R. C. Sage has resigned as manager of the Woodstock Gas Light Co., and leaves shortly for Toronto where he will take a position with a publishing house.

A Business That Has Developed

WHEN Mono-Lino moved into their new premises in Brigden Building, some one happened to look around one day and find out that they had some 31 people on the payroll. Quite a growth from the time in 1912 when the concern had its start in a one-machine plant. Wm. R. Adamson, the manager of the plant, worked first with the West Toronto *Tribune*, then with Warwick Brothers and Rutter, later going to South-am Press, where he operated a keyboard. In 1912 he started on an agreement with Addison and Mainprice to operate a monotype equipment. This grew into a small trade plant. In July of 1917 the Mono-Lino Co. came into existence, Mr. Addison being president and W. R. Adamson manager. They took 600 feet in the Brigden Building. Six months after they had more than doubled this space. Of course this space has been left behind long ago and now there is an equipment of five monotypes, two linotypes and an Elrod lead and rule.

S. F. McMURRAY   WM. R. ADAMSON

caster. Last spring Mr. Adamson bought the entire stock of the company, and now has associated with him as assistant manager S. F. McMurray. Mr. "Mac" knows the publishing fraternity well, having been with the Toronto Type for some time, also with Linotype and Monotype Companies.

The U.T.A. cost system is used in the establishment, and most of the time the plant operates night and day shifts.

A make-up department is also in operation at the plant, and work is sent out ready for the press.

Editor Wins Yale Seat

J. A. McKELVIE, editor of the Vernon *News*, signs it J. A. McKelvie, M.P., having been successful in the bye-election for Yale, B.C., in the seat formerly held by Martin Burrell, which he won by acclamation in 1917. On account of the former election having gone by acclamation, there was no organization to help Mr. McKelvie at the start, but he came out of the rumpus with a majority of 381. His newspaper experience has been confined to the Vernon *News*, where he went in 1893. His uncle, the late John Livingstone, was in his day a prominent Canadian journalist, having been editor of the St. John *Sun*, Montreal *Herald*, Toronto *Empire* and the Calgary *Herald*. "Who's Who in Western Canada" gives the following information:—

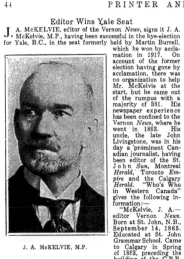

J. A. McKELVIE, M.P.

"McKelvie, J. A.—editor Vernon *News*. Born at St. John, N.B., September 14, 1865. Educated at St. John Grammar School. Came to Calgary in Spring of 1883, preceding the building of the C.P.R. to that point. Served in the Riel Rebellion 1885 with the Alberta Mounted Rifles. Came to Vancouver 1888, and to Vernon 1889. Married. Conservative. Presbyterian. Lodge A.F. &A.M. and I.O.O.F. Became editor of Vernon *News* in 1893. Has been President of Yale Conservative Association. Was a member of Royal Labor Commission appointed in 1912."

Mr. Burns is now city circulation manager of the Toronto *Globe*, previous to which he was with the *Border Cities Star*. He was also on the Toronto *News* some years ago.

F. Douglas Reville, for many years editor of the Brantford *Courier*, has completed the work on the history of Brant County, on which he has been engaged for the past two years.

Max B. Cody has taken the position of night editor of the *Border Cities Sun*. He was on the Hamilton *Times* as news editor, going there from the London *Free Press*, where he had been for a number of years.

G. C. Grant is now on the city copy desk at the *Globe*, coming there when the Hamilton *Times* broke. He had been at the *Times* only a few days, having gone there from the West when the reorganization took place.

John H. Thompson, of the Thorold *Post*, has been on a trip through Western Canada. In a series of letters to his paper he shows that he understands people and news, for instead of writing about western conditions in general he tells of former Thorold people who are living in the West, what they are doing and how they are getting along.

Messrs. J. R. Robinson, Irving E. Robertson, Douglas Robertson and Alfred T. Chadwick, trustees of the estate of the late John Ross Robertson and managers of the Toronto *Evening Telegram*, were served with notice of complaint under the Libel and Slander Act, by I. F. Hellmuth, K.C., of the firm of Hellmuth, Cattanach and Meredith, acting for Mr. E. W. Backus. The notice of action is the outcome of certain articles appearing in the Toronto *Telegram* on November 6 and 8.

The Canadian Weekly Newspaper Association started with nothing at the first of the year, and although there have been heavy drains on the finances, the Association will end its first year without a deficit. The Weekly men looked for about $1,800 in the hole as a starter. Friend Sayles may have imbibed some of his "how to make the thing go" ideas from his early days on the Brantford *Expositor* when he used to make enough money at 8 cents a thousand on the old typograph to wear silk shirts. All of which leads to the remark that type doesn't grow for eight cents any more.

One of the oldest newspapers in the Dominion, the Amherstburg *Echo*, celebrates its forty-sixth birthday, never missing an issue during the 2,386 weeks it has served Essex county. A record unique among Canadian publications is the fact that five of the *Echo's* employees have been with it in the aggregate 149 years. John Auld, editor, has 46 years service to his credit. The *Echo* has lived and thrived through the administration of practically every Government Canada has had. It was founded shortly after Confederation.

After a day's illness of paralysis, Walter R. Scace, counties jailer, died at Brockville. For 28 years prior to appointment to that office, he was business manager of the Brockville *Times*, and previously served as a printer on Brantford, Welland and Winnipeg papers. In 1912 he was appointed jailer. Surviving are his widow, formerly Miss Bella Fennell, of Brockville, and two sons. Among his brothers is F. G. Scace, Inspector of Customs, Toronto. Mr. Scace was born in Dundas. He was also secretary of the Public School Board and a leading Freemason.

Harry Anderson has been appointed assistant managing editor of the Toronto *Globe*, this promotion going into effect a few days ago. He will have charge of the news departments, Stewart Lyon, the managing editor, devoting himself more to matters of policy and editorial work. Harry Anderson started newspaper work at Chatham, and from there went to the Toronto *News* before it was tombstoned. It is about twelve years since he went to the Globe, at first doing the Ontario Legislature, and after that the Dominion House. He has a very wide political acquaintance at the capital, knowing members on both sides of politics. At various times he has been on the city desk at the *Globe*, and latterly news editor and editorial writer.

Rev. R. Douglas Fraser, D.D., formally relinquishes his position as business manager and editor of Presbyterian Publications, and Rev. D. M. Solandt, B.D., succeeds to the position of business manager. Dr. Fraser was educated at Bradford and Newburgh High Schools and the University of Toronto. He studied for the ministry at Knox College, Toronto, and at the Presbyterian College Montreal. He was ordained in 1873 and held charges at Cookstown, Toronto, Claude and Bowmanville. At the inception of the Publications Department of the Presbyterian Church in 1898, Dr. Fraser was chosen as business manager and editor. One of the last acts of business carried out by Dr. Fraser was the establishment of an official Church weekly paper by the purchase and amalgamation of the *Presbyterian Witness* and the *Presbyterian and Westminster*. Rev. D. M. Solandt, B.D., is the newly-appointed successor to Dr. Fraser as business manager.

JAMES G. WILSON, for the past thirteen years foreman at *Saturday Night Press*, Toronto, has resigned and taken over the W. R. Maxwell printing plant at 84 Adelaide street East. Mr. Wilson started with *Saturday Night* when there were three cylinder presses looking after the trade there, while now the plant has sixteen cylinders, and other departments have expanded accordingly. Mr. Wilson served his time on the Galt *Reporter*, when Jaffray Brothers were running that paper, and after finishing there went to Toronto, where he started with the R. G. McLean Co., leaving there to go to the *Saturday Night*. He has always been a close student of good typography, good

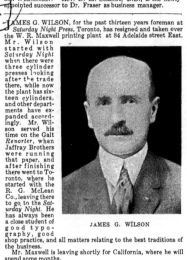

JAMES G. WILSON

shop practice, and all matters relating to the best traditions of the business.

Mr. Maxwell is leaving shortly for California, where he will spend some months.

Three New Appointments for Newspaper Men

J. O. HERITY,
Industrial Commissioner, Belleville.

CAPT. WILLIAM WALLACE.
Manager C.D.N.A.

M. J. HUTCHINSON,
Manager National Newspapers.

J. O. Herity, managing editor of the *Daily Ontario*, Belleville, who is retiring from that position to become industrial commissioner and managing secretary of the Chamber of Commerce at Belleville, is a native of Hastings County, Ontario. After receiving his education at Stirling High School and Toronto University, he spent three years in the teaching profession. He then entered the publishing business by purchasing the Markham *Sun* (since amalgamated with the Markham *Economist*.) He remained in Markham eight years. In April, 1910, in company with his brother-in-law, Mr. W. H. Morton, he purchased from T. G. Carman & Son the printing and publishing business conducted by them under the name of the *Daily and Weekly Ontario*. Mr. Herity entered the partnership as managing editor and editorial writer and has continued to occupy that position up to the time of his retirement. He has also been secretary-treasurer of the Bay of Quinte Press Association since that body was organized in November, 1913. Mr. Herity has taken a deep interest in better city government and it was largely because of his leadership in several important municipal developments that he was selected unanimously by the city council and the Chamber of Commerce for this responsible position.

William Wallace, who was private secretary to the Hon. N. W. Rowell, K.C., during his presidency of the Privy Council, and more recently secretary of the Canadian committee in charge of arrangements for the Imperial Press Conference, has been appointed manager of the Canadian Daily Newspapers' Association.

Mr. Wallace was a member of the editorial staff of the Toronto *Star* for some years prior to July, 1915, when he enlisted, and afterwards served in France with the 75th Battalion. He was awarded the Military Cross in March, 1917, and invalided home three months later. In September, 1917, he was appointed officer in charge for Canada of the Canadian Daily Record, supplying home news by cable for the newspaper that was issued to Canadians at the front.

In 1918 he became private secretary to the president of the Privy Council and in March, 1920, he was appointed secretary of the special commisson of the Canadian Press Association Inc., which had charge of the arrangements for the Imperial Press Conference, accompanying the delegates in their tour across Canada.

Mr. Wallace will take up his new work about Dec. 15.

The increase in the price of newsprint is causing many newspapers to raise their rates. Practically every newspaper in Halton County has announced that its subscription price will be $2.00 for the coming year instead of $1.50.

M. J. Hutchinson has been appointed manager of the Canadian National Newspapers and Periodicals Association. Speaking of this appointment the Edmonton *Bulletin* states:— Edmonton is shortly to lose a well known and public-spirited citizen in the person of M. J. Hutchinson, who has just received

the appointment of manager of the Canadian National News and Periodical Association with headquarters at Toronto. The association is composed of the publishers of trade and technical papers and magazines of Canada. He will enter upon his new duties Dec. 1st. Before coming to Edmonton to assume the managership of the *Bulletin* in 1914, Mr. Hutchinson had been for three years advertising manager of the Regina *Leader*. Previous to that he was in Toronto where for five years he was associated with trade papers. The work on which he was engaged then gave him an experience which will serve him well in his new position. During his six years' residence in this city Mr. Hutchinson has been largely identified with many lines of activity. He has been on the council of the board of trade since 1916 and last year was one of its vice-presidents. He is a charter member of the Edmonton Rotary Club, a director four years and district governor one year with jurisdiction over all Rotary Clubs of Western Canada. In addition he has been a member of the board of McDougall Methodist church and a director of the Y.M.C.A. Mrs. Hutchinson as well has been largely identified with the life of the community and now occupies the position of regent of the Duchess of Sutherland chapter I.O.D.E., besides engaging in many church and other activities. Mr. Hutchinson recently accepted an offer to become sales manager of the North West Mill and Feed Company, a subsidiary to the North West Biscuit Company, but through the courtesy of Harvey Shaw, president of these companies, he has been released from that engagement to take up this offer from Toronto.

Forest *Standard*:—The other day Jack Hall, 6th Warwick, asked us if we knew Jack Hunter, of Kincardine, and wanted to know if he was a real newspaper man or was he putting up a bluff. We informed him that J. H. was proprietor and editor of a paper also that he began his career as "devil" and has worked up on the job ever since. "Well," said Mr. Hall, "you can take it from me he is willing to work on a farm, look a good horse over, teach a Sunday School class and generally make himself useful. The other day at Charlie Smith's, Warwick, you should have seen him help fill a silo. When he finished that he went home to milk Bannister's cows. This is the story of Kincardine's Mayor. He leaves home for a week's holiday and does hard work on a farm. When he bid us good-bye before returning home he didn't look as if he had been doing all that hard work. They say a change is as good as a rest, but Jack's newspaper friends will never credit him with having really helped on the farm."

Miss Mona Cleaver, ("Polly Peele" of the Toronto *Globe*) has resigned from that paper, and her marriage took place lately. As a token of their regard and regret, her fellow-workers at the *Globe* presented her with a beautiful oil painting, "Autumn Meadows," by H. S. Palmer, A.R.C.A. The presentation was made by the Managing Editor, Mr. Stewart Lyon, who paid a warm tribute to the work done by Miss Cleaver,

THOSE who have come in contact with Sir Campbell Stuart, will endorse his appointment to the position of Managing Director of the *Times*. During the war he served in Ireland; after that he was assistant military attache at Washington and then once more crossed the Atlantic to become military secretary to the British War Mission to the U.S.A. His gifts were soon appreciated by Lord Northcliffe and each task which was found for him was carried out with 100 per cent. efficiency. "The Secrets of the Crewe House" which was written by Campbell Stuart explains many of the mysteries developed in that mansion. When the Labor delegation from U.S.A. visited England it was he who played the part of host and the party went home full of admiration for him and

SIR CAMPBELL STUART

they had witnessed. Lord Northcliffe, not being able to be present himself at the Imperial Press Conference, made no mistake in sending as his representative Campbell Stuart, who represented the *Times* and other allied papers, at Ottawa. With all his responsibilities he is the cheeriest soul imaginable, and strong minded people accept his point of view, even after deciding not to do so. He has a very keen sense of humor— in short he is a good fellow and his friends rejoice in his success and are convinced that his future will redound to the credit of Canada. He is a Montreal boy.

alluding particularly to her bright personality, which has endeared her to all her professional associates and to hundreds of her public. Further words of appreciation were spoken by Miss White of the Women's Department and by Mr. Harry Anderson, Assistant Managing Editor. During the nine years that Miss Cleaver has served the *Globe* she has become known to many by her articles signed "Polly Peel." Every Monday she appeared as "Mrs. Buylow" keeping the public informed as to prices at St. Lawrence Market. For two years she was editor of the weekly page for juniors, "The Circle of Young Canada," and to her must also be credited frequent and valuable notes on "Art and Artists." In addition to all this she has been an expert reporter, giving most of her attention to recording women's activities.

Maritime

E. E. Kelly, of the editorial staff, Halifax *Herald*, spent a short vacation in Lunenburg recently.

Dr. J. D. Logan's latest book, *Twilight Litanies*, is now in the bookstores and promises to have a good Christmas sale.

C. V. Havrill, of the Printers Supplies Ltd., Halifax, was on a trip through New Brunswick the latter part of November.

The Maritime Printing Co., of Halifax, have slightly enlarged their premises and installed a 12x19 Gordon Press.

Chas. MacCauley, formerly caster-man on the *Evening Mail*, Halifax, is now in charge of the Monotypes at the Ross Print.

It is stated that the Nova Print, of Halifax, are considering the installation of Monotype equipment, and will do work for the trade.

The *Presbyterian Witness*, which for a number of years has been printed at the Imperial Pub. Co., Halifax, is now being done in Toronto.

A. F. McDonald, managing editor of the *Morning Chronicle* at Halifax, has been elected president of the North British Society of Halifax.

Arthur Hughes, of the *Chronicle* staff, has returned to Halifax after spending a three weeks' vacation in New York, Chicago and other American centres.

Leo Hanlon, assistant manager of the Canadian Railway News Company, Halifax, spent his vacation in Montreal, Toronto and other Canadian cities.

The Halifax Typo. Union, No. 130, at their December meeting, endorsed the proposition of holding a Maritime conference to further the interests of the trade.

The *Citizen*, labor press of Halifax, is at present compiling a Trades Union Directory, which is to contain much valuable

information. It is expected to be off the press some time in January.

J. T. McBride, late of the New York *Marine Register*, has accepted a position with the Halifax *Herald*. Mr. McBride was formerly connected with the *Herald*, but left Halifax shortly after the explosion in 1917.

J. R. Smallwood, formerly of the reporting staff of the Halifax *Herald*, was in the city recently from New York, where he has been employed with the *Call* of that city. Mr. Smallwood was on his way to his home in Newfoundland.

Kenneth Clarke, who has been reporting for the *Chronicle* during the past eighteen months, has severed his connection with this paper to accept a position with A. D. Merkle, the Canadian Press superintendent for the Maritimes.

Jack McDonald, of the Glace Bay *Gazette*, was in Halifax with the Caledonia football team when they played a losing game with Dalhousie College for the championship of the Province. Jack was among the guests who attended the banquet given by Senator Crosby after the game at the Queen Hotel. v

A. G. MacIntyre, manager of the Clarke Company Pulp Mills, at Bear River, was in Halifax recently in connection with some promises made by the provincial government regarding hydro development at Bear River. It is felt that the company may move to St. John should the Government promises not be adhered to.

Halifax was visited recently by Dr. Crossly Batt, D. Sc., O.B.E., lady journalist, who is touring the Maritimes studying the industrial conditions for the London *Times*. This lady has already toured Canada, west of Montreal, also Australia and New Zealand.

Rev. George S. Carson of Halifax, has been appointed as one of the Associate Editors of the *Presbyterian Witness* of Toronto. Dr. Carson has for fourteen years been editor-in-chief of the *Presbyterian Witness*, which has been published in Halifax, but has now been amalgamated with the *Presbyterian and Westminster* of Toronto. Dr. Robert Haddow of Toronto was also appointed to be associated with Mr. Carson.

British Columbia

Commencing with the first of December the rate for transient advertising in the *Herald*, Penticton, will be 75 cents an inch.

The *Star*, Princeton, which less than three years ago was printed on a 10 x 15 Gordon press, is now turning out a six-page six-column paper, linotype set.

Miss L. Sloan, an employee of the *Free Press*, Fernie, is liable to lose one of the fingers of her right hand, due to a mishap while operating a stitching machine.

Editor Jordan, of the *Review*, Revelstoke, was out of luck entirely in the way of business in the recent election. In the Revelstoke riding the Liberal candidate was elected by acclamation.

There will be at least one newspaperman in the new B. C. legislature, in W. K. Esling, Conservative-elect for Rossland. Mr. Esling, until lately, owned the *Miner*, Rossland, and *News*, Trail.

Almost the first engagement J. A. McKelvie, editor of the *News*, Vernon, and M.P.-elect for Yale, had after his election, was to present Burt R. Campbell, for fifteen years on the *News* staff, with a silver teapot suitably engraved.

Trail *News*:—The mayor of Kamloops should supply his local editors with boxing gloves and insist that they use them. From the amount of shadow boxing they have been doing lately, the bout should be a good one.

Okanagan *Commoner*:—F. E. Simpson died in Kamloops last week. Long years ago Mr. Simpson started publishing newspapers in British Columbia. He was known as "Dad" by every weekly newspaper publisher in the Province. And this prefix was one of endearment.

Every paper in the province got its share of the provincial Liberal campaign advertising in connection with the recent election; 120 inches was the minimum contract. Robb Sutherland lately of the *Daily News*, and a past president of the B. C. Press Association, was in charge of the publicity end of the campaign.

Trail *News*:—The Penticton *Herald* last week contained 74 columns of advertising in its 16 pages and the editor is growing so affluent that safe crackers have been tampering with his safe. Most newspapermen have no use for a safe anyhow,

Our New Address: 130 *Wellington St. W.*

PRE-WAR PRICES
ON
REBUILT MACHINERY TO CLEAR

We are offering machines from the following list at pre-war prices for cash, in order to reduce our large stock of rebuilt machines. Write us for prices.

No. 460—39x55 New Series Cottrell Two-Revolution Press, four rollers, four distributors, interchangeable, sheet and fly delivery, first-class press.

No. 376—Six-column Quarto Two-Revolution Campbell, table distribution, front fly delivery, four form rollers, four distributors.

No. 432—13x19 Colts Press.

No. 396—¾" New Jersey Stitcher.

No. 424—No. 7 Wire Stitcher.

No. 446—10" Hand Perforator.

No. 442—24" Rosback Perforator.

No. 461—32" Cloth Ruling Machine.

No. 463—10x15 Westman & Baker Gordon.

No. 464—10x15 Westman & Baker Gordon.

No. 465—10x15 Westman & Baker Gordon.

No. 466—10x15 Westman & Baker Gordon.

No. 467—10x15 Challenge Gordon.

No. 443—30" Oswego Lever Cutter.

No. 434—19" Westman & Baker Lever Cutter

No. 461—32" Cloth Faint Line Ruling Machine.

No. 456—No. 7 Brehmer Wire Stitcher.

No. 235—10" Bradley Card Cutter.

No. 447—No. 1 Golding Padding Press.

No. 407—500 lb. Metal Pot with gas burner.

STEPHENSON, BLAKE & CO.
C. H. CREIGHTON
Manager
130 **Wellington Street West, TORONTO**

---

*Brass Rule Made
to Order*

*Roller Composition
and Casting*

GEO. M. STEWART

PRINTING and
BOOKBINDING
MACHINERY

TYPE and
SUPPLIES

92 McGILL STREET, MONTREAL

PHONE MAIN 1892

Thoroughly Rebuilt Cylinder and Platen Presses, Paper Cutters and Machinery of all kinds for Printers, Bookbinders, Box Makers, etc. Write and state your requirements.

The Albion
SILKY COTTON
CORDS

The Cords of a hundred uses for the Artistic and Progressive Stationer and Printer.

A wide range of sizes and colours always in stock.

Send your enquiries direct or through indent agent to

THE ALBION SEWING COTTON CO., LTD.

Fawley Mills,   Tottenham Hale,
LONDON, N. 17

---

but Mr. McDougall must now have a place in which to store his government bonds, cash, diamonds and eggs.

"Dad" Simpson established publications along the Crow's Nest district years ago where he founded the Wardner *International*, the Marysville *Tribune*, and the Wattsburg *Wrinkle*. He also established and edited papers in Lethbridge, Alta., and Cranbrook, B.C. Then he went to Victoria and started the *Victorian*, which was discontinued in 1917. Mr. Simpson then moved with his family to Kamloops, where he was managing editor of the Kamloops *Standard* until the spring of the present year, when he retired from the newspaper field, and with his son entered private business. Mr. Simpson was prominent in I.O.O.F. circles, being a past grand master of the order in British Columbia, while Mrs. Simpson is past president of the Rebekah Assembly of this province. He is survived by his widow and one son, Donald, who enlisted with the artillery in Victoria and saw much service overseas.

Technical Training Worth While

Speaking of the work being done in a technical school for printing, *Printer and Publisher* asked Mr. F. H. Atkinson, instructor of the printing department at the Hamilton Technical School, if he could furnish a concrete case of the value of such training. , We wanted to know if, in this work, there were such

JAMES TODD

things as direct results. Mr. Atkinson was able to come back very quickly with the following:—

"The subject of this sketch, James Todd, enlisted in the 120th Battalion in Hamilton in 1915 and served four years in the army, being invalided home in 1919. After convalescing, he was placed by the Soldiers' Civil Re-Establishment in the Hamilton Technical School where he took a six months' course in printing which was later supplemented by an extra three months. He proved an apt pupil, missing but one or two days in the entire course.

"Starting at the 'case' he was soon able to set small jobs and feed the press and by the time his course was finished he could handle any job that was given to him, both manuscript and tabular matter, and he had a good idea of tone harmony, shape harmony, type appropriations, grouping, etc.

"Mr. Todd is now employed by the National Paper Goods Co., of Hamilton, Ontario, and is earning a salary equal to that of an apprentice in the last six months of his time—twenty-five dollars per week.

"What the printing trade needs more than anything is a better grade of boy. A higher standard of education should be asked for and if the drudgery of sweeping floors and putting

away material could be lessened, and the wages raised to six or seven dollars per week, there is no doubt that the printing trade would be benefited thereby. The present scarcity of apprentices is just the outcome of the practice followed for years of taking any kind of boy, regardless of qualifications, as long as he was cheap. Then, in the course of time, he had to make good. He was, to use a slang phrase, 'up against it.' Every employing printer should insist that an apprentice be of entrance standing and see that he is physically fit before taking him on. Thus, he would benefit, not only himself, but the boy also, and help to raise the standard of the craft."

Ottawa Valley Meet at Ottawa

A meeting of the members of the Ottawa Valley Press Association and the publishers of Eastern Ontario and those located along the northern shores of the Ottawa river, was called for Nov. 15, at the Chateau Laurier, Ottawa.

There was a very representative gathering present, Mr. E. Roy Sayles, manager of the Canadian Weekly Newspapers Association, Toronto, being one of the number. He stated that one of the objects of the meeting was to perfect some organization of the publishers in the district who are not members of any District Press Association.

A motion was introduced by Mr. C. W. Young, of the Free-holder, Cornwall, seconded by Mr. Duncan, of the *Review*, Vankleek Hill, that the Eastern Ontario publishers and those located on the Quebec side of the Ottawa Valley affiliate with the Ottawa Valley Press Association. Carried unanimously.

The President of the O. V. P. A., Mr. D. A. Jones, of the *Observer*, Pembroke, then took the chair and called for nominations for the several offices, the result of the election being as follows:

President, D. A. Jones, Pembroke.
Vice-president, C. W. Young, Cornwall.
Secy.-treasurer, F. A. J. Davis, *Central Canadian*, Carleton Place.
Executive committee, Edgar Laberge, *Le Spectateur*, Hull, Que.; A. G. F. Macdonald, *News*, Alexandria, and G. F. McKimm, *Record-News*, Smith's Falls.

Addresses were delivered by Mr. W. R. Davies, the *Mercury*, Renfrew, president of the C.W.N.A., and by Mr. E. Roy Sayles, manager of the C.W.N.A., on Association matters, particular stress being laid on the several benefits which accrue to the weekly publishers through their membership in the C.W.N.A. That the free zone had been retained by weekly publishers was entirely due to the efforts of the C.W.N.A. Progress was reported in the extension of the $2.00 subscription rate, the majority of the members of the old O.V.P.A. having already adopted this rate, while others present at the meeting expressed their determination to put this rate into effect at an early date.

A fee of $1.00 per year was agreed upon for membership in the O.V.P.A. and seventeen members were registered as having paid.

A Job Printing Price List was introduced by the secretary and on motion of Mr. Jeffery, of the *Chronicle*, Arnprior, seconded by Mr. James Muir, of the *Gazette*, Almonte, it was recommended for use by the several offices in the Association until the next meeting which will likely be held in Ottawa in February next.

Mr. E. R. Sayles reported at the close of the meeting that the membership in the C.W.N.A. had now reached 404, some new members having been secured at this meeting.

The members registered at the meeting were:

Jas. H. Ross, the *Press*, Winchester; C. W. Young, *Freeholder*, Cornwall; D. C. McFarlane, *Sun*, Cobden; W. R. Davies, *Mercury*, Renfrew; B. O. Britton, *Reporter*, Gananoque; J. H. Laurin, *Echo*, Hawkesbury; Edgar Laberge, *Le Spectateur*, Hull, Que.; H. E. Lemieux, *La Voix du Sol*, Ottawa; A. G. F. Macdonald, *Glengarry News*, Alexandria; E. Roy Sayles, manager C.W.N.A., Toronto; James Muir, *Gazette*, Almonte; G. F. McKimm, *Record-News*, Smith's Falls; D. A. Jones, *Observer*, Pembroke; R. A. Jeffery, *Chronicle*, Arnprior; F. A. J. Davis, *Central Canadian*, Carleton Place; Thos. Whalley, *Standard*, Pembroke; W. J. Duncan, *Review*, Vankleek Hill; Harry Sutton, *Record-News*, Smith's Falls.

Money-Saving Information

"The most useful information contained in any paper I get"—so a Western banker writes in to-day's mail, renewing his subscription for FINANCIAL POST.

"Very often," his letter goes on to say, "I am called on to suggest investments for small amounts, sometimes as low as a few hundreds, and I find your Investors' Inquiry Service a reliable partner to consult. If every investor knew there was such service at his call it would surely lessen the losses of many of these people."

The Investors' Inquiry Service fills just that need. Unless you are perfectly sure of your investments write us before you buy.

It costs FINANCIAL POST subscribers nothing to be sure before placing hard-earned savings in stocks that may never have a chance of paying dividends. Trained service men will give you the benefit of keen analysis based on the facts behind the securities you are considering. This is one of many features enjoyed by our readers.

The Financial Post
143 University Avenue
Toronto, Canada

Send me for one year (52 issues) The Financial Post. I attached $5.00—commence at once.

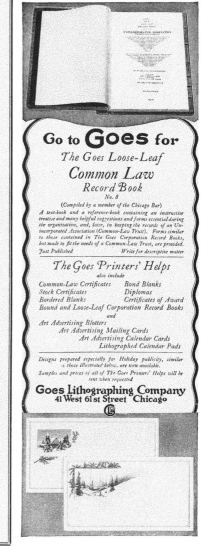

Go to **Goes** for

The Goes Loose-Leaf

Common Law
Record Book
No. 8
(Compiled by a member of the Chicago Bar)

A text-book and a reference-book containing an instructive treatise and many helpful suggestions and forms essential during the organization, and, later, in keeping the records of an Unincorporated Association (Common-Law Trust). Forms similar to those contained in The Goes Corporation Record Books, but made to fit the needs of a Common-Law Trust, are provided.
Just Published   Write for descriptive matter

The Goes Printers' Helps
also include

Common-Law Certificates   Bond Blanks
Stock Certificates   Diplomas
Bordered Blanks   Certificates of Award
Bound and Loose-Leaf Corporation Record Books
and
Art Advertising Blotters
        Art Advertising Mailing Cards
            Art Advertising Calendar Cards
                Lithographed Calendar Pads

Designs prepared especially for Holiday publicity, similar to those illustrated below, are now available.
Samples and prices of all of The Goes Printers' Helps will be sent when requested

Goes Lithographing Company
41 West 61st Street   Chicago

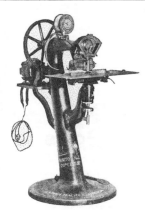
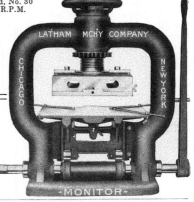

NET OUTPUT IS WHAT COUNTS TO-DAY

In these times of heavy operating expenses, economy and efficiency are the prime requisites of success.

HOE PRESSES

give the maximum net output and combine quality with quantity of product.

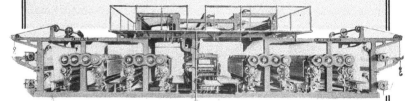

Hoe Unit-Type Octuple Press recently installed for the Springfield (Mass.) Republican and Daily News.

The publisher who relies upon Hoe printing and stereotyping machinery has FEWER WORRIES.

R. HOE & CO.

504-520 GRAND STREET, NEW YORK

7 Water Street
BOSTON, MASS.

109-112 Borough Road
LONDON, S.E. 1, ENG.

827 Tribune Building
CHICAGO, ILL.

Say you saw it in PRINTER AND PUBLISHER

Wilson-Munroe Co., LIMITED
TORONTO

The Management and Staff take this opportunity to wish you the Compliments of the Season and to express thanks for past favors accorded them.

WHOLESALE PAPER DEALERS
PRINTERS BOOKBINDERS & BOXMAKERS SUPPLIES

LET'S GO!

A record-breaking year is ahead of every live printer.

Business houses everywhere will need trade literature to captivate trade that had suddenly become coy and hard to please.

You Must Have Every Modern Convenience To Keep Pace with the Enlarged Demand.

will speed-up your output and reduce your operating costs.

Send for our Catalog.

GREAT WEST ELECTRIC CO., LTD., 57 Albert Street, Winnipeg, Man., for all points west of Port Arthur and Fort William.

MASCO COMPANY, LTD., 78 East Richmond Street, Toronto, Canada, for all points east of Port Arthur and Fort William.

Job press motors
Cylinder press motors
Motors for folders
Stitchers, cutters, monotype machines and other printing plant equipment.

KIMBLE ELECTRIC CO.
2403 West Erie Street
CHICAGO, U.S.A.

Say you saw it in PRINTER AND PUBLISHER

Many Thanks!

What Will Santa Claus
Bring Our Politicians

"**S**ANTA'S POLITICAL STOCKING" is the title of J. K. Munro's feature article in MACLEAN'S December 15th issue. Mr. Munro thinks old Kris Kringle should bring Premier Meighen a "cap that will pull down over his ears, so that he can't hear what his Cabinet colleagues are saying about him"; a hobby horse for Crerar; a tin sword for Ballantyne; a "white plume" for Lapointe; a case of grape juice for Rowell, and a pair of long trousers for Mackenzie King.

Mr. Munro also sizes up the East Elgin farmers' victory, and lets you know its real significance.

Dr. Wilfred T. Grenfell, C.M.G.

THE famous physician of Labrador has contributed a striking piece of graphic fact-fiction for the Christmas issue—"Deeds of 'Derring Do'," which describes the brave fight waged by Skipper Loveday, his crew and wife—in the dismantled Silver Queen. They expected to find a watery grave that Christmas week, but the wife's dauntless spirit put so much courage into the men that they won a fearful fight against the December gales.

Christmas Issue of Maclean's, December 15th

"THE EMANCIPATION OF POLLY MacCRAE"
By F. B. M. Collier.
The so-human story of two spinster sisters in Old Ontario and how the crippled one won a husband.

"THE JEST OF CIRCUMSTANCE"
By Gertrude Arnold.
Phyllis lands in a Canadian city, fresh from England, and there is no fiancé to meet her. The girl ultimately finds happiness just as the Christmas Carols commence—but how?

"OUR GOLDEN FLOOD ROARS EAST"
By Nicholas North.
Every few minutes a train loads up at one of our many mammoth grain elevators, taking our wheat to the seaboard.

"THE CITY OF PERIL"
By Arthur Stringer.
The largest instalment yet published of this sensational dramatic serial of Bolshevistic plotting in New York.

"—AND ALL POINTS NORTH."
By Nellie L. McClung.
A gripping story of the pioneer men and women of the Peace River country—many even out of the reach of railroads, telephones and doctors. Read what trained nurses are doing in the pioneer settlements.

"OF CHRISTMASES AND GOVERNORS"
By Colonel George Ham.
The "Colonel" has spent Christmas in some peculiar places. His experiences form the foundation of a great story. Also, Col. Ham tells of the human side of some of our Governors-General.

"WHO GETS OUR PAPER PROFITS?"
By Agnes C. Laut.
The real facts of our paper, pulp and sulphite products, and some information as to where the biggest slices of the melon go.

"THE YULETIDE GLOW"
By Charles Christopher Jenkins.
What converts Scrooges into human beings, 'round about December each year? Get in a crowd with "Jenk" and you'll find out.

"BUTTERED SIDE UP"
By C. W. Stephens.
The hero of this story loses his job a few days before Christmas. But he doesn't lose the girl, and lands a real job Christmas Eve.

"ORATORS I HAVE ENJOYED"
By "Margot" Asquith.
The wife of the ex-Premier tells what she thinks of Lloyd-George, as an orator, and others.

Review of Reviews Section

"The War Spirit in the World"—By Sisley Huddleston.
"The Irresistible Thing"—By Sir Gilbert Parker.
"German Universities Hard Up"—By Allen W. Porterfield.
"The Bleeding Statues of Tipperary"—By Edwin E. Slosson.

"A Modern Burton"—By Charles A. Merrill.
"Lansdowne's Memories"—By Marquis of Lansdowne, K.G.
"Flesh and Blood Inspired Barrie"—By William de Wagstaffe.
"Doctors Dupes of Fashion?"—London Lancet.

SECURE YOUR COPY EARLY---THE SUPPLY IS LIMITED.

MACLEAN'S
"CANADA'S NATIONAL MAGAZINE"

DECEMBER 15th ISSUE On All News-stands **20c**

Or Send $3.00 for a Year's Subscription to MACLEAN'S MAGAZINE, 143-153 University Avenue, Toronto, Canada

PRINTER AND PUBLISHER 61

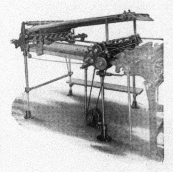 

CLASSIFIED ADVERTISEMENT SECTION

TWO CENTS A WORD, Box Number as five words ; minimum charge is $1.00 per insertion, for 50 words or less, set in 6 pt. type. Each figure counts as a word. Display ads., or ads. set in border, are at the card rates.

FOR SALE

FOR SALE — NO. 11 IMPROVED PEARL Press (new) complete with friction belt drive and quarter horsepower A-K motor, 25 cycle A.C. G. Davis, 185 Richmond West, Toronto. (p12p)

ELECTRIC PROOF PRESS, SIZE 10x26, complete with 115 volt Sprague motor, in first-class condition. Apply Supt. at Saturday Night Press, Richmond and Sheppard Sts., Toronto. (p12p)

FOR SALE—WEEKLY NEWSPAPER AND job printing plant in a prosperous British Columbia mining, fruit growing and lumbering district. Good schools, fine fishing and hunting with ideal climate the year round. $3,000. $1,000 down, balance on very easy terms. For particulars write H. W. Power, Box 532, Nelson, B.C. (pt9p)

SITUATION WANTED

ADVERTISING MAN OF TWO YEARS' EXperience is open to discuss proposition with publisher or agency, who seeks earnest and energetic worker. Write Box 111220, Printer and Publisher. (pfp)

WANTED—POSITION OF SUPERINTENDent or assistant superintendent or manager of job printing plant. Practical in every line. Wide experience and thorough knowledge of business. Estimating and meeting customers, paper expert. Best of references. Apply to E. J. Armstrong. 136 First Avenue, Ottawa. (p12p)

ADVERTISING MAN WITH VALUABLE Eastern and Western newspaper training and experience, and first-rate war record, is open to discuss new proposition with publisher who seeks live, earnest worker for either local or foreign departments, or manager of both. Has all essential qualifications—soliciting, advising, preparation lay-outs, copy, etc. Box 354, Postal Station H, Montreal, Que. (pfp)

EQUIPMENT WANTED

WANTED — SEVEN-COLUMN QUARTO press in good condition. Apply Box 10820, Printer and Publisher. (pfp)

DIRECT CURRENT MOTORS—ONE 2 H.P., 220 Volts, with Cutler-Hammer controller; two ¾ H.P., 220 Volts; one Monotype keyboard, Reliance; one paper cutter, interlocking, 28½-inch cut; about 100 type cases, upper and lower ; a number of California job cases ; about one ton Eddystone newsprint, 31x44, 51 lbs.; three imposing stones, size about thirty-six inches by forty-six inches, for $25 each. Box 102720, Printer and Publisher. (p11p)

Sell Your Idle Equipment!

If you have anything you wish to sell, use Printer and Publisher classified advertising section.

SITUATIONS VACANT

Notice that "I" is at the centre of w-i-n.

APPRENTICES—LOOK—I CAN HELP YOU make money in your spare time. Right in your own town. No experience necessary. Box 102720, Printer and Publisher. (pfp)

PRINTING SALESMAN—WANTED FOR A real, live, job printing office. State experience, if any. Am willing to consider ambitious young man now in mechanical department. Box 102120, Printer and Publisher. (pfp)

WANTED — LITHOGRAPHIC TRANSFERrers, pressmen and artists ; non-union and not at present employed; competent men only need apply; steady work guaranteed. Apply to Mortimer Co., Ltd., Ottawa, mentioning "Printer and Publisher." (pfp)

SUPERINTENDENT WANTED FOR JOB printing plant. Must understand the business in all branches, be able to meet customers and estimate. Franklin Price List used. Apply stating age, qualifications and salary to the Review Printing Co., Ltd., Peterboro. (p11p)

BY MONTREAL PRINTING AND LITHOgraphing firm, experienced young man, capable of planning, preparing and selling direct-by-mail advertising. Good opportunity for development and advancement. First-class art and mechanical facilities. State extent of education, training and experience, and salary expected. Box 12220, Printer and Publisher. (pfp)

WHY BE A MACHINE? MAKE THE MAchine do the work. Learn to operate the Monotype Keyboard. Free schools in Philadelphia, New York, Chicago and Toronto. Apply to the nearest city. Keyboard operators of ability are always in demand, where good wages, permanent positions and the best of working conditions are assured. Lanston Monotype Machine Company. (p12p)

COLLECTIONS

SEND US YOUR LIST OF DELINQUENTS. We will turn Debit into Credit. Publishers' Protective Association. Toronto. (pfp)

PRESSES

BOOKBINDING

BOX and SPECIAL

MACHINERY

BARGAINS SOLD OUT

ROYAL MACHINE WORKS

738 St. Paul West   Montreal

Write us regarding your requirements
Prompt attention.   Best service

SITUATIONS VACANT—Con.

LINOTYPE OPERATOR — PERMANENT position for good man. Apply, mentioning "Printer and Publisher," to Review, Niagara Falls. (pfp)

ALL-ROUND PRINTER WANTED — AT once ; permanent position. Phone, mentioning "Printer and Publisher," The World, Beeton, Ont. (pfp)

PRINTER — FOR JOB OR PRESSWORK. Write or telephone; state wages. Apply, mentioning "Printer and Publisher," to Advance, Niagara-on-the-Lake. (pfp)

REPORTER — DAILY ONTARIO, BELLEville ; state salary and experience; situation open now. Apply, mentioning "Printer and Publisher," to Morton & Herity. (pfp)

PRINTER—GOOD TWO-THIRDER WOULD suit, for general work around job office. Phone or wire, mentioning "Printer and Publisher," C. A. Goodfellow & Son, Whitby. (pfp)

EDITOR—FOR DAILY ONTARIO; POSItion open now; state salary and experience. Apply, mentioning "Printer and Publisher," to Morton & Herity, Belleville, Ont. (pfp)

PRINTER WANTED FOR COUNTRY NEWS and job office, to do job and press work. $25.00 per week the year round. Railroad fare refunded on arrival. Wire at our expense. "The Advocate," Thessalon, Ont.

GOOD HAND COMPOSITOR WHO UNDERstands linotype ; steady work ; 49-hour week; good wages to reliable man. State experience and wages wanted. Apply, mentioning "Printer and Publisher," to The Progress, Preston, Ont. (pfp)

HOE CYLINDER NEWSPAPER PRESS— Bed 31 X 45 inches ; a good, serviceable press in good shape. Eclipse folder in good running order; two tables; four folds. These machines will be sold cheap. Address A. W. Wright, Mount Forest, Ont.

GORDON PRESSES—ONE 13 X 19 WESTman & Baker, one 9 X 13, both re-built and equipped with new individual A.C. variable speed motors, push button control, also Chandler & Price lever quitter, 26 inch, one galley proof press and other equipment. We are over equipped. Printers, move quickly. Box 12820, Printer and Publisher. (p12p)

AGENTS WANTED — SEE ADVERTISEment on page 57 of this issue of "Printer and Publisher." (p12p)

READER'S NOTICE

Regarding

CHANGE OF ADDRESS

A REQUEST FOR CHANGE OF ADDRESS must reach us at least thirty days before the date of the issue with which it is to take effect. Duplicate copies cannot be sent to replace those undelivered through failure to send this advance notice. Be sure to give your old address as well as the new one.

Subscribe Today for "Printer and Publisher," $3.00 per year.

Buyers' Guide

Newspaper and Magazine Accounts
EVERYWHERE

Send us your delinquent accounts. Let us turn them into cash for you.

No Collection, No Charge—Prompt Returns.

Reult - Reult

REFERENCES—The Bank of Nova Scotia and over 200 satisfied Canadian publishers for whom we have been collecting for the last nine years.

The Canadian Mercantile Agency
OTTAWA, CANADA

GREAT WESTERN SMELTING
and Refining Co.,
P.O. Box - 1060
Vancouver, B. C.

TYPE METAL for All Purposes
Linotype Combination, Stereotype, Monotype, Electrotype.

Quality, Cleanliness and Analysis Guaranteed.

J. L. PEPPER
Printing Plant Production

Accurate Appraisals
Efficiency Reports

38 TORONTO STREET
TORONTO, ONT.

---

*T*HE firms listed in this Buyers' Guide are all advertisers in PRINTER AND PUBLISHER. Refer to the ads. by consulting the Index. Our interests are mutual—tell the advertisers you read their ad. in PRINTER AND PUBLISHER. Patronize PRINTER AND PUBLISHER advertisers—they are all definitely interested in the promotion of efficiency in equipment and service in Canada's allied printing trades.

ADDRESSING MACHINES
The Challenge Machinery Co., Grand Haven, Mich.
Westman & Baker Limited, Toronto.

BALERS FOR WASTE PAPER
Golding Mfg. Co., Franklin, Mass.
Logan, H. J., 114 Adelaide St. W., Toronto.
Stephenson, Blake & Co., Toronto.
Stewart, Geo. M., 92 McGill St., Montreal.
Westman & Baker Limited, Toronto.

BINDERY EQUIPMENT AND SUPPLIES
(See also CUTTING MACHINES)
Albion Sewing Cotton Co., Ltd., London, Eng.
Berry Machine Co., St. Louis, Mo.
Christensen Machine Co., Racine, Wis.
Dexter Folder Co., New York.
Golding Mfg. Co., Franklin, Mass.
Kallstrom, J., New York City.
Logan, H. J., 114 Adelaide St. W., Toronto.
Miller & Richard, Toronto and Winnipeg.
Morrison Co., J. L., Toronto, Ont.
Royal Machine Works, Montreal.
Steel Co. of Canada, The, Hamilton (wire).
Stephenson, Blake & Co., Toronto.
Stewart, Geo. M., 92 McGill St., Montreal.
Westman & Baker Limited, Toronto.

BINDERS—LOOSE LEAF
Luckett Loose Co., Toronto.

COMPOSING ROOM EQUIPMENT
(See also LEADS, SLUGS AND TYPE)
The following list covers Iron Furniture—
Eastern Brass & Wood Type Co., New York.
Hamilton Mfg. Co., Two Rivers, Wisconsin.
Stephenson, Blake & Co., Toronto.
The Challenge Machinery Co., Grand Haven, Mich.
The Toronto Type Foundry Co., Ltd., Toronto.
Westman & Baker Limited, Toronto.

CORDS, SILK, ETC.
Albion Sewing Cotton Co., Ltd., London, Eng.

COUNTING MACHINES
Stephenson, Blake & Co., Toronto.
Westman & Baker Limited, Toronto.

CUTTING MACHINES—PAPER
Golding Mfg. Co., Franklin, Mass.
Morrison Co., J. L., 445 King St. W., Toronto.
Stephenson, Blake & Co., Toronto.
The Challenge Machinery Co., Grand Haven, Mich.
Westman & Baker Limited, Toronto.

COLLECTION AGENCIES
Canadian Mercantile Agency, Ottawa.
Publishers' Protective Association, Toronto.
Nagle Mercantile Agency, Laprairie, Montreal.

EFFICIENCY EXPERT
Pepper, J. L., 38 Toronto St., Toronto.

ELECTROTYPING AND STEREOTYPING
Rapid Electrotype Co. of Canada, Toronto.
Toronto Electrotype & Stereotype Co., Toronto.

ELECTROTYPE AND STEREOTYPE BASES
The Challenge Machinery Co., Grand Haven, Mich.
Westman & Baker Limited, Toronto.

ELECTROTYPE METAL
British Smelting & Refining Co., Ltd., Montreal.
Canada Metal Co., Limited, Toronto.
Hoyt Metal Co., Limited, Toronto.

EMBOSSING EQUIPMENT
Automatic Ptg. Devices Co., San Francisco, Cal.
Ellis New Method Embossing, Hamilton, Ont.
Golding Mfg. Co., Franklin, Mass.
Stephenson, Blake & Co., Toronto.
Westman & Baker Limited, Toronto.

ENGRAVERS
Legge Bros., Ltd., Toronto.
Reliance Eng. Co., Toronto.

ENVELOPE MANUFACTURERS
Toronto Envelope Co., Toronto.
Dawson Ltd., W. V., Montreal and Toronto.

McFarlane, Son & Hodgson, Limited

WHOLESALE
PAPER DEALERS
AND
STATIONERS

14 ST. ALEXANDER STREET
MONTREAL

KILLED

On the first of the month several hundred dollars' worth of subscriptions were struck off a publisher's list.

Had he turned them over to us there would have been no reason for such action.

We collect where others fail.

Publishers' Protective Association
Goodyear Building, Toronto, Canada

BERRY ROUND HOLE CUTTER

Drills or "cuts" clean holes through any paper or pasteboard stock ten times as fast as a die punch.

One to two inches drilled at an operation. Ask for proof.

Berry Machine Co.
300 N. Third St., St. Louis, Mo.

WE PAY
SPOT CASH
FOR
Type Metal Drosses
Old Small Type
Electros and Stereos

CANADA METAL CO.
LIMITED
Reclaiming Department
TORONTO

Buyers' Guide

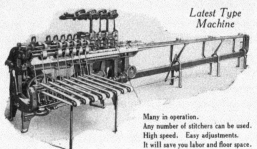

INDEX TO ADVERTISERS

The season prompts us to extend our thanks to our many business friends for their steady and increasing patronage.

During the year 1921 we shall endeavor to show our appreciation by giving you the best service within our power.

❧ ❧ ❧ ❧

CANADA PRINTING INK CO.
LIMITED
15 DUNCAN STREET, TORONTO

THE SIGNIFICANCE OF THE SLUG–II

THE RUN-AROUND
PRESENTS NO PROBLEM TO THE LINOTYPE

The run-around, a bugbear in the one-type-at-a-time shop, presents no problem to the LINOTYPE, which quickly sets each required line to its correct measure and delivers the job in solid slugs that make for security, ease, and swiftness in all subsequent manipulations of make-up and lock-up.

CANADIAN LINOTYPE LIMITED
68 Temperance Street
TORONTO

This advertisement, including border ornaments, is composed entirely of LINOTYPE material

as made
by
RYRIE
BROS'
LIMITED
TORONTO

THIS reproduction of a Booklet Cover in three colors from zinc plates is from the press of CROFT & WRIGHT, Toronto.

Christmas Bells

I heard the bells on Christmas day
Their old familiar carols play,
    And wild and sweet
    The words repeat
Of peace on earth, good-will to men.

    And thought how, as the day had come,
    The belfries of all Christendom
        Had rolled along
        The unbroken song
    Of peace on earth, good-will to men.

Till ringing, singing on its way,
The world revolved from night to day,
    A voice, a chime,
    A chant sublime,
Of peace on earth, good-will to men.

    Then from each black, accursed mouth
    The cannon thundered in the south,
        And with the sound
        The carols drowned
    Of peace on earth, good-will to men.

It was as if an earthquake rent
The hearth-stones of a continent,
    And made forlorn
    The households born
Of peace on earth, good-will to men.

    And in despair I bowed my head.
    "There is no peace on earth," I said;
        "For hate is strong
        And mocks the song
    Of peace on earth, good-will to men."

Then pealed the bells more loud and deep;
"God is not dead, nor doth He sleep;
    The Wrong shall fail
    The Right prevail,
With peace on earth, good-will to men."

           —H. W. LONGFELLOW.

Lightning Source UK Ltd.
Milton Keynes UK
UKHW011956201118
332601UK00012B/1990/P